The Relations of
Milton Snavely HERSHEY

by
Lawrence Knorr

an imprint of Sunbury Press, Inc.
Mechanicsburg, PA USA

an imprint of Sunbury Press, Inc.
Mechanicsburg, PA USA

Copyright © 2004, 2005, 2006, 2007 by Lawrence Knorr.
Cover Copyright © 2025 by Sunbury Press, Inc.

Sunbury Press supports copyright. Copyright fuels creativity, encourages diverse voices, promotes free speech, and creates a vibrant culture. Thank you for buying an authorized edition of this book and for complying with copyright laws. Except for the quotation of short passages for the purpose of criticism and review, no part of this publication may be reproduced, scanned, or distributed in any form without permission. You are supporting writers and allowing Sunbury Press to continue to publish books for every reader. For information contact Sunbury Press, Inc., Subsidiary Rights Dept., PO Box 548, Boiling Springs, PA 17007 USA or legal@sunburypress.com.

For information about special discounts for bulk purchases, please contact Sunbury Press Orders Dept. at (855) 338-8359 or orders@sunburypress.com.

To request one of our authors for speaking engagements or book signings, please contact Sunbury Press Publicity Dept. at publicity@sunburypress.com.

FIRST DISTELFINK PRESS EDITION: April 2025

Set in Adobe Garamond | Interior design by Lawrence Knorr | Cover design by Lawrence Knorr | Edited by Lawrence Knorr.

Publisher's Cataloging-in-Publication Data
Names: Knorr, Lawrence, author.
Title: The relations of Milton Snavely Hershey / Lawrence Knorr.
Description: First trade paperback edition. | Mechanicsburg, PA : Distelfink Press, 2025.
Summary: Nearly 10,000 relations of the chocolate baron, Milton Hershey, are detailed, from his earliest roots in Germany and Switzerland to present.
Identifiers: ISBN : 1-978-1-93459-700-2 (softcover) | LCCN : 2007942169.
Subjects: REFERENCE / Genealogy & Heraldry | HISTORY / Europe / Germany | HISTORY / United States / State & Local / Middle Atlantic.

Designed in the USA
0 1 1 2 3 5 8 13 21 34 55

For the Love of Books!

To Taylor and Abbey

Table of Contents

Introduction 5

Ancestry of Milton Snavely Hershey 6

Photographs of Milton Hershey 22

The Descendants of Hans Stouffer 24

The Descendants of George Weber 291

The Great Train Wreck of Republic, Ohio - 1887 - Photos 363

The Great Train Wreck of Republic, Ohio - 1887 364

Interesting Notes on the Kin of Milton Hershey 366

Kinship Report of Milton Snavely Hershey 367

Mr. & Mrs. Andrew Baer Hackman 514

Mr. & Mrs. Willis Brenner Hackman 515

About the Author 516

Index 417

Introduction

Milton Snavely Hershey (1857-1945) was best known as the entrepreneur who founded the great American chocolate candy company that bears his name. Descended from Pennsylvania Mennonite roots, Milton succeeded in becoming one of the great tycoons of the Gilded Age. However, unlike many of his wealthy contemporaries, he always maintained a sense of respectable humility—ever mindful of the "little guy." Ultimately, Milton was also one of the great philanthropists in American history. Childless, his fortune was left to the care of trustees to manage a school for orphans that bears his name. To this day, the Milton Hershey School remains one of the best-endowed institutions of learning in the nation. Additionally, the community he founded and designed to surround his factories remains a wonderful place to live for many—and a tourist or entertainment destination for millions more.

This book attempts to draw together many of the relations of Milton Hershey. Like any genealogy, this study is incomplete. While many of Milton's ancestral lines are included, there are likely more relatives from those lines left out of this work than included. An attempt has been made to include as many descendants from these lines as possible. As mentioned previously, there are no direct descendants of Milton Hershey. Thus, those mentioned in this tome are either ancestors or cousins of some degree.

Sources for this book include several "subset" genealogies. These have been blended to attempt to be comprehensive. One might also note some of the odd twists and turns the genealogy takes. My siblings and I are related to Milton Hershey at least five different ways—finding connections on my mother's side through both of her parents. It was not unusual for our Mennonite kin—especially in the earlier times—to marry second or third cousins. In fact, many of the Lancaster Mennonite families came from the same or nearby villages in the German Palatinate & Switzerland in previous centuries. For the sake of space, only the closest relationship to Milton is recorded.

The focus of this book is genealogical information. No attempt is made to recount the life and times of our great cousin. Many others have succeeded at this in the past. Rather, the focus is on an accurate and comprehensive compilation of relations. I hope that this effort is but the beginning of a much larger compilation—to include the contributions of many readers—who are themselves kin to the great Milton Hershey.

"Cousin" Lawrence Knorr
April 2004

Ancestors of Milton Snavely Hershey

Generation No. 1

1. Milton Snavely Hershey, born September 13, 1857 in Derry Twp, PA; died October 13, 1945 in Hershey, PA. He was the son of **2. Henry Hershey Hershey** and **3. Veronica Buckwalter Snavely**. He married **(1) Catherine Elizabeth Sweeney** May 25, 1898 in St. Patrick's Rectory, New York, NY. She was born July 06, 1872 in Jamestown, NY, and died March 25, 1915 in Philadelphia, PA.

Generation No. 2

2. Henry Hershey Hershey, born January 04, 1829 in Derry Twp, Dauphin Co, PA; died February 18, 1904. He was the son of **4. Jacob Frantz Hershey** and **5. Nancy Hershey**. He married **3. Veronica Buckwalter Snavely** January 15, 1856 in Parsonage at Holy Trinity Lutheran Church, Lancaster, PA.
3. Veronica Buckwalter Snavely, born September 04, 1835 in Pequea Twp, Lancaster Co, PA; died March 11, 1920. She was the daughter of **6. Abraham Barr Snavely** and **7. Elizabeth Buckwalter**.

Children of Henry Hershey and Veronica Snavely are:
- 1 i. Milton Snavely Hershey, born September 13, 1857 in Derry Twp, PA; died October 13, 1945 in Hershey, PA; married Catherine Elizabeth Sweeney May 25, 1898 in St. Patrick's Rectory, New York, NY.
-     ii. Sarena Hershey, born April 12, 1862; died March 31, 1867.

Generation No. 3

4. Jacob Frantz Hershey, born September 22, 1802; died May 15, 1877. He was the son of **8. Isaac Hernley Hershey** and **9. Anna Hostetter Frantz**. He married **5. Nancy Hershey**.
5. Nancy Hershey, born January 22, 1808; died September 03, 1869. She was the daughter of **10. Christian Hershey** and **11. Susanna Hershey**.

Children of Jacob Hershey and Nancy Hershey are:
- 2 i. Henry Hershey Hershey, born January 04, 1829 in Derry Twp, Dauphin Co, PA; died February 18, 1904; married Veronica Buckwalter Snavely January 15, 1856 in Parsonage at Holy Trinity Lutheran Church, Lancaster, PA.
-     ii. Joseph Hershey, born January 19, 1830; died August 04, 1855.
-     iii. Elizabeth Hershey, born September 26, 1832.
-     iv. Christian Hershey, born March 16, 1836; died September 29, 1884; married Barbara Good; born Abt. 1835.
-     v. Jacob H Hershey, born October 09, 1839; married Barbara B Light; born February 13, 1840.
-     vi. Elias H Hershey, born December 12, 1841; died November 16, 1925; married Elizabeth Miller Frantz 1868; born December 13, 1844; died July 09, 1906.
-     vii. Isaac Hershey, born May 06, 1846; died March 26, 1848.

6. Abraham Barr Snavely, born May 03, 1787; died March 01, 1866. He was the son of **12. John Snavely** and **13. Elizabeth Barr**. He married **7. Elizabeth Buckwalter** January 18, 1809.
7. Elizabeth Buckwalter, born March 09, 1789; died February 03, 1865. She was the daughter of **14. Benjamin Buckwalter** and **15. Barabara Herr**.

Children of Abraham Snavely and Elizabeth Buckwalter are:
-     i. Benjamin Snavely
-     ii. Martha B Snavely, born 1831.
-     iii. Elizabeth Snavely, born May 11, 1820; died January 19, 1848; married Abraham S Mylin; born August 09, 1812; died October 31, 1893.
-     iv. Abraham B Snavely, born December 15, 1824; died November 20, 1901; married Catherine Rohrer; born August 29, 1828.
- 3   v. Veronica Buckwalter Snavely, born September 04, 1835 in Pequea Twp, Lancaster Co, PA; died March 11, 1920; married Henry Hershey Hershey January 15, 1856 in Parsonage at Holy Trinity Lutheran Church, Lancaster, PA.

The Relations of Milton Snavely Hershey, 4th Ed.

Generation No. 4

8. Isaac Hernley Hershey, born February 06, 1773 in Warwick Twp., Lancaster Co, PA; died January 17, 1831 in Dauphin Co, PA. He was the son of **16. Christian Hershey** and **17. Anna Hernley**. He married **9. Anna Hostetter Frantz**.

9. Anna Hostetter Frantz, born September 22, 1774 in Lancaster Co, PA; died August 09, 1861 in Dauphin Co, PA. She was the daughter of **18. John Frantz** and **19. Elisabeth Maria Hostetter**.

Children of Isaac Hershey and Anna Frantz are:

- i. Elizabeth Hershey, born January 06, 1799; died October 03, 1867.
- ii. John Frantz Hershey, born June 28, 1800 in Derry Twp, Dauphin Co, PA; died May 28, 1851 in Derry Twp, Dauphin Co, PA; married Nancy S Frick February 19, 1824; born August 08, 1800; died October 08, 1853.
- 4 iii. Jacob Frantz Hershey, born September 22, 1802; died May 15, 1877; married Nancy Hershey.
- iv. Samuel Hershey, born 1804; died February 27, 1885; married Elizabeth Harnish September 06, 1829; born March 27, 1806; died October 17, 1891.
- v. Mary Hershey, born November 04, 1806; died January 16, 1869.
- vi. Isaac Hershey, born June 25, 1809; died September 01, 1879; married Mary Landis; born January 10, 1810; died February 18, 1900.
- vii. Christian Hershey, born December 24, 1812 in Derry Twp, Dauphin Co, PA; died May 06, 1875; married Frances Eshelman January 02, 1840; born July 26, 1818 in Greenland, Lancaster Co, PA; died November 11, 1900.
- viii. Nancy Hershey, born July 07, 1815; died September 18, 1867.

10. Christian Hershey, born June 20, 1780; died August 05, 1843. He was the son of **20. Jacob Snavely Hershey** and **21. Anna Weber Newcomer**. He married **11. Susanna Hershey**.

11. Susanna Hershey, born November 08, 1785; died February 08, 1858. She was the daughter of **22. Jacob Hershey** and **23. Elizabeth Eby**.

Children of Christian Hershey and Susanna Hershey are:

- 5 i. Nancy Hershey, born January 22, 1808; died September 03, 1869; married Jacob Frantz Hershey.
- ii. Benjamin Hershey, born July 18, 1809.
- iii. Jacob L Hershey, born May 03, 1811.
- iv. Jacob Hershey, born November 27, 1812; died August 24, 1889; married Maria Martin; born November 17, 1811; died December 11, 1844.
- v. Christian Hershey, born May 07, 1813.
- vi. John Hershey, born April 17, 1815.
- vii. Elizabeth Hershey, born September 16, 1817.
- viii. Abraham Hershey, born August 16, 1819; died December 18, 1886; married Martha; born 1824.
- ix. Susanna Hershey, born July 06, 1822.

12. John Snavely, born 1745; died April 19, 1794. He was the son of **24. Jacob Snavely** and **25. Veronica Kreider**. He married **13. Elizabeth Barr** February 02, 1774 in St. James Episcopal Church, Lanc, PA.

13. Elizabeth Barr, born February 28, 1750/51; died January 17, 1828. She was the daughter of **26. Jacob Barr** and **27. Elizabeth Anna Brubaker**.

Children of John Snavely and Elizabeth Barr are:

- i. Susanna Snavely
- ii. Veronica Snavely, married Samuel Buckwalter.
- iii. Barbara Snavely, born October 05, 1779; died December 25, 1854; married Johannes Landis May 16, 1797; born July 03, 1766; died August 11, 1826.
- iv. Henry Snavely, born June 25, 1781; died December 16, 1849; married Anna Shenk April 29, 1809.
- v. Margaretta Snavely, born August 19, 1783 in Manheim Twp, Lancaster Co, PA; died August 24, 1855 in Manheim Twp, Lanaster Co, PA; married John Erb Landis May 20, 1800 in 1st Reformed Church, Lancaster, PA; born April 18, 1779 in Manheim Twp, Lancaster Co, PA; died January 23, 1858 in Manheim Twp, Lancaster Co, PA.
- vi. Christian Snavely, born April 27, 1784; died August 31, 1863; married Veronica Herr March 23, 1809.
- vii. Elizabeth Snavely, born March 19, 1786; died July 04, 1878; married David Harnish March 20, 1804; born June 01, 1781; died April 11, 1867.
- 6 viii. Abraham Barr Snavely, born May 03, 1787; died March 01, 1866; married Elizabeth Buckwalter January 18, 1809.
- ix. Martin Snavely, born February 16, 1790; died November 02, 1877; married Anna Huber; born April 04, 1795; died August 12, 1837.
- x. Daniel Snavely, born Abt. 1791; died 1823; married Barbara Meyer October 13, 1813; born February 01,

1797; died February 07, 1824.
- xi. David Snavely, born March 26, 1792; died May 10, 1873; married Prudence Miller.

14. Benjamin Buckwalter, born 1764 in East Lampeter Twp, Lancaster Co, PA; died 1804 in East Lampeter Twp, Lancaster Co, PA. He was the son of **28. Abraham Buckwalter** and **29. Mary Landis**. He married **15. Barabara Herr**.
15. Barabara Herr, born 1775; died 1850 in East Lampeter Twp, Lancaster Co, PA.

Children of Benjamin Buckwalter and Barabara Herr are:
- 7   i. Elizabeth Buckwalter, born March 09, 1789; died February 03, 1865; married Abraham Barr Snavely January 18, 1809.
- ii. Jacob Buckwalter, born 1790.
- iii. Abraham Buckwalter, born December 24, 1792.
- iv. Mary Buckwalter, born June 12, 1796.
- v. Ann Buckwalter, born March 11, 1798.
- vi. Benjamin Buckwalter, born May 22, 1804.

Generation No. 5

16. Christian Hershey, born February 01, 1718/19; died November 21, 1782. He was the son of **32. Benjamin Stauffer Hershey** and **33. Mary Rhode**. He married **17. Anna Hernley**.
17. Anna Hernley, born June 15, 1737; died March 15, 1812.

Children of Christian Hershey and Anna Hernley are:
- i. Veronica Hershey, born November 19, 1766.
- ii. Benjamin Hershey, born March 11, 1768 in Manheim, Lanc Co, PA; died March 07, 1842; married Veronica Snyder; born July 24, 1767 in Manheim, Lanc Co, PA; died May 15, 1856.
- iii. Esther Hershey, born September 14, 1769; died November 12, 1824; married John Hess 1788; born November 09, 1768 in Warwick Twp., Lancaster Co, PA; died November 27, 1830.
- 8   iv. Isaac Hernley Hershey, born February 06, 1773 in Warwick Twp., Lancaster Co, PA; died January 17, 1831 in Dauphin Co, PA; married Anna Hostetter Frantz.
- v. John Hershey, born September 14, 1775; died November 01, 1865; married Elizabeth Frantz; born November 20, 1780; died December 02, 1839.

18. John Frantz, born December 15, 1749; died October 1821 in Warwick Twp, Lancaster County, Pa. He was the son of **36. John Frantz** and **37. Catharine Unknown**. He married **19. Elisabeth Maria Hostetter**.
19. Elisabeth Maria Hostetter, born Abt. 1750. She was the daughter of **38. Jacob Hostetter** and **39. Ann Elisabeth Hershey**.

Children of John Frantz and Elisabeth Hostetter are:
- i. Jacob Frantz, born March 01, 1773; died 1840; married Elizabeth Hershey; born Abt. 1775.
- 9   ii. Anna Hostetter Frantz, born September 22, 1774 in Lancaster Co, PA; died August 09, 1861 in Dauphin Co, PA; married Isaac Hernley Hershey.
- iii. John Frantz, born March 13, 1778; married Elizabeth Hershey; born August 20, 1780.
- iv. Elisabeth Frantz, born November 02, 1780.
- v. Barbara Frantz, born November 09, 1784.
- vi. Christian H Frantz, born December 17, 1786.
- vii. Maria Frantz, born June 12, 1788.

20. Jacob Snavely Hershey, born 1742 in Hempfield Twp, Lancaster Co, PA; died April 11, 1825. He was the son of **40. Rev. Andrew Stauffer Hershey** and **41. Mary Catharine Schnabley**. He married **21. Anna Weber Newcomer** Abt. 1771 in Pennsylvania.
21. Anna Weber Newcomer, born July 25, 1752; died January 08, 1832. She was the daughter of **42. Wolfgang Newcomer** and **43. Elizabeth Weber**.

Children of Jacob Hershey and Anna Newcomer are:
- i. John Hershey, born May 21, 1772 in Derry Twp, Dauphin Co, PA; died November 23, 1850; married (1) Anna Horst; married (2) Anna Horst March 20, 1802; born October 03, 1778 in Leacock Twp., Lancaster Co., Pa.; died August 28, 1861.
- ii. Jacob Hershey, born 1775 in Derry Twp, Dauphin Co, PA; died 1829.
- 10   iii. Christian Hershey, born June 20, 1780; died August 05, 1843; married Susanna Hershey.
- iv. Elizabeth Hershey, born May 19, 1783 in Derry Twp, Dauphin Co, PA; died June 12, 1875; married (1) Benedict Brackbill; born June 03, 1779; died May 15, 1827; married (2) Benedict Brackbill February 12, 1805; born June 08, 1779; died May 15, 1827.

v. Abraham Hershey, born January 24, 1787 in Derry Twp, Dauphin Co, PA; died January 09, 1844; married (1) Maria Siegrist; born 1794; died January 22, 1820; married (2) Anna Eby; born December 15, 1800; died February 29, 1896.
vi. Andrew Hershey, born January 24, 1787; died Abt. January 24, 1787.
vii. Abraham Hershey, born June 21, 1787 in Derry Twp, Lancaster, PA; died January 09, 1844; married Anna Eby; born December 15, 1800; died February 29, 1896.
viii. Joseph Hershey, born October 10, 1791 in Derry Twp, Dauphin Co, PA; died April 12, 1856; married Magdelene Rupp; born June 07, 1791; died April 19, 1887.

22. Jacob Hershey, born December 13, 1747; died October 12, 1819. He was the son of **16. Christian Hershey** and **45. Barbara Hostetter.** He married **23. Elizabeth Eby.**

23. Elizabeth Eby, born August 12, 1751; died January 21, 1835. She was the daughter of **46. Christian Eby** and **47. Elizabeth Mayer.**

Children of Jacob Hershey and Elizabeth Eby are:
  i. Anna Hershey, born July 27, 1779; died January 09, 1864; married Jr Benjamin Long; born July 17, 1775; died January 27, 1851.
11 ii. Susanna Hershey, born November 08, 1785; died February 08, 1858; married Christian Hershey.

24. Jacob Snavely, born Abt. 1710 in Europe; died April 01, 1781. He married **25. Veronica Kreider.**
25. Veronica Kreider, born Abt. 1704; died November 04, 1789.

Children of Jacob Snavely and Veronica Kreider are:
  i. Veronica Snavely, born 1731; died Abt. 1776; married Christian Graff; born in York Co, PA.
  ii. Anna Snavely, born 1735; died 1817; married Melchior Brenneman; born May 10, 1726; died December 06, 1809 in Donegal Twp, Lanc Co, PA.
  iii. Mary Snavely, born 1740; died Abt. 1776; married John Steinman.
12 iv. John Snavely, born 1745; died April 19, 1794; married (1) Esther Herr; married (2) Elizabeth Barr February 02, 1774 in St. James Episcopal Church, Lanc, PA.

26. Jacob Barr, born January 08, 1722/23 in Bart Twp, Lancaster Co, PA; died November 01, 1803 in Bart Twp, Lancaster Co, PA. He was the son of **52. John Martin Baer** and **53. Anna Elizabeth Groff.** He married **27. Elizabeth Anna Brubaker.**

27. Elizabeth Anna Brubaker, born Abt. 1725; died Abt. 1754. She was the daughter of **54. Hans Brubaker.**

Children of Jacob Barr and Elizabeth Brubaker are:
13 i. Elizabeth Barr, born February 28, 1750/51; died January 17, 1828; married John Snavely February 02, 1774 in St. James Episcopal Church, Lanc, PA.

28. Abraham Buckwalter, born August 27, 1738; died January 08, 1820. He was the son of **56. Joseph Buckwalter** and **57. Barbara Landis.** He married **29. Mary Landis** 1756 in Strasburg, Lancaster Co, PA.

29. Mary Landis, born 1738; died January 29, 1804. She was the daughter of **58. Benjamin Landis** and **59. Maria Weber.**

Children of Abraham Buckwalter and Mary Landis are:
  i. Mary Buckwalter, born 1757.
  ii. Abraham Buckwalter, born September 24, 1759.
  iii. Susan Buckwalter, born 1763.
14 iv. Benjamin Buckwalter, born 1764 in East Lampeter Twp, Lancaster Co, PA; died 1804 in East Lampeter Twp, Lancaster Co, PA; married Barabara Herr.

Generation No. 6

32. Benjamin Stauffer Hershey, born 1696; died July 29, 1789. He was the son of **64. Christian Schmidt Hershey** and **65. Adelheid Galle Stouffer.** He married **33. Mary Rhode.**
33. Mary Rhode

Children of Benjamin Hershey and Mary Rhode are:
16 i. Christian Hershey, born February 01, 1718/19; died November 21, 1782; married (1) Anna Hernley; married (2) Barbara Hostetter.
  ii. Ann Elisabeth Hershey, born 1724; died February 01, 1790; married Jacob Hostetter; born 1719 in Lancaster County, Pa; died January 31, 1796 in Manor Twp, Lancaster County, Pa.
  iii. Benjamin Hershey, born 1730; died 1812; married Magdalena Roadt.

iv. Mary Hershey, married (1) Jacob Musser; married (2) Benedict Mellinger October 31, 1756; born 1715; died 1795.

36. John Frantz, born Abt. 1720; died 1787 in Manor Twp, Lancaster Co, PA. He married **37. Catharine Unknown**.
37. Catharine Unknown, born Abt. 1720.

Children of John Frantz and Catharine Unknown are:
- i. Michael Frantz, born Abt. 1745.
- ii. Elizabeth Frantz, born Abt. 1747.
- 18 iii. John Frantz, born December 15, 1749; died October 1821 in Warwick Twp, Lancaster County, Pa; married Elisabeth Maria Hostetter.
- iv. Christian Frantz, born 1752.
- v. Jacob Frantz, born September 25, 1755; died May 14, 1799; married (1) Maria Nissley; born Abt. 1760; married (2) Barbara Hostetter; born October 28, 1752; died October 04, 1791; married (3) Barbara Hostetter; born 1752; died 1844.

38. Jacob Hostetter, born 1719 in Lancaster County, Pa; died January 31, 1796 in Manor Twp, Lancaster County, Pa. He was the son of **76. Jacob Hostetter** and **77. Anna Kreider**. He married **39. Ann Elisabeth Hershey**.
39. Ann Elisabeth Hershey, born 1724; died February 01, 1790. She was the daughter of **32. Benjamin Stauffer Hershey** and **33. Mary Rhode**.

Children of Jacob Hostetter and Ann Hershey are:
- i. Anna Hostetter, married Abraham Herr.
- 19 ii. Elisabeth Maria Hostetter, born Abt. 1750; married John Frantz.
- iii. Esther Hostetter, married John Reist; born 1758; died 1815.
- iv. Maria Hostetter, married Isaac Hernley.
- v. Jacob Hostetter, born September 11, 1745 in Lancaster County, Pa; died February 12, 1826 in Manheim, Pa; married Maria Metzler June 24, 1770 in Lancaster County, Pa; born November 05, 1750 in Lancaster County, Pa; died December 27, 1822 in Manheim, Pa.
- vi. Barbara Hostetter, born October 28, 1752; died October 04, 1791; married Jacob Frantz; born September 25, 1755; died May 14, 1799.
- vii. Benjamin Hostetter, born March 12, 1755 in Lancaster County, Pa; died February 11, 1844 in Manor Twp, Lancaster County, Pa; married Magdalena Wissler; born July 11, 1759.
- viii. Abraham Hostetter, born October 12, 1763 in Lancaster County, Pa; died January 19, 1834 in Manor Twp, Lancaster Cty, Pa; married Ann Hiestand; born November 28, 1769; died September 06, 1841 in Lancaster County, Pa.
- ix. Anna Hostetter, married Abraham Herr.
- x. Elizabeth Hostetter, married John Frantz.
- xi. Maria Hostetter, married Isaac Hernly.
- xii. Esther Hostetter, married John Reist.
- xiii. Barbara Hostetter, born 1752; died 1844; married Jacob Frantz; born September 25, 1755; died May 14, 1799.
- xiv. Benjamin Hostetter, born 1759; died 1844; married Magdalena Wissler; born July 11, 1759.
- xv. Abraham Hostetter, born 1763; died 1834; married Ann Heistand.

40. Rev. Andrew Stauffer Hershey, born February 11, 1697/98 in Apenzell Switzerland; died December 24, 1754. He was the son of **64. Christian Schmidt Hershey** and **65. Adelheid Galle Stouffer**. He married **41. Mary Catharine Schnabley** 1725 in Lancaster Co, PA.
41. Mary Catharine Schnabley, born 1702 in Boisenbiesen, Alsace; died 1759. She was the daughter of **82. Johann Jacob Schnebele** and **83. Unknown Unknown**.

Children of Andrew Hershey and Mary Schnabley are:
- i. Maria Hershey, born August 31, 1730 in Lancaster Co, PA; died April 1798 in Pennsylvania; married Jacob Bauman Schneider April 01, 1755 in Lancaster Co, PA; born April 02, 1727 in Germany; died April 09, 1803 in Pennsylvania.
- ii. Christian Hershey, born 1734 in East Hempfield Twp, Lanc Co, PA; died November 1806 in Manor Twp, Lanc Co, PA; married (1) Elizabeth Heistand; married (2) Elizabeth Hiestand.
- iii. Andrew Hershey, born 1736 in Lancaster, PA; died July 16, 1806 in PA; married (1) Magdalena Bauchman; born Abt. 1738; died Bef. 1763 in Hempfield Twp, Lancaster Co, PA; married (2) Maria Acker; born September 26, 1743; died September 13, 1831.
- iv. Benjamin Hershey, born Abt. 1737 in Lancaster Co, PA; died April 07, 1817 in Londonderry Twp., Lebanon Co., PA; married Barbara Schmutz Abt. 1774 in Pennsylvania; born Abt. 1750 in Lancaster Co, PA.

The Relations of Milton Snavely Hershey, 4th Ed.

       v. Adli Hershey, born Abt. 1740.
     vi. Catharine Hershey, born Abt. 1740.
    vii. John Hershey, born March 11, 1740/41 in Conestoga Twp., Lancaster Co., PA; died April 04, 1811 in Hagerstown, Washington Co., MD; married Magdalena Hoover Abt. 1764 in Lancaster Co, PA; born December 16, 1744; died January 16, 1808 in Hagerstown, Washington Co., MD.
20   viii. Jacob Snavely Hershey, born 1742 in Hempfield Twp, Lancaster Co, PA; died April 11, 1825; married Anna Weber Newcomer Abt. 1771 in Pennsylvania.
     ix. Rev. Abraham Hershey, born 1743 in East Hempfield Twp, Lanc Co, PA; died October 1821 in Lancaster Co, PA; married Veronica Greider.
      x. Isaac Hershey, born 1745 in W. Hempfield Twp., Lancaster Co., PA; died 1814 in Hagerstown, Washington Co., MD; married Barbara Stauffer Abt. 1775 in Pennsylvania; born 1756 in W. Hempfield Twp., Lancaster Co., PA; died October 23, 1845 in Hagerstown, Washington Co., MD.
     xi. Henry Hershey, born Bet. 1746 - 1748 in Hemphill Twp., Lancaster Co, PA; died 1838 in Swatara Creek, PA; married Zook Elizabeth Greider.
    xii. Peter Hershey, born 1750 in Hempfield Twp, Lancaster Co, PA; died June 20, 1819 in Williamsville, Erie Co., NY; married Mary E. Kauffman March 25, 1783 in hempfield Twp., Lancaster Co., PA; born Abt. 1766 in hempfield Twp., Lancaster Co., PA; died September 15, 1840 in Williamsville, Erie Co., NY.

42. Wolfgang Newcomer, born Bef. 1710; died March 04, 1771. He was the son of **84. Peter Newcomer** and **85. Unknown Unknown**. He married **43. Elizabeth Weber**.
    43. Elizabeth Weber, died Aft. March 04, 1771. She was the daughter of **86. Henry Weber** and **87. Maudlin Kendig**.

Children of Wolfgang Newcomer and Elizabeth Weber are:
      i. Elizabeth Newcomer
     ii. Magdalena Newcomer
    iii. Peter Newcomer, married Unknown Houser.
    iv. Henry Newcomer, born December 31, 1744; died May 14, 1795; married Barbara Garver; born December 25, 1746; died February 01, 1818.
     v. Barbara Newcomer, born 1747; died January 26, 1820; married Abraham Buckwalter; born 1741; died January 07, 1819.
     vi. Christian Newcomer, born January 21, 1748/49; died March 12, 1830; married Elizabeth Bear March 31, 1772 in Zeltenreich Reformed Church; born 1752; died April 22, 1811.
21   vii. Anna Weber Newcomer, born July 25, 1752; died January 08, 1832; married Jacob Snavely Hershey Abt. 1771 in Pennsylvania.

16. Christian Hershey, born February 01, 1718/19; died November 21, 1782. He was the son of **32. Benjamin Stauffer Hershey** and **33. Mary Rhode**. He married **45. Barbara Hostetter**.
    45. Barbara Hostetter, born Abt. 1720; died 1752 in Lancaster County, Pa. She was the daughter of **76. Jacob Hostetter** and **77. Anna Kreider**.

Children of Christian Hershey and Barbara Hostetter are:
      i. Maria Hershey, born 1746.
22   ii. Jacob Hershey, born December 13, 1747; died October 12, 1819; married Elizabeth Eby.
    iii. Barbara Hostetter Hershey, born August 22, 1750 in Lancaster Pa; died July 14, 1795 in Lancaster Pa; married Abraham Hess Stauffer; born January 07, 1746/47 in Lancaster Pa, Warwick Twp; died March 11, 1809 in Franklin Pa.

46. Christian Eby, born February 12, 1697/98; died September 15, 1756 in Warwick Twp, Lanc Co, PA. He was the son of **92. Theodorus (Durst) Eby**. He married **47. Elizabeth Mayer** April 26, 1730 in Earl Twp, Lanc Co, PA.
    47. Elizabeth Mayer, born Abt. 1712 in Hammer Creek, Lancaster, PA; died December 12, 1787 in Warwick Twp, Lanc Co, PA. She was the daughter of **94. John Meyer** and **95. Barbara Landis**.

Children of Christian Eby and Elizabeth Mayer are:
      i. Christian Eby, born February 22, 1733/34; died September 14, 1807; married Catherine Bricker; born 1743; died March 16, 1810.
     ii. Barabara Eby, born December 14, 1740 in Warwick, Lancaster, PA; died May 27, 1816; married Jacob Hershey; born 1738; died 1798.
    iii. Peter Eby, born November 11, 1742.
    iv. Anna Eby, born January 04, 1744/45; died January 30, 1826 in Elizabeth Twp Lancaster Co, PA; married Christian Stauffer; born December 06, 1736 in Pa.
     v. Andrew Eby, born January 11, 1746/47.

	vi.	George Eby, born December 11, 1748.
23	vii.	Elizabeth Eby, born August 12, 1751; died January 21, 1835; married Jacob Hershey.
	viii.	Samuel Eby, born December 20, 1752.
	ix.	Michael Eby, born December 29, 1755.

52. John Martin Baer, born Abt. 1686 in Ittlingen, Heidelberg, Baden, Germany; died February 1758 in Lampeter Twp, Lancaster Co, PA. He was the son of **104. Martin Baer** and **105. Anna Magdalena Meyer**. He married **53. Anna Elizabeth Groff**.
53. Anna Elizabeth Groff, born 1691.

Child of John Baer and Anna Groff is:
26   i. Jacob Barr, born January 08, 1722/23 in Bart Twp, Lancaster Co, PA; died November 01, 1803 in Bart Twp, Lancaster Co, PA; married (2) Elizabeth Anna Brubaker.

54. Hans Brubaker

Child of Hans Brubaker is:
27   i. Elizabeth Anna Brubaker, born Abt. 1725; died Abt. 1754; married Jacob Barr.

56. Joseph Buckwalter, born 1692; died April 02, 1748. He was the son of **112. Francis Buckwalter** and **113. Mary Unknown**. He married **57. Barbara Landis**.
57. Barbara Landis

Child of Joseph Buckwalter and Barbara Landis is:
28   i. Abraham Buckwalter, born August 27, 1738; died January 08, 1820; married Mary Landis 1756 in Strasburg, Lancaster Co, PA.

58. Benjamin Landis, born 1697 in Switzerland; died 1781 in Lancaster Co, PA. He was the son of **116. Jacob Landes** and **117. Ann Witmer**. He married **59. Maria Weber**.
59. Maria Weber, born 1695. She was the daughter of **118. Johann Anton Weber** and **119. Maria Margaretha Herr**.

Children of Benjamin Landis and Maria Weber are:
	i.	Benjamin Landis, born 1730; died October 01, 1787; married Anna Snavely.
	ii.	Anna Landis, born January 28, 1729/30; died May 30, 1760; married John Brackbill; born January 06, 1727/28; died August 20, 1813.
29	iii.	Mary Landis, born 1738; died January 29, 1804; married Abraham Buckwalter 1756 in Strasburg, Lancaster Co, PA.
	iv.	Abraham Landis, born 1739; died 1790; married Maria Barr; born 1732; died 1802.
	v.	Jacob Landis, born 1740; died April 08, 1794; married Esther Barr; born Abt. 1745.
	vi.	Barbara Landis, born 1747; died 1820; married Abraham Buckwalter; born August 27, 1740; died January 07, 1819.
	vii.	Henry Landis, born April 10, 1744 in East Lampeter Township, Lancaster County, Pennsylvania; died March 04, 1825 in East Lampeter Township, Lancaster County, Pennsylvania; married Maria Brubaker; born February 08, 1746/47 in Manheim Township, Lancaster County, Pennsylvania; died September 18, 1828 in East Lampeter Township, Lancaster County, Pennsylvania.

Generation No. 7

64. Christian Schmidt Hershey, born 1664 in Emmental Switzerland; died 1729 in Conestoga Twp, Lancaster Co, PA. He married **65. Adelheid Galle Stouffer** 1692.
65. Adelheid Galle Stouffer, born February 12, 1659/60. She was the daughter of **130. Daniel Stouffer** and **131. Barbara Neukommet Galli**.

Children of Christian Hershey and Adelheid Stouffer are:
	i.	Christian Stauffer Hershey, born 1694; died Abt. 1745; married (1) Maria Stoneman; married (2) Esther Egle; born Abt. 1690; died 1792.
32	ii.	Benjamin Stauffer Hershey, born 1696; died July 29, 1789; married Mary Rhode.
	iii.	Anna Hershey, born 1698 in Appenzell, Switzerland; died 1754 in Lancaster Co, PA; married Herman Long; born Abt. 1694; died Abt. 1773.
40	iv.	Rev. Andrew Stauffer Hershey, born February 11, 1697/98 in Apenzell Switzerland; died December 24, 1754; married Mary Catharine Schnabley 1725 in Lancaster Co, PA.

76. Jacob Hostetter, born 1695 in Germany; died 1761 in Lancaster County, Pa. He was the son of **152. Oswald Hostetter.** He married **77. Anna Kreider.**

77. Anna Kreider, born 1700 in Germany. She was the daughter of **154. Jacob Kreider** and **155. Barbara Schenk.**

Children of Jacob Hostetter and Anna Kreider are:
- i. John Hostetter, died 1765 in Lancaster County, Pa; married Elisabeth Schenk; born 1730.
- ii. Margaret Hostetter, died 1808 in Lititz, Lancaster County, PA; married John Kreider; born 1732 in Lancaster County, Pa; died 1784 in Lancaster County, Pa.
- 45 iii. Barbara Hostetter, born Abt. 1720; died 1752 in Lancaster County, Pa; married Christian Hershey.
- iv. Anna Hostetter, died 1787 in Lancaster County, Pa; married John Brubaker; born 1712 in Germany; died 1785 in Manheim Twp, Lancaster County, Pa.
- v. Catherine Hostetter
- 38 vi. Jacob Hostetter, born 1719 in Lancaster County, Pa; died January 31, 1796 in Manor Twp, Lancaster County, Pa; married Ann Elisabeth Hershey.
- vii. Elisabeth Hostetter, born 1722; died 1798 in Warwick Twp, Lancaster Cty, PA; married Christian Bomberger November 11, 1746; born 1719; died 1787.
- viii. Abraham Hostetter, born 1723 in Lancaster County, Pa; died 1796 in Lancaster County, Pa; married Catharine Long.

82. Johann Jacob Schnebele, born 1659 in Baldenheim, Alsace; died 1743. He was the son of **164. Jakob Schnebele** and **165. Unknown Unknown.** He married **83. Unknown Unknown.**

83. Unknown Unknown

Children of Johann Schnebele and Unknown Unknown are:
- i. Eva Schnebele, born in Boisenbiesen, Alsace; married Jacob Kauffman; died 1767.
- ii. John Schnebele, born Abt. 1690 in Boisenbiesen, Alsace; died Abt. January 1746/47; married Anna Unknown.
- iii. Johann Jacob Schnebele, born December 21, 1694; died August 24, 1766; married (1) Unknown Unknown; married (2) Barbara Eberle April 14, 1736.
- iv. Anna Schnebele, born January 1705/06 in Boisenbiesen, Alsace; died Aft. 1764; married Johannes Lang Abt. 1722; born June 10, 1693 in Zennern, Hesse, Germany; died Bef. September 24, 1767.
- 41 v. Mary Catharine Schnabley, born 1702 in Boisenbiesen, Alsace; died 1759; married Rev. Andrew Stauffer Hershey 1725 in Lancaster Co, PA.

84. Peter Newcomer, died Aft. January 29, 1731/32. He was the son of **168. Peter Newkommet** and **169. Unknown Unknown.** He married **85. Unknown Unknown.**

85. Unknown Unknown

Child of Peter Newcomer and Unknown Unknown is:
- 42 i. Wolfgang Newcomer, born Bef. 1710; died March 04, 1771; married (1) Elizabeth Weber; married (2) Unknown Baer.

86. Henry Weber, born 1690; died June 1745. He was the son of **118. Johann Anton Weber** and **119. Maria Margaretha Herr.** He married **87. Maudlin Kendig.**

87. Maudlin Kendig, born Abt. 1703; died Aft. 1744. She was the daughter of **174. Hans Jacob Kundig** and **175. Susanna Wymann.**

Children of Henry Weber and Maudlin Kendig are:
- i. Anna Weber, died 1784; married John Carpenter; born 1720; died 1786.
- 43 ii. Elizabeth Weber, died Aft. March 04, 1771; married (1) Wolfgang Newcomer; married (2) Vincent Meyer.
- iii. Mary Weber, married John Wanner.
- iv. Beverly Weber, died October 1788 in Lancaster Co, PA; married George Anthony Mummah; born 1722; died 1786 in Hempfield Twp, Lancaster Co, PA.
- v. Eva Weber, married John Wistler.
- vi. Christian Weber, born December 25, 1731 in Earl Twp, Lanc Co, PA; died February 13, 1820; married Magdalena Rutt September 30, 1749; born September 30, 1733; died February 16, 1804.
- vii. Heine Weber, born 1736; died March 20, 1826; married Eve Wenger; born January 07, 1736/37; died May 07, 1799.
- viii. Magdalena Weber, born October 28, 1738; died May 28, 1819; married Frantz Buckwalter; born April 05, 1732; died March 06, 1816.

92. **Theodorus (Durst) Eby,** born April 25, 1663 in Emmental, Canton Berne, Switzerlan; died December 17, 1727.

Children of Theodorus (Durst) Eby are:
- i. Johannes Eby, born 1685 in Emmental, Canton Berne, Switzerlan; died 1744.
- ii. Peter Eby, born Abt. 1690 in Emmental, Canton Berne, Switzerlan; died Abt. 1749; married (1) Anna Mylin; born Abt. 1703; died Abt. 1740; married (2) Barbara Groff.
- iii. George Eby, born 1694 in Emmental, Canton Berne, Switzerlan; died April 27, 1743; married Barbara Neff.
- iv. Jacob Eby, born 1698 in Emmental, Canton Berne, Switzerlan; died 1745.
- 46 v. Christian Eby, born February 12, 1697/98; died September 15, 1756 in Warwick Twp, Lanc Co, PA; married Elizabeth Mayer April 26, 1730 in Earl Twp, Lanc Co, PA.

94. **John Meyer,** born 1684. He was the son of **188. Hans Meyer** and **189. Unknown Unknown**. He married **95. Barbara Landis** 1709.
95. **Barbara Landis**

Children of John Meyer and Barbara Landis are:
- i. Elias Meyer, born Abt. 1710; died Aft. December 10, 1761 in Lancaster Co, PA; married Barbara Unknown Bef. 1760.
- 47 ii. Elizabeth Mayer, born Abt. 1712 in Hammer Creek, Lancaster, PA; died December 12, 1787 in Warwick Twp, Lanc Co, PA; married Christian Eby April 26, 1730 in Earl Twp, Lanc Co, PA.
- iii. John Mayer, born Abt. 1714; died Bef. 1759; married Unknown Unknown; died Aft. 1759.
- iv. Vincent Meyer, born 1721; died 1797; married (1) Elizabeth Weber; died Aft. March 04, 1771; married (2) Anna Huber; born May 16, 1727; died September 16, 1773.

104. **Martin Baer,** born Bef. 1660 in Reihen, Heidelberg, Baden, Germany. He married **105. Anna Magdalena Meyer**.
105. **Anna Magdalena Meyer,** born Abt. 1660. She was the daughter of **210. Vincenz Meyer** and **211. Elizabeth Hasler**.

Child of Martin Baer and Anna Meyer is:
- 52 i. John Martin Baer, born Abt. 1686 in Ittlingen, Heidelberg, Baden, Germany; died February 1758 in Lampeter Twp, Lancaster Co, PA; married Anna Elizabeth Groff.

112. **Francis Buckwalter,** born 1665; died 1723. He married **113. Mary Unknown**.
113. **Mary Unknown**

Children of Francis Buckwalter and Mary Unknown are:
- i. Jacob Buckwalter
- ii. Mary Buckwalter
- 56 iii. Joseph Buckwalter, born 1692; died April 02, 1748; married (1) Barbara Landis; married (2) Magdalena Fritz.
- iv. Johannes Buckwalter, born 1698; died August 1776; married Magdelena Clotz Longenecker Abt. 1740; born 1706 in Chester County, Pennsylvania; died 1804 in Chester County, Pennsylvania.
- v. Theodorus Buckwalter, born 1702; died July 1782 in Lancaster Co, PA; married Barbara Landis 1724 in Lancaster, PA; born 1705 in Zurich, Switzerland; died 1788 in Lampeter Twp, Lancaster Co, PA.

116. **Jacob Landes,** born 1667; died 1730 in Lancaster Co, PA. He was the son of **232. Hans Heinrich Landis** and **233. Barbara Bueler**. He married **117. Ann Witmer**.
117. **Ann Witmer,** born 1671.

Children of Jacob Landes and Ann Witmer are:
- 58 i. Benjamin Landis, born 1697 in Switzerland; died 1781 in Lancaster Co, PA; married Maria Weber.
- ii. Barbara Landis, born 1705 in Zurich, Switzerland; died 1788 in Lampeter Twp, Lancaster Co, PA; married Theodorus Buckwalter 1724 in Lancaster, PA; born 1702; died July 1782 in Lancaster Co, PA.
- iii. Anna Landis, born Abt. 1704; married (1) Christian Mosser; died 1741; married (2) Henry Tinkey.

118. **Johann Anton Weber,** died December 17, 1724 in Lancaster Co, PA. He was the son of **236. Heinrich Weber** and **237. Elsbeth Ruggin**. He married **119. Maria Margaretha Herr**.
119. **Maria Margaretha Herr,** died Aft. November 1725.

Children of Johann Weber and Maria Herr are:

      i. John Weber, born Abt. 1685; died 1755 in West Lampeter Twp., Lanc Co, Pa; married Barbara Hauser; died Aft. 1721.
     ii. Jacob Weber, born 1688; died January 1746/47; married Anna Bauman Abt. 1721; born Abt. 1705; died February 11, 1771 in Ephrata Cloisters, Ephrata, PA.
    iii. Henry Weber, born 1690; died June 1745; married Maudlin Kendig; born Abt. 1703; died Aft. 1744.
    iv. George Weber, born 1693; died 1772; married Barbara Guth 1726; born Abt. 1693; died 1782.

59   v. Maria Weber, born 1695; married Benjamin Landis.
    vi. Anna Weber, born Abt. 1700; died 1727 in at sea on Molly; married David Martin Bef. 1727; born Abt. 1700; died November 10, 1784 in Earl Twp., Lanc. Co., PA.

Marriage Notes for Anna Weber and David Martin:
[jweaver..FTW]

Family tradition said that his first wife who died at sea on the Molly was Anna Weaver, sister of Henry, George, Jacob, and John Weber of Weber's Thal. However, Darvin Martin argues that this is highly unlikely. He argues in his article that the families probably never knew each other and that it is highly improbable that if he had a wife who was lost at sea, her name was Anna Weber.

I would like to see more proof before I throw away this wonderful tale which M. G. Weaver quotes in his book. Jay Weaver..

Generation No. 8

130. Daniel Stouffer, born 1631 in Eggiwil, Near Zurich, Switzerland; died Abt. 1700 in Germany. He was the son of **260. Christian Stouffer** and **261. Adelfried Oppliger**. He married **131. Barbara Neukommet Galli** May 08, 1652.
    131. Barbara Neukommet Galli, born 1628; died Aft. 1672. She was the daughter of **262. Ulrich Galli** and **263. Barbara Neukommet**.

Children of Daniel Stouffer and Barbara Galli are:
      i. Ulrich Galle Stouffer, born Abt. 1654.
     ii. Margareth Galle Stouffer, born Abt. 1656.
    iii. Barbara Galle Stouffer, born Abt. 1658.
    iv. Daniel Galle Stouffer, born 1660.

65   v. Adelheid Galle Stouffer, born February 12, 1659/60; married Christian Schmidt Hershey 1692.
    vi. Christian Stauffer, born March 29, 1663 in Switzerland; died Abt. 1715 in Germany; married Magdalena Brubacher WFT Est. 1682-1714; born Abt. 1665.
    vii. Madlena Galle Stouffer, born Abt. 1665.
   viii. Abraham Galle Stouffer, born 1672.

152. Oswald Hostetter, born March 12, 1670/71 in Mettmenstetten, Switzerland. He was the son of **304. Heinrich Hoffstetter** and **305. Margaret Vollenweider**.

Children of Oswald Hostetter are:
76   i. Jacob Hostetter, born 1695 in Germany; died 1761 in Lancaster County, Pa; married Anna Kreider.
    ii. Oswald Hostetter, born 1702 in Germany; died 1749 in Lancaster Cty, PA; married Maria Unknown.

154. Jacob Kreider, born 1664. He was the son of **308. Michael Kreider**. He married **155. Barbara Schenk**.
    155. Barbara Schenk, born April 14, 1667 in Eggiwil, Switzerland. She was the daughter of **310. Michael Schenk** and **311. Anna Stauffer**.

Children of Jacob Kreider and Barbara Schenk are:
      i. Michael Kreider, born 1691 in Ittlingen Germany; died 1739 in Lancaster County, Pa; married Barbara Graff.
     ii. Jacob Kreider, born 1693 in Germany; died 1758 in Lancaster County, Pa.
    iii. Hans Jacob Kreider, born 1695.
    iv. Barbara Kreider, born 1702.
    v. Martin Kreider, born 1706.
77   vi. Anna Kreider, born 1700 in Germany; married (2) Jacob Hostetter.

164. Jakob Schnebele, born 1624 in Affoltern am Albis, Zurich, Switzerland. He was the son of **328. Jacob Schnebele** and **329. Anna Melchiorin**. He married **165. Unknown Unknown**.

165. Unknown Unknown

Child of Jakob Schnebele and Unknown Unknown is:
- 82   i. Johann Jacob Schnebele, born 1659 in Baldenheim, Alsace; died 1743; married Unknown Unknown.

168. Peter Newkommet He married **169. Unknown Unknown**.
169. Unknown Unknown

Child of Peter Newkommet and Unknown Unknown is:
- 84   i. Peter Newcomer, died Aft. January 29, 1731/32; married Unknown Unknown.

174. Hans Jacob Kundig, died Bef. November 28, 1735 in Strasburg Twp, Lanc Co, PA. He was the son of **348. Hans Heinrich Kundig** and **349. Dorothea Scharer**. He married **175. Susanna Wymann** April 24, 1703 in Dubendorf.
175. Susanna Wymann, born in Alstetten near Zurich; died Aft. January 01, 1713/14.

Children of Hans Kundig and Susanna Wymann are:
- i. Heinrich Kendig, died Bef. February 09, 1756 in Strasburg, Lanc Co, PA; married Mary Wolf; died Aft. 1756.
- ii. Verena Kundig, died December 10, 1711 in Pfaffikon.
- iii. Jacob Kundig
- iv. Mary Kendig, died Aft. 1751; married Christian Herr; born February 20, 1716/17; died May 18, 1772 in Lampeter Twp., PA.
- 87   v. Maudlin Kendig, born Abt. 1703; died Aft. 1744; married Henry Weber.
- vi. Veronica Kendig, born Abt. 1703; married Jacob Lichty; died Bef. 1751.
- vii. Anna Kendig, born Abt. 1704.
- viii. Barbara Kendig, born Abt. 1705; married Abraham Burkholder; died Bef. 1776.
- ix. Elizabeth Kendig, born Abt. 1709; married John Longenecker Bef. 1736.
- x. Ester Kendig, born Abt. 1712.
- xi. Eva Kendig, born Abt. 1714.

188. Hans Meyer, born 1666 in Bussenhausen, Pfaffikon, Zurich, Switzerland; died 1722 in Conestoga Township, Lancaster County, Pennsylvania. He was the son of **210. Vincenz Meyer** and **211. Elizabeth Hasler**. He married **189. Unknown Unknown**.
189. Unknown Unknown

Children of Hans Meyer and Unknown Unknown are:
- 94   i. John Meyer, born 1684; married Barbara Landis 1709.
- ii. Elisabeth Mayer, born Abt. 1690; married Johannes Herr August 10, 1710 in Mauer, Germany.
- iii. Veronica Meyer, born Abt. 1692; married Jacob Hochstetter May 13, 1714.
- iv. Heinrich Mayer, born Abt. 1700 in Mauer, Germany; died September 08, 1781 in Conestoga Twp, Lanc Co, PA.

210. Vincenz Meyer, born Abt. 1628; died Aft. 1685. He was the son of **420. Vincenz Meyer** and **421. Elsbeth Muller**. He married **211. Elizabeth Hasler**.
211. Elizabeth Hasler

Children of Vincenz Meyer and Elizabeth Hasler are:
- i. Mayer, born Abt. 1657; married Jacob Gut February 18, 1678/79 in Steinsfurt Reformed; born Abt. 1657; died Bef. April 22, 1730 in Conestoga Twp, Lanc Co, PA.
- ii. Maria Mayer, born Abt. 1659; married Abraham Deutsch June 21, 1680 in Steinsfurt.
- 105   iii. Anna Magdalena Meyer, born Abt. 1660; married (1) Martin Baer; married (2) Martin Bar Abt. 1680.
- iv. Michael Meyer, born Abt. 1667; died Bet. 1724 - 1731; married Unknown Unknown.
- v. Samuel Meyer, born Bef. February 27, 1669/70; died Aft. 1739.
- vi. Hans Meyer, born 1666 in Bussenhausen, Pfaffikon, Zurich, Switzerland; died 1722 in Conestoga Township, Lancaster County, Pennsylvania; married (1) Anna Hiestand Brubaker; born 1669 in Ibersheim, Germany; died Abt. 1730 in Conestoga Township, Lancaster County, Pennsylvania; married (2) Unknown Unknown.

232. Hans Heinrich Landis, died Bef. 1670. He was the son of **464. Hans Landis** and **465. Elizabeth Ertzinger**. He married **233. Barbara Bueler** February 14, 1642/43 in Hirzel, Switzerland.
233. Barbara Bueler

Children of Hans Landis and Barbara Bueler are:
- i. Jacob Landis, died March 20, 1645/46.
- ii. Catharina Landis
- iii. Barbara Landis, married Jacob Stocker September 28, 1670.
- iv. Hans Heinrich Landis
- v. Hans Jacob Landis, born Abt. 1648; died January 30, 1711/12 in Rohrbach; married Verena Schneider; born Abt. 1649; died October 16, 1713 in Rohrbach.
- vi. Rudolf Landis, born Abt. 1662; died April 05, 1705 in Steinsfurt.
- vii. Child Landis, born Abt. 1664; died September 1665.
- viii. Hans Landis, born 1664 in Germany or Switzerland; died December 02, 1727 in Earl Twp., Lanc. Co., PA; married Unknown Unknown.
- 116 ix. Jacob Landes, born 1667; died 1730 in Lancaster Co, PA; married Ann Witmer.

236. Heinrich Weber, died Aft. 1670. He was the son of **472. George Weber** and **473. Elsbeth Schnebli**. He married **237. Elsbeth Ruggin** January 26, 1640/41 in Baretswil, Switzerland.
237. Elsbeth Ruggin, died Bef. 1670. She was the daughter of **474. Uli Ruggin** and **475. Anna Ruegg**.

Children of Heinrich Weber and Elsbeth Ruggin are:
- 118 i. Johann Anton Weber, died December 17, 1724 in Lancaster Co, PA; married Maria Margaretha Herr.
- ii. Jagli Weber
- iii. Samuel Weber, died Aft. 1700; married (1) Barbara Pfenniger Bef. 1670; died Bef. 1700; married (2) Verena Meyer Bef. 1700.
- iv. Anna Weber
- v. Elsbeth Weber
- vi. Heinrich Weber
- vii. Barbeli Weber
- viii. Georg Weber
- ix. Hans Rudolf Weber, born 1660; married Adelheit Pfenniger Bef. 1689.
- x. Verena Weber, born 1664.

Generation No. 9

260. Christian Stouffer, born 1582 in Rothenbach; died WFT Est. 1632-1651. He was the son of **520. Hans Stouffer**. He married **261. Adelfried Oppliger** June 18, 1610.
261. Adelfried Oppliger, born Abt. 1588; died 1632. She was the daughter of **522. Peter Oppliger** and **523. Adelheed Blanier**.

Child of Christian Stouffer and Adelfried Oppliger is:
- 130 i. Daniel Stouffer, born 1631 in Eggiwil, Near Zurich, Switzerland; died Abt. 1700 in Germany; married Barbara Neukommet Galli May 08, 1652.

262. Ulrich Galli He married **263. Barbara Neukommet**.
263. Barbara Neukommet

Child of Ulrich Galli and Barbara Neukommet is:
- 131 i. Barbara Neukommet Galli, born 1628; died Aft. 1672; married Daniel Stouffer May 08, 1652.

304. Heinrich Hoffstetter, born February 02, 1628/29 in Mettmenstetten, Switzerland. He was the son of **608. Heinrich Hoffstetter**. He married **305. Margaret Vollenweider**.
305. Margaret Vollenweider

Children of Heinrich Hoffstetter and Margaret Vollenweider are:
- i. Jacob Hostetter, born 1648.
- ii. Anna Hostetter, born 1650.
- iii. Hans Hostetter, born 1656.
- iv. Cathri Hostetter, born 1658.
- v. Hans Jagli Hostetter, born September 23, 1660.
- vi. Hans Heinrich Hostetter, born August 16, 1663.
- vii. Elsbeth Hostetter, born 1668.
- 152 viii. Oswald Hostetter, born March 12, 1670/71 in Mettmenstetten, Switzerland.
- ix. Jageli Hostetter, born July 22, 1677.

308. Michael Kreider, born 1640.

Children of Michael Kreider are:
- i. Hans Kreider, born 1670.
- 154 ii. Jacob Kreider, born 1664; married Barbara Schenk.

310. Michael Schenk, born 1639 in Eggiwil, Switzerland. He was the son of **620. Michael Schenk** and **621. Anna Stauffer**. He married **311. Anna Stauffer** September 21, 1660 in Switzerland.
311. Anna Stauffer, born 1643 in Eggiwil, Switzerland. She was the daughter of **622. Hans Stauffer** and **623. Madlena Neuenschwander**.

Children of Michael Schenk and Anna Stauffer are:
- i. Christian Schenk, born June 15, 1662.
- ii. Hans Schenk, born December 04, 1664.
- 155 iii. Barbara Schenk, born April 14, 1667 in Eggiwil, Switzerland; married Jacob Kreider.
- iv. Michael Schenk, born January 04, 1669/70 in Eggiwil, Switzerland.

328. Jacob Schnebele, born Abt. 1590 in Affoltern am Albis, Zurich, Switzerland; died Abt. 1660. He married **329. Anna Melchiorin**.
329. Anna Melchiorin

Children of Jacob Schnebele and Anna Melchiorin are:
- i. Heinrich Schnebele
- ii. Johann Jacob Schnebele
- iii. Regula Schnebele, died Bef. 1693; married Gregorius Gropp.
- iv. Felix Schnebele, born 1622 in Affoltern am Albis, Zurich, Switzerland.
- 164 v. Jakob Schnebele, born 1624 in Affoltern am Albis, Zurich, Switzerland; married Unknown Unknown.
- vi. Philip Schnebel, born Abt. 1625 in Affoltern am Albis, Zurich, Switzerland.

348. Hans Heinrich Kundig, died April 06, 1720 in Pfaffikon. He was the son of **696. Jorg Kundig** and **697. Barbel Huffellberg**. He married **349. Dorothea Scharer** March 30, 1663 in Pfaffikon.
349. Dorothea Scharer, died Bef. 1680.

Children of Hans Kundig and Dorothea Scharer are:
- i. Jacob Kundig, married Anna Saylor May 15, 1688; died Aft. 1707.
- ii. Jorg Kundig, died Bef. May 21, 1755 in Conestoga Twp, Lanc Co, PA; married (1) Barbara Unknown; died Aft. 1754; married (2) Ursula Muller April 20, 1697 in Pfaffikon; born Abt. 1679 in Dubendorf.
- iii. Barbel Kundig
- 174 iv. Hans Jacob Kundig, died Bef. November 28, 1735 in Strasburg Twp, Lanc Co, PA; married (1) Susanna Wymann April 24, 1703 in Dubendorf; married (2) Elisabeth Unknown Bef. 1715.
- v. Anna Kundig
- vi. Elsbeth Kundig

420. Vincenz Meyer, born Abt. 1598 in Schleitheim. He was the son of **840. Melchior Meyer**. He married **421. Elsbeth Muller**.
421. Elsbeth Muller

Children of Vincenz Meyer and Elsbeth Muller are:
- i. Verena Meyer, born Bef. December 26, 1624 in Schleitheim.
- 210 ii. Vincenz Meyer, born Abt. 1628; died Aft. 1685; married Elizabeth Hasler.

464. Hans Landis He was the son of **928. Hans Landis** and **929. Barbara Hochstrasser**. He married **465. Elizabeth Ertzinger**.
465. Elizabeth Ertzinger, born in Eggerberg, Zurich, Switzerland. She was the daughter of **930. Uli Ertzinger** and **931. Unknown Unknown**.

Children of Hans Landis and Elizabeth Ertzinger are:
- i. Rudolf Landis, died Bef. 1670; married Christine Mettler September 01, 1646.
- ii. Margaretha Landis, married Joseph Casson.
- 232 iii. Hans Heinrich Landis, died Bef. 1670; married Barbara Bueler February 14, 1642/43 in Hirzel, Switzerland.
- iv. Anna Landis

- v. Jacob Landis
- vi. Verena Landis
- vii. Barbara Landis
- viii. Hans Rudolf Landis
- ix. Elisabeth Landis, died July 04, 1637 in Hirzel, Switzerland.
- x. Margaret Landis, married Joseph Casson June 23, 1664 in Markirch.
- xi. Caspar Landis, born Abt. 1614; married (1) Susanna Pfister July 22, 1634 in Hirzel, Switzerland; born Abt. 1613; married (2) Catharina Danherr June 02, 1661 in Durrenentzen, Alsace; died February 15, 1686/87 in Durrenentzen, Alsace.
- xii. Hans Landis, born 1615.
- xiii. Elsbeth Landis, born Abt. 1620.

472. George Weber, born Abt. 1578; died Aft. 1649. He married **473. Elsbeth Schnebli** Bef. 1621.
473. Elsbeth Schnebli, died Bef. 1633.

Marriage Notes for George Weber and Elsbeth Schnebli:
[jweaver..FTW]

Marriage was probably before 1617 since oldest child was born abt 1617.

Children of George Weber and Elsbeth Schnebli are:
- 236 i. Heinrich Weber, died Aft. 1670; married Elsbeth Ruggin January 26, 1640/41 in Baretswil, Switzerland.
- ii. Sara Weber, born Abt. 1617.
- iii. Georg Weber, born Abt. 1623.

474. Uli Ruggin, died in Hinterberg. He married **475. Anna Ruegg.**
475. Anna Ruegg, died in Hinterberg.

Child of Uli Ruggin and Anna Ruegg is:
- 237 i. Elsbeth Ruggin, died Bef. 1670; married Heinrich Weber January 26, 1640/41 in Baretswil, Switzerland.

Generation No. 10

520. Hans Stouffer, born 1534 in Rotenbock; died WFT Est. 1553-1625. He was the son of **1040. Hans Stouffer.**

Child of Hans Stouffer is:
- 260 i. Christian Stouffer, born 1582 in Rothenbach; died WFT Est. 1632-1651; married Adelfried Oppliger June 18, 1610.

522. Peter Oppliger, born WFT Est. 1537-1566; died WFT Est. 1591-1651. He married **523. Adelheed Blanier** WFT Est. 1563-1606.
523. Adelheed Blanier, born WFT Est. 1546-1569; died WFT Est. 1591-1657.

Child of Peter Oppliger and Adelheed Blanier is:
- 261 i. Adelfried Oppliger, born Abt. 1588; died 1632; married Christian Stouffer June 18, 1610.

608. Heinrich Hoffstetter, born 1610 in Niedermettmenstetten, Switzerland. He was the son of **1216. Mr Hoffstetter.**

Children of Heinrich Hoffstetter are:
- 304 i. Heinrich Hoffstetter, born February 02, 1628/29 in Mettmenstetten, Switzerland; married (1) Margaret Vollenweider; married (2) Anna Bar.
- ii. Maria Hoffstetter, born 1630.
- iii. Anna Hoffstetter, born 1633.
- iv. Barbel Hoffstetter, born 1635.
- v. Elsi Hoffstetter, born 1637.
- vi. Georg Hoffstetter, born 1642.
- vii. Hans Jacob Hoffstetter, born 1644.
- viii. Anna Hoffstetter, born 1648.
- ix. Oswald Hoffstetter, born 1655.

620. Michael Schenk, born 1590 in Bern, Switzerland. He was the son of **1240. Ulrich Schenk** and **1241. Annali Rytz**. He married **621. Anna Stauffer**.

621. Anna Stauffer, born 1602.

Children of Michael Schenk and Anna Stauffer are:
- i. Niklaus Schenk
- ii. Ulrich Schenk, born 1622.
- iii. Christian Schenk, born 1624.
- iv. Margaret Schenk, born 1631.
- 310 v. Michael Schenk, born 1639 in Eggiwil, Switzerland; married Anna Stauffer September 21, 1660 in Switzerland.
- vi. Barbara Schenk, born 1640.
- vii. Johannes Schenk, born 1642.

622. Hans Stauffer, born April 18, 1613 in Rothenbach, Switzerland. He married **623. Madlena Neuenschwander.**

623. Madlena Neuenschwander

Children of Hans Stauffer and Madlena Neuenschwander are:
- i. Christian Stauffer, born 1637.
- ii. Barbara Stauffer, born 1639.
- 311 iii. Anna Stauffer, born 1643 in Eggiwil, Switzerland; married Michael Schenk September 21, 1660 in Switzerland.
- iv. Hans Stauffer, born 1644.
- v. Ulrich Stauffer, born 1647.
- vi. Catherina Stauffer, born 1648.

696. Jorg Kundig, died Aft. 1650. He was the son of **1392. Peter Kundig**. He married **697. Barbel Huffellberg** Bef. 1636.

697. Barbel Huffellberg, died Aft. 1650.

Children of Jorg Kundig and Barbel Huffellberg are:
- i. Hans Jagli Kundig, married Elsbeth Meili Bef. 1666; born 1636.
- 348 ii. Hans Heinrich Kundig, died April 06, 1720 in Pfaffikon; married (1) Dorothea Scharer March 30, 1663 in Pfaffikon; married (2) Barbel Weyner October 26, 1680 in Pfaffikon.
- iii. Heinrich Kundig
- iv. Barbel Kundig, born Abt. 1643.

840. Melchior Meyer, born Abt. 1555.

Children of Melchior Meyer are:
- i. Christian Meyer, born Abt. 1590 in Schleitheim; married Anna Russenberger.
- 420 ii. Vincenz Meyer, born Abt. 1598 in Schleitheim; married Elsbeth Muller.
- iii. Hans Meyer, born Abt. 1580; married (1) Barbel/Cherl Unknown; married (2) Barbel Egli Bef. 1603; married (3) Barbel Frey February 24, 1604/05 in Pfaffikon; born in Kempten.

928. Hans Landis, born Abt. 1544; died September 30, 1614. He was the son of **1856. Hans Landis** and **1857. Katharina Schinz**. He married **929. Barbara Hochstrasser** Bef. 1580.

929. Barbara Hochstrasser

Children of Hans Landis and Barbara Hochstrasser are:
- 464 i. Hans Landis, married Elizabeth Ertzinger.
- ii. Margreth Landis

930. Uli Ertzinger He married **931. Unknown Unknown.**

931. Unknown Unknown

Child of Uli Ertzinger and Unknown Unknown is:
- 465 i. Elizabeth Ertzinger, born in Eggerberg, Zurich, Switzerland; married Hans Landis.

Generation No. 11

1040. Hans Stouffer, born 1500; died WFT Est. 1537-1591.

Child of Hans Stouffer is:
- 520   i. Hans Stouffer, born 1534 in Rotenbock; died WFT Est. 1553-1625; married WFT Est. 1553-1585.

1216. Mr Hoffstetter, born 1580.

Children of Mr Hoffstetter are:
- i. Jacob Hoffstetter, born 1609 in Switzerland; married Anna Huber.
- 608   ii. Heinrich Hoffstetter, born 1610 in Niedermettmenstetten, Switzerland.

1240. Ulrich Schenk, born in Switzerland. He married **1241. Annali Rytz**.
1241. Annali Rytz

Child of Ulrich Schenk and Annali Rytz is:
- 620   i. Michael Schenk, born 1590 in Bern, Switzerland; married Anna Stauffer.

1392. Peter Kundig, born Abt. 1565; died Aft. 1601. He was the son of **2784. Felix Kundig**.

Children of Peter Kundig are:
- i. Adrian Kundig, married (1) Barbel Tobel December 18, 1628 in Baretswil, Switzerland; married (2) Regel Walder April 20, 1630 in Baretswil, Switzerland; died Bef. 1649 in 2.
- 696   ii. Jorg Kundig, died Aft. 1650; married (1) Anna Meyer Bef. 1626; married (2) Barbel Huffellberg Bef. 1636.
- iii. Elsbet Kundig
- iv. Hans Kundig, born Bef. October 20, 1594 in Baretswil, Switzerland; died Bef. 1649; married Elsbeth Zupinger Bef. 1649.

1856. Hans Landis, born Abt. 1520. He married **1857. Katharina Schinz**.
1857. Katharina Schinz, born Abt. 1524.

Children of Hans Landis and Katharina Schinz are:
- i. Anna Landis
- ii. Anna Landis
- iii. Hans Heinrich (Heini) Landis, died July 01, 1622 in Hirzel, Switzerland; married Verena Berschinger Abt. 1585.
- iv. Agta Landis
- v. Ludi Landis
- vi. Anna Landis
- 928   vii. Hans Landis, born Abt. 1544; died September 30, 1614; married (1) Barbara Hochstrasser Bef. 1580; married (2) Margaretha Hochstrasser Bef. 1582.
- viii. Ulrich Landis, born 1546.
- ix. Rudolf Landis, born 1547; married Anna Bruppacher Abt. 1570.

Generation No. 12

2784. Felix Kundig

Child of Felix Kundig is:
- 1392   i. Peter Kundig, born Abt. 1565; died Aft. 1601.

Above Left: Young Milton Hershey ca. 1885, Middle: Milton & wife Katherine (Sweeney) ca. 1900. Above Right: Milton in his late 40's.

Photos Below: Milton in his later years.

Upper Left: Katherine Sweeney, Upper Right: Milton in Egypt, Middle Left: Milton with Youths, Middle Right: Old Litho of the factory, Lower Left: Old Hershey Postcard, Lower Right: Photo of early Hershey Delivery Truck

The Relations of Milton Snavely Hershey, 4th Ed.

Descendants of Hans Stouffer

Generation No. 1

1. Hans¹ Stouffer was born 1500, and died WFT Est. 1537-1591.

Child of Hans Stouffer is:
+   2   i.   Hans² Stouffer, born 1534 in Rotenbock; died WFT Est. 1553-1625.

Generation No. 2

2. Hans² Stouffer (Hans¹) was born 1534 in Rotenbock, and died WFT Est. 1553-1625.

Child of Hans Stouffer is:
+   3   i.   Christian³ Stouffer, born 1582 in Rothenbach; died WFT Est. 1632-1651.

Generation No. 3

3. Christian³ Stouffer (Hans², Hans¹) was born 1582 in Rothenbach, and died WFT Est. 1632-1651. He married **Adelfried Oppliger** June 18, 1610, daughter of Peter Oppliger and Adelheed Blanier. She was born Abt. 1588, and died 1632.

Child of Christian Stouffer and Adelfried Oppliger is:
+   4   i.   Daniel⁴ Stouffer, born 1631 in Eggiwil, Near Zurich, Switzerland; died Abt. 1700 in Germany.

Generation No. 4

4. Daniel⁴ Stouffer (Christian³, Hans², Hans¹) was born 1631 in Eggiwil, Near Zurich, Switzerland, and died Abt. 1700 in Germany. He married **Barbara Neukommet Galli** May 08, 1652, daughter of Ulrich Galli and Barbara Neukommet. She was born 1628, and died Aft. 1672.

Children of Daniel Stouffer and Barbara Galli are:
    5   i.   Ulrich Galle⁵ Stouffer, born Abt. 1654.
    6   ii.   Margareth Galle Stouffer, born Abt. 1656.
    7   iii.   Barbara Galle Stouffer, born Abt. 1658.
    8   iv.   Daniel Galle Stouffer, born 1660.
+   9   v.   Adelheid Galle Stouffer, born February 12, 1659/60.
+   10   vi.   Christian Stauffer, born March 29, 1663 in Switzerland; died Abt. 1715 in Germany.
    11   vii.   Madlena Galle Stouffer, born Abt. 1665.
    12   viii.   Abraham Galle Stouffer, born 1672.

Generation No. 5

9. Adelheid Galle⁵ Stouffer (Daniel⁴, Christian³, Hans², Hans¹) was born February 12, 1659/60. She married **Christian Schmidt Hershey** 1692. He was born 1664 in Emmental Switzerland, and died 1729 in Conestoga Twp, Lancaster Co, PA.

Children of Adelheid Stouffer and Christian Hershey are:
+   13   i.   Christian Stauffer⁶ Hershey, born 1694; died Abt. 1745.
+   14   ii.   Benjamin Stauffer Hershey, born 1696; died July 29, 1789.
+   15   iii.   Anna Hershey, born 1698 in Appenzell, Switzerland; died 1754 in Lancaster Co, PA.
+   16   iv.   Rev. Andrew Stauffer Hershey, born February 11, 1697/98 in Apenzell Switzerland; died December 24, 1754.

10. Christian⁵ Stauffer (Daniel⁴ Stouffer, Christian³, Hans², Hans¹) was born March 29, 1663 in Switzerland, and died Abt. 1715 in Germany. He married **Magdalena Brubacher** WFT Est. 1682-1714. She was born Abt. 1665.

Children of Christian Stauffer and Magdalena Brubacher are:

+	17	i.	Daniel[6] Stouffer, born Abt. 1685 in Ibersheim, Germany.
	18	ii.	Jacob Stouffer, born 1685.
+	19	iii.	Hans Stauffer, born 1687.
	20	iv.	Ulrich Stouffer, born Abt. 1689.
	21	v.	Christian Stouffer, born Abt. 1691.
	22	vi.	Agnes Stouffer, born Abt. 1693.

Generation No. 6

13. Christian Stauffer[6] Hershey (Adelheid Galle[5] Stouffer, Daniel[4], Christian[3], Hans[2], Hans[1]) was born 1694, and died Abt. 1745. He married **(1) Maria Stoneman**. He married **(2) Esther Egle**. She was born Abt. 1690, and died 1792.

Children of Christian Hershey and Esther Egle are:

+	23	i.	Elisabeth[7] Hershey, born Abt. 1714 in Friedelsheim, GER; died Abt. 1786.
+	24	ii.	Barbara Hershey, born Abt. 1720; died March 04, 1805.
	25	iii.	Mary Hershey, born Abt. 1728; died Abt. 1799. She married Abraham Neff; born Abt. 1719 in PA; died Abt. 1793 in PA.
+	26	iv.	Christian Hershey, born July 24, 1730; died January 24, 1825.
	27	v.	Esther (Hester) Hershey, born Abt. 1732; died 1780. She married Henry Herr; born Abt. 1725 in PA; died July 26, 1780 in PA.
+	28	vi.	Anna Elizabeth Hershey, born Abt. 1734.
+	29	vii.	Abraham Hershey, born 1740; died 1811 in Manheim Twp, Lanc Co, PA.
+	30	viii.	Benjamin Hershey, born 1741 in Lancaster, PA; died 1820 in Bertie Twp, Welland, ONT, CAN.
	31	ix.	Adah (Ada) Hershey, born Abt. 1742. She married Jacob Erisman.

14. Benjamin Stauffer[6] Hershey (Adelheid Galle[5] Stouffer, Daniel[4], Christian[3], Hans[2], Hans[1]) was born 1696, and died July 29, 1789. He married **Mary Rhode**.

Children of Benjamin Hershey and Mary Rhode are:

+	32	i.	Christian[7] Hershey, born February 01, 1718/19; died November 21, 1782.
+	33	ii.	Ann Elisabeth Hershey, born 1724; died February 01, 1790.
+	34	iii.	Benjamin Hershey, born 1730; died 1812.
+	35	iv.	Mary Hershey.

15. Anna[6] Hershey (Adelheid Galle[5] Stouffer, Daniel[4], Christian[3], Hans[2], Hans[1]) was born 1698 in Appenzell, Switzerland, and died 1754 in Lancaster Co, PA. She married **Herman Long**. He was born Abt. 1694, and died Abt. 1773.

Children of Anna Hershey and Herman Long are:

	36	i.	Christian[7] Long.
	37	ii.	Addah Long. She married Peter Swart.
	38	iii.	Anna Long, died 1792. She married Michael Witmer; born Abt. 1718; died 1789.
	39	iv.	Elizabeth Long.
	40	v.	Maria Long.
	41	vi.	Magdalena Long.
	42	vii.	Herman Long.
	43	viii.	Esther Long.
+	44	ix.	John Long, died 1782.
	45	x.	Barbara Long. She married Abraham Heistand; born 1739; died 1772.
+	46	xi.	Susanna Long.
	47	xii.	Fronica Long. She married John Rohrer.
+	48	xiii.	Catharine Long.

16. Rev. Andrew Stauffer[6] Hershey (Adelheid Galle[5] Stouffer, Daniel[4], Christian[3], Hans[2], Hans[1]) was born February 11, 1697/98 in Apenzell Switzerland, and died December 24, 1754. He married **Mary Catharine Schnabley** 1725 in Lancaster Co, PA, daughter of Johann Schnebele and Unknown Unknown. She was born 1702 in Boisenbiesen, Alsace, and died 1759.

Children of Andrew Hershey and Mary Schnabley are:

	49	i.	Maria[7] Hershey, born August 31, 1730 in Lancaster Co, PA; died April 1798 in Pennsylvania. She married Jacob Bauman Schneider April 01, 1755 in Lancaster Co, PA; born April 02, 1727 in Germany; died April 09, 1803 in Pennsylvania.
	50	ii.	Christian Hershey, born 1734 in East Hempfield Twp, Lanc Co, PA; died November 1806 in Manor

Twp, Lanc Co, PA. He married (1) Elizabeth Heistand. He married (2) Elizabeth Hiestand.
+ 51   iii. Andrew Hershey, born 1736 in Lancaster, PA; died July 16, 1806 in PA.
   52   iv. Benjamin Hershey, born Abt. 1737 in Lancaster Co, PA; died April 07, 1817 in Londonderry Twp., Lebanon Co., PA. He married Barbara Schmutz Abt. 1774 in Pennsylvania; born Abt. 1750 in Lancaster Co, PA.
   53   v. Adli Hershey, born Abt. 1740.
   54   vi. Catharine Hershey, born Abt. 1740.
+ 55   vii. John Hershey, born March 11, 1740/41 in Conestoga Twp., Lancaster Co., PA; died April 04, 1811 in Hagerstown, Washington Co., MD.
+ 56   viii. Jacob Snavely Hershey, born 1742 in Hempfield Twp, Lancaster Co, PA; died April 11, 1825.
+ 57   ix. Rev. Abraham Hershey, born 1743 in East Hempfield Twp, Lanc Co, PA; died October 1821 in Lancaster Co, PA.
   58   x. Isaac Hershey, born 1745 in W. Hempfield Twp., Lancaster Co., PA; died 1814 in Hagerstown, Washington Co., MD. He married Barbara Stauffer Abt. 1775 in Pennsylvania; born 1756 in W. Hempfield Twp., Lancaster Co., PA; died October 23, 1845 in Hagerstown, Washington Co., MD.
+ 59   xi. Henry Hershey, born Bet. 1746 - 1748 in Hemphill Twp., Lancaster Co, PA; died 1838 in Swatara Creek, PA.
   60   xii. Peter Hershey, born 1750 in Hempfield Twp, Lancaster Co, PA; died June 20, 1819 in Williamsville, Erie Co., NY. He married Mary E. Kauffman March 25, 1783 in hempfield Twp., Lancaster Co., PA; born Abt. 1766 in hempfield Twp., Lancaster Co., PA; died September 15, 1840 in Williamsville, Erie Co., NY.

17. Daniel[6] Stouffer (Christian[5] Stauffer, Daniel[4] Stouffer, Christian[3], Hans[2], Hans[1]) was born Abt. 1685 in Ibersheim, Germany. He married **Magdalena Brubashcher** WFT Est. 1700-1734. She was born Abt. 1690.

Children of Daniel Stouffer and Magdalena Brubashcher are:
   61   i. Christian[7] Stauffer, born 1709.
   62   ii. Barbara Virginia Stauffer, born 1711.
   63   iii. Jacob Stauffer, born 1712.
+ 64   iv. Johannes Stauffer, born August 06, 1715 in Wartenberg, Germany; died December 30, 1766 in Warwick Twp, Lancaster Co, PA.
   65   v. Magdalena Stauffer, born Abt. 1717.

19. Hans[6] Stauffer (Christian[5], Daniel[4] Stouffer, Christian[3], Hans[2], Hans[1]) was born 1687. He married **Elizabeth Risser** June 10, 1713.

Children of Hans Stauffer and Elizabeth Risser are:
   66   i. Martin[7] Stauffer.
   67   ii. Anna Stauffer.
   68   iii. Madelena Stauffer.
+ 69   iv. Henry Jacob Stauffer, born 1712 in Muckenhauserhof, Germany; died 1775.

Generation No. 7

23. Elisabeth[7] Hershey (Christian Stauffer[6], Adelheid Galle[5] Stouffer, Daniel[4], Christian[3], Hans[2], Hans[1]) was born Abt. 1714 in Friedelsheim, GER, and died Abt. 1786. She married **Peter Risser** 1736 in Friedelsheim, GER. He was born September 03, 1713 in Friedelsheim, GER, and died February 1804 in Lancaster, PA.

Children of Elisabeth Hershey and Peter Risser are:
   70   i. Esther[8] Risser, born 1737 in Friedelsheim, GER.
   71   ii. John Risser, born 1739 in Friedelsheim, GER.
   72   iii. Catherine Risser, born 1741 in Lancaster, PA.
   73   iv. Elizabeth Risser, born 1742 in Lancaster, PA.
   74   v. Barbara Risser, born 1745 in Lancaster, PA.
   75   vi. Christian Reesor, born August 26, 1747 in Lancaster, PA; died March 16, 1806 in Markham Twp, York, Ontario, CAN.
   76   vii. Peter Risser, born November 05, 1750 in Lancaster, PA.
+ 77   viii. Abraham H. Risser, born 1755 in Lancaster, PA.
   78   ix. Magdalena H. Risser, born December 08, 1758 in Lancaster, PA; died November 16, 1806.
   79   x. Jacob H. Risser, born October 19, 1764 in Lancaster, PA; died September 18, 1835 in Mt. Joy Twp, Lancaster, PA.

24. Barbara[7] Hershey (Christian Stauffer[6], Adelheid Galle[5] Stouffer, Daniel[4], Christian[3], Hans[2], Hans[1]) was born Abt. 1720, and died March 04, 1805. She married **David Herr**. He was born 1722, and died January 11, 1772 in Lancaster Co, PA.

Child of Barbara Hershey and David Herr is:
+ 80   i. Fanny[8] Herr, born January 06, 1745/46.

26. Christian[7] Hershey (Christian Stauffer[6], Adelheid Galle[5] Stouffer, Daniel[4], Christian[3], Hans[2], Hans[1]) was born July 24, 1730, and died January 24, 1825. He married **Magdalena Kauffman**. She was born 1767, and died 1847.

Child of Christian Hershey and Magdalena Kauffman is:
+ 81   i. Rudolph[8] Hershey, born December 30, 1814 in Heidelburg Twp, York, PA; died December 22, 1862 in Washington Twp, Shelby, OH.

28. Anna Elizabeth[7] Hershey (Christian Stauffer[6], Adelheid Galle[5] Stouffer, Daniel[4], Christian[3], Hans[2], Hans[1]) was born Abt. 1734. She married **Samuel Herr**. He was born February 1721/22, and died Bef. June 12, 1787.

Child of Anna Hershey and Samuel Herr is:
82   i. Fronica[8] Herr.

29. Abraham[7] Hershey (Christian Stauffer[6], Adelheid Galle[5] Stouffer, Daniel[4], Christian[3], Hans[2], Hans[1]) was born 1740, and died 1811 in Manheim Twp, Lanc Co, PA. He married **Elizabeth Landis** 1764 in Mannheim Twp, Lancaster, PA, daughter of Henry Landis and Fronica Groff. She was born October 09, 1743, and died December 12, 1781.

Children of Abraham Hershey and Elizabeth Landis are:
    83   i. Anna[8] Hershey, born Abt. 1765. She married John Frick.
    84   ii. Esther Hershey, born Abt. 1767. She married Jacob Shumaker.
+ 85   iii. Barbara Hershey, born March 01, 1769; died December 09, 1828.
    86   iv. Catherine Hershey, born July 13, 1771; died September 25, 1849. She married David Long.
+ 87   v. Elizabeth Hershey, born Abt. 1772; died 1857.
+ 88   vi. Abraham Hershey, born March 03, 1774 in Manheim Twp, Lancaster, PA; died May 06, 1839.
+ 89   vii. Christian Hershey, born January 16, 1777 in Lancaster, PA; died August 03, 1853 in Lisbon, Linn, IA.
    90   viii. Mary Hershey, born Abt. 1779; died Abt. 1856. She married John Long.
    91   ix. Unnamed Infant Hershey, born 1781; died 1781.
    92   x. Unnamed Infant Hershey, born 1781; died 1781.

30. Benjamin[7] Hershey (Christian Stauffer[6], Adelheid Galle[5] Stouffer, Daniel[4], Christian[3], Hans[2], Hans[1]) was born 1741 in Lancaster, PA, and died 1820 in Bertie Twp, Welland, ONT, CAN. He married **Catherine Landis**, daughter of Henry Landis and Fronica Groff. She was born 1747.

Children of Benjamin Hershey and Catherine Landis are:
    93   i. Christian[8] Hershey, born 1768.
    94   ii. Abraham Hershey, born 1770.
    95   iii. Catherine Hershey, born 1772.
    96   iv. Benjamin Hershey, born 1776.
    97   v. Mary Hershey, born 1782.
    98   vi. Esther Hershey, born Abt. 1784.
+ 99   vii. Henry Hershey, born 1786.
    100   viii. John Hershey, born 1788.

32. Christian[7] Hershey (Benjamin Stauffer[6], Adelheid Galle[5] Stouffer, Daniel[4], Christian[3], Hans[2], Hans[1]) was born February 01, 1718/19, and died November 21, 1782. He married **(1) Anna Hernley**. She was born June 15, 1737, and died March 15, 1812. He married **(2) Barbara Hostetter**, daughter of Jacob Hostetter and Anna Kreider. She was born Abt. 1720, and died 1752 in Lancaster County, Pa.

Children of Christian Hershey and Anna Hernley are:
    101   i. Veronica[8] Hershey, born November 19, 1766.
    102   ii. Benjamin Hershey, born March 11, 1768 in Manheim, Lanc Co, PA; died March 07, 1842. He married Veronica Snyder; born July 24, 1767 in Manheim, Lanc Co, PA; died May 15, 1856.
+ 103   iii. Esther Hershey, born September 14, 1769; died November 12, 1824.
+ 104   iv. Isaac Hernley Hershey, born February 06, 1773 in Warwick Twp., Lancaster Co, PA; died January 17, 1831 in Dauphin Co, PA.

105   v. John Hershey, born September 14, 1775; died November 01, 1865. He married Elizabeth Frantz; born November 20, 1780; died December 02, 1839.

Children of Christian Hershey and Barbara Hostetter are:
- 106   i. Maria[8] Hershey, born 1746.
- \+ 107   ii. Jacob Hershey, born December 13, 1747; died October 12, 1819.
- \+ 108   iii. Barbara Hostetter Hershey, born August 22, 1750 in Lancaster Pa; died July 14, 1795 in Lancaster Pa.

33. Ann Elisabeth[7] Hershey (Benjamin Stauffer[6], Adelheid Galle[5] Stouffer, Daniel[4], Christian[3], Hans[2], Hans[1]) was born 1724, and died February 01, 1790. She married **Jacob Hostetter**, son of Jacob Hostetter and Anna Kreider. He was born 1719 in Lancaster County, Pa, and died January 31, 1796 in Manor Twp, Lancaster County, Pa.

Children of Ann Hershey and Jacob Hostetter are:
- \+ 109   i. Anna[8] Hostetter.
- \+ 110   ii. Elisabeth Maria Hostetter, born Abt. 1750.
- \+ 111   iii. Esther Hostetter.
- \+ 112   iv. Maria Hostetter.
- \+ 113   v. Jacob Hostetter, born September 11, 1745 in Lancaster County, Pa; died February 12, 1826 in Manheim, Pa.
- \+ 114   vi. Barbara Hostetter, born October 28, 1752; died October 04, 1791.
- \+ 115   vii. Benjamin Hostetter, born March 12, 1755 in Lancaster County, Pa; died February 11, 1844 in Manor Twp, Lancaster County, Pa.
- \+ 116   viii. Abraham Hostetter, born October 12, 1763 in Lancaster County, Pa; died January 19, 1834 in Manor Twp, Lancaster Cty, Pa.
- 117   ix. Anna Hostetter. She married Abraham Herr.
- 118   x. Elizabeth Hostetter. She married John Frantz.
- 119   xi. Maria Hostetter. She married Isaac Hernly.
- 120   xii. Esther Hostetter. She married John Reist.
- \+ 121   xiii. Barbara Hostetter, born 1752; died 1844.
- 122   xiv. Benjamin Hostetter, born 1759; died 1844. He married Magdalena Wissler; born July 11, 1759.
- \+ 123   xv. Abraham Hostetter, born 1763; died 1834.

34. Benjamin[7] Hershey (Benjamin Stauffer[6], Adelheid Galle[5] Stouffer, Daniel[4], Christian[3], Hans[2], Hans[1]) was born 1730, and died 1812. He married **Magdalena Roadt**.

Children of Benjamin Hershey and Magdalena Roadt are:
- 124   i. Benjamin[8] Hershey.
- 125   ii. Christian Hershey.
- 126   iii. Magdalen Hershey. She married Christian Brubaker.
- 127   iv. Mary Hershey. She married Christian Brubaker.
- 128   v. Ann Hershey, born 1766; died 1830. She married Henry Weber; born 1758; died 1816.
- 129   vi. Feronica Hershey, born 1766; died 1830. She married Henry Weber; born December 16, 1758; died April 20, 1816.

35. Mary[7] Hershey (Benjamin Stauffer[6], Adelheid Galle[5] Stouffer, Daniel[4], Christian[3], Hans[2], Hans[1]) She married **(1) Jacob Musser**. She married **(2) Benedict Mellinger** October 31, 1756. He was born 1715, and died 1795.

Children of Mary Hershey and Benedict Mellinger are:
- 130   i. Franni[8] Mellinger, born October 09, 1757.
- 131   ii. Freni Mellinger, born January 15, 1759.
- \+ 132   iii. David Mellinger, born December 01, 1760.
- 133   iv. Christian Mellinger, born September 05, 1762.
- \+ 134   v. John Mellinger, born July 13, 1764; died September 21, 1844.

44. John[7] Long (Anna[6] Hershey, Adelheid Galle[5] Stouffer, Daniel[4], Christian[3], Hans[2], Hans[1]) died 1782. He married **Maria Bachman**.

Children of John Long and Maria Bachman are:
- 135   i. Herman[8] Long.
- 136   ii. John Long.

137		iii.	Christian Long.
138		iv.	Ann Long.
139		v.	Mary Long.
140		vi.	Elizabeth Long.
141		vii.	Joseph Long.
142		viii.	Abraham Long, born April 20, 1778 in E. Hempfield Twp, Lancaster, PA; died December 28, 1846.

46. Susanna[7] Long (Anna[6] Hershey, Adelheid Galle[5] Stouffer, Daniel[4], Christian[3], Hans[2], Hans[1]) She married **Jacob Kreider**. He was born Abt. 1742, and died Abt. 1822.

Children of Susanna Long and Jacob Kreider are:

	143	i.	Elizabeth[8] Kreider.
	144	ii.	Maria Kreider.
	145	iii.	Barbara Kreider, born Abt. 1765. She married Henry Dohner; born 1764 in Dauphin, PA.
	146	iv.	Jacob Kreider, born August 17, 1771; died February 17, 1853. He married Maria "Mary" Stauffer; born 1777; died February 07, 1850.
	147	v.	Henry Kreider, born September 12, 1774; died April 09, 1835. He married Christiana Widemoyer; born July 11, 1777; died August 03, 1864.
	148	vi.	John Kreider, born January 12, 1777; died August 03, 1864. He married Catherine Dohner; born 1771 in Dauphin, PA; died 1821.
+	149	vii.	Anna Kreider, born 1778.

48. Catharine[7] Long (Anna[6] Hershey, Adelheid Galle[5] Stouffer, Daniel[4], Christian[3], Hans[2], Hans[1]) She married **Abraham Hostetter**, son of Jacob Hostetter and Anna Kreider. He was born 1723 in Lancaster County, Pa, and died 1796 in Lancaster County, Pa.

Children of Catharine Long and Abraham Hostetter are:

+	150	i.	Henry[8] Hostetter.
+	151	ii.	Abraham Hostetter, born in Manor Twp Lancaster County, Pa; died in Lancaster County, Pa.
+	152	iii.	Jacob Hostetter, born 1752 in Manor Twp, Lancaster County, Pa; died 1823 in Hempfield Twp, Lancaster County, Pa.
+	153	iv.	Herman Hostetter, born October 02, 1753 in Lancaster County, Pa; died December 10, 1812 in Canada.
+	154	v.	John Hostetter, born October 28, 1754 in Manor Twp, Lancaster Cty, Pa; died May 06, 1818 in Manor Twp, Lancaster County, Pa.
+	155	vi.	Anna Hostetter, born September 1757; died March 1821.
+	156	vii.	Christian Hostetter, born 1762; died 1838 in Warwick Twp Lancaster Cty, Pa.
+	157	viii.	Barbara Hostetter, born Abt. 1760.
+	158	ix.	Abraham Hostetter, died 1834.
	159	x.	Barbara Hostetter.
	160	xi.	Henry Hostetter.
	161	xii.	Anna Hostetter, born 1751; died 1821. She married Christian Herr; born December 25, 1753; died March 21, 1821.
+	162	xiii.	John Hostetter, born 1754; died 1854.
+	163	xiv.	Christian Hostetter, born 1762; died 1838.

51. Andrew[7] Hershey (Andrew Stauffer[6], Adelheid Galle[5] Stouffer, Daniel[4], Christian[3], Hans[2], Hans[1]) was born 1736 in Lancaster, PA, and died July 16, 1806 in PA. He married **(1) Magdalena Bauchman**. She was born Abt. 1738, and died Bef. 1763 in Hempfield Twp, Lancaster Co, PA. He married **(2) Maria Acker**. She was born September 26, 1743, and died September 13, 1831.

Child of Andrew Hershey and Magdalena Bauchman is:

	164	i.	Catharine[8] Hershey, born 1760; died July 16, 1833. She married Martin Bear; born February 26, 1753; died in Cumberland, PA.

Children of Andrew Hershey and Maria Acker are:

	165	i.	Anna[8] Hershey, born February 27, 1762; died March 05, 1855.
+	166	ii.	Jacob Hershey, born October 02, 1765; died May 30, 1821.
	167	iii.	Maria Hershey, born May 23, 1768; died December 05, 1849.
+	168	iv.	Andrew Hershey, born September 14, 1770; died August 01, 1835.
	169	v.	Henry Hershey, born December 19, 1772; died April 24, 1838.
	170	vi.	Elizabeth Hershey, born December 05, 1775; died August 17, 1870.
	171	vii.	John Hershey, born March 31, 1783; died July 16, 1831.

55. John[7] **Hershey** (Andrew Stauffer[6], Adelheid Galle[5] Stouffer, Daniel[4], Christian[3], Hans[2], Hans[1]) was born March 11, 1740/41 in Conestoga Twp., Lancaster Co., PA, and died April 04, 1811 in Hagerstown, Washington Co., MD. He married **Magdalena Hoover** Abt. 1764 in Lancaster Co, PA. She was born December 16, 1744, and died January 16, 1808 in Hagerstown, Washington Co., MD.

Child of John Hershey and Magdalena Hoover is:
+ 172   i.   Anna[8] Hershey, born February 23, 1765 in Lancaster, PA; died February 18, 1850 in Cumberland, PA.

56. Jacob Snavely[7] **Hershey** (Andrew Stauffer[6], Adelheid Galle[5] Stouffer, Daniel[4], Christian[3], Hans[2], Hans[1]) was born 1742 in Hempfield Twp, Lancaster Co, PA, and died April 11, 1825. He married **Anna Weber Newcomer** Abt. 1771 in Pennsylvania, daughter of Wolfgang Newcomer and Elizabeth Weber. She was born July 25, 1752, and died January 08, 1832.

Children of Jacob Hershey and Anna Newcomer are:
+ 173   i.   John[8] Hershey, born May 21, 1772 in Derry Twp, Dauphin Co, PA; died November 23, 1850.
    174   ii.   Jacob Hershey, born 1775 in Derry Twp, Dauphin Co, PA; died 1829.
+ 175   iii.   Christian Hershey, born June 20, 1780; died August 05, 1843.
    176   iv.   Elizabeth Hershey, born May 19, 1783 in Derry Twp, Dauphin Co, PA; died June 12, 1875. She married (1) Benedict Brackbill; born June 03, 1779; died May 15, 1827. She married (2) Benedict Brackbill February 12, 1805; born June 08, 1779; died May 15, 1827.
+ 177   v.   Abraham Hershey, born January 24, 1787 in Derry Twp, Dauphin Co, PA; died January 09, 1844.
    178   vi.   Andrew Hershey, born January 24, 1787; died Abt. January 24, 1787.
    179   vii.   Abraham Hershey, born June 21, 1787 in Derry Twp, Lancaster, PA; died January 09, 1844. He married Anna Eby; born December 15, 1800; died February 29, 1896.
    180   viii.   Joseph Hershey, born October 10, 1791 in Derry Twp, Dauphin Co, PA; died April 12, 1856. He married Magdelene Rupp; born June 07, 1791; died April 19, 1887.

57. Rev. Abraham[7] **Hershey** (Andrew Stauffer[6], Adelheid Galle[5] Stouffer, Daniel[4], Christian[3], Hans[2], Hans[1]) was born 1743 in East Hempfield Twp, Lanc Co, PA, and died October 1821 in Lancaster Co, PA. He married **Veronica Greider**.

Child of Abraham Hershey and Veronica Greider is:
+ 181   i.   Elizabeth[8] Hershey, born August 20, 1780.

59. Henry[7] **Hershey** (Andrew Stauffer[6], Adelheid Galle[5] Stouffer, Daniel[4], Christian[3], Hans[2], Hans[1]) was born Bet. 1746 - 1748 in Hemphill Twp., Lancaster Co, PA, and died 1838 in Swatara Creek, PA. He married **Zook Elizabeth Greider**.

Child of Henry Hershey and Elizabeth Greider is:
+ 182   i.   Martin[8] Hershey, born October 20, 1771; died August 25, 1825 in near Bindnagle's Church, Dauphin Co, PA.

64. Johannes[7] **Stauffer** (Daniel[6] Stouffer, Christian[5] Stauffer, Daniel[4] Stouffer, Christian[3], Hans[2], Hans[1]) was born August 06, 1715 in Wartenberg, Germany, and died December 30, 1766 in Warwick Twp, Lancaster Co, PA. He married **(1) Katherine Katrina Schenk** October 1738. She was born April 1720 in Conestoga Twp, Lancaster Co, and died November 29, 1760 in Lancaster Co, Pa. He married **(2) Catherine Stauffer** Abt. 1761.

Children of Johannes Stauffer and Katherine Schenk are:
+ 183   i.   Anna Barbara[8] Stauffer, born August 1739; died February 02, 1808.
+ 184   ii.   Elizabeth Stauffer, born August 09, 1741 in Warwick Twp., Lancaster Cty., PA; died 1777.
+ 185   iii.   Veronica " Frany " Stauffer, born July 31, 1742; died WFT Est. 1758-1836.
    186   iv.   Christian Stauffer, born July 31, 1744. He married Veronica Hostetter.
    187   v.   Jacob Stauffer, born May 07, 1745. He married Elizabeth Brubacker.
    188   vi.   Ann Stauffer, born September 30, 1746. She married Michael Laber.
    189   vii.   Christina Stauffer, born February 02, 1747/48. She married Isaac Eshelman.
    190   viii.   Catherine Stauffer, born February 26, 1749/50.
    191   ix.   Eva Stauffer, born April 12, 1751. She married Abraham Ebersole.
    192   x.   Henry Stauffer, born March 29, 1754; died April 1754.
    193   xi.   John Stauffer, born March 29, 1754. He married Ann Unknown.
    194   xii.   Marie Stauffer, born 1756. She married Christian Hagey; born in Rapho Twp, Lancaster Co.
    195   xiii.   Michael Stauffer, born December 18, 1758.

Children of Johannes Stauffer and Catherine Stauffer are:
    196   i.   Susanna[8] Stauffer, born Abt. 1761.

197 ii. Magdalena Stauffer, born Abt. 1761.

69. Henry Jacob[7] Stauffer (Hans[6], Christian[5], Daniel[4] Stouffer, Christian[3], Hans[2], Hans[1]) was born 1712 in Muckenhauserhof, Germany, and died 1775. He married **Magdalena Hess** 1735. She was born March 28, 1717, and died 1784.

Children of Henry Stauffer and Magdalena Hess are:
- + 198 i. Elizabeth[8] Stauffer, born December 07, 1735 in Warwick Twp., Lancaster Co, PA; died in Mt. Joy, PA.
- + 199 ii. Christian Stauffer, born December 06, 1736 in Pa.
- 200 iii. Veronica Frena Stauffer, born May 03, 1738 in Pa Westmoreland Co. She married Jacob Berg.
- + 201 iv. Jacob Stauffer, born 1740; died 1793.
- 202 v. Magdalena Stauffer, born March 01, 1742/43 in Pa. She married John Shearer.
- + 203 vi. Abraham Hess Stauffer, born January 07, 1746/47 in Lancaster Pa, Warwick Twp; died March 11, 1809 in Franklin Pa.
- 204 vii. Daniel Stauffer, born September 01, 1749; died September 15, 1818. He married Eva Unknown.
- 205 viii. Barbara Stauffer, born Abt. 1751 in Pa. She married Jacob Ebersole.
- 206 ix. Eva Stauffer, born Abt. 1753. She married John Poorman.
- 207 x. Mary Stauffer, born Abt. 1755. She married Christian Hershberger.
- 208 xi. Peter Stauffer, born Abt. 1757.
- 209 xii. Henry Stauffer, born January 07, 1757.
- 210 xiii. Susanna Stauffer, born Abt. 1759.
- + 211 xiv. Anna Marie Stauffer, born January 24, 1759 in Pa; died Abt. 1789 in Md.

Generation No. 8

77. Abraham H.[8] Risser (Elisabeth[7] Hershey, Christian Stauffer[6], Adelheid Galle[5] Stouffer, Daniel[4], Christian[3], Hans[2], Hans[1]) was born 1755 in Lancaster, PA. He married **Elizabeth Hackman** 1784. She was born 1761, and died 1843.

Child of Abraham Risser and Elizabeth Hackman is:
- + 212 i. Elizabeth H.[9] Risser, born 1789; died 1872.

80. Fanny[8] Herr (Barbara[7] Hershey, Christian Stauffer[6], Adelheid Galle[5] Stouffer, Daniel[4], Christian[3], Hans[2], Hans[1]) was born January 06, 1745/46. She married **(1) Henry Binkley**. She married **(2) Baltzer Shertzer**.

Child of Fanny Herr and Henry Binkley is:
- 213 i. David[9] Binkley, born in Millersville, Lancaster, PA. He married Mary Yordy.

Children of Fanny Herr and Baltzer Shertzer are:
- 214 i. Elizabeth[9] Shertzer.
- 215 ii. Barbara Shertzer.

81. Rudolph[8] Hershey (Christian[7], Christian Stauffer[6], Adelheid Galle[5] Stouffer, Daniel[4], Christian[3], Hans[2], Hans[1]) was born December 30, 1814 in Heidelburg Twp, York, PA, and died December 22, 1862 in Washington Twp, Shelby, OH. He married **Mary Erhart** September 15, 1839 in Montgomery, OH. She was born September 09, 1819 in Montgomery, OH, and died November 02, 1871 in Washington Twp, Shelby, OH.

Children of Rudolph Hershey and Mary Erhart are:
- 216 i. Lavina[9] Hershey, born June 15, 1840 in Butler Twp, Montgomery, OH; died April 26, 1870 in OH.
- 217 ii. Catharine Hershey, born May 10, 1842 in Butler Twp, Montgomery, OH; died December 01, 1874 in Owatonna, Steele, MN.
- 218 iii. Jacob Hershey, born March 09, 1844 in Butler Twp, Montgomery, OH; died October 02, 1922 in DeGraff, OH.
- 219 iv. Christian Hershey, born March 09, 1844 in Butler Twp, Montgomery, OH; died July 28, 1844 in Butler Twp, Montgomery, OH.
- + 220 v. Daniel Webster Hershey, born February 11, 1847 in Butler Twp, Montgomery, OH; died January 27, 1884 in IN.
- 221 vi. Abraham L. Hershey, born May 09, 1849 in Butler Twp, Montgomery, OH; died May 1924.
- 222 vii. Mary Elizabeth Hershey, born December 25, 1853 in Butler Twp, Montgomery, OH; died November 20, 1873 in Butler Twp, Montgomery, OH.

85. Barbara[8] Hershey (Abraham[7], Christian Stauffer[6], Adelheid Galle[5] Stouffer, Daniel[4], Christian[3], Hans[2], Hans[1]) was born March 01, 1769, and died December 09, 1828. She married **David Herr**. He was born 1722, and died January 11, 1772 in Lancaster Co, PA.

Children of Barbara Hershey and David Herr are:
- \+ 223   i. Fanny[9] Herr, born January 19, 1745/46.
- \+ 224   ii. Esther Herr, born July 30, 1750; died 1750.
- \+ 225   iii. Abraham Herr, born October 07, 1751; died November 26, 1823.
- 226   iv. John Herr, born December 30, 1753. He married Anna Hershey.
- \+ 227   v. Esther Herr, born July 18, 1755.
- 228   vi. David Herr, born August 25, 1758; died 1846. He married (1) Susan Yertz. He married (2) Anna Shenk.
- 229   vii. Unnamed Herr, born 1760; died 1760.
- 230   viii. Benjamin Herr, born December 07, 1760; died May 09, 1846. He married Magdalena Lichte April 29, 1794; born 1769; died October 13, 1842.

87. Elizabeth[8] Hershey (Abraham[7], Christian Stauffer[6], Adelheid Galle[5] Stouffer, Daniel[4], Christian[3], Hans[2], Hans[1]) was born Abt. 1772, and died 1857. She married **Christian Erb**.

Child of Elizabeth Hershey and Christian Erb is:
- 231   i. Jacob[9] Erb.

88. Abraham[8] Hershey (Abraham[7], Christian Stauffer[6], Adelheid Galle[5] Stouffer, Daniel[4], Christian[3], Hans[2], Hans[1]) was born March 03, 1774 in Manheim Twp, Lancaster, PA, and died May 06, 1839. He married **Mary Herr**. She was born April 19, 1784, and died March 22, 1855.

Children of Abraham Hershey and Mary Herr are:
- 232   i. Barbara[9] Hershey. She married Daniel Peiffer.
- 233   ii. Elizabeth Hershey, born November 18, 1802; died September 13, 1844.
- 234   iii. David Hershey, born May 19, 1815; died December 22, 1815.
- 235   iv. Esther Hershey, born August 09, 1816; died September 19, 1816.

89. Christian[8] Hershey (Abraham[7], Christian Stauffer[6], Adelheid Galle[5] Stouffer, Daniel[4], Christian[3], Hans[2], Hans[1]) was born January 16, 1777 in Lancaster, PA, and died August 03, 1853 in Lisbon, Linn, IA. He married **Elizabeth Yordy** 1795 in PA. She was born March 15, 1776 in Lampeter Twp, Lancaster, PA, and died September 06, 1863 in Lisbon, Linn, IA.

Children of Christian Hershey and Elizabeth Yordy are:
- 236   i. Catharine[9] Hershey. She married Jonathan Neidig 1833; born April 03, 1811 in Dauphin, PA; died February 20, 1868 in Lancaster, PA.
- \+ 237   ii. Mary Katherine Eby Hershey, born October 30, 1803 in Lancaster, PA; died May 15, 1877 in Lisbon, Linn, IA.
- \+ 238   iii. Nancy Ann Hershey, born December 03, 1805 in PA; died November 03, 1874.
- \+ 239   iv. Abraham Hershey, born 1807 in Mannheim Twp, Lancaster, PA; died June 13, 1864 in Carrollton, LA.
- \+ 240   v. Elizabeth Hershey, born 1812.
- \+ 241   vi. Hester (Esther) Hershey, born June 08, 1815 in Lancaster, PA; died February 04, 1876 in Lisbon, Linn, IA.

99. Henry[8] Hershey (Benjamin[7], Christian Stauffer[6], Adelheid Galle[5] Stouffer, Daniel[4], Christian[3], Hans[2], Hans[1]) was born 1786. He married **Mary House**. She was born 1796.

Children of Henry Hershey and Mary House are:
- 242   i. Elizabeth[9] Hershey, born 1814.
- 243   ii. Catherine Hershey, born 1815.
- 244   iii. Benjamin Hershey, born 1817.
- 245   iv. Henry Hershey, born 1819.
- 246   v. Henry Hershey, born 1821.
- 247   vi. Frederick Hershey, born 1824.
- \+ 248   vii. George Hershey, born August 12, 1826 in Bertie, Lincoln, Ontario, Canada.
- 249   viii. John Hershey, born 1829.
- 250   ix. Margaret Hershey, born 1831.
- \+ 251   x. Mary Hershey, born March 07, 1834 in Bertie Twp, Welland, Ontario, Canada.
- 252   xi. Sarah Hershey, born 1837.
- 253   xii. David Hershey, born 1840.

103. Esther[8] Hershey (Christian[7], Benjamin Stauffer[6], Adelheid Galle[5] Stouffer, Daniel[4], Christian[3], Hans[2], Hans[1]) was born September 14, 1769, and died November 12, 1824. She married **John Hess** 1788, son of John Hess and Susanna Landis. He was born November 09, 1768 in Warwick Twp., Lancaster Co, PA, and died November 27, 1830.

Children of Esther Hershey and John Hess are:
+ 254 i. Christian[9] Hess, born October 11, 1789 in Warwick Twp, Lanc Co, PA; died August 03, 1855.
   255 ii. John Hess, born September 24, 1791; died July 30, 1831.
+ 256 iii. Henry Hess, born January 17, 1794 in Warwick Twp, Lanc Co, PA; died June 13, 1867.
   257 iv. Susanna Hess, born December 29, 1795; died May 28, 1868.
   258 v. Esther Hess, born July 24, 1798; died 1814.
   259 vi. Annie Hess, born October 06, 1800; died September 02, 1870 in near Bitzer's Mill, Earl Twp, Lancaster.
   260 vii. Barbara Hess, born March 18, 1803; died 1811.
+ 261 viii. Martha H. Hess, born July 17, 1805; died April 27, 1861.
   262 ix. Elizabeth Hess, born November 19, 1807 in Warwick Twp, Lanc Co, PA; died January 12, 1839 in Hammer Creek, Lancaster Co, PA, USA.
   263 x. Samuel Hess, born 1810; died 1811.

104. Isaac Hernley[8] Hershey (Christian[7], Benjamin Stauffer[6], Adelheid Galle[5] Stouffer, Daniel[4], Christian[3], Hans[2], Hans[1]) was born February 06, 1773 in Warwick Twp., Lancaster Co, PA, and died January 17, 1831 in Dauphin Co, PA. He married **Anna Hostetter Frantz**, daughter of John Frantz and Elisabeth Hostetter. She was born September 22, 1774 in Lancaster Co, PA, and died August 09, 1861 in Dauphin Co, PA.

Children of Isaac Hershey and Anna Frantz are:
   264 i. Elizabeth[9] Hershey, born January 06, 1799; died October 03, 1867.
+ 265 ii. John Frantz Hershey, born June 28, 1800 in Derry Twp, Dauphin Co, PA; died May 28, 1851 in Derry Twp, Dauphin Co, PA.
+ 266 iii. Jacob Frantz Hershey, born September 22, 1802; died May 15, 1877.
+ 267 iv. Samuel Hershey, born 1804; died February 27, 1885.
   268 v. Mary Hershey, born November 04, 1806; died January 16, 1869.
   269 vi. Isaac Hershey, born June 25, 1809; died September 01, 1879. He married Mary Landis; born January 10, 1810; died February 18, 1900.
+ 270 vii. Christian Hershey, born December 24, 1812 in Derry Twp, Dauphin Co, PA; died May 06, 1875.
   271 viii. Nancy Hershey, born July 07, 1815; died September 18, 1867.

107. Jacob[8] Hershey (Christian[7], Benjamin Stauffer[6], Adelheid Galle[5] Stouffer, Daniel[4], Christian[3], Hans[2], Hans[1]) was born December 13, 1747, and died October 12, 1819. He married **Elizabeth Eby**, daughter of Christian Eby and Elizabeth Mayer. She was born August 12, 1751, and died January 21, 1835.

Children of Jacob Hershey and Elizabeth Eby are:
+ 272 i. Anna[9] Hershey, born July 27, 1779; died January 09, 1864.
+ 273 ii. Susanna Hershey, born November 08, 1785; died February 08, 1858.

108. Barbara Hostetter[8] Hershey (Christian[7], Benjamin Stauffer[6], Adelheid Galle[5] Stouffer, Daniel[4], Christian[3], Hans[2], Hans[1]) was born August 22, 1750 in Lancaster Pa, and died July 14, 1795 in Lancaster Pa. She married **Abraham Hess Stauffer**, son of Henry Stauffer and Magdalena Hess. He was born January 07, 1746/47 in Lancaster Pa, Warwick Twp, and died March 11, 1809 in Franklin Pa.

Children of Barbara Hershey and Abraham Stauffer are:
   274 i. Anna[9] Stauffer, born November 16, 1769 in Landcaster Pa; died July 10, 1848 in Franklin Pa.
   275 ii. Magdalena Stauffer, born April 19, 1771 in Lancaster Pa; died December 22, 1851 in Lancaster Pa.
   276 iii. Jacob Stauffer, born May 04, 1773 in Lancaster Pa; died July 03, 1843 in Lancaster Pa. He married Elizabeth Brubaker; born 1773.
+ 277 iv. Abraham Hershey Stauffer, born January 09, 1780 in Warwick Twp., Lancaster Co, PA; died October 21, 1851 in Blair Ontario.
   278 v. John Stauffer, born November 30, 1787 in Lancaster Pa; died July 22, 1867 in Lancaster Pa. He married Hannah Price.
   279 vi. Barbara Stauffer, born August 26, 1790 in Lancaster Pa; died November 05, 1802 in Lancaster Pa.

109. Anna[8] Hostetter (Ann Elisabeth[7] Hershey, Benjamin Stauffer[6], Adelheid Galle[5] Stouffer, Daniel[4], Christian[3], Hans[2], Hans[1]) She married **Abraham Herr**.

Children of Anna Hostetter and Abraham Herr are:
- 280   i.   Abraham[9] Herr.
- 281   ii. Barbara Herr, born 1764.
- 282   iii. Christian Herr, born 1767.
- 283   iv. Mary Herr, born 1769.
- 284   v.   Elisabeth Herr, born 1772.
- 285   vi. Anna Herr, born 1776.
- 286   vii. Esther Herr, born 1779.

110. Elisabeth Maria[8] Hostetter (Ann Elisabeth[7] Hershey, Benjamin Stauffer[6], Adelheid Galle[5] Stouffer, Daniel[4], Christian[3], Hans[2], Hans[1]) was born Abt. 1750. She married **John Frantz**, son of John Frantz and Catharine Unknown. He was born December 15, 1749, and died October 1821 in Warwick Twp, Lancaster County, Pa.

Children of Elisabeth Hostetter and John Frantz are:
- + 287   i.   Jacob[9] Frantz, born March 01, 1773; died 1840.
- + 288   ii. Anna Hostetter Frantz, born September 22, 1774 in Lancaster Co, PA; died August 09, 1861 in Dauphin Co, PA.
- + 289   iii. John Frantz, born March 13, 1778.
-   290   iv. Elisabeth Frantz, born November 02, 1780.
-   291   v.   Barbara Frantz, born November 09, 1784.
-   292   vi. Christian H Frantz, born December 17, 1786.
-   293   vii. Maria Frantz, born June 12, 1788.

111. Esther[8] Hostetter (Ann Elisabeth[7] Hershey, Benjamin Stauffer[6], Adelheid Galle[5] Stouffer, Daniel[4], Christian[3], Hans[2], Hans[1]) She married **John Reist**. He was born 1758, and died 1815.

Children of Esther Hostetter and John Reist are:
- 294   i.   John[9] Reist.
- 295   ii. Esther Reist.
- 296   iii. Annie Reist.
- 297   iv. Maria Reist.

112. Maria[8] Hostetter (Ann Elisabeth[7] Hershey, Benjamin Stauffer[6], Adelheid Galle[5] Stouffer, Daniel[4], Christian[3], Hans[2], Hans[1]) She married **Isaac Hernley**.

Children of Maria Hostetter and Isaac Hernley are:
- 298   i.   John[9] Hernley.
- 299   ii. Abraham Hernley.

113. Jacob[8] Hostetter (Ann Elisabeth[7] Hershey, Benjamin Stauffer[6], Adelheid Galle[5] Stouffer, Daniel[4], Christian[3], Hans[2], Hans[1]) was born September 11, 1745 in Lancaster County, Pa, and died February 12, 1826 in Manheim, Pa. He married **Maria Metzler** June 24, 1770 in Lancaster County, Pa. She was born November 05, 1750 in Lancaster County, Pa, and died December 27, 1822 in Manheim, Pa.

Children of Jacob Hostetter and Maria Metzler are:
-   300   i.   Joseph[9] Hostetter.
- + 301   ii.   Anna Hostetter, born June 13, 1772.
- + 302   iii. Jacob Hostetter, born August 13, 1774 in Manheim, Pa; died April 06, 1865 in Manheim, Pa.
- + 303   iv.   Abraham Hostetter, born December 20, 1777 in Manheim, Pa; died February 24, 1831 in Manheim, Pa.
-   304   v.   Maria Hostetter, born November 26, 1780. She married Christian Miller.
-   305   vi.   Elisabeth Hostetter, born April 06, 1783.
- + 306   vii. Barbara Hostetter, born February 11, 1786; died January 15, 1845.
- + 307   viii. Barbara Hostetter.
-   308   ix.   Anna Hostetter. She married Johannes Snyder.
-   309   x.   Maria Hostetter. She married Christian Miller.
- + 310   xi.   Jacob Hostetter, born August 13, 1774; died April 09, 1865.
- + 311   xii. Abraham Hostetter, born 1777; died 1831.

114. Barbara[8] Hostetter (Ann Elisabeth[7] Hershey, Benjamin Stauffer[6], Adelheid Galle[5] Stouffer, Daniel[4], Christian[3], Hans[2], Hans[1]) was born October 28, 1752, and died October 04, 1791. She married **Jacob Frantz**, son of John Frantz and Catharine Unknown. He was born September 25, 1755, and died May 14, 1799.

Children of Barbara Hostetter and Jacob Frantz are:
+ 312   i. Anna[9] Frantz, born February 23, 1779; died 1850.
    313   ii. John Frantz, born September 1781.
    314   iii. Jacob Frantz, born January 09, 1786.

115. Benjamin[8] Hostetter (Ann Elisabeth[7] Hershey, Benjamin Stauffer[6], Adelheid Galle[5] Stouffer, Daniel[4], Christian[3], Hans[2], Hans[1]) was born March 12, 1755 in Lancaster County, Pa, and died February 11, 1844 in Manor Twp, Lancaster County, Pa. He married **Magdalena Wissler**. She was born July 11, 1759.

Children of Benjamin Hostetter and Magdalena Wissler are:
    315   i. Maria[9] Hostetter.
    316   ii. Anna Hostetter.
    317   iii. Magdalena Hostetter.
    318   iv. Catharine Hostetter.
    319   v. Esther Hostetter.
+ 320   vi. Rudolph Hostetter, born January 01, 1789 in Lancaster County, Pa; died September 13, 1844 in Lancaster County, Pa.
+ 321   vii. Benjamin Hostetter, born October 16, 1796 in Lancaster County, Pa; died March 22, 1858 in Lancaster County, Pa.

116. Abraham[8] Hostetter (Ann Elisabeth[7] Hershey, Benjamin Stauffer[6], Adelheid Galle[5] Stouffer, Daniel[4], Christian[3], Hans[2], Hans[1]) was born October 12, 1763 in Lancaster County, Pa, and died January 19, 1834 in Manor Twp, Lancaster Cty, Pa. He married **Ann Hiestand**. She was born November 28, 1769, and died September 06, 1841 in Lancaster County, Pa.

Children of Abraham Hostetter and Ann Hiestand are:
    322   i. Jacob[9] Hostetter.
+ 323   ii. Elisabeth Hostetter, born May 13, 1799 in lancaster County, Pa; died November 04, 1841 in lancaster County, Pa.

121. Barbara[8] Hostetter (Ann Elisabeth[7] Hershey, Benjamin Stauffer[6], Adelheid Galle[5] Stouffer, Daniel[4], Christian[3], Hans[2], Hans[1]) was born 1752, and died 1844. She married **Jacob Frantz**, son of John Frantz and Catharine Unknown. He was born September 25, 1755, and died May 14, 1799.

Child of Barbara Hostetter and Jacob Frantz is:
+ 324   i. Jacob Hostetter[9] Frantz, born January 09, 1789; died January 30, 1860.

123. Abraham[8] Hostetter (Ann Elisabeth[7] Hershey, Benjamin Stauffer[6], Adelheid Galle[5] Stouffer, Daniel[4], Christian[3], Hans[2], Hans[1]) was born 1763, and died 1834. He married **Ann Heistand**.

Children of Abraham Hostetter and Ann Heistand are:
    325   i. Elizabeth[9] Hostetter. She married Mathias Groff.
    326   ii. Jacob Hostetter. He married Anna Swarr.

132. David[8] Mellinger (Mary[7] Hershey, Benjamin Stauffer[6], Adelheid Galle[5] Stouffer, Daniel[4], Christian[3], Hans[2], Hans[1]) was born December 01, 1760. He married **Ann Newcomer**.

Child of David Mellinger and Ann Newcomer is:
+ 327   i. David[9] Mellinger, born April 19, 1809.

134. John[8] Mellinger (Mary[7] Hershey, Benjamin Stauffer[6], Adelheid Galle[5] Stouffer, Daniel[4], Christian[3], Hans[2], Hans[1]) was born July 13, 1764, and died September 21, 1844. He married **Elizabeth Dills**. She was born February 08, 1762, and died August 12, 1825.

Children of John Mellinger and Elizabeth Dills are:
    328   i. Benjamin[9] Mellinger, born October 22, 1785 in Indiantown, Lancaster, PA; died June 04, 1862.
    329   ii. John Mellinger, born October 19, 1790; died September 12, 1885.
    330   iii. Christian Mellinger, born November 11, 1792; died August 29, 1849.
    331   iv. David Mellinger, born February 1795; died April 09, 1878.
    332   v. Henry Mellinger, born January 20, 1797; died February 27, 1879.
+ 333   vi. Martin Mellinger, born May 11, 1800; died August 18, 1888.
    334   vii. Jacob Mellinger, born 1803; died April 1888.

335 viii. Elizabeth Mellinger, born March 01, 1806.

149. Anna[8] Kreider (Susanna[7] Long, Anna[6] Hershey, Adelheid Galle[5] Stouffer, Daniel[4], Christian[3], Hans[2], Hans[1]) was born 1778. She married **Joseph Dohner**. He was born 1774 in Dauphin, PA, and died 1848.

Children of Anna Kreider and Joseph Dohner are:
- 336   i.   Susan[9] Dohner, born 1792.
- 337   ii.   John Dohner, born 1794.
- 338   iii.   Joseph Dohner, born 1796.
- \+ 339   iv.   Mary Elizabeth Dohner, born 1797; died Abt. 1832.
- 340   v.   Susannah Dohner, born 1798.
- 341   vi.   Jacob Dohner, born 1806.
- \+ 342   vii.   Moses Dohner, born 1808; died June 04, 1850 in West Milton, OH.
- 343   viii.   Catherine Dohner, born 1810.
- 344   ix.   Elizabeth Dohner, born 1812.
- 345   x.   Lydia Dohner, born 1814.

150. Henry[8] Hostetter (Catharine[7] Long, Anna[6] Hershey, Adelheid Galle[5] Stouffer, Daniel[4], Christian[3], Hans[2], Hans[1]) He married **Maria Erb**, daughter of Christian Erb and Anna Bomberger. She was born 1785.

Children of Henry Hostetter and Maria Erb are:
- 346   i.   John[9] Hostetter.
- 347   ii.   Rachel Hostetter.
- 348   iii.   Polly Hostetter.
- 349   iv.   Sarah Hostetter.
- 350   v.   Catherine Hostetter.
- 351   vi.   Elisabeth Hostetter.
- 352   vii.   Christian Hostetter.
- 353   viii.   Anna Hostetter.
- \+ 354   ix.   George Hostetter, born March 03, 1799 in Lancaster County, Pa; died in Ohio.

151. Abraham[8] Hostetter (Catharine[7] Long, Anna[6] Hershey, Adelheid Galle[5] Stouffer, Daniel[4], Christian[3], Hans[2], Hans[1]) was born in Manor Twp Lancaster County, Pa, and died in Lancaster County, Pa. He married **Elisabeth Strickler**. She was born 1777.

Children of Abraham Hostetter and Elisabeth Strickler are:
- 355   i.   Abraham[9] Hostetter.
- \+ 356   ii.   John Hostetter, born January 26, 1791 in Lancaster County, Pa; died October 05, 1866 in Adams Cty, PA.
- \+ 357   iii.   Ulrich Hostetter, born November 12, 1793 in Lancaster County, Pa; died March 15, 1866 in Lancaster County, Pa.

152. Jacob[8] Hostetter (Catharine[7] Long, Anna[6] Hershey, Adelheid Galle[5] Stouffer, Daniel[4], Christian[3], Hans[2], Hans[1]) was born 1752 in Manor Twp, Lancaster County, Pa, and died 1823 in Hempfield Twp, Lancaster County, Pa. He married **Barbara Funk**. She was born 1755 in Lancaster County, Pa, and died 1828 in Lancaster County, Pa.

Children of Jacob Hostetter and Barbara Funk are:
- 358   i.   Catherine[9] Hostetter.
- 359   ii.   Elisabeth Hostetter, born 1776.
- \+ 360   iii.   Abraham Hostetter, born January 26, 1777 in Lancaster County, Pa; died April 13, 1843 in Lancaster County, Pa.
- 361   iv.   Anna Hostetter, born 1779.
- 362   v.   Barbara Hostetter, born 1781.
- 363   vi.   Maria Hostetter, born 1783.
- \+ 364   vii.   Magdalena Hostetter, born December 01, 1789; died 1829.
- \+ 365   viii.   Jacob Hostetter, born 1791 in Lancaster County, Pa; died 1859.
- \+ 366   ix.   Susanna Hostetter, born February 21, 1797 in Lancaster County, Pa; died 1874 in Lancaster County, Pa.
- 367   x.   Elizabeth Hostetter. She married Jacob Shenk.
- 368   xi.   Barbara Hostetter. She married Christian Shenk.
- 369   xii.   Anna Hostetter. She married Christian Weldy.
- 370   xiii.   Maria Hostetter. She married Christian Smith.
- 371   xiv.   Catherine Hostetter. She married Jacob Rohrer.

372	xv.	Magdalena Hostetter. She married Martin Kreider.
373	xvi.	Susanna Hostetter. She married John Summy.
+ 374	xvii.	Abraham Hostetter, born June 02, 1777; died April 13, 1843.
+ 375	xviii.	Jacob Hostetter, born 1791; died 1859.

153. Herman[8] Hostetter (Catharine[7] Long, Anna[6] Hershey, Adelheid Galle[5] Stouffer, Daniel[4], Christian[3], Hans[2], Hans[1]) was born October 02, 1753 in Lancaster County, Pa, and died December 10, 1812 in Canada. He married **(1) Ann Newman Kennedy**. She was born August 14, 1757, and died January 03, 1851 in Canada. He married **(2) Ann Newman Kennedy**.

Children of Herman Hostetter and Ann Kennedy are:

376	i.	Deborah[9] Hostetter. She married Thomas Gilleland.
+ 377	ii.	Catherine Hostetter, born 1784 in Shelburne, Nova Scotia; died 1828 in Canada.
+ 378	iii.	Abraham Hostetter, born 1786 in Nova Scotia; died September 07, 1868 in Grantham Twp, Canada.
+ 379	iv.	Ann Hostetter, born April 14, 1786 in Shelburne, Nova Scotia; died June 01, 1850 in Niagara Township, Canada.
+ 380	v.	Elisabeth Hostetter, born 1790; died 1862 in Canada.
+ 381	vi.	Jacob Hostetter, born 1792 in Canada; died 1854 in Canada.
382	vii.	Mary Hostetter, born 1794.
383	viii.	Sarah Hostetter, born 1797. She married John Gilleland.
384	ix.	Rebecca Hostetter, born 1799. She married Jeremiah Forrester.
385	x.	Charlotte Hostetter, born 1803.
+ 386	xi.	Herman Hostetter, born 1805 in Canada; died 1871 in Canada.

Children of Herman Hostetter and Ann Kennedy are:

387	i.	Catherine[9] Hostetter. She married William Westover; born October 13, 1769 in Sheffield, Massachusetts; died 1836 in Canada.
388	ii.	Ann Hostetter. She married Frederick Goring.
389	iii.	Elizabeth Hostetter. She married Jacob Ball; born 1777; died 1820.
390	iv.	Jacob Hostetter.
391	v.	Mary Hostetter. She married William Miller.
392	vi.	Charlotte Hostetter. She married Lewis Travers.
393	vii.	Herman Hostetter.
+ 394	viii.	Abraham Hostetter, born 1753; died 1868.

154. John[8] Hostetter (Catharine[7] Long, Anna[6] Hershey, Adelheid Galle[5] Stouffer, Daniel[4], Christian[3], Hans[2], Hans[1]) was born October 28, 1754 in Manor Twp, Lancaster Cty, Pa, and died May 06, 1818 in Manor Twp, Lancaster County, Pa. He married **(1) Magdalena Resh**. She was born February 13, 1755, and died May 31, 1841.

Children of John Hostetter and Magdalena Resh are:

+ 395	i.	Maria[9] Hostetter.
+ 396	ii.	Anna Hostetter, born September 26, 1796; died September 28, 1884.
397	iii.	Magdalena Hostetter.
398	iv.	Barbara Hostetter.
399	v.	Susanna Hostetter.
400	vi.	Catherine Hostetter.
+ 401	vii.	Abraham Hostetter, born September 15, 1779 in Lancaster County, Pa; died February 13, 1858 in Lancaster County, Pa.
+ 402	viii.	John Hostetter, born January 16, 1787 in Manor Twp, Lancaster Cty, PA; died September 24, 1854 in Lancaster County, Pa.

155. Anna[8] Hostetter (Catharine[7] Long, Anna[6] Hershey, Adelheid Galle[5] Stouffer, Daniel[4], Christian[3], Hans[2], Hans[1]) was born September 1757, and died March 1821. She married **Christian Herr**. He was born December 25, 1753, and died March 21, 1821.

Children of Anna Hostetter and Christian Herr are:

403	i.	Catherine[9] Herr.
404	ii.	David Herr.
405	iii.	Christian Herr.
406	iv.	Anna Herr.
407	v.	Abraham Herr.

156. Christian[8] Hostetter (Catharine[7] Long, Anna[6] Hershey, Adelheid Galle[5] Stouffer, Daniel[4], Christian[3], Hans[2], Hans[1]) was born 1762, and died 1838 in Warwick Twp Lancaster Cty, Pa. He married **Barbara Reist**. She was born 1763, and died 1838.

Children of Christian Hostetter and Barbara Reist are:
- \+ 408   i. John[9] Hostetter, born August 16, 1788 in Lancaster County, Pa; died September 02, 1879 in Lebanon Cty, PA.
- \+ 409   ii. Daniel Hostetter, born January 09, 1791 in Lancaster County, Pa; died January 25, 1824 in Lancaster County, Pa.
- \+ 410   iii. Jacob Hostetter, born February 20, 1794 in Lancaster County, Pa; died February 04, 1863 in Lancaster County, Pa.
- 411   iv. Henry Hostetter, born 1796.
- 412   v. Christian Hostetter, born 1800.
- \+ 413   vi. Isaac Hostetter, born November 30, 1810 in Lancaster County, Pa; died March 02, 1861 in Ohio.

157. Barbara[8] Hostetter (Catharine[7] Long, Anna[6] Hershey, Adelheid Galle[5] Stouffer, Daniel[4], Christian[3], Hans[2], Hans[1]) was born Abt. 1760. She married **Henry Schenk**, son of John Schenk and Barbara Gingrich. He was born January 14, 1756, and died September 13, 1853 in Manor Twp, Lancaster Cty, PA.

Children of Barbara Hostetter and Henry Schenk are:
- 414   i. Abraham[9] Schenk.
- 415   ii. Christian Schenk.
- 416   iii. Elisabeth Schenk.
- 417   iv. Henry Schenk.
- 418   v. John Schenk.

158. Abraham[8] Hostetter (Catharine[7] Long, Anna[6] Hershey, Adelheid Galle[5] Stouffer, Daniel[4], Christian[3], Hans[2], Hans[1]) died 1834. He married **Elizabeth Strickler**.

Children of Abraham Hostetter and Elizabeth Strickler are:
- \+ 419   i. John[9] Hostetter, born 1791; died 1866.
- 420   ii. Abraham Hostetter, born 1792; died 1871. He married Veronica Schock.

162. John[8] Hostetter (Catharine[7] Long, Anna[6] Hershey, Adelheid Galle[5] Stouffer, Daniel[4], Christian[3], Hans[2], Hans[1]) was born 1754, and died 1854. He married **Magdalena Resh**. She was born February 13, 1755, and died May 31, 1841.

Children of John Hostetter and Magdalena Resh are:
- \+ 421   i. Abraham[9] Hostetter.
- \+ 422   ii. John Hostetter.
- 423   iii. Catherine Hostetter. She married John Markley.
- 424   iv. Barbara Hostetter. She married Martin Kreider.
- 425   v. Susanna Hostetter. She married John Herr.
- 426   vi. Magdalena Hostetter.
- 427   vii. Anna Hostetter. She married Rudolph Herr; born May 10, 1801; died March 23, 1888.
- 428   viii. Maria Hostetter. She married Abraham Strickler; born July 26, 1769; died February 20, 1830.

163. Christian[8] Hostetter (Catharine[7] Long, Anna[6] Hershey, Adelheid Galle[5] Stouffer, Daniel[4], Christian[3], Hans[2], Hans[1]) was born 1762, and died 1838. He married **Barbara Reist**.

Children of Christian Hostetter and Barbara Reist are:
- 429   i. Christian[9] Hostetter. He married Esther Overholtzer.
- 430   ii. Henry Hostetter. He married Susan good.
- \+ 431   iii. Jacob Hostetter.
- \+ 432   iv. John Hostetter, born 1788; died 1879.

166. Jacob[8] Hershey (Andrew[7], Andrew Stauffer[6], Adelheid Galle[5] Stouffer, Daniel[4], Christian[3], Hans[2], Hans[1]) was born October 02, 1765, and died May 30, 1821.

Children of Jacob Hershey are:
- 433   i. Jacob[9] Hershey.
- 434   ii. John Hershey.
- 435   iii. Benjamin Hershey.

436 iv. Henry Hershey.
437 v. Anna Hershey.
438 vi. Elizabeth Hershey.
+ 439 vii. Andreas Hershey, born December 16, 1795; died March 23, 1837.

168. Andrew[8] Hershey (Andrew[7], Andrew Stauffer[6], Adelheid Galle[5] Stouffer, Daniel[4], Christian[3], Hans[2], Hans[1]) was born September 14, 1770, and died August 01, 1835. He married **Esther Kauffman**. She was born May 31, 1776, and died March 03, 1829.

Children of Andrew Hershey and Esther Kauffman are:
440 i. Christian[9] Hershey, born December 28, 1796; died September 05, 1834.
441 ii. Anna Hershey, born July 15, 1799; died June 27, 1874.
442 iii. Andrew Hershey, born January 15, 1802; died December 31, 1839.
443 iv. Maria Hershey, born December 09, 1804.
444 v. Catherine Hershey, born January 15, 1809; died January 15, 1872.
445 vi. Esther Hershey, born September 11, 1811; died March 09, 1848.
446 vii. Barbara Hershey, born December 09, 1814.
447 viii. Elizabeth Hershey, born December 09, 1814; died December 30, 1825.
448 ix. John Hershey, born March 14, 1818; died October 07, 1821.
449 x. Magdalena Hershey, born March 20, 1821; died November 01, 1861.

172. Anna[8] Hershey (John[7], Andrew Stauffer[6], Adelheid Galle[5] Stouffer, Daniel[4], Christian[3], Hans[2], Hans[1]) was born February 23, 1765 in Lancaster, PA, and died February 18, 1850 in Cumberland, PA. She married **Johannes Shopp** 1786. He was born 1761.

Child of Anna Hershey and Johannes Shopp is:
450 i. Christian[9] Shopp.

173. John[8] Hershey (Jacob Snavely[7], Andrew Stauffer[6], Adelheid Galle[5] Stouffer, Daniel[4], Christian[3], Hans[2], Hans[1]) was born May 21, 1772 in Derry Twp, Dauphin Co, PA, and died November 23, 1850. He married **(1) Anna Horst**. He married **(2) Anna Horst** March 20, 1802, daughter of John Horst and Ann Strickler. She was born October 03, 1778 in Leacock Twp., Lancaster Co., Pa., and died August 28, 1861.

Children of John Hershey and Anna Horst are:
+ 451 i. Jacob[9] Hershey, born May 09, 1803 in Lancaster, PA; died July 12, 1883 in Paradise Twp, Lancaster, PA.
452 ii. Fronica Hershey, born 1808 in Lancaster, PA; died 1881.
453 iii. John Hershey, born 1810 in Lancaster, PA; died 1869.
454 iv. Benjamin Hershey, born 1812 in Lancaster, PA; died 1875.
455 v. Joseph Hershey, born 1916 in Lancaster, PA; died 1891.

Children of John Hershey and Anna Horst are:
+ 456 i. Jacob[9] Hershey, born March 09, 1803 in Paradise Twp., Lancaster Co., PA; died July 12, 1883 in Paradise Twp., Lancaster Co., PA.
457 ii. Magdalena Hershey, born August 15, 1804 in Lancaster Co, PA; died July 04, 1857. She married Joseph Snavely; born 1801; died 1871.
+ 458 iii. Nancy Ann Hershey, born October 22, 1805; died September 13, 1885.
+ 459 iv. Veronica Hershey, born August 31, 1808 in Leacock Twp., Lancaster Co., Pa.; died March 19, 1881 in East Earl Twp., Lancaster Co., Pa..
460 v. John Hershey, born October 01, 1810 in Salisbury township, Lancaster, PA, USA; died March 19, 1869 in Rohrerstown, Lancaster Co., PA. He married Margaret Musser; born September 06, 1807 in Lancaster Co, PA; died February 24, 1862 in Lancaster Co, PA.
461 vi. Benjamin Hershey, born April 12, 1812 in Lancaster Co, PA; died February 22, 1875. He married Veronica Musser; born October 26, 1811; died March 15, 1890.
+ 462 vii. Joseph Hershey, born November 20, 1816; died July 17, 1891.

175. Christian[8] Hershey (Jacob Snavely[7], Andrew Stauffer[6], Adelheid Galle[5] Stouffer, Daniel[4], Christian[3], Hans[2], Hans[1]) was born June 20, 1780, and died August 05, 1843. He married **Susanna Hershey**, daughter of Jacob Hershey and Elizabeth Eby. She was born November 08, 1785, and died February 08, 1858.

Children of Christian Hershey and Susanna Hershey are:
+ 463 i. Nancy[9] Hershey, born January 22, 1808; died September 03, 1869.
464 ii. Benjamin Hershey, born July 18, 1809.

	465	iii.	Jacob L Hershey, born May 03, 1811.
+	466	iv.	Jacob Hershey, born November 27, 1812; died August 24, 1889.
	467	v.	Christian Hershey, born May 07, 1813.
	468	vi.	John Hershey, born April 17, 1815.
	469	vii.	Elizabeth Hershey, born September 16, 1817.
+	470	viii.	Abraham Hershey, born August 16, 1819; died December 18, 1886.
	471	ix.	Susanna Hershey, born July 06, 1822.

177. Abraham[8] Hershey (Jacob Snavely[7], Andrew Stauffer[6], Adelheid Galle[5] Stouffer, Daniel[4], Christian[3], Hans[2], Hans[1]) was born January 24, 1787 in Derry Twp, Dauphin Co, PA, and died January 09, 1844. He married **(1) Maria Siegrist**. She was born 1794, and died January 22, 1820. He married **(2) Anna Eby**. She was born December 15, 1800, and died February 29, 1896.

Child of Abraham Hershey and Anna Eby is:

+	472	i.	Peter E.[9] Hershey, born February 05, 1826; died August 31, 1911.

181. Elizabeth[8] Hershey (Abraham[7], Andrew Stauffer[6], Adelheid Galle[5] Stouffer, Daniel[4], Christian[3], Hans[2], Hans[1]) was born August 20, 1780. She married **John Frantz**, son of John Frantz and Elisabeth Hostetter. He was born March 13, 1778.

Child of Elizabeth Hershey and John Frantz is:

+	473	i.	Elizabeth[9] Frantz, born March 13, 1816; died September 13, 1863.

182. Martin[8] Hershey (Henry[7], Andrew Stauffer[6], Adelheid Galle[5] Stouffer, Daniel[4], Christian[3], Hans[2], Hans[1]) was born October 20, 1771, and died August 25, 1825 in near Bindnagle's Church, Dauphin Co, PA. He married **(1) Catharine Windsor**. He married **(2) Elizabeth Landis**. She was born May 25, 1781, and died September 27, 1811. He married **(3) Catharine Denninger**.

Children of Martin Hershey and Elizabeth Landis are:

	474	i.	John[9] Hershey, born September 27, 1799 in Derry Twp, Dauphin Co, PA.
+	475	ii.	Henry Hershey, born September 01, 1803; died January 13, 1854.
	476	iii.	Jacob Hershey, born October 12, 1807.
	477	iv.	Joseph Hershey, born December 03, 1809.
	478	v.	Isaac Hershey, born September 16, 1805. He married Anna Abt. 1840.
	479	vi.	Martin Hershey, born August 20, 1801.
	480	vii.	John Hershey, born September 27, 1799 in Derry Twp, Dauphin Co, PA.
+	481	viii.	Henry Hershey, born September 01, 1803; died January 13, 1854 in Hummelstown, PA.
	482	ix.	Jacob Hershey, born October 12, 1807.
	483	x.	Joseph Hershey, born December 03, 1809.

183. Anna Barbara[8] Stauffer (Johannes[7], Daniel[6] Stouffer, Christian[5] Stauffer, Daniel[4] Stouffer, Christian[3], Hans[2], Hans[1]) was born August 1739, and died February 02, 1808. She married **(1) John Ebersole**. He died June 10, 1802. She married **(2) John Hostetter** WFT Est. 1752-1773. He was born WFT Est. 1705-1738 in Londonderry Twp, Lancaster Co, and died February 27, 1777 in Lancaster Co, Pa..

Child of Anna Stauffer and John Hostetter is:

+	484	i.	Christiana[9] Hastetter, born Abt. 1752; died Bef. 1806.

184. Elizabeth[8] Stauffer (Johannes[7], Daniel[6] Stouffer, Christian[5] Stauffer, Daniel[4] Stouffer, Christian[3], Hans[2], Hans[1]) was born August 09, 1741 in Warwick Twp., Lancaster Cty., PA, and died 1777. She married **Jacob Ober** WFT Est. 1753-1783, son of Jacob Ober. He was born 1729 in aboard the Martonhouse en route to America, and died 1804 in Rapho Twp., Lancaster Cty., PA.

Children of Elizabeth Stauffer and Jacob Ober are:

+	485	i.	Peter[9] Ober, born WFT Est. 1758-1776; died WFT Est. 1791-1861.
+	486	ii.	Christian Ober, born September 29, 1762 in Running Pump, W. Donegal Twp., Lancaster Co., PA; died November 27, 1840.
+	487	iii.	Henry Ober, born 1771; died March 03, 1839 in W. Donegal Twp., Lancaster Cty., PA.
+	488	iv.	David S Ober, born 1774 in Lancaster, Rapho Township, PA; died 1843 in Lancaster, PA.

185. Veronica " Frany "[8] Stauffer (Johannes[7], Daniel[6] Stouffer, Christian[5] Stauffer, Daniel[4] Stouffer, Christian[3], Hans[2], Hans[1]) was born July 31, 1742, and died WFT Est. 1758-1836. She married **Henry Ober** WFT Est. 1758-1790, son of Jacob Ober. He was born 1742 in Rapho Twp, Lancaster Co, PA, and died July 13, 1822 in Donegal Twp, Lancaster Co, PA.

Children of Veronica Stauffer and Henry Ober are:

+	489	i.	Henry[9] Ober, born 1769; died 1843 in Bedford County, Pennsylvania.
+	490	ii.	Michael Ober, died Abt. 1806.
	491	iii.	Jacob Ober.
+	492	iv.	Peter Ober, died Bef. 1847.
+	493	v.	Christian Ober, born 1765; died 1824.
+	494	vi.	John Ober, born 1767; died 1821.
+	495	vii.	Elizabeth Ober, born 1777; died Bef. 1821.
+	496	viii.	Veronica Ober, born January 19, 1784; died April 23, 1856.
+	497	ix.	Benjamin Ober, born Abt. 1786; died April 22, 1839.

198. Elizabeth[8] Stauffer (Henry Jacob[7], Hans[6], Christian[5], Daniel[4] Stouffer, Christian[3], Hans[2], Hans[1]) was born December 07, 1735 in Warwick Twp., Lancaster Co, PA, and died in Mt. Joy, PA. She married **(1) Abraham Hackman**. He was born Abt. 1730 in Warwick Twp., Lancaster Co, PA. She married **(2) ABRAHAM HERR HACKMAN**. He was born 1733 in Ibersheim, Germany, and died 1776 in York County, PA.

Children of Elizabeth Stauffer and ABRAHAM HACKMAN are:

	498	i.	Christian Stauffer[9] Hackman.
+	499	ii.	Henry Stauffer (Hockman) Hackman, born 1760 in Warwick Township, Lancaster County, Pennsylvania; died March 17, 1831 in Shenandoah County, Virginia.
+	500	iii.	Abraham Hackman, born Abt. 1770.
	501	iv.	Samuel Hackman, born Abt. 1773.
	502	v.	John Hackman, born Abt. 1776.

199. Christian[8] Stauffer (Henry Jacob[7], Hans[6], Christian[5], Daniel[4] Stouffer, Christian[3], Hans[2], Hans[1]) was born December 06, 1736 in Pa. He married **(1) Veronica Poorman**. He married **(2) Anna Eby**, daughter of Christian Eby and Elizabeth Mayer. She was born January 04, 1744/45, and died January 30, 1826 in Elizabeth Twp Lancaster Co, PA.

Child of Christian Stauffer and Veronica Poorman is:
    503   i.   Barbara[9] Stauffer. She married Michael Schenk.

Child of Christian Stauffer and Anna Eby is:
+   504   i.   Elizabeth[9] Stauffer, born October 01, 1765 in Donegal Twp., Lancaster County, Pennsylvania; died March 07, 1828 in Lancaster County, Pennsylvania.

201. Jacob[8] Stauffer (Henry Jacob[7], Hans[6], Christian[5], Daniel[4] Stouffer, Christian[3], Hans[2], Hans[1]) was born 1740, and died 1793. He married **Elizabeth Kuntz**.

Children of Jacob Stauffer and Elizabeth Kuntz are:

	505	i.	Peter[9] Stoffer, born Bet. 1770 - 1773.
+	506	ii.	Jacob Stoffer, born August 09, 1780 in New Castle, Lawrence Co, Penna; died April 1850 in Knox Township, Columbiana County, Ohio.

203. Abraham Hess[8] Stauffer (Henry Jacob[7], Hans[6], Christian[5], Daniel[4] Stouffer, Christian[3], Hans[2], Hans[1]) was born January 07, 1746/47 in Lancaster Pa, Warwick Twp, and died March 11, 1809 in Franklin Pa. He married **(1) Elizabeth Boyer**. She was born August 14, 1760, and died June 15, 1819. He married **(2) Barbara Hostetter Hershey**, daughter of Christian Hershey and Barbara Hostetter. She was born August 22, 1750 in Lancaster Pa, and died July 14, 1795 in Lancaster Pa.

Children are listed above under (108) Barbara Hostetter Hershey.

211. Anna Marie[8] Stauffer (Henry Jacob[7], Hans[6], Christian[5], Daniel[4] Stouffer, Christian[3], Hans[2], Hans[1]) was born January 24, 1759 in Pa, and died Abt. 1789 in Md. She married **Jacob Brunk**. He was born 1730 in Germany, and died 1787 in Md.

Children of Anna Stauffer and Jacob Brunk are:

507	i.	Ann Mary[9] Brunk.
508	ii.	Susanna Brunk.
509	iii.	Elizabeth Brunk.
510	iv.	John Brunk.
511	v.	Jacob Jr Brunk.
512	vi.	Barbara Brunk.
513	vii.	George Brunk.
514	viii.	David Brunk.

Generation No. 9

212. Elizabeth H.⁹ Risser (Abraham H.⁸, Elisabeth⁷ Hershey, Christian Stauffer⁶, Adelheid Galle⁵ Stouffer, Daniel⁴, Christian³, Hans², Hans¹) was born 1789, and died 1872. She married **Benjamin Hoover** 1807. He was born 1784, and died 1872.

Children of Elizabeth Risser and Benjamin Hoover are:
- 517   i.   Benjamin¹⁰ Hoover.
- 518   ii.   Elizabeth R. Hoover.
- 519   iii. Nancy R. Hoover.
- 520   iv.   Stephen R. Hoover.
- 521   v.   Abraham Hoover, born 1808; died 1876.
- 522   vi.   John R. Hoover, born 1809; died 1902.
- 523   vii. Samuel R. Hoover, born 1817; died 1893.
- 524   viii. Esther R. Hoover, born 1820; died 1885.
- 525   ix.   Risser Hoover, born 1827; died 1893.

220. Daniel Webster⁹ Hershey (Rudolph⁸, Christian⁷, Christian Stauffer⁶, Adelheid Galle⁵ Stouffer, Daniel⁴, Christian³, Hans², Hans¹) was born February 11, 1847 in Butler Twp, Montgomery, OH, and died January 27, 1884 in IN. He married **Charlotte Elizabeth Gray** February 06, 1873 in Troy, OH. She was born September 09, 1841 in Miami, OH, and died March 14, 1918 in Des Moines, IA.

Children of Daniel Hershey and Charlotte Gray are:
- 526   i.   Mary Clyde¹⁰ Hershey, born November 14, 1873 in Shelby, OH; died December 04, 1951 in Tyler, TX.
- 527   ii.   John Rudy Hershey, born October 02, 1875 in Shelby, OH; died February 28, 1960 in Elwood, IN.
- 528   iii. George Daniel Hershey, born August 18, 1877 in Shelby, OH; died May 02, 1932 in Elwood, IN.
- 529   iv.   Adah Louisa Hershey, born November 28, 1880 in Shelby, OH; died January 08, 1947 in Los Angeles, Los Angeles, CA.
- 530   v.   Cloyd Gray Hershey, born June 18, 1883 in Lease's Corner, Cass, IN; died November 06, 1908 in Boston, MA.

223. Fanny⁹ Herr (Barbara⁸ Hershey, Abraham⁷, Christian Stauffer⁶, Adelheid Galle⁵ Stouffer, Daniel⁴, Christian³, Hans², Hans¹) was born January 19, 1745/46. She married **(1) Henry Binkley**. She married **(2) Baltzer Shertzer**.

Child of Fanny Herr and Henry Binkley is:
- 531   i.   David¹⁰ Binkley, born in Millersville, Lancaster, PA.

Children of Fanny Herr and Baltzer Shertzer are:
- 532   i.   Elizabeth¹⁰ Shertzer.
- 533   ii.   Barbara Shertzer.

224. Esther⁹ Herr (Barbara⁸ Hershey, Abraham⁷, Christian Stauffer⁶, Adelheid Galle⁵ Stouffer, Daniel⁴, Christian³, Hans², Hans¹) was born July 30, 1750, and died 1750. She married **Christian Habecker**. He was born September 17, 1747, and died October 27, 1822.

Children of Esther Herr and Christian Habecker are:
- 534   i.   Esther¹⁰ Habecker.
- 535   ii.   Christian Habecker, born April 05, 1789 in Manor Twp, Lancaster, PA; died November 06, 1860.

225. Abraham⁹ Herr (Barbara⁸ Hershey, Abraham⁷, Christian Stauffer⁶, Adelheid Galle⁵ Stouffer, Daniel⁴, Christian³, Hans², Hans¹) was born October 07, 1751, and died November 26, 1823. He married **Barbara Eshleman**. She was born May 22, 1757, and died September 16, 1839.

Children of Abraham Herr and Barbara Eshleman are:
- 536   i.   Barbara¹⁰ Herr.
- 537   ii.   Abraham Herr.
- 538   iii. Hettie Herr.
- 539   iv.   John Herr.
- 540   v.   Nancy Herr.
- 541   vi.   Mary Herr.

542	vii.	Benjamin Herr, born November 20, 1776; died March 1849.
543	viii.	Elizabeth Herr, born January 18, 1783; died June 28, 1827.
544	ix.	Fanny Herr, born April 13, 1790; died December 05, 1849.

227. Esther[9] Herr (Barbara[8] Hershey, Abraham[7], Christian Stauffer[6], Adelheid Galle[5] Stouffer, Daniel[4], Christian[3], Hans[2], Hans[1]) was born July 18, 1755. She married **Christian Habecker**. He was born September 17, 1747, and died October 27, 1822.

Children of Esther Herr and Christian Habecker are:

545	i.	Esther[10] Habecker.
546	ii.	Christian Habecker, born April 05, 1789 in Manor Twp, Lancaster, PA; died November 06, 1860.

237. Mary Katherine Eby[9] Hershey (Christian[8], Abraham[7], Christian Stauffer[6], Adelheid Galle[5] Stouffer, Daniel[4], Christian[3], Hans[2], Hans[1]) was born October 30, 1803 in Lancaster, PA, and died May 15, 1877 in Lisbon, Linn, IA. She married **(1) John Eby** October 09, 1821. He was born March 07, 1800, and died August 14, 1822. She married **(2) Michael Hoover** February 10, 1826 in Dauphin, PA. He was born July 04, 1803 in Dauphin, PA, and died December 24, 1888 in Lisbon, Linn, IA.

Child of Mary Hershey and John Eby is:

547	i.	John Hershey[10] Eby, born February 13, 1823 in Conestoga Twp, Lancaster, PA; died March 26, 1917 in Newark, NJ.

Children of Mary Hershey and Michael Hoover are:

548	i.	Benjamin[10] Hoover, born April 17, 1827 in Dauphin, PA; died February 01, 1897 in Lisbon, Linn, IA.
549	ii.	Nancy Ann Hoover, born March 24, 1828 in Dauphin, PA; died September 28, 1871 in Muscatine, Muscatine, IA.
550	iii.	Christian Hoover, born June 12, 1830 in PA; died September 28, 1831 in PA.
551	iv.	Henry Hoover, born September 20, 1831 in PA; died February 27, 1882.
552	v.	Jonathan Hoover, born February 27, 1833 in Dauphin, PA; died January 14, 1897 in Lisbon, Linn, IA.
553	vi.	Elizabeth Hoover, born September 26, 1835 in Lancaster, PA; died March 07, 1922 in Lisbon, Linn, IA.
554	vii.	Michael Hoover, born February 29, 1840 in Harrisburg, Dauphin, PA; died May 21, 1928 in Tama, Tama, IA.
555	viii.	Christian H. Hoover, born July 25, 1842 in Lancaster, PA; died April 02, 1901 in Lincoln, NE.
556	ix.	Mary Catherine Hoover, born November 06, 1844 in Conestoga Twp, Lancaster, PA; died August 26, 1922 in Portland, Multnomah, OR.

238. Nancy Ann[9] Hershey (Christian[8], Abraham[7], Christian Stauffer[6], Adelheid Galle[5] Stouffer, Daniel[4], Christian[3], Hans[2], Hans[1]) was born December 03, 1805 in PA, and died November 03, 1874. She married **John Neidig** February 10, 1825 in PA. He was born January 18, 1797 in Dauphin, PA, and died December 20, 1871 in Lisbon, Linn, IA.

Children of Nancy Hershey and John Neidig are:

557	i.	Elizabeth[10] Neidig, born January 31, 1828 in PA; died February 27, 1913.
558	ii.	Christian H. Neidig, born November 24, 1829 in Lancaster, PA; died July 21, 1890 in Mt. Vernon, Linn, IA.

239. Abraham[9] Hershey (Christian[8], Abraham[7], Christian Stauffer[6], Adelheid Galle[5] Stouffer, Daniel[4], Christian[3], Hans[2], Hans[1]) was born 1807 in Mannheim Twp, Lancaster, PA, and died June 13, 1864 in Carrollton, LA. He married **Anna Bassler** April 13, 1831 in Lancaster, PA, daughter of John Bossler and Barbara Hostetter. She was born 1812 in Mannheim Twp, Lancaster, PA, and died April 29, 1886.

Children of Abraham Hershey and Anna Bassler are:

559	i.	Christian B.[10] Hershey, born January 30, 1832; died June 01, 1868.
560	ii.	Elizabeth Hershey, born December 20, 1833; died September 09, 1890.
561	iii.	Barbara Ann Hershey, born August 02, 1834 in Lancaster, PA; died January 02, 1925 in Los Angeles, Los Angeles, CA.
562	iv.	John Hershey, born November 13, 1836 in PA; died September 19, 1913 in Cedar Rapids, Linn, IA.
563	v.	Hester Hershey, born April 30, 1839; died October 1926.
564	vi.	Henry Hershey, born November 25, 1840; died March 07, 1919.
565	vii.	Maria Hershey, born December 11, 1842; died 1858.
566	viii.	Anna Hershey, born June 02, 1846; died September 21, 1850.
567	ix.	Abraham Hershey, born April 21, 1849 in Lisbon, Linn, IA; died 1854.
568	x.	Jacob Hershey, born January 03, 1852; died 1852.
569	xi.	Benjamin Hershey, born January 09, 1853; died March 25, 1927.

570   xii.   Emma Hershey, born March 02, 1867; died 1920.

240. Elizabeth[9] Hershey (Christian[8], Abraham[7], Christian Stauffer[6], Adelheid Galle[5] Stouffer, Daniel[4], Christian[3], Hans[2], Hans[1]) was born 1812. She married **Jacob Brenneman**.

Child of Elizabeth Hershey and Jacob Brenneman is:
571   i.   Amos[10] Breneman, born April 15, 1834 in Lancaster, PA.

241. Hester (Esther)[9] Hershey (Christian[8], Abraham[7], Christian Stauffer[6], Adelheid Galle[5] Stouffer, Daniel[4], Christian[3], Hans[2], Hans[1]) was born June 08, 1815 in Lancaster, PA, and died February 04, 1876 in Lisbon, Linn, IA. She married **John Erb Kurtz** November 08, 1838. He was born September 05, 1817 in Lancaster, PA, and died May 14, 1900 in Lisbon, Linn, IA.

Children of Hester Hershey and John Kurtz are:
572   i.   Christian H.[10] Kurtz, born March 29, 1840 in Lancaster, Lancaster, PA; died July 01, 1925.
573   ii.   John H. Kurtz, born July 25, 1841 in PA; died December 13, 1861.
574   iii.   Barbara Ann Kurtz, born September 06, 1842 in Lancaster, PA; died August 17, 1914 in Linn, IA.
575   iv.   Henry Clay Kurtz, born August 01, 1844 in PA; died September 30, 1920.
576   v.   Abraham Kurtz, born May 10, 1846 in PA.
577   vi.   David Harrison Kurtz, born October 06, 1848 in IA; died November 22, 1928.
578   vii.   Elizabeth Kurtz, born February 05, 1850 in IA.
579   viii.   Mary Kurtz, born April 09, 1852; died February 20, 1857.
580   ix.   Samuel Albert Kurtz, born December 15, 1854 in IA; died October 26, 1937.

248. George[9] Hershey (Henry[8], Benjamin[7], Christian Stauffer[6], Adelheid Galle[5] Stouffer, Daniel[4], Christian[3], Hans[2], Hans[1]) was born August 12, 1826 in Bertie, Lincoln, Ontario, Canada. He married **Sarah Bullock**. She was born March 21, 1830 in Nelson, Halton, Ontario, Canada.

Children of George Hershey and Sarah Bullock are:
581   i.   Emily Jane[10] Hershey, born December 14, 1849 in Nelson, Halton, Ontario, Canada.
582   ii.   Ida Anne Hershey, born October 28, 1851 in Nelson, Halton, Ontario, Canada.
583   iii.   Spencer Hershey, born November 03, 1855 in Nelson, Halton, Ontario, Canada.
584   iv.   Louisa Hershey, born January 13, 1858 in Bertie, Lincoln, Ontario, Canada.
585   v.   Malcolm Clarence Hershey, born January 19, 1873 in Bertie, Lincoln, Ontario, Canada.

251. Mary[9] Hershey (Henry[8], Benjamin[7], Christian Stauffer[6], Adelheid Galle[5] Stouffer, Daniel[4], Christian[3], Hans[2], Hans[1]) was born March 07, 1834 in Bertie Twp, Welland, Ontario, Canada. She married **Peter Learn**. He was born April 20, 1836 in Bertie Twp, Welland, Ontario, Canada.

Children of Mary Hershey and Peter Learn are:
586   i.   Evelyn Hershey[10] Learn, born May 09, 1863 in Bertie Twp, Welland, Ontario, Canada.
587   ii.   Hershey David Learn, born March 12, 1868 in Bertie Twp, Welland, Ontario, Canada.

254. Christian[9] Hess (Esther[8] Hershey, Christian[7], Benjamin Stauffer[6], Adelheid Galle[5] Stouffer, Daniel[4], Christian[3], Hans[2], Hans[1]) was born October 11, 1789 in Warwick Twp, Lanc Co, PA, and died August 03, 1855. He married **Barbara Huber** 1811. She was born September 12, 1791 in Warwick Twp, Lanc Co, PA, and died April 05, 1848.

Children of Christian Hess and Barbara Huber are:
+   588   i.   Joseph H[10] Hess, born September 27, 1824 in Warwick Twp, Lanc Co, PA; died June 13, 1895.
+   589   ii.   Barbara Hess, born December 25, 1829; died March 11, 1901 in Warwick Twp., Lancaster Co., PA.

256. Henry[9] Hess (Esther[8] Hershey, Christian[7], Benjamin Stauffer[6], Adelheid Galle[5] Stouffer, Daniel[4], Christian[3], Hans[2], Hans[1]) was born January 17, 1794 in Warwick Twp, Lanc Co, PA, and died June 13, 1867. He married **Catherine Huber** November 22, 1814. She was born September 28, 1796 in Warwick Twp, Lanc Co, PA, and died September 19, 1879.

Child of Henry Hess and Catherine Huber is:
+   590   i.   Samuel H[10] Hess, born November 19, 1830 in Elizabeth Twp Lancaster Co, PA; died December 10, 1871 in Willow Bank Mills, Elizabeth Twp., Lancaster Co., PA.

261. Martha H.[9] Hess (Esther[8] Hershey, Christian[7], Benjamin Stauffer[6], Adelheid Galle[5] Stouffer, Daniel[4], Christian[3], Hans[2], Hans[1]) was born July 17, 1805, and died April 27, 1861. She married **Samuel Oberholtzer** May 1824. He was born December 25, 1802, and died June 10, 1875.

Children of Martha Hess and Samuel Oberholtzer are:

    591   i.   Esther H.[10] Oberholtzer, born February 25, 1825; died April 13, 1865. She married Michael Martin; born August 29, 1823; died October 17, 1875.

    592   ii.   Jacob H. Oberholtzer, born June 25, 1826; died May 21, 1888. He married Maria Hostetter; born May 16, 1830; died February 07, 1882.

+   593   iii.   Martha H. Oberholtzer, born August 03, 1828; died June 05, 1869.

+   594   iv.   Catharine Oberholtzer, born September 26, 1830; died July 17, 1918.

    595   v.   Elizabeth H. Oberholtzer, born September 22, 1832; died April 24, 1877. She married Christian Nolt; born December 03, 1831; died January 26, 1907.

    596   vi.   Anna H. Oberholtzer, born November 14, 1834; died January 18, 1864.

    597   vii.   Samuel H. Oberholtzer, born April 28, 1836; died November 02, 1885. He married Maria E. Reist September 29, 1859; born December 29, 1839; died December 18, 1864.

    598   viii.   John H. Oberholtzer, born November 21, 1839; died May 14, 1913. He married (1) Fianna Burkholder December 02, 1862; born December 29, 1838; died August 22, 1891. He married (2) Elizabeth Weaver December 21, 1893; born August 06, 1842; died May 05, 1905.

    599   ix.   Joseph H. Oberholtzer, born August 17, 1842; died August 21, 1904. He married Mary M. Risser October 08, 1863; born April 05, 1844; died June 04, 1921.

    600   x.   Henry H. Oberholtzer, born October 29, 1845; died September 17, 1925. He married Susanna Stauffer October 27, 1868; born December 12, 1847; died May 20, 1925.

    601   xi.   Susanna H. Oberholtzer, born August 11, 1849; died January 19, 1914. She married Abraham Huber September 23, 1869; born May 24, 1847; died May 24, 1882.

265. John Frantz[9] Hershey (Isaac Hernley[8], Christian[7], Benjamin Stauffer[6], Adelheid Galle[5] Stouffer, Daniel[4], Christian[3], Hans[2], Hans[1]) was born June 28, 1800 in Derry Twp, Dauphin Co, PA, and died May 28, 1851 in Derry Twp, Dauphin Co, PA. He married **Nancy S Frick** February 19, 1824. She was born August 08, 1800, and died October 08, 1853.

Children of John Hershey and Nancy Frick are:

    602   i.   Annie[10] Hershey.

    603   ii.   Martin Hershey, born 1829.

+   604   iii.   Elizabeth Frick Hershey, born March 21, 1831 in Hummelstown, PA; died December 16, 1882.

    605   iv.   Fanny Hershey, born 1833.

    606   v.   Priscilla Hershey, born 1834.

    607   vi.   Lydia Hershey, born 1836.

    608   vii.   Menno Frick Hershey, born December 09, 1838.

    609   viii.   Leah Hershey, born 1840.

    610   ix.   Maria Hershey, born 1842.

266. Jacob Frantz[9] Hershey (Isaac Hernley[8], Christian[7], Benjamin Stauffer[6], Adelheid Galle[5] Stouffer, Daniel[4], Christian[3], Hans[2], Hans[1]) was born September 22, 1802, and died May 15, 1877. He married **Nancy Hershey**, daughter of Christian Hershey and Susanna Hershey. She was born January 22, 1808, and died September 03, 1869.

Children of Jacob Hershey and Nancy Hershey are:

+   611   i.   Henry Hershey[10] Hershey, born January 04, 1829 in Derry Twp, Dauphin Co, PA; died February 18, 1904.

    612   ii.   Joseph Hershey, born January 19, 1830; died August 04, 1855.

    613   iii.   Elizabeth Hershey, born September 26, 1832.

+   614   iv.   Christian Hershey, born March 16, 1836; died September 29, 1884.

+   615   v.   Jacob H Hershey, born October 09, 1839.

+   616   vi.   Elias H Hershey, born December 12, 1841; died November 16, 1925.

    617   vii.   Isaac Hershey, born May 06, 1846; died March 26, 1848.

267. Samuel[9] Hershey (Isaac Hernley[8], Christian[7], Benjamin Stauffer[6], Adelheid Galle[5] Stouffer, Daniel[4], Christian[3], Hans[2], Hans[1]) was born 1804, and died February 27, 1885. He married **Elizabeth Harnish** September 06, 1829. She was born March 27, 1806, and died October 17, 1891.

Children of Samuel Hershey and Elizabeth Harnish are:

    618   i.   Francis[10] Hershey, born August 18, 1832.

    619   ii.   Isaac Hershey, born October 24, 1837.

+   620   iii.   Samuel Harnish Hershey, born September 05, 1841.

621   iv.   Jacob Hershey, born October 25, 1843.
+   622   v.   Elizabeth Hershey, born December 11, 1851.

270. Christian[9] Hershey (Isaac Hernley[8], Christian[7], Benjamin Stauffer[6], Adelheid Galle[5] Stouffer, Daniel[4], Christian[3], Hans[2], Hans[1]) was born December 24, 1812 in Derry Twp, Dauphin Co, PA, and died May 06, 1875. He married **Frances Eshelman** January 02, 1840. She was born July 26, 1818 in Greenland, Lancaster Co, PA, and died November 11, 1900.

Children of Christian Hershey and Frances Eshelman are:
+   623   i.   Fianna[10] Hershey, born March 17, 1841 in Waynesboro, Franklin Co, PA; died January 29, 1925.
    624   ii.   Naomi Hershey, born August 12, 1842.
+   625   iii.   John F Hershey, born August 12, 1842 in Waynesboro, Franklin Co, PA.
+   626   iv.   Amos F Hershey, born August 15, 1845 in Waynesboro, Franklin Co, PA.
+   627   v.   Martin F Hershey, born January 24, 1847 in Waynesboro, Franklin Co, PA.
    628   vi.   Daniel F Hershey, born December 14, 1850 in Waynesboro, Franklin Co, PA. He married Henrietta Kramer.

272. Anna[9] Hershey (Jacob[8], Christian[7], Benjamin Stauffer[6], Adelheid Galle[5] Stouffer, Daniel[4], Christian[3], Hans[2], Hans[1]) was born July 27, 1779, and died January 09, 1864. She married **Jr Benjamin Long**, son of Benjamin Long and Christina Rudy. He was born July 17, 1775, and died January 27, 1851.

Child of Anna Hershey and Benjamin Long is:
+   629   i.   Anna[10] Long, born May 29, 1800 in Manheim Twp, Lanc Co, PA; died May 19, 1885.

273. Susanna[9] Hershey (Jacob[8], Christian[7], Benjamin Stauffer[6], Adelheid Galle[5] Stouffer, Daniel[4], Christian[3], Hans[2], Hans[1]) was born November 08, 1785, and died February 08, 1858. She married **Christian Hershey**, son of Jacob Hershey and Anna Newcomer. He was born June 20, 1780, and died August 05, 1843.

Children are listed above under (175) Christian Hershey.

277. Abraham Hershey[9] Stauffer (Abraham Hess[8], Henry Jacob[7], Hans[6], Christian[5], Daniel[4] Stouffer, Christian[3], Hans[2], Hans[1]) was born January 09, 1780 in Warwick Twp., Lancaster Co, PA, and died October 21, 1851 in Blair Ontario. He married **Elizabeth Reesor**. She was born 1774 in Lancaster County, Pennsylvania, and died 1835 in Markham Twp., Ork Co., Ont., Canada.

Children of Abraham Stauffer and Elizabeth Reesor are:
+   630   i.   Elizabeth[10] Stouffer.
    631   ii.   Fanny Stouffer.
    632   iii.   Jacob Stouffer.
    633   iv.   John Stouffer.
+   634   v.   Christian Stauffer, born January 17, 1799 in Chambersburg, PA; died 1868.
+   635   vi.   Abraham Stouffer, born 1806; died 1878.

287. Jacob[9] Frantz (Elisabeth Maria[8] Hostetter, Ann Elisabeth[7] Hershey, Benjamin Stauffer[6], Adelheid Galle[5] Stouffer, Daniel[4], Christian[3], Hans[2], Hans[1]) was born March 01, 1773, and died 1840. He married **Elizabeth Hershey**. She was born Abt. 1775.

Child of Jacob Frantz and Elizabeth Hershey is:
    636   i.   Anna[10] Frantz, born November 22, 1810.

288. Anna Hostetter[9] Frantz (Elisabeth Maria[8] Hostetter, Ann Elisabeth[7] Hershey, Benjamin Stauffer[6], Adelheid Galle[5] Stouffer, Daniel[4], Christian[3], Hans[2], Hans[1]) was born September 22, 1774 in Lancaster Co, PA, and died August 09, 1861 in Dauphin Co, PA. She married **Isaac Hernley Hershey**, son of Christian Hershey and Anna Hernley. He was born February 06, 1773 in Warwick Twp., Lancaster Co, PA, and died January 17, 1831 in Dauphin Co, PA.

Children are listed above under (104) Isaac Hernley Hershey.

289. John[9] Frantz (Elisabeth Maria[8] Hostetter, Ann Elisabeth[7] Hershey, Benjamin Stauffer[6], Adelheid Galle[5] Stouffer, Daniel[4], Christian[3], Hans[2], Hans[1]) was born March 13, 1778. He married **Elizabeth Hershey**, daughter of Abraham Hershey and Veronica Greider. She was born August 20, 1780.

Child is listed above under (181) Elizabeth Hershey.

301. Anna[9] Hostetter (Jacob[8], Ann Elisabeth[7] Hershey, Benjamin Stauffer[6], Adelheid Galle[5] Stouffer, Daniel[4], Christian[3], Hans[2], Hans[1]) was born June 13, 1772. She married **Johannes Snyder**.

Children of Anna Hostetter and Johannes Snyder are:
- 637 i. Samuel[10] Snyder.
- 638 ii. John Henry Snyder.

302. Jacob[9] Hostetter (Jacob[8], Ann Elisabeth[7] Hershey, Benjamin Stauffer[6], Adelheid Galle[5] Stouffer, Daniel[4], Christian[3], Hans[2], Hans[1]) was born August 13, 1774 in Manheim, Pa, and died April 06, 1865 in Manheim, Pa. He married **Elisabeth Miller**. She was born September 30, 1781, and died July 03, 1873 in Manheim, Pa.

Children of Jacob Hostetter and Elisabeth Miller are:
- + 639 i.   Martha[10] Hostetter.
-   640 ii.   Magdalene Hostetter.
- + 641 iii. John Hostetter, born July 15, 1801 in Penn Twp, Lancaster Cty, PA; died September 23, 1866 in Lancaster County, Pa.
-   642 iv.   Mary Hostetter, born 1802.
- + 643 v.   Jacob Hostetter, born August 25, 1805 in Lancaster County, Pa; died 1853 in Lancaster County, Pa.
-   644 vi.   Elizabeth Hostetter, born 1807.
- + 645 vii. Ann Hostetter, born 1807 in Lancaster County, Pa; died 1895 in Lancaster County, Pa.
- + 646 viii. Susan Hostetter, born 1809 in Lancaster County, Pa; died 1866.
- + 647 ix.   Barbara Hostetter, born 1811.
- + 648 x.   David Hostetter, born January 27, 1816 in Lancaster County, Pa; died May 19, 1885 in Lancaster County, Pa.
- + 649 xi.   Catherine Hostetter, born 1818.
- + 650 xii. Fanny Hostetter, born August 28, 1820; died December 12, 1893.

303. Abraham[9] Hostetter (Jacob[8], Ann Elisabeth[7] Hershey, Benjamin Stauffer[6], Adelheid Galle[5] Stouffer, Daniel[4], Christian[3], Hans[2], Hans[1]) was born December 20, 1777 in Manheim, Pa, and died February 24, 1831 in Manheim, Pa. He married **Anna Bucher**. She was born October 16, 1780 in Lancaster Cty, Pa, and died December 11, 1831 in Manheim, Pa.

Children of Abraham Hostetter and Anna Bucher are:
-   651 i.   Samuel[10] Hostetter.
-   652 ii.   Anney Hostetter.
- + 653 iii. Joseph Hostetter, born January 29, 1801 in Manheim, Pa; died September 10, 1872 in Ashland County, Ohio.
-   654 iv.   Maria Hostetter, born May 03, 1807. He married John Mumma.
- + 655 v.   Abraham Hostetter, born November 01, 1809 in Manheim, Pa; died May 24, 1881 in Lancaster, Pa.
-   656 vi.   Jacob Hostetter, born November 01, 1809.
- + 657 vii. David Hostetter, born June 03, 1815 in Manheim, Pa; died October 09, 1887 in Lancaster, Pa.

306. Barbara[9] Hostetter (Jacob[8], Ann Elisabeth[7] Hershey, Benjamin Stauffer[6], Adelheid Galle[5] Stouffer, Daniel[4], Christian[3], Hans[2], Hans[1]) was born February 11, 1786, and died January 15, 1845. She married **John Bossler**. He was born May 22, 1778, and died October 14, 1839.

Children of Barbara Hostetter and John Bossler are:
-   658 i.   Henry[10] Bassler.
-   659 ii.   John Bassler.
-   660 iii. Maria Bassler. She married Emanuel Weidler.
-   661 iv.   Christian Bassler.
-   662 v.   Jacob Bassler.
- + 663 vi.   Anna Bassler, born 1812 in Mannheim Twp, Lancaster, PA; died April 29, 1886.

307. Barbara[9] Hostetter (Jacob[8], Ann Elisabeth[7] Hershey, Benjamin Stauffer[6], Adelheid Galle[5] Stouffer, Daniel[4], Christian[3], Hans[2], Hans[1]) She married **John Bassler**.

Child of Barbara Hostetter and John Bassler is:
- 664 i. Anna[10] Hostetter.

310. Jacob[9] Hostetter (Jacob[8], Ann Elisabeth[7] Hershey, Benjamin Stauffer[6], Adelheid Galle[5] Stouffer, Daniel[4], Christian[3], Hans[2], Hans[1]) was born August 13, 1774, and died April 09, 1865. He married **Elizabeth Miller**. She was born September 30, 1781, and died July 03, 1873.

Children of Jacob Hostetter and Elizabeth Miller are:
- 665 i. David[10] Hostetter.
- 666 ii. Mary Hostetter.
- 667 iii. Jacob Hostetter.
- 668 iv. Elizabeth Hostetter.
- 669 v. Ann Hostetter.
- 670 vi. Susan Hostetter.
- 671 vii. Barbara Hostetter.
- 672 viii. John Hostetter.
- 673 ix. Magdalena Hostetter.
- 674 x. Martha Hostetter.

311. Abraham[9] Hostetter (Jacob[8], Ann Elisabeth[7] Hershey, Benjamin Stauffer[6], Adelheid Galle[5] Stouffer, Daniel[4], Christian[3], Hans[2], Hans[1]) was born 1777, and died 1831. He married **Anna Bucher**. She was born October 16, 1780 in Lancaster Cty, Pa, and died December 11, 1831 in Manheim, Pa.

Children of Abraham Hostetter and Anna Bucher are:
- 675 i. Annie[10] Hostetter.
- 676 ii. Maria Hostetter, born 1807.
- 677 iii. Abraham Hostetter, born 1809; died 1881.
- 678 iv. Jacob Hostetter, born 1809; died 1831.
- 679 v. Samuel Hostetter, born 1812.
- 680 vi. David Hostetter, born 1815; died 1887.

312. Anna[9] Frantz (Barbara[8] Hostetter, Ann Elisabeth[7] Hershey, Benjamin Stauffer[6], Adelheid Galle[5] Stouffer, Daniel[4], Christian[3], Hans[2], Hans[1]) was born February 23, 1779, and died 1850. She married **Johannes Baer**. He was born December 10, 1776, and died September 01, 1822.

Children of Anna Frantz and Johannes Baer are:
- 681 i. Maria[10] Bear, born Abt. 1800; died 1839. She married Samuel Brubaker; born Abt. 1800.
- 682 ii. Elizabeth Bear, born Abt. 1800. She married Charles Rudy; born Abt. 1800.
- + 683 iii. Lea Bear, born Abt. 1800.
- + 684 iv. Susanna Frantz Bear, born January 16, 1804; died January 21, 1886 in Hammercreek Cemetery.
- 685 v. Veronica Bear, born 1809; died June 18, 1885.
- 686 vi. Ephriam Bear, born 1810; died 1822.
- + 687 vii. Isaac F Bear, born January 15, 1815; died 1858.
- 688 viii. David Bear, born 1819; died 1822.

320. Rudolph[9] Hostetter (Benjamin[8], Ann Elisabeth[7] Hershey, Benjamin Stauffer[6], Adelheid Galle[5] Stouffer, Daniel[4], Christian[3], Hans[2], Hans[1]) was born January 01, 1789 in Lancaster County, Pa, and died September 13, 1844 in Lancaster County, Pa. He married **Elizabeth Eshelman** February 29, 1816 in Trinity Lutheran, Lancaster, Lancaster, PA. She was born November 23, 1794, and died May 19, 1893.

Children of Rudolph Hostetter and Elizabeth Eshelman are:
- 689 i. Benjamin[10] Hostetter.
- 690 ii. Rudolph Hostetter.
- 691 iii. Lydia Hostetter.
- 692 iv. Fronica Hostetter.
- 693 v. Elizabeth Hostetter.
- + 694 vi. Emmanuel Hostetter, born March 08, 1817 in Lancaster County, Pa; died May 26, 1890 in Lancaster County, Pa.
- 695 vii. Elizabeth Hostetter.
- 696 viii. Emmanuel Hostetter.
- 697 ix. Feronica Hostetter.
- 698 x. Lydia Hostetter.

321. Benjamin[9] Hostetter (Benjamin[8], Ann Elisabeth[7] Hershey, Benjamin Stauffer[6], Adelheid Galle[5] Stouffer, Daniel[4], Christian[3], Hans[2], Hans[1]) was born October 16, 1796 in Lancaster County, Pa, and died March 22, 1858 in Lancaster County, Pa. He married **(1) Elizabeth Miller**. He married **(2) Elizabeth Miller**.

Children of Benjamin Hostetter and Elizabeth Miller are:
- + 699 i. Ezra[10] Hostetter, born December 20, 1838 in Manor Twp, Lancaster Cty, PA; died October 14, 1919 in

			Lancaster County, Pa.
+	700	ii.	Jacob H Hostetter, born January 27, 1841 in Lancaster County, Pa; died April 04, 1932 in Lancaster County, Pa.
	701	iii.	Christian Hostetter, born 1842.

Children of Benjamin Hostetter and Elizabeth Miller are:
- 702   i.   Christian[10] Hostetter.
- 703   ii.   Jacob Hostetter.

323. Elisabeth[9] Hostetter (Abraham[8], Ann Elisabeth[7] Hershey, Benjamin Stauffer[6], Adelheid Galle[5] Stouffer, Daniel[4], Christian[3], Hans[2], Hans[1]) was born May 13, 1799 in lancaster County, Pa, and died November 04, 1841 in lancaster County, Pa. She married **Mathias Graeff**. He was born August 30, 1793, and died April 29, 1887 in Lancaster County, Pa.

Children of Elisabeth Hostetter and Mathias Graeff are:
- 704   i.   Abraham[10] Graeff.
- 705   ii.   Elizabeth Graeff.
- 706   iii.   Kate Graeff.
- 707   iv.   Maria Graeff.
- 708   v.   Susan Graeff.
- 709   vi.   Mathias Graeff.
- 710   vii.   Jacob Graeff.

324. Jacob Hostetter[9] Frantz (Barbara[8] Hostetter, Ann Elisabeth[7] Hershey, Benjamin Stauffer[6], Adelheid Galle[5] Stouffer, Daniel[4], Christian[3], Hans[2], Hans[1]) was born January 09, 1789, and died January 30, 1860. He married **Anna Miller**.

Child of Jacob Frantz and Anna Miller is:
- 711   i.   John Miller[10] Frantz, born December 29, 1812 in Lancaster, PA; died August 13, 1881.

327. David[9] Mellinger (David[8], Mary[7] Hershey, Benjamin Stauffer[6], Adelheid Galle[5] Stouffer, Daniel[4], Christian[3], Hans[2], Hans[1]) was born April 19, 1809.

Children of David Mellinger are:
- 712   i.   Benjamin[10] Mellinger, born January 31, 1831.
- 713   ii.   David Mellinger, born October 20, 1833.

333. Martin[9] Mellinger (John[8], Mary[7] Hershey, Benjamin Stauffer[6], Adelheid Galle[5] Stouffer, Daniel[4], Christian[3], Hans[2], Hans[1]) was born May 11, 1800, and died August 18, 1888. He married **Anna K. Kauffman**. She was born October 25, 1805, and died November 18, 1875.

Children of Martin Mellinger and Anna Kauffman are:
- 714   i.   John Kauffman[10] Mellinger.
- 715   ii.   Magdalena Kauffman Mellinger.
- 716   iii.   David Kauffman Mellinger.
- 717   iv.   Christian Kauffman Mellinger.
- 718   v.   Elizabeth Kauffman Mellinger.
- 719   vi.   Martin Kauffman Mellinger, born October 20, 1830; died December 30, 1870.
- 720   vii.   Anna Kauffman Mellinger, born June 12, 1835; died February 22, 1907.
- 721   viii.   Benjamin Kauffman Mellinger, born April 06, 1837; died July 05, 1865.
- 722   ix.   Abraham Kauffman Mellinger, born March 18, 1841; died July 12, 1917.
- 723   x.   Henry Kauffman Mellinger, born May 31, 1843; died 1922.
- 724   xi.   Jacob Kauffman Mellinger, born January 22, 1845; died March 15, 1864.
- 725   xii.   Fannie Kauffman Mellinger, born August 10, 1848 in Manor Twp, Lancaster, PA; died March 1939.

339. Mary Elizabeth[9] Dohner (Anna[8] Kreider, Susanna[7] Long, Anna[6] Hershey, Adelheid Galle[5] Stouffer, Daniel[4], Christian[3], Hans[2], Hans[1]) was born 1797, and died Abt. 1832. She married **John Hoover** 1828. He was born January 21, 1808 in Lancaster, PA, and died March 30, 1888 in Laporte, Laporte, IN.

Children of Mary Dohner and John Hoover are:
- 726   i.   Isaac[10] Hoover, born Abt. 1830.
- 727   ii.   John D. Hoover, born Abt. 1830.

342. Moses[9] **Dohner** (Anna[8] Kreider, Susanna[7] Long, Anna[6] Hershey, Adelheid Galle[5] Stouffer, Daniel[4], Christian[3], Hans[2], Hans[1]) was born 1808, and died June 04, 1850 in West Milton, OH. He married **Catherine Hoover**. She was born 1815, and died February 15, 1887 in Lebanon, Lancaster, Pa.

Children of Moses Dohner and Catherine Hoover are:
- 728   i.   Mary Elizabeth[10] Dohner, born June 17, 1834; died February 22, 1925.
- 729   ii.   Joseph Dohner, born 1835.
- 730   iii.   Lydia Dohner, born 1838.
- 731   iv.   Noah Dohner, born 1839.
- 732   v.   Anna Dohner, born 1842.
- 733   vi.   Moses Dohner, born 1844.
- 734   vii.   Christian Dohner, born 1846.
- 735   viii.   Michael Dohner, born 1849.

354. George[9] **Hostetter** (Henry[8], Catharine[7] Long, Anna[6] Hershey, Adelheid Galle[5] Stouffer, Daniel[4], Christian[3], Hans[2], Hans[1]) was born March 03, 1799 in Lancaster County, Pa, and died in Ohio. He married **Susanna Keplinger**.

Children of George Hostetter and Susanna Keplinger are:
- 736   i.   Peter[10] Hostetter.
- 737   ii.   Isaac Hostetter.
- 738   iii.   Emanuel Hostetter.
- 739   iv.   Maria Hostetter, born 1828.

356. John[9] **Hostetter** (Abraham[8], Catharine[7] Long, Anna[6] Hershey, Adelheid Galle[5] Stouffer, Daniel[4], Christian[3], Hans[2], Hans[1]) was born January 26, 1791 in Lancaster County, Pa, and died October 05, 1866 in Adams Cty, PA. He married **(1) Maria Bair**. She was born September 13, 1795, and died January 17, 1817. He married **(2) Anna Keagy**. She was born August 02, 1794, and died August 17, 1876 in Adams Cty, PA.

Children of John Hostetter and Maria Bair are:
- 740   i.   Judith[10] Hostetter, born 1812; died 1815.
- 741   ii.   Lidi Hostetter, born 1814; died 1815.
- + 742   iii.   John Hostetter, born January 11, 1817 in Adams Cty, PA; died February 13, 1872 in Adams Cty, PA.

Children of John Hostetter and Anna Keagy are:
- + 743   i.   Abraham F.[10] Hostetter, born October 05, 1820 in Adams Cty, PA; died February 14, 1868 in Adams Cty, PA.
- 744   ii.   Anna Hostetter, born 1822.
- + 745   iii.   Jacob K. Hostetter, born October 05, 1824 in Adams Cty, PA; died November 18, 1898 in Adams Cty, PA.
- + 746   iv.   Elisabeth Hostetter, born February 26, 1827 in Adams Cty, PA; died July 13, 1894.
- + 747   v.   Mary Hostetter, born January 29, 1829 in Adams Cty, PA; died November 09, 1910.
- 748   vi.   Susan Hostetter, born 1830.
- + 749   vii.   Benjamin Hostetter, born September 25, 1832 in Adams Cty, PA; died July 25, 1882 in Adams Cty, PA.

357. Ulrich[9] **Hostetter** (Abraham[8], Catharine[7] Long, Anna[6] Hershey, Adelheid Galle[5] Stouffer, Daniel[4], Christian[3], Hans[2], Hans[1]) was born November 12, 1793 in Lancaster County, Pa, and died March 15, 1866 in Lancaster County, Pa. He married **Maria Eshelman**. She was born September 26, 1799, and died September 06, 1884 in Lancaster County, Pa.

Children of Ulrich Hostetter and Maria Eshelman are:
- 750   i.   Elisabeth[10] Hostetter, born 1821.
- + 751   ii.   Christian Hostetter, born August 16, 1823 in Lancaster County, Pa; died February 27, 1879 in Lancaster County, Pa.
- + 752   iii.   Anna Hostetter, born November 07, 1827 in Lancaster County, Pa; died October 08, 1854 in Lancaster County, Pa.
- 753   iv.   Abraham Hostetter, born 1830.
- 754   v.   Elizabeth Hostetter, born 1821; died 1842.
- 755   vi.   Christian Hostetter, born 1823; died 1879.
- 756   vii.   Anna Hostetter, born 1827; died 1854.
- 757   viii.   Abraham Hostetter, born 1830; died 1887.

360. Abraham[9] Hostetter (Jacob[8], Catharine[7] Long, Anna[6] Hershey, Adelheid Galle[5] Stouffer, Daniel[4], Christian[3], Hans[2], Hans[1]) was born January 26, 1777 in Lancaster County, Pa, and died April 13, 1843 in Lancaster County, Pa. He married **Magdalena Lichty**. She was born December 24, 1793 in Lancaster County, Pa, and died March 22, 1835 in Lancaster County, Pa.

Children of Abraham Hostetter and Magdalena Lichty are:
- 758   i.   Susan[10] Hostetter, born 1812.
- + 759   ii.   Jacob Hostetter, born April 24, 1814 in Lancaster County, Pa; died February 23, 1879 in Lancaster County, Pa.
- + 760   iii.   Abraham Hostetter, born September 26, 1818 in Lancaster County, Pa; died July 12, 1873 in Mt. Carroll, Il..
- 761   iv.   John Hostetter, born 1821.
- 762   v.   Noah Hostetter, born 1824.
- 763   vi.   Anna Hostetter, born 1828.

364. Magdalena[9] Hostetter (Jacob[8], Catharine[7] Long, Anna[6] Hershey, Adelheid Galle[5] Stouffer, Daniel[4], Christian[3], Hans[2], Hans[1]) was born December 01, 1789, and died 1829. She married **Martin Kreider**.

Children of Magdalena Hostetter and Martin Kreider are:
- 764   i.   Jacob[10] Kreider.
- 765   ii.   Martin Kreider.
- 766   iii.   David Kreider.
- 767   iv.   Magdalena Kreider.
- 768   v.   Barbara Kreider.
- 769   vi.   Abraham Kreider.
- 770   vii.   Elizabeth Kreider.
- 771   viii.   John Kreider.

365. Jacob[9] Hostetter (Jacob[8], Catharine[7] Long, Anna[6] Hershey, Adelheid Galle[5] Stouffer, Daniel[4], Christian[3], Hans[2], Hans[1]) was born 1791 in Lancaster County, Pa, and died 1859. He married **Mary Landis**. She was born 1798, and died 1824.

Children of Jacob Hostetter and Mary Landis are:
- 772   i.   Mary Ann[10] Hostetter.
- 773   ii.   Elizabeth Hostetter.
- + 774   iii.   David Hostetter, born January 23, 1819; died November 06, 1888 in Pennsylvania.

366. Susanna[9] Hostetter (Jacob[8], Catharine[7] Long, Anna[6] Hershey, Adelheid Galle[5] Stouffer, Daniel[4], Christian[3], Hans[2], Hans[1]) was born February 21, 1797 in Lancaster County, Pa, and died 1874 in Lancaster County, Pa. She married **John Summy**.

Children of Susanna Hostetter and John Summy are:
- 775   i.   Jacob[10] Summy.
- 776   ii.   John H Summy.
- 777   iii.   Peter Summy.
- 778   iv.   Maria Summy.
- 779   v.   Abram Summy.
- 780   vi.   Aaron Summy.
- 781   vii.   David Summy.

374. Abraham[9] Hostetter (Jacob[8], Catharine[7] Long, Anna[6] Hershey, Adelheid Galle[5] Stouffer, Daniel[4], Christian[3], Hans[2], Hans[1]) was born June 02, 1777, and died April 13, 1843. He married **Magdalena Lichty**. She was born December 24, 1793 in Lancaster County, Pa, and died March 22, 1835 in Lancaster County, Pa.

Children of Abraham Hostetter and Magdalena Lichty are:
- 782   i.   Susan[10] Hostetter.
- 783   ii.   Anna Hostetter.
- 784   iii.   Jacob Hostetter, born 1814; died 1879.
- 785   iv.   Abraham Hostetter, born 1818; died 1873.
- 786   v.   John Hostetter, born 1821; died 1877.

375. Jacob[9] Hostetter (Jacob[8], Catharine[7] Long, Anna[6] Hershey, Adelheid Galle[5] Stouffer, Daniel[4], Christian[3], Hans[2], Hans[1]) was born 1791, and died 1859. He married **Mary Landis**.

Children of Jacob Hostetter and Mary Landis are:
- 787   i.   David[10] Hostetter.
- 788   ii.   Mary Ann Hostetter.
- 789   iii.   Elizabeth Hostetter.

377. Catherine[9] Hostetter (Herman[8], Catharine[7] Long, Anna[6] Hershey, Adelheid Galle[5] Stouffer, Daniel[4], Christian[3], Hans[2], Hans[1]) was born 1784 in Shelburne, Nova Scotia, and died 1828 in Canada. She married **William Westover** 1805 in Canada. He was born October 13, 1769 in Sheffield, Massachusetts, and died 1836 in Canada.

Children of Catherine Hostetter and William Westover are:
- 790   i.   Isaac[10] Westover.
- 791   ii.   Hiram Westover.
- 792   iii.   Jacob Westover.
- 793   iv.   Charlotte Westover.
- 794   v.   William Westover.
- 795   vi.   Mahetable Westover.
- 796   vii.   John Westover, born 1806.
- 797   viii.   Ann Westover, born 1807.
- 798   ix.   Herman Westover, born 1808.
- 799   x.   Elizabeth Westover, born 1814.
- 800   xi.   Ruffus Westover, born 1816.
- 801   xii.   George Westover, born 1819.
- 802   xiii.   Horace Westover, born 1825.
- 803   xiv.   Barbara Westover, born March 14, 1825.

378. Abraham[9] Hostetter (Herman[8], Catharine[7] Long, Anna[6] Hershey, Adelheid Galle[5] Stouffer, Daniel[4], Christian[3], Hans[2], Hans[1]) was born 1786 in Nova Scotia, and died September 07, 1868 in Grantham Twp, Canada. He married **Mary Donaldson** November 11, 1817. She was born 1795, and died February 14, 1862 in Canada.

Children of Abraham Hostetter and Mary Donaldson are:
- 804   i.   Helen[10] Hostetter.
- 805   ii.   Herman Robert Hostetter, born 1821.
- + 806   iii.   Thomas Hostetter, born 1825 in Canada; died 1870 in Canada.
- 807   iv.   Margaret Hostetter, born 1830.

379. Ann[9] Hostetter (Herman[8], Catharine[7] Long, Anna[6] Hershey, Adelheid Galle[5] Stouffer, Daniel[4], Christian[3], Hans[2], Hans[1]) was born April 14, 1786 in Shelburne, Nova Scotia, and died June 01, 1850 in Niagara Township, Canada. She married **Frederick Augustus Goring** November 05, 1805 in St Catharine's, Canada. He was born February 15, 1785 in Niagara, Canada, and died November 02, 1868 in St Catharine's, Canada.

Children of Ann Hostetter and Frederick Goring are:
- 808   i.   Lucretia Caroline[10] Goring.
- 809   ii.   James Goring.
- 810   iii.   Sarah Goring.
- 811   iv.   William Goring.
- 812   v.   John Goring.
- 813   vi.   Francis Goring, born 1806.
- 814   vii.   Frederick Augustus Goring, born 1812.
- 815   viii.   Harmon Goring, born 1817.
- 816   ix.   Charlotte Goring, born 1822.

380. Elisabeth[9] Hostetter (Herman[8], Catharine[7] Long, Anna[6] Hershey, Adelheid Galle[5] Stouffer, Daniel[4], Christian[3], Hans[2], Hans[1]) was born 1790, and died 1862 in Canada. She married **Jacob Ball**. He was born 1777, and died 1820.

Children of Elisabeth Hostetter and Jacob Ball are:
- 817   i.   Jacob[10] Ball, born 1817.
- 818   ii.   Peter Herman Ball, born 1818.
- 819   iii.   Ann Elizabeth Ball, born 1819.
- 820   iv.   Gertrude Amelia Ball, born 1820.

381. Jacob[9] **Hostetter** (Herman[8], Catharine[7] Long, Anna[6] Hershey, Adelheid Galle[5] Stouffer, Daniel[4], Christian[3], Hans[2], Hans[1]) was born 1792 in Canada, and died 1854 in Canada. He married **Catherine Gould**. She was born 1792, and died 1865.

Children of Jacob Hostetter and Catherine Gould are:
- 821   i.   James[10] Hostetter, born 1816.
- 822   ii.   Hiram Hostetter, born 1818.
- 823   iii.   Herman Hostetter, born 1821.
- 824   iv.   Elisabeth Jane Hostetter, born 1823.
- 825   v.   Ann Hostetter, born 1824.
- 826   vi.   Margaret Hostetter, born 1826.
- 827   vii.   Jacob Hostetter, born 1828 in Canada; died 1862. He married Dinah Van Every; born 1831; died 1861.
- 828   viii.   Mary Hostetter, born 1831.
- 829   ix.   John Hostetter, born 1832.
- 830   x.   Catherine Hostetter, born 1835.

386. Herman[9] **Hostetter** (Herman[8], Catharine[7] Long, Anna[6] Hershey, Adelheid Galle[5] Stouffer, Daniel[4], Christian[3], Hans[2], Hans[1]) was born 1805 in Canada, and died 1871 in Canada. He married **Catherine Carroll**.

Children of Herman Hostetter and Catherine Carroll are:
- 831   i.   David[10] Hostetter.
- 832   ii.   Luke Hostetter, born 1828.
- 833   iii.   Ann Hostetter, born 1831.
- 834   iv.   Herman Hostetter, born 1834.
- 835   v.   Lewis Hostetter, born 1840.
- 836   vi.   John Hostetter, born 1841.
- 837   vii.   Catherine Hostetter, born 1843.

394. Abraham[9] **Hostetter** (Herman[8], Catharine[7] Long, Anna[6] Hershey, Adelheid Galle[5] Stouffer, Daniel[4], Christian[3], Hans[2], Hans[1]) was born 1753, and died 1868. He married **Mary Donaldson**.

Children of Abraham Hostetter and Mary Donaldson are:
- 838   i.   Herman Robert[10] Hostetter.
- 839   ii.   Thomas Hostetter.
- 840   iii.   Margaret Hostetter.
- 841   iv.   Helen Hostetter.

395. Maria[9] **Hostetter** (John[8], Catharine[7] Long, Anna[6] Hershey, Adelheid Galle[5] Stouffer, Daniel[4], Christian[3], Hans[2], Hans[1]) She married **Abraham Strickler**. He was born July 26, 1769, and died February 20, 1830.

Children of Maria Hostetter and Abraham Strickler are:
- 842   i.   Mary[10] Strickler.
- 843   ii.   Elisabeth Strickler, born December 29, 1805.
- 844   iii.   Abraham Strickler, born 1809.
- 845   iv.   John Strickler, born September 02, 1811.
- 846   v.   Henry Strickler, born April 22, 1814.
- 847   vi.   Martha Strickler, born December 10, 1815.
- 848   vii.   Jacob Strickler, born 1818.
- 849   viii.   Susan Strickler, born 1821.
- 850   ix.   Annie Strickler, born 1825.
- 851   x.   Fannie Strickler, born 1825.

396. Anna[9] **Hostetter** (John[8], Catharine[7] Long, Anna[6] Hershey, Adelheid Galle[5] Stouffer, Daniel[4], Christian[3], Hans[2], Hans[1]) was born September 26, 1796, and died September 28, 1884. She married **Rudolph Herr**. He was born May 10, 1801, and died March 23, 1888.

Children of Anna Hostetter and Rudolph Herr are:
- +   852   i.   John[10] Herr, born January 11, 1834.
-      853   ii.   Abraham Herr, born 1824.

401. Abraham[9] **Hostetter** (John[8], Catharine[7] Long, Anna[6] Hershey, Adelheid Galle[5] Stouffer, Daniel[4], Christian[3], Hans[2], Hans[1]) was born September 15, 1779 in Lancaster County, Pa, and died February 13, 1858 in Lancaster County, Pa. He married **Elisabeth Buckwalter**. She died August 18, 1840.

Children of Abraham Hostetter and Elisabeth Buckwalter are:
+ 854 i. Barbara[10] Hostetter.
  855 ii. Elisabeth Hostetter.
+ 856 iii. David Hostetter, born 1808 in Lancaster County, Pa; died 1872 in Lancaster County, Pa.
  857 iv. Susan Hostetter, born 1812.
  858 v. Martha Hostetter, born 1814.

402. John[9] Hostetter (John[8], Catharine[7] Long, Anna[6] Hershey, Adelheid Galle[5] Stouffer, Daniel[4], Christian[3], Hans[2], Hans[1]) was born January 16, 1787 in Manor Twp, Lancaster Cty, PA, and died September 24, 1854 in Lancaster County, Pa. He married **Catherine Eby**. She was born August 12, 1795, and died March 06, 1848 in Lancaster County, Pa.

Children of John Hostetter and Catherine Eby are:
  859 i. Catharine[10] Hostetter.
  860 ii. Henry Hostetter.
  861 iii. Elias Hostetter.
  862 iv. Magdalena Hostetter, born 1817.
  863 v. Mary Hostetter, born 1820.
+ 864 vi. John E. Hostetter, born February 02, 1823 in Lancaster County, Pa; died April 08, 1908 in Lancaster County, Pa.
+ 865 vii. Jonas E. Hostetter, born January 13, 1833 in Lancaster County, Pa; died August 15, 1803 in Lancaster County, Pa.
+ 866 viii. Abraham Hostetter, born 1835 in Lancaster County, Pa; died in Lancaster County, Pa.

408. John[9] Hostetter (Christian[8], Catharine[7] Long, Anna[6] Hershey, Adelheid Galle[5] Stouffer, Daniel[4], Christian[3], Hans[2], Hans[1]) was born August 16, 1788 in Lancaster County, Pa, and died September 02, 1879 in Lebanon Cty, PA. He married **Veronica Huber**. She was born November 26, 1790, and died July 17, 1854.

Children of John Hostetter and Veronica Huber are:
  867 i. Lydia[10] Hostetter.
  868 ii. Jacob Hostetter.
+ 869 iii. Maria Hostetter, born October 06, 1812; died August 21, 1860.
  870 iv. Catherine Hostetter, born 1814.
+ 871 v. Samuel Hostetter, born October 26, 1816 in Lancaster County, Pa; died February 16, 1860 in Lebanon Cty, PA.
+ 872 vi. Christian Hostetter, born October 21, 1819; died February 08, 1897 in Lebanon Cty, PA.
+ 873 vii. John Hostetter, born November 30, 1821; died March 03, 1907 in Lebanon Cty, PA.
  874 viii. Henry Hostetter, born 1823.
  875 ix. Daniel Hostetter, born 1830.

409. Daniel[9] Hostetter (Christian[8], Catharine[7] Long, Anna[6] Hershey, Adelheid Galle[5] Stouffer, Daniel[4], Christian[3], Hans[2], Hans[1]) was born January 09, 1791 in Lancaster County, Pa, and died January 25, 1824 in Lancaster County, Pa. He married **Susanna Rudy**. She was born July 08, 1794, and died August 27, 1875.

Children of Daniel Hostetter and Susanna Rudy are:
  876 i. Isaac R.[10] Hostetter.
  877 ii. Emmanuel Hostetter.
  878 iii. Annie Hostetter.
  879 iv. Charles Hostetter, born 1815.
  880 v. Isaac Hostetter.
  881 vi. Emmanuel Hostetter.
  882 vii. Annie Hostetter.

410. Jacob[9] Hostetter (Christian[8], Catharine[7] Long, Anna[6] Hershey, Adelheid Galle[5] Stouffer, Daniel[4], Christian[3], Hans[2], Hans[1]) was born February 20, 1794 in Lancaster County, Pa, and died February 04, 1863 in Lancaster County, Pa. He married **Barbara Hertzler** January 23, 1817 in First Reformed Church, Lancaster, PA. She was born November 13, 1797, and died July 16, 1875 in Lancaster County, Pa.

Children of Jacob Hostetter and Barbara Hertzler are:
  883 i. Daniel[10] Hostetter.
  884 ii. Simon Hostetter, born 1821.
  885 iii. John H. Hostetter, born 1828.

413. Isaac⁹ Hostetter (Christian⁸, Catharine⁷ Long, Anna⁶ Hershey, Adelheid Galle⁵ Stouffer, Daniel⁴, Christian³, Hans², Hans¹) was born November 30, 1810 in Lancaster County, Pa, and died March 02, 1861 in Ohio. He married **Hannah Hagar**. She was born 1814, and died 1866.

Children of Isaac Hostetter and Hannah Hagar are:
- 886   i.   Elisabeth¹⁰ Hostetter.
- 887   ii.   Samuel A. Hostetter.
- 888   iii.   Thomas Hostetter.
- 889   iv.   Franklin Hostetter.
- 890   v.   Hiram H. Hostetter, born 1842.
- 891   vi.   Salinda Hostetter, born 1843.

419. John⁹ Hostetter (Abraham⁸, Catharine⁷ Long, Anna⁶ Hershey, Adelheid Galle⁵ Stouffer, Daniel⁴, Christian³, Hans², Hans¹) was born 1791, and died 1866. He married **(1) Anna Keagy**. She was born August 02, 1794, and died August 17, 1876 in Adams Cty, PA. He married **(2) Maria Bair**. She was born September 13, 1795, and died January 17, 1817.

Children of John Hostetter and Maria Bair are:
- 892   i.   Elizabeth K.¹⁰ Hostetter.
- 893   ii.   Mary Hostetter.
- 894   iii.   John Hostetter, born 1817; died 1872.
- 895   iv.   Abraham Hostetter, born 1820; died 1868.
- 896   v.   Anna Hostetter, born 1822; died 1893.
- 897   vi.   Jacob Hostetter, born 1824; died 1898.
- 898   vii.   Susan Hostetter, born 1830; died 1893.
- 899   viii.   Benjamin Hostetter, born 1832; died 1882.

421. Abraham⁹ Hostetter (John⁸, Catharine⁷ Long, Anna⁶ Hershey, Adelheid Galle⁵ Stouffer, Daniel⁴, Christian³, Hans², Hans¹) He married **Elizabeth Barbara Buckwalter**.

Children of Abraham Hostetter and Elizabeth Buckwalter are:
- 900   i.   David¹⁰ Hostetter, died 1872.
- 901   ii.   Barbara Hostetter.
- 902   iii.   Elizabeth Hostetter.
- 903   iv.   Susan Hostetter.
- 904   v.   Martha Hostetter.

422. John⁹ Hostetter (John⁸, Catharine⁷ Long, Anna⁶ Hershey, Adelheid Galle⁵ Stouffer, Daniel⁴, Christian³, Hans², Hans¹) He married **Catherine Eby**. She was born August 12, 1795, and died March 06, 1848 in Lancaster County, Pa.

Children of John Hostetter and Catherine Eby are:
- 905   i.   Magdalena¹⁰ Hostetter.
- 906   ii.   Mary Hostetter.
- 907   iii.   John E. Hostetter.
- 908   iv.   Catherine Hostetter.
- 909   v.   Henry Hostetter.
- 910   vi.   Abraham Hostetter.

431. Jacob⁹ Hostetter (Christian⁸, Catharine⁷ Long, Anna⁶ Hershey, Adelheid Galle⁵ Stouffer, Daniel⁴, Christian³, Hans², Hans¹) He married **Barbara " Hostetter**.

Children of Jacob Hostetter and Barbara Hostetter are:
- 911   i.   Daniel¹⁰ Hostetter.
- 912   ii.   John Hostetter.

432. John⁹ Hostetter (Christian⁸, Catharine⁷ Long, Anna⁶ Hershey, Adelheid Galle⁵ Stouffer, Daniel⁴, Christian³, Hans², Hans¹) was born 1788, and died 1879. He married **Veronica Huber**. She was born November 26, 1790, and died July 17, 1854.

Children of John Hostetter and Veronica Huber are:
- 913   i.   Christian A.¹⁰ Hostetter.

914	ii.	Catherine Hostetter.
915	iii.	Jacob Hostetter.
916	iv.	Samuel Hostetter.
917	v.	Henry Hostetter.
918	vi.	Lydia Hostetter.
919	vii.	John Hostetter, born 1821; died 1907.
920	viii.	Daniel Hostetter, born September 07, 1830; died 1922.

439. Andreas[9] Hershey (Jacob[8], Andrew[7], Andrew Stauffer[6], Adelheid Galle[5] Stouffer, Daniel[4], Christian[3], Hans[2], Hans[1]) was born December 16, 1795, and died March 23, 1837.

Children of Andreas Hershey are:
921	i.	Benjamin[10] Hershey.
922	ii.	Barbara Hershey.
923	iii.	Anna Hershey.
924	iv.	Jacob Hershey, born June 04, 1826.

451. Jacob[9] Hershey (John[8], Jacob Snavely[7], Andrew Stauffer[6], Adelheid Galle[5] Stouffer, Daniel[4], Christian[3], Hans[2], Hans[1]) was born May 09, 1803 in Lancaster, PA, and died July 12, 1883 in Paradise Twp, Lancaster, PA. He married **Elizabeth Eby**. She was born June 12, 1807 in Paradise Twp., Lancaster Co., PA, and died May 31, 1897 in Paradise Twp., Lancaster Co., PA.

Children of Jacob Hershey and Elizabeth Eby are:
925	i.	Anna[10] Hershey, born 1824; died 1842.
926	ii.	Susan Hershey, born 1843; died 1927.
927	iii.	Unnamed Hershey, born 1851; died 1851.

456. Jacob[9] Hershey (John[8], Jacob Snavely[7], Andrew Stauffer[6], Adelheid Galle[5] Stouffer, Daniel[4], Christian[3], Hans[2], Hans[1]) was born March 09, 1803 in Paradise Twp., Lancaster Co., PA, and died July 12, 1883 in Paradise Twp., Lancaster Co., PA. He married **Elizabeth Eby**. She was born June 12, 1807 in Paradise Twp., Lancaster Co., PA, and died May 31, 1897 in Paradise Twp., Lancaster Co., PA.

Children of Jacob Hershey and Elizabeth Eby are:
	928	i.	Anna[10] Hershey, born November 18, 1824; died August 09, 1842.
	929	ii.	Margaret Hershey, born June 23, 1827; died April 14, 1906.
	930	iii.	John Eby Hershey, born January 16, 1830; died May 08, 1906.
	931	iv.	Elizabeth Hershey, born March 08, 1831; died February 13, 1916.
	932	v.	Peter Hershey, born December 25, 1835; died May 27, 1836.
	933	vi.	Elias Hershey, born March 15, 1837; died January 12, 1911.
+	934	vii.	Peter Hershey, born August 02, 1839; died December 17, 1922.
	935	viii.	Maria Hershey, born September 20, 1841; died August 15, 1842.
	936	ix.	Susan Hershey, born January 30, 1843; died May 19, 1927.
	937	x.	David Hershey, born June 01, 1845; died December 20, 1846.
	938	xi.	Jacob Menno Hershey, born October 16, 1847; died December 06, 1923.

458. Nancy Ann[9] Hershey (John[8], Jacob Snavely[7], Andrew Stauffer[6], Adelheid Galle[5] Stouffer, Daniel[4], Christian[3], Hans[2], Hans[1]) was born October 22, 1805, and died September 13, 1885. She married **Jonas S. Martin**. He was born January 30, 1806, and died September 11, 1874.

Child of Nancy Hershey and Jonas Martin is:
939	i.	Frances[10] Martin, born October 27, 1831 in Caernarvon Twp, Lanc Co, PA; died 1861. She married Levi Weaver; born May 30, 1832; died March 29, 1913.

459. Veronica[9] Hershey (John[8], Jacob Snavely[7], Andrew Stauffer[6], Adelheid Galle[5] Stouffer, Daniel[4], Christian[3], Hans[2], Hans[1]) was born August 31, 1808 in Leacock Twp., Lancaster Co., Pa., and died March 19, 1881 in East Earl Twp., Lancaster Co., Pa.. She married **Abraham Reiff**, son of Joseph Reiff and Barbara Nolt. He was born November 15, 1803 in West Earl Twp, Lanc Co, PA, and died September 28, 1874.

Children of Veronica Hershey and Abraham Reiff are:
	940	i.	Fanny H.[10] Rife, born February 11, 1836; died March 14, 1900. She married John M. Sauder; born June 29, 1833; died June 11, 1878.
+	941	ii.	Annie Reiff, born October 24, 1842 in West Earl Twp, Lanc Co, PA; died February 23, 1917.

942   iii.   John A. Reiff, born July 20, 1846; died June 07, 1900.
943   iv.   Magdalena Reiff, born November 28, 1852; died October 28, 1856.

462. Joseph[9] Hershey (John[8], Jacob Snavely[7], Andrew Stauffer[6], Adelheid Galle[5] Stouffer, Daniel[4], Christian[3], Hans[2], Hans[1]) was born November 20, 1816, and died July 17, 1891. He married **Fannie Hartman** January 01, 1839. She was born November 03, 1819, and died April 14, 1894.

Children of Joseph Hershey and Fannie Hartman are:
944   i.   John[10] Hershey.
945   ii.   Annie Hershey.
946   iii.   Henry H Hershey.
947   iv.   Lydia Hershey.
948   v.   Catherine Hershey.
949   vi.   Joseph Hershey.
950   vii.   Fannie Hershey.
951   viii.   Magdalena Hershey.
952   ix.   Elizabeth Hershey.
953   x.   Margaret Hershey.
954   xi.   Amos H Hershey, born June 01, 1858; died February 27, 1933.
955   xii.   Amanda Hershey.

463. Nancy[9] Hershey (Christian[8], Jacob Snavely[7], Andrew Stauffer[6], Adelheid Galle[5] Stouffer, Daniel[4], Christian[3], Hans[2], Hans[1]) was born January 22, 1808, and died September 03, 1869. She married **Jacob Frantz Hershey**, son of Isaac Hershey and Anna Frantz. He was born September 22, 1802, and died May 15, 1877.

Children are listed above under (266) Jacob Frantz Hershey.

466. Jacob[9] Hershey (Christian[8], Jacob Snavely[7], Andrew Stauffer[6], Adelheid Galle[5] Stouffer, Daniel[4], Christian[3], Hans[2], Hans[1]) was born November 27, 1812, and died August 24, 1889. He married **Maria Martin**. She was born November 17, 1811, and died December 11, 1844.

Child of Jacob Hershey and Maria Martin is:
956   i.   Elizabeth[10] Hershey, born May 27, 1835; died October 06, 1863.

470. Abraham[9] Hershey (Christian[8], Jacob Snavely[7], Andrew Stauffer[6], Adelheid Galle[5] Stouffer, Daniel[4], Christian[3], Hans[2], Hans[1]) was born August 16, 1819, and died December 18, 1886. He married **Martha**. She was born 1824.

Children of Abraham Hershey and Martha are:
957   i.   Enos[10] Hershey, born 1847.
+ 958   ii.   Susan Hershey, born January 14, 1852; died November 24, 1915.
959   iii.   Levi Hershey, born 1854.
960   iv.   Mary Hershey, born 1858.
961   v.   Henry Hershey, born 1862.

472. Peter E.[9] Hershey (Abraham[8], Jacob Snavely[7], Andrew Stauffer[6], Adelheid Galle[5] Stouffer, Daniel[4], Christian[3], Hans[2], Hans[1]) was born February 05, 1826, and died August 31, 1911. He married **(1) Annie L. Landis** December 05, 1848, daughter of Christian Landis and Mary Landis. She was born December 22, 1829, and died June 04, 1918. He married **(2) Anna Landis** December 05, 1848. She was born December 22, 1829, and died June 04, 1918.

Children of Peter Hershey and Anna Landis are:
962   i.   Christian L.[10] Hershey, born May 27, 1850; died January 25, 1868.
963   ii.   Anna L. Hershey, born August 31, 1852; died September 16, 1877.
964   iii.   Henry Hershey, born May 19, 1855.
965   iv.   Mary Hershey, born March 25, 1858.
966   v.   Landes L. Hershey, born August 24, 1867; died December 14, 1962.

473. Elizabeth[9] Frantz (John[9], Elisabeth Maria[8] Hostetter, Ann Elisabeth[7] Hershey, Benjamin Stauffer[6], Adelheid Galle[5] Stouffer, Daniel[4], Christian[3], Hans[2], Hans[1]) was born March 13, 1816, and died September 13, 1863. She married **Benjamin B Root**. He was born March 14, 1815.

Child of Elizabeth Frantz and Benjamin Root is:

The Relations of Milton Snavely Hershey, 4th Ed.

    967   i.   Adam Frantz[10] Root, born May 20, 1836.

475. Henry[9] Hershey (Martin[8], Henry[7], Andrew Stauffer[6], Adelheid Galle[5] Stouffer, Daniel[4], Christian[3], Hans[2], Hans[1]) was born September 01, 1803, and died January 13, 1854. He married **Mary (Nancy) Landis** Abt. 1830. She was born December 17, 1812 in Dauphin Co, PA, and died May 04, 1880 in Harrisburg, PA.

Children of Henry Hershey and Mary Landis are:
    968   i.   Christian[10] Landis, born February 24, 1833; died May 03, 1908. He married Fanny Mumma May 11, 1852.
    969   ii.   Elizabeth Hershey, born 1837; died September 09, 1895 in Asbury Park, NJ. She married Israel Groff " Dr in Ephrata, PA.
    970   iii.   John Hershey, born 1838.

481. Henry[9] Hershey (Martin[8], Henry[7], Andrew Stauffer[6], Adelheid Galle[5] Stouffer, Daniel[4], Christian[3], Hans[2], Hans[1]) was born September 01, 1803, and died January 13, 1854 in Hummelstown, PA. He married **Mary Nancy Landis**. She was born December 17, 1812 in Dauphin Co, PA, and died May 04, 1880 in Harrisburg, PA.

Children of Henry Hershey and Mary Landis are:
+   971   i.   Diana[10] Hershey, born August 12, 1831 in Derry Twp, Dauphin Co, PA; died August 12, 1904 in Hummelstown, PA.
    972   ii.   Christian Hershey, born February 24, 1833.
    973   iii.   Elizabeth Hershey, born 1837.
    974   iv.   John Hershey, born 1838.
    975   v.   Mary A Hershey, born 1841; died November 13, 1906. She married Witmer C. Rounck Abt. 1869.
    976   vi.   Henrietta Hershey, born 1845. She married George W. Boyd Abt. 1868.
    977   vii.   Henry L Hershey, born July 07, 1852 in Hummelstown, PA; died 1931 in Harrisburtg, PA. He married Mary Gertrude Buehler 1880.

484. Christiana[9] Hastetter (Anna Barbara[8] Stauffer, Johannes[7], Daniel[6] Stouffer, Christian[5] Stauffer, Daniel[4] Stouffer, Christian[3], Hans[2], Hans[1]) was born Abt. 1752, and died Bef. 1806. She married **George Nickey** 1774. He was born 1746 in Rapho Twp, Lancaster Co, Pa., and died August 27, 1839 in Frankford Twp, Cumb Co, Pa..

Child of Christiana Hastetter and George Nickey is:
+   978   i.   Samuel[10] Nickey, born October 10, 1789 in Rapho Twp, Lancaster Co, Pa.; died July 05, 1875 in Cumberland Co, Pa. Buried Pa. German Baptist Churchyard, Huntsdale, Pa..

485. Peter[9] Ober (Elizabeth[8] Stauffer, Johannes[7], Daniel[6] Stouffer, Christian[5] Stauffer, Daniel[4] Stouffer, Christian[3], Hans[2], Hans[1]) was born WFT Est. 1758-1776, and died WFT Est. 1791-1861. He married **Franey Farney** WFT Est. 1767-1813. She was born WFT Est. 1745-1768, and died WFT Est. 1790-1856.

Child of Peter Ober and Franey Farney is:
+   979   i.   Elizabeth[10] Owens, born February 13, 1787; died July 18, 1862.

486. Christian[9] Ober (Elizabeth[8] Stauffer, Johannes[7], Daniel[6] Stouffer, Christian[5] Stauffer, Daniel[4] Stouffer, Christian[3], Hans[2], Hans[1]) was born September 29, 1762 in Running Pump, W. Donegal Twp., Lancaster Co., PA, and died November 27, 1840. He married **Elizabeth Hunsperger** 1784. She was born November 19, 1764 in PA, and died June 12, 1845 in Mt. Ober, Lancaster, PA.

Children of Christian Ober and Elizabeth Hunsperger are:
    980   i.   Jacob[10] Ober, born August 10, 1786; died 1839. He married Barbara Calle; born 1791; died 1841.
+   981   ii.   Isaac Huntsberger Ober, born February 13, 1790 in Conewago Twp, Lancaster Co, PA; died January 22, 1863 in Conewago Twp, Dauphin Co, PA.
    982   iii.   Mary Ober, born April 17, 1800; died April 02, 1878. She married Elias Foster; born 1787; died 1830.
    983   iv.   Sarah Ober, born February 28, 1802; died 1837. She married Henry Myers; born 1803; died 1890.
    984   v.   Elizabeth Ober, born February 04, 1804. She married Samuel Shelly; born Abt. 1800.

487. Henry[9] Ober (Elizabeth[8] Stauffer, Johannes[7], Daniel[6] Stouffer, Christian[5] Stauffer, Daniel[4] Stouffer, Christian[3], Hans[2], Hans[1]) was born 1771, and died March 03, 1839 in W. Donegal Twp., Lancaster Cty., PA. He married **Maria Delebaugh**. She was born 1771, and died 1849 in W. Donegal Twp., Lancaster Cty., PA.

Child of Henry Ober and Maria Delebaugh is:

+ 985 i. Michael[10] Ober, born May 25, 1794; died May 21, 1854 in W. Donegal Twp., Lancester Cty., PA.

488. David S[9] Ober (Elizabeth[8] Stauffer, Johannes[7], Daniel[6] Stouffer, Christian[5] Stauffer, Daniel[4] Stouffer, Christian[3], Hans[2], Hans[1]) was born 1774 in Lancaster, Rapho Township, PA, and died 1843 in Lancaster, PA. He married **Elizabeth Longenecker**. She was born Abt. 1775, and died Abt. 1860.

Children of David Ober and Elizabeth Longenecker are:
  986 i. Marshall[10] Ober, born 1802 in Lancaster, PA; died 1803 in Lancaster, PA.
+ 987 ii. Christian Longnecker Ober, born 1805 in Lancaster, PA; died 1806 in Lancaster, PA.

489. Henry[9] Ober (Veronica " Frany "[8] Stauffer, Johannes[7], Daniel[6] Stouffer, Christian[5] Stauffer, Daniel[4] Stouffer, Christian[3], Hans[2], Hans[1]) was born 1769, and died 1843 in Bedford County, Pennsylvania. He married **Barbara Hertzler**. She was born Abt. 1770, and died in Bedford County, Pennsylvania.

Children of Henry Ober and Barbara Hertzler are:
  988 i. Henry[10] Ober, born Abt. 1798; died 1840.
+ 989 ii. John Ober, born February 09, 1799; died September 29, 1851.
+ 990 iii. Susannah Ober, born Abt. 1800 in Maryland; died Bef. 1853.
+ 991 iv. Jacob Ober, born February 20, 1801; died September 09, 1855 in Pennsylvania.
  992 v. Elizabeth Ober, born 1803; died Aft. 1880. She married Jacob Livengood; born March 20, 1803; died January 04, 1885.
+ 993 vi. Joseph Ober, born January 1805; died April 29, 1869.
+ 994 vii. Franey Ober, born 1809.
+ 995 viii. Christian Ober, born July 08, 1812; died May 12, 1880 in Pennsylvania.
+ 996 ix. Samuel Ober, born 1815.
+ 997 x. Mary Ober, born Abt. 1818; died 1912.

490. Michael[9] Ober (Veronica " Frany "[8] Stauffer, Johannes[7], Daniel[6] Stouffer, Christian[5] Stauffer, Daniel[4] Stouffer, Christian[3], Hans[2], Hans[1]) died Abt. 1806. He married **Catherine Oberholtzer**. She died Abt. 1823.

Children of Michael Ober and Catherine Oberholtzer are:
+ 998 i. Ann[10] Ober, born Abt. 1780; died Abt. 1840.
+ 999 ii. Barbara Ober, born Abt. 1789; died May 10, 1859.
+ 1000 iii. Catherine Ober, born Abt. 1790; died Bef. February 1825.
+ 1001 iv. Jacob Ober, born June 30, 1793; died August 15, 1854.
+ 1002 v. Elizabeth Ober, born Abt. 1794; died Bef. May 09, 1826.
+ 1003 vi. Samuel Ober, born Abt. 1797.
  1004 vii. Fronica Ober, born Abt. 1799; died Abt. 1825.
+ 1005 viii. Magdalena Ober, born November 04, 1801; died July 02, 1840.

492. Peter[9] Ober (Veronica " Frany "[8] Stauffer, Johannes[7], Daniel[6] Stouffer, Christian[5] Stauffer, Daniel[4] Stouffer, Christian[3], Hans[2], Hans[1]) died Bef. 1847. He married **Hannah Unknown**. She was born Abt. 1776, and died Abt. 1847.

Children of Peter Ober and Hannah Unknown are:
  1006 i. Cyrus Henry[10] Ober.
  1007 ii. Sarah Jane Ober. She married Milton Young.
  1008 iii. Rosanna Ober. She married Charles Reen.
  1009 iv. Eliza Ober. She married George A. Garnes.
  1010 v. Harrison Jackson Ober.
  1011 vi. Hannah Ober.
  1012 vii. Chambers Ober.
  1013 viii. Oliver Francis Ober.

493. Christian[9] Ober (Veronica " Frany "[8] Stauffer, Johannes[7], Daniel[6] Stouffer, Christian[5] Stauffer, Daniel[4] Stouffer, Christian[3], Hans[2], Hans[1]) was born 1765, and died 1824. He married **(1) Sarah Unknown**. She was born Abt. 1794. He married **(2) Catherine Unknown**. She was born Aft. 1830. He married **(3) Barbara Berg**. She was born Abt. 1776.

Children of Christian Ober and Sarah Unknown are:
  1014 i. James C.[10] Ober, born 1811; died 1919.
  1015 ii. William Ober, born March 10, 1816.
+ 1016 iii. Lewis Ober, born 1818; died December 1897.

+ 1017 iv. John C. Ober, born January 25, 1818; died February 21, 1898.

Children of Christian Ober and Catherine Unknown are:
    1018 i. Henry[10] Ober.
+ 1019 ii. Barbara Ober.
+ 1020 iii. Nancy Ober, born October 02, 1799; died September 13, 1879.

494. John[9] Ober (Veronica " Frany "[8] Stauffer, Johannes[7], Daniel[6] Stouffer, Christian[5] Stauffer, Daniel[4] Stouffer, Christian[3], Hans[2], Hans[1]) was born 1767, and died 1821. He married **(1) Unknown Unknown**. He married **(2) Ann Oberholtzer**.

Children of John Ober and Unknown Unknown are:
    1021 i. Magdalena[10] Ober. She married Henry Brechbill.
+ 1022 ii. Henry Ober, born Aft. 1788.
+ 1023 iii. Veronica Francis Ober, born Abt. 1790; died Aft. 1853.
+ 1024 iv. Nancy Catherine Ober, born 1793; died March 05, 1862.
+ 1025 v. Jacob Ober, born 1794; died 1866.
+ 1026 vi. Anna Nancy Ober, born March 30, 1796; died January 26, 1852.
+ 1027 vii. Elizabeth Ober, born 1799; died July 26, 1864.
+ 1028 viii. John Ober, born Abt. 1800.
+ 1029 ix. Benjamin Ober, born January 30, 1803; died February 24, 1870.

495. Elizabeth[9] Ober (Veronica " Frany "[8] Stauffer, Johannes[7], Daniel[6] Stouffer, Christian[5] Stauffer, Daniel[4] Stouffer, Christian[3], Hans[2], Hans[1]) was born 1777, and died Bef. 1821. She married **David Brubacher**. He was born 1763, and died Abt. 1847.

Children of Elizabeth Ober and David Brubacher are:
+ 1030 i. John O.[10] Brubacher, born 1792; died October 12, 1868.
+ 1031 ii. Jacob O. Brubacher, born May 08, 1796; died April 28, 1839.
+ 1032 iii. Peter O. Brubacher, born May 11, 1798; died May 20, 1871.
+ 1033 iv. David O. Brubacher, born February 08, 1805; died March 12, 1888.
+ 1034 v. Augustus Brubacher, born January 22, 1819; died September 16, 1870.

496. Veronica[9] Ober (Veronica " Frany "[8] Stauffer, Johannes[7], Daniel[6] Stouffer, Christian[5] Stauffer, Daniel[4] Stouffer, Christian[3], Hans[2], Hans[1]) was born January 19, 1784, and died April 23, 1856. She married **Joseph Shenk**. He was born October 12, 1779, and died December 27, 1857.

Children of Veronica Ober and Joseph Shenk are:
    1035 i. John[10] Shenk, born February 02, 1803; died October 27, 1804.
+ 1036 ii. Barbara Shenk, born September 16, 1804; died Bef. 1857.
+ 1037 iii. Jacob Shenk, born December 1806; died June 13, 1874.
+ 1038 iv. Elizabeth Shenk, born April 05, 1807; died June 08, 1884.
    1039 v. Henry Shenk, born July 10, 1808; died December 22, 1810.
    1040 vi. Maria Shenk, born September 23, 1809; died July 26, 1811.
+ 1041 vii. Veronica Shenk, born November 04, 1812; died April 03, 1887.
+ 1042 viii. Joseph Shenk, born March 23, 1814; died July 28, 1893.
+ 1043 ix. Maria Shenk, born December 13, 1814; died August 11, 1892.
+ 1044 x. Magdalena Shenk, born April 02, 1817; died January 30, 1894.
+ 1045 xi. Catherine Shenk, born November 19, 1818; died August 26, 1883.
+ 1046 xii. Nancy Shenk, born January 27, 1820; died March 01, 1842.
    1047 xiii. Lydia Shenk, born Aft. 1829.
    1048 xiv. Sarah Shenk, born Aft. 1829.
    1049 xv. Susanna Shenk, born Aft. 1829.

497. Benjamin[9] Ober (Veronica " Frany "[8] Stauffer, Johannes[7], Daniel[6] Stouffer, Christian[5] Stauffer, Daniel[4] Stouffer, Christian[3], Hans[2], Hans[1]) was born Abt. 1786, and died April 22, 1839. He married **(1) Elizabeth Margaret Messersmith**. She was born February 14, 1774, and died March 07, 1826. He married **(2) Sarah Hambright**. She was born March 28, 1791, and died November 22, 1866.

Child of Benjamin Ober and Elizabeth Messersmith is:
+ 1050 i. Cecelia O.[10] Ober, born June 07, 1820; died June 01, 1887.

Children of Benjamin Ober and Sarah Hambright are:

1051   i.   Susan[10] Ober, born 1828.
1052   ii. Benjamin H. Ober, born Abt. 1829.
1053   iii. James B. Ober, born Aft. 1830.

499. Henry Stauffer (Hockman)[9] Hackman (Elizabeth[8] Stauffer, Henry Jacob[7], Hans[6], Christian[5], Daniel[4] Stouffer, Christian[3], Hans[2], Hans[1]) was born 1760 in Warwick Township, Lancaster County, Pennsylvania, and died March 17, 1831 in Shenandoah County, Virginia. He married **Catherine Hockman Beidler** October 24, 1786 in Lancaster, Pennsylvania. She was born July 15, 1770 in Shenandoah County, Virginia, and died October 13, 1832 in Shenandoah County, Virginia.

Children of Henry Hackman and Catherine Beidler are:
1054   i.   John Beidler[10] Hackman. He married Mary Maphis.
1055   ii. Benjamin Beidler Hackman.
1056   iii. Abraham Beidler Hackman, born March 02, 1794. He married Catherine Stover Hottel; born February 06, 1800.

500. Abraham[9] Hackman (Elizabeth[8] Stauffer, Henry Jacob[7], Hans[6], Christian[5], Daniel[4] Stouffer, Christian[3], Hans[2], Hans[1]) was born Abt. 1770. He married **Elizabeth Unknown**.

Children of Abraham Hackman and Elizabeth Unknown are:
1057   i.   Anna Maria[10] Hackman, born Abt. 1794. She married John Kurtz Zook; born Abt. 1794.
1058   ii. Elizabeth Hackman, born Abt. 1796. She married George M. Bachman/Bauman; born Abt. 1796.
1059   iii. Anna Hackman, born Abt. 1798. She married Henry Musselman; born Abt. 1798.

504. Elizabeth[9] Stauffer (Christian[8], Henry Jacob[7], Hans[6], Christian[5], Daniel[4] Stouffer, Christian[3], Hans[2], Hans[1]) was born October 01, 1765 in Donegal Twp., Lancaster County, Pennsylvania, and died March 07, 1828 in Lancaster County, Pennsylvania. She married **Daniel Brubaker**. He was born April 15, 1762 in Lancaster County, Pennsylvania, and died August 29, 1821 in Lancaster County, Pennsylvania.

Children of Elizabeth Stauffer and Daniel Brubaker are:
+ 1060   i.   Christian[10] Brubaker, born March 30, 1787 in Lancaster County, Pennsylvania; died July 04, 1863 in Lebanon County, Pennsylvania.
+ 1061   ii. Peter Brubaker, born March 08, 1791 in Buffalo Springs, Heidelberg Township, Lebanon County, Pennsylvania; died August 08, 1827 in Heidelberg Township, Lebanon County, Pennsylvania.

506. Jacob[9] Stoffer (Jacob[8] Stauffer, Henry Jacob[7], Hans[6], Christian[5], Daniel[4] Stouffer, Christian[3], Hans[2], Hans[1]) was born August 09, 1780 in New Castle, Lawrence Co, Penna, and died April 1850 in Knox Township, Columbiana County, Ohio. He married **Christina Keister** Abt. September 1805 in Westmoreland County, Penna.. She was born August 20, 1781 in Westmoreland County, Penna., and died November 03, 1870 in Knox Township, Columbiana County, Ohio.

Marriage Notes for Jacob Stoffer and Christina Keister:
[chrststauffer1663.ged]

Custom Field:<_FA#> 1850Columbiana County, Ohio@S03361@Reading Brethren Church Records
_MENDDeath of one spouse

Custom Field:<_FA#> 1850Columbiana County, Ohio@S03361@Reading Brethren Church Records
_MENDDeath of one spouse

1 _M END Death of one spouse

Children of Jacob Stoffer and Christina Keister are:
1062   i.   Elizabeth[10] Stoffer, born May 02, 1801 in Pa   Westmoreland Co.
+ 1063   ii.   Catherine Stoffer, born October 10, 1802 in Pa   Westmoreland Co; died 1851 in Columbiana   Co Ohio.
+ 1064   iii. Jacob S Stoffer, born October 26, 1803 in Westmoreland Pa; died March 02, 1844 in Columbiana   Co Ohio.
1065   iv.   LewisStoffer, born January 27, 1804 in Westmoreland County, Penna.; died February 23, 1885 in Knox Township, Columbiana County, Ohio.
+ 1066   v.   Louis J Stoffer, born January 27, 1804 in Westmoreland Cty Pa; died February 23, 1885 in Columbiana Co Ohio.
1067   vi.   Stoffer Jacob, born October 26, 1805 in Westmoreland County, Penna.; died May 02, 1866 in Carey, Wyandot County, Ohio.
+ 1068   vii. Samuel Stoffer, born January 25, 1806 in Knox Township, Columbiana County, Ohio; died February 14,

1878 in Knox Township, Columbiana County, Ohio.
+ 1069 viii. Margaret Stoffer, born December 15, 1808 in Columbiana Cty, Ohio; died November 15, 1885 in Columbiana Cty, Ohio.
+ 1070 ix. John Stoffer, born 1813 in Knox Township, Columbiana County, Ohio; died 1895 in Richland Ohio, Springfeild Twp.
+ 1071 x. Leah Stoffer, born November 10, 1817 in Knox Township, Columbiana County, Ohio; died February 01, 1898 in Columbiana County, Ohio.
+ 1072 xi. George Stoffer, born July 25, 1820 in Knox Township, Columbiana County, Ohio; died April 21, 1899 in Knox Township, Columbiana County, Ohio.
1073 xii. David Stoffer, born July 25, 1825 in Knox Township, Columbiana County, Ohio.

Generation No. 10

588. Joseph H^{10} Hess (Christian^9, Esther^8 Hershey, Christian^7, Benjamin Stauffer^6, Adelheid Galle^5 Stouffer, Daniel^4, Christian^3, Hans^2, Hans^1) was born September 27, 1824 in Warwick Twp, Lanc Co, PA, and died June 13, 1895. He married **Elizabeth Weidler** October 03, 1848. She was born December 12, 1831 in Warwick Twp, Lanc Co, PA, and died October 25, 1906.

Child of Joseph Hess and Elizabeth Weidler is:
+ 1074 i. Sarah Weidler^{11} Hess, born February 10, 1859 in Warwick Twp, Lanc Co, PA; died September 14, 1926.

589. Barbara^{10} Hess (Christian^9, Esther^8 Hershey, Christian^7, Benjamin Stauffer^6, Adelheid Galle^5 Stouffer, Daniel^4, Christian^3, Hans^2, Hans^1) was born December 25, 1829, and died March 11, 1901 in Warwick Twp., Lancaster Co., PA. She married **Jacob Bomberger**. He was born October 15, 1821, and died May 15, 1885.

Child of Barbara Hess and Jacob Bomberger is:
+ 1075 i. Annie H^{11} Bomberger, born November 20, 1849.

590. Samuel H^{10} Hess (Henry^9, Esther^8 Hershey, Christian^7, Benjamin Stauffer^6, Adelheid Galle^5 Stouffer, Daniel^4, Christian^3, Hans^2, Hans^1) was born November 19, 1830 in Elizabeth Twp Lancaster Co, PA, and died December 10, 1871 in Willow Bank Mills, Elizabeth Twp., Lancaster Co., PA. He married **Fanny Long Landis**, daughter of Benjamin Landis and Anna Long. She was born August 26, 1833 in Manheim Twp, Lanc Co, PA, and died July 16, 1898.

Child of Samuel Hess and Fanny Landis is:
+ 1076 i. Henry L^{11} Hess, born January 28, 1857 in Elizabeth Twp Lancaster Co, PA; died December 10, 1919.

593. Martha H.^{10} Oberholtzer (Martha H.^{9} Hess, Esther^8 Hershey, Christian^7, Benjamin Stauffer^6, Adelheid Galle^5 Stouffer, Daniel^4, Christian^3, Hans^2, Hans^1) was born August 03, 1828, and died June 05, 1869. She married **Joseph Horst Martin** January 18, 1846, son of Abraham Martin and Elizabeth Horst. He was born December 28, 1823, and died September 24, 1900.

Children of Martha Oberholtzer and Joseph Martin are:
1077 i. Elizabeth O.^{11} Martin, born January 15, 1848; died January 10, 1921. She married John B. Keener October 04, 1869; born October 18, 1845.
+ 1078 ii. Magdalena O. Martin, born August 15, 1850; died May 09, 1886.
1079 iii. Anna O. Martin, born August 14, 1853. She married Benjamin Brackbill November 05, 1878; born September 19, 1848.
1080 iv. Samuel O. Martin, born January 29, 1855; died February 27, 1936. He married Amanda Landis; born September 22, 1854; died August 30, 1931.
1081 v. Abraham O. Martin, born January 23, 1857; died May 03, 1858.
1082 vi. Infant1 Martin, born February 19, 1859; died February 24, 1859.
1083 vii. Joseph O. Martin, born February 24, 1860; died October 31, 1861.
1084 viii. Henry O. Martin, born June 19, 1862; died December 30, 1876.
1085 ix. Isaac O. Martin, born October 10, 1864; died October 01, 1872.
1086 x. David O. Martin, born November 29, 1866; died March 13, 1875.
1087 xi. Infant2 Martin, born June 03, 1869; died June 03, 1869.

594. Catharine^{10} Oberholtzer (Martha H.^{9} Hess, Esther^8 Hershey, Christian^7, Benjamin Stauffer^6, Adelheid Galle^5 Stouffer, Daniel^4, Christian^3, Hans^2, Hans^1) was born September 26, 1830, and died July 17, 1918. She married **Joseph Horst Martin** September 06, 1870, son of Abraham Martin and Elizabeth Horst. He was born December 28, 1823, and died September 24, 1900.

Child of Catharine Oberholtzer and Joseph Martin is:
1088 i. Susanna^{11} Martin, born September 06, 1871; died March 30, 1872.

604. Elizabeth Frick[10] Hershey (John Frantz[9], Isaac Hernley[8], Christian[7], Benjamin Stauffer[6], Adelheid Galle[5] Stouffer, Daniel[4], Christian[3], Hans[2], Hans[1]) was born March 21, 1831 in Hummelstown, PA, and died December 16, 1882. She married **Martin Hoover**.

Children of Elizabeth Hershey and Martin Hoover are:
    1089   i.   Annie[11] Hoover.
    1090   ii.   Leah Hoover.

611. Henry Hershey[10] Hershey (Jacob Frantz[9], Isaac Hernley[8], Christian[7], Benjamin Stauffer[6], Adelheid Galle[5] Stouffer, Daniel[4], Christian[3], Hans[2], Hans[1]) was born January 04, 1829 in Derry Twp, Dauphin Co, PA, and died February 18, 1904. He married **Veronica Buckwalter Snavely** January 15, 1856 in Parsonage at Holy Trinity Lutheran Church, Lancaster, PA, daughter of Abraham Snavely and Elizabeth Buckwalter. She was born September 04, 1835 in Pequea Twp, Lancaster Co, PA, and died March 11, 1920.

Children of Henry Hershey and Veronica Snavely are:
    1091   i.   Milton Snavely[11] Hershey, born September 13, 1857 in Derry Twp, PA; died October 13, 1945 in Hershey, PA. He married Catherine Elizabeth Sweeney May 25, 1898 in St. Patrick's Rectory, New York, NY; born July 06, 1872 in Jamestown, NY; died March 25, 1915 in Philadelphia, PA.
    1092   ii.   Sarena Hershey, born April 12, 1862; died March 31, 1867.

614. Christian[10] Hershey (Jacob Frantz[9], Isaac Hernley[8], Christian[7], Benjamin Stauffer[6], Adelheid Galle[5] Stouffer, Daniel[4], Christian[3], Hans[2], Hans[1]) was born March 16, 1836, and died September 29, 1884. He married **Barbara Good**. She was born Abt. 1835.

Children of Christian Hershey and Barbara Good are:
    1093   i.   Virginia[11] Hershey, born 1866; died 1886.
+   1094   ii.   Lorena Hershey, born October 02, 1868.
    1095   iii.   Bessie M Hershey, born April 13, 1874; died August 11, 1911.

615. Jacob H[10] Hershey (Jacob Frantz[9], Isaac Hernley[8], Christian[7], Benjamin Stauffer[6], Adelheid Galle[5] Stouffer, Daniel[4], Christian[3], Hans[2], Hans[1]) was born October 09, 1839. He married **Barbara B Light**. She was born February 13, 1840.

Children of Jacob Hershey and Barbara Light are:
    1096   i.   Morris Light[11] Hershey, born March 04, 1866; died February 05, 1867.
    1097   ii.   Dr. Elmer Light Hershey, born October 27, 1868.
    1098   iii.   Laura Light Hershey, born December 17, 1870; died February 11, 1872.
    1099   iv.   Katie Light Hershey, born July 16, 1872; died August 25, 1918.
    1100   v.   John Adam Light Hershey, born January 22, 1876.
    1101   vi.   Monroe Light Hershey, born January 03, 1878; died March 1907.
+   1102   vii.   Eugene Light Hershey, born October 02, 1880; died August 1966 in 17083 Quentin, Lebanon, PA.
    1103   viii.   Alice Light Hershey, born May 15, 1884; died July 22, 1885.

616. Elias H[10] Hershey (Jacob Frantz[9], Isaac Hernley[8], Christian[7], Benjamin Stauffer[6], Adelheid Galle[5] Stouffer, Daniel[4], Christian[3], Hans[2], Hans[1]) was born December 12, 1841, and died November 16, 1925. He married **Elizabeth Miller Frantz** 1868. She was born December 13, 1844, and died July 09, 1906.

Children of Elias Hershey and Elizabeth Frantz are:
+   1104   i.   Annie[11] Hershey, born November 14, 1869; died May 15, 1916.
+   1105   ii.   Mary Hershey, born November 17, 1872.
    1106   iii.   Jacob Hershey, born March 08, 1876.
    1107   iv.   Christian Hershey, born April 26, 1878.
+   1108   v.   Ezra Frantz Hershey, born September 01, 1879; died 1949.

620. Samuel Harnish[10] Hershey (Samuel[9], Isaac Hernley[8], Christian[7], Benjamin Stauffer[6], Adelheid Galle[5] Stouffer, Daniel[4], Christian[3], Hans[2], Hans[1]) was born September 05, 1841. He married **Mary Bachman** November 18, 1869. She was born August 08, 1847.

Children of Samuel Hershey and Mary Bachman are:
+   1109   i.   Chauncey[11] Hershey, born August 28, 1870.
    1110   ii.   Cora Hershey, born 1872.
    1111   iii.   Elizabeth B Hershey, born 1874.
    1112   iv.   Samuel Mark Hershey, born 1884.

622. Elizabeth[10] Hershey (Samuel[9], Isaac Hernley[8], Christian[7], Benjamin Stauffer[6], Adelheid Galle[5] Stouffer, Daniel[4], Christian[3], Hans[2], Hans[1]) was born December 11, 1851. She married **Franklin Frick Landis**.

Children of Elizabeth Hershey and Franklin Landis are:
- 1113   i.   Ida May[11] Landis, born 1870.
- 1114   ii.   Benjamin F Landis.
- 1115   iii.   Mary Hershey Landis, born 1873.
- + 1116   iv.   Elizabeth H Landis, born 1875 in Franklin Co, PA.
- 1117   v.   Annie E Landis, born 1878.
- 1118   vi.   Adria Landis.
- 1119   vii.   Frank H Landis.
- 1120   viii.   Mark H Landis.

623. Fianna[10] Hershey (Christian[9], Isaac Hernley[8], Christian[7], Benjamin Stauffer[6], Adelheid Galle[5] Stouffer, Daniel[4], Christian[3], Hans[2], Hans[1]) was born March 17, 1841 in Waynesboro, Franklin Co, PA, and died January 29, 1925. She married **Henry B Strickler** December 09, 1866. He died April 04, 1900.

Children of Fianna Hershey and Henry Strickler are:
- 1121   i.   Emerson[11] Strickler.
- 1122   ii.   Ambrose Strickler.
- 1123   iii.   Fannie Strickler.

625. John F[10] Hershey (Christian[9], Isaac Hernley[8], Christian[7], Benjamin Stauffer[6], Adelheid Galle[5] Stouffer, Daniel[4], Christian[3], Hans[2], Hans[1]) was born August 12, 1842 in Waynesboro, Franklin Co, PA. He married **(1) Sarah Mumma**. He married **(2) Mary V Neff** October 11, 1868.

Children of John Hershey and Mary Neff are:
- 1124   i.   Aldus[11] Hershey.
- 1125   ii.   Mary Hershey.

626. Amos F[10] Hershey (Christian[9], Isaac Hernley[8], Christian[7], Benjamin Stauffer[6], Adelheid Galle[5] Stouffer, Daniel[4], Christian[3], Hans[2], Hans[1]) was born August 15, 1845 in Waynesboro, Franklin Co, PA. He married **Frances Beam** November 12, 1867. She was born July 26, 1846.

Children of Amos Hershey and Frances Beam are:
- 1126   i.   Jacob[11] Hershey, born Abt. 1868; died Abt. 1868.
- + 1127   ii.   Naomi B Hershey.
- 1128   iii.   May B Hershey.

627. Martin F[10] Hershey (Christian[9], Isaac Hernley[8], Christian[7], Benjamin Stauffer[6], Adelheid Galle[5] Stouffer, Daniel[4], Christian[3], Hans[2], Hans[1]) was born January 24, 1847 in Waynesboro, Franklin Co, PA. He married **Grace Muench** November 20, 1884. She was born March 1860.

Children of Martin Hershey and Grace Muench are:
- 1129   i.   Mary F[11] Hershey, born August 1886.
- 1130   ii.   Esther G Hershey, born January 1884.

629. Anna[10] Long (Anna[9] Hershey, Jacob[8], Christian[7], Benjamin Stauffer[6], Adelheid Galle[5] Stouffer, Daniel[4], Christian[3], Hans[2], Hans[1]) was born May 29, 1800 in Manheim Twp, Lanc Co, PA, and died May 19, 1885. She married **Benjamin L. Landis** January 01, 1818, son of Henry Landis and Anna Long. He was born November 06, 1791 in Manheim Twp, Lanc Co, PA, and died December 10, 1849.

Child of Anna Long and Benjamin Landis is:
- + 1131   i.   Fanny Long[11] Landis, born August 26, 1833 in Manheim Twp, Lanc Co, PA; died July 16, 1898.

630. Elizabeth[10] Stouffer (Abraham Hershey[9] Stouffer, Abraham Hess[8], Henry Jacob[7], Hans[6], Christian[5], Daniel[4] Stouffer, Christian[3], Hans[2], Hans[1]) She married **David Betzner**.

Children of Elizabeth Stouffer and David Betzner are:
- + 1132   i.   Samuel[11] Betzner, born 1828; died 1914.

+	1133	ii.	Abraham Betzner, born 1829; died 1912.
+	1134	iii.	Jacob Betzner, born 1831; died 1906.
+	1135	iv.	David S. Betzner, born 1835; died 1906.
+	1136	v.	John Weir Betzner, born 1837; died 1906.

634. Christian[10] Stauffer (Abraham Hershey[9], Abraham Hess[8], Henry Jacob[7], Hans[6], Christian[5], Daniel[4] Stouffer, Christian[3], Hans[2], Hans[1]) was born January 17, 1799 in Chambersburg, PA, and died 1868. He married **Magdalena Raymer**.

Children of Christian Stauffer and Magdalena Raymer are:
+	1137	i.	Abraham[11] Stauffer, born May 09, 1826 in Canada.
+	1138	ii.	Elizabeth Stouffer.
+	1139	iii.	Jacob Stouffer.
+	1140	iv.	Martha Stouffer.
+	1141	v.	Christian Stouffer.
+	1142	vi.	John Reesor Stouffer.
+	1143	vii.	Susan Stouffer.
+	1144	viii.	Peter Stouffer.

635. Abraham[10] Stouffer (Abraham Hershey[9] Stauffer, Abraham Hess[8], Henry Jacob[7], Hans[6], Christian[5], Daniel[4] Stouffer, Christian[3], Hans[2], Hans[1]) was born 1806, and died 1878. He married **Esther Lehman**.

Children of Abraham Stouffer and Esther Lehman are:
+	1145	i.	John[11] Stouffer.
+	1146	ii.	Samuel Stouffer.
+	1147	iii.	Jacob Stouffer.
+	1148	iv.	Elizabeth Stouffer.
+	1149	v.	Simeon Stouffer.
+	1150	vi.	Abraham Stouffer, born 1830; died 1909.
+	1151	vii.	Christian Stouffer, born 1839; died 1924.
+	1152	viii.	David Stouffer, born 1844; died 1933.

639. Martha[10] Hostetter (Jacob[9], Jacob[8], Ann Elisabeth[7] Hershey, Benjamin Stauffer[6], Adelheid Galle[5] Stouffer, Daniel[4], Christian[3], Hans[2], Hans[1]) She married **John Stauffer**.

Children of Martha Hostetter and John Stauffer are:
| | 1153 | i. | Elisabeth[11] Stauffer. |
| | 1154 | ii. | David Stauffer. |

641. John[10] Hostetter (Jacob[9], Jacob[8], Ann Elisabeth[7] Hershey, Benjamin Stauffer[6], Adelheid Galle[5] Stouffer, Daniel[4], Christian[3], Hans[2], Hans[1]) was born July 15, 1801 in Penn Twp, Lancaster Cty, PA, and died September 23, 1866 in Lancaster County, Pa. He married **(1) Maria Stauffer**. He married **(2) Elisabeth Forney**.

Children of John Hostetter and Maria Stauffer are:
	1155	i.	Henry[11] Hostetter.
	1156	ii.	Elisabeth Hostetter.
	1157	iii.	Sarah Hostetter.
	1158	iv.	Emanuel F Hostetter.
	1159	v.	Ephraim Hostetter.
	1160	vi.	Maria Hostetter.
	1161	vii.	Benjamin Hostetter, born 1837.
	1162	viii.	John F Hostetter, born 1838.

643. Jacob[10] Hostetter (Jacob[9], Jacob[8], Ann Elisabeth[7] Hershey, Benjamin Stauffer[6], Adelheid Galle[5] Stouffer, Daniel[4], Christian[3], Hans[2], Hans[1]) was born August 25, 1805 in Lancaster County, Pa, and died 1853 in Lancaster County, Pa. He married **Mary Cassel**.

Children of Jacob Hostetter and Mary Cassel are:
	1163	i.	Harriet[11] Hostetter, born 1836.
	1164	ii.	Joseph Hostetter, born 1838.
	1165	iii.	Anna Hostetter, born 1841.

645. Ann[10] **Hostetter** (Jacob[9], Jacob[8], Ann Elisabeth[7] Hershey, Benjamin Stauffer[6], Adelheid Galle[5] Stouffer, Daniel[4], Christian[3], Hans[2], Hans[1]) was born 1807 in Lancaster County, Pa, and died 1895 in Lancaster County, Pa. She married **Christian Wissler**. He was born 1805, and died 1878.

Children of Ann Hostetter and Christian Wissler are:
- 1166   i.   Elisabeth[11] Wissler, born 1832.
- 1167   ii.   Benjamin Wissler, born 1838.
- 1168   iii. Jacob Wissler, born 1842.
- 1169   iv.   Mary Wissler, born 1845.

646. Susan[10] **Hostetter** (Jacob[9], Jacob[8], Ann Elisabeth[7] Hershey, Benjamin Stauffer[6], Adelheid Galle[5] Stouffer, Daniel[4], Christian[3], Hans[2], Hans[1]) was born 1809 in Lancaster County, Pa, and died 1866. She married **John Sheaffer**.

Child of Susan Hostetter and John Sheaffer is:
- 1170   i.   Josiah[11] Sheaffer.

647. Barbara[10] **Hostetter** (Jacob[9], Jacob[8], Ann Elisabeth[7] Hershey, Benjamin Stauffer[6], Adelheid Galle[5] Stouffer, Daniel[4], Christian[3], Hans[2], Hans[1]) was born 1811. She married **Joseph Hershey**.

Children of Barbara Hostetter and Joseph Hershey are:
- 1171   i.   Ephraim[11] Hershey.
- 1172   ii.   Benjamin Hershey.
- 1173   iii. Joseph Hershey.
- 1174   iv.   Esther Hershey.
- 1175   v.   Anna Hershey.

648. David[10] **Hostetter** (Jacob[9], Jacob[8], Ann Elisabeth[7] Hershey, Benjamin Stauffer[6], Adelheid Galle[5] Stouffer, Daniel[4], Christian[3], Hans[2], Hans[1]) was born January 27, 1816 in Lancaster County, Pa, and died May 19, 1885 in Lancaster County, Pa. He married **Maria Peifer**. She was born 1819, and died 1898.

Children of David Hostetter and Maria Peifer are:
- 1176   i.   Pharus[11] Hostetter.
- 1177   ii.   Martha Hostetter.
- 1178   iii. Lizzie Hostetter.
- 1179   iv.   David M Hostetter.
- 1180   v.   Sarah A Hostetter.
- 1181   vi.   Jacob P Hostetter, born 1840.
- 1182   vii. Josiah Hostetter, born 1845.
- 1183   viii. Abraham Hostetter, born 1847.
- 1184   ix.   Nathan Hostetter, born 1854.
- 1185   x.   Emanuel P Hostetter, born 1856.
- 1186   xi.   Cephas Hostetter, born 1859.
- 1187   xii. Benjamin F Hostetter, born 1862.

649. Catherine[10] **Hostetter** (Jacob[9], Jacob[8], Ann Elisabeth[7] Hershey, Benjamin Stauffer[6], Adelheid Galle[5] Stouffer, Daniel[4], Christian[3], Hans[2], Hans[1]) was born 1818. She married **Christian Erisman**.

Children of Catherine Hostetter and Christian Erisman are:
- 1188   i.   Susan[11] Erisman.
- 1189   ii.   Elizabeth Erisman.
- 1190   iii. Metz Erisman.
- 1191   iv.   Sarah Erisman.
- 1192   v.   Albert Erisman.
- 1193   vi.   Mary Erisman.
- 1194   vii. Elnora Erisman.
- 1195   viii. Amelia Erisman.

650. Fanny[10] **Hostetter** (Jacob[9], Jacob[8], Ann Elisabeth[7] Hershey, Benjamin Stauffer[6], Adelheid Galle[5] Stouffer, Daniel[4], Christian[3], Hans[2], Hans[1]) was born August 28, 1820, and died December 12, 1893. She married **David Hershey**. He was born January 08, 1817, and died December 07, 1898.

Children of Fanny Hostetter and David Hershey are:
- 1196 i. Benjamin H[11] Hershey.
- 1197 ii. Susan Hershey.
- 1198 iii. Amos H Hershey.
- 1199 iv. David C Hershey.

653. Joseph[10] Hostetter (Abraham[9], Jacob[8], Ann Elisabeth[7] Hershey, Benjamin Stauffer[6], Adelheid Galle[5] Stouffer, Daniel[4], Christian[3], Hans[2], Hans[1]) was born January 29, 1801 in Manheim, Pa, and died September 10, 1872 in Ashland County, Ohio. He married **Elisabeth Hershey**. She was born September 11, 1805 in Lancaster County, Pa, and died May 04, 1883 in Ashland County, Pa.

Children of Joseph Hostetter and Elisabeth Hershey are:
- 1200 i. Oliver[11] Hostetter.
- 1201 ii. Cecilia Hostetter, born 1826.
- 1202 iii. Elisabeth Hostetter, born 1828.
- 1203 iv. Benjamin Hostetter, born 1830.
- + 1204 v. Joseph Hostetter, born March 02, 1832; died February 23, 1928 in Ashland County, Ohio.
- + 1205 vi. Henry Hostetter, born September 08, 1834; died 1894 in Ohio.
- + 1206 vii. David Hostetter, born September 15, 1838; died March 01, 1917 in Ohio.
- 1207 viii. Elisabeth Hostetter, born 1840.
- 1208 ix. Ann Marie Hostetter, born 1843.
- 1209 x. Harriet Ester Hostetter, born 1849.

655. Abraham[10] Hostetter (Abraham[9], Jacob[8], Ann Elisabeth[7] Hershey, Benjamin Stauffer[6], Adelheid Galle[5] Stouffer, Daniel[4], Christian[3], Hans[2], Hans[1]) was born November 01, 1809 in Manheim, Pa, and died May 24, 1881 in Lancaster, Pa. He married **Lydia White** September 27, 1832 in Manheim, Pa. She was born March 07, 1813 in Cumru Twp, Berks County, Pa, and died July 20, 1868 in Shippensberg, Pa.

Children of Abraham Hostetter and Lydia White are:
- + 1210 i. Fianna[11] Hostetter, born August 11, 1833 in Lancaster County, Pa; died September 11, 1913 in Lancaster County, Pa.
- 1211 ii. Bert Hostetter, born July 27, 1835.
- + 1212 iii. Susan A Hostetter, born August 17, 1836.
- + 1213 iv. Harriet A Hostetter, born July 14, 1838 in Lancaster County, Pa; died June 30, 1903 in Cedar Rapids, Iowa.
- + 1214 v. Lucinda Hostetter, born October 15, 1840 in Lancaster County, Pa.
- 1215 vi. Elizabeth Hostetter, born November 05, 1842.
- + 1216 vii. Christina Hostetter, born June 11, 1843 in Lancaster County, Pa; died February 14, 1909.
- + 1217 viii. Isabella Victoria Hostetter, born July 12, 1845.
- + 1218 ix. Clement Hostetter, born November 20, 1847 in Lancaster County, Pa; died March 07, 1921 in Cedar Rapids, Iowa.
- 1219 x. Lydia Ann Hostetter, born July 11, 1849.
- + 1220 xi. Abraham Webster Hostetter, born October 20, 1851 in Lancaster County, Pa; died January 29, 1935 in Minnesota.
- + 1221 xii. Taylor T Hostetter, born November 02, 1853 in Lancaster, pa; died September 22, 1912 in Reading, Pa.

657. David[10] Hostetter (Abraham[9], Jacob[8], Ann Elisabeth[7] Hershey, Benjamin Stauffer[6], Adelheid Galle[5] Stouffer, Daniel[4], Christian[3], Hans[2], Hans[1]) was born June 03, 1815 in Manheim, Pa, and died October 09, 1887 in Lancaster, Pa. He married **(1) Maria Reinohl**. He married **(2) Unknown Rebecca**. She was born 1821, and died 1850.

Children of David Hostetter and Unknown Rebecca are:
- 1222 i. Lillie[11] Hostetter.
- 1223 ii. Mary Hostetter.
- 1224 iii. Alice M Hostetter.
- 1225 iv. Frank L Hostetter.
- 1226 v. David R Hostetter.
- 1227 vi. William H Hostetter, born 1841.
- 1228 vii. Hiram C. Hostetter, born 1844; died 1863 in White Plains, VA.
- + 1229 viii. Annie Hostetter, born January 1853 in Lancaster County, Pa.

663. Anna[10] Bassler (Barbara[9] Hostetter, Jacob[8], Ann Elisabeth[7] Hershey, Benjamin Stauffer[6], Adelheid Galle[5] Stouffer, Daniel[4],

Christian[3], Hans[2], Hans[1]) was born 1812 in Mannheim Twp, Lancaster, PA, and died April 29, 1886. She married **(1) John Ringer**. She married **(2) Abraham Hershey** April 13, 1831 in Lancaster, PA, son of Christian Hershey and Elizabeth Yordy. He was born 1807 in Mannheim Twp, Lancaster, PA, and died June 13, 1864 in Carrollton, LA.

Children are listed above under (239) Abraham Hershey.

683. Lea[10] Bear (Anna[9] Frantz, Barbara[8] Hostetter, Ann Elisabeth[7] Hershey, Benjamin Stauffer[6], Adelheid Galle[5] Stouffer, Daniel[4], Christian[3], Hans[2], Hans[1]) was born Abt. 1800. She married **Unknown Martin**. He was born Abt. 1800.

Children of Lea Bear and Unknown Martin are:
- 1230   i. Rolandis[11] Martin, born Abt. 1825.
- 1231   ii. Wayne Martin, born Abt. 1825.

684. Susanna Frantz[10] Bear (Anna[9] Frantz, Barbara[8] Hostetter, Ann Elisabeth[7] Hershey, Benjamin Stauffer[6], Adelheid Galle[5] Stouffer, Daniel[4], Christian[3], Hans[2], Hans[1]) was born January 16, 1804, and died January 21, 1886 in Hammercreek Cemetery. She married **(1) David Hiestand Hackman**. He was born September 21, 1801, and died December 29, 1831 in Elizabeth Township, Lancaster County, Pennsylvania. She married **(2) John Gesell Brubaker**. He was born November 10, 1797, and died February 27, 1884 in Hammercreek Cemetery.

Children of Susanna Bear and David Hackman are:
- \+ 1232   i. Jacob Baer[11] Hackman, born March 26, 1825; died January 20, 1899.
- \+ 1233   ii. David Baer Hackman, born March 19, 1827; died November 16, 1896.
- \+ 1234   iii. Andrew Baer Hackman, born July 05, 1828; died July 27, 1916.
- 1235   iv. Anna Hackman, born November 27, 1829; died April 10, 1830.

Children of Susanna Bear and John Brubaker are:
- 1236   i. Susan B[11] Brubaker, born August 14, 1840; died August 18, 1860 in Hammercreek Cemetery.
- 1237   ii. Fanny Brubaker, born July 03, 1843; died August 16, 1935. She married Benjamin N Bollinger; born May 15, 1838; died October 28, 1906.
- 1238   iii. Mary Brubaker, born 1844. She married Richard Rickert; born Abt. 1840 in Warwick Township, Lancaster County, PA.
- 1239   iv. Isaac Brubaker, born October 25, 1846; died August 24, 1867 in Hammercreek Cemetery.

687. Isaac F[10] Bear (Anna[9] Frantz, Barbara[8] Hostetter, Ann Elisabeth[7] Hershey, Benjamin Stauffer[6], Adelheid Galle[5] Stouffer, Daniel[4], Christian[3], Hans[2], Hans[1]) was born January 15, 1815, and died 1858.

Children of Isaac F Bear are:
- 1240   i. John[11] Bear, born Aft. 1835.
- 1241   ii. Gabriel Bear, born Aft. 1835.

694. Emmanuel[10] Hostetter (Rudolph[9], Benjamin[8], Ann Elisabeth[7] Hershey, Benjamin Stauffer[6], Adelheid Galle[5] Stouffer, Daniel[4], Christian[3], Hans[2], Hans[1]) was born March 08, 1817 in Lancaster County, Pa, and died May 26, 1890 in Lancaster County, Pa. He married **Mina Unknown**.

Children of Emmanuel Hostetter and Mina Unknown are:
- 1242   i. Edward[11] Hostetter, born 1857.
- 1243   ii. Hettie Hostetter, born 1861.
- 1244   iii. Benjamin Hostetter, born 1864.
- 1245   iv. Wilhelmina Hostetter, born 1867.

699. Ezra[10] Hostetter (Benjamin[9], Benjamin[8], Ann Elisabeth[7] Hershey, Benjamin Stauffer[6], Adelheid Galle[5] Stouffer, Daniel[4], Christian[3], Hans[2], Hans[1]) was born December 20, 1838 in Manor Twp, Lancaster Cty, PA, and died October 14, 1919 in Lancaster County, Pa. He married **Susan Dietrich**. She was born December 16, 1834, and died January 26, 1910 in Lancaster County, Pa.

Children of Ezra Hostetter and Susan Dietrich are:
- \+ 1246   i. Kathryn[11] Hostetter, born in Lancaster County, Pa.
- 1247   ii. Mary Elisabeth Hostetter.
- 1248   iii. Benjamin D. Hostetter, born 1861.
- \+ 1249   iv. Jacob D. Hostetter, born October 06, 1863 in Lancaster County, Pa; died May 04, 1951 in Lancaster County, Pa.

700. Jacob H[10] Hostetter (Benjamin[9], Benjamin[8], Ann Elisabeth[7] Hershey, Benjamin Stauffer[6], Adelheid Galle[5] Stouffer, Daniel[4], Christian[3], Hans[2], Hans[1]) was born January 27, 1841 in Lancaster County, Pa, and died April 04, 1932 in Lancaster County, Pa. He married **Mary Rebecca Miller**. She was born 1851, and died May 20, 1922.

Children of Jacob Hostetter and Mary Miller are:
- 1250   i.   Bessie Grace[11] Hostetter, born 1874.
- 1251   ii. W. Clyde Hostetter, born 1876.
- 1252   iii. Mary Edith Hostetter, born 1878.
- 1253   iv. Lida Garber Hostetter, born 1881.
- 1254   v.   Maude Gertrude Hostetter, born 1884.
- 1255   vi. Adele Hostetter, born 1889.

742. John[10] Hostetter (John[9], Abraham[8], Catharine[7] Long, Anna[6] Hershey, Adelheid Galle[5] Stouffer, Daniel[4], Christian[3], Hans[2], Hans[1]) was born January 11, 1817 in Adams Cty, PA, and died February 13, 1872 in Adams Cty, PA. He married **Anna Kindig**. She was born April 30, 1821, and died August 13, 1887 in Adams Cty, PA.

Children of John Hostetter and Anna Kindig are:
- 1256   i.   Daniel M[11] Hostetter, born 1848.
- 1257   ii. Sarah J Hostetter, born 1851.
- 1258   iii. Mary C Hostetter, born 1861.

743. Abraham F.[10] Hostetter (John[9], Abraham[8], Catharine[7] Long, Anna[6] Hershey, Adelheid Galle[5] Stouffer, Daniel[4], Christian[3], Hans[2], Hans[1]) was born October 05, 1820 in Adams Cty, PA, and died February 14, 1868 in Adams Cty, PA. He married **(1) Anna Forry**. She was born November 21, 1817, and died July 13, 1845 in Adams Cty, PA. He married **(2) Mary Huber**. She was born August 14, 1825, and died February 20, 1875 in Adams Cty, PA.

Child of Abraham Hostetter and Anna Forry is:
- 1259   i.   Barbara[11] Hostetter, born 1843.

Children of Abraham Hostetter and Mary Huber are:
- 1260   i.   Jacob H[11] Hostetter.
- 1261   ii.   Samuel H Hostetter, born 1849.
- 1262   iii. Anna Magdalena Hostetter, born 1854.
- 1263   iv.   Emanuel H Hostetter, born 1856.
- 1264   v.   Mary Elisabeth Hostetter, born 1861.
- 1265   vi.   Emma Jane Hostetter, born 1861.
- 1266   vii. Emma Jane Hostetter, born 1863.
- 1267   viii. Aaron Hostetter, born 1866.
- 1268   ix.   Alverta Hostetter, born 1867.

745. Jacob K.[10] Hostetter (John[9], Abraham[8], Catharine[7] Long, Anna[6] Hershey, Adelheid Galle[5] Stouffer, Daniel[4], Christian[3], Hans[2], Hans[1]) was born October 05, 1824 in Adams Cty, PA, and died November 18, 1898 in Adams Cty, PA. He married **(1) Mary Swope Weikert**. He married **(2) Catherine Lohr**.

Children of Jacob Hostetter and Mary Weikert are:
- 1269   i.   John Henry[11] Hostetter, born 1852.
- 1270   ii.   Ann R Hostetter, born 1854.
- 1271   iii. Mary Ellen Hostetter, born 1855.
- 1272   iv.   Emma J Hostetter, born 1857.
- 1273   v.   Catherine Hostetter, born 1859.
- 1274   vi.   Susan Alice Hostetter, born 1861.
- 1275   vii. Sarah E Hostetter, born 1863.
- 1276   viii. Amos J Hostetter, born 1865.
- 1277   ix.   Abraham Hostetter, born 1867.
- 1278   x.   Samuel E Hostetter, born 1868.
- 1279   xi.   Margaret Hostetter, born 1871.

Child of Jacob Hostetter and Catherine Lohr is:
- 1280   i.   Minnie[11] Hostetter, born 1877.

746. Elisabeth[10] **Hostetter** (John[9], Abraham[8], Catharine[7] Long, Anna[6] Hershey, Adelheid Galle[5] Stouffer, Daniel[4], Christian[3], Hans[2], Hans[1]) was born February 26, 1827 in Adams Cty, PA, and died July 13, 1894. She married **Samuel Grove**. He was born November 12, 1824, and died March 28, 1894.

Children of Elisabeth Hostetter and Samuel Grove are:
- 1281 i. John[11] Grove.
- 1282 ii. Daniel Grove.
- 1283 iii. Samuel Grove.
- 1284 iv. Mary Grove.
- 1285 v. George Grove.
- 1286 vi. Martin Grove.
- 1287 vii. Annie Grove.
- 1288 viii. Abraham Grove.
- 1289 ix. Henry Grove.

747. Mary[10] **Hostetter** (John[9], Abraham[8], Catharine[7] Long, Anna[6] Hershey, Adelheid Galle[5] Stouffer, Daniel[4], Christian[3], Hans[2], Hans[1]) was born January 29, 1829 in Adams Cty, PA, and died November 09, 1910. She married **Martin Grove**. He was born April 02, 1827, and died June 21, 1883.

Child of Mary Hostetter and Martin Grove is:
- 1290 i. Mary[11] Grove.

749. Benjamin[10] **Hostetter** (John[9], Abraham[8], Catharine[7] Long, Anna[6] Hershey, Adelheid Galle[5] Stouffer, Daniel[4], Christian[3], Hans[2], Hans[1]) was born September 25, 1832 in Adams Cty, PA, and died July 25, 1882 in Adams Cty, PA. He married **Maria Forry**. She was born August 14, 1833, and died August 29, 1911.

Children of Benjamin Hostetter and Maria Forry are:
- 1291 i. Ezra[11] Hostetter.
- 1292 ii. Henry Hostetter.
- 1293 iii. Benjamin Hostetter.
- 1294 iv. Abraham Hostetter, born 1868.
- 1295 v. John Hostetter, born 1877.

751. Christian[10] **Hostetter** (Ulrich[9], Abraham[8], Catharine[7] Long, Anna[6] Hershey, Adelheid Galle[5] Stouffer, Daniel[4], Christian[3], Hans[2], Hans[1]) was born August 16, 1823 in Lancaster County, Pa, and died February 27, 1879 in Lancaster County, Pa. He married **(1) Maria Haverstick**. She was born 1830, and died 1864 in Lancaster County, Pa. He married **(2) Magdalena Herr** February 14, 1865. She was born November 20, 1830 in Millersville, PA.

Children of Christian Hostetter and Maria Haverstick are:
- 1296 i. John[11] Hostetter.
- 1297 ii. Catherine Hostetter.
- 1298 iii. Aaron Hostetter, born 1850.
- 1299 iv. Ephraim Hostetter, born 1853.
- 1300 v. Jacob H Hostetter, born 1855.
- 1301 vi. Emma Hostetter, born 1866.

Child of Christian Hostetter and Magdalena Herr is:
- 1302 i. Emma M[11] Hostetter, born January 16, 1866. She married Elmer Erisman.

752. Anna[10] **Hostetter** (Ulrich[9], Abraham[8], Catharine[7] Long, Anna[6] Hershey, Adelheid Galle[5] Stouffer, Daniel[4], Christian[3], Hans[2], Hans[1]) was born November 07, 1827 in Lancaster County, Pa, and died October 08, 1854 in Lancaster County, Pa. She married **Benjamin Neff**. He was born August 23, 1821 in Lancaster County, Pa, and died June 29, 1879 in Lancaster County, Pa.

Children of Anna Hostetter and Benjamin Neff are:
- 1303 i. Cyrus[11] Hostetter.
- 1304 ii. Benjamin Hostetter.

759. Jacob[10] **Hostetter** (Abraham[9], Jacob[8], Catharine[7] Long, Anna[6] Hershey, Adelheid Galle[5] Stouffer, Daniel[4], Christian[3], Hans[2], Hans[1]) was born April 24, 1814 in Lancaster County, Pa, and died February 23, 1879 in Lancaster County, Pa. He married **Marie Witmer**. She was born October 25, 1812, and died May 20, 1897 in Lancaster County, Pa.

Children of Jacob Hostetter and Marie Witmer are:
+ 1305 i. Amos[11] Hostetter.
+ 1306 ii. Anna Hostetter.
   1307 iii. John Hostetter.

760. Abraham[10] Hostetter (Abraham[9], Jacob[8], Catharine[7] Long, Anna[6] Hershey, Adelheid Galle[5] Stouffer, Daniel[4], Christian[3], Hans[2], Hans[1]) was born September 26, 1818 in Lancaster County, Pa, and died July 12, 1873 in Mt. Carroll, Il.. He married **Catherine Bowman** November 25, 1841.

Children of Abraham Hostetter and Catherine Bowman are:
+ 1308 i. Linnaeus[11] Hostetter, born 1842 in Lancaster County, Pa; died in Illinois.
+ 1309 ii. Abram Hostetter, born June 01, 1847 in Lancaster County, Pa; died October 21, 1921 in Illinois.
+ 1310 iii. Ross Hostetter, born 1852 in Lancaster County, Pa; died in Illinois.
   1311 iv. Sarah Hostetter, born 1856.
   1312 v. Susan Hostetter, born 1860.

774. David[10] Hostetter (Jacob[9], Jacob[8], Catharine[7] Long, Anna[6] Hershey, Adelheid Galle[5] Stouffer, Daniel[4], Christian[3], Hans[2], Hans[1]) was born January 23, 1819, and died November 06, 1888 in Pennsylvania. He married **Rosetta Cobb Richey** July 13, 1854. She was born October 06, 1829, and died July 03, 1904.

Children of David Hostetter and Rosetta Richey are:
   1313 i. Harry H.[11] Hostetter.
   1314 ii. Wilfred Hostetter.
+ 1315 iii. Amy Susette Hostetter, born 1858; died in Pennsylvania.
+ 1316 iv. David H. Hostetter, born 1859.
   1317 v. Theodore Hostetter, born 1869.

806. Thomas[10] Hostetter (Abraham[9], Herman[8], Catharine[7] Long, Anna[6] Hershey, Adelheid Galle[5] Stouffer, Daniel[4], Christian[3], Hans[2], Hans[1]) was born 1825 in Canada, and died 1870 in Canada. He married **Emma Jane Smith**. She was born 1840, and died 1895.

Children of Thomas Hostetter and Emma Smith are:
+ 1318 i. Emma Elisabeth[11] Hostetter, born 1860; died 1906.
   1319 ii. Louisa Jane Hostetter, born 1862. She married William Hamilton; born 1866.

852. John[10] Herr (Anna[9] Hostetter, John[8], Catharine[7] Long, Anna[6] Hershey, Adelheid Galle[5] Stouffer, Daniel[4], Christian[3], Hans[2], Hans[1]) was born January 11, 1834. He married **Barbara Peters**. She was born October 02, 1838.

Children of John Herr and Barbara Peters are:
+ 1320 i. Minnie P[11] Herr, born 1878; died Aft. 1930.
   1321 ii. Henry P Herr, born 1860.
   1322 iii. Jacob P Herr, born 1869.

854. Barbara[10] Hostetter (Abraham[9], John[8], Catharine[7] Long, Anna[6] Hershey, Adelheid Galle[5] Stouffer, Daniel[4], Christian[3], Hans[2], Hans[1]) She married **Abram Herr**.

Child of Barbara Hostetter and Abram Herr is:
   1323 i. Mary[11] Herr.

856. David[10] Hostetter (Abraham[9], John[8], Catharine[7] Long, Anna[6] Hershey, Adelheid Galle[5] Stouffer, Daniel[4], Christian[3], Hans[2], Hans[1]) was born 1808 in Lancaster County, Pa, and died 1872 in Lancaster County, Pa. He married **(1) Esther Bossler**. He married **(2) Catherine Miller**. She was born 1804, and died 1885 in Lancaster County, Pa.

Child of David Hostetter and Esther Bossler is:
   1324 i. Hetty[11] Hostetter, born 1831.

Children of David Hostetter and Catherine Miller are:
   1325 i. Elisabeth[11] Hostetter.
   1326 ii. Eva Hostetter.

1327 iii. Hannah Hostetter.
1328 iv. John Hostetter.
1329 v. Abraham Hostetter, born 1834.
1330 vi. Jacob Hostetter, born 1835.
1331 vii. David M Hostetter, born 1836.
1332 viii. Joseph Hostetter, born 1839.
1333 ix. Catharine Hostetter, born 1842.
1334 x. Amos Hostetter, born 1846.

864. John E.[10] Hostetter (John[9], John[8], Catharine[7] Long, Anna[6] Hershey, Adelheid Galle[5] Stouffer, Daniel[4], Christian[3], Hans[2], Hans[1]) was born February 02, 1823 in Lancaster County, Pa, and died April 08, 1908 in Lancaster County, Pa. He married **Elisabeth Stehman**. She was born July 18, 1831 in Lancaster County, Pa, and died May 14, 1909 in Lancaster County, Pa.

Children of John Hostetter and Elisabeth Stehman are:
1335 i. Lizzie[11] Hostetter.
1336 ii. Mary Hostetter.
1337 iii. John Hostetter.
1338 iv. Anna Hostetter, born 1855.
1339 v. Kathryn Hostetter, born 1864.
1340 vi. Amos Hostetter, born 1869.
1341 vii. Jonas Hostetter, born 1871.
1342 viii. Ella Hostetter, born 1875.

865. Jonas E.[10] Hostetter (John[9], John[8], Catharine[7] Long, Anna[6] Hershey, Adelheid Galle[5] Stouffer, Daniel[4], Christian[3], Hans[2], Hans[1]) was born January 13, 1833 in Lancaster County, Pa, and died August 15, 1803 in Lancaster County, Pa. He married **Barbara Nissley**. She was born January 07, 1837, and died April 14, 1920 in Lancaster County, Pa.

Children of Jonas Hostetter and Barbara Nissley are:
1343 i. Jacob[11] Hostetter.
1344 ii. Levi Hostetter.
1345 iii. Elam Hostetter.
1346 iv. Jonas Hostetter.
1347 v. Tilman N Hostetter, born 1858.
1348 vi. Mary Hostetter, born 1864.
1349 vii. Amos Hostetter, born 1866.
1350 viii. Abner Hostetter, born 1873.
1351 ix. Simon Hostetter, born 1876.

866. Abraham[10] Hostetter (John[9], John[8], Catharine[7] Long, Anna[6] Hershey, Adelheid Galle[5] Stouffer, Daniel[4], Christian[3], Hans[2], Hans[1]) was born 1835 in Lancaster County, Pa, and died in Lancaster County, Pa. He married **Rose Hogendobler**.

Children of Abraham Hostetter and Rose Hogendobler are:
1352 i. Alice[11] Hostetter.
1353 ii. Fannie Hostetter.

869. Maria[10] Hostetter (John[9], Christian[8], Catharine[7] Long, Anna[6] Hershey, Adelheid Galle[5] Stouffer, Daniel[4], Christian[3], Hans[2], Hans[1]) was born October 06, 1812, and died August 21, 1860. She married **Jacob Royer**. He was born November 10, 1805, and died December 26, 1862.

Children of Maria Hostetter and Jacob Royer are:
1354 i. Samuel[11] Royer.
1355 ii. Susannah Royer.
1356 iii. Ephraim Royer, born 1833.
1357 iv. Jonas Royer, born 1836.
1358 v. Mary Royer, born 1837.
1359 vi. John Royer, born 1839.
1360 vii. Leah Royer, born 1842.
1361 viii. Jacob Royer, born 1849.
1362 ix. William Royer, born 1852.

871. Samuel[10] **Hostetter** (John[9], Christian[8], Catharine[7] Long, Anna[6] Hershey, Adelheid Galle[5] Stouffer, Daniel[4], Christian[3], Hans[2], Hans[1]) was born October 26, 1816 in Lancaster County, Pa, and died February 16, 1860 in Lebanon Cty, PA. He married **Catharine Leffler**. She was born April 03, 1812, and died December 31, 1880.

Children of Samuel Hostetter and Catharine Leffler are:
- 1363　　i.　　Levi[11] Hostetter.
- 1364　　ii.　　Lydia Hostetter.
- 1365　　iii.　　Mary Hostetter.
- 1366　　iv.　　Catharine Hostetter.
- 1367　　v.　　Elisabeth Ann Hostetter, born 1844.
- 1368　　vi.　　Samuel G Hostetter, born 1854.

872. Christian[10] **Hostetter** (John[9], Christian[8], Catharine[7] Long, Anna[6] Hershey, Adelheid Galle[5] Stouffer, Daniel[4], Christian[3], Hans[2], Hans[1]) was born October 21, 1819, and died February 08, 1897 in Lebanon Cty, PA. He married **Sarah Hibshman**. She was born 1824, and died 1860.

Children of Christian Hostetter and Sarah Hibshman are:
- 1369　　i.　　John H[11] Hostetter.
- 1370　　ii.　　William H Hostetter, born 1842.

873. John[10] **Hostetter** (John[9], Christian[8], Catharine[7] Long, Anna[6] Hershey, Adelheid Galle[5] Stouffer, Daniel[4], Christian[3], Hans[2], Hans[1]) was born November 30, 1821, and died March 03, 1907 in Lebanon Cty, PA. He married **Sarah Gockley**. She was born October 19, 1821, and died August 21, 1891.

Children of John Hostetter and Sarah Gockley are:
- 1371　　i.　　Levi[11] Hostetter.
- 1372　　ii.　　Fanny Hostetter, born 1851.

934. Peter[10] **Hershey** (Jacob[9], John[8], Jacob Snavely[7], Andrew Stauffer[6], Adelheid Galle[5] Stouffer, Daniel[4], Christian[3], Hans[2], Hans[1]) was born August 02, 1839, and died December 17, 1922. He married **Barbara Neff Buckwalter**, daughter of Henry Buckwalter and Barbara Neff. She was born January 23, 1840, and died March 29, 1911.

Children of Peter Hershey and Barbara Buckwalter are:
- 　　1373　　i.　　Infant[11] Hershey, born May 10, 1862; died May 10, 1862.
- +　1374　　ii.　　Sarah Lucinda Hershey, born September 09, 1863; died December 22, 1942.
- +　1375　　iii.　　Isaiah B. Hershey, born June 28, 1865; died October 09, 1919.
- +　1376　　iv.　　Enos Jacob Hershey, born November 02, 1866; died March 20, 1939.
- +　1377　　v.　　Elizabeth Hershey, born September 09, 1868; died September 06, 1934.
- 　　1378　　vi.　　Mary Hershey, born January 01, 1870; died April 08, 1878.
- +　1379　　vii.　　Henry Peter Hershey, born March 14, 1872; died December 10, 1949.
- +　1380　　viii.　　Martin Eby Hershey, born December 20, 1873; died June 13, 1953.
- 　　1381　　ix.　　Ellen Hershey, born March 29, 1875; died April 16, 1878.
- 　　1382　　x.　　Martha A. Hershey, born August 12, 1876; died August 19, 1968. She married Amos H. Hoover; born November 21, 1852; died October 12, 1941.
- 　　1383　　xi.　　Barbara Hershey, born June 25, 1878; died July 26, 1896.
- 　　1384　　xii.　　Infant Hershey, born December 24, 1879; died December 24, 1879.
- +　1385　　xiii.　　Silas N. Hershey, born March 22, 1881; died November 20, 1970.

941. Annie[10] **Reiff** (Veronica[9] Hershey, John[8], Jacob Snavely[7], Andrew Stauffer[6], Adelheid Galle[5] Stouffer, Daniel[4], Christian[3], Hans[2], Hans[1]) was born October 24, 1842 in West Earl Twp, Lanc Co, PA, and died February 23, 1917. She married **Chambers U. Sweigart**. He was born August 23, 1841 in Lancaster Co, PA, and died August 24, 1923.

Children of Annie Reiff and Chambers Sweigart are:
- 　　1386　　i.　　Amos R.[11] Sweigart, born October 06, 1864; died July 15, 1865.
- 　　1387　　ii.　　Abraham R. Sweigart, born November 28, 1865; died October 24, 1934. He married (1) Mary C. Heiney; born September 26, 1863; died March 31, 1895. He married (2) Mary Ann Wenger; born July 29, 1871; died November 16, 1956.
- 　　1388　　iii.　　John R. Sweigart, born June 25, 1867; died November 07, 1928. He married Wynaria M. Geist; born September 07, 1866; died November 15, 1937.
- +　1389　　iv.　　Frances Reiff Sweigart, born November 03, 1868 in Earl Twp, Lanc Co, PA; died December 12, 1947.
- 　　1390　　v.　　Martin R. Sweigart, born April 21, 1870; died May 03, 1929. He married Lydia Ann Sauder; born April 20, 1870; died April 05, 1922.

1391	vi.	Anna R. Sweigart, born January 28, 1872; died January 27, 1948. She married John B. Rutt; born April 27, 1872; died July 13, 1951.
1392	vii.	Elizabeth R. Sweigart, born September 03, 1873; died May 12, 1936. She married John Kilhefner; born July 19, 1871; died December 16, 1943.
1393	viii.	Jacob R. Sweigart, born May 18, 1876; died July 20, 1963. He married Hannah G. Shirk; born August 07, 1881; died 1963.
1394	ix.	Lydia R. Sweigart, born March 25, 1878; died March 08, 1949. She married Frank Kilhefner; born October 02, 1874; died February 21, 1939.
1395	x.	Amanda R. Sweigart, born February 15, 1879; died November 13, 1940. She married (1) Phares B. Gehman; born September 06, 1875; died March 12, 1898. She married (2) John L. Gockley; born February 26, 1855; died October 03, 1936.
1396	xi.	Eli R. Sweigart, born October 19, 1885; died August 16, 1957. He married Mary E. Leicy; born February 02, 1889; died September 22, 1968.

958. Susan[10] **Hershey** (Abraham[9], Christian[8], Jacob Snavely[7], Andrew Stauffer[6], Adelheid Galle[5] Stouffer, Daniel[4], Christian[3], Hans[2], Hans[1]) was born January 14, 1852, and died November 24, 1915. She married **Oliver Burkholder**, son of Ulrich Burkholder and Mary Kauffman. He was born November 17, 1844, and died March 12, 1921.

Children of Susan Hershey and Oliver Burkholder are:
1397	i.	Annie[11] Burkholder, born 1877.
1398	ii.	Felix Burkholder, born 1879.
+ 1399	iii.	Abraham H Burkholder, born August 02, 1885; died January 06, 1935.
1400	iv.	Harry Hershey Burkholder, born 1880.

971. Diana[10] **Hershey** (Henry[9], Martin[8], Henry[7], Andrew Stauffer[6], Adelheid Galle[5] Stouffer, Daniel[4], Christian[3], Hans[2], Hans[1]) was born August 12, 1831 in Derry Twp, Dauphin Co, PA, and died August 12, 1904 in Hummelstown, PA. She married **Thomas George Fox** May 11, 1852 in Derry Twp., Dauphin Co., PA. He was born July 19, 1827 in Derry Twp, Dauphin Co, PA, and died June 18, 1914 in Hummelstown, Dauphin Co., PA.

Children of Diana Hershey and Thomas Fox are:
+ 1401	i.	Webster Fox Lawrence "[11] Lafayette, born March 19, 1853 in Hummelstown, Dauphin Co., PA; died June 02, 1931 in Ardmore, PA.
1402	ii.	Elizabeth "Lillie" Fox, born 1856 in Hummelstown, Dauphin Co., PA; died July 21, 1918 in Hummelstown, Dauphin Co., PA.
1403	iii.	Robert Thomas Fox, born January 21, 1857 in Hummelstown, Dauphin Co., PA; died December 06, 1860 in Hummelstown, Dauphin Co., PA.
+ 1404	iv.	James George Fox, born November 05, 1858 in Hummelstown, Dauphin Co., PA; died August 07, 1933 in Union Deposit, Dauphin Co., PA.
+ 1405	v.	Fox John Edgar " Eshenauer, born November 27, 1860 in Hummelstown, Dauphin Co., PA; died August 07, 1942 in Harrisburg, PA.
+ 1406	vi.	Adelaide Fox, born September 05, 1862 in Hummelstown, Dauphin Co., PA; died March 04, 1948 in Philadelphia, PA.
1407	vii.	Mary Hershey Fox, born February 11, 1865 in Hummelstown, Dauphin Co., PA; died May 08, 1954 in Hummelstown, Dauphin Co., PA.
+ 1408	viii.	Caroline Lee Fox, born November 17, 1869 in Hummelstown, Dauphin Co., PA; died October 11, 1948.
+ 1409	ix.	George Hershey Fox, born May 09, 1872 in Hummelstown, Dauphin Co., PA; died April 14, 1910 in Mt. Alto TB San., PA.

978. Samuel[10] **Nickey** (Christiana[9] Hastetter, Anna Barbara[8] Stauffer, Johannes[7], Daniel[6] Stouffer, Christian[5] Stauffer, Daniel[4] Stouffer, Christian[3], Hans[2], Hans[1]) was born October 10, 1789 in Rapho Twp, Lancaster Co, Pa., and died July 05, 1875 in Cumberland Co, Pa. Buried Pa. German Baptist Churchyard, Huntsdale, Pa..

Children of Samuel Nickey are:
+ 1410	i.	Nancy[11] Nickey, born February 02, 1819 in Perry County, Pa.; died March 28, 1891 in Huntsdale, Pa. buried Pa. German Baptist Church, Huntsdale, Pa..
+ 1411	ii.	Edward Nickey, born 1829; died 1860.

979. Elizabeth[10] **Owens** (Peter[9] Ober, Elizabeth[8] Stauffer, Johannes[7], Daniel[6] Stouffer, Christian[5] Stauffer, Daniel[4] Stouffer, Christian[3], Hans[2], Hans[1]) was born February 13, 1787, and died July 18, 1862. She married **David Farner** February 28, 1805. He was born 1783, and died 1833.

Children of Elizabeth Owens and David Farner are:

- 1412 i. Solomon[11] Farner, born August 29, 1805; died WFT Est. 1806-1895.
- 1413 ii. Mary Farner, born June 25, 1807; died WFT Est. 1808-1901.
- 1414 iii. Catharine Farner, born November 20, 1808; died WFT Est. 1809-1902.
- 1415 iv. John Farner, born July 19, 1811; died WFT Est. 1812-1901.
- 1416 v. Daniel Farner, born June 20, 1813; died WFT Est. 1814-1903.
- 1417 vi. Peter Farner, born November 16, 1814; died WFT Est. 1815-1904.
- 1418 vii. Elizabeth Farner, born November 16, 1816; died WFT Est. 1817-1910.
- 1419 viii. Fanny Farner, born March 20, 1818; died WFT Est. 1819-1912.
- 1420 ix. Conrad Farner, born November 16, 1820; died WFT Est. 1821-1910.
- 1421 x. Mariah Farner, born September 05, 1821; died WFT Est. 1822-1915.
- 1422 xi. Gabriel Farner, born April 1823; died WFT Est. 1824-1913.
- + 1423 xii. Charlotte Farner, born June 15, 1827 in Franklin Co, Pa.; died November 15, 1892 in Buried in Presbyterian Churchyard, Dickensen, Pa..
- + 1424 xiii. Susannah Farner, born October 02, 1829; died 1910 in buried Upper Cem, Newville, Pa..
- 1425 xiv. Henry Farner, born October 02, 1829; died September 18, 1905 in buried Oakville Cem, Cumberland Co, Pa..

981. Isaac Huntsberger[10] Ober (Christian[9], Elizabeth[8] Stauffer, Johannes[7], Daniel[6] Stouffer, Christian[5] Stauffer, Daniel[4] Stouffer, Christian[3], Hans[2], Hans[1]) was born February 13, 1790 in Conewago Twp, Lancaster Co, PA, and died January 22, 1863 in Conewago Twp, Dauphin Co, PA. He married **Catherine Myers**. She was born September 04, 1795, and died July 28, 1879.

Children of Isaac Ober and Catherine Myers are:

- 1426 i. Samuel[11] Ober, born 1815; died 1841.
- 1427 ii. Jeremiah Ober, born 1819; died 1833.
- 1428 iii. Barbara Ober, born Abt. 1820. She married Abraham Hoffer; born Abt. 1820.
- 1429 iv. Christian Ober, born 1821; died 1822.
- 1430 v. Isaac Ober, born 1824; died 1854. He married Annie Nissley; born Abt. 1820.
- + 1431 vi. David Ober, born March 01, 1827 in Lancaster, West Donegal Twp, PA; died January 04, 1887 in Train wreck near Republic, Ohio.
- 1432 vii. Elizabeth Anna Ober, born 1830; died 1847. She married Benjamin Hoffer; born Abt. 1820.
- 1433 viii. Annie Ober, born January 11, 1830; died April 14, 1909. She married Rev Joseph Nissley; born September 15, 1830; died April 09, 1921.
- 1434 ix. Henry Ober, born 1834; died 1844.
- 1435 x. Catherine Ober, born 1835; died 1836.

985. Michael[10] Ober (Henry[9], Elizabeth[8] Stauffer, Johannes[7], Daniel[6] Stouffer, Christian[5] Stauffer, Daniel[4] Stouffer, Christian[3], Hans[2], Hans[1]) was born May 25, 1794, and died May 21, 1854 in W. Donegal Twp., Lancester Cty., PA. He married **Mary Cramer**. She was born September 02, 1804, and died March 29, 1844 in W. Donegal Twp., Lancester Cty., PA.

Child of Michael Ober and Mary Cramer is:

- + 1436 i. Michael Cramer[11] Ober, born 1827; died 1872 in Donegal Twp., Lancester Cty., PA.

987. Christian Longnecker[10] Ober (David S[9], Elizabeth[8] Stauffer, Johannes[7], Daniel[6] Stouffer, Christian[5] Stauffer, Daniel[4] Stouffer, Christian[3], Hans[2], Hans[1]) was born 1805 in Lancaster, PA, and died 1806 in Lancaster, PA. He married **Barbara Ruhl**. She was born January 17, 1816, and died January 27, 1877.

Children of Christian Ober and Barbara Ruhl are:

- 1437 i. Mary Or Mattie[11] Ober.
- 1438 ii. Michael Ober, born 1836.
- + 1439 iii. Moses Ruhl Ober, born January 21, 1838; died December 07, 1907.
- 1440 iv. Barbara Ober, born 1840.
- 1441 v. Anne Ober, born 1842.
- + 1442 vi. Henry E. Ober, born September 13, 1844 in Rapho Twsp, PA; died January 16, 1906.
- 1443 vii. Christian Ober, born 1846 in Rapho Twsp, PA.
- 1444 viii. Aaron Ober, born 1847.

989. John[10] Ober (Henry[9], Veronica " Frany "[8] Stauffer, Johannes[7], Daniel[6] Stouffer, Christian[5] Stauffer, Daniel[4] Stouffer, Christian[3], Hans[2], Hans[1]) was born February 09, 1799, and died September 29, 1851. He married **Nancy Bechtal**. She was born Abt. 1800, and died August 13, 1879.

Children of John Ober and Nancy Bechtal are:
- 1445 i. Henry[11] Ober, born June 26, 1822. He married Elizabeth Diehl; born Abt. 1821.
- 1446 ii. John Ober, born Abt. 1829; died Bef. 1851.
- 1447 iii. Nancy Ober, born Abt. 1834. She married George Diehl; died November 22, 1899.
- 1448 iv. Daniel Ober, born January 21, 1835. He married (1) Christiana Keagy; born December 10, 1839; died February 15, 1872. He married (2) Elizabeth Holderbaum; born August 14, 1838; died February 22, 1911.
- 1449 v. Elizabeth Ober, born 1839.
- 1450 vi. Sarah Ober, born August 12, 1839; died November 02, 1908. She married Jacob Brechbill; born September 02, 1832; died February 21, 1902.

990. Susannah[10] Ober (Henry[9], Veronica " Frany "[8] Stauffer, Johannes[7], Daniel[6] Stouffer, Christian[5] Stauffer, Daniel[4] Stouffer, Christian[3], Hans[2], Hans[1]) was born Abt. 1800 in Maryland, and died Bef. 1853. She married **John Bower**. He was born Abt. 1800, and died 1844 in North Woodbury Twp. Bedford County, Pennsylvania.

Children of Susannah Ober and John Bower are:
- 1451 i. Barbara[11] Bowers, born Abt. 1820.
- 1452 ii. Nancy Bowers, born Abt. 1822.
- + 1453 iii. Sarah Rebecca Bowers, born April 18, 1825 in Huntington County, Pennsylvania; died November 01, 1896 in Elkhorn, Ray County, Missouri.
- 1454 iv. Susan Bowers, born Abt. 1829 in Pennsylvania.
- 1455 v. Andrew Bowers, born Abt. 1832; died April 20, 1865 in Stark County, Ohio.

991. Jacob[10] Ober (Henry[9], Veronica " Frany "[8] Stauffer, Johannes[7], Daniel[6] Stouffer, Christian[5] Stauffer, Daniel[4] Stouffer, Christian[3], Hans[2], Hans[1]) was born February 20, 1801, and died September 09, 1855 in Pennsylvania. He married **Hannah Stevens**. She was born April 20, 1809, and died July 25, 1851.

Children of Jacob Ober and Hannah Stevens are:
- 1456 i. Cyrus Stevens[11] Ober, born April 14, 1831; died May 12, 1903. She married Leah Steffy; born January 10, 1834; died February 26, 1911.
- 1457 ii. Henry Ober, born June 08, 1832; died October 07, 1837.
- 1458 iii. Caroline Ober, born September 28, 1833; died January 30, 1901. She married Abraham Reighart; born January 04, 1831; died September 06, 1906.
- 1459 iv. Christian J. Ober, born May 18, 1835; died November 02, 1907. He married Fannie Carper; born April 21, 1842; died February 01, 1902.
- 1460 v. Obadiah S. Ober, born April 18, 1837; died April 22, 1918. He married Sophia Amanda Buck; born March 11, 1841; died June 05, 1929.
- 1461 vi. Delilah O. Ober, born January 18, 1839; died January 24, 1921. She married John Snyder Brumbaugh; born June 16, 1832; died February 20, 1903.
- 1462 vii. David H. Ober, born January 23, 1841; died March 01, 1903. He married Elizabeth Zook; born January 01, 1850; died July 11, 1926.
- 1463 viii. Alfred S. Ober, born June 20, 1843; died May 24, 1860.
- 1464 ix. Hannah Amanda Ober, born 1845; died November 21, 1916. She married Charles L. Buck; born July 01, 1843; died 1912.
- 1465 x. Mary Sue Ober, born 1847. She married Gideon C. Long; born January 03, 1849; died 1910.
- 1466 xi. Harriet S. Ober, born 1851; died May 1925. She married Andrew Zook Kagarise; born July 21, 1853; died March 20, 1932.

993. Joseph[10] Ober (Henry[9], Veronica " Frany "[8] Stauffer, Johannes[7], Daniel[6] Stouffer, Christian[5] Stauffer, Daniel[4] Stouffer, Christian[3], Hans[2], Hans[1]) was born January 1805, and died April 29, 1869. He married **Anna Smith**. She was born July 15, 1812, and died July 13, 1898.

Children of Joseph Ober and Anna Smith are:
- 1467 i. Elizabeth[11] Ober, born January 08, 1831.
- 1468 ii. Barbara Ober, born January 27, 1833; died February 16, 1833.
- 1469 iii. Esther Ober, born January 27, 1835; died November 19, 1902. She married Levi H. Biddle; born December 27, 1832; died November 14, 1907.
- 1470 iv. Levi Ober, born June 20, 1836; died December 05, 1913. He married Elizabeth Teeters; born January 10, 1839; died May 05, 1905.
- 1471 v. William S. Ober, born July 17, 1838; died August 06, 1839.
- 1472 vi. Rebecca Ober, born February 27, 1841; died March 15, 1841.
- 1473 vii. Joseph Ober, born June 10, 1842; died June 10, 1842.

1474 viii. William Ober, born February 15, 1844; died April 30, 1911. He married Mary Snider; born January 18, 1842; died January 25, 1925.

1475 ix. David S. Ober, born March 01, 1845. He married (1) Harriet Ditmars; born Abt. 1848. He married (2) Mildred L. Buck.

1476 x. Drusannah Ober, born October 09, 1846; died April 08, 1921. She married (1) David S. Stayer; born November 03, 1845; died November 24, 1925. She married (2) Emanuel Bechtel; born August 11, 1842; died April 15, 1871.

1477 xi. Joseph S. Ober, born October 06, 1853; died February 18, 1921. He married Annice Hall Jones; born April 09, 1856; died September 28, 1936.

994. Franey[10] Ober (Henry[9], Veronica " Frany "[8] Stauffer, Johannes[7], Daniel[6] Stouffer, Christian[5] Stauffer, Daniel[4] Stouffer, Christian[3], Hans[2], Hans[1]) was born 1809. She married **John Myers**. He was born Abt. 1805.

Children of Franey Ober and John Myers are:
1478 i. Susannah[11] Myers, born Abt. 1830.
1479 ii. Elisabeth Myers, born Abt. 1831.
1480 iii. Rebecca Myers, born Abt. 1832.
1481 iv. Mary A. Myers, born Abt. 1834.
1482 v. Henry O. Myers, born Abt. 1836.
1483 vi. Daniel Myers, born Abt. 1837.
1484 vii. John O. Myers, born Abt. 1838. He married Elizabeth Unknown; born Abt. 1847.
1485 viii. Margaret Myers, born Abt. 1840.
1486 ix. William O. Myers, born Abt. 1841. He married Lottie Unknown; born Abt. 1851.
1487 x. Peter Myers, born Abt. 1843.
1488 xi. Caroline Myers, born Abt. 1844.
1489 xii. Matilda Myers, born Abt. 1847.

995. Christian[10] Ober (Henry[9], Veronica " Frany "[8] Stauffer, Johannes[7], Daniel[6] Stouffer, Christian[5] Stauffer, Daniel[4] Stouffer, Christian[3], Hans[2], Hans[1]) was born July 08, 1812, and died May 12, 1880 in Pennsylvania. He married **Mary Barbara Saylor**. She was born October 23, 1818, and died October 23, 1872.

Children of Christian Ober and Mary Saylor are:
1490 i. Joseph[11] Ober, died January 15, 1912. He married Elizabeth Dick; born September 15, 1886.
1491 ii. Elizabeth B. Ober, born October 08, 1845; died 1924. She married Ephraim K. Brant; born May 28, 1851; died 1928.
1492 iii. Jacob Ober, born April 13, 1848; died October 24, 1945. He married Anna M. Smith; born July 29, 1846; died April 17, 1948.
1493 iv. Mary A. Ober, born June 08, 1850. She married David M. Pletcher; born November 12, 1856.
1494 v. Henry Saylor Ober, born January 31, 1853; died 1928. He married Mary Rebecca Blackburn; born January 03, 1854; died 1930.
1495 vi. Cyrus Ober, born May 09, 1855; died April 12, 1936. He married Matilda Agnes Darr; born September 26, 1861; died July 1942.
1496 vii. Lucy Ober, born July 22, 1858; died December 29, 1860.
1497 viii. Missouri Ober, born November 09, 1860; died November 26, 1860.
1498 ix. Sarah E. Ober, born June 23, 1862; died 1910. She married (1) Henry S. Berkey; born April 05, 1841; died May 31, 1889. She married (2) Jerome Crouse; born March 03, 1856; died 1930.
1499 x. Joseph Ober, born February 04, 1866; died November 26, 1876.

996. Samuel[10] Ober (Henry[9], Veronica " Frany "[8] Stauffer, Johannes[7], Daniel[6] Stouffer, Christian[5] Stauffer, Daniel[4] Stouffer, Christian[3], Hans[2], Hans[1]) was born 1815. He married **Mary Lichty**. She was born June 18, 1821.

Children of Samuel Ober and Mary Lichty are:
1500 i. Unknown[11] Ober. She married Cyrus Miller; born Abt. 1838.
1501 ii. Elizabeth Ober, born Abt. 1840.
1502 iii. Jacob Ober, born Abt. 1847.

997. Mary[10] Ober (Henry[9], Veronica " Frany "[8] Stauffer, Johannes[7], Daniel[6] Stouffer, Christian[5] Stauffer, Daniel[4] Stouffer, Christian[3], Hans[2], Hans[1]) was born Abt. 1818, and died 1912. She married **Solomon Imler**. He was born 1817, and died 1878.

Children of Mary Ober and Solomon Imler are:
1503 i. William[11] Imler, born Abt. 1842.

1504	ii.	Mathias Imler, born Abt. 1843.
1505	iii.	Sarah Imler, born Abt. 1846.
1506	iv.	Hannah Imler, born Abt. 1848.
1507	v.	Thomas O. Imler, born 1849; died 1908.
1508	vi.	Elizabeth Imler, born Abt. 1851.
1509	vii.	Margaret Imler, born Abt. 1853.
1510	viii.	Joseph Imler, born Abt. 1856.

998. Ann[10] Ober (Michael[9], Veronica " Frany "[8] Stauffer, Johannes[7], Daniel[6] Stouffer, Christian[5] Stauffer, Daniel[4] Stouffer, Christian[3], Hans[2], Hans[1]) was born Abt. 1780, and died Abt. 1840. She married **Henry Bear**. He was born Abt. 1754, and died 1830.

Children of Ann Ober and Henry Bear are:
- 1511　i.　Lydia[11] Bear. She married Jacob Sangree.
- 1512　ii.　Sophia Bear.
- 1513　iii.　Elizabeth Bear, born Abt. 1805; died Abt. 1870. She married Peter Summy; born Abt. 1800.
- 1514　iv.　Nancy Bear, born Abt. 1809; died Bef. 1870. She married Henry Heffleblower; born April 01, 1801; died July 31, 1872.
- 1515　v.　Catherine Bear, born January 14, 1814; died November 27, 1868. She married David Spencer; born May 25, 1801; died October 13, 1883.
- 1516　vi.　Magdalena Bear, born January 14, 1814; died November 27, 1868. She married David Spencer; born May 25, 1801; died October 13, 1883.
- 1517　vii.　David Bear, born Abt. 1818; died October 08, 1892. He married Sarah Unknown; born Abt. 1822; died April 01, 1904.
- 1518　viii.　Barbara Bear, born Abt. 1818. She married Joseph C. Lindsey; born Abt. 1802; died February 18, 1879.
- 1519　ix.　Sarah Bear, born Abt. 1823. She married James Parker; born Abt. 1816.

999. Barbara[10] Ober (Michael[9], Veronica " Frany "[8] Stauffer, Johannes[7], Daniel[6] Stouffer, Christian[5] Stauffer, Daniel[4] Stouffer, Christian[3], Hans[2], Hans[1]) was born Abt. 1789, and died May 10, 1859. She married **David Lesher**. He was born Abt. 1785, and died May 03, 1857.

Children of Barbara Ober and David Lesher are:
- 1520　i.　Jacob[11] Lesher, born October 02, 1808; died May 25, 1867. He married Rachel Unknown; born May 01, 1814; died April 08, 1842.
- 1521　ii.　Catherine Lesher, born July 17, 1810; died March 13, 1868. She married Hugh Smith; born December 14, 1805; died December 22, 1883.
- 1522　iii.　Mary Lesher, born Bef. 1816; died August 23, 1881. She married John Powders; born Abt. 1817; died August 04, 1886.
- + 1523　iv.　David Lesher, born May 02, 1817 in Pennsylvania; died October 20, 1889 in Iowa.
- 1524　v.　Ann Lesher, born Abt. 1822; died Aft. 1890. She married Jacob Myers Ober; born March 28, 1825; died September 11, 1855.
- 1525　vi.　Barbara A. Lesher, born July 25, 1826; died December 23, 1881. She married Elias Stouffer; born December 20, 1821; died April 01, 1900.
- 1526　vii.　Fanny Lesher, born Abt. 1827. She married John Stevick; born Abt. 1815.
- 1527　viii.　Caspar Lesher, born Abt. 1828. He married Margaret Unknown; born Abt. 1828.
- 1528　ix.　John Lesher, born November 03, 1829; died November 10, 1902. He married Mary A. Hollar; born July 27, 1834.
- 1529　x.　Peter Lesher, born Bef. 1857. He married Elizabeth Unknown.
- 1530　xi.　Elizabeth Lesher, born Bef. 1857. She married Michael T. Miller; born Bef. 1857.

1000. Catherine[10] Ober (Michael[9], Veronica " Frany "[8] Stauffer, Johannes[7], Daniel[6] Stouffer, Christian[5] Stauffer, Daniel[4] Stouffer, Christian[3], Hans[2], Hans[1]) was born Abt. 1790, and died Bef. February 1825. She married **John Powder**.

Children of Catherine Ober and John Powder are:
- 1531　i.　Jacob[11] Powder.
- 1532　ii.　John Powder.
- 1533　iii.　Catherine Powder.
- 1534　iv.　Michael Powder.

1001. Jacob[10] Ober (Michael[9], Veronica " Frany "[8] Stauffer, Johannes[7], Daniel[6] Stouffer, Christian[5] Stauffer, Daniel[4] Stouffer, Christian[3], Hans[2], Hans[1]) was born June 30, 1793, and died August 15, 1854. He married **Catherine Myers** June 30, 1793. She was born December 11, 1798, and died April 20, 1875.

Children of Jacob Ober and Catherine Myers are:
- 1535   i.   David[11] Ober.
- 1536   ii.   Jacob Myers Ober, born March 28, 1825; died September 11, 1855. He married Ann Lesher; born Abt. 1822; died Aft. 1890.
- 1537   iii.   John J. Ober, born 1828; died 1904. He married Mary Ann Unknown; born February 13, 1826; died March 27, 1892.
- + 1538   iv.   Catherine A. Ober, born February 11, 1831 in Hopewell Township, Cumberland County, Pennsylvania; died June 26, 1892 in Bloom Township, Wood County, Ohio.
- 1539   v.   Ephraim B. Ober, born October 23, 1833; died June 19, 1863. He married Margaret Reed.
- 1540   vi.   Mary Ober, born Abt. 1836.

1002. Elizabeth[10] Ober (Michael[9], Veronica " Frany "[8] Stauffer, Johannes[7], Daniel[6] Stouffer, Christian[5] Stauffer, Daniel[4] Stouffer, Christian[3], Hans[2], Hans[1]) was born Abt. 1794, and died Bef. May 09, 1826. She married **Christian Stouffer**. He was born Abt. 1794.

Children of Elizabeth Ober and Christian Stouffer are:
- 1541   i.   Molly[11] Stouffer.
- 1542   ii.   Jacob Stouffer.
- 1543   iii.   John Stouffer.
- 1544   iv.   Elizabeth Stouffer.

1003. Samuel[10] Ober (Michael[9], Veronica " Frany "[8] Stauffer, Johannes[7], Daniel[6] Stouffer, Christian[5] Stauffer, Daniel[4] Stouffer, Christian[3], Hans[2], Hans[1]) was born Abt. 1797. He married **Kesiah Unknown**. She was born September 23, 1800, and died July 28, 1861.

Children of Samuel Ober and Kesiah Unknown are:
- 1545   i.   Adaline[11] Ober, born June 26, 1838; died October 19, 1849.
- 1546   ii.   Daniel Ober, born Abt. 1842.

1005. Magdalena[10] Ober (Michael[9], Veronica " Frany "[8] Stauffer, Johannes[7], Daniel[6] Stouffer, Christian[5] Stauffer, Daniel[4] Stouffer, Christian[3], Hans[2], Hans[1]) was born November 04, 1801, and died July 02, 1840. She married **John Stouffer**. He was born January 25, 1798, and died September 25, 1857.

Children of Magdalena Ober and John Stouffer are:
- 1547   i.   John O.[11] Stouffer, born January 11, 1820; died March 07, 1885. He married Elizabeth Unknown; died September 13, 1877.
- 1548   ii.   Catharine Stouffer, born August 19, 1820; died September 09, 1875. She married Henry S. Fisher; born February 13, 1815; died May 29, 1875.
- 1549   iii.   David K. Stouffer, born March 25, 1827; died May 26, 1899. He married Anna C. Unknown; born Abt. 1826.
- 1550   iv.   Christian C. Stouffer, born Abt. 1831; died October 05, 1898. He married Margaret D. Unknown; born Abt. 1839; died December 23, 1882.
- 1551   v.   Jacob Stouffer, born Abt. 1833.
- 1552   vi.   Andrew Stouffer, born 1835.
- 1553   vii.   William Stouffer, born 1837.

1016. Lewis[10] Ober (Christian[9], Veronica " Frany "[8] Stauffer, Johannes[7], Daniel[6] Stouffer, Christian[5] Stauffer, Daniel[4] Stouffer, Christian[3], Hans[2], Hans[1]) was born 1818, and died December 1897. He married **Maria Catherine Unknown**. She was born 1819, and died 1897.

Children of Lewis Ober and Maria Unknown are:
- 1554   i.   Sarah Jane[11] Ober, born November 04, 1845.
- 1555   ii.   Edward K. Ober, born 1848; died 1919. He married Ellen C. Crouse; born 1849; died 1919.
- 1556   iii.   Martha E. Ober, born Abt. 1850.
- 1557   iv.   John F. Ober, born Abt. 1856.

1017. John C.[10] Ober (Christian[9], Veronica " Frany "[8] Stauffer, Johannes[7], Daniel[6] Stouffer, Christian[5] Stauffer, Daniel[4] Stouffer, Christian[3], Hans[2], Hans[1]) was born January 25, 1818, and died February 21, 1898. He married **(1) Susan Kimmel**. She was born 1813, and died September 18, 1859. He married **(2) Ann Elizabeth Berkeybile**. She was born February 13, 1838, and died October 15, 1908.

Children of John Ober and Susan Kimmel are:
- 1558   i.   Theodore[11] Ober, born December 04, 1842; died February 18, 1915. He married Martha Garrett; born

		May 10, 1853.
1559	ii.	Elizabeth Ober, born September 11, 1845; died February 27, 1922. She married Adam Cleveland Berkeybile; born January 16, 1843; died August 23, 1922.
1560	iii.	George Ober, born Abt. 1846.
1561	iv.	William Ober, born September 26, 1847; died August 16, 1923. He married Cora Alice Leabo; born October 13, 1859; died September 02, 1948.
1562	v.	Daniel S. Ober, born 1848; died 1915. He married Sarah Brandt; born June 27, 1850; died June 13, 1941.
1563	vi.	Rebecca Ober, born Abt. 1851.
1564	vii.	Kain Ober, born March 29, 1852; died May 29, 1937. He married (1) Harriet M. Shaffer. He married (2) Civilla Lambert; born January 28, 1859; died May 10, 1945.
1565	viii.	John J. Ober, born Abt. 1854. He married Lucinda Davis; born August 16, 1853; died February 17, 1888.
1566	ix.	Gabrielle Ober, born 1855; died 1927. He married Margaret Berkey Clark /.
1567	x.	Sarah J. Ober, born Abt. 1857.

Children of John Ober and Ann Berkeybile are:

1568	i.	James C.[11] Ober, born October 09, 1861; died April 30, 1954. He married Mary M. Ash; born January 1864; died 1915.
1569	ii.	Robert H. Ober, born April 10, 1863; died Bef. 1919. He married Joella Davis; died March 12, 1919.
1570	iii.	Wilhelmia Ober, born June 15, 1865; died July 25, 1865.
1571	iv.	Margaret Ober, born June 04, 1866; died October 1949.
1572	v.	Horatio Seymour Ober, born June 15, 1868; died 1938. He married Anna Mary Kline; born January 1870; died 1950.
1573	vi.	Augustine Ober, born June 06, 1870.
1574	vii.	Mary Adella Ober, born March 17, 1872; died 1956. She married Harry Weible; born June 1879; died 1956.

1019. Barbara[10] Ober (Christian[9], Veronica " Frany "[8] Stauffer, Johannes[7], Daniel[6] Stouffer, Christian[5] Stauffer, Daniel[4] Stouffer, Christian[3], Hans[2], Hans[1]) She married **Absalom Hale**.

Child of Barbara Ober and Absalom Hale is:
1575   i.   John[11] Hale. He married Sarah Corle.

1020. Nancy[10] Ober (Christian[9], Veronica " Frany "[8] Stauffer, Johannes[7], Daniel[6] Stouffer, Christian[5] Stauffer, Daniel[4] Stouffer, Christian[3], Hans[2], Hans[1]) was born October 02, 1799, and died September 13, 1879. She married **Peter Gardner**. He was born March 04, 1786, and died April 19, 1849.

Children of Nancy Ober and Peter Gardner are:

1576	i.	Mary[11] Gardner, born June 27, 1815; died May 29, 1884. She married Daniel Malone; died October 29, 1873.
1577	ii.	Eliza Gardner, born March 13, 1819; died March 08, 1876. She married George W. Baush; born Abt. 1815; died July 30, 1880.
1578	iii.	George Gardner, born June 09, 1823; died November 25, 1890. He married Mary Blough; born Abt. 1829; died January 15, 1895.
1579	iv.	Henry Gardner, born August 25, 1825; died December 12, 1892. He married Amanda Unknown; born Abt. 1828; died December 12, 1892.
1580	v.	Peter Frederick Gardner, born September 16, 1827; died November 14, 1901. He married Susan N. Lohr; born September 07, 1831; died April 13, 1909.
1581	vi.	Cyrus Gardner, born October 28, 1829; died August 15, 1844.
1582	vii.	Benjamin Gardner, born January 29, 1832; died September 20, 1894. He married Margaret L. Taylor; born November 22, 1841; died February 22, 1908.
1583	viii.	John W. Gardner, born April 28, 1832; died May 15, 1895. He married Matilda Unknown; born 1840; died 1929.
1584	ix.	James Gardner, born 1838.
1585	x.	Lewis Gardner, born May 16, 1840; died July 25, 1842.
1586	xi.	Leah Gardner, born 1842; died May 30, 1889. She married John Leitenberger.
1587	xii.	Julia Gardner, born December 25, 1843; died May 14, 1902.
1588	xiii.	Nancy Gardner, born July 21, 1845; died May 12, 1906.
1589	xiv.	Rosanna Gardner, born Abt. 1847; died December 01, 1875. She married George F. Barron; born May 02, 1840; died May 10, 1933.

1022. Henry[10] Ober (John[9], Veronica " Frany "[8] Stauffer, Johannes[7], Daniel[6] Stouffer, Christian[5] Stauffer, Daniel[4] Stouffer, Christian[3], Hans[2], Hans[1]) was born Aft. 1788. He married **Elizabeth Hoover**. She was born Abt. 1792, and died Aft. 1860.

Children of Henry Ober and Elizabeth Hoover are:
- 1590　i.　David[11] Ober, born Abt. 1810. He married Sarah Unknown; born Abt. 1823.
- 1591　ii.　Elizabeth Ober, born Abt. 1811.
- 1592　iii.　John H. Ober, born Abt. 1812; died November 12, 1881. He married Julia Ann Unknown; born January 29, 1821; died August 12, 1893.
- 1593　iv.　Henry Ober, born 1821. He married (1) Susan Irvin; born Abt. 1825; died Bef. 1860. He married (2) Mary Pote.

1023. Veronica Francis[10] Ober (John[9], Veronica " Frany "[8] Stauffer, Johannes[7], Daniel[6] Stouffer, Christian[5] Stauffer, Daniel[4] Stouffer, Christian[3], Hans[2], Hans[1]) was born Abt. 1790, and died Aft. 1853. She married **Benjamin Barricks**. He was born Abt. 1787, and died Abt. 1853.

Children of Veronica Ober and Benjamin Barricks are:
- 1594　i.　Mary[11] Barricks, born Abt. 1832.
- 1595　ii.　Abraham Barricks, born Abt. 1841.

1024. Nancy Catherine[10] Ober (John[9], Veronica " Frany "[8] Stauffer, Johannes[7], Daniel[6] Stouffer, Christian[5] Stauffer, Daniel[4] Stouffer, Christian[3], Hans[2], Hans[1]) was born 1793, and died March 05, 1862. She married **(1) Jacob Brechbill**. He was born September 10, 1777, and died September 01, 1863. She married **(2) Emanuel Hoover**. He was born 1800, and died 1825.

Child of Nancy Ober and Jacob Brechbill is:
- 1596　i.　Fannie[11] Brechbill, born July 20, 1833; died October 01, 1914. She married George R. Metz; born Abt. 1832; died December 30, 1900.

Children of Nancy Ober and Emanuel Hoover are:
- 1597　i.　John[11] Hoover.
- 1598　ii.　Christian Hoover.
- 1599　iii.　David Hoover.
- 1600　iv.　Anna Hoover.
- 1601　v.　Barbara Hoover.
- 1602　vi.　Catharine Hoover.
- 1603　vii.　Mary A. Hoover, born May 26, 1824; died June 08, 1909. She married Jacob Snowberger Detwiler; born May 06, 1815; died March 20, 1864.

1025. Jacob[10] Ober (John[9], Veronica " Frany "[8] Stauffer, Johannes[7], Daniel[6] Stouffer, Christian[5] Stauffer, Daniel[4] Stouffer, Christian[3], Hans[2], Hans[1]) was born 1794, and died 1866. He married **Sarah Feighter**. She was born February 24, 1805, and died Aft. 1880.

Children of Jacob Ober and Sarah Feighter are:
- 1604　i.　John[11] Ober, born Abt. 1823; died Bef. 1865. He married Margaret Unknown; born Abt. 1824.
- 1605　ii.　Benjamin Franklin Ober, born January 08, 1824; died September 26, 1911. He married Elizabeth Barnet; born Abt. 1822.
- 1606　iii.　Jacob Ober, born Abt. 1825.
- 1607　iv.　Martin Ober, born Abt. 1827. He married Susan Unknown; born Abt. 1823.
- 1608　v.　Joseph Ober, born Abt. 1828. He married Ella Unknown; born Abt. 1844.
- 1609　vi.　Henry Ober, born Abt. 1832. He married Lydia Unknown; born Abt. 1825.
- 1610　vii.　Ann Ober, born Abt. 1833. She married John Widdowson; born October 30, 1823; died February 09, 1904.
- 1611　viii.　Rebecca Ober, born Abt. 1835. She married Unknown Shadrick.
- 1612　ix.　George Ober, born Abt. 1838.
- 1613　x.　Sarah Ober, born Abt. 1842. She married Henry McGaw.

1026. Anna Nancy[10] Ober (John[9], Veronica " Frany "[8] Stauffer, Johannes[7], Daniel[6] Stouffer, Christian[5] Stauffer, Daniel[4] Stouffer, Christian[3], Hans[2], Hans[1]) was born March 30, 1796, and died January 26, 1852. She married **John Weisel**. He was born April 14, 1790, and died April 11, 1854.

Children of Anna Ober and John Weisel are:

1614   i. Israel[11] Weisel, born December 13, 1821.
1615   ii. Eliza Weisel, born September 19, 1824; died June 09, 1885. She married Joseph S. Doughtery.
1616   iii. Levi Weisel, born December 11, 1830. He married Catharine Hoover; born March 17, 1832; died February 27, 1854.

1027. Elizabeth[10] Ober (John[9], Veronica " Frany "[8] Stauffer, Johannes[7], Daniel[6] Stouffer, Christian[5] Stauffer, Daniel[4] Stouffer, Christian[3], Hans[2], Hans[1]) was born 1799, and died July 26, 1864. She married **John Hoffman**. He was born Abt. 1801, and died September 19, 1863.

Children of Elizabeth Ober and John Hoffman are:
1617   i. Nancy[11] Hoffman, born Abt. 1830.
1618   ii. Susan Hoffman, born Abt. 1831.
1619   iii. Elisabeth Hoffman, born Abt. 1833.

1028. John[10] Ober (John[9], Veronica " Frany "[8] Stauffer, Johannes[7], Daniel[6] Stouffer, Christian[5] Stauffer, Daniel[4] Stouffer, Christian[3], Hans[2], Hans[1]) was born Abt. 1800. He married **Mary Pote**. She was born 1798.

Children of John Ober and Mary Pote are:
1620   i. Emanuel[11] Ober, born June 17, 1826; died May 30, 1912. He married Barbara Mock; born September 19, 1834; died December 01, 1919.
1621   ii. Elizabeth Ober, born Abt. 1830.
1622   iii. Susan Ober, born Abt. 1831.
1623   iv. Mary Ober, born Abt. 1835.
1624   v. Margaret Ober, born Abt. 1838.
1625   vi. Catherine Ober, born Abt. 1839.
1626   vii. John Ober, born Abt. 1840.

1029. Benjamin[10] Ober (John[9], Veronica " Frany "[8] Stauffer, Johannes[7], Daniel[6] Stouffer, Christian[5] Stauffer, Daniel[4] Stouffer, Christian[3], Hans[2], Hans[1]) was born January 30, 1803, and died February 24, 1870. He married **Sarah Garretson**. She was born June 1798, and died November 09, 1839.

Children of Benjamin Ober and Sarah Garretson are:
1627   i. Abraham[11] Ober, born December 19, 1824; died December 02, 1855. He married Nancy Anna Keagy; born March 13, 1823; died December 20, 1909.
1628   ii. Levi S. Ober, born March 23, 1826; died December 05, 1913. He married Elizabeth Williams; born Abt. 1828; died May 05, 1905.
1629   iii. Aaron G. Ober, born October 28, 1827. He married Lovina Truby; born Abt. 1838.
1630   iv. William Ober, born Bef. 1828.
1631   v. Margaret Ober, born Bef. 1828.
1632   vi. Charlotte Ober, born Bef. 1828.
1633   vii. Susannah Ober, born Bef. 1828.
1634   viii. Mary G. Ober, born August 17, 1829; died November 29, 1916. She married John Brallier Fluck; born September 24, 1824; died January 06, 1915.
1635   ix. Nancy Ann Ober, born June 16, 1832; died August 16, 1896. She married Enos Ellis Rogers; born February 26, 1834.
1636   x. Ober Benjamin, born June 06, 1836.
1637   xi. Elizabeth Ober, born October 27, 1838; died February 23, 1914.

1030. John O.[10] Brubacher (Elizabeth[9] Ober, Veronica " Frany "[8] Stauffer, Johannes[7], Daniel[6] Stouffer, Christian[5] Stauffer, Daniel[4] Stouffer, Christian[3], Hans[2], Hans[1]) was born 1792, and died October 12, 1868. He married **Catharine Dissinger**. She died August 13, 1876.

Children of John Brubacher and Catharine Dissinger are:
1638   i. Joseph D.[11] Brubacher. He married Elizabeth Nusbaum.
1639   ii. Polly Brubacher.
1640   iii. Henry W. Brubacher, born June 02, 1824; died February 20, 1881. He married Elizabeth Unknown; born March 27, 1837; died June 10, 1898.
1641   iv. Elizabeth D. Brubacher, born June 06, 1826; died March 28, 1834.
1642   v. John D. Brubacher, born Abt. 1830; died July 06, 1865. He married Elizabeth Rohland; born 1831; died 1902.
1643   vi. David F. Brubacher, born September 04, 1841; died June 02, 1914. He married Mary L. Taylor; born

		Abt. 1850.
1644	vii.	Jacob D. Brubacher, born 1843; died 1915. He married Agnes R. Hummerhouser; born 1848; died 1915.
1645	viii.	Catharine D. Brubacher, born 1843; died 1915. She married Samuel Heckman; born 1840; died 1930.

1031. Jacob O.[10] **Brubacher** (Elizabeth[9] Ober, Veronica " Frany "[8] Stauffer, Johannes[7], Daniel[6] Stouffer, Christian[5] Stauffer, Daniel[4] Stouffer, Christian[3], Hans[2], Hans[1]) was born May 08, 1796, and died April 28, 1839. He married **Sarah Mark**. She was born February 17, 1803, and died January 18.

Children of Jacob Brubacher and Sarah Mark are:
1646	i.	George M.[11] Brubacher, born July 19, 1824; died October 26, 1891. He married (1) Eliza Bever; born February 22, 1829; died July 11, 1856. He married (2) Mary J. Lime; born November 02, 1833; died January 10, 1923.
1647	ii.	Margaret Brubacher, born June 16, 1829; died 1909. She married Simon Eberly; born 1826; died 1895.

1032. Peter O.[10] **Brubacher** (Elizabeth[9] Ober, Veronica " Frany "[8] Stauffer, Johannes[7], Daniel[6] Stouffer, Christian[5] Stauffer, Daniel[4] Stouffer, Christian[3], Hans[2], Hans[1]) was born May 11, 1798, and died May 20, 1871. He married **Mary Crall**. She was born February 07, 1803, and died November 05, 1888.

Children of Peter Brubacher and Mary Crall are:
1648	i.	David[11] Brubacher, born October 24, 1826; died December 03, 1901. He married Sarah Krall; born January 17, 1827; died December 01, 1900.
1649	ii.	John Brubacher, born Abt. 1827. He married Martha Burd; born Abt. 1840.
1650	iii.	Peter Brubacher, born Abt. 1831. He married Catharine Behney; born Abt. 1837.
1651	iv.	Carolina Brubacher, born 1833; died 1911. She married Samuel Lehman; born January 30, 1830; died April 16, 1911.
1652	v.	Elizabeth Brubacher, born Abt. 1834. She married Andrew Yuengt.

1033. David O.[10] **Brubacher** (Elizabeth[9] Ober, Veronica " Frany "[8] Stauffer, Johannes[7], Daniel[6] Stouffer, Christian[5] Stauffer, Daniel[4] Stouffer, Christian[3], Hans[2], Hans[1]) was born February 08, 1805, and died March 12, 1888. He married **(1) Ann Elizabeth Nauman**. She was born August 10, 1807, and died July 03, 1842. He married **(2) Lucinda Bishop**. She was born November 01, 1808, and died February 28, 1880.

Children of David Brubacher and Ann Nauman are:
1653	i.	Caroline[11] Brubacher.
1654	ii.	Eliza N. Brubacher, born Abt. 1831; died November 08, 1890. She married Joseph Greenawald; born Abt. 1808; died October 22, 1887.
1655	iii.	David N. Brubacher, born December 10, 1833; died January 06, 1877. He married Victoria Dollar; born February 22, 1838; died January 03, 1926.
1656	iv.	Susan N. Brubacher, born March 24, 1836; died March 25, 1909. She married Abraham Shelly Bradley; born June 07, 1839; died December 28, 1914.
1657	v.	Samuel N. Brubacher, born January 22, 1837; died March 16, 1914. He married (1) Elizabeth Ackerman; born November 06, 1836; died December 19, 1878. He married (2) Margaret A. Unknown.
1658	vi.	Jacob N. Brubacher, born 1840; died April 26, 1919. He married Mary Elizabeth Wert; born January 05, 1849; died April 27, 1927.

Child of David Brubacher and Lucinda Bishop is:
1659	i.	Isaac B.[11] Brubacher, born May 07, 1850; died January 13, 1927. He married Anna Hoyt; born January 08, 1858; died January 30, 1940.

1034. Augustus[10] **Brubacher** (Elizabeth[9] Ober, Veronica " Frany "[8] Stauffer, Johannes[7], Daniel[6] Stouffer, Christian[5] Stauffer, Daniel[4] Stouffer, Christian[3], Hans[2], Hans[1]) was born January 22, 1819, and died September 16, 1870. He married **Susannah Farsht**. She was born January 05, 1823, and died February 26, 1895.

Children of Augustus Brubacher and Susannah Farsht are:
1660	i.	Priscilla[11] Brubacher, born January 16, 1843; died January 02, 1886. She married Aaron Bayleat; born March 15, 1827; died January 10, 1903.
1661	ii.	John H. Brubacher, born May 21, 1845; died May 21, 1852.
1662	iii.	Sarah Brubacher, born February 14, 1847; died October 11, 1911.
1663	iv.	Samuel F. Brubacher, born November 02, 1849; died February 04, 1912. He married Florence A. Fuller.
1664	v.	Jacob F. Brubacher, born September 24, 1852; died July 26, 1854.
1665	vi.	David A. Judson Brubacher, born June 17, 1858; died 1936.

1036. Barbara[10] Shenk (Veronica[9] Ober, Veronica " Frany "[8] Stauffer, Johannes[7], Daniel[6] Stouffer, Christian[5] Stauffer, Daniel[4] Stouffer, Christian[3], Hans[2], Hans[1]) was born September 16, 1804, and died Bef. 1857. She married **Joseph Horst**. He was born Abt. 1797.

Children of Barbara Shenk and Joseph Horst are:
- 1666   i.   Joseph Shenk[11] Horst, born October 17, 1833; died August 07, 1897. He married Mary S. Brubaker; born June 07, 1839; died July 20, 1938.
- 1667   ii.   Barbara Horst, born Abt. 1835.
- 1668   iii.   Catharine Horst, born Abt. 1837.
- 1669   iv.   Anna Horst, born Abt. 1842.
- 1670   v.   Eliza Horst, born Abt. 1844.
- 1671   vi.   Samuel Horst, born Abt. 1845.

1037. Jacob[10] Shenk (Veronica[9] Ober, Veronica " Frany "[8] Stauffer, Johannes[7], Daniel[6] Stouffer, Christian[5] Stauffer, Daniel[4] Stouffer, Christian[3], Hans[2], Hans[1]) was born December 1806, and died June 13, 1874. He married **(1) Magdalene Miller**. She was born November 04, 1810, and died Aft. 1860. He married **(2) Catharine Unknown**. She was born 1818.

Children of Jacob Shenk and Magdalene Miller are:
- 1672   i.   Henry[11] Shenk, born August 05, 1828. He married Elizabeth Groh; born 1830; died 1896.
- 1673   ii.   Joseph M. Shenk, born Abt. 1831; died Abt. 1902. He married (1) Mary Unknown. He married (2) Malinda B. Unknown. He married (3) Sarah Kurtz.
- 1674   iii.   Veronica Shenk, born Abt. 1832; died Abt. 1900.
- 1675   iv.   John S. Shenk, born Abt. 1833. He married Malinda Unknown.
- 1676   v.   Christian M. Shenk, born November 16, 1836; died February 23, 1916. He married Harriet Few; born Abt. 1845; died February 23, 1916.
- 1677   vi.   Catherine Shenk, born Abt. 1843. She married Abraham Oberholtzer; born Abt. 1839.
- 1678   vii.   Jacob M. Shenk, born January 31, 1847; died 1882. He married Lydia A. Stitcher; born 1847; died June 10, 1883.
- 1679   viii.   Michael M. Shenk, born 1852; died 1925. He married Sarah Bomberger; born December 03, 1853; died November 07, 1923.

1038. Elizabeth[10] Shenk (Veronica[9] Ober, Veronica " Frany "[8] Stauffer, Johannes[7], Daniel[6] Stouffer, Christian[5] Stauffer, Daniel[4] Stouffer, Christian[3], Hans[2], Hans[1]) was born April 05, 1807, and died June 08, 1884. She married **Christian B. Herr**. He was born October 25, 1801, and died April 22, 1843.

Children of Elizabeth Shenk and Christian Herr are:
- 1680   i.   Nancy[11] Herr, born March 28, 1824; died August 19, 1906. She married Reuben Reist; born July 29, 1820; died March 08, 1894.
- 1681   ii.   Joseph Herr, born Abt. 1825. He married Anna Unknown; born Abt. 1822.
- 1682   iii.   Veronica Herr, born July 30, 1827; died November 19, 1875. She married Elias Brubaker; born December 26, 1835; died May 07, 1894.
- 1683   iv.   Christian Herr, born August 04, 1828; died June 27, 1904. He married Sabina Snyder; born August 03, 1836; died January 19, 1911.
- 1684   v.   Elizabeth Herr, born 1830; died 1903. She married Moses S. Brubaker; born August 20, 1822; died May 23, 1901.
- 1685   vi.   Abraham Herr, born 1831; died 1906. He married Sarah Mark; born Abt. 1831.
- 1686   vii.   Maria Herr, born 1833; died 1906. She married John Flickinger; born December 15, 1831; died November 04, 1904.
- 1687   viii.   Samuel Herr, born January 25, 1836. He married Louisa Brittenstine; born June 28, 1840.
- 1688   ix.   Magdalena Herr, born May 14, 1838; died August 06, 1861.
- 1689   x.   Barbara M. Herr, born May 27, 1841; died February 26, 1925.
- 1690   xi.   Lydia Herr, born August 17, 1842; died October 20, 1895. She married Jonas Snyder; born 1841; died 1920.

1041. Veronica[10] Shenk (Veronica[9] Ober, Veronica " Frany "[8] Stauffer, Johannes[7], Daniel[6] Stouffer, Christian[5] Stauffer, Daniel[4] Stouffer, Christian[3], Hans[2], Hans[1]) was born November 04, 1812, and died April 03, 1887. She married **Samuel Kettering**. He was born October 31, 1808, and died September 04, 1885.

Children of Veronica Shenk and Samuel Kettering are:
- 1691   i.   Mary[11] Kettering, born July 29, 1832; died March 09, 1921. She married Michael Naftzinger; born February 04, 1828; died September 20, 1909.

1692	ii.	Joseph Kettering, born December 26, 1833; died May 16, 1894. He married (1) Leah Sherk; born June 28, 1837; died October 18, 1857. He married (2) Elizabeth Sherk; born February 13, 1839; died April 08, 1901.
1693	iii.	Samuel Kettering, born August 24, 1835; died January 14, 1837.
1694	iv.	Jacob Kettering, born July 14, 1837; died July 01, 1918. He married (1) Lydia Kreider; born July 14, 1840; died June 06, 1869. He married (2) Catherine L. Gingerich; born September 05, 1844; died July 11, 1915.
1695	v.	Veronica Kettering, born April 15, 1840; died November 06, 1902. She married John S. Sprecher; born July 30, 1837; died October 06, 1918.
1696	vi.	Rebecca Kettering, born February 08, 1842; died March 25, 1919. She married John Kreider; born November 08, 1839; died November 01, 1898.
1697	vii.	Samuel A. Kettering, born November 24, 1843; died January 17, 1925. He married Amanda Light; born May 25, 1847; died May 12, 1911.
1698	viii.	John S. Kettering, born November 18, 1845; died February 14, 1915. He married Elizabeth Bucher; born January 17, 1849; died April 08, 1920.
1699	ix.	Lydia Kettering, born January 18, 1848; died August 19, 1936. She married John Zinn Bachman; born April 14, 1843; died September 01, 1921.
1700	x.	Philip Kettering, born March 04, 1850; died October 23, 1927. He married Mary Kiefer; born April 14, 1858; died June 27, 1915.
1701	xi.	Henry Kettering, born December 02, 1851; died June 19, 1902. He married Lydia Shenk Kreider; born October 17, 1857; died April 02, 1935.
1702	xii.	Amanda Kettering, born August 08, 1853; died July 16, 1928. She married Ezra Meyer Wenger; born December 11, 1852; died June 29, 1930.
1703	xiii.	Elizabeth Kettering, born September 02, 1858; died January 17, 1924. She married John Wenger; born August 31, 1858; died November 18, 1936.

1042. Joseph[10] Shenk (Veronica[9] Ober, Veronica " Frany "[8] Stauffer, Johannes[7], Daniel[6] Stouffer, Christian[5] Stauffer, Daniel[4] Stouffer, Christian[3], Hans[2], Hans[1]) was born March 23, 1814, and died July 28, 1893. He married **Elizabeth Risser**. She was born November 15, 1810, and died February 18, 1893.

Children of Joseph Shenk and Elizabeth Risser are:
1704	i.	Peter[11] Shenk, born Abt. 1838.
1705	ii.	Joseph Shenk, born Abt. 1840.
1706	iii.	Samuel Shenk, born Abt. 1843.
1707	iv.	Abraham Shenk, born Abt. 1847.

1043. Maria[10] Shenk (Veronica[9] Ober, Veronica " Frany "[8] Stauffer, Johannes[7], Daniel[6] Stouffer, Christian[5] Stauffer, Daniel[4] Stouffer, Christian[3], Hans[2], Hans[1]) was born December 13, 1814, and died August 11, 1892. She married **John Risser**. He was born January 27, 1809, and died December 06, 1869.

Children of Maria Shenk and John Risser are:
1708	i.	Veronica[11] Risser, born August 06, 1835; died November 04, 1907. She married John H. Risser; born February 21, 1834; died November 05, 1901.
1709	ii.	Joseph L. Risser, born December 28, 1836; died June 09, 1925. He married Annie L. Garber; born June 11, 1842; died September 24, 1888.
1710	iii.	Abraham S. Risser, born October 20, 1838; died December 25, 1876. He married Annie Ebersole; born June 24, 1843; died October 03, 1908.
1711	iv.	John S. Risser, born May 24, 1842; died September 14, 1922. He married Mary Ann Shenk; born April 12, 1843; died October 27, 1915.
1712	v.	Samuel S. Risser, born March 01, 1849; died February 22, 1929. He married Mary A. Kuhns.

1044. Magdalena[10] Shenk (Veronica[9] Ober, Veronica " Frany "[8] Stauffer, Johannes[7], Daniel[6] Stouffer, Christian[5] Stauffer, Daniel[4] Stouffer, Christian[3], Hans[2], Hans[1]) was born April 02, 1817, and died January 30, 1894. She married **Levi Light**. He was born May 14, 1816, and died March 03, 1901.

Children of Magdalena Shenk and Levi Light are:
| 1713 | i. | Veronica[11] Light, born November 30, 1844; died January 12, 1894. She married Jeremiah Stoever; born January 15, 1836. |
| 1714 | ii. | Elizabeth Light, born May 18, 1847; died January 12, 1894. |

1045. Catherine[10] Shenk (Veronica[9] Ober, Veronica " Frany "[8] Stauffer, Johannes[7], Daniel[6] Stouffer, Christian[5] Stauffer, Daniel[4]

Stouffer, Christian[3], Hans[2], Hans[1]) was born November 19, 1818, and died August 26, 1883. She married **Jacob Erb**. He was born December 1803, and died 1866.

Children of Catherine Shenk and Jacob Erb are:
- 1715   i.   Isaac[11] Erb, born September 04, 1839; died August 21, 1903. He married Barbara Burkholder; born February 11, 1839; died July 12, 1906.
- 1716   ii.   Fanny Erb, born September 26, 1841. She married George Graby; born Abt. 1841.
- 1717   iii.   Gabrial Erb, born January 06, 1843; died 1895.
- 1718   iv.   Peter Erb, born November 07, 1844; died 1918.
- 1719   v.   Mary Louise Erb, born December 22, 1846; died May 20, 1920. She married Elias Kettering Schaak; born June 10, 1835; died August 06, 1890.
- 1720   vi.   Fianna Erb, born November 30, 1855; died 1928.

1046. Nancy[10] Shenk (Veronica[9] Ober, Veronica " Frany "[8] Stauffer, Johannes[7], Daniel[6] Stouffer, Christian[5] Stauffer, Daniel[4] Stouffer, Christian[3], Hans[2], Hans[1]) was born January 27, 1820, and died March 01, 1842. She married **Joseph Bucher**, son of Jonas Bucher and Susan Witwer. He was born May 20, 1820, and died February 03, 1894.

Child of Nancy Shenk and Joseph Bucher is:
- 1721   i.   Veronica S.[11] Bucher, born October 07, 1841; died December 24, 1910. She married Simon B. Snyder; born January 05, 1836; died June 05, 1907.

1050. Cecelia O.[10] Ober (Benjamin[9], Veronica " Frany "[8] Stauffer, Johannes[7], Daniel[6] Stouffer, Christian[5] Stauffer, Daniel[4] Stouffer, Christian[3], Hans[2], Hans[1]) was born June 07, 1820, and died June 01, 1887. She married **John H. Pearsol**. He was born January 12, 1818, and died October 10, 1887.

Children of Cecelia Ober and John Pearsol are:
- 1722   i.   Unknown[11] Pearsol.
- 1723   ii.   Charles Pearsol.
- 1724   iii.   William H. Pearsol, born Abt. 1846; died November 20, 1863.
- 1725   iv.   Ellen Pearsol, born Abt. 1848.
- 1726   v.   Agnes Keys Pearsol, born September 24, 1850. She married Luther Reily Kelker; born February 29, 1848.
- 1727   vi.   Anna Pearsol, born Abt. 1855.
- 1728   vii.   John H. Pearsol, born Abt. 1860.

1060. Christian[10] Brubaker (Elizabeth[9] Stauffer, Christian[8], Henry Jacob[7], Hans[6], Christian[5], Daniel[4] Stouffer, Christian[3], Hans[2], Hans[1]) was born March 30, 1787 in Lancaster County, Pennsylvania, and died July 04, 1863 in Lebanon County, Pennsylvania. He married **Elizabeth Eberly**. She was born February 17, 1786 in Lancaster County, Pennsylvania, and died January 19, 1863 in Lebanon County, Pennsylvania.

Children of Christian Brubaker and Elizabeth Eberly are:
- +   1729   i.   Isaac[11] Brubaker, born 1815 in Lebannon County, Pennsylvania; died 1866 in Lebannon County, Pennsylvania.
- +   1730   ii.   Susanna Brubaker, born March 22, 1822 in Lebanon Township, Lebanon County, Pennsylvania; died August 10, 1867 in Campbelltown, Lebanon County, Pennsylvania.
- +   1731   iii.   Christian Brubaker, born 1819; died Aft. 1880.

1061. Peter[10] Brubaker (Elizabeth[9] Stauffer, Christian[8], Henry Jacob[7], Hans[6], Christian[5], Daniel[4] Stouffer, Christian[3], Hans[2], Hans[1]) was born March 08, 1791 in Buffalo Springs, Heidelberg Township, Lebanon County, Pennsylvania, and died August 08, 1827 in Heidelberg Township, Lebanon County, Pennsylvania. He married **Anna Hershberger**. She was born October 04, 1789 in Cocalico Township, Lancaster County, Pennsylvania, and died February 03, 1851 in Heidelberg Township, Lebanon County, Pennsylvania.

Child of Peter Brubaker and Anna Hershberger is:
- +   1732   i.   Magdalena[11] Brubaker, born August 22, 1824 in Heidelberg Township, Lebanon County, Pennsylvania; died April 15, 1900 in South Lebanon Township, Lancaster County, Pennsylvania.

1063. Catherine[10] Stoffer (Jacob[9], Jacob[8] Stauffer, Henry Jacob[7], Hans[6], Christian[5], Daniel[4] Stouffer, Christian[3], Hans[2], Hans[1]) was born October 10, 1802 in Pa Westmoreland Co, and died 1851 in Columbiana Co Ohio. She married **Henry Newcomer** March 18, 1834 in Columbiana Cty, Ohio. He was born March 31, 1787 in Penn., and died November 03, 1870 in Columbiana Co Ohio.

Children of Catherine Stoffer and Henry Newcomer are:

	1733	i.	Jacob[11] Newcomer, born 1835 in Columbiana County, Ohio.
	1734	ii.	Elizabeth Newcomer, born 1837 in Columbiana Cty Ohio; died 1913 in Columbiana Cty Ohio. She married James Reed July 27, 1854 in Columbiana Cty, Ohio; born 1833 in Columbiana Cty Ohio; died 1907 in Columbiana Cty Ohio.
	1735	iii.	Mary Newcomer, born 1838 in Columbiana County, Ohio.
	1736	iv.	Levi Newcomer, born 1842 in Columbiana County, Ohio. He married Rebecca Longanecker August 16, 1863 in Columbiana County, Ohio.

1064. Jacob S[10] Stoffer (Jacob[9], Jacob[8] Stauffer, Henry Jacob[7], Hans[6], Christian[5], Daniel[4] Stouffer, Christian[3], Hans[2], Hans[1]) was born October 26, 1803 in Westmoreland Pa, and died March 02, 1844 in Columbiana Co Ohio. He married **Elizabeth Hoffman** April 15, 1824 in Columbiana Co Ohio. She was born October 06, 1805, and died March 20, 1875 in Columbiana Co Ohio.

Children of Jacob Stoffer and Elizabeth Hoffman are:

	1737	i.	James[11] Stoffer.
	1738	ii.	Silvia Stoffer.
	1739	iii.	Eli Stoffer.
	1740	iv.	David Stoffer.
+	1741	v.	John Stoffer, born December 15, 1828 in Columbiana Cty, Ohio; died November 12, 1920 in Nappanee, Elkhart Ind.
	1742	vi.	Sarah Stoffer, born June 17, 1848; died December 17, 1866 in Carey, Ohio.

1066. Louis J[10] Stoffer (Jacob[9], Jacob[8] Stauffer, Henry Jacob[7], Hans[6], Christian[5], Daniel[4] Stouffer, Christian[3], Hans[2], Hans[1]) was born January 27, 1804 in Westmoreland Cty Pa, and died February 23, 1885 in Columbiana Co Ohio. He married **Katherine Wolf** September 07, 1826 in Columbiana Co Ohio. She was born December 03, 1809 in Pa, and died February 21, 1896 in Columbiana Co Ohio.

Children of Louis Stoffer and Katherine Wolf are:

	1743	i.	Christine[11] Stoffer, born October 07, 1828 in Columbiana Co Ohio; died November 13, 1901 in Canal Fulton, Stark Cty Ohio. She married Henry Ickes September 27, 1845 in Columbiana Co Ohio; born July 06, 1819 in New Oxford, Adams Cty PA; died February 13, 1902 in Canal Fulton, Stark Cty, Ohio.
+	1744	ii.	Nancy Stoffer, born 1830 in Columbiana Co ohio.
	1745	iii.	Eliza A Stoffer, born 1832 in Columbiana Co Ohio; died April 26, 1905 in Columbiana Co Ohio. She married Samuel K Sanor March 31, 1853 in Columbiana Co Ohio; born 1833 in Columbiana Co Ohio; died 1913 in Columbiana Co Ohio.
+	1746	iv.	Mary Ann Stoffer, born April 23, 1836 in Columbiana Cty Ohio; died September 19, 1906 in Columbiana Cty Ohio.
	1747	v.	Samuel J Stoffer, born 1839 in Columbiana Co, Ohio; died February 13, 1878 in Columbiana Co, Ohio. He married Mary A Bowman December 31, 1863; born 1818; died October 28, 1875 in Columbiana Co Ohio.
+	1748	vi.	Jesse A Stoffer, born 1841 in Columbiana Co, Ohio; died August 17, 1900 in Stark Co Ohio.
+	1749	vii.	Barbara Ellen Stoffer, born 1844 in Columbiana Co, Ohio.
+	1750	viii.	Lewis Jr Stoffer, born December 24, 1848 in Columbiana Co Ohio; died March 12, 1916 in Columbiana Co Ohio.

1068. Samuel[10] Stoffer (Jacob[9], Jacob[8] Stauffer, Henry Jacob[7], Hans[6], Christian[5], Daniel[4] Stouffer, Christian[3], Hans[2], Hans[1]) was born January 25, 1806 in Knox Township, Columbiana County, Ohio, and died February 14, 1878 in Knox Township, Columbiana County, Ohio. He married **(1) Catharine Mizner** November 09, 1826 in Columbiana Co Ohio. She was born 1811, and died March 22, 1835 in Columbiana Co Ohio. He married **(2) Mary Ann Wolf** July 19, 1835 in Columbiana Co Ohio. She was born March 25, 1818, and died October 28, 1875 in Columbiana Cty, Ohio.

Children of Samuel Stoffer and Catharine Mizner are:

+	1751	i.	Peter[11] Stoffer, born 1828 in Columbiana Co Ohio; died October 15, 1886 in Columbiana Co Ohio.
+	1752	ii.	Christina Stoffer, born October 27, 1828 in Canton Ohio, Stark Cty; died December 13, 1901 in Canal Fulton, Stark Cty ohio.
+	1753	iii.	Jacob L Stoffer, born March 08, 1830 in Columbiana Co Ohio; died February 12, 1919 in Columbiana Co Ohio.

Children of Samuel Stoffer and Mary Wolf are:

+	1754	i.	Eli[11] Stoffer, born 1836 in Columbiana Co, Ohio.
+	1755	ii.	Nancy Stoffer, born December 07, 1838 in Columbiana Co Ohio; died February 09, 1889 in Columbiana Co Ohio.
+	1756	iii.	Melinda J Stoffer, born December 28, 1840 in Columbiana Cty Ohio; died December 21, 1888 in

	1757	iv.	Catherine Ann Stoffer, born 1842 in Columbiana Cty, Ohio; died September 16, 1873 in Columbiana Cty, Ohio.
+			Columbiana Cty Ohio.
+	1758	v.	Samuel Jr Stoffer, born 1843 in Columbiana Co Ohio; died March 12, 1932 in Stark Cty, Ohio.
	1759	vi.	Rachel A Stoffer, born March 27, 1845 in Columbiana Cty, Ohio; died April 08, 1895 in Columbiana Cty, Ohio. She married John W Glass March 11, 1866 in Columbiana Cty Ohio; born December 26, 1837 in Columbiana Cty Ohio; died July 03, 1902 in Columbiana Cty, Ohio.
+	1760	vii.	Eliza Stoffer, born December 1849; died 1905.

1069. Margaret[10] Stoffer (Jacob[9], Jacob[8] Stauffer, Henry Jacob[7], Hans[6], Christian[5], Daniel[4] Stouffer, Christian[3], Hans[2], Hans[1]) was born December 15, 1808 in Columbiana Cty, Ohio, and died November 15, 1885 in Columbiana Cty, Ohio. She married **(1) Henry Wolf** November 02, 1826 in Columbiana Cty Ohio. He was born November 02, 1826 in Columbiana Cty, Ohio, and died 1854 in Columbiana Cty, Ohio. She married **(2) George Sanor** August 07, 1858 in Columbiana Cty, Ohio. He was born October 15, 1797, and died July 23, 1886 in Columbiana Cty Ohio.

Marriage Notes for Margaret Stoffer and Henry Wolf:
[chrststauffer1663.ged]

1 _FA1
2 DATE 1858
2 PLAC Columbiana county , Ohio
1 _MEND Divorce

Children of Margaret Stoffer and Henry Wolf are:
	1761	i.	Collin[11] Wolf, born 1828.
	1762	ii.	Catherine Wolf, born May 11, 1830 in Columbiana Cty; died November 10, 1894 in Columbiana Cty. She married David Sanor October 30, 1849 in Columbiana Cty, Ohio; born September 30, 1825 in Columbiana Cty Ohio; died August 22, 1903 in Columbiana Cty.
	1763	iii.	George B II Wolf, born 1834.
	1764	iv.	Christena Wolf, born 1838; died December 12, 1867.
	1765	v.	Lewis Wolf, born 1840.

1070. John[10] Stoffer (Jacob[9], Jacob[8] Stauffer, Henry Jacob[7], Hans[6], Christian[5], Daniel[4] Stouffer, Christian[3], Hans[2], Hans[1]) was born 1813 in Knox Township, Columbiana County, Ohio, and died 1895 in Richland Ohio, Springfeild Twp. He married **Eliza Fried** March 20, 1832 in Columbiana Co Ohio, West Twp. She was born 1815 in Maryland.

Children of John Stoffer and Eliza Fried are:
	1766	i.	David[11] Stoffer, born 1835. He married Mary Yeager March 23, 1854 in Columbiana Co Ohio; born 1837.
	1767	ii.	Levi Stoffer, born 1837 in Columbiana Co Ohio.
	1768	iii.	Christena Stoffer, born 1840 in Columbiana Co Ohio.
	1769	iv.	George Stoffer, born 1842 in Columbiana Co Ohio.
	1770	v.	Daniel D Stoffer, born 1843 in Columbiana Co Ohio; died July 29, 1910.
	1771	vi.	Enos Stoffer, born November 1844 in Columbiana Cty Ohio; died February 17, 1917 in Erie Cty Ohio. He married Sarah A Garber October 07, 1876 in Richland Cty, Ohio.
+	1772	vii.	Dennis Stoffer, born November 1844 in Columbiana County, Ohio; died 1922.
+	1773	viii.	John Jacob Stoffer, born August 11, 1846 in Columbiana Co Ohio; died April 19, 1921 in Ohio, Richland Co.
	1774	ix.	Joseph Stoffer, born 1848 in Columbiana County, Ohio.
	1775	x.	Albert Stoffer, born 1850 in Columbiana County, Ohio.
	1776	xi.	Elizabeth Rose Stoffer, born 1854 in Columbiana Cty Ohio; died 1912 in Richland Cty, Ohio. She married (1) A C Hettinger. She married (2) R Butterbaugh August 13, 1876 in Richland Cty Ohio.
	1777	xii.	Catherine Stoffer, born 1854.
	1778	xiii.	Nehariah Stoffer, born 1858.

1071. Leah[10] Stoffer (Jacob[9], Jacob[8] Stauffer, Henry Jacob[7], Hans[6], Christian[5], Daniel[4] Stouffer, Christian[3], Hans[2], Hans[1]) was born November 10, 1817 in Knox Township, Columbiana County, Ohio, and died February 01, 1898 in Columbiana County, Ohio. She married **Abraham Heestand** October 21, 1838 in Columbiana Co Ohio. He was born May 22, 1816 in Columbiana Co Ohio, and died August 24, 1892 in Columbiana Co Ohio.

Children of Leah Stoffer and Abraham Heestand are:
	1779	i.	Levi[11] Heestand, born 1839; died 1913 in Knox Township, Columbiana County, Ohio. He married Catherine Lower.

1780	ii.	Joseph Heestand, born 1841 in Columbiana Co, Ohio.
1781	iii.	Samuel Heestand, born January 16, 1842 in Knox Twp, Columbiana CO, Ohio; died September 14, 1933 in Knox Twp, Columbiana CO, Ohio. He married (1) Sarah Summers. He married (2) Clementine Summers; born 1851; died 1915 in Knox Twp, Columbiana Cty, Ohio.
1782	iv.	Issac S Heestand, born October 12, 1843 in Columbiana Co, Ohio; died November 09, 1862 in Civil War.
1783	v.	Anna Heestand, born 1845 in Columbiana Co, Ohio.
1784	vi.	Infant Heestand, born July 10, 1854 in Knox Township, Columbiana County, Ohio; died July 29, 1854 in Knox Township, Columbiana County, Ohio.

1072. George[10] Stoffer (Jacob[9], Jacob[8] Stauffer, Henry Jacob[7], Hans[6], Christian[5], Daniel[4] Stouffer, Christian[3], Hans[2], Hans[1]) was born July 25, 1820 in Knox Township, Columbiana County, Ohio, and died April 21, 1899 in Knox Township, Columbiana County, Ohio. He married **(1) Catherine Fox** January 27, 1842 in Columbiana County, Ohio. She was born October 18, 1828 in Columbiana County, Ohio, and died October 08, 1866 in Knox Township, Columbiana County, Ohio. He married **(2) Catherine Weaver** February 27, 1868 in Columbiana County, Ohio. She was born August 26, 1831 in Knox Township, Columbiana County, Ohio, and died March 08, 1874 in Knox Township, Columbiana County, Ohio. He married **(3) Elizabeth Catherine Weaver Baier** March 12, 1868 in Columbiana Cty, Ohio. She was born December 04, 1822, and died February 20, 1910 in Ohio. He married **(4) Anna Margaret Bowman** August 29, 1877 in Stark County, Ohio. She was born October 03, 1834 in Ohio, and died January 21, 1919 in Columbiana County, Ohio. He married **(5) Margaret Anna Bowman** August 29, 1877 in Stark Co, Ohio-Rev P. Herbruck. She was born October 03, 1835 in Penna., Bedford Co, and died January 21, 1919.

Children of George Stoffer and Catherine Fox are:

	1785	i.	Louella I[11] Stoffer, born in Columbiana Co Ohio.
+	1786	ii.	Levi Stoffer, born June 16, 1845 in Ohio; died July 09, 1932 in Ohio.
	1787	iii.	David M. Stoffer, born December 20, 1850 in Columbiana County, Ohio; died December 07, 1869 in Wisconsin.
	1788	iv.	David M Stoffer, born December 10, 1851 in Ohio; died December 07, 1869 in Columbiana Co Ohio.
+	1789	v.	Laurtis W. Stoffer, born December 02, 1854 in Columbiana County, Ohio; died August 24, 1913 in Columbiana County, Ohio.
+	1790	vi.	Simon Henry Stoffer, born May 21, 1856 in Columbiana County, Ohio; died April 06, 1944 in Orange County, Texas.
+	1791	vii.	Rolandus Stoffer, born May 27, 1858 in Columbiana County, Ohio; died January 13, 1934 in Columbiana County, Ohio.
+	1792	viii.	George D Stoffer, born April 01, 1860 in Columbiana County, Ohio; died November 09, 1940 in Columbiana Cty, Ohio.
+	1793	ix.	Stanton Uriah Stoffer, born October 27, 1861 in Columbiana Co Ohio; died March 16, 1940 in Ohio.
+	1794	x.	Sherman Stoffer, born May 21, 1865 in Columbiana Co Ohio; died March 31, 1926 in Ohio, Portage Cty.
+	1795	xi.	Leander Stoffer, born September 19, 1866 in Columbiana County, Ohio; died March 30, 1942 in Columbiana County, Ohio.

Children of George Stoffer and Catherine Weaver are:

1796	i.	Clara M.[11] Stoffer, born March 11, 1869 in Knox Township, Columbiana County, Ohio; died January 21, 1919 in Columbiana County, Ohio.
1797	ii.	Louella Stoffer, born August 07, 1871 in Knox Township, Columbiana County, Ohio; died September 1872 in Knox Township, Columbiana County, Ohio.

Child of George Stoffer and Elizabeth Baier is:

1798	i.	Clara M[11] Stoffer, born March 12, 1870 in Columbiana Co Ohio; died March 07, 1958 in Ohio.

Generation No. 11

1074. Sarah Weidler[11] Hess (Joseph H[10], Christian[9], Esther[8] Hershey, Christian[7], Benjamin Stauffer[6], Adelheid Galle[5] Stouffer, Daniel[4], Christian[3], Hans[2], Hans[1]) was born February 10, 1859 in Warwick Twp, Lanc Co, PA, and died September 14, 1926. She married **Henry L Hess** November 12, 1876, son of Samuel Hess and Fanny Landis. He was born January 28, 1857 in Elizabeth Twp Lancaster Co, PA, and died December 10, 1919.

Child of Sarah Hess and Henry Hess is:

+	1799	i.	Harry H[12] Hess, born July 20, 1884 in Manheim Twp, Lanc Co, PA; died January 17, 1958.

1075. Annie H[11] Bomberger (Barbara[10] Hess, Christian[9], Esther[8] Hershey, Christian[7], Benjamin Stauffer[6], Adelheid Galle[5] Stouffer,

Daniel[4], Christian[3], Hans[2], Hans[1]) was born November 20, 1849. She married **Henry G Snyder** November 14, 1872. He was born May 28, 1849.

Children of Annie Bomberger and Henry Snyder are:
- 1800   i.   Jacob B[12] Snyder, born October 02, 1873.
- 1801   ii.   Mary B Snyder, born November 23, 1875.
- 1802   iii.   Barbara B Snyder, born August 23, 1877.
- 1803   iv.   Lizzie B Snyder, born August 23, 1877.
- 1804   v.   Christian B Snyder, born October 16, 1879.
- + 1805   vi.   Amos B Snyder, born February 21, 1883.
- 1806   vii.   Annie B Snyder, born February 26, 1892.

1076. Henry L[11] Hess (Samuel H[10], Henry[9], Esther[8] Hershey, Christian[7], Benjamin Stauffer[6], Adelheid Galle[5] Stouffer, Daniel[4], Christian[3], Hans[2], Hans[1]) was born January 28, 1857 in Elizabeth Twp Lancaster Co, PA, and died December 10, 1919. He married **Sarah Weidler Hess** November 12, 1876, daughter of Joseph Hess and Elizabeth Weidler. She was born February 10, 1859 in Warwick Twp, Lanc Co, PA, and died September 14, 1926.

Child is listed above under (1074) Sarah Weidler Hess.

1078. Magdalena O.[11] Martin (Martha H.[10] Oberholtzer, Martha H.[9] Hess, Esther[8] Hershey, Christian[7], Benjamin Stauffer[6], Adelheid Galle[5] Stouffer, Daniel[4], Christian[3], Hans[2], Hans[1]) was born August 15, 1850, and died May 09, 1886. She married **Elam B. Landis** November 25, 1875, son of Levi Landis and Mary Buckwalter. He was born October 06, 1850, and died May 06, 1938 in Ephrata Twp, Lanc Co, PA.

Children of Magdalena Martin and Elam Landis are:
- 1807   i.   Mary M.[12] Landis, born September 07, 1876. She married Benjamin E. Martin June 09, 1900; born June 27, 1875; died February 16, 1927.
- 1808   ii.   Annie M. Landis, born June 22, 1878; died April 28, 1896.
- 1809   iii.   Emma M. Landis, born September 13, 1880; died September 17, 1963. She married Michael W. Sensenig January 01, 1899; born December 17, 1877; died 1953.
- + 1810   iv.   Magdalena M. Landis, born December 22, 1881 in Intercourse, Lanc Co, PA; died October 17, 1946 in Akron, Lancaster Co, PA.
- 1811   v.   Ada Cathrine Landis, born January 29, 1884; died August 17, 1895.
- 1812   vi.   Harry M. Landis, born March 28, 1886; died June 21, 1968. He married Emma W. Myers June 03, 1909; born October 24, 1885; died February 18, 1951.

1094. Lorena[11] Hershey (Christian[10], Jacob Frantz[9], Isaac Hernley[8], Christian[7], Benjamin Stauffer[6], Adelheid Galle[5] Stouffer, Daniel[4], Christian[3], Hans[2], Hans[1]) was born October 02, 1868. She married **James B Leithiser**.

Child of Lorena Hershey and James Leithiser is:
- 1813   i.   Margaret[12] Leithiser, born June 02, 1893.

1102. Eugene Light[11] Hershey (Jacob H[10], Jacob Frantz[9], Isaac Hernley[8], Christian[7], Benjamin Stauffer[6], Adelheid Galle[5] Stouffer, Daniel[4], Christian[3], Hans[2], Hans[1]) was born October 02, 1880, and died August 1966 in 17083 Quentin, Lebanon, PA. He married **Elizabeth Unknown** 1908. She was born 1883.

Children of Eugene Hershey and Elizabeth Unknown are:
- 1814   i.   Jacob B[12] Hershey, born February 02, 1911; died November 12, 1990.
- 1815   ii.   Leona R Hershey, born 1913.
- 1816   iii.   Freda M Hershey, born 1922.

1104. Annie[11] Hershey (Elias H[10], Jacob Frantz[9], Isaac Hernley[8], Christian[7], Benjamin Stauffer[6], Adelheid Galle[5] Stouffer, Daniel[4], Christian[3], Hans[2], Hans[1]) was born November 14, 1869, and died May 15, 1916. She married **Harvey Bitzer**. He was born May 22, 1870.

Children of Annie Hershey and Harvey Bitzer are:
- + 1817   i.   Helen Virginia[12] Bitzer, born February 21, 1891.
- 1818   ii.   Elizabeth Gertrude Bitzer, born December 17, 1894.

1105. Mary[11] Hershey (Elias H[10], Jacob Frantz[9], Isaac Hernley[8], Christian[7], Benjamin Stauffer[6], Adelheid Galle[5] Stouffer, Daniel[4], Christian[3], Hans[2], Hans[1]) was born November 17, 1872. She married **Monroe Pfautz**. He was born 1857.

Child of Mary Hershey and Monroe Pfautz is:

1819   i.   Mildred[12] Pfautz, born November 24, 1896. She married Allen Hammond; born 1894.

1108. Ezra Frantz[11] Hershey (Elias H[10], Jacob Frantz[9], Isaac Hernley[8], Christian[7], Benjamin Stauffer[6], Adelheid Galle[5] Stouffer, Daniel[4], Christian[3], Hans[2], Hans[1]) was born September 01, 1879, and died 1949. He married **Mary Amanda Rohrer**. She was born August 04, 1883, and died Aft. 1960.

Children of Ezra Hershey and Mary Rohrer are:
   1820   i.   Katherine Rohrer[12] Hershey, born September 30, 1911.
+ 1821   ii.   Maria Elizabeth Hershey, born June 05, 1913.
   1822 iii.   Ezra Frantz Hershey, born March 24, 1916; died May 21, 2003 in Richmond, Henrico, VA.

1109. Chauncey[11] Hershey (Samuel Harnish[10], Samuel[9], Isaac Hernley[8], Christian[7], Benjamin Stauffer[6], Adelheid Galle[5] Stouffer, Daniel[4], Christian[3], Hans[2], Hans[1]) was born August 28, 1870. He married **Elizabeth H Landis**, daughter of Franklin Landis and Elizabeth Hershey. She was born 1875 in Franklin Co, PA.

Children of Chauncey Hershey and Elizabeth Landis are:
   1823   i.   Robert Landis[12] Hershey, born 1902.
   1824   ii.   Samuel F Hershey, born 1904.

1116. Elizabeth H[11] Landis (Elizabeth[10] Hershey, Samuel[9], Isaac Hernley[8], Christian[7], Benjamin Stauffer[6], Adelheid Galle[5] Stouffer, Daniel[4], Christian[3], Hans[2], Hans[1]) was born 1875 in Franklin Co, PA. She married **Chauncey Hershey**, son of Samuel Hershey and Mary Bachman. He was born August 28, 1870.

Children are listed above under (1109) Chauncey Hershey.

1127. Naomi B[11] Hershey (Amos F[10], Christian[9], Isaac Hernley[8], Christian[7], Benjamin Stauffer[6], Adelheid Galle[5] Stouffer, Daniel[4], Christian[3], Hans[2], Hans[1]) She married **William Gingrich**.

Children of Naomi Hershey and William Gingrich are:
   1825   i.   Katie[12] Gingrich.
   1826   ii.   Charles Gingrich.
   1827 iii.   Fannie Gingrich.
   1828   iv.   LeRoy Gingrich.
   1829   v.   Ruth Gingrich.
   1830   vi.   Harry Gingrich.

1131. Fanny Long[11] Landis (Anna[10] Long, Anna[9] Hershey, Jacob[8], Christian[7], Benjamin Stauffer[6], Adelheid Galle[5] Stouffer, Daniel[4], Christian[3], Hans[2], Hans[1]) was born August 26, 1833 in Manheim Twp, Lanc Co, PA, and died July 16, 1898. She married **Samuel H Hess**, son of Henry Hess and Catherine Huber. He was born November 19, 1830 in Elizabeth Twp Lancaster Co, PA, and died December 10, 1871 in Willow Bank Mills, Elizabeth Twp., Lancaster Co., PA.

Child is listed above under (590) Samuel H Hess.

1132. Samuel[11] Betzner (Elizabeth[10] Stouffer, Abraham Hershey[9] Stauffer, Abraham Hess[8], Henry Jacob[7], Hans[6], Christian[5], Daniel[4] Stouffer, Christian[3], Hans[2], Hans[1]) was born 1828, and died 1914. He married **Sarah Surerus** December 29, 1852. She was born 1834, and died 1905.

Children of Samuel Betzner and Sarah Surerus are:
   1831   i.   William[12] Betzner.
+ 1832   ii.   Wesley Betzner, born July 02, 1855; died December 15, 1941.
   1833 iii.   Jacob Betzner, born May 13, 1857; died December 05, 1857.
+ 1834   iv.   Mary Elizabeth Betzner, born December 22, 1858; died September 29, 1940.
+ 1835   v.   Andrew Betzner, born December 10, 1865.
   1836   vi.   Emma Louise Betzner, born June 20, 1867; died January 29, 1939. She married John Baird; died 1903.

1133. Abraham[11] Betzner (Elizabeth[10] Stouffer, Abraham Hershey[9] Stauffer, Abraham Hess[8], Henry Jacob[7], Hans[6], Christian[5], Daniel[4] Stouffer, Christian[3], Hans[2], Hans[1]) was born 1829, and died 1912. He married **(1) Mary Beemer Ward**. She was born 1829, and died 1920. He married **(2) Ellan Beemer** November 05, 1850. She died 1932.

Children of Abraham Betzner and Ellan Beemer are:
+ 1837   i.   Elizabeth[12] Betzner, born September 06, 1851; died August 30, 1934.
   1838   ii.   Fanny Betzner, born February 18, 1853; died September 05, 1906.

+ 1839 iii. George Washington Betzner, born October 17, 1855; died May 07, 1934.
+ 1840 iv. Joseph Betzner, born 1859; died November 09, 1934.

1134. Jacob[11] Betzner (Elizabeth[10] Stouffer, Abraham Hershey[9] Stauffer, Abraham Hess[8], Henry Jacob[7], Hans[6], Christian[5], Daniel[4] Stouffer, Christian[3], Hans[2], Hans[1]) was born 1831, and died 1906. He married **(1) Mary Jones**. He married **(2) Lydia Clemons** October 04, 1852. She was born January 04, 1831.

Children of Jacob Betzner and Lydia Clemons are:
    1841 i. William[12] Betzner. He married Mary Anderson.
    1842 ii. David Betzner, born 1850; died 1908.
+ 1843 iii. Alice Betzner, born October 01, 1863; died May 26, 1929.

1135. David S.[11] Betzner (Elizabeth[10] Stouffer, Abraham Hershey[9] Stauffer, Abraham Hess[8], Henry Jacob[7], Hans[6], Christian[5], Daniel[4] Stouffer, Christian[3], Hans[2], Hans[1]) was born 1835, and died 1906. He married **(1) Emma Halla**. She was born 1851, and died 1916. He married **(2) Ann Marshall** August 25, 1857. She was born 1836, and died 1883.

Child of David Betzner and Emma Halla is:
+ 1844 i. Etta[12] Betzner, born February 17, 1884; died May 29, 1937.

Child of David Betzner and Ann Marshall is:
+ 1845 i. David Thomas[12] Betzner, born September 08, 1861; died March 20, 1940.

1136. John Weir[11] Betzner (Elizabeth[10] Stouffer, Abraham Hershey[9] Stauffer, Abraham Hess[8], Henry Jacob[7], Hans[6], Christian[5], Daniel[4] Stouffer, Christian[3], Hans[2], Hans[1]) was born 1837, and died 1906. He married **Dorothy Jones** January 19, 1859. She was born 1837, and died 1903.

Children of John Betzner and Dorothy Jones are:
    1846 i. Rachel Elizabeth[12] Betzner, born April 20, 1860.
+ 1847 ii. John Abram Betzner, born February 11, 1862; died February 15, 1942.
+ 1848 iii. George David Betzner, born February 15, 1865.
+ 1849 iv. Albert E. Betzner, born June 16, 1867.

1137. Abraham[11] Stauffer (Christian[10], Abraham Hershey[9], Abraham Hess[8], Henry Jacob[7], Hans[6], Christian[5], Daniel[4] Stouffer, Christian[3], Hans[2], Hans[1]) was born May 09, 1826 in Canada. He married **Elizabeth Reynolds**. She was born Abt. 1830.

Children of Abraham Stauffer and Elizabeth Reynolds are:
    1850 i. Wellington[12] Stouffer.
    1851 ii. Maria Stouffer.
    1852 iii. John Stouffer.
    1853 iv. Roxa Stouffer.
    1854 v. Infant Stouffer.
+ 1855 vi. Nancy Jane Stauffer, born August 12, 1853; died July 17, 1950 in Spokane, WA.

1138. Elizabeth[11] Stouffer (Christian[10] Stauffer, Abraham Hershey[9], Abraham Hess[8], Henry Jacob[7], Hans[6], Christian[5], Daniel[4] Stouffer, Christian[3], Hans[2], Hans[1]) She married **Adam Sherk**.

Children of Elizabeth Stouffer and Adam Sherk are:
    1856 i. Adgeline[12] Sherk.
    1857 ii. Caroline Sherk.
    1858 iii. Franklin Sherk.
    1859 iv. Martha Sherk.

1139. Jacob[11] Stouffer (Christian[10] Stauffer, Abraham Hershey[9], Abraham Hess[8], Henry Jacob[7], Hans[6], Christian[5], Daniel[4] Stouffer, Christian[3], Hans[2], Hans[1]) He married **Maria Sanborn**.

Children of Jacob Stouffer and Maria Sanborn are:
    1860 i. William[12] Stoffer.
    1861 ii. Nancy Stoffer.
    1862 iii. Maggie Stoffer.

1863   iv.   Samuel Stoffer.
1864   v.   Elizabeth Stoffer.

1140. Martha[11] Stouffer (Christian[10] Stauffer, Abraham Hershey[9], Abraham Hess[8], Henry Jacob[7], Hans[6], Christian[5], Daniel[4] Stouffer, Christian[3], Hans[2], Hans[1]) She married **Amos Sherk**.

Children of Martha Stouffer and Amos Sherk are:
- 1865   i.   Matilda[12] Sherk.
- 1866   ii.   Maria Sherk.
- 1867   iii.   Albert Sherk.
- 1868   iv.   Amanda Sherk.
- 1869   v.   Elizabeth Sherk.
- 1870   vi.   Reuben Sherk.
- 1871   vii.   Arvilla Sherk.
- 1872   viii.   Luella Sherk.
- 1873   ix.   Edward Sherk.

1141. Christian[11] Stouffer (Christian[10] Stauffer, Abraham Hershey[9], Abraham Hess[8], Henry Jacob[7], Hans[6], Christian[5], Daniel[4] Stouffer, Christian[3], Hans[2], Hans[1]) He married **Rebecca Motheral**.

Children of Christian Stouffer and Rebecca Motheral are:
- 1874   i.   Francis[12] Stouffer.
- 1875   ii.   Ephraim Stouffer.
- 1876   iii.   Albert Stouffer.

1142. John Reesor[11] Stouffer (Christian[10] Stauffer, Abraham Hershey[9], Abraham Hess[8], Henry Jacob[7], Hans[6], Christian[5], Daniel[4] Stouffer, Christian[3], Hans[2], Hans[1]) He married **(1) Mary Strome**. He married **(2) Rosa Hughes**.

Children of John Stouffer and Mary Strome are:
- 1877   i.   Drusilla[12] Stouffer.
- 1878   ii.   Jared Stouffer.
- 1879   iii.   Flora Stouffer.
- 1880   iv.   Martha Stouffer.
- 1881   v.   Annie Stouffer.
- 1882   vi.   John Stouffer.

Children of John Stouffer and Rosa Hughes are:
- 1883   i.   Alonz[12] Stouffer.
- 1884   ii.   Clara Stouffer.

1143. Susan[11] Stouffer (Christian[10] Stauffer, Abraham Hershey[9], Abraham Hess[8], Henry Jacob[7], Hans[6], Christian[5], Daniel[4] Stouffer, Christian[3], Hans[2], Hans[1]) She married **Moses Brown**.

Children of Susan Stouffer and Moses Brown are:
- 1885   i.   Marietta[12] Brown.
- 1886   ii.   Eliza Brown.
- 1887   iii.   Anna Brown.
- 1888   iv.   Rosa Brown.

1144. Peter[11] Stouffer (Christian[10] Stauffer, Abraham Hershey[9], Abraham Hess[8], Henry Jacob[7], Hans[6], Christian[5], Daniel[4] Stouffer, Christian[3], Hans[2], Hans[1]) He married **Hannah Johnson**.

Children of Peter Stouffer and Hannah Johnson are:
- 1889   i.   Minnie[12] Stouffer.
- 1890   ii.   Alden Stouffer.

1145. John[11] Stouffer (Abraham[10], Abraham Hershey[9] Stauffer, Abraham Hess[8], Henry Jacob[7], Hans[6], Christian[5], Daniel[4] Stouffer, Christian[3], Hans[2], Hans[1]) He married **Sarah Hare**.

Children of John Stouffer and Sarah Hare are:
+ 1891 i. Matilda[12] Stouffer.
  1892 ii. Elias Stouffer, died 1922.
  1893 iii. John Stouffer, died 1924.
+ 1894 iv. Esther Stouffer, died 1938.
  1895 v. Sarah Stouffer, died 1930. She married Unknown Barcome.
+ 1896 vi. Bertha Stouffer.
  1897 vii. Mary Stouffer.
+ 1898 viii. Aaron Stouffer, born 1859; died 1891.

1146. Samuel[11] Stouffer (Abraham[10], Abraham Hershey[9] Stauffer, Abraham Hess[8], Henry Jacob[7], Hans[6], Christian[5], Daniel[4] Stouffer, Christian[3], Hans[2], Hans[1]) He married **Lavilla Woolman**.

Children of Samuel Stouffer and Lavilla Woolman are:
+ 1899 i. Eli[12] Stouffer.
+ 1900 ii. Hannah Stouffer.
+ 1901 iii. Elizabeth Stouffer.
  1902 iv. Esther Stouffer.
  1903 v. Matilda Stouffer.
+ 1904 vi. Lavilla Stouffer.

1147. Jacob[11] Stouffer (Abraham[10], Abraham Hershey[9] Stauffer, Abraham Hess[8], Henry Jacob[7], Hans[6], Christian[5], Daniel[4] Stouffer, Christian[3], Hans[2], Hans[1]) He married **Anna Reesor**.

Children of Jacob Stouffer and Anna Reesor are:
+ 1905 i. John Franklin[12] Stouffer.
+ 1906 ii. David Wesley Stouffer.
  1907 iii. Mary Stouffer. She married John Patterson.
+ 1908 iv. Abraham Stouffer.
  1909 v. Esther Stouffer.
  1910 vi. Isaac Stouffer. He married Charolette Hoover.
+ 1911 vii. Keturah Stouffer, born February 06, 1859.
+ 1912 viii. Flavius Jacob Stouffer, born July 26, 1875; died January 10, 1941.
  1913 ix. Clayton Stouffer, born 1887. He married Martha Forsyth.

1148. Elizabeth[11] Stouffer (Abraham[10], Abraham Hershey[9] Stauffer, Abraham Hess[8], Henry Jacob[7], Hans[6], Christian[5], Daniel[4] Stouffer, Christian[3], Hans[2], Hans[1]) She married **(1) David Wideman**. She married **(2) Henry Woodburn**.

Children of Elizabeth Stouffer and David Wideman are:
+ 1914 i. Esther[12] Wideman.
  1915 ii. Abraham Henry Wideman, died in Died In Infancy.
+ 1916 iii. Jacob S. Wideman, born 1867.

Child of Elizabeth Stouffer and Henry Woodburn is:
  1917 i. Ed[12] Woodburn.

1149. Simeon[11] Stouffer (Abraham[10], Abraham Hershey[9] Stauffer, Abraham Hess[8], Henry Jacob[7], Hans[6], Christian[5], Daniel[4] Stouffer, Christian[3], Hans[2], Hans[1]) He married **Sarah Webb**.

Children of Simeon Stouffer and Sarah Webb are:
+ 1918 i. Laura[12] Stouffer, born May 13, 1869; died 1942.
  1919 ii. Luella Stouffer, born 1871. She married Ernest Doughtery.
  1920 iii. Jean Stouffer, born 1872. She married Alton Perkins.
+ 1921 iv. Fred Stouffer, born 1875.

1150. Abraham[11] Stouffer (Abraham[10], Abraham Hershey[9] Stauffer, Abraham Hess[8], Henry Jacob[7], Hans[6], Christian[5], Daniel[4] Stouffer, Christian[3], Hans[2], Hans[1]) was born 1830, and died 1909. He married **Elizabeth Sherrick** October 14, 1852. She was born 1828, and died 1915.

Children of Abraham Stouffer and Elizabeth Sherrick are:

	1922	i.	Esther[12] Stouffer, died June 15, 1860 in Died In Infancy.
+	1923	ii.	Christina Stouffer, born November 20, 1853; died 1935.
+	1924	iii.	Frances Stouffer, born May 23, 1855; died 1940.
	1925	iv.	Elizabeth Stouffer, born August 27, 1856; died 1940.
+	1926	v.	Noah Stouffer, born June 26, 1858; died 1931.
	1927	vi.	Adeline Stouffer, born July 28, 1862; died 1932.
	1928	vii.	Mary Ann Stouffer, born August 29, 1864; died 1931. She married James Bruce.
+	1929	viii.	Josephuine Stouffer, born September 11, 1866; died 1937.
+	1930	ix.	Martha Stouffer, born August 05, 1868; died 1947.
+	1931	x.	Abraham Stouffer, born June 23, 1872.

1151. Christian[11] Stouffer (Abraham[10], Abraham Hershey[9] Stauffer, Abraham Hess[8], Henry Jacob[7], Hans[6], Christian[5], Daniel[4] Stouffer, Christian[3], Hans[2], Hans[1]) was born 1839, and died 1924. He married **Jane Macklem**. She was born 1862, and died 1913.

Children of Christian Stouffer and Jane Macklem are:

+	1932	i.	Wellington[12] Stouffer.
+	1933	ii.	Andrew Stouffer.
	1934	iii.	Edward Stouffer, died 1949. He married Mary Patterson.
+	1935	iv.	Thomas Stouffer.
	1936	v.	Esther Stouffer. She married (1) Lorne Kester. She married (2) Jesse Cook.
+	1937	vi.	Alberta Stouffer.
	1938	vii.	Christian Stouffer. He married Helen Probert.
+	1939	viii.	David Stouffer.

1152. David[11] Stouffer (Abraham[10], Abraham Hershey[9] Stauffer, Abraham Hess[8], Henry Jacob[7], Hans[6], Christian[5], Daniel[4] Stouffer, Christian[3], Hans[2], Hans[1]) was born 1844, and died 1933. He married **(1) Ellen Parsons**. He married **(2) Mary Revis**. He married **(3) Margaret Ann Stephenson**.

Child of David Stouffer and Ellen Parsons is:
    1940   i.   Revis Parsons[12] Stouffer, born March 24, 1891. He married Ethel Robertson.

1204. Joseph[11] Hostetter (Joseph[10], Abraham[9], Jacob[8], Ann Elisabeth[7] Hershey, Benjamin Stauffer[6], Adelheid Galle[5] Stouffer, Daniel[4], Christian[3], Hans[2], Hans[1]) was born March 02, 1832, and died February 23, 1928 in Ashland County, Ohio. He married **Harriet Hershey**. She was born 1835, and died 1904 in Ohio.

Children of Joseph Hostetter and Harriet Hershey are:
    1941   i.   Benjamin[12] Hostetter, born 1857.
    1942   ii.   Adaline Hostetter, born 1861.
    1943   iii.   Mary Belle Hostetter, born 1865.

1205. Henry[11] Hostetter (Joseph[10], Abraham[9], Jacob[8], Ann Elisabeth[7] Hershey, Benjamin Stauffer[6], Adelheid Galle[5] Stouffer, Daniel[4], Christian[3], Hans[2], Hans[1]) was born September 08, 1834, and died 1894 in Ohio. He married **Harriet Scott**.

Children of Henry Hostetter and Harriet Scott are:
    1944   i.   Florence[12] Hostetter.
    1945   ii.   Venich Hostetter.
    1946   iii.   Adella Hostetter, born 1866.
    1947   iv.   David Hostetter, born 1869.

1206. David[11] Hostetter (Joseph[10], Abraham[9], Jacob[8], Ann Elisabeth[7] Hershey, Benjamin Stauffer[6], Adelheid Galle[5] Stouffer, Daniel[4], Christian[3], Hans[2], Hans[1]) was born September 15, 1838, and died March 01, 1917 in Ohio. He married **(1) Jamina Sanders**. He married **(2) Emma Strickland**. She was born January 28, 1853, and died October 28, 1893 in Ohio.

Children of David Hostetter and Emma Strickland are:
    1948   i.   William F[12] Hostetter, born 1873.
    1949   ii.   Jenny E Hostetter, born 1876.
    1950   iii.   Roy Grant Hostetter, born 1881.

1210. Fianna[11] Hostetter (Abraham[10], Abraham[9], Jacob[8], Ann Elisabeth[7] Hershey, Benjamin Stauffer[6], Adelheid Galle[5] Stouffer, Daniel[4], Christian[3], Hans[2], Hans[1]) was born August 11, 1833 in Lancaster County, Pa, and died September 11, 1913 in Lancaster County,

Pa. She married **Edwin Eshelman** February 19, 1852. He was born April 02, 1822, and died October 03, 1864 in Washington, DC.

Children of Fianna Hostetter and Edwin Eshelman are:

1951	i.	Abraham[12] Eshelman.
1952	ii.	Susan Eshelman.
1953	iii.	Alice Eshelman, born 1852.
1954	iv.	Lydia Eshelman, born March 25, 1855; died May 03, 1876.
1955	v.	Hagar Eshelman, born April 1858; died October 17, 1935.

1212. Susan A[11] Hostetter (Abraham[10], Abraham[9], Jacob[8], Ann Elisabeth[7] Hershey, Benjamin Stauffer[6], Adelheid Galle[5] Stouffer, Daniel[4], Christian[3], Hans[2], Hans[1]) was born August 17, 1836. She married **Jacob Shreiner**.

Children of Susan Hostetter and Jacob Shreiner are:
    1956   i.   Charles[12] Shreiner.
    1957   ii.   Mary Shreiner.

1213. Harriet A[11] Hostetter (Abraham[10], Abraham[9], Jacob[8], Ann Elisabeth[7] Hershey, Benjamin Stauffer[6], Adelheid Galle[5] Stouffer, Daniel[4], Christian[3], Hans[2], Hans[1]) was born July 14, 1838 in Lancaster County, Pa, and died June 30, 1903 in Cedar Rapids, Iowa. She married **Joseph Stauffer Brubaker**. He was born March 18, 1830 in Lancaster County, Pa, and died May 20, 1919 in Vinton, Iowa.

Children of Harriet Hostetter and Joseph Brubaker are:
    1958   i.   Stauffer Joseph[12] Brubaker, born May 16, 1859 in Carlisle, Pa; died March 20, 1942 in Cedar Rapids, Iowa. He married Margery Eckels February 16, 1881 in Cedar Rapids, Iowa; born December 21, 1862 in Carlisle, Pa; died August 02, 1913 in Cedar Rapids, Iowa.
    1959   ii.   Frank Hostetter Brubaker, born January 10, 1861 in Carlisle, Pa; died January 06, 1933 in Cedar Rapids, Iowa.
    1960   iii. Charles White Brubaker, born August 18, 1865; died November 24, 1924 in Cedar Rapids, Iowa.

1214. Lucinda[11] Hostetter (Abraham[10], Abraham[9], Jacob[8], Ann Elisabeth[7] Hershey, Benjamin Stauffer[6], Adelheid Galle[5] Stouffer, Daniel[4], Christian[3], Hans[2], Hans[1]) was born October 15, 1840 in Lancaster County, Pa. She married **Joab Martin**.

Children of Lucinda Hostetter and Joab Martin are:
    1961   i.   Nancy[12] Martin.
    1962   ii.   Margaret Martin.
    1963   iii. Rose Martin.
    1964   iv. Mary Martin.
    1965   v.   Paul Martin.
    1966   vi. Dorcus Lucinda Martin, born 1878 in Shippensburg, Pa; died 1966 in Ambler, Pa.

1216. Christina[11] Hostetter (Abraham[10], Abraham[9], Jacob[8], Ann Elisabeth[7] Hershey, Benjamin Stauffer[6], Adelheid Galle[5] Stouffer, Daniel[4], Christian[3], Hans[2], Hans[1]) was born June 11, 1843 in Lancaster County, Pa, and died February 14, 1909. She married **Charles Eckels**.

Children of Christina Hostetter and Charles Eckels are:
    1967   i.   Margery[12] Eckels, born December 21, 1862 in Carlisle, Pa; died August 02, 1913 in Cedar Rapids, Iowa. She married Stauffer Joseph Brubaker February 16, 1881 in Cedar Rapids, Iowa; born May 16, 1859 in Carlisle, Pa; died March 20, 1942 in Cedar Rapids, Iowa.
    1968   ii.   Grace Eckels, born 1865.

1217. Isabella Victoria[11] Hostetter (Abraham[10], Abraham[9], Jacob[8], Ann Elisabeth[7] Hershey, Benjamin Stauffer[6], Adelheid Galle[5] Stouffer, Daniel[4], Christian[3], Hans[2], Hans[1]) was born July 12, 1845. She married **Andrew Jackson**.

Child of Isabella Hostetter and Andrew Jackson is:
    1969   i.   John[12] Jackson.

1218. Clement[11] Hostetter (Abraham[10], Abraham[9], Jacob[8], Ann Elisabeth[7] Hershey, Benjamin Stauffer[6], Adelheid Galle[5] Stouffer, Daniel[4], Christian[3], Hans[2], Hans[1]) was born November 20, 1847 in Lancaster County, Pa, and died March 07, 1921 in Cedar Rapids, Iowa. He married **Belle Stone**.

Children of Clement Hostetter and Belle Stone are:

1970   i.   Bella[12] Hostetter, born 1873.
1971   ii.   Robert White Hostetter, born 1875.

1220. Abraham Webster[11] Hostetter (Abraham[10], Abraham[9], Jacob[8], Ann Elisabeth[7] Hershey, Benjamin Stauffer[6], Adelheid Galle[5] Stouffer, Daniel[4], Christian[3], Hans[2], Hans[1]) was born October 20, 1851 in Lancaster County, Pa, and died January 29, 1935 in Minnesota. He married **Martha Asenath Coburn** November 03, 1873. She died June 14, 1927.

Children of Abraham Hostetter and Martha Coburn are:
1972   i.   Florence Ethel[12] Hostetter, born August 22, 1874; died July 14, 1943.
1973   ii.   Jessie Olive Hostetter, born October 14, 1878; died October 14, 1916.
1974   iii.   Ervilla Hostetter, born April 28, 1880.

1221. Taylor T[11] Hostetter (Abraham[10], Abraham[9], Jacob[8], Ann Elisabeth[7] Hershey, Benjamin Stauffer[6], Adelheid Galle[5] Stouffer, Daniel[4], Christian[3], Hans[2], Hans[1]) was born November 02, 1853 in Lancaster, pa, and died September 22, 1912 in Reading, Pa. He married **Mary Elizabeth Stoudt** March 11, 1877 in Trinity Lutheran Church Reading, Pa. She was born September 15, 1854 in Womelsdorf, Pa, and died February 26, 1908 in Reading, Pa.

Children of Taylor Hostetter and Mary Stoudt are:
1975   i.   William S[12] Hostetter, born in Reading, Pa.
1976   ii.   Floyd R Hostetter.
1977   iii.   Harry Jacob Hostetter, born April 03, 1878 in Berks County, Pa; died January 28, 1940 in Reading, Pa.
1978   iv.   Charles E Hostetter, born 1880.
1979   v.   John E Hostetter, born 1882 in Reading, Pa; died 1951 in Reading, Pa.
1980   vi.   Earl W Hostetter, born February 16, 1885 in Reading, Pa; died 1917 in Philadelphia, Pa.
1981   vii.   Clarence White Hostetter, born August 15, 1887 in Pottsville, Pa; died March 16, 1973 in Ashtubula, Ohio.
1982   viii.   George Washington Hostetter, born August 15, 1887 in Pottsville, Pa; died January 27, 1946 in Pottsville, pa.
1983   ix.   Grace E Hostetter, born December 03, 1889; died May 1945 in Philadelphia, Pa.
1984   x.   Robert Lynne Hostetter, born October 12, 1891.

1229. Annie[11] Hostetter (David[10], Abraham[9], Jacob[8], Ann Elisabeth[7] Hershey, Benjamin Stauffer[6], Adelheid Galle[5] Stouffer, Daniel[4], Christian[3], Hans[2], Hans[1]) was born January 1853 in Lancaster County, Pa. She married **Abraham C. Bitner**. He was born July 1834, and died 1877.

Children of Annie Hostetter and Abraham Bitner are:
1985   i.   Grace[12] Bitner, born January 1878.
1986   ii.   Herbert Bitner, born January 1880.
1987   iii.   Walter Bitner, born June 1882.
1988   iv.   Clarence Bitner, born February 1885.
1989   v.   Anna Bitner, born February 1888.
1990   vi.   Robert Bitner, born March 1891.
1991   vii.   Charles Eby Bitner, born July 23, 1894 in Lancaster County, Pa; died October 06, 1974 in Lafayette, Contra Costa Cty, CA..

1232. Jacob Baer[11] Hackman (Susanna Frantz[10] Bear, Anna[9] Frantz, Barbara[8] Hostetter, Ann Elisabeth[7] Hershey, Benjamin Stauffer[6], Adelheid Galle[5] Stouffer, Daniel[4], Christian[3], Hans[2], Hans[1]) was born March 26, 1825, and died January 20, 1899. He married **Maria Unknown**. She was born August 26, 1830, and died May 09, 1897.

Children of Jacob Hackman and Maria Unknown are:
1992   i.   Henry[12] Hackman, born 1850.
1993   ii.   Aaron Hackman, born 1852.
1994   iii.   David Hackman, born 1856.
1995   iv.   Andrew Hackman, born 1859.
1996   v.   Jacob Hackman, born 1862.
1997   vi.   Joseph Hackman, born 1865.
1998   vii.   Leonard Hackman, born April 1870.

1233. David Baer[11] Hackman (Susanna Frantz[10] Bear, Anna[9] Frantz, Barbara[8] Hostetter, Ann Elisabeth[7] Hershey, Benjamin Stauffer[6], Adelheid Galle[5] Stouffer, Daniel[4], Christian[3], Hans[2], Hans[1]) was born March 19, 1827, and died November 16, 1896. He married **(1) Ella C**. She was born April 26, 1851, and died February 02, 1907. He married **(2) Harriet B Miller** 1854. She was born February 05,

1829, and died December 09, 1870.

Child of David Hackman and Harriet Miller is:
    1999   i.   Augustus Miller[12] Hackman, born Abt. 1855.

1234. Andrew Baer[11] Hackman (Susanna Frantz[10] Bear, Anna[9] Frantz, Barbara[8] Hostetter, Ann Elisabeth[7] Hershey, Benjamin Stauffer[6], Adelheid Galle[5] Stouffer, Daniel[4], Christian[3], Hans[2], Hans[1]) was born July 05, 1828, and died July 27, 1916. He married **Martha Eschbach Brenner** September 05, 1861 in B Kauffman's Tavern. She was born February 15, 1839 in Millersville, PA, and died July 17, 1913.

Marriage Notes for Andrew Hackman and Martha Brenner:
Andrew & Martha were married by the Reverend Jacob Reinhold

Children of Andrew Hackman and Martha Brenner are:
    2000   i.   Alice Ann B[12] Hackman, born January 01, 1862; died June 26, 1894. She married John E Leed; born September 11, 1854; died September 13, 1948.
    2001   ii.   Emma Amelia Hackman, born February 13, 1868. She married John Grube; born Abt. 1860.
    2002   iii.   Romanus Andrew B Hackman, born November 30, 1871; died January 18, 1873.
+   2003   iv.   Willis Brenner Hackman, born February 21, 1877; died August 11, 1947 in Lancaster, PA.

1246. Kathryn[11] Hostetter (Ezra[10], Benjamin[9], Benjamin[8], Ann Elisabeth[7] Hershey, Benjamin Stauffer[6], Adelheid Galle[5] Stouffer, Daniel[4], Christian[3], Hans[2], Hans[1]) was born in Lancaster County, Pa. She married **John G. Reist**.

Children of Kathryn Hostetter and John Reist are:
    2004   i.   Florence[12] Reist, born 1891.
    2005   ii.   Naomi Reist, born 1896.
    2006   iii.   John H. Reist, born 1898.

1249. Jacob D.[11] Hostetter (Ezra[10], Benjamin[9], Benjamin[8], Ann Elisabeth[7] Hershey, Benjamin Stauffer[6], Adelheid Galle[5] Stouffer, Daniel[4], Christian[3], Hans[2], Hans[1]) was born October 06, 1863 in Lancaster County, Pa, and died May 04, 1951 in Lancaster County, Pa. He married **Alta Herr**. She was born December 11, 1874, and died June 18, 1960.

Children of Jacob Hostetter and Alta Herr are:
    2007   i.   Private[12] Hostetter.
    2008   ii.   Private Hostetter.
    2009   iii.   Private Hostetter.
    2010   iv.   Private Hostetter.
    2011   v.   E. Maurice Hostetter, born 1896.

1305. Amos[11] Hostetter (Jacob[10], Abraham[9], Jacob[8], Catharine[7] Long, Anna[6] Hershey, Adelheid Galle[5] Stouffer, Daniel[4], Christian[3], Hans[2], Hans[1])

Child of Amos Hostetter is:
    2012   i.   Amos[12] Hostetter.

1306. Anna[11] Hostetter (Jacob[10], Abraham[9], Jacob[8], Catharine[7] Long, Anna[6] Hershey, Adelheid Galle[5] Stouffer, Daniel[4], Christian[3], Hans[2], Hans[1]) She married **C. Bachman Herr**.

Children of Anna Hostetter and C. Herr are:
    2013   i.   Benjamin[12] Herr.
    2014   ii.   Charles S. Herr.

1308. Linnaeus[11] Hostetter (Abraham[10], Abraham[9], Jacob[8], Catharine[7] Long, Anna[6] Hershey, Adelheid Galle[5] Stouffer, Daniel[4], Christian[3], Hans[2], Hans[1]) was born 1842 in Lancaster County, Pa, and died in Illinois. He married **Mary Peart**.

Child of Linnaeus Hostetter and Mary Peart is:
    2015   i.   Heber[12] Hostetter, born 1886.

1309. Abram[11] Hostetter (Abraham[10], Abraham[9], Jacob[8], Catharine[7] Long, Anna[6] Hershey, Adelheid Galle[5] Stouffer, Daniel[4], Christian[3], Hans[2], Hans[1]) was born June 01, 1847 in Lancaster County, Pa, and died October 21, 1921 in Illinois. He married **Harriet**

Irvine.

Child of Abram Hostetter and Harriet Irvine is:
    2016   i.   Adaline[12] Hostetter, born 1877.

1310. Ross[11] Hostetter (Abraham[10], Abraham[9], Jacob[8], Catharine[7] Long, Anna[6] Hershey, Adelheid Galle[5] Stouffer, Daniel[4], Christian[3], Hans[2], Hans[1]) was born 1852 in Lancaster County, Pa, and died in Illinois. He married **Elisabeth Barber**.

Children of Ross Hostetter and Elisabeth Barber are:
    2017   i.   Abram[12] Hostetter.
    2018   ii.   Beth Hostetter.
    2019   iii.   Ross Hostetter.

1315. Amy Susette[11] Hostetter (David[10], Jacob[9], Jacob[8], Catharine[7] Long, Anna[6] Hershey, Adelheid Galle[5] Stouffer, Daniel[4], Christian[3], Hans[2], Hans[1]) was born 1858, and died in Pennsylvania. She married **Herbert Dupuy**. He died in Pennsylvania.

Children of Amy Hostetter and Herbert Dupuy are:
    2020   i.   Harry Wilford[12] Dupuy.
    2021   ii.   Eleanor Dupuy.
    2022   iii.   Amy Dupuy.
    2023   iv.   Rosetta Dupuy.
    2024   v.   Charles Dupuy.

1316. David H.[11] Hostetter (David[10], Jacob[9], Jacob[8], Catharine[7] Long, Anna[6] Hershey, Adelheid Galle[5] Stouffer, Daniel[4], Christian[3], Hans[2], Hans[1]) was born 1859. He married **Miriam Gerdes**.

Children of David Hostetter and Miriam Gerdes are:
    2025   i.   D. Herbert[12] Hostetter.
    2026   ii.   Frederick Hostetter.
    2027   iii.   Miriam Virginia Hostetter.
    2028   iv.   Helen Hostetter.

1318. Emma Elisabeth[11] Hostetter (Thomas[10], Abraham[9], Herman[8], Catharine[7] Long, Anna[6] Hershey, Adelheid Galle[5] Stouffer, Daniel[4], Christian[3], Hans[2], Hans[1]) was born 1860, and died 1906. She married **William Gallagher**. He was born 1854, and died 1904.

Children of Emma Hostetter and William Gallagher are:
    2029   i.   Arthur E[12] Gallagher, born 1885.
    2030   ii.   Sherald George Gallagher, born 1891.
    2031   iii.   Louise E Gallagher, born 1893.

1320. Minnie P[11] Herr (John[10], Anna[9] Hostetter, John[8], Catharine[7] Long, Anna[6] Hershey, Adelheid Galle[5] Stouffer, Daniel[4], Christian[3], Hans[2], Hans[1]) was born 1878, and died Aft. 1930. She married **Peter G Brubaker**. He was born October 24, 1874, and died Aft. 1930 in Elizabethtown, Lancaster Co., PA.

Children of Minnie Herr and Peter Brubaker are:
    2032   i.   Rheta H[12] Brubaker, born Abt. 1900. She married Walter F Brubaker Aft. 1930; born September 09, 1902; died December 1977.
    2033   ii.   Katie Brubaker, born September 08, 1899. She married Unknown (spouse of Katie Brubaker) Brandt.
+   2034   iii.   Paul M Brubaker, born October 21, 1914; died May 16, 1991.

1374. Sarah Lucinda[11] Hershey (Peter[10], Jacob[9], John[8], Jacob Snavely[7], Andrew Stauffer[6], Adelheid Galle[5] Stouffer, Daniel[4], Christian[3], Hans[2], Hans[1]) was born September 09, 1863, and died December 22, 1942. She married **Henry John Eby**. He was born April 07, 1858, and died September 30, 1922 in New Holland PA.

Children of Sarah Hershey and Henry Eby are:
+   2035   i.   Ella Barbara[12] Eby, born December 27, 1884; died May 06, 1959.
+   2036   ii.   Elizabeth Hershey Eby, born September 15, 1886; died February 16, 1944.
+   2037   iii.   Peter Hershey Eby, born August 09, 1889; died February 11, 1919.
+   2038   iv.   Enos Jacob Eby, born June 20, 1891; died April 27, 1974.
+   2039   v.   Sarah Lucinda Eby, born February 25, 1893; died January 04, 1946.

| | 2040 | vi. | John Silas Eby, born October 21, 1894; died December 04, 1912. |

- 2040 vi.   John Silas Eby, born October 21, 1894; died December 04, 1912.
+ 2041 vii. Henry Musser Eby, born July 14, 1896; died June 15, 1974.
+ 2042 viii. Anna Martha Eby, born April 29, 1898; died November 27, 1980.
- 2043 ix.   Isaac Isaiah Eby, born August 23, 1899; died August 01, 1906.
- 2044 x.   Mary Edith Eby, born August 26, 1901. She married Ivan M. Sensenig; born March 20, 1898; died August 08, 1983.
+ 2045 xi.   Aaron Buckwalter Eby, born February 02, 1904; died April 06, 1975.
+ 2046 xii. Menno Hershey Eby, born October 27, 1905; died June 22, 1974.
+ 2047 xiii. Martin Christian Eby, born July 10, 1910; died March 02, 1986.

1375. Isaiah B.[11] Hershey (Peter[10], Jacob[9], John[8], Jacob Snavely[7], Andrew Stauffer[6], Adelheid Galle[5] Stouffer, Daniel[4], Christian[3], Hans[2], Hans[1]) was born June 28, 1865, and died October 09, 1919. He married **Katharine Sauder**. She was born July 11, 1863, and died April 04, 1919.

Child of Isaiah Hershey and Katharine Sauder is:
+ 2048 i. Galen Warren[12] Hershey, born October 31, 1886; died April 17, 1988.

1376. Enos Jacob[11] Hershey (Peter[10], Jacob[9], John[8], Jacob Snavely[7], Andrew Stauffer[6], Adelheid Galle[5] Stouffer, Daniel[4], Christian[3], Hans[2], Hans[1]) was born November 02, 1866, and died March 20, 1939. He married **Susan Eby**. She was born September 29, 1865, and died April 08, 1948.

Children of Enos Hershey and Susan Eby are:
  2049 i.   Edith May[12] Hershey, born July 28, 1890; died July 20, 1912.
+ 2050 ii. Henry Clay Hershey, born September 01, 1892; died February 20, 1946.
  2051 iii. Grace Elizabeth Hershey, born January 15, 1895. She married Roy Eby Smith; born November 11, 1899; died January 06, 1971.
+ 2052 iv. Mark Eby Hershey, born April 13, 1897; died December 19, 1983.
+ 2053 v.   David Warren Hershey, born November 25, 1899; died July 23, 1985.
+ 2054 vi. Mary Helen Hershey, born January 06, 1903.
  2055 vii. Ethel Pauline Hershey, born October 21, 1904; died January 24, 1987. She married (1) Harry R. Lichty; born May 24, 1891; died June 17, 1957. She married (2) Milton S. Horst; born December 23, 1899.

1377. Elizabeth[11] Hershey (Peter[10], Jacob[9], John[8], Jacob Snavely[7], Andrew Stauffer[6], Adelheid Galle[5] Stouffer, Daniel[4], Christian[3], Hans[2], Hans[1]) was born September 09, 1868, and died September 06, 1934. She married **Henry H. Hess**. He was born April 03, 1862, and died February 07, 1918.

Children of Elizabeth Hershey and Henry Hess are:
+ 2056 i.   Clyde C.[12] Hess, born April 22, 1888; died March 06, 1957.
+ 2057 ii. Harry Hershey Hess, born April 01, 1890; died August 14, 1949.
  2058 iii. Willis Rutter Hess, born December 17, 1891; died March 19, 1968. He married Wilhelmina G. Wederman; born May 18, 1889; died April 22, 1966.
  2059 iv. Harriet Ann Hess, born September 06, 1898.
  2060 v.   Mildred Elizabeth Hess, born February 26, 1908; died November 14, 1957. She married Norman Lincoln Towle; born November 24, 1895; died May 15, 1963.

1379. Henry Peter[11] Hershey (Peter[10], Jacob[9], John[8], Jacob Snavely[7], Andrew Stauffer[6], Adelheid Galle[5] Stouffer, Daniel[4], Christian[3], Hans[2], Hans[1]) was born March 14, 1872, and died December 10, 1949. He married **Anna Keene**. She was born September 05, 1875, and died December 17, 1951.

Children of Henry Hershey and Anna Keene are:
+ 2061 i. Paul Keene[12] Hershey, born September 06, 1900; died July 13, 1968.
  2062 ii. Erma Elizabeth Hershey, born August 12, 1904. She married Charles Wesley Appler; born June 07, 1905.

1380. Martin Eby[11] Hershey (Peter[10], Jacob[9], John[8], Jacob Snavely[7], Andrew Stauffer[6], Adelheid Galle[5] Stouffer, Daniel[4], Christian[3], Hans[2], Hans[1]) was born December 20, 1873, and died June 13, 1953. He married **Cora Etta Eaby**. She was born February 27, 1874, and died August 08, 1926.

Children of Martin Hershey and Cora Eaby are:
+ 2063 i. Esther Elizabeth[12] Hershey, born May 27, 1905.
+ 2064 ii. Miriam Clara Hershey, born February 06, 1909; died June 27, 1998.

1385. Silas N.[11] Hershey (Peter[10], Jacob[9], John[8], Jacob Snavely[7], Andrew Stauffer[6], Adelheid Galle[5] Stouffer, Daniel[4], Christian[3], Hans[2], Hans[1]) was born March 22, 1881, and died November 20, 1970. He married **Lillie Landis Denlinger**. She was born April 13, 1884.

Children of Silas Hershey and Lillie Denlinger are:
- + 2065 i. Elsie D.[12] Hershey, born December 24, 1905; died July 31, 1987.
- + 2066 ii. Frances Hershey, born August 30, 1907.
- + 2067 iii. Lester D. Hershey, born February 22, 1910.
- + 2068 iv. Barbara Elizabeth Hershey, born March 24, 1912.
- + 2069 v. Willis Daniel Hershey, born June 26, 1916; died July 19, 1994.
- + 2070 vi. Reba L. Hershey, born July 09, 1922.
- + 2071 vii. Doris Mae Hershey, born May 11, 1925.
-   2072 viii. Mary Emily Hershey, born January 26, 1928; died March 25, 1928.

1389. Frances Reiff[11] Sweigart (Annie[10] Reiff, Veronica[9] Hershey, John[8], Jacob Snavely[7], Andrew Stauffer[6], Adelheid Galle[5] Stouffer, Daniel[4], Christian[3], Hans[2], Hans[1]) was born November 03, 1868 in Earl Twp, Lanc Co, PA, and died December 12, 1947. She married **Reuben Weaver Horst** November 18, 1888, son of Jacob Horst and Lydia Weaver. He was born December 05, 1868 in West Earl Twp, Lanc Co, PA, and died June 22, 1941.

Children of Frances Sweigart and Reuben Horst are:
- + 2073 i. Elam Sweigart[12] Horst, born January 16, 1890; died March 23, 1977.
- + 2074 ii. Reuben Sweigart Horst, born August 14, 1891.
- + 2075 iii. Amos Sweigart Horst, born July 19, 1893; died January 01, 1963.
- + 2076 iv. Eli Sweigart Horst, born January 14, 1896; died September 23, 1980 in Tampa, FL.
-   2077 v. Jacob Sweigart Horst, born October 18, 1897; died May 11, 1898.
- + 2078 vi. Titus Sweigart Horst, born May 10, 1899; died June 17, 1976.
- + 2079 vii. Frances Sweigart Horst, born May 23, 1901; died October 09, 1982.
- + 2080 viii. Phares Sweigart Horst, born March 14, 1903.
- + 2081 ix. Noah Sweigart Horst, born June 05, 1905; died August 07, 1964.
-   2082 x. Anna Sweigart Horst, born July 06, 1907; died November 14, 1999 in Landis Homes, Lancaster Co., PA. She married (1) George Wolf July 1947; born May 10, 1889; died January 01, 1952. She married (2) Jacob G. Herr December 16, 1952; born June 08, 1895 in Lancaster Twp, Lanc Co, PA; died October 15, 1991.
- + 2083 xi. Walter Sweigart Horst, born September 04, 1909.
- + 2084 xii. Ada Sweigart Horst, born May 30, 1911 in West Earl Twp, Lanc Co, PA; died July 03, 1979 in Akron, Lancaster Co, PA.
- + 2085 xiii. Katie Sweigart Horst, born May 30, 1911; died August 20, 1994 in Manheim Twp, Lanc Co, PA.
- + 2086 xiv. Lloyd Sweigart Horst, born August 16, 1913.

1399. Abraham H[11] Burkholder (Susan[10] Hershey, Abraham[9], Christian[8], Jacob Snavely[7], Andrew Stauffer[6], Adelheid Galle[5] Stouffer, Daniel[4], Christian[3], Hans[2], Hans[1]) was born August 02, 1885, and died January 06, 1935. He married **Mabel E Ebersole**. She was born June 05, 1887, and died June 16, 1965.

Children of Abraham Burkholder and Mabel Ebersole are:
-   2087 i. Marie[12] Burkholder.
- + 2088 ii. Melvin E Burkholder, born January 1909; died 1971.
-   2089 iii. Marlin Burkholder.
-   2090 iv. A M Burkholder.
-   2091 v. Clark A Burkholder.
-   2092 vi. Dorothy M Burkholder, born September 17, 1919.
-   2093 vii. E J Burkholder.
-   2094 viii. George R Burkholder, born 1926.

1401. Webster Fox Lawrence "[11] Lafayette (Diana[10] Hershey, Henry[9], Martin[8], Henry[7], Andrew Stauffer[6], Adelheid Galle[5] Stouffer, Daniel[4], Christian[3], Hans[2], Hans[1]) was born March 19, 1853 in Hummelstown, Dauphin Co., PA, and died June 02, 1931 in Ardmore, PA. He married **Cecelia Beatrice Bickerton** September 1889 in Liverpool, England. She was born May 25, 1860 in London, England, and died October 12, 1933.

Children of Lawrence Lafayette and Cecelia Bickerton are:
-   2095 i. Cecelia Beatrice[12] Fox, born August 06, 1890; died December 04, 1968. She married Charles Francis Griffith February 27, 1919; born January 14, 1876; died October 18, 1954.

	2096	ii.	Thomas Bickerton Fox, born May 04, 1892; died December 1894.
+	2097	iii.	Jr. Lawrence Webster Fox, born January 05, 1895; died November 1969.

1404. James George[11] **Fox** (Diana[10] Hershey, Henry[9], Martin[8], Henry[7], Andrew Stauffer[6], Adelheid Galle[5] Stouffer, Daniel[4], Christian[3], Hans[2], Hans[1]) was born November 05, 1858 in Hummelstown, Dauphin Co., PA, and died August 07, 1933 in Union Deposit, Dauphin Co., PA. He married **Emma Brightbill Strickler** February 09, 1881 in Swatara Station, PA. She was born May 08, 1861 in Swatara Station, PA, and died October 12, 1917 in Derry Township, Dauphin Co., PA.

Children of James Fox and Emma Strickler are:

	2098	i.	George Francis[12] Fox, born March 20, 1882 in Derry Township, Dauphin Co., PA; died November 22, 1956 in Union Deposit, Dauphin Co., PA.
+	2099	ii.	Robert Thomas Fox, born August 30, 1883 in Derry Township, Dauphin Co., PA; died October 28, 1966 in Hummelstown, Dauphin Co., PA.
	2100	iii.	James Walter Fox, born October 11, 1884; died August 23, 1948 in Darby, PA. He married Mabel McCreary 1909; born 1887; died 1963.
+	2101	iv.	Charles Adam Fox, born March 27, 1886 in Derry Township, Dauphin Co., PA; died January 28, 1954 in Seattle, WA.
+	2102	v.	John Edward Fox, born May 14, 1887 in Hummelstown, PA; died October 09, 1967 in Hummelstown, PA.
	2103	vi.	William Webster Fox, born March 24, 1889 in Derry Township, Dauphin Co., PA; died August 06, 1903 in Chester Co., PA.
+	2104	vii.	Mary Virginia Fox, born June 29, 1891 in Hummelstown, PA; died August 09, 1964 in Vancouver, BC.
	2105	viii.	Ethel Elizabeth Fox, born October 19, 1893 in Caln Township, Chester Co., PA; died January 29, 1895 in Caln Township, Chester Co., PA.
+	2106	ix.	Thomas G. Fox, born February 08, 1896 in Downingtown, Chester Co., PA; died July 15, 1945 in Philadelphia, PA.
+	2107	x.	Sara Diana Fox, born January 05, 1899 in Caln Township, Chester Co., PA; died January 29, 1989 in Seattle, WA.
+	2108	xi.	Jr. James George Fox, born April 20, 1905 in Caln Township, Chester Co., PA; died January 23, 1975 in Newark, Essex Co., NJ.

1405. Fox John Edgar "[11] **Eshenauer** (Diana[10] Hershey, Henry[9], Martin[8], Henry[7], Andrew Stauffer[6], Adelheid Galle[5] Stouffer, Daniel[4], Christian[3], Hans[2], Hans[1]) was born November 27, 1860 in Hummelstown, Dauphin Co., PA, and died August 07, 1942 in Harrisburg, PA. He married **Rachel Beverlina Kunkel** September 04, 1907. She was born October 17, 1882, and died January 24, 1968.

Children of John Eshenauer and Rachel Kunkel are:

	2109	i.	Charles Kunkel[12] Fox.
	2110	ii.	Jr. Private Fox. He married Private Wallower.
+	2111	iii.	Rachel Virginia Fox.
+	2112	iv.	Private Fox.
	2113	v.	Private Fox. He married Private Brignom.
	2114	vi.	Mary Elizabeth Fox, born September 29, 1911; died January 16, 1969.

1406. Adelaide[11] **Fox** (Diana[10] Hershey, Henry[9], Martin[8], Henry[7], Andrew Stauffer[6], Adelheid Galle[5] Stouffer, Daniel[4], Christian[3], Hans[2], Hans[1]) was born September 05, 1862 in Hummelstown, Dauphin Co., PA, and died March 04, 1948 in Philadelphia, PA. She married **John Howard Gay** February 16, 1888 in Hummelstown, Dauphin Co., PA. He was born March 19, 1866 in Philadelphia, PA, and died November 13, 1929.

Children of Adelaide Fox and John Gay are:

	2115	i.	Jr. John Howard[12] Gay, born January 19, 1889; died March 05, 1947.
+	2116	ii.	Gertrude Gay, born December 14, 1891; died June 17, 1970.
	2117	iii.	Adelaide Gay, born April 01, 1893. She married (1) Louis Will; born Abt. 1886. She married (2) Douglas Drummond; born Abt. 1886.

1408. Caroline Lee[11] **Fox** (Diana[10] Hershey, Henry[9], Martin[8], Henry[7], Andrew Stauffer[6], Adelheid Galle[5] Stouffer, Daniel[4], Christian[3], Hans[2], Hans[1]) was born November 17, 1869 in Hummelstown, Dauphin Co., PA, and died October 11, 1948. She married **John Paul Nissley** February 22, 1894 in Hummelstown, Dauphin Co., PA. He was born 1869 in Hummelstown, Dauphin Co., PA, and died August 15, 1914.

Child of Caroline Fox and John Nissley is:

+	2118	i.	Katherine[12] Nissley, born July 07, 1895; died November 08, 1977.

The Relations of Milton Snavely Hershey, 4th Ed.

1409. George Hershey[11] Fox (Diana[10] Hershey, Henry[9], Martin[8], Henry[7], Andrew Stauffer[6], Adelheid Galle[5] Stouffer, Daniel[4], Christian[3], Hans[2], Hans[1]) was born May 09, 1872 in Hummelstown, Dauphin Co., PA, and died April 14, 1910 in Mt. Alto TB San., PA. He married **Emilie Karthaus**. She was born Abt. 1882.

Children of George Fox and Emilie Karthaus are:
+ 2119   i.   Emilie Karthaus[12] Fox.
+ 2120   ii.   Karolyn Diana Fox.

1410. Nancy[11] Nickey (Samuel[10], Christiana[9] Hastetter, Anna Barbara[8] Stauffer, Johannes[7], Daniel[6] Stouffer, Christian[5] Stauffer, Daniel[4] Stouffer, Christian[3], Hans[2], Hans[1]) was born February 02, 1819 in Perry County, Pa., and died March 28, 1891 in Huntsdale, Pa. buried Pa. German Baptist Church, Huntsdale, Pa.. She married **Peter Tritt** June 10, 1845. He was born June 24, 1821 in Huntsdale, Pa., and died March 16, 1887 in Huntsdale, Pa. buried Pa. German Baptist Church, Huntsdale,Pa..

Children of Nancy Nickey and Peter Tritt are:
   2121   i.   Christian[12] Tritt, born July 08, 1846; died July 12, 1846 in buried Centerville, Pa..
+ 2122   ii.   John A. Tritt, born September 23, 1847; died September 18, 1929 in Buried Centerville, Pa..
+ 2123   iii.   Samuel John Tritt, born 1849; died 1917.
+ 2124   iv.   Lydia Jane Tritt, born August 10, 1851 in Huntsdale, Pa; died April 25, 1900 in Greason, Pa. buried Presbyterian Churchyard Dickesen, Pa..
+ 2125   v.   Elizabeth Tritt, born October 23, 1854; died WFT Est. 1872-1948.
   2126   vi.   Maggie T. Tritt, born 1857; died November 09, 1864 in buried Centerville, Pa..
+ 2127   vii.   Peter Stough Tritt, born March 08, 1860; died June 03, 1896 in (of Pnuemonia) buried Huntsdale, Pa..

1411. Edward[11] Nickey (Samuel[10], Christiana[9] Hastetter, Anna Barbara[8] Stauffer, Johannes[7], Daniel[6] Stouffer, Christian[5] Stauffer, Daniel[4] Stouffer, Christian[3], Hans[2], Hans[1]) was born 1829, and died 1860. He married **Elizabeth Mumall** WFT Est. 1845-1858. She was born 1829, and died WFT Est. 1848-1923.

Child of Edward Nickey and Elizabeth Mumall is:
   2128   i.   Mary Jane[12] Nickey, born WFT Est. 1848-1861; died WFT Est. 1863-1950. She married William Finkey WFT Est. 1863-1902; born WFT Est. 1837-1861; died WFT Est. 1863-1945.

1423. Charlotte[11] Farner (Elizabeth[10] Owens, Peter[9] Ober, Elizabeth[8] Stauffer, Johannes[7], Daniel[6] Stouffer, Christian[5] Stauffer, Daniel[4] Stouffer, Christian[3], Hans[2], Hans[1]) was born June 15, 1827 in Franklin Co, Pa., and died November 15, 1892 in Buried in Presbyterian Churchyard, Dickensen, Pa.. She married **Lewis Goodhart** April 09, 1846. He was born April 15, 1822 in Cumberland Co, Pa., and died June 18, 1891 in Buried in Presbyterian Churchyard,Dickensen, Pa..

Children of Charlotte Farner and Lewis Goodhart are:
   2129   i.   Infant[12] Goodhart, born WFT Est. 1844-1870; died WFT Est. 1849-1953.
   2130   ii.   Frances Emma Goodhart, born April 11, 1848; died July 08, 1860 in Buried Presbyterian Churchyard, Dickensen, Pa..
   2131   iii.   Marion Anson Goodhart, born October 22, 1849 in Penn Twp, Pa.; died 1927.
+ 2132   iv.   Mary Elizabeth Goodhart, born June 06, 1851; died November 13, 1892 in buried Prospect Hill Cem, Newville, pa..
+ 2133   v.   Agnes Bordilla Goodhart, born October 20, 1853; died 1940.
+ 2134   vi.   Calvin Goodhart, born March 11, 1856; died February 19, 1941 in buried Spring Hill Cem, Shippensburg, Pa..
+ 2135   vii.   Theodore Goodhart, born April 24, 1858 in Penn Twp, Cumberland Co; died December 26, 1945 in buried Dickeson, Pa..
   2136   viii.   George Grove Goodhart, born July 21, 1865; died June 26, 1872 in buried Pres. Churchyard, Dickensen, Pa..
+ 2137   ix.   David Grier McClelland Goodhart, born July 21, 1865; died November 09, 1931 in buried Lutheran Cem, Centerville, Pa..
   2138   x.   Clarence Eugene Goodhart, born December 15, 1869; died July 18, 1936 in buried Upper Cem,Newville, Pa.. He married Agnes Druscilla Goodhart June 27, 1899; born November 13, 1865; died March 03, 1938 in buried Upper Cem, Newville, Pa..

1424. Susannah[11] Farner (Elizabeth[10] Owens, Peter[9] Ober, Elizabeth[8] Stauffer, Johannes[7], Daniel[6] Stouffer, Christian[5] Stauffer, Daniel[4] Stouffer, Christian[3], Hans[2], Hans[1]) was born October 02, 1829, and died 1910 in buried Upper Cem, Newville, Pa.. She married **William Goodhart** WFT Est. 1841-1871. He was born February 23, 1820, and died June 23, 1897 in buried Upper Cem, Newville, Pa..

Children of Susannah Farner and William Goodhart are:

	2139	i.	Oberdick[12] Goodhart, born WFT Est. 1843-1869; died WFT Est. 1878-1951 in buried New Kingston. He married Clara Belle Palm WFT Est. 1875-1908; born 1862; died 1933 in buried New Kingston.
+	2140	ii.	Nora Griffin Goodhart, born WFT Est. 1843-1870; died WFT Est. 1865-1953.
+	2141	iii.	Elizabeth Trough Goodhart, born WFT Est. 1843-1870; died WFT Est. 1865-1953.
+	2142	iv.	Newton Goodhart, born 1855; died 1918.
	2143	v.	Agnes Druscilla Goodhart, born November 13, 1865; died March 03, 1938 in buried Upper Cem, Newville, Pa.. She married Clarence Eugene Goodhart June 27, 1899; born December 15, 1869; died July 18, 1936 in buried Upper Cem,Newville, Pa..

1431. David[11] Ober (Isaac Huntsberger[10], Christian[9], Elizabeth[8] Stauffer, Johannes[7], Daniel[6] Stouffer, Christian[5] Stauffer, Daniel[4] Stouffer, Christian[3], Hans[2], Hans[1]) was born March 01, 1827 in Lancaster, West Donegal Twp, PA, and died January 04, 1887 in Train wreck near Republic, Ohio. He married **Anna Barabara Brenner**. She was born June 28, 1834 in Churchville, Northampton Twp., Bucks Co.,Pennsylvania, and died April 04, 1876 in Oberlin, PA.

Children of David Ober and Anna Brenner are:

+	2144	i.	Emma Barbara[12] Ober, born 1856; died 1931.
+	2145	ii.	Catherine Rebecca Ober, born April 29, 1857; died February 09, 1943 in Highspire, PA.
+	2146	iii.	Benjamin Franklin Ober, born February 17, 1859; died March 30, 1938.
+	2147	iv.	Agnes Eda Ober, born 1861; died in Noblesville, IN.
+	2148	v.	Annie Elizabeth Ober, born July 10, 1862; died October 22, 1948 in Penbrook.
	2149	vi.	Solomon Henry Ober, born 1863; died 1864.
	2150	vii.	John Motter Ober, born June 30, 1868 in Oberlin, PA; died October 11, 1952 in Oberlin, PA. He married Elizabeth Myers; born December 31, 1868; died December 26, 1934 in Oberlin, PA.
	2151	viii.	Julia Irene Ober, born 1870; died 1873.
+	2152	ix.	David W Ober, born 1871; died 1938.
+	2153	x.	Isaac Newton Ober, born July 29, 1872; died May 1970 in Indianapolis, IN.
+	2154	xi.	Bernard Farren Ober, born 1873.
	2155	xii.	Mary Alice Ober, born 1873; died 1880 in Oberlin, PA.
+	2156	xiii.	Florence May Ober, born 1875; died in Penbrook.
+	2157	xiv.	Barbara Estella Ober, born 1876; died in Michigan.

1436. Michael Cramer[11] Ober (Michael[10], Henry[9], Elizabeth[8] Stauffer, Johannes[7], Daniel[6] Stouffer, Christian[5] Stauffer, Daniel[4] Stouffer, Christian[3], Hans[2], Hans[1]) was born 1827, and died 1872 in Donegal Twp., Lancaster Cty., PA. He married **Harriet Weber**. She was born 1830, and died 1908 in W. Donegal Twp., Lancaster Cty., PA.

Child of Michael Ober and Harriet Weber is:

+	2158	i.	Annie[12] Ober, born 1856 in Lancaster Cty., PA; died 1929 in Lancaster Cty., PA.

1439. Moses Ruhl[11] Ober (Christian Longnecker[10], David S[9], Elizabeth[8] Stauffer, Johannes[7], Daniel[6] Stouffer, Christian[5] Stauffer, Daniel[4] Stouffer, Christian[3], Hans[2], Hans[1]) was born January 21, 1838, and died December 07, 1907. He married **Barbara Heagy**. She was born July 26, 1838, and died September 03, 1911.

Children of Moses Ober and Barbara Heagy are:

	2159	i.	Edward[12] Ober.
	2160	ii.	Jacob Ober.
+	2161	iii.	Moses Heagly Ober, born January 31, 1860 in Rapho Twsp, PA; died February 25, 1916.
	2162	iv.	Annie Ober, born 1862 in Rapho Twsp, PA.
	2163	v.	Maryann Ober, born 1864.
	2164	vi.	Emma Ober, born 1867 in Rapho Twsp, PA.

1442. Henry E.[11] Ober (Christian Longnecker[10], David S[9], Elizabeth[8] Stauffer, Johannes[7], Daniel[6] Stouffer, Christian[5] Stauffer, Daniel[4] Stouffer, Christian[3], Hans[2], Hans[1]) was born September 13, 1844 in Rapho Twsp, PA, and died January 16, 1906. He married **Mary Anne Metzler**. She was born November 20, 1844.

Child of Henry Ober and Mary Metzler is:

	2165	i.	Agnes[12] Ober, born April 26, 1869; died May 12, 1946.

1453. Sarah Rebecca[11] Bowers (Susannah[10] Ober, Henry[9], Veronica " Frany "[8] Stauffer, Johannes[7], Daniel[6] Stouffer, Christian[5] Stauffer, Daniel[4] Stouffer, Christian[3], Hans[2], Hans[1]) was born April 18, 1825 in Huntington County, Pennsylvania, and died November 01, 1896 in Elkhorn , Ray County, Missouri. She married **Stephen R. Richardson** January 25, 1846 in Lancaster County, Pennsylvania. He was born March 20, 1820 in Lancaster County, Pennsylvania, and died December 15, 1894 in Perry, Noble County, Oklahoma.

Children of Sarah Bowers and Stephen Richardson are:
+ 2166 i. Mary Jane[12] Richardson, born October 22, 1846 in Lancaster County, Pennsylvania; died February 23, 1912 in Upland, California.
+ 2167 ii. Susan Ann Richardson, born May 11, 1849 in Lancaster County, Pennsylvania; died January 02, 1877 in Pine Creek, Illinois.
  2168 iii. Nancy Ann Richardson, born September 22, 1850 in Lancaster County, Pennsylvania; died January 04, 1872.
+ 2169 iv. Rebecca Jane Richardson, born April 10, 1853 in Stark County, Ohio; died October 18, 1934 in Polo, Illinois.
+ 2170 v. Sarah B. Richardson, born July 09, 1855 in Stark County, Ohio; died March 02, 1894 in Sedgwick, Kansas.
+ 2171 vi. Andrew Jackson Richardson, born June 05, 1859 in Canton, Stark County, Ohio; died December 11, 1931 in Belle Plaine, Kansas.
+ 2172 vii. Stephen E. Richardson, born March 10, 1862 in Stark County, Ohio; died April 04, 1929 in Topeka, KS..
+ 2173 viii. Harriet May Richardson, born September 14, 1864 in Canton, Stark County, Ohio; died November 17, 1944 in Dayton, Montgomery County, Ohio.
  2174 ix. Infant Daughter, born December 27, 1867 in Ogle County, Illinois; died December 27, 1867 in Ogle County, Illinois.
+ 2175 x. Martha Richardson, born August 26, 1870 in Ogle County, Illinois; died February 22, 1921 in Sedgwick, Kansas.
  2176 xi. Anna Richardson, born August 26, 1870 in Ogle County, Illinois; died January 04, 1871.

1523. David[11] Lesher (Barbara[10] Ober, Michael[9], Veronica " Frany "[8] Stauffer, Johannes[7], Daniel[6] Stouffer, Christian[5] Stauffer, Daniel[4] Stouffer, Christian[3], Hans[2], Hans[1]) was born May 02, 1817 in Pennsylvania, and died October 20, 1889 in Iowa. He married **Elizabeth Strickler**. She was born October 20, 1824, and died February 1914.

Children of David Lesher and Elizabeth Strickler are:
  2177 i. Jeremiah[12] Lesher, born August 16, 1845.
  2178 ii. Benjamin Franklin Lesher, born August 09, 1847; died June 1933.
  2179 iii. Christian Hertzler Lesher, born February 01, 1849.
  2180 iv. Susan Alice Lesher, born March 10, 1854.
  2181 v. Ida Elizabeth Lesher, born May 11, 1860; died December 1930.
+ 2182 vi. Mary Ann Lesher, born June 13, 1866; died May 29, 1946.
+ 2183 vii. Naomi Jane Lesher, born August 27, 1867; died February 11, 1946.

1538. Catherine A.[11] Ober (Jacob[10], Michael[9], Veronica " Frany "[8] Stauffer, Johannes[7], Daniel[6] Stouffer, Christian[5] Stauffer, Daniel[4] Stouffer, Christian[3], Hans[2], Hans[1]) was born February 11, 1831 in Hopewell Township, Cumberland County, Pennsylvania, and died June 26, 1892 in Bloom Township, Wood County, Ohio. She married **John Reuben Diehl** November 28, 1850 in Cumberland County, Pennsylvania. He was born August 1827 in Middle Spring, Shippensburg Township, Cumberland County, Pennsylvania, and died January 28, 1906 in Morrison, Illinois.

Marriage Notes for Catherine Ober and John Diehl:
[Henry Ober 1742.ged]

_STATMARRIED

Children of Catherine Ober and John Diehl are:
+ 2184 i. David Alfred[12] Diehl, born May 1852 in Pennsylvania; died 1920 in Kasson Township.
  2185 ii. Charles A. Diehl, born December 1854 in Pennsylvania; died Aft. 1910.
+ 2186 iii. Ida M. Diehl, born June 17, 1858 in Chambersburg, Franklin County, Pennsylvania; died June 11, 1935 in Bloom Township, Wood County, Ohio.
  2187 iv. Elmer E. Diehl, born April 1861 in Pennsylvania; died September 28, 1901 in Bloomdale, Bloom Township, Wood County, Ohio.
  2188 v. Lillian Diehl, born Abt. 1864. She married Unknown Schraeder.

   Marriage Notes for Lillian Diehl and Unknown Schraeder:
   [Henry Ober 1742.ged]

   _STATMARRIED

+ 2189 vi. John Reuben, Diehl, born 1866 in Pennsylvania; died Aft. 1935 in Ohio.

2190 vii. Anna C. Diehl, born Abt. 1868.
2191 viii. Thomas E. Diehl, born Abt. 1871.
2192 ix. Harry Lee Diehl, born Abt. 1874 in Pennsylvania; died January 29, 1903 in New Martinsville, West Virginia. He married Ora Price.

Marriage Notes for Harry Diehl and Ora Price:
[Henry Ober 1742.ged]

_STATMARRIED

+ 2193 x. Kathryn Diehl, born Abt. 1875 in Pennsylvania; died Aft. 1935.

1729. Isaac[11] Brubaker (Christian[10], Elizabeth[9] Stauffer, Christian[8], Henry Jacob[7], Hans[6], Christian[5], Daniel[4] Stouffer, Christian[3], Hans[2], Hans[1]) was born 1815 in Lebannon County, Pennsylvania, and died 1866 in Lebannon County, Pennsylvania. He married **Elizabeth Bucher**. She was born Abt. 1815 in Lancaster County, Pennsylvania, and died in Lebannon County, Pennsylvania.

Child of Isaac Brubaker and Elizabeth Bucher is:
+ 2194 i. Isaac[12] Brubaker, born 1857 in Lebannon County, Pennsylvania; died 1939 in Unknown.

1730. Susanna[11] Brubaker (Christian[10], Elizabeth[9] Stauffer, Christian[8], Henry Jacob[7], Hans[6], Christian[5], Daniel[4] Stouffer, Christian[3], Hans[2], Hans[1]) was born March 22, 1822 in Lebanon Township, Lebanon County, Pennsylvania, and died August 10, 1867 in Campbelltown, Lebanon County, Pennsylvania. She married **Henry Widemoyer Kreider**. He was born June 22, 1815 in Lebanon Township, Lebanon County, Pennsylvania, and died October 11, 1910 in Campbelltown, Lebanon County, Pennsylvania.

Child of Susanna Brubaker and Henry Kreider is:
+ 2195 i. Mary Brubaker[12] Kreider, born October 30, 1840 in Campbelltown, Lebanon County, Pennsylvania; died July 02, 1912 in Campbelltown, Lebanon County, Pennsylvania.

1731. Christian[11] Brubaker (Christian[10], Elizabeth[9] Stauffer, Christian[8], Henry Jacob[7], Hans[6], Christian[5], Daniel[4] Stouffer, Christian[3], Hans[2], Hans[1]) was born 1819, and died Aft. 1880. He married **Barbara Becker Longenecker**. She was born September 09, 1822 in Warwick Twp., Lancaster Co, PA, and died May 22, 1900.

Children of Christian Brubaker and Barbara Longenecker are:
+ 2196 i. Ezra[12] Brubaker, born 1845; died Bef. 1880.
  2197 ii. Nathan Brubaker, born 1852. He married Sarah Unknown; born 1855.
  2198 iii. Fannie Brubaker, born 1852.

1732. Magdalena[11] Brubaker (Peter[10], Elizabeth[9] Stauffer, Christian[8], Henry Jacob[7], Hans[6], Christian[5], Daniel[4] Stouffer, Christian[3], Hans[2], Hans[1]) was born August 22, 1824 in Heidelberg Township, Lebanon County, Pennsylvania, and died April 15, 1900 in South Lebanon Township, Lancaster County, Pennsylvania. She married **Moses Breitenstein** September 05, 1843. He was born December 04, 1822 in South Lebanon Township, Lancaster County, Pennsylvania, and died December 19, 1901 in South Lebanon Township, Lancaster County, Pennsylvania.

Child of Magdalena Brubaker and Moses Breitenstein is:
+ 2199 i. Mary[12] Breitenstein, born August 22, 1851 in South Lebanon Township, Lancaster County, Pennsylvania; died March 17, 1921 in Myerstown, Lebanon County, Pennsylvania.

1741. John[11] Stoffer (Jacob S[10], Jacob[9], Jacob[8] Stauffer, Henry Jacob[7], Hans[6], Christian[5], Daniel[4] Stouffer, Christian[3], Hans[2], Hans[1]) was born December 15, 1828 in Columbiana Cty, Ohio, and died November 12, 1920 in Nappanee, Elkhart Ind. He married **Abigale Winder** October 29, 1854 in Elkhart Ind. She was born October 15, 1833 in Ohio, Portage Cty, and died June 16, 1893.

Children of John Stoffer and Abigale Winder are:
  2200 i. Florence Eudora[12] Stoffer, born June 06, 1855 in Elkhart Ind; died March 22, 1922.
  2201 ii. Horace Raymond Stoffer, born March 08, 1858 in Elkhart Ind.
  2202 iii. Wallace Winder Stoffer, born September 03, 1861 in Elkhart Ind; died August 23, 1938 in Akron Ind.
  2203 iv. Cora Alice Stoffer, born April 04, 1868 in Elkhart Ind.
  2204 v. Nellie Ione Stoffer, born December 22, 1871.

1744. Nancy[11] Stoffer (Louis J[10], Jacob[9], Jacob[8] Stauffer, Henry Jacob[7], Hans[6], Christian[5], Daniel[4] Stouffer, Christian[3], Hans[2], Hans[1]) was born 1830 in Columbiana Co ohio. She married **William Ickes** January 01, 1849 in Columbiana Co Ohio. He was born

The Relations of Milton Snavely Hershey, 4th Ed.

November 15, 1827 in New Oxford, Adams Cty PA, and died December 08, 1902 in Columbiana Coo ohio.

Children of Nancy Stoffer and William Ickes are:
- 2205   i.   William II[12] Ickes, born June 1852 in Ohio; died July 1853 in Ohio.
- + 2206   ii.   Carolyn Ickes, born December 24, 1867; died February 02, 1956 in Stark Cty, Ohio.

1746. Mary Ann[11] Stoffer (Louis J[10], Jacob[9], Jacob[8] Stauffer, Henry Jacob[7], Hans[6], Christian[5], Daniel[4] Stouffer, Christian[3], Hans[2], Hans[1]) was born April 23, 1836 in Columbiana Cty Ohio, and died September 19, 1906 in Columbiana Cty Ohio. She married **Hiram Ruff** November 05, 1855 in Columbiana Cty, Ohio. He was born April 29, 1837 in Columbiana Cty Ohio, and died October 13, 1909 in Columbiana Cty Ohio.

Child of Mary Stoffer and Hiram Ruff is:
- + 2207   i.   Nancy[12] Ruff, born August 28, 1854 in Columbiana County, Ohio; died March 06, 1930 in Columbiana County, Ohio.

1748. Jesse A[11] Stoffer (Louis J[10], Jacob[9], Jacob[8] Stauffer, Henry Jacob[7], Hans[6], Christian[5], Daniel[4] Stouffer, Christian[3], Hans[2], Hans[1]) was born 1841 in Columbiana Co, Ohio, and died August 17, 1900 in Stark Co Ohio. He married **Elizabeth Dice** April 30, 1863 in Ohio, Stark Co.

Children of Jesse Stoffer and Elizabeth Dice are:
- 2208   i.   Jerome[12] Stoffer, born 1864.
- 2209   ii.   Herman Stoffer, born 1866; died October 13, 1892.
- 2210   iii.   Homer Stoffer, born 1866.
- 2211   iv.   Owen Stoffer, born March 31, 1873 in Columbiana Co Ohio.
- 2212   v.   Warren Stoffer, born April 16, 1874 in Columbian Co Ohio.
- 2213   vi.   Allie Stoffer, born 1876.
- 2214   vii.   Royal Stoffer, born February 07, 1880 in Columbiana Co Ohio.

1749. Barbara Ellen[11] Stoffer (Louis J[10], Jacob[9], Jacob[8] Stauffer, Henry Jacob[7], Hans[6], Christian[5], Daniel[4] Stouffer, Christian[3], Hans[2], Hans[1]) was born 1844 in Columbiana Co, Ohio. She married **Sylvester Hardy** February 22, 1864 in Columbiana Co Ohio.

Children of Barbara Stoffer and Sylvester Hardy are:
- 2215   i.   Henry Franklin[12] Hardy.
- 2216   ii.   Alice Loretta Hardy.
- 2217   iii.   William S Hardy.
- 2218   iv.   Ida May Hardy, born Bef. 1880.

1750. Lewis Jr[11] Stoffer (Louis J[10], Jacob[9], Jacob[8] Stauffer, Henry Jacob[7], Hans[6], Christian[5], Daniel[4] Stouffer, Christian[3], Hans[2], Hans[1]) was born December 24, 1848 in Columbiana Co Ohio, and died March 12, 1916 in Columbiana Co Ohio. He married **Amanda E Dice** February 16, 1868 in Columbiana Co Ohio. She was born May 07, 1849 in Columbiana Co Ohio, and died July 18, 1924 in Columbiana Co Ohio.

Marriage Notes for Lewis Stoffer and Amanda Dice:
[chrststauffer1663.ged]

[DATA FILE.FBK.FTW]

Children of Lewis Stoffer and Amanda Dice are:
- + 2219   i.   Howard H.[12] Stoffer, born January 15, 1869 in Columbiana Cty, Ohio; died September 05, 1934 in Stark Cty Ohio.
- + 2220   ii.   Ida J. Stoffer, born June 12, 1870 in Columbiana Co Ohio; died March 15, 1973 in West View Manor, Wooster, Ohio.
- + 2221   iii.   Walter George Stoffer, born May 13, 1872 in Columbiana Cty, Ohio; died May 14, 1950 in Columbiana Cty, Ohio.
- 2222   iv.   Cora Stoffer, born February 14, 1874 in Columbiana Cty Ohio. She married John Campbell.
- + 2223   v.   Mary Catherine Stoffer, born May 03, 1878 in Columbiana Co Ohio; died April 07, 1970 in Minerva, Stark Co Ohio.
- + 2224   vi.   Albert Lewis Stoffer, born May 03, 1881 in Columbiana Co Ohio; died April 19, 1982 in Copeland Oaks Nursing Home, Sebring, Ohio.
- 2225   vii.   Emmet Stoffer, born December 17, 1886 in Columbiana Cty Ohio; died January 12, 1887 in Columbiana Cty Ohio.

1751. Peter[11] **Stoffer** (Samuel[10], Jacob[9], Jacob[8] Stauffer, Henry Jacob[7], Hans[6], Christian[5], Daniel[4] Stouffer, Christian[3], Hans[2], Hans[1]) was born 1828 in Columbiana Co Ohio, and died October 15, 1886 in Columbiana Co Ohio. He married **Barbara Sanor** February 10, 1848 in Columbiana Co Ohio. She was born June 28, 1828 in Ohio.

Children of Peter Stoffer and Barbara Sanor are:
- 2226   i.   Daniel[12] Stoffer, born 1849 in Columbiana Co, Ohio.
- 2227   ii.   Samantha Stoffer, born 1852 in Columbiana Co, Ohio.
- 2228   iii.   William Stoffer, born 1855 in Columbiana Co, Ohio.
- 2229   iv.   Solomon Stoffer, born 1857 in Ohio; died July 21, 1857 in Ohio.
- + 2230   v.   Peter Stoffer, born August 1862 in Ohio.

1752. Christina[11] **Stoffer** (Samuel[10], Jacob[9], Jacob[8] Stauffer, Henry Jacob[7], Hans[6], Christian[5], Daniel[4] Stouffer, Christian[3], Hans[2], Hans[1]) was born October 27, 1828 in Canton Ohio, Stark Cty, and died December 13, 1901 in Canal Fulton, Stark Cty ohio. She married **William Baer** December 25, 1852 in Columbiana County, Ohio.

Children of Christina Stoffer and William Baer are:
- 2231   i.   Samuel[12] Baer.
- 2232   ii.   Charles Baer.
- 2233   iii.   Jesse Baer.
- 2234   iv.   Alice Baer.
- 2235   v.   John Baer.

1753. Jacob L[11] **Stoffer** (Samuel[10], Jacob[9], Jacob[8] Stauffer, Henry Jacob[7], Hans[6], Christian[5], Daniel[4] Stouffer, Christian[3], Hans[2], Hans[1]) was born March 08, 1830 in Columbiana Co Ohio, and died February 12, 1919 in Columbiana Co Ohio. He married **Susanna Ickis** October 20, 1853 in Columbiana Co Ohio. She was born May 1836 in Columbiana Co Ohio, and died 1913 in Columbiana Co Ohio.

Children of Jacob Stoffer and Susanna Ickis are:
- + 2236   i.   David[12] Stoffer, born September 1861; died 1919 in Ohio.
- 2237   ii.   Sarah Stoffer, born October 1862.
- 2238   iii.   Marion Stoffer, born 1865.
- 2239   iv.   Harvey Stoffer, born 1868.
- + 2240   v.   John Stoffer, born June 1870 in Columbiana Co Ohio; died November 04, 1918 in Columbiana Co Ohio.
- 2241   vi.   Elmer Stoffer, born June 19, 1870 in Columbiana Cty, Ohio.
- 2242   vii.   Lydia Stoffer, born October 31, 1872 in Columbiana Cty Ohio; died December 06, 1959 in Columbiana Cty, Ohio.
- 2243   viii.   Corda Stoffer, born May 1881 in Ohio.

1754. Eli[11] **Stoffer** (Samuel[10], Jacob[9], Jacob[8] Stauffer, Henry Jacob[7], Hans[6], Christian[5], Daniel[4] Stouffer, Christian[3], Hans[2], Hans[1]) was born 1836 in Columbiana Co, Ohio. He married **Elisabeth Weaver** January 27, 1856 in Columbiana Co Ohio. She was born August 06, 1836 in Columbiana Co, Ohio, and died January 14, 1914.

Children of Eli Stoffer and Elisabeth Weaver are:
- 2244   i.   Ella[12] Stoffer.
- 2245   ii.   Oliver Stoffer, born 1857 in Columbiana Co, Ohio.
- 2246   iii.   Delilah Stoffer, born 1858 in Columbiana Co, Ohio.
- 2247   iv.   Amanda J Stoffer, born 1860 in Columbiana Co, Ohio.

1755. Nancy[11] **Stoffer** (Samuel[10], Jacob[9], Jacob[8] Stauffer, Henry Jacob[7], Hans[6], Christian[5], Daniel[4] Stouffer, Christian[3], Hans[2], Hans[1]) was born December 07, 1838 in Columbiana Co Ohio, and died February 09, 1889 in Columbiana Co Ohio. She married **John W Weaver** December 13, 1855 in Columbiana Cty Ohio. He was born August 24, 1832 in Columbiana Co Ohio, and died April 15, 1906 in Columbiana Co Ohio.

Child of Nancy Stoffer and John Weaver is:
- 2248   i.   Marietta[12] Weaver, born 1857; died 1928. She married Unknown Liber.

1756. Melinda J[11] **Stoffer** (Samuel[10], Jacob[9], Jacob[8] Stauffer, Henry Jacob[7], Hans[6], Christian[5], Daniel[4] Stouffer, Christian[3], Hans[2], Hans[1]) was born December 28, 1840 in Columbiana Cty Ohio, and died December 21, 1888 in Columbiana Cty Ohio. She married

The Relations of Milton Snavely Hershey, 4th Ed.

John Pentz August 29, 1863 in Columbiana Cty, Ohio. He was born January 02, 1837 in Columbiana Cty Ohio, and died April 25, 1887 in Columbiana Cty Ohio.

Children of Melinda Stoffer and John Pentz are:
- 2249   i.   William[12] Pentz, born 1868.
- 2250   ii.   Samuel Pentz, born 1871.
- 2251   iii.   Mary Ann Pentz, born 1875.

1757. Catherine Ann[11] Stoffer (Samuel[10], Jacob[9], Jacob[8] Stauffer, Henry Jacob[7], Hans[6], Christian[5], Daniel[4] Stouffer, Christian[3], Hans[2], Hans[1]) was born 1842 in Columbiana Cty, Ohio, and died September 16, 1873 in Columbiana Cty, Ohio. She married **Daniel Borton** September 18, 1866 in Columbiana Cty Ohio. He was born January 03, 1843 in Columbiana Cty, Ohio, and died June 10, 1931 in Columbiana Cty, Ohio.

Children of Catherine Stoffer and Daniel Borton are:
- 2252   i.   Samuel[12] Borton, born March 04, 1867 in Columbiana Cty ohio; died October 14, 1946. He married Metta S. Sinclair; born September 1865 in Ohio; died February 19, 1932 in Ohio.
- 2253   ii.   Ellis Borton, born 1871 in Columbiana County, Ohio; died April 23, 1936 in Alliance, Ohio. He married Jessie Davis.
- 2254   iii.   Katherine Ann Borton, born September 1873 in Ohio. She married Eugene Perry.

1758. Samuel Jr[11] Stoffer (Samuel[10], Jacob[9], Jacob[8] Stauffer, Henry Jacob[7], Hans[6], Christian[5], Daniel[4] Stouffer, Christian[3], Hans[2], Hans[1]) was born 1843 in Columbiana Co Ohio, and died March 12, 1932 in Stark Cty, Ohio. He married **(1) Laura Reece**. She was born 1853, and died December 03, 1936 in Stark Cty, Ohio. He married **(2) Mary Louise Bowman** December 31, 1863 in Columbiana Co Ohio. She was born July 09, 1843 in Knox Twp, Columbiana Co Ohio, and died February 26, 1878 in Knox Twp, Columbiana Co Ohio.

Children of Samuel Stoffer and Laura Reece are:
- + 2255   i.   Homer E[12] Stoffer, born February 27, 1880 in Columbiana Cty, Ohio; died January 24, 1954 in Ohio.
- 2256   ii.   Cora Stoffer, born January 1881 in Columbiana Cty, Ohio; died April 06, 1882 in Stark Cty Ohio.

Children of Samuel Stoffer and Mary Bowman are:
- 2257   i.   George[12] Stoffer, born 1868.
- 2258   ii.   Leslie A Stoffer, born June 28, 1871 in Columbiana Cty; died October 03, 1896 in Columbiana Cty.
- 2259   iii.   John Arthur Stoffer, born October 14, 1876 in Columbiana Co, Ohio; died January 25, 1878 in Columbiana Co, Ohio.

1760. Eliza[11] Stoffer (Samuel[10], Jacob[9], Jacob[8] Stauffer, Henry Jacob[7], Hans[6], Christian[5], Daniel[4] Stouffer, Christian[3], Hans[2], Hans[1]) was born December 1849, and died 1905. She married **John Fultz** March 10, 1874 in Columbiana Cty, Ohio. He was born February 1850 in Columbiana Cty ohio, and died 1920 in Columbiana Cty ohio.

Children of Eliza Stoffer and John Fultz are:
- 2260   i.   Samuel[12] Fultz.
- 2261   ii.   Mark Fultz.

1772. Dennis[11] Stoffer (John[10], Jacob[9], Jacob[8] Stauffer, Henry Jacob[7], Hans[6], Christian[5], Daniel[4] Stouffer, Christian[3], Hans[2], Hans[1]) was born November 1844 in Columbiana County, Ohio, and died 1922. He married **Isabelle Stoffer Grubb**. She was born 1855 in Ohio, and died 1927.

Children of Dennis Stoffer and Isabelle Grubb are:
- 2262   i.   Clinton[12] Stoffer, born 1871.
- 2263   ii.   Mildred Stoffer, born 1886.

1773. John Jacob[11] Stoffer (John[10], Jacob[9], Jacob[8] Stauffer, Henry Jacob[7], Hans[6], Christian[5], Daniel[4] Stouffer, Christian[3], Hans[2], Hans[1]) was born August 11, 1846 in Columbiana Co Ohio, and died April 19, 1921 in Ohio, Richland Co. He married **Mary Marilla Gatton** August 31, 1872 in Richland Ohio. She was born March 05, 1854 in Butler, Richland Co. Ohio, and died July 11, 1921 in Shelby Ohio. Richland Co.

Children of John Stoffer and Mary Gatton are:
- + 2264   i.   Cynthia Idella[12] Stoffer, born November 13, 1872; died March 16, 1953 in Bellville Ohio, Richland Co.
- 2265   ii.   George O Stoffer, born January 13, 1875; died June 04, 1944. He married Anna Hettinger.
- 2266   iii.   Elurtus Gatton Stoffer, born December 29, 1877.
- 2267   iv.   Willard Edson Stoffer, born November 11, 1882; died March 12, 1951 in Shelby Ohio, Richland Co. He

The Relations of Milton Snavely Hershey, 4th Ed.

married (1) Pearl Whipple. He married (2) Daisy Grace Cross March 1902.
- 2268 v. Millard Stoffer, born November 11, 1882; died November 11, 1882.
- 2269 vi. Mary Luella Stoffer, born January 16, 1885; died September 13, 1911. She married Burt Johnson.
- 2270 vii. Lida Marrilla Stoffer, born October 13, 1888. She married Stark Ball.
- 2271 viii. Flora Ann Stoffer, born July 13, 1889. She married Frank Ashley Wheeler January 14, 1961.
- 2272 ix. Walter Leon Stoffer, born June 04, 1892; died June 20, 1956. He married Etta Lucinda Huston.

1786. Levi[11] Stoffer (George[10], Jacob[9], Jacob[8] Stauffer, Henry Jacob[7], Hans[6], Christian[5], Daniel[4] Stouffer, Christian[3], Hans[2], Hans[1]) was born June 16, 1845 in Ohio, and died July 09, 1932 in Ohio. He married **Sarah Ann Dice** September 20, 1866 in Columbiana Co Ohio. She was born 1847 in Columbiana Co Ohio, and died May 30, 1907 in Columbiana Co Ohio.

Children of Levi Stoffer and Sarah Dice are:
- 2273 i. Milton C[12] Stoffer, born June 09, 1867 in Columbiana Cty Ohio; died February 04, 1870 in Alliance, Columbiana Cty Ohio.
- 2274 ii. Marion (Nick) Stoffer, born January 14, 1869 in Columbiana Co Ohio; died October 11, 1962 in Alliance, Ohio. He married Mary Jane Weaver October 25, 1894; born May 08, 1876 in Reading, Columbiana Co Ohio; died March 12, 1973 in Valley Nursing Home, Damascus Ohio.
- + 2275 iii. Ada Stoffer, born March 02, 1871 in Columbiana Cty, Ohio; died December 14, 1950.
- + 2276 iv. Laurance L Stoffer, born August 29, 1874 in Columbiana Cty, Ohio; died October 11, 1947.
- + 2277 v. Idella Stoffer, born May 12, 1877 in Columbiana Cty, Ohio; died 1900.
- 2278 vi. Windfield Stoffer, born November 07, 1879 in Columbiana Cty, Ohio.
- 2279 vii. Raymond Stoffer, born September 11, 1881 in North Georgetown Ohio, Columbiana Co; died April 11, 1962 in Damascus, Columbiana Co Ohio.
- 2280 viii. Myrtle Stoffer, born September 17, 1883 in Columbiana Co Ohio; died July 08, 1961.
- + 2281 ix. Pearl Stoffer, born April 12, 1886 in Columbiana Co Ohio; died March 11, 1958.
- + 2282 x. Erwin William Stoffer, born March 29, 1889 in Columbiana Cty, Ohio; died June 27, 1917 in Columbiana Cty, Ohio.

1789. Laurtis W.[11] Stoffer (George[10], Jacob[9], Jacob[8] Stauffer, Henry Jacob[7], Hans[6], Christian[5], Daniel[4] Stouffer, Christian[3], Hans[2], Hans[1]) was born December 02, 1854 in Columbiana County, Ohio, and died August 24, 1913 in Columbiana County, Ohio. He married **Analiza Eliza Woolf** January 10, 1875 in Columbiana Co Ohio. She was born January 01, 1857 in Columbiana Co Ohio, and died April 26, 1940 in Columbiana Co Ohio.

Children of Laurtis Stoffer and Analiza Woolf are:
- + 2283 i. William Franklin[12] Stoffer, born November 09, 1876 in Columbiana Co Ohio; died March 10, 1942 in Parry Sound, Ontario Canada.
- 2284 ii. Harvey W Stoffer, born August 18, 1878 in Columbiana Co Ohio; died September 07, 1910 in Columbiana Co Ohio.
- 2285 iii. Eva Stoffer, born June 26, 1880 in Columbiana Co Ohio; died June 30, 1880 in Columbiana Co Ohio.
- 2286 iv. Nora Olive Stoffer, born September 05, 1881 in Columbiana Co Ohio; died February 02, 1882 in Columbiana Co Ohio.
- + 2287 v. John Wallace Stoffer, born April 12, 1883 in Columbiana Co Ohio; died December 06, 1967 in Beloit Ohio, Mahoning Cty.
- 2288 vi. Elmer E Stoffer, born April 09, 1885 in Columbiana Co Ohio; died May 21, 1913 in Canton, Stark Cty Ohio.
- + 2289 vii. Lester Clyde Stoffer, born February 07, 1887 in North Georgetown Ohio, Columbiana Co; died November 29, 1973 in Lisbon, Columbiana Co Ohio.
- 2290 viii. Carrie M Stoffer, born March 07, 1889 in Columbiana Co ohio; died December 20, 1957 in Jackson, Breathitt, Kentucky.
- + 2291 ix. Gladys Alice Stoffer, born October 10, 1889 in Columbiana Co Ohio.
- + 2292 x. Veron Roy Stoffer, born May 10, 1891 in Columbiana Co. Ohio; died April 1970 in Carroll Co Indiana.
- + 2293 xi. Mary Catherine Stoffer, born September 04, 1891 in Columbiana Cty ohio; died October 14, 1975 in Columbiana Cty ohio.
- + 2294 xii. Charles G Stoffer, born March 24, 1893 in Columbiana Co Ohio; died March 29, 1988 in Alliance Ohio.
- 2295 xiii. Elbert R Stoffer, born September 08, 1894 in Columbiana Co, Ohio; died August 11, 1954 in Hudson Ohio, Summit Co. He married Eva Graber Hubbard December 31, 1940; born February 19, 1900 in Hudson Ohio, Summit Co; died April 1982 in Hudson Ohio, Summit Co.
- + 2296 xiv. Bryan Sewell Stoffer, born July 27, 1896 in North Georgetown Ohio, Columbiana Co; died March 19, 1961 in Topeka, Kansas.

1790. Simon Henry[11] Stoffer (George[10], Jacob[9], Jacob[8] Stauffer, Henry Jacob[7], Hans[6], Christian[5], Daniel[4] Stouffer, Christian[3],

The Relations of Milton Snavely Hershey, 4th Ed.

Hans[2], Hans[1]) was born May 21, 1856 in Columbiana County, Ohio, and died April 06, 1944 in Orange County, Texas. He married **Alice Phillipa Hyde** September 23, 1880 in Hays City, Kansas. She was born June 19, 1864 in Wisconsin Grant Cty, and died December 08, 1944 in Ohio.

Children of Simon Stoffer and Alice Hyde are:

	2297	i.	Mable Catherine[12] Stoffer, born June 13, 1881 in Kansas, Ellis or Pawnee Co; died August 06, 1980 in Orange Co., Texas. She married Thomas Creighton November 10, 1917 in Inez, Texas.
+	2298	ii.	George Allen Stoffer, born July 09, 1883 in Kansas, Ellis Cty; died August 18, 1942 in Aline Okla..
	2299	iii.	Fannie Pearl Stoffer, born June 09, 1886 in Kansas, Ellis or Pawnee Co; died February 09, 1947 in Orange Co., Texas. She married Joseph M Spring February 04, 1903 in Agusta, Oklahoma.
	2300	iv.	Earl Eugene Stoffer, born July 25, 1888 in Kansas, Ellis or Pawnee Co. He married Mary Berridge October 23, 1915 in Victoria, Texas.
	2301	v.	Lena Viola Stoffer, born February 16, 1891 in Kansas, Ellis or Pawnee Co. She married Clarence Hedrick April 28, 1908 in Alva, Oklahoma.
+	2302	vi.	Simon Levi Stoffer, born February 20, 1893 in Kansas, Ellis or Pawnee Co; died December 26, 1967 in Orange Cty Tx.
	2303	vii.	Mary Dora Stoffer, born August 04, 1895 in Oklahoma, Wood Co; died February 11, 1911 in Aline Okla.
+	2304	viii.	Alice Ellen Stoffer, born October 18, 1900 in Oklahoma; died November 1990 in Orange Co., Texas.
	2305	ix.	John Ralph Stoffer, born October 03, 1903 in Oklahoma, Wood Co; died November 24, 1972 in Orange Co., Texas.
	2306	x.	Eva Lola Stoffer, born February 24, 1908 in Oklahoma, Wood Co; died 1996 in Orange Cty, Texas. She married Horace Peveto June 08, 1929 in Orange County, Texas.

1791. Rolandus[11] Stoffer (George[10], Jacob[9], Jacob[8] Stauffer, Henry Jacob[7], Hans[6], Christian[5], Daniel[4] Stouffer, Christian[3], Hans[2], Hans[1]) was born May 27, 1858 in Columbiana County, Ohio, and died January 13, 1934 in Columbiana County, Ohio. He married **Anna Miriam Miller** 1880 in Columbiana Co Ohio. She was born February 16, 1861, and died August 27, 1911 in Columbiana Co Ohio.

Children of Rolandus Stoffer and Anna Miller are:

	2307	i.	Nettie Pearl[12] Stoffer, born October 05, 1883 in Columbiana Co Ohio; died May 17, 1973. She married Gail Stark February 28, 1914.
+	2308	ii.	Claire Daniel Stoffer, born June 08, 1893 in Columbiana Cty Ohio; died April 27, 1959 in Calif.
+	2309	iii.	Vera Lucille Stoffer, born April 17, 1896 in Ohio; died January 18, 1982 in Columbiana Cty ohio.

1792. George D[11] Stoffer (George[10], Jacob[9], Jacob[8] Stauffer, Henry Jacob[7], Hans[6], Christian[5], Daniel[4] Stouffer, Christian[3], Hans[2], Hans[1]) was born April 01, 1860 in Columbiana County, Ohio, and died November 09, 1940 in Columbiana Cty, Ohio. He married **(1) Ida M. Koffel**. She was born May 1861 in Columbiana Cty, Ohio, and died March 11, 1884 in Columbiana Cty, Ohio. He married **(2) Alverda Randels** March 04, 1885 in Columbiana Cty, Ohio. She was born December 04, 1861, and died December 23, 1908 in Columbiana Cty, Ohio.

Child of George Stoffer and Ida Koffel is:

+	2310	i.	Bertha Lorena[12] Stoffer, born June 23, 1882 in Columbiana Cty, Ohio; died December 23, 1962.

Children of George Stoffer and Alverda Randels are:

	2311	i.	Roy Lester[12] Stoffer, born February 21, 1886 in Columbiana Co Ohio; died February 27, 1966 in Homeworth, Columbiana Co Ohio.
	2312	ii.	Lula Nora Stoffer, born September 14, 1887 in Columbiana Cty ohio; died August 07, 1888 in Columbiana Cty ohio.
+	2313	iii.	Zella May Stoffer, born April 18, 1889 in Columbiana Co Ohio; died December 02, 1972.
+	2314	iv.	Chester A Stoffer, born January 12, 1891 in Columbiana Cty Ohio; died November 12, 1933 in Columbiana Cty Ohio.
+	2315	v.	Wesley Emerson Stoffer, born December 22, 1892 in Homeworth, Knox Twp, Columbiana Co, Ohio; died July 08, 1979 in Louisville, Ohio, Nist Nursing Home.
+	2316	vi.	Russell D Stoffer, born October 09, 1897 in Columbiana Co Ohio; died February 15, 1982 in Cuyahoga Falls, Ohio.

1793. Stanton Uriah[11] Stoffer (George[10], Jacob[9], Jacob[8] Stauffer, Henry Jacob[7], Hans[6], Christian[5], Daniel[4] Stouffer, Christian[3], Hans[2], Hans[1]) was born October 27, 1861 in Columbiana Co Ohio, and died March 16, 1940 in Ohio. He married **Sarah Regina Sturgeon** March 22, 1883 in Ohio. She was born January 01, 1864 in Columbiana County, Ohio, and died March 10, 1944 in Columbiana County, Ohio.

Marriage Notes for Stanton Stoffer and Sarah Sturgeon:

[chrststauffer1663.ged]

_STATMARRIED
1 _MEND Death of one spouse

Children of Stanton Stoffer and Sarah Sturgeon are:
+ 2317 i. Ora Deliah[12] Stoffer, born November 10, 1883 in Columbiana County, Ohio; died June 01, 1941 in Salem, Columbiana County, Ohio.
+ 2318 ii. Benjamine Franklin Stoffer, born July 23, 1885 in Columbiana Co Ohio; died June 17, 1967 in Canton Ohio, Stark Co.
  2319 iii. Charles Henry Stoffer, born August 30, 1887 in Knox Township, Columbiana County, Ohio; died September 12, 1888 in Columbiana County, Ohio.
+ 2320 iv. Roscoe "Ross" Stoffer, born October 14, 1889 in Knox Township, Columbiana County, Ohio; died March 07, 1969 in Ohio.
+ 2321 v. Curtis Homer Stoffer, born June 17, 1892 in Knox Township, Columbiana County, Ohio; died December 01, 1983 in Salem, Columbiana County, Ohio.
  2322 vi. Ralph Leo Stoffer, born September 08, 1894 in Columbiana Cty ohio; died 1895 in Columbiana Cty ohio.
+ 2323 vii. Ruthanna Stoffer, born September 28, 1896 in Ohio; died June 12, 1961 in Ohio.
+ 2324 viii. Ruth Anna Stoffer, born September 28, 1896 in Columbiana Co. Ohio; died June 12, 1961 in Ohio, Stark Co.
  2325 ix. Milan Leroy Stoffer, born June 30, 1899 in Hanover Township, Columbiana County, Ohio; died September 11, 1901 in Butler Township, Columbiana County, Ohio.
+ 2326 x. Bertha Cleo Stoffer, born January 10, 1902 in Knox Township, Columbiana County, Ohio; died March 04, 1986 in Columbiana County, Ohio.
  2327 xi. Helen Naomi Stoffer, born December 13, 1905 in Columbiana Cty, Ohio; died March 25, 1924 in Columbiana Cty, Ohio.

1794. Sherman[11] **Stoffer** (George[10], Jacob[9], Jacob[8] Stauffer, Henry Jacob[7], Hans[6], Christian[5], Daniel[4] Stouffer, Christian[3], Hans[2], Hans[1]) was born May 21, 1865 in Columbiana Co Ohio, and died March 31, 1926 in Ohio, Portage Cty. He married **Susanna Justina Oesch** November 01, 1885. She was born 1864 in Ohio, and died Aft. 1910.

Marriage Notes for Sherman Stoffer and Susanna Oesch:
[chrststauffer1663.ged]

1 _MEND Death of one spouse

Children of Sherman Stoffer and Susanna Oesch are:
  2328 i. Earl[12] Stoffer.
  2329 ii. Leona Rosa Stoffer, born Abt. January 08, 1885 in Ohio; died Abt. March 05, 1885 in Okla.
  2330 iii. Elgie Stoffer, born May 01, 1886 in Columbiana Co Ohio; died January 02, 1962 in Youngstown Ohio.
  2331 iv. Edward W Stoffer, born June 10, 1887 in Columbiana Co Ohio; died April 21, 1961 in Columbiana Co Ohio.
  2332 v. Orietta Stoffer, born October 11, 1888 in Columbiana Co Ohio.
  2333 vi. Ross Stoffer, born October 30, 1889 in Columbiana Co Ohio.
  2334 vii. Blanche Mae Stoffer, born May 14, 1892 in Columbiana Co Ohio; died December 1984 in Baton RougeLouisana. She married (1) Vincent Jacobs. She married (2) Walter E Bolinger 1920; born December 1893 in Grafton W Va.
  2335 viii. Sylvia Stoffer, born January 15, 1894 in Columbiana Co, Ohio. She married Unknown Lonagher.
  2336 ix. Odessa Stoffer, born April 28, 1896 in Columbiana Co Ohio. She married Unknown Auker.
+ 2337 x. Leo Lesile Stoffer, born October 01, 1905 in Ohio; died August 1985 in Columbiana Co Ohio, Leetonoia.
  2338 xi. Eileen M Stoffer, born 1907 in Ohio. She married Unknown Williams.
  2339 xii. Ethel Stoffer, born 1911 in Ohio. She married Unknown Dicky.

1795. Leander[11] **Stoffer** (George[10], Jacob[9], Jacob[8] Stauffer, Henry Jacob[7], Hans[6], Christian[5], Daniel[4] Stouffer, Christian[3], Hans[2], Hans[1]) was born September 19, 1866 in Columbiana County, Ohio, and died March 30, 1942 in Columbiana County, Ohio. He married **(1) Laura Yeagley** October 31, 1883 in Columbiana County, Ohio. He married **(2) Mary Newcomer** June 03, 1892. She was born 1866 in Columbiana Co Ohio, and died November 11, 1933 in Columbiana Co Ohio.

Marriage Notes for Leander Stoffer and Laura Yeagley:
[chrststauffer1663.ged]

The Relations of Milton Snavely Hershey, 4th Ed.

1 _MEND Divorce

Children of Leander Stoffer and Laura Yeagley are:
- 2340   i.   Charles Floyd[12] Stoffer, born April 23, 1884 in Columbiana Cty, Ohio; died June 20, 1907 in Columbiana Cty, Ohio.
- 2341   ii.   Maud E Stoffer, born September 10, 1885 in Columbiana County, Ohio.
- + 2342   iii.   Anson Oscar Stoffer, born September 18, 1888 in Columbiana Cty, Ohio; died February 19, 1980.

Children of Leander Stoffer and Mary Newcomer are:
- 2343   i.   Maude Eve[12] Stoffer, born September 10, 1885 in Columbiana Co Ohio.
- + 2344   ii.   Glen Wilson Stoffer, born June 19, 1893 in Columbiana Co, Ohio; died May 01, 1972 in Columbiana Co, Ohio.
- 2345   iii.   Eldon Stoffer, born July 02, 1895 in Columbiana Cty, Ohio.
- 2346   iv.   Mabel Alice Stoffer, born February 28, 1898 in Columbiana Cty, Ohio; died April 05, 1959. She married (1) Ward L Sox; born August 12, 1896; died December 23, 1967. She married (2) Edward L Cox; born August 12, 1896; died December 23, 1967.
- + 2347   v.   Goldie Marie Stoffer, born June 06, 1901 in Columbiana Cty, Ohio; died April 01, 1975.
- + 2348   vi.   Wade Orla Stoffer, born June 14, 1903 in Columbian Co Ohio; died August 12, 1976.
- + 2349   vii.   Darl Lincoln Stoffer, born February 12, 1910 in Columbiana Co Ohio; died February 27, 1999 in Mansfield, Richland Co, Ohio.

Generation No. 12

1799. Harry H[12] **Hess** (Henry L[11], Samuel H[10], Henry[9], Esther[8] Hershey, Christian[7], Benjamin Stauffer[6], Adelheid Galle[5] Stouffer, Daniel[4], Christian[3], Hans[2], Hans[1]) was born July 20, 1884 in Manheim Twp, Lanc Co, PA, and died January 17, 1958. He married **Anna Rupp Wolf** August 18, 1910. She was born December 31, 1884 in Millway, Warwick Twp, Lancaster Co, PA, and died October 10, 1958.

Child of Harry Hess and Anna Wolf is:
- 2350   i.   Ruth Wolf[13] Hess, born December 05, 1921 in Millway, Warwick Twp, Lancaster Co, PA. She married Archie L Good May 15, 1943.

1805. Amos B[12] **Snyder** (Annie H[11] Bomberger, Barbara[10] Hess, Christian[9], Esther[8] Hershey, Christian[7], Benjamin Stauffer[6], Adelheid Galle[5] Stouffer, Daniel[4], Christian[3], Hans[2], Hans[1]) was born February 21, 1883. He married **Amy Landis Hershey**, daughter of Andrew Hershey and Martha Landis. She was born January 07, 1889.

Children of Amos Snyder and Amy Hershey are:
- 2351   i.   Wanda H[13] Snyder, born October 05, 1917. She married Harold B Hess; born October 14, 1917.
- 2352   ii.   Melvin H Snyder, born May 02, 1922.
- 2353   iii.   Arlene Snyder, born October 12, 1923.

1810. Magdalena M.[12] **Landis** (Magdalena O.[11] Martin, Martha H.[10] Oberholtzer, Martha H.[9] Hess, Esther[8] Hershey, Christian[7], Benjamin Stauffer[6], Adelheid Galle[5] Stouffer, Daniel[4], Christian[3], Hans[2], Hans[1]) was born December 22, 1881 in Intercourse, Lanc Co, PA, and died October 17, 1946 in Akron, Lancaster Co, PA. She married **John Hollinger Weaver** August 23, 1903 in Murrel, PA, son of Christian Weaver and Susanna Hollinger. He was born February 23, 1881, and died June 06, 1946 in Akron, Lancaster Co, PA.

Children of Magdalena Landis and John Weaver are:
- 2354   i.   Mabel L.[13] Weaver, born April 12, 1905; died February 25, 2000 in Landis Homes, Lancaster Co., PA. She married Emanuel Marner March 09, 1956; born September 28, 1896 in Kokomo, IN; died February 01, 1983 in Manheim Twp, Lanc Co, PA.
- + 2355   ii.   John Landis Weaver, born September 04, 1909 in Earl Twp, Lanc Co, PA; died April 30, 1991 in Akron, Lancaster Co, PA.

1817. Helen Virginia[12] **Bitzer** (Annie[11] Hershey, Elias H[10], Jacob Frantz[9], Isaac Hernley[8], Christian[7], Benjamin Stauffer[6], Adelheid Galle[5] Stouffer, Daniel[4], Christian[3], Hans[2], Hans[1]) was born February 21, 1891. She married **Edward W Sigler**. He was born July 15, 1885.

Child of Helen Bitzer and Edward Sigler is:
- 2356   i.   Anna Elizabeth[13] Sigler, born February 15, 1922.

1821. Maria Elizabeth[12] **Hershey** (Ezra Frantz[11], Elias H[10], Jacob Frantz[9], Isaac Hernley[8], Christian[7], Benjamin Stauffer[6], Adelheid

Galle[5] Stouffer, Daniel[4], Christian[3], Hans[2], Hans[1]) was born June 05, 1913. She married **Walter Lutz**.

Child of Maria Hershey and Walter Lutz is:
    2357   i.   James Hershey[13] Lutz, born Abt. 1940.

1832. Wesley[12] Betzner (Samuel[11], Elizabeth[10] Stouffer, Abraham Hershey[9] Stauffer, Abraham Hess[8], Henry Jacob[7], Hans[6], Christian[5], Daniel[4] Stouffer, Christian[3], Hans[2], Hans[1]) was born July 02, 1855, and died December 15, 1941. He married **Rachael Green** January 11, 1883. She was born March 04, 1861, and died April 10, 1915.

Children of Wesley Betzner and Rachael Green are:
    2358   i.   Mary Claude[13] Betzner, born November 26, 1883.
+   2359   ii.   Harvey Andrew Betzner, born August 04, 1886.

1834. Mary Elizabeth[12] Betzner (Samuel[11], Elizabeth[10] Stouffer, Abraham Hershey[9] Stauffer, Abraham Hess[8], Henry Jacob[7], Hans[6], Christian[5], Daniel[4] Stouffer, Christian[3], Hans[2], Hans[1]) was born December 22, 1858, and died September 29, 1940. She married **Peter Augustus Neff** October 27, 1881. He was born November 08, 1857, and died October 17, 1935.

Child of Mary Betzner and Peter Neff is:
+   2360   i.   Nellie Louise[13] Neff, born February 22, 1886.

1835. Andrew[12] Betzner (Samuel[11], Elizabeth[10] Stouffer, Abraham Hershey[9] Stauffer, Abraham Hess[8], Henry Jacob[7], Hans[6], Christian[5], Daniel[4] Stouffer, Christian[3], Hans[2], Hans[1]) was born December 10, 1865. He married **Edith Maria Kelly** September 26, 1895. She was born April 18, 1866, and died March 12, 1947.

Children of Andrew Betzner and Edith Kelly are:
+   2361   i.   Nellie Elizabeth[13] Betzner.
+   2362   ii.   Clancey K. Betzner, born November 12, 1899.

1837. Elizabeth[12] Betzner (Abraham[11], Elizabeth[10] Stouffer, Abraham Hershey[9] Stauffer, Abraham Hess[8], Henry Jacob[7], Hans[6], Christian[5], Daniel[4] Stouffer, Christian[3], Hans[2], Hans[1]) was born September 06, 1851, and died August 30, 1934. She married **Drake Kitchen** January 01, 1873. He was born October 04, 1847, and died April 07, 1895.

Children of Elizabeth Betzner and Drake Kitchen are:
    2363   i.   Amos Abraham[13] Kitchen, died March 17, 1912.
+   2364   ii.   Ellen Ruletta Kitchen, born July 24, 1874; died May 07, 1920.
    2365   iii.   Mary Edith Kitchen, born February 07, 1878; died February 14, 1897.
+   2366   iv.   Mabel Gertrude Kitchen, born July 03, 1881.
    2367   v.   Harry Milton Kitchen, born June 01, 1888.
    2368   vi.   Lottie Augusta Kitchen, born July 26, 1890.

1839. George Washington[12] Betzner (Abraham[11], Elizabeth[10] Stouffer, Abraham Hershey[9] Stauffer, Abraham Hess[8], Henry Jacob[7], Hans[6], Christian[5], Daniel[4] Stouffer, Christian[3], Hans[2], Hans[1]) was born October 17, 1855, and died May 07, 1934. He married **Harriett Kitchen** 1873. She was born February 05, 1855, and died January 31, 1922.

Child of George Betzner and Harriett Kitchen is:
+   2369   i.   Henry Franklin[13] Betzner, born May 20, 1882; died December 28, 1945.

1840. Joseph[12] Betzner (Abraham[11], Elizabeth[10] Stouffer, Abraham Hershey[9] Stauffer, Abraham Hess[8], Henry Jacob[7], Hans[6], Christian[5], Daniel[4] Stouffer, Christian[3], Hans[2], Hans[1]) was born 1859, and died November 09, 1934. He married **Zilpha Horning** December 21, 1881. She was born December 21, 1856.

Child of Joseph Betzner and Zilpha Horning is:
+   2370   i.   Roy Sylvester[13] Betzner, born April 03, 1885.

1843. Alice[12] Betzner (Jacob[11], Elizabeth[10] Stouffer, Abraham Hershey[9] Stauffer, Abraham Hess[8], Henry Jacob[7], Hans[6], Christian[5], Daniel[4] Stouffer, Christian[3], Hans[2], Hans[1]) was born October 01, 1863, and died May 26, 1929. She married **W. J. Stutt** October 04, 1883. He was born February 07, 1858.

Children of Alice Betzner and W. Stutt are:
    2371   i.   H. Gordon[13] Stutt, born August 05, 1885.

2372   ii.   H. Gertrude Stutt, born September 22, 1888. She married W. Evart Young February 04, 1920; born March 27, 1886.
+ 2373   iii.   A. Katharine Stutt, born May 07, 1893.
2374   iv.   James E. Stutt, born July 17, 1898. He married Claire Wallace.

1844. Etta[12] Betzner (David S.[11], Elizabeth[10] Stouffer, Abraham Hershey[9] Stauffer, Abraham Hess[8], Henry Jacob[7], Hans[6], Christian[5], Daniel[4] Stouffer, Christian[3], Hans[2], Hans[1]) was born February 17, 1884, and died May 29, 1937. She married **John Marlow** March 08, 1911. He was born May 08, 1872.

Children of Etta Betzner and John Marlow are:
2375   i.   Andy[13] Marlow.
2376   ii.   Sarah Marlow.
2377   iii.   Jack Marlow, born March 16, 1917; died May 01, 1949.

1845. David Thomas[12] Betzner (David S.[11], Elizabeth[10] Stouffer, Abraham Hershey[9] Stauffer, Abraham Hess[8], Henry Jacob[7], Hans[6], Christian[5], Daniel[4] Stouffer, Christian[3], Hans[2], Hans[1]) was born September 08, 1861, and died March 20, 1940. He married **Elsie Ann Davidson** December 27, 1882. She was born May 18, 1862.

Children of David Betzner and Elsie Davidson are:
2378   i.   Annie Agnes[13] Betzner, born September 22, 1883. She married Lloyd Hoover Sisson November 27, 1913; born May 04, 1890.
+ 2379   ii.   Isabella D. Betzner, born June 28, 1885.
2380   iii.   Jean Betzner, born March 22, 1888.

1847. John Abram[12] Betzner (John Weir[11], Elizabeth[10] Stouffer, Abraham Hershey[9] Stauffer, Abraham Hess[8], Henry Jacob[7], Hans[6], Christian[5], Daniel[4] Stouffer, Christian[3], Hans[2], Hans[1]) was born February 11, 1862, and died February 15, 1942. He married **Mary Thompson** January 05, 1887. She was born April 13, 1862, and died July 31, 1940.

Children of John Betzner and Mary Thompson are:
2381   i.   Clarence[13] Betzner.
2382   ii.   Mabel T. Betzner, born October 29, 1887. She married Albert Shepherd February 08, 1930; born July 31, 1875.
+ 2383   iii.   Ethel May Betzner, born July 01, 1892.

1848. George David[12] Betzner (John Weir[11], Elizabeth[10] Stouffer, Abraham Hershey[9] Stauffer, Abraham Hess[8], Henry Jacob[7], Hans[6], Christian[5], Daniel[4] Stouffer, Christian[3], Hans[2], Hans[1]) was born February 15, 1865. He married **Alice Celesta Horning** March 07, 1889. She was born May 24, 1864, and died October 20, 1929.

Children of George Betzner and Alice Horning are:
2384   i.   Norman Edwin[13] Betzner, born May 05, 1890. He married Anna O. Dounell.
+ 2385   ii.   Ina Louisa Betzner, born May 20, 1893.
+ 2386   iii.   Laura G. Betzner, born April 22, 1899.

1849. Albert E.[12] Betzner (John Weir[11], Elizabeth[10] Stouffer, Abraham Hershey[9] Stauffer, Abraham Hess[8], Henry Jacob[7], Hans[6], Christian[5], Daniel[4] Stouffer, Christian[3], Hans[2], Hans[1]) was born June 16, 1867. He married **Ida E. Horning** September 20, 1894. She was born October 16, 1869.

Children of Albert Betzner and Ida Horning are:
+ 2387   i.   Evelyn A.[13] Betzner.
+ 2388   ii.   Erland S. Betzner, born November 17, 1896.

1855. Nancy Jane[12] Stauffer (Abraham[11], Christian[10], Abraham Hershey[9], Abraham Hess[8], Henry Jacob[7], Hans[6], Christian[5], Daniel[4] Stouffer, Christian[3], Hans[2], Hans[1]) was born August 12, 1853, and died July 17, 1950 in Spokane, WA. She married **Alfred DeWitt Frost** in Grand Rapids, MI. He was born September 16, 1851 in Michigan, and died September 21, 1932 in North Dakota.

Child of Nancy Stauffer and Alfred Frost is:
+ 2389   i.   Oliver[13] Frost, born January 05, 1878 in Fort Worth, TX; died May 15, 1961 in Hastings, Dakota Co, MN.

1891. Matilda[12] Stouffer (John[11], Abraham[10], Abraham Hershey[9] Stauffer, Abraham Hess[8], Henry Jacob[7], Hans[6], Christian[5], Daniel[4] Stouffer, Christian[3], Hans[2], Hans[1]) She married **Unknown Gardner**.

Children of Matilda Stouffer and Unknown Gardner are:
    2390   i.   Infant[13] Gardner.
    2391   ii.   John Gardner, died 1945.
    2392   iii.   William Gardner.

1894. Esther[12] Stouffer (John[11], Abraham[10], Abraham Hershey[9] Stauffer, Abraham Hess[8], Henry Jacob[7], Hans[6], Christian[5], Daniel[4] Stouffer, Christian[3], Hans[2], Hans[1]) died 1938. She married **(1) Unknown Hoist**. She married **(2) Unknown Kendall**.

Children of Esther Stouffer and Unknown Kendall are:
    2393   i.   William[13] Kendall.
    2394   ii.   John Kendall.

1896. Bertha[12] Stouffer (John[11], Abraham[10], Abraham Hershey[9] Stauffer, Abraham Hess[8], Henry Jacob[7], Hans[6], Christian[5], Daniel[4] Stouffer, Christian[3], Hans[2], Hans[1]) She married **Unknown Cooley**.

Children of Bertha Stouffer and Unknown Cooley are:
+   2395   i.   Clayton[13] Cooley.
    2396   ii.   Myron Cooley.
    2397   iii.   Bruce Cooley, born 1890; died 1927.
    2398   iv.   Fern Cooley, born 1891; died 1894.
+   2399   v.   Nina Cooley, born 1894.
+   2400   vi.   Marie Cooley, born 1895.
    2401   vii.   Jay Cooley, born 1906; died 1906.
    2402   viii.   Harold Cooley, born 1908; died 1908.
    2403   ix.   Gerald Cooley, born 1908; died 1908.

1898. Aaron[12] Stouffer (John[11], Abraham[10], Abraham Hershey[9] Stauffer, Abraham Hess[8], Henry Jacob[7], Hans[6], Christian[5], Daniel[4] Stouffer, Christian[3], Hans[2], Hans[1]) was born 1859, and died 1891. He married **Sarah Barkey**. She was born 1860, and died 1935.

Children of Aaron Stouffer and Sarah Barkey are:
    2404   i.   Clarence[13] Stouffer, died 1936. He married Tillie Burkholder.
+   2405   ii.   Ida Stouffer, born 1884; died 1974.
    2406   iii.   Willis Stouffer, born 1888. He married Dora Ingram.

1899. Eli[12] Stouffer (Samuel[11], Abraham[10], Abraham Hershey[9] Stauffer, Abraham Hess[8], Henry Jacob[7], Hans[6], Christian[5], Daniel[4] Stouffer, Christian[3], Hans[2], Hans[1]) He married **Cordelia Abigail Hall**.

Children of Eli Stouffer and Cordelia Hall are:
    2407   i.   Ernest[13] Stouffer.
+   2408   ii.   Jason Stouffer.
    2409   iii.   Miline Stouffer.
+   2410   iv.   May Stouffer.
+   2411   v.   Blanche Stouffer.
+   2412   vi.   Samuel Stouffer.

1900. Hannah[12] Stouffer (Samuel[11], Abraham[10], Abraham Hershey[9] Stauffer, Abraham Hess[8], Henry Jacob[7], Hans[6], Christian[5], Daniel[4] Stouffer, Christian[3], Hans[2], Hans[1]) She married **Benjamin Hall**.

Children of Hannah Stouffer and Benjamin Hall are:
+   2413   i.   Nellie[13] Hall.
+   2414   ii.   Nettie Hall.
    2415   iii.   Mildred Hall. She married Lloyd Oscar.
+   2416   iv.   Lola Hall.
+   2417   v.   Vera Hall.
    2418   vi.   Verna Hall.
    2419   vii.   Faye Hall. She married Archie McLeod.

1901. Elizabeth[12] Stouffer (Samuel[11], Abraham[10], Abraham Hershey[9] Stauffer, Abraham Hess[8], Henry Jacob[7], Hans[6], Christian[5], Daniel[4] Stouffer, Christian[3], Hans[2], Hans[1]) She married **I. L. Bateman**.

Children of Elizabeth Stouffer and I. Bateman are:
    2420   i.   Lydia[13] Bateman. She married George Daley.
+   2421   ii.   Nellie Bateman.
    2422   iii. Mary Bateman.
    2423   iv. May Bateman.
    2424   v.   Della Bateman.

1904. Lavilla[12] Stouffer (Samuel[11], Abraham[10], Abraham Hershey[9] Stauffer, Abraham Hess[8], Henry Jacob[7], Hans[6], Christian[5], Daniel[4] Stouffer, Christian[3], Hans[2], Hans[1]) She married **Charles Murrell**.

Children of Lavilla Stouffer and Charles Murrell are:
    2425   i.   Ernest[13] Murrell.
+   2426   ii.   Alpha Murrell.

1905. John Franklin[12] Stouffer (Jacob[11], Abraham[10], Abraham Hershey[9] Stauffer, Abraham Hess[8], Henry Jacob[7], Hans[6], Christian[5], Daniel[4] Stouffer, Christian[3], Hans[2], Hans[1]) He married **Jennie Adelia Yando**.

Children of John Stouffer and Jennie Yando are:
+   2427   i.   Edna[13] Stouffer.
    2428   ii.   Leslie Stouffer.
+   2429   iii. Stanley Stouffer.
+   2430   iv. Edwin Stouffer.
    2431   v.   Llewellyn Stouffer, died in France.
+   2432   vi. Isobel Stouffer.
+   2433   vii. Kathleen Stouffer.
+   2434   viii. Kenneth Stouffer.
+   2435   ix. Evelyn Stouffer.

1906. David Wesley[12] Stouffer (Jacob[11], Abraham[10], Abraham Hershey[9] Stauffer, Abraham Hess[8], Henry Jacob[7], Hans[6], Christian[5], Daniel[4] Stouffer, Christian[3], Hans[2], Hans[1]) He married **(1) Mabel Bowman**. He married **(2) Eleanor Gillson Pick**.

Children of David Stouffer and Mabel Bowman are:
    2436   i.   Erman[13] Stouffer.
+   2437   ii.   Wesley Adrian Stouffer.
+   2438   iii. Jacob Karl Stouffer.
    2439   iv. Ruth Stouffer.

Children of David Stouffer and Eleanor Pick are:
    2440   i.   Phyllis[13] Stouffer. She married Jason Howard Barger.
+   2441   ii.   Wilbert Gillson Stouffer.
+   2442   iii. Conrad Ulrick Stouffer.

1908. Abraham[12] Stouffer (Jacob[11], Abraham[10], Abraham Hershey[9] Stauffer, Abraham Hess[8], Henry Jacob[7], Hans[6], Christian[5], Daniel[4] Stouffer, Christian[3], Hans[2], Hans[1]) He married **Louise Konshak**.

Children of Abraham Stouffer and Louise Konshak are:
+   2443   i.   Ernest Albert[13] Stouffer.
+   2444   ii.   Lloyd Arthur Stouffer.
+   2445   iii. Anna Helena Stouffer.
    2446   iv. Myrtle Inez Stouffer. She married George Oliver.
+   2447   v.   Ora Hilda Stouffer.

1911. Keturah[12] Stouffer (Jacob[11], Abraham[10], Abraham Hershey[9] Stauffer, Abraham Hess[8], Henry Jacob[7], Hans[6], Christian[5], Daniel[4] Stouffer, Christian[3], Hans[2], Hans[1]) was born February 06, 1859. She married **James Murison**.

Children of Keturah Stouffer and James Murison are:
    2448   i.   Anna[13] Murison.

	2449	ii.	William Jacob Murison, born July 25, 1891; died February 02, 1892.
+	2450	iii.	Gordon Ernest Murison, born February 05, 1893.
	2451	iv.	Wilfrid Charles Murison, born December 17, 1896; died May 02, 1918 in World War I.
+	2452	v.	Bessie Louise Murison, born December 24, 1898.

1912. Flavius Jacob[12] Stouffer (Jacob[11], Abraham[10], Abraham Hershey[9] Stauffer, Abraham Hess[8], Henry Jacob[7], Hans[6], Christian[5], Daniel[4] Stouffer, Christian[3], Hans[2], Hans[1]) was born July 26, 1875, and died January 10, 1941. He married **Rachel Edith Parker**.

Children of Flavius Stouffer and Rachel Parker are:
+	2453	i.	Clayton Parker[13] Stouffer.
+	2454	ii.	Jennie Grace Stouffer.
+	2455	iii.	Martha May Stouffer.
	2456	iv.	Harry Norman Stouffer.

1914. Esther[12] Wideman (Elizabeth[11] Stouffer, Abraham[10], Abraham Hershey[9] Stauffer, Abraham Hess[8], Henry Jacob[7], Hans[6], Christian[5], Daniel[4] Stouffer, Christian[3], Hans[2], Hans[1]) She married **Samuel George**.

Children of Esther Wideman and Samuel George are:
+	2457	i.	Nellie Almina[13] George.
	2458	ii.	Clarence Judson George, died May 19, 1926.
+	2459	iii.	Elizabeth Ann George, died May 23, 1949.
	2460	iv.	Harold Wideman George. He married Blanche Folliott.

1916. Jacob S.[12] Wideman (Elizabeth[11] Stouffer, Abraham[10], Abraham Hershey[9] Stauffer, Abraham Hess[8], Henry Jacob[7], Hans[6], Christian[5], Daniel[4] Stouffer, Christian[3], Hans[2], Hans[1]) was born 1867. He married **Sarah Lehman**.

Children of Jacob Wideman and Sarah Lehman are:
+	2461	i.	Harry[13] Wideman.
+	2462	ii.	Clarence Wideman.
	2463	iii.	Lorne Wideman. He married Mildred Foote.
+	2464	iv.	Elizabeth Wideman, born August 11, 1894.
+	2465	v.	Carson Wideman, born August 06, 1899.

1918. Laura[12] Stouffer (Simeon[11], Abraham[10], Abraham Hershey[9] Stauffer, Abraham Hess[8], Henry Jacob[7], Hans[6], Christian[5], Daniel[4] Stouffer, Christian[3], Hans[2], Hans[1]) was born May 13, 1869, and died 1942. She married **George Collard** 1903. He was born 1868, and died 1948.

Children of Laura Stouffer and George Collard are:
+	2466	i.	Alan[13] Collard.
+	2467	ii.	Jean Collard.
+	2468	iii.	Eric Collard.
	2469	iv.	Isabel Collard.

1921. Fred[12] Stouffer (Simeon[11], Abraham[10], Abraham Hershey[9] Stauffer, Abraham Hess[8], Henry Jacob[7], Hans[6], Christian[5], Daniel[4] Stouffer, Christian[3], Hans[2], Hans[1]) was born 1875.

Children of Fred Stouffer are:
2470	i.	Walter[13] Stouffer.
2471	ii.	Harold Stouffer.
2472	iii.	Maude Stouffer. She married Otto Wellan.
2473	iv.	Leonard Stouffer.

1923. Christina[12] Stouffer (Abraham[11], Abraham[10], Abraham Hershey[9] Stauffer, Abraham Hess[8], Henry Jacob[7], Hans[6], Christian[5], Daniel[4] Stouffer, Christian[3], Hans[2], Hans[1]) was born November 20, 1853, and died 1935. She married **Christian Raymer**. He died 1933.

Children of Christina Stouffer and Christian Raymer are:
+	2474	i.	Ruth[13] Raymer, died 1943.
+	2475	ii.	Elmina Raymer.
	2476	iii.	Bertie Raymer. She married John Lehman.

1924. Frances[12] **Stouffer** (Abraham[11], Abraham[10], Abraham Hershey[9] Stauffer, Abraham Hess[8], Henry Jacob[7], Hans[6], Christian[5], Daniel[4] Stouffer, Christian[3], Hans[2], Hans[1]) was born May 23, 1855, and died 1940. She married **Martin Wideman**.

Children of Frances Stouffer and Martin Wideman are:
- \+ 2477   i.   Wilmot[13] Wideman.
- \+ 2478   ii.   Herbert Wideman.
- \+ 2479   iii.   Mabel Wideman.
- \+ 2480   iv.   Martha Wideman.
-     2481   v.   Wesley Wideman. He married Agnes Warkentine.
-     2482   vi.   Elizabeth Wideman.
- \+ 2483   vii.   Joseph Wideman.

1926. Noah[12] **Stouffer** (Abraham[11], Abraham[10], Abraham Hershey[9] Stauffer, Abraham Hess[8], Henry Jacob[7], Hans[6], Christian[5], Daniel[4] Stouffer, Christian[3], Hans[2], Hans[1]) was born June 26, 1858, and died 1931. He married **Alice Hamilton**.

Children of Noah Stouffer and Alice Hamilton are:
- \+ 2484   i.   Louie[13] Stouffer.
- \+ 2485   ii.   Harry Stouffer.
-     2486   iii.   Ernest Stouffer.

1929. Josephuine[12] **Stouffer** (Abraham[11], Abraham[10], Abraham Hershey[9] Stauffer, Abraham Hess[8], Henry Jacob[7], Hans[6], Christian[5], Daniel[4] Stouffer, Christian[3], Hans[2], Hans[1]) was born September 11, 1866, and died 1937. She married **Simeon Hoover**.

Children of Josephuine Stouffer and Simeon Hoover are:
- \+ 2487   i.   Jennie[13] Hoover.
- \+ 2488   ii.   George Hoover.
- \+ 2489   iii.   Bella Hoover.
- \+ 2490   iv.   Ruth Hoover.
- \+ 2491   v.   Flora Hoover.
- \+ 2492   vi.   Edith Hoover.

1930. Martha[12] **Stouffer** (Abraham[11], Abraham[10], Abraham Hershey[9] Stauffer, Abraham Hess[8], Henry Jacob[7], Hans[6], Christian[5], Daniel[4] Stouffer, Christian[3], Hans[2], Hans[1]) was born August 05, 1868, and died 1947. She married **Wilmot Barkey**.

Children of Martha Stouffer and Wilmot Barkey are:
-     2493   i.   Mildred[13] Barkey.
- \+ 2494   ii.   Charles Barkey.
-     2495   iii.   William Barkey.
-     2496   iv.   Ella Barkey.
- \+ 2497   v.   Mary Barkey.

1931. Abraham[12] **Stouffer** (Abraham[11], Abraham[10], Abraham Hershey[9] Stauffer, Abraham Hess[8], Henry Jacob[7], Hans[6], Christian[5], Daniel[4] Stouffer, Christian[3], Hans[2], Hans[1]) was born June 23, 1872. He married **Emma Shank**.

Children of Abraham Stouffer and Emma Shank are:
-     2498   i.   Bertha[13] Stouffer.
- \+ 2499   ii.   Lambert Stouffer.
- \+ 2500   iii.   Abraham Stouffer.
- \+ 2501   iv.   Reginald Stouffer.
- \+ 2502   v.   Luella Stouffer.
-     2503   vi.   Walter Stouffer, born March 30, 1892. He married Ethel Learn.
- \+ 2504   vii.   Archibald Stouffer, born December 24, 1895.

1932. Wellington[12] **Stouffer** (Christian[11], Abraham[10], Abraham Hershey[9] Stauffer, Abraham Hess[8], Henry Jacob[7], Hans[6], Christian[5], Daniel[4] Stouffer, Christian[3], Hans[2], Hans[1]) He married **Minnie Grieves**.

Children of Wellington Stouffer and Minnie Grieves are:
-     2505   i.   Charles[13] Stouffer.
- \+ 2506   ii.   Jean Stouffer.
- \+ 2507   iii.   Stewart W. Stouffer.

+ 2508 iv. Edward Bruce Stouffer.

1933. Andrew[12] Stouffer (Christian[11], Abraham[10], Abraham Hershey[9] Stauffer, Abraham Hess[8], Henry Jacob[7], Hans[6], Christian[5], Daniel[4] Stouffer, Christian[3], Hans[2], Hans[1]) He married **(1) Lily O'Brian**. He married **(2) Florence Parsons**.

Children of Andrew Stouffer and Lily O'Brian are:
    2509   i. Arthur[13] Stouffer. He married Gladys Lemon.
    2510   ii. Carl Stouffer. He married Jean Lightbody.
+ 2511   iii. Florence Stouffer.

Child of Andrew Stouffer and Florence Parsons is:
    2512   i. Victor[13] Stouffer. He married Helen Mellow.

1935. Thomas[12] Stouffer (Christian[11], Abraham[10], Abraham Hershey[9] Stauffer, Abraham Hess[8], Henry Jacob[7], Hans[6], Christian[5], Daniel[4] Stouffer, Christian[3], Hans[2], Hans[1]) He married **Jennie Bedford**.

Children of Thomas Stouffer and Jennie Bedford are:
    2513   i. Robert[13] Stouffer, died in Died In Infancy.
+ 2514   ii. David Stouffer.

1937. Alberta[12] Stouffer (Christian[11], Abraham[10], Abraham Hershey[9] Stauffer, Abraham Hess[8], Henry Jacob[7], Hans[6], Christian[5], Daniel[4] Stouffer, Christian[3], Hans[2], Hans[1]) She married **George Barkey**.

Children of Alberta Stouffer and George Barkey are:
    2515   i. Evelyn Maude[13] Barkey.
    2516   ii. Howard Barkey.

1939. David[12] Stouffer (Christian[11], Abraham[10], Abraham Hershey[9] Stauffer, Abraham Hess[8], Henry Jacob[7], Hans[6], Christian[5], Daniel[4] Stouffer, Christian[3], Hans[2], Hans[1]) He married **Frances Hoover**.

Children of David Stouffer and Frances Hoover are:
+ 2517   i. Marion[13] Stouffer.
+ 2518   ii. Helen Stouffer.

2003. Willis Brenner[12] Hackman (Andrew Baer[11], Susanna Frantz[10] Bear, Anna[9] Frantz, Barbara[8] Hostetter, Ann Elisabeth[7] Hershey, Benjamin Stauffer[6], Adelheid Galle[5] Stouffer, Daniel[4], Christian[3], Hans[2], Hans[1]) was born February 21, 1877, and died August 11, 1947 in Lancaster, PA. He married **(1) Anna Hess Hess** April 03, 1902 in Neffsville, PA. She was born October 12, 1879, and died August 27, 1917 in Millport, PA. He married **(2) Emma Earhart Geib** Abt. 1918. She was born September 05, 1880, and died October 06, 1958 in Bickerville, PA.

Marriage Notes for Willis Hackman and Anna Hess:
According to Henry H Hackman:

Anna Hess Hess & Willis Brenner Hackman were married by the Rev. John M. Lefever, at his residence in Neffsville, Lancaster Co., PA.

Children of Willis Hackman and Anna Hess are:
    2519   i. Myrtle[13] Hackman, born December 11, 1902 in Millport, Warwick Township, Lancaster County, PA; died February 11, 1903 in Millport, Warwick Township, Lancaster County, PA.
    2520   ii. Andrew Hess Hackman, born December 17, 1903 in Millport, Warwick Township, Lancaster County, PA; died June 29, 1964. He married Ada Horst January 01, 1925 in New Holland, PA; born November 16, 1903 in West Earl Township, Lancaster County; died January 01, 1978 in Lititz, PA.
+ 2521   iii. Henry Hess Hackman, born July 27, 1908 in Millport, Warwick Township, Lancaster County, PA; died September 24, 1987.
+ 2522   iv. Willis Hess Hackman, born November 21, 1909 in Millport, Warwick Township, Lancaster County, PA; died August 20, 1989 in Elizabethtown, PA.
+ 2523   v. Walter Hess Hackman, born April 07, 1911 in Millport, Warwick Township, Lancaster County, PA.
+ 2524   vi. Richard Hess Hackman, born August 25, 1913 in Millport, Warwick Township, Lancaster County, PA.
    2525   vii. Baby Hackman, born 1917 in Millport, Warwick Township, Lancaster County, PA; died 1917 in Millport, Warwick Township, Lancaster County, PA.

Children of Willis Hackman and Emma Geib are:
+ 2526 i. Violet Gertrude[13] Hackman, born July 07, 1919 in Millport, Warwick Township, Lancaster County, PA.
+ 2527 ii. Emma Amelia Hackman, born May 28, 1921 in Millport, Warwick Township, Lancaster County, PA; died November 03, 1994 in Elizabethtown, PA.

2034. Paul M[12] Brubaker (Minnie P[11] Herr, John[10], Anna[9] Hostetter, John[8], Catharine[7] Long, Anna[6] Hershey, Adelheid Galle[5] Stouffer, Daniel[4], Christian[3], Hans[2], Hans[1]) was born October 21, 1914, and died May 16, 1991. He married **Anna F Longenecker**. She was born 1920 in Palmyra, PA.

Child of Paul Brubaker and Anna Longenecker is:
+ 2528 i. Robert Lee[13] Brubaker, born July 15, 1943; died December 25, 1999 in Lancaster Co, PA.

2035. Ella Barbara[12] Eby (Sarah Lucinda[11] Hershey, Peter[10], Jacob[9], John[8], Jacob Snavely[7], Andrew Stauffer[6], Adelheid Galle[5] Stouffer, Daniel[4], Christian[3], Hans[2], Hans[1]) was born December 27, 1884, and died May 06, 1959. She married **Daniel M. Fox**. He was born May 12, 1879, and died June 30, 1971.

Children of Ella Eby and Daniel Fox are:
+ 2529 i. Willis Eby[13] Fox, born May 17, 1907.
+ 2530 ii. Henry Peter Fox, born September 16, 1909.
+ 2531 iii. Sarah Lucinda Fox, born July 06, 1911; died October 19, 1971.
   2532 iv. John David Fox, born June 19, 1913; died January 10, 1971.
   2533 v. Anna Elizabeth Fox, born July 14, 1915.
+ 2534 vi. Daniel Hershey Fox, born August 19, 1917; died June 10, 1986.
   2535 vii. Elmer Eby Fox, born May 19, 1920; died February 08, 1921.
   2536 viii. Mary Eby Fox, born September 18, 1923. She married Leo Richard Grant; born February 10, 1925.
+ 2537 ix. Ivan Martin Fox, born October 23, 1925; died February 13, 1987.

2036. Elizabeth Hershey[12] Eby (Sarah Lucinda[11] Hershey, Peter[10], Jacob[9], John[8], Jacob Snavely[7], Andrew Stauffer[6], Adelheid Galle[5] Stouffer, Daniel[4], Christian[3], Hans[2], Hans[1]) was born September 15, 1886, and died February 16, 1944. She married **Frank W. Mohler**. He was born December 07, 1894, and died February 26, 1967.

Child of Elizabeth Eby and Frank Mohler is:
   2538 i. Graybill Eby[13] Mohler, born March 28, 1922. He married Helen Louise Kochel; born November 19, 1925.

2037. Peter Hershey[12] Eby (Sarah Lucinda[11] Hershey, Peter[10], Jacob[9], John[8], Jacob Snavely[7], Andrew Stauffer[6], Adelheid Galle[5] Stouffer, Daniel[4], Christian[3], Hans[2], Hans[1]) was born August 09, 1889, and died February 11, 1919. He married **Anna M. Weaver**. She was born August 18, 1890, and died January 23, 1982.

Children of Peter Eby and Anna Weaver are:
+ 2539 i. Franklin W.[13] Eby, born January 31, 1915; died November 14, 1968.
+ 2540 ii. Susan W. Eby, born November 16, 1916.
+ 2541 iii. Emma Mae Eby, born October 27, 1918.

2038. Enos Jacob[12] Eby (Sarah Lucinda[11] Hershey, Peter[10], Jacob[9], John[8], Jacob Snavely[7], Andrew Stauffer[6], Adelheid Galle[5] Stouffer, Daniel[4], Christian[3], Hans[2], Hans[1]) was born June 20, 1891, and died April 27, 1974. He married **Esther Weaver Shirk**. She was born March 13, 1894, and died May 18, 1966.

Children of Enos Eby and Esther Shirk are:
   2542 i. Isaac S.[13] Eby, born November 12, 1916.
+ 2543 ii. Rhoda S. Eby, born August 22, 1918.
+ 2544 iii. Henry S. Eby, born July 21, 1920.
+ 2545 iv. Ezra S. Eby, born October 31, 1922.
+ 2546 v. Eli S. Eby, born March 19, 1925; died December 12, 1985.
+ 2547 vi. Lydia S. Eby, born March 31, 1927.
   2548 vii. Aaron S. Eby, born August 02, 1929; died October 16, 1929.
   2549 viii. John S. Eby, born March 25, 1932; died March 25, 1932.
   2550 ix. Sarah S. Eby, born January 30, 1935; died April 22, 1960.

2039. Sarah Lucinda[12] Eby (Sarah Lucinda[11] Hershey, Peter[10], Jacob[9], John[8], Jacob Snavely[7], Andrew Stauffer[6], Adelheid Galle[5] Stouffer, Daniel[4], Christian[3], Hans[2], Hans[1]) was born February 25, 1893, and died January 04, 1946. She married **Harry H. Gehman**. He was born June 26, 1890, and died March 26, 1947.

Children of Sarah Eby and Harry Gehman are:
+ 2551 i. Private[13] Gehman.
+ 2552 ii. Private Gehman.
+ 2553 iii. Arthur E. Gehman, born January 19, 1920.
+ 2554 iv. John E. Gehman, born October 18, 1921.
+ 2555 v. Edith Elizabeth Gehman, born March 31, 1923.
+ 2556 vi. Lucy E. Gehman, born November 19, 1924.
    2557 vii. Grace Gehman, born October 30, 1926.
+ 2558 viii. Harry Jacob Gehman, born November 25, 1929.

2041. Henry Musser[12] Eby (Sarah Lucinda[11] Hershey, Peter[10], Jacob[9], John[8], Jacob Snavely[7], Andrew Stauffer[6], Adelheid Galle[5] Stouffer, Daniel[4], Christian[3], Hans[2], Hans[1]) was born July 14, 1896, and died June 15, 1974. He married **Anna Mae Zeiset**. She was born January 01, 1900.

Children of Henry Eby and Anna Zeiset are:
+ 2559 i. Private[13] Eby.
+ 2560 ii. Private Eby.
+ 2561 iii. Private Eby.
+ 2562 iv. Private Eby.
+ 2563 v. Private Eby.
+ 2564 vi. Martin Z. Eby, born December 25, 1921.
+ 2565 vii. Ethel Z. Eby, born November 25, 1923.
    2566 viii. Warren Z. Eby, born September 23, 1925.
+ 2567 ix. Roy Z. Eby, born September 20, 1927.
+ 2568 x. Mary Z. Eby, born June 11, 1929.

2042. Anna Martha[12] Eby (Sarah Lucinda[11] Hershey, Peter[10], Jacob[9], John[8], Jacob Snavely[7], Andrew Stauffer[6], Adelheid Galle[5] Stouffer, Daniel[4], Christian[3], Hans[2], Hans[1]) was born April 29, 1898, and died November 27, 1980. She married **Walter M. Martin**. He was born April 03, 1897, and died April 22, 1975.

Children of Anna Eby and Walter Martin are:
+ 2569 i. Private[13] Martin.
+ 2570 ii. Private Martin.
+ 2571 iii. Clarence E. Martin, born November 13, 1919.
+ 2572 iv. Mary E. Martin, born December 22, 1921.
+ 2573 v. Paul E. Martin, born September 29, 1923.
+ 2574 vi. Earl E. Martin, born November 28, 1926.
+ 2575 vii. Wilmer E. Martin, born June 05, 1929.

2045. Aaron Buckwalter[12] Eby (Sarah Lucinda[11] Hershey, Peter[10], Jacob[9], John[8], Jacob Snavely[7], Andrew Stauffer[6], Adelheid Galle[5] Stouffer, Daniel[4], Christian[3], Hans[2], Hans[1]) was born February 02, 1904, and died April 06, 1975. He married **Edna M. Sensenig**. She was born September 09, 1904.

Children of Aaron Eby and Edna Sensenig are:
+ 2576 i. Private[13] Eby.
+ 2577 ii. Private Eby.
+ 2578 iii. Private Eby.
+ 2579 iv. Private Eby.
+ 2580 v. Richard S. Eby, born October 08, 1928.
+ 2581 vi. Clyde S. Eby, born November 29, 1937; died October 08, 1974.

2046. Menno Hershey[12] Eby (Sarah Lucinda[11] Hershey, Peter[10], Jacob[9], John[8], Jacob Snavely[7], Andrew Stauffer[6], Adelheid Galle[5] Stouffer, Daniel[4], Christian[3], Hans[2], Hans[1]) was born October 27, 1905, and died June 22, 1974. He married **Helen V. Weaver**. She was born October 11, 1911.

Children of Menno Eby and Helen Weaver are:
+ 2582 i. Private[13] Eby.
+ 2583 ii. Private Eby.

\+ 2584 iii. Private Eby.

2047. Martin Christian[12] **Eby** (Sarah Lucinda[11] Hershey, Peter[10], Jacob[9], John[8], Jacob Snavely[7], Andrew Stauffer[6], Adelheid Galle[5] Stouffer, Daniel[4], Christian[3], Hans[2], Hans[1]) was born July 10, 1910, and died March 02, 1986. He married **(1) Helen Stauffer Wenger**. She was born January 20, 1916, and died June 04, 1960. He married **(2) Esta Mae Hershey**. She was born May 13, 1916.

Children of Martin Eby and Helen Wenger are:
\+ 2585 i. Private[13] Eby.
\+ 2586 ii. Private Eby.
\+ 2587 iii. Private Eby.
    2588 iv. Private Eby.
\+ 2589 v. Private Eby.

2048. Galen Warren[12] **Hershey** (Isaiah B.[11], Peter[10], Jacob[9], John[8], Jacob Snavely[7], Andrew Stauffer[6], Adelheid Galle[5] Stouffer, Daniel[4], Christian[3], Hans[2], Hans[1]) was born October 31, 1886, and died April 17, 1988. He married **Margie Eby**. She was born March 30, 1890, and died February 22, 1986.

Children of Galen Hershey and Margie Eby are:
\+ 2590 i. Erma E.[13] Hershey, born March 08, 1910.
\+ 2591 ii. Galen Clair Hershey, born February 10, 1914; died July 15, 1992.

2050. Henry Clay[12] **Hershey** (Enos Jacob[11], Peter[10], Jacob[9], John[8], Jacob Snavely[7], Andrew Stauffer[6], Adelheid Galle[5] Stouffer, Daniel[4], Christian[3], Hans[2], Hans[1]) was born September 01, 1892, and died February 20, 1946. He married **Edna Hershey**. She was born August 25, 1893, and died April 04, 1939.

Children of Henry Hershey and Edna Hershey are:
\+ 2592 i. Private[13] Hershey.
\+ 2593 ii. Private Hershey.
\+ 2594 iii. Private Hershey.
\+ 2595 iv. Private Hershey.
\+ 2596 v. Hazel Pauline Hershey, born August 15, 1914; died March 08, 1985.
    2597 vi. Mildred L. Hershey, born December 22, 1916; died October 31, 1961.
\+ 2598 vii. Ralph Glenn Hershey, born December 15, 1918; died March 12, 1988.
    2599 viii. William Nelson Hershey, born September 20, 1925.
\+ 2600 ix. Gladys Edna Hershey, born August 08, 1927.
\+ 2601 x. Clifford Eby Hershey, born November 17, 1928; died February 06, 1969.

2052. Mark Eby[12] **Hershey** (Enos Jacob[11], Peter[10], Jacob[9], John[8], Jacob Snavely[7], Andrew Stauffer[6], Adelheid Galle[5] Stouffer, Daniel[4], Christian[3], Hans[2], Hans[1]) was born April 13, 1897, and died December 19, 1983. He married **Anna Kreider Hershey**. She was born August 10, 1901.

Children of Mark Hershey and Anna Hershey are:
\+ 2602 i. Private[13] Hershey.
\+ 2603 ii. Private Hershey.
\+ 2604 iii. Private Hershey.
\+ 2605 iv. Private Hershey.
\+ 2606 v. Private Hershey.
\+ 2607 vi. Private Hershey.
\+ 2608 vii. Private Hershey.
    2609 viii. Jean Lois Hershey, born March 23, 1928.

2053. David Warren[12] **Hershey** (Enos Jacob[11], Peter[10], Jacob[9], John[8], Jacob Snavely[7], Andrew Stauffer[6], Adelheid Galle[5] Stouffer, Daniel[4], Christian[3], Hans[2], Hans[1]) was born November 25, 1899, and died July 23, 1985. He married **Celeste Edith Denlinger**. She was born October 01, 1901.

Children of David Hershey and Celeste Denlinger are:
\+ 2610 i. Private[13] Hershey.
\+ 2611 ii. Vincent Denlinger Hershey, born September 20, 1925.
    2612 iii. Victor Eby Hershey, born April 21, 1927. He married Private Weaver.
    2613 iv. Edith Celeste Hershey, born January 19, 1929. She married Stanley Howard Thomas; born March 21, 1928.

2054. Mary Helen[12] Hershey (Enos Jacob[11], Peter[10], Jacob[9], John[8], Jacob Snavely[7], Andrew Stauffer[6], Adelheid Galle[5] Stouffer, Daniel[4], Christian[3], Hans[2], Hans[1]) was born January 06, 1903. She married **Edwin Guy Ranck**. He was born January 25, 1902, and died February 03, 1932.

Children of Mary Hershey and Edwin Ranck are:
+ 2614 i. Private[13] Ranck.
+ 2615 ii. Lester Hershey Ranck, born April 21, 1924.
+ 2616 iii. Arthur Eby Ranck, born September 06, 1925.
+ 2617 iv. Donald Edwin Ranck, born June 26, 1927.
   2618 v. Enos Raymond Ranck, born December 13, 1929; died August 05, 1930.

2056. Clyde C.[12] Hess (Elizabeth[11] Hershey, Peter[10], Jacob[9], John[8], Jacob Snavely[7], Andrew Stauffer[6], Adelheid Galle[5] Stouffer, Daniel[4], Christian[3], Hans[2], Hans[1]) was born April 22, 1888, and died March 06, 1957. He married **Catherine L. Price**. She was born June 29, 1888.

Child of Clyde Hess and Catherine Price is:
+ 2619 i. Janet Potter[13] Hess, born July 10, 1924.

2057. Harry Hershey[12] Hess (Elizabeth[11] Hershey, Peter[10], Jacob[9], John[8], Jacob Snavely[7], Andrew Stauffer[6], Adelheid Galle[5] Stouffer, Daniel[4], Christian[3], Hans[2], Hans[1]) was born April 01, 1890, and died August 14, 1949. He married **Manilla Tolemie**. She was born May 20, 1898.

Children of Harry Hess and Manilla Tolemie are:
   2620 i. Private[13] Hess.
+ 2621 ii. Rhoda Gregory Hess, born September 12, 1926.

2061. Paul Keene[12] Hershey (Henry Peter[11], Peter[10], Jacob[9], John[8], Jacob Snavely[7], Andrew Stauffer[6], Adelheid Galle[5] Stouffer, Daniel[4], Christian[3], Hans[2], Hans[1]) was born September 06, 1900, and died July 13, 1968. He married **Mabel Corinne Appler**. She was born May 14, 1904, and died December 31, 1987.

Children of Paul Hershey and Mabel Appler are:
+ 2622 i. Richard Henry[13] Hershey, born January 10, 1928.
+ 2623 ii. Paul Kenneth Hershey, born October 14, 1929.
   2624 iii. John Alan Hershey, born June 30, 1931; died September 22, 1958.

2063. Esther Elizabeth[12] Hershey (Martin Eby[11], Peter[10], Jacob[9], John[8], Jacob Snavely[7], Andrew Stauffer[6], Adelheid Galle[5] Stouffer, Daniel[4], Christian[3], Hans[2], Hans[1]) was born May 27, 1905. She married **William Ralph Pennock**. He was born July 18, 1904, and died March 13, 1984.

Children of Esther Hershey and William Pennock are:
   2625 i. Private[13] Pennock.
+ 2626 ii. Private Pennock.
+ 2627 iii. Betty Louise Pennock, born October 18, 1929.

2064. Miriam Clara[12] Hershey (Martin Eby[11], Peter[10], Jacob[9], John[8], Jacob Snavely[7], Andrew Stauffer[6], Adelheid Galle[5] Stouffer, Daniel[4], Christian[3], Hans[2], Hans[1]) was born February 06, 1909, and died June 27, 1998. She married **Donald Fink Rodgers**. He was born May 27, 1905, and died October 24, 1966.

Child of Miriam Hershey and Donald Rodgers is:
+ 2628 i. Private[13] Rodgers.

2065. Elsie D.[12] Hershey (Silas N.[11], Peter[10], Jacob[9], John[8], Jacob Snavely[7], Andrew Stauffer[6], Adelheid Galle[5] Stouffer, Daniel[4], Christian[3], Hans[2], Hans[1]) was born December 24, 1905, and died July 31, 1987. She married **Miles Eby Harsh**. He was born February 26, 1893.

Child of Elsie Hershey and Miles Harsh is:
   2629 i. Private[13] Harsh.

The Relations of Milton Snavely Hershey, 4th Ed.

2066. Frances[12] Hershey (Silas N.[11], Peter[10], Jacob[9], John[8], Jacob Snavely[7], Andrew Stauffer[6], Adelheid Galle[5] Stouffer, Daniel[4], Christian[3], Hans[2], Hans[1]) was born August 30, 1907. She married **Clarence William Stambaugh**. He was born March 01, 1910.

Child of Frances Hershey and Clarence Stambaugh is:
    2630   i.   Private[13] Stambaugh. She married John Harold Retallack; born November 24, 1928.

2067. Lester D.[12] Hershey (Silas N.[11], Peter[10], Jacob[9], John[8], Jacob Snavely[7], Andrew Stauffer[6], Adelheid Galle[5] Stouffer, Daniel[4], Christian[3], Hans[2], Hans[1]) was born February 22, 1910. He married **Mary R. Groff**. She was born March 05, 1924.

Children of Lester Hershey and Mary Groff are:
    2631   i.   Private[13] Hershey.
+   2632   ii.   Private Hershey.

2068. Barbara Elizabeth[12] Hershey (Silas N.[11], Peter[10], Jacob[9], John[8], Jacob Snavely[7], Andrew Stauffer[6], Adelheid Galle[5] Stouffer, Daniel[4], Christian[3], Hans[2], Hans[1]) was born March 24, 1912. She married **Elmer Denlinger Zimmerman**. He was born April 18, 1912.

Children of Barbara Hershey and Elmer Zimmerman are:
+   2633   i.   Private[13] Zimmerman.
+   2634   ii.   Private Zimmerman.
+   2635   iii. Private Zimmerman.

2069. Willis Daniel[12] Hershey (Silas N.[11], Peter[10], Jacob[9], John[8], Jacob Snavely[7], Andrew Stauffer[6], Adelheid Galle[5] Stouffer, Daniel[4], Christian[3], Hans[2], Hans[1]) was born June 26, 1916, and died July 19, 1994. He married **Ella Margaret Newswanger**. She was born October 30, 1918.

Children of Willis Hershey and Ella Newswanger are:
+   2636   i.   Private[13] Hershey.
+   2637   ii.   Private Hershey.
+   2638   iii. Private Hershey.
+   2639   iv. Private Hershey.
+   2640   v.   Private Hershey.
+   2641   vi. Jay Paul Hershey, born April 27, 1941; died November 02, 1996.

2070. Reba L.[12] Hershey (Silas N.[11], Peter[10], Jacob[9], John[8], Jacob Snavely[7], Andrew Stauffer[6], Adelheid Galle[5] Stouffer, Daniel[4], Christian[3], Hans[2], Hans[1]) was born July 09, 1922. She married **Chester B. Nolt**. He was born September 29, 1919.

Children of Reba Hershey and Chester Nolt are:
+   2642   i.   Private[13] Nolt.
+   2643   ii.   Private Nolt.
    2644   iii. Private Nolt.

2071. Doris Mae[12] Hershey (Silas N.[11], Peter[10], Jacob[9], John[8], Jacob Snavely[7], Andrew Stauffer[6], Adelheid Galle[5] Stouffer, Daniel[4], Christian[3], Hans[2], Hans[1]) was born May 11, 1925. She married **(1) Benjamin Franklin Kauffman**. He was born December 15, 1913. She married **(2) Robert Warren Lowry**. He was born March 17, 1920.

Children of Doris Hershey and Benjamin Kauffman are:
+   2645   i.   Private[13] Kauffman.
+   2646   ii.   Private Kauffman.

Child of Doris Hershey and Robert Lowry is:
+   2647   i.   Private[13] Lowry.

2073. Elam Sweigart[12] Horst (Frances Reiff[11] Sweigart, Annie[10] Reiff, Veronica[9] Hershey, John[8], Jacob Snavely[7], Andrew Stauffer[6], Adelheid Galle[5] Stouffer, Daniel[4], Christian[3], Hans[2], Hans[1]) was born January 16, 1890, and died March 23, 1977. He married **(1) Alice Parmer Steffy** November 11, 1911. She was born July 07, 1889, and died November 06, 1952. He married **(2) Rebecca L. Zook** November 25, 1954. She was born May 03, 1919.

Children of Elam Horst and Alice Steffy are:
    2648   i.   Martha Steffy[13] Horst, born July 29, 1912; died August 19, 1912.
+   2649   ii.   Paul Steffy Horst, born July 26, 1914.

+ 2650 iii. William Prichard Horst, born October 03, 1917.
+ 2651 iv. Erma Steffy Horst, born April 25, 1924.
+ 2652 v. Gordon Steffy Horst, born March 30, 1929.

Children of Elam Horst and Rebecca Zook are:
2653 i. Carl Zook[13] Horst, born August 14, 1955. He married Charlene Tiffany September 11, 1976; born March 12, 1955 in California.
2654 ii. Blaine Zook Horst, born October 24, 1957.

2074. Reuben Sweigart[12] Horst (Frances Reiff[11] Sweigart, Annie[10] Reiff, Veronica[9] Hershey, John[8], Jacob Snavely[7], Andrew Stauffer[6], Adelheid Galle[5] Stouffer, Daniel[4], Christian[3], Hans[2], Hans[1]) was born August 14, 1891. He married **Ida Snyder Stoner** November 12, 1914. She was born March 05, 1891, and died November 13, 1978.

Children of Reuben Horst and Ida Stoner are:
2655 i. Ruth Naomi[13] Horst, born September 28, 1915.
2656 ii. Lois Esther Horst, born June 14, 1917.
2657 iii. John Alton Horst, born November 08, 1924.

2075. Amos Sweigart[12] Horst (Frances Reiff[11] Sweigart, Annie[10] Reiff, Veronica[9] Hershey, John[8], Jacob Snavely[7], Andrew Stauffer[6], Adelheid Galle[5] Stouffer, Daniel[4], Christian[3], Hans[2], Hans[1]) was born July 19, 1893, and died January 01, 1963. He married **Nora Snyder Stoner** December 12, 1918. She was born February 12, 1895, and died July 08, 1990.

Children of Amos Horst and Nora Stoner are:
2658 i. John Mark[13] Horst, born December 04, 1919; died February 02, 1935.
2659 ii. James Albert Horst, born August 01, 1926; died February 22, 1930.

2076. Eli Sweigart[12] Horst (Frances Reiff[11] Sweigart, Annie[10] Reiff, Veronica[9] Hershey, John[8], Jacob Snavely[7], Andrew Stauffer[6], Adelheid Galle[5] Stouffer, Daniel[4], Christian[3], Hans[2], Hans[1]) was born January 14, 1896, and died September 23, 1980 in Tampa, FL. He married **(1) Ruth Campbell**. She died April 10, 1962. He married **(2) Elizabeth Oberholtzer** June 19, 1920.

Children of Eli Horst and Ruth Campbell are:
2660 i. Henry Reuben[13] Horst, born June 13, 1944.
2661 ii. Douglas Clyde Horst, born June 06, 1947.
2662 iii. David Campbell Horst, born June 13, 1951.

Children of Eli Horst and Elizabeth Oberholtzer are:
2663 i. Quintis[13] Horst, born August 02, 1924; died September 09, 1932.
2664 ii. Miriam Elizabeth Horst, born August 21, 1927.

2078. Titus Sweigart[12] Horst (Frances Reiff[11] Sweigart, Annie[10] Reiff, Veronica[9] Hershey, John[8], Jacob Snavely[7], Andrew Stauffer[6], Adelheid Galle[5] Stouffer, Daniel[4], Christian[3], Hans[2], Hans[1]) was born May 10, 1899, and died June 17, 1976. He married **Mary Buckwalter Landis** November 24, 1921. She was born January 09, 1899 in Union Grove, Earl Twp, Lanc Co, PA, and died November 18, 1987 in West Earl Twp, Lanc Co, PA.

Children of Titus Horst and Mary Landis are:
2665 i. John Landis[13] Horst, born January 10, 1923.
2666 ii. Ray Ernest Horst, born April 23, 1924.
2667 iii. Martha Frances Horst, born July 22, 1928.
2668 iv. Titus Glenn Horst, born June 06, 1932.

2079. Frances Sweigart[12] Horst (Frances Reiff[11] Sweigart, Annie[10] Reiff, Veronica[9] Hershey, John[8], Jacob Snavely[7], Andrew Stauffer[6], Adelheid Galle[5] Stouffer, Daniel[4], Christian[3], Hans[2], Hans[1]) was born May 23, 1901, and died October 09, 1982. She married **Lehman Herr Lefever** August 04, 1920. He was born February 22, 1898, and died February 11, 1987.

Children of Frances Horst and Lehman Lefever are:
2669 i. Harold Horst[13] Lefever, born July 17, 1921.
2670 ii. Titus Horst Lefever, born April 11, 1923.
2671 iii. Miriam Horst Lefever, born August 18, 1925.
2672 iv. Jay Lehman Lefever, born February 22, 1927.

2673   v.   Merle Horst Lefever, born February 22, 1929.
2674   vi.   Frances Violet Lefever, born September 19, 1933.

2080. Phares Sweigart[12] Horst (Frances Reiff[11] Sweigart, Annie[10] Reiff, Veronica[9] Hershey, John[8], Jacob Snavely[7], Andrew Stauffer[6], Adelheid Galle[5] Stouffer, Daniel[4], Christian[3], Hans[2], Hans[1]) was born March 14, 1903. He married **Magdalena Moseman** December 25, 1929. She was born November 01, 1904.

Children of Phares Horst and Magdalena Moseman are:
2675   i.   Jeanne Loraine[13] Horst, born September 16, 1931.
2676   ii.   Lee Sterling Horst, born April 15, 1934.

2081. Noah Sweigart[12] Horst (Frances Reiff[11] Sweigart, Annie[10] Reiff, Veronica[9] Hershey, John[8], Jacob Snavely[7], Andrew Stauffer[6], Adelheid Galle[5] Stouffer, Daniel[4], Christian[3], Hans[2], Hans[1]) was born June 05, 1905, and died August 07, 1964. He married **Ruth Myer** September 19, 1929. She was born September 01, 1906.

Children of Noah Horst and Ruth Myer are:
2677   i.   Richard M.[13] Horst, born March 30, 1938.
2678   ii.   Dorothy A. Horst, born July 18, 1944.

2083. Walter Sweigart[12] Horst (Frances Reiff[11] Sweigart, Annie[10] Reiff, Veronica[9] Hershey, John[8], Jacob Snavely[7], Andrew Stauffer[6], Adelheid Galle[5] Stouffer, Daniel[4], Christian[3], Hans[2], Hans[1]) was born September 04, 1909. He married **(1) Miriam Mosemann** February 29, 1932. She was born June 27, 1912, and died October 03, 1976. He married **(2) Lucy S. Brubaker** December 13, 1979. She was born November 22, 1932.

Children of Walter Horst and Miriam Mosemann are:
2679   i.   Kenneth Moseman[13] Horst, born January 07, 1933.
2680   ii.   Walter Dale Horst, born January 27, 1936.
2681   iii.   Lois Jean Horst, born April 26, 1942.
2682   iv.   Miriam Darlene Horst, born March 01, 1947.
2683   v.   Janet Elaine Horst, born June 07, 1949.

2084. Ada Sweigart[12] Horst (Frances Reiff[11] Sweigart, Annie[10] Reiff, Veronica[9] Hershey, John[8], Jacob Snavely[7], Andrew Stauffer[6], Adelheid Galle[5] Stouffer, Daniel[4], Christian[3], Hans[2], Hans[1]) was born May 30, 1911 in West Earl Twp, Lanc Co, PA, and died July 03, 1979 in Akron, Lancaster Co, PA. She married **John Landis Weaver** January 07, 1932, son of John Weaver and Magdalena Landis. He was born September 04, 1909 in Earl Twp, Lanc Co, PA, and died April 30, 1991 in Akron, Lancaster Co, PA.

Children of Ada Horst and John Weaver are:
+   2684   i.   Jay Donald[13] Weaver, born April 20, 1933 in Ephrata Twp, Lanc Co, PA.
+   2685   ii.   Arvilla Weaver, born July 21, 1934 in Ephrata Twp, Lanc Co, PA.
+   2686   iii.   Donna Lou Weaver, born July 11, 1942 in Akron, Lancaster Co, PA.
+   2687   iv.   John Eric Weaver, born February 11, 1945 in Ephrata, PA.
       2688   v.   Elizabeth Ann Weaver, born January 01, 1947 in Ephrata Twp, Lanc Co, PA. She married (1) Frank Espich. She married (2) James Mcelhenny June 17, 1972 in Ephrata, PA.
+   2689   vi.   Ronald Lee Weaver, born August 16, 1950 in Ephrata, PA.

2085. Katie Sweigart[12] Horst (Frances Reiff[11] Sweigart, Annie[10] Reiff, Veronica[9] Hershey, John[8], Jacob Snavely[7], Andrew Stauffer[6], Adelheid Galle[5] Stouffer, Daniel[4], Christian[3], Hans[2], Hans[1]) was born May 30, 1911, and died August 20, 1994 in Manheim Twp, Lanc Co, PA. She married **John Kauffman Shenk** June 15, 1930. He was born March 07, 1906 in Penn Twp, Lanc Co, PA, and died December 20, 1986.

Children of Katie Horst and John Shenk are:
2690   i.   Florence LaVerne[13] Shenk, born March 30, 1932.
2691   ii.   Frances Geraldine Shenk, born May 08, 1933.
2692   iii.   John Marlin Shenk, born September 24, 1936.
2693   iv.   Donald Reuben Shenk, born March 17, 1939.

2086. Lloyd Sweigart[12] Horst (Frances Reiff[11] Sweigart, Annie[10] Reiff, Veronica[9] Hershey, John[8], Jacob Snavely[7], Andrew Stauffer[6], Adelheid Galle[5] Stouffer, Daniel[4], Christian[3], Hans[2], Hans[1]) was born August 16, 1913. He married **Alice Virginia Heatwole** February 29, 1936. She was born June 14, 1912, and died January 05, 1997.

Children of Lloyd Horst and Alice Heatwole are:

2694	i.	Joseph Franklin[13] Horst, born March 14, 1938.
2695	ii.	James Daniel Horst, born July 15, 1940.
2696	iii.	Amos David Horst, born October 16, 1941.
2697	iv.	Enos Heatwole Horst, born November 21, 1943.
2698	v.	Rachel Frances Horst, born November 30, 1945.
2699	vi.	Reuben Walter Horst, born August 08, 1947.
2700	vii.	Anna Lois Horst, born November 18, 1950.

2088. Melvin E[12] Burkholder (Abraham H[11], Susan[10] Hershey, Abraham[9], Christian[8], Jacob Snavely[7], Andrew Stauffer[6], Adelheid Galle[5] Stouffer, Daniel[4], Christian[3], Hans[2], Hans[1]) was born January 1909, and died 1971. He married **Marcella Wealand**. She was born January 1910, and died June 1991.

Child of Melvin Burkholder and Marcella Wealand is:
+   2701   i.   Robert Melvin[13] Burkholder, born March 03, 1935.

2097. Jr. Lawrence Webster[12] Fox (Lawrence "[11] Lafayette, Diana[10] Hershey, Henry[9], Martin[8], Henry[7], Andrew Stauffer[6], Adelheid Galle[5] Stouffer, Daniel[4], Christian[3], Hans[2], Hans[1]) was born January 05, 1895, and died November 1969. He married **Bettie Cary** May 15, 1919. She was born September 04, 1898.

Children of Lawrence Fox and Bettie Cary are:
  2702   i.   III Private[13] Fox.
  2703   ii. Private Fox. She married Jr. Private Downs.
  2704   iii. Private Fox. She married Private Fisher.

2098. George Francis[12] Fox (James George[11], Diana[10] Hershey, Henry[9], Martin[8], Henry[7], Andrew Stauffer[6], Adelheid Galle[5] Stouffer, Daniel[4], Christian[3], Hans[2], Hans[1]) was born March 20, 1882 in Derry Township, Dauphin Co., PA, and died November 22, 1956 in Union Deposit, Dauphin Co., PA. He married **(1) Jessica Keene** 1910 in Shanghai, China. She was born Abt. 1887, and died 1933. He married **(2) Mabel Osborne** 1926. She was born Abt. 1887, and died 1945.

Children of George Fox and Jessica Keene are:
  2705   i.   Beverly[13] Fox. She married C.W. Mason.
  2706   ii. Jr. Private Fox.

Child of George Fox and Mabel Osborne is:
  2707   i.   Private[13] Fox.

2099. Robert Thomas[12] Fox (James George[11], Diana[10] Hershey, Henry[9], Martin[8], Henry[7], Andrew Stauffer[6], Adelheid Galle[5] Stouffer, Daniel[4], Christian[3], Hans[2], Hans[1]) was born August 30, 1883 in Derry Township, Dauphin Co., PA, and died October 28, 1966 in Hummelstown, Dauphin Co., PA. He married **Lillie Sophia Walton** November 17, 1914 in Hummelstown, Dauphin Co., PA. She was born November 27, 1888, and died August 28, 1952 in PA.

Children of Robert Fox and Lillie Walton are:
+ 2708   i.   Private[13] Fox.
  2709   ii. Unnamed Fox, born 1916 in Hummelstown, Dauphin Co., PA; died 1916 in Hummelstown, Dauphin Co., PA.
  2710   iii. Jr. Robert Thomas Fox, born June 02, 1916 in Hummelstown, Dauphin Co., PA; died April 28, 1991 in Harrisburg, PA.

2101. Charles Adam[12] Fox (James George[11], Diana[10] Hershey, Henry[9], Martin[8], Henry[7], Andrew Stauffer[6], Adelheid Galle[5] Stouffer, Daniel[4], Christian[3], Hans[2], Hans[1]) was born March 27, 1886 in Derry Township, Dauphin Co., PA, and died January 28, 1954 in Seattle, WA. He married **Sarah Edna Black** April 10, 1912. She was born July 21, 1887, and died October 03, 1982.

Children of Charles Fox and Sarah Black are:
+ 2711   i.   Private[13] Fox.
+ 2712   ii. Private Fox.

2102. John Edward[12] Fox (James George[11], Diana[10] Hershey, Henry[9], Martin[8], Henry[7], Andrew Stauffer[6], Adelheid Galle[5] Stouffer, Daniel[4], Christian[3], Hans[2], Hans[1]) was born May 14, 1887 in Hummelstown, PA, and died October 09, 1967 in Hummelstown, PA. He married **Jeanette Fredricka Bryan** April 12, 1913 in Wilmington, DE. She was born February 07, 1893 in Christ Ch Rectory, Eddington,

The Relations of Milton Snavely Hershey, 4th Ed.

Phil., PA, and died May 29, 1974 in Harrisburg, PA.

Children of John Fox and Jeanette Bryan are:
+ 2713 i. Private[13] Fox.
+ 2714 ii. Private Fox.
   2715 iii. John Edward Fox, born February 01, 1913 in West Chester, PA; died September 20, 1935 in Ellston, MD.
   2716 iv. Webster Fox, born March 14, 1914 in West Chester, PA; died January 23, 1970 in Palmyra, PA. He married (1) Jenny Shay; born Abt. 1919. He married (2) Betty Knoll Snyder; born 1907; died August 23, 1994 in Lincoln, NE.
+ 2717 v. Bryan Fox, born October 05, 1916 in West Chester, PA; died November 17, 1983.
+ 2718 vi. Jeanette Fredricka Fox, born April 03, 1919 in Downingtown, PA; died June 08, 1992 in Hershey, PA.
+ 2719 vii. Dorothy Fox, born July 14, 1922 in Downingtown, Chester Co., PA; died February 07, 1989.
+ 2720 viii. Marjorie Fox, born June 12, 1924 in Downingtown, Chester Co., PA; died August 22, 1997 in Landsdale, PA.
+ 2721 ix. Fox Mary Eliza " Molly, born September 16, 1928 in Downingtown, PA; died February 21, 2002 in Harrisburg, PA.
   2722 x. George Henry Fox, born February 05, 1932 in Sand Beach, Dauphin Co, PA; died June 21, 1932 in Sand Beach, Dauphin Co, PA.

2104. Mary Virginia[12] Fox (James George[11], Diana[10] Hershey, Henry[9], Martin[8], Henry[7], Andrew Stauffer[6], Adelheid Galle[5] Stouffer, Daniel[4], Christian[3], Hans[2], Hans[1]) was born June 29, 1891 in Hummelstown, PA, and died August 09, 1964 in Vancouver, BC. She married **(1) Paul Jay Sykes** November 30, 1917 in Lutheran Church, Hummelstown, PA. He was born 1889, and died October 12, 1918. She married **(2) Bertrand Bampton** June 18, 1924 in Seattle, WA. He was born December 23, 1885 in LaChute, Quebec, Canada, and died April 07, 1965 in Vancouver, BC.

Child of Mary Fox and Paul Sykes is:
+ 2723 i. Jr. Private[13] Sykes.

Children of Mary Fox and Bertrand Bampton are:
+ 2724 i. Private[13] Bampton.
   2725 ii. Private Bampton. She married (1) Lawrence Robertson Munroe; born July 10, 1923; died January 12, 1970. She married (2) Private Belhouse.

2106. Thomas G.[12] Fox (James George[11], Diana[10] Hershey, Henry[9], Martin[8], Henry[7], Andrew Stauffer[6], Adelheid Galle[5] Stouffer, Daniel[4], Christian[3], Hans[2], Hans[1]) was born February 08, 1896 in Downingtown, Chester Co., PA, and died July 15, 1945 in Philadelphia, PA. He married **Kathryn Romaine Fasnacht** April 19, 1920 in Union Deposit, Dauphin Co., PA. She was born March 07, 1901, and died October 21, 1977.

Children of Thomas Fox and Kathryn Fasnacht are:
+ 2726 i. Private[13] Fox.
+ 2727 ii. Private Fox.
+ 2728 iii. Private Fox.
+ 2729 iv. Private Fox.
   2730 v. Private Fox. She married Jr. Private Mascutti.
+ 2731 vi. Jr. Thomas G. Fox, born February 19, 1921; died November 28, 1977.
+ 2732 vii. Virginia Romaine Fox, born July 20, 1922; died April 11, 1981.
+ 2733 viii. Diana Lucille Fox, born April 15, 1934; died March 03, 1996 in Sunbury, PA.

2107. Sara Diana[12] Fox (James George[11], Diana[10] Hershey, Henry[9], Martin[8], Henry[7], Andrew Stauffer[6], Adelheid Galle[5] Stouffer, Daniel[4], Christian[3], Hans[2], Hans[1]) was born January 05, 1899 in Caln Township, Chester Co., PA, and died January 29, 1989 in Seattle, WA. She married **Julian Hawthorne Bair** June 13, 1928 in Tacoma, WA. He was born September 01, 1897, and died May 08, 1952.

Child of Sara Fox and Julian Bair is:
+ 2734 i. Private[13] Bair.

2108. Jr. James George[12] Fox (James George[11], Diana[10] Hershey, Henry[9], Martin[8], Henry[7], Andrew Stauffer[6], Adelheid Galle[5] Stouffer, Daniel[4], Christian[3], Hans[2], Hans[1]) was born April 20, 1905 in Caln Township, Chester Co., PA, and died January 23, 1975 in Newark, Essex Co., NJ. He married **Edna Snyder Ziegler** September 15, 1930 in Philadelphia, PA. She was born May 05, 1905 in Philadelphia, PA, and died July 22, 1985.

Children of James Fox and Edna Ziegler are:
+ 2735 i. III Private[13] Fox.
+ 2736 ii. Private Fox.

2109. Charles Kunkel[12] Fox (John Edgar "[11] Eshenauer, Diana[10] Hershey, Henry[9], Martin[8], Henry[7], Andrew Stauffer[6], Adelheid Galle[5] Stouffer, Daniel[4], Christian[3], Hans[2], Hans[1]) He married **Gladford Doris Machamer**.

Children of Charles Fox and Gladford Machamer are:
2737 i. Private[13] Fox.
2738 ii. Private Fox.

2111. Rachel Virginia[12] Fox (John Edgar "[11] Eshenauer, Diana[10] Hershey, Henry[9], Martin[8], Henry[7], Andrew Stauffer[6], Adelheid Galle[5] Stouffer, Daniel[4], Christian[3], Hans[2], Hans[1]) She married **Frederick W. Uihlein**.

Children of Rachel Fox and Frederick Uihlein are:
2739 i. Jr. Private[13] Uihlein.
2740 ii. Private Uihlein.

2112. Private[12] Fox (John Edgar "[11] Eshenauer, Diana[10] Hershey, Henry[9], Martin[8], Henry[7], Andrew Stauffer[6], Adelheid Galle[5] Stouffer, Daniel[4], Christian[3], Hans[2], Hans[1]) She married **David Jenkins Gerhardt**.

Children of Private Fox and David Gerhardt are:
2741 i. Private[13] Gerhardt.
2742 ii. Private Gerhardt.

2115. Jr. John Howard[12] Gay (Adelaide[11] Fox, Diana[10] Hershey, Henry[9], Martin[8], Henry[7], Andrew Stauffer[6], Adelheid Galle[5] Stouffer, Daniel[4], Christian[3], Hans[2], Hans[1]) was born January 19, 1889, and died March 05, 1947. He married **Margaret Rowland**. She was born Abt. 1894, and died January 05, 1945.

Children of John Gay and Margaret Rowland are:
+ 2743 i. Private[13] Gay.
+ 2744 ii. III Private Gay.
2745 iii. Margaret Gay, born Abt. 1915; died Abt. 1916.

2116. Gertrude[12] Gay (Adelaide[11] Fox, Diana[10] Hershey, Henry[9], Martin[8], Henry[7], Andrew Stauffer[6], Adelheid Galle[5] Stouffer, Daniel[4], Christian[3], Hans[2], Hans[1]) was born December 14, 1891, and died June 17, 1970. She married **(1) Harry Foster Lee** October 29, 1911. He was born Abt. 1886, and died Abt. 1914. She married **(2) Arthur Charles Friedel** October 18, 1921. He was born 1885, and died November 1969.

Child of Gertrude Gay and Harry Lee is:
+ 2746 i. Jr. Private[13] Lee.

Children of Gertrude Gay and Arthur Friedel are:
+ 2747 i. Jr. Private[13] Friedel.
2748 ii. Private Friedel. He married Private Benham.

2118. Katherine[12] Nissley (Caroline Lee[11] Fox, Diana[10] Hershey, Henry[9], Martin[8], Henry[7], Andrew Stauffer[6], Adelheid Galle[5] Stouffer, Daniel[4], Christian[3], Hans[2], Hans[1]) was born July 07, 1895, and died November 08, 1977. She married **III Samuel Arnold** April 04, 1919. He was born August 16, 1892, and died April 06, 1977.

Children of Katherine Nissley and Samuel Arnold are:
2749 i. Private[13] Arnold.
+ 2750 ii. II Private Arnold.

2119. Emilie Karthaus[12] Fox (George Hershey[11], Diana[10] Hershey, Henry[9], Martin[8], Henry[7], Andrew Stauffer[6], Adelheid Galle[5] Stouffer, Daniel[4], Christian[3], Hans[2], Hans[1]) She married **Albert Nathan Wolff**.

Children of Emilie Fox and Albert Wolff are:
+ 2751 i. Private[13] Wolff.

+   2752   ii.   Private Wolff.

2120. Karolyn Diana[12] Fox (George Hershey[11], Diana[10] Hershey, Henry[9], Martin[8], Henry[7], Andrew Stauffer[6], Adelheid Galle[5] Stouffer, Daniel[4], Christian[3], Hans[2], Hans[1]) She married **James Alfred Taylor**.

Children of Karolyn Fox and James Taylor are:
+   2753   i.   Private[13] Taylor.
+   2754   ii.   Private Taylor.
+   2755   iii.   Jr. James Alfred Taylor, born July 10, 1932; died July 24, 1960.

2122. John A.[12] Tritt (Nancy[11] Nickey, Samuel[10], Christiana[9] Hastetter, Anna Barbara[8] Stauffer, Johannes[7], Daniel[6] Stouffer, Christian[5] Stauffer, Daniel[4] Stouffer, Christian[3], Hans[2], Hans[1]) was born September 23, 1847, and died September 18, 1929 in Buried Centerville, Pa.. He married **Jennie E. Tobias** WFT Est. 1862-1894. She was born July 25, 1845, and died October 17, 1920 in Buried Centerville, Pa..

Children of John Tritt and Jennie Tobias are:
      2756   i.   Alice E.[13] Tritt, born WFT Est. 1864-1893; died WFT Est. 1870-1975.
      2757   ii.   Edgar P. Tritt, born WFT Est. 1864-1893; died WFT Est. 1871-1972.
      2758   iii.   Florence E. Tritt, born WFT Est. 1864-1893; died WFT Est. 1870-1975.
      2759   iv.   Maud T. Tritt, born WFT Est. 1864-1893; died WFT Est. 1870-1975.
      2760   v.   Melvin J. Tritt, born WFT Est. 1864-1893; died WFT Est. 1871-1972.
      2761   vi.   Clarence E. Tritt, born WFT Est. 1864-1893; died WFT Est. 1871-1972.

2123. Samuel John[12] Tritt (Nancy[11] Nickey, Samuel[10], Christiana[9] Hastetter, Anna Barbara[8] Stauffer, Johannes[7], Daniel[6] Stouffer, Christian[5] Stauffer, Daniel[4] Stouffer, Christian[3], Hans[2], Hans[1]) was born 1849, and died 1917. He married **Mary Lacey** WFT Est. 1868-1891. She was born 1852, and died 1901.

Child of Samuel Tritt and Mary Lacey is:
      2762   i.   Clarence Ziegler[13] Tritt, born April 30, 1884; died 1891 in Huntsdale, Pa..

2124. Lydia Jane[12] Tritt (Nancy[11] Nickey, Samuel[10], Christiana[9] Hastetter, Anna Barbara[8] Stauffer, Johannes[7], Daniel[6] Stouffer, Christian[5] Stauffer, Daniel[4] Stouffer, Christian[3], Hans[2], Hans[1]) was born August 10, 1851 in Huntsdale, Pa, and died April 25, 1900 in Greason, Pa. buried Presbyterian Churchyard Dickesen, Pa.. She married **J. Marion Sheaffer** WFT Est. 1864-1889. He was born May 15, 1843 in Huntsdale, Pa., and died November 24, 1927 in Carlisle, buried Westminster Cem..

Children of Lydia Tritt and J. Sheaffer are:
      2763   i.   Bertie F.[13] Sheaffer, born January 03, 1867; died February 07, 1862 in buried Pa. German Baptist
                      Churchyard, Huntsdale, Pa..
+   2764   ii.   Alice Margaret Sheaffer, born October 26, 1869 in Craighead, Cumberlan Co, Pa.; died September 07,
                      1930 in Dickesen, Pa..
+   2765   iii.   Charles M. Sheaffer, born January 14, 1874 in Huntsdale, Pa.; died October 02, 1965 in Utica, New
                      York buried St. Agnes Cem, Utica, NY.

2125. Elizabeth[12] Tritt (Nancy[11] Nickey, Samuel[10], Christiana[9] Hastetter, Anna Barbara[8] Stauffer, Johannes[7], Daniel[6] Stouffer, Christian[5] Stauffer, Daniel[4] Stouffer, Christian[3], Hans[2], Hans[1]) was born October 23, 1854, and died WFT Est. 1872-1948. She married **Thomas Ferree** WFT Est. 1870-1900. He was born December 28, 1852, and died WFT Est. 1872-1943.

Child of Elizabeth Tritt and Thomas Ferree is:
      2766   i.   Alice[13] Ferree, born WFT Est. 1872-1899; died WFT Est. 1878-1982. She married Mr. Bowman.

2127. Peter Stough[12] Tritt (Nancy[11] Nickey, Samuel[10], Christiana[9] Hastetter, Anna Barbara[8] Stauffer, Johannes[7], Daniel[6] Stouffer, Christian[5] Stauffer, Daniel[4] Stouffer, Christian[3], Hans[2], Hans[1]) was born March 08, 1860, and died June 03, 1896 in (of Pnuemonia) buried Huntsdale, Pa.. He married **Annie McMonus** WFT Est. 1877-1893. She was born 1861, and died 1953.

Child of Peter Tritt and Annie McMonus is:
      2767   i.   Alice Bell[13] Tritt, born September 20, 1881; died 1883 in buried Huntsdale, Pa.

2132. Mary Elizabeth[12] Goodhart (Charlotte[11] Farner, Elizabeth[10] Owens, Peter[9] Ober, Elizabeth[8] Stauffer, Johannes[7], Daniel[6] Stouffer, Christian[5] Stauffer, Daniel[4] Stouffer, Christian[3], Hans[2], Hans[1]) was born June 06, 1851, and died November 13, 1892 in buried Prospect Hill Cem, Newville, pa.. She married **James Alexander Mitten** WFT Est. 1868-1888. He was born 1855, and died 1913 in buried

Prospect Hill Cem, Newville, Pa..

Children of Mary Goodhart and James Mitten are:
- 2768 i. Clarence Edward[13] Mitten, born April 06, 1870; died September 09, 1954 in Clairmont Farm.
- 2769 ii. William L. Mitten, born WFT Est. 1871-1891; died WFT Est. 1877-1975.
- 2770 iii. Charlotte Mitten, born 1880; died 1947 in buried Presbyterian Churchyard, Dickensen, Pa.. She married Charles A. Wardecker WFT Est. 1896-1924; born 1877; died 1958 in buried Presbyterian Churchyard, Dickensen, Pa..
- 2771 iv. Agnes Alverdia Mitten, born September 18, 1892; died December 11, 1983. She married Miley Le Mont Miller WFT Est. 1912-1939; born 1872; died 1953.

2133. Agnes Bordilla[12] Goodhart (Charlotte[11] Farner, Elizabeth[10] Owens, Peter[9] Ober, Elizabeth[8] Stauffer, Johannes[7], Daniel[6] Stouffer, Christian[5] Stauffer, Daniel[4] Stouffer, Christian[3], Hans[2], Hans[1]) was born October 20, 1853, and died 1940. She married **William H. Brandt** WFT Est. 1874-1909. He was born 1862, and died 1936.

Child of Agnes Goodhart and William Brandt is:
- + 2772 i. Edna[13] Brandt, born WFT Est. 1865-1888; died WFT Est. 1888-1975.

2134. Calvin[12] Goodhart (Charlotte[11] Farner, Elizabeth[10] Owens, Peter[9] Ober, Elizabeth[8] Stauffer, Johannes[7], Daniel[6] Stouffer, Christian[5] Stauffer, Daniel[4] Stouffer, Christian[3], Hans[2], Hans[1]) was born March 11, 1856, and died February 19, 1941 in buried Spring Hill Cem, Shippensburg, Pa.. He married **Anna Bell Allen** 1878. She was born 1859, and died 1920 in buried Spring Hill Cem, Shippensburg, Pa..

Children of Calvin Goodhart and Anna Allen are:
- 2773 i. Henry[13] Goodhart, born WFT Est. 1877-1903; died WFT Est. 1883-1983.
- 2774 ii. Lettie Goodhart, born WFT Est. 1877-1903; died WFT Est. 1882-1986.
- 2775 iii. Allan Goodhart, born WFT Est. 1877-1903; died WFT Est. 1883-1983.
- 2776 iv. Dellie Goodhart, born WFT Est. 1877-1903; died WFT Est. 1882-1986.
- 2777 v. Theodore Goodhart, born WFT Est. 1877-1903; died WFT Est. 1883-1983.
- 2778 vi. Ray Goodhart, born WFT Est. 1877-1903; died WFT Est. 1883-1983.
- 2779 vii. Carl Goodhart, born WFT Est. 1877-1903; died WFT Est. 1883-1983.
- 2780 viii. Martha Goodhart, born WFT Est. 1877-1903; died WFT Est. 1882-1986.
- 2781 ix. Wilbur Goodhart, born WFT Est. 1877-1903; died WFT Est. 1883-1983.

2135. Theodore[12] Goodhart (Charlotte[11] Farner, Elizabeth[10] Owens, Peter[9] Ober, Elizabeth[8] Stauffer, Johannes[7], Daniel[6] Stouffer, Christian[5] Stauffer, Daniel[4] Stouffer, Christian[3], Hans[2], Hans[1]) was born April 24, 1858 in Penn Twp, Cumberland Co, and died December 26, 1945 in buried Dickeson, Pa.. He married **Alice Margaret Sheaffer** November 14, 1889 in Mechanicsburg, Pa., daughter of J. Sheaffer and Lydia Tritt. She was born October 26, 1869 in Craighead, Cumberlan Co, Pa., and died September 07, 1930 in Dickesen, Pa..

Children of Theodore Goodhart and Alice Sheaffer are:
- + 2782 i. Pearle Viola[13] Goodhart, born January 31, 1891 in Greason, Pa.; died July 30, 1972 in Carlisle, Pa. Buried Ashland Cem, Carlisle, Pa..
- 2783 ii. Marian Esther Goodhart, born April 25, 1893 in Greason, Pa.; died March 12, 1896 in Greason, Pa. of Diptheria buried Pres. Churchyard, Dickesen, Pa..
- 2784 iii. Charles Floyd Goodhart, born March 28, 1897 in Greason, Pa.; died June 26, 1974 in buried in Upper Cem, Newville, Pa.. He married Mary Grace Weaver July 19, 1932; born October 12, 1901; died March 19, 1974 in Carlisle, Pa. Buried Upper Cem, Newville, Pa..
- + 2785 iv. Margaret Elizabeth Alice Goodhart, born June 27, 1899 in Greason, Pa; died June 28, 1994 in Union Twp, Leb. Co, buried Ft.Indiantown Gap National Cem.
- + 2786 v. Theodore Riley Goodhart, born May 12, 1902 in Kerrsville, Pa.; died December 17, 1936 in Carlisle, Pa. buried Westminster Cem, near Carlisle, Pa..
- 2787 vi. Flora Pauline Goodhart, born December 14, 1904 in Kerrsville, Pa.; died November 27, 1976 in Plainfield, Pa. buried Westminster Cem, near Carlisle, Pa.. He married Lawrence Delmar Calaman February 21, 1931 in Greason, Pa.; born October 07, 1899 in Boiling Springs, Pa; died January 20, 1965 in Carlisle, Pa. buried Westminster Cem, near Carlisle, Pa..
- + 2788 vii. Clarence Eugene Goodhart, born Private.
- + 2789 viii. Lester Sheaffer Goodhart, born Private.

2137. David Grier McClelland[12] Goodhart (Charlotte[11] Farner, Elizabeth[10] Owens, Peter[9] Ober, Elizabeth[8] Stauffer, Johannes[7], Daniel[6] Stouffer, Christian[5] Stauffer, Daniel[4] Stouffer, Christian[3], Hans[2], Hans[1]) was born July 21, 1865, and died November 09, 1931 in buried Lutheran Cem, Centerville, Pa.. He married **Margaret Jane Smith** November 20, 1886. She was born WFT Est. 1851-1875, and died WFT Est. 1902-1963 in buried Lutheran Cem, Centerville, Pa..

Children of David Goodhart and Margaret Smith are:
+ 2790 i. Lewis[13] Goodhart, born Private.
  2791 ii. Lorretta Goodhart, born Private. She married Fulton Kelse Private; born WFT Est. 1882-1902; died WFT Est. 1916-1988.
  2792 iii. Clair Goodhart, born Private. She married Chambers.
  2793 iv. Della Goodhart, born Private.
  2794 v. Ada Goodhart, born Private.
  2795 vi. Marion Goodhart, born Private.
  2796 vii. Argus Goodhart, born Private.
  2797 viii. Ray Goodhart, born Private.

2140. Nora Griffin[12] Goodhart (Susannah[11] Farner, Elizabeth[10] Owens, Peter[9] Ober, Elizabeth[8] Stauffer, Johannes[7], Daniel[6] Stouffer, Christian[5] Stauffer, Daniel[4] Stouffer, Christian[3], Hans[2], Hans[1]) was born WFT Est. 1843-1870, and died WFT Est. 1865-1953.

Children of Nora Griffin Goodhart are:
  2798 i. Lester[13], born WFT Est. 1865-1903; died WFT Est. 1875-1981.
  2799 ii. Frances, born WFT Est. 1865-1903; died WFT Est. 1875-1981.

2141. Elizabeth Trough[12] Goodhart (Susannah[11] Farner, Elizabeth[10] Owens, Peter[9] Ober, Elizabeth[8] Stauffer, Johannes[7], Daniel[6] Stouffer, Christian[5] Stauffer, Daniel[4] Stouffer, Christian[3], Hans[2], Hans[1]) was born WFT Est. 1843-1870, and died WFT Est. 1865-1953.

Child of Elizabeth Trough Goodhart is:
  2800 i. Rhoda[13], born WFT Est. 1865-1903; died WFT Est. 1883-1984. She married Christopher Oiler WFT Est. 1883-1935; born WFT Est. 1858-1901; died WFT Est. 1883-1979.

2142. Newton[12] Goodhart (Susannah[11] Farner, Elizabeth[10] Owens, Peter[9] Ober, Elizabeth[8] Stauffer, Johannes[7], Daniel[6] Stouffer, Christian[5] Stauffer, Daniel[4] Stouffer, Christian[3], Hans[2], Hans[1]) was born 1855, and died 1918. He married **Anna** WFT Est. 1874-1902. She was born 1861, and died 1929.

Children of Newton Goodhart and Anna are:
  2801 i. Ruth[13] Goodhart, born WFT Est. 1877-1903; died WFT Est. 1883-1986.
  2802 ii. Mildred Goodhart, born WFT Est. 1877-1903; died WFT Est. 1883-1986.
  2803 iii. George Goodhart, born 1891; died 1894.

2144. Emma Barbara[12] Ober (David[11], Isaac Huntsberger[10], Christian[9], Elizabeth[8] Stauffer, Johannes[7], Daniel[6] Stouffer, Christian[5] Stauffer, Daniel[4] Stouffer, Christian[3], Hans[2], Hans[1]) was born 1856, and died 1931. She married **Edward M Hursh**. He was born 1854, and died 1942.

Children of Emma Ober and Edward Hursh are:
  2804 i. Clarence B[13] Hursh, born 1874; died 1943. He married Emma B Hursh; born Abt. 1875; died 1948.
+ 2805 ii. Lillie E Hursh, born 1876.
+ 2806 iii. Agnes E Hursh, born 1877.
+ 2807 iv. Edna R Hursh, born 1879; died 1943.
+ 2808 v. Jay B Hursh, born 1885; died 1930.

2145. Catherine Rebecca[12] Ober (David[11], Isaac Huntsberger[10], Christian[9], Elizabeth[8] Stauffer, Johannes[7], Daniel[6] Stouffer, Christian[5] Stauffer, Daniel[4] Stouffer, Christian[3], Hans[2], Hans[1]) was born April 29, 1857, and died February 09, 1943 in Highspire, PA. She married **(1) William Malcolm Duncan**. He was born Abt. 1855, and died Bef. 1880. She married **(2) Franklin LeFevere Wolf** 1884. He was born December 29, 1849 in York County, PA, and died March 02, 1933 in Highspire, PA.

Children of Catherine Ober and William Duncan are:
  2809 i. William Malcolm[13] Duncan, born Abt. 1875. He married Asenath Stephens September 08, 1902 in New York, NY; born Abt. 1880.
+ 2810 ii. Margaret Ann Duncan, born May 24, 1877; died July 14, 1953 in Hummelstown, PA.

Children of Catherine Ober and Franklin Wolf are:
+ 2811 i. Clarence R[13] Wolf, born 1886 in Highspire, PA; died Abt. 1970 in Millville, NJ.
  2812 ii. Anna B Wolf, born 1888; died in Hummelstown, PA. She married Joseph B Hershey; born July 09, 1884; died September 28, 1966 in Hummelstown, PA.

	2813	iii.	David Ober Wolf, born 1890 in Highspire, PA; died October 09, 1975 in Highspire, PA.
+			
	2814	iv.	Nellie I Wolf, born 1891; died Bef. 1910.
+	2815	v.	Mary Estelle Wolf, born 1893 in Highspire, PA; died 1930 in Highspire, PA.
+	2816	vi.	Franklin Earl Wolf, born January 15, 1897 in Highspire, PA; died December 07, 1958 in Highspire, PA.
+	2817	vii.	George Edgar Wolf, born January 15, 1897; died May 1977 in Hannibal, MO.
+	2818	viii.	Catherine Rebecca Wolf, born April 30, 1898 in Highspire, PA; died June 10, 1986 in Highspire, PA.

2146. Benjamin Franklin[12] Ober (David[11], Isaac Huntsberger[10], Christian[9], Elizabeth[8] Stauffer, Johannes[7], Daniel[6] Stouffer, Christian[5] Stauffer, Daniel[4] Stouffer, Christian[3], Hans[2], Hans[1]) was born February 17, 1859, and died March 30, 1938. He married **Rachel H Nisley**. She was born 1857, and died 1946.

Child of Benjamin Ober and Rachel Nisley is:
+ 2819   i.   Fannie O[13] Ober, born 1894.

2147. Agnes Eda[12] Ober (David[11], Isaac Huntsberger[10], Christian[9], Elizabeth[8] Stauffer, Johannes[7], Daniel[6] Stouffer, Christian[5] Stauffer, Daniel[4] Stouffer, Christian[3], Hans[2], Hans[1]) was born 1861, and died in Noblesville, IN. She married **William Murphy**. He was born Abt. 1860.

Child of Agnes Ober and William Murphy is:
+ 2820   i.   Eda R[13] Murphy, born Abt. 1885.

2148. Annie Elizabeth[12] Ober (David[11], Isaac Huntsberger[10], Christian[9], Elizabeth[8] Stauffer, Johannes[7], Daniel[6] Stouffer, Christian[5] Stauffer, Daniel[4] Stouffer, Christian[3], Hans[2], Hans[1]) was born July 10, 1862, and died October 22, 1948 in Penbrook. She married **John Duncan**. He was born 1859, and died 1906.

Children of Annie Ober and John Duncan are:
+ 2821   i.   Rachael Agnes[13] Duncan, born March 16, 1881; died August 19, 1963 in Oberlin, PA.
+ 2822   ii. Alvid O Duncan, born 1883; died 1933.
+ 2823   iii. Katherine M Duncan, born 1887.
+ 2824   iv. Anna B Duncan, born 1897; died 1958.

2152. David W[12] Ober (David[11], Isaac Huntsberger[10], Christian[9], Elizabeth[8] Stauffer, Johannes[7], Daniel[6] Stouffer, Christian[5] Stauffer, Daniel[4] Stouffer, Christian[3], Hans[2], Hans[1]) was born 1871, and died 1938. He married **Mary Dubert**. She was born 1875.

Children of David Ober and Mary Dubert are:
+ 2825   i.   Wilbur C[13] Ober, born Abt. 1900.
+ 2826   ii. David W Ober, Jr, born Abt. 1910.
+ 2827   iii. John D Ober, born Abt. 1910.

2153. Isaac Newton[12] Ober (David[11], Isaac Huntsberger[10], Christian[9], Elizabeth[8] Stauffer, Johannes[7], Daniel[6] Stouffer, Christian[5] Stauffer, Daniel[4] Stouffer, Christian[3], Hans[2], Hans[1]) was born July 29, 1872, and died May 1970 in Indianapolis, IN. He married **Millmy Strauss**. She was born Abt. 1880.

Children of Isaac Ober and Millmy Strauss are:
+ 2828   i.   Cecil S[13] Ober, born Abt. 1900.
+ 2829   ii. Merritt L Ober, born May 11, 1900; died July 1982 in Indianapolis, IN.
+ 2830   iii. Arden G Ober, born Abt. 1900.
  2831   iv. Melissa G Ober, born Abt. 1900.
+ 2832   v.   C Kiefer Ober, born Abt. 1900.

2154. Bernard Farren[12] Ober (David[11], Isaac Huntsberger[10], Christian[9], Elizabeth[8] Stauffer, Johannes[7], Daniel[6] Stouffer, Christian[5] Stauffer, Daniel[4] Stouffer, Christian[3], Hans[2], Hans[1]) was born 1873. He married **Nellie M Ramsey**. She was born Abt. 1875.

Children of Bernard Ober and Nellie Ramsey are:
  2833   i.   Arthur[13] Ober, born Abt. 1900.
  2834   ii. Harold Ober, born Abt. 1900. He married Bonnie K Perry; born Abt. 1900.

2156. Florence May[12] Ober (David[11], Isaac Huntsberger[10], Christian[9], Elizabeth[8] Stauffer, Johannes[7], Daniel[6] Stouffer, Christian[5] Stauffer, Daniel[4] Stouffer, Christian[3], Hans[2], Hans[1]) was born 1875, and died in Penbrook. She married **George Smith**. He was born Abt.

1870.

Children of Florence Ober and George Smith are:
+ 2835 i. Edna M[13] Smith, born 1891.
+ 2836 ii. Emma R Smith, born 1893.
   2837 iii. Ober Smith, born 1895.
   2838 iv. Anna G Smith, born 1898.
   2839 v. George L Smith, born 1900; died 1918.

2157. Barbara Estella[12] Ober (David[11], Isaac Huntsberger[10], Christian[9], Elizabeth[8] Stauffer, Johannes[7], Daniel[6] Stouffer, Christian[5] Stauffer, Daniel[4] Stouffer, Christian[3], Hans[2], Hans[1]) was born 1876, and died in Michigan. She married **Charles Hubert**. He was born Abt. 1870.

Children of Barbara Ober and Charles Hubert are:
+ 2840 i. Frank[13] Hubert, born 1904.
+ 2841 ii. Mildred M Hubert, born 1906.
   2842 iii. Edgar C Hubert, born 1909.
+ 2843 iv. Helen B Hubert, born 1912.

2158. Annie[12] Ober (Michael Cramer[11], Michael[10], Henry[9], Elizabeth[8] Stauffer, Johannes[7], Daniel[6] Stouffer, Christian[5] Stauffer, Daniel[4] Stouffer, Christian[3], Hans[2], Hans[1]) was born 1856 in Lancaster Cty., PA, and died 1929 in Lancaster Cty., PA. She married **William A. Morning**. He was born 1851, and died 1934 in Lancaster Cty., PA.

Child of Annie Ober and William Morning is:
+ 2844 i. Mary L.[13] Morning, born October 05, 1889 in Elizabethtown, PA; died August 1973 in Harrisburg, PA.

2161. Moses Heagly[12] Ober (Moses Ruhl[11], Christian Longnecker[10], David S[9], Elizabeth[8] Stauffer, Johannes[7], Daniel[6] Stouffer, Christian[5] Stauffer, Daniel[4] Stouffer, Christian[3], Hans[2], Hans[1]) was born January 31, 1860 in Rapho Twsp, PA, and died February 25, 1916. He married **Elizabeth S Myers**. She was born January 04, 1861, and died April 06, 1932.

Children of Moses Ober and Elizabeth Myers are:
   2845 i. Moses M.[13] Ober, born April 05, 1883; died March 22, 1968. He married Lottie Gottschall April 1907; born May 17, 1882; died February 14, 1970.
   2846 ii. Mary Ann Or Sue Ober, born February 17, 1885 in Rapho Twsp, PA.
   2847 iii. Daniel M Ober, born October 01, 1886; died January 13, 1963. He married Minnie Sauder September 19, 1916.
   2848 iv. Elmer M. Ober, born November 23, 1888 in Rapho Twsp, PA; died August 04, 1946. He married Minnie Johnson March 1922; born November 30, 1895; died September 1987.
+ 2849 v. Daisy Meyers Ober, born April 30, 1892 in Rapho Twsp, PA; died March 06, 1964.
   2850 vi. Harry F. Ober, born April 06, 1896 in Rapho Twsp, PA; died September 06, 1971. He married Stella Kaufer; born June 09, 1891; died May 24, 1952.
+ 2851 vii. Stella M Ober, born August 17, 1898; died January 09, 1965.
   2852 viii. George A Ober, born October 07, 1900; died April 23, 1937. He married Mary Smith April 1922; born March 02, 1903.

2166. Mary Jane[12] Richardson (Sarah Rebecca[11] Bowers, Susannah[10] Ober, Henry[9], Veronica " Frany "[8] Stauffer, Johannes[7], Daniel[6] Stouffer, Christian[5] Stauffer, Daniel[4] Stouffer, Christian[3], Hans[2], Hans[1]) was born October 22, 1846 in Lancaster County, Pennsylvania, and died February 23, 1912 in Upland, California. She married **John Wesley Stauffer** September 24, 1867 in Pine Creek, Ogle County, Illinois. He was born January 24, 1846 in Finley, Ohio, and died February 08, 1923 in Phoenix, Arizona.

Children of Mary Richardson and John Stauffer are:
+ 2853 i. Ella May[13] Stauffer, born June 23, 1868 in Pine Creek, Illinois; died October 04, 1927 in Upland, California.
   2854 ii. William E. Stauffer, born November 29, 1869 in Pine Creek, Illinois.
+ 2855 iii. Andrew Grant Stauffer, born November 16, 1871 in Pine Creek, Illinois; died November 06, 1953.
   2856 iv. John Milton Stauffer, born August 30, 1873 in Hamilton, Kansas; died October 15, 1873 in Hamilton, Kansas.
   2857 v. Stephen Stauffer, born November 23, 1874 in Pine Creek, Illinois; died March 26, 1879 in Sedgwick, Kansas.
+ 2858 vi. Elias Richardson Stauffer, born July 23, 1877 in Pine Creek, Illinois; died March 30, 1940 in Prescott, Arizona.
+ 2859 vii. Charles Albert Stauffer, born March 23, 1880 in Sedgwick, Kansas.

| | 2860 | viii. | Ray Franklin Stauffer, born February 11, 1882 in Sedgwick, Kansas; died December 12, 1939 in Phoenix, Arizona. |
+ | 2861 | ix. | Sara Rebecca Stauffer, born January 02, 1884 in Sedgwick, Kansas; died March 30, 1970 in Phoenix, Arizona.
+ | 2862 | x. | Mary Lemmie Ann Stauffer, born May 27, 1886 in Sedgwick, Kansas; died January 12, 1976 in Tuscon, Arizona.
+ | 2863 | xi. | Anna Pearl Stauffer, born March 17, 1889 in Sedgwick, Kansas.
| 2864 | xii. | Beulah Bell Stauffer, born November 20, 1892 in Glendale, Arizona; died June 1969 in Phoenix, Arizona. She married (1) Bart Thomas; died February 10, 1970 in Phoenix, Arizona. She married (2) William Baird McLemore November 29, 1921 in Phoenix, Arizona.

2167. Susan Ann[12] Richardson (Sarah Rebecca[11] Bowers, Susannah[10] Ober, Henry[9], Veronica " Frany "[8] Stauffer, Johannes[7], Daniel[6] Stouffer, Christian[5] Stauffer, Daniel[4] Stouffer, Christian[3], Hans[2], Hans[1]) was born May 11, 1849 in Lancaster County, Pennsylvania, and died January 02, 1877 in Pine Creek, Illinois. She married **Jacob S. Shelly** December 09, 1869 in Ogle County, Illinois. He was born April 14, 1847 in Blair County, Pennsylvania, and died May 09, 1929 in Wheaton, Illinois.

Children of Susan Richardson and Jacob Shelly are:
+ 2865   i.   Ellis Clinton[13] Shelly, born January 22, 1872 in Haldane, Illinois; died December 30, 1939 in Chicago, Illinois.
  2866   ii. John Willis Shelly, born September 01, 1873 in Shannon, Illinois; died April 17, 1907 in Shannon, Illinois.
  2867   iii. Infant Son, born September 01, 1873 in Shannon, Illinois; died September 01, 1873 in Shannon, Illinois.

2169. Rebecca Jane[12] Richardson (Sarah Rebecca[11] Bowers, Susannah[10] Ober, Henry[9], Veronica " Frany "[8] Stauffer, Johannes[7], Daniel[6] Stouffer, Christian[5] Stauffer, Daniel[4] Stouffer, Christian[3], Hans[2], Hans[1]) was born April 10, 1853 in Stark County, Ohio, and died October 18, 1934 in Polo, Illinois. She married **Jerimiah Washington Trump** March 09, 1876 in Pine Creek Twp.-Ogle County, Illinois. He was born June 09, 1855 in Canton, Ohio, and died July 01, 1936 in Polo, Illinois.

Children of Rebecca Richardson and Jerimiah Trump are:
  2868   i.   Mary May[13] Trump, born May 09, 1877 in Olgle County, IL.; died September 30, 1879 in Polo, IL..
+ 2869   ii. Emma Elizabeth Trump, born October 27, 1879 in Sedgwick, Kansas; died in Polo, Illinois.
+ 2870   iii. Oliver Garfield Trump, born November 11, 1880 in Sedgwick, Kansas; died March 18, 1956 in Polo, Illinois (Fairmont Cemetery).
+ 2871   iv. Oscar A. Trump, born December 13, 1881 in Sedgwick, Kansas; died August 16, 1948 in Polo, Illinois (Buffalo Grove Cemetery).
  2872   v.   Bessie Pearl Trump, born November 04, 1883 in Sedgwick, Kansas; died in Polo, Illinois - Fairmount Cemetery. She married Guy Elmer Donaldson April 20, 1902 in Polo, Illinois; born April 14, 1872 in Polo, Illinois.
+ 2873   vi. John Henry Trump, born July 30, 1887 in Polo, Illinois; died December 01, 1935 in Hutchinson, Kansas.
  2874   vii. Clarence R. Trump, born October 05, 1894 in Sedgwick, Kansas; died November 28, 1927 in Polo, Illinois.

2170. Sarah B.[12] Richardson (Sarah Rebecca[11] Bowers, Susannah[10] Ober, Henry[9], Veronica " Frany "[8] Stauffer, Johannes[7], Daniel[6] Stouffer, Christian[5] Stauffer, Daniel[4] Stouffer, Christian[3], Hans[2], Hans[1]) was born July 09, 1855 in Stark County, Ohio, and died March 02, 1894 in Sedgwick, Kansas. She married **Elias L. Snyder** January 15, 1874 in Polo, Illinois. He was born July 26, 1851 in Lehigh County, Pennsylvania, and died January 15, 1944.

Children of Sarah Richardson and Elias Snyder are:
+ 2875   i.   Goldie May[13] Snyder, born November 17, 1874 in Polo, Illinois.
+ 2876   ii. Sarah Jane Snyder, born October 27, 1876 in Polo, Illinois.
+ 2877   iii. Harriet Lucretia Snyder, born September 05, 1882 in Sedgwick, Kansas.

2171. Andrew Jackson[12] Richardson (Sarah Rebecca[11] Bowers, Susannah[10] Ober, Henry[9], Veronica " Frany "[8] Stauffer, Johannes[7], Daniel[6] Stouffer, Christian[5] Stauffer, Daniel[4] Stouffer, Christian[3], Hans[2], Hans[1]) was born June 05, 1859 in Canton, Stark County, Ohio, and died December 11, 1931 in Belle Plaine, Kansas. He married **Ada Ann Lucretia Martin** October 05, 1880 in Plum Grove, Kansas. She was born May 01, 1860 in Easley, South Carolina, and died September 18, 1927 in Belle Plaine, Kansas.

Children of Andrew Richardson and Ada Martin are:
  2878   i.   Emily Pearl[13] Richardson, born September 10, 1881 in Sedgwick, Kansas; died March 25, 1885 in Sedgwick, Kansas.
+ 2879   ii. Stephen Andrew Richardson, born August 13, 1882 in Sedgwick, Kansas.
  2880   iii. Sarah Ruby Richardson, born October 01, 1882; died July 19, 1883 in Sedgwick, Kansas.

	2881	iv.	Ada Lucretia Richardson, born December 26, 1883 in Sedgwick, Kansas.
+	2881	iv.	Ada Lucretia Richardson, born December 26, 1883 in Sedgwick, Kansas.
+	2882	v.	Mattie Beulah Richardson, born November 15, 1885 in Sedgwick, Kansas.
+	2883	vi.	Melville Jackson Richardson, born March 25, 1889 in Sedgwick, Kansas.
+	2884	vii.	Margaret Ella Blanch Richardson, born May 09, 1892 in Newton, Kansas.
+	2885	viii.	Eva Beatrice Richardson, born October 20, 1894 in Sedgwick, Kansas.
	2886	ix.	Alice Vivian Richardson, born June 13, 1898 in Rondo, Missouri; died October 03, 1898 in Elkhorn, Missouri.
+	2887	x.	Leslie Martin Richardson, born April 13, 1902 in Corbin, Kansas.

2172. Stephen E.[12] Richardson (Sarah Rebecca[11] Bowers, Susannah[10] Ober, Henry[9], Veronica " Frany "[8] Stauffer, Johannes[7], Daniel[6] Stouffer, Christian[5] Stauffer, Daniel[4] Stouffer, Christian[3], Hans[2], Hans[1]) was born March 10, 1862 in Stark County, Ohio, and died April 04, 1929 in Topeka, KS.. He married **Florence Anna Cafferty** October 26, 1883 in Sedgwick, Kansas. She was born August 17, 1865 in Owego, New York.

Children of Stephen Richardson and Florence Cafferty are:

	2888	i.	Florence Mildred[13] Richardson, born March 14, 1885 in Sedgwick, Kansas.
+	2888	i.	Florence Mildred[13] Richardson, born March 14, 1885 in Sedgwick, Kansas.
+	2889	ii.	Sydney Robert Richardson, born September 12, 1887 in Sedgwick, Kansas.
	2890	iii.	Harold Richardson, born October 06, 1889 in Newton, Kansas; died February 03, 1899 in Perry, Oklahoma.
+	2891	iv.	Stephen Roscoe Richardson, born June 01, 1895 in Perry, Oklahoma.
	2892	v.	Reginold Richardson, born December 18, 1896 in Perry, Oklahoma; died December 25, 1896 in Perry, Oklahoma.
	2893	vi.	Dolores Elaine Richardson, born September 13, 1898 in Perry, Oklahoma; died February 02, 1902 in Perry, Oklahoma.
+	2894	vii.	Charlotte B. Richardson, born November 05, 1900 in Perry, Oklahoma.

2173. Harriet May[12] Richardson (Sarah Rebecca[11] Bowers, Susannah[10] Ober, Henry[9], Veronica " Frany "[8] Stauffer, Johannes[7], Daniel[6] Stouffer, Christian[5] Stauffer, Daniel[4] Stouffer, Christian[3], Hans[2], Hans[1]) was born September 14, 1864 in Canton, Stark County, Ohio, and died November 17, 1944 in Dayton, Montgomery County, Ohio. She married **Zelorah J. Line** December 15, 1881 in Newton, Kansas. He was born July 02, 1857 in Sidney, Shelby County, Ohio, and died January 13, 1921 in Germantown, Montgomery County, Ohio.

Children of Harriet Richardson and Zelorah Line are:

	2895	i.	Fauntis May[13] Line, born August 08, 1883 in Kingman, Kansas; died August 15, 1883 in Newton, Kansas.
	2895	i.	Fauntis May[13] Line, born August 08, 1883 in Kingman, Kansas; died August 15, 1883 in Newton, Kansas.
+	2896	ii.	Stephen Clyde Line, born March 08, 1885 in Kingman, Kansas; died January 12, 1959 in Preble County, Ohio.
+	2897	iii.	Mabel Beatrice Line, born August 16, 1887 in Jetmore, Kansas; died May 02, 1960 in Dayton, Montgomery County, Ohio.
+	2898	iv.	Golda Gladys Line, born September 02, 1892 in Kingman, Kansas; died April 1977.
+	2899	v.	Sara Margaret Line, born August 21, 1896 in Kingman, Kansas; died May 1978 in Dayton, Montgomery County, Ohio.

2175. Martha[12] Richardson (Sarah Rebecca[11] Bowers, Susannah[10] Ober, Henry[9], Veronica " Frany "[8] Stauffer, Johannes[7], Daniel[6] Stouffer, Christian[5] Stauffer, Daniel[4] Stouffer, Christian[3], Hans[2], Hans[1]) was born August 26, 1870 in Ogle County, Illinois, and died February 22, 1921 in Sedgwick, Kansas. She married **Albert W. Haynes** January 22, 1890 in Sedgwick, Kansas. He was born May 06, 1869 in Granville, Ohio.

Children of Martha Richardson and Albert Haynes are:

	2900	i.	Agatha E.[13] Haynes, born October 21, 1890 in Sedgwick, Kansas.
+	2900	i.	Agatha E.[13] Haynes, born October 21, 1890 in Sedgwick, Kansas.
	2901	ii.	Ethel Haynes, born May 30, 1892 in Bancroft, Missouri; died September 23, 1935 in Newton, Kansas. She married Cecil E. Dick March 26, 1916 in Sedgwick, Kansas; born October 08, 1888 in Sedwick, Kansas; died July 1953 in Newton, Kansas.
+	2902	iii.	Dorothy Haynes, born April 30, 1895 in Humesville, Missouri.
+	2903	iv.	Marjorie Haynes, born December 15, 1898 in Sedgwick, Kansas.
	2904	v.	Alberta Haynes, born September 12, 1903 in Sedgwick, Kansas. She married (1) Everett McMurray; died June 25, 1929 in Little Rock, Arkansas. She married (2) Rev. Charles Hanna June 29, 1939 in Little Roch, Arkansas; born March 26, 1910 in Canton, Ohio.
	2905	vi.	Josephine Haynes, born April 14, 1906 in Sedgwick, Kansas; died July 04, 1931 in Traverse, Michigan.

2182. Mary Ann[12] Lesher (David[11], Barbara[10] Ober, Michael[9], Veronica " Frany "[8] Stauffer, Johannes[7], Daniel[6] Stouffer, Christian[5] Stauffer, Daniel[4] Stouffer, Christian[3], Hans[2], Hans[1]) was born June 13, 1866, and died May 29, 1946. She married **James William Level**.

He was born 1863 in Wisconsin.

Children of Mary Lesher and James Level are:
- 2906   i.   Unknown[13] Level.
- 2907   ii.   Annie Eliza Level, born March 25, 1888. She married William Pultz.
- 2908   iii.   Frank Marshall Level, born July 27, 1890.
- + 2909   iv.   Burgess Coleman Level, born October 21, 1892.
- + 2910   v.   Cloyd Irwin Level, born May 23, 1895.
- 2911   vi.   Ida Mae Level, born May 08, 1899.
- + 2912   vii.   John Howard Level, born February 06, 1909 in Odebolt, Iowa; died September 06, 1949 in Martinez, California.

2183. Naomi Jane[12] Lesher (David[11], Barbara[10] Ober, Michael[9], Veronica " Frany "[8] Stauffer, Johannes[7], Daniel[6] Stouffer, Christian[5] Stauffer, Daniel[4] Stouffer, Christian[3], Hans[2], Hans[1]) was born August 27, 1867, and died February 11, 1946. She married **Charles F. Starr** 1890.

Children of Naomi Lesher and Charles Starr are:
- 2913   i.   Verne E.[13] Starr.
- 2914   ii.   Ronald(Unknown) Starr.
- 2915   iii.   Mabel Starr, born 1927.

2184. David Alfred[12] Diehl (Catherine A.[11] Ober, Jacob[10], Michael[9], Veronica " Frany "[8] Stauffer, Johannes[7], Daniel[6] Stouffer, Christian[5] Stauffer, Daniel[4] Stouffer, Christian[3], Hans[2], Hans[1]) was born May 1852 in Pennsylvania, and died 1920 in Kasson Township. He married **(1) Belenia Simon** January 03, 1875 in Wood County, Ohio. She was born March 06, 1852 in Bloom Township, Wood County, Ohio, and died November 11, 1884 in Bloom Township, Wood County, Ohio. He married **(2) Amanda Alice Borough** May 06, 1888 in Wood County, Ohio. She was born 1867 in Ohio, and died December 07, 1946 in Grand Rapids, Michigan.

Marriage Notes for David Diehl and Amanda Borough:
[Henry Ober 1742.ged]

_STATMARRIED
_STATMARRIED

Children of David Diehl and Belenia Simon are:
- 2916   i.   Howard B.[13] Deihl.
- + 2917   ii.   Myrtle Liliom D. Diehl, born April 17, 1877 in Pennsylvania; died April 05, 1931 in Findlay, Hancock County, Ohio.
- + 2918   iii.   James Alfred Deihl, born February 23, 1880 in Bloom Township, Wood County, Ohio; died March 15, 1944 in Pandora, Wood County, Ohio.
- + 2919   iv.   Harvey A. Deihl, born June 06, 1881 in Wood County, Ohio; died Aft. 1931.
- + 2920   v.   Gideon S. Deihl, born December 27, 1882 in Bloom Township, Wood County, Ohio; died Aft. 1944.

Children of David Diehl and Amanda Borough are:
- + 2921   i.   Zelda F.[13] Diehl, born May 1890 in Wood County, Ohio.
- + 2922   ii.   Percy Ellsworth Diehl, born November 18, 1893 in Wood County, Ohio; died August 01, 1987 in Traverse City, Michigan.
- 2923   iii.   Winifred N. Diehl, born October 1898 in Wood County, Ohio; died February 18, 1914 in Belmont County, Ohio.
- 2924   iv.   Virginia May Diehl, born June 27, 1900 in Wood County, Ohio; died October 13, 1998 in Hudsonville, Michigan. She married (1) John Gebraad; born April 18, 1890; died March 1977 in Grand Rapids, Kent County, Michigan. She married (2) Quincy Edward Boughey II Abt. 1920; born 1895; died 1922 in Grand Rapids, Kent County, Michigan.

2186. Ida M.[12] Diehl (Catherine A.[11] Ober, Jacob[10], Michael[9], Veronica " Frany "[8] Stauffer, Johannes[7], Daniel[6] Stouffer, Christian[5] Stauffer, Daniel[4] Stouffer, Christian[3], Hans[2], Hans[1]) was born June 17, 1858 in Chambersburg, Franklin County, Pennsylvania, and died June 11, 1935 in Bloom Township, Wood County, Ohio. She married **Adam Carbaugh** December 01, 1885 in Hancock County, Ohio. He was born October 01, 1858 in Middle Spring, Shippensburg Township, Cumberland County, Pennsylvania, and died March 23, 1928 in Bloomdale, Bloom Township, Wood County, Ohio.

Marriage Notes for Ida Diehl and Adam Carbaugh:
[Henry Ober 1742.ged]

_STATMARRIED

Child of Ida Diehl and Adam Carbaugh is:
- 2925   i.   Unknown[13] Carbaugh.

2189. John[12] Reuben, Diehl (Catherine A.[11] Ober, Jacob[10], Michael[9], Veronica " Frany "[8] Stauffer, Johannes[7], Daniel[6] Stouffer, Christian[5] Stauffer, Daniel[4] Stouffer, Christian[3], Hans[2], Hans[1]) was born 1866 in Pennsylvania, and died Aft. 1935 in Ohio. He married **Georgiann Unknown**.

Marriage Notes for John Reuben and Georgiann Unknown:
[Henry Ober 1742.ged]

_STATMARRIED

Children of John Reuben and Georgiann Unknown are:
- 2926   i.   Unknown[13] Deihl.
- 2927   ii.   Unknown Deihl.
- 2928   iii. Unknown Deihl.
- 2929   iv.   Unknown Deihl.

2193. Kathryn[12] Diehl (Catherine A.[11] Ober, Jacob[10], Michael[9], Veronica " Frany "[8] Stauffer, Johannes[7], Daniel[6] Stouffer, Christian[5] Stauffer, Daniel[4] Stouffer, Christian[3], Hans[2], Hans[1]) was born Abt. 1875 in Pennsylvania, and died Aft. 1935. She married **Henry D. LeGron** October 06, 1896 in Wood County, Ohio. He died Abt. 1916 in Toledo, Lucas County, Ohio.

Marriage Notes for Kathryn Diehl and Henry LeGron:
[Henry Ober 1742.ged]

_STATMARRIED

Children of Kathryn Diehl and Henry LeGron are:
- 2930   i.   Unknown[13] LeGron.
- 2931   ii.   Unknown LeGron.
- 2932   iii. Unknown LeGron.
- 2933   iv.   Unknown LeGron.

2194. Isaac[12] Brubaker (Isaac[11], Christian[10], Elizabeth[9] Stauffer, Christian[8], Henry Jacob[7], Hans[6], Christian[5], Daniel[4] Stouffer, Christian[3], Hans[2], Hans[1]) was born 1857 in Lebannon County, Pennsylvania, and died 1939 in Unknown. He married **Sarah Royer**. She was born Abt. 1860 in Pennsylvania, and died in Unknown.

Child of Isaac Brubaker and Sarah Royer is:
- 2934   i.   Warren W.[13] Brubaker, born Abt. 1890 in Pennsylvania; died in Unknown.

2195. Mary Brubaker[12] Kreider (Susanna[11] Brubaker, Christian[10], Elizabeth[9] Stauffer, Christian[8], Henry Jacob[7], Hans[6], Christian[5], Daniel[4] Stouffer, Christian[3], Hans[2], Hans[1]) was born October 30, 1840 in Campbelltown, Lebanon County, Pennsylvania, and died July 02, 1912 in Campbelltown, Lebanon County, Pennsylvania. She married **John Funk Kreider**. He was born October 01, 1838 in Fairland, Lebanon County, Pennsylvania, and died June 26, 1880 in Campbelltown, Lebanon County, Pennsylvania.

Child of Mary Kreider and John Kreider is:
- 2935   i.   Henry[13] Kreider, born January 10, 1873 in Campbelltown, Lebanon County, Pennsylvania; died April 22, 1947 in Campbelltown, Lebanon County, Pennsylvania.

2196. Ezra[12] Brubaker (Christian[11], Christian[10], Elizabeth[9] Stauffer, Christian[8], Henry Jacob[7], Hans[6], Christian[5], Daniel[4] Stouffer, Christian[3], Hans[2], Hans[1]) was born 1845, and died Bef. 1880. He married **Serena Longenecker**. She was born 1850, and died Bef. 1880.

Child of Ezra Brubaker and Serena Longenecker is:
- + 2936   i.   Allen L[13] Brubaker, born 1868; died Aft. 1930.

2199. Mary[12] Breitenstein (Magdalena[11] Brubaker, Peter[10], Elizabeth[9] Stauffer, Christian[8], Henry Jacob[7], Hans[6], Christian[5], Daniel[4] Stouffer, Christian[3], Hans[2], Hans[1]) was born August 22, 1851 in South Lebanon Township, Lancaster County, Pennsylvania, and died March 17, 1921 in Myerstown, Lebanon County, Pennsylvania. She married **John Koehler** May 16, 1874. He was born March 22, 1851 in Elizabeth Township, Lancaster County, Pennsylvania, and died June 02, 1936 in Myerstown, Lebanon County, Pennsylvania.

Child of Mary Breitenstein and John Koehler is:

2937 i. Clayton[13] Koehler, born May 08, 1877 in South Lebanon Township, Lancaster County, Pennsylvania; died June 15, 1953 in Cleona, Lebanon County, Pennsylvania.

2206. Carolyn[12] Ickes (Nancy[11] Stoffer, Louis J[10], Jacob[9], Jacob[8] Stauffer, Henry Jacob[7], Hans[6], Christian[5], Daniel[4] Stouffer, Christian[3], Hans[2], Hans[1]) was born December 24, 1867, and died February 02, 1956 in Stark Cty, Ohio. She married **Howard H. Stoffer**, son of Lewis Stoffer and Amanda Dice. He was born January 15, 1869 in Columbiana Cty, Ohio, and died September 05, 1934 in Stark Cty Ohio.

Children of Carolyn Ickes and Howard Stoffer are:
- 2938 i. Alveida[13] Stoffer, born August 16, 1891 in Columbiana Cty, Ohio.
- 2939 ii. Emmett Stoffer, born July 28, 1893 in Columbiana Cty, Ohio.
- 2940 iii. Ida Stoffer, born July 1895; died April 20, 1903.
- 2941 iv. Mauda Stoffer, born April 22, 1897 in Columbiana Co Ohio.
- 2942 v. Mabel Stoffer, born July 23, 1899 in Columbiana Cty, Ohio.

2207. Nancy[12] Ruff (Mary Ann[11] Stoffer, Louis J[10], Jacob[9], Jacob[8] Stauffer, Henry Jacob[7], Hans[6], Christian[5], Daniel[4] Stouffer, Christian[3], Hans[2], Hans[1]) was born August 28, 1854 in Columbiana County, Ohio, and died March 06, 1930 in Columbiana County, Ohio. She married **James Little Scott** March 23, 1882 in Columbiana County, Ohio. He was born August 06, 1855 in Columbiana County, Ohio, and died February 12, 1946 in Columbiana County, Ohio.

Children of Nancy Ruff and James Scott are:
- + 2943 i. John C[13] Scott, born December 12, 1882 in Columbiana County, Ohio; died December 06, 1971 in Columbiana County, Ohio.
- + 2944 ii. Ralph L Scott, born April 12, 1889 in Columbiana County, Ohio; died 1988 in Columbiana County, Ohio.
- 2945 iii. Aruthur G Scott, born September 08, 1891 in Columbiana County, Ohio; died November 24, 1983 in Columbiana County, Ohio. He married Anna Mary Hoffman.
- + 2946 iv. Mary A Scott, born June 04, 1894 in Columbiana County, Ohio; died October 17, 1982 in Columbiana County, Ohio.
- + 2947 v. Ruth Isabel Scott, born January 04, 1898 in Columbiana County, Ohio; died October 15, 1924 in Columbiana County, Ohio.

2219. Howard H.[12] Stoffer (Lewis Jr[11], Louis J[10], Jacob[9], Jacob[8] Stauffer, Henry Jacob[7], Hans[6], Christian[5], Daniel[4] Stouffer, Christian[3], Hans[2], Hans[1]) was born January 15, 1869 in Columbiana Cty, Ohio, and died September 05, 1934 in Stark Cty Ohio. He married **Carolyn Ickes**, daughter of William Ickes and Nancy Stoffer. She was born December 24, 1867, and died February 02, 1956 in Stark Cty, Ohio.

Children are listed above under (2206) Carolyn Ickes.

2220. Ida J.[12] Stoffer (Lewis Jr[11], Louis J[10], Jacob[9], Jacob[8] Stauffer, Henry Jacob[7], Hans[6], Christian[5], Daniel[4] Stouffer, Christian[3], Hans[2], Hans[1]) was born June 12, 1870 in Columbiana Co Ohio, and died March 15, 1973 in West View Manor, Wooster, Ohio. She married **William W. Stroup** June 04, 1891 in Columbiana Co Ohio. He was born April 20, 1866 in Columbiana Cty Ohio, and died February 13, 1931 in Columbiana Cty Ohio.

Marriage Notes for Ida Stoffer and William Stroup:
[chrststauffer1663.ged]

[DATA FILE.FBK.FTW]

_DETS13 Feb 1931Ohio

Children of Ida Stoffer and William Stroup are:
- + 2948 i. Earl[13] Stroup, born May 28, 1892 in Columbiana County, Ohio; died May 22, 1979 in Shreve, Wayne County, Ohio.
- + 2949 ii. Nellie F. Stroup, born September 26, 1896 in Columbiana County, Ohio; died February 05, 1986 in Copeland Oaks Nursing Home, Sebring, Ohio.

2221. Walter George[12] Stoffer (Lewis Jr[11], Louis J[10], Jacob[9], Jacob[8] Stauffer, Henry Jacob[7], Hans[6], Christian[5], Daniel[4] Stouffer, Christian[3], Hans[2], Hans[1]) was born May 13, 1872 in Columbiana Cty, Ohio, and died May 14, 1950 in Columbiana Cty, Ohio. He married **Odessa May Weaver** October 12, 1893 in Columbiana Cty, Ohio. She was born February 20, 1874 in Columbiana Cty, Ohio, and died

The Relations of Milton Snavely Hershey, 4th Ed.

October 07, 1943 in Columbiana Cty, Ohio.

Marriage Notes for Walter Stoffer and Odessa Weaver:
[chrststauffer1663.ged]

[DATA FILE.FBK.FTW]

[

_DETS7 Oct 1943Columbiana County, OhioFamily Member sJim StofferCencus RecordsFa mily Bible

Children of Walter Stoffer and Odessa Weaver are:
+   2950   i.   Inez Genesta[13] Stoffer, born February 27, 1897 in Columbiana Cty, Ohio; died August 09, 1970 in Alliance, Ohio.
+   2951   ii.   Virgil Forest Stoffer, born July 24, 1899 in Columbiana Cty, Ohio; died January 16, 1984 in Copeland Oaks Retirement Center, Sebring, Ohio.
+   2952   iii.   Beulah Fern Stoffer, born March 05, 1903 in Columbiana Cty, Ohio; died May 15, 1973 in Eustis, Florida.
    2953   iv.   Erma Armada Stoffer, born April 24, 1906 in Columbiana Cty, Ohio; died May 21, 1982 in Columbiana Cty, Ohio. She married Virgil Walton Jackson February 12, 1927 in Columbiana Cty, Ohio; born October 20, 1905 in Columbiana Cty, Ohio; died February 27, 1999 in Alliance, Ohio.

Marriage Notes for Erma Stoffer and Virgil Jackson:
[chrststauffer1663.ged]

[DATA FILE.FBK.FTW]

_DETS21 May 1982Homeworth, Columbiana County, Ohio

+   2954   v.   Dorothy Ada Stoffer, born February 11, 1912 in Columbiana County, Homeworth Ohio.

2223. Mary Catherine[12] Stoffer (Lewis Jr[11], Louis J[10], Jacob[9], Jacob[8] Stauffer, Henry Jacob[7], Hans[6], Christian[5], Daniel[4] Stouffer, Christian[3], Hans[2], Hans[1]) was born May 03, 1878 in Columbiana Co Ohio, and died April 07, 1970 in Minerva, Stark Co Ohio. She married **Jay Alexander** March 06, 1900 in Columbiana Co Ohio. He died July 22, 1958 in Minerva, Stark Cty Ohio.

Marriage Notes for Mary Stoffer and Jay Alexander:
[chrststauffer1663.ged]

[DATA FILE.FBK.FTW]

[STOFFER FAMILY !!.GED]

[test2.FTW]

_DETS22 Jul 1 958Minerva, Stark County, Ohio[STOFFERS.GED]

[STOFFER FAMILY !!.GED]

[te st2.FTW]

_DETS22 Jul 1958Minerva, Stark County, Ohio[STOFFERS.GED]

[STOFF ER FAMILY !!.GED]

[test2.FTW]

_DETS22 Jul 1958Minerva, Stark County, Ohi

Child of Mary Stoffer and Jay Alexander is:
    2955   i.   Herbert "Jack"[13] Alexander.

2224. Albert Lewis[12] Stoffer (Lewis Jr[11], Louis J[10], Jacob[9], Jacob[8] Stauffer, Henry Jacob[7], Hans[6], Christian[5], Daniel[4] Stouffer, Christian[3], Hans[2], Hans[1]) was born May 03, 1881 in Columbiana Co Ohio, and died April 19, 1982 in Copeland Oaks Nursing Home,

Sebring, Ohio. He married **Ada louella Stroup** March 29, 1900 in Columbiana Co Ohio. She was born February 11, 1880 in Columbiana Co Ohio, and died May 13, 1958 in Columbiana Co Ohio.

Marriage Notes for Albert Stoffer and Ada Stroup:
[chrststauffer1663.ged]

[DATA FILE.FBK.FTW]

[STOFFER FAMILY !!.GED]

[test2.FTW]

_DETS13 May 1 958Homeworth, Columbiana County, Ohio[STOFFERS.GED]

[STOFFER FAMILY !!.GED]

[test2.FTW]

_DETS13 May 1958Homeworth, Columbiana County, Ohio[STOFFERS. GED]

[STOFFER FAMILY !!.GED]

[test2.FTW]

_DETS13 May 1958Homeworth, C olumbiana County, Ohio

Child of Albert Stoffer and Ada Stroup is:
    2956   i.   Lela Catherine[13] Stoffer, born June 30, 1900 in Columbiana Cty, Ohio. She married Kenneth Cope.

2230. Peter[12] Stoffer (Peter[11], Samuel[10], Jacob[9], Jacob[8] Stauffer, Henry Jacob[7], Hans[6], Christian[5], Daniel[4] Stouffer, Christian[3], Hans[2], Hans[1]) was born August 1862 in Ohio. He married **Sorama Unknown**. She was born August 1863 in Ohio.

Child of Peter Stoffer and Sorama Unknown is:
    2957   i.   Carl T[13] Stoffer.

2236. David[12] Stoffer (Jacob L[11], Samuel[10], Jacob[9], Jacob[8] Stauffer, Henry Jacob[7], Hans[6], Christian[5], Daniel[4] Stouffer, Christian[3], Hans[2], Hans[1]) was born September 1861, and died 1919 in Ohio. He married **Louisa C Buchs**. She was born 1861, and died 1943 in Ohio.

Children of David Stoffer and Louisa Buchs are:
    2958   i.   Earl[13] Stoffer.
    2959   ii.   Edward Stoffer.
    2960   iii.   John A Stoffer, born 1881 in Ohio; died Bef. 1962.
+   2961   iv.   Frank Stoffer, born December 31, 1886 in North Georgetown Ohio, Columbiana Co; died April 25, 1982 in Alliance Ohio.
+   2962   v.   Harry B Stoffer, born March 10, 1898 in North Georgetown Ohio, Columbiana Co.

2240. John[12] Stoffer (Jacob L[11], Samuel[10], Jacob[9], Jacob[8] Stauffer, Henry Jacob[7], Hans[6], Christian[5], Daniel[4] Stouffer, Christian[3], Hans[2], Hans[1]) was born June 1870 in Columbiana Co Ohio, and died November 04, 1918 in Columbiana Co Ohio. He married **Elizabeth Catherine Ruff**. She was born August 25, 1885 in Columbiana Co Ohio, Knox Twp, and died May 15, 1974 in Westlake, Mahoning Co Ohio.

Children of John Stoffer and Elizabeth Ruff are:
    2963   i.   Thelma R[13] Stoffer. She married Unknown Barnes.
    2964   ii.   Otis R Stoffer.
    2965   iii.   Leland L Stoffer.

2255. Homer E[12] Stoffer (Samuel Jr[11], Samuel[10], Jacob[9], Jacob[8] Stauffer, Henry Jacob[7], Hans[6], Christian[5], Daniel[4] Stouffer, Christian[3], Hans[2], Hans[1]) was born February 27, 1880 in Columbiana Cty, Ohio, and died January 24, 1954 in Ohio. He married **Leola M Stroup**. She was born May 13, 1882 in Homeworth, Columbiana Cty, Ohio, and died May 21, 1956 in Ohio.

Child of Homer Stoffer and Leola Stroup is:
    2966   i.   Raymond[13] Stoffer, born August 24, 1910 in Paris Ohio; died October 06, 1992 in Ohio. He married Wilma S Sukosd; born October 09, 1912 in Canton Ohio, Stark Co; died November 20, 1999 in Ohio.

2264. Cynthia Idella[12] Stoffer (John Jacob[11], John[10], Jacob[9], Jacob[8] Stauffer, Henry Jacob[7], Hans[6], Christian[5], Daniel[4] Stouffer, Christian[3], Hans[2], Hans[1]) was born November 13, 1872, and died March 16, 1953 in Bellville Ohio, Richland Co. She married **William Franklin Gearhart** November 04, 1891 in Bellville Ohio, Richland Co. He was born November 23, 1860, and died October 12, 1933 in Bellville Ohio, Richland Co.

Children of Cynthia Stoffer and William Gearhart are:
- 2967   i.   Mable Althea[13] Gearhart, born February 09, 1893; died November 05, 1896.
- 2968   ii. Gladys Estella Gearhart, born May 15, 1895; died November 21, 1972. She married George Irving Armstrong December 20, 1914.
- 2969   iii. Ralph Elretus Gearhart, born February 17, 1897; died October 06, 1962. He married (1) Bessie Bell Page. He married (2) Josephine J Maglott September 01, 1920.
- 2970   iv. John Fredrick Gearhart, born October 04, 1899.
- 2971   v.   Lyle Franklin Gearhart, born September 08, 1902; died February 27, 1973. He married Bertha Etta Spiesterbach November 08, 1924.
- + 2972 vi. Dayle Kermit Gearhart, born August 22, 1905 in Ohio, Richland Co; died January 12, 1976 in Ohio, Richland Co.
- 2973   vii. Vance Leon Gearhart, born December 21, 1906.
- 2974   viii. Mary Elizabeth Gearhart, born October 19, 1908; died November 20, 1975. She married Wilbur Ray Bowers October 27, 1928.
- 2975   ix. Carroll Gearhart, born November 29, 1910.
- 2976   x.   Geneva Lucille Gearhart, born June 11, 1913 in Bellville Ohio, Richland Co; died May 27, 1978 in Mansfeild Ohio, Richland Co. She married Harry Thomas Robinson March 12, 1931 in Johnsville, Ohio.
- 2977   xi. Mildred Louise Gearhart, born November 03, 1915 in Bellville Ohio, Richland Co; died August 23, 2001 in Ohio. She married Virgile Lewis Schroeder April 18, 1936 in Johnsville, Ohio.

2275. Ada[12] Stoffer (Levi[11], George[10], Jacob[9], Jacob[8] Stauffer, Henry Jacob[7], Hans[6], Christian[5], Daniel[4] Stouffer, Christian[3], Hans[2], Hans[1]) was born March 02, 1871 in Columbiana Cty, Ohio, and died December 14, 1950. She married **(1) Adolph Moser**. She married **(2) David Keister**. He was born January 1856 in Ohio, and died 1947. She married **(3) Emmet Newcomer**.

Child of Ada Stoffer and Adolph Moser is:
- + 2978 i.   Stella[13] Moser, born May 30, 1890 in Columbiana County, Ohio; died May 27, 1907.

Child of Ada Stoffer and David Keister is:
- 2979   i.   Wilson[13] Keister, born July 1895 in Ohio.

Child of Ada Stoffer and Emmet Newcomer is:
- 2980   i.   Pearlie[13] Newcomer.

2276. Laurance L[12] Stoffer (Levi[11], George[10], Jacob[9], Jacob[8] Stauffer, Henry Jacob[7], Hans[6], Christian[5], Daniel[4] Stouffer, Christian[3], Hans[2], Hans[1]) was born August 29, 1874 in Columbiana Cty, Ohio, and died October 11, 1947. He married **Jessie Bell Harding** 1895. She was born October 29, 1875, and died May 22, 1938.

Children of Laurance Stoffer and Jessie Harding are:
- 2981   i.   Carl Levy[13] Stoffer, born May 08, 1896 in Columbiana Cty, Ohio; died April 13, 1964.
- 2982   ii. Ralph Norman Stoffer, born February 27, 1898 in Ohio; died March 1980 in Salem, Columbiana Cty, Ohio. He married Ann Zing.
- 2983   iii. Ethel Stoffer, born November 10, 1899 in Columbiana Co Ohio. She married Elwood E. Calvin; born March 20, 1901; died January 20, 1958.
- 2984   iv. Ester Stoffer, born November 11, 1899. She married Elwood E. Calvin; born March 20, 1901; died January 20, 1958.
- 2985   v.   Hazel M Stoffer, born January 13, 1902 in Salem, Ohio; died April 26, 1968 in Salem Ohio, Columbiana Co.
- 2986   vi. Paul Elmer Stoffer, born November 16, 1904 in Columbiana Co Ohio; died August 07, 1963.
- 2987   vii. Harold James Stoffer, born February 04, 1908 in Columbiana Cty, Ohio; died December 10, 1976.
- 2988   viii. Helen Stoffer, born February 04, 1908 in Columbiana Cty, Ohio; died 1941.
- + 2989 ix. Harold Walter Stoffer, born September 28, 1914 in Columbiana Cty, Ohio; died August 27, 1979 in Alliance City Hospital, Alliance, Ohio.

2277. Idella[12] Stoffer (Levi[11], George[10], Jacob[9], Jacob[8] Stauffer, Henry Jacob[7], Hans[6], Christian[5], Daniel[4] Stouffer, Christian[3], Hans[2], Hans[1]) was born May 12, 1877 in Columbiana Cty, Ohio, and died 1900. She married **George W Shively**. He was born August 22, 1876, and died March 03, 1960.

Children of Idella Stoffer and George Shively are:
    2990   i.   Florence[13] Shively, born August 10, 1898. She married Argus Summer.
+   2991   ii.   Ray Shively, born October 27, 1898; died November 27, 1925.

2281. Pearl[12] Stoffer (Levi[11], George[10], Jacob[9], Jacob[8] Stauffer, Henry Jacob[7], Hans[6], Christian[5], Daniel[4] Stouffer, Christian[3], Hans[2], Hans[1]) was born April 12, 1886 in Columbiana Co Ohio, and died March 11, 1958. She married **Bert E Mercer** May 01, 1901. He was born December 14, 1878, and died May 01, 1968.

Children of Pearl Stoffer and Bert Mercer are:
+   2992   i.   Orvie W[13] Mercer, born October 17, 1901.
+   2993   ii.   Chester Mercer, born December 28, 1907.
+   2994   iii.   Herbert Russell Mercer, born March 22, 1913.
+   2995   iv.   Hazel Debra Mercer, born January 23, 1919.
+   2996   v.   Helen M Mercer, born April 05, 1923.
+   2997   vi.   Glenn A Mercer, born February 13, 1925; died January 19, 1981.

2282. Erwin William[12] Stoffer (Levi[11], George[10], Jacob[9], Jacob[8] Stauffer, Henry Jacob[7], Hans[6], Christian[5], Daniel[4] Stouffer, Christian[3], Hans[2], Hans[1]) was born March 29, 1889 in Columbiana Cty, Ohio, and died June 27, 1917 in Columbiana Cty, Ohio. He married **Myrtle Olive John** January 04, 1911. She was born October 18, 1892 in East Rodchester Ohio, and died January 30, 1974 in Malvern Ohio.

Children of Erwin Stoffer and Myrtle John are:
    2998   i.   Esther[13] Stoffer. She married Unknown Lucas.
    2999   ii.   Ethel Stoffer. She married Victor Ferguson.
    3000   iii.   Jean Stoffer. She married Robert Grogg.
    3001   iv.   Blanche Stoffer. She married Ervin Freitag.
+   3002   v.   Loyal Stoffer, born September 18, 1911 in North Georgetown Ohio, Columbiana Co; died 1978 in Canton Ohio, Stark Co.

2283. William Franklin[12] Stoffer (Laurtis W.[11], George[10], Jacob[9], Jacob[8] Stauffer, Henry Jacob[7], Hans[6], Christian[5], Daniel[4] Stouffer, Christian[3], Hans[2], Hans[1]) was born November 09, 1876 in Columbiana Co Ohio, and died March 10, 1942 in Parry Sound, Ontario Canada. He married **Elizabeth Celesta Connell** October 16, 1898. She was born June 02, 1880 in Columbiana Co Ohio, and died June 03, 1948.

Children of William Stoffer and Elizabeth Connell are:
    3003   i.   Nora[13] Stoffer.
    3004   ii.   Harvey Stoffer.
    3005   iii.   Eva Stoffer.
    3006   iv.   Ethel Marie Stoffer, born December 03, 1898 in Columbiana Co Ohio; died February 23, 1920 in Columbiana Co Ohio. She married Unknown Ward.
+   3007   v.   Paul Lawrence Stoffer, born June 29, 1901 in North Georgetown Ohio, Columbiana Co; died November 01, 1944 in Columbiana Co Ohio.

2287. John Wallace[12] Stoffer (Laurtis W.[11], George[10], Jacob[9], Jacob[8] Stauffer, Henry Jacob[7], Hans[6], Christian[5], Daniel[4] Stouffer, Christian[3], Hans[2], Hans[1]) was born April 12, 1883 in Columbiana Co Ohio, and died December 06, 1967 in Beloit Ohio, Mahoning Cty. He married **Nellie Virginia Bartley** July 12, 1911 in Columbiana Co Ohio, Lisbon. She was born July 24, 1890 in Columbian Co Ohio, Butler Twp, and died December 07, 1972 in Beloit Ohio, Mahoning Cty.

Children of John Stoffer and Nellie Bartley are:
+   3008   i.   Virginia[13] Stoffer.
+   3009   ii.   Gorman H Stoffer, born December 26, 1914 in Columbiana Co Ohio; died July 28, 1999 in Salem, Columbiana Cty, Ohio.

2289. Lester Clyde[12] Stoffer (Laurtis W.[11], George[10], Jacob[9], Jacob[8] Stauffer, Henry Jacob[7], Hans[6], Christian[5], Daniel[4] Stouffer, Christian[3], Hans[2], Hans[1]) was born February 07, 1887 in North Georgetown Ohio, Columbiana Co, and died November 29, 1973 in Lisbon, Columbiana Co Ohio. He married **Grace Walters** November 21, 1911 in Columbiana Co Ohio. She was born December 30, 1886 in Bayard Ohio, Columbiana Co, and died October 19, 1941.

Children of Lester Stoffer and Grace Walters are:
+ 3010 i. Ester[13] Stoffer.
+ 3011 ii. Floyd W Stoffer, born June 14, 1912 in Bayard Ohio, Columbiana Co; died July 09, 1969 in Ohio, Stark Co.
+ 3012 iii. Cecil F Stoffer, born April 05, 1916 in Bayard Ohio, Columbiana Co; died April 1987 in Mahoning Co Ohio.

2291. Gladys Alice[12] Stoffer (Laurtis W.[11], George[10], Jacob[9], Jacob[8] Stauffer, Henry Jacob[7], Hans[6], Christian[5], Daniel[4] Stouffer, Christian[3], Hans[2], Hans[1]) was born October 10, 1889 in Columbiana Co Ohio. She married **(1) Allen L Freshley** September 30, 1917. He was born September 20, 1896. She married **(2) William Wyss** September 22, 1946. He was born December 20, 1900 in Columbian Co Ohio, and died August 02, 1953 in North Georgetown, Columbiana Cty ohio.

Marriage Notes for Gladys Stoffer and Allen Freshley:
[chrststauffer1663.ged]

1 _FA1
2 PLAC 10/13/1943
1 _MEND Divorce

Children of Gladys Stoffer and Allen Freshley are:
+ 3013 i. Robert[13] Freshley.
  3014 ii. William Freshley. He married Ruth Brownlee.
+ 3015 iii. Marjorie Freshley.
+ 3016 iv. Eugene A Freshley, born January 02, 1920.
+ 3017 v. June Freshley, born October 19, 1921.

2292. Veron Roy[12] Stoffer (Laurtis W.[11], George[10], Jacob[9], Jacob[8] Stauffer, Henry Jacob[7], Hans[6], Christian[5], Daniel[4] Stouffer, Christian[3], Hans[2], Hans[1]) was born May 10, 1891 in Columbiana Co. Ohio, and died April 1970 in Carroll Co Indiana. He married **Dessie Young** September 02, 1916 in Columbiana Co Ohio. She was born March 21, 1891 in Roanoke, Hunting Ind.

Children of Veron Stoffer and Dessie Young are:
+ 3018 i. Martha[13] Stoffer, born January 10, 1918.
+ 3019 ii. Dwight Stoffer, born February 10, 1920.

2293. Mary Catherine[12] Stoffer (Laurtis W.[11], George[10], Jacob[9], Jacob[8] Stauffer, Henry Jacob[7], Hans[6], Christian[5], Daniel[4] Stouffer, Christian[3], Hans[2], Hans[1]) was born September 04, 1891 in Columbiana Cty ohio, and died October 14, 1975 in Columbiana Cty ohio. She married **Cornelius Hall Randall**. He was born August 05, 1889, and died November 01, 1956 in Columbiana Cty ohio.

Child of Mary Stoffer and Cornelius Randall is:
+ 3020 i. Lowell Orland[13] Randall, born September 11, 1910.

2294. Charles G[12] Stoffer (Laurtis W.[11], George[10], Jacob[9], Jacob[8] Stauffer, Henry Jacob[7], Hans[6], Christian[5], Daniel[4] Stouffer, Christian[3], Hans[2], Hans[1]) was born March 24, 1893 in Columbiana Co Ohio, and died March 29, 1988 in Alliance Ohio. He married **Mildred R Werteberger** May 31, 1928 in Columbiana Co, Ohio. She was born March 14, 1906 in Stark Co Ohio, and died February 05, 1962 in Homeworth Ohio.

Children of Charles Stoffer and Mildred Werteberger are:
+ 3021 i. Private[13] Stoffer.
+ 3022 ii. Private Stoffer.
+ 3023 iii. Private Stoffer.
+ 3024 iv. Elmer L Stoffer, born 1929.
  3025 v. Joseph C Stoffer, born November 25, 1938 in Columbiana Cty, Ohio; died December 25, 1938 in Columbiana Cty, Ohio.
  3026 vi. Jacob H Stoffer, born November 12, 1939 in Columbiana Cty ohio; died January 04, 1952 in Columbiana Cty ohio.

2296. Bryan Sewell[12] Stoffer (Laurtis W.[11], George[10], Jacob[9], Jacob[8] Stauffer, Henry Jacob[7], Hans[6], Christian[5], Daniel[4] Stouffer, Christian[3], Hans[2], Hans[1]) was born July 27, 1896 in North Georgetown Ohio, Columbiana Co, and died March 19, 1961 in Topeka, Kansas. He married **Freda Elizabeth Price** September 01, 1923 in Nappanee In. She was born July 05, 1895 in Napnee Ind, and died December 26, 1984 in Topeka, Kansas.

Children of Bryan Stoffer and Freda Price are:
- 3027   i.   Private[13] Stoffer.
- + 3028   ii.   Robert Price Stoffer, born 1926.
- 3029   iii.   Thomas Fredric Stoffer, born September 26, 1931 in Madura India; died October 21, 1933 in Madura India.

2298. George Allen[12] Stoffer (Simon Henry[11], George[10], Jacob[9], Jacob[8] Stauffer, Henry Jacob[7], Hans[6], Christian[5], Daniel[4] Stouffer, Christian[3], Hans[2], Hans[1]) was born July 09, 1883 in Kansas, Ellis Cty, and died August 18, 1942 in Aline Okla.. He married **(1) Ethel Miller** February 04, 1906 in Wisby, Oklahoma. He married **(2) Hazel Leona (Dollie) Blackwell** August 11, 1926 in Aline Okla.. She was born February 21, 1910 in Aline Okla., and died March 26, 1998 in Hobbs New Mexico.

Children of George Stoffer and Hazel Blackwell are:
- + 3030   i.   Private[13] Stoffer.
- + 3031   ii.   Lola Mae Stoffer, born July 05, 1927 in Aline Okla.; died July 01, 1994 in Wichita Kansas.
- + 3032   iii.   Roy Dean Stoffer, born September 28, 1928 in Aline Okla..

2302. Simon Levi[12] Stoffer (Simon Henry[11], George[10], Jacob[9], Jacob[8] Stauffer, Henry Jacob[7], Hans[6], Christian[5], Daniel[4] Stouffer, Christian[3], Hans[2], Hans[1]) was born February 20, 1893 in Kansas, Ellis or Pawnee Co, and died December 26, 1967 in Orange Cty Tx. He married **Jennie M Wilson** January 30, 1917 in Texas. She was born September 23, 1895, and died September 26, 1967 in Orange Cty Tx.

Children of Simon Stoffer and Jennie Wilson are:
- + 3033   i.   Private[13] Stoffer.
- 3034   ii.   Private Stoffer.
- 3035   iii.   Private Stoffer.

2304. Alice Ellen[12] Stoffer (Simon Henry[11], George[10], Jacob[9], Jacob[8] Stauffer, Henry Jacob[7], Hans[6], Christian[5], Daniel[4] Stouffer, Christian[3], Hans[2], Hans[1]) was born October 18, 1900 in Oklahoma, and died November 1990 in Orange Co., Texas. She married **Raymond Niles Moore** May 19, 1923 in Victoria, Texas. He was born February 09, 1895 in Springfeild Illonois, and died September 1981 in Orange Texas.

Children of Alice Stoffer and Raymond Moore are:
- 3036   i.   Henry Daniel[13] Moore. He married Reba A Scogun July 03, 1947 in Orange Co Tx.
- 3037   ii.   Richard N Moore.
- 3038   iii.   Robert Moore.
- + 3039   iv.   John Raymond Moore, born August 05, 1925 in Victoria Texas.
- 3040   v.   Mary Alice Moore, born October 28, 1928.

2308. Claire Daniel[12] Stoffer (Rolandus[11], George[10], Jacob[9], Jacob[8] Stauffer, Henry Jacob[7], Hans[6], Christian[5], Daniel[4] Stouffer, Christian[3], Hans[2], Hans[1]) was born June 08, 1893 in Columbiana Cty Ohio, and died April 27, 1959 in Calif. He married **(1) Dorothy Winschell**. She was born in Idaho, and died 1997 in Calif. He married **(2) Hazel Howell** February 28, 1914. She was born in Oregon.

Children of Claire Stoffer and Hazel Howell are:
- 3041   i.   Don[13] Stoffer.
- 3042   ii.   Lloyd Stoffer.
- 3043   iii.   Rex Stoffer, born Abt. 1914.

2309. Vera Lucille[12] Stoffer (Rolandus[11], George[10], Jacob[9], Jacob[8] Stauffer, Henry Jacob[7], Hans[6], Christian[5], Daniel[4] Stouffer, Christian[3], Hans[2], Hans[1]) was born April 17, 1896 in Ohio, and died January 18, 1982 in Columbiana Cty ohio. She married **Paul Eugene Barnett** February 25, 1914. He was born January 13, 1892, and died November 17, 1964 in Columbiana Cty ohio.

Children of Vera Stoffer and Paul Barnett are:
- + 3044   i.   Dale Eugene[13] Barnett, born December 13, 1914; died June 25, 1965.
- + 3045   ii.   Theda Fay Barnett, born December 30, 1916.
- + 3046   iii.   Jay Melvin Barnett, born December 20, 1919.

2310. Bertha Lorena[12] Stoffer (George D[11], George[10], Jacob[9], Jacob[8] Stauffer, Henry Jacob[7], Hans[6], Christian[5], Daniel[4] Stouffer, Christian[3], Hans[2], Hans[1]) was born June 23, 1882 in Columbiana Cty, Ohio, and died December 23, 1962. She married **Jesse Mountz** November 28, 1901. He was born November 06, 1880, and died May 29, 1955.

Children of Bertha Stoffer and Jesse Mountz are:

+	3047	i.	Alta[13] Mountz, born June 23, 1902.
	3048	ii.	Malvern Mountz, born December 13, 1913. He married Nellie Halwell August 17, 1951; born July 09, 1924.
+	3049	iii.	Wilfred Mountz, born January 08, 1915.
+	3050	iv.	Mary Mountz, born May 17, 1917.
+	3051	v.	Kathryn Mountz, born October 12, 1918.

2313. Zella May[12] Stoffer (George D[11], George[10], Jacob[9], Jacob[8] Stauffer, Henry Jacob[7], Hans[6], Christian[5], Daniel[4] Stouffer, Christian[3], Hans[2], Hans[1]) was born April 18, 1889 in Columbiana Co Ohio, and died December 02, 1972. She married **Vernon Stuart** September 25, 1913. He was born April 11, 1889.

Children of Zella Stoffer and Vernon Stuart are:

+	3052	i.	Private[13] Stuart.
	3053	ii.	Neil Stuart, born July 20, 1914. He married Audrey Francis Barker July 06, 1949; born February 04, 1914.
+	3054	iii.	Russell Stuart, born September 04, 1918.
+	3055	iv.	Dean Stuart, born November 18, 1919.

2314. Chester A[12] Stoffer (George D[11], George[10], Jacob[9], Jacob[8] Stauffer, Henry Jacob[7], Hans[6], Christian[5], Daniel[4] Stouffer, Christian[3], Hans[2], Hans[1]) was born January 12, 1891 in Columbiana Cty Ohio, and died November 12, 1933 in Columbiana Cty Ohio. He married **Ellen Freshley** April 17, 1914 in Columbiana Cty, Ohio. She was born September 30, 1896 in Columbiana Cty Ohio, and died 1939 in Columbiana Cty, Ohio.

Children of Chester Stoffer and Ellen Freshley are:

	3056	i.	Wilma E[13] Stoffer, born 1915 in Columbiana Cty Ohio; died 1939 in Columbiana Cty Ohio.
	3057	ii.	Gwendolyn G Stoffer, born 1916 in Columbiana Cty Ohio; died 1939 in Columbiana Cty Ohio.

2315. Wesley Emerson[12] Stoffer (George D[11], George[10], Jacob[9], Jacob[8] Stauffer, Henry Jacob[7], Hans[6], Christian[5], Daniel[4] Stouffer, Christian[3], Hans[2], Hans[1]) was born December 22, 1892 in Homeworth, Knox Twp, Columbiana Co, Ohio, and died July 08, 1979 in Louisville, Ohio, Nist Nursing Home. He married **Pearl R Harlan** December 24, 1913 in Columbiana Cty, Ohio. She was born August 13, 1895 in Columbiana Cty, Ohio, and died February 27, 1972 in Columbiana Cty, Ohio.

Children of Wesley Stoffer and Pearl Harlan are:

+	3058	i.	Orlan Clifford[13] Stoffer, born August 03, 1917 in NortGeorgetown, Columbiana Co Ohio; died October 15, 1975 in Minerva, Ohio.
+	3059	ii.	Verma Adella Stoffer, born September 29, 1922 in North Georgetown <Columbiana Cty Ohio; died August 15, 2000 in Ohio.

2316. Russell D[12] Stoffer (George D[11], George[10], Jacob[9], Jacob[8] Stauffer, Henry Jacob[7], Hans[6], Christian[5], Daniel[4] Stouffer, Christian[3], Hans[2], Hans[1]) was born October 09, 1897 in Columbiana Co Ohio, and died February 15, 1982 in Cuyahoga Falls, Ohio. He married **Addie Jane Sherman Stoffer** February 28, 1925. She was born March 08, 1896, and died March 1980.

Children of Russell Stoffer and Addie Stoffer are:

+	3060	i.	Private[13] Stoffer.
	3061	ii.	Jimmie Dale Stoffer, born November 11, 1926.

2317. Ora Deliah[12] Stoffer (Stanton Uriah[11], George[10], Jacob[9], Jacob[8] Stauffer, Henry Jacob[7], Hans[6], Christian[5], Daniel[4] Stouffer, Christian[3], Hans[2], Hans[1]) was born November 10, 1883 in Columbiana County, Ohio, and died June 01, 1941 in Salem, Columbiana County, Ohio. She married **(1) Cleveland Samuel Wyss** November 20, 1907. He was born December 29, 1885, and died October 02, 1952 in Columbiana Co Ohio. She married **(2) Joe Blyth** February 21, 1930.

Children of Ora Stoffer and Cleveland Wyss are:

	3062	i.	Evelyn[13] Wyss.
+	3063	ii.	Ralph Leroy Wyss, born June 10, 1908 in Columbian Co Ohio; died November 05, 1952 in Ohio.
+	3064	iii.	Florian F. Wyss, born May 20, 1911; died November 05, 1988 in Ohio.
+	3065	iv.	Naomi B. Wyss, born June 29, 1913 in Ohio; died March 04, 1999 in Ohio.
	3066	v.	Woodrow Wyss, born November 17, 1916; died March 09, 1999.
+	3067	vi.	Audrey Odessa "Audey" Wyss, born December 22, 1921 in Ohio.

2318. Benjamine Franklin[12] Stoffer (Stanton Uriah[11], George[10], Jacob[9], Jacob[8] Stauffer, Henry Jacob[7], Hans[6], Christian[5], Daniel[4]

Stouffer, Christian[3], Hans[2], Hans[1]) was born July 23, 1885 in Columbiana Co Ohio, and died June 17, 1967 in Canton Ohio, Stark Co. He married **Martha Jane Leipper** August 04, 1906 in Columbiana Co Ohio. She was born July 10, 1889 in Westville Ohio, and died July 09, 1957 in Massillon Ohio.

Marriage Notes for Benjamine Stoffer and Martha Leipper:
[chrststauffer1663.ged]

1 _MEND Death of one spouse

Children of Benjamine Stoffer and Martha Leipper are:

	3068	i.	Adaline[13] Stoffer, born 1906 in Columbiana Co Ohio; died 1906 in Columbiana Co Ohio.
+	3069	ii.	Clarence Leward Stoffer, born September 20, 1907 in North Georgetown Ohio, Columbiana Co; died March 02, 1970 in Salem Ohio.
+	3070	iii.	Clifford Lewis Stoffer, born November 09, 1909 in Paris Ohio; died October 14, 1991 in Canton Ohio, Stark Co.
+	3071	iv.	William Stanton Stoffer, born February 18, 1912 in Ohio; died September 04, 1964 in Ohio.
+	3072	v.	Milan Benjamin Stoffer, born April 30, 1914 in Ohio; died November 16, 1954 in Canton, Ohio.
+	3073	vi.	Ray Arnold Stoffer, born September 20, 1916 in Ohio; died September 23, 1944 in Italy WW ll.
+	3074	vii.	Alva Orlan Stoffer, born March 24, 1919 in Ohio; died May 14, 1993 in Ohio.
+	3075	viii.	Cleo Ruth Stoffer, born June 15, 1921 in Ohio.
+	3076	ix.	Donald Andrew Stoffer, born August 19, 1924 in Ohio; died November 11, 1980 in Canton, Stark Co., Ohio.
+	3077	x.	Margaret Louise Stoffer, born November 13, 1926 in Moultrie, Ohio; died September 19, 1996 in Canton, Ohio.
+	3078	xi.	Rollin Jr Stoffer, born June 12, 1929 in Ohio.
+	3079	xii.	Franklin Eugene Stoffer, born August 21, 1933 in Beloit, Ohio; died July 21, 1995 in Canton, Stark Co., Ohio.

2320. Roscoe "Ross"[12] Stoffer (Stanton Uriah[11], George[10], Jacob[9], Jacob[8] Stauffer, Henry Jacob[7], Hans[6], Christian[5], Daniel[4] Stoffer, Christian[3], Hans[2], Hans[1]) was born October 14, 1889 in Knox Township, Columbiana County, Ohio, and died March 07, 1969 in Ohio. He married **Mabel M Berger** November 22, 1912 in Columbiana County, Ohio. She was born May 14, 1889 in North Georgetown Ohio, Columbiana Co, and died April 17, 1972 in SalemOhio.

Marriage Notes for Roscoe Stoffer and Mabel Berger:
[chrststauffer1663.ged]

_STATMARRIED

Children of Roscoe Stoffer and Mabel Berger are:

	3080	i.	Private[13] Stoffer. She married Private Lewis.
	3081	ii.	Private Stoffer.
+	3082	iii.	Lorin Albert Stoffer, born May 03, 1914 in North Georgetown Ohio, Columbiana Co; died March 05, 1988 in Beloit Ohio, Mahoning Co.
+	3083	iv.	Edith Stoffer, born March 24, 1919.
	3084	v.	Kenny Stoffer, born 1922. He married Rose Spinelli.
	3085	vi.	Kenneth Lee Stoffer, born March 11, 1922 in Columbiana Cty, Ohio. He married Rose Spinelli.
	3086	vii.	Buddy Ross Stoffer, born March 24, 1934 in Ohio, Knox Twp, Columbiana Co; died June 01, 1990 in Salem Ohio.

2321. Curtis Homer[12] Stoffer (Stanton Uriah[11], George[10], Jacob[9], Jacob[8] Stauffer, Henry Jacob[7], Hans[6], Christian[5], Daniel[4] Stoffer, Christian[3], Hans[2], Hans[1]) was born June 17, 1892 in Knox Township, Columbiana County, Ohio, and died December 01, 1983 in Salem, Columbiana County, Ohio. He married **Florence John**. She was born November 18, 1900, and died October 04, 1973 in Columbiana Co Ohio.

Children of Curtis Stoffer and Florence John are:

	3087	i.	Leward[13] Stoffer, died in Killed WW II.
	3088	ii.	Thomas Stoffer.
+	3089	iii.	Clyde C. Stoffer, born March 20, 1918 in Salem Ohio; died September 1985 in Ohio.
	3090	iv.	Arnold Leroy Stoffer, born January 25, 1920; died April 28, 1953.
+	3091	v.	Leonard Stoffer, born October 10, 1923 in Salem Ohio; died October 29, 1996 in Magadore Ohio.
	3092	vi.	Martha Ellen Stoffer, born June 04, 1925 in Ohio; died January 03, 1931 in Ohio.

2323. Ruthanna[12] Stoffer (Stanton Uriah[11], George[10], Jacob[9], Jacob[8] Stauffer, Henry Jacob[7], Hans[6], Christian[5], Daniel[4] Stoffer,

Christian³, Hans², Hans¹) was born September 28, 1896 in Ohio, and died June 12, 1961 in Ohio. She married **Chris W. Krause**. He was born April 18, 1904, and died March 1981 in Ohio.

Children of Ruthanna Stoffer and Chris Krause are:
+ 3093   i. Private¹³ Krause.
    3094   ii. Private Krause.
    3095   iii. Private Krause.

2324. Ruth Anna¹² Stoffer (Stanton Uriah¹¹, George¹⁰, Jacob⁹, Jacob⁸ Stauffer, Henry Jacob⁷, Hans⁶, Christian⁵, Daniel⁴ Stouffer, Christian³, Hans², Hans¹) was born September 28, 1896 in Columbiana Co. Ohio, and died June 12, 1961 in Ohio, Stark Co. She married **Chris W. Krause**. He was born April 18, 1904, and died March 1981 in Ohio.

Children of Ruth Stoffer and Chris Krause are:
    3096   i. Willard D¹³ Krause. He married Private Rice.
    3097   ii. Glen Krause.
+ 3098   iii. Herbert Stanton Krause, born July 17, 1927 in Beloit Ohio; died September 11, 2000 in Beloit Ohio.

2326. Bertha Cleo¹² Stoffer (Stanton Uriah¹¹, George¹⁰, Jacob⁹, Jacob⁸ Stauffer, Henry Jacob⁷, Hans⁶, Christian⁵, Daniel⁴ Stouffer, Christian³, Hans², Hans¹) was born January 10, 1902 in Knox Township, Columbiana County, Ohio, and died March 04, 1986 in Columbiana County, Ohio. She married **Earl D. Hahn**. He was born 1898, and died 1950 in Ohio.

Children of Bertha Stoffer and Earl Hahn are:
+ 3099   i. Wayne¹³ Hahn, died June 08, 1999 in OHIO.
    3100   ii. Leland Eugene Hahn.
    3101   iii. Bobby Hahn.

2337. Leo Lesile¹² Stoffer (Sherman¹¹, George¹⁰, Jacob⁹, Jacob⁸ Stauffer, Henry Jacob⁷, Hans⁶, Christian⁵, Daniel⁴ Stouffer, Christian³, Hans², Hans¹) was born October 01, 1905 in Ohio, and died August 1985 in Columbiana Co Ohio, Leetonoia. He married **Mona V Deffenbaugh** March 31, 1924. She was born February 06, 1908 in Bellaire Ohio, and died September 02, 1997 in Sebbring Ohio.

Children of Leo Stoffer and Mona Deffenbaugh are:
    3102   i. Daniel¹³ Stoffer.
    3103   ii. Donald Stoffer.
    3104   iii. Private Stoffer. She married Unknown Wilde.
+ 3105   iv. Earl L Stoffer, born March 30, 1925 in Sebring Ohio; died September 19, 1997 in Alliance Ohio.

2342. Anson Oscar¹² Stoffer (Leander¹¹, George¹⁰, Jacob⁹, Jacob⁸ Stauffer, Henry Jacob⁷, Hans⁶, Christian⁵, Daniel⁴ Stouffer, Christian³, Hans², Hans¹) was born September 18, 1888 in Columbiana Cty, Ohio, and died February 19, 1980. He married **Neveda Bada Mc Vay** April 16, 1910. She was born April 16, 1889, and died March 17, 1969 in Sanford, Florida.

Children of Anson Stoffer and Neveda Mc Vay are:
+ 3106   i. Ester Leah¹³ Stoffer, born November 07, 1912.
+ 3107   ii. Wilma Ruth Stoffer, born June 15, 1915.
+ 3108   iii. Homer Stoffer, born April 18, 1921.

2344. Glen Wilson¹² Stoffer (Leander¹¹, George¹⁰, Jacob⁹, Jacob⁸ Stauffer, Henry Jacob⁷, Hans⁶, Christian⁵, Daniel⁴ Stouffer, Christian³, Hans², Hans¹) was born June 19, 1893 in Columbiana Co, Ohio, and died May 01, 1972 in Columbiana Co, Ohio. He married **Iva Martha Harlan** June 28, 1913 in Lisbon, Ohio, Columbiana Co. She was born September 27, 1893 in Columbiana Co, Ohio, and died August 25, 1972 in Columbiana Co, Ohio.

Children of Glen Stoffer and Iva Harlan are:
+ 3109   i. Donald Lowell¹³ Stoffer, born August 27, 1914 in Alliance Ohio, Columbiana Co Ohio; died January 17, 1998 in Carson City Nev.
+ 3110   ii. Lucille Naomi Stoffer, born March 10, 1916 in Columbiana Co Ohio.
    3111   iii. Mildred Marjorie Stoffer, born July 21, 1917 in Columbiana Co, Ohio.
+ 3112   iv. Evelyn Ora Stoffer, born May 14, 1920 in Columbiana County, Ohio; died December 27, 1992 in Alliance Ohio.
+ 3113   v. Doris May Stoffer, born October 15, 1923.
+ 3114   vi. Iona Eleanor Stoffer, born February 28, 1927.

2347. Goldie Marie[12] Stoffer (Leander[11], George[10], Jacob[9], Jacob[8] Stauffer, Henry Jacob[7], Hans[6], Christian[5], Daniel[4] Stouffer, Christian[3], Hans[2], Hans[1]) was born June 06, 1901 in Columbiana Cty, Ohio, and died April 01, 1975. She married **(1) Alton Samuel Bye**. He was born June 28, 1895, and died September 24, 1976. She married **(2) Ward Geiger** April 30, 1920.

Marriage Notes for Goldie Stoffer and Ward Geiger:
[chrststauffer1663.ged]

1 _FA1
2 DATE 1931
1 _MEND Divorce

Child of Goldie Stoffer and Ward Geiger is:
+ 3115   i.   Barbara Ann[13] Geiger, born December 20, 1924.

2348. Wade Orla[12] Stoffer (Leander[11], George[10], Jacob[9], Jacob[8] Stauffer, Henry Jacob[7], Hans[6], Christian[5], Daniel[4] Stouffer, Christian[3], Hans[2], Hans[1]) was born June 14, 1903 in Columbian Co Ohio, and died August 12, 1976. He married **(1) Julia Amidon**. She was born January 22, 1919. He married **(2) Trulah Keener** April 1926. She was born August 09, 1901, and died May 17, 2000 in Ohio.

Marriage Notes for Wade Stoffer and Trulah Keener:
[chrststauffer1663.ged]

1 _MEND Divorce

Child of Wade Stoffer and Trulah Keener is:
+ 3116   i.   Private[13] Stoffer.

2349. Darl Lincoln[12] Stoffer (Leander[11], George[10], Jacob[9], Jacob[8] Stauffer, Henry Jacob[7], Hans[6], Christian[5], Daniel[4] Stouffer, Christian[3], Hans[2], Hans[1]) was born February 12, 1910 in Columbiana Co Ohio, and died February 27, 1999 in Mansfield, Richland Co, Ohio. He married **Lucille Elizabeth Koppler** January 31, 1931. She was born May 08, 1909, and died December 30, 1983 in Florida.

Children of Darl Stoffer and Lucille Koppler are:
+ 3117   i.   Private[13] Stoffer.
+ 3118   ii.   Private Stoffer.
+ 3119   iii.   Private Stoffer.

Generation No. 13

2355. John Landis[13] Weaver (Magdalena M.[12] Landis, Magdalena O.[11] Martin, Martha H.[10] Oberholtzer, Martha H.[9] Hess, Esther[8] Hershey, Christian[7], Benjamin Stauffer[6], Adelheid Galle[5] Stouffer, Daniel[4], Christian[3], Hans[2], Hans[1]) was born September 04, 1909 in Earl Twp, Lanc Co, PA, and died April 30, 1991 in Akron, Lancaster Co, PA. He married **Ada Sweigart Horst** January 07, 1932, daughter of Reuben Horst and Frances Sweigart. She was born May 30, 1911 in West Earl Twp, Lanc Co, PA, and died July 03, 1979 in Akron, Lancaster Co, PA.

Children are listed above under (2084) Ada Sweigart Horst.

2359. Harvey Andrew[13] Betzner (Wesley[12], Samuel[11], Elizabeth[10] Stouffer, Abraham Hershey[9] Stauffer, Abraham Hess[8], Henry Jacob[7], Hans[6], Christian[5], Daniel[4] Stouffer, Christian[3], Hans[2], Hans[1]) was born August 04, 1886. He married **Pearl E. Anderson**.

Children of Harvey Betzner and Pearl Anderson are:
+ 3120   i.   John Elwood[14] Betzner.
    3121   ii.   Stanley Bertram Betzner, born September 24, 1916; died March 21, 1922.

2360. Nellie Louise[13] Neff (Mary Elizabeth[12] Betzner, Samuel[11], Elizabeth[10] Stouffer, Abraham Hershey[9] Stauffer, Abraham Hess[8], Henry Jacob[7], Hans[6], Christian[5], Daniel[4] Stouffer, Christian[3], Hans[2], Hans[1]) was born February 22, 1886. She married **William Arthur Begg**. He was born August 25, 1882, and died August 30, 1924.

Children of Nellie Neff and William Begg are:
    3122   i.   Phyllis Beatrice Mary[14] Begg.
    3123   ii.   Mildred Louise Begg.
    3124   iii.   Robert Arthur Begg.
    3125   iv.   John Cameron Begg.

2361. Nellie Elizabeth[13] **Betzner** (Andrew[12], Samuel[11], Elizabeth[10] Stouffer, Abraham Hershey[9] Stauffer, Abraham Hess[8], Henry Jacob[7], Hans[6], Christian[5], Daniel[4] Stouffer, Christian[3], Hans[2], Hans[1]) She married **Ralph Sheldon Murry**. He was born 1897, and died 1949.

Children of Nellie Betzner and Ralph Murry are:
- 3126 i. Marguerite Elizabeth[14] Murry.
- 3127 ii. Jean Marie Murry.

2362. Clancey K.[13] **Betzner** (Andrew[12], Samuel[11], Elizabeth[10] Stouffer, Abraham Hershey[9] Stauffer, Abraham Hess[8], Henry Jacob[7], Hans[6], Christian[5], Daniel[4] Stouffer, Christian[3], Hans[2], Hans[1]) was born November 12, 1899. He married **Dorothy E. Temple**.

Children of Clancey Betzner and Dorothy Temple are:
- 3128 i. Donald Temple[14] Betzner.
- 3129 ii. Eleanor Ruth Betzner.

2364. Ellen Ruletta[13] **Kitchen** (Elizabeth[12] Betzner, Abraham[11], Elizabeth[10] Stouffer, Abraham Hershey[9] Stauffer, Abraham Hess[8], Henry Jacob[7], Hans[6], Christian[5], Daniel[4] Stouffer, Christian[3], Hans[2], Hans[1]) was born July 24, 1874, and died May 07, 1920. She married **Evert Dunham**.

Children of Ellen Kitchen and Evert Dunham are:
- 3130 i. Gertie Gibson[14] Dunham. She married Cecil Burt Govier.
- + 3131 ii. Norman Nelson Dunham.
- + 3132 iii. Jessie Jean Dunham.
- + 3133 iv. Frederick Fielding Dunham.
- + 3134 v. Bertha Beatrice Dunham, born February 03, 1896.
- + 3135 vi. Eleanor Elizabeth Dunham, born August 30, 1898.
- + 3136 vii. Watson William Dunham, born April 14, 1900; died January 06, 1947.

2366. Mabel Gertrude[13] **Kitchen** (Elizabeth[12] Betzner, Abraham[11], Elizabeth[10] Stouffer, Abraham Hershey[9] Stauffer, Abraham Hess[8], Henry Jacob[7], Hans[6], Christian[5], Daniel[4] Stouffer, Christian[3], Hans[2], Hans[1]) was born July 03, 1881. She married **Freedman Dunham**.

Children of Mabel Kitchen and Freedman Dunham are:
- + 3137 i. William Kitchen[14] Dunham.
- + 3138 ii. Mildred Elizabeth Dunham.
- + 3139 iii. Elmer Ray Dunham.
- 3140 iv. Lorne Milton Dunham, born February 27, 1904; died October 20, 1904.

2369. Henry Franklin[13] **Betzner** (George Washington[12], Abraham[11], Elizabeth[10] Stouffer, Abraham Hershey[9] Stauffer, Abraham Hess[8], Henry Jacob[7], Hans[6], Christian[5], Daniel[4] Stouffer, Christian[3], Hans[2], Hans[1]) was born May 20, 1882, and died December 28, 1945. He married **Mable Weaver**.

Children of Henry Betzner and Mable Weaver are:
- + 3141 i. Clare Sadie[14] Betzner.
- 3142 ii. Cecila La Verne Betzner. He married Vera Luella Barlow.
- + 3143 iii. Muriel Verna Betzner.

2370. Roy Sylvester[13] **Betzner** (Joseph[12], Abraham[11], Elizabeth[10] Stouffer, Abraham Hershey[9] Stauffer, Abraham Hess[8], Henry Jacob[7], Hans[6], Christian[5], Daniel[4] Stouffer, Christian[3], Hans[2], Hans[1]) was born April 03, 1885. He married **Annetta Echlin** April 07, 1909. She was born February 14, 1890.

Children of Roy Betzner and Annetta Echlin are:
- 3144 i. Doris Madeline[14] Betzner. She married Bertram Charles Patterson.
- + 3145 ii. Murry Abram Betzner.
- + 3146 iii. Bruce Echlin Betzner.

2373. A. Katharine[13] **Stutt** (Alice[12] Betzner, Jacob[11], Elizabeth[10] Stouffer, Abraham Hershey[9] Stauffer, Abraham Hess[8], Henry Jacob[7], Hans[6], Christian[5], Daniel[4] Stouffer, Christian[3], Hans[2], Hans[1]) was born May 07, 1893. She married **J. S. Clark** November 22, 1930. He was born March 20, 1892.

Child of A. Stutt and J. Clark is:

3147 i. Private[14] Clark.

2379. Isabella D.[13] **Betzner** (David Thomas[12], David S.[11], Elizabeth[10] Stouffer, Abraham Hershey[9] Stauffer, Abraham Hess[8], Henry Jacob[7], Hans[6], Christian[5], Daniel[4] Stouffer, Christian[3], Hans[2], Hans[1]) was born June 28, 1885. She married **Ralph W. Howe** February 07, 1912. He was born August 22, 1885, and died October 23, 1935.

Children of Isabella Betzner and Ralph Howe are:
+ 3148 i. Jean Marie[14] Howe.
   3149 ii. Ralph Howe.

2383. Ethel May[13] **Betzner** (John Abram[12], John Weir[11], Elizabeth[10] Stouffer, Abraham Hershey[9] Stauffer, Abraham Hess[8], Henry Jacob[7], Hans[6], Christian[5], Daniel[4] Stouffer, Christian[3], Hans[2], Hans[1]) was born July 01, 1892. She married **William J. Veith** September 04, 1919. He was born May 10, 1877.

Child of Ethel Betzner and William Veith is:
   3150 i. Robert John[14] Veith. He married Doris M. Sparks.

2385. Ina Louisa[13] **Betzner** (George David[12], John Weir[11], Elizabeth[10] Stouffer, Abraham Hershey[9] Stauffer, Abraham Hess[8], Henry Jacob[7], Hans[6], Christian[5], Daniel[4] Stouffer, Christian[3], Hans[2], Hans[1]) was born May 20, 1893. She married **Ross Herbert Edworthy**.

Child of Ina Betzner and Ross Edworthy is:
+ 3151 i. Louise Norman[14] Edworthy, born May 19, 1923.

2386. Laura G.[13] **Betzner** (George David[12], John Weir[11], Elizabeth[10] Stouffer, Abraham Hershey[9] Stauffer, Abraham Hess[8], Henry Jacob[7], Hans[6], Christian[5], Daniel[4] Stouffer, Christian[3], Hans[2], Hans[1]) was born April 22, 1899. She married **Gordon Charles Harper**.

Children of Laura Betzner and Gordon Harper are:
   3152 i. Eleanor Jean[14] Harper.
   3153 ii. Lois Marjorie Harper.

2387. Evelyn A.[13] **Betzner** (Albert E.[12], John Weir[11], Elizabeth[10] Stouffer, Abraham Hershey[9] Stauffer, Abraham Hess[8], Henry Jacob[7], Hans[6], Christian[5], Daniel[4] Stouffer, Christian[3], Hans[2], Hans[1]) She married **Sanford K. Bonham**. He was born October 02, 1896.

Children of Evelyn Betzner and Sanford Bonham are:
   3154 i. Marion I.[14] Bonham. She married Gordon E. Brooks.
   3155 ii. Margaret Jean Bonham.
   3156 iii. Ruth Bonham.

2388. Erland S.[13] **Betzner** (Albert E.[12], John Weir[11], Elizabeth[10] Stouffer, Abraham Hershey[9] Stauffer, Abraham Hess[8], Henry Jacob[7], Hans[6], Christian[5], Daniel[4] Stouffer, Christian[3], Hans[2], Hans[1]) was born November 17, 1896. He married **Gladys B. Edworthy** September 03, 1921. She was born April 04, 1895.

Children of Erland Betzner and Gladys Edworthy are:
   3157 i. Elizabeth Grace[14] Betzner.
+ 3158 ii. Erland Lloyd Betzner.

2389. Oliver[13] **Frost** (Nancy Jane[12] Stauffer, Abraham[11], Christian[10], Abraham Hershey[9], Abraham Hess[8], Henry Jacob[7], Hans[6], Christian[5], Daniel[4] Stouffer, Christian[3], Hans[2], Hans[1]) was born January 05, 1878 in Fort Worth, TX, and died May 15, 1961 in Hastings, Dakota Co, MN. He married **Margaret Cecilia O'Connor**. She was born March 15, 1877, and died May 18, 1973 in Hastings, Dakota Co, MN.

Child of Oliver Frost and Margaret O'Connor is:
+ 3159 i. Reginald Joseph[14] Frost, born November 14, 1905 in Harvey, ND; died June 14, 1975 in Hastings, Dakota Co, MN.

2395. Clayton[13] **Cooley** (Bertha[12] Stouffer, John[11], Abraham[10], Abraham Hershey[9] Stauffer, Abraham Hess[8], Henry Jacob[7], Hans[6], Christian[5], Daniel[4] Stouffer, Christian[3], Hans[2], Hans[1])

Children of Clayton Cooley are:

+   3160   i.   Delores[14] Cooley.
+   3161   ii. Audrey Cooley.
+   3162   iii. Virginia Cooley.

2399. Nina[13] Cooley (Bertha[12] Stouffer, John[11], Abraham[10], Abraham Hershey[9] Stauffer, Abraham Hess[8], Henry Jacob[7], Hans[6], Christian[5], Daniel[4] Stouffer, Christian[3], Hans[2], Hans[1]) was born 1894. She married **Unknown Santee**.

Children of Nina Cooley and Unknown Santee are:
    3163   i.   Dorothy[14] Santee. She married Unknown Krammer.
+   3164   ii. Betty Jane Santee.
    3165   iii. Kenneth Santee.

2400. Marie[13] Cooley (Bertha[12] Stouffer, John[11], Abraham[10], Abraham Hershey[9] Stauffer, Abraham Hess[8], Henry Jacob[7], Hans[6], Christian[5], Daniel[4] Stouffer, Christian[3], Hans[2], Hans[1]) was born 1895. She married **Unknown Sharick**.

Children of Marie Cooley and Unknown Sharick are:
+   3166   i.   Mary Elizabeth[14] Sharick.
+   3167   ii. Patricia Sharick.
    3168   iii. Douglas Sharick.
    3169   iv. Earl Sharick.
    3170   v.   June Sharick.

2405. Ida[13] Stouffer (Aaron[12], John[11], Abraham[10], Abraham Hershey[9] Stauffer, Abraham Hess[8], Henry Jacob[7], Hans[6], Christian[5], Daniel[4] Stouffer, Christian[3], Hans[2], Hans[1]) was born 1884, and died 1974. She married **James Cook**. He died 1949.

Children of Ida Stouffer and James Cook are:
    3171   i.   Fern[14] Cook. She married Robert Gray.
+   3172   ii. Claud Cook.
+   3173   iii. Lola Cook.
+   3174   iv. Ernest Cook.

2408. Jason[13] Stouffer (Eli[12], Samuel[11], Abraham[10], Abraham Hershey[9] Stauffer, Abraham Hess[8], Henry Jacob[7], Hans[6], Christian[5], Daniel[4] Stouffer, Christian[3], Hans[2], Hans[1]) He married **Annie Law**.

Children of Jason Stouffer and Annie Law are:
    3175   i.   Florence[14] Stouffer.
    3176   ii. Eldon Stouffer.
    3177   iii. Madeline Stouffer.

2410. May[13] Stouffer (Eli[12], Samuel[11], Abraham[10], Abraham Hershey[9] Stauffer, Abraham Hess[8], Henry Jacob[7], Hans[6], Christian[5], Daniel[4] Stouffer, Christian[3], Hans[2], Hans[1]) She married **Angus Campbell**.

Children of May Stouffer and Angus Campbell are:
    3178   i.   James[14] Campbell.
    3179   ii. Bruce Campbell.
    3180   iii. Blanche Campbell.

2411. Blanche[13] Stouffer (Eli[12], Samuel[11], Abraham[10], Abraham Hershey[9] Stauffer, Abraham Hess[8], Henry Jacob[7], Hans[6], Christian[5], Daniel[4] Stouffer, Christian[3], Hans[2], Hans[1]) She married **John Devlin**.

Children of Blanche Stouffer and John Devlin are:
    3181   i.   Norman[14] Devlin.
    3182   ii. John Devlin.
    3183   iii. Harry Devlin.
    3184   iv. Gordon Devlin.

2412. Samuel[13] Stouffer (Eli[12], Samuel[11], Abraham[10], Abraham Hershey[9] Stauffer, Abraham Hess[8], Henry Jacob[7], Hans[6], Christian[5], Daniel[4] Stouffer, Christian[3], Hans[2], Hans[1]) He married **(1) Elizabeth Williams**. He married **(2) Ruby Radley**.

Children of Samuel Stouffer and Elizabeth Williams are:
- 3185   i. Marion[14] Stouffer.
- 3186   ii. Carson Stouffer.

2413. Nellie[13] Hall (Hannah[12] Stouffer, Samuel[11], Abraham[10], Abraham Hershey[9] Stauffer, Abraham Hess[8], Henry Jacob[7], Hans[6], Christian[5], Daniel[4] Stouffer, Christian[3], Hans[2], Hans[1]) She married **Henry Johnson**.

Children of Nellie Hall and Henry Johnson are:
- 3187   i. Geneva[14] Johnson.
- 3188   ii. Harold Johnson.

2414. Nettie[13] Hall (Hannah[12] Stouffer, Samuel[11], Abraham[10], Abraham Hershey[9] Stauffer, Abraham Hess[8], Henry Jacob[7], Hans[6], Christian[5], Daniel[4] Stouffer, Christian[3], Hans[2], Hans[1]) She married **Jesse McLeod**.

Children of Nettie Hall and Jesse McLeod are:
- 3189   i. Gerald[14] McLeod.
- 3190   ii. Fern McLeod.
- 3191   iii. Nina McLeod.

2416. Lola[13] Hall (Hannah[12] Stouffer, Samuel[11], Abraham[10], Abraham Hershey[9] Stauffer, Abraham Hess[8], Henry Jacob[7], Hans[6], Christian[5], Daniel[4] Stouffer, Christian[3], Hans[2], Hans[1]) She married **Charles Hunter**.

Children of Lola Hall and Charles Hunter are:
- 3192   i. Francis M.[14] Hunter.
- 3193   ii. Vera Hunter.
- 3194   iii. Shirley Hunter.

2417. Vera[13] Hall (Hannah[12] Stouffer, Samuel[11], Abraham[10], Abraham Hershey[9] Stauffer, Abraham Hess[8], Henry Jacob[7], Hans[6], Christian[5], Daniel[4] Stouffer, Christian[3], Hans[2], Hans[1]) She married **George Grant**.

Children of Vera Hall and George Grant are:
- 3195   i. Lola[14] Grant.
- 3196   ii. Doris May Grant.

2421. Nellie[13] Bateman (Elizabeth[12] Stouffer, Samuel[11], Abraham[10], Abraham Hershey[9] Stauffer, Abraham Hess[8], Henry Jacob[7], Hans[6], Christian[5], Daniel[4] Stouffer, Christian[3], Hans[2], Hans[1]) She married **Matthew Lightbody**.

Child of Nellie Bateman and Matthew Lightbody is:
- 3197   i. Ila[14] Lightbody.

2426. Alpha[13] Murrell (Lavilla[12] Stouffer, Samuel[11], Abraham[10], Abraham Hershey[9] Stauffer, Abraham Hess[8], Henry Jacob[7], Hans[6], Christian[5], Daniel[4] Stouffer, Christian[3], Hans[2], Hans[1]) She married **John Jones**.

Children of Alpha Murrell and John Jones are:
- 3198   i. George[14] Jones.
- 3199   ii. Overton Jones.
- 3200   iii. Laura Jones.

2427. Edna[13] Stouffer (John Franklin[12], Jacob[11], Abraham[10], Abraham Hershey[9] Stauffer, Abraham Hess[8], Henry Jacob[7], Hans[6], Christian[5], Daniel[4] Stouffer, Christian[3], Hans[2], Hans[1]) She married **William Allen**.

Children of Edna Stouffer and William Allen are:
- 3201   i. Ronald[14] Allen.
- 3202   ii. Jean Allen.
- 3203   iii. Jennie Allen.
- 3204   iv. Phyllis Allen.
- 3205   v. Hugh Allen.
- 3206   vi. David Allen.
- 3207   vii. Marjorie Allen.

2429. Stanley[13] **Stouffer** (John Franklin[12], Jacob[11], Abraham[10], Abraham Hershey[9] Stauffer, Abraham Hess[8], Henry Jacob[7], Hans[6], Christian[5], Daniel[4] Stouffer, Christian[3], Hans[2], Hans[1]) He married **Margaret McLasty**.

Children of Stanley Stouffer and Margaret McLasty are:
- 3208   i.   Donald[14] Stouffer.
- 3209   ii.   Phyllis Stouffer.
- 3210   iii.   Llewellyn Stouffer.
- 3211   iv.   Wilfrid Stouffer.
- 3212   v.   Alice Stouffer.

2430. Edwin[13] **Stouffer** (John Franklin[12], Jacob[11], Abraham[10], Abraham Hershey[9] Stauffer, Abraham Hess[8], Henry Jacob[7], Hans[6], Christian[5], Daniel[4] Stouffer, Christian[3], Hans[2], Hans[1]) He married **Alberta McKenzie**.

Children of Edwin Stouffer and Alberta McKenzie are:
- 3213   i.   Garth[14] Stouffer.
- 3214   ii.   Neil Stouffer.
- 3215   iii.   Franklin Stouffer.
- 3216   iv.   Bruce Stouffer.

2432. Isobel[13] **Stouffer** (John Franklin[12], Jacob[11], Abraham[10], Abraham Hershey[9] Stauffer, Abraham Hess[8], Henry Jacob[7], Hans[6], Christian[5], Daniel[4] Stouffer, Christian[3], Hans[2], Hans[1]) She married **Edwin Oliver**.

Children of Isobel Stouffer and Edwin Oliver are:
- 3217   i.   David[14] Oliver.
- 3218   ii.   Gerald Oliver. He married Beryl Unknown.
- 3219   iii.   Edith Oliver.
- 3220   iv.   Gladys Oliver.
- 3221   v.   Jane Oliver.
- 3222   vi.   Earl Oliver.

2433. Kathleen[13] **Stouffer** (John Franklin[12], Jacob[11], Abraham[10], Abraham Hershey[9] Stauffer, Abraham Hess[8], Henry Jacob[7], Hans[6], Christian[5], Daniel[4] Stouffer, Christian[3], Hans[2], Hans[1]) She married **Roy Porter**.

Children of Kathleen Stouffer and Roy Porter are:
- 3223   i.   Verna[14] Porter.
- 3224   ii.   Kenneth Porter.
- 3225   iii.   Keith Porter.

2434. Kenneth[13] **Stouffer** (John Franklin[12], Jacob[11], Abraham[10], Abraham Hershey[9] Stauffer, Abraham Hess[8], Henry Jacob[7], Hans[6], Christian[5], Daniel[4] Stouffer, Christian[3], Hans[2], Hans[1]) He married **Myrtle Porter**.

Children of Kenneth Stouffer and Myrtle Porter are:
- 3226   i.   Lloyd[14] Stouffer.
- 3227   ii.   Louis Stouffer.
- 3228   iii.   Private Stouffer.

2435. Evelyn[13] **Stouffer** (John Franklin[12], Jacob[11], Abraham[10], Abraham Hershey[9] Stauffer, Abraham Hess[8], Henry Jacob[7], Hans[6], Christian[5], Daniel[4] Stouffer, Christian[3], Hans[2], Hans[1]) She married **(1) B. W. Sager**. She married **(2) Joe Forsyth**.

Children of Evelyn Stouffer and B. Sager are:
- 3229   i.   Beverly[14] Sager.
- 3230   ii.   Edwin Sager.
- 3231   iii.   Philip Sager.

2437. Wesley Adrian[13] **Stouffer** (David Wesley[12], Jacob[11], Abraham[10], Abraham Hershey[9] Stauffer, Abraham Hess[8], Henry Jacob[7], Hans[6], Christian[5], Daniel[4] Stouffer, Christian[3], Hans[2], Hans[1]) He married **Anna Marie Gilboyne**.

Child of Wesley Stouffer and Anna Gilboyne is:

3232 i. Mary Adrienne[14] Stouffer.

2438. Jacob Karl[13] Stouffer (David Wesley[12], Jacob[11], Abraham[10], Abraham Hershey[9] Stauffer, Abraham Hess[8], Henry Jacob[7], Hans[6], Christian[5], Daniel[4] Stouffer, Christian[3], Hans[2], Hans[1]) He married **Emma Unknown**.

Children of Jacob Stouffer and Emma Unknown are:
- 3233 i. Carlton Lee[14] Stouffer.
+ 3234 ii. Emma Ruth Stouffer.
- 3235 iii. Wesley Stouffer.

2441. Wilbert Gillson[13] Stouffer (David Wesley[12], Jacob[11], Abraham[10], Abraham Hershey[9] Stauffer, Abraham Hess[8], Henry Jacob[7], Hans[6], Christian[5], Daniel[4] Stouffer, Christian[3], Hans[2], Hans[1]) He married **Lena May Patterson**.

Child of Wilbert Stouffer and Lena Patterson is:
- 3236 i. Donna Maxine[14] Stouffer.

2442. Conrad Ulrick[13] Stouffer (David Wesley[12], Jacob[11], Abraham[10], Abraham Hershey[9] Stauffer, Abraham Hess[8], Henry Jacob[7], Hans[6], Christian[5], Daniel[4] Stouffer, Christian[3], Hans[2], Hans[1]) He married **Jewell Dean Hawkins**.

Child of Conrad Stouffer and Jewell Hawkins is:
- 3237 i. Joe Karl[14] Stouffer.

2443. Ernest Albert[13] Stouffer (Abraham[12], Jacob[11], Abraham[10], Abraham Hershey[9] Stauffer, Abraham Hess[8], Henry Jacob[7], Hans[6], Christian[5], Daniel[4] Stouffer, Christian[3], Hans[2], Hans[1]) He married **(1) Grace Wallace**.   He married **(2) Ann Lahodny**.

Child of Ernest Stouffer and Grace Wallace is:
- 3238 i. Daniel Ernest[14] Stouffer.

2444. Lloyd Arthur[13] Stouffer (Abraham[12], Jacob[11], Abraham[10], Abraham Hershey[9] Stauffer, Abraham Hess[8], Henry Jacob[7], Hans[6], Christian[5], Daniel[4] Stouffer, Christian[3], Hans[2], Hans[1]) He married **Ann Giesbrecht**.

Children of Lloyd Stouffer and Ann Giesbrecht are:
- 3239 i. Dianne Louise[14] Stouffer.
- 3240 ii. Jean Carol Stouffer.

2445. Anna Helena[13] Stouffer (Abraham[12], Jacob[11], Abraham[10], Abraham Hershey[9] Stauffer, Abraham Hess[8], Henry Jacob[7], Hans[6], Christian[5], Daniel[4] Stouffer, Christian[3], Hans[2], Hans[1]) She married **Archie Judson Palmer**.

Children of Anna Stouffer and Archie Palmer are:
- 3241 i. Marjorie Ann[14] Palmer.
- 3242 ii. Darrel Archie Palmer.

2447. Ora Hilda[13] Stouffer (Abraham[12], Jacob[11], Abraham[10], Abraham Hershey[9] Stauffer, Abraham Hess[8], Henry Jacob[7], Hans[6], Christian[5], Daniel[4] Stouffer, Christian[3], Hans[2], Hans[1]) She married **Mason Simon Shutt**.

Children of Ora Stouffer and Mason Shutt are:
- 3243 i. Janet Kaye[14] Shutt.
- 3244 ii. Sandra Lee Shutt.

2450. Gordon Ernest[13] Murison (Keturah[12] Stouffer, Jacob[11], Abraham[10], Abraham Hershey[9] Stauffer, Abraham Hess[8], Henry Jacob[7], Hans[6], Christian[5], Daniel[4] Stouffer, Christian[3], Hans[2], Hans[1]) was born February 05, 1893. He married **Bertha Lotton**.

Children of Gordon Murison and Bertha Lotton are:
- 3245 i. Isobel Anna[14] Murison.
- 3246 ii. Aileen Ruth Murison. She married Frank Robb.
- 3247 iii. William Gordon Murison.
- 3248 iv. James Wilfred Murison.
- 3249 v. John Alexander Murison.

3250   vi. Audrey Jean Murison.
3251   vii. Private Murison.

2452. Bessie Louise[13] **Murison** (Keturah[12] Stouffer, Jacob[11], Abraham[10], Abraham Hershey[9] Stauffer, Abraham Hess[8], Henry Jacob[7], Hans[6], Christian[5], Daniel[4] Stouffer, Christian[3], Hans[2], Hans[1]) was born December 24, 1898. She married **William Hewlett**.

Children of Bessie Murison and William Hewlett are:
3252   i. Wilfred Murison[14] Hewlett.
3253   ii. James Edward Hewlett.
3254   iii. Barbara Rye Hewlett.

2453. Clayton Parker[13] **Stouffer** (Flavius Jacob[12], Jacob[11], Abraham[10], Abraham Hershey[9] Stauffer, Abraham Hess[8], Henry Jacob[7], Hans[6], Christian[5], Daniel[4] Stouffer, Christian[3], Hans[2], Hans[1]) He married **Tressie Deola Docksteader**.

Children of Clayton Stouffer and Tressie Docksteader are:
3255   i. Ralph Clayton[14] Stouffer. He married Private Wenzel.
+ 3256   ii. Delma Izetta Stouffer.
3257   iii. Private Stouffer. She married William Dalton Foot.
3258   iv. Private Stouffer.
3259   v. Private Stouffer.

2454. Jennie Grace[13] **Stouffer** (Flavius Jacob[12], Jacob[11], Abraham[10], Abraham Hershey[9] Stauffer, Abraham Hess[8], Henry Jacob[7], Hans[6], Christian[5], Daniel[4] Stouffer, Christian[3], Hans[2], Hans[1]) She married **Cecil Wilfred Dafoe**.

Children of Jennie Stouffer and Cecil Dafoe are:
3260   i. Kenneth Cecil[14] Dafoe.
3261   ii. Private Dafoe.
3262   iii. Private Dafoe.
3263   iv. Private Dafoe.
3264   v. Private Dafoe.
3265   vi. Private Dafoe.
3266   vii. Mavis Ruth Dafoe, born January 14, 1933; died March 21, 1944.

2455. Martha May[13] **Stouffer** (Flavius Jacob[12], Jacob[11], Abraham[10], Abraham Hershey[9] Stauffer, Abraham Hess[8], Henry Jacob[7], Hans[6], Christian[5], Daniel[4] Stouffer, Christian[3], Hans[2], Hans[1]) She married **Nicholas Sigrid Johnson**.

Children of Martha Stouffer and Nicholas Johnson are:
3267   i. Garth Wilson[14] Johnson.
3268   ii. Barbara May Johnson.
3269   iii. Private Johnson.
3270   iv. Private Johnson.

2457. Nellie Almina[13] **George** (Esther[12] Wideman, Elizabeth[11] Stouffer, Abraham[10], Abraham Hershey[9] Stauffer, Abraham Hess[8], Henry Jacob[7], Hans[6], Christian[5], Daniel[4] Stouffer, Christian[3], Hans[2], Hans[1]) She married **Richard Warmington**.

Child of Nellie George and Richard Warmington is:
3271   i. Richard George[14] Warmington. He married Dorothy Coulter.

2459. Elizabeth Ann[13] **George** (Esther[12] Wideman, Elizabeth[11] Stouffer, Abraham[10], Abraham Hershey[9] Stauffer, Abraham Hess[8], Henry Jacob[7], Hans[6], Christian[5], Daniel[4] Stouffer, Christian[3], Hans[2], Hans[1]) died May 23, 1949. She married **William G. Whyle**.

Children of Elizabeth George and William Whyle are:
3272   i. William George[14] Whyle. He married Grace Robertson.
3273   ii. Lola Whyle.

2461. Harry[13] **Wideman** (Jacob S.[12], Elizabeth[11] Stouffer, Abraham[10], Abraham Hershey[9] Stauffer, Abraham Hess[8], Henry Jacob[7], Hans[6], Christian[5], Daniel[4] Stouffer, Christian[3], Hans[2], Hans[1]) He married **Nellie Morgan**.

Children of Harry Wideman and Nellie Morgan are:

3274 i. Carol[14] Wideman.
3275 ii. Glen Wideman.

2462. Clarence[13] **Wideman** (Jacob S.[12], Elizabeth[11] Stouffer, Abraham[10], Abraham Hershey[9] Stauffer, Abraham Hess[8], Henry Jacob[7], Hans[6], Christian[5], Daniel[4] Stouffer, Christian[3], Hans[2], Hans[1]) He married **Jean Mustard**. She was born September 07, 1912, and died 1938.

Child of Clarence Wideman and Jean Mustard is:
3276 i. Unknown[14] Wideman, died in Died In Infancy.

2464. Elizabeth[13] **Wideman** (Jacob S.[12], Elizabeth[11] Stouffer, Abraham[10], Abraham Hershey[9] Stauffer, Abraham Hess[8], Henry Jacob[7], Hans[6], Christian[5], Daniel[4] Stouffer, Christian[3], Hans[2], Hans[1]) was born August 11, 1894. She married **Ed Nigh**. He was born July 09, 1885.

Children of Elizabeth Wideman and Ed Nigh are:
3277 i. Frances[14] Nigh. She married Norman O'Boyle.
+ 3278 ii. Jack Nigh.
3279 iii. William Nigh.

2465. Carson[13] **Wideman** (Jacob S.[12], Elizabeth[11] Stouffer, Abraham[10], Abraham Hershey[9] Stauffer, Abraham Hess[8], Henry Jacob[7], Hans[6], Christian[5], Daniel[4] Stouffer, Christian[3], Hans[2], Hans[1]) was born August 06, 1899. He married **Grace Byers**.

Children of Carson Wideman and Grace Byers are:
3280 i. Robert[14] Wideman.
3281 ii. John Wideman.
3282 iii. James Wideman.

2466. Alan[13] **Collard** (Laura[12] Stouffer, Simeon[11], Abraham[10], Abraham Hershey[9] Stauffer, Abraham Hess[8], Henry Jacob[7], Hans[6], Christian[5], Daniel[4] Stouffer, Christian[3], Hans[2], Hans[1]) He married **Margaret Hillman**.

Child of Alan Collard and Margaret Hillman is:
3283 i. Private[14] Collard.

2467. Jean[13] **Collard** (Laura[12] Stouffer, Simeon[11], Abraham[10], Abraham Hershey[9] Stauffer, Abraham Hess[8], Henry Jacob[7], Hans[6], Christian[5], Daniel[4] Stouffer, Christian[3], Hans[2], Hans[1]) She married **Alex Macleod**.

Children of Jean Collard and Alex Macleod are:
3284 i. Douglas[14] Macleod.
3285 ii. Private Macleod.

2468. Eric[13] **Collard** (Laura[12] Stouffer, Simeon[11], Abraham[10], Abraham Hershey[9] Stauffer, Abraham Hess[8], Henry Jacob[7], Hans[6], Christian[5], Daniel[4] Stouffer, Christian[3], Hans[2], Hans[1]) She married **Earl Robertson**.

Children of Eric Collard and Earl Robertson are:
3286 i. Private[14] Robertson.
3287 ii. Private Robertson.

2474. Ruth[13] **Raymer** (Christina[12] Stouffer, Abraham[11], Abraham[10], Abraham Hershey[9] Stauffer, Abraham Hess[8], Henry Jacob[7], Hans[6], Christian[5], Daniel[4] Stouffer, Christian[3], Hans[2], Hans[1]) died 1943. She married **Edward Hoover**.

Child of Ruth Raymer and Edward Hoover is:
+ 3288 i. Herbert[14] Hoover.

2475. Elmina[13] **Raymer** (Christina[12] Stouffer, Abraham[11], Abraham[10], Abraham Hershey[9] Stauffer, Abraham Hess[8], Henry Jacob[7], Hans[6], Christian[5], Daniel[4] Stouffer, Christian[3], Hans[2], Hans[1]) She married **Bruno Wiancko**.

Children of Elmina Raymer and Bruno Wiancko are:
+ 3289 i. Redford[14] Wiancko.

+ 3290 ii. Margaret Wiancko.
  3291 iii. Eldon Wiancko.

2477. Wilmot[13] Wideman (Frances[12] Stouffer, Abraham[11], Abraham[10], Abraham Hershey[9] Stauffer, Abraham Hess[8], Henry Jacob[7], Hans[6], Christian[5], Daniel[4] Stouffer, Christian[3], Hans[2], Hans[1]) He married **Sarah Moyer**.

Children of Wilmot Wideman and Sarah Moyer are:
  3292 i. Ruby[14] Wideman.
  3293 ii. Frances Wideman.
+ 3294 iii. Muriel Wideman.

2478. Herbert[13] Wideman (Frances[12] Stouffer, Abraham[11], Abraham[10], Abraham Hershey[9] Stauffer, Abraham Hess[8], Henry Jacob[7], Hans[6], Christian[5], Daniel[4] Stouffer, Christian[3], Hans[2], Hans[1]) He married **Myrtle Grove**.

Children of Herbert Wideman and Myrtle Grove are:
+ 3295 i. Harley[14] Wideman.
  3296 ii. Ross Wideman.
  3297 iii. Bruce Wideman. He married Alice Hachborn.
  3298 iv. Lloyd Wideman. He married Margaret Eby.
  3299 v. Frances E. Wideman.

2479. Mabel[13] Wideman (Frances[12] Stouffer, Abraham[11], Abraham[10], Abraham Hershey[9] Stauffer, Abraham Hess[8], Henry Jacob[7], Hans[6], Christian[5], Daniel[4] Stouffer, Christian[3], Hans[2], Hans[1]) She married **(1) Wilmont Schell**. She married **(2) Arthur C. Barkey**.

Children of Mabel Wideman and Wilmont Schell are:
+ 3300 i. Miriam[14] Schell.
  3301 ii. Gordon Schell.
  3302 iii. Clifford Schell. He married Gwen Cockburn.
  3303 iv. Robert Schell.
  3304 v. Shirley Schell.

2480. Martha[13] Wideman (Frances[12] Stouffer, Abraham[11], Abraham[10], Abraham Hershey[9] Stauffer, Abraham Hess[8], Henry Jacob[7], Hans[6], Christian[5], Daniel[4] Stouffer, Christian[3], Hans[2], Hans[1]) She married **Clare Bolender**.

Children of Martha Wideman and Clare Bolender are:
  3305 i. Gladys[14] Bolender.
  3306 ii. Lloyd Bolender. He married Delma Atkinson.
  3307 iii. Paul Bolender.
  3308 iv. Grace Bolender.
  3309 v. Louie Bolender.
  3310 vi. Arlene Bolender.
  3311 vii. Florence Bolender.
  3312 viii. Howard Bolender.

2483. Joseph[13] Wideman (Frances[12] Stouffer, Abraham[11], Abraham[10], Abraham Hershey[9] Stauffer, Abraham Hess[8], Henry Jacob[7], Hans[6], Christian[5], Daniel[4] Stouffer, Christian[3], Hans[2], Hans[1]) He married **Nettie Miller**.

Children of Joseph Wideman and Nettie Miller are:
+ 3313 i. Harvey[14] Wideman.
+ 3314 ii. Alan Wideman.
+ 3315 iii. Vera Wideman.

2484. Louie[13] Stouffer (Noah[12], Abraham[11], Abraham[10], Abraham Hershey[9] Stauffer, Abraham Hess[8], Henry Jacob[7], Hans[6], Christian[5], Daniel[4] Stouffer, Christian[3], Hans[2], Hans[1]) She married **Levi Forsythe**.

Children of Louie Stouffer and Levi Forsythe are:
+ 3316 i. Floyd[14] Forsythe.
+ 3317 ii. Lola Jean Forsythe.
  3318 iii. Vera Irene Forsythe.
  3319 iv. Alice Morene Forsythe. She married Lloyd Hamm.

The Relations of Milton Snavely Hershey, 4th Ed.

2485. Harry[13] **Stouffer** (Noah[12], Abraham[11], Abraham[10], Abraham Hershey[9] Stauffer, Abraham Hess[8], Henry Jacob[7], Hans[6], Christian[5], Daniel[4] Stouffer, Christian[3], Hans[2], Hans[1]) He married **(1) Geraldine Thoman**.   He married **(2) Mildred Lehman**.

Child of Harry Stouffer and Geraldine Thoman is:
    3320   i.   Geraldine[14] Stouffer.

2487. Jennie[13] **Hoover** (Josephuine[12] Stouffer, Abraham[11], Abraham[10], Abraham Hershey[9] Stauffer, Abraham Hess[8], Henry Jacob[7], Hans[6], Christian[5], Daniel[4] Stouffer, Christian[3], Hans[2], Hans[1]) She married **Roy Moyer**.

Children of Jennie Hoover and Roy Moyer are:
    3321   i.   Eleanor[14] Moyer.
+ 3322   ii.   Katherine Moyer.
    3323   iii. Margaret Moyer.
    3324   iv. Lillian Moyer. She married Robert McDowell.
    3325   v.   Warren Moyer.
    3326   vi. Willard Moyer.

2488. George[13] **Hoover** (Josephuine[12] Stouffer, Abraham[11], Abraham[10], Abraham Hershey[9] Stauffer, Abraham Hess[8], Henry Jacob[7], Hans[6], Christian[5], Daniel[4] Stouffer, Christian[3], Hans[2], Hans[1]) He married **Esther Schell**.

Children of George Hoover and Esther Schell are:
    3327   i.   Betty[14] Hoover. She married Herbert Constable.
    3328   ii.   Helen Hoover.

2489. Bella[13] **Hoover** (Josephuine[12] Stouffer, Abraham[11], Abraham[10], Abraham Hershey[9] Stauffer, Abraham Hess[8], Henry Jacob[7], Hans[6], Christian[5], Daniel[4] Stouffer, Christian[3], Hans[2], Hans[1]) She married **Charles Hoover**.

Children of Bella Hoover and Charles Hoover are:
    3329   i.   Doris[14] Hoover.
    3330   ii.   Blanche Hoover.

2490. Ruth[13] **Hoover** (Josephuine[12] Stouffer, Abraham[11], Abraham[10], Abraham Hershey[9] Stauffer, Abraham Hess[8], Henry Jacob[7], Hans[6], Christian[5], Daniel[4] Stouffer, Christian[3], Hans[2], Hans[1]) She married **(1) Clarence Barkey**.   She married **(2) Maurice Eby**.

Children of Ruth Hoover and Clarence Barkey are:
    3331   i.   Marian[14] Barkey.
+ 3332   ii.   Norma Barkey.
    3333   iii. Pauline Barkey.

2491. Flora[13] **Hoover** (Josephuine[12] Stouffer, Abraham[11], Abraham[10], Abraham Hershey[9] Stauffer, Abraham Hess[8], Henry Jacob[7], Hans[6], Christian[5], Daniel[4] Stouffer, Christian[3], Hans[2], Hans[1]) She married **Elmore Barkey**.

Children of Flora Hoover and Elmore Barkey are:
    3334   i.   Lawrence[14] Barkey.
    3335   ii.   Alice Barkey.
    3336   iii. Gordon Barkey.

2492. Edith[13] **Hoover** (Josephuine[12] Stouffer, Abraham[11], Abraham[10], Abraham Hershey[9] Stauffer, Abraham Hess[8], Henry Jacob[7], Hans[6], Christian[5], Daniel[4] Stouffer, Christian[3], Hans[2], Hans[1]) She married **Reginald Gibbins**.

Children of Edith Hoover and Reginald Gibbins are:
    3337   i.   Patricia[14] Gibbins.
    3338   ii.   Peter Gibbins.

2494. Charles[13] **Barkey** (Martha[12] Stouffer, Abraham[11], Abraham[10], Abraham Hershey[9] Stauffer, Abraham Hess[8], Henry Jacob[7], Hans[6], Christian[5], Daniel[4] Stouffer, Christian[3], Hans[2], Hans[1]) He married **Bessie Mowder**.

Children of Charles Barkey and Bessie Mowder are:
+ 3339 i. Clifford[14] Barkey.
  3340 ii. Barbara Barkey. She married Arthur Adams.

2497. Mary[13] Barkey (Martha[12] Stouffer, Abraham[11], Abraham[10], Abraham Hershey[9] Stauffer, Abraham Hess[8], Henry Jacob[7], Hans[6], Christian[5], Daniel[4] Stouffer, Christian[3], Hans[2], Hans[1]) She married **Clarence Hoover**.

Children of Mary Barkey and Clarence Hoover are:
3341 i. Florence[14] Hoover. She married Jacob Broadway.
3342 ii. Donald Hoover.

2499. Lambert[13] Stouffer (Abraham[12], Abraham[11], Abraham[10], Abraham Hershey[9] Stauffer, Abraham Hess[8], Henry Jacob[7], Hans[6], Christian[5], Daniel[4] Stouffer, Christian[3], Hans[2], Hans[1]) He married **Alma Valentine**.

Children of Lambert Stouffer and Alma Valentine are:
3343 i. Bert Grenfell[14] Stouffer.
3344 ii. Donna Stouffer.
3345 iii. Alan Stouffer.
3346 iv. Private Stouffer.

2500. Abraham[13] Stouffer (Abraham[12], Abraham[11], Abraham[10], Abraham Hershey[9] Stauffer, Abraham Hess[8], Henry Jacob[7], Hans[6], Christian[5], Daniel[4] Stouffer, Christian[3], Hans[2], Hans[1]) He married **Margaret Barkey**.

Children of Abraham Stouffer and Margaret Barkey are:
3347 i. Miline[14] Stouffer.
3348 ii. Marian Stouffer.
3349 iii. Private Stouffer.
3350 iv. Private Stouffer.
3351 v. Private Stouffer.

2501. Reginald[13] Stouffer (Abraham[12], Abraham[11], Abraham[10], Abraham Hershey[9] Stauffer, Abraham Hess[8], Henry Jacob[7], Hans[6], Christian[5], Daniel[4] Stouffer, Christian[3], Hans[2], Hans[1]) He married **Mary Lewis**.

Child of Reginald Stouffer and Mary Lewis is:
3352 i. David Abraham[14] Stouffer.

2502. Luella[13] Stouffer (Abraham[12], Abraham[11], Abraham[10], Abraham Hershey[9] Stauffer, Abraham Hess[8], Henry Jacob[7], Hans[6], Christian[5], Daniel[4] Stouffer, Christian[3], Hans[2], Hans[1]) She married **James Tompkins**.

Children of Luella Stouffer and James Tompkins are:
3353 i. Bertha Jeanne[14] Tompkins.
3354 ii. J. Daniel S. Tompkins.

2504. Archibald[13] Stouffer (Abraham[12], Abraham[11], Abraham[10], Abraham Hershey[9] Stauffer, Abraham Hess[8], Henry Jacob[7], Hans[6], Christian[5], Daniel[4] Stouffer, Christian[3], Hans[2], Hans[1]) was born December 24, 1895. He married **Candance Eby**.

Children of Archibald Stouffer and Candance Eby are:
3355 i. Katherine E.[14] Stouffer.
3356 ii. H. Elgin Stouffer.
3357 iii. Mary Stouffer.
3358 iv. John Stouffer.

2506. Jean[13] Stouffer (Wellington[12], Christian[11], Abraham[10], Abraham Hershey[9] Stauffer, Abraham Hess[8], Henry Jacob[7], Hans[6], Christian[5], Daniel[4] Stouffer, Christian[3], Hans[2], Hans[1]) She married **Gordon Boyd**.

Child of Jean Stouffer and Gordon Boyd is:
3359 i. Private[14] Boyd.

2507. Stewart W.[13] Stouffer (Wellington[12], Christian[11], Abraham[10], Abraham Hershey[9] Stauffer, Abraham Hess[8], Henry Jacob[7], Hans[6], Christian[5], Daniel[4] Stouffer, Christian[3], Hans[2], Hans[1]) He married **Jean Grove**.

Child of Stewart Stouffer and Jean Grove is:
- 3360   i.   Private[14] Stouffer.

2508. Edward Bruce[13] Stouffer (Wellington[12], Christian[11], Abraham[10], Abraham Hershey[9] Stauffer, Abraham Hess[8], Henry Jacob[7], Hans[6], Christian[5], Daniel[4] Stouffer, Christian[3], Hans[2], Hans[1]) He married **Joyce Filyer**.

Children of Edward Stouffer and Joyce Filyer are:
- 3361   i.   Private[14] Stouffer.
- 3362   ii. Private Stouffer.
- 3363   iii. Private Stouffer.

2511. Florence[13] Stouffer (Andrew[12], Christian[11], Abraham[10], Abraham Hershey[9] Stauffer, Abraham Hess[8], Henry Jacob[7], Hans[6], Christian[5], Daniel[4] Stouffer, Christian[3], Hans[2], Hans[1]) She married **Fred Henry**.

Children of Florence Stouffer and Fred Henry are:
- 3364   i.   Private[14] Henry.
- 3365   ii. Private Henry.

2514. David[13] Stouffer (Thomas[12], Christian[11], Abraham[10], Abraham Hershey[9] Stauffer, Abraham Hess[8], Henry Jacob[7], Hans[6], Christian[5], Daniel[4] Stouffer, Christian[3], Hans[2], Hans[1])

Children of David Stouffer are:
- 3366   i.   Private[14] Stouffer.
- 3367   ii. Private Stouffer.

2517. Marion[13] Stouffer (David[12], Christian[11], Abraham[10], Abraham Hershey[9] Stauffer, Abraham Hess[8], Henry Jacob[7], Hans[6], Christian[5], Daniel[4] Stouffer, Christian[3], Hans[2], Hans[1]) She married **Fred Nicely**.

Child of Marion Stouffer and Fred Nicely is:
- 3368   i.   Private[14] Nicely.

2518. Helen[13] Stouffer (David[12], Christian[11], Abraham[10], Abraham Hershey[9] Stauffer, Abraham Hess[8], Henry Jacob[7], Hans[6], Christian[5], Daniel[4] Stouffer, Christian[3], Hans[2], Hans[1]) She married **Belfry Hamilton**.

Children of Helen Stouffer and Belfry Hamilton are:
- 3369   i.   Private[14] Hamilton.
- 3370   ii. Private Hamilton.
- 3371   iii. Private Hamilton.

2521. Henry Hess[13] Hackman (Willis Brenner[12], Andrew Baer[11], Susanna Frantz[10] Bear, Anna[9] Frantz, Barbara[8] Hostetter, Ann Elisabeth[7] Hershey, Benjamin Stauffer[6], Adelheid Galle[5] Stouffer, Daniel[4], Christian[3], Hans[2], Hans[1]) was born July 27, 1908 in Millport, Warwick Township, Lancaster County, PA, and died September 24, 1987. He married **(1) Minnie Mae Becker** May 28, 1933 in Lititz, PA. She was born May 01, 1913 in Rapho Township, PA, and died May 06, 1982. He married **(2) Mildred Burkholder McDonnel** July 16, 1983 in Elizabethtown, PA. She was born Abt. 1910.

Marriage Notes for Henry Hackman and Minnie Becker:
Married at the Lititz Church of the Brethern by Dr A C Baugher.

Children of Henry Hackman and Minnie Becker are:
- + 3372   i.   Dorothy Elaine[14] Hackman, born June 06, 1934 in Newville, Cumberland Co., PA.
- + 3373   ii. Willard Henry Hackman, born June 29, 1938 in Newville, Cumberland Co., PA.
-   3374   iii. John Allen Hackman, born May 19, 1947 in Runnymede Farm, Rapho Twp, Lancaster Co, PA. He married (1) Margaret Sue Yoder April 28, 1973; born February 28, 1954 in Goshen, Indiana. He married (2) Joann Taber August 20, 1983 in Lancaster, PA; born Abt. 1950.

2522. Willis Hess[13] Hackman (Willis Brenner[12], Andrew Baer[11], Susanna Frantz[10] Bear, Anna[9] Frantz, Barbara[8] Hostetter, Ann Elisabeth[7] Hershey, Benjamin Stauffer[6], Adelheid Galle[5] Stouffer, Daniel[4], Christian[3], Hans[2], Hans[1]) was born November 21, 1909 in

Millport, Warwick Township, Lancaster County, PA, and died August 20, 1989 in Elizabethtown, PA. He married **Mary Ebersole Martin** December 19, 1931. She was born February 06, 1914 in New Holland, PA.

Children of Willis Hackman and Mary Martin are:

+	3375	i.	Ray Donald[14] Hackman, born May 05, 1933.
+	3376	ii.	Kenneth Lee Hackman, born September 03, 1934.
+	3377	iii.	Annie Marian Hackman, born November 20, 1937.
+	3378	iv.	Margaret Ann Hackman, born March 11, 1939.
+	3379	v.	Alice Lorraine Hackman, born February 06, 1942.
+	3380	vi.	Willis Martin Hackman, born January 08, 1946.

2523. Walter Hess[13] Hackman (Willis Brenner[12], Andrew Baer[11], Susanna Frantz[10] Bear, Anna[9] Frantz, Barbara[8] Hostetter, Ann Elisabeth[7] Hershey, Benjamin Stauffer[6], Adelheid Galle[5] Stouffer, Daniel[4], Christian[3], Hans[2], Hans[1]) was born April 07, 1911 in Millport, Warwick Township, Lancaster County, PA. He married **Margaret Bucher Boose** April 06, 1935. She was born October 01, 1917 in West Cocalico Township, PA.

Child of Walter Hackman and Margaret Boose is:
+ 3381 i. Robert Lorin[14] Hackman, born October 20, 1935.

2524. Richard Hess[13] Hackman (Willis Brenner[12], Andrew Baer[11], Susanna Frantz[10] Bear, Anna[9] Frantz, Barbara[8] Hostetter, Ann Elisabeth[7] Hershey, Benjamin Stauffer[6], Adelheid Galle[5] Stouffer, Daniel[4], Christian[3], Hans[2], Hans[1]) was born August 25, 1913 in Millport, Warwick Township, Lancaster County, PA. He married **(1) Betty Forney** August 25, 1934. She was born April 23, 1909 in Neffsville, PA, and died November 29, 1989 in Lititz, PA. He married **(2) Mary Dubble** August 19, 1990. She was born Abt. 1915.

Children of Richard Hackman and Betty Forney are:
+ 3382 i. Betty Lou[14] Hackman, born May 27, 1935.
+ 3383 ii. Richard Forney Hackman, born January 24, 1940.
  3384 iii. Robert Forney Hackman, born September 10, 1946. He married Janice Marie Breneman June 26, 1970; born November 02, 1948 in Lancaster, PA.

2526. Violet Gertrude[13] Hackman (Willis Brenner[12], Andrew Baer[11], Susanna Frantz[10] Bear, Anna[9] Frantz, Barbara[8] Hostetter, Ann Elisabeth[7] Hershey, Benjamin Stauffer[6], Adelheid Galle[5] Stouffer, Daniel[4], Christian[3], Hans[2], Hans[1]) was born July 07, 1919 in Millport, Warwick Township, Lancaster County, PA. She married **Roy Edward Pfaltzgraff**. He was born 1917 in Manchester, York Co, PA.

Children of Violet Hackman and Roy Pfaltzgraff are:
+ 3385 i. Roy Edward[14] Pfaltzgraff, Jr, born September 08, 1943 in Philadelphia, PA.
+ 3386 ii. George Hackman Pfaltzgraff, born April 22, 1945 in Garkida, Nigeria.
+ 3387 iii. David Jasini Pfaltzgraff, born September 11, 1946 in Lasa, Nigeria.
  3388 iv. Kathryn Joyce Pfaltzgraff, born October 22, 1953 in Lasa, Nigeria. She married David A Williford; born Abt. 1950 in Dandridge, TN.
  3389 v. Nevin Mark Pfaltzgraff, born November 13, 1955 in Garkida, Nigeria. He married Antonia Marie Parry; born Abt. 1955.

2527. Emma Amelia[13] Hackman (Willis Brenner[12], Andrew Baer[11], Susanna Frantz[10] Bear, Anna[9] Frantz, Barbara[8] Hostetter, Ann Elisabeth[7] Hershey, Benjamin Stauffer[6], Adelheid Galle[5] Stouffer, Daniel[4], Christian[3], Hans[2], Hans[1]) was born May 28, 1921 in Millport, Warwick Township, Lancaster County, PA, and died November 03, 1994 in Elizabethtown, PA. She married **William Walter White** August 07, 1942 in St. Peter's Lutheran Church, Highspire, PA, son of William White and Catherine Wolf. He was born May 31, 1923 in Highspire, PA, and died August 31, 1998 in Highspire, PA.

Children of Emma Hackman and William White are:
+ 3390 i. Emily Faline[14] White, born February 16, 1943 in Lititz, PA.
+ 3391 ii. William Walter White, born December 12, 1944.

2528. Robert Lee[13] Brubaker (Paul M[12], Minnie P[11] Herr, John[10], Anna[9] Hostetter, John[8], Catharine[7] Long, Anna[6] Hershey, Adelheid Galle[5] Stouffer, Daniel[4], Christian[3], Hans[2], Hans[1]) was born July 15, 1943, and died December 25, 1999 in Lancaster Co, PA. He married **Carol Shank**.

Children of Robert Brubaker and Carol Shank are:
  3392 i. Christopher Scott[14] Brubaker, born December 30, 1963.
  3393 ii. Nathan Brubaker, born Abt. 1970.

2529. Willis Eby[13] Fox (Ella Barbara[12] Eby, Sarah Lucinda[11] Hershey, Peter[10], Jacob[9], John[8], Jacob Snavely[7], Andrew Stauffer[6], Adelheid Galle[5] Stouffer, Daniel[4], Christian[3], Hans[2], Hans[1]) was born May 17, 1907. He married **Vera Weaver Wise**. She was born April 07, 1916.

Children of Willis Fox and Vera Wise are:
```
      3394    i.    Private[14] Fox.  She married Private Hartranft.
+     3395    ii.   Private Fox.
+     3396    iii.  Private Fox.
+     3397    iv.   Private Fox.
      3398    v.    Private Fox.
      3399    vi.   Private Fox.
+     3400    vii.  Private Fox.
      3401    viii. Alta Mae Fox, born September 20, 1959; died September 20, 1959.
```

2530. Henry Peter[13] Fox (Ella Barbara[12] Eby, Sarah Lucinda[11] Hershey, Peter[10], Jacob[9], John[8], Jacob Snavely[7], Andrew Stauffer[6], Adelheid Galle[5] Stouffer, Daniel[4], Christian[3], Hans[2], Hans[1]) was born September 16, 1909. He married **Ellen Mary Martin**. She was born January 26, 1911.

Children of Henry Fox and Ellen Martin are:
```
+     3402    i.    Private[14] Fox.
      3403    ii.   Private Fox.  She married Private Gaffney.
+     3404    iii.  Private Fox.
+     3405    iv.   Private Fox.
      3406    v.    Private Fox.  She married Private Fellabaum.
+     3407    vi.   Private Fox.
      3408    vii.  Private Fox.
+     3409    viii. Private Fox.
+     3410    ix.   Private Fox.
+     3411    x.    Private Fox.
+     3412    xi.   Private Fox.
```

2531. Sarah Lucinda[13] Fox (Ella Barbara[12] Eby, Sarah Lucinda[11] Hershey, Peter[10], Jacob[9], John[8], Jacob Snavely[7], Andrew Stauffer[6], Adelheid Galle[5] Stouffer, Daniel[4], Christian[3], Hans[2], Hans[1]) was born July 06, 1911, and died October 19, 1971. She married **Noah Hoover Zimmerman**. He was born October 13, 1907.

Children of Sarah Fox and Noah Zimmerman are:
```
+     3413    i.    Private[14] Zimmerman.
+     3414    ii.   Private Zimmerman.
+     3415    iii.  Private Zimmerman.
+     3416    iv.   Private Zimmerman.
```

2534. Daniel Hershey[13] Fox (Ella Barbara[12] Eby, Sarah Lucinda[11] Hershey, Peter[10], Jacob[9], John[8], Jacob Snavely[7], Andrew Stauffer[6], Adelheid Galle[5] Stouffer, Daniel[4], Christian[3], Hans[2], Hans[1]) was born August 19, 1917, and died June 10, 1986. He married **Ruth Esther Winey**. She was born May 12, 1918.

Children of Daniel Fox and Ruth Winey are:
```
+     3417    i.    Private[14] Fox.
+     3418    ii.   Private Fox.
+     3419    iii.  Private Fox.
```

2537. Ivan Martin[13] Fox (Ella Barbara[12] Eby, Sarah Lucinda[11] Hershey, Peter[10], Jacob[9], John[8], Jacob Snavely[7], Andrew Stauffer[6], Adelheid Galle[5] Stouffer, Daniel[4], Christian[3], Hans[2], Hans[1]) was born October 23, 1925, and died February 13, 1987. He married **Private Bollinger**.

Children of Ivan Fox and Private Bollinger are:
```
      3420    i.    Private[14] Fox.
+     3421    ii.   Private Fox.
+     3422    iii.  Private Fox.
```

2539. Franklin W.[13] Eby (Peter Hershey[12], Sarah Lucinda[11] Hershey, Peter[10], Jacob[9], John[8], Jacob Snavely[7], Andrew Stauffer[6], Adelheid Galle[5] Stouffer, Daniel[4], Christian[3], Hans[2], Hans[1]) was born January 31, 1915, and died November 14, 1968. He married **Mary**

Martin. She was born March 26, 1914.

Child of Franklin Eby and Mary Martin is:
+ 3423 i. Private[14] Eby.

2540. Susan W.[13] Eby (Peter Hershey[12], Sarah Lucinda[11] Hershey, Peter[10], Jacob[9], John[8], Jacob Snavely[7], Andrew Stauffer[6], Adelheid Galle[5] Stouffer, Daniel[4], Christian[3], Hans[2], Hans[1]) was born November 16, 1916. She married **Aaron K. Martin**. He was born February 24, 1916.

Children of Susan Eby and Aaron Martin are:
  3424 i. Private[14] Martin.
+ 3425 ii. Private Martin.
+ 3426 iii. Private Martin.
+ 3427 iv. Private Martin.
+ 3428 v. Private Martin.
+ 3429 vi. Private Martin.
+ 3430 vii. Private Martin.
+ 3431 viii. Private Martin.
+ 3432 ix. John E. Martin, born May 25, 1949; died February 11, 1984.

2541. Emma Mae[13] Eby (Peter Hershey[12], Sarah Lucinda[11] Hershey, Peter[10], Jacob[9], John[8], Jacob Snavely[7], Andrew Stauffer[6], Adelheid Galle[5] Stouffer, Daniel[4], Christian[3], Hans[2], Hans[1]) was born October 27, 1918. She married **Carmi R. Stauffer**. He was born November 20, 1913.

Children of Emma Eby and Carmi Stauffer are:
+ 3433 i. Private[14] Stauffer.
+ 3434 ii. Private Stauffer.
+ 3435 iii. Private Stauffer.
+ 3436 iv. Private Stauffer.

2543. Rhoda S.[13] Eby (Enos Jacob[12], Sarah Lucinda[11] Hershey, Peter[10], Jacob[9], John[8], Jacob Snavely[7], Andrew Stauffer[6], Adelheid Galle[5] Stouffer, Daniel[4], Christian[3], Hans[2], Hans[1]) was born August 22, 1918. She married **Daniel B. Stauffer**. He was born September 28, 1920.

Children of Rhoda Eby and Daniel Stauffer are:
  3437 i. Private[14] Stauffer.
+ 3438 ii. Private Stauffer.
+ 3439 iii. Private Stauffer.
  3440 iv. Private Stauffer.
  3441 v. Private Stauffer.
  3442 vi. Private Stauffer.
  3443 vii. Private Stauffer.
  3444 viii. Joe E. Stauffer, born November 14, 1950; died June 04, 1979.

2544. Henry S.[13] Eby (Enos Jacob[12], Sarah Lucinda[11] Hershey, Peter[10], Jacob[9], John[8], Jacob Snavely[7], Andrew Stauffer[6], Adelheid Galle[5] Stouffer, Daniel[4], Christian[3], Hans[2], Hans[1]) was born July 21, 1920. He married **Emma E. Zeiset**. She was born November 03, 1927.

Children of Henry Eby and Emma Zeiset are:
+ 3445 i. Private[14] Eby.
+ 3446 ii. Private Eby.
+ 3447 iii. Private Eby.
+ 3448 iv. Private Eby.
+ 3449 v. Private Eby.
+ 3450 vi. Private Eby.
  3451 vii. Private Eby.
  3452 viii. James Z. Eby, born August 31, 1960; died February 19, 1961.

2545. Ezra S.[13] Eby (Enos Jacob[12], Sarah Lucinda[11] Hershey, Peter[10], Jacob[9], John[8], Jacob Snavely[7], Andrew Stauffer[6], Adelheid Galle[5] Stouffer, Daniel[4], Christian[3], Hans[2], Hans[1]) was born October 31, 1922. He married **Ada Zimmerman**. She was born February 02, 1926.

Children of Ezra Eby and Ada Zimmerman are:
	3453	i.	Private[14] Eby.
+	3454	ii.	Private Eby.
	3455	iii.	Private Eby.
+	3456	iv.	Private Eby.
+	3457	v.	Private Eby.
	3458	vi.	Private Eby.
+	3459	vii.	Private Eby.
+	3460	viii.	Private Eby.

2546. Eli S.[13] Eby (Enos Jacob[12], Sarah Lucinda[11] Hershey, Peter[10], Jacob[9], John[8], Jacob Snavely[7], Andrew Stauffer[6], Adelheid Galle[5] Stouffer, Daniel[4], Christian[3], Hans[2], Hans[1]) was born March 19, 1925, and died December 12, 1985. He married **Private Zimmerman**.

Children of Eli Eby and Private Zimmerman are:
	3461	i.	Private[14] Eby.
	3462	ii.	Private Eby.
	3463	iii.	Private Eby.
+	3464	iv.	Private Eby.
+	3465	v.	Private Eby.
+	3466	vi.	Private Eby.

2547. Lydia S.[13] Eby (Enos Jacob[12], Sarah Lucinda[11] Hershey, Peter[10], Jacob[9], John[8], Jacob Snavely[7], Andrew Stauffer[6], Adelheid Galle[5] Stouffer, Daniel[4], Christian[3], Hans[2], Hans[1]) was born March 31, 1927. She married **Private Bauman**.

Child of Lydia Eby and Private Bauman is:
3467	i.	Private[14] Bauman. She married Private Gehman.

2551. Private[13] Gehman (Sarah Lucinda[12] Eby, Sarah Lucinda[11] Hershey, Peter[10], Jacob[9], John[8], Jacob Snavely[7], Andrew Stauffer[6], Adelheid Galle[5] Stouffer, Daniel[4], Christian[3], Hans[2], Hans[1]) He married **Private Barnhill**.

Children of Private Gehman and Private Barnhill are:
	3468	i.	Private[14] Gehman.
	3469	ii.	Private Gehman.
+	3470	iii.	Private Gehman.
+	3471	iv.	Private Gehman.
+	3472	v.	Private Gehman.

2552. Private[13] Gehman (Sarah Lucinda[12] Eby, Sarah Lucinda[11] Hershey, Peter[10], Jacob[9], John[8], Jacob Snavely[7], Andrew Stauffer[6], Adelheid Galle[5] Stouffer, Daniel[4], Christian[3], Hans[2], Hans[1]) He married **Mildrfed K. Ebersole**. She was born July 15, 1929.

Children of Private Gehman and Mildrfed Ebersole are:
+	3473	i.	Private[14] Gehman.
+	3474	ii.	Private Gehman.
	3475	iii.	Private Gehman. She married Private Brackbill.
+	3476	iv.	Private Gehman.
	3477	v.	Private Gehman.

2553. Arthur E.[13] Gehman (Sarah Lucinda[12] Eby, Sarah Lucinda[11] Hershey, Peter[10], Jacob[9], John[8], Jacob Snavely[7], Andrew Stauffer[6], Adelheid Galle[5] Stouffer, Daniel[4], Christian[3], Hans[2], Hans[1]) was born January 19, 1920. He married **Martha Helen Shafer**. She was born February 13, 1919, and died April 21, 1990.

Children of Arthur Gehman and Martha Shafer are:
+	3478	i.	Private[14] Gehman.
+	3479	ii.	Private Gehman.
+	3480	iii.	Private Gehman.

2554. John E.[13] Gehman (Sarah Lucinda[12] Eby, Sarah Lucinda[11] Hershey, Peter[10], Jacob[9], John[8], Jacob Snavely[7], Andrew Stauffer[6], Adelheid Galle[5] Stouffer, Daniel[4], Christian[3], Hans[2], Hans[1]) was born October 18, 1921. He married **Anna Mae Mull**. She was born July

26, 1920.

Children of John Gehman and Anna Mull are:
	3481	i.	Private[14] Gehman.
+	3482	ii.	Private Gehman.
	3483	iii.	Private Gehman.
+	3484	iv.	Private Gehman.
+	3485	v.	Private Gehman.
	3486	vi.	Private Gehman. She married Private Graybill.
+	3487	vii.	Private Gehman.

2555. Edith Elizabeth[13] Gehman (Sarah Lucinda[12] Eby, Sarah Lucinda[11] Hershey, Peter[10], Jacob[9], John[8], Jacob Snavely[7], Andrew Stauffer[6], Adelheid Galle[5] Stouffer, Daniel[4], Christian[3], Hans[2], Hans[1]) was born March 31, 1923. She married **Norman Myer Groff**. He was born March 24, 1924.

Children of Edith Gehman and Norman Groff are:
+	3488	i.	Private[14] Groff.
+	3489	ii.	Private Groff.
+	3490	iii.	Private Groff.
+	3491	iv.	Private Groff.
+	3492	v.	Private Groff.
+	3493	vi.	Private Groff.

2556. Lucy E.[13] Gehman (Sarah Lucinda[12] Eby, Sarah Lucinda[11] Hershey, Peter[10], Jacob[9], John[8], Jacob Snavely[7], Andrew Stauffer[6], Adelheid Galle[5] Stouffer, Daniel[4], Christian[3], Hans[2], Hans[1]) was born November 19, 1924. She married **John Henry Rudy**. He was born March 06, 1924.

Children of Lucy Gehman and John Rudy are:
	3494	i.	Private[14] Rudy.
+	3495	ii.	Private Rudy.
	3496	iii.	Private Rudy. He married Private Kiriyama.
	3497	iv.	Marjorie Elaine Rudy, born June 16, 1948; died July 19, 1948.

2558. Harry Jacob[13] Gehman (Sarah Lucinda[12] Eby, Sarah Lucinda[11] Hershey, Peter[10], Jacob[9], John[8], Jacob Snavely[7], Andrew Stauffer[6], Adelheid Galle[5] Stouffer, Daniel[4], Christian[3], Hans[2], Hans[1]) was born November 25, 1929. He married **Private Graybill**.

Children of Harry Gehman and Private Graybill are:
	3498	i.	Private[14] Gehman.
	3499	ii.	Private Gehman.
+	3500	iii.	Private Gehman.
+	3501	iv.	Private Gehman.
+	3502	v.	Private Gehman.
+	3503	vi.	Private Gehman.
+	3504	vii.	Private Gehman.

2559. Private[13] Eby (Henry Musser[12], Sarah Lucinda[11] Hershey, Peter[10], Jacob[9], John[8], Jacob Snavely[7], Andrew Stauffer[6], Adelheid Galle[5] Stouffer, Daniel[4], Christian[3], Hans[2], Hans[1]) He married **Private Martin**.

Children of Private Eby and Private Martin are:
3505	i.	Private[14] Eby.
3506	ii.	Private Eby.
3507	iii.	Private Eby.
3508	iv.	Private Eby.

2560. Private[13] Eby (Henry Musser[12], Sarah Lucinda[11] Hershey, Peter[10], Jacob[9], John[8], Jacob Snavely[7], Andrew Stauffer[6], Adelheid Galle[5] Stouffer, Daniel[4], Christian[3], Hans[2], Hans[1]) She married **Private Penner**.

Children of Private Eby and Private Penner are:
| 3509 | i. | Private[14] Penner. |
| 3510 | ii. | Private Penner. |

2561. Private[13] Eby (Henry Musser[12], Sarah Lucinda[11] Hershey, Peter[10], Jacob[9], John[8], Jacob Snavely[7], Andrew Stauffer[6], Adelheid Galle[5] Stouffer, Daniel[4], Christian[3], Hans[2], Hans[1]) She married **Private Hennelly**.

Child of Private Eby and Private Hennelly is:
    3511   i.   Private[14] Hennelly.

2562. Private[13] Eby (Henry Musser[12], Sarah Lucinda[11] Hershey, Peter[10], Jacob[9], John[8], Jacob Snavely[7], Andrew Stauffer[6], Adelheid Galle[5] Stouffer, Daniel[4], Christian[3], Hans[2], Hans[1]) He married **Private Beachy**.

Children of Private Eby and Private Beachy are:
    3512   i.   Private[14] Eby.
    3513   ii.   Private Eby.
    3514   iii.   Private Eby.

2563. Private[13] Eby (Henry Musser[12], Sarah Lucinda[11] Hershey, Peter[10], Jacob[9], John[8], Jacob Snavely[7], Andrew Stauffer[6], Adelheid Galle[5] Stouffer, Daniel[4], Christian[3], Hans[2], Hans[1]) He married **Private Stephens**.

Children of Private Eby and Private Stephens are:
    3515   i.   Private[14] Eby.
    3516   ii.   Private Reeves.

2564. Martin Z.[13] Eby (Henry Musser[12], Sarah Lucinda[11] Hershey, Peter[10], Jacob[9], John[8], Jacob Snavely[7], Andrew Stauffer[6], Adelheid Galle[5] Stouffer, Daniel[4], Christian[3], Hans[2], Hans[1]) was born December 25, 1921. He married **Lydia Pearl Heishman**. She was born July 07, 1921.

Children of Martin Eby and Lydia Heishman are:
+   3517   i.   Private[14] Eby.
    3518   ii.   Private Eby. He married Private Coakley.

2565. Ethel Z.[13] Eby (Henry Musser[12], Sarah Lucinda[11] Hershey, Peter[10], Jacob[9], John[8], Jacob Snavely[7], Andrew Stauffer[6], Adelheid Galle[5] Stouffer, Daniel[4], Christian[3], Hans[2], Hans[1]) was born November 25, 1923. She married **Edward J. Miller**. He was born November 25, 1921.

Children of Ethel Eby and Edward Miller are:
    3519   i.   Private[14] Miller.
+   3520   ii.   Private Miller.
+   3521   iii.   Private Miller.
    3522   iv.   Private Miller.

2567. Roy Z.[13] Eby (Henry Musser[12], Sarah Lucinda[11] Hershey, Peter[10], Jacob[9], John[8], Jacob Snavely[7], Andrew Stauffer[6], Adelheid Galle[5] Stouffer, Daniel[4], Christian[3], Hans[2], Hans[1]) was born September 20, 1927. He married **Private Schrock**.

Children of Roy Eby and Private Schrock are:
    3523   i.   Private[14] Eby.
    3524   ii.   Private Eby.
    3525   iii.   Private Eby.
    3526   iv.   Private Eby.

2568. Mary Z.[13] Eby (Henry Musser[12], Sarah Lucinda[11] Hershey, Peter[10], Jacob[9], John[8], Jacob Snavely[7], Andrew Stauffer[6], Adelheid Galle[5] Stouffer, Daniel[4], Christian[3], Hans[2], Hans[1]) was born June 11, 1929. She married **Henry D. Weaver**. He was born May 05, 1928.

Children of Mary Eby and Henry Weaver are:
    3527   i.   Private[14] Weaver.
    3528   ii.   Private Weaver. She married Private Miller.
+   3529   iii.   Private Weaver.
+   3530   iv.   Private Weaver.

2569. Private[13] Martin (Anna Martha[12] Eby, Sarah Lucinda[11] Hershey, Peter[10], Jacob[9], John[8], Jacob Snavely[7], Andrew Stauffer[6],

Adelheid Galle[5] Stouffer, Daniel[4], Christian[3], Hans[2], Hans[1]) He married **Private Unruh**.

Children of Private Martin and Private Unruh are:
    3531   i.   Private[14] Martin.
    3532   ii.   Private Martin.
    3533   iii.   Private Martin.

2570. Private[13] Martin (Anna Martha[12] Eby, Sarah Lucinda[11] Hershey, Peter[10], Jacob[9], John[8], Jacob Snavely[7], Andrew Stauffer[6], Adelheid Galle[5] Stouffer, Daniel[4], Christian[3], Hans[2], Hans[1]) She married **Private Zeiset**.

Child of Private Martin and Private Zeiset is:
+   3534   i.   Private[14] Zeiset.

2571. Clarence E.[13] Martin (Anna Martha[12] Eby, Sarah Lucinda[11] Hershey, Peter[10], Jacob[9], John[8], Jacob Snavely[7], Andrew Stauffer[6], Adelheid Galle[5] Stouffer, Daniel[4], Christian[3], Hans[2], Hans[1]) was born November 13, 1919. He married **Lydia Weaver**. She was born May 19, 1920.

Children of Clarence Martin and Lydia Weaver are:
    3535   i.   Private[14] Martin.
    3536   ii.   Private Martin.
+   3537   iii.   Private Martin.
+   3538   iv.   Private Martin.
+   3539   v.   Private Martin.
+   3540   vi.   Private Martin.
+   3541   vii.   Private Martin.

2572. Mary E.[13] Martin (Anna Martha[12] Eby, Sarah Lucinda[11] Hershey, Peter[10], Jacob[9], John[8], Jacob Snavely[7], Andrew Stauffer[6], Adelheid Galle[5] Stouffer, Daniel[4], Christian[3], Hans[2], Hans[1]) was born December 22, 1921. She married **Clarence H. Martin**. He was born December 15, 1919.

Children of Mary Martin and Clarence Martin are:
    3542   i.   Private[14] Martin. He married Private Freed.
+   3543   ii.   Private Martin.

2573. Paul E.[13] Martin (Anna Martha[12] Eby, Sarah Lucinda[11] Hershey, Peter[10], Jacob[9], John[8], Jacob Snavely[7], Andrew Stauffer[6], Adelheid Galle[5] Stouffer, Daniel[4], Christian[3], Hans[2], Hans[1]) was born September 29, 1923. He married **Private High**.

Children of Paul Martin and Private High are:
+   3544   i.   Private[14] Martin.
+   3545   ii.   Private Martin.
+   3546   iii.   Private Martin.

2574. Earl E.[13] Martin (Anna Martha[12] Eby, Sarah Lucinda[11] Hershey, Peter[10], Jacob[9], John[8], Jacob Snavely[7], Andrew Stauffer[6], Adelheid Galle[5] Stouffer, Daniel[4], Christian[3], Hans[2], Hans[1]) was born November 28, 1926. He married **Private Petersheim**.

Children of Earl Martin and Private Petersheim are:
+   3547   i.   Private[14] Martin.
+   3548   ii.   Private Martin.

2575. Wilmer E.[13] Martin (Anna Martha[12] Eby, Sarah Lucinda[11] Hershey, Peter[10], Jacob[9], John[8], Jacob Snavely[7], Andrew Stauffer[6], Adelheid Galle[5] Stouffer, Daniel[4], Christian[3], Hans[2], Hans[1]) was born June 05, 1929. He married **Private Bollinger**.

Children of Wilmer Martin and Private Bollinger are:
    3549   i.   Private[14] Martin.
    3550   ii.   Private Martin.

2576. Private[13] Eby (Aaron Buckwalter[12], Sarah Lucinda[11] Hershey, Peter[10], Jacob[9], John[8], Jacob Snavely[7], Andrew Stauffer[6], Adelheid Galle[5] Stouffer, Daniel[4], Christian[3], Hans[2], Hans[1]) She married **Private Martin**.

Children of Private Eby and Private Martin are:
- 3551   i.   Private[14] Martin.
- 3552   ii.   Thomas Dean Martin, born September 30, 1967; died December 28, 1983.

2577. Private[13] Eby (Aaron Buckwalter[12], Sarah Lucinda[11] Hershey, Peter[10], Jacob[9], John[8], Jacob Snavely[7], Andrew Stauffer[6], Adelheid Galle[5] Stouffer, Daniel[4], Christian[3], Hans[2], Hans[1]) He married **Private Brubaker**.

Children of Private Eby and Private Brubaker are:
- 3553   i.   Private[14] Eby.
- 3554   ii.   Private Eby.

2578. Private[13] Eby (Aaron Buckwalter[12], Sarah Lucinda[11] Hershey, Peter[10], Jacob[9], John[8], Jacob Snavely[7], Andrew Stauffer[6], Adelheid Galle[5] Stouffer, Daniel[4], Christian[3], Hans[2], Hans[1]) He married **Private Stoltzfus**.

Children of Private Eby and Private Stoltzfus are:
- + 3555   i.   Private[14] Eby.
-     3556   ii.   Private Eby.
-     3557   iii.   Private Eby.
-     3558   iv.   Private Eby. She married Private Buckwalter.

2579. Private[13] Eby (Aaron Buckwalter[12], Sarah Lucinda[11] Hershey, Peter[10], Jacob[9], John[8], Jacob Snavely[7], Andrew Stauffer[6], Adelheid Galle[5] Stouffer, Daniel[4], Christian[3], Hans[2], Hans[1]) He married **Private Lynch**.

Children of Private Eby and Private Lynch are:
-     3559   i.   Private[14] Eby.
-     3560   ii.   Private Eby.
-     3561   iii.   Private Eby. She married Private Breneman.
- + 3562   iv.   Private Eby.
-     3563   v.   Eileen Marie Eby, born March 26, 1958; died October 07, 1967.

2580. Richard S.[13] Eby (Aaron Buckwalter[12], Sarah Lucinda[11] Hershey, Peter[10], Jacob[9], John[8], Jacob Snavely[7], Andrew Stauffer[6], Adelheid Galle[5] Stouffer, Daniel[4], Christian[3], Hans[2], Hans[1]) was born October 08, 1928. He married **Private Buckwalter**.

Children of Richard Eby and Private Buckwalter are:
- + 3564   i.   Private[14] Eby.
-     3565   ii.   Private Eby.
- + 3566   iii.   Private Eby.
- + 3567   iv.   Private Eby.
- + 3568   v.   Private Eby.
- + 3569   vi.   Private Eby.

2581. Clyde S.[13] Eby (Aaron Buckwalter[12], Sarah Lucinda[11] Hershey, Peter[10], Jacob[9], John[8], Jacob Snavely[7], Andrew Stauffer[6], Adelheid Galle[5] Stouffer, Daniel[4], Christian[3], Hans[2], Hans[1]) was born November 29, 1937, and died October 08, 1974. He married **Private Nauman**.

Children of Clyde Eby and Private Nauman are:
- 3570   i.   Private[14] Eby.
- 3571   ii.   Private Eby.
- 3572   iii.   Private Eby.

2582. Private[13] Eby (Menno Hershey[12], Sarah Lucinda[11] Hershey, Peter[10], Jacob[9], John[8], Jacob Snavely[7], Andrew Stauffer[6], Adelheid Galle[5] Stouffer, Daniel[4], Christian[3], Hans[2], Hans[1]) He married **Private Kuipers**.

Children of Private Eby and Private Kuipers are:
- 3573   i.   Private[14] Eby.
- 3574   ii.   Private Eby.
- 3575   iii.   Private Eby.

2583. Private[13] Eby (Menno Hershey[12], Sarah Lucinda[11] Hershey, Peter[10], Jacob[9], John[8], Jacob Snavely[7], Andrew Stauffer[6],

Adelheid Galle[5] Stouffer, Daniel[4], Christian[3], Hans[2], Hans[1]) She married **Private Baker**.

Children of Private Eby and Private Baker are:
    3576   i.   Private[14] Baker.
    3577   ii.   Private Baker.

2584. Private[13] Eby (Menno Hershey[12], Sarah Lucinda[11] Hershey, Peter[10], Jacob[9], John[8], Jacob Snavely[7], Andrew Stauffer[6], Adelheid Galle[5] Stouffer, Daniel[4], Christian[3], Hans[2], Hans[1]) He married **Private Peters**.

Child of Private Eby and Private Peters is:
    3578   i.   Private[14] Eby.

2585. Private[13] Eby (Martin Christian[12], Sarah Lucinda[11] Hershey, Peter[10], Jacob[9], John[8], Jacob Snavely[7], Andrew Stauffer[6], Adelheid Galle[5] Stouffer, Daniel[4], Christian[3], Hans[2], Hans[1]) He married **Private Martin**.

Children of Private Eby and Private Martin are:
    3579   i.   Private[14] Eby.
    3580   ii.   Private Eby.

2586. Private[13] Eby (Martin Christian[12], Sarah Lucinda[11] Hershey, Peter[10], Jacob[9], John[8], Jacob Snavely[7], Andrew Stauffer[6], Adelheid Galle[5] Stouffer, Daniel[4], Christian[3], Hans[2], Hans[1]) He married **Private Stoltzfus**.

Children of Private Eby and Private Stoltzfus are:
    3581   i.   Private[14] Eby.
    3582   ii.   Private Eby.

2587. Private[13] Eby (Martin Christian[12], Sarah Lucinda[11] Hershey, Peter[10], Jacob[9], John[8], Jacob Snavely[7], Andrew Stauffer[6], Adelheid Galle[5] Stouffer, Daniel[4], Christian[3], Hans[2], Hans[1]) She married **Private Ebersole**.

Children of Private Eby and Private Ebersole are:
    3583   i.   Private[14] Ebersole.
    3584   ii.   Private Ebersole.

2589. Private[13] Eby (Martin Christian[12], Sarah Lucinda[11] Hershey, Peter[10], Jacob[9], John[8], Jacob Snavely[7], Andrew Stauffer[6], Adelheid Galle[5] Stouffer, Daniel[4], Christian[3], Hans[2], Hans[1]) He married **Private Landis**.

Children of Private Eby and Private Landis are:
    3585   i.   Private[14] Eby.
    3586   ii.   Private Eby.
    3587   iii.   Private Eby.

2590. Erma E.[13] Hershey (Galen Warren[12], Isaiah B.[11], Peter[10], Jacob[9], John[8], Jacob Snavely[7], Andrew Stauffer[6], Adelheid Galle[5] Stouffer, Daniel[4], Christian[3], Hans[2], Hans[1]) was born March 08, 1910. She married **Leo Trostle Crouthamel**. He was born June 22, 1909, and died September 28, 1989.

Children of Erma Hershey and Leo Crouthamel are:
+   3588   i.   Private[14] Crouthamel.
+   3589   ii.   Private Crouthamel.
+   3590   iii.   Private Crouthamel.

2591. Galen Clair[13] Hershey (Galen Warren[12], Isaiah B.[11], Peter[10], Jacob[9], John[8], Jacob Snavely[7], Andrew Stauffer[6], Adelheid Galle[5] Stouffer, Daniel[4], Christian[3], Hans[2], Hans[1]) was born February 10, 1914, and died July 15, 1992. He married **Martha Louise Acker**. She was born October 25, 1920, and died 1973.

Children of Galen Hershey and Martha Acker are:
+   3591   i.   Private[14] Hershey.
+   3592   ii.   Private Hershey.

2592. Private[13] Hershey (Henry Clay[12], Enos Jacob[11], Peter[10], Jacob[9], John[8], Jacob Snavely[7], Andrew Stauffer[6], Adelheid Galle[5] Stouffer, Daniel[4], Christian[3], Hans[2], Hans[1]) He married **Private Wenger**.

Children of Private Hershey and Private Wenger are:
- 3593   i. Private[14] Hershey.
- + 3594   ii. Private Hershey.
- 3595   iii. Private Hershey. He married Private Earhart.

2593. Private[13] Hershey (Henry Clay[12], Enos Jacob[11], Peter[10], Jacob[9], John[8], Jacob Snavely[7], Andrew Stauffer[6], Adelheid Galle[5] Stouffer, Daniel[4], Christian[3], Hans[2], Hans[1]) He married **Private Alter**.

Children of Private Hershey and Private Alter are:
- 3596   i. Private[14] Hershey.
- 3597   ii. Private Hershey.
- 3598   iii. Private Hershey.
- 3599   iv. Private Hershey.

2594. Private[13] Hershey (Henry Clay[12], Enos Jacob[11], Peter[10], Jacob[9], John[8], Jacob Snavely[7], Andrew Stauffer[6], Adelheid Galle[5] Stouffer, Daniel[4], Christian[3], Hans[2], Hans[1]) He married **Private Lefever**.

Children of Private Hershey and Private Lefever are:
- + 3600   i. Private[14] Hershey.
- + 3601   ii. Private Hershey.

2595. Private[13] Hershey (Henry Clay[12], Enos Jacob[11], Peter[10], Jacob[9], John[8], Jacob Snavely[7], Andrew Stauffer[6], Adelheid Galle[5] Stouffer, Daniel[4], Christian[3], Hans[2], Hans[1]) She married **Private Damiani**.

Children of Private Hershey and Private Damiani are:
- 3602   i. Private[14] Damiani.
- 3603   ii. Private Damiani.

2596. Hazel Pauline[13] Hershey (Henry Clay[12], Enos Jacob[11], Peter[10], Jacob[9], John[8], Jacob Snavely[7], Andrew Stauffer[6], Adelheid Galle[5] Stouffer, Daniel[4], Christian[3], Hans[2], Hans[1]) was born August 15, 1914, and died March 08, 1985. She married **Elmer Metzler**. He was born March 16, 1916.

Children of Hazel Hershey and Elmer Metzler are:
- 3604   i. Private[14] Metzler. She married Private Franklin.
- + 3605   ii. Private Metzler.
- 3606   iii. Private Metzler. She married Private Markovich.

2598. Ralph Glenn[13] Hershey (Henry Clay[12], Enos Jacob[11], Peter[10], Jacob[9], John[8], Jacob Snavely[7], Andrew Stauffer[6], Adelheid Galle[5] Stouffer, Daniel[4], Christian[3], Hans[2], Hans[1]) was born December 15, 1918, and died March 12, 1988. He married **Miriam Lengenecker**. She was born October 15, 1922.

Children of Ralph Hershey and Miriam Lengenecker are:
- + 3607   i. Private[14] Hershey.
- + 3608   ii. Private Hershey.
- + 3609   iii. Private Hershey.

2600. Gladys Edna[13] Hershey (Henry Clay[12], Enos Jacob[11], Peter[10], Jacob[9], John[8], Jacob Snavely[7], Andrew Stauffer[6], Adelheid Galle[5] Stouffer, Daniel[4], Christian[3], Hans[2], Hans[1]) was born August 08, 1927. She married **Eby Kreider**. He was born April 22, 1926.

Children of Gladys Hershey and Eby Kreider are:
- + 3610   i. Private[14] Kreider.
- 3611   ii. Private Kreider. She married Private Sherid.
- + 3612   iii. Private Kreider.
- + 3613   iv. Private Kreider.
- 3614   v. Unknown Kreider, born November 07, 1949; died November 07, 1949.

2601. Clifford Eby[13] **Hershey** (Henry Clay[12], Enos Jacob[11], Peter[10], Jacob[9], John[8], Jacob Snavely[7], Andrew Stauffer[6], Adelheid Galle[5] Stouffer, Daniel[4], Christian[3], Hans[2], Hans[1]) was born November 17, 1928, and died February 06, 1969. He married **Private Feister**.

Children of Clifford Hershey and Private Feister are:
	3615	i.	Private[14] Hershey.
	3616	ii.	Private Hershey.
	3617	iii.	Private Hershey.
+	3618	iv.	Private Hershey.
+	3619	v.	Private Hershey.

2602. Private[13] **Hershey** (Mark Eby[12], Enos Jacob[11], Peter[10], Jacob[9], John[8], Jacob Snavely[7], Andrew Stauffer[6], Adelheid Galle[5] Stouffer, Daniel[4], Christian[3], Hans[2], Hans[1]) He married **Private Lehigh**.

Children of Private Hershey and Private Lehigh are:
- 3620 i. Private[14] Hershey.
- 3621 ii. Private Hershey.

2603. Private[13] **Hershey** (Mark Eby[12], Enos Jacob[11], Peter[10], Jacob[9], John[8], Jacob Snavely[7], Andrew Stauffer[6], Adelheid Galle[5] Stouffer, Daniel[4], Christian[3], Hans[2], Hans[1]) She married **Private Peachey**.

Children of Private Hershey and Private Peachey are:
- 3622 i. Private[14] Peachey.
- 3623 ii. Private Peachey.
- 3624 iii. Private Peachey.
- 3625 iv. Private Peachey.

2604. Private[13] **Hershey** (Mark Eby[12], Enos Jacob[11], Peter[10], Jacob[9], John[8], Jacob Snavely[7], Andrew Stauffer[6], Adelheid Galle[5] Stouffer, Daniel[4], Christian[3], Hans[2], Hans[1]) She married **Private Lichty**.

Children of Private Hershey and Private Lichty are:
- 3626 i. Private[14] Lichty.
- 3627 ii. Private Lichty.
- 3628 iii. Private Lichty.

2605. Private[13] **Hershey** (Mark Eby[12], Enos Jacob[11], Peter[10], Jacob[9], John[8], Jacob Snavely[7], Andrew Stauffer[6], Adelheid Galle[5] Stouffer, Daniel[4], Christian[3], Hans[2], Hans[1]) She married **Private Martin**.

Children of Private Hershey and Private Martin are:
	3629	i.	Private[14] Martin.
	3630	ii.	Private Martin. She married Private Frey.
	3631	iii.	Private Martin. He married Private Yoder.
+	3632	iv.	Private Martin.

2606. Private[13] **Hershey** (Mark Eby[12], Enos Jacob[11], Peter[10], Jacob[9], John[8], Jacob Snavely[7], Andrew Stauffer[6], Adelheid Galle[5] Stouffer, Daniel[4], Christian[3], Hans[2], Hans[1]) He married **Private Kauffman**.

Children of Private Hershey and Private Kauffman are:
- 3633 i. Private[14] Hershey.
- 3634 ii. Private Hershey.
- 3635 iii. Private Hershey. He married Private Unknown.
- 3636 iv. Private Hershey.
- 3637 v. Private Hershey.

2607. Private[13] **Hershey** (Mark Eby[12], Enos Jacob[11], Peter[10], Jacob[9], John[8], Jacob Snavely[7], Andrew Stauffer[6], Adelheid Galle[5] Stouffer, Daniel[4], Christian[3], Hans[2], Hans[1]) She married **Martin L. Bender**. He was born June 03, 1928.

Children of Private Hershey and Martin Bender are:
- 3638 i. Private[14] Bender.
- 3639 ii. Private Bender.
- 3640 iii. Private Bender.

	3641	iv.	Private Bender.
+	3642	v.	Private Bender.

2608. Private[13] Hershey (Mark Eby[12], Enos Jacob[11], Peter[10], Jacob[9], John[8], Jacob Snavely[7], Andrew Stauffer[6], Adelheid Galle[5] Stouffer, Daniel[4], Christian[3], Hans[2], Hans[1]) He married **Private Singer**.

Children of Private Hershey and Private Singer are:
	3643	i.	Private[14] Hershey.
+	3644	ii.	Private Hershey.
+	3645	iii.	Private Hershey.
+	3646	iv.	Private Hershey.

2610. Private[13] Hershey (David Warren[12], Enos Jacob[11], Peter[10], Jacob[9], John[8], Jacob Snavely[7], Andrew Stauffer[6], Adelheid Galle[5] Stouffer, Daniel[4], Christian[3], Hans[2], Hans[1]) She married **Private Herr**.

Children of Private Hershey and Private Herr are:
	3647	i.	Private[14] Herr.
	3648	ii.	Private Herr.

2611. Vincent Denlinger[13] Hershey (David Warren[12], Enos Jacob[11], Peter[10], Jacob[9], John[8], Jacob Snavely[7], Andrew Stauffer[6], Adelheid Galle[5] Stouffer, Daniel[4], Christian[3], Hans[2], Hans[1]) was born September 20, 1925. He married **Mary Ethel Brackbill**. She was born July 24, 1925.

Children of Vincent Hershey and Mary Brackbill are:
	3649	i.	Private[14] Hershey.
+	3650	ii.	Private Hershey.
	3651	iii.	Private Hershey.
+	3652	iv.	Private Hershey.
+	3653	v.	Private Hershey.

2614. Private[13] Ranck (Mary Helen[12] Hershey, Enos Jacob[11], Peter[10], Jacob[9], John[8], Jacob Snavely[7], Andrew Stauffer[6], Adelheid Galle[5] Stouffer, Daniel[4], Christian[3], Hans[2], Hans[1]) He married **Private Wynia**.

Child of Private Ranck and Private Wynia is:
3654	i.	Private[14] Ranck.

2615. Lester Hershey[13] Ranck (Mary Helen[12] Hershey, Enos Jacob[11], Peter[10], Jacob[9], John[8], Jacob Snavely[7], Andrew Stauffer[6], Adelheid Galle[5] Stouffer, Daniel[4], Christian[3], Hans[2], Hans[1]) was born April 21, 1924. He married **Mary Root Todd**. She was born March 05, 1924.

Children of Lester Ranck and Mary Todd are:
	3655	i.	Private[14] Ranck. He married Private Groff.
+	3656	ii.	Private Ranck.
+	3657	iii.	Private Ranck.
	3658	iv.	Private Ranck.

2616. Arthur Eby[13] Ranck (Mary Helen[12] Hershey, Enos Jacob[11], Peter[10], Jacob[9], John[8], Jacob Snavely[7], Andrew Stauffer[6], Adelheid Galle[5] Stouffer, Daniel[4], Christian[3], Hans[2], Hans[1]) was born September 06, 1925. He married **Phoebe Kennel**. She was born February 27, 1926.

Children of Arthur Ranck and Phoebe Kennel are:
	3659	i.	Private[14] Ranck.
+	3660	ii.	Private Ranck.
	3661	iii.	Private Ranck. He married Private Horst.
	3662	iv.	Jane Elizabeth Ranck, born December 15, 1957; died December 15, 1957.

2617. Donald Edwin[13] Ranck (Mary Helen[12] Hershey, Enos Jacob[11], Peter[10], Jacob[9], John[8], Jacob Snavely[7], Andrew Stauffer[6], Adelheid Galle[5] Stouffer, Daniel[4], Christian[3], Hans[2], Hans[1]) was born June 26, 1927. He married **Kathleen Martin**. She was born May 07, 1927.

Children of Donald Ranck and Kathleen Martin are:
- 3663   i.   Private[14] Ranck.
- + 3664   ii.   Private Ranck.

2619. Janet Potter[13] Hess (Clyde C.[12], Elizabeth[11] Hershey, Peter[10], Jacob[9], John[8], Jacob Snavely[7], Andrew Stauffer[6], Adelheid Galle[5] Stouffer, Daniel[4], Christian[3], Hans[2], Hans[1]) was born July 10, 1924. She married **Ernest Ludwig Daman**. He was born March 14, 1923.

Children of Janet Hess and Ernest Daman are:
- 3665   i.   Private[14] Daman.
- + 3666   ii.   Private Daman.
- + 3667   iii.   Private Daman.

2621. Rhoda Gregory[13] Hess (Harry Hershey[12], Elizabeth[11] Hershey, Peter[10], Jacob[9], John[8], Jacob Snavely[7], Andrew Stauffer[6], Adelheid Galle[5] Stouffer, Daniel[4], Christian[3], Hans[2], Hans[1]) was born September 12, 1926. She married **Lyle Andrew Briggs**.

Children of Rhoda Hess and Lyle Briggs are:
- 3668   i.   Private[14] Briggs.
- 3669   ii.   Private Briggs. She married Private Heilman.
- 3670   iii.   Private Briggs. She married Private vanWormer.

2622. Richard Henry[13] Hershey (Paul Keene[12], Henry Peter[11], Peter[10], Jacob[9], John[8], Jacob Snavely[7], Andrew Stauffer[6], Adelheid Galle[5] Stouffer, Daniel[4], Christian[3], Hans[2], Hans[1]) was born January 10, 1928. He married **Private Roush**.

Children of Richard Hershey and Private Roush are:
- 3671   i.   Private[14] Hershey.
- 3672   ii.   Private Hershey.

2623. Paul Kenneth[13] Hershey (Paul Keene[12], Henry Peter[11], Peter[10], Jacob[9], John[8], Jacob Snavely[7], Andrew Stauffer[6], Adelheid Galle[5] Stouffer, Daniel[4], Christian[3], Hans[2], Hans[1]) was born October 14, 1929. He married **(1) Private Dotts**. He married **(2) Private Hails**.

Children of Paul Hershey and Private Dotts are:
- + 3673   i.   Private[14] Hershey.
- 3674   ii.   Private Hershey.

Children of Paul Hershey and Private Hails are:
- 3675   i.   Private[14] Hershey.
- 3676   ii.   Private Hershey.

2626. Private[13] Pennock (Esther Elizabeth[12] Hershey, Martin Eby[11], Peter[10], Jacob[9], John[8], Jacob Snavely[7], Andrew Stauffer[6], Adelheid Galle[5] Stouffer, Daniel[4], Christian[3], Hans[2], Hans[1]) She married **Thomas Garrett Hewes**. He was born November 02, 1928.

Children of Private Pennock and Thomas Hewes are:
- + 3677   i.   Private[14] Hewes.
- + 3678   ii.   Private Hewes.
- + 3679   iii.   Private Hewes.
- 3680   iv.   Private Hewes.
- 3681   v.   Private Hewes.
- 3682   vi.   John Martin Hewes, born July 04, 1956; died May 20, 1987. He married Private Unknown.

2627. Betty Louise[13] Pennock (Esther Elizabeth[12] Hershey, Martin Eby[11], Peter[10], Jacob[9], John[8], Jacob Snavely[7], Andrew Stauffer[6], Adelheid Galle[5] Stouffer, Daniel[4], Christian[3], Hans[2], Hans[1]) was born October 18, 1929. She married **Harry Brisbin Skiles**. He was born January 04, 1929, and died July 09, 1988.

Children of Betty Pennock and Harry Skiles are:
- + 3683   i.   Private[14] Skiles.
- + 3684   ii.   Private Skiles.

2628. Private[13] **Rodgers** (Miriam Clara[12] Hershey, Martin Eby[11], Peter[10], Jacob[9], John[8], Jacob Snavely[7], Andrew Stauffer[6], Adelheid Galle[5] Stouffer, Daniel[4], Christian[3], Hans[2], Hans[1]) He married **Private McSeveney**.

Children of Private Rodgers and Private McSeveney are:
- 3685   i.   Private[14] Rodgers.
- + 3686   ii.   Private Rodgers.
- 3687   iii.   Private Rodgers.
- 3688   iv.   Private Rodgers.
- 3689   v.   Private Rodgers.

2632. Private[13] **Hershey** (Lester D.[12], Silas N.[11], Peter[10], Jacob[9], John[8], Jacob Snavely[7], Andrew Stauffer[6], Adelheid Galle[5] Stouffer, Daniel[4], Christian[3], Hans[2], Hans[1]) She married **Private Weaver**.

Children of Private Hershey and Private Weaver are:
- 3690   i.   Private[14] Weaver.
- 3691   ii.   Private Weaver.
- 3692   iii.   Private Weaver.
- 3693   iv.   Private Weaver.
- 3694   v.   Private Weaver.

2633. Private[13] **Zimmerman** (Barbara Elizabeth[12] Hershey, Silas N.[11], Peter[10], Jacob[9], John[8], Jacob Snavely[7], Andrew Stauffer[6], Adelheid Galle[5] Stouffer, Daniel[4], Christian[3], Hans[2], Hans[1]) She married **Private Stauffer**.

Children of Private Zimmerman and Private Stauffer are:
- 3695   i.   Private[14] Stauffer.
- 3696   ii.   Private Stauffer.

2634. Private[13] **Zimmerman** (Barbara Elizabeth[12] Hershey, Silas N.[11], Peter[10], Jacob[9], John[8], Jacob Snavely[7], Andrew Stauffer[6], Adelheid Galle[5] Stouffer, Daniel[4], Christian[3], Hans[2], Hans[1]) He married **Private Lutz**.

Children of Private Zimmerman and Private Lutz are:
- 3697   i.   Private[14] Zimmerman.
- 3698   ii.   Private Zimmerman.
- 3699   iii.   Private Zimmerman.

2635. Private[13] **Zimmerman** (Barbara Elizabeth[12] Hershey, Silas N.[11], Peter[10], Jacob[9], John[8], Jacob Snavely[7], Andrew Stauffer[6], Adelheid Galle[5] Stouffer, Daniel[4], Christian[3], Hans[2], Hans[1]) He married **Private Smoker**.

Children of Private Zimmerman and Private Smoker are:
- 3700   i.   Private[14] Zimmerman.
- 3701   ii.   Private Zimmerman.

2636. Private[13] **Hershey** (Willis Daniel[12], Silas N.[11], Peter[10], Jacob[9], John[8], Jacob Snavely[7], Andrew Stauffer[6], Adelheid Galle[5] Stouffer, Daniel[4], Christian[3], Hans[2], Hans[1]) She married **(1) Private Richardson**. She married **(2) Private Alexander**.

Children of Private Hershey and Private Richardson are:
- + 3702   i.   Private[14] Richardson.
- + 3703   ii.   Private Richardson.
- 3704   iii.   Private Richardson.

2637. Private[13] **Hershey** (Willis Daniel[12], Silas N.[11], Peter[10], Jacob[9], John[8], Jacob Snavely[7], Andrew Stauffer[6], Adelheid Galle[5] Stouffer, Daniel[4], Christian[3], Hans[2], Hans[1]) She married **Private Summers**.

Children of Private Hershey and Private Summers are:
- + 3705   i.   Private[14] Summers.
- + 3706   ii.   Private Summers.

2638. Private[13] Hershey (Willis Daniel[12], Silas N.[11], Peter[10], Jacob[9], John[8], Jacob Snavely[7], Andrew Stauffer[6], Adelheid Galle[5] Stouffer, Daniel[4], Christian[3], Hans[2], Hans[1]) He married **(1) Private Myers**. He married **(2) Private Gregg**.

Child of Private Hershey and Private Myers is:
+ 3707   i.   Private[14] Bomberger.

Child of Private Hershey and Private Gregg is:
+ 3708   i.   Private[14] Hershey.

2639. Private[13] Hershey (Willis Daniel[12], Silas N.[11], Peter[10], Jacob[9], John[8], Jacob Snavely[7], Andrew Stauffer[6], Adelheid Galle[5] Stouffer, Daniel[4], Christian[3], Hans[2], Hans[1]) He married **Private Hoober**.

Children of Private Hershey and Private Hoober are:
+ 3709   i.   Private[14] Hershey.
    3710   ii.   Private Hershey. He married Private Landis.

2640. Private[13] Hershey (Willis Daniel[12], Silas N.[11], Peter[10], Jacob[9], John[8], Jacob Snavely[7], Andrew Stauffer[6], Adelheid Galle[5] Stouffer, Daniel[4], Christian[3], Hans[2], Hans[1]) She married **Private Miller**.

Children of Private Hershey and Private Miller are:
    3711   i.   Private[14] Miller.
    3712   ii.   Private Miller.

2641. Jay Paul[13] Hershey (Willis Daniel[12], Silas N.[11], Peter[10], Jacob[9], John[8], Jacob Snavely[7], Andrew Stauffer[6], Adelheid Galle[5] Stouffer, Daniel[4], Christian[3], Hans[2], Hans[1]) was born April 27, 1941, and died November 02, 1996. He married **Private Boohar**.

Children of Jay Hershey and Private Boohar are:
+ 3713   i.   Private[14] Hershey.
+ 3714   ii.   Private Hershey.
+ 3715   iii.   Private Hershey.

2642. Private[13] Nolt (Reba L.[12] Hershey, Silas N.[11], Peter[10], Jacob[9], John[8], Jacob Snavely[7], Andrew Stauffer[6], Adelheid Galle[5] Stouffer, Daniel[4], Christian[3], Hans[2], Hans[1]) She married **(1) Private Clymer**. She married **(2) Private Swartzendruber**.

Child of Private Nolt and Private Clymer is:
    3716   i.   Private[14] Clymer.

Child of Private Nolt and Private Swartzendruber is:
    3717   i.   Private[14] Swartzendruber.

2643. Private[13] Nolt (Reba L.[12] Hershey, Silas N.[11], Peter[10], Jacob[9], John[8], Jacob Snavely[7], Andrew Stauffer[6], Adelheid Galle[5] Stouffer, Daniel[4], Christian[3], Hans[2], Hans[1]) She married **(1) Private Harmon**. She married **(2) Private Kranz**.

Child of Private Nolt and Private Harmon is:
    3718   i.   Private[14] Harmon.

2645. Private[13] Kauffman (Doris Mae[12] Hershey, Silas N.[11], Peter[10], Jacob[9], John[8], Jacob Snavely[7], Andrew Stauffer[6], Adelheid Galle[5] Stouffer, Daniel[4], Christian[3], Hans[2], Hans[1]) She married **Private Barth**.

Children of Private Kauffman and Private Barth are:
    3719   i.   Private[14] Barth.
    3720   ii.   Private Barth.
    3721   iii.   Private Barth.

2646. Private[13] Kauffman (Doris Mae[12] Hershey, Silas N.[11], Peter[10], Jacob[9], John[8], Jacob Snavely[7], Andrew Stauffer[6], Adelheid Galle[5] Stouffer, Daniel[4], Christian[3], Hans[2], Hans[1]) She married **(1) Private Stover**. She married **(2) Private Haldeman**.

Child of Private Kauffman and Private Stover is:

3722 i. Private[14] Stover.

2647. Private[13] Lowry (Doris Mae[12] Hershey, Silas N.[11], Peter[10], Jacob[9], John[8], Jacob Snavely[7], Andrew Stauffer[6], Adelheid Galle[5] Stouffer, Daniel[4], Christian[3], Hans[2], Hans[1]) She married **Private Wanner**.

Children of Private Lowry and Private Wanner are:
 3723 i. Private[14] Wanner.
 3724 ii. Private Wanner.

2649. Paul Steffy[13] Horst (Elam Sweigart[12], Frances Reiff[11] Sweigart, Annie[10] Reiff, Veronica[9] Hershey, John[8], Jacob Snavely[7], Andrew Stauffer[6], Adelheid Galle[5] Stouffer, Daniel[4], Christian[3], Hans[2], Hans[1]) was born July 26, 1914. He married **Sylvia Kauffman**. She was born December 10, 1919.

Children of Paul Horst and Sylvia Kauffman are:
+ 3725 i. Cedric Linn[14] Horst, born March 13, 1942.
 3726 ii. Joan Elaine Horst, born July 27, 1943.
+ 3727 iii. Joann Louise Horst, born July 27, 1943.
+ 3728 iv. Paul Gary Horst, born February 08, 1950.

2650. William Prichard[13] Horst (Elam Sweigart[12], Frances Reiff[11] Sweigart, Annie[10] Reiff, Veronica[9] Hershey, John[8], Jacob Snavely[7], Andrew Stauffer[6], Adelheid Galle[5] Stouffer, Daniel[4], Christian[3], Hans[2], Hans[1]) was born October 03, 1917. He married **Emma Zimmerman Weber** February 06, 1937. She was born June 12, 1916.

Children of William Horst and Emma Weber are:
 3729 i. James Richard[14] Horst, born October 08, 1942.
+ 3730 ii. Mary Louise Horst, born January 27, 1944.
+ 3731 iii. Mark William Horst, born November 08, 1948.

2651. Erma Steffy[13] Horst (Elam Sweigart[12], Frances Reiff[11] Sweigart, Annie[10] Reiff, Veronica[9] Hershey, John[8], Jacob Snavely[7], Andrew Stauffer[6], Adelheid Galle[5] Stouffer, Daniel[4], Christian[3], Hans[2], Hans[1]) was born April 25, 1924. She married **Luke Carvell** February 09, 1946. He was born April 02, 1926.

Children of Erma Horst and Luke Carvell are:
+ 3732 i. Vici Mae[14] Carvell, born March 24, 1948.
+ 3733 ii. Audrey Nadine Carvell, born May 07, 1949.
 3734 iii. Glee Eileen Carvell, born July 29, 1952. She married C. William Usmar March 26, 1977; born September 15, 1934.

2652. Gordon Steffy[13] Horst (Elam Sweigart[12], Frances Reiff[11] Sweigart, Annie[10] Reiff, Veronica[9] Hershey, John[8], Jacob Snavely[7], Andrew Stauffer[6], Adelheid Galle[5] Stouffer, Daniel[4], Christian[3], Hans[2], Hans[1]) was born March 30, 1929. He married **(1) Miriam Galebach** 1947. He married **(2) Barbara Dyer** 1956. He married **(3) Evelyn Mae Neidermyer Shaub** July 17, 1971.

Children of Gordon Horst and Barbara Dyer are:
 3735 i. Diane L.[14] Horst, born October 09, 1956. She married Scott Lee Bachman.
 3736 ii. Randy Paul Horst, born October 07, 1957.
 3737 iii. Rodney William Horst, born February 23, 1959.
 3738 iv. Ronald Gregory Horst, born January 20, 1960.

2684. Jay Donald[13] Weaver (John Landis[13], Magdalena M.[12] Landis, Magdalena O.[11] Martin, Martha H.[10] Oberholtzer, Martha H.[9] Hess, Esther[8] Hershey, Christian[7], Benjamin Stauffer[6], Adelheid Galle[5] Stouffer, Daniel[4], Christian[3], Hans[2], Hans[1]) was born April 20, 1933 in Ephrata Twp, Lanc Co, PA. He married **Mary Naomi Musser** July 16, 1955 in East Petersburg, PA, daughter of Christian Musser and Martha Livengood. She was born April 21, 1934 in East Hempfield Twp, Lanc Co, PA.

Children of Jay Weaver and Mary Musser are:
 3739 i. Ellen Sue[14] Weaver, born December 04, 1956 in Reading, Berks Co, PA.
+ 3740 ii. James Edward Weaver, born November 10, 1960 in Lancaster, PA.

2685. Arvilla[13] Weaver (John Landis[13], Magdalena M.[12] Landis, Magdalena O.[11] Martin, Martha H.[10] Oberholtzer, Martha H.[9] Hess, Esther[8] Hershey, Christian[7], Benjamin Stauffer[6], Adelheid Galle[5] Stouffer, Daniel[4], Christian[3], Hans[2], Hans[1]) was born July 21, 1934 in

Ephrata Twp, Lanc Co, PA. She married **Robert T. Langsdale** March 02, 1958 in Kalamazoo, MI. He was born April 02, 1930 in Pittsburgh, PA.

Children of Arvilla Weaver and Robert Langsdale are:
+   3741   i.   Rae Elizabeth[14] Langsdale, born December 23, 1958 in Ephrata, PA.
       3742   ii.   Edward Jay Langsdale, born June 29, 1960 in Buffalo, NY.
+   3743   iii.   Robert John Langsdale, born September 05, 1965.

2686. Donna Lou[13] Weaver (John Landis[13], Magdalena M.[12] Landis, Magdalena O.[11] Martin, Martha H.[10] Oberholtzer, Martha H.[9] Hess, Esther[8] Hershey, Christian[7], Benjamin Stauffer[6], Adelheid Galle[5] Stouffer, Daniel[4], Christian[3], Hans[2], Hans[1]) was born July 11, 1942 in Akron, Lancaster Co, PA. She married **(1) Jerry Foster**. He was born October 25, 1942 in Hartford, CT. She married **(2) David Arthur Bucove** November 05, 1960 in Brownstown, Lancaster Co., PA. He was born January 15, 1941.

Children of Donna Weaver and David Bucove are:
       3744   i.   Andre Maurice[14] Bucove, born August 15, 1961.
+   3745   ii.   Rachel Naomi Bucove, born July 13, 1971.

2687. John Eric[13] Weaver (John Landis[13], Magdalena M.[12] Landis, Magdalena O.[11] Martin, Martha H.[10] Oberholtzer, Martha H.[9] Hess, Esther[8] Hershey, Christian[7], Benjamin Stauffer[6], Adelheid Galle[5] Stouffer, Daniel[4], Christian[3], Hans[2], Hans[1]) was born February 11, 1945 in Ephrata, PA. He married **Sandra M. Fritz** October 09, 1965 in Akron, Lancaster Co, PA. She was born December 09, 1944.

Children of John Weaver and Sandra Fritz are:
+   3746   i.   John Michael[14] Weaver, born June 19, 1968 in Ephrata, Lancaster Co., PA.
       3747   ii.   Lisa Rene Weaver, born November 28, 1970.

2689. Ronald Lee[13] Weaver (John Landis[13], Magdalena M.[12] Landis, Magdalena O.[11] Martin, Martha H.[10] Oberholtzer, Martha H.[9] Hess, Esther[8] Hershey, Christian[7], Benjamin Stauffer[6], Adelheid Galle[5] Stouffer, Daniel[4], Christian[3], Hans[2], Hans[1]) was born August 16, 1950 in Ephrata, PA. He married **Carolyn Jean Weaver** October 21, 1972. She was born December 21, 1950.

Children of Ronald Weaver and Carolyn Weaver are:
       3748   i.   John Matthew[14] Weaver, born November 29, 1974 in Ephrata, Lancaster Co., PA. He married Krista J. Weber; born March 02, 1974 in Ephrata, Lancaster Co., PA.
       3749   ii.   Jennifer Lynn Weaver, born December 14, 1977 in Ephrata, Lancaster Co., PA. She married Corby M. Burkholder May 16, 1998 in Neffsville Mennonite Church, Manheim Twp., Lancaster Co., PA; born November 09, 1977 in Lancaster, Lancaster Co., PA.
       3750   iii.   Andrew S. Weaver, born July 20, 1979 in Ephrata, Lancaster Co., PA.

2701. Robert Melvin[13] Burkholder (Melvin E[12], Abraham H[11], Susan[10] Hershey, Abraham[9], Christian[8], Jacob Snavely[7], Andrew Stauffer[6], Adelheid Galle[5] Stouffer, Daniel[4], Christian[3], Hans[2], Hans[1]) was born March 03, 1935. He married **Justina Miller**. She was born March 30, 1935.

Children of Robert Burkholder and Justina Miller are:
       3751   i.   Robert[14] Burkholder, born February 03, 1957.
       3752   ii.   Kathleen Burkholder, born February 05, 1959.
       3753   iii.   Thomas Burkholder, born July 20, 1962.
       3754   iv.   Lisa Burkholder, born August 07, 1964.
       3755   v.   Kevin Burkholder, born July 04, 1970. He married Gina Marie D'Ginto.

2708. Private[13] Fox (Robert Thomas[12], James George[11], Diana[10] Hershey, Henry[9], Martin[8], Henry[7], Andrew Stauffer[6], Adelheid Galle[5] Stouffer, Daniel[4], Christian[3], Hans[2], Hans[1]) She married **Private Miller**.

Children of Private Fox and Private Miller are:
+   3756   i.   Private[14] Miller.
+   3757   ii.   Private Miller.

2711. Private[13] Fox (Charles Adam[12], James George[11], Diana[10] Hershey, Henry[9], Martin[8], Henry[7], Andrew Stauffer[6], Adelheid Galle[5] Stouffer, Daniel[4], Christian[3], Hans[2], Hans[1]) She married **John Rutherford**. He was born March 07, 1907, and died December 30, 1976.

Children of Private Fox and John Rutherford are:
+   3758   i.   Private[14] Rutherford.

+ 3759 ii. Private Rutherford.

2712. Private[13] Fox (Charles Adam[12], James George[11], Diana[10] Hershey, Henry[9], Martin[8], Henry[7], Andrew Stauffer[6], Adelheid Galle[5] Stouffer, Daniel[4], Christian[3], Hans[2], Hans[1]) She married **(1) John Keith Soper**. She married **(2) James Drumheller**.

Children of Private Fox and John Soper are:
+ 3760 i. Private[14] Soper.
   3761 ii. Private Soper. She married Private Cottam.

2713. Private[13] Fox (John Edward[12], James George[11], Diana[10] Hershey, Henry[9], Martin[8], Henry[7], Andrew Stauffer[6], Adelheid Galle[5] Stouffer, Daniel[4], Christian[3], Hans[2], Hans[1]) He married **Private Teets**.

Children of Private Fox and Private Teets are:
+ 3762 i. Private[14] Fox.
   3763 ii. Private Fox.

2714. Private[13] Fox (John Edward[12], James George[11], Diana[10] Hershey, Henry[9], Martin[8], Henry[7], Andrew Stauffer[6], Adelheid Galle[5] Stouffer, Daniel[4], Christian[3], Hans[2], Hans[1]) He married **Alice Gordon King**. She was born March 28, 1920, and died December 26, 1969.

Children of Private Fox and Alice King are:
   3764 i. Private[14] Fox.
   3765 ii. Jr. Richard Thomas Fox, born July 28, 1947 in Hershey, PA; died August 20, 1978.

2717. Bryan[13] Fox (John Edward[12], James George[11], Diana[10] Hershey, Henry[9], Martin[8], Henry[7], Andrew Stauffer[6], Adelheid Galle[5] Stouffer, Daniel[4], Christian[3], Hans[2], Hans[1]) was born October 05, 1916 in West Chester, PA, and died November 17, 1983. He married **Private Shiffler**.

Children of Bryan Fox and Private Shiffler are:
   3766 i. Private[14] Fox.
+ 3767 ii. Private Fox.

2718. Jeanette Fredricka[13] Fox (John Edward[12], James George[11], Diana[10] Hershey, Henry[9], Martin[8], Henry[7], Andrew Stauffer[6], Adelheid Galle[5] Stouffer, Daniel[4], Christian[3], Hans[2], Hans[1]) was born April 03, 1919 in Downingtown, PA, and died June 08, 1992 in Hershey, PA. She married **(1) Elmer Clifton Daniels** February 20, 1938 in St. Andrew's Episc., Harrisburg, PA. He was born March 07, 1917 in Jennerstown, Westmoreland Co, PA, and died May 14, 1965 in Hershey Hosp, Hershey, PA. She married **(2) Fred D. Hesse** February 05, 1972 in All Saints, Hershey, PA. He died July 1992 in Hershey, PA.

Children of Jeanette Fox and Elmer Daniels are:
+ 3768 i. Private[14] Daniels.
+ 3769 ii. Private Daniels.
+ 3770 iii. Private Daniels.

2719. Dorothy[13] Fox (John Edward[12], James George[11], Diana[10] Hershey, Henry[9], Martin[8], Henry[7], Andrew Stauffer[6], Adelheid Galle[5] Stouffer, Daniel[4], Christian[3], Hans[2], Hans[1]) was born July 14, 1922 in Downingtown, Chester Co., PA, and died February 07, 1989. She married **(1) Private Vanasco**. She married **(2) Private Stone**.

Children of Dorothy Fox and Private Vanasco are:
   3771 i. Private[14] Vanasco.
+ 3772 ii. Private Vanasco.
+ 3773 iii. Private Vanasco.
   3774 iv. Deanna Vanasco, born September 27, 1946; died September 27, 1946.
   3775 v. Laureen Vanasco, born September 27, 1946; died September 27, 1946.
   3776 vi. James Marten Vanasco, born August 29, 1948; died June 21, 1964.
   3777 vii. John Michael Vanasco, born August 29, 1948; died November 01, 1962.

2720. Marjorie[13] Fox (John Edward[12], James George[11], Diana[10] Hershey, Henry[9], Martin[8], Henry[7], Andrew Stauffer[6], Adelheid Galle[5] Stouffer, Daniel[4], Christian[3], Hans[2], Hans[1]) was born June 12, 1924 in Downingtown, Chester Co., PA, and died August 22, 1997 in Landsdale, PA. She married **Private Fountain**.

Children of Marjorie Fox and Private Fountain are:

+	3778	i.	Private[14] Fountain.
	3779	ii.	Private Fountain.
+	3780	iii.	Private Fountain.
+	3781	iv.	Private Fountain.
	3782	v.	Kristina Diane Fountain, born November 11, 1951; died January 15, 1952.
	3783	vi.	Kathryn Dorothea Fountain, born November 11, 1951; died December 25, 1951.

2721. Fox Mary Eliza "[13] Molly (John Edward[12] Fox, James George[11], Diana[10] Hershey, Henry[9], Martin[8], Henry[7], Andrew Stauffer[6], Adelheid Galle[5] Stouffer, Daniel[4], Christian[3], Hans[2], Hans[1]) was born September 16, 1928 in Downingtown, PA, and died February 21, 2002 in Harrisburg, PA. She married **(1) John Vincent Dolan** December 17, 1955 in Harrisburg, PA. He was born February 02, 1922, and died July 18, 1975. She married **(2) Paul Grubb** March 20, 1993. He was born Abt. 1923, and died June 02, 1994.

Children of Mary Molly and John Dolan are:

+	3784	i.	Private[14] Dolan.
	3785	ii.	Private Dolan. He married Private Smith.
+	3786	iii.	Private Dolan.
	3787	iv.	Private Dolan.
	3788	v.	Private Dolan. He married Private Glunt.

2723. Jr. Private[13] Sykes (Mary Virginia[12] Fox, James George[11], Diana[10] Hershey, Henry[9], Martin[8], Henry[7], Andrew Stauffer[6], Adelheid Galle[5] Stouffer, Daniel[4], Christian[3], Hans[2], Hans[1]) He married **(1) Private Keys**. He married **(2) Private Kendrick**.

Child of Private Sykes and Private Keys is:
    3789   i.   Private[14] Grill.

2724. Private[13] Bampton (Mary Virginia[12] Fox, James George[11], Diana[10] Hershey, Henry[9], Martin[8], Henry[7], Andrew Stauffer[6], Adelheid Galle[5] Stouffer, Daniel[4], Christian[3], Hans[2], Hans[1]) She married **Private Reiffer**.

Child of Private Bampton and Private Reiffer is:
    3790   i.   Private[14] Reiffer. He married Private Minishka.

2726. Private[13] Fox (Thomas G.[12], James George[11], Diana[10] Hershey, Henry[9], Martin[8], Henry[7], Andrew Stauffer[6], Adelheid Galle[5] Stouffer, Daniel[4], Christian[3], Hans[2], Hans[1]) She married **Private McKitrick**.

Children of Private Fox and Private McKitrick are:

+	3791	i.	Private[14] McKitrick.
	3792	ii.	Jr. Private McKitrick. He married Private Uhl.
	3793	iii.	Private McKitrick. He married Private Hines.

2727. Private[13] Fox (Thomas G.[12], James George[11], Diana[10] Hershey, Henry[9], Martin[8], Henry[7], Andrew Stauffer[6], Adelheid Galle[5] Stouffer, Daniel[4], Christian[3], Hans[2], Hans[1]) He married **Private Fulleman**.

Children of Private Fox and Private Fulleman are:

+	3794	i.	Private[14] Fox.
+	3795	ii.	Private Fox.

2728. Private[13] Fox (Thomas G.[12], James George[11], Diana[10] Hershey, Henry[9], Martin[8], Henry[7], Andrew Stauffer[6], Adelheid Galle[5] Stouffer, Daniel[4], Christian[3], Hans[2], Hans[1]) He married **Private Boyer**.

Children of Private Fox and Private Boyer are:

+	3796	i.	Private[14] Fox.
+	3797	ii.	Private Fox.

2729. Private[13] Fox (Thomas G.[12], James George[11], Diana[10] Hershey, Henry[9], Martin[8], Henry[7], Andrew Stauffer[6], Adelheid Galle[5] Stouffer, Daniel[4], Christian[3], Hans[2], Hans[1]) She married **Jr. Private Seachrist**.

Children of Private Fox and Private Seachrist are:

+	3798	i.	Private[14] Seachrist.
+	3799	ii.	Private Seachrist.

+ 3800 iii. III Private Seachrist.
+ 3801 iv. Private Seachrist.
+ 3802 v. Private Seachrist.
+ 3803 vi. Private Seachrist.

2731. Jr. Thomas G.[13] Fox (Thomas G.[12], James George[11], Diana[10] Hershey, Henry[9], Martin[8], Henry[7], Andrew Stauffer[6], Adelheid Galle[5] Stouffer, Daniel[4], Christian[3], Hans[2], Hans[1]) was born February 19, 1921, and died November 28, 1977. He married **(1) Private Cake**. He married **(2) Private MacCallum**.

Children of Thomas Fox and Private Cake are:
    3804 i. Private[14] Fox.
+ 3805 ii. Private Fox.
    3806 iii. Joyce Melinda Fox, born September 28, 1951; died April 20, 1970.

2732. Virginia Romaine[13] Fox (Thomas G.[12], James George[11], Diana[10] Hershey, Henry[9], Martin[8], Henry[7], Andrew Stauffer[6], Adelheid Galle[5] Stouffer, Daniel[4], Christian[3], Hans[2], Hans[1]) was born July 20, 1922, and died April 11, 1981. She married **Private Mengel**.

Child of Virginia Fox and Private Mengel is:
+ 3807 i. Private[14] Mengel.

2733. Diana Lucille[13] Fox (Thomas G.[12], James George[11], Diana[10] Hershey, Henry[9], Martin[8], Henry[7], Andrew Stauffer[6], Adelheid Galle[5] Stouffer, Daniel[4], Christian[3], Hans[2], Hans[1]) was born April 15, 1934, and died March 03, 1996 in Sunbury, PA. She married **Private Allamong**.

Children of Diana Fox and Private Allamong are:
    3808 i. Private[14] Allamong.
+ 3809 ii. Private Allamong.

2734. Private[13] Bair (Sara Diana[12] Fox, James George[11], Diana[10] Hershey, Henry[9], Martin[8], Henry[7], Andrew Stauffer[6], Adelheid Galle[5] Stouffer, Daniel[4], Christian[3], Hans[2], Hans[1]) He married **(1) Private Wild**. He married **(2) Pearl Lorraine Wolk**. She was born March 25, 1929 in Omaha, NE, and died 1992 in Sedro Woolley, WA.

Children of Private Bair and Private Wild are:
+ 3810 i. Private[14] Bair.
+ 3811 ii. Private Bair.
+ 3812 iii. Private Bair.
    3813 iv. James Dean Bair, born February 06, 1957; died February 06, 1957.

2735. III Private[13] Fox (James George[12], James George[11], Diana[10] Hershey, Henry[9], Martin[8], Henry[7], Andrew Stauffer[6], Adelheid Galle[5] Stouffer, Daniel[4], Christian[3], Hans[2], Hans[1]) He married **Private Barrett**.

Children of Private Fox and Private Barrett are:
    3814 i. Private[14] Fox.
    3815 ii. Private Fox.
    3816 iii. IV Private Fox.
    3817 iv. Private Fox.

2736. Private[13] Fox (James George[12], James George[11], Diana[10] Hershey, Henry[9], Martin[8], Henry[7], Andrew Stauffer[6], Adelheid Galle[5] Stouffer, Daniel[4], Christian[3], Hans[2], Hans[1]) She married **Private Silver**.

Children of Private Fox and Private Silver are:
+ 3818 i. Private[14] Silver.
+ 3819 ii. Private Silver.
    3820 iii. Private Silver. He married Private Hanrahan.

2743. Private[13] Gay (John Howard[12], Adelaide[11] Fox, Diana[10] Hershey, Henry[9], Martin[8], Henry[7], Andrew Stauffer[6], Adelheid Galle[5] Stouffer, Daniel[4], Christian[3], Hans[2], Hans[1]) She married **Private Hawkins**.

Child of Private Gay and Private Hawkins is:

+ 3821 i. Jr. Private[14] Hawkins.

2744. III Private[13] Gay (John Howard[12], Adelaide[11] Fox, Diana[10] Hershey, Henry[9], Martin[8], Henry[7], Andrew Stauffer[6], Adelheid Galle[5] Stouffer, Daniel[4], Christian[3], Hans[2], Hans[1]) He married **Private Dodson**.

Children of Private Gay and Private Dodson are:
+ 3822 i. Private[14] Gay.
+ 3823 ii. Private Gay.
+ 3824 iii. Private Gay.

2746. Jr. Private[13] Lee (Gertrude[12] Gay, Adelaide[11] Fox, Diana[10] Hershey, Henry[9], Martin[8], Henry[7], Andrew Stauffer[6], Adelheid Galle[5] Stouffer, Daniel[4], Christian[3], Hans[2], Hans[1]) He married **Private Pohl**.

Children of Private Lee and Private Pohl are:
+ 3825 i. Private[14] Lee.
   3826 ii. Private Lee.

2747. Jr. Private[13] Friedel (Gertrude[12] Gay, Adelaide[11] Fox, Diana[10] Hershey, Henry[9], Martin[8], Henry[7], Andrew Stauffer[6], Adelheid Galle[5] Stouffer, Daniel[4], Christian[3], Hans[2], Hans[1]) He married **Private DeWitt**.

Children of Private Friedel and Private DeWitt are:
   3827 i. III Private[14] Friedel.
   3828 ii. Private Friedel.

2750. II Private[13] Arnold (Katherine[12] Nissley, Caroline Lee[11] Fox, Diana[10] Hershey, Henry[9], Martin[8], Henry[7], Andrew Stauffer[6], Adelheid Galle[5] Stouffer, Daniel[4], Christian[3], Hans[2], Hans[1]) He married **(1) Private Forman**.   He married **(2) Private Bivins**.

Children of Private Arnold and Private Bivins are:
+ 3829 i. Private[14] Arnold.
+ 3830 ii. Private Arnold.

2751. Private[13] Wolff (Emilie Karthaus[12] Fox, George Hershey[11], Diana[10] Hershey, Henry[9], Martin[8], Henry[7], Andrew Stauffer[6], Adelheid Galle[5] Stouffer, Daniel[4], Christian[3], Hans[2], Hans[1]) He married **Private Condie**.

Children of Private Wolff and Private Condie are:
   3831 i. Private[14] Wolff.
   3832 ii. Private Wolff.
   3833 iii. Private Wolff.

2752. Private[13] Wolff (Emilie Karthaus[12] Fox, George Hershey[11], Diana[10] Hershey, Henry[9], Martin[8], Henry[7], Andrew Stauffer[6], Adelheid Galle[5] Stouffer, Daniel[4], Christian[3], Hans[2], Hans[1]) She married **Private Fleming**.

Children of Private Wolff and Private Fleming are:
   3834 i. Jr. Private[14] Fleming.
+ 3835 ii. Private Fleming.
   3836 iii. Private Fleming.
   3837 iv. Private Fleming. She married Private Hawthorne.

2753. Private[13] Taylor (Karolyn Diana[12] Fox, George Hershey[11], Diana[10] Hershey, Henry[9], Martin[8], Henry[7], Andrew Stauffer[6], Adelheid Galle[5] Stouffer, Daniel[4], Christian[3], Hans[2], Hans[1]) He married **Private Meacham**.

Children of Private Taylor and Private Meacham are:
   3838 i. Jr. Private[14] Taylor.
+ 3839 ii. Private Taylor.

2754. Private[13] Taylor (Karolyn Diana[12] Fox, George Hershey[11], Diana[10] Hershey, Henry[9], Martin[8], Henry[7], Andrew Stauffer[6], Adelheid Galle[5] Stouffer, Daniel[4], Christian[3], Hans[2], Hans[1]) She married **Jr. Private Barringer**.

Children of Private Taylor and Private Barringer are:
- 3840   i.   III Private[14] Barringer.
- 3841   ii.   Private Barringer.
- 3842   iii. Private Barringer.

2755.   Jr. James Alfred[13] Taylor (Karolyn Diana[12] Fox, George Hershey[11], Diana[10] Hershey, Henry[9], Martin[8], Henry[7], Andrew Stauffer[6], Adelheid Galle[5] Stouffer, Daniel[4], Christian[3], Hans[2], Hans[1]) was born July 10, 1932, and died July 24, 1960. He married **Private Allan**.

Children of James Taylor and Private Allan are:
+ 3843   i.   Private[14] Taylor.
+ 3844   ii.   Private Taylor.

2764.   Alice Margaret[13] Sheaffer (Lydia Jane[12] Tritt, Nancy[11] Nickey, Samuel[10], Christiana[9] Hastetter, Anna Barbara[8] Stauffer, Johannes[7], Daniel[6] Stouffer, Christian[5] Stauffer, Daniel[4] Stouffer, Christian[3], Hans[2], Hans[1]) was born October 26, 1869 in Craighead, Cumberlan Co, Pa., and died September 07, 1930 in Dickesen, Pa.. She married **Theodore Goodhart** November 14, 1889 in Mechanicsburg, Pa., son of Lewis Goodhart and Charlotte Farner. He was born April 24, 1858 in Penn Twp, Cumberland Co, and died December 26, 1945 in buried Dickeson, Pa..

Children are listed above under (2135) Theodore Goodhart.

2765.   Charles M.[13] Sheaffer (Lydia Jane[12] Tritt, Nancy[11] Nickey, Samuel[10], Christiana[9] Hastetter, Anna Barbara[8] Stauffer, Johannes[7], Daniel[6] Stouffer, Christian[5] Stauffer, Daniel[4] Stouffer, Christian[3], Hans[2], Hans[1]) was born January 14, 1874 in Huntsdale, Pa., and died October 02, 1965 in Utica, New York buried St. Agnes Cem, Utica, NY. He married **Rose Frances Kane** September 07, 1912 in St.Frances De Sales Church, Utica, New York. She was born April 03, 1885 in Utica New York, and died February 11, 1947 in Yonkers, New York buried St. Agnes Cem, Utica,NY.

Child of Charles Sheaffer and Rose Kane is:
+ 3845   i.   Doris Madeline[14] Sheaffer, born November 08, 1913; died January 25, 1980 in Utica, N.Y..

2772.   Edna[13] Brandt (Agnes Bordilla[12] Goodhart, Charlotte[11] Farner, Elizabeth[10] Owens, Peter[9] Ober, Elizabeth[8] Stauffer, Johannes[7], Daniel[6] Stouffer, Christian[5] Stauffer, Daniel[4] Stouffer, Christian[3], Hans[2], Hans[1]) was born WFT Est. 1865-1888, and died WFT Est. 1888-1975. She married **Elmer Reese** WFT Est. 1861-1917. He was born WFT Est. 1834-1863, and died WFT Est. 1888-1948.

Children of Edna Brandt and Elmer Reese are:
- 3846   i.   Marion H.[14] Reese, born WFT Est. 1870-1923; died April 17, 1959.
- 3847   ii.   Neola Reese, born 1885; died 1899.
- 3848   iii. Adam George Reese, born Private. He married Margaret Lefoon Private; born Private.
- 3849   iv.   Dana Everett Reese, born Private.
- 3850   v.   Ola Reese, born Private.
+ 3851   vi.   Velva Grace Reese, born Private.
+ 3852   vii. Herman Wilson Reese, born Private.
+ 3853   viii. Mary Esther Katherine Reese, born Private.

2782.   Pearle Viola[13] Goodhart (Theodore[12], Charlotte[11] Farner, Elizabeth[10] Owens, Peter[9] Ober, Elizabeth[8] Stauffer, Johannes[7], Daniel[6] Stouffer, Christian[5] Stauffer, Daniel[4] Stouffer, Christian[3], Hans[2], Hans[1]) was born January 31, 1891 in Greason, Pa., and died July 30, 1972 in Carlisle, Pa. Buried Ashland Cem, Carlisle, Pa.. She married **William Shively Weaver** October 03, 1928 in Cadiz, Ohio. He was born February 18, 1899, and died March 15, 1978 in Carlisle, Pa. Buried Ashland Cem, Carlisle, Pa..

Child of Pearle Goodhart and William Weaver is:
- 3854   i.   Theodore Floyd[14] Weaver, born Private.

2785.   Margaret Elizabeth Alice[13] Goodhart (Theodore[12], Charlotte[11] Farner, Elizabeth[10] Owens, Peter[9] Ober, Elizabeth[8] Stauffer, Johannes[7], Daniel[6] Stouffer, Christian[5] Stauffer, Daniel[4] Stouffer, Christian[3], Hans[2], Hans[1]) was born June 27, 1899 in Greason, Pa, and died June 28, 1994 in Union Twp, Leb. Co, buried Ft.Indiantown Gap National Cem. She married **Robert William Hippensteel** March 26, 1920 in Harrisburg, Pa.. He was born September 28, 1896 in Mt. Rock, Cumberland Co, Pa., and died November 03, 1990 in Union Twp, Leb. Co, buried Ft. Indiantown Gap National Cem..

Children of Margaret Goodhart and Robert Hippensteel are:
+ 3855   i.   Robert Goodhart[14] Hippensteel, born Private.
+ 3856   ii.   Dorothy Jean Hippensteel, born Private.
+ 3857   iii. Doris Madeline Hippensteel, born Private.

+   3858   iv.   Margaret Joanne Hippensteel, born Private.

2786. Theodore Riley[13] Goodhart (Theodore[12], Charlotte[11] Farner, Elizabeth[10] Owens, Peter[9] Ober, Elizabeth[8] Stauffer, Johannes[7], Daniel[6] Stouffer, Christian[5] Stauffer, Daniel[4] Stouffer, Christian[3], Hans[2], Hans[1]) was born May 12, 1902 in Kerrsville, Pa., and died December 17, 1936 in Carlisle, Pa. buried Westminster Cem, near Carlisle, Pa.. He married **Anna Mabel Rice** June 16, 1927 in Phoenixville, Pa.. She was born August 10, 1902, and died 1994 in buried Westminster Cem, near Carlisle, Pa..

Child of Theodore Goodhart and Anna Rice is:
   3859   i.   Theodore Rice[14] Goodhart, born January 15, 1935; died October 03, 1987.

2788. Clarence Eugene[13] Goodhart (Theodore[12], Charlotte[11] Farner, Elizabeth[10] Owens, Peter[9] Ober, Elizabeth[8] Stauffer, Johannes[7], Daniel[6] Stouffer, Christian[5] Stauffer, Daniel[4] Stouffer, Christian[3], Hans[2], Hans[1]) was born Private. He married **Mary Mildred Piper** Private. She was born September 07, 1907, and died 1994.

Children of Clarence Goodhart and Mary Piper are:
+   3860   i.   Charles Dale[14] Goodhart, born Private.
+   3861   ii. Lee Piper Goodhart, born Private.

2789. Lester Sheaffer[13] Goodhart (Theodore[12], Charlotte[11] Farner, Elizabeth[10] Owens, Peter[9] Ober, Elizabeth[8] Stauffer, Johannes[7], Daniel[6] Stouffer, Christian[5] Stauffer, Daniel[4] Stouffer, Christian[3], Hans[2], Hans[1]) was born Private. He married **Blanche Shotzer** Private. She was born Private.

Children of Lester Goodhart and Blanche Shotzer are:
   3862   i.   Edward Sheaffer[14] Goodhart, born Private. He married Mary Jane Ramsies Private; born Private.
+   3863   ii. Robert Michael Goodhart, born Private.
   3864   iii. Ann Betta Goodhart, born Private.

2790. Lewis[13] Goodhart (David Grier McClelland[12], Charlotte[11] Farner, Elizabeth[10] Owens, Peter[9] Ober, Elizabeth[8] Stauffer, Johannes[7], Daniel[6] Stouffer, Christian[5] Stauffer, Daniel[4] Stouffer, Christian[3], Hans[2], Hans[1]) was born Private. He married **Maybelle Noble** Private. She was born Private.

Children of Lewis Goodhart and Maybelle Noble are:
   3865   i.   Homer[14] Goodhart, born Private.
   3866   ii. Lois Goodhart, born Private.

2805. Lillie E[13] Hursh (Emma Barbara[12] Ober, David[11], Isaac Huntsberger[10], Christian[9], Elizabeth[8] Stauffer, Johannes[7], Daniel[6] Stouffer, Christian[5] Stauffer, Daniel[4] Stouffer, Christian[3], Hans[2], Hans[1]) was born 1876. She married **Frank B Harrington**. He was born 1877.

Children of Lillie Hursh and Frank Harrington are:
+   3867   i.   Almer H[14] Harrington, born 1896; died 1923.
+   3868   ii. Beryl F Harrington, born 1901.
+   3869   iii. Lillian R Harrington, born 1911.

2806. Agnes E[13] Hursh (Emma Barbara[12] Ober, David[11], Isaac Huntsberger[10], Christian[9], Elizabeth[8] Stauffer, Johannes[7], Daniel[6] Stouffer, Christian[5] Stauffer, Daniel[4] Stouffer, Christian[3], Hans[2], Hans[1]) was born 1877. She married **Robert Haggert**. He was born Abt. 1875.

Children of Agnes Hursh and Robert Haggert are:
   3870   i.   Gertrude[14] Haggert, born Abt. 1900. She married Frazier Fusilier; born Abt. 1900.
   3871   ii. Glen Haggert, born Abt. 1900.

2807. Edna R[13] Hursh (Emma Barbara[12] Ober, David[11], Isaac Huntsberger[10], Christian[9], Elizabeth[8] Stauffer, Johannes[7], Daniel[6] Stouffer, Christian[5] Stauffer, Daniel[4] Stouffer, Christian[3], Hans[2], Hans[1]) was born 1879, and died 1943. She married **Fred Harrington**. He was born 1879, and died 1934.

Children of Edna Hursh and Fred Harrington are:
+   3872   i.   Alfred[14] Harrington, born 1899.
+   3873   ii. Grace Harrington, born 1904.
+   3874   iii. Lucile Harrington, born 1907.

3875 iv. Frances Harrington, born 1909. She married Peter Auks; born Abt. 1900.

2808. Jay B[13] Hursh (Emma Barbara[12] Ober, David[11], Isaac Huntsberger[10], Christian[9], Elizabeth[8] Stauffer, Johannes[7], Daniel[6] Stouffer, Christian[5] Stauffer, Daniel[4] Stouffer, Christian[3], Hans[2], Hans[1]) was born 1885, and died 1930. He married **Frances Allen**. She was born 1884.

Children of Jay Hursh and Frances Allen are:
+ 3876 i. Brenner P[14] Hursh, born 1911; died 1944.
   3877 ii. Odille Anne Hursh, born 1914. She married James W May; born 1915.
   3878 iii. Margery B Hursh, born 1916. She married Kyle S McMichael; born Abt. 1915.

2810. Margaret Ann[13] Duncan (Catherine Rebecca[12] Ober, David[11], Isaac Huntsberger[10], Christian[9], Elizabeth[8] Stauffer, Johannes[7], Daniel[6] Stouffer, Christian[5] Stauffer, Daniel[4] Stouffer, Christian[3], Hans[2], Hans[1]) was born May 24, 1877, and died July 14, 1953 in Hummelstown, PA. She married **Solomon S Balsbaugh**. He was born March 16, 1873, and died July 10, 1961 in Hummelstown, PA.

Children of Margaret Duncan and Solomon Balsbaugh are:
   3879 i. Edgar F[14] Balsbaugh, born 1898; died 1906.
   3880 ii. William D Balsbaugh, born 1900; died 1920.
+ 3881 iii. Jayson C Balsbaugh, born 1902.
+ 3882 iv. Kathryn S Balsbaugh, born 1903.
   3883 v. Ober S Balsbaugh, born 1905; died 1907.
   3884 vi. Margaret A Balsbaugh, born 1907.
   3885 vii. Clarence Balsbaugh, born 1910.
+ 3886 viii. Erlo R Balsbaugh, born 1911.

2811. Clarence R[13] Wolf (Catherine Rebecca[12] Ober, David[11], Isaac Huntsberger[10], Christian[9], Elizabeth[8] Stauffer, Johannes[7], Daniel[6] Stouffer, Christian[5] Stauffer, Daniel[4] Stouffer, Christian[3], Hans[2], Hans[1]) was born 1886 in Highspire, PA, and died Abt. 1970 in Millville, NJ. He married **Mary M Miller**. She was born 1893.

Children of Clarence Wolf and Mary Miller are:
+ 3887 i. Clarence Franklin[14] Wolf, born 1912.
   3888 ii. Mary E Wolf, born 1917. She married Marvin L Howard; born Abt. 1910.
   3889 iii. David O Wolf, born 1919; died Abt. 1960.
   3890 iv. Alice K Wolf, born 1924; died Abt. 1960.
+ 3891 v. John S Wolf, born 1926.
   3892 vi. Barbara Ann Wolf, born 1928. She married Krenar Shapllo June 14, 1952 in Millville, NJ; born Abt. 1910.

2813. David Ober[13] Wolf (Catherine Rebecca[12] Ober, David[11], Isaac Huntsberger[10], Christian[9], Elizabeth[8] Stauffer, Johannes[7], Daniel[6] Stouffer, Christian[5] Stauffer, Daniel[4] Stouffer, Christian[3], Hans[2], Hans[1]) was born 1890 in Highspire, PA, and died October 09, 1975 in Highspire, PA. He married **Marian Taylor Steele** April 07, 1923 in Pittsburgh, PA. She was born Abt. 1890, and died December 28, 1950.

Children of David Wolf and Marian Steele are:
   3893 i. Marian Elizabeth[14] Wolf, born Aft. 1923; died in Storrs, CT. She married Carl William Rettenmeyer June 26 in Ann Arbor, MI.
+ 3894 ii. Marjorie Ann Wolf, born Abt. 1928 in Pittsburgh, PA; died September 30, 1970 in Glastonbury, CT.

2815. Mary Estelle[13] Wolf (Catherine Rebecca[12] Ober, David[11], Isaac Huntsberger[10], Christian[9], Elizabeth[8] Stauffer, Johannes[7], Daniel[6] Stouffer, Christian[5] Stauffer, Daniel[4] Stouffer, Christian[3], Hans[2], Hans[1]) was born 1893 in Highspire, PA, and died 1930 in Highspire, PA. She married **Howard Jones Williams** December 09, 1922 in Pittsburgh, PA. He was born June 16, 1893 in Plymouth, PA, and died 1958 in Millville, NJ.

Children of Mary Wolf and Howard Williams are:
   3895 i. Howard Jones[14] Williams, born 1924; died in Macon, GA. He married Mary Dorris Tidwell December 28 in Douglassville, GA.
   3896 ii. Ruth L Williams, born 1927; died in Union, NJ. She married Howard Forrest; born Aft. 1900.
   3897 iii. Ober Wolf Williams, born 1929; died in Cincinnati, OH. He married Marceline Elodia Colle August 18, 1956 in Rochester, NY.

2816. Franklin Earl¹³ Wolf (Catherine Rebecca¹² Ober, David¹¹, Isaac Huntsberger¹⁰, Christian⁹, Elizabeth⁸ Stauffer, Johannes⁷, Daniel⁶ Stouffer, Christian⁵ Stauffer, Daniel⁴ Stouffer, Christian³, Hans², Hans¹) was born January 15, 1897 in Highspire, PA, and died December 07, 1958 in Highspire, PA. He married **Helen Gene Lancaster** August 01, 1924 in West Chester, PA. She was born Abt. 1900.

Child of Franklin Wolf and Helen Lancaster is:
+ 3898   i.   Franklin Earl¹⁴ Wolf, born Abt. 1930.

2817. George Edgar¹³ Wolf (Catherine Rebecca¹² Ober, David¹¹, Isaac Huntsberger¹⁰, Christian⁹, Elizabeth⁸ Stauffer, Johannes⁷, Daniel⁶ Stouffer, Christian⁵ Stauffer, Daniel⁴ Stouffer, Christian³, Hans², Hans¹) was born January 15, 1897, and died May 1977 in Hannibal, MO. He married **Lela Berneice Burnham** April 17, 1926 in Springfield, IL. She was born Abt. 1880.

Children of George Wolf and Lela Burnham are:
+ 3899   i.   Barbara J¹⁴ Wolf, born Aft. 1900.
+ 3900   ii.   Mary L Wolf, born Aft. 1900.
   3901   iii.   Edgar Wolf, born Aft. 1900.

2818. Catherine Rebecca¹³ Wolf (Catherine Rebecca¹² Ober, David¹¹, Isaac Huntsberger¹⁰, Christian⁹, Elizabeth⁸ Stauffer, Johannes⁷, Daniel⁶ Stouffer, Christian⁵ Stauffer, Daniel⁴ Stouffer, Christian³, Hans², Hans¹) was born April 30, 1898 in Highspire, PA, and died June 10, 1986 in Highspire, PA. She married **William Walter White** July 05, 1920 in Highspire, PA. He was born March 05, 1895 in Highspire, PA, and died October 23, 1974 in Highspire, PA.

Child of Catherine Wolf and William White is:
+ 3902   i.   William Walter¹⁴ White, born May 31, 1923 in Highspire, PA; died August 31, 1998 in Highspire, PA.

2819. Fannie O¹³ Ober (Benjamin Franklin¹², David¹¹, Isaac Huntsberger¹⁰, Christian⁹, Elizabeth⁸ Stauffer, Johannes⁷, Daniel⁶ Stouffer, Christian⁵ Stauffer, Daniel⁴ Stouffer, Christian³, Hans², Hans¹) was born 1894. She married **Elmer A Kirkpatrick**. He was born 1889, and died 1922.

Child of Fannie Ober and Elmer Kirkpatrick is:
+ 3903   i.   Barbara¹⁴ Kirkpatrick, born 1919.

2820. Eda R¹³ Murphy (Agnes Eda¹² Ober, David¹¹, Isaac Huntsberger¹⁰, Christian⁹, Elizabeth⁸ Stauffer, Johannes⁷, Daniel⁶ Stouffer, Christian⁵ Stauffer, Daniel⁴ Stouffer, Christian³, Hans², Hans¹) was born Abt. 1885. She married **Walter A Sharpe**. He was born Abt. 1885.

Children of Eda Murphy and Walter Sharpe are:
+ 3904   i.   Vernon W¹⁴ Sharpe, born 1909.
+ 3905   ii.   Ruth B Sharpe, born 1912.

2821. Rachael Agnes¹³ Duncan (Annie Elizabeth¹² Ober, David¹¹, Isaac Huntsberger¹⁰, Christian⁹, Elizabeth⁸ Stauffer, Johannes⁷, Daniel⁶ Stouffer, Christian⁵ Stauffer, Daniel⁴ Stouffer, Christian³, Hans², Hans¹) was born March 16, 1881, and died August 19, 1963 in Oberlin, PA. She married **William O Stevens**. He was born 1881, and died 1935.

Children of Rachael Duncan and William Stevens are:
   3906   i.   F Clair¹⁴ Stevens, born 1903; died 1903.
+ 3907   ii.   B Marie Stevens, born 1904.
+ 3908   iii.   Arthur W Stevens, born 1907.
+ 3909   iv.   Marlin O Stevens, born 1911.
+ 3910   v.   J Donald Stevens, born 1914.
   3911   vi.   Carrell D Stevens, born 1916. He married Clarise Stevens; born Abt. 1920.
   3912   vii.   Wilbur A Stevens, born 1918. He married Elizabeth Troutman; born 1923.

2822. Alvid O¹³ Duncan (Annie Elizabeth¹² Ober, David¹¹, Isaac Huntsberger¹⁰, Christian⁹, Elizabeth⁸ Stauffer, Johannes⁷, Daniel⁶ Stouffer, Christian⁵ Stauffer, Daniel⁴ Stouffer, Christian³, Hans², Hans¹) was born 1883, and died 1933. He married **Gertrude Y Sarciner**. She was born 1885.

Children of Alvid Duncan and Gertrude Sarciner are:
+ 3913   i.   Adrian E¹⁴ Duncan, born 1913.
+ 3914   ii.   Delmar M Duncan, born 1918.

2823. Katherine M[13] **Duncan** (Annie Elizabeth[12] Ober, David[11], Isaac Huntsberger[10], Christian[9], Elizabeth[8] Stauffer, Johannes[7], Daniel[6] Stouffer, Christian[5] Stauffer, Daniel[4] Stouffer, Christian[3], Hans[2], Hans[1]) was born 1887. She married **Harry S Smolizer**. He was born 1883, and died 1946.

Child of Katherine Duncan and Harry Smolizer is:
+ 3915   i.   Charlotte E[14] Smolizer, born 1911.

2824. Anna B[13] **Duncan** (Annie Elizabeth[12] Ober, David[11], Isaac Huntsberger[10], Christian[9], Elizabeth[8] Stauffer, Johannes[7], Daniel[6] Stouffer, Christian[5] Stauffer, Daniel[4] Stouffer, Christian[3], Hans[2], Hans[1]) was born 1897, and died 1958. She married **Ira S Murray**. He was born 1898.

Children of Anna Duncan and Ira Murray are:
+ 3916   i.   Sylvan E[14] Murray, born 1917.
    3917   ii.   Richard A Murray, born 1920. He married Valerie Rishel Beck; born Aft. 1920.
+ 3918   iii.   Donald E Murray, born 1926.
    3919   iv.   Jack O Murray, born 1927.

2825. Wilbur C[13] **Ober** (David W[12], David[11], Isaac Huntsberger[10], Christian[9], Elizabeth[8] Stauffer, Johannes[7], Daniel[6] Stouffer, Christian[5] Stauffer, Daniel[4] Stouffer, Christian[3], Hans[2], Hans[1]) was born Abt. 1900. He married **Ruth J Dowdell**. She was born Abt. 1900.

Children of Wilbur Ober and Ruth Dowdell are:
+ 3920   i.   Mary E[14] Ober, born 1924.
+ 3921   ii.   Wilbur C Ober, Jr, born 1926.

2826. David W[13] **Ober, Jr** (David W[12], David[11], Isaac Huntsberger[10], Christian[9], Elizabeth[8] Stauffer, Johannes[7], Daniel[6] Stouffer, Christian[5] Stauffer, Daniel[4] Stouffer, Christian[3], Hans[2], Hans[1]) was born Abt. 1910. He married **Catherine Holehan**. She was born Abt. 1920.

Children of David Ober and Catherine Holehan are:
    3922   i.   Edward[14] Ober, born Aft. 1940.
    3923   ii.   David W Ober III, born 1945.
    3924   iii.   Marilyn E Ober, born 1946.

2827. John D[13] **Ober** (David W[12], David[11], Isaac Huntsberger[10], Christian[9], Elizabeth[8] Stauffer, Johannes[7], Daniel[6] Stouffer, Christian[5] Stauffer, Daniel[4] Stouffer, Christian[3], Hans[2], Hans[1]) was born Abt. 1910. He married **Marion Rider**. She was born Abt. 1910.

Child of John Ober and Marion Rider is:
    3925   i.   John D[14] Ober II, born 1943.

2828. Cecil S[13] **Ober** (Isaac Newton[12], David[11], Isaac Huntsberger[10], Christian[9], Elizabeth[8] Stauffer, Johannes[7], Daniel[6] Stouffer, Christian[5] Stauffer, Daniel[4] Stouffer, Christian[3], Hans[2], Hans[1]) was born Abt. 1900. He married **(1) Helen A MenMuir**. She was born Abt. 1900. He married **(2) Mary E Edwards**. She was born Abt. 1900.

Children of Cecil Ober and Helen MenMuir are:
    3926   i.   Jean[14] Ober, born Abt. 1925.
+ 3927   ii.   Joan Ober, born Abt. 1925.
    3928   iii.   John Ober, born Abt. 1925. He married Betty L Kreigbaum; born Abt. 1925.

Child of Cecil Ober and Mary Edwards is:
    3929   i.   Mary A[14] Ober, born Aft. 1920.

2829. Merritt L[13] **Ober** (Isaac Newton[12], David[11], Isaac Huntsberger[10], Christian[9], Elizabeth[8] Stauffer, Johannes[7], Daniel[6] Stouffer, Christian[5] Stauffer, Daniel[4] Stouffer, Christian[3], Hans[2], Hans[1]) was born May 11, 1900, and died July 1982 in Indianapolis, IN. He married **(1) Edith Martin**. She was born Abt. 1900. He married **(2) Frances Fisher** September 14, 1947. She was born June 28, 1911, and died February 25, 1998.

Child of Merritt Ober and Edith Martin is:
    3930   i.   David W[14] Ober, born Abt. 1925.

2830. Arden G^{13} Ober (Isaac Newton^{12}, David^{11}, Isaac Huntsberger^{10}, Christian^9, Elizabeth^8 Stauffer, Johannes^7, Daniel^6 Stouffer, Christian^5 Stauffer, Daniel^4 Stouffer, Christian^3, Hans^2, Hans^1) was born Abt. 1900. He married **Emma A Horn**. She was born Abt. 1900.

Children of Arden Ober and Emma Horn are:
- \+ 3931 i. Arden G^{14} Ober, Jr, born Aft. 1920.
- \+ 3932 ii. Elaine C Ober, born Aft. 1920.
- 3933 iii. Geraldine L Ober, born Aft. 1920.
- 3934 iv. Evelyn M Ober, born Aft. 1920.
- 3935 v. Marilyn M Ober, born Aft. 1920.

2832. C Kiefer^{13} Ober (Isaac Newton^{12}, David^{11}, Isaac Huntsberger^{10}, Christian^9, Elizabeth^8 Stauffer, Johannes^7, Daniel^6 Stouffer, Christian^5 Stauffer, Daniel^4 Stouffer, Christian^3, Hans^2, Hans^1) was born Abt. 1900. He married **E Virginia Adams**. She was born Abt. 1900.

Children of C Ober and E Adams are:
- 3936 i. Chandra Kay^{14} Ober, born Abt. 1920.
- 3937 ii. Eleanor V Ober, born Abt. 1920.

2835. Edna M^{13} Smith (Florence May^{12} Ober, David^{11}, Isaac Huntsberger^{10}, Christian^9, Elizabeth^8 Stauffer, Johannes^7, Daniel^6 Stouffer, Christian^5 Stauffer, Daniel^4 Stouffer, Christian^3, Hans^2, Hans^1) was born 1891. She married **Cloyd R Knupp**. He was born Abt. 1890.

Children of Edna Smith and Cloyd Knupp are:
- \+ 3938 i. Edna M^{14} Knupp, born 1911.
- 3939 ii. Cloyd R Knupp, Jr, born 1913.
- 3940 iii. Florence W Knupp, born 1915. She married Unknown Bauer; born Aft. 1900.
- \+ 3941 iv. Muriel R Knupp, born 1917.
- 3942 v. John H Knupp, born 1919.
- 3943 vi. Robert O Knupp, born 1923.
- 3944 vii. June A Knupp, born 1927.
- 3945 viii. Jane L Knupp, born 1930.

2836. Emma R^{13} Smith (Florence May^{12} Ober, David^{11}, Isaac Huntsberger^{10}, Christian^9, Elizabeth^8 Stauffer, Johannes^7, Daniel^6 Stouffer, Christian^5 Stauffer, Daniel^4 Stouffer, Christian^3, Hans^2, Hans^1) was born 1893. She married **(1) Martin Feeser**. He was born Abt. 1880, and died 1914. She married **(2) Robert Murphy**. He was born Abt. 1890.

Children of Emma Smith and Martin Feeser are:
- 3946 i. John E^{14} Feeser, born 1913; died 1913.
- 3947 ii. Anna E Feeser, born 1914; died 1919.

Child of Emma Smith and Robert Murphy is:
- 3948 i. Richard W^{14} Murphy, born 1930.

2840. Frank^{13} Hubert (Barbara Estella^{12} Ober, David^{11}, Isaac Huntsberger^{10}, Christian^9, Elizabeth^8 Stauffer, Johannes^7, Daniel^6 Stouffer, Christian^5 Stauffer, Daniel^4 Stouffer, Christian^3, Hans^2, Hans^1) was born 1904. He married **Gertrude Drover**. She was born Abt. 1905.

Children of Frank Hubert and Gertrude Drover are:
- 3949 i. Arden^{14} Hubert, born Abt. 1930.
- 3950 ii. Leonard Hubert, born Abt. 1930.

2841. Mildred M^{13} Hubert (Barbara Estella^{12} Ober, David^{11}, Isaac Huntsberger^{10}, Christian^9, Elizabeth^8 Stauffer, Johannes^7, Daniel^6 Stouffer, Christian^5 Stauffer, Daniel^4 Stouffer, Christian^3, Hans^2, Hans^1) was born 1906. She married **Harvey Miller**. He was born Abt. 1900.

Children of Mildred Hubert and Harvey Miller are:
- 3951 i. Barbara^{14} Miller, born Abt. 1925.
- 3952 ii. Kenneth Miller, born Abt. 1925.

2843. Helen B[13] **Hubert** (Barbara Estella[12] Ober, David[11], Isaac Huntsberger[10], Christian[9], Elizabeth[8] Stauffer, Johannes[7], Daniel[6] Stouffer, Christian[5] Stauffer, Daniel[4] Stouffer, Christian[3], Hans[2], Hans[1]) was born 1912. She married **Wilbur Pullin**. He was born Abt. 1910.

Children of Helen Hubert and Wilbur Pullin are:
- 3953 i. George[14] Pullin, born Abt. 1935.
- 3954 ii. Richard Pullin, born Abt. 1935.
- 3955 iii. Janet Pullin, born Abt. 1935.

2844. Mary L.[13] **Morning** (Annie[12] Ober, Michael Cramer[11], Michael[10], Henry[9], Elizabeth[8] Stauffer, Johannes[7], Daniel[6] Stouffer, Christian[5] Stauffer, Daniel[4] Stouffer, Christian[3], Hans[2], Hans[1]) was born October 05, 1889 in Elizabethtown, PA, and died August 1973 in Harrisburg, PA. She married **George A. Brinser**. He was born September 11, 1889 in Elizabethtown, PA, and died April 1964 in Harrisburg, PA.

Child of Mary Morning and George Brinser is:
- + 3956 i. Elinor L.[14] Brinser, born June 11, 1914 in Elizabethtown, PA; died October 16, 1987 in Rochester, NY.

2849. Daisy Meyers[13] **Ober** (Moses Heagly[12], Moses Ruhl[11], Christian Longnecker[10], David S[9], Elizabeth[8] Stauffer, Johannes[7], Daniel[6] Stouffer, Christian[5] Stauffer, Daniel[4] Stouffer, Christian[3], Hans[2], Hans[1]) was born April 30, 1892 in Rapho Twsp, PA, and died March 06, 1964. She married **John Miller Ober**. He was born October 24, 1886 in Mt. Hope, PA, and died December 1967 in Elizabethtown PA.

Child of Daisy Ober and John Ober is:
- + 3957 i. Minnie[14] Ober, born January 23, 1910 in PA; died May 21, 1977 in Lancaster, PA.

2851. Stella M[13] **Ober** (Moses Heagly[12], Moses Ruhl[11], Christian Longnecker[10], David S[9], Elizabeth[8] Stauffer, Johannes[7], Daniel[6] Stouffer, Christian[5] Stauffer, Daniel[4] Stouffer, Christian[3], Hans[2], Hans[1]) was born August 17, 1898, and died January 09, 1965. She married **Amos G Hitz** January 19, 1918. He was born November 06, 1891, and died October 29, 1971.

Children of Stella Ober and Amos Hitz are:
- 3958 i. Amanda Elizabeth[14] Hitz, born June 25, 1918. She married Wilbur McAfee November 23, 1942; born February 05, 1916.
- + 3959 ii. Elmer Ezra Hitz, born June 13, 1920.
- 3960 iii. Jacob Amos Hitz, born December 27, 1921. He married Mary Aldinger November 12, 1944; born January 24, 1924.
- 3961 iv. Mary Kathryn Hitz, born December 17, 1925. She married Fern Hartman November 10, 1956; born March 14, 1917; died July 21, 1976.
- 3962 v. Florence Mae Hitz, born September 16, 1927. She married Glen Shank October 30, 1947; born April 22, 1924.
- 3963 vi. George Richard Hitz, born March 16, 1931. He married Eva Yeager January 12, 1952; born September 29, 1932.
- 3964 vii. Jay Mark Hitz, born December 10, 1941. He married Leslie Kessler January 19, 1963; born November 27, 1943.

2853. Ella May[13] **Stauffer** (Mary Jane[12] Richardson, Sarah Rebecca[11] Bowers, Susannah[10] Ober, Henry[9], Veronica " Frany "[8] Stauffer, Johannes[7], Daniel[6] Stouffer, Christian[5] Stauffer, Daniel[4] Stouffer, Christian[3], Hans[2], Hans[1]) was born June 23, 1868 in Pine Creek, Illinois, and died October 04, 1927 in Upland, California. She married **Isaac Eyers** December 12, 1885 in Sedgwick, Kansas. He was born January 07, 1857 in Hedford, Ontario, Canada, and died October 23, 1938 in Upland, California.

Children of Ella Stauffer and Isaac Eyers are:
- + 3965 i. Mary Belle[14] Eyer, born November 18, 1886 in Pine Creek Illinois; died October 04, 1922 in Upland, California.
- + 3966 ii. Lewis Benjamin Eyer, born May 26, 1889 in Hamlin, Kansas; died July 22, 1939 in Los Angeles, California.
- + 3967 iii. Harold Ray Eyer, born January 28, 1896 in Glendale, Arizona.
- + 3968 iv. John Paul Eyer, born November 14, 1899 in Glendale, Arizona.
- + 3969 v. Katherine Lucile Eyer, born July 02, 1903 in Glendale, Arizona.

2855. Andrew Grant[13] **Stauffer** (Mary Jane[12] Richardson, Sarah Rebecca[11] Bowers, Susannah[10] Ober, Henry[9], Veronica " Frany "[8] Stauffer, Johannes[7], Daniel[6] Stouffer, Christian[5] Stauffer, Daniel[4] Stouffer, Christian[3], Hans[2], Hans[1]) was born November 16, 1871 in Pine Creek, Illinois, and died November 06, 1953. He married **Ida Ota Uts** December 11, 1892 in Sedgwick, Kansas. She was born October 15,

1874 in Frankfort, Indiana, and died March 08, 1962.

Children of Andrew Stauffer and Ida Uts are:
+ 3970 i. Private[14] Stauffer.
+ 3971 ii. Paul J. Stauffer, born April 08, 1896 in Sedgwick, Kansas; died July 29, 1922 in Newton, Kansas.
+ 3972 iii. Aesta Blanch Staufer, born June 28, 1897 in Glendale, Arizona; died September 03, 1982 in Wichita, Kansas.
+ 3973 iv. Charles Lloyd Stauffer, born August 11, 1899 in Sedgwick, Kansas; died February 16, 1983.
  3974 v. Russell Lee Stauffer, born March 08, 1904 in Sedgwick, Kansas; died July 11, 1904 in Sedgwick, Kansas.
+ 3975 vi. Alice Pearl Stauffer, born October 18, 1905 in Valley Center, Kansas; died July 11, 1958 in Newton, Kansas.
  3976 vii. Leah Mayford Stauffer, born November 14, 1908 in Valley Center, Kansas; died February 22, 1918 in Valley Center, Kansas.
  3977 viii. Andrew Neal Stauffer, born December 04, 1914 in Valley Center, Kansas; died December 17, 1927 in Valley Center, Kansas.

2858. Elias Richardson[13] Stauffer (Mary Jane[12] Richardson, Sarah Rebecca[11] Bowers, Susannah[10] Ober, Henry[9], Veronica " Frany "[8] Stauffer, Johannes[7], Daniel[6] Stouffer, Christian[5] Stauffer, Daniel[4] Stouffer, Christian[3], Hans[2], Hans[1]) was born July 23, 1877 in Pine Creek, Illinois, and died March 30, 1940 in Prescott, Arizona. He married **(1) Emma Lively** January 30, 1900 in Prescott, Arizona. She was born November 21, 1881 in Wichita, Kansas. He married **(2) Lillian Jackson** September 20, 1906 in Prescott, Arizona. He married **(3) Dessie May Starns** March 20, 1934 in Prescott, Arizona.

Child of Elias Stauffer and Emma Lively is:
+ 3978 i. Mary Helen[14] Stauffer, born March 19, 1901 in Prescott, Arizona.

Child of Elias Stauffer and Lillian Jackson is:
  3979 i. Wesley Richard[14] Stauffer, born May 31, 1907 in Prescott, Arizona; died June 01, 1907 in Prescott, Arizona.

2859. Charles Albert[13] Stauffer (Mary Jane[12] Richardson, Sarah Rebecca[11] Bowers, Susannah[10] Ober, Henry[9], Veronica " Frany "[8] Stauffer, Johannes[7], Daniel[6] Stouffer, Christian[5] Stauffer, Daniel[4] Stouffer, Christian[3], Hans[2], Hans[1]) was born March 23, 1880 in Sedgwick, Kansas. He married **Edith Louise Bennett** April 10, 1909 in Phoenix, Arizona. She was born June 10, 1885 in El Paso, Illinois.

Children of Charles Stauffer and Edith Bennett are:
+ 3980 i. Private[14] Stauffer.
  3981 ii. Eleanor Stauffer, born October 08, 1916 in Phoenix, Arizona.
  3982 iii. Sylvia Stauffer, born November 24, 1919 in Phoenix, Arizona.
  3983 iv. Charles Bennett Stauffer, born December 04, 1923 in Phoenix, Arizona; died December 27, 1970.

2860. Ray Franklin[13] Stauffer (Mary Jane[12] Richardson, Sarah Rebecca[11] Bowers, Susannah[10] Ober, Henry[9], Veronica " Frany "[8] Stauffer, Johannes[7], Daniel[6] Stouffer, Christian[5] Stauffer, Daniel[4] Stouffer, Christian[3], Hans[2], Hans[1]) was born February 11, 1882 in Sedgwick, Kansas, and died December 12, 1939 in Phoenix, Arizona. He married **(1) Clair McClaughry** August 15, 1909 in Glendale, Arizona. She was born in Coffeyville, Kansas, and died March 06, 1919 in Glendale, Arizona. He married **(2) Julia Segal** March 23, 1923 in El Centro, California. She was born January 01, 1903 in Ragsdale, Texas.

Children of Ray Stauffer and Clair McClaughry are:
+ 3984 i. Private[14] Stauffer.
  3985 ii. Ray Franklin Stauffer, born December 17, 1917 in Glendale, Arizona; died November 08, 1918.

Children of Ray Stauffer and Julia Segal are:
  3986 i. Private[14] Stauffer.
  3987 ii. Private Stauffer.

2861. Sara Rebecca[13] Stauffer (Mary Jane[12] Richardson, Sarah Rebecca[11] Bowers, Susannah[10] Ober, Henry[9], Veronica " Frany "[8] Stauffer, Johannes[7], Daniel[6] Stouffer, Christian[5] Stauffer, Daniel[4] Stouffer, Christian[3], Hans[2], Hans[1]) was born January 02, 1884 in Sedgwick, Kansas, and died March 30, 1970 in Phoenix, Arizona. She married **Frank Webb Griffen** April 22, 1909 in Glendale, Arizona. He was born November 21, 1883 in Sabetha, Kansas.

Children of Sara Stauffer and Frank Griffen are:
+ 3988 i. Private[14] Griffen.

3989 ii. Frank Webb Griffen, born March 04, 1919 in Phoenix, Arizona.

2862. Mary Lemmie Ann[13] Stauffer (Mary Jane[12] Richardson, Sarah Rebecca[11] Bowers, Susannah[10] Ober, Henry[9], Veronica " Frany "[8] Stauffer, Johannes[7], Daniel[6] Stouffer, Christian[5] Stauffer, Daniel[4] Stouffer, Christian[3], Hans[2], Hans[1]) was born May 27, 1886 in Sedgwick, Kansas, and died January 12, 1976 in Tuscon, Arizona. She married **Thomas Henson Higley** August 05, 1911 in Portland, Oregon. He was born October 22, 1888 in Carrolton, Missouri, and died 1961.

Child of Mary Stauffer and Thomas Higley is:
+ 3990 i. Private[14] Higley.

2863. Anna Pearl[13] Stauffer (Mary Jane[12] Richardson, Sarah Rebecca[11] Bowers, Susannah[10] Ober, Henry[9], Veronica " Frany "[8] Stauffer, Johannes[7], Daniel[6] Stouffer, Christian[5] Stauffer, Daniel[4] Stouffer, Christian[3], Hans[2], Hans[1]) was born March 17, 1889 in Sedgwick, Kansas. She married **Walter Wesley Knorpp**. He was born May 19, 1891 in Chicago, Illinois.

Children of Anna Stauffer and Walter Knorpp are:
3991 i. Betty Ann[14] Knorpp, born September 06, 1921 in Phoenix, Arizona; died August 27, 1923 in Phoenix, Arizona.
3992 ii. Mary Jane Knorpp, born February 27, 1923 in Phoenix, Arizona; died December 08, 1987.
3993 iii. Margaret Eda Knorpp, born January 02, 1926.

2865. Ellis Clinton[13] Shelly (Susan Ann[12] Richardson, Sarah Rebecca[11] Bowers, Susannah[10] Ober, Henry[9], Veronica " Frany "[8] Stauffer, Johannes[7], Daniel[6] Stouffer, Christian[5] Stauffer, Daniel[4] Stouffer, Christian[3], Hans[2], Hans[1]) was born January 22, 1872 in Haldane, Illinois, and died December 30, 1939 in Chicago, Illinois. He married **Anna Theresa Thometz** July 10, 1900 in Chicago, Illinois. She was born March 04, 1871 in Shannon, Illinois.

Children of Ellis Shelly and Anna Thometz are:
+ 3994 i. Magdalene Katherine[14] Shelly, born August 18, 1901 in Chicago, Illinois.
3995 ii. Viola Lou Shelly, born October 15, 1908 in Chicago, Illinois. She married William Martin Herbster May 11, 1935 in Chicago, Illinois; born August 15, 1909 in Chicago, Illinois.

2869. Emma Elizabeth[13] Trump (Rebecca Jane[12] Richardson, Sarah Rebecca[11] Bowers, Susannah[10] Ober, Henry[9], Veronica " Frany "[8] Stauffer, Johannes[7], Daniel[6] Stouffer, Christian[5] Stauffer, Daniel[4] Stouffer, Christian[3], Hans[2], Hans[1]) was born October 27, 1879 in Sedgwick, Kansas, and died in Polo, Illinois. She married **Irwin Lee Paul** January 26, 1902 in Polo, Illinois. He was born April 21, 1879 in Polo, Illinois.

Children of Emma Trump and Irwin Paul are:
+ 3996 i. Private[14] Paul.
+ 3997 ii. Bessie Norene Paul, born February 05, 1906.

2870. Oliver Garfield[13] Trump (Rebecca Jane[12] Richardson, Sarah Rebecca[11] Bowers, Susannah[10] Ober, Henry[9], Veronica " Frany "[8] Stauffer, Johannes[7], Daniel[6] Stouffer, Christian[5] Stauffer, Daniel[4] Stouffer, Christian[3], Hans[2], Hans[1]) was born November 11, 1880 in Sedgwick, Kansas, and died March 18, 1956 in Polo, Illinois (Fairmont Cemetery). He married **Luella N. Stees** February 28, 1904 in Polo, Illinois. She was born April 09, 1884 in Buena Vista, Illinois.

Children of Oliver Trump and Luella Stees are:
+ 3998 i. Private[14] Trump.
3999 ii. Private Trump. She married Private Boddiger.

2871. Oscar A.[13] Trump (Rebecca Jane[12] Richardson, Sarah Rebecca[11] Bowers, Susannah[10] Ober, Henry[9], Veronica " Frany "[8] Stauffer, Johannes[7], Daniel[6] Stouffer, Christian[5] Stauffer, Daniel[4] Stouffer, Christian[3], Hans[2], Hans[1]) was born December 13, 1881 in Sedgwick, Kansas, and died August 16, 1948 in Polo, Illinois (Buffalo Grove Cemetery). He married **Eva Katherine Wilder** May 30, 1903. She was born August 16, 1886 in Polo, Illinois.

Child of Oscar Trump and Eva Wilder is:
4000 i. Harold[14] Trump, born August 28, 1904 in Polo, Illinois; died May 28, 1923 in Polo, Illinois.

2873. John Henry[13] Trump (Rebecca Jane[12] Richardson, Sarah Rebecca[11] Bowers, Susannah[10] Ober, Henry[9], Veronica " Frany "[8] Stauffer, Johannes[7], Daniel[6] Stouffer, Christian[5] Stauffer, Daniel[4] Stouffer, Christian[3], Hans[2], Hans[1]) was born July 30, 1887 in Polo, Illinois, and died December 01, 1935 in Hutchinson, Kansas. He married **Helen Edith Thrope** January 29, 1902 in Polo, IL.. She was born September 11, 1883 in Jennings, Michigan, and died September 12, 1947 in Pasadena, CA..

Children of John Trump and Helen Thrope are:
- 4001   i. Private[14] Trump. She married Private Harter.
- + 4002   ii. Private Trump.
- + 4003   iii. Jerry Roosevelt Trump, born December 12, 1902 in Polo, Illinois; died June 27, 1989 in Arcadia, CA - 4076 Daines Dr. (Home).
- 4004   iv. Charles Clifford Trump, born April 28, 1904 in Polo, IL.; died October 29, 1935 in Waterville, MN..
- + 4005   v. Anita Trump, born July 02, 1909 in Sedgwick, Kansas.
- 4006   vi. John Duane Trump, born October 08, 1917 in Wichita, Kansas; died December 12, 1917 in Burton, Kansas.
- 4007   vii. Charles Clifford Trump, born April 29, 1935 in Polo, Illinois; died October 29, 1935 in Waterville, Minnesota.

2875. Goldie May[13] **Snyder** (Sarah B.[12] Richardson, Sarah Rebecca[11] Bowers, Susannah[10] Ober, Henry[9], Veronica " Frany "[8] Stauffer, Johannes[7], Daniel[6] Stouffer, Christian[5] Stauffer, Daniel[4] Stouffer, Christian[3], Hans[2], Hans[1]) was born November 17, 1874 in Polo, Illinois. She married **Alfred Lafayette Kinzer** May 02, 1894 in Sedgwick, Kansas. He was born May 09, 1868 in Fulton County, Illinois.

Children of Goldie Snyder and Alfred Kinzer are:
- + 4008   i. Wanda Naomi[14] Kinzer, born May 10, 1895 in Mulvane, Kansas.
- 4009   ii. Alfred Glenn Kinzer, born May 28, 1897 in Sedgwick, Kansas. He married Edna Voelker December 03, 1930 in Edwardsville, Illinois; born November 26, 1894 in Edwardsville, Illinois.
- + 4010   iii. Jesse Arden Kinzer, born February 03, 1907 in New Douglas, Illinois.

2876. Sarah Jane[13] **Snyder** (Sarah B.[12] Richardson, Sarah Rebecca[11] Bowers, Susannah[10] Ober, Henry[9], Veronica " Frany "[8] Stauffer, Johannes[7], Daniel[6] Stouffer, Christian[5] Stauffer, Daniel[4] Stouffer, Christian[3], Hans[2], Hans[1]) was born October 27, 1876 in Polo, Illinois. She married **(1) Charles R. Frost** October 27, 1897 in Sedgwick, Kansas. She married **(2) Clayton E. Youtsey** September 26, 1914 in Kearney, Nebraska. He was born February 23, 1880 in Loveland, Colorado.

Children of Sarah Snyder and Charles Frost are:
- 4011   i. Infant[14] Frost, born 1889 in Sedgwick, Kansas; died 1889 in Sedgwick, Kansas.
- 4012   ii. Harry Frost, born Abt. 1899; died Abt. 1899.
- + 4013   iii. Charles Snyder Frost, born April 10, 1900 in Wichita, Kansas.

2877. Harriet Lucretia[13] **Snyder** (Sarah B.[12] Richardson, Sarah Rebecca[11] Bowers, Susannah[10] Ober, Henry[9], Veronica " Frany "[8] Stauffer, Johannes[7], Daniel[6] Stouffer, Christian[5] Stauffer, Daniel[4] Stouffer, Christian[3], Hans[2], Hans[1]) was born September 05, 1882 in Sedgwick, Kansas. She married **Charles Wesley Hamilton** December 21, 1902 in Sedgwick, Kansas. He was born March 20, 1880 in Indianola, Iowa.

Children of Harriet Snyder and Charles Hamilton are:
- + 4014   i. Private[14] Hamilton.
- 4015   ii. Private Hamilton. She married Private Smith.
- 4016   iii. Aura Titus Hamilton, born November 05, 1903 in Indianola, Iowa; died July 28, 1904 in Cave, Kansas.
- + 4017   iv. Elton Kenneth Hamilton, born July 14, 1906 in Dodge City, Kansas.
- 4018   v. Vera Lucretia Hamilton, born June 23, 1910 in Fowler, Kansas; died January 29, 1911 in Wichita, Kansas.
- 4019   vi. Harold Leon Hamilton, born December 15, 1922 in Los Angeles, California; died March 24, 1923 in Los Angeles, California.

2879. Stephen Andrew[13] **Richardson** (Andrew Jackson[12], Sarah Rebecca[11] Bowers, Susannah[10] Ober, Henry[9], Veronica " Frany "[8] Stauffer, Johannes[7], Daniel[6] Stouffer, Christian[5] Stauffer, Daniel[4] Stouffer, Christian[3], Hans[2], Hans[1]) was born August 13, 1882 in Sedgwick, Kansas. He married **(1) Nellie Hatfield** February 14, 1907 in Belle Plaine, Kansas. She was born in Belle Plaine, Kansas. He married **(2) Mable Waugh** October 03, 1915. She was born October 15, 1898 in South Haven, Kansas.

Child of Stephen Richardson and Nellie Hatfield is:
- + 4020   i. Carl Andrew[14] Richardson, born July 26, 1908 in Belle Plaine, Kansas.

2881. Ada Lucretia[13] **Richardson** (Andrew Jackson[12], Sarah Rebecca[11] Bowers, Susannah[10] Ober, Henry[9], Veronica " Frany "[8] Stauffer, Johannes[7], Daniel[6] Stouffer, Christian[5] Stauffer, Daniel[4] Stouffer, Christian[3], Hans[2], Hans[1]) was born December 26, 1883 in Sedgwick, Kansas. She married **Sidney Lincoln Miller** July 29, 1914 in Belle Plaine, Kansas. He was born March 17, 1890 in Cimarron, Kansas.

Children of Ada Richardson and Sidney Miller are:
- 4021   i.   Private[14] Miller. She married Private Waples.
- 4022   ii.   Private Miller.
- 4023   iii.   Private Miller.

2882. Mattie Beulah[13] Richardson (Andrew Jackson[12], Sarah Rebecca[11] Bowers, Susannah[10] Ober, Henry[9], Veronica " Frany "[8] Stauffer, Johannes[7], Daniel[6] Stouffer, Christian[5] Stauffer, Daniel[4] Stouffer, Christian[3], Hans[2], Hans[1]) was born November 15, 1885 in Sedgwick, Kansas. She married **Ray J. Barner** November 19, 1906 in Wichita, Kansas. He was born November 12, 1884 in Belle Plaine, Kansas.

Children of Mattie Richardson and Ray Barner are:
- +   4024   i.   Private[14] Barner.
-      4025   ii.   Private Barner. He married Private Pergrem.
-      4026   iii.   Private Barner.
- +   4027   iv.   Ramona Lee Barner, born October 06, 1907 in Belle Plaine, Kansas.
- +   4028   v.   Charles Merle Barner, born September 23, 1909 in Belle Plaine, Kansas.

2883. Melville Jackson[13] Richardson (Andrew Jackson[12], Sarah Rebecca[11] Bowers, Susannah[10] Ober, Henry[9], Veronica " Frany "[8] Stauffer, Johannes[7], Daniel[6] Stouffer, Christian[5] Stauffer, Daniel[4] Stouffer, Christian[3], Hans[2], Hans[1]) was born March 25, 1889 in Sedgwick, Kansas. He married **Ada Howard** 1912. She was born February 17, 1896, and died February 15, 1918 in Belle Plaine, Kansas.

Children of Melville Richardson and Ada Howard are:
- +   4029   i.   Private[14] Richardson.
- +   4030   ii.   Private Richardson.

2884. Margaret Ella Blanch[13] Richardson (Andrew Jackson[12], Sarah Rebecca[11] Bowers, Susannah[10] Ober, Henry[9], Veronica " Frany "[8] Stauffer, Johannes[7], Daniel[6] Stouffer, Christian[5] Stauffer, Daniel[4] Stouffer, Christian[3], Hans[2], Hans[1]) was born May 09, 1892 in Newton, Kansas. She married **(1) John Graham Alter** November 15, 1911 in Belle Plaine, Kansas. He was born January 29, 1884, and died December 08, 1918 in Belle Plaine, Kansas. She married **(2) Walter Walker** April 01, 1934 in Los Angeles, California. He was born July 23, 1896 in Baird, Texas.

Child of Margaret Richardson and John Alter is:
- +   4031   i.   Private[14] Alter.

2885. Eva Beatrice[13] Richardson (Andrew Jackson[12], Sarah Rebecca[11] Bowers, Susannah[10] Ober, Henry[9], Veronica " Frany "[8] Stauffer, Johannes[7], Daniel[6] Stouffer, Christian[5] Stauffer, Daniel[4] Stouffer, Christian[3], Hans[2], Hans[1]) was born October 20, 1894 in Sedgwick, Kansas. She married **Otto Laurence Lane** June 19, 1913 in Belle Plaine, Kansas. He was born April 11, 1891 in Belle Plaine, Kansas.

Children of Eva Richardson and Otto Lane are:
- +   4032   i.   Private[14] Lane.
-      4033   ii.   Private Lane. He married Private Lawless.
-      4034   iii.   Private Lane.

2887. Leslie Martin[13] Richardson (Andrew Jackson[12], Sarah Rebecca[11] Bowers, Susannah[10] Ober, Henry[9], Veronica " Frany "[8] Stauffer, Johannes[7], Daniel[6] Stouffer, Christian[5] Stauffer, Daniel[4] Stouffer, Christian[3], Hans[2], Hans[1]) was born April 13, 1902 in Corbin, Kansas. He married **Velma Donelda Brooks** February 07, 1931 in Belle Plaine, Kansas. She was born September 16, 1911 in Belle Plaine, Kansas.

Children of Leslie Richardson and Velma Brooks are:
- 4035   i.   Private[14] Richardson.
- 4036   ii.   Private Richardson.

2888. Florence Mildred[13] Richardson (Stephen E.[12], Sarah Rebecca[11] Bowers, Susannah[10] Ober, Henry[9], Veronica " Frany "[8] Stauffer, Johannes[7], Daniel[6] Stouffer, Christian[5] Stauffer, Daniel[4] Stouffer, Christian[3], Hans[2], Hans[1]) was born March 14, 1885 in Sedgwick, Kansas. She married **Halleck Charles Davis** December 26, 1905 in Morrison, Oklahoma. He was born September 18, 1878 in Burnaide, Kentucky.

Child of Florence Richardson and Halleck Davis is:
- 4037   i.   Private[14] Davis. He married (1) Unknown. He married (2) Private Howe.

2889. Sydney Robert[13] Richardson (Stephen E.[12], Sarah Rebecca[11] Bowers, Susannah[10] Ober, Henry[9], Veronica " Frany "[8] Stauffer, Johannes[7], Daniel[6] Stouffer, Christian[5] Stauffer, Daniel[4] Stouffer, Christian[3], Hans[2], Hans[1]) was born September 12, 1887 in Sedgwick, Kansas. He married **Abbie Mae Jennings** September 15, 1921 in Leona, Iowa. She was born October 29, 1892 in Boone, Iowa.

Children of Sydney Richardson and Abbie Jennings are:
- 4038 i. Private[14] Richardson.
- 4039 ii. Private Richardson.
- 4040 iii. Private Richardson.

2891. Stephen Roscoe[13] Richardson (Stephen E.[12], Sarah Rebecca[11] Bowers, Susannah[10] Ober, Henry[9], Veronica " Frany "[8] Stauffer, Johannes[7], Daniel[6] Stouffer, Christian[5] Stauffer, Daniel[4] Stouffer, Christian[3], Hans[2], Hans[1]) was born June 01, 1895 in Perry, Oklahoma. He married **(1) Edna Silver** September 19, 1913 in Perry, Oklahoma. She was born September 10, 1897 in Perry, Oklahoma. He married **(2) Cora Bell Shoemaker** July 03, 1928 in Bayard, Nebraska. She was born July 03, 1908.

Children of Stephen Richardson and Edna Silver are:
- 4041 i. Private[14] Richardson.
- 4042 ii. Private Richardson.

Children of Stephen Richardson and Cora Shoemaker are:
- 4043 i. Private[14] Richardson.
- 4044 ii. Private Richardson.
- 4045 iii. Private Richardson.
- 4046 iv. Private Richardson.
- 4047 v. Private Richardson.
- 4048 vi. Private Richardson.

2894. Charlotte B.[13] Richardson (Stephen E.[12], Sarah Rebecca[11] Bowers, Susannah[10] Ober, Henry[9], Veronica " Frany "[8] Stauffer, Johannes[7], Daniel[6] Stouffer, Christian[5] Stauffer, Daniel[4] Stouffer, Christian[3], Hans[2], Hans[1]) was born November 05, 1900 in Perry, Oklahoma. She married **(1) Sumner Bowers Cragin** August 19, 1918 in Percell, Oklahoma. He was born April 04, 1899 in Anthony, Kansas. She married **(2) Edgar Paul Hawk** October 24, 1932. He was born August 02, 1909.

Children of Charlotte Richardson and Sumner Cragin are:
- 4049 i. Private[14] Craign.
- 4050 ii. Private Cragin.

Children of Charlotte Richardson and Edgar Hawk are:
- 4051 i. Private[14] Hawk.
- 4052 ii. Private Hawk.

2896. Stephen Clyde[13] Line (Harriet May[12] Richardson, Sarah Rebecca[11] Bowers, Susannah[10] Ober, Henry[9], Veronica " Frany "[8] Stauffer, Johannes[7], Daniel[6] Stouffer, Christian[5] Stauffer, Daniel[4] Stouffer, Christian[3], Hans[2], Hans[1]) was born March 08, 1885 in Kingman, Kansas, and died January 12, 1959 in Preble County, Ohio. He married **Emma Iona Arnold** June 14, 1905 in Dayton, Ohio. She was born January 27, 1884 in Trotwood, Ohio, and died July 10, 1975 in Lebanon, Warren County, Ohio.

Children of Stephen Line and Emma Arnold are:
- 4053 i. Clayton Merle[14] Line, born April 26, 1907 in Dayton, Ohio; died April 1977 in Weslaco, Hidalgo County, Texas. He married Alda Pope; born March 19, 1903; died March 06, 1992.
- + 4054 ii. Thora Isabelle Line, born October 24, 1910 in Dayton, Ohio; died December 30, 1990 in West Palm Beach, Florida.

2897. Mabel Beatrice[13] Line (Harriet May[12] Richardson, Sarah Rebecca[11] Bowers, Susannah[10] Ober, Henry[9], Veronica " Frany "[8] Stauffer, Johannes[7], Daniel[6] Stouffer, Christian[5] Stauffer, Daniel[4] Stouffer, Christian[3], Hans[2], Hans[1]) was born August 16, 1887 in Jetmore, Kansas, and died May 02, 1960 in Dayton, Montgomery County, Ohio. She married **Carl Gordon Loose** February 26, 1910 in Dayton, Ohio. He was born February 15, 1884 in Terre Haute, Indiana, and died December 1970.

Children of Mabel Line and Carl Loose are:
- + 4055 i. Private[14] Loose.
- + 4056 ii. Private Loose.
- + 4057 iii. Carl Maurice Loose, born February 26, 1911 in Dayton, Ohio; died September 1991.

2898. Golda Gladys[13] Line (Harriet May[12] Richardson, Sarah Rebecca[11] Bowers, Susannah[10] Ober, Henry[9], Veronica " Frany "[8] Stauffer, Johannes[7], Daniel[6] Stouffer, Christian[5] Stauffer, Daniel[4] Stouffer, Christian[3], Hans[2], Hans[1]) was born September 02, 1892 in Kingman, Kansas, and died April 1977. She married **Dr. John Robert Arthur** November 16, 1916 in Dayton, Ohio. He was born June 14, 1892 in Cedarville, Ohio, and died March 16, 1965 in Dayton, Montgomery County, Ohio.

Children of Golda Line and John Arthur are:
- 4058   i.   Private[14] Arthur.
- 4059   ii.   Private Arthur.
- 4060   iii.   Private Arthur.

2899. Sara Margaret[13] Line (Harriet May[12] Richardson, Sarah Rebecca[11] Bowers, Susannah[10] Ober, Henry[9], Veronica " Frany "[8] Stauffer, Johannes[7], Daniel[6] Stouffer, Christian[5] Stauffer, Daniel[4] Stouffer, Christian[3], Hans[2], Hans[1]) was born August 21, 1896 in Kingman, Kansas, and died May 1978 in Dayton, Montgomery County, Ohio. She married **Wilbert John Harnish** May 30, 1917 in Dayton, Ohio. He was born January 06, 1894 in Dayton, Ohio, and died May 1992 in Dayton, Montgomery County, Ohio.

Children of Sara Line and Wilbert Harnish are:
- +   4061   i.   Private[14] Harnish.
-     4062   ii.   Private Harnish.
-     4063   iii.   Private Harnish.
-     4064   iv.   Private Harnish.
-     4065   v.   Private Harnish.

2900. Agatha E.[13] Haynes (Martha[12] Richardson, Sarah Rebecca[11] Bowers, Susannah[10] Ober, Henry[9], Veronica " Frany "[8] Stauffer, Johannes[7], Daniel[6] Stouffer, Christian[5] Stauffer, Daniel[4] Stouffer, Christian[3], Hans[2], Hans[1]) was born October 21, 1890 in Sedgwick, Kansas. She married **Carl Mornhingweig** January 22, 1913 in Wichita, Kansas.

Children of Agatha Haynes and Carl Mornhingweig are:
- +   4066   i.   Private[14] Mornhengweig.
-     4067   ii.   Private Mornhengweig.
- +   4068   iii.   Private Mornhengweig.
-     4069   iv.   Private Mornhengweig.

2902. Dorothy[13] Haynes (Martha[12] Richardson, Sarah Rebecca[11] Bowers, Susannah[10] Ober, Henry[9], Veronica " Frany "[8] Stauffer, Johannes[7], Daniel[6] Stouffer, Christian[5] Stauffer, Daniel[4] Stouffer, Christian[3], Hans[2], Hans[1]) was born April 30, 1895 in Humesville, Missouri. She married **Clyde Seibert** April 14, 1929 in Phoenix, Arizona. He was born August 09, 1895 in Perris, California.

Children of Dorothy Haynes and Clyde Seibert are:
- 4070   i.   Private[14] Seibert.
- 4071   ii.   Private Seibert.

2903. Marjorie[13] Haynes (Martha[12] Richardson, Sarah Rebecca[11] Bowers, Susannah[10] Ober, Henry[9], Veronica " Frany "[8] Stauffer, Johannes[7], Daniel[6] Stouffer, Christian[5] Stauffer, Daniel[4] Stouffer, Christian[3], Hans[2], Hans[1]) was born December 15, 1898 in Sedgwick, Kansas. She married **(1) Wilmer Wood** Abt. 1920. She married **(2) Jolly A. Hendrix** December 07, 1925 in Sedgwick, Kansas. He was born January 10, 1898 in Chelsea, Oklahoma.

Children of Marjorie Haynes and Jolly Hendrix are:
- 4072   i.   Private[14] Hendrix.
- 4073   ii.   Private Hendrix.

2909. Burgess Coleman[13] Level (Mary Ann[12] Lesher, David[11], Barbara[10] Ober, Michael[9], Veronica " Frany "[8] Stauffer, Johannes[7], Daniel[6] Stouffer, Christian[5] Stauffer, Daniel[4] Stouffer, Christian[3], Hans[2], Hans[1]) was born October 21, 1892. He married **Mae Unknown**.

Child of Burgess Level and Mae Unknown is:
- 4074   i.   Unknown[14] Level.

2910. Cloyd Irwin[13] Level (Mary Ann[12] Lesher, David[11], Barbara[10] Ober, Michael[9], Veronica " Frany "[8] Stauffer, Johannes[7], Daniel[6] Stouffer, Christian[5] Stauffer, Daniel[4] Stouffer, Christian[3], Hans[2], Hans[1]) was born May 23, 1895. He married **Ethelda Unknown**.

Children of Cloyd Level and Ethelda Unknown are:
- 4075   i.   Unknown[14] Level.

4076   ii.   Unknown Level.
4077   iii.   Unknown Level.

2912. John Howard[13] **Level** (Mary Ann[12] Lesher, David[11], Barbara[10] Ober, Michael[9], Veronica " Frany "[8] Stauffer, Johannes[7], Daniel[6] Stouffer, Christian[5] Stauffer, Daniel[4] Stouffer, Christian[3], Hans[2], Hans[1]) was born February 06, 1909 in Odebolt, Iowa, and died September 06, 1949 in Martinez, California. He married **Leone Elizabeth Lakers**. She was born March 14, 1914 in Manila, Iowa, and died February 06, 1989.

Children of John Level and Leone Lakers are:
+   4078   i.   Private[14] Level.
+   4079   ii.   Private Level.
+   4080   iii.   Private Level.
    4081   iv.   Elizabeth Leone Level, born December 12, 1944; died 1995.

2917. Myrtle Liliom D.[13] **Diehl** (David Alfred[12], Catherine A.[11] Ober, Jacob[10], Michael[9], Veronica " Frany "[8] Stauffer, Johannes[7], Daniel[6] Stouffer, Christian[5] Stauffer, Daniel[4] Stouffer, Christian[3], Hans[2], Hans[1]) was born April 17, 1877 in Pennsylvania, and died April 05, 1931 in Findlay, Hancock County, Ohio. She married **Homer Tyner** December 19, 1900 in Wood County, Ohio. He died 1943.

Marriage Notes for Myrtle Diehl and Homer Tyner:
[Henry Ober 1742.ged]

_STATMARRIED

Children of Myrtle Diehl and Homer Tyner are:
    4082   i.   Kenneth A[14] Tyner.
    4083   ii.   Saint Elmo Parlette Tyner.
+   4084   iii.   Bethel Leone Tyner.

2918. James Alfred[13] **Deihl** (David Alfred[12] Diehl, Catherine A.[11] Ober, Jacob[10], Michael[9], Veronica " Frany "[8] Stauffer, Johannes[7], Daniel[6] Stouffer, Christian[5] Stauffer, Daniel[4] Stouffer, Christian[3], Hans[2], Hans[1]) was born February 23, 1880 in Bloom Township, Wood County, Ohio, and died March 15, 1944 in Pandora, Wood County, Ohio. He married **Minnie B. Alexander**.

Marriage Notes for James Deihl and Minnie Alexander:
[Henry Ober 1742.ged]

_STATMARRIED

Children of James Deihl and Minnie Alexander are:
    4085   i.   Unknown[14] Deihl.
    4086   ii.   Unknown Deihl.
    4087   iii.   Unknown Deihl.
    4088   iv.   Miriam Deihl, born Bef. 1912 in Ohio.

2919. Harvey A.[13] **Deihl** (David Alfred[12] Diehl, Catherine A.[11] Ober, Jacob[10], Michael[9], Veronica " Frany "[8] Stauffer, Johannes[7], Daniel[6] Stouffer, Christian[5] Stauffer, Daniel[4] Stouffer, Christian[3], Hans[2], Hans[1]) was born June 06, 1881 in Wood County, Ohio, and died Aft. 1931. He married **Mamie Dell Gamell**.

Marriage Notes for Harvey Deihl and Mamie Gamell:
[Henry Ober 1742.ged]

_STATMARRIED

Children of Harvey Deihl and Mamie Gamell are:
    4089   i.   Unknown[14] Deihl.
    4090   ii.   Unknown Deihl.
    4091   iii.   Unknown Deihl.
    4092   iv.   Unknown Deihl.

2920. Gideon S.[13] **Deihl** (David Alfred[12] Diehl, Catherine A.[11] Ober, Jacob[10], Michael[9], Veronica " Frany "[8] Stauffer, Johannes[7], Daniel[6] Stouffer, Christian[5] Stauffer, Daniel[4] Stouffer, Christian[3], Hans[2], Hans[1]) was born December 27, 1882 in Bloom Township, Wood County, Ohio, and died Aft. 1944. He married **Jennie M. Unknown**.

Marriage Notes for Gideon Deihl and Jennie Unknown:
[Henry Ober 1742.ged]

_STATMARRIED

Children of Gideon Deihl and Jennie Unknown are:
- 4093 i. Unknown[14] Deihl.
- 4094 ii. Unknown Deihl.

2921. Zelda F.[13] **Diehl** (David Alfred[12], Catherine A.[11] Ober, Jacob[10], Michael[9], Veronica " Frany "[8] Stauffer, Johannes[7], Daniel[6] Stouffer, Christian[5] Stauffer, Daniel[4] Stouffer, Christian[3], Hans[2], Hans[1]) was born May 1890 in Wood County, Ohio. She married **Monroe E. Amidon**. He was born August 28, 1877 in Michigan, and died January 1963 in New York.

Children of Zelda Diehl and Monroe Amidon are:
- 4095 i. Mary L.[14] Amidon, born 1899 in Michigan.
- 4096 ii. James A. Amidon, born 1909 in Michigan.
- 4097 iii. Mary L. Amidon, born 1928 in Michigan.

2922. Percy Ellsworth[13] **Diehl** (David Alfred[12], Catherine A.[11] Ober, Jacob[10], Michael[9], Veronica " Frany "[8] Stauffer, Johannes[7], Daniel[6] Stouffer, Christian[5] Stauffer, Daniel[4] Stouffer, Christian[3], Hans[2], Hans[1]) was born November 18, 1893 in Wood County, Ohio, and died August 01, 1987 in Traverse City, Michigan. He married **Albena May Tousignant** 1921 in Munising, Michigan. She was born July 31, 1900 in Marquette, Chocolay Township, Marquette County, Michigan, and died April 08, 1988 in Traverse City, Michigan.

Marriage Notes for Percy Diehl and Albena Tousignant:
[Henry Ober 1742.ged]

_STATMARRIED

Children of Percy Diehl and Albena Tousignant are:
- + 4098 i. Private[14] Diehl.
- + 4099 ii. Private Diehl.
- + 4100 iii. Private Diehl.
- + 4101 iv. Juanita Glada Diehl, born December 09, 1921 in Maple City, Michigan; died February 19, 2002 in Traverse City, Michigan.
- + 4102 v. David R. Diehl, born November 15, 1922 in Maple City, Michigan; died August 02, 1994 in Lakeview, Michigan.
- 4103 vi. Harold James Diehl, born November 25, 1926 in Maple City, Kasson Township, Leelanau County, Michigan; died March 28, 2002 in Sebring, Florida. He married (1) Private Bush. He married (2) Private Unknown. He married (3) Private Unknown. He married (4) Private Unknown.
- 4104 vii. Lorraine Louise Diehl, born January 17, 1929 in Leelanau County, Michigan; died May 21, 1929 in Leelanau County, Michigan.
- + 4105 viii. Donald Diehl, born August 23, 1930 in Maple City, Michigan; died September 29, 1990 in Traverse City, Michigan.
- 4106 ix. John Daniel Diehl, born January 09, 1934 in Maple City, Michigan; died January 1935 in Maple City, Michigan.

2936. Allen L[13] **Brubaker** (Ezra[12], Christian[11], Christian[10], Elizabeth[9] Stauffer, Christian[8], Henry Jacob[7], Hans[6], Christian[5], Daniel[4] Stouffer, Christian[3], Hans[2], Hans[1]) was born 1868, and died Aft. 1930. He married **Lizzie Risser Franck**. She was born 1871, and died Aft. 1930.

Children of Allen Brubaker and Lizzie Franck are:
- 4107 i. Mary F[14] Brubaker, born 1893.
- 4108 ii. Elsie Brubaker, born 1895.
- 4109 iii. Florence Brubaker, born 1896.
- 4110 iv. Helen Brubaker, born 1897.
- 4111 v. Walter F Brubaker, born September 09, 1902; died December 1977. He married Rheta H Brubaker Aft. 1930; born Abt. 1900.
- 4112 vi. Harold F Brubaker, born 1905.
- 4113 vii. Warren E Brubaker, born 1908.
- 4114 viii. Fanny Elizabeth Brubaker, born 1909.
- + 4115 ix. Arlene Celeste Brubaker, born January 08, 1911.
- 4116 x. Charles E Brubaker, born 1912.
- 4117 xi. Arthur J Brubaker, born 1914.

2943. John C[13] Scott (Nancy[12] Ruff, Mary Ann[11] Stoffer, Louis J[10], Jacob[9], Jacob[8] Stauffer, Henry Jacob[7], Hans[6], Christian[5], Daniel[4] Stouffer, Christian[3], Hans[2], Hans[1]) was born December 12, 1882 in Columbiana County, Ohio, and died December 06, 1971 in Columbiana County, Ohio. He married **Bertha Bartchey**. She was born March 08, 1886 in Columbiana County, Ohio.

Child of John Scott and Bertha Bartchey is:
    4118   i.   Ruth[14] Scott.

2944. Ralph L[13] Scott (Nancy[12] Ruff, Mary Ann[11] Stoffer, Louis J[10], Jacob[9], Jacob[8] Stauffer, Henry Jacob[7], Hans[6], Christian[5], Daniel[4] Stouffer, Christian[3], Hans[2], Hans[1]) was born April 12, 1889 in Columbiana County, Ohio, and died 1988 in Columbiana County, Ohio. He married **Jean O'Brien**.

Children of Ralph Scott and Jean O'Brien are:
    4119   i.   James[14] Scott.
    4120   ii.   William Scott.

2946. Mary A[13] Scott (Nancy[12] Ruff, Mary Ann[11] Stoffer, Louis J[10], Jacob[9], Jacob[8] Stauffer, Henry Jacob[7], Hans[6], Christian[5], Daniel[4] Stouffer, Christian[3], Hans[2], Hans[1]) was born June 04, 1894 in Columbiana County, Ohio, and died October 17, 1982 in Columbiana County, Ohio. She married **Evan Byers**.

Children of Mary Scott and Evan Byers are:
    4121   i.   Hazel[14] Byers.
    4122   ii.   Ralph Byers.
    4123   iii.   James Byers.
    4124   iv.   Robert Byers.
    4125   v.   Phyllis Byers.
    4126   vi.   Dwight Byers.

2947. Ruth Isabel[13] Scott (Nancy[12] Ruff, Mary Ann[11] Stoffer, Louis J[10], Jacob[9], Jacob[8] Stauffer, Henry Jacob[7], Hans[6], Christian[5], Daniel[4] Stouffer, Christian[3], Hans[2], Hans[1]) was born January 04, 1898 in Columbiana County, Ohio, and died October 15, 1924 in Columbiana County, Ohio. She married **Irvin Emmanuel Yaggi**.

Children of Ruth Scott and Irvin Yaggi are:
+   4127   i.   Lois Jean[14] Yaggi.
+   4128   ii.   Agnes Ruth Yaggi.
+   4129   iii.   Mary Elizabeth Yaggi, born June 23, 1919 in Columbiana County, Ohio; died November 26, 1980.

2948. Earl[13] Stroup (Ida J.[12] Stoffer, Lewis Jr[11], Louis J[10], Jacob[9], Jacob[8] Stauffer, Henry Jacob[7], Hans[6], Christian[5], Daniel[4] Stouffer, Christian[3], Hans[2], Hans[1]) was born May 28, 1892 in Columbiana County, Ohio, and died May 22, 1979 in Shreve, Wayne County, Ohio. He married **(1) Carrie Sutton** November 26, 1917 in Columbiana County, Ohio. She was born January 13, 1895 in Columbiana County, Ohio, and died May 02, 1930 in Columbiana County, Ohio. He married **(2) Alice Kniveton** 1932 in Columbiana County, Ohio.

Children of Earl Stroup and Carrie Sutton are:
    4130   i.   Russell[14] Stroup.
    4131   ii.   Lowell Stroup.
    4132   iii.   June Stroup.
    4133   iv.   Julia Faye Stroup.
    4134   v.   Atlee Stroup, born November 03, 1918.

Children of Earl Stroup and Alice Kniveton are:
    4135   i.   Private[14] Stroup.
    4136   ii.   Private Stroup.
    4137   iii.   Private Stroup.

2949. Nellie F.[13] Stroup (Ida J.[12] Stoffer, Lewis Jr[11], Louis J[10], Jacob[9], Jacob[8] Stauffer, Henry Jacob[7], Hans[6], Christian[5], Daniel[4] Stouffer, Christian[3], Hans[2], Hans[1]) was born September 26, 1896 in Columbiana County, Ohio, and died February 05, 1986 in Copeland Oaks Nursing Home, Sebring, Ohio. She married **J. Maynard Hummel** September 01, 1928 in Columbiana County, Ohio. He died 1972.

Child of Nellie Stroup and J. Hummel is:

4138 i. Julia[14] Hummel.

2950. Inez Genesta[13] **Stoffer** (Walter George[12], Lewis Jr[11], Louis J[10], Jacob[9], Jacob[8] Stauffer, Henry Jacob[7], Hans[6], Christian[5], Daniel[4] Stouffer, Christian[3], Hans[2], Hans[1]) was born February 27, 1897 in Columbiana Cty, Ohio, and died August 09, 1970 in Alliance, Ohio. She married **John Norman Baker** December 23, 1915 in Columbiana Cty, Ohio. He was born July 28, 1884 in Bachmansville, Penn, and died January 31, 1962 in Columbiana Cty, Ohio.

Marriage Notes for Inez Stoffer and John Baker:
[chrststauffer1663.ged]

[DATA FILE.FBK.FTW]

_DETS31 Jan 1962Homeworth, Columbiana County, Ohio

Child of Inez Stoffer and John Baker is:
+ 4139 i. Lowell[14] Baker.

2951. Virgil Forest[13] **Stoffer** (Walter George[12], Lewis Jr[11], Louis J[10], Jacob[9], Jacob[8] Stauffer, Henry Jacob[7], Hans[6], Christian[5], Daniel[4] Stouffer, Christian[3], Hans[2], Hans[1]) was born July 24, 1899 in Columbiana Cty, Ohio, and died January 16, 1984 in Copeland Oaks Retirement Center, Sebring, Ohio. He married **Bernice Winifred Summer** April 12, 1921 in New Lisbon, Ohio. She was born July 05, 1901 in Columbiana Cty, Ohio, and died October 02, 1978 in Alliance, Stark Cty Ohio.

Marriage Notes for Virgil Stoffer and Bernice Summer:
[chrststauffer1663.ged]

[DATA FILE.FBK.FTW]

_DETS2 Oct 1978Alliance, Stark County, Ohio

Children of Virgil Stoffer and Bernice Summer are:
+ 4140 i. Lewis John[14] Stoffer.
+ 4141 ii. Kenneth George Stoffer, born February 22, 1922.
+ 4142 iii. Barbara Sue Stoffer, born March 04, 1924.
+ 4143 iv. Kathryn Olive Stoffer, born March 25, 1924 in Columbiana County, Ohio; died December 31, 1995 in California.

2952. Beulah Fern[13] **Stoffer** (Walter George[12], Lewis Jr[11], Louis J[10], Jacob[9], Jacob[8] Stauffer, Henry Jacob[7], Hans[6], Christian[5], Daniel[4] Stouffer, Christian[3], Hans[2], Hans[1]) was born March 05, 1903 in Columbiana Cty, Ohio, and died May 15, 1973 in Eustis, Florida. She married **Chester Larue Knoll** June 06, 1922 in Columbiana Cty, Ohio. He was born January 08, 1901 in Columbiana Cty, Ohio, and died August 01, 1988 in Eustis, Florida.

Marriage Notes for Beulah Stoffer and Chester Knoll:
[chrststauffer1663.ged]

[DATA FILE.FBK.FTW]

_DETS15 May 1973Eustis, Florida

Children of Beulah Stoffer and Chester Knoll are:
4144 i. Richard Lee[14] Knoll.
+ 4145 ii. Dorothy Mae Knoll.
4146 iii. June Elizabeth Knoll, born June 28, 1927 in Columbiana Cty, Ohio; died July 11, 1939 in Columbiana Cty, Ohio.

2954. Dorothy Ada[13] **Stoffer** (Walter George[12], Lewis Jr[11], Louis J[10], Jacob[9], Jacob[8] Stauffer, Henry Jacob[7], Hans[6], Christian[5], Daniel[4] Stouffer, Christian[3], Hans[2], Hans[1]) was born February 11, 1912 in Columbiana County, Homeworth Ohio. She married **(1) Private Sylvester**. She married **(2) Albert Ray Ward** June 06, 1936 in Columbiana County, Ohio. He was born July 09, 1907 in Columbiana County, Winona Ohio, and died February 12, 1967 in Indianapolis, Indiana.

Marriage Notes for Dorothy Stoffer and Albert Ward:

The Relations of Milton Snavely Hershey, 4th Ed.

[chrststauffer1663.ged]

[DATA FILE.FBK.FTW]

[

_DETS16 Feb 1967

Children of Dorothy Stoffer and Albert Ward are:
+   4147   i.   Private[14] Ward.
+   4148   ii.   Private Ward.

2961. Frank[13] Stoffer (David[12], Jacob L[11], Samuel[10], Jacob[9], Jacob[8] Stauffer, Henry Jacob[7], Hans[6], Christian[5], Daniel[4] Stouffer, Christian[3], Hans[2], Hans[1]) was born December 31, 1886 in North Georgetown Ohio, Columbiana Co, and died April 25, 1982 in Alliance Ohio. He married **(1) Helen Liber**. She was born 1897, and died January 20, 1960. He married **(2) Blanche M Weaver** October 16, 1907 in Columbiana Co, Ohio. She was born July 10, 1886 in Columbiana Co, Ohio, and died June 13, 1913 in Columbiana Co, Ohio.

Children of Frank Stoffer and Helen Liber are:
    4149   i.   Gladys[14] Stoffer. She married Vaughn Caufield.
    4150   ii.   Iris Stoffer. She married Harold Behner.
    4151   iii.   Private Stoffer. She married George M Gloss.
+   4152   iv.   Frank JR Stoffer, born September 27, 1933; died September 17, 1995 in Ohio.

Children of Frank Stoffer and Blanche Weaver are:
    4153   i.   Mildred Louisa[14] Stoffer, born May 07, 1909; died August 08, 1994 in Stark Cty Ohio. She married Florian Charles"Dutch" Woolf 1929; born 1908; died 1975 in Columbiana Cty, Ohio.
+   4154   ii.   C Robert Stoffer, born February 19, 1912 in Columbiana Cty, Ohio; died January 25, 1999 in Salem, Columbiana Cty, Ohio.

2962. Harry B[13] Stoffer (David[12], Jacob L[11], Samuel[10], Jacob[9], Jacob[8] Stauffer, Henry Jacob[7], Hans[6], Christian[5], Daniel[4] Stouffer, Christian[3], Hans[2], Hans[1]) was born March 10, 1898 in North Georgetown Ohio, Columbiana Co. He married **Esther Smith** January 19, 1945. She was born September 13, 1912, and died June 14, 1994 in Salem, Ohio.

Children of Harry Stoffer and Esther Smith are:
    4155   i.   William[14] Stoffer, died Bef. 1994.
    4156   ii.   Private Stoffer.
    4157   iii.   Private Stoffer. She married Private Robb.
    4158   iv.   Private Stoffer.

2972. Dayle Kermit[13] Gearhart (Cynthia Idella[12] Stoffer, John Jacob[11], John[10], Jacob[9], Jacob[8] Stauffer, Henry Jacob[7], Hans[6], Christian[5], Daniel[4] Stouffer, Christian[3], Hans[2], Hans[1]) was born August 22, 1905 in Ohio, Richland Co, and died January 12, 1976 in Ohio, Richland Co. He married **Blanche Pauline Leedy** October 19, 1932 in Johnsville, Ohio. She was born May 08, 1914 in Williamsport Ohio, and died July 01, 1970 in Ohio, Richland Co.

Children of Dayle Gearhart and Blanche Leedy are:
    4159   i.   Private[14] Gearhart. He married Private Rinehart.
    4160   ii.   Private Gearhart. He married (1) Private Morgan. He married (2) Private Snyder.
+   4161   iii.   Private Gearhart.
    4162   iv.   Pauline Lucille Gearhart, born September 09, 1933 in Bellville Ohio, Richland Co; died June 23, 1941 in Bellville Ohio, Richland Co.
    4163   v.   Don Leedy Gearhart, born August 26, 1936; died April 25, 1997 in Fla. He married (1) Private Graves. He married (2) Private Hart. He married (3) Private Migliorsis. He married (4) Private Kilgore.

2978. Stella[13] Moser (Ada[12] Stoffer, Levi[11], George[10], Jacob[9], Jacob[8] Stauffer, Henry Jacob[7], Hans[6], Christian[5], Daniel[4] Stouffer, Christian[3], Hans[2], Hans[1]) was born May 30, 1890 in Columbiana County, Ohio, and died May 27, 1907. She married **Harry Agnew**. He was born December 13, 1882, and died June 18, 1958.

Children of Stella Moser and Harry Agnew are:
+   4164   i.   Mary Elizabeth[14] Agnew.
    4165   ii.   Harold Agnew, born June 18, 1908.
    4166   iii.   John Agnew, born September 30, 1909.
+   4167   iv.   Charles Agnew, born June 23, 1911; died September 16, 1958.

+ 4168 v. Donald Robert Agnew, born June 14, 1917.

2989. Harold Walter[13] Stoffer (Laurance L[12], Levi[11], George[10], Jacob[9], Jacob[8] Stauffer, Henry Jacob[7], Hans[6], Christian[5], Daniel[4] Stouffer, Christian[3], Hans[2], Hans[1]) was born September 28, 1914 in Columbiana Cty, Ohio, and died August 27, 1979 in Alliance City Hospital, Alliance, Ohio. He married **Ruth Ann Borton** June 10, 1939 in Columbiana Cty, Ohio. She was born September 19, 1918 in Columbiana Cty, Ohio, and died September 12, 1997 in Alliance, Ohio.

Marriage Notes for Harold Stoffer and Ruth Borton:
[chrststauffer1663.ged]

[DATA FILE.FBK.FTW]

_DETS29 Aug 1979Homeworth, Ohio
Harold and Ruth Ann were married at the home of Ruth Ann. The home is located on Buck Road, south of Alliance, Ohio in Columbiana County. The maid of honor was Edna Stanley Cunningham, best friend of the bride, and the best man was Lowell Baker, nephew of the groom. They took a honeymoon to Niagara Falls. When they returned home, they rented a house in Homeworth for two years before buying their home on Cherry Street in Homeworth. Ruth Ann sold that home in the spring of 1995 and moved to an apartment in Liberty Heights, Alliance, Ohio

Child of Harold Stoffer and Ruth Borton is:
+ 4169 i. Private[14] Stoffer.

2991. Ray[13] Shively (Idella[12] Stoffer, Levi[11], George[10], Jacob[9], Jacob[8] Stauffer, Henry Jacob[7], Hans[6], Christian[5], Daniel[4] Stouffer, Christian[3], Hans[2], Hans[1]) was born October 27, 1898, and died November 27, 1925. He married **Lela Walker** May 20, 1903. She was born May 20, 1903.

Child of Ray Shively and Lela Walker is:
4170 i. Bonnie Walker[14] Shively. She married Bill Summers.

2992. Orvie W[13] Mercer (Pearl[12] Stoffer, Levi[11], George[10], Jacob[9], Jacob[8] Stauffer, Henry Jacob[7], Hans[6], Christian[5], Daniel[4] Stouffer, Christian[3], Hans[2], Hans[1]) was born October 17, 1901. He married **Bernice Christen** March 28, 1921. She was born March 16, 1905.

Children of Orvie Mercer and Bernice Christen are:
+ 4171 i. Private[14] Mercer.
  4172 ii. Private Mercer.
+ 4173 iii. Ruth Mercer, born March 20, 1922.
+ 4174 iv. Ruby Mercer, born May 21, 1923.

2993. Chester[13] Mercer (Pearl[12] Stoffer, Levi[11], George[10], Jacob[9], Jacob[8] Stauffer, Henry Jacob[7], Hans[6], Christian[5], Daniel[4] Stouffer, Christian[3], Hans[2], Hans[1]) was born December 28, 1907. He married **Virginia Stoudt** February 07, 1933.

Children of Chester Mercer and Virginia Stoudt are:
+ 4175 i. Private[14] Mercer.
+ 4176 ii. Private Mercer.
+ 4177 iii. Private Mercer.
+ 4178 iv. Private Mercer.

2994. Herbert Russell[13] Mercer (Pearl[12] Stoffer, Levi[11], George[10], Jacob[9], Jacob[8] Stauffer, Henry Jacob[7], Hans[6], Christian[5], Daniel[4] Stouffer, Christian[3], Hans[2], Hans[1]) was born March 22, 1913. He married **Kathleen Lucille Summers** June 24, 1939. She was born March 31, 1921.

Child of Herbert Mercer and Kathleen Summers is:
+ 4179 i. Private[14] Mercer.

2995. Hazel Debra[13] Mercer (Pearl[12] Stoffer, Levi[11], George[10], Jacob[9], Jacob[8] Stauffer, Henry Jacob[7], Hans[6], Christian[5], Daniel[4] Stouffer, Christian[3], Hans[2], Hans[1]) was born January 23, 1919. She married **Joseph Sneltzer** May 23, 1936. He was born December 12, 1906, and died March 14, 1973.

Children of Hazel Mercer and Joseph Sneltzer are:
+ 4180 i. Private[14] Sneltzer.
+ 4181 ii. Private Sneltzer.
+ 4182 iii. Private Sneltzer.
+ 4183 iv. Private Sneltzer.

2996. Helen M[13] Mercer (Pearl[12] Stoffer, Levi[11], George[10], Jacob[9], Jacob[8] Stauffer, Henry Jacob[7], Hans[6], Christian[5], Daniel[4] Stouffer, Christian[3], Hans[2], Hans[1]) was born April 05, 1923. She married **Louren E Arnold** May 06, 1946. He was born March 22, 1925.

Children of Helen Mercer and Louren Arnold are:
 4184 i. Private[14] Arnold.
 4185 ii. Private Arnold.
 4186 iii. Private Arnold.

2997. Glenn A[13] Mercer (Pearl[12] Stoffer, Levi[11], George[10], Jacob[9], Jacob[8] Stauffer, Henry Jacob[7], Hans[6], Christian[5], Daniel[4] Stouffer, Christian[3], Hans[2], Hans[1]) was born February 13, 1925, and died January 19, 1981. He married **Barbara Roberts** June 29, 1946. She was born April 23, 1926.

Child of Glenn Mercer and Barbara Roberts is:
+ 4187 i. Private[14] Mercer.

3002. Loyal[13] Stoffer (Erwin William[12], Levi[11], George[10], Jacob[9], Jacob[8] Stauffer, Henry Jacob[7], Hans[6], Christian[5], Daniel[4] Stouffer, Christian[3], Hans[2], Hans[1]) was born September 18, 1911 in North Georgetown Ohio, Columbiana Co, and died 1978 in Canton Ohio, Stark Co. He married **(1) Anna Mae Geckler**. She died 1959. He married **(2) Iva Leida**.

Marriage Notes for Loyal Stoffer and Anna Geckler:
[chrststauffer1663.ged]

1 _MEND Death of one spouse

Children of Loyal Stoffer and Anna Geckler are:
 4188 i. Private[14] Stoffer.
 4189 ii. Private Stoffer. She married Private Snyder.
 4190 iii. Private Stoffer.

3007. Paul Lawrence[13] Stoffer (William Franklin[12], Laurtis W.[11], George[10], Jacob[9], Jacob[8] Stauffer, Henry Jacob[7], Hans[6], Christian[5], Daniel[4] Stouffer, Christian[3], Hans[2], Hans[1]) was born June 29, 1901 in North Georgetown Ohio, Columbiana Co, and died November 01, 1944 in Columbiana Co Ohio. He married **Lavinia Daugherty** April 25, 1921. She was born October 03, 1900 in Coshoton Ohio, and died January 13, 1996 in Mahoning Co Ohio.

Children of Paul Stoffer and Lavinia Daugherty are:
+ 4191 i. Thomas Lawrence[14] Stoffer, born December 21, 1922 in North Georgetown.
+ 4192 ii. Ellen Ann Stoffer, born May 05, 1925.
+ 4193 iii. Robert Liewellyn Stoffer, born September 16, 1927.

3008. Virginia[13] Stoffer (John Wallace[12], Laurtis W.[11], George[10], Jacob[9], Jacob[8] Stauffer, Henry Jacob[7], Hans[6], Christian[5], Daniel[4] Stouffer, Christian[3], Hans[2], Hans[1]) She married **Thpmas Sr Rill**.

Children of Virginia Stoffer and Thpmas Rill are:
 4194 i. Private[14] Rill.
 4195 ii. Private Rill.
 4196 iii. Private Rill.

3009. Gorman H[13] Stoffer (John Wallace[12], Laurtis W.[11], George[10], Jacob[9], Jacob[8] Stauffer, Henry Jacob[7], Hans[6], Christian[5], Daniel[4] Stouffer, Christian[3], Hans[2], Hans[1]) was born December 26, 1914 in Columbiana Co Ohio, and died July 28, 1999 in Salem, Columbiana Cty, Ohio. He married **Virginia M Court** July 21, 1934. She was born August 18, 1915 in Sebring Ohio, and died October 12, 1982 in Columbiana County, Ohio.

Children of Gorman Stoffer and Virginia Court are:
 4197 i. Private[14] Stoffer.

4198 ii. Private Stoffer.
4199 iii. Private Stoffer.
4200 iv. Private Stoffer.

3010. Ester[13] Stoffer (Lester Clyde[12], Laurtis W.[11], George[10], Jacob[9], Jacob[8] Stauffer, Henry Jacob[7], Hans[6], Christian[5], Daniel[4] Stouffer, Christian[3], Hans[2], Hans[1]) She married **Edwin Evans**.

Children of Ester Stoffer and Edwin Evans are:
4201 i. Private[14] Evans.
4202 ii. Private Evans.
4203 iii. Private Evans.
4204 iv. Private Evans.
4205 v. Private Evans.

3011. Floyd W[13] Stoffer (Lester Clyde[12], Laurtis W.[11], George[10], Jacob[9], Jacob[8] Stauffer, Henry Jacob[7], Hans[6], Christian[5], Daniel[4] Stouffer, Christian[3], Hans[2], Hans[1]) was born June 14, 1912 in Bayard Ohio, Columbiana Co, and died July 09, 1969 in Ohio, Stark Co. He married **June Felger** August 17, 1934.

Children of Floyd Stoffer and June Felger are:
4206 i. Private[14] Stoffer.
4207 ii. Private Stoffer.

3012. Cecil F[13] Stoffer (Lester Clyde[12], Laurtis W.[11], George[10], Jacob[9], Jacob[8] Stauffer, Henry Jacob[7], Hans[6], Christian[5], Daniel[4] Stouffer, Christian[3], Hans[2], Hans[1]) was born April 05, 1916 in Bayard Ohio, Columbiana Co, and died April 1987 in Mahoning Co Ohio. He married **Dorothy Temple**. She was born 1921.

Child of Cecil Stoffer and Dorothy Temple is:
4208 i. Private[14] Stoffer.

3013. Robert[13] Freshley (Gladys Alice[12] Stoffer, Laurtis W.[11], George[10], Jacob[9], Jacob[8] Stauffer, Henry Jacob[7], Hans[6], Christian[5], Daniel[4] Stouffer, Christian[3], Hans[2], Hans[1]) He married **Patricia Mann**.

Children of Robert Freshley and Patricia Mann are:
4209 i. Private[14] Freshley.
4210 ii. Private Freshley.

3015. Marjorie[13] Freshley (Gladys Alice[12] Stoffer, Laurtis W.[11], George[10], Jacob[9], Jacob[8] Stauffer, Henry Jacob[7], Hans[6], Christian[5], Daniel[4] Stouffer, Christian[3], Hans[2], Hans[1]) She married **William H Stroup**.

Children of Marjorie Freshley and William Stroup are:
4211 i. Private[14] Stroup.
4212 ii. Private Stroup.

3016. Eugene A[13] Freshley (Gladys Alice[12] Stoffer, Laurtis W.[11], George[10], Jacob[9], Jacob[8] Stauffer, Henry Jacob[7], Hans[6], Christian[5], Daniel[4] Stouffer, Christian[3], Hans[2], Hans[1]) was born January 02, 1920. He married **Dorothy J Summers**. She was born 1924, and died 1973.

Children of Eugene Freshley and Dorothy Summers are:
4213 i. Private[14] Freshley. He married (1) Private Mc Kacken. He married (2) Private McKracken.
4214 ii. Private Freshley. He married Private Hanesworth.
4215 iii. Private Freshley. He married (1) Private Crefro. He married (2) Private Cefro.
4216 iv. Private Freshley. She married Private Bennett.
4217 v. Private Freshley. He married Private Eiklor.
4218 vi. Private Freshley. He married Private Steen.

3017. June[13] Freshley (Gladys Alice[12] Stoffer, Laurtis W.[11], George[10], Jacob[9], Jacob[8] Stauffer, Henry Jacob[7], Hans[6], Christian[5], Daniel[4] Stouffer, Christian[3], Hans[2], Hans[1]) was born October 19, 1921. She married **William Livingston**. He was born March 07, 1918, and died May 07, 1979.

Children of June Freshley and William Livingston are:
- 4219   i. Private[14] Livingston. She married Private Green.
- 4220   ii. Private Livingston.
- 4221   iii. Private Livingston. She married Private Blickenderfer.

3018. Martha[13] Stoffer (Veron Roy[12], Laurtis W.[11], George[10], Jacob[9], Jacob[8] Stauffer, Henry Jacob[7], Hans[6], Christian[5], Daniel[4] Stouffer, Christian[3], Hans[2], Hans[1]) was born January 10, 1918. She married **John Wagoner**.

Children of Martha Stoffer and John Wagoner are:
- 4222   i. Private[14] Wagoner.
- 4223   ii. Private Wagoner.
- 4224   iii. Private Wagoner.

3019. Dwight[13] Stoffer (Veron Roy[12], Laurtis W.[11], George[10], Jacob[9], Jacob[8] Stauffer, Henry Jacob[7], Hans[6], Christian[5], Daniel[4] Stouffer, Christian[3], Hans[2], Hans[1]) was born February 10, 1920. He married **Dolly Fleming**.

Children of Dwight Stoffer and Dolly Fleming are:
- 4225   i. Private[14] Stoffer.
- 4226   ii. Private Stoffer.
- 4227   iii. Private Stoffer.
- 4228   iv. Private Stoffer.
- 4229   v. Private Stoffer.

3020. Lowell Orland[13] Randall (Mary Catherine[12] Stoffer, Laurtis W.[11], George[10], Jacob[9], Jacob[8] Stauffer, Henry Jacob[7], Hans[6], Christian[5], Daniel[4] Stouffer, Christian[3], Hans[2], Hans[1]) was born September 11, 1910. He married **Margaret Leary** September 16, 1936. She was born September 18, 1912.

Children of Lowell Randall and Margaret Leary are:
- + 4230   i. Private[14] Randall.
- + 4231   ii. Private Randall.

3021. Private[13] Stoffer (Charles G[12], Laurtis W.[11], George[10], Jacob[9], Jacob[8] Stauffer, Henry Jacob[7], Hans[6], Christian[5], Daniel[4] Stouffer, Christian[3], Hans[2], Hans[1]) She married **Rev Kenneth Choflet**.

Children of Private Stoffer and Rev Choflet are:
- 4232   i. Private[14] Choflet.
- 4233   ii. Private Choflet.
- 4234   iii. Private Choflet.
- 4235   iv. Private Choflet.

3022. Private[13] Stoffer (Charles G[12], Laurtis W.[11], George[10], Jacob[9], Jacob[8] Stauffer, Henry Jacob[7], Hans[6], Christian[5], Daniel[4] Stouffer, Christian[3], Hans[2], Hans[1]) He married **Private Precise**.

Children of Private Stoffer and Private Precise are:
- 4236   i. Private[14] Stoffer.
- 4237   ii. Private Stoffer.

3023. Private[13] Stoffer (Charles G[12], Laurtis W.[11], George[10], Jacob[9], Jacob[8] Stauffer, Henry Jacob[7], Hans[6], Christian[5], Daniel[4] Stouffer, Christian[3], Hans[2], Hans[1]) She married **Private Novak**.

Children of Private Stoffer and Private Novak are:
- 4238   i. Private[14] Novak.
- 4239   ii. Private Novak.

3024. Elmer L[13] Stoffer (Charles G[12], Laurtis W.[11], George[10], Jacob[9], Jacob[8] Stauffer, Henry Jacob[7], Hans[6], Christian[5], Daniel[4] Stouffer, Christian[3], Hans[2], Hans[1]) was born 1929. He married **Hilda Garren**. She was born 1924.

Child of Elmer Stoffer and Hilda Garren is:
- 4240   i. Private[14] Stoffer.

3028. Robert Price[13] Stoffer (Bryan Sewell[12], Laurtis W.[11], George[10], Jacob[9], Jacob[8] Stauffer, Henry Jacob[7], Hans[6], Christian[5], Daniel[4] Stouffer, Christian[3], Hans[2], Hans[1]) was born 1926. He married **Lucinda Stanton**.

Child of Robert Stoffer and Lucinda Stanton is:
+   4241   i.   Private[14] Stoffer.

3030. Private[13] Stoffer (George Allen[12], Simon Henry[11], George[10], Jacob[9], Jacob[8] Stauffer, Henry Jacob[7], Hans[6], Christian[5], Daniel[4] Stouffer, Christian[3], Hans[2], Hans[1]) He married **Jeanne D Anderegg**. She was born February 09, 1934 in Wichita Kansas, and died April 28, 2000 in Lubbock Texas.

Children of Private Stoffer and Jeanne Anderegg are:
      4242   i.   Private[14] Stoffer. She married Private McKenzie.
+   4243   ii.   Private Stoffer.
+   4244   iii.   Private Stoffer.
+   4245   iv.   Private Stoffer.
+   4246   v.   Private Stoffer.
+   4247   vi.   Private Stoffer.
+   4248   vii.   Private Stoffer.
+   4249   viii.   Private Stoffer.

3031. Lola Mae[13] Stoffer (George Allen[12], Simon Henry[11], George[10], Jacob[9], Jacob[8] Stauffer, Henry Jacob[7], Hans[6], Christian[5], Daniel[4] Stouffer, Christian[3], Hans[2], Hans[1]) was born July 05, 1927 in Aline Okla., and died July 01, 1994 in Wichita Kansas. She married **Henry Burt Burns** July 05, 1942 in Enid Okla.. He was born July 21, 1923 in Hugo Okla., and died June 25, 2002 in Wichita Kansas.

Children of Lola Stoffer and Henry Burns are:
+   4250   i.   Private[14] Burns.
+   4251   ii.   Private Burns.

3032. Roy Dean[13] Stoffer (George Allen[12], Simon Henry[11], George[10], Jacob[9], Jacob[8] Stauffer, Henry Jacob[7], Hans[6], Christian[5], Daniel[4] Stouffer, Christian[3], Hans[2], Hans[1]) was born September 28, 1928 in Aline Okla.. He married **Private Reitober**.

Children of Roy Stoffer and Private Reitober are:
+   4252   i.   Private[14] Stoffer.
      4253   ii.   Private Stoffer. He married Private Nelson.
+   4254   iii.   Private Stoffer.

3033. Private[13] Stoffer (Simon Levi[12], Simon Henry[11], George[10], Jacob[9], Jacob[8] Stauffer, Henry Jacob[7], Hans[6], Christian[5], Daniel[4] Stouffer, Christian[3], Hans[2], Hans[1]) He married **Private Joiner**.

Children of Private Stoffer and Private Joiner are:
      4255   i.   Private[14] Stoffer.
      4256   ii.   Private Stoffer?.

3039. John Raymond[13] Moore (Alice Ellen[12] Stoffer, Simon Henry[11], George[10], Jacob[9], Jacob[8] Stauffer, Henry Jacob[7], Hans[6], Christian[5], Daniel[4] Stouffer, Christian[3], Hans[2], Hans[1]) was born August 05, 1925 in Victoria Texas. He married **(1) Gladys Marie Gray**. He married **(2) Katrina Faye Outlaw**.

Children of John Moore and Gladys Gray are:
      4257   i.   Private[14] Moore.
      4258   ii.   Private Moore.
      4259   iii.   Private Moore.
      4260   iv.   Private Moore.
      4261   v.   Private Moore.
      4262   vi.   Private Moore. He married Private Skinner.

3044. Dale Eugene[13] Barnett (Vera Lucille[12] Stoffer, Rolandus[11], George[10], Jacob[9], Jacob[8] Stauffer, Henry Jacob[7], Hans[6], Christian[5], Daniel[4] Stouffer, Christian[3], Hans[2], Hans[1]) was born December 13, 1914, and died June 25, 1965. He married **Eva Berger** April 22, 1934. She was born March 27, 1914.

Children of Dale Barnett and Eva Berger are:
+ 4263 i. Private[14] Barnett.
+ 4264 ii. Private Barnett.

3045. Theda Fay[13] **Barnett** (Vera Lucille[12] Stoffer, Rolandus[11], George[10], Jacob[9], Jacob[8] Stauffer, Henry Jacob[7], Hans[6], Christian[5], Daniel[4] Stouffer, Christian[3], Hans[2], Hans[1]) was born December 30, 1916. She married **Roy Thornton**. He was born November 10, 1912.

Children of Theda Barnett and Roy Thornton are:
    4265 i. Private[14] Thornton.
    4266 ii. Private Thornton.

3046. Jay Melvin[13] **Barnett** (Vera Lucille[12] Stoffer, Rolandus[11], George[10], Jacob[9], Jacob[8] Stauffer, Henry Jacob[7], Hans[6], Christian[5], Daniel[4] Stouffer, Christian[3], Hans[2], Hans[1]) was born December 20, 1919. He married **Lucille Stoffer** March 21, 1941. She was born May 17, 1918.

Children of Jay Barnett and Lucille Stoffer are:
+ 4267 i. Private[14] Barnett.
+ 4268 ii. Private Barnett.

3047. Alta[13] **Mountz** (Bertha Lorena[12] Stoffer, George D[11], George[10], Jacob[9], Jacob[8] Stauffer, Henry Jacob[7], Hans[6], Christian[5], Daniel[4] Stouffer, Christian[3], Hans[2], Hans[1]) was born June 23, 1902. She married **Charles Kibler** November 17, 1923. He was born February 18, 1896.

Children of Alta Mountz and Charles Kibler are:
    4269 i. Harold[14] Kibler.
+ 4270 ii. Carl Kibler.
+ 4271 iii. Robert Kibler, born February 06, 1924.
+ 4272 iv. Joyce Kibler, born May 20, 1925.
+ 4273 v. Lolyd Kibler, born July 25, 1926.
+ 4274 vi. June Kibler, born November 06, 1927.

3049. Wilfred[13] **Mountz** (Bertha Lorena[12] Stoffer, George D[11], George[10], Jacob[9], Jacob[8] Stauffer, Henry Jacob[7], Hans[6], Christian[5], Daniel[4] Stouffer, Christian[3], Hans[2], Hans[1]) was born January 08, 1915. He married **Edith Bruderly** August 27, 1938. She was born May 16, 1920.

Children of Wilfred Mountz and Edith Bruderly are:
+ 4275 i. Private[14] Mountz.
+ 4276 ii. Private Mountz.
    4277 iii. Private Mountz. She married Private Carsey.
+ 4278 iv. Private Mountz.

3050. Mary[13] **Mountz** (Bertha Lorena[12] Stoffer, George D[11], George[10], Jacob[9], Jacob[8] Stauffer, Henry Jacob[7], Hans[6], Christian[5], Daniel[4] Stouffer, Christian[3], Hans[2], Hans[1]) was born May 17, 1917. She married **Dan Planchock** December 27, 1935. He was born June 21, 1913.

Children of Mary Mountz and Dan Planchock are:
+ 4279 i. Private[14] Planchock.
+ 4280 ii. Private Planchock.
    4281 iii. Private Planchock. She married Private Levison.
+ 4282 iv. Private Planchock.
    4283 v. Private Planchock. He married Private Hamrick.
    4284 vi. Private Planchock.

3051. Kathryn[13] **Mountz** (Bertha Lorena[12] Stoffer, George D[11], George[10], Jacob[9], Jacob[8] Stauffer, Henry Jacob[7], Hans[6], Christian[5], Daniel[4] Stouffer, Christian[3], Hans[2], Hans[1]) was born October 12, 1918. She married **Paul Martig** May 17, 1941. He was born December 02, 1913.

Children of Kathryn Mountz and Paul Martig are:
+ 4285 i. Private[14] Martig.

+ 4286 ii. Private Martig.
4287 iii. Private Martig. He married Private Heinemann.

3052. Private[13] **Stuart** (Zella May[12] Stoffer, George D[11], George[10], Jacob[9], Jacob[8] Stauffer, Henry Jacob[7], Hans[6], Christian[5], Daniel[4] Stouffer, Christian[3], Hans[2], Hans[1]) He married **Private Mori**.

Child of Private Stuart and Private Mori is:
4288 i. Private[14] Stuart.

3054. Russell[13] **Stuart** (Zella May[12] Stoffer, George D[11], George[10], Jacob[9], Jacob[8] Stauffer, Henry Jacob[7], Hans[6], Christian[5], Daniel[4] Stouffer, Christian[3], Hans[2], Hans[1]) was born September 04, 1918. He married **Wilma Ethelyn Leichlite** June 03, 1943. She was born October 06, 1922.

Children of Russell Stuart and Wilma Leichlite are:
4289 i. Private[14] Stuart.
4290 ii. Private Stuart.
4291 iii. Private Stuart.

3055. Dean[13] **Stuart** (Zella May[12] Stoffer, George D[11], George[10], Jacob[9], Jacob[8] Stauffer, Henry Jacob[7], Hans[6], Christian[5], Daniel[4] Stouffer, Christian[3], Hans[2], Hans[1]) was born November 18, 1919. He married **Mary Louise Brown** April 24, 1947. She was born June 19, 1919.

Children of Dean Stuart and Mary Brown are:
4292 i. Private[14] Stuart.
4293 ii. Private Stuart.
4294 iii. Private Stuart.

3058. Orlan Clifford[13] **Stoffer** (Wesley Emerson[12], George D[11], George[10], Jacob[9], Jacob[8] Stauffer, Henry Jacob[7], Hans[6], Christian[5], Daniel[4] Stouffer, Christian[3], Hans[2], Hans[1]) was born August 03, 1917 in NortGeorgetown, Columbiana Co Ohio, and died October 15, 1975 in Minerva, Ohio. He married **Dorothy Eileen Hawkins Widener** August 15, 1943. She was born August 04, 1921.

Children of Orlan Stoffer and Dorothy Widener are:
+ 4295 i. Private[14] Stoffer.
+ 4296 ii. Private Stoffer.
+ 4297 iii. Private Stoffer.

3059. Verma Adella[13] **Stoffer** (Wesley Emerson[12], George D[11], George[10], Jacob[9], Jacob[8] Stauffer, Henry Jacob[7], Hans[6], Christian[5], Daniel[4] Stouffer, Christian[3], Hans[2], Hans[1]) was born September 29, 1922 in North Georgetown <Columbiana Cty Ohio, and died August 15, 2000 in Ohio. She married **(1) Thomas Phillip Coughen** July 28, 1945. He was born August 12, 1921, and died February 03, 1975. She married **(2) Maurice William Bayer** May 14, 1977. He was born April 04, 1921, and died May 23, 1998.

Children of Verma Stoffer and Thomas Coughen are:
4298 i. Private[14] Coughen. She married Private Stoner.
+ 4299 ii. Private Coughen.
+ 4300 iii. Private Coughen.
4301 iv. Nancy Ann Coughen, born June 05, 1946; died June 05, 1946 in Columbiana County, Ohio.

3060. Private[13] **Stoffer** (Russell D[12], George D[11], George[10], Jacob[9], Jacob[8] Stauffer, Henry Jacob[7], Hans[6], Christian[5], Daniel[4] Stouffer, Christian[3], Hans[2], Hans[1]) She married **Private Willis**.

Child of Private Stoffer and Private Willis is:
4302 i. Private[14] Willis.

3063. Ralph Leroy[13] **Wyss** (Ora Deliah[12] Stoffer, Stanton Uriah[11], George[10], Jacob[9], Jacob[8] Stauffer, Henry Jacob[7], Hans[6], Christian[5], Daniel[4] Stouffer, Christian[3], Hans[2], Hans[1]) was born June 10, 1908 in Columbian Co Ohio, and died November 05, 1952 in Ohio. He married **Thelma Ruth Parsons** September 23, 1931. She was born November 22, 1910 in Salem, Columbiana Co., Ohio, and died September 09, 1985 in Homeworth, Ohio.

Children of Ralph Wyss and Thelma Parsons are:
4303 i. Private[14] Wyss. She married Private McQuilkin.

4304	ii.	Private Isenschmid. She married Private Whinery.
4305	iii.	Private Wyss.
4306	iv.	Richard Adelbert Wyss, born March 16, 1932; died June 15, 1994.
4307	v.	Daryl Leroy "Cork" Wyss, born January 06, 1934; died September 28, 1984.
4308	vi.	Darly Leroy Wyss, born January 06, 1934; died September 28, 1984.
4309	vii.	Shirley Ruth Wyss, born July 16, 1935; died January 15, 2000. She married (1) Private Goss. She married (2) Private Gross.
4310	viii.	Wayne Ralph Wyss, born July 20, 1947; died November 13, 1993.

3064. Florian F.[13] **Wyss** (Ora Deliah[12] Stoffer, Stanton Uriah[11], George[10], Jacob[9], Jacob[8] Stauffer, Henry Jacob[7], Hans[6], Christian[5], Daniel[4] Stouffer, Christian[3], Hans[2], Hans[1]) was born May 20, 1911, and died November 05, 1988 in Ohio. He married **Freda I Owens**. She was born 1911.

Child of Florian Wyss and Freda Owens is:
    4311   i.   Private[14] Wyss.

3065. Naomi B.[13] **Wyss** (Ora Deliah[12] Stoffer, Stanton Uriah[11], George[10], Jacob[9], Jacob[8] Stauffer, Henry Jacob[7], Hans[6], Christian[5], Daniel[4] Stouffer, Christian[3], Hans[2], Hans[1]) was born June 29, 1913 in Ohio, and died March 04, 1999 in Ohio. She married **Elgie M Boyle** August 13, 1930. He was born January 19, 1911, and died October 14, 1994 in Ohio.

Child of Naomi Wyss and Elgie Boyle is:
    4312   i.   Private[14] Boyle.

3067. Audrey Odessa "Audey"[13] **Wyss** (Ora Deliah[12] Stoffer, Stanton Uriah[11], George[10], Jacob[9], Jacob[8] Stauffer, Henry Jacob[7], Hans[6], Christian[5], Daniel[4] Stouffer, Christian[3], Hans[2], Hans[1]) was born December 22, 1921 in Ohio. She married **(2) Carl Isenschmid** May 17, 1941. He was born December 16, 1916, and died October 25, 1943 in Ohio. She married **(3) Car W Isenschmid** May 17, 1941. He was born December 16, 1916, and died October 25, 1943 in OHIO. She married **(4) George Hardy** November 08, 1946. He was born April 12, 1925.

Child of Audrey Odessa "Audey" Wyss is:
    4313   i.   Gary[14] Isenschmid, died Abt. April 23, 1964.

Children of Audrey Wyss and George Hardy are:
    4314   i.   Private[14] Hardy.
    4315   ii.   Private Hardy.
    4316   iii.   Private Hardy.
    4317   iv.   Private Hardy.
    4318   v.   Private Hardy.

3069. Clarence Leward[13] **Stoffer** (Benjamine Franklin[12], Stanton Uriah[11], George[10], Jacob[9], Jacob[8] Stauffer, Henry Jacob[7], Hans[6], Christian[5], Daniel[4] Stouffer, Christian[3], Hans[2], Hans[1]) was born September 20, 1907 in North Georgetown Ohio, Columbiana Co, and died March 02, 1970 in Salem Ohio. He married **Ethel Miller** May 31, 1930. She was born August 18, 1909 in Canton Ohio, Stark Co, and died July 1971 in Salem, Ohio.

Children of Clarence Stoffer and Ethel Miller are:
+   4319   i.   Private[14] Stoffer.
+   4320   ii.   Larry Lee Stoffer, born November 04, 1937 in Ohio; died January 24, 1992 in Las Vegas, Clark Co., Nevada.

3070. Clifford Lewis[13] **Stoffer** (Benjamine Franklin[12], Stanton Uriah[11], George[10], Jacob[9], Jacob[8] Stauffer, Henry Jacob[7], Hans[6], Christian[5], Daniel[4] Stouffer, Christian[3], Hans[2], Hans[1]) was born November 09, 1909 in Paris Ohio, and died October 14, 1991 in Canton Ohio, Stark Co. He married **Cordella Pittman** 1930. She was born September 12, 1912 in Temperanceville, Ohio, and died June 01, 1984 in Canton, Ohio.

Children of Clifford Stoffer and Cordella Pittman are:
+   4321   i.   Private[14] Stoffer.
+   4322   ii.   Private Stoffer.

3071. William Stanton[13] **Stoffer** (Benjamine Franklin[12], Stanton Uriah[11], George[10], Jacob[9], Jacob[8] Stauffer, Henry Jacob[7], Hans[6],

Christian[5], Daniel[4] Stoffer, Christian[3], Hans[2], Hans[1]) was born February 18, 1912 in Ohio, and died September 04, 1964 in Ohio. He married **Ada Grove**. She was born November 15, 1914.

Children of William Stoffer and Ada Grove are:
- 4323   i.   Private[14] Stoffer. She married Private Mossey.
- 4324   ii.   Private Stoffer. She married Private Kibler.
- 4325   iii.   Private Stoffer. She married Private Gallins.

3072. Milan Benjamin[13] Stoffer (Benjamine Franklin[12], Stanton Uriah[11], George[10], Jacob[9], Jacob[8] Stauffer, Henry Jacob[7], Hans[6], Christian[5], Daniel[4] Stouffer, Christian[3], Hans[2], Hans[1]) was born April 30, 1914 in Ohio, and died November 16, 1954 in Canton, Ohio. He married **Wilma Mae Owen**. She was born February 20, 1916, and died November 19, 1988 in Salem Ohio.

Children of Milan Stoffer and Wilma Owen are:
- 4326   i.   Private[14] Stoffer.
- 4327   ii.   Private Stoffer. She married Private Rockman.
- + 4328   iii.   Private Stoffer.
- + 4329   iv.   Private Stoffer.
- + 4330   v.   Dale Milan Stoffer, born September 20, 1934 in Ohio; died November 18, 2000 in Lithia Springs Ga, Douglas Co.

3073. Ray Arnold[13] Stoffer (Benjamine Franklin[12], Stanton Uriah[11], George[10], Jacob[9], Jacob[8] Stauffer, Henry Jacob[7], Hans[6], Christian[5], Daniel[4] Stouffer, Christian[3], Hans[2], Hans[1]) was born September 20, 1916 in Ohio, and died September 23, 1944 in Italy WW ll. He married **Wilma Canfield**.

Child of Ray Stoffer and Wilma Canfield is:
- + 4331   i.   Private[14] Stoffer.

3074. Alva Orlan[13] Stoffer (Benjamine Franklin[12], Stanton Uriah[11], George[10], Jacob[9], Jacob[8] Stauffer, Henry Jacob[7], Hans[6], Christian[5], Daniel[4] Stouffer, Christian[3], Hans[2], Hans[1]) was born March 24, 1919 in Ohio, and died May 14, 1993 in Ohio. He married **Delores Miller** in Ohio. She was born in Ohio.

Children of Alva Stoffer and Delores Miller are:
- 4332   i.   Private[14] Stoffer. She married Private Kenneth?Unknown.
- 4333   ii.   Private Stoffer.
- 4334   iii.   Private Stoffer.
- 4335   iv.   Private Stoffer.
- 4336   v.   Private Stoffer.
- 4337   vi.   Private Stoffer.

3075. Cleo Ruth[13] Stoffer (Benjamine Franklin[12], Stanton Uriah[11], George[10], Jacob[9], Jacob[8] Stauffer, Henry Jacob[7], Hans[6], Christian[5], Daniel[4] Stouffer, Christian[3], Hans[2], Hans[1]) was born June 15, 1921 in Ohio. She married **Ernest DePalmo** July 19, 1944 in Ohio. She was born September 18, 1918, and died February 04, 1994 in Minerva, Ohio.

Children of Cleo Stoffer and Ernest DePalmo are:
- + 4338   i.   Private[14] DePalmo.
- + 4339   ii.   Private DePalmo.
- + 4340   iii.   Private DePalmo.
- + 4341   iv.   Private DePalmo.
- + 4342   v.   Private DePalmo.
- + 4343   vi.   Private DePalmo.
- 4344   vii.   Private DePalmo. She married (1) Private Hamilton. She married (2) Private Renfro. She married (3) Private Johnson.

3076. Donald Andrew[13] Stoffer (Benjamine Franklin[12], Stanton Uriah[11], George[10], Jacob[9], Jacob[8] Stauffer, Henry Jacob[7], Hans[6], Christian[5], Daniel[4] Stouffer, Christian[3], Hans[2], Hans[1]) was born August 19, 1924 in Ohio, and died November 11, 1980 in Canton, Stark Co., Ohio. He married **Shirley Sleeman**.

Children of Donald Stoffer and Shirley Sleeman are:
- 4345   i.   Private[14] Stoffer.
- 4346   ii.   Private Stoffer.
- 4347   iii.   Private Stoffer.

4348 iv. Private Stoffer.

3077. Margaret Louise[13] Stoffer (Benjamine Franklin[12], Stanton Uriah[11], George[10], Jacob[9], Jacob[8] Stauffer, Henry Jacob[7], Hans[6], Christian[5], Daniel[4] Stoffer, Christian[3], Hans[2], Hans[1]) was born November 13, 1926 in Moultrie, Ohio, and died September 19, 1996 in Canton, Ohio. She married **Clifford Jesse Prater** July 03, 1947 in Cattlesburg Ky. He was born April 08, 1922 in Logan West Virginia, and died May 07, 1969 in Canton Ohio.

Marriage Notes for Margaret Stoffer and Clifford Prater:
[chrststauffer1663.ged]

1 _MEND Death of one spouse

Child of Margaret Stoffer and Clifford Prater is:
    4349   i.   Private[14] Prater. She married Keith John Asp; born November 02, 1944 in San Metago Calif; died May 15, 1996 in Canton Ohio, Stark Co.

3078. Rollin Jr[13] Stoffer (Benjamine Franklin[12], Stanton Uriah[11], George[10], Jacob[9], Jacob[8] Stauffer, Henry Jacob[7], Hans[6], Christian[5], Daniel[4] Stoffer, Christian[3], Hans[2], Hans[1]) was born June 12, 1929 in Ohio. He married **(1) Private Plock**. He married **(2) Sophi Elifdities**. He married **(3) Sophi Eleftheriades** October 23, 1948 in Ohio.

Children of Rollin Stoffer and Private Plock are:
+   4350   i.   Private[14] Stoffer.
+   4351   ii.   Private Stoffer.
+   4352   iii. Private Stoffer.
    4353   iv.   Debara Ann Stoffer, born December 16, 1957 in Canton Ohio, Stark Co; died November 16, 1973 in Ohio.

Children of Rollin Stoffer and Sophi Eleftheriades are:
+   4354   i.   Private[14] Stoffer.
    4355   ii.   Benjamin Franklin II Stoffer, born October 03, 1950 in Canton Ohio; died February 26, 1979 in Viet - Nam--Quan Tri Providence.

3079. Franklin Eugene[13] Stoffer (Benjamine Franklin[12], Stanton Uriah[11], George[10], Jacob[9], Jacob[8] Stauffer, Henry Jacob[7], Hans[6], Christian[5], Daniel[4] Stoffer, Christian[3], Hans[2], Hans[1]) was born August 21, 1933 in Beloit, Ohio, and died July 21, 1995 in Canton, Stark Co., Ohio. He married **(1) Private Locy**. He married **(2) Private French**.

Child of Franklin Stoffer and Private French is:
+   4356   i.   Private[14] Stoffer.

3082. Lorin Albert[13] Stoffer (Roscoe "Ross"[12], Stanton Uriah[11], George[10], Jacob[9], Jacob[8] Stauffer, Henry Jacob[7], Hans[6], Christian[5], Daniel[4] Stoffer, Christian[3], Hans[2], Hans[1]) was born May 03, 1914 in North Georgetown Ohio, Columbiana Co, and died March 05, 1988 in Beloit Ohio, Mahoning Co. He married **(1) Goldie Lutechia "Lou" Wood**. He married **(2) Sahra Polly Strain** June 22, 1936. She died March 17, 1941. He married **(3) Delores J Yohe** May 02, 1968. She was born April 12, 1928.

Marriage Notes for Lorin Stoffer and Goldie Wood:
[chrststauffer1663.ged]

_STATMARRIED

Marriage Notes for Lorin Stoffer and Delores Yohe:
[chrststauffer1663.ged]

_STATMARRIED

Children of Lorin Stoffer and Goldie Wood are:
    4357   i.   Private[14] Stoffer. She married Arnie Crew; born May 06.
+   4358   ii.   Private Stoffer.
+   4359   iii. Private Stoffer.
    4360   iv.   Private Stoffer.
    4361   v.   Private Stoffer.
+   4362   vi.   2nd Private Stoffer.
    4363   vii. Susan Stoffer, born May 21, 1921. She married Arnold Crew; born May 06.

Children of Lorin Stoffer and Sahra Strain are:
+ 4364 i. Private[14] Stoffer.
+ 4365 ii. Private Stoffer.

Children of Lorin Stoffer and Delores Yohe are:
4366 i. Private[14] Stoffer.
4367 ii. Private Stoffer. She married Private Chisholm.

3083. Edith[13] Stoffer (Roscoe "Ross"[12], Stanton Uriah[11], George[10], Jacob[9], Jacob[8] Stauffer, Henry Jacob[7], Hans[6], Christian[5], Daniel[4] Stouffer, Christian[3], Hans[2], Hans[1]) was born March 24, 1919. She married **(1) Steve Burkheart**. She married **(2) Ronald Teaque**.

Children of Edith Stoffer and Steve Burkheart are:
4368 i. Private[14] Burkheart.
4369 ii. Private Burkheart.
4370 iii. Private Burkheart.

Child of Edith Stoffer and Ronald Teaque is:
4371 i. Private[14] Teaque.

3089. Clyde C.[13] Stoffer (Curtis Homer[12], Stanton Uriah[11], George[10], Jacob[9], Jacob[8] Stauffer, Henry Jacob[7], Hans[6], Christian[5], Daniel[4] Stouffer, Christian[3], Hans[2], Hans[1]) was born March 20, 1918 in Salem Ohio, and died September 1985 in Ohio. He married **(1) Delores Miller**. She was born in Ohio. He married **(2) Private (stoffer)**.

Child of Clyde Stoffer and Delores Miller is:
4372 i. Clyde[14] C., Jr Stoffer, born October 12, 1946; died March 17, 1998.

3091. Leonard[13] Stoffer (Curtis Homer[12], Stanton Uriah[11], George[10], Jacob[9], Jacob[8] Stauffer, Henry Jacob[7], Hans[6], Christian[5], Daniel[4] Stouffer, Christian[3], Hans[2], Hans[1]) was born October 10, 1923 in Salem Ohio, and died October 29, 1996 in Magadore Ohio. He married **Betty J Unknown**.

Children of Leonard Stoffer and Betty Unknown are:
4373 i. Private[14] Stoffer.
4374 ii. Private Stoffer. She married Private Armstrong.

3093. Private[13] Krause (Ruthanna[12] Stoffer, Stanton Uriah[11], George[10], Jacob[9], Jacob[8] Stauffer, Henry Jacob[7], Hans[6], Christian[5], Daniel[4] Stouffer, Christian[3], Hans[2], Hans[1]) He married **Private Rice**.

Children of Private Krause and Private Rice are:
4375 i. Private[14] Krause. She married Private Unknown.
4376 ii. Private Krause.
4377 iii. Private Krause.

3098. Herbert Stanton[13] Krause (Ruth Anna[12] Stoffer, Stanton Uriah[11], George[10], Jacob[9], Jacob[8] Stauffer, Henry Jacob[7], Hans[6], Christian[5], Daniel[4] Stouffer, Christian[3], Hans[2], Hans[1]) was born July 17, 1927 in Beloit Ohio, and died September 11, 2000 in Beloit Ohio. He married **Private Galbreath**.

Children of Herbert Krause and Private Galbreath are:
4378 i. Private[14] Krause.
4379 ii. Private Krause.

3099. Wayne[13] Hahn (Bertha Cleo[12] Stoffer, Stanton Uriah[11], George[10], Jacob[9], Jacob[8] Stauffer, Henry Jacob[7], Hans[6], Christian[5], Daniel[4] Stouffer, Christian[3], Hans[2], Hans[1]) died June 08, 1999 in OHIO.

Children of Wayne Hahn are:
4380 i. Private[14] Hahn.
4381 ii. Private Hahn.
4382 iii. Private Hahn.

3105. Earl L[13] Stoffer (Leo Lesile[12], Sherman[11], George[10], Jacob[9], Jacob[8] Stauffer, Henry Jacob[7], Hans[6], Christian[5], Daniel[4] Stouffer, Christian[3], Hans[2], Hans[1]) was born March 30, 1925 in Sebring Ohio, and died September 19, 1997 in Alliance Ohio. He married **Betty A Runion** December 16, 1945.

Children of Earl Stoffer and Betty Runion are:
- 4383   i.   Private[14] Stoffer.
- 4384   ii. Private Stoffer.
- 4385   iii. Private Stoffer.
- 4386   iv. Private Stoffer.
- 4387   v.   Private Stoffer. She married Private Franklin.
- 4388   vi. Private Stoffer. She married Private Parks.

3106. Ester Leah[13] Stoffer (Anson Oscar[12], Leander[11], George[10], Jacob[9], Jacob[8] Stauffer, Henry Jacob[7], Hans[6], Christian[5], Daniel[4] Stouffer, Christian[3], Hans[2], Hans[1]) was born November 07, 1912. She married **Orin Wesley Thompson** June 21, 1930. He was born November 10, 1906.

Child of Ester Stoffer and Orin Thompson is:
- + 4389   i.   Private[14] Thompson.

3107. Wilma Ruth[13] Stoffer (Anson Oscar[12], Leander[11], George[10], Jacob[9], Jacob[8] Stauffer, Henry Jacob[7], Hans[6], Christian[5], Daniel[4] Stouffer, Christian[3], Hans[2], Hans[1]) was born June 15, 1915. She married **Donald Crantson** July 09, 1931.

Children of Wilma Stoffer and Donald Crantson are:
- + 4390   i.   Private[14] Crantson.
- + 4391   ii. Private Crantson.

3108. Homer[13] Stoffer (Anson Oscar[12], Leander[11], George[10], Jacob[9], Jacob[8] Stauffer, Henry Jacob[7], Hans[6], Christian[5], Daniel[4] Stouffer, Christian[3], Hans[2], Hans[1]) was born April 18, 1921. He married **(1) Unknown Mary**.   He married **(2) Amelia Rockie** September 20, 1941.

Marriage Notes for Homer Stoffer and Amelia Rockie:
[chrststauffer1663.ged]

1 _MEND Divorce

Children of Homer Stoffer and Amelia Rockie are:
- 4392   i.   Private[14] Stoffer.
- 4393   ii. Private Stoffer.
- 4394   iii. Private Stoffer.

3109. Donald Lowell[13] Stoffer (Glen Wilson[12], Leander[11], George[10], Jacob[9], Jacob[8] Stauffer, Henry Jacob[7], Hans[6], Christian[5], Daniel[4] Stouffer, Christian[3], Hans[2], Hans[1]) was born August 27, 1914 in Alliance Ohio, Columbiana Co Ohio, and died January 17, 1998 in Carson City Nev. He married **(1) Madge Hessel Johnson** June 25, 1938 in Columbiana Cty, Ohio.   He married **(2) Helen Josephine Grew Bailey** November 15, 1946. She was born June 15, 1917, and died 1996.

Marriage Notes for Donald Stoffer and Madge Johnson:
[chrststauffer1663.ged]

1 _MEND Divorce

Children of Donald Stoffer and Madge Johnson are:
- + 4395   i.   Private[14] Stoffer.
- 4396   ii. Private Stoffer.
- 4397   iii. Private Stoffer.

Children of Donald Stoffer and Helen Bailey are:
- 4398   i.   Private[14] Stoffer. He married Private Spencer.
- + 4399   ii. Private Stoffer.

3110. Lucille Naomi[13] Stoffer (Glen Wilson[12], Leander[11], George[10], Jacob[9], Jacob[8] Stauffer, Henry Jacob[7], Hans[6], Christian[5], Daniel[4] Stoffer, Christian[3], Hans[2], Hans[1]) was born March 10, 1916 in Columbiana Co Ohio. She married **Raymond Hunter Ernst** January 23, 1937 in Columbiana Co Ohio. He was born March 09, 1915.

Children of Lucille Stoffer and Raymond Ernst are:
+ 4400   i.   Private[14] Ernst.
+ 4401   ii.   Private Ernst.
+ 4402   iii.   Private Ernst.
   4403   iv.   Private Ernst. She married Private Woods.

3112. Evelyn Ora[13] Stoffer (Glen Wilson[12], Leander[11], George[10], Jacob[9], Jacob[8] Stauffer, Henry Jacob[7], Hans[6], Christian[5], Daniel[4] Stoffer, Christian[3], Hans[2], Hans[1]) was born May 14, 1920 in Columbiana County, Ohio, and died December 27, 1992 in Alliance Ohio. She married **Wilford McKinley Mercer** November 11, 1941. He was born December 21, 1918, and died June 13, 1999 in Alliance Ohio.

Children of Evelyn Stoffer and Wilford Mercer are:
+ 4404   i.   Private[14] Mercer.
+ 4405   ii.   Private Mercer.
   4406   iii.   Private Mercer. He married Private Crowe.

3113. Doris May[13] Stoffer (Glen Wilson[12], Leander[11], George[10], Jacob[9], Jacob[8] Stauffer, Henry Jacob[7], Hans[6], Christian[5], Daniel[4] Stoffer, Christian[3], Hans[2], Hans[1]) was born October 15, 1923. She married **Gale Emery Ray** December 12, 1941. He was born February 03, 1922.

Children of Doris Stoffer and Gale Ray are:
+ 4407   i.   Private[14] Ray.
+ 4408   ii.   Private Ray.
+ 4409   iii.   Private Ray.
+ 4410   iv.   Private Ray.
+ 4411   v.   Private Ray.
+ 4412   vi.   Private Ray.
+ 4413   vii.   Private Ray.
+ 4414   viii.   Private Ray.
   4415   ix.   Private Ray.

3114. Iona Eleanor[13] Stoffer (Glen Wilson[12], Leander[11], George[10], Jacob[9], Jacob[8] Stauffer, Henry Jacob[7], Hans[6], Christian[5], Daniel[4] Stoffer, Christian[3], Hans[2], Hans[1]) was born February 28, 1927. She married **Veron Montell Stiffler** August 15, 1948. He was born September 26, 1923.

Children of Iona Stoffer and Veron Stiffler are:
+ 4416   i.   Private[14] Stiffler.
+ 4417   ii.   Private Stiffler.

3115. Barbara Ann[13] Geiger (Goldie Marie[12] Stoffer, Leander[11], George[10], Jacob[9], Jacob[8] Stauffer, Henry Jacob[7], Hans[6], Christian[5], Daniel[4] Stoffer, Christian[3], Hans[2], Hans[1]) was born December 20, 1924. She married **Ross Earl Wagner** April 09, 1948. He was born August 16, 1923.

Children of Barbara Geiger and Ross Wagner are:
   4418   i.   Private[14] Wagner. He married Private Break.
   4419   ii.   Private Wagner. He married Private Mercer.
   4420   iii.   Private Wagner. She married Private Patterson.

3116. Private[13] Stoffer (Wade Orla[12], Leander[11], George[10], Jacob[9], Jacob[8] Stauffer, Henry Jacob[7], Hans[6], Christian[5], Daniel[4] Stoffer, Christian[3], Hans[2], Hans[1]) He married **Private Gitters**.

Children of Private Stoffer and Private Gitters are:
   4421   i.   Private[14] Stoffer. She married Private Bower.
   4422   ii.   Private Stoffer.
   4423   iii.   Private Stoffer. She married Private Rudo.
   4424   iv.   Private Stoffer.

3117. Private[13] Stoffer (Darl Lincoln[12], Leander[11], George[10], Jacob[9], Jacob[8] Stauffer, Henry Jacob[7], Hans[6], Christian[5], Daniel[4] Stouffer, Christian[3], Hans[2], Hans[1]) She married **David Edward Gruen**. He was born 1928.

Children of Private Stoffer and David Gruen are:
- 4425   i.   Private[14] Gruen.
- 4426   ii. Private Gruen.
- 4427   iii. Private Gruen.
- 4428   iv. Private Gruen.
- 4429   v.   Private Gruen.

3118. Private[13] Stoffer (Darl Lincoln[12], Leander[11], George[10], Jacob[9], Jacob[8] Stauffer, Henry Jacob[7], Hans[6], Christian[5], Daniel[4] Stouffer, Christian[3], Hans[2], Hans[1]) He married **Private Yarman**.

Children of Private Stoffer and Private Yarman are:
- 4430   i.   Private[14] Stoffer.
- 4431   ii. Private Stoffer.
- 4432   iii. Private Stoffer.
- 4433   iv. Private Stoffer.

3119. Private[13] Stoffer (Darl Lincoln[12], Leander[11], George[10], Jacob[9], Jacob[8] Stauffer, Henry Jacob[7], Hans[6], Christian[5], Daniel[4] Stouffer, Christian[3], Hans[2], Hans[1]) She married **Private Knox**.

Children of Private Stoffer and Private Knox are:
- 4434   i.   Private[14] Knox.
- 4435   ii. Private Knox.

Generation No. 14

3120. John Elwood[14] Betzner (Harvey Andrew[13], Wesley[12], Samuel[11], Elizabeth[10] Stouffer, Abraham Hershey[9] Stauffer, Abraham Hess[8], Henry Jacob[7], Hans[6], Christian[5], Daniel[4] Stouffer, Christian[3], Hans[2], Hans[1]) He married **Elizabeth Richards**.

Children of John Betzner and Elizabeth Richards are:
- 4436   i.   Private[15] Betzner.
- 4437   ii. Private Betzner.

3131. Norman Nelson[14] Dunham (Ellen Ruletta[13] Kitchen, Elizabeth[12] Betzner, Abraham[11], Elizabeth[10] Stouffer, Abraham Hershey[9] Stauffer, Abraham Hess[8], Henry Jacob[7], Hans[6], Christian[5], Daniel[4] Stouffer, Christian[3], Hans[2], Hans[1]) He married **Mabel Olive Harding**.

Child of Norman Dunham and Mabel Harding is:
- 4438   i.   Private[15] Dunham.

3132. Jessie Jean[14] Dunham (Ellen Ruletta[13] Kitchen, Elizabeth[12] Betzner, Abraham[11], Elizabeth[10] Stouffer, Abraham Hershey[9] Stauffer, Abraham Hess[8], Henry Jacob[7], Hans[6], Christian[5], Daniel[4] Stouffer, Christian[3], Hans[2], Hans[1]) She married **Roy St. Clair Bacon**.

Children of Jessie Dunham and Roy Bacon are:
- 4439   i.   Lloyd Frederick[15] Bacon.
- 4440   ii. Private Bacon.
- 4441   iii. Private Bacon.

3133. Frederick Fielding[14] Dunham (Ellen Ruletta[13] Kitchen, Elizabeth[12] Betzner, Abraham[11], Elizabeth[10] Stouffer, Abraham Hershey[9] Stauffer, Abraham Hess[8], Henry Jacob[7], Hans[6], Christian[5], Daniel[4] Stouffer, Christian[3], Hans[2], Hans[1]) He married **Elizabeth Mezurick**.

Children of Frederick Dunham and Elizabeth Mezurick are:
- 4442   i.   Private[15] Dunham.
- 4443   ii. Private Dunham.

3134. Bertha Beatrice[14] Dunham (Ellen Ruletta[13] Kitchen, Elizabeth[12] Betzner, Abraham[11], Elizabeth[10] Stouffer, Abraham Hershey[9] Stauffer, Abraham Hess[8], Henry Jacob[7], Hans[6], Christian[5], Daniel[4] Stouffer, Christian[3], Hans[2], Hans[1]) was born February 03, 1896. She married **Charles Samuel Gilbert** July 14, 1920. He was born September 01, 1896.

Children of Bertha Dunham and Charles Gilbert are:
+ 4444 i. Annielaurie Ruletta[15] Gilbert.
   4445 ii. George Evert Gilbert. He married Alice Masterson.

3135. Eleanor Elizabeth[14] Dunham (Ellen Ruletta[13] Kitchen, Elizabeth[12] Betzner, Abraham[11], Elizabeth[10] Stouffer, Abraham Hershey[9] Stauffer, Abraham Hess[8], Henry Jacob[7], Hans[6], Christian[5], Daniel[4] Stouffer, Christian[3], Hans[2], Hans[1]) was born August 30, 1898. She married **Nelson William Everett** February 23, 1916. He was born February 05, 1895.

Children of Eleanor Dunham and Nelson Everett are:
+ 4446 i. Hugh Munson[15] Everett.
+ 4447 ii. Ralph Avon Everett.

3136. Watson William[14] Dunham (Ellen Ruletta[13] Kitchen, Elizabeth[12] Betzner, Abraham[11], Elizabeth[10] Stouffer, Abraham Hershey[9] Stauffer, Abraham Hess[8], Henry Jacob[7], Hans[6], Christian[5], Daniel[4] Stouffer, Christian[3], Hans[2], Hans[1]) was born April 14, 1900, and died January 06, 1947. He married **Ethel Lillian Thompson**.

Children of Watson Dunham and Ethel Thompson are:
   4448 i. Alvin William[15] Dunham.
   4449 ii. James Orval Dunham.
   4450 iii. Private Dunham.
   4451 iv. Private Dunham.

3137. William Kitchen[14] Dunham (Mabel Gertrude[13] Kitchen, Elizabeth[12] Betzner, Abraham[11], Elizabeth[10] Stouffer, Abraham Hershey[9] Stauffer, Abraham Hess[8], Henry Jacob[7], Hans[6], Christian[5], Daniel[4] Stouffer, Christian[3], Hans[2], Hans[1]) He married **Jean Knox**.

Child of William Dunham and Jean Knox is:
+ 4452 i. Betty Jean Mabel[15] Dunham.

3138. Mildred Elizabeth[14] Dunham (Mabel Gertrude[13] Kitchen, Elizabeth[12] Betzner, Abraham[11], Elizabeth[10] Stouffer, Abraham Hershey[9] Stauffer, Abraham Hess[8], Henry Jacob[7], Hans[6], Christian[5], Daniel[4] Stouffer, Christian[3], Hans[2], Hans[1]) She married **Abram Vansickle**.

Child of Mildred Dunham and Abram Vansickle is:
   4453 i. Lloyd[15] Vansickle.

3139. Elmer Ray[14] Dunham (Mabel Gertrude[13] Kitchen, Elizabeth[12] Betzner, Abraham[11], Elizabeth[10] Stouffer, Abraham Hershey[9] Stauffer, Abraham Hess[8], Henry Jacob[7], Hans[6], Christian[5], Daniel[4] Stouffer, Christian[3], Hans[2], Hans[1]) He married **Lilliam Arnold**.

Child of Elmer Dunham and Lilliam Arnold is:
   4454 i. Private[15] Dunham.

3141. Clare Sadie[14] Betzner (Henry Franklin[13], George Washington[12], Abraham[11], Elizabeth[10] Stouffer, Abraham Hershey[9] Stauffer, Abraham Hess[8], Henry Jacob[7], Hans[6], Christian[5], Daniel[4] Stouffer, Christian[3], Hans[2], Hans[1]) She married **Frederick Henry Brooks**.

Children of Clare Betzner and Frederick Brooks are:
   4455 i. Private[15] Brooks.
   4456 ii. Private Brooks.
   4457 iii. Private Brooks.

3143. Muriel Verna[14] Betzner (Henry Franklin[13], George Washington[12], Abraham[11], Elizabeth[10] Stouffer, Abraham Hershey[9] Stauffer, Abraham Hess[8], Henry Jacob[7], Hans[6], Christian[5], Daniel[4] Stouffer, Christian[3], Hans[2], Hans[1]) She married **Calvin Learoy Vansickle**.

Child of Muriel Betzner and Calvin Vansickle is:
   4458 i. Barry Learoy[15] Vansickle, died January 20, 1943.

3145. Murry Abram[14] Betzner (Roy Sylvester[13], Joseph[12], Abraham[11], Elizabeth[10] Stouffer, Abraham Hershey[9] Stauffer, Abraham

Hess[8], Henry Jacob[7], Hans[6], Christian[5], Daniel[4] Stouffer, Christian[3], Hans[2], Hans[1]) He married **Helen Ruth Parker**.

Child of Murry Betzner and Helen Parker is:
 4459 i. Private[15] Betzner.

3146. Bruce Echlin[14] Betzner (Roy Sylvester[13], Joseph[12], Abraham[11], Elizabeth[10] Stouffer, Abraham Hershey[9] Stauffer, Abraham Hess[8], Henry Jacob[7], Hans[6], Christian[5], Daniel[4] Stouffer, Christian[3], Hans[2], Hans[1]) He married **Winnifred Iva Frances Green**.

Children of Bruce Betzner and Winnifred Green are:
 4460 i. Private[15] Betzner.
 4461 ii. Private Betzner.

3148. Jean Marie[14] Howe (Isabella D.[13] Betzner, David Thomas[12], David S.[11], Elizabeth[10] Stouffer, Abraham Hershey[9] Stauffer, Abraham Hess[8], Henry Jacob[7], Hans[6], Christian[5], Daniel[4] Stouffer, Christian[3], Hans[2], Hans[1]) She married **Herman M. Hall**.

Children of Jean Howe and Herman Hall are:
 4462 i. Private[15] Hall.
 4463 ii. Private Hall.

3151. Louise Norman[14] Edworthy (Ina Louisa[13] Betzner, George David[12], John Weir[11], Elizabeth[10] Stouffer, Abraham Hershey[9] Stauffer, Abraham Hess[8], Henry Jacob[7], Hans[6], Christian[5], Daniel[4] Stouffer, Christian[3], Hans[2], Hans[1]) was born May 19, 1923. She married **(1) Shore**. She married **(2) Samuel Ross George** September 25, 1948. He was born April 19, 1920, and died October 14, 1959.

Child of Louise Edworthy and Shore is:
+ 4464 i. Private[15] Shore.

Children of Louise Edworthy and Samuel George are:
+ 4465 i. Private[15] Shore.
+ 4466 ii. Private Shore.

3158. Erland Lloyd[14] Betzner (Erland S.[13], Albert E.[12], John Weir[11], Elizabeth[10] Stouffer, Abraham Hershey[9] Stauffer, Abraham Hess[8], Henry Jacob[7], Hans[6], Christian[5], Daniel[4] Stouffer, Christian[3], Hans[2], Hans[1]) He married **Jean Jamieson**.

Child of Erland Betzner and Jean Jamieson is:
 4467 i. Private[15] Betzner.

3159. Reginald Joseph[14] Frost (Oliver[13], Nancy Jane[12] Stauffer, Abraham[11], Christian[10], Abraham Hershey[9], Abraham Hess[8], Henry Jacob[7], Hans[6], Christian[5], Daniel[4] Stouffer, Christian[3], Hans[2], Hans[1]) was born November 14, 1905 in Harvey, ND, and died June 14, 1975 in Hastings, Dakota Co, MN. He married **Rosella Catherine Reuter**. She was born January 14, 1913 in Hastings, Dakota Co, MN, and died December 06, 1999 in Hastings, Dakota Co, MN.

Child of Reginald Frost and Rosella Reuter is:
 4468 i. Reginald Joseph[15] Frost, born January 27, 1950.

3160. Delores[14] Cooley (Clayton[13], Bertha[12] Stouffer, John[11], Abraham[10], Abraham Hershey[9] Stauffer, Abraham Hess[8], Henry Jacob[7], Hans[6], Christian[5], Daniel[4] Stouffer, Christian[3], Hans[2], Hans[1]) She married **Unknown Weeden**.

Child of Delores Cooley and Unknown Weeden is:
 4469 i. Private[15] Weeden.

3161. Audrey[14] Cooley (Clayton[13], Bertha[12] Stouffer, John[11], Abraham[10], Abraham Hershey[9] Stauffer, Abraham Hess[8], Henry Jacob[7], Hans[6], Christian[5], Daniel[4] Stouffer, Christian[3], Hans[2], Hans[1]) She married **Cordell**.

Child of Audrey Cooley and Cordell is:
 4470 i. Private[15] Cordell.

3162. Virginia[14] Cooley (Clayton[13], Bertha[12] Stouffer, John[11], Abraham[10], Abraham Hershey[9] Stauffer, Abraham Hess[8], Henry Jacob[7], Hans[6], Christian[5], Daniel[4] Stouffer, Christian[3], Hans[2], Hans[1]) She married **Unknown Williamson**.

Children of Virginia Cooley and Unknown Williamson are:
  4471 i. Private[15] Williamson.
  4472 ii. Private Williamson.

3164. Betty Jane[14] Santee (Nina[13] Cooley, Bertha[12] Stouffer, John[11], Abraham[10], Abraham Hershey[9] Stauffer, Abraham Hess[8], Henry Jacob[7], Hans[6], Christian[5], Daniel[4] Stouffer, Christian[3], Hans[2], Hans[1]) She married **Unknown Meredith**.

Child of Betty Santee and Unknown Meredith is:
  4473 i. Private[15] Meredith.

3166. Mary Elizabeth[14] Sharick (Marie[13] Cooley, Bertha[12] Stouffer, John[11], Abraham[10], Abraham Hershey[9] Stauffer, Abraham Hess[8], Henry Jacob[7], Hans[6], Christian[5], Daniel[4] Stouffer, Christian[3], Hans[2], Hans[1]) She married **Unknown Matthews**.

Child of Mary Sharick and Unknown Matthews is:
  4474 i. Private[15] Sharick.

3167. Patricia[14] Sharick (Marie[13] Cooley, Bertha[12] Stouffer, John[11], Abraham[10], Abraham Hershey[9] Stauffer, Abraham Hess[8], Henry Jacob[7], Hans[6], Christian[5], Daniel[4] Stouffer, Christian[3], Hans[2], Hans[1]) She married **Unknown Mount**.

Children of Patricia Sharick and Unknown Mount are:
  4475 i. Private[15] Mount.
  4476 ii. Private Mount.

3172. Claud[14] Cook (Ida[13] Stouffer, Aaron[12], John[11], Abraham[10], Abraham Hershey[9] Stauffer, Abraham Hess[8], Henry Jacob[7], Hans[6], Christian[5], Daniel[4] Stouffer, Christian[3], Hans[2], Hans[1]) He married **Lulu Thorpe**.

Children of Claud Cook and Lulu Thorpe are:
  4477 i. Private[15] Cook.
  4478 ii. Private Cook.

3173. Lola[14] Cook (Ida[13] Stouffer, Aaron[12], John[11], Abraham[10], Abraham Hershey[9] Stauffer, Abraham Hess[8], Henry Jacob[7], Hans[6], Christian[5], Daniel[4] Stouffer, Christian[3], Hans[2], Hans[1]) She married **Roy Smith**.

Child of Lola Cook and Roy Smith is:
  4479 i. Private[15] Smith.

3174. Ernest[14] Cook (Ida[13] Stouffer, Aaron[12], John[11], Abraham[10], Abraham Hershey[9] Stauffer, Abraham Hess[8], Henry Jacob[7], Hans[6], Christian[5], Daniel[4] Stouffer, Christian[3], Hans[2], Hans[1]) He married **Ruth Nichol**.

Children of Ernest Cook and Ruth Nichol are:
  4480 i. Private[15] Cook.
  4481 ii. Private Cook.

3234. Emma Ruth[14] Stouffer (Jacob Karl[13], David Wesley[12], Jacob[11], Abraham[10], Abraham Hershey[9] Stauffer, Abraham Hess[8], Henry Jacob[7], Hans[6], Christian[5], Daniel[4] Stouffer, Christian[3], Hans[2], Hans[1]) She married **Patrick Boyle**.

Child of Emma Stouffer and Patrick Boyle is:
  4482 i. Private[15] Boyle.

3256. Delma Izetta[14] Stouffer (Clayton Parker[13], Flavius Jacob[12], Jacob[11], Abraham[10], Abraham Hershey[9] Stauffer, Abraham Hess[8], Henry Jacob[7], Hans[6], Christian[5], Daniel[4] Stouffer, Christian[3], Hans[2], Hans[1]) She married **Frank Frederick Foot**.

Child of Delma Stouffer and Frank Foot is:
  4483 i. Private[15] Foot.

3278. Jack[14] Nigh (Elizabeth[13] Wideman, Jacob S.[12], Elizabeth[11] Stouffer, Abraham[10], Abraham Hershey[9] Stauffer, Abraham Hess[8], Henry Jacob[7], Hans[6], Christian[5], Daniel[4] Stouffer, Christian[3], Hans[2], Hans[1]) He married **Isobel Fleming**.

Children of Jack Nigh and Isobel Fleming are:
- 4484 i. Private[15] Nigh.
- 4485 ii. Private Nigh.
- 4486 iii. Private Nigh.

3288. Herbert[14] Hoover (Ruth[13] Raymer, Christina[12] Stouffer, Abraham[11], Abraham[10], Abraham Hershey[9] Stauffer, Abraham Hess[8], Henry Jacob[7], Hans[6], Christian[5], Daniel[4] Stouffer, Christian[3], Hans[2], Hans[1]) He married **Agnes Offert**.

Child of Herbert Hoover and Agnes Offert is:
- 4487 i. Wesley[15] Hoover.

3289. Redford[14] Wiancko (Elmina[13] Raymer, Christina[12] Stouffer, Abraham[11], Abraham[10], Abraham Hershey[9] Stauffer, Abraham Hess[8], Henry Jacob[7], Hans[6], Christian[5], Daniel[4] Stouffer, Christian[3], Hans[2], Hans[1]) He married **Mary Harrop**.

Children of Redford Wiancko and Mary Harrop are:
- 4488 i. Paul[15] Wiancko.
- 4489 ii. Elmina Jane Wiancko.

3290. Margaret[14] Wiancko (Elmina[13] Raymer, Christina[12] Stouffer, Abraham[11], Abraham[10], Abraham Hershey[9] Stauffer, Abraham Hess[8], Henry Jacob[7], Hans[6], Christian[5], Daniel[4] Stouffer, Christian[3], Hans[2], Hans[1]) She married **William Barnes**.

Child of Margaret Wiancko and William Barnes is:
- 4490 i. Christina Margaret[15] Barnes.

3294. Muriel[14] Wideman (Wilmot[13], Frances[12] Stouffer, Abraham[11], Abraham[10], Abraham Hershey[9] Stauffer, Abraham Hess[8], Henry Jacob[7], Hans[6], Christian[5], Daniel[4] Stouffer, Christian[3], Hans[2], Hans[1]) She married **William Annett**.

Child of Muriel Wideman and William Annett is:
- 4491 i. David[15] Annett.

3295. Harley[14] Wideman (Herbert[13], Frances[12] Stouffer, Abraham[11], Abraham[10], Abraham Hershey[9] Stauffer, Abraham Hess[8], Henry Jacob[7], Hans[6], Christian[5], Daniel[4] Stouffer, Christian[3], Hans[2], Hans[1]) He married **Lena Weber**.

Children of Harley Wideman and Lena Weber are:
- 4492 i. Private[15] Wideman.
- 4493 ii. Private Wideman.

3300. Miriam[14] Schell (Mabel[13] Wideman, Frances[12] Stouffer, Abraham[11], Abraham[10], Abraham Hershey[9] Stauffer, Abraham Hess[8], Henry Jacob[7], Hans[6], Christian[5], Daniel[4] Stouffer, Christian[3], Hans[2], Hans[1]) She married **Ray Hiscox**.

Children of Miriam Schell and Ray Hiscox are:
- 4494 i. Yvonne[15] Hiscox.
- 4495 ii. Carl Hiscox.
- 4496 iii. Sharon Hiscox.

3313. Harvey[14] Wideman (Joseph[13], Frances[12] Stouffer, Abraham[11], Abraham[10], Abraham Hershey[9] Stauffer, Abraham Hess[8], Henry Jacob[7], Hans[6], Christian[5], Daniel[4] Stouffer, Christian[3], Hans[2], Hans[1]) He married **Ruby Snyder**.

Children of Harvey Wideman and Ruby Snyder are:
- 4497 i. Private[15] Wideman.
- 4498 ii. Private Wideman.
- 4499 iii. Private Wideman.
- 4500 iv. Private Wideman.
- 4501 v. Evelyn Wideman, born 1936; died 1948.

3314. Alan[14] Wideman (Joseph[13], Frances[12] Stouffer, Abraham[11], Abraham[10], Abraham Hershey[9] Stauffer, Abraham Hess[8], Henry Jacob[7], Hans[6], Christian[5], Daniel[4] Stouffer, Christian[3], Hans[2], Hans[1]) He married **Helene Annett**.

Children of Alan Wideman and Helene Annett are:
- 4502 i. Private[15] Wideman.
- 4503 ii. Private Wideman.
- 4504 iii. Private Wideman.

3315. Vera[14] Wideman (Joseph[13], Frances[12] Stouffer, Abraham[11], Abraham[10], Abraham Hershey[9] Stauffer, Abraham Hess[8], Henry Jacob[7], Hans[6], Christian[5], Daniel[4] Stouffer, Christian[3], Hans[2], Hans[1]) She married **John Annett**.

Children of Vera Wideman and John Annett are:
- 4505 i. Private[15] Annett.
- 4506 ii. Private Annett.
- 4507 iii. Private Annett.

3316. Floyd[14] Forsythe (Louie[13] Stouffer, Noah[12], Abraham[11], Abraham[10], Abraham Hershey[9] Stauffer, Abraham Hess[8], Henry Jacob[7], Hans[6], Christian[5], Daniel[4] Stouffer, Christian[3], Hans[2], Hans[1]) He married **Reta Wells**.

Child of Floyd Forsythe and Reta Wells is:
- 4508 i. Private[15] Forsythe.

3317. Lola Jean[14] Forsythe (Louie[13] Stouffer, Noah[12], Abraham[11], Abraham[10], Abraham Hershey[9] Stauffer, Abraham Hess[8], Henry Jacob[7], Hans[6], Christian[5], Daniel[4] Stouffer, Christian[3], Hans[2], Hans[1]) She married **Earl Hoover**.

Child of Lola Forsythe and Earl Hoover is:
- 4509 i. Private[15] Hoover.

3322. Katherine[14] Moyer (Jennie[13] Hoover, Josephuine[12] Stouffer, Abraham[11], Abraham[10], Abraham Hershey[9] Stauffer, Abraham Hess[8], Henry Jacob[7], Hans[6], Christian[5], Daniel[4] Stouffer, Christian[3], Hans[2], Hans[1]) She married **Clarence McDowell**.

Children of Katherine Moyer and Clarence McDowell are:
- 4510 i. Private[15] McDowell.
- 4511 ii. Private McDowell.
- 4512 iii. Private McDowell.

3332. Norma[14] Barkey (Ruth[13] Hoover, Josephuine[12] Stouffer, Abraham[11], Abraham[10], Abraham Hershey[9] Stauffer, Abraham Hess[8], Henry Jacob[7], Hans[6], Christian[5], Daniel[4] Stouffer, Christian[3], Hans[2], Hans[1]) She married **Bruce Clarke**.

Child of Norma Barkey and Bruce Clarke is:
- 4513 i. Private[15] Clarke.

3339. Clifford[14] Barkey (Charles[13], Martha[12] Stouffer, Abraham[11], Abraham[10], Abraham Hershey[9] Stauffer, Abraham Hess[8], Henry Jacob[7], Hans[6], Christian[5], Daniel[4] Stouffer, Christian[3], Hans[2], Hans[1]) He married **Mary Graham**.

Children of Clifford Barkey and Mary Graham are:
- 4514 i. Private[15] Barkey.
- 4515 ii. Private Barkey.
- 4516 iii. Private Barkey.

3372. Dorothy Elaine[14] Hackman (Henry Hess[13], Willis Brenner[12], Andrew Baer[11], Susanna Frantz[10] Bear, Anna[9] Frantz, Barbara[8] Hostetter, Ann Elisabeth[7] Hershey, Benjamin Stauffer[6], Adelheid Galle[5] Stouffer, Daniel[4], Christian[3], Hans[2], Hans[1]) was born June 06, 1934 in Newville, Cumberland Co., PA. She married **Dorman John Grace** June 07, 1953 in Church of the Brethern, Palmyra, PA. He was born September 04, 1933 in Hershey, Dauphin Co, PA.

Children of Dorothy Hackman and Dorman Grace are:
- + 4517 i. Dorman John[15] Grace III, born October 27, 1955 in Good Samaritan Hospital, Lebanon, PA.
- + 4518 ii. Nancy Anne Grace, born August 30, 1958 in Good Samaritan Hospital, Lebanon, PA.
- 4519 iii. Kathleen Kay Grace, born August 11, 1959 in Good Samaritan Hospital, Lebanon, PA.

The Relations of Milton Snavely Hershey, 4th Ed.

3373. Willard Henry[14] Hackman (Henry Hess[13], Willis Brenner[12], Andrew Baer[11], Susanna Frantz[10] Bear, Anna[9] Frantz, Barbara[8] Hostetter, Ann Elisabeth[7] Hershey, Benjamin Stauffer[6], Adelheid Galle[5] Stouffer, Daniel[4], Christian[3], Hans[2], Hans[1]) was born June 29, 1938 in Newville, Cumberland Co., PA. He married **Shelby Sensenderfer** November 27, 1958. She was born October 11, 1938 in Manheim, PA.

Children of Willard Hackman and Shelby Sensenderfer are:
- 4520 i. Michael Frederick[15] Hackman, born June 08, 1964. He married Dona Lynn McFarland December 22, 1984; born Abt. 1965.
- 4521 ii. Christopher Allen Hackman, born September 24, 1965. He married Colleen Hollinger August 06, 1988; born Abt. 1965.

3375. Ray Donald[14] Hackman (Willis Hess[13], Willis Brenner[12], Andrew Baer[11], Susanna Frantz[10] Bear, Anna[9] Frantz, Barbara[8] Hostetter, Ann Elisabeth[7] Hershey, Benjamin Stauffer[6], Adelheid Galle[5] Stouffer, Daniel[4], Christian[3], Hans[2], Hans[1]) was born May 05, 1933. He married **(1) Unknown Unknown**. She was born Abt. 1933. He married **(2) Karen Ann Fortney** June 24, 1972. She was born March 12, 1949.

Children of Ray Hackman and Unknown Unknown are:
- 4522 i. Dennis Ray[15] Hackman, born November 24, 1953 in Hershey, Dauphin Co, PA.
- 4523 ii. Gerald Allen Hackman, born October 24, 1954 in Hershey, Dauphin Co, PA. He married Candace M Kraybill June 1978; born Abt. 1955.
- 4524 iii. Randall Lee Hackman, born December 10, 1955 in Hershey, Dauphin Co, PA. He married Lori A Good May 16, 1981 in Elizabethtown, PA; born Abt. 1955.
- 4525 iv. Gary Jay Hackman, born November 23, 1957 in Hershey, Dauphin Co, PA.
- 4526 v. Cindy Lynn Hackman, born March 16, 1959 in Hershey, Dauphin Co, PA.
- 4527 vi. Thomas Jon Hackman, born June 29, 1960 in Hershey, Dauphin Co, PA.
- 4528 vii. Daniel Michael Hackman, born January 16, 1966 in Corning, NY.
- 4529 viii. Tammy Sue Hackman, born May 29, 1969 in Williamsport, PA.
- 4530 ix. Terry Lee Hackman, born May 29, 1969 in Williamsport, PA.

Child of Ray Hackman and Karen Fortney is:
- 4531 i. Rea Ann[15] Hackman, born July 15, 1976 in Elizabethtown, PA.

3376. Kenneth Lee[14] Hackman (Willis Hess[13], Willis Brenner[12], Andrew Baer[11], Susanna Frantz[10] Bear, Anna[9] Frantz, Barbara[8] Hostetter, Ann Elisabeth[7] Hershey, Benjamin Stauffer[6], Adelheid Galle[5] Stouffer, Daniel[4], Christian[3], Hans[2], Hans[1]) was born September 03, 1934. He married **Marian Arlene Baker** February 04, 1956. She was born January 29, 1935 in Conewago Twp, Dauphin Co, PA.

Children of Kenneth Hackman and Marian Baker are:
- 4532 i. Brenda Kay[15] Hackman, born July 09, 1956 in Elizabethtown, PA.
- 4533 ii. Wanda Jean Hackman, born December 08, 1957 in Elizabethtown, PA.
- 4534 iii. Kenneth Lee Hackman, born January 31, 1960 in Elizabethtown, PA.

3377. Annie Marian[14] Hackman (Willis Hess[13], Willis Brenner[12], Andrew Baer[11], Susanna Frantz[10] Bear, Anna[9] Frantz, Barbara[8] Hostetter, Ann Elisabeth[7] Hershey, Benjamin Stauffer[6], Adelheid Galle[5] Stouffer, Daniel[4], Christian[3], Hans[2], Hans[1]) was born November 20, 1937. She married **Harold LeRoy McKain** November 20, 1959. He was born September 25, 1932 in Marietta, Lancaster Co, PA.

Children of Annie Hackman and Harold McKain are:
- + 4535 i. Tracy Louise[15] McKain, born May 24, 1969 in Lancaster, PA.
- 4536 ii. Sheila Nadine McKain, born March 20, 1971 in Lancaster, PA.

3378. Margaret Ann[14] Hackman (Willis Hess[13], Willis Brenner[12], Andrew Baer[11], Susanna Frantz[10] Bear, Anna[9] Frantz, Barbara[8] Hostetter, Ann Elisabeth[7] Hershey, Benjamin Stauffer[6], Adelheid Galle[5] Stouffer, Daniel[4], Christian[3], Hans[2], Hans[1]) was born March 11, 1939. She married **John Kennedy Gill** September 10, 1960. He was born October 03, 1935 in Manchester, Lancashire, England.

Children of Margaret Hackman and John Gill are:
- 4537 i. Terry Lee[15] Gill, born June 13, 1961 in Plattsburg, NY.
- 4538 ii. Tina Lynn Gill, born August 03, 1962 in Lancaster, PA.
- 4539 iii. Dawn Marie Gill, born July 24, 1970 in Lakenheath, England.

3379. Alice Lorraine[14] Hackman (Willis Hess[13], Willis Brenner[12], Andrew Baer[11], Susanna Frantz[10] Bear, Anna[9] Frantz, Barbara[8] Hostetter, Ann Elisabeth[7] Hershey, Benjamin Stauffer[6], Adelheid Galle[5] Stouffer, Daniel[4], Christian[3], Hans[2], Hans[1]) was born February 06, 1942. She married **John Henry Gerlach** September 09, 1976. He was born January 21, 1939 in Elizabethtown, PA.

Children of Alice Hackman and John Gerlach are:
- 4540   i.   Carol Ann[15] Gerlach, born April 29, 1965 in Lancaster, PA.
- 4541   ii.   Daryl Eugene Gerlach, born December 19, 1967 in Lancaster, PA.
- 4542   iii.   Douglas Scott Gerlach, born April 10, 1970 in Lancaster, PA.

3380. Willis Martin[14] Hackman (Willis Hess[13], Willis Brenner[12], Andrew Baer[11], Susanna Frantz[10] Bear, Anna[9] Frantz, Barbara[8] Hostetter, Ann Elisabeth[7] Hershey, Benjamin Stauffer[6], Adelheid Galle[5] Stouffer, Daniel[4], Christian[3], Hans[2], Hans[1]) was born January 08, 1946. He married **Rosetta Brubaker** October 05, 1968. She was born March 16, 1949.

Child of Willis Hackman and Rosetta Brubaker is:
- 4543   i.   Tony Robert[15] Hackman, born March 20, 1973 in Lancaster, PA.

3381. Robert Lorin[14] Hackman (Walter Hess[13], Willis Brenner[12], Andrew Baer[11], Susanna Frantz[10] Bear, Anna[9] Frantz, Barbara[8] Hostetter, Ann Elisabeth[7] Hershey, Benjamin Stauffer[6], Adelheid Galle[5] Stouffer, Daniel[4], Christian[3], Hans[2], Hans[1]) was born October 20, 1935. He married **Florence Mildred Stuber** January 07, 1956. She was born February 05, 1935 in Ephrata Twp, Lancaster Co, PA.

Children of Robert Hackman and Florence Stuber are:
- 4544   i.   Karen Lee[15] Hackman, born August 02, 1956 in Ephrata Twp, Lancaster Co, PA.
- 4545   ii.   Steven Dean Hackman, born November 26, 1958 in Ephrata Twp, Lancaster Co, PA.
- 4546   iii.   Mitchell Keith Hackman, born September 04, 1962.

3382. Betty Lou[14] Hackman (Richard Hess[13], Willis Brenner[12], Andrew Baer[11], Susanna Frantz[10] Bear, Anna[9] Frantz, Barbara[8] Hostetter, Ann Elisabeth[7] Hershey, Benjamin Stauffer[6], Adelheid Galle[5] Stouffer, Daniel[4], Christian[3], Hans[2], Hans[1]) was born May 27, 1935. She married **Thomas William Williams III** June 24, 1956. He was born October 07, 1935 in Northampton Co, PA.

Children of Betty Hackman and Thomas Williams are:
- 4547   i.   Douglas Thomas[15] Williams, born June 26, 1957 in Lancaster, PA.
- 4548   ii.   Donald Everett Williams, born August 23, 1959 in Lancaster, PA.
- 4549   iii.   Dee Ann Williams, born July 28, 1963 in Lancaster, PA.

3383. Richard Forney[14] Hackman (Richard Hess[13], Willis Brenner[12], Andrew Baer[11], Susanna Frantz[10] Bear, Anna[9] Frantz, Barbara[8] Hostetter, Ann Elisabeth[7] Hershey, Benjamin Stauffer[6], Adelheid Galle[5] Stouffer, Daniel[4], Christian[3], Hans[2], Hans[1]) was born January 24, 1940. He married **Bonadine Marie Bucher** June 21, 1969. She was born March 25, 1945 in Lebanon, PA.

Child of Richard Hackman and Bonadine Bucher is:
- 4550   i.   Amy Lynn[15] Hackman, born December 05, 1970 in Lancaster, PA.

3385. Roy Edward[14] Pfaltzgraff, Jr (Violet Gertrude[13] Hackman, Willis Brenner[12], Andrew Baer[11], Susanna Frantz[10] Bear, Anna[9] Frantz, Barbara[8] Hostetter, Ann Elisabeth[7] Hershey, Benjamin Stauffer[6], Adelheid Galle[5] Stouffer, Daniel[4], Christian[3], Hans[2], Hans[1]) was born September 08, 1943 in Philadelphia, PA. He married **Kathryn Krehmeyer**. She was born Abt. 1945 in Haxtun Co, CO.

Children of Roy Pfaltzgraff and Kathryn Krehmeyer are:
- 4551   i.   Renee[15] Pfaltzgraff, born Abt. 1970.
- 4552   ii.   Rhonda Pfaltzgraff, born Abt. 1970.
- 4553   iii.   Rebecca Pfaltzgraff, born Abt. 1970.
- 4554   iv.   Roberta Pfaltzgraff, born Abt. 1970.

3386. George Hackman[14] Pfaltzgraff (Violet Gertrude[13] Hackman, Willis Brenner[12], Andrew Baer[11], Susanna Frantz[10] Bear, Anna[9] Frantz, Barbara[8] Hostetter, Ann Elisabeth[7] Hershey, Benjamin Stauffer[6], Adelheid Galle[5] Stouffer, Daniel[4], Christian[3], Hans[2], Hans[1]) was born April 22, 1945 in Garkida, Nigeria. He married **(1) Cynthia Porter**. She was born Abt. 1945 in Manchester, IN. He married **(2) Peggie**. She was born Abt. 1945 in Cincinnati, OH.

Child of George Pfaltzgraff and Cynthia Porter is:
- 4555   i.   Christina Catherine[15] Pfaltzgraff, born Abt. 1970.

3387. David Jasini[14] Pfaltzgraff (Violet Gertrude[13] Hackman, Willis Brenner[12], Andrew Baer[11], Susanna Frantz[10] Bear, Anna[9] Frantz, Barbara[8] Hostetter, Ann Elisabeth[7] Hershey, Benjamin Stauffer[6], Adelheid Galle[5] Stouffer, Daniel[4], Christian[3], Hans[2], Hans[1]) was born September 11, 1946 in Lasa, Nigeria. He married **Ruth Susanna Kehr**. She was born Abt. 1950 in York, PA.

Children of David Pfaltzgraff and Ruth Kehr are:
- 4556   i.   Timothy David[15] Pfaltzgraff, born Abt. 1975.
- 4557   ii.   Michael Jasini Pfaltzgraff, born Abt. 1975.

3390. Emily Faline[14] White (Emma Amelia[13] Hackman, Willis Brenner[12], Andrew Baer[11], Susanna Frantz[10] Bear, Anna[9] Frantz, Barbara[8] Hostetter, Ann Elisabeth[7] Hershey, Benjamin Stauffer[6], Adelheid Galle[5] Stouffer, Daniel[4], Christian[3], Hans[2], Hans[1]) was born February 16, 1943 in Lititz, PA. She married **Lawrence David Knorr** August 03, 1963 in Church of the Brethern, Elizabethtown, PA. He was born May 04, 1943 in Reading, PA.

Children of Emily White and Lawrence Knorr are:
- +   4558   i.   Lawrence Kevin[15] Knorr, born May 05, 1964 in Reading Hostpital, Reading, PA.
- +   4559   ii.   Alice Kathleen Knorr, born August 11, 1965 in Reading, PA.
-      4560   iii.   David Brian Knorr, born April 07, 1968 in Reading, PA. He married Tara Phillips May 19, 1995 in Gulfport, MS; born Abt. 1972.

3391. William Walter[14] White (Emma Amelia[13] Hackman, Willis Brenner[12], Andrew Baer[11], Susanna Frantz[10] Bear, Anna[9] Frantz, Barbara[8] Hostetter, Ann Elisabeth[7] Hershey, Benjamin Stauffer[6], Adelheid Galle[5] Stouffer, Daniel[4], Christian[3], Hans[2], Hans[1]) was born December 12, 1944. He married **Dorothy Krafft**. She was born 1955.

Children of William White and Dorothy Krafft are:
- 4561   i.   Shelby[15] White, born February 19, 1986.
- 4562   ii.   McKenzie White, born March 09, 1988.

3395. Private[14] Fox (Willis Eby[13], Ella Barbara[12] Eby, Sarah Lucinda[11] Hershey, Peter[10], Jacob[9], John[8], Jacob Snavely[7], Andrew Stauffer[6], Adelheid Galle[5] Stouffer, Daniel[4], Christian[3], Hans[2], Hans[1]) She married **Private Zimmerman**.

Children of Private Fox and Private Zimmerman are:
- 4563   i.   Private[15] Zimmerman.
- 4564   ii.   Private Zimmerman.
- 4565   iii.   Christine Renee Zimmerman, born January 19, 1975; died April 17, 1975.
- 4566   iv.   Neil Brian Zimmerman, born August 15, 1977; died October 26, 1977.

3396. Private[14] Fox (Willis Eby[13], Ella Barbara[12] Eby, Sarah Lucinda[11] Hershey, Peter[10], Jacob[9], John[8], Jacob Snavely[7], Andrew Stauffer[6], Adelheid Galle[5] Stouffer, Daniel[4], Christian[3], Hans[2], Hans[1]) He married **Private Trupe**.

Children of Private Fox and Private Trupe are:
- 4567   i.   Private[15] Fox.
- 4568   ii.   Private Fox.
- 4569   iii.   Private Fox.

3397. Private[14] Fox (Willis Eby[13], Ella Barbara[12] Eby, Sarah Lucinda[11] Hershey, Peter[10], Jacob[9], John[8], Jacob Snavely[7], Andrew Stauffer[6], Adelheid Galle[5] Stouffer, Daniel[4], Christian[3], Hans[2], Hans[1]) She married **Private Newswanger**.

Child of Private Fox and Private Newswanger is:
- 4570   i.   Private[15] Newswanger.

3400. Private[14] Fox (Willis Eby[13], Ella Barbara[12] Eby, Sarah Lucinda[11] Hershey, Peter[10], Jacob[9], John[8], Jacob Snavely[7], Andrew Stauffer[6], Adelheid Galle[5] Stouffer, Daniel[4], Christian[3], Hans[2], Hans[1]) He married **Private Weaver**.

Children of Private Fox and Private Weaver are:
-      4571   i.   Private[15] Fox.
-      4572   ii.   Private Fox. She married Private Martin.
- +   4573   iii.   Private Fox.
- +   4574   iv.   Private Fox.
-      4575   v.   Marvin Lamar Fox, born December 13, 1962; died March 20, 1980.

3402. Private[14] Fox (Henry Peter[13], Ella Barbara[12] Eby, Sarah Lucinda[11] Hershey, Peter[10], Jacob[9], John[8], Jacob Snavely[7], Andrew Stauffer[6], Adelheid Galle[5] Stouffer, Daniel[4], Christian[3], Hans[2], Hans[1]) She married **Private Evans**.

Children of Private Fox and Private Evans are:
- 4576　　i.　　Private[15] Evans.
- 4577　　ii.　　Private Evans.
- 4578　　iii.　　Private Evans.
- 4579　　iv.　　Cecile Loren Evans, born July 18, 1985; died November 04, 1985.

3404. Private[14] Fox (Henry Peter[13], Ella Barbara[12] Eby, Sarah Lucinda[11] Hershey, Peter[10], Jacob[9], John[8], Jacob Snavely[7], Andrew Stauffer[6], Adelheid Galle[5] Stouffer, Daniel[4], Christian[3], Hans[2], Hans[1])　He married **Private Kennel**.

Children of Private Fox and Private Kennel are:
- 4580　　i.　　Private[15] Fox.
- 4581　　ii.　　Private Fox.

3405. Private[14] Fox (Henry Peter[13], Ella Barbara[12] Eby, Sarah Lucinda[11] Hershey, Peter[10], Jacob[9], John[8], Jacob Snavely[7], Andrew Stauffer[6], Adelheid Galle[5] Stouffer, Daniel[4], Christian[3], Hans[2], Hans[1])　He married **Private Felpel**.

Children of Private Fox and Private Felpel are:
- 4582　　i.　　Private[15] Fox.
- 4583　　ii.　　Private Fox.
- 4584　　iii.　　Private Fox.
- 4585　　iv.　　Private Fox.

3407. Private[14] Fox (Henry Peter[13], Ella Barbara[12] Eby, Sarah Lucinda[11] Hershey, Peter[10], Jacob[9], John[8], Jacob Snavely[7], Andrew Stauffer[6], Adelheid Galle[5] Stouffer, Daniel[4], Christian[3], Hans[2], Hans[1])　He married **Private Heisey**.

Children of Private Fox and Private Heisey are:
- 4586　　i.　　Private[15] Fox.
- 4587　　ii.　　Private Fox.　He married Private Fryberger.

3409. Private[14] Fox (Henry Peter[13], Ella Barbara[12] Eby, Sarah Lucinda[11] Hershey, Peter[10], Jacob[9], John[8], Jacob Snavely[7], Andrew Stauffer[6], Adelheid Galle[5] Stouffer, Daniel[4], Christian[3], Hans[2], Hans[1])　She married **Private Augsburger**.

Children of Private Fox and Private Augsburger are:
- 　4588　　i.　　Private[15] Augsburger.　He married Private Denlinger.
- + 4589　　ii.　　Private Augsburger.
- + 4590　　iii.　　Private Augsburger.
- 　4591　　iv.　　Private Augsburger.　He married Private Hollinger.

3410. Private[14] Fox (Henry Peter[13], Ella Barbara[12] Eby, Sarah Lucinda[11] Hershey, Peter[10], Jacob[9], John[8], Jacob Snavely[7], Andrew Stauffer[6], Adelheid Galle[5] Stouffer, Daniel[4], Christian[3], Hans[2], Hans[1])　She married **Private Eberly**.

Children of Private Fox and Private Eberly are:
- 　4592　　i.　　Private[15] Eberly.　He married Private Balmer.
- + 4593　　ii.　　Private Eberly.
- 　4594　　iii.　　Private Eberly.　She married Private Hurst.

3411. Private[14] Fox (Henry Peter[13], Ella Barbara[12] Eby, Sarah Lucinda[11] Hershey, Peter[10], Jacob[9], John[8], Jacob Snavely[7], Andrew Stauffer[6], Adelheid Galle[5] Stouffer, Daniel[4], Christian[3], Hans[2], Hans[1])　She married **Private Good**.

Children of Private Fox and Private Good are:
- 　4595　　i.　　Private[15] Good.
- 　4596　　ii.　　Private Good.
- + 4597　　iii.　　Private Good.
- + 4598　　iv.　　Private Good.

3412. Private[14] Fox (Henry Peter[13], Ella Barbara[12] Eby, Sarah Lucinda[11] Hershey, Peter[10], Jacob[9], John[8], Jacob Snavely[7], Andrew Stauffer[6], Adelheid Galle[5] Stouffer, Daniel[4], Christian[3], Hans[2], Hans[1])　She married **Private Zimmerman**.

Children of Private Fox and Private Zimmerman are:

	4599	i.	Private[15] Zimmerman.
+	4600	ii.	Private Zimmerman.
+	4601	iii.	Private Zimmerman.

3413. Private[14] Zimmerman (Sarah Lucinda[13] Fox, Ella Barbara[12] Eby, Sarah Lucinda[11] Hershey, Peter[10], Jacob[9], John[8], Jacob Snavely[7], Andrew Stauffer[6], Adelheid Galle[5] Stouffer, Daniel[4], Christian[3], Hans[2], Hans[1]) He married **Private Long**.

Children of Private Zimmerman and Private Long are:
- 4602   i.   Private[15] Zimmerman.
- 4603   ii. Private Zimmerman.

3414. Private[14] Zimmerman (Sarah Lucinda[13] Fox, Ella Barbara[12] Eby, Sarah Lucinda[11] Hershey, Peter[10], Jacob[9], John[8], Jacob Snavely[7], Andrew Stauffer[6], Adelheid Galle[5] Stouffer, Daniel[4], Christian[3], Hans[2], Hans[1]) She married **Private Groff**.

Children of Private Zimmerman and Private Groff are:
- 4604   i.   Private[15] Groff.
- 4605   ii.   Private Groff.
- 4606   iii. Private Groff.
- 4607   iv.   Private Groff.

3415. Private[14] Zimmerman (Sarah Lucinda[13] Fox, Ella Barbara[12] Eby, Sarah Lucinda[11] Hershey, Peter[10], Jacob[9], John[8], Jacob Snavely[7], Andrew Stauffer[6], Adelheid Galle[5] Stouffer, Daniel[4], Christian[3], Hans[2], Hans[1]) He married **Private Hostetter**.

Children of Private Zimmerman and Private Hostetter are:
- 4608   i.   Private[15] Zimmerman.
- 4609   ii.   Private Zimmerman.
- 4610   iii. Private Zimmerman.
- 4611   iv.   Private Zimmerman.
- 4612   v.   Private Zimmerman.
- 4613   vi.   Private Zimmerman.
- 4614   vii. Private Zimmerman.

3416. Private[14] Zimmerman (Sarah Lucinda[13] Fox, Ella Barbara[12] Eby, Sarah Lucinda[11] Hershey, Peter[10], Jacob[9], John[8], Jacob Snavely[7], Andrew Stauffer[6], Adelheid Galle[5] Stouffer, Daniel[4], Christian[3], Hans[2], Hans[1]) He married **Private Wenger**.

Children of Private Zimmerman and Private Wenger are:
- 4615   i.   Private[15] Zimmerman.
- 4616   ii.   Private Zimmerman.
- 4617   iii.   Private Zimmerman.
- 4618   iv.   Private Zimmerman.
- 4619   v.   Private Zimmerman.
- 4620   vi.   Private Zimmerman.
- 4621   vii.   Private Zimmerman.
- 4622   viii. Private Zimmerman.
- 4623   ix.   Private Zimmerman.
- 4624   x.   Private Zimmerman.
- 4625   xi.   Private Zimmerman.
- + 4626   xii.   Private Zimmerman.
- 4627   xiii. Private Zimmerman. She married Private Hoover.
- 4628   xiv.   Private Zimmerman.
- + 4629   xv.   Private Zimmerman.

3417. Private[14] Fox (Daniel Hershey[13], Ella Barbara[12] Eby, Sarah Lucinda[11] Hershey, Peter[10], Jacob[9], John[8], Jacob Snavely[7], Andrew Stauffer[6], Adelheid Galle[5] Stouffer, Daniel[4], Christian[3], Hans[2], Hans[1]) She married **Private Mall**.

Child of Private Fox and Private Mall is:
- 4630   i.   Private[15] Mall.

3418. Private[14] Fox (Daniel Hershey[13], Ella Barbara[12] Eby, Sarah Lucinda[11] Hershey, Peter[10], Jacob[9], John[8], Jacob Snavely[7], Andrew

Stauffer[6], Adelheid Galle[5] Stouffer, Daniel[4], Christian[3], Hans[2], Hans[1]) She married **Private Kilmer**.

Children of Private Fox and Private Kilmer are:
- 4631 i. Private[15] Kilmer.
- 4632 ii. Private Kilmer.
- 4633 iii. Private Kilmer.

3419. Private[14] Fox (Daniel Hershey[13], Ella Barbara[12] Eby, Sarah Lucinda[11] Hershey, Peter[10], Jacob[9], John[8], Jacob Snavely[7], Andrew Stauffer[6], Adelheid Galle[5] Stouffer, Daniel[4], Christian[3], Hans[2], Hans[1])

Child of Private Fox is:
- 4634 i. Private[15] Fox.

3421. Private[14] Fox (Ivan Martin[13], Ella Barbara[12] Eby, Sarah Lucinda[11] Hershey, Peter[10], Jacob[9], John[8], Jacob Snavely[7], Andrew Stauffer[6], Adelheid Galle[5] Stouffer, Daniel[4], Christian[3], Hans[2], Hans[1]) He married **Private Myers**.

Children of Private Fox and Private Myers are:
- 4635 i. Private[15] Brown.
- 4636 ii. Private Brown.

3422. Private[14] Fox (Ivan Martin[13], Ella Barbara[12] Eby, Sarah Lucinda[11] Hershey, Peter[10], Jacob[9], John[8], Jacob Snavely[7], Andrew Stauffer[6], Adelheid Galle[5] Stouffer, Daniel[4], Christian[3], Hans[2], Hans[1]) He married **Private Tangvald**.

Children of Private Fox and Private Tangvald are:
- 4637 i. Private[15] Fox.
- 4638 ii. Private Fox.
- 4639 iii. Private Fox.

3423. Private[14] Eby (Franklin W.[13], Peter Hershey[12], Sarah Lucinda[11] Hershey, Peter[10], Jacob[9], John[8], Jacob Snavely[7], Andrew Stauffer[6], Adelheid Galle[5] Stouffer, Daniel[4], Christian[3], Hans[2], Hans[1]) She married **(1) Private Groff**.   She married **(2) Private Malin**.

Child of Private Eby and Private Groff is:
- 4640 i. Private[15] Groff.

Child of Private Eby and Private Malin is:
- 4641 i. Private[15] Malin.

3425. Private[14] Martin (Susan W.[13] Eby, Peter Hershey[12], Sarah Lucinda[11] Hershey, Peter[10], Jacob[9], John[8], Jacob Snavely[7], Andrew Stauffer[6], Adelheid Galle[5] Stouffer, Daniel[4], Christian[3], Hans[2], Hans[1]) He married **Private Nolt**.

Children of Private Martin and Private Nolt are:
- 4642 i. Private[15] Martin.
- 4643 ii. Private Martin.
- 4644 iii. Private Martin.

3426. Private[14] Martin (Susan W.[13] Eby, Peter Hershey[12], Sarah Lucinda[11] Hershey, Peter[10], Jacob[9], John[8], Jacob Snavely[7], Andrew Stauffer[6], Adelheid Galle[5] Stouffer, Daniel[4], Christian[3], Hans[2], Hans[1]) She married **Private Martin**.

Children of Private Martin and Private Martin are:
- 4645 i. Private[15] Martin.
- 4646 ii. Private Martin.
- 4647 iii. Private Martin.

3427. Private[14] Martin (Susan W.[13] Eby, Peter Hershey[12], Sarah Lucinda[11] Hershey, Peter[10], Jacob[9], John[8], Jacob Snavely[7], Andrew Stauffer[6], Adelheid Galle[5] Stouffer, Daniel[4], Christian[3], Hans[2], Hans[1]) She married **Private Weber**.

Children of Private Martin and Private Weber are:
- 4648 i. Private[15] Weber.

4649 ii. Private Weber.

3428. Private[14] Martin (Susan W.[13] Eby, Peter Hershey[12], Sarah Lucinda[11] Hershey, Peter[10], Jacob[9], John[8], Jacob Snavely[7], Andrew Stauffer[6], Adelheid Galle[5] Stouffer, Daniel[4], Christian[3], Hans[2], Hans[1]) He married **Private Nolt**.

Children of Private Martin and Private Nolt are:
- 4650 i. Private[15] Martin.
- 4651 ii. Private Martin.
- 4652 iii. Private Martin.
- 4653 iv. Private Martin.
- 4654 v. Private Martin.
- 4655 vi. Private Martin.
- 4656 vii. Private Martin.
- 4657 viii. Private Martin. She married Private Good.

3429. Private[14] Martin (Susan W.[13] Eby, Peter Hershey[12], Sarah Lucinda[11] Hershey, Peter[10], Jacob[9], John[8], Jacob Snavely[7], Andrew Stauffer[6], Adelheid Galle[5] Stouffer, Daniel[4], Christian[3], Hans[2], Hans[1]) He married **Private Nolt**.

Children of Private Martin and Private Nolt are:
- 4658 i. Private[15] Martin.
- 4659 ii. Private Martin.
- 4660 iii. Private Martin.
- 4661 iv. Private Martin.
- 4662 v. Private Martin.
- 4663 vi. Private Martin.
- + 4664 vii. Private Martin.
- 4665 viii. Rosalea Joy Martin, born January 25, 1979; died January 25, 1979.

3430. Private[14] Martin (Susan W.[13] Eby, Peter Hershey[12], Sarah Lucinda[11] Hershey, Peter[10], Jacob[9], John[8], Jacob Snavely[7], Andrew Stauffer[6], Adelheid Galle[5] Stouffer, Daniel[4], Christian[3], Hans[2], Hans[1]) He married **Private Mitchell**.

Children of Private Martin and Private Mitchell are:
- 4666 i. Private[15] Martin.
- 4667 ii. Private Martin.
- 4668 iii. Private Martin. She married Private Gehman.

3431. Private[14] Martin (Susan W.[13] Eby, Peter Hershey[12], Sarah Lucinda[11] Hershey, Peter[10], Jacob[9], John[8], Jacob Snavely[7], Andrew Stauffer[6], Adelheid Galle[5] Stouffer, Daniel[4], Christian[3], Hans[2], Hans[1]) He married **Private Weaver**.

Children of Private Martin and Private Weaver are:
- 4669 i. Private[15] Martin.
- 4670 ii. Private Martin.
- 4671 iii. Private Martin.
- 4672 iv. Private Martin.
- 4673 v. Private Martin.
- 4674 vi. Private Martin.
- 4675 vii. Private Martin.
- 4676 viii. Private Martin. She married Private Stauffer.
- 4677 ix. Lavone W. Martin, born October 02, 1961; died October 02, 1961.
- 4678 x. Vernon W. Martin, born October 10, 1962; died October 10, 1962.

3432. John E.[14] Martin (Susan W.[13] Eby, Peter Hershey[12], Sarah Lucinda[11] Hershey, Peter[10], Jacob[9], John[8], Jacob Snavely[7], Andrew Stauffer[6], Adelheid Galle[5] Stouffer, Daniel[4], Christian[3], Hans[2], Hans[1]) was born May 25, 1949, and died February 11, 1984. He married **Private Good**.

Children of John Martin and Private Good are:
- 4679 i. Private[15] Martin.
- 4680 ii. Private Martin.
- 4681 iii. Private Martin.

3433. Private[14] Stauffer (Emma Mae[13] Eby, Peter Hershey[12], Sarah Lucinda[11] Hershey, Peter[10], Jacob[9], John[8], Jacob Snavely[7], Andrew Stauffer[6], Adelheid Galle[5] Stouffer, Daniel[4], Christian[3], Hans[2], Hans[1]) He married **Private Nolt**.

Children of Private Stauffer and Private Nolt are:
- 4682 i. Private[15] Stauffer.
- 4683 ii. Private Stauffer.
- 4684 iii. Private Stauffer.
- 4685 iv. Private Stauffer.

3434. Private[14] Stauffer (Emma Mae[13] Eby, Peter Hershey[12], Sarah Lucinda[11] Hershey, Peter[10], Jacob[9], John[8], Jacob Snavely[7], Andrew Stauffer[6], Adelheid Galle[5] Stouffer, Daniel[4], Christian[3], Hans[2], Hans[1]) She married **Private Horst**.

Children of Private Stauffer and Private Horst are:
- 4686 i. Private[15] Horst.
- 4687 ii. Private Horst.
- 4688 iii. Private Horst.
- 4689 iv. Private Horst.
- 4690 v. Private Horst.
- 4691 vi. Private Horst.
- 4692 vii. Private Horst.
- 4693 viii. Private Horst.
- 4694 ix. Private Horst.

3435. Private[14] Stauffer (Emma Mae[13] Eby, Peter Hershey[12], Sarah Lucinda[11] Hershey, Peter[10], Jacob[9], John[8], Jacob Snavely[7], Andrew Stauffer[6], Adelheid Galle[5] Stouffer, Daniel[4], Christian[3], Hans[2], Hans[1]) She married **Private Horning**.

Children of Private Stauffer and Private Horning are:
- 4695 i. Private[15] Horning.
- 4696 ii. Private Horning.
- 4697 iii. Private Horning.
- 4698 iv. Private Horning.
- 4699 v. Private Horning.
- 4700 vi. Private Horning.
- 4701 vii. Private Horning.
- 4702 viii. Private Horning.
- 4703 ix. Private Horning.
- 4704 x. Esther Mae Horning, born January 27, 1981; died July 10, 1984.

3436. Private[14] Stauffer (Emma Mae[13] Eby, Peter Hershey[12], Sarah Lucinda[11] Hershey, Peter[10], Jacob[9], John[8], Jacob Snavely[7], Andrew Stauffer[6], Adelheid Galle[5] Stouffer, Daniel[4], Christian[3], Hans[2], Hans[1]) She married **Private Zimmerman**.

Children of Private Stauffer and Private Zimmerman are:
- 4705 i. Private[15] Zimmerman.
- 4706 ii. Private Zimmerman.
- 4707 iii. Private Zimmerman.
- 4708 iv. Private Zimmerman.
- 4709 v. Private Zimmerman.
- + 4710 vi. Private Zimmerman.
- + 4711 vii. Private Zimmerman.
- + 4712 viii. Private Zimmerman.
- + 4713 ix. Private Zimmerman.

3438. Private[14] Stauffer (Rhoda S.[13] Eby, Enos Jacob[12], Sarah Lucinda[11] Hershey, Peter[10], Jacob[9], John[8], Jacob Snavely[7], Andrew Stauffer[6], Adelheid Galle[5] Stouffer, Daniel[4], Christian[3], Hans[2], Hans[1]) She married **Private Martin**.

Children of Private Stauffer and Private Martin are:
- 4714 i. Private[15] Martin.
- 4715 ii. Private Martin.
- 4716 iii. Private Martin.
- 4717 iv. Private Martin.

3439. Private[14] Stauffer (Rhoda S.[13] Eby, Enos Jacob[12], Sarah Lucinda[11] Hershey, Peter[10], Jacob[9], John[8], Jacob Snavely[7], Andrew Stauffer[6], Adelheid Galle[5] Stouffer, Daniel[4], Christian[3], Hans[2], Hans[1]) He married **Private Good**.

Children of Private Stauffer and Private Good are:
- 4718   i.   Private[15] Stauffer.
- 4719   ii.   Private Stauffer.
- 4720   iii.   Private Stauffer.
- 4721   iv.   Private Stauffer.
- 4722   v.   Private Stauffer.
- 4723   vi.   Private Stauffer.

3445. Private[14] Eby (Henry S.[13], Enos Jacob[12], Sarah Lucinda[11] Hershey, Peter[10], Jacob[9], John[8], Jacob Snavely[7], Andrew Stauffer[6], Adelheid Galle[5] Stouffer, Daniel[4], Christian[3], Hans[2], Hans[1]) She married **Private Weaver**.

Child of Private Eby and Private Weaver is:
- 4724   i.   Private[15] Weaver.

3446. Private[14] Eby (Henry S.[13], Enos Jacob[12], Sarah Lucinda[11] Hershey, Peter[10], Jacob[9], John[8], Jacob Snavely[7], Andrew Stauffer[6], Adelheid Galle[5] Stouffer, Daniel[4], Christian[3], Hans[2], Hans[1]) He married **Private Zimmerman**.

Child of Private Eby and Private Zimmerman is:
- 4725   i.   Private[15] Eby.

3447. Private[14] Eby (Henry S.[13], Enos Jacob[12], Sarah Lucinda[11] Hershey, Peter[10], Jacob[9], John[8], Jacob Snavely[7], Andrew Stauffer[6], Adelheid Galle[5] Stouffer, Daniel[4], Christian[3], Hans[2], Hans[1]) He married **Private Zimmerman**.

Children of Private Eby and Private Zimmerman are:
- 4726   i.   Private[15] Eby.
- 4727   ii.   Private Eby.

3448. Private[14] Eby (Henry S.[13], Enos Jacob[12], Sarah Lucinda[11] Hershey, Peter[10], Jacob[9], John[8], Jacob Snavely[7], Andrew Stauffer[6], Adelheid Galle[5] Stouffer, Daniel[4], Christian[3], Hans[2], Hans[1]) He married **Private Zimmerman**.

Child of Private Eby and Private Zimmerman is:
- 4728   i.   Private[15] Eby.

3449. Private[14] Eby (Henry S.[13], Enos Jacob[12], Sarah Lucinda[11] Hershey, Peter[10], Jacob[9], John[8], Jacob Snavely[7], Andrew Stauffer[6], Adelheid Galle[5] Stouffer, Daniel[4], Christian[3], Hans[2], Hans[1]) He married **Private Auker**.

Children of Private Eby and Private Auker are:
- 4729   i.   Private[15] Eby.
- 4730   ii.   Private Eby.

3450. Private[14] Eby (Henry S.[13], Enos Jacob[12], Sarah Lucinda[11] Hershey, Peter[10], Jacob[9], John[8], Jacob Snavely[7], Andrew Stauffer[6], Adelheid Galle[5] Stouffer, Daniel[4], Christian[3], Hans[2], Hans[1]) She married **Private Hartzler**.

Child of Private Eby and Private Hartzler is:
- 4731   i.   Private[15] Hartzler.

3454. Private[14] Eby (Ezra S.[13], Enos Jacob[12], Sarah Lucinda[11] Hershey, Peter[10], Jacob[9], John[8], Jacob Snavely[7], Andrew Stauffer[6], Adelheid Galle[5] Stouffer, Daniel[4], Christian[3], Hans[2], Hans[1]) She married **Private Rissler**.

Child of Private Eby and Private Rissler is:
- 4732   i.   Private[15] Rissler.

3456. Private[14] Eby (Ezra S.[13], Enos Jacob[12], Sarah Lucinda[11] Hershey, Peter[10], Jacob[9], John[8], Jacob Snavely[7], Andrew Stauffer[6],

Adelheid Galle[5] Stouffer, Daniel[4], Christian[3], Hans[2], Hans[1]) He married **Private Horst**.

Child of Private Eby and Private Horst is:
    4733   i.   Private[15] Eby.

3457. Private[14] Eby (Ezra S.[13], Enos Jacob[12], Sarah Lucinda[11] Hershey, Peter[10], Jacob[9], John[8], Jacob Snavely[7], Andrew Stauffer[6], Adelheid Galle[5] Stouffer, Daniel[4], Christian[3], Hans[2], Hans[1]) He married **Private Burkholder**.

Children of Private Eby and Private Burkholder are:
    4734   i.   Private[15] Eby.
    4735   ii.   Private Eby.
    4736   iii.   Private Eby.

3459. Private[14] Eby (Ezra S.[13], Enos Jacob[12], Sarah Lucinda[11] Hershey, Peter[10], Jacob[9], John[8], Jacob Snavely[7], Andrew Stauffer[6], Adelheid Galle[5] Stouffer, Daniel[4], Christian[3], Hans[2], Hans[1]) He married **Private Martin**.

Children of Private Eby and Private Martin are:
    4737   i.   Private[15] Eby.
    4738   ii.   Private Eby.
    4739   iii.   Private Eby.
    4740   iv.   Private Eby.

3460. Private[14] Eby (Ezra S.[13], Enos Jacob[12], Sarah Lucinda[11] Hershey, Peter[10], Jacob[9], John[8], Jacob Snavely[7], Andrew Stauffer[6], Adelheid Galle[5] Stouffer, Daniel[4], Christian[3], Hans[2], Hans[1]) He married **Private Sensenig**.

Children of Private Eby and Private Sensenig are:
    4741   i.   Private[15] Eby.
    4742   ii.   Private Eby.
    4743   iii.   Private Eby.
    4744   iv.   Private Eby.
    4745   v.   Marsha Eby, born August 18, 1975; died August 18, 1975.

3464. Private[14] Eby (Eli S.[13], Enos Jacob[12], Sarah Lucinda[11] Hershey, Peter[10], Jacob[9], John[8], Jacob Snavely[7], Andrew Stauffer[6], Adelheid Galle[5] Stouffer, Daniel[4], Christian[3], Hans[2], Hans[1]) She married **Private Sensenig**.

Child of Private Eby and Private Sensenig is:
    4746   i.   Private[15] Sensenig.

3465. Private[14] Eby (Eli S.[13], Enos Jacob[12], Sarah Lucinda[11] Hershey, Peter[10], Jacob[9], John[8], Jacob Snavely[7], Andrew Stauffer[6], Adelheid Galle[5] Stouffer, Daniel[4], Christian[3], Hans[2], Hans[1]) He married **Private Horning**.

Children of Private Eby and Private Horning are:
    4747   i.   Private[15] Eby.
    4748   ii.   Private Eby.
    4749   iii.   Private Eby.
    4750   iv.   Private Eby.

3466. Private[14] Eby (Eli S.[13], Enos Jacob[12], Sarah Lucinda[11] Hershey, Peter[10], Jacob[9], John[8], Jacob Snavely[7], Andrew Stauffer[6], Adelheid Galle[5] Stouffer, Daniel[4], Christian[3], Hans[2], Hans[1]) She married **Private Kurtz**.

Children of Private Eby and Private Kurtz are:
    4751   i.   Private[15] Kurtz.
    4752   ii.   Private Kurtz.
    4753   iii.   Private Kurtz.
    4754   iv.   Private Kurtz.

3470. Private[14] Gehman (Private[13], Sarah Lucinda[12] Eby, Sarah Lucinda[11] Hershey, Peter[10], Jacob[9], John[8], Jacob Snavely[7], Andrew Stauffer[6], Adelheid Galle[5] Stouffer, Daniel[4], Christian[3], Hans[2], Hans[1]) He married **Private Burkett**.

Child of Private Gehman and Private Burkett is:
+ 4755 i. Private[15] Gehman.

3471. Private[14] Gehman (Private[13], Sarah Lucinda[12] Eby, Sarah Lucinda[11] Hershey, Peter[10], Jacob[9], John[8], Jacob Snavely[7], Andrew Stauffer[6], Adelheid Galle[5] Stouffer, Daniel[4], Christian[3], Hans[2], Hans[1]) He married **Private Beachy**.

Child of Private Gehman and Private Beachy is:
+ 4756 i. Private[15] Gehman.

3472. Private[14] Gehman (Private[13], Sarah Lucinda[12] Eby, Sarah Lucinda[11] Hershey, Peter[10], Jacob[9], John[8], Jacob Snavely[7], Andrew Stauffer[6], Adelheid Galle[5] Stouffer, Daniel[4], Christian[3], Hans[2], Hans[1]) He married **Private Horst**.

Child of Private Gehman and Private Horst is:
+ 4757 i. Private[15] Gehman.

3473. Private[14] Gehman (Private[13], Sarah Lucinda[12] Eby, Sarah Lucinda[11] Hershey, Peter[10], Jacob[9], John[8], Jacob Snavely[7], Andrew Stauffer[6], Adelheid Galle[5] Stouffer, Daniel[4], Christian[3], Hans[2], Hans[1]) She married **Private Martin**.

Child of Private Gehman and Private Martin is:
+ 4758 i. Private[15] Martin.

3474. Private[14] Gehman (Private[13], Sarah Lucinda[12] Eby, Sarah Lucinda[11] Hershey, Peter[10], Jacob[9], John[8], Jacob Snavely[7], Andrew Stauffer[6], Adelheid Galle[5] Stouffer, Daniel[4], Christian[3], Hans[2], Hans[1]) She married **Private Heimbach**.

Child of Private Gehman and Private Heimbach is:
+ 4759 i. Private[15] Heimbach.

3476. Private[14] Gehman (Private[13], Sarah Lucinda[12] Eby, Sarah Lucinda[11] Hershey, Peter[10], Jacob[9], John[8], Jacob Snavely[7], Andrew Stauffer[6], Adelheid Galle[5] Stouffer, Daniel[4], Christian[3], Hans[2], Hans[1]) He married **Private Metzler**.

Children of Private Gehman and Private Metzler are:
+ 4760 i. Private[15] Gehman.
+ 4761 ii. Private Gehman.
+ 4762 iii. Private Gehman.

3478. Private[14] Gehman (Arthur E.[13], Sarah Lucinda[12] Eby, Sarah Lucinda[11] Hershey, Peter[10], Jacob[9], John[8], Jacob Snavely[7], Andrew Stauffer[6], Adelheid Galle[5] Stouffer, Daniel[4], Christian[3], Hans[2], Hans[1]) He married **Private Rice**.

Children of Private Gehman and Private Rice are:
+ 4763 i. Private[15] Gehman.
+ 4764 ii. Private Gehman.

3479. Private[14] Gehman (Arthur E.[13], Sarah Lucinda[12] Eby, Sarah Lucinda[11] Hershey, Peter[10], Jacob[9], John[8], Jacob Snavely[7], Andrew Stauffer[6], Adelheid Galle[5] Stouffer, Daniel[4], Christian[3], Hans[2], Hans[1]) He married **Private Brendle**.

Child of Private Gehman and Private Brendle is:
+ 4765 i. Todd Matthew[15] Gehman, born July 26, 1984; died July 26, 1984.

3480. Private[14] Gehman (Arthur E.[13], Sarah Lucinda[12] Eby, Sarah Lucinda[11] Hershey, Peter[10], Jacob[9], John[8], Jacob Snavely[7], Andrew Stauffer[6], Adelheid Galle[5] Stouffer, Daniel[4], Christian[3], Hans[2], Hans[1]) She married **Private Landis**.

Children of Private Gehman and Private Landis are:
+ 4766 i. Private[15] Landis.
+ 4767 ii. Private Landis.

3482. Private[14] Gehman (John E.[13], Sarah Lucinda[12] Eby, Sarah Lucinda[11] Hershey, Peter[10], Jacob[9], John[8], Jacob Snavely[7], Andrew Stauffer[6], Adelheid Galle[5] Stouffer, Daniel[4], Christian[3], Hans[2], Hans[1]) She married **Private Lauver**.

Children of Private Gehman and Private Lauver are:
- 4768   i. Private[15] Lauver.
- 4769   ii. Private Lauver.

3484. Private[14] Gehman (John E.[13], Sarah Lucinda[12] Eby, Sarah Lucinda[11] Hershey, Peter[10], Jacob[9], John[8], Jacob Snavely[7], Andrew Stauffer[6], Adelheid Galle[5] Stouffer, Daniel[4], Christian[3], Hans[2], Hans[1]) He married **Private Dien**.

Children of Private Gehman and Private Dien are:
- 4770   i. Private[15] Gehman.
- 4771   ii. Private Gehman.

3485. Private[14] Gehman (John E.[13], Sarah Lucinda[12] Eby, Sarah Lucinda[11] Hershey, Peter[10], Jacob[9], John[8], Jacob Snavely[7], Andrew Stauffer[6], Adelheid Galle[5] Stouffer, Daniel[4], Christian[3], Hans[2], Hans[1]) He married **Private Metzler**.

Children of Private Gehman and Private Metzler are:
- 4772   i. Private[15] Gehman.
- 4773   ii. Private Gehman.
- 4774   iii. Private Gehman.

3487. Private[14] Gehman (John E.[13], Sarah Lucinda[12] Eby, Sarah Lucinda[11] Hershey, Peter[10], Jacob[9], John[8], Jacob Snavely[7], Andrew Stauffer[6], Adelheid Galle[5] Stouffer, Daniel[4], Christian[3], Hans[2], Hans[1]) She married **Private Eicher**.

Child of Private Gehman and Private Eicher is:
- 4775   i. Private[15] Eicher.

3488. Private[14] Groff (Edith Elizabeth[13] Gehman, Sarah Lucinda[12] Eby, Sarah Lucinda[11] Hershey, Peter[10], Jacob[9], John[8], Jacob Snavely[7], Andrew Stauffer[6], Adelheid Galle[5] Stouffer, Daniel[4], Christian[3], Hans[2], Hans[1]) He married **Private Heimbach**.

Child of Private Groff and Private Heimbach is:
- 4776   i. Private[15] Groff.

3489. Private[14] Groff (Edith Elizabeth[13] Gehman, Sarah Lucinda[12] Eby, Sarah Lucinda[11] Hershey, Peter[10], Jacob[9], John[8], Jacob Snavely[7], Andrew Stauffer[6], Adelheid Galle[5] Stouffer, Daniel[4], Christian[3], Hans[2], Hans[1]) She married **Private Yoder**.

Children of Private Groff and Private Yoder are:
- 4777   i. Private[15] Yoder.
- 4778   ii. Private Yoder.
- 4779   iii. Private Yoder.
- 4780   iv. Private Yoder.

3490. Private[14] Groff (Edith Elizabeth[13] Gehman, Sarah Lucinda[12] Eby, Sarah Lucinda[11] Hershey, Peter[10], Jacob[9], John[8], Jacob Snavely[7], Andrew Stauffer[6], Adelheid Galle[5] Stouffer, Daniel[4], Christian[3], Hans[2], Hans[1]) He married **Private Yoder**.

Children of Private Groff and Private Yoder are:
- 4781   i. Private[15] Groff.
- 4782   ii. Private Groff.
- 4783   iii. Private Groff.

3491. Private[14] Groff (Edith Elizabeth[13] Gehman, Sarah Lucinda[12] Eby, Sarah Lucinda[11] Hershey, Peter[10], Jacob[9], John[8], Jacob Snavely[7], Andrew Stauffer[6], Adelheid Galle[5] Stouffer, Daniel[4], Christian[3], Hans[2], Hans[1]) He married **Private Jutzi**.

Children of Private Groff and Private Jutzi are:
- 4784   i. Private[15] Groff.
- 4785   ii. Private Groff.
- 4786   iii. Private Groff.
- 4787   iv. Private Groff.

3492. Private[14] Groff (Edith Elizabeth[13] Gehman, Sarah Lucinda[12] Eby, Sarah Lucinda[11] Hershey, Peter[10], Jacob[9], John[8], Jacob

Snavely[7], Andrew Stauffer[6], Adelheid Galle[5] Stouffer, Daniel[4], Christian[3], Hans[2], Hans[1]) He married **Private Weaver**.

Children of Private Groff and Private Weaver are:

4788	i.	Private[15] Groff.
4789	ii.	Private Groff.
4790	iii.	Private Groff.
4791	iv.	Private Groff.

3493. Private[14] Groff (Edith Elizabeth[13] Gehman, Sarah Lucinda[12] Eby, Sarah Lucinda[11] Hershey, Peter[10], Jacob[9], John[8], Jacob Snavely[7], Andrew Stauffer[6], Adelheid Galle[5] Stouffer, Daniel[4], Christian[3], Hans[2], Hans[1]) He married **Private Bomberger**.

Children of Private Groff and Private Bomberger are:
- 4792   i. Private[15] Groff.
- 4793   ii. Private Groff.
- 4794   iii. Private Groff.

3495. Private[14] Rudy (Lucy E.[13] Gehman, Sarah Lucinda[12] Eby, Sarah Lucinda[11] Hershey, Peter[10], Jacob[9], John[8], Jacob Snavely[7], Andrew Stauffer[6], Adelheid Galle[5] Stouffer, Daniel[4], Christian[3], Hans[2], Hans[1]) He married **Private Jantzi**.

Child of Private Rudy and Private Jantzi is:
- 4795   i. Private[15] Rudy.

3500. Private[14] Gehman (Harry Jacob[13], Sarah Lucinda[12] Eby, Sarah Lucinda[11] Hershey, Peter[10], Jacob[9], John[8], Jacob Snavely[7], Andrew Stauffer[6], Adelheid Galle[5] Stouffer, Daniel[4], Christian[3], Hans[2], Hans[1]) He married **Private High**.

Child of Private Gehman and Private High is:
- 4796   i. Private[15] Gehman.

3501. Private[14] Gehman (Harry Jacob[13], Sarah Lucinda[12] Eby, Sarah Lucinda[11] Hershey, Peter[10], Jacob[9], John[8], Jacob Snavely[7], Andrew Stauffer[6], Adelheid Galle[5] Stouffer, Daniel[4], Christian[3], Hans[2], Hans[1]) She married **Private Kreider**.

Children of Private Gehman and Private Kreider are:
- 4797   i. Private[15] Kreider.
- 4798   ii. Private Kreider.
- 4799   iii. Private Kreider.
- 4800   iv. Private Kreider.

3502. Private[14] Gehman (Harry Jacob[13], Sarah Lucinda[12] Eby, Sarah Lucinda[11] Hershey, Peter[10], Jacob[9], John[8], Jacob Snavely[7], Andrew Stauffer[6], Adelheid Galle[5] Stouffer, Daniel[4], Christian[3], Hans[2], Hans[1]) He married **Private Kreider**.

Children of Private Gehman and Private Kreider are:
- 4801   i. Private[15] Gehman.
- 4802   ii. Private Gehman.

3503. Private[14] Gehman (Harry Jacob[13], Sarah Lucinda[12] Eby, Sarah Lucinda[11] Hershey, Peter[10], Jacob[9], John[8], Jacob Snavely[7], Andrew Stauffer[6], Adelheid Galle[5] Stouffer, Daniel[4], Christian[3], Hans[2], Hans[1]) He married **Private High**.

Children of Private Gehman and Private High are:
- 4803   i. Private[15] Gehman.
- 4804   ii. Private Gehman.

3504. Private[14] Gehman (Harry Jacob[13], Sarah Lucinda[12] Eby, Sarah Lucinda[11] Hershey, Peter[10], Jacob[9], John[8], Jacob Snavely[7], Andrew Stauffer[6], Adelheid Galle[5] Stouffer, Daniel[4], Christian[3], Hans[2], Hans[1]) He married **Private Shertzer**.

Children of Private Gehman and Private Shertzer are:
- 4805   i. Private[15] Gehman.
- 4806   ii. Private Gehman.
- 4807   iii. Private Gehman.
- 4808   iv. Private Gehman.

4809   v.   Private Gehman.
4810   vi.   Private Gehman.

3517. Private[14] Eby (Martin Z.[13], Henry Musser[12], Sarah Lucinda[11] Hershey, Peter[10], Jacob[9], John[8], Jacob Snavely[7], Andrew Stauffer[6], Adelheid Galle[5] Stouffer, Daniel[4], Christian[3], Hans[2], Hans[1]) He married **Private Greiser**.

Children of Private Eby and Private Greiser are:
4811   i.   Private[15] Eby.
4812   ii.   Private Eby.

3520. Private[14] Miller (Ethel Z.[13] Eby, Henry Musser[12], Sarah Lucinda[11] Hershey, Peter[10], Jacob[9], John[8], Jacob Snavely[7], Andrew Stauffer[6], Adelheid Galle[5] Stouffer, Daniel[4], Christian[3], Hans[2], Hans[1]) He married **Private Pickel**.

Children of Private Miller and Private Pickel are:
4813   i.   Private[15] Miller.
4814   ii.   Private Simpson.
4815   iii.   Private Short.
4816   iv.   Private Short.

3521. Private[14] Miller (Ethel Z.[13] Eby, Henry Musser[12], Sarah Lucinda[11] Hershey, Peter[10], Jacob[9], John[8], Jacob Snavely[7], Andrew Stauffer[6], Adelheid Galle[5] Stouffer, Daniel[4], Christian[3], Hans[2], Hans[1]) He married **Private Weng**.

Children of Private Miller and Private Weng are:
4817   i.   Private[15] Miller.
4818   ii.   Private Miller.
4819   iii.   Private Miller.

3529. Private[14] Weaver (Mary Z.[13] Eby, Henry Musser[12], Sarah Lucinda[11] Hershey, Peter[10], Jacob[9], John[8], Jacob Snavely[7], Andrew Stauffer[6], Adelheid Galle[5] Stouffer, Daniel[4], Christian[3], Hans[2], Hans[1]) She married **Private Aguirre**.

Children of Private Weaver and Private Aguirre are:
4820   i.   Private[15] Aguirre.
4821   ii.   Private Aguirre.

3530. Private[14] Weaver (Mary Z.[13] Eby, Henry Musser[12], Sarah Lucinda[11] Hershey, Peter[10], Jacob[9], John[8], Jacob Snavely[7], Andrew Stauffer[6], Adelheid Galle[5] Stouffer, Daniel[4], Christian[3], Hans[2], Hans[1]) She married **Private Glick**.

Children of Private Weaver and Private Glick are:
4822   i.   Private[15] Glick.
4823   ii.   Private Glick.

3534. Private[14] Zeiset (Private[13] Martin, Anna Martha[12] Eby, Sarah Lucinda[11] Hershey, Peter[10], Jacob[9], John[8], Jacob Snavely[7], Andrew Stauffer[6], Adelheid Galle[5] Stouffer, Daniel[4], Christian[3], Hans[2], Hans[1]) He married **Private Dombach**.

Child of Private Zeiset and Private Dombach is:
4824   i.   Private[15] Zeiset.

3537. Private[14] Martin (Clarence E.[13], Anna Martha[12] Eby, Sarah Lucinda[11] Hershey, Peter[10], Jacob[9], John[8], Jacob Snavely[7], Andrew Stauffer[6], Adelheid Galle[5] Stouffer, Daniel[4], Christian[3], Hans[2], Hans[1]) She married **Private Weaver**.

Children of Private Martin and Private Weaver are:
4825   i.   Private[15] Weaver.
4826   ii.   Private Weaver.

3538. Private[14] Martin (Clarence E.[13], Anna Martha[12] Eby, Sarah Lucinda[11] Hershey, Peter[10], Jacob[9], John[8], Jacob Snavely[7], Andrew Stauffer[6], Adelheid Galle[5] Stouffer, Daniel[4], Christian[3], Hans[2], Hans[1]) He married **Private Zimmerman**.

Children of Private Martin and Private Zimmerman are:

4827   i.   Private[15] Martin.
4828   ii.   Private Martin.
4829   iii.   Private Martin.
4830   iv.   Private Martin.

3539. Private[14] Martin (Clarence E.[13], Anna Martha[12] Eby, Sarah Lucinda[11] Hershey, Peter[10], Jacob[9], John[8], Jacob Snavely[7], Andrew Stauffer[6], Adelheid Galle[5] Stouffer, Daniel[4], Christian[3], Hans[2], Hans[1]) She married **Private Kurtz**.

Children of Private Martin and Private Kurtz are:
4831   i.   Private[15] Kurtz.
4832   ii.   Private Kurtz.

3540. Private[14] Martin (Clarence E.[13], Anna Martha[12] Eby, Sarah Lucinda[11] Hershey, Peter[10], Jacob[9], John[8], Jacob Snavely[7], Andrew Stauffer[6], Adelheid Galle[5] Stouffer, Daniel[4], Christian[3], Hans[2], Hans[1]) He married **Private Hoover**.

Children of Private Martin and Private Hoover are:
4833   i.   Private[15] Martin.
4834   ii.   Private Martin.
4835   iii.   Private Martin.
4836   iv.   Private Martin.

3541. Private[14] Martin (Clarence E.[13], Anna Martha[12] Eby, Sarah Lucinda[11] Hershey, Peter[10], Jacob[9], John[8], Jacob Snavely[7], Andrew Stauffer[6], Adelheid Galle[5] Stouffer, Daniel[4], Christian[3], Hans[2], Hans[1]) He married **Private Good**.

Children of Private Martin and Private Good are:
4837   i.   Private[15] Martin.
4838   ii.   Private Martin. He married Private Steffy.
4839   iii.   Private Martin.

3543. Private[14] Martin (Mary E.[13], Anna Martha[12] Eby, Sarah Lucinda[11] Hershey, Peter[10], Jacob[9], John[8], Jacob Snavely[7], Andrew Stauffer[6], Adelheid Galle[5] Stouffer, Daniel[4], Christian[3], Hans[2], Hans[1]) She married **Private Thomas**.

Children of Private Martin and Private Thomas are:
4840   i.   Private[15] Thomas.
4841   ii.   Private Thomas.

3544. Private[14] Martin (Paul E.[13], Anna Martha[12] Eby, Sarah Lucinda[11] Hershey, Peter[10], Jacob[9], John[8], Jacob Snavely[7], Andrew Stauffer[6], Adelheid Galle[5] Stouffer, Daniel[4], Christian[3], Hans[2], Hans[1]) He married **Private Nolt**.

Child of Private Martin and Private Nolt is:
4842   i.   Private[15] Martin.

3545. Private[14] Martin (Paul E.[13], Anna Martha[12] Eby, Sarah Lucinda[11] Hershey, Peter[10], Jacob[9], John[8], Jacob Snavely[7], Andrew Stauffer[6], Adelheid Galle[5] Stouffer, Daniel[4], Christian[3], Hans[2], Hans[1]) She married **Private Hurst**.

Children of Private Martin and Private Hurst are:
4843   i.   Private[15] Hurst.
4844   ii.   Private Hurst.
4845   iii.   Private Hurst.

3546. Private[14] Martin (Paul E.[13], Anna Martha[12] Eby, Sarah Lucinda[11] Hershey, Peter[10], Jacob[9], John[8], Jacob Snavely[7], Andrew Stauffer[6], Adelheid Galle[5] Stouffer, Daniel[4], Christian[3], Hans[2], Hans[1]) He married **Private Ziegler**.

Children of Private Martin and Private Ziegler are:
4846   i.   Private[15] Martin.
4847   ii.   Private Martin.
4848   iii.   Private Martin.

3547. Private[14] Martin (Earl E.[13], Anna Martha[12] Eby, Sarah Lucinda[11] Hershey, Peter[10], Jacob[9], John[8], Jacob Snavely[7], Andrew Stauffer[6], Adelheid Galle[5] Stouffer, Daniel[4], Christian[3], Hans[2], Hans[1]) She married **Private Good**.

Child of Private Martin and Private Good is:
- 4849   i.   Private[15] Good.

3548. Private[14] Martin (Earl E.[13], Anna Martha[12] Eby, Sarah Lucinda[11] Hershey, Peter[10], Jacob[9], John[8], Jacob Snavely[7], Andrew Stauffer[6], Adelheid Galle[5] Stouffer, Daniel[4], Christian[3], Hans[2], Hans[1]) She married **Private Eberly**.

Children of Private Martin and Private Eberly are:
- 4850   i.   Private[15] Eberly.
- 4851   ii.   Private Eberly.

3555. Private[14] Eby (Private[13], Aaron Buckwalter[12], Sarah Lucinda[11] Hershey, Peter[10], Jacob[9], John[8], Jacob Snavely[7], Andrew Stauffer[6], Adelheid Galle[5] Stouffer, Daniel[4], Christian[3], Hans[2], Hans[1]) She married **Private Groff**.

Child of Private Eby and Private Groff is:
- 4852   i.   Private[15] Groff.

3562. Private[14] Eby (Private[13], Aaron Buckwalter[12], Sarah Lucinda[11] Hershey, Peter[10], Jacob[9], John[8], Jacob Snavely[7], Andrew Stauffer[6], Adelheid Galle[5] Stouffer, Daniel[4], Christian[3], Hans[2], Hans[1]) She married **Private Nolt**.

Children of Private Eby and Private Nolt are:
- 4853   i.   Private[15] Nolt.
- 4854   ii.   Private Nolt.

3564. Private[14] Eby (Richard S.[13], Aaron Buckwalter[12], Sarah Lucinda[11] Hershey, Peter[10], Jacob[9], John[8], Jacob Snavely[7], Andrew Stauffer[6], Adelheid Galle[5] Stouffer, Daniel[4], Christian[3], Hans[2], Hans[1]) He married **Private Hershey**.

Children of Private Eby and Private Hershey are:
- 4855   i.   Private[15] Eby.
- 4856   ii.   Private Eby.
- 4857   iii.   Private Eby.

3566. Private[14] Eby (Richard S.[13], Aaron Buckwalter[12], Sarah Lucinda[11] Hershey, Peter[10], Jacob[9], John[8], Jacob Snavely[7], Andrew Stauffer[6], Adelheid Galle[5] Stouffer, Daniel[4], Christian[3], Hans[2], Hans[1]) She married **Private Delgado**.

Children of Private Eby and Private Delgado are:
- 4858   i.   Private[15] Delgado.
- 4859   ii.   Private Delgado.

3567. Private[14] Eby (Richard S.[13], Aaron Buckwalter[12], Sarah Lucinda[11] Hershey, Peter[10], Jacob[9], John[8], Jacob Snavely[7], Andrew Stauffer[6], Adelheid Galle[5] Stouffer, Daniel[4], Christian[3], Hans[2], Hans[1]) He married **Private Beachy**.

Child of Private Eby and Private Beachy is:
- 4860   i.   Private[15] Eby.

3568. Private[14] Eby (Richard S.[13], Aaron Buckwalter[12], Sarah Lucinda[11] Hershey, Peter[10], Jacob[9], John[8], Jacob Snavely[7], Andrew Stauffer[6], Adelheid Galle[5] Stouffer, Daniel[4], Christian[3], Hans[2], Hans[1]) He married **Private Zimmerman**.

Children of Private Eby and Private Zimmerman are:
- 4861   i.   Private[15] Eby.
- 4862   ii.   Private Eby.

3569. Private[14] Eby (Richard S.[13], Aaron Buckwalter[12], Sarah Lucinda[11] Hershey, Peter[10], Jacob[9], John[8], Jacob Snavely[7], Andrew Stauffer[6], Adelheid Galle[5] Stouffer, Daniel[4], Christian[3], Hans[2], Hans[1]) She married **Private Ober**.

Children of Private Eby and Private Ober are:
- 4863   i.   Private[15] Ober.

4864 ii. Private Ober.
4865 iii. Private Ober.

3588. Private[14] Crouthamel (Erma E.[13] Hershey, Galen Warren[12], Isaiah B.[11], Peter[10], Jacob[9], John[8], Jacob Snavely[7], Andrew Stauffer[6], Adelheid Galle[5] Stouffer, Daniel[4], Christian[3], Hans[2], Hans[1]) She married **Private Moyer**.

Children of Private Crouthamel and Private Moyer are:
4866 i. Private[15] Moyer.
4867 ii. Private Moyer. She married Private Wood.

3589. Private[14] Crouthamel (Erma E.[13] Hershey, Galen Warren[12], Isaiah B.[11], Peter[10], Jacob[9], John[8], Jacob Snavely[7], Andrew Stauffer[6], Adelheid Galle[5] Stouffer, Daniel[4], Christian[3], Hans[2], Hans[1]) She married **(1) Private Pier**.   She married **(2) Private O'Connell**.

Child of Private Crouthamel and Private Pier is:
4868 i. Private[15] Pier.

Child of Private Crouthamel and Private O'Connell is:
4869 i. Private[15] O'Connell.

3590. Private[14] Crouthamel (Erma E.[13] Hershey, Galen Warren[12], Isaiah B.[11], Peter[10], Jacob[9], John[8], Jacob Snavely[7], Andrew Stauffer[6], Adelheid Galle[5] Stouffer, Daniel[4], Christian[3], Hans[2], Hans[1]) He married **Private Baum**.

Children of Private Crouthamel and Private Baum are:
4870 i. Private[15] Crouthamel.
4871 ii. Private Crouthamel.

3591. Private[14] Hershey (Galen Clair[13], Galen Warren[12], Isaiah B.[11], Peter[10], Jacob[9], John[8], Jacob Snavely[7], Andrew Stauffer[6], Adelheid Galle[5] Stouffer, Daniel[4], Christian[3], Hans[2], Hans[1]) He married **Private Manley**.

Children of Private Hershey and Private Manley are:
4872 i. Private[15] Hershey.
4873 ii. Private Hershey.

3592. Private[14] Hershey (Galen Clair[13], Galen Warren[12], Isaiah B.[11], Peter[10], Jacob[9], John[8], Jacob Snavely[7], Andrew Stauffer[6], Adelheid Galle[5] Stouffer, Daniel[4], Christian[3], Hans[2], Hans[1]) She married **Private Glancey**.

Children of Private Hershey and Private Glancey are:
4874 i. Private[15] Glancey.
4875 ii. Private Glancey.

3594. Private[14] Hershey (Private[13], Henry Clay[12], Enos Jacob[11], Peter[10], Jacob[9], John[8], Jacob Snavely[7], Andrew Stauffer[6], Adelheid Galle[5] Stouffer, Daniel[4], Christian[3], Hans[2], Hans[1]) She married **Private Nyeholt**.

Child of Private Hershey and Private Nyeholt is:
4876 i. Private[15] Nyeholt.

3600. Private[14] Hershey (Private[13], Henry Clay[12], Enos Jacob[11], Peter[10], Jacob[9], John[8], Jacob Snavely[7], Andrew Stauffer[6], Adelheid Galle[5] Stouffer, Daniel[4], Christian[3], Hans[2], Hans[1]) She married **Private Miller**.

Child of Private Hershey and Private Miller is:
4877 i. Private[15] Miller.

3601. Private[14] Hershey (Private[13], Henry Clay[12], Enos Jacob[11], Peter[10], Jacob[9], John[8], Jacob Snavely[7], Andrew Stauffer[6], Adelheid Galle[5] Stouffer, Daniel[4], Christian[3], Hans[2], Hans[1]) He married **Private Johnson**.

Children of Private Hershey and Private Johnson are:
4878 i. Private[15] Hershey.

4879   ii.   Private Hershey.

3605. Private[14] **Metzler** (Hazel Pauline[13] Hershey, Henry Clay[12], Enos Jacob[11], Peter[10], Jacob[9], John[8], Jacob Snavely[7], Andrew Stauffer[6], Adelheid Galle[5] Stouffer, Daniel[4], Christian[3], Hans[2], Hans[1]) He married **Private Grason**.

Children of Private Metzler and Private Grason are:
4880   i.   Private[15] Metzler.
4881   ii.   Private Metzler.

3607. Private[14] **Hershey** (Ralph Glenn[13], Henry Clay[12], Enos Jacob[11], Peter[10], Jacob[9], John[8], Jacob Snavely[7], Andrew Stauffer[6], Adelheid Galle[5] Stouffer, Daniel[4], Christian[3], Hans[2], Hans[1]) He married **Private McSparron**.

Children of Private Hershey and Private McSparron are:
4882   i.   Private[15] Hershey.
4883   ii.   Private Hershey.
4884   iii.   Private Hershey.

3608. Private[14] **Hershey** (Ralph Glenn[13], Henry Clay[12], Enos Jacob[11], Peter[10], Jacob[9], John[8], Jacob Snavely[7], Andrew Stauffer[6], Adelheid Galle[5] Stouffer, Daniel[4], Christian[3], Hans[2], Hans[1]) She married **Private Hershey**.

Children of Private Hershey and Private Hershey are:
4885   i.   Private[15] Hershey.
4886   ii.   Private Hershey.

3609. Private[14] **Hershey** (Ralph Glenn[13], Henry Clay[12], Enos Jacob[11], Peter[10], Jacob[9], John[8], Jacob Snavely[7], Andrew Stauffer[6], Adelheid Galle[5] Stouffer, Daniel[4], Christian[3], Hans[2], Hans[1]) He married **Private Long**.

Children of Private Hershey and Private Long are:
4887   i.   Private[15] Hershey.
4888   ii.   Private Hershey.
4889   iii.   Private Hershey.

3610. Private[14] **Kreider** (Gladys Edna[13] Hershey, Henry Clay[12], Enos Jacob[11], Peter[10], Jacob[9], John[8], Jacob Snavely[7], Andrew Stauffer[6], Adelheid Galle[5] Stouffer, Daniel[4], Christian[3], Hans[2], Hans[1]) She married **Private Hoffman**.

Children of Private Kreider and Private Hoffman are:
4890   i.   Private[15] Hoffman.
4891   ii.   Private Hoffman.
4892   iii.   Private Hoffman.

3612. Private[14] **Kreider** (Gladys Edna[13] Hershey, Henry Clay[12], Enos Jacob[11], Peter[10], Jacob[9], John[8], Jacob Snavely[7], Andrew Stauffer[6], Adelheid Galle[5] Stouffer, Daniel[4], Christian[3], Hans[2], Hans[1]) He married **Private Wenger**.

Children of Private Kreider and Private Wenger are:
4893   i.   Private[15] Kreider.
4894   ii.   Private Kreider.
4895   iii.   Private Kreider.

3613. Private[14] **Kreider** (Gladys Edna[13] Hershey, Henry Clay[12], Enos Jacob[11], Peter[10], Jacob[9], John[8], Jacob Snavely[7], Andrew Stauffer[6], Adelheid Galle[5] Stouffer, Daniel[4], Christian[3], Hans[2], Hans[1]) She married **Private Gordley**.

Children of Private Kreider and Private Gordley are:
4896   i.   Private[15] Gordley.
4897   ii.   Private Gordley.
4898   iii.   Private Gordley.

3618. Private[14] **Hershey** (Clifford Eby[13], Henry Clay[12], Enos Jacob[11], Peter[10], Jacob[9], John[8], Jacob Snavely[7], Andrew Stauffer[6], Adelheid Galle[5] Stouffer, Daniel[4], Christian[3], Hans[2], Hans[1]) He married **Private Rutter**.

Children of Private Hershey and Private Rutter are:
- 4899 i. Private[15] Hershey.
- 4900 ii. Private Hershey.

3619. Private[14] Hershey (Clifford Eby[13], Henry Clay[12], Enos Jacob[11], Peter[10], Jacob[9], John[8], Jacob Snavely[7], Andrew Stauffer[6], Adelheid Galle[5] Stouffer, Daniel[4], Christian[3], Hans[2], Hans[1]) He married **Private Napoli**.

Children of Private Hershey and Private Napoli are:
- 4901 i. Private[15] Hershey.
- 4902 ii. Private Hershey.

3632. Private[14] Martin (Private[13] Hershey, Mark Eby[12], Enos Jacob[11], Peter[10], Jacob[9], John[8], Jacob Snavely[7], Andrew Stauffer[6], Adelheid Galle[5] Stouffer, Daniel[4], Christian[3], Hans[2], Hans[1]) He married **Private Groff**.

Children of Private Martin and Private Groff are:
- 4903 i. Private[15] Martin.
- 4904 ii. Private Martin.

3642. Private[14] Bender (Private[13] Hershey, Mark Eby[12], Enos Jacob[11], Peter[10], Jacob[9], John[8], Jacob Snavely[7], Andrew Stauffer[6], Adelheid Galle[5] Stouffer, Daniel[4], Christian[3], Hans[2], Hans[1]) She married **Private Brenneman**.

Children of Private Bender and Private Brenneman are:
- 4905 i. Private[15] Brenneman.
- 4906 ii. Private Brenneman.

3643. Private[14] Hershey (Private[13], Mark Eby[12], Enos Jacob[11], Peter[10], Jacob[9], John[8], Jacob Snavely[7], Andrew Stauffer[6], Adelheid Galle[5] Stouffer, Daniel[4], Christian[3], Hans[2], Hans[1]) She married **Private Yoder**.

Children of Private Hershey and Private Yoder are:
- 4907 i. Private[15] Yoder.
- 4908 ii. Private Yoder.

3644. Private[14] Hershey (Private[13], Mark Eby[12], Enos Jacob[11], Peter[10], Jacob[9], John[8], Jacob Snavely[7], Andrew Stauffer[6], Adelheid Galle[5] Stouffer, Daniel[4], Christian[3], Hans[2], Hans[1]) She married **Private Rohrer**.

Children of Private Hershey and Private Rohrer are:
- 4909 i. Private[15] Rohrer.
- 4910 ii. Private Rohrer.

3645. Private[14] Hershey (Private[13], Mark Eby[12], Enos Jacob[11], Peter[10], Jacob[9], John[8], Jacob Snavely[7], Andrew Stauffer[6], Adelheid Galle[5] Stouffer, Daniel[4], Christian[3], Hans[2], Hans[1]) She married **Private Lapp**.

Children of Private Hershey and Private Lapp are:
- 4911 i. Private[15] Lapp.
- 4912 ii. Private Lapp.

3646. Private[14] Hershey (Private[13], Mark Eby[12], Enos Jacob[11], Peter[10], Jacob[9], John[8], Jacob Snavely[7], Andrew Stauffer[6], Adelheid Galle[5] Stouffer, Daniel[4], Christian[3], Hans[2], Hans[1]) He married **Private Saxton**.

Children of Private Hershey and Private Saxton are:
- 4913 i. Private[15] Hershey.
- 4914 ii. Private Hershey.

3647. Private[14] Herr (Private[13] Hershey, David Warren[12], Enos Jacob[11], Peter[10], Jacob[9], John[8], Jacob Snavely[7], Andrew Stauffer[6], Adelheid Galle[5] Stouffer, Daniel[4], Christian[3], Hans[2], Hans[1]) He married **Private Newlin**.

Child of Private Herr and Private Newlin is:

4915 i. Private[15] Herr.

3650. Private[14] Hershey (Vincent Denlinger[13], David Warren[12], Enos Jacob[11], Peter[10], Jacob[9], John[8], Jacob Snavely[7], Andrew Stauffer[6], Adelheid Galle[5] Stouffer, Daniel[4], Christian[3], Hans[2], Hans[1]) He married **Private Stauffer**.

Child of Private Hershey and Private Stauffer is:
 4916 i. Private[15] Hershey.

3652. Private[14] Hershey (Vincent Denlinger[13], David Warren[12], Enos Jacob[11], Peter[10], Jacob[9], John[8], Jacob Snavely[7], Andrew Stauffer[6], Adelheid Galle[5] Stouffer, Daniel[4], Christian[3], Hans[2], Hans[1]) He married **Private Coates**.

Child of Private Hershey and Private Coates is:
 4917 i. Private[15] Hershey.

3653. Private[14] Hershey (Vincent Denlinger[13], David Warren[12], Enos Jacob[11], Peter[10], Jacob[9], John[8], Jacob Snavely[7], Andrew Stauffer[6], Adelheid Galle[5] Stouffer, Daniel[4], Christian[3], Hans[2], Hans[1]) He married **Private Buzzard**.

Children of Private Hershey and Private Buzzard are:
 4918 i. Private[15] Hershey.
 4919 ii. Private Hershey.
 4920 iii. Private Hershey.

3656. Private[14] Ranck (Lester Hershey[13], Mary Helen[12] Hershey, Enos Jacob[11], Peter[10], Jacob[9], John[8], Jacob Snavely[7], Andrew Stauffer[6], Adelheid Galle[5] Stouffer, Daniel[4], Christian[3], Hans[2], Hans[1]) He married **Private Nissley**.

Children of Private Ranck and Private Nissley are:
 4921 i. Private[15] Ranck.
 4922 ii. Private Ranck.
 4923 iii. Private Ranck.

3657. Private[14] Ranck (Lester Hershey[13], Mary Helen[12] Hershey, Enos Jacob[11], Peter[10], Jacob[9], John[8], Jacob Snavely[7], Andrew Stauffer[6], Adelheid Galle[5] Stouffer, Daniel[4], Christian[3], Hans[2], Hans[1]) She married **Private Thomas**.

Children of Private Ranck and Private Thomas are:
 4924 i. Private[15] Thomas.
 4925 ii. Private Thomas.
 4926 iii. Private Thomas.

3660. Private[14] Ranck (Arthur Eby[13], Mary Helen[12] Hershey, Enos Jacob[11], Peter[10], Jacob[9], John[8], Jacob Snavely[7], Andrew Stauffer[6], Adelheid Galle[5] Stouffer, Daniel[4], Christian[3], Hans[2], Hans[1]) He married **Private Showalter**.

Children of Private Ranck and Private Showalter are:
 4927 i. Private[15] Ranck.
 4928 ii. Private Ranck.

3664. Private[14] Ranck (Donald Edwin[13], Mary Helen[12] Hershey, Enos Jacob[11], Peter[10], Jacob[9], John[8], Jacob Snavely[7], Andrew Stauffer[6], Adelheid Galle[5] Stouffer, Daniel[4], Christian[3], Hans[2], Hans[1]) She married **Private Yoder**.

Child of Private Ranck and Private Yoder is:
 4929 i. Private[15] Yoder.

3666. Private[14] Daman (Janet Potter[13] Hess, Clyde C.[12], Elizabeth[11] Hershey, Peter[10], Jacob[9], John[8], Jacob Snavely[7], Andrew Stauffer[6], Adelheid Galle[5] Stouffer, Daniel[4], Christian[3], Hans[2], Hans[1]) She married **Private Hauch**.

Child of Private Daman and Private Hauch is:
 4930 i. Private[15] Hauch.

3667. Private[14] Daman (Janet Potter[13] Hess, Clyde C.[12], Elizabeth[11] Hershey, Peter[10], Jacob[9], John[8], Jacob Snavely[7], Andrew Stauffer[6], Adelheid Galle[5] Stouffer, Daniel[4], Christian[3], Hans[2], Hans[1]) She married **Private Gates**.

Children of Private Daman and Private Gates are:
- 4931 i. Private[15] Gates.
- 4932 ii. Private Gates.

3673. Private[14] Hershey (Paul Kenneth[13], Paul Keene[12], Henry Peter[11], Peter[10], Jacob[9], John[8], Jacob Snavely[7], Andrew Stauffer[6], Adelheid Galle[5] Stouffer, Daniel[4], Christian[3], Hans[2], Hans[1]) She married **Private Murphy**.

Child of Private Hershey and Private Murphy is:
- 4933 i. Private[15] Murphy.

3677. Private[14] Hewes (Private[13] Pennock, Esther Elizabeth[12] Hershey, Martin Eby[11], Peter[10], Jacob[9], John[8], Jacob Snavely[7], Andrew Stauffer[6], Adelheid Galle[5] Stouffer, Daniel[4], Christian[3], Hans[2], Hans[1]) She married **Private Printz**.

Child of Private Hewes and Private Printz is:
- 4934 i. Private[15] Printz.

3678. Private[14] Hewes (Private[13] Pennock, Esther Elizabeth[12] Hershey, Martin Eby[11], Peter[10], Jacob[9], John[8], Jacob Snavely[7], Andrew Stauffer[6], Adelheid Galle[5] Stouffer, Daniel[4], Christian[3], Hans[2], Hans[1]) He married **Private Lichty**.

Children of Private Hewes and Private Lichty are:
- 4935 i. Private[15] Hewes.
- 4936 ii. Private Hewes.

3679. Private[14] Hewes (Private[13] Pennock, Esther Elizabeth[12] Hershey, Martin Eby[11], Peter[10], Jacob[9], John[8], Jacob Snavely[7], Andrew Stauffer[6], Adelheid Galle[5] Stouffer, Daniel[4], Christian[3], Hans[2], Hans[1]) She married **Private Mohr**.

Child of Private Hewes and Private Mohr is:
- 4937 i. Private[15] Mohr.

3683. Private[14] Skiles (Betty Louise[13] Pennock, Esther Elizabeth[12] Hershey, Martin Eby[11], Peter[10], Jacob[9], John[8], Jacob Snavely[7], Andrew Stauffer[6], Adelheid Galle[5] Stouffer, Daniel[4], Christian[3], Hans[2], Hans[1]) He married **Private Loriencz**.

Children of Private Skiles and Private Loriencz are:
- 4938 i. Private[15] Skiles.
- 4939 ii. Private Skiles.
- 4940 iii. Private Skiles.

3684. Private[14] Skiles (Betty Louise[13] Pennock, Esther Elizabeth[12] Hershey, Martin Eby[11], Peter[10], Jacob[9], John[8], Jacob Snavely[7], Andrew Stauffer[6], Adelheid Galle[5] Stouffer, Daniel[4], Christian[3], Hans[2], Hans[1]) He married **Private Johndrow**.

Child of Private Skiles and Private Johndrow is:
- 4941 i. Private[15] Skiles.

3686. Private[14] Rodgers (Private[13], Miriam Clara[12] Hershey, Martin Eby[11], Peter[10], Jacob[9], John[8], Jacob Snavely[7], Andrew Stauffer[6], Adelheid Galle[5] Stouffer, Daniel[4], Christian[3], Hans[2], Hans[1]) He married **Private Canning**.

Children of Private Rodgers and Private Canning are:
- 4942 i. Private[15] Rodgers.
- 4943 ii. Private Rodgers.

3702. Private[14] Richardson (Private[13] Hershey, Willis Daniel[12], Silas N.[11], Peter[10], Jacob[9], John[8], Jacob Snavely[7], Andrew Stauffer[6], Adelheid Galle[5] Stouffer, Daniel[4], Christian[3], Hans[2], Hans[1]) She married **Private Woods**.

Children of Private Richardson and Private Woods are:
- 4944 i. Private[15] Woods.
- 4945 ii. Private Woods.

3703. Private[14] Richardson (Private[13] Hershey, Willis Daniel[12], Silas N.[11], Peter[10], Jacob[9], John[8], Jacob Snavely[7], Andrew Stauffer[6], Adelheid Galle[5] Stouffer, Daniel[4], Christian[3], Hans[2], Hans[1]) She married **Private Mercer**.

Children of Private Richardson and Private Mercer are:
- 4946   i. Private[15] Mercer.
- 4947   ii. Private Mercer.
- 4948   iii. Private Mercer.

3705. Private[14] Summers (Private[13] Hershey, Willis Daniel[12], Silas N.[11], Peter[10], Jacob[9], John[8], Jacob Snavely[7], Andrew Stauffer[6], Adelheid Galle[5] Stouffer, Daniel[4], Christian[3], Hans[2], Hans[1]) She married **Private Shirk**.

Children of Private Summers and Private Shirk are:
- 4949   i. Private[15] Shirk.
- 4950   ii. Private Shirk.

3706. Private[14] Summers (Private[13] Hershey, Willis Daniel[12], Silas N.[11], Peter[10], Jacob[9], John[8], Jacob Snavely[7], Andrew Stauffer[6], Adelheid Galle[5] Stouffer, Daniel[4], Christian[3], Hans[2], Hans[1]) He married **Private Weston**.

Child of Private Summers and Private Weston is:
- 4951   i. Private[15] Summers.

3707. Private[14] Bomberger (Private[13] Hershey, Willis Daniel[12], Silas N.[11], Peter[10], Jacob[9], John[8], Jacob Snavely[7], Andrew Stauffer[6], Adelheid Galle[5] Stouffer, Daniel[4], Christian[3], Hans[2], Hans[1]) He married **Private Unknown**.

Children of Private Bomberger and Private Unknown are:
- 4952   i. Private[15] Bomberger.
- 4953   ii. Private Bomberger.

3708. Private[14] Hershey (Private[13], Willis Daniel[12], Silas N.[11], Peter[10], Jacob[9], John[8], Jacob Snavely[7], Andrew Stauffer[6], Adelheid Galle[5] Stouffer, Daniel[4], Christian[3], Hans[2], Hans[1]) She married **Private Dick**.

Children of Private Hershey and Private Dick are:
- 4954   i. Private[15] Hershey.
- 4955   ii. Private Hershey.

3709. Private[14] Hershey (Private[13], Willis Daniel[12], Silas N.[11], Peter[10], Jacob[9], John[8], Jacob Snavely[7], Andrew Stauffer[6], Adelheid Galle[5] Stouffer, Daniel[4], Christian[3], Hans[2], Hans[1]) He married **Private Wance**.

Children of Private Hershey and Private Wance are:
- 4956   i. Private[15] Hershey.
- 4957   ii. Private Hershey.
- 4958   iii. Private Hershey.

3713. Private[14] Hershey (Jay Paul[13], Willis Daniel[12], Silas N.[11], Peter[10], Jacob[9], John[8], Jacob Snavely[7], Andrew Stauffer[6], Adelheid Galle[5] Stouffer, Daniel[4], Christian[3], Hans[2], Hans[1]) She married **Private Eby**.

Children of Private Hershey and Private Eby are:
- 4959   i. Private[15] Eby.
- 4960   ii. Private Eby.
- 4961   iii. Private Eby.

3714. Private[14] Hershey (Jay Paul[13], Willis Daniel[12], Silas N.[11], Peter[10], Jacob[9], John[8], Jacob Snavely[7], Andrew Stauffer[6], Adelheid Galle[5] Stouffer, Daniel[4], Christian[3], Hans[2], Hans[1]) She married **Private Gatto**.

Child of Private Hershey and Private Gatto is:
- 4962   i. Private[15] Gatto.

3715. Private[14] Hershey (Jay Paul[13], Willis Daniel[12], Silas N.[11], Peter[10], Jacob[9], John[8], Jacob Snavely[7], Andrew Stauffer[6], Adelheid Galle[5] Stouffer, Daniel[4], Christian[3], Hans[2], Hans[1]) He married **Private Unknown**.

Children of Private Hershey and Private Unknown are:
- 4963   i. Private[15] Hershey.
- 4964   ii. Private Hershey.

3725. Cedric Linn[14] Horst (Paul Steffy[13], Elam Sweigart[12], Frances Reiff[11] Sweigart, Annie[10] Reiff, Veronica[9] Hershey, John[8], Jacob Snavely[7], Andrew Stauffer[6], Adelheid Galle[5] Stouffer, Daniel[4], Christian[3], Hans[2], Hans[1]) was born March 13, 1942. He married **(1) Barbara Carrithers**. She was born March 07, 1951. He married **(2) Cheryl Ann Campbell**. She was born August 28, 1957 in Georgia. He married **(3) Diane Kay Staub** July 07, 1962. She was born December 26, 1945.

Child of Cedric Horst and Barbara Carrithers is:
- 4965   i. Misty Dawn[15] Horst, born September 22, 1972.

Child of Cedric Horst and Cheryl Campbell is:
- 4966   i. Jonathan Lynn[15] Horst, born October 22, 1974.

Children of Cedric Horst and Diane Staub are:
- 4967   i. Paul Howard[15] Horst, born August 17, 1964 in Ohio.
- 4968   ii. Shelby Lynn Horst, born September 15, 1965 in Ohio.

3727. Joann Louise[14] Horst (Paul Steffy[13], Elam Sweigart[12], Frances Reiff[11] Sweigart, Annie[10] Reiff, Veronica[9] Hershey, John[8], Jacob Snavely[7], Andrew Stauffer[6], Adelheid Galle[5] Stouffer, Daniel[4], Christian[3], Hans[2], Hans[1]) was born July 27, 1943. She married **Thomas Lyle Adams** July 27, 1962. He was born October 14, 1940 in Ohio.

Child of Joann Horst and Thomas Adams is:
- 4969   i. Thomas Lyle[15] Adams, born July 30, 1963 in Ohio.

3728. Paul Gary[14] Horst (Paul Steffy[13], Elam Sweigart[12], Frances Reiff[11] Sweigart, Annie[10] Reiff, Veronica[9] Hershey, John[8], Jacob Snavely[7], Andrew Stauffer[6], Adelheid Galle[5] Stouffer, Daniel[4], Christian[3], Hans[2], Hans[1]) was born February 08, 1950. He married **(1) Milene Sue Ruple Brynmor**. She was born December 30, 1951. He married **(2) Janie Monte Lang** February 04, 1968. She was born December 11, 1951.

Children of Paul Horst and Milene Brynmor are:
- 4970   i. John Ruple[15] Brynmor, born May 07, 1970 in Ohio.
- 4971   ii. Shannon Lea Horst, born August 02, 1974 in Pennsylvania.

Children of Paul Horst and Janie Lang are:
- 4972   i. Gail Marie[15] Horst, born May 16, 1969.
- 4973   ii. Gary Paul Horst, born June 29, 1972.

3730. Mary Louise[14] Horst (William Prichard[13], Elam Sweigart[12], Frances Reiff[11] Sweigart, Annie[10] Reiff, Veronica[9] Hershey, John[8], Jacob Snavely[7], Andrew Stauffer[6], Adelheid Galle[5] Stouffer, Daniel[4], Christian[3], Hans[2], Hans[1]) was born January 27, 1944. She married **John W. Farmer** June 17, 1961. He was born July 17, 1937 in Virginia.

Children of Mary Horst and John Farmer are:
- 4974   i. Mary Elizabeth[15] Farmer, born August 23, 1962.
- 4975   ii. Cindy Hope Farmer, born February 18, 1968.

3731. Mark William[14] Horst (William Prichard[13], Elam Sweigart[12], Frances Reiff[11] Sweigart, Annie[10] Reiff, Veronica[9] Hershey, John[8], Jacob Snavely[7], Andrew Stauffer[6], Adelheid Galle[5] Stouffer, Daniel[4], Christian[3], Hans[2], Hans[1]) was born November 08, 1948. He married **Lenora May Gordon** August 05, 1967. She was born November 27, 1946.

Children of Mark Horst and Lenora Gordon are:
- 4976   i. Christine Marie[15] Horst, born August 23, 1971.
- 4977   ii. William Mark Horst, born August 09, 1974.

3732. Vici Mae[14] Carvell (Erma Steffy[13] Horst, Elam Sweigart[12], Frances Reiff[11] Sweigart, Annie[10] Reiff, Veronica[9] Hershey, John[8], Jacob Snavely[7], Andrew Stauffer[6], Adelheid Galle[5] Stouffer, Daniel[4], Christian[3], Hans[2], Hans[1]) was born March 24, 1948. She married **David M. McGowan** September 02, 1967. He was born May 30, 1947 in Massachusets.

Child of Vici Carvell and David McGowan is:
    4978   i.   Debra Lynne[15] McGown, born June 15, 1973 in New Hampshire.

3733. Audrey Nadine[14] Carvell (Erma Steffy[13] Horst, Elam Sweigart[12], Frances Reiff[11] Sweigart, Annie[10] Reiff, Veronica[9] Hershey, John[8], Jacob Snavely[7], Andrew Stauffer[6], Adelheid Galle[5] Stouffer, Daniel[4], Christian[3], Hans[2], Hans[1]) was born May 07, 1949. She married **Leon Eugene Buckwalter** July 07, 1973. He was born June 29, 1948.

Child of Audrey Carvell and Leon Buckwalter is:
    4979   i.   Heidi Rene[15] Buckwalter, born August 02, 1978.

3740. James Edward[14] Weaver (Jay Donald[14], John Landis[13], Magdalena M.[12] Landis, Magdalena O.[11] Martin, Martha H.[10] Oberholtzer, Martha H.[9] Hess, Esther[8] Hershey, Christian[7], Benjamin Stauffer[6], Adelheid Galle[5] Stouffer, Daniel[4], Christian[3], Hans[2], Hans[1]) was born November 10, 1960 in Lancaster, PA. He married **Sherry Rittenhouse** May 25, 1985 in Manheim Twp, Lanc Co, PA. She was born in Lancaster, PA.

Child of James Weaver and Sherry Rittenhouse is:
    4980   i.   Joshua Alan[15] Weaver, born July 18, 1990 in Lancaster, PA.

3741. Rae Elizabeth[14] Langsdale (Arvilla[14] Weaver, John Landis[13], Magdalena M.[12] Landis, Magdalena O.[11] Martin, Martha H.[10] Oberholtzer, Martha H.[9] Hess, Esther[8] Hershey, Christian[7], Benjamin Stauffer[6], Adelheid Galle[5] Stouffer, Daniel[4], Christian[3], Hans[2], Hans[1]) was born December 23, 1958 in Ephrata, PA. She married **David A. Burt** April 17, 1990 in Pittsfield, MA.

Child of Rae Langsdale and David Burt is:
    4981   i.   Caitlin Ann[15] Burt, born October 15, 1991 in Pittsfield, MA.

3743. Robert John[14] Langsdale (Arvilla[14] Weaver, John Landis[13], Magdalena M.[12] Landis, Magdalena O.[11] Martin, Martha H.[10] Oberholtzer, Martha H.[9] Hess, Esther[8] Hershey, Christian[7], Benjamin Stauffer[6], Adelheid Galle[5] Stouffer, Daniel[4], Christian[3], Hans[2], Hans[1]) was born September 05, 1965. He married **Ann Marie Giannopolo** September 07, 1991 in Pittsfield, MA. She was born April 16, 1965 in Pittsfield, MA.

Child of Robert Langsdale and Ann Giannopolo is:
    4982   i.   Tessa Maria[15] Langsdale, born May 28, 1999 in Pittsfield, MA.

3745. Rachel Naomi[14] Bucove (Donna Lou[14] Weaver, John Landis[13], Magdalena M.[12] Landis, Magdalena O.[11] Martin, Martha H.[10] Oberholtzer, Martha H.[9] Hess, Esther[8] Hershey, Christian[7], Benjamin Stauffer[6], Adelheid Galle[5] Stouffer, Daniel[4], Christian[3], Hans[2], Hans[1]) was born July 13, 1971. She married **Michael David Hitchcock**. He was born September 17, 1966 in New Haven, CT.

Children of Rachel Bucove and Michael Hitchcock are:
    4983   i.   Alexander Milton[15] Hitchcock, born January 13, 1993 in Portland, OR.
    4984   ii.   Zachary Falcon Hitchcock, born September 07, 1995 in Portland, OR.
    4985   iii.   Jonathan Elliot Hitchcock, born June 07, 1998 in Portland, OR.

3746. John Michael[14] Weaver (John Eric[14], John Landis[13], Magdalena M.[12] Landis, Magdalena O.[11] Martin, Martha H.[10] Oberholtzer, Martha H.[9] Hess, Esther[8] Hershey, Christian[7], Benjamin Stauffer[6], Adelheid Galle[5] Stouffer, Daniel[4], Christian[3], Hans[2], Hans[1]) was born June 19, 1968 in Ephrata, Lancaster Co., PA. He married **Jodi Lynn Lied** April 14, 1991.

Children of John Weaver and Jodi Lied are:
    4986   i.   Rachel Anne[15] Weaver, born January 20, 1998 in Chesapeake, VA.
    4987   ii.   Benjamin Michael Weaver, born January 26, 2000 in Portsmouth, VA.

3756. Private[14] Miller (Private[13] Fox, Robert Thomas[12], James George[11], Diana[10] Hershey, Henry[9], Martin[8], Henry[7], Andrew Stauffer[6], Adelheid Galle[5] Stouffer, Daniel[4], Christian[3], Hans[2], Hans[1]) He married **Private Roach**.

Child of Private Miller and Private Roach is:
    4988   i.   Private[15] Miller.

3757. Private[14] Miller (Private[13] Fox, Robert Thomas[12], James George[11], Diana[10] Hershey, Henry[9], Martin[8], Henry[7], Andrew Stauffer[6], Adelheid Galle[5] Stouffer, Daniel[4], Christian[3], Hans[2], Hans[1]) She married **Jr. Private Fortini**.

Children of Private Miller and Private Fortini are:
- 4989   i. Private[15] Fortini.
- 4990   ii. Private Fortini.

3758. Private[14] Rutherford (Private[13] Fox, Charles Adam[12], James George[11], Diana[10] Hershey, Henry[9], Martin[8], Henry[7], Andrew Stauffer[6], Adelheid Galle[5] Stouffer, Daniel[4], Christian[3], Hans[2], Hans[1]) He married **Private Walley**.

Children of Private Rutherford and Private Walley are:
- 4991   i. Private[15] Rutherford.
- 4992   ii. Private Rutherford.

3759. Private[14] Rutherford (Private[13] Fox, Charles Adam[12], James George[11], Diana[10] Hershey, Henry[9], Martin[8], Henry[7], Andrew Stauffer[6], Adelheid Galle[5] Stouffer, Daniel[4], Christian[3], Hans[2], Hans[1]) He married **Private Solga**.

Children of Private Rutherford and Private Solga are:
- 4993   i. Private[15] Rutherford.
- 4994   ii. Private Rutherford.
- 4995   iii. Private Rutherford.

3760. Private[14] Soper (Private[13] Fox, Charles Adam[12], James George[11], Diana[10] Hershey, Henry[9], Martin[8], Henry[7], Andrew Stauffer[6], Adelheid Galle[5] Stouffer, Daniel[4], Christian[3], Hans[2], Hans[1]) He married **(1) Private Klein**.   He married **(2) Private Byrne**.

Children of Private Soper and Private Byrne are:
- 4996   i. Private[15] Soper.
- 4997   ii. Private Soper.

3762. Private[14] Fox (Private[13], John Edward[12], James George[11], Diana[10] Hershey, Henry[9], Martin[8], Henry[7], Andrew Stauffer[6], Adelheid Galle[5] Stouffer, Daniel[4], Christian[3], Hans[2], Hans[1]) He married **Private Confer**.

Child of Private Fox and Private Confer is:
- 4998   i. Private[15] Fox.

3767. Private[14] Fox (Bryan[13], John Edward[12], James George[11], Diana[10] Hershey, Henry[9], Martin[8], Henry[7], Andrew Stauffer[6], Adelheid Galle[5] Stouffer, Daniel[4], Christian[3], Hans[2], Hans[1]) He married **Private Toomey**.

Children of Private Fox and Private Toomey are:
- 4999   i. Private[15] Fox.
- 5000   ii. Private Fox.
- 5001   iii. Private Fox.

3768. Private[14] Daniels (Jeanette Fredricka[13] Fox, John Edward[12], James George[11], Diana[10] Hershey, Henry[9], Martin[8], Henry[7], Andrew Stauffer[6], Adelheid Galle[5] Stouffer, Daniel[4], Christian[3], Hans[2], Hans[1]) She married **(1) Private Shope**.   She married **(2) Private Walton**.

Children of Private Daniels and Private Shope are:
- 5002   i. Private[15] Shope.
- 5003   ii. Private Shope.

3769. Private[14] Daniels (Jeanette Fredricka[13] Fox, John Edward[12], James George[11], Diana[10] Hershey, Henry[9], Martin[8], Henry[7], Andrew Stauffer[6], Adelheid Galle[5] Stouffer, Daniel[4], Christian[3], Hans[2], Hans[1]) He married **Private Conrad**.

Children of Private Daniels and Private Conrad are:
- 5004   i. Private[15] Daniels.
- 5005   ii. Private Daniels.

5006 iii. Private Daniels.
5007 iv. Private Daniels.

3770. Private[14] Daniels (Jeanette Fredricka[13] Fox, John Edward[12], James George[11], Diana[10] Hershey, Henry[9], Martin[8], Henry[7], Andrew Stauffer[6], Adelheid Galle[5] Stouffer, Daniel[4], Christian[3], Hans[2], Hans[1]) She married **Private Greiner**.

Children of Private Daniels and Private Greiner are:
5008 i. Private[15] Greiner.
5009 ii. Private Greiner.
5010 iii. Private Greiner.
5011 iv. Private Greiner.

3772. Private[14] Vanasco (Dorothy[13] Fox, John Edward[12], James George[11], Diana[10] Hershey, Henry[9], Martin[8], Henry[7], Andrew Stauffer[6], Adelheid Galle[5] Stouffer, Daniel[4], Christian[3], Hans[2], Hans[1]) She married **Private Glass**.

Children of Private Vanasco and Private Glass are:
5012 i. Private[15] Glass.
5013 ii. Private Glass.
5014 iii. Private Glass.
5015 iv. Private Glass.
5016 v. Jr. Private Glass.

3773. Private[14] Vanasco (Dorothy[13] Fox, John Edward[12], James George[11], Diana[10] Hershey, Henry[9], Martin[8], Henry[7], Andrew Stauffer[6], Adelheid Galle[5] Stouffer, Daniel[4], Christian[3], Hans[2], Hans[1]) She married **(1) Private Bretz**.   She married **(2) Private Mutch**.

Child of Private Vanasco and Private Bretz is:
5017 i. Private[15] Bretz.

Children of Private Vanasco and Private Mutch are:
5018 i. Private[15] Mutch.
5019 ii. Private Mutch.

3778. Private[14] Fountain (Marjorie[13] Fox, John Edward[12], James George[11], Diana[10] Hershey, Henry[9], Martin[8], Henry[7], Andrew Stauffer[6], Adelheid Galle[5] Stouffer, Daniel[4], Christian[3], Hans[2], Hans[1]) She married **Private Baugher**.

Children of Private Fountain and Private Baugher are:
5020 i. Private[15] Baugher.
5021 ii. Private Baugher.
5022 iii. Private Baugher.

3780. Private[14] Fountain (Marjorie[13] Fox, John Edward[12], James George[11], Diana[10] Hershey, Henry[9], Martin[8], Henry[7], Andrew Stauffer[6], Adelheid Galle[5] Stouffer, Daniel[4], Christian[3], Hans[2], Hans[1]) She married **Private Crandell**.

Child of Private Fountain and Private Crandell is:
5023 i. Jr. Private[15] Crandell.

3781. Private[14] Fountain (Marjorie[13] Fox, John Edward[12], James George[11], Diana[10] Hershey, Henry[9], Martin[8], Henry[7], Andrew Stauffer[6], Adelheid Galle[5] Stouffer, Daniel[4], Christian[3], Hans[2], Hans[1]) He married **Private Gallagher**.

Child of Private Fountain and Private Gallagher is:
5024 i. Private[15] Fountain.

3784. Private[14] Dolan (Mary Eliza "[13] Molly, John Edward[12] Fox, James George[11], Diana[10] Hershey, Henry[9], Martin[8], Henry[7], Andrew Stauffer[6], Adelheid Galle[5] Stouffer, Daniel[4], Christian[3], Hans[2], Hans[1]) She married **Private Mooseberger**.

Child of Private Dolan and Private Mooseberger is:
5025 i. Private[15] Mooseberger.

3786. Private[14] Dolan (Mary Eliza "[13] Molly, John Edward[12] Fox, James George[11], Diana[10] Hershey, Henry[9], Martin[8], Henry[7], Andrew Stauffer[6], Adelheid Galle[5] Stouffer, Daniel[4], Christian[3], Hans[2], Hans[1]) She married **(1) Private Harrison**. She married **(2) Private Schmidt**.

Child of Private Dolan and Private Harrison is:
    5026   i.   Private[15] Harrison.

Children of Private Dolan are:
    5027   i.   Private[15] Harrison.
    5028   ii.   Private Harrison.

3791. Private[14] McKitrick (Private[13] Fox, Thomas G.[12], James George[11], Diana[10] Hershey, Henry[9], Martin[8], Henry[7], Andrew Stauffer[6], Adelheid Galle[5] Stouffer, Daniel[4], Christian[3], Hans[2], Hans[1]) She married **Private Grimes**.

Children of Private McKitrick and Private Grimes are:
    5029   i.   Private[15] Grimes.
    5030   ii.   Private Grimes.
    5031   iii.   Private Grimes.

3794. Private[14] Fox (Private[13], Thomas G.[12], James George[11], Diana[10] Hershey, Henry[9], Martin[8], Henry[7], Andrew Stauffer[6], Adelheid Galle[5] Stouffer, Daniel[4], Christian[3], Hans[2], Hans[1]) He married **Private Wada**.

Children of Private Fox and Private Wada are:
    5032   i.   Private[15] Fox.
    5033   ii.   Private Fox.

3795. Private[14] Fox (Private[13], Thomas G.[12], James George[11], Diana[10] Hershey, Henry[9], Martin[8], Henry[7], Andrew Stauffer[6], Adelheid Galle[5] Stouffer, Daniel[4], Christian[3], Hans[2], Hans[1]) She married **Private Shirley**.

Children of Private Fox and Private Shirley are:
    5034   i.   Private[15] Shirley.
    5035   ii.   Private Shirley.

3796. Private[14] Fox (Private[13], Thomas G.[12], James George[11], Diana[10] Hershey, Henry[9], Martin[8], Henry[7], Andrew Stauffer[6], Adelheid Galle[5] Stouffer, Daniel[4], Christian[3], Hans[2], Hans[1]) She married **Private Cornelius**.

Children of Private Fox and Private Cornelius are:
    5036   i.   Private[15] Cornelius.
    5037   ii.   Private Cornelius.

3797. Private[14] Fox (Private[13], Thomas G.[12], James George[11], Diana[10] Hershey, Henry[9], Martin[8], Henry[7], Andrew Stauffer[6], Adelheid Galle[5] Stouffer, Daniel[4], Christian[3], Hans[2], Hans[1]) He married **Private Slothour**.

Child of Private Fox and Private Slothour is:
    5038   i.   Private[15] Fox.

3798. Private[14] Seachrist (Private[13] Fox, Thomas G.[12], James George[11], Diana[10] Hershey, Henry[9], Martin[8], Henry[7], Andrew Stauffer[6], Adelheid Galle[5] Stouffer, Daniel[4], Christian[3], Hans[2], Hans[1]) She married **Private Aldridge**.

Child of Private Seachrist and Private Aldridge is:
    5039   i.   Private[15] Aldridge.

3799. Private[14] Seachrist (Private[13] Fox, Thomas G.[12], James George[11], Diana[10] Hershey, Henry[9], Martin[8], Henry[7], Andrew Stauffer[6], Adelheid Galle[5] Stouffer, Daniel[4], Christian[3], Hans[2], Hans[1]) She married **Private Lesher**.

Children of Private Seachrist and Private Lesher are:
    5040   i.   Private[15] Lesher.
    5041   ii.   Private Lesher.

3800. III Private[14] Seachrist (Private[13] Fox, Thomas G.[12], James George[11], Diana[10] Hershey, Henry[9], Martin[8], Henry[7], Andrew Stauffer[6], Adelheid Galle[5] Stouffer, Daniel[4], Christian[3], Hans[2], Hans[1]) He married **Private Bunora**.

Children of Private Seachrist and Private Bunora are:
- 5042   i. Private[15] Seachrist.
- 5043   ii. Private Seachrist.

3801. Private[14] Seachrist (Private[13] Fox, Thomas G.[12], James George[11], Diana[10] Hershey, Henry[9], Martin[8], Henry[7], Andrew Stauffer[6], Adelheid Galle[5] Stouffer, Daniel[4], Christian[3], Hans[2], Hans[1]) He married **Private Hunsicker**.

Child of Private Seachrist and Private Hunsicker is:
- 5044   i. Private[15] Seachrist.

3802. Private[14] Seachrist (Private[13] Fox, Thomas G.[12], James George[11], Diana[10] Hershey, Henry[9], Martin[8], Henry[7], Andrew Stauffer[6], Adelheid Galle[5] Stouffer, Daniel[4], Christian[3], Hans[2], Hans[1]) He married **Private Smith**.

Child of Private Seachrist and Private Smith is:
- 5045   i. Private[15] Seachrist.

3803. Private[14] Seachrist (Private[13] Fox, Thomas G.[12], James George[11], Diana[10] Hershey, Henry[9], Martin[8], Henry[7], Andrew Stauffer[6], Adelheid Galle[5] Stouffer, Daniel[4], Christian[3], Hans[2], Hans[1]) She married **Private Yohn**.

Child of Private Seachrist and Private Yohn is:
- 5046   i. Private[15] Yohn.

3805. Private[14] Fox (Thomas G.[13], Thomas G.[12], James George[11], Diana[10] Hershey, Henry[9], Martin[8], Henry[7], Andrew Stauffer[6], Adelheid Galle[5] Stouffer, Daniel[4], Christian[3], Hans[2], Hans[1]) She married **Private Cooke**.

Children of Private Fox and Private Cooke are:
- 5047   i. Private[15] Cooke.
- 5048   ii. Private Cooke.

3807. Private[14] Mengel (Virginia Romaine[13] Fox, Thomas G.[12], James George[11], Diana[10] Hershey, Henry[9], Martin[8], Henry[7], Andrew Stauffer[6], Adelheid Galle[5] Stouffer, Daniel[4], Christian[3], Hans[2], Hans[1]) He married **(1) Private Moore**. He married **(2) Private Gray**.

Child of Private Mengel and Private Moore is:
- 5049   i. Private[15] Mengel.

Children of Private Mengel and Private Gray are:
- 5050   i. Private[15] Mengel.
- 5051   ii. Private Mengel.

3809. Private[14] Allamong (Diana Lucille[13] Fox, Thomas G.[12], James George[11], Diana[10] Hershey, Henry[9], Martin[8], Henry[7], Andrew Stauffer[6], Adelheid Galle[5] Stouffer, Daniel[4], Christian[3], Hans[2], Hans[1]) He married **Private Emory**.

Child of Private Allamong and Private Emory is:
- 5052   i. Private[15] Allamong.

3810. Private[14] Bair (Private[13], Sara Diana[12] Fox, James George[11], Diana[10] Hershey, Henry[9], Martin[8], Henry[7], Andrew Stauffer[6], Adelheid Galle[5] Stouffer, Daniel[4], Christian[3], Hans[2], Hans[1]) She married **Private Tolman**.

Children of Private Bair and Private Tolman are:
- 5053   i.   Private[15] Tolman.
- 5054   ii. Private Tolman.
- 5055   iii. Private Tolman.

3811. Private[14] Bair (Private[13], Sara Diana[12] Fox, James George[11], Diana[10] Hershey, Henry[9], Martin[8], Henry[7], Andrew Stauffer[6], Adelheid Galle[5] Stouffer, Daniel[4], Christian[3], Hans[2], Hans[1]) She married **(1) Private Stengel**.   She married **(2) Private Mohr**.

Children of Private Bair and Private Stengel are:
   5056   i.   Private[15] Stengel.
   5057   ii. Private Stengel.

Child of Private Bair and Private Mohr is:
   5058   i.   Private[15] Mohr.

3812. Private[14] Bair (Private[13], Sara Diana[12] Fox, James George[11], Diana[10] Hershey, Henry[9], Martin[8], Henry[7], Andrew Stauffer[6], Adelheid Galle[5] Stouffer, Daniel[4], Christian[3], Hans[2], Hans[1]) She married **Private Allen**.

Children of Private Bair and Private Allen are:
   5059   i.   Private[15] Allen.
   5060   ii. Private Allen.

3818. Private[14] Silver (Private[13] Fox, James George[12], James George[11], Diana[10] Hershey, Henry[9], Martin[8], Henry[7], Andrew Stauffer[6], Adelheid Galle[5] Stouffer, Daniel[4], Christian[3], Hans[2], Hans[1]) She married **Private Boyer**.

Children of Private Silver and Private Boyer are:
   5061   i.   Private[15] Boyer.
   5062   ii. Private Boyer.

3819. Private[14] Silver (Private[13] Fox, James George[12], James George[11], Diana[10] Hershey, Henry[9], Martin[8], Henry[7], Andrew Stauffer[6], Adelheid Galle[5] Stouffer, Daniel[4], Christian[3], Hans[2], Hans[1]) He married **Private Lotrek**.

Children of Private Silver and Private Lotrek are:
   5063   i.   Private[15] Silver.
   5064   ii.   Private Silver.
   5065   iii. Private Silver.

3821. Jr. Private[14] Hawkins (Private[13] Gay, John Howard[12], Adelaide[11] Fox, Diana[10] Hershey, Henry[9], Martin[8], Henry[7], Andrew Stauffer[6], Adelheid Galle[5] Stouffer, Daniel[4], Christian[3], Hans[2], Hans[1])

Child of Jr. Private Hawkins is:
   5066   i.   Private[15] Hawkins.

3822. Private[14] Gay (Private[13], John Howard[12], Adelaide[11] Fox, Diana[10] Hershey, Henry[9], Martin[8], Henry[7], Andrew Stauffer[6], Adelheid Galle[5] Stouffer, Daniel[4], Christian[3], Hans[2], Hans[1]) She married **Private Lavender**.

Child of Private Gay and Private Lavender is:
   5067   i.   Private[15] Lavender.

3823. Private[14] Gay (Private[13], John Howard[12], Adelaide[11] Fox, Diana[10] Hershey, Henry[9], Martin[8], Henry[7], Andrew Stauffer[6], Adelheid Galle[5] Stouffer, Daniel[4], Christian[3], Hans[2], Hans[1]) She married **Private Stackhouse**.

Children of Private Gay and Private Stackhouse are:
   5068   i.   Private[15] Stackhouse.
   5069   ii. Private Stackhouse.

3824. Private[14] Gay (Private[13], John Howard[12], Adelaide[11] Fox, Diana[10] Hershey, Henry[9], Martin[8], Henry[7], Andrew Stauffer[6], Adelheid Galle[5] Stouffer, Daniel[4], Christian[3], Hans[2], Hans[1]) She married **Jr. Private Newell**.

Children of Private Gay and Private Newell are:
   5070   i.   Private[15] Newell.
   5071   ii. Private Newell.

5072   iii.   Private Newell.

3825. Private[14] Lee (Private[13], Gertrude[12] Gay, Adelaide[11] Fox, Diana[10] Hershey, Henry[9], Martin[8], Henry[7], Andrew Stauffer[6], Adelheid Galle[5] Stouffer, Daniel[4], Christian[3], Hans[2], Hans[1]) He married **Private Stetson**.

Children of Private Lee and Private Stetson are:
5073   i.   Private[15] Lee.
5074   ii.   Private Lee.

3829. Private[14] Arnold (Private[13], Katherine[12] Nissley, Caroline Lee[11] Fox, Diana[10] Hershey, Henry[9], Martin[8], Henry[7], Andrew Stauffer[6], Adelheid Galle[5] Stouffer, Daniel[4], Christian[3], Hans[2], Hans[1]) He married **Private Newberry**.

Child of Private Arnold and Private Newberry is:
5075   i.   Private[15] Arnold.

3830. Private[14] Arnold (Private[13], Katherine[12] Nissley, Caroline Lee[11] Fox, Diana[10] Hershey, Henry[9], Martin[8], Henry[7], Andrew Stauffer[6], Adelheid Galle[5] Stouffer, Daniel[4], Christian[3], Hans[2], Hans[1]) She married **(1) Private McNulty**.   She married **(2) Private Kinney**.

Child of Private Arnold and Private McNulty is:
5076   i.   Private[15] McNulty.

3835. Private[14] Fleming (Private[13] Wolff, Emilie Karthaus[12] Fox, George Hershey[11], Diana[10] Hershey, Henry[9], Martin[8], Henry[7], Andrew Stauffer[6], Adelheid Galle[5] Stouffer, Daniel[4], Christian[3], Hans[2], Hans[1]) She married **Private Hinton**.

Child of Private Fleming and Private Hinton is:
5077   i.   Private[15] Hinton.

3839. Private[14] Taylor (Private[13], Karolyn Diana[12] Fox, George Hershey[11], Diana[10] Hershey, Henry[9], Martin[8], Henry[7], Andrew Stauffer[6], Adelheid Galle[5] Stouffer, Daniel[4], Christian[3], Hans[2], Hans[1]) He married **Private**.

Child of Private Taylor and Private is:
5078   i.   Jr. Private[15] Taylor.

3843. Private[14] Taylor (James Alfred[13], Karolyn Diana[12] Fox, George Hershey[11], Diana[10] Hershey, Henry[9], Martin[8], Henry[7], Andrew Stauffer[6], Adelheid Galle[5] Stouffer, Daniel[4], Christian[3], Hans[2], Hans[1]) She married **Private Palmer**.

Child of Private Taylor and Private Palmer is:
5079   i.   Private[15] Palmer.

3844. Private[14] Taylor (James Alfred[13], Karolyn Diana[12] Fox, George Hershey[11], Diana[10] Hershey, Henry[9], Martin[8], Henry[7], Andrew Stauffer[6], Adelheid Galle[5] Stouffer, Daniel[4], Christian[3], Hans[2], Hans[1]) She married **Private Byram**.

Child of Private Taylor and Private Byram is:
5080   i.   Private[15] Byram.

3845. Doris Madeline[14] Sheaffer (Charles M.[13], Lydia Jane[12] Tritt, Nancy[11] Nickey, Samuel[10], Christiana[9] Hastetter, Anna Barbara[8] Stauffer, Johannes[7], Daniel[6] Stouffer, Christian[5] Stauffer, Daniel[4] Stouffer, Christian[3], Hans[2], Hans[1]) was born November 08, 1913, and died January 25, 1980 in Utica, N.Y.. She married **Carmen Joseph Lucenti** WFT Est. 1934-1965. He was born February 18, 1922, and died August 27, 1986 in Utica, N.Y,.

Children of Doris Sheaffer and Carmen Lucenti are:
+   5081   i.   Teresa Rose Charlene[15] Lucenti, born Private.
+   5082   ii.   Sandra Marie Lucenti, born Private.

3851. Velva Grace[14] Reese (Edna[13] Brandt, Agnes Bordilla[12] Goodhart, Charlotte[11] Farner, Elizabeth[10] Owens, Peter[9] Ober, Elizabeth[8] Stauffer, Johannes[7], Daniel[6] Stouffer, Christian[5] Stauffer, Daniel[4] Stouffer, Christian[3], Hans[2], Hans[1]) was born Private. She married **George Schuyler** Private. He was born Private.

Children of Velva Reese and George Schuyler are:
- 5083   i.   George[15] Schuyler, born Private.
- 5084   ii.   Grace Schuyler, born Private.

3852. Herman Wilson[14] Reese (Edna[13] Brandt, Agnes Bordilla[12] Goodhart, Charlotte[11] Farner, Elizabeth[10] Owens, Peter[9] Ober, Elizabeth[8] Stauffer, Johannes[7], Daniel[6] Stouffer, Christian[5] Stauffer, Daniel[4] Stouffer, Christian[3], Hans[2], Hans[1]) was born Private.

Child of Herman Wilson Reese is:
- 5085   i.   Ricky[15] Reese, born Private.

3853. Mary Esther Katherine[14] Reese (Edna[13] Brandt, Agnes Bordilla[12] Goodhart, Charlotte[11] Farner, Elizabeth[10] Owens, Peter[9] Ober, Elizabeth[8] Stauffer, Johannes[7], Daniel[6] Stouffer, Christian[5] Stauffer, Daniel[4] Stouffer, Christian[3], Hans[2], Hans[1]) was born Private. She married **Norman Eaken** Private. He was born Private.

Children of Mary Reese and Norman Eaken are:
- 5086   i.   John[15] Eaken, born Private.
- 5087   ii.   Susan Eaken, born Private.

3855. Robert Goodhart[14] Hippensteel (Margaret Elizabeth Alice[13] Goodhart, Theodore[12], Charlotte[11] Farner, Elizabeth[10] Owens, Peter[9] Ober, Elizabeth[8] Stauffer, Johannes[7], Daniel[6] Stouffer, Christian[5] Stauffer, Daniel[4] Stouffer, Christian[3], Hans[2], Hans[1]) was born Private. He married **Carolyn Ann Weigle** Private. She was born October 03, 1926, and died December 02, 1988.

Children of Robert Hippensteel and Carolyn Weigle are:
- 5088   i.   Sandra Lee[15] Hippensteel, born Private. She married Robert Tomilson Private; born Private.
- 5089   ii.   Judy Ann Hippensteel, born Private. She married (1) James Copley Private; born Private. She married (2) Robert Rourke Private; born Private.
- 5090   iii.   Infant Son Hippensteel, born Private.

3856. Dorothy Jean[14] Hippensteel (Margaret Elizabeth Alice[13] Goodhart, Theodore[12], Charlotte[11] Farner, Elizabeth[10] Owens, Peter[9] Ober, Elizabeth[8] Stauffer, Johannes[7], Daniel[6] Stouffer, Christian[5] Stauffer, Daniel[4] Stouffer, Christian[3], Hans[2], Hans[1]) was born Private. She married **Ralph E. Mohler** Private. He was born Private.

Children of Dorothy Hippensteel and Ralph Mohler are:
- +   5091   i.   Kathryn Ann[15] Mohler, born Private.
- +   5092   ii.   John Robert Mohler, born Private.
-      5093   iii.   David Ralph Mohler, born Private. He married (1) Carolyn Rogers Private; born Private. He married (2) Susan Wakely Private; born Private.

3857. Doris Madeline[14] Hippensteel (Margaret Elizabeth Alice[13] Goodhart, Theodore[12], Charlotte[11] Farner, Elizabeth[10] Owens, Peter[9] Ober, Elizabeth[8] Stauffer, Johannes[7], Daniel[6] Stouffer, Christian[5] Stauffer, Daniel[4] Stouffer, Christian[3], Hans[2], Hans[1]) was born Private. She married **Adam Leroy West** Private. He was born June 11, 1924 in Fayetteville, Franklin County, Pa., and died March 18, 1987 in Clarksville, Tennesee.

Children of Doris Hippensteel and Adam West are:
- +   5094   i.   Diane Elizabeth[15] West, born Private.
- +   5095   ii.   Barbara Elaine West, born Private.

3858. Margaret Joanne[14] Hippensteel (Margaret Elizabeth Alice[13] Goodhart, Theodore[12], Charlotte[11] Farner, Elizabeth[10] Owens, Peter[9] Ober, Elizabeth[8] Stauffer, Johannes[7], Daniel[6] Stouffer, Christian[5] Stauffer, Daniel[4] Stouffer, Christian[3], Hans[2], Hans[1]) was born Private. She married **(1) Walter J. Bernheisel** Private. He was born Private. She married **(2) O. P. Stancer** Private. He was born Private.

Children of Margaret Hippensteel and Walter Bernheisel are:
- 5096   i.   Michael Scott[15] Bernheisel, born Private.
- 5097   ii.   Patrick Alan Bernheisel, born Private.
- 5098   iii.   Toni Karen Bernheisel, born Private.

3860. Charles Dale[14] Goodhart (Clarence Eugene[13], Theodore[12], Charlotte[11] Farner, Elizabeth[10] Owens, Peter[9] Ober, Elizabeth[8] Stauffer, Johannes[7], Daniel[6] Stouffer, Christian[5] Stauffer, Daniel[4] Stouffer, Christian[3], Hans[2], Hans[1]) was born Private. He married **Betty Jane Cahill** Private. She was born Private.

Children of Charles Goodhart and Betty Cahill are:
- 5099　　i.　James Lee[15] Goodhart, born Private. He married Glenda Vogelsong Private; born Private.
- + 5100　　ii.　John Charles Goodhart, born Private.

3861. Lee Piper[14] **Goodhart** (Clarence Eugene[13], Theodore[12], Charlotte[11] Farner, Elizabeth[10] Owens, Peter[9] Ober, Elizabeth[8] Stauffer, Johannes[7], Daniel[6] Stouffer, Christian[5] Stauffer, Daniel[4] Stouffer, Christian[3], Hans[2], Hans[1]) was born Private. He married **(1) Isabelle Line** Private. She was born Private. He married **(2) Sandra Rissinger** Private. She was born Private. He married **(3) Irene Flickinger** Private. She was born Private. He married **(4) Helen Julia Jackson** Private. She was born Private.

Children of Lee Goodhart and Sandra Rissinger are:
- 5101　　i.　Winifred Sue[15] Goodhart, born Private. She married Hockley.
- 5102　　ii.　Sharon Agnes Goodhart, born Private. She married Rakestron.

3863. Robert Michael[14] **Goodhart** (Lester Sheaffer[13], Theodore[12], Charlotte[11] Farner, Elizabeth[10] Owens, Peter[9] Ober, Elizabeth[8] Stauffer, Johannes[7], Daniel[6] Stouffer, Christian[5] Stauffer, Daniel[4] Stouffer, Christian[3], Hans[2], Hans[1]) was born Private. He married **Diane Wengert** Private. She was born Private.

Children of Robert Goodhart and Diane Wengert are:
- 5103　　i.　Traci Diane[15] Goodhart, born Private.
- 5104　　ii.　Erik Michael Goodhart, born Private.

3867. Almer H[14] **Harrington** (Lillie E[13] Hursh, Emma Barbara[12] Ober, David[11], Isaac Huntsberger[10], Christian[9], Elizabeth[8] Stauffer, Johannes[7], Daniel[6] Stouffer, Christian[5] Stauffer, Daniel[4] Stouffer, Christian[3], Hans[2], Hans[1]) was born 1896, and died 1923. He married **Ruth Sewell**. She was born Abt. 1900.

Child of Almer Harrington and Ruth Sewell is:
- + 5105　　i.　Margaret H[15] Harrington, born 1918.

3868. Beryl F[14] **Harrington** (Lillie E[13] Hursh, Emma Barbara[12] Ober, David[11], Isaac Huntsberger[10], Christian[9], Elizabeth[8] Stauffer, Johannes[7], Daniel[6] Stouffer, Christian[5] Stauffer, Daniel[4] Stouffer, Christian[3], Hans[2], Hans[1]) was born 1901. He married **Margaret Tichenon**. She was born Abt. 1900.

Children of Beryl Harrington and Margaret Tichenon are:
- 5106　　i.　Doris J[15] Harrington, born 1926. She married William Blackman; born Aft. 1920.
- 5107　　ii.　Frances Anne Harrington, born 1934.
- 5108　　iii.　Jack A Harrington, born 1940.

3869. Lillian R[14] **Harrington** (Lillie E[13] Hursh, Emma Barbara[12] Ober, David[11], Isaac Huntsberger[10], Christian[9], Elizabeth[8] Stauffer, Johannes[7], Daniel[6] Stouffer, Christian[5] Stauffer, Daniel[4] Stouffer, Christian[3], Hans[2], Hans[1]) was born 1911. She married **Richard Stoll**. He was born Abt. 1910.

Children of Lillian Harrington and Richard Stoll are:
- 5109　　i.　Susan L[15] Stoll, born Abt. 1940.
- 5110　　ii.　Michael H Stoll, born 1943.

3872. Alfred[14] **Harrington** (Edna R[13] Hursh, Emma Barbara[12] Ober, David[11], Isaac Huntsberger[10], Christian[9], Elizabeth[8] Stauffer, Johannes[7], Daniel[6] Stouffer, Christian[5] Stauffer, Daniel[4] Stouffer, Christian[3], Hans[2], Hans[1]) was born 1899. He married **Lorene Harrington**. She was born 1906.

Child of Alfred Harrington and Lorene Harrington is:
- 5111　　i.　Lynn[15] Harrington, born 1934.

3873. Grace[14] **Harrington** (Edna R[13] Hursh, Emma Barbara[12] Ober, David[11], Isaac Huntsberger[10], Christian[9], Elizabeth[8] Stauffer, Johannes[7], Daniel[6] Stouffer, Christian[5] Stauffer, Daniel[4] Stouffer, Christian[3], Hans[2], Hans[1]) was born 1904. She married **Howard Fox**. He was born 1893.

Children of Grace Harrington and Howard Fox are:
- 5112　　i.　Donald[15] Fox, born 1930.
- 5113　　ii.　Richard Fox, born 1936.

3874. Lucile[14] Harrington (Edna R[13] Hursh, Emma Barbara[12] Ober, David[11], Isaac Huntsberger[10], Christian[9], Elizabeth[8] Stauffer, Johannes[7], Daniel[6] Stouffer, Christian[5] Stauffer, Daniel[4] Stouffer, Christian[3], Hans[2], Hans[1]) was born 1907. She married **Clifford Conrad**. He was born 1902.

Children of Lucile Harrington and Clifford Conrad are:
- 5114   i.   Gerald[15] Conrad, born 1932.
- 5115   ii.   Marilyn Conrad, born 1936.
- 5116   iii.   Glenn Conrad, born 1940.

3876. Brenner P[14] Hursh (Jay B[13], Emma Barbara[12] Ober, David[11], Isaac Huntsberger[10], Christian[9], Elizabeth[8] Stauffer, Johannes[7], Daniel[6] Stouffer, Christian[5] Stauffer, Daniel[4] Stouffer, Christian[3], Hans[2], Hans[1]) was born 1911, and died 1944. He married **Frances M Hursh**. She was born 1919.

Child of Brenner Hursh and Frances Hursh is:
- 5117   i.   Diane A[15] Hursh, born 1939.

3881. Jayson C[14] Balsbaugh (Margaret Ann[13] Duncan, Catherine Rebecca[12] Ober, David[11], Isaac Huntsberger[10], Christian[9], Elizabeth[8] Stauffer, Johannes[7], Daniel[6] Stouffer, Christian[5] Stauffer, Daniel[4] Stouffer, Christian[3], Hans[2], Hans[1]) was born 1902. He married **Elizabeth Rodgers**. She was born Aft. 1900.

Children of Jayson Balsbaugh and Elizabeth Rodgers are:
- 5118   i.   Sidney[15] Balsbaugh, born Aft. 1920.
- 5119   ii.   Allen Balsbaugh, born Aft. 1920.

3882. Kathryn S[14] Balsbaugh (Margaret Ann[13] Duncan, Catherine Rebecca[12] Ober, David[11], Isaac Huntsberger[10], Christian[9], Elizabeth[8] Stauffer, Johannes[7], Daniel[6] Stouffer, Christian[5] Stauffer, Daniel[4] Stouffer, Christian[3], Hans[2], Hans[1]) was born 1903. She married **Richard H Lackey, Jr**. He was born Abt. 1900.

Children of Kathryn Balsbaugh and Richard Lackey are:
- 5120   i.   Patricia A[15] Lackey, born Abt. 1925.
- 5121   ii.   Susan J Lackey, born Abt. 1925.

3886. Erlo R[14] Balsbaugh (Margaret Ann[13] Duncan, Catherine Rebecca[12] Ober, David[11], Isaac Huntsberger[10], Christian[9], Elizabeth[8] Stauffer, Johannes[7], Daniel[6] Stouffer, Christian[5] Stauffer, Daniel[4] Stouffer, Christian[3], Hans[2], Hans[1]) was born 1911. She married **Irvin Gruber**. He was born Abt. 1910.

Children of Erlo Balsbaugh and Irvin Gruber are:
- 5122   i.   Jihn B[15] Gruber, born Abt. 1935.
- 5123   ii.   James D Gruber, born Abt. 1935.

3887. Clarence Franklin[14] Wolf (Clarence R[13], Catherine Rebecca[12] Ober, David[11], Isaac Huntsberger[10], Christian[9], Elizabeth[8] Stauffer, Johannes[7], Daniel[6] Stouffer, Christian[5] Stauffer, Daniel[4] Stouffer, Christian[3], Hans[2], Hans[1]) was born 1912. He married **Verna Dilks**. She was born Abt. 1910.

Children of Clarence Wolf and Verna Dilks are:
- 5124   i.   Ray[15] Wolf, born Abt. 1930.
- 5125   ii.   Alice K Wolf, born Abt. 1930.
- 5126   iii.   Margaret M Wolf, born Abt. 1930.

3891. John S[14] Wolf (Clarence R[13], Catherine Rebecca[12] Ober, David[11], Isaac Huntsberger[10], Christian[9], Elizabeth[8] Stauffer, Johannes[7], Daniel[6] Stouffer, Christian[5] Stauffer, Daniel[4] Stouffer, Christian[3], Hans[2], Hans[1]) was born 1926. He married **Dorothy Kasper**. She was born Abt. 1910.

Children of John Wolf and Dorothy Kasper are:
- 5127   i.   Holly Ann[15] Wolf, born Aft. 1930.
- 5128   ii.   Mary E Wolf, born Aft. 1930.

3894. Marjorie Ann[14] Wolf (David Ober[13], Catherine Rebecca[12] Ober, David[11], Isaac Huntsberger[10], Christian[9], Elizabeth[8] Stauffer,

Johannes[7], Daniel[6] Stouffer, Christian[5] Stauffer, Daniel[4] Stouffer, Christian[3], Hans[2], Hans[1]) was born Abt. 1928 in Pittsburgh, PA, and died September 30, 1970 in Glastonbury, CT. She married **Allan Baker Partridge** June 25, 1955 in Durham, NH.

Children of Marjorie Wolf and Allan Partridge are:
    5129   i.   Charles Allan[15] Partridge.
    5130   ii. Diane Louise Partridge.

3898. Franklin Earl[14] Wolf (Franklin Earl[13], Catherine Rebecca[12] Ober, David[11], Isaac Huntsberger[10], Christian[9], Elizabeth[8] Stauffer, Johannes[7], Daniel[6] Stouffer, Christian[5] Stauffer, Daniel[4] Stouffer, Christian[3], Hans[2], Hans[1]) was born Abt. 1930. He married **Hilda Gonzalez**. She was born Abt. 1930.

Child of Franklin Wolf and Hilda Gonzalez is:
    5131   i.   Maria[15] Wolf, born 1963.

3899. Barbara J[14] Wolf (George Edgar[13], Catherine Rebecca[12] Ober, David[11], Isaac Huntsberger[10], Christian[9], Elizabeth[8] Stauffer, Johannes[7], Daniel[6] Stouffer, Christian[5] Stauffer, Daniel[4] Stouffer, Christian[3], Hans[2], Hans[1]) was born Aft. 1900. She married **Richard Wilson**. He was born Abt. 1900.

Children of Barbara Wolf and Richard Wilson are:
    5132   i.   Patricia A[15] Wilson, born Abt. 1925.
    5133   ii. Richard Wilson, Jr, born Abt. 1925.

3900. Mary L[14] Wolf (George Edgar[13], Catherine Rebecca[12] Ober, David[11], Isaac Huntsberger[10], Christian[9], Elizabeth[8] Stauffer, Johannes[7], Daniel[6] Stouffer, Christian[5] Stauffer, Daniel[4] Stouffer, Christian[3], Hans[2], Hans[1]) was born Aft. 1900. She married **William T Hassler**. He was born Aft. 1900.

Child of Mary Wolf and William Hassler is:
    5134   i.   Michael[15] Hassler, born Abt. 1930.

3902. William Walter[14] White (Catherine Rebecca[13] Wolf, Catherine Rebecca[12] Ober, David[11], Isaac Huntsberger[10], Christian[9], Elizabeth[8] Stauffer, Johannes[7], Daniel[6] Stouffer, Christian[5] Stauffer, Daniel[4] Stouffer, Christian[3], Hans[2], Hans[1]) was born May 31, 1923 in Highspire, PA, and died August 31, 1998 in Highspire, PA. He married **(1) Emma Amelia Hackman** August 07, 1942 in St. Peter's Lutheran Church, Highspire, PA, daughter of Willis Hackman and Emma Geib. She was born May 28, 1921 in Millport, Warwick Township, Lancaster County, PA, and died November 03, 1994 in Elizabethtown, PA. He married **(2) Christabel J Deimler** October 1994. She was born Abt. 1945 in Perry County.

Children are listed above under (2527) Emma Amelia Hackman.

3903. Barbara[14] Kirkpatrick (Fannie O[13] Ober, Benjamin Franklin[12], David[11], Isaac Huntsberger[10], Christian[9], Elizabeth[8] Stauffer, Johannes[7], Daniel[6] Stouffer, Christian[5] Stauffer, Daniel[4] Stouffer, Christian[3], Hans[2], Hans[1]) was born 1919. She married **Herbert W Strong, Jr**. He was born Abt. 1910.

Child of Barbara Kirkpatrick and Herbert Strong is:
    5135   i.   Kirk M[15] Strong, born 1951.

3904. Vernon W[14] Sharpe (Eda R[13] Murphy, Agnes Eda[12] Ober, David[11], Isaac Huntsberger[10], Christian[9], Elizabeth[8] Stauffer, Johannes[7], Daniel[6] Stouffer, Christian[5] Stauffer, Daniel[4] Stouffer, Christian[3], Hans[2], Hans[1]) was born 1909. He married **Margaret B Atz**. She was born 1908.

Children of Vernon Sharpe and Margaret Atz are:
    5136   i.   Marjorie Ann[15] Sharpe, born 1931.
    5137   ii.   James W Sharpe, born 1933.
    5138   iii. Charles V Sharpe, born 1935.
    5139   iv. Mary C Sharpe, born 1945.

3905. Ruth B[14] Sharpe (Eda R[13] Murphy, Agnes Eda[12] Ober, David[11], Isaac Huntsberger[10], Christian[9], Elizabeth[8] Stauffer, Johannes[7], Daniel[6] Stouffer, Christian[5] Stauffer, Daniel[4] Stouffer, Christian[3], Hans[2], Hans[1]) was born 1912. She married **Morris B Cooper**. He was born 1912.

Children of Ruth Sharpe and Morris Cooper are:
    5140   i.   Donald W[15] Cooper, born 1939.

5141 ii. Jerold M Cooper, born 1942.
5142 iii. Alan C Cooper, born 1945.

3907. B Marie[14] Stevens (Rachael Agnes[13] Duncan, Annie Elizabeth[12] Ober, David[11], Isaac Huntsberger[10], Christian[9], Elizabeth[8] Stauffer, Johannes[7], Daniel[6] Stouffer, Christian[5] Stauffer, Daniel[4] Stouffer, Christian[3], Hans[2], Hans[1]) was born 1904. She married **George M Bingaman**. He was born 1901.

Children of B Stevens and George Bingaman are:
+ 5143 i. Nancy L[15] Bingaman, born 1927.
  5144 ii. John D Bingaman, born 1934.

3908. Arthur W[14] Stevens (Rachael Agnes[13] Duncan, Annie Elizabeth[12] Ober, David[11], Isaac Huntsberger[10], Christian[9], Elizabeth[8] Stauffer, Johannes[7], Daniel[6] Stouffer, Christian[5] Stauffer, Daniel[4] Stouffer, Christian[3], Hans[2], Hans[1]) was born 1907. He married **Hazel Peck**. She was born Abt. 1906.

Children of Arthur Stevens and Hazel Peck are:
5145 i. Arthur W[15] Stevens, Jr, born 1926.
5146 ii. John E Stevens, born 1935.

3909. Marlin O[14] Stevens (Rachael Agnes[13] Duncan, Annie Elizabeth[12] Ober, David[11], Isaac Huntsberger[10], Christian[9], Elizabeth[8] Stauffer, Johannes[7], Daniel[6] Stouffer, Christian[5] Stauffer, Daniel[4] Stouffer, Christian[3], Hans[2], Hans[1]) was born 1911. He married **Parthena S Valient**. She was born Abt. 1915.

Children of Marlin Stevens and Parthena Valient are:
5147 i. Kitty[15] Stevens, born 1933.
5148 ii. Arthur W Stevens, born 1936.
5149 iii. Marlin O Stevens, Jr, born 1938.
5150 iv. Paul A Stevens, born 1940.

3910. J Donald[14] Stevens (Rachael Agnes[13] Duncan, Annie Elizabeth[12] Ober, David[11], Isaac Huntsberger[10], Christian[9], Elizabeth[8] Stauffer, Johannes[7], Daniel[6] Stouffer, Christian[5] Stauffer, Daniel[4] Stouffer, Christian[3], Hans[2], Hans[1]) was born 1914. He married **Alva Kline**. She was born Abt. 1915.

Children of J Stevens and Alva Kline are:
5151 i. Mary E[15] Stevens, born 1943.
5152 ii. Richard L Stevens, born 1946.
5153 iii. Linda K Stevens, born 1948.
5154 iv. Virginia A Stevens, born 1949.
5155 v. Donna A Stevens, born 1952.

3913. Adrian E[14] Duncan (Alvid O[13], Annie Elizabeth[12] Ober, David[11], Isaac Huntsberger[10], Christian[9], Elizabeth[8] Stauffer, Johannes[7], Daniel[6] Stouffer, Christian[5] Stauffer, Daniel[4] Stouffer, Christian[3], Hans[2], Hans[1]) was born 1913. She married **Joseph C Fink**. He was born 1910.

Children of Adrian Duncan and Joseph Fink are:
+ 5156 i. Patricia L[15] Fink, born 1933.
  5157 ii. Joseph A Fink, born 1935.
  5158 iii. Barbara D Fink, born 1937; died 1937.
  5159 iv. James E Fink, born 1942.
  5160 v. Richard E Fink, born 1946.

3914. Delmar M[14] Duncan (Alvid O[13], Annie Elizabeth[12] Ober, David[11], Isaac Huntsberger[10], Christian[9], Elizabeth[8] Stauffer, Johannes[7], Daniel[6] Stouffer, Christian[5] Stauffer, Daniel[4] Stouffer, Christian[3], Hans[2], Hans[1]) was born 1918. He married **Marian A Rudy**. She was born Abt. 1920.

Children of Delmar Duncan and Marian Rudy are:
5161 i. Delmar A[15] Duncan, born 1940.
5162 ii. Shirley A Duncan, born 1942.
5163 iii. Lucille M Duncan, born 1944.

3915. Charlotte E[14] **Smolizer** (Katherine M[13] Duncan, Annie Elizabeth[12] Ober, David[11], Isaac Huntsberger[10], Christian[9], Elizabeth[8] Stauffer, Johannes[7], Daniel[6] Stouffer, Christian[5] Stauffer, Daniel[4] Stouffer, Christian[3], Hans[2], Hans[1]) was born 1911. She married **Myers W Knight**. He was born 1909.

Children of Charlotte Smolizer and Myers Knight are:
    5164   i.   Barbara J[15] Knight, born 1939.
    5165   ii.   Beverly A Knight, born 1946.

3916. Sylvan E[14] **Murray** (Anna B[13] Duncan, Annie Elizabeth[12] Ober, David[11], Isaac Huntsberger[10], Christian[9], Elizabeth[8] Stauffer, Johannes[7], Daniel[6] Stouffer, Christian[5] Stauffer, Daniel[4] Stouffer, Christian[3], Hans[2], Hans[1]) was born 1917. He married **Ruth R Pavlovich**. She was born 1928.

Child of Sylvan Murray and Ruth Pavlovich is:
    5166   i.   Judy A[15] Murray, born 1949.

3918. Donald E[14] **Murray** (Anna B[13] Duncan, Annie Elizabeth[12] Ober, David[11], Isaac Huntsberger[10], Christian[9], Elizabeth[8] Stauffer, Johannes[7], Daniel[6] Stouffer, Christian[5] Stauffer, Daniel[4] Stouffer, Christian[3], Hans[2], Hans[1]) was born 1926. He married **Betty J Clare**. She was born 1926.

Child of Donald Murray and Betty Clare is:
    5167   i.   Terry L[15] Murray, born 1950.

3920. Mary E[14] **Ober** (Wilbur C[13], David W[12], David[11], Isaac Huntsberger[10], Christian[9], Elizabeth[8] Stauffer, Johannes[7], Daniel[6] Stouffer, Christian[5] Stauffer, Daniel[4] Stouffer, Christian[3], Hans[2], Hans[1]) was born 1924. She married **A Morris Todd, Jr**. He was born Abt. 1920.

Children of Mary Ober and A Todd are:
    5168   i.   Michael M[15] Todd, born 1951.
    5169   ii.   Marc D Todd, born 1952.

3921. Wilbur C[14] **Ober, Jr** (Wilbur C[13], David W[12], David[11], Isaac Huntsberger[10], Christian[9], Elizabeth[8] Stauffer, Johannes[7], Daniel[6] Stouffer, Christian[5] Stauffer, Daniel[4] Stouffer, Christian[3], Hans[2], Hans[1]) was born 1926. He married **Betty Nussey**. She was born Abt. 1926.

Children of Wilbur Ober and Betty Nussey are:
    5170   i.   Kathleen P[15] Ober, born 1948.
    5171   ii.   Margaret R Ober, born 1950.

3927. Joan[14] **Ober** (Cecil S[13], Isaac Newton[12], David[11], Isaac Huntsberger[10], Christian[9], Elizabeth[8] Stauffer, Johannes[7], Daniel[6] Stouffer, Christian[5] Stauffer, Daniel[4] Stouffer, Christian[3], Hans[2], Hans[1]) was born Abt. 1925. She married **Howard Thomas**. He was born Abt. 1925.

Child of Joan Ober and Howard Thomas is:
    5172   i.   Carol J[15] Thomas, born Abt. 1950.

3931. Arden G[14] **Ober, Jr** (Arden G[13], Isaac Newton[12], David[11], Isaac Huntsberger[10], Christian[9], Elizabeth[8] Stauffer, Johannes[7], Daniel[6] Stouffer, Christian[5] Stauffer, Daniel[4] Stouffer, Christian[3], Hans[2], Hans[1]) was born Aft. 1920. He married **Fredrico Cox**. She was born Aft. 1920.

Child of Arden Ober and Fredrico Cox is:
    5173   i.   Vicky Lee[15] Ober, born Abt. 1945.

3932. Elaine C[14] **Ober** (Arden G[13], Isaac Newton[12], David[11], Isaac Huntsberger[10], Christian[9], Elizabeth[8] Stauffer, Johannes[7], Daniel[6] Stouffer, Christian[5] Stauffer, Daniel[4] Stouffer, Christian[3], Hans[2], Hans[1]) was born Aft. 1920. She married **James R Bell**. He was born Aft. 1920.

Child of Elaine Ober and James Bell is:
    5174   i.   Cynthia Ann[15] Bell, born Aft. 1940.

3938. Edna M[14] Knupp (Edna M[13] Smith, Florence May[12] Ober, David[11], Isaac Huntsberger[10], Christian[9], Elizabeth[8] Stauffer, Johannes[7], Daniel[6] Stouffer, Christian[5] Stauffer, Daniel[4] Stouffer, Christian[3], Hans[2], Hans[1]) was born 1911. She married **Unknown Rode**. He was born Abt. 1910, and died 1940.

Child of Edna Knupp and Unknown Rode is:
    5175   i.   Murial A[15] Rode, born 1938.

3941. Muriel R[14] Knupp (Edna M[13] Smith, Florence May[12] Ober, David[11], Isaac Huntsberger[10], Christian[9], Elizabeth[8] Stauffer, Johannes[7], Daniel[6] Stouffer, Christian[5] Stauffer, Daniel[4] Stouffer, Christian[3], Hans[2], Hans[1]) was born 1917. She married **Unknown Hopkins**. He was born Abt. 1915.

Children of Muriel Knupp and Unknown Hopkins are:
    5176   i.   Barbara G[15] Hopkins, born 1943.
    5177   ii.   Gary Lee Hopkins, born 1948.

3956. Elinor L.[14] Brinser (Mary L.[13] Morning, Annie[12] Ober, Michael Cramer[11], Michael[10], Henry[9], Elizabeth[8] Stauffer, Johannes[7], Daniel[6] Stouffer, Christian[5] Stauffer, Daniel[4] Stouffer, Christian[3], Hans[2], Hans[1]) was born June 11, 1914 in Elizabethtown, PA, and died October 16, 1987 in Rochester, NY. She married **James C. Rhoads** June 1937 in Harrisburg, PA. He was born July 17, 1912 in New York, N.Y., and died September 30, 1960 in At sea.

Children of Elinor Brinser and James Rhoads are:
+   5178   i.   Private[15] Rhoads.
    5179   ii.   Private Rhoads.
    5180   iii.   Private Rhoads.

3957. Minnie[14] Ober (Daisy Meyers[13], Moses Heagly[12], Moses Ruhl[11], Christian Longnecker[10], David S[9], Elizabeth[8] Stauffer, Johannes[7], Daniel[6] Stouffer, Christian[5] Stauffer, Daniel[4] Stouffer, Christian[3], Hans[2], Hans[1]) was born January 23, 1910 in PA, and died May 21, 1977 in Lancaster, PA. She married **Cyrus Derr** December 22, 1929. He was born February 29, 1904 in Maryland, and died March 10, 1995 in Mount Joy, PA.

Children of Minnie Ober and Cyrus Derr are:
    5181   i.   Living[15] Derr.
    5182   ii.   Living Derr. She married Oscar John Jumper.
    5183   iii.   Living Derr. She married Living Dunk.
    5184   iv.   Living Derr. She married Living Hartman.
    5185   v.   Luella Mae Ober Anthony Derr, born May 29, 1927; died July 26, 2002. She married Anthony ?.
+   5186   vi.   Jay Earl Franklin Derr, born March 24, 1930 in Susquehanna, PA; died November 17, 1981 in Lewistown, MT.
+   5187   vii.   Elizabeth Jane Feldser Derr, born August 06, 1934 in Lancaster, PA; died April 13, 2000 in New Bloomfield, PA.
    5188   viii.   Goldie Annabell Derr, born March 03, 1937 in PA; died May 1978 in Lancaster, PA.

3959. Elmer Ezra[14] Hitz (Stella M[13] Ober, Moses Heagly[12], Moses Ruhl[11], Christian Longnecker[10], David S[9], Elizabeth[8] Stauffer, Johannes[7], Daniel[6] Stouffer, Christian[5] Stauffer, Daniel[4] Stouffer, Christian[3], Hans[2], Hans[1]) was born June 13, 1920. He married **Emma Meashey Landis** June 30, 1941. She was born May 15, 1918.

Children of Elmer Hitz and Emma Landis are:
    5189   i.   Ann Marie[15] Hitz, born August 16, 1943.
+   5190   ii.   Elvin Ezra Hitz, born July 01, 1946.
+   5191   iii.   Galen D Hitz, born February 13, 1948.
+   5192   iv.   Jacob Landis Hitz, born January 24, 1953.
    5193   v.   John Amos Hitz, born December 22, 1955.
    5194   vi.   Katherine Jane Hitz, born June 06, 1968.

3965. Mary Belle[14] Eyer (Ella May[13] Stauffer, Mary Jane[12] Richardson, Sarah Rebecca[11] Bowers, Susannah[10] Ober, Henry[9], Veronica " Frany "[8] Stauffer, Johannes[7], Daniel[6] Stouffer, Christian[5] Stauffer, Daniel[4] Stouffer, Christian[3], Hans[2], Hans[1]) was born November 18, 1886 in Pine Creek Illinois, and died October 04, 1922 in Upland, California. She married **Ray C. Lehman** December 12, 1885 in Sedgwick, Kansas. He was born January 14, 1884 in Marcus, Iowa.

Children of Mary Eyer and Ray Lehman are:

5195 i. Private[15] Lehman.
5196 ii. Private Lehman.
5197 iii. Harold Ray Lehman, born February 28, 1909 in Glendale, Arizona.

3966. Lewis Benjamin[14] Eyer (Ella May[13] Stauffer, Mary Jane[12] Richardson, Sarah Rebecca[11] Bowers, Susannah[10] Ober, Henry[9], Veronica " Frany "[8] Stauffer, Johannes[7], Daniel[6] Stouffer, Christian[5] Stauffer, Daniel[4] Stouffer, Christian[3], Hans[2], Hans[1]) was born May 26, 1889 in Hamlin, Kansas, and died July 22, 1939 in Los Angeles, California. He married **Elsie Maye Grube** May 29, 1915 in Los Angeles, California. She was born May 15, 1890 in Council Hill, Illinois.

Children of Lewis Eyer and Elsie Grube are:
5198 i. Private[15] Eyer.
5199 ii. Private Eyer.
5200 iii. Private Eyer.

3967. Harold Ray[14] Eyer (Ella May[13] Stauffer, Mary Jane[12] Richardson, Sarah Rebecca[11] Bowers, Susannah[10] Ober, Henry[9], Veronica " Frany "[8] Stauffer, Johannes[7], Daniel[6] Stouffer, Christian[5] Stauffer, Daniel[4] Stouffer, Christian[3], Hans[2], Hans[1]) was born January 28, 1896 in Glendale, Arizona. He married **Elizabeth I. Turner** February 21, 1921 in Los Angeles, California. She was born October 03, 1895 in Camp Verde, Arizona.

Children of Harold Eyer and Elizabeth Turner are:
5201 i. Private[15] Eyer.
5202 ii. Private Eyer.

3968. John Paul[14] Eyer (Ella May[13] Stauffer, Mary Jane[12] Richardson, Sarah Rebecca[11] Bowers, Susannah[10] Ober, Henry[9], Veronica " Frany "[8] Stauffer, Johannes[7], Daniel[6] Stouffer, Christian[5] Stauffer, Daniel[4] Stouffer, Christian[3], Hans[2], Hans[1]) was born November 14, 1899 in Glendale, Arizona. He married **Irene Loretta Roth** March 01, 1919 in San Bernardino, California. She was born May 11, 1899 in Ste. Marie, Illinois.

Children of John Eyer and Irene Roth are:
5203 i. Private[15] Eyer.
5204 ii. Private Eyer.
5205 iii. Private Eyer.
5206 iv. Private Eyer.

3969. Katherine Lucile[14] Eyer (Ella May[13] Stauffer, Mary Jane[12] Richardson, Sarah Rebecca[11] Bowers, Susannah[10] Ober, Henry[9], Veronica " Frany "[8] Stauffer, Johannes[7], Daniel[6] Stouffer, Christian[5] Stauffer, Daniel[4] Stouffer, Christian[3], Hans[2], Hans[1]) was born July 02, 1903 in Glendale, Arizona. She married **Charles C. Engle** November 23, 1922 in Upland, California.

Children of Katherine Eyer and Charles Engle are:
5207 i. Private[15] Engle.
5208 ii. Private Engle.
5209 iii. Private Engle.

3970. Private[14] Stauffer (Andrew Grant[13], Mary Jane[12] Richardson, Sarah Rebecca[11] Bowers, Susannah[10] Ober, Henry[9], Veronica " Frany "[8] Stauffer, Johannes[7], Daniel[6] Stouffer, Christian[5] Stauffer, Daniel[4] Stouffer, Christian[3], Hans[2], Hans[1]) She married **Millard H. Patterson**. He was born September 16, 1920, and died November 04, 1984.

Child of Private Stauffer and Millard Patterson is:
5210 i. Private[15] Patterson.

3971. Paul J.[14] Stauffer (Andrew Grant[13], Mary Jane[12] Richardson, Sarah Rebecca[11] Bowers, Susannah[10] Ober, Henry[9], Veronica " Frany "[8] Stauffer, Johannes[7], Daniel[6] Stouffer, Christian[5] Stauffer, Daniel[4] Stouffer, Christian[3], Hans[2], Hans[1]) was born April 08, 1896 in Sedgwick, Kansas, and died July 29, 1922 in Newton, Kansas. He married **Viola E. Evans** September 10, 1916 in Valley Center, Kansas. She was born September 19, 1894 in New Murdock, Kansas, and died September 05, 1956.

Children of Paul Stauffer and Viola Evans are:
5211 i. Private[15] Stauffer.
5212 ii. Earl Evans Stauffer, born August 18, 1917 in Valley Center, Kansas; died July 27, 1966.
5213 iii. Agnes Pauline Stauffer, born May 08, 1919 in Valley Center, Kansas.

The Relations of Milton Snavely Hershey, 4th Ed.

3972. Aesta Blanch[14] **Staufer** (Andrew Grant[13] Stauffer, Mary Jane[12] Richardson, Sarah Rebecca[11] Bowers, Susannah[10] Ober, Henry[9], Veronica " Frany "[8] Stauffer, Johannes[7], Daniel[6] Stouffer, Christian[5] Stauffer, Daniel[4] Stouffer, Christian[3], Hans[2], Hans[1]) was born June 28, 1897 in Glendale, Arizona, and died September 03, 1982 in Wichita, Kansas. She married **Cecil E. Dick** March 12, 1939 in Vally center, Kansas. He was born October 08, 1888 in Sedwick, Kansas, and died July 1953 in Newton, Kansas.

Child of Aesta Staufer and Cecil Dick is:
    5214   i. Private[15] Dick.

3973. Charles Lloyd[14] **Stauffer** (Andrew Grant[13], Mary Jane[12] Richardson, Sarah Rebecca[11] Bowers, Susannah[10] Ober, Henry[9], Veronica " Frany "[8] Stauffer, Johannes[7], Daniel[6] Stouffer, Christian[5] Stauffer, Daniel[4] Stouffer, Christian[3], Hans[2], Hans[1]) was born August 11, 1899 in Sedgwick, Kansas, and died February 16, 1983. He married **(1) Bessie Sitier Lavender**. She was born October 08, 1906, and died October 08, 1988. He married **(2) Mary Dunn** September 02, 1922 in Valley Center, Kansas. She was born April 10, 1902 in Flushing, Ohio, and died November 26, 1963.

Children of Charles Stauffer and Mary Dunn are:
    5215   i. Private[15] Stauffer.
    5216   ii. Private Stauffer.

3975. Alice Pearl[14] **Stauffer** (Andrew Grant[13], Mary Jane[12] Richardson, Sarah Rebecca[11] Bowers, Susannah[10] Ober, Henry[9], Veronica " Frany "[8] Stauffer, Johannes[7], Daniel[6] Stouffer, Christian[5] Stauffer, Daniel[4] Stouffer, Christian[3], Hans[2], Hans[1]) was born October 18, 1905 in Valley Center, Kansas, and died July 11, 1958 in Newton, Kansas. She married **Lewin Guthrie** October 16, 1926 in Valley Center, Kansas. He was born July 29, 1902 in Sedgwick, Kansas.

Children of Alice Stauffer and Lewin Guthrie are:
    5217   i. Private[15] Guthrie.
    5218   ii. Private Guthrie.
    5219   iii. Private Guthrie.

3978. Mary Helen[14] **Stauffer** (Elias Richardson[13], Mary Jane[12] Richardson, Sarah Rebecca[11] Bowers, Susannah[10] Ober, Henry[9], Veronica " Frany "[8] Stauffer, Johannes[7], Daniel[6] Stouffer, Christian[5] Stauffer, Daniel[4] Stouffer, Christian[3], Hans[2], Hans[1]) was born March 19, 1901 in Prescott, Arizona. She married **Lloyd Archer Wall** December 10, 1924 in Prescott, Arizona. He was born May 23, 1895 in Alta, Iowa.

Children of Mary Stauffer and Lloyd Wall are:
    5220   i. Private[15] Wall.
    5221   ii. Private Wall.
    5222   iii. Private Wall.

3980. Private[14] **Stauffer** (Charles Albert[13], Mary Jane[12] Richardson, Sarah Rebecca[11] Bowers, Susannah[10] Ober, Henry[9], Veronica " Frany "[8] Stauffer, Johannes[7], Daniel[6] Stouffer, Christian[5] Stauffer, Daniel[4] Stouffer, Christian[3], Hans[2], Hans[1]) She married **Private Fahlen**.

Child of Private Stauffer and Private Fahlen is:
    5223   i. Private[15] Fahlen.

3984. Private[14] **Stauffer** (Ray Franklin[13], Mary Jane[12] Richardson, Sarah Rebecca[11] Bowers, Susannah[10] Ober, Henry[9], Veronica " Frany "[8] Stauffer, Johannes[7], Daniel[6] Stouffer, Christian[5] Stauffer, Daniel[4] Stouffer, Christian[3], Hans[2], Hans[1]) She married **(1) John Pendergast**. He was born in Phoenox, Arizona. She married **(2) Private Schwarting**. She married **(3) Private Morgan**.

Child of Private Stauffer and John Pendergast is:
    5224   i. Private[15] Pendergast.

3988. Private[14] **Griffen** (Sara Rebecca[13] Stauffer, Mary Jane[12] Richardson, Sarah Rebecca[11] Bowers, Susannah[10] Ober, Henry[9], Veronica " Frany "[8] Stauffer, Johannes[7], Daniel[6] Stouffer, Christian[5] Stauffer, Daniel[4] Stouffer, Christian[3], Hans[2], Hans[1]) She married **Private Rockwell**.

Children of Private Griffen and Private Rockwell are:
    5225   i. Private[15] Rockwell.
    5226   ii. Private Rockwell.

3990. Private[14] **Higley** (Mary Lemmie Ann[13] Stauffer, Mary Jane[12] Richardson, Sarah Rebecca[11] Bowers, Susannah[10] Ober, Henry[9],

Veronica " Frany "[8] Stauffer, Johannes[7], Daniel[6] Stouffer, Christian[5] Stauffer, Daniel[4] Stouffer, Christian[3], Hans[2], Hans[1]) He married **Private Fauher**.

Child of Private Higley and Private Fauher is:
    5227   i.   II Private[15] Higley.

3994. Magdalene Katherine[14] **Shelly** (Ellis Clinton[13], Susan Ann[12] Richardson, Sarah Rebecca[11] Bowers, Susannah[10] Ober, Henry[9], Veronica " Frany "[8] Stauffer, Johannes[7], Daniel[6] Stouffer, Christian[5] Stauffer, Daniel[4] Stouffer, Christian[3], Hans[2], Hans[1]) was born August 18, 1901 in Chicago, Illinois. She married **Joseph Edward Hartigan** July 10, 1923 in Chicago, Illinois. He was born January 01, 1896 in St. Joseph, Missouri.

Children of Magdalene Shelly and Joseph Hartigan are:
    5228   i.   Private[15] Hartigan.
    5229   ii.   Private Hartigan.
    5230   iii. Private Hartigan.

3996. Private[14] **Paul** (Emma Elizabeth[13] Trump, Rebecca Jane[12] Richardson, Sarah Rebecca[11] Bowers, Susannah[10] Ober, Henry[9], Veronica " Frany "[8] Stauffer, Johannes[7], Daniel[6] Stouffer, Christian[5] Stauffer, Daniel[4] Stouffer, Christian[3], Hans[2], Hans[1]) She married **Private Webb**.

Child of Private Paul and Private Webb is:
    5231   i.   Private[15] Webb.

3997. Bessie Norene[14] **Paul** (Emma Elizabeth[13] Trump, Rebecca Jane[12] Richardson, Sarah Rebecca[11] Bowers, Susannah[10] Ober, Henry[9], Veronica " Frany "[8] Stauffer, Johannes[7], Daniel[6] Stouffer, Christian[5] Stauffer, Daniel[4] Stouffer, Christian[3], Hans[2], Hans[1]) was born February 05, 1906. She married **Howard M. Dennis** July 24, 1924 in Polo, Illinois. He was born December 09, 1899 in Polo, Illinois.

Child of Bessie Paul and Howard Dennis is:
    5232   i.   Private[15] Dennis.

3998. Private[14] **Trump** (Oliver Garfield[13], Rebecca Jane[12] Richardson, Sarah Rebecca[11] Bowers, Susannah[10] Ober, Henry[9], Veronica " Frany "[8] Stauffer, Johannes[7], Daniel[6] Stouffer, Christian[5] Stauffer, Daniel[4] Stouffer, Christian[3], Hans[2], Hans[1]) She married **Private Hedrix**.

Children of Private Trump and Private Hedrix are:
    5233   i.   Private[15] Hendrix.
    5234   ii.   Private Hendrix.

4002. Private[14] **Trump** (John Henry[13], Rebecca Jane[12] Richardson, Sarah Rebecca[11] Bowers, Susannah[10] Ober, Henry[9], Veronica " Frany "[8] Stauffer, Johannes[7], Daniel[6] Stouffer, Christian[5] Stauffer, Daniel[4] Stouffer, Christian[3], Hans[2], Hans[1]) She married **(1) Private Harter**. She married **(2) Leighton Robert Taylor**. He was born April 03, 1908 in Chicago, IL., and died December 17, 1992 in Phenix, AZ.

Children of Private Trump and Private Harter are:
    5235   i.   Private[15] Harter.
    5236   ii.   Private Harter.
    5237   iii. Private Harter.

4003. Jerry Roosevelt[14] **Trump** (John Henry[13], Rebecca Jane[12] Richardson, Sarah Rebecca[11] Bowers, Susannah[10] Ober, Henry[9], Veronica " Frany "[8] Stauffer, Johannes[7], Daniel[6] Stouffer, Christian[5] Stauffer, Daniel[4] Stouffer, Christian[3], Hans[2], Hans[1]) was born December 12, 1902 in Polo, Illinois, and died June 27, 1989 in Arcadia, CA - 4076 Daines Dr. (Home). He married **Thelma Lucille Steele** June 08, 1925 in Stafford, Kansas. She was born April 14, 1906 in Newton, Kansas, and died April 04, 1989 in Arcadia, California.

Children of Jerry Trump and Thelma Steele are:
    5238   i.   Private[15] Trump.
    5239   ii.   Private Trump.
    5240   iii. Private Trump.

4005. Anita[14] **Trump** (John Henry[13], Rebecca Jane[12] Richardson, Sarah Rebecca[11] Bowers, Susannah[10] Ober, Henry[9], Veronica " Frany "[8] Stauffer, Johannes[7], Daniel[6] Stouffer, Christian[5] Stauffer, Daniel[4] Stouffer, Christian[3], Hans[2], Hans[1]) was born July 02, 1909 in

Sedgwick, Kansas. She married **Virgil William Cochran** April 08, 1928 in Hutchinson, Kansas. He was born August 10, 1906 in Peaxe Valley, Missouri.

Children of Anita Trump and Virgil Cochran are:
- 5241 i. Private[15] Cochran.
- 5242 ii. Private Cochran.

4008. Wanda Naomi[14] **Kinzer** (Goldie May[13] Snyder, Sarah B.[12] Richardson, Sarah Rebecca[11] Bowers, Susannah[10] Ober, Henry[9], Veronica " Frany "[8] Stauffer, Johannes[7], Daniel[6] Stouffer, Christian[5] Stauffer, Daniel[4] Stouffer, Christian[3], Hans[2], Hans[1]) was born May 10, 1895 in Mulvane, Kansas. She married **Robb E. Isaacs** January 02, 1915 in New Douglas, Illinois. He was born June 05, 1893 in New Douglas, Illinois.

Children of Wanda Kinzer and Robb Isaacs are:
- 5243 i. Private[15] Isaacs.
- 5244 ii. Private Isaacs.
- 5245 iii. Private Isaacs.
- 5246 iv. Kenneth Eugene Isaacs, born May 05, 1923 in New Douglas, Illinois; died May 05, 1923 in New Douglas, Illinois.

4010. Jesse Arden[14] **Kinzer** (Goldie May[13] Snyder, Sarah B.[12] Richardson, Sarah Rebecca[11] Bowers, Susannah[10] Ober, Henry[9], Veronica " Frany "[8] Stauffer, Johannes[7], Daniel[6] Stouffer, Christian[5] Stauffer, Daniel[4] Stouffer, Christian[3], Hans[2], Hans[1]) was born February 03, 1907 in New Douglas, Illinois. He married **Leanore Williams** November 12, 1927 in New Douglas, Illinois. She was born June 06, 1908 in Panama, Illinois.

Children of Jesse Kinzer and Leanore Williams are:
- 5247 i. Private[15] Kinzer.
- 5248 ii. Private Kinzer.

4013. Charles Snyder[14] **Frost** (Sarah Jane[13] Snyder, Sarah B.[12] Richardson, Sarah Rebecca[11] Bowers, Susannah[10] Ober, Henry[9], Veronica " Frany "[8] Stauffer, Johannes[7], Daniel[6] Stouffer, Christian[5] Stauffer, Daniel[4] Stouffer, Christian[3], Hans[2], Hans[1]) was born April 10, 1900 in Wichita, Kansas. She married **Edith Marie Bergren** April 18, 1922 in St. Paul, Minnesota. He was born April 20, 1898 in Lindstrom, Minnesota.

Child of Charles Frost and Edith Bergren is:
- 5249 i. Private[15] Frost.

4014. Private[14] **Hamilton** (Harriet Lucretia[13] Snyder, Sarah B.[12] Richardson, Sarah Rebecca[11] Bowers, Susannah[10] Ober, Henry[9], Veronica " Frany "[8] Stauffer, Johannes[7], Daniel[6] Stouffer, Christian[5] Stauffer, Daniel[4] Stouffer, Christian[3], Hans[2], Hans[1]) She married **Private Dukart**.

Child of Private Hamilton and Private Dukart is:
- 5250 i. Private[15] Dukart.

4017. Elton Kenneth[14] **Hamilton** (Harriet Lucretia[13] Snyder, Sarah B.[12] Richardson, Sarah Rebecca[11] Bowers, Susannah[10] Ober, Henry[9], Veronica " Frany "[8] Stauffer, Johannes[7], Daniel[6] Stouffer, Christian[5] Stauffer, Daniel[4] Stouffer, Christian[3], Hans[2], Hans[1]) was born July 14, 1906 in Dodge City, Kansas. He married **Elvera E. Johnson** April 09, 1929 in Los Angeles, California. She was born August 17, 1909 in Dayton, Ohio.

Children of Elton Hamilton and Elvera Johnson are:
- 5251 i. Private[15] Hamilton.
- 5252 ii. Private Hamilton.

4020. Carl Andrew[14] **Richardson** (Stephen Andrew[13], Andrew Jackson[12], Sarah Rebecca[11] Bowers, Susannah[10] Ober, Henry[9], Veronica " Frany "[8] Stauffer, Johannes[7], Daniel[6] Stouffer, Christian[5] Stauffer, Daniel[4] Stouffer, Christian[3], Hans[2], Hans[1]) was born July 26, 1908 in Belle Plaine, Kansas. He married **Bealah Verdie Woolridge** February 06, 1926 in Wellington, Kansas. She was born June 02, 1904.

Children of Carl Richardson and Bealah Woolridge are:
- 5253 i. Private[15] Richardson.
- 5254 ii. Private Richardson.
- 5255 iii. Private Richardson.

5256   iv.   Private Richardson.
5257   v.   Private Richardson.

4024. Private[14] Barner (Mattie Beulah[13] Richardson, Andrew Jackson[12], Sarah Rebecca[11] Bowers, Susannah[10] Ober, Henry[9], Veronica " Frany "[8] Stauffer, Johannes[7], Daniel[6] Stouffer, Christian[5] Stauffer, Daniel[4] Stouffer, Christian[3], Hans[2], Hans[1]) He married **Private Oitman**.

Children of Private Barner and Private Oitman are:
5258   i.   Private[15] Barner.
5259   ii.   Private Barner.

4027. Ramona Lee[14] Barner (Mattie Beulah[13] Richardson, Andrew Jackson[12], Sarah Rebecca[11] Bowers, Susannah[10] Ober, Henry[9], Veronica " Frany "[8] Stauffer, Johannes[7], Daniel[6] Stouffer, Christian[5] Stauffer, Daniel[4] Stouffer, Christian[3], Hans[2], Hans[1]) was born October 06, 1907 in Belle Plaine, Kansas. She married **Andrew Jackson Turner** September 04, 1931 in Long Beach, California. He was born September 14, 1905 in Linden, Texas.

Child of Ramona Barner and Andrew Turner is:
5260   i.   Private[15] Turner.

4028. Charles Merle[14] Barner (Mattie Beulah[13] Richardson, Andrew Jackson[12], Sarah Rebecca[11] Bowers, Susannah[10] Ober, Henry[9], Veronica " Frany "[8] Stauffer, Johannes[7], Daniel[6] Stouffer, Christian[5] Stauffer, Daniel[4] Stouffer, Christian[3], Hans[2], Hans[1]) was born September 23, 1909 in Belle Plaine, Kansas. He married **Private Reeves**.

Children of Charles Barner and Private Reeves are:
5261   i.   Private[15] Barner.
5262   ii.   Private Barner.
5263   iii.   Private Barner.
5264   iv.   Private Barner.

4029. Private[14] Richardson (Melville Jackson[13], Andrew Jackson[12], Sarah Rebecca[11] Bowers, Susannah[10] Ober, Henry[9], Veronica " Frany "[8] Stauffer, Johannes[7], Daniel[6] Stouffer, Christian[5] Stauffer, Daniel[4] Stouffer, Christian[3], Hans[2], Hans[1]) She married **Private McDaniel**.

Child of Private Richardson and Private McDaniel is:
5265   i.   Private[15] McDanill.

4030. Private[14] Richardson (Melville Jackson[13], Andrew Jackson[12], Sarah Rebecca[11] Bowers, Susannah[10] Ober, Henry[9], Veronica " Frany "[8] Stauffer, Johannes[7], Daniel[6] Stouffer, Christian[5] Stauffer, Daniel[4] Stouffer, Christian[3], Hans[2], Hans[1]) He married **Private Applying**.

Child of Private Richardson and Private Applying is:
5266   i.   Private[15] Richardson.

4031. Private[14] Alter (Margaret Ella Blanch[13] Richardson, Andrew Jackson[12], Sarah Rebecca[11] Bowers, Susannah[10] Ober, Henry[9], Veronica " Frany "[8] Stauffer, Johannes[7], Daniel[6] Stouffer, Christian[5] Stauffer, Daniel[4] Stouffer, Christian[3], Hans[2], Hans[1]) She married **Private Reiter**.

Children of Private Alter and Private Reiter are:
5267   i.   Private[15] Reiter.
5268   ii.   Private Reiter.

4032. Private[14] Lane (Eva Beatrice[13] Richardson, Andrew Jackson[12], Sarah Rebecca[11] Bowers, Susannah[10] Ober, Henry[9], Veronica " Frany "[8] Stauffer, Johannes[7], Daniel[6] Stouffer, Christian[5] Stauffer, Daniel[4] Stouffer, Christian[3], Hans[2], Hans[1]) She married **Private Osborn**.

Children of Private Lane and Private Osborn are:
5269   i.   Private[15] Osborn.
5270   ii.   Private Osborn.

4054. Thora Isabelle[14] Line (Stephen Clyde[13], Harriet May[12] Richardson, Sarah Rebecca[11] Bowers, Susannah[10] Ober, Henry[9], Veronica " Frany "[8] Stauffer, Johannes[7], Daniel[6] Stouffer, Christian[5] Stauffer, Daniel[4] Stouffer, Christian[3], Hans[2], Hans[1]) was born October 24, 1910 in Dayton, Ohio, and died December 30, 1990 in West Palm Beach, Florida. She married **Stuart Joseph Odin Heavyside** June 20, 1935 in Richmond, Indiana. He was born November 02, 1904 in Edgware, England, and died April 07, 1988 in West Palm Beach, Florida.

Children of Thora Line and Stuart Heavyside are:
- 5271 i. Private[15] Heavyside.
- 5272 ii. Joan Elizabeth Heavyside, born July 16, 1938 in Dayton, Ohio; died July 10, 1976 in Virginia Beach, Virginia.

4055. Private[14] Loose (Mabel Beatrice[13] Line, Harriet May[12] Richardson, Sarah Rebecca[11] Bowers, Susannah[10] Ober, Henry[9], Veronica " Frany "[8] Stauffer, Johannes[7], Daniel[6] Stouffer, Christian[5] Stauffer, Daniel[4] Stouffer, Christian[3], Hans[2], Hans[1]) She married **Charles David Cooper**. He was born August 22, 1911 in Cincinnatti, Ohio, and died September 1979.

Child of Private Loose and Charles Cooper is:
- 5273 i. Private[15] Cooper.

4056. Private[14] Loose (Mabel Beatrice[13] Line, Harriet May[12] Richardson, Sarah Rebecca[11] Bowers, Susannah[10] Ober, Henry[9], Veronica " Frany "[8] Stauffer, Johannes[7], Daniel[6] Stouffer, Christian[5] Stauffer, Daniel[4] Stouffer, Christian[3], Hans[2], Hans[1]) He married **Private Wiggins**.

Child of Private Loose and Private Wiggins is:
- 5274 i. Private[15] Loose.

4057. Carl Maurice[14] Loose (Mabel Beatrice[13] Line, Harriet May[12] Richardson, Sarah Rebecca[11] Bowers, Susannah[10] Ober, Henry[9], Veronica " Frany "[8] Stauffer, Johannes[7], Daniel[6] Stouffer, Christian[5] Stauffer, Daniel[4] Stouffer, Christian[3], Hans[2], Hans[1]) was born February 26, 1911 in Dayton, Ohio, and died September 1991. He married **Barbara M. Light** July 28, 1934 in Dayton, Ohio. She was born November 15, 1902 in Dayton, Ohio, and died May 1983.

Children of Carl Loose and Barbara Light are:
- 5275 i. Private[15] Loose.
- 5276 ii. Private Loose.

4061. Private[14] Harnish (Sara Margaret[13] Line, Harriet May[12] Richardson, Sarah Rebecca[11] Bowers, Susannah[10] Ober, Henry[9], Veronica " Frany "[8] Stauffer, Johannes[7], Daniel[6] Stouffer, Christian[5] Stauffer, Daniel[4] Stouffer, Christian[3], Hans[2], Hans[1]) She married **James Signor Ward**. He was born January 30, 1914 in Dayton, Ohio, and died January 30, 1996.

Child of Private Harnish and James Ward is:
- 5277 i. Private[15] Ward.

4066. Private[14] Mornhengweig (Agatha E.[13] Haynes, Martha[12] Richardson, Sarah Rebecca[11] Bowers, Susannah[10] Ober, Henry[9], Veronica " Frany "[8] Stauffer, Johannes[7], Daniel[6] Stouffer, Christian[5] Stauffer, Daniel[4] Stouffer, Christian[3], Hans[2], Hans[1])

Child of Private Mornhengweig is:
- 5278 i. Private[15] Mornhengweig.

4068. Private[14] Mornhengweig (Agatha E.[13] Haynes, Martha[12] Richardson, Sarah Rebecca[11] Bowers, Susannah[10] Ober, Henry[9], Veronica " Frany "[8] Stauffer, Johannes[7], Daniel[6] Stouffer, Christian[5] Stauffer, Daniel[4] Stouffer, Christian[3], Hans[2], Hans[1]) She married **Private Buller**.

Child of Private Mornhengweig and Private Buller is:
- 5279 i. Private[15] Miller.

4078. Private[14] Level (John Howard[13], Mary Ann[12] Lesher, David[11], Barbara[10] Ober, Michael[9], Veronica " Frany "[8] Stauffer, Johannes[7], Daniel[6] Stouffer, Christian[5] Stauffer, Daniel[4] Stouffer, Christian[3], Hans[2], Hans[1]) She married **Private Burdett**.

Child of Private Level and Private Burdett is:
- 5280 i. Private[15] Burdett.

4079. Private[14] Level (John Howard[13], Mary Ann[12] Lesher, David[11], Barbara[10] Ober, Michael[9], Veronica " Frany "[8] Stauffer, Johannes[7], Daniel[6] Stouffer, Christian[5] Stauffer, Daniel[4] Stouffer, Christian[3], Hans[2], Hans[1]) She married **Private Morris**.

Children of Private Level and Private Morris are:
- 5281 i. Private[15] Morris.
- 5282 ii. Private Morris.
- 5283 iii. Private Morris.
- 5284 iv. Private Morris.

4080. Private[14] Level (John Howard[13], Mary Ann[12] Lesher, David[11], Barbara[10] Ober, Michael[9], Veronica " Frany "[8] Stauffer, Johannes[7], Daniel[6] Stouffer, Christian[5] Stauffer, Daniel[4] Stouffer, Christian[3], Hans[2], Hans[1]) She married **Private Griffith**.

Child of Private Level and Private Griffith is:
- 5285 i. Private[15] Griffith.

4084. Bethel Leone[14] Tyner (Myrtle Liliom D.[13] Diehl, David Alfred[12], Catherine A.[11] Ober, Jacob[10], Michael[9], Veronica " Frany "[8] Stauffer, Johannes[7], Daniel[6] Stouffer, Christian[5] Stauffer, Daniel[4] Stouffer, Christian[3], Hans[2], Hans[1])

Child of Bethel Leone Tyner is:
- 5286 i. Lew[15].

4098. Private[14] Diehl (Percy Ellsworth[13], David Alfred[12], Catherine A.[11] Ober, Jacob[10], Michael[9], Veronica " Frany "[8] Stauffer, Johannes[7], Daniel[6] Stouffer, Christian[5] Stauffer, Daniel[4] Stouffer, Christian[3], Hans[2], Hans[1]) He married **Private Sherman**.

Children of Private Diehl and Private Sherman are:
- + 5287 i. Private[15] Diehl.
- + 5288 ii. Private Diehl.
- + 5289 iii. Private Diehl.

4099. Private[14] Diehl (Percy Ellsworth[13], David Alfred[12], Catherine A.[11] Ober, Jacob[10], Michael[9], Veronica " Frany "[8] Stauffer, Johannes[7], Daniel[6] Stouffer, Christian[5] Stauffer, Daniel[4] Stouffer, Christian[3], Hans[2], Hans[1]) He married **(1) Private Zimmer**. He married **(2) Private Unknown**. He married **(3) Private Unknown**.

Child of Private Diehl and Private Zimmer is:
- 5290 i. Private[15] Diehl.

Children of Private Diehl and Private Unknown are:
- + 5291 i. Private[15] Diehl.
- + 5292 ii. Private Diehl.
- + 5293 iii. Private Diehl.
- + 5294 iv. Private Diehl.

4100. Private[14] Diehl (Percy Ellsworth[13], David Alfred[12], Catherine A.[11] Ober, Jacob[10], Michael[9], Veronica " Frany "[8] Stauffer, Johannes[7], Daniel[6] Stouffer, Christian[5] Stauffer, Daniel[4] Stouffer, Christian[3], Hans[2], Hans[1]) She married **Private Pike**.

Children of Private Diehl and Private Pike are:
- + 5295 i. Private[15] Pike.
- + 5296 ii. Private Pike.
- 5297 iii. Brian K. Pike, born December 14, 1973 in Traverse City, Grand Traverse County, Michigan; died May 12, 1999 in Munson Medical Ctr., Traverse City, Grand Traverse County, Michigan. He married Private Bennett.

4101. Juanita Glada[14] Diehl (Percy Ellsworth[13], David Alfred[12], Catherine A.[11] Ober, Jacob[10], Michael[9], Veronica " Frany "[8] Stauffer, Johannes[7], Daniel[6] Stouffer, Christian[5] Stauffer, Daniel[4] Stouffer, Christian[3], Hans[2], Hans[1]) was born December 09, 1921 in Maple City, Michigan, and died February 19, 2002 in Traverse City, Michigan. She married **William Martin Bright** October 15, 1940 in Traverse City, Michigan. He was born August 08, 1918 in East Kasson Township, and died March 16, 2001 in Traverse City, Michigan.

Marriage Notes for Juanita Diehl and William Bright:
[Henry Ober 1742.ged]

The Relations of Milton Snavely Hershey, 4th Ed.

_STATMARRIED

Children of Juanita Diehl and William Bright are:
+ 5298 i. Private[15] Bright.
+ 5299 ii. Private Bright.

4102. David R.[14] Diehl (Percy Ellsworth[13], David Alfred[12], Catherine A.[11] Ober, Jacob[10], Michael[9], Veronica " Frany "[8] Stauffer, Johannes[7], Daniel[6] Stouffer, Christian[5] Stauffer, Daniel[4] Stouffer, Christian[3], Hans[2], Hans[1]) was born November 15, 1922 in Maple City, Michigan, and died August 02, 1994 in Lakeview, Michigan. He married **Marie Highers(Unknown)** December 04, 1959 in Germany.

Marriage Notes for David Diehl and Marie Highers(Unknown):
[Henry Ober 1742.ged]

_STATMARRIED

Children of David Diehl and Marie Highers(Unknown) are:
  5300 i. Private[15] Diehl.
  5301 ii. Private Diehl.

4105. Donald[14] Diehl (Percy Ellsworth[13], David Alfred[12], Catherine A.[11] Ober, Jacob[10], Michael[9], Veronica " Frany "[8] Stauffer, Johannes[7], Daniel[6] Stouffer, Christian[5] Stauffer, Daniel[4] Stouffer, Christian[3], Hans[2], Hans[1]) was born August 23, 1930 in Maple City, Michigan, and died September 29, 1990 in Traverse City, Michigan. He married **Private Manger**.

Children of Donald Diehl and Private Manger are:
+ 5302 i. Private[15] Diehl.
  5303 ii. Private Diehl. She married Private Eager.
  5304 iii. Private Diehl. She married Private Josline.
  5305 iv. Private Diehl. She married Private Zimmerman.
  5306 v. Private Diehl. He married (1) Private Radcliffe. He married (2) Private Tvardek.
  5307 vi. Private Diehl.
  5308 vii. Private Diehl. He married Private Abbey.
  5309 viii. Private Diehl. She married Private Gauthier.

4115. Arlene Celeste[14] Brubaker (Allen L[13], Ezra[12], Christian[11], Christian[10], Elizabeth[9] Stauffer, Christian[8], Henry Jacob[7], Hans[6], Christian[5], Daniel[4] Stouffer, Christian[3], Hans[2], Hans[1]) was born January 08, 1911. She married **Luke Musser Mosemann** September 20, 1934. He was born July 29, 1908, and died September 26, 1986.

Children of Arlene Brubaker and Luke Mosemann are:
  5310 i. Private[15] Mosemann, born Abt. 1936.
  5311 ii. Private Mosemann, born Abt. 1938.
  5312 iii. Private Mosemann, born Abt. 1940.
+ 5313 iv. Private Mosemann, born Abt. 1942.

4127. Lois Jean[14] Yaggi (Ruth Isabel[13] Scott, Nancy[12] Ruff, Mary Ann[11] Stoffer, Louis J[10], Jacob[9], Jacob[8] Stauffer, Henry Jacob[7], Hans[6], Christian[5], Daniel[4] Stouffer, Christian[3], Hans[2], Hans[1]) She married **John Hofer**. He was born May 22, 1915, and died April 16, 1974.

Children of Lois Yaggi and John Hofer are:
  5314 i. Private[15] Hofer.
  5315 ii. Private Hofer.
  5316 iii. Private Hofer.
  5317 iv. Private Hofer.
  5318 v. Private Hofer.
  5319 vi. Private Hofer.
  5320 vii. Private Hofer.
  5321 viii. Private Hofer.
  5322 ix. Private Hofer.
  5323 x. Private Hofer.

4128. Agnes Ruth[14] Yaggi (Ruth Isabel[13] Scott, Nancy[12] Ruff, Mary Ann[11] Stoffer, Louis J[10], Jacob[9], Jacob[8] Stauffer, Henry Jacob[7], Hans[6], Christian[5], Daniel[4] Stouffer, Christian[3], Hans[2], Hans[1]) She married **Kertes Joseph**. He was born January 28, 1914.

Children of Agnes Yaggi and Kertes Joseph are:
- 5324   i. Private[15] Kertes.
- 5325   ii. Private Kertes.
- 5326   iii. Private Kertes.

4129. Mary Elizabeth[14] Yaggi (Ruth Isabel[13] Scott, Nancy[12] Ruff, Mary Ann[11] Stoffer, Louis J[10], Jacob[9], Jacob[8] Stauffer, Henry Jacob[7], Hans[6], Christian[5], Daniel[4] Stouffer, Christian[3], Hans[2], Hans[1]) was born June 23, 1919 in Columbiana County, Ohio, and died November 26, 1980. She married **McCelland Edward Miller**. He was born May 02, 1918, and died April 02, 1964.

Children of Mary Yaggi and McCelland Miller are:
- 5327   i. Private[15] Miller.
- 5328   ii. Private Miller.

4139. Lowell[14] Baker (Inez Genesta[13] Stoffer, Walter George[12], Lewis Jr[11], Louis J[10], Jacob[9], Jacob[8] Stauffer, Henry Jacob[7], Hans[6], Christian[5], Daniel[4] Stouffer, Christian[3], Hans[2], Hans[1]) He married **Marjorie Jean Beck**. She was born February 17, 1923 in Columbiana County, Ohio, and died April 05, 1997 in Columbiana County, Ohio.

Children of Lowell Baker and Marjorie Beck are:
- 5329   i. Private[15] Baker.
- 5330   ii. Private Baker.
- 5331   iii. Private Baker.
- 5332   iv. Private Baker.
- 5333   v. Private Baker.
- 5334   vi. Private Baker.
- 5335   vii. Private Baker.

4140. Lewis John[14] Stoffer (Virgil Forest[13], Walter George[12], Lewis Jr[11], Louis J[10], Jacob[9], Jacob[8] Stauffer, Henry Jacob[7], Hans[6], Christian[5], Daniel[4] Stouffer, Christian[3], Hans[2], Hans[1]) He married **Private Buck**.

Children of Lewis Stoffer and Private Buck are:
- 5336   i. Private[15] Stoffer.
- 5337   ii. Private Stoffer.
- 5338   iii. Private Stoffer.
- 5339   iv. Private Stoffer.

4141. Kenneth George[14] Stoffer (Virgil Forest[13], Walter George[12], Lewis Jr[11], Louis J[10], Jacob[9], Jacob[8] Stauffer, Henry Jacob[7], Hans[6], Christian[5], Daniel[4] Stouffer, Christian[3], Hans[2], Hans[1]) was born February 22, 1922. He married **Mary Angela Meng**.

Children of Kenneth Stoffer and Mary Meng are:
- 5340   i. Private[15] Stoffer.
- 5341   ii. Private Stoffer.
- 5342   iii. Private Stoffer.
- 5343   iv. Private Stoffer.

4142. Barbara Sue[14] Stoffer (Virgil Forest[13], Walter George[12], Lewis Jr[11], Louis J[10], Jacob[9], Jacob[8] Stauffer, Henry Jacob[7], Hans[6], Christian[5], Daniel[4] Stouffer, Christian[3], Hans[2], Hans[1]) was born March 04, 1924. She married **Arthur "Murray" Cunningham**.

Children of Barbara Stoffer and Arthur Cunningham are:
- 5344   i. Private[15] Cunningham.
- 5345   ii. Private Cunningham.
- 5346   iii. Private Cunningham.

4143. Kathryn Olive[14] Stoffer (Virgil Forest[13], Walter George[12], Lewis Jr[11], Louis J[10], Jacob[9], Jacob[8] Stauffer, Henry Jacob[7], Hans[6], Christian[5], Daniel[4] Stouffer, Christian[3], Hans[2], Hans[1]) was born March 25, 1924 in Columbiana County, Ohio, and died December 31, 1995 in California. She married **Robert Cope Brown** January 22, 1944. He was born October 12, 1921 in Greenfield, Ohio, and died December 07, 1993 in California.

Children of Kathryn Stoffer and Robert Brown are:
- 5347   i. Private[15] Brown.

5348 ii. Private Brown.
5349 iii. Private Brown.
5350 iv. Private Brown.

4145. Dorothy Mae[14] Knoll (Beulah Fern[13] Stoffer, Walter George[12], Lewis Jr[11], Louis J[10], Jacob[9], Jacob[8] Stauffer, Henry Jacob[7], Hans[6], Christian[5], Daniel[4] Stouffer, Christian[3], Hans[2], Hans[1]) She married **Robert Oliver Pickens**.

Children of Dorothy Knoll and Robert Pickens are:
5351 i. Private[15] Pickens.
5352 ii. Private Pickens.
5353 iii. Private Pickens.

4147. Private[14] Ward (Dorothy Ada[13] Stoffer, Walter George[12], Lewis Jr[11], Louis J[10], Jacob[9], Jacob[8] Stauffer, Henry Jacob[7], Hans[6], Christian[5], Daniel[4] Stouffer, Christian[3], Hans[2], Hans[1]) He married **Private Jacoby**.

Children of Private Ward and Private Jacoby are:
5354 i. Private[15] Ward.
5355 ii. Private Ward.
5356 iii. Private Ward.

4148. Private[14] Ward (Dorothy Ada[13] Stoffer, Walter George[12], Lewis Jr[11], Louis J[10], Jacob[9], Jacob[8] Stauffer, Henry Jacob[7], Hans[6], Christian[5], Daniel[4] Stouffer, Christian[3], Hans[2], Hans[1]) She married **Private Salisbury**.

Children of Private Ward and Private Salisbury are:
5357 i. Private[15] Salisbury.
5358 ii. Private Salisbury.
5359 iii. Private Salisbury.

4152. Frank JR[14] Stoffer (Frank[13], David[12], Jacob L[11], Samuel[10], Jacob[9], Jacob[8] Stauffer, Henry Jacob[7], Hans[6], Christian[5], Daniel[4] Stouffer, Christian[3], Hans[2], Hans[1]) was born September 27, 1933, and died September 17, 1995 in Ohio. He married **Connie L Gaverick**. She was born 1938.

Children of Frank Stoffer and Connie Gaverick are:
5360 i. Private[15] Stoffer.
5361 ii. Private Stoffer.

4154. C Robert[14] Stoffer (Frank[13], David[12], Jacob L[11], Samuel[10], Jacob[9], Jacob[8] Stauffer, Henry Jacob[7], Hans[6], Christian[5], Daniel[4] Stouffer, Christian[3], Hans[2], Hans[1]) was born February 19, 1912 in Columbiana Cty, Ohio, and died January 25, 1999 in Salem, Columbiana Cty, Ohio. He married **Isabelle L Mercer** August 05, 1941. She was born July 16, 1921.

Children of C Stoffer and Isabelle Mercer are:
5362 i. Private[15] Stoffer.
5363 ii. Private Stoffer.
5364 iii. Private Stoffer.
5365 iv. Private Stoffer.
5366 v. Private Stoffer.

4161. Private[14] Gearhart (Dayle Kermit[13], Cynthia Idella[12] Stoffer, John Jacob[11], John[10], Jacob[9], Jacob[8] Stauffer, Henry Jacob[7], Hans[6], Christian[5], Daniel[4] Stouffer, Christian[3], Hans[2], Hans[1]) She married **Roger William Stevens**. He was born January 03, 1944 in Ky, Boyd Co, and died May 10, 1995 in Ohio, Richland Co.

Children of Private Gearhart and Roger Stevens are:
5367 i. Private[15] Stevens.
5368 ii. Private Stevens.
5369 iii. Private Stevens.
5370 iv. Bryan Keith Stevens, born June 01, 1968 in Ky, Boyd Co; died June 01, 1968 in Ky, Boyd Co.

4164. Mary Elizabeth[14] Agnew (Stella[13] Moser, Ada[12] Stoffer, Levi[11], George[10], Jacob[9], Jacob[8] Stauffer, Henry Jacob[7], Hans[6], Christian[5], Daniel[4] Stouffer, Christian[3], Hans[2], Hans[1]) She married **Lloyd Abney**.

Child of Mary Agnew and Lloyd Abney is:
5371 i. Neil[15] Abney.

4167. Charles[14] Agnew (Stella[13] Moser, Ada[12] Stoffer, Levi[11], George[10], Jacob[9], Jacob[8] Stauffer, Henry Jacob[7], Hans[6], Christian[5], Daniel[4] Stouffer, Christian[3], Hans[2], Hans[1]) was born June 23, 1911, and died September 16, 1958. He married **Lucille Martin**.

Children of Charles Agnew and Lucille Martin are:
5372 i. Private[15] Agnew.
5373 ii. Private Agnew.

4168. Donald Robert[14] Agnew (Stella[13] Moser, Ada[12] Stoffer, Levi[11], George[10], Jacob[9], Jacob[8] Stauffer, Henry Jacob[7], Hans[6], Christian[5], Daniel[4] Stouffer, Christian[3], Hans[2], Hans[1]) was born June 14, 1917. He married **Louise Huges** December 08, 1939. She was born March 14, 1920.

Child of Donald Agnew and Louise Huges is:
5374 i. Private[15] Agnew.

4169. Private[14] Stoffer (Harold Walter[13], Laurance L[12], Levi[11], George[10], Jacob[9], Jacob[8] Stauffer, Henry Jacob[7], Hans[6], Christian[5], Daniel[4] Stouffer, Christian[3], Hans[2], Hans[1]) He married **Private Allshouse**.

Children of Private Stoffer and Private Allshouse are:
5375 i. Private[15] Stoffer.
5376 ii. Private Stoffer.
5377 iii. Matthew Alan Stoffer, born January 09, 1974 in Barberton Citizens Hosptial, Barberton, Ohio; died September 01, 2000 in Twinsburg, Summit County, Ohio.

4171. Private[14] Mercer (Orvie W[13], Pearl[12] Stoffer, Levi[11], George[10], Jacob[9], Jacob[8] Stauffer, Henry Jacob[7], Hans[6], Christian[5], Daniel[4] Stouffer, Christian[3], Hans[2], Hans[1]) He married **(1) Private Unknown**. He married **(2) Private Myrna**.

Children of Private Mercer and Private Unknown are:
5378 i. Private[15] Mercer.
5379 ii. Private Mercer.
5380 iii. Private Mercer.
5381 iv. Private Mercer.

4173. Ruth[14] Mercer (Orvie W[13], Pearl[12] Stoffer, Levi[11], George[10], Jacob[9], Jacob[8] Stauffer, Henry Jacob[7], Hans[6], Christian[5], Daniel[4] Stouffer, Christian[3], Hans[2], Hans[1]) was born March 20, 1922. She married **Bob Pancake** November 25, 1942. He was born January 23, 1921.

Children of Ruth Mercer and Bob Pancake are:
5382 i. Private[15] Pancake.
5383 ii. Private Pancake.
5384 iii. Private Pancake.
5385 iv. Private Pancake.

4174. Ruby[14] Mercer (Orvie W[13], Pearl[12] Stoffer, Levi[11], George[10], Jacob[9], Jacob[8] Stauffer, Henry Jacob[7], Hans[6], Christian[5], Daniel[4] Stouffer, Christian[3], Hans[2], Hans[1]) was born May 21, 1923. She married **(1) Oscar Roof**. She married **(2) Orian Brown**.

Child of Ruby Mercer and Oscar Roof is:
5386 i. Private[15] Roof.

Child of Ruby Mercer and Orian Brown is:
5387 i. Private[15] Brown.

4175. Private[14] Mercer (Chester[13], Pearl[12] Stoffer, Levi[11], George[10], Jacob[9], Jacob[8] Stauffer, Henry Jacob[7], Hans[6], Christian[5], Daniel[4] Stouffer, Christian[3], Hans[2], Hans[1]) She married **Private Hardgrove**.

Children of Private Mercer and Private Hardgrove are:

5388 i. Private[15] Hardgrove.
5389 ii. Private Hardgrove.
5390 iii. Private Hardgrove.
5391 iv. Private Hardgrove.
5392 v. Private Hardgrove.

4176. Private[14] Mercer (Chester[13], Pearl[12] Stoffer, Levi[11], George[10], Jacob[9], Jacob[8] Stauffer, Henry Jacob[7], Hans[6], Christian[5], Daniel[4] Stouffer, Christian[3], Hans[2], Hans[1]) He married **Private Jane**.

Children of Private Mercer and Private Jane are:
5393 i. Private[15] Mercer.
5394 ii. Private Mercer.
5395 iii. Private Mercer.

4177. Private[14] Mercer (Chester[13], Pearl[12] Stoffer, Levi[11], George[10], Jacob[9], Jacob[8] Stauffer, Henry Jacob[7], Hans[6], Christian[5], Daniel[4] Stouffer, Christian[3], Hans[2], Hans[1]) He married **Private Denny**.

Child of Private Mercer and Private Denny is:
5396 i. Private[15] Mercer.

4178. Private[14] Mercer (Chester[13], Pearl[12] Stoffer, Levi[11], George[10], Jacob[9], Jacob[8] Stauffer, Henry Jacob[7], Hans[6], Christian[5], Daniel[4] Stouffer, Christian[3], Hans[2], Hans[1]) She married **Private Butch**.

Child of Private Mercer and Private Butch is:
5397 i. Private[15] Butch.

4179. Private[14] Mercer (Herbert Russell[13], Pearl[12] Stoffer, Levi[11], George[10], Jacob[9], Jacob[8] Stauffer, Henry Jacob[7], Hans[6], Christian[5], Daniel[4] Stouffer, Christian[3], Hans[2], Hans[1]) She married **Kenneth Allen Baumgartner**. He was born July 15, 1929.

Children of Private Mercer and Kenneth Baumgartner are:
5398 i. Private[15] Baumgartner.
5399 ii. Private Baumgartner.
5400 iii. Private Baumgartner.
5401 iv. Private Baumgartner.

4180. Private[14] Sneltzer (Hazel Debra[13] Mercer, Pearl[12] Stoffer, Levi[11], George[10], Jacob[9], Jacob[8] Stauffer, Henry Jacob[7], Hans[6], Christian[5], Daniel[4] Stouffer, Christian[3], Hans[2], Hans[1]) She married **Private Hrovatic**.

Children of Private Sneltzer and Private Hrovatic are:
5402 i. Private[15] Hrovatic.
5403 ii. Private Hrovatic.

4181. Private[14] Sneltzer (Hazel Debra[13] Mercer, Pearl[12] Stoffer, Levi[11], George[10], Jacob[9], Jacob[8] Stauffer, Henry Jacob[7], Hans[6], Christian[5], Daniel[4] Stouffer, Christian[3], Hans[2], Hans[1]) He married **Private Fleming**.

Children of Private Sneltzer and Private Fleming are:
5404 i. Private[15] Sneltzer.
5405 ii. Private Sneltzer.
5406 iii. Private Sneltzer.

4182. Private[14] Sneltzer (Hazel Debra[13] Mercer, Pearl[12] Stoffer, Levi[11], George[10], Jacob[9], Jacob[8] Stauffer, Henry Jacob[7], Hans[6], Christian[5], Daniel[4] Stouffer, Christian[3], Hans[2], Hans[1]) He married **Private Keeler**.

Child of Private Sneltzer and Private Keeler is:
5407 i. Private[15] Sneltzer.

4183. Private[14] Sneltzer (Hazel Debra[13] Mercer, Pearl[12] Stoffer, Levi[11], George[10], Jacob[9], Jacob[8] Stauffer, Henry Jacob[7], Hans[6], Christian[5], Daniel[4] Stouffer, Christian[3], Hans[2], Hans[1]) She married **Private Mapes**.

Children of Private Sneltzer and Private Mapes are:
5408 i. Private[15] lll.
5409 ii. Private Mapes.

4187. Private[14] Mercer (Glenn A[13], Pearl[12] Stoffer, Levi[11], George[10], Jacob[9], Jacob[8] Stauffer, Henry Jacob[7], Hans[6], Christian[5], Daniel[4] Stouffer, Christian[3], Hans[2], Hans[1]) She married **Private Reese**.

Children of Private Mercer and Private Reese are:
5410 i. Private[15] Reese.
5411 ii. Private Reese.

4191. Thomas Lawrence[14] Stoffer (Paul Lawrence[13], William Franklin[12], Laurtis W.[11], George[10], Jacob[9], Jacob[8] Stauffer, Henry Jacob[7], Hans[6], Christian[5], Daniel[4] Stouffer, Christian[3], Hans[2], Hans[1]) was born December 21, 1922 in North Georgetown. He married **Donna Rupert** August 18, 1946 in Greenwich Ohio. She was born August 11, 1921 in Savannah Ohio.

Children of Thomas Stoffer and Donna Rupert are:
5412 i. Private[15] Stoffer.
5413 ii. Private Stoffer.
5414 iii. Private Stoffer.
5415 iv. Private Stoffer.

4192. Ellen Ann[14] Stoffer (Paul Lawrence[13], William Franklin[12], Laurtis W.[11], George[10], Jacob[9], Jacob[8] Stauffer, Henry Jacob[7], Hans[6], Christian[5], Daniel[4] Stouffer, Christian[3], Hans[2], Hans[1]) was born May 05, 1925. She married **Ray Sluss**.

Children of Ellen Stoffer and Ray Sluss are:
5416 i. Private[15] Sluss.
5417 ii. Private Sluss.
5418 iii. Private Sluss.

4193. Robert Liewellyn[14] Stoffer (Paul Lawrence[13], William Franklin[12], Laurtis W.[11], George[10], Jacob[9], Jacob[8] Stauffer, Henry Jacob[7], Hans[6], Christian[5], Daniel[4] Stouffer, Christian[3], Hans[2], Hans[1]) was born September 16, 1927. He married **Private Selby**.

Children of Robert Stoffer and Private Selby are:
5419 i. Private[15] Stoffer.
5420 ii. Private Stoffer.
5421 iii. Private Stoffer.

4230. Private[14] Randall (Lowell Orland[13], Mary Catherine[12] Stoffer, Laurtis W.[11], George[10], Jacob[9], Jacob[8] Stauffer, Henry Jacob[7], Hans[6], Christian[5], Daniel[4] Stouffer, Christian[3], Hans[2], Hans[1]) She married **Private Shackleton**.

Children of Private Randall and Private Shackleton are:
5422 i. Private[15] Shackleton.
5423 ii. Private Shackleton.
5424 iii. Private Shackleton.

4231. Private[14] Randall (Lowell Orland[13], Mary Catherine[12] Stoffer, Laurtis W.[11], George[10], Jacob[9], Jacob[8] Stauffer, Henry Jacob[7], Hans[6], Christian[5], Daniel[4] Stouffer, Christian[3], Hans[2], Hans[1]) He married **Private Censky**.

Children of Private Randall and Private Censky are:
5425 i. Private[15] Randall.
5426 ii. Private Randall.

4241. Private[14] Stoffer (Robert Price[13], Bryan Sewell[12], Laurtis W.[11], George[10], Jacob[9], Jacob[8] Stauffer, Henry Jacob[7], Hans[6], Christian[5], Daniel[4] Stouffer, Christian[3], Hans[2], Hans[1]) He married **Private Beer**.

Child of Private Stoffer and Private Beer is:
5427 i. Private[15] Stoffer.

4243. Private[14] Stoffer (Private[13], George Allen[12], Simon Henry[11], George[10], Jacob[9], Jacob[8] Stauffer, Henry Jacob[7], Hans[6], Christian[5], Daniel[4] Stouffer, Christian[3], Hans[2], Hans[1]) She married **Private Cruce**.

Children of Private Stoffer and Private Cruce are:
- 5428   i.   Private[15] Cruce.
- 5429   ii. Private Cruce.
- 5430   iii. Private Cruce.
- 5431   iv. Private Cruce.

4244. Private[14] Stoffer (Private[13], George Allen[12], Simon Henry[11], George[10], Jacob[9], Jacob[8] Stauffer, Henry Jacob[7], Hans[6], Christian[5], Daniel[4] Stouffer, Christian[3], Hans[2], Hans[1]) He married **(1) Private Truesdale**.   He married **(2) Private St Armond**.

Children of Private Stoffer and Private Truesdale are:
- 5432   i.   Private[15] Stoffer.
- 5433   ii. Private Stoffer.

4245. Private[14] Stoffer (Private[13], George Allen[12], Simon Henry[11], George[10], Jacob[9], Jacob[8] Stauffer, Henry Jacob[7], Hans[6], Christian[5], Daniel[4] Stouffer, Christian[3], Hans[2], Hans[1]) He married **Private King**.

Children of Private Stoffer and Private King are:
- 5434   i.   Private[15] Stoffer.
- 5435   ii. Private Stoffer.
- 5436   iii. Private Stoffer.

4246. Private[14] Stoffer (Private[13], George Allen[12], Simon Henry[11], George[10], Jacob[9], Jacob[8] Stauffer, Henry Jacob[7], Hans[6], Christian[5], Daniel[4] Stouffer, Christian[3], Hans[2], Hans[1]) She married **Private Martenize**.

Child of Private Stoffer and Private Martenize is:
- 5437   i.   Private[15] Martenize.

4247. Private[14] Stoffer (Private[13], George Allen[12], Simon Henry[11], George[10], Jacob[9], Jacob[8] Stauffer, Henry Jacob[7], Hans[6], Christian[5], Daniel[4] Stouffer, Christian[3], Hans[2], Hans[1]) She married **(1) Private Burns**.   She married **(2) Private Hardy**.

Children of Private Stoffer and Private Burns are:
- 5438   i.   Private[15] Burns.
- 5439   ii. Private Burns.
- 5440   iii. Private Burns.

4248. Private[14] Stoffer (Private[13], George Allen[12], Simon Henry[11], George[10], Jacob[9], Jacob[8] Stauffer, Henry Jacob[7], Hans[6], Christian[5], Daniel[4] Stouffer, Christian[3], Hans[2], Hans[1]) She married **Private Tedford**.

Children of Private Stoffer and Private Tedford are:
- 5441   i.   Private[15] Tedford.
- 5442   ii. Private Tedford.

4249. Private[14] Stoffer (Private[13], George Allen[12], Simon Henry[11], George[10], Jacob[9], Jacob[8] Stauffer, Henry Jacob[7], Hans[6], Christian[5], Daniel[4] Stouffer, Christian[3], Hans[2], Hans[1]) He married **Private Allison**.

Children of Private Stoffer and Private Allison are:
- 5443   i.   Private[15] Stoffer.
- 5444   ii. Private Stoffer.

4250. Private[14] Burns (Lola Mae[13] Stoffer, George Allen[12], Simon Henry[11], George[10], Jacob[9], Jacob[8] Stauffer, Henry Jacob[7], Hans[6], Christian[5], Daniel[4] Stouffer, Christian[3], Hans[2], Hans[1]) He married **Private Unknown**.

Children of Private Burns and Private Unknown are:
- 5445   i.   Private[15] Burns.
- 5446   ii. Private Burns.

5447	iii.	Private Burns.
5448	iv.	Private Burns.
5449	v.	Private Burns.

4251. Private[14] **Burns** (Lola Mae[13] Stoffer, George Allen[12], Simon Henry[11], George[10], Jacob[9], Jacob[8] Stauffer, Henry Jacob[7], Hans[6], Christian[5], Daniel[4] Stouffer, Christian[3], Hans[2], Hans[1]) He married **(1) Private Unknown**. He married **(2) Private Unknown**.

Children of Private Burns and Private Unknown are:
5450	i.	Private[15] Burns.
5451	ii.	Private Burns.

Child of Private Burns and Private Unknown is:
5452	i.	Private[15] Burns.

4252. Private[14] **Stoffer** (Roy Dean[13], George Allen[12], Simon Henry[11], George[10], Jacob[9], Jacob[8] Stauffer, Henry Jacob[7], Hans[6], Christian[5], Daniel[4] Stouffer, Christian[3], Hans[2], Hans[1]) She married **(1) Thomas Elijah Evans**. He was born July 20, 1952 in Purcell Okla., and died August 12, 1992 in Wilson Okla.. She married **(2) Private Baxter**.

Child of Private Stoffer and Thomas Evans is:
5453	i.	Private[15] Evans.

Child of Private Stoffer and Private Baxter is:
5454	i.	Private[15] Baxter.

4254. Private[14] **Stoffer** (Roy Dean[13], George Allen[12], Simon Henry[11], George[10], Jacob[9], Jacob[8] Stauffer, Henry Jacob[7], Hans[6], Christian[5], Daniel[4] Stouffer, Christian[3], Hans[2], Hans[1]) She married **Private Beasley**.

Children of Private Stoffer and Private Beasley are:
5455	i.	Private[15] Beasley.
5456	ii.	Private Jr.

4263. Private[14] **Barnett** (Dale Eugene[13], Vera Lucille[12] Stoffer, Rolandus[11], George[10], Jacob[9], Jacob[8] Stauffer, Henry Jacob[7], Hans[6], Christian[5], Daniel[4] Stouffer, Christian[3], Hans[2], Hans[1]) She married **Private Shanks**.

Children of Private Barnett and Private Shanks are:
5457	i.	Private[15] Shanks.
5458	ii.	Private Shanks.

4264. Private[14] **Barnett** (Dale Eugene[13], Vera Lucille[12] Stoffer, Rolandus[11], George[10], Jacob[9], Jacob[8] Stauffer, Henry Jacob[7], Hans[6], Christian[5], Daniel[4] Stouffer, Christian[3], Hans[2], Hans[1]) She married **Private Burrier**.

Children of Private Barnett and Private Burrier are:
5459	i.	Private[15] Burrier.
5460	ii.	Private Burrier.

4267. Private[14] **Barnett** (Jay Melvin[13], Vera Lucille[12] Stoffer, Rolandus[11], George[10], Jacob[9], Jacob[8] Stauffer, Henry Jacob[7], Hans[6], Christian[5], Daniel[4] Stouffer, Christian[3], Hans[2], Hans[1]) He married **Beatrice Loos**. She was born July 10.

Children of Private Barnett and Beatrice Loos are:
5461	i.	Private[15] Barnett.
5462	ii.	Private Barnett.

4268. Private[14] **Barnett** (Jay Melvin[13], Vera Lucille[12] Stoffer, Rolandus[11], George[10], Jacob[9], Jacob[8] Stauffer, Henry Jacob[7], Hans[6], Christian[5], Daniel[4] Stouffer, Christian[3], Hans[2], Hans[1]) She married **Private Jones**.

Children of Private Barnett and Private Jones are:
5463	i.	Private[15] Jones.

5464   ii.   Private Jones.

4270. Carl[14] Kibler (Alta[13] Mountz, Bertha Lorena[12] Stoffer, George D[11], George[10], Jacob[9], Jacob[8] Stauffer, Henry Jacob[7], Hans[6], Christian[5], Daniel[4] Stouffer, Christian[3], Hans[2], Hans[1]) He married **Betty Powell** August 07, 1949.

Children of Carl Kibler and Betty Powell are:
5465   i.   Private[15] Kibler.
5466   ii.   Private Kibler.
5467   iii. Private Kibler.
5468   iv.   Private Kibler.
5469   v.   Private Kibler.
5470   vi.   Private Kibler.
5471   vii. Private Kibler.
5472   viii. Private Kibler.
5473   ix.   Private Kibler.
5474   x.   Private Kibler.

4271. Robert[14] Kibler (Alta[13] Mountz, Bertha Lorena[12] Stoffer, George D[11], George[10], Jacob[9], Jacob[8] Stauffer, Henry Jacob[7], Hans[6], Christian[5], Daniel[4] Stouffer, Christian[3], Hans[2], Hans[1]) was born February 06, 1924. He married **Betty Cain** June 07, 1947. She was born May 07, 1929.

Children of Robert Kibler and Betty Cain are:
5475   i.   Private[15] Kibler.
5476   ii.   Private Kibler.
5477   iii. Private Kibler.
5478   iv.   Private Kibler.
5479   v.   Private Kibler.

4272. Joyce[14] Kibler (Alta[13] Mountz, Bertha Lorena[12] Stoffer, George D[11], George[10], Jacob[9], Jacob[8] Stauffer, Henry Jacob[7], Hans[6], Christian[5], Daniel[4] Stouffer, Christian[3], Hans[2], Hans[1]) was born May 20, 1925. She married **Elmer A Orsbirn** March 31, 1942. He was born June 16, 1922.

Children of Joyce Kibler and Elmer Orsbirn are:
5480   i.   Private[15] Orsbirn.
5481   ii.   Private Orsbirn.
5482   iii. Private Orsbirn.
5483   iv.   Private Orsbirn.
5484   v.   Private Orsbirn.
5485   vi.   Private Orsbirn.

4273. Lolyd[14] Kibler (Alta[13] Mountz, Bertha Lorena[12] Stoffer, George D[11], George[10], Jacob[9], Jacob[8] Stauffer, Henry Jacob[7], Hans[6], Christian[5], Daniel[4] Stouffer, Christian[3], Hans[2], Hans[1]) was born July 25, 1926. He married **Betty Mc Manas** July 20, 1957. She was born March 18, 1927.

Child of Lolyd Kibler and Betty Mc Manas is:
5486   i.   Private[15] Kibler.

4274. June[14] Kibler (Alta[13] Mountz, Bertha Lorena[12] Stoffer, George D[11], George[10], Jacob[9], Jacob[8] Stauffer, Henry Jacob[7], Hans[6], Christian[5], Daniel[4] Stouffer, Christian[3], Hans[2], Hans[1]) was born November 06, 1927. She married **Leroy Rodgers**. He was born September 12, 1926.

Children of June Kibler and Leroy Rodgers are:
5487   i.   Private[15] Rodgers.
5488   ii.   Private Rodgers.

4275. Private[14] Mountz (Wilfred[13], Bertha Lorena[12] Stoffer, George D[11], George[10], Jacob[9], Jacob[8] Stauffer, Henry Jacob[7], Hans[6], Christian[5], Daniel[4] Stouffer, Christian[3], Hans[2], Hans[1]) He married **Private Smith**.

Children of Private Mountz and Private Smith are:
5489   i.   Private[15] Mountz.

5490 ii. Private Mountz.

4276. Private[14] **Mountz** (Wilfred[13], Bertha Lorena[12] Stoffer, George D[11], George[10], Jacob[9], Jacob[8] Stauffer, Henry Jacob[7], Hans[6], Christian[5], Daniel[4] Stouffer, Christian[3], Hans[2], Hans[1]) She married **Private Cummings**.

Children of Private Mountz and Private Cummings are:
5491 i. Private[15] Cummings.
5492 ii. Private Cummings.

4278. Private[14] **Mountz** (Wilfred[13], Bertha Lorena[12] Stoffer, George D[11], George[10], Jacob[9], Jacob[8] Stauffer, Henry Jacob[7], Hans[6], Christian[5], Daniel[4] Stouffer, Christian[3], Hans[2], Hans[1]) She married **Private Bardo**.

Child of Private Mountz and Private Bardo is:
5493 i. Private[15] Bardo.

4279. Private[14] **Planchock** (Mary[13] Mountz, Bertha Lorena[12] Stoffer, George D[11], George[10], Jacob[9], Jacob[8] Stauffer, Henry Jacob[7], Hans[6], Christian[5], Daniel[4] Stouffer, Christian[3], Hans[2], Hans[1]) She married **Private Hepler**.

Children of Private Planchock and Private Hepler are:
5494 i. Private[15] Hepler.
5495 ii. Private Hepler.

4280. Private[14] **Planchock** (Mary[13] Mountz, Bertha Lorena[12] Stoffer, George D[11], George[10], Jacob[9], Jacob[8] Stauffer, Henry Jacob[7], Hans[6], Christian[5], Daniel[4] Stouffer, Christian[3], Hans[2], Hans[1]) He married **Private Yanosh**.

Children of Private Planchock and Private Yanosh are:
5496 i. Private[15] Planchock.
5497 ii. Private Planchock.

4282. Private[14] **Planchock** (Mary[13] Mountz, Bertha Lorena[12] Stoffer, George D[11], George[10], Jacob[9], Jacob[8] Stauffer, Henry Jacob[7], Hans[6], Christian[5], Daniel[4] Stouffer, Christian[3], Hans[2], Hans[1]) She married **Private Fidoe**.

Child of Private Planchock and Private Fidoe is:
5498 i. Private[15] Fidoe.

4285. Private[14] **Martig** (Kathryn[13] Mountz, Bertha Lorena[12] Stoffer, George D[11], George[10], Jacob[9], Jacob[8] Stauffer, Henry Jacob[7], Hans[6], Christian[5], Daniel[4] Stouffer, Christian[3], Hans[2], Hans[1]) He married **Private Paxon**.

Children of Private Martig and Private Paxon are:
5499 i. Private[15] Martig.
5500 ii. Private Martig.
5501 iii. Private Martig.
5502 iv. Private Martig.

4286. Private[14] **Martig** (Kathryn[13] Mountz, Bertha Lorena[12] Stoffer, George D[11], George[10], Jacob[9], Jacob[8] Stauffer, Henry Jacob[7], Hans[6], Christian[5], Daniel[4] Stouffer, Christian[3], Hans[2], Hans[1]) She married **Private Sartwell**.

Child of Private Martig and Private Sartwell is:
5503 i. Private[15] Sartwell.

4295. Private[14] **Stoffer** (Orlan Clifford[13], Wesley Emerson[12], George D[11], George[10], Jacob[9], Jacob[8] Stauffer, Henry Jacob[7], Hans[6], Christian[5], Daniel[4] Stouffer, Christian[3], Hans[2], Hans[1]) She married **(1) Private McLaughlin**.   She married **(2) Private Kail**.

Children of Private Stoffer and Private Kail are:
5504 i. Private[15] Kail.
5505 ii. Private Kail.
5506 iii. Private Kail.

4296. Private[14] Stoffer (Orlan Clifford[13], Wesley Emerson[12], George D[11], George[10], Jacob[9], Jacob[8] Stauffer, Henry Jacob[7], Hans[6], Christian[5], Daniel[4] Stouffer, Christian[3], Hans[2], Hans[1]) She married **(1) Private Stitch**.   She married **(2) Private Mc Laughlin**.

Child of Private Stoffer and Private Stitch is:
    5507   i.   Private[15] Stitch.

4297. Private[14] Stoffer (Orlan Clifford[13], Wesley Emerson[12], George D[11], George[10], Jacob[9], Jacob[8] Stauffer, Henry Jacob[7], Hans[6], Christian[5], Daniel[4] Stouffer, Christian[3], Hans[2], Hans[1]) He married **Private Cole**.

Children of Private Stoffer and Private Cole are:
    5508   i.   Private[15] Stoffer.
    5509   ii.   Private Stoffer.

4299. Private[14] Coughen (Verma Adella[13] Stoffer, Wesley Emerson[12], George D[11], George[10], Jacob[9], Jacob[8] Stauffer, Henry Jacob[7], Hans[6], Christian[5], Daniel[4] Stouffer, Christian[3], Hans[2], Hans[1]) She married **Private Van Hiner**.

Child of Private Coughen and Private Van Hiner is:
    5510   i.   Private[15] Van Hiner.

4300. Private[14] Coughen (Verma Adella[13] Stoffer, Wesley Emerson[12], George D[11], George[10], Jacob[9], Jacob[8] Stauffer, Henry Jacob[7], Hans[6], Christian[5], Daniel[4] Stouffer, Christian[3], Hans[2], Hans[1]) She married **Private Adams**.

Child of Private Coughen and Private Adams is:
    5511   i.   Private[15] Adams.

4319. Private[14] Stoffer (Clarence Leward[13], Benjamine Franklin[12], Stanton Uriah[11], George[10], Jacob[9], Jacob[8] Stauffer, Henry Jacob[7], Hans[6], Christian[5], Daniel[4] Stouffer, Christian[3], Hans[2], Hans[1]) She married **(1) Private Popa**.   She married **(2) Private Popa**.

Child of Private Stoffer and Private Popa is:
    5512   i.   Private[15] Popa.

Child of Private Stoffer and Private Popa is:
    5513   i.   Private[15] Popa.

4320. Larry Lee[14] Stoffer (Clarence Leward[13], Benjamine Franklin[12], Stanton Uriah[11], George[10], Jacob[9], Jacob[8] Stauffer, Henry Jacob[7], Hans[6], Christian[5], Daniel[4] Stouffer, Christian[3], Hans[2], Hans[1]) was born November 04, 1937 in Ohio, and died January 24, 1992 in Las Vegas, Clark Co., Nevada. He married **Private Fenell**.

Children of Larry Stoffer and Private Fenell are:
    5514   i.   Private[15] Stoffer.
    5515   ii.   Private Stoffer.

4321. Private[14] Stoffer (Clifford Lewis[13], Benjamine Franklin[12], Stanton Uriah[11], George[10], Jacob[9], Jacob[8] Stauffer, Henry Jacob[7], Hans[6], Christian[5], Daniel[4] Stouffer, Christian[3], Hans[2], Hans[1]) He married **(1) Private Unknown**.   He married **(2) Private M(Sargent)**.

Children of Private Stoffer and Private Unknown are:
    5516   i.   Private[15] Stoffer.
    5517   ii.   Private Stoffer.
    5518   iii.   Private Stoffer.
    5519   iv.   Private Stoffer.

Children of Private Stoffer and Private M(Sargent) are:
    5520   i.   Private[15] Stoffer.
    5521   ii.   Private Stoffer.
    5522   iii.   Private Stoffer.
    5523   iv.   Private Stoffer.

4322. Private[14] **Stoffer** (Clifford Lewis[13], Benjamine Franklin[12], Stanton Uriah[11], George[10], Jacob[9], Jacob[8] Stauffer, Henry Jacob[7], Hans[6], Christian[5], Daniel[4] Stouffer, Christian[3], Hans[2], Hans[1]) She married **Ralph Kettering**. He was born June 08, 1929, and died November 19, 1995 in Ohio.

Children of Private Stoffer and Ralph Kettering are:
- 5524 i. Private[15] Kettering.
- 5525 ii. Private Kettering.
- 5526 iii. Private Kettering.

4328. Private[14] **Stoffer** (Milan Benjamin[13], Benjamine Franklin[12], Stanton Uriah[11], George[10], Jacob[9], Jacob[8] Stauffer, Henry Jacob[7], Hans[6], Christian[5], Daniel[4] Stouffer, Christian[3], Hans[2], Hans[1]) He married **Private Miller**.

Children of Private Stoffer and Private Miller are:
- 5527 i. Private[15] Stoffer.
- 5528 ii. Private Stoffer.
- 5529 iii. Private Stoffer.
- 5530 iv. Private Stoffer.

4329. Private[14] **Stoffer** (Milan Benjamin[13], Benjamine Franklin[12], Stanton Uriah[11], George[10], Jacob[9], Jacob[8] Stauffer, Henry Jacob[7], Hans[6], Christian[5], Daniel[4] Stouffer, Christian[3], Hans[2], Hans[1]) She married **Private Mordeau**.

Child of Private Stoffer and Private Mordeau is:
- 5531 i. Private[15] Mordeau.

4330. Dale Milan[14] **Stoffer** (Milan Benjamin[13], Benjamine Franklin[12], Stanton Uriah[11], George[10], Jacob[9], Jacob[8] Stauffer, Henry Jacob[7], Hans[6], Christian[5], Daniel[4] Stouffer, Christian[3], Hans[2], Hans[1]) was born September 20, 1934 in Ohio, and died November 18, 2000 in Lithia Springs Ga, Douglas Co. He married **(1) Private Unknown**. He married **(2) Private Chastine**.

Children of Dale Stoffer and Private Chastine are:
- 5532 i. Private[15] Stoffer.
- 5533 ii. Private Stoffer.
- 5534 iii. Private Stoffer.

4331. Private[14] **Stoffer** (Ray Arnold[13], Benjamine Franklin[12], Stanton Uriah[11], George[10], Jacob[9], Jacob[8] Stauffer, Henry Jacob[7], Hans[6], Christian[5], Daniel[4] Stouffer, Christian[3], Hans[2], Hans[1]) She married **Private Myers**.

Children of Private Stoffer and Private Myers are:
- 5535 i. Private[15] Myers.
- 5536 ii. Private Myers.

4338. Private[14] **DePalmo** (Cleo Ruth[13] Stoffer, Benjamine Franklin[12], Stanton Uriah[11], George[10], Jacob[9], Jacob[8] Stauffer, Henry Jacob[7], Hans[6], Christian[5], Daniel[4] Stouffer, Christian[3], Hans[2], Hans[1]) She married **(1) Private Walker**. She married **(2) Oscar Edward Collingsworth**. He was born January 23, 1934 in Duck Run, Portsmith Ohio, and died May 14, 1992 in Canton Ohio.

Children of Private DePalmo and Private Walker are:
- 5537 i. Private[15] DePalmo.
- 5538 ii. Private DePalmo.

4339. Private[14] **DePalmo** (Cleo Ruth[13] Stoffer, Benjamine Franklin[12], Stanton Uriah[11], George[10], Jacob[9], Jacob[8] Stauffer, Henry Jacob[7], Hans[6], Christian[5], Daniel[4] Stouffer, Christian[3], Hans[2], Hans[1]) He married **(1) Private Unknown**. He married **(2) Private Grogg**. He married **(3) Private Germonoff**. He married **(4) Private Wiley**.

Child of Private DePalmo and Private Unknown is:
- 5539 i. Private[15] DePalmo.

Child of Private DePalmo and Private Grogg is:
- 5540 i. Private[15] DePalmo.

Child of Private DePalmo and Private Germonoff is:
    5541   i. Private[15] DePalmo.

Child of Private DePalmo and Private Wiley is:
    5542   i. Private[15] DePalmo.

4340. Private[14] DePalmo (Cleo Ruth[13] Stoffer, Benjamine Franklin[12], Stanton Uriah[11], George[10], Jacob[9], Jacob[8] Stauffer, Henry Jacob[7], Hans[6], Christian[5], Daniel[4] Stouffer, Christian[3], Hans[2], Hans[1]) He married **(1) Private Chadwick**. He married **(2) Private Grogg**. He married **(3) Private Phillips**.

Children of Private DePalmo and Private Grogg are:
    5543   i. Private[15] DePalmo.
    5544   ii. Private DePalmo.

Child of Private DePalmo and Private Phillips is:
    5545   i. Private[15] DePalmo.

4341. Private[14] DePalmo (Cleo Ruth[13] Stoffer, Benjamine Franklin[12], Stanton Uriah[11], George[10], Jacob[9], Jacob[8] Stauffer, Henry Jacob[7], Hans[6], Christian[5], Daniel[4] Stouffer, Christian[3], Hans[2], Hans[1]) She married **(1) Private Renfro**. She married **(2) Private Hamilton**. She married **(3) Private Johnson**.

Children of Private DePalmo and Private Hamilton are:
    5546   i. Private[15] Hamilton.
    5547   ii. Private Hamilton.

4342. Private[14] DePalmo (Cleo Ruth[13] Stoffer, Benjamine Franklin[12], Stanton Uriah[11], George[10], Jacob[9], Jacob[8] Stauffer, Henry Jacob[7], Hans[6], Christian[5], Daniel[4] Stouffer, Christian[3], Hans[2], Hans[1]) He married **(1) Private Wiley**. He married **(2) Private Linda**. He married **(3) Private Germonoff**. He married **(4) Private Grogg**.

Child of Private DePalmo and Private Wiley is:
    5548   i. Private[15] DePalmo.

Child of Private DePalmo and Private Linda is:
    5549   i. Private[15] DePalmo.

Child of Private DePalmo and Private Germonoff is:
    5550   i. Private[15] DePalmo.

Child of Private DePalmo and Private Grogg is:
    5551   i. Private[15] DePalmo.

4343. Private[14] DePalmo (Cleo Ruth[13] Stoffer, Benjamine Franklin[12], Stanton Uriah[11], George[10], Jacob[9], Jacob[8] Stauffer, Henry Jacob[7], Hans[6], Christian[5], Daniel[4] Stouffer, Christian[3], Hans[2], Hans[1]) He married **(1) Private Grogg**. He married **(2) Private Phillips**. He married **(3) Private Chadwick**.

Children of Private DePalmo and Private Grogg are:
    5552   i. Private[15] DePalmo.
    5553   ii. Private DePalmo.

Child of Private DePalmo and Private Phillips is:
    5554   i. Private[15] DePalmo.

4350. Private[14] Stoffer (Rollin Jr[13], Benjamine Franklin[12], Stanton Uriah[11], George[10], Jacob[9], Jacob[8] Stauffer, Henry Jacob[7], Hans[6], Christian[5], Daniel[4] Stouffer, Christian[3], Hans[2], Hans[1]) She married **Private Russell**.

Children of Private Stoffer and Private Russell are:

5555   i.   Private[15] Russell.
5556   ii.   Private Russell.
5557   iii.   Private Russell.

4351. Private[14] Stoffer (Rollin Jr[13], Benjamine Franklin[12], Stanton Uriah[11], George[10], Jacob[9], Jacob[8] Stauffer, Henry Jacob[7], Hans[6], Christian[5], Daniel[4] Stouffer, Christian[3], Hans[2], Hans[1])

Children of Private Stoffer are:
5558   i.   Private[15] Stoffer.
5559   ii.   Private Stoffer.
5560   iii.   Private Stoffer.

4352. Private[14] Stoffer (Rollin Jr[13], Benjamine Franklin[12], Stanton Uriah[11], George[10], Jacob[9], Jacob[8] Stauffer, Henry Jacob[7], Hans[6], Christian[5], Daniel[4] Stouffer, Christian[3], Hans[2], Hans[1])

Child of Private Stoffer is:
5561   i.   Private[15] Stoffer.

4354. Private[14] Stoffer (Rollin Jr[13], Benjamine Franklin[12], Stanton Uriah[11], George[10], Jacob[9], Jacob[8] Stauffer, Henry Jacob[7], Hans[6], Christian[5], Daniel[4] Stouffer, Christian[3], Hans[2], Hans[1]) He married **(1) Private Snowd**. He married **(2) Private Long**.

Children of Private Stoffer and Private Snowd are:
5562   i.   Private[15] Stoffer.
5563   ii.   Private Stoffer.

Child of Private Stoffer and Private Long is:
5564   i.   Private[15] Stoffer.

4356. Private[14] Stoffer (Franklin Eugene[13], Benjamine Franklin[12], Stanton Uriah[11], George[10], Jacob[9], Jacob[8] Stauffer, Henry Jacob[7], Hans[6], Christian[5], Daniel[4] Stouffer, Christian[3], Hans[2], Hans[1])

Child of Private Stoffer is:
5565   i.   Private[15] Stoffer.

4358. Private[14] Stoffer (Lorin Albert[13], Roscoe "Ross"[12], Stanton Uriah[11], George[10], Jacob[9], Jacob[8] Stauffer, Henry Jacob[7], Hans[6], Christian[5], Daniel[4] Stouffer, Christian[3], Hans[2], Hans[1]) He married **Private Martin**.

Children of Private Stoffer and Private Martin are:
5566   i.   Private[15] Stoffer.
5567   ii.   Private Stoffer.

4359. Private[14] Stoffer (Lorin Albert[13], Roscoe "Ross"[12], Stanton Uriah[11], George[10], Jacob[9], Jacob[8] Stauffer, Henry Jacob[7], Hans[6], Christian[5], Daniel[4] Stouffer, Christian[3], Hans[2], Hans[1])

Child of Private Stoffer is:
5568   i.   Shannon M. Smith[15] Stoffer, born January 02, 1980 in Ohio; died December 03, 1996 in Columbiana Co., Ohio.

4362. 2nd Private[14] Stoffer (Lorin Albert[13], Roscoe "Ross"[12], Stanton Uriah[11], George[10], Jacob[9], Jacob[8] Stauffer, Henry Jacob[7], Hans[6], Christian[5], Daniel[4] Stouffer, Christian[3], Hans[2], Hans[1]) He married **Private Hoopes**.

Children of Private Stoffer and Private Hoopes are:
5569   i.   Private[15] Stoffer.
5570   ii.   Private Stoffer.
5571   iii.   3rd Private Stoffer.
5572   iv.   Private Stoffer.

4364. Private[14] Stoffer (Lorin Albert[13], Roscoe "Ross"[12], Stanton Uriah[11], George[10], Jacob[9], Jacob[8] Stauffer, Henry Jacob[7], Hans[6], Christian[5], Daniel[4] Stouffer, Christian[3], Hans[2], Hans[1]) She married **Private Huges**.

Children of Private Stoffer and Private Huges are:
- 5573   i.   Private[15] Huges.
- 5574   ii.   Private Huges.

4365. Private[14] Stoffer (Lorin Albert[13], Roscoe "Ross"[12], Stanton Uriah[11], George[10], Jacob[9], Jacob[8] Stauffer, Henry Jacob[7], Hans[6], Christian[5], Daniel[4] Stouffer, Christian[3], Hans[2], Hans[1]) She married **(1) Private Minagay**. She married **(2) Private Schreckengast**.

Children of Private Stoffer and Private Minagay are:
- 5575   i.   Private[15] Minagay.
- 5576   ii.   Private Minagay.
- 5577   iii.   Private Minagay.

4389. Private[14] Thompson (Ester Leah[13] Stoffer, Anson Oscar[12], Leander[11], George[10], Jacob[9], Jacob[8] Stauffer, Henry Jacob[7], Hans[6], Christian[5], Daniel[4] Stouffer, Christian[3], Hans[2], Hans[1]) She married **Rev. John Joseph Hinton**. He was born January 24, 1927.

Children of Private Thompson and Rev Hinton are:
- 5578   i.   Private[15] Hinton.
- 5579   ii.   Private Hinton.
- 5580   iii.   Private Hinton.
- 5581   iv.   Private Hinton.

4390. Private[14] Crantson (Wilma Ruth[13] Stoffer, Anson Oscar[12], Leander[11], George[10], Jacob[9], Jacob[8] Stauffer, Henry Jacob[7], Hans[6], Christian[5], Daniel[4] Stouffer, Christian[3], Hans[2], Hans[1]) She married **Earl Barrett**.

Child of Private Crantson and Earl Barrett is:
- 5582   i.   Private[15] Barrett.

4391. Private[14] Crantson (Wilma Ruth[13] Stoffer, Anson Oscar[12], Leander[11], George[10], Jacob[9], Jacob[8] Stauffer, Henry Jacob[7], Hans[6], Christian[5], Daniel[4] Stouffer, Christian[3], Hans[2], Hans[1]) She married **Private Pengotti**.

Child of Private Crantson and Private Pengotti is:
- 5583   i.   Private[15] Pengotti.

4395. Private[14] Stoffer (Donald Lowell[13], Glen Wilson[12], Leander[11], George[10], Jacob[9], Jacob[8] Stauffer, Henry Jacob[7], Hans[6], Christian[5], Daniel[4] Stouffer, Christian[3], Hans[2], Hans[1]) He married **Private Mathews**.

Children of Private Stoffer and Private Mathews are:
- 5584   i.   Private[15] Stoffer.
- 5585   ii.   Private Stoffer.

4399. Private[14] Stoffer (Donald Lowell[13], Glen Wilson[12], Leander[11], George[10], Jacob[9], Jacob[8] Stauffer, Henry Jacob[7], Hans[6], Christian[5], Daniel[4] Stouffer, Christian[3], Hans[2], Hans[1]) She married **Private Ventura**.

Child of Private Stoffer and Private Ventura is:
- 5586   i.   Private[15] Ventura.

4400. Private[14] Ernst (Lucille Naomi[13] Stoffer, Glen Wilson[12], Leander[11], George[10], Jacob[9], Jacob[8] Stauffer, Henry Jacob[7], Hans[6], Christian[5], Daniel[4] Stouffer, Christian[3], Hans[2], Hans[1]) He married **Private Kellner**.

Child of Private Ernst and Private Kellner is:
- 5587   i.   Private[15] Ernst.

4401. Private[14] Ernst (Lucille Naomi[13] Stoffer, Glen Wilson[12], Leander[11], George[10], Jacob[9], Jacob[8] Stauffer, Henry Jacob[7], Hans[6], Christian[5], Daniel[4] Stouffer, Christian[3], Hans[2], Hans[1]) She married **Private Shultz**.

Children of Private Ernst and Private Shultz are:

5588 i. Private[15] Shultz.
5589 ii. Private Shultz.

4402. Private[14] Ernst (Lucille Naomi[13] Stoffer, Glen Wilson[12], Leander[11], George[10], Jacob[9], Jacob[8] Stauffer, Henry Jacob[7], Hans[6], Christian[5], Daniel[4] Stouffer, Christian[3], Hans[2], Hans[1]) He married **(1) Private White**. He married **(2) Private Rohaley**.

Children of Private Ernst and Private Rohaley are:
5590 i. Private[15] Ernest.
5591 ii. Private Ernst.

4404. Private[14] Mercer (Evelyn Ora[13] Stoffer, Glen Wilson[12], Leander[11], George[10], Jacob[9], Jacob[8] Stauffer, Henry Jacob[7], Hans[6], Christian[5], Daniel[4] Stouffer, Christian[3], Hans[2], Hans[1]) He married **Private Greenwalt**.

Children of Private Mercer and Private Greenwalt are:
5592 i. Private[15] Mercer.
5593 ii. Private Mercer.
5594 iii. Private Mercer.

4405. Private[14] Mercer (Evelyn Ora[13] Stoffer, Glen Wilson[12], Leander[11], George[10], Jacob[9], Jacob[8] Stauffer, Henry Jacob[7], Hans[6], Christian[5], Daniel[4] Stouffer, Christian[3], Hans[2], Hans[1]) She married **Private Powell**.

Children of Private Mercer and Private Powell are:
5595 i. Private[15] Powell.
5596 ii. Private Powell.
5597 iii. Private Powell.

4407. Private[14] Ray (Doris May[13] Stoffer, Glen Wilson[12], Leander[11], George[10], Jacob[9], Jacob[8] Stauffer, Henry Jacob[7], Hans[6], Christian[5], Daniel[4] Stouffer, Christian[3], Hans[2], Hans[1]) He married **Private Hardy**.

Children of Private Ray and Private Hardy are:
5598 i. Private[15] Ray.
5599 ii. Private Ray.

4408. Private[14] Ray (Doris May[13] Stoffer, Glen Wilson[12], Leander[11], George[10], Jacob[9], Jacob[8] Stauffer, Henry Jacob[7], Hans[6], Christian[5], Daniel[4] Stouffer, Christian[3], Hans[2], Hans[1]) She married **Private Davis**.

Children of Private Ray and Private Davis are:
5600 i. Private[15] Davis.
5601 ii. Private Davis.
5602 iii. Private Davis.

4409. Private[14] Ray (Doris May[13] Stoffer, Glen Wilson[12], Leander[11], George[10], Jacob[9], Jacob[8] Stauffer, Henry Jacob[7], Hans[6], Christian[5], Daniel[4] Stouffer, Christian[3], Hans[2], Hans[1]) He married **Private Crist**.

Children of Private Ray and Private Crist are:
5603 i. Private[15] Ray.
5604 ii. Private Ray.

4410. Private[14] Ray (Doris May[13] Stoffer, Glen Wilson[12], Leander[11], George[10], Jacob[9], Jacob[8] Stauffer, Henry Jacob[7], Hans[6], Christian[5], Daniel[4] Stouffer, Christian[3], Hans[2], Hans[1]) She married **(1) Private Salter**. She married **(2) Private Smith**.

Children of Private Ray and Private Salter are:
5605 i. Private[15] Salter.
5606 ii. Private Salter.
5607 iii. Private Salter.

4411. Private[14] Ray (Doris May[13] Stoffer, Glen Wilson[12], Leander[11], George[10], Jacob[9], Jacob[8] Stauffer, Henry Jacob[7], Hans[6], Christian[5], Daniel[4] Stouffer, Christian[3], Hans[2], Hans[1]) She married **Private Prickett**.

Children of Private Ray and Private Prickett are:
  5608 i. Private[15] Prickett.
  5609 ii. Private Prickett.

4412. Private[14] Ray (Doris May[13] Stoffer, Glen Wilson[12], Leander[11], George[10], Jacob[9], Jacob[8] Stauffer, Henry Jacob[7], Hans[6], Christian[5], Daniel[4] Stouffer, Christian[3], Hans[2], Hans[1]) She married **Private Wilk**.

Children of Private Ray and Private Wilk are:
  5610 i. Private[15] Wilk.
  5611 ii. Private Wilk.

4413. Private[14] Ray (Doris May[13] Stoffer, Glen Wilson[12], Leander[11], George[10], Jacob[9], Jacob[8] Stauffer, Henry Jacob[7], Hans[6], Christian[5], Daniel[4] Stouffer, Christian[3], Hans[2], Hans[1]) She married **Private Danner**.

Child of Private Ray and Private Danner is:
  5612 i. Private[15] Danner.

4414. Private[14] Ray (Doris May[13] Stoffer, Glen Wilson[12], Leander[11], George[10], Jacob[9], Jacob[8] Stauffer, Henry Jacob[7], Hans[6], Christian[5], Daniel[4] Stouffer, Christian[3], Hans[2], Hans[1]) She married **(1) Private Benson**. She married **(2) Private Danson**.

Children of Private Ray and Private Benson are:
  5613 i. Private[15] Benson.
  5614 ii. Private Benson.

Children of Private Ray and Private Danson are:
  5615 i. Private[15] Danson.
  5616 ii. Private Danson.

4416. Private[14] Stiffler (Iona Eleanor[13] Stoffer, Glen Wilson[12], Leander[11], George[10], Jacob[9], Jacob[8] Stauffer, Henry Jacob[7], Hans[6], Christian[5], Daniel[4] Stouffer, Christian[3], Hans[2], Hans[1]) She married **(1) Private Rout**. She married **(2) Private Ruesga**.

Child of Private Stiffler and Private Ruesga is:
  5617 i. Private[15] Ruesga.

4417. Private[14] Stiffler (Iona Eleanor[13] Stoffer, Glen Wilson[12], Leander[11], George[10], Jacob[9], Jacob[8] Stauffer, Henry Jacob[7], Hans[6], Christian[5], Daniel[4] Stouffer, Christian[3], Hans[2], Hans[1]) She married **(1) Private Maples**. She married **(2) Private Naples**.

Child of Private Stiffler and Private Maples is:
  5618 i. Private[15] Maples.

Child of Private Stiffler and Private Naples is:
  5619 i. Private[15] Naples.

Generation No. 15

4444. Annielaurie Ruletta[15] Gilbert (Bertha Beatrice[14] Dunham, Ellen Ruletta[13] Kitchen, Elizabeth[12] Betzner, Abraham[11], Elizabeth[10] Stouffer, Abraham Hershey[9] Stauffer, Abraham Hess[8], Henry Jacob[7], Hans[6], Christian[5], Daniel[4] Stouffer, Christian[3], Hans[2], Hans[1]) She married **George Peters**.

Child of Annielaurie Gilbert and George Peters is:
  5620 i. Private[16] Peters.

4446. Hugh Munson[15] Everett (Eleanor Elizabeth[14] Dunham, Ellen Ruletta[13] Kitchen, Elizabeth[12] Betzner, Abraham[11], Elizabeth[10] Stouffer, Abraham Hershey[9] Stauffer, Abraham Hess[8], Henry Jacob[7], Hans[6], Christian[5], Daniel[4] Stouffer, Christian[3], Hans[2], Hans[1]) He married **Edna Joyce Davenport**.

Children of Hugh Everett and Edna Davenport are:
- 5621 i. Private[16] Everett.
- 5622 ii. Private Everett.

4447. Ralph Avon[15] **Everett** (Eleanor Elizabeth[14] Dunham, Ellen Ruletta[13] Kitchen, Elizabeth[12] Betzner, Abraham[11], Elizabeth[10] Stouffer, Abraham Hershey[9] Stauffer, Abraham Hess[8], Henry Jacob[7], Hans[6], Christian[5], Daniel[4] Stouffer, Christian[3], Hans[2], Hans[1]) He married **Jean Barclay Burnside**.

Children of Ralph Everett and Jean Burnside are:
- 5623 i. Private[16] Everett.
- 5624 ii. Private Everett.

4452. Betty Jean Mabel[15] **Dunham** (William Kitchen[14], Mabel Gertrude[13] Kitchen, Elizabeth[12] Betzner, Abraham[11], Elizabeth[10] Stouffer, Abraham Hershey[9] Stauffer, Abraham Hess[8], Henry Jacob[7], Hans[6], Christian[5], Daniel[4] Stouffer, Christian[3], Hans[2], Hans[1]) She married **Kenneth Alexander Forester**.

Child of Betty Dunham and Kenneth Forester is:
- 5625 i. Private[16] Forester.

4464. Private[15] **Shore** (Louise Norman[14] Edworthy, Ina Louisa[13] Betzner, George David[12], John Weir[11], Elizabeth[10] Stouffer, Abraham Hershey[9] Stauffer, Abraham Hess[8], Henry Jacob[7], Hans[6], Christian[5], Daniel[4] Stouffer, Christian[3], Hans[2], Hans[1]) He married **(1) Private Drexler**. He married **(2) Private Brock**.

Child of Private Shore and Private Drexler is:
- 5626 i. Private[16] Shore.

Child of Private Shore and Private Brock is:
- 5627 i. Private[16] Shore.

4465. Private[15] **Shore** (Louise Norman[14] Edworthy, Ina Louisa[13] Betzner, George David[12], John Weir[11], Elizabeth[10] Stouffer, Abraham Hershey[9] Stauffer, Abraham Hess[8], Henry Jacob[7], Hans[6], Christian[5], Daniel[4] Stouffer, Christian[3], Hans[2], Hans[1]) He married **(1) Private McGee**. He married **(2) Private Fixter**.

Child of Private Shore and Private McGee is:
- 5628 i. Private[16] Shore.

4466. Private[15] **Shore** (Louise Norman[14] Edworthy, Ina Louisa[13] Betzner, George David[12], John Weir[11], Elizabeth[10] Stouffer, Abraham Hershey[9] Stauffer, Abraham Hess[8], Henry Jacob[7], Hans[6], Christian[5], Daniel[4] Stouffer, Christian[3], Hans[2], Hans[1]) She married **Private Pryde**.

Child of Private Shore and Private Pryde is:
- 5629 i. Private[16] Pryde.

4517. Dorman John[15] **Grace III** (Dorothy Elaine[14] Hackman, Henry Hess[13], Willis Brenner[12], Andrew Baer[11], Susanna Frantz[10] Bear, Anna[9] Frantz, Barbara[8] Hostetter, Ann Elisabeth[7] Hershey, Benjamin Stauffer[6], Adelheid Galle[5] Stouffer, Daniel[4], Christian[3], Hans[2], Hans[1]) was born October 27, 1955 in Good Samaritan Hospital, Lebanon, PA. He married **Sandra Boale** August 20, 1977 in New Castle, PA. She was born May 21, 1958.

Children of Dorman Grace and Sandra Boale are:
- 5630 i. Robert Joseph[16] Grace, born May 11, 1979.
- 5631 ii. Daniel Sverre Grace, born February 15, 1981.

4518. Nancy Anne[15] **Grace** (Dorothy Elaine[14] Hackman, Henry Hess[13], Willis Brenner[12], Andrew Baer[11], Susanna Frantz[10] Bear, Anna[9] Frantz, Barbara[8] Hostetter, Ann Elisabeth[7] Hershey, Benjamin Stauffer[6], Adelheid Galle[5] Stouffer, Daniel[4], Christian[3], Hans[2], Hans[1]) was born August 30, 1958 in Good Samaritan Hospital, Lebanon, PA. She married **David L Bogdonoff** May 22, 1983 in Hershey, Dauphin Co, PA. He was born September 15, 1955.

Children of Nancy Grace and David Bogdonoff are:
- 5632 i. Jacob Alan[16] Bogdonoff, born April 08, 1989 in Charlottesville, VA.

5633 ii. Eleanor Kate Bogdonoff, born February 17, 1992 in Charlottesville, VA.

4535. Tracy Louise[15] McKain (Annie Marian[14] Hackman, Willis Hess[13], Willis Brenner[12], Andrew Baer[11], Susanna Frantz[10] Bear, Anna[9] Frantz, Barbara[8] Hostetter, Ann Elisabeth[7] Hershey, Benjamin Stauffer[6], Adelheid Galle[5] Stouffer, Daniel[4], Christian[3], Hans[2], Hans[1]) was born May 24, 1969 in Lancaster, PA. She married **(1) Jason Funk**. She married **(2) Joseph Murgas**.

Children of Tracy McKain and Jason Funk are:
5634 i. Jazmond Hess[16] Funk.
5635 ii. Tyler Ray Funk.

Child of Tracy McKain and Joseph Murgas is:
5636 i. Joseph[16] Murgas.

4558. Lawrence Kevin[15] Knorr (Emily Faline[15] White, William Walter[14], Catherine Rebecca[13] Wolf, Catherine Rebecca[12] Ober, David[11], Isaac Huntsberger[10], Christian[9], Elizabeth[8] Stauffer, Johannes[7], Daniel[6] Stouffer, Christian[5] Stauffer, Daniel[4] Stouffer, Christian[3], Hans[2], Hans[1]) was born May 05, 1964 in Reading Hostpital, Reading, PA. He married **Dr Ann Louise Berger** November 05, 1994 in Palm Island Resort, Englewood, Florida. She was born July 25, 1965 in Reading Hospital, Reading, PA.

Children of Lawrence Knorr and Ann Berger are:
5637 i. Taylor[16] Berger-Knorr, born June 22, 1998 in Reading Hospital, Reading, PA.
5638 ii. Abbey Berger-Knorr, born May 04, 2002 in Reading Hostpital, Reading, PA.

4559. Alice Kathleen[15] Knorr (Emily Faline[15] White, William Walter[14], Catherine Rebecca[13] Wolf, Catherine Rebecca[12] Ober, David[11], Isaac Huntsberger[10], Christian[9], Elizabeth[8] Stauffer, Johannes[7], Daniel[6] Stouffer, Christian[5] Stauffer, Daniel[4] Stouffer, Christian[3], Hans[2], Hans[1]) was born August 11, 1965 in Reading, PA. She met **(1) Gary Fidler** in Pennside, PA. He was born Abt. 1955 in Reading, PA. She married **(2) Glenn Buchman** June 23, 1990 in Reading, PA. He was born Abt. 1953 in Kutztown, PA.

Child of Alice Knorr and Gary Fidler is:
5639 i. Gary Kyle[16] Buchman, born April 30, 1983.

4573. Private[15] Fox (Private[14], Willis Eby[13], Ella Barbara[12] Eby, Sarah Lucinda[11] Hershey, Peter[10], Jacob[9], John[8], Jacob Snavely[7], Andrew Stauffer[6], Adelheid Galle[5] Stouffer, Daniel[4], Christian[3], Hans[2], Hans[1]) He married **Private Eberly**.

Child of Private Fox and Private Eberly is:
5640 i. Private[16] Fox.

4574. Private[15] Fox (Private[14], Willis Eby[13], Ella Barbara[12] Eby, Sarah Lucinda[11] Hershey, Peter[10], Jacob[9], John[8], Jacob Snavely[7], Andrew Stauffer[6], Adelheid Galle[5] Stouffer, Daniel[4], Christian[3], Hans[2], Hans[1]) She married **Private Stauffer**.

Children of Private Fox and Private Stauffer are:
5641 i. Private[16] Stauffer.
5642 ii. Private Stauffer.

4589. Private[15] Augsburger (Private[14] Fox, Henry Peter[13], Ella Barbara[12] Eby, Sarah Lucinda[11] Hershey, Peter[10], Jacob[9], John[8], Jacob Snavely[7], Andrew Stauffer[6], Adelheid Galle[5] Stouffer, Daniel[4], Christian[3], Hans[2], Hans[1]) She married **Private Hostetter**.

Children of Private Augsburger and Private Hostetter are:
5643 i. Private[16] Hostetter.
5644 ii. Private Hostetter.

4590. Private[15] Augsburger (Private[14] Fox, Henry Peter[13], Ella Barbara[12] Eby, Sarah Lucinda[11] Hershey, Peter[10], Jacob[9], John[8], Jacob Snavely[7], Andrew Stauffer[6], Adelheid Galle[5] Stouffer, Daniel[4], Christian[3], Hans[2], Hans[1]) She married **Private Groff**.

Children of Private Augsburger and Private Groff are:
5645 i. Private[16] Groff.
5646 ii. Private Groff.

4593. Private[15] Eberly (Private[14] Fox, Henry Peter[13], Ella Barbara[12] Eby, Sarah Lucinda[11] Hershey, Peter[10], Jacob[9], John[8], Jacob

The Relations of Milton Snavely Hershey, 4th Ed.

Snavely[7], Andrew Stauffer[6], Adelheid Galle[5] Stouffer, Daniel[4], Christian[3], Hans[2], Hans[1]) He married **Private Nafziger**.

Children of Private Eberly and Private Nafziger are:
- 5647   i. Private[16] Eberly.
- 5648   ii. Private Eberly.

4597. Private[15] Good (Private[14] Fox, Henry Peter[13], Ella Barbara[12] Eby, Sarah Lucinda[11] Hershey, Peter[10], Jacob[9], John[8], Jacob Snavely[7], Andrew Stauffer[6], Adelheid Galle[5] Stouffer, Daniel[4], Christian[3], Hans[2], Hans[1]) He married **Private Weaver**.

Child of Private Good and Private Weaver is:
- 5649   i. Private[16] Good.

4598. Private[15] Good (Private[14] Fox, Henry Peter[13], Ella Barbara[12] Eby, Sarah Lucinda[11] Hershey, Peter[10], Jacob[9], John[8], Jacob Snavely[7], Andrew Stauffer[6], Adelheid Galle[5] Stouffer, Daniel[4], Christian[3], Hans[2], Hans[1]) She married **Private Denlinger**.

Children of Private Good and Private Denlinger are:
- 5650   i. Private[16] Denlinger.
- 5651   ii. Private Denlinger.

4599. Private[15] Zimmerman (Private[14] Fox, Henry Peter[13], Ella Barbara[12] Eby, Sarah Lucinda[11] Hershey, Peter[10], Jacob[9], John[8], Jacob Snavely[7], Andrew Stauffer[6], Adelheid Galle[5] Stouffer, Daniel[4], Christian[3], Hans[2], Hans[1]) She married **Private Kauffman**.

Child of Private Zimmerman and Private Kauffman is:
- 5652   i. Private[16] Kauffman.

4600. Private[15] Zimmerman (Private[14] Fox, Henry Peter[13], Ella Barbara[12] Eby, Sarah Lucinda[11] Hershey, Peter[10], Jacob[9], John[8], Jacob Snavely[7], Andrew Stauffer[6], Adelheid Galle[5] Stouffer, Daniel[4], Christian[3], Hans[2], Hans[1]) He married **Private Bucher**.

Children of Private Zimmerman and Private Bucher are:
- 5653   i. Private[16] Zimmerman.
- 5654   ii. Private Zimmerman.

4601. Private[15] Zimmerman (Private[14] Fox, Henry Peter[13], Ella Barbara[12] Eby, Sarah Lucinda[11] Hershey, Peter[10], Jacob[9], John[8], Jacob Snavely[7], Andrew Stauffer[6], Adelheid Galle[5] Stouffer, Daniel[4], Christian[3], Hans[2], Hans[1]) She married **Private Buckwalter**.

Children of Private Zimmerman and Private Buckwalter are:
- 5655   i. Private[16] Buckwalter.
- 5656   ii. Private Buckwalter.
- 5657   iii. Private Buckwalter.

4626. Private[15] Zimmerman (Private[14], Sarah Lucinda[13] Fox, Ella Barbara[12] Eby, Sarah Lucinda[11] Hershey, Peter[10], Jacob[9], John[8], Jacob Snavely[7], Andrew Stauffer[6], Adelheid Galle[5] Stouffer, Daniel[4], Christian[3], Hans[2], Hans[1]) She married **Private Hostetter**.

Child of Private Zimmerman and Private Hostetter is:
- 5658   i. Private[16] Hostetter.

4629. Private[15] Zimmerman (Private[14], Sarah Lucinda[13] Fox, Ella Barbara[12] Eby, Sarah Lucinda[11] Hershey, Peter[10], Jacob[9], John[8], Jacob Snavely[7], Andrew Stauffer[6], Adelheid Galle[5] Stouffer, Daniel[4], Christian[3], Hans[2], Hans[1]) She married **Private Hostetter**.

Children of Private Zimmerman and Private Hostetter are:
- 5659   i. Private[16] Hostetter.
- 5660   ii. Private Hostetter.
- 5661   iii. Private Hostetter.
- 5662   iv. Private Hostetter.

4664. Private[15] Martin (Private[14], Susan W.[13] Eby, Peter Hershey[12], Sarah Lucinda[11] Hershey, Peter[10], Jacob[9], John[8], Jacob Snavely[7], Andrew Stauffer[6], Adelheid Galle[5] Stouffer, Daniel[4], Christian[3], Hans[2], Hans[1]) She married **Private Ebersole**.

Child of Private Martin and Private Ebersole is:

The Relations of Milton Snavely Hershey, 4th Ed.

    5663   i.   Private[16] Ebersole.

4710. Private[15] Zimmerman (Private[14] Stauffer, Emma Mae[13] Eby, Peter Hershey[12], Sarah Lucinda[11] Hershey, Peter[10], Jacob[9], John[8], Jacob Snavely[7], Andrew Stauffer[6], Adelheid Galle[5] Stouffer, Daniel[4], Christian[3], Hans[2], Hans[1]) She married **Private Garman**.

Child of Private Zimmerman and Private Garman is:
    5664   i.   Private[16] Garman.

4711. Private[15] Zimmerman (Private[14] Stauffer, Emma Mae[13] Eby, Peter Hershey[12], Sarah Lucinda[11] Hershey, Peter[10], Jacob[9], John[8], Jacob Snavely[7], Andrew Stauffer[6], Adelheid Galle[5] Stouffer, Daniel[4], Christian[3], Hans[2], Hans[1]) She married **Private Shirk**.

Children of Private Zimmerman and Private Shirk are:
    5665   i.   Private[16] Shirk.
    5666   ii. Private Shirk.

4712. Private[15] Zimmerman (Private[14] Stauffer, Emma Mae[13] Eby, Peter Hershey[12], Sarah Lucinda[11] Hershey, Peter[10], Jacob[9], John[8], Jacob Snavely[7], Andrew Stauffer[6], Adelheid Galle[5] Stouffer, Daniel[4], Christian[3], Hans[2], Hans[1]) She married **Private Zimmerman**.

Children of Private Zimmerman and Private Zimmerman are:
    5667   i.   Private[16] Zimmerman.
    5668   ii. Private Zimmerman.

4713. Private[15] Zimmerman (Private[14] Stauffer, Emma Mae[13] Eby, Peter Hershey[12], Sarah Lucinda[11] Hershey, Peter[10], Jacob[9], John[8], Jacob Snavely[7], Andrew Stauffer[6], Adelheid Galle[5] Stouffer, Daniel[4], Christian[3], Hans[2], Hans[1]) She married **Private Burkholder**.

Children of Private Zimmerman and Private Burkholder are:
    5669   i.   Private[16] Burkholder.
    5670   ii. Private Burkholder.
    5671   iii. Private Burkholder.

5081. Teresa Rose Charlene[15] Lucenti (Doris Madeline[14] Sheaffer, Charles M.[13], Lydia Jane[12] Tritt, Nancy[11] Nickey, Samuel[10], Christiana[9] Hastetter, Anna Barbara[8] Stauffer, Johannes[7], Daniel[6] Stouffer, Christian[5] Stauffer, Daniel[4] Stouffer, Christian[3], Hans[2], Hans[1]) was born Private. She married **Lawrence R. Taylor** Private. He was born Private.

Child of Teresa Lucenti and Lawrence Taylor is:
    5672   i.   Traci Ann[16] Taylor, born Private.

5082. Sandra Marie[15] Lucenti (Doris Madeline[14] Sheaffer, Charles M.[13], Lydia Jane[12] Tritt, Nancy[11] Nickey, Samuel[10], Christiana[9] Hastetter, Anna Barbara[8] Stauffer, Johannes[7], Daniel[6] Stouffer, Christian[5] Stauffer, Daniel[4] Stouffer, Christian[3], Hans[2], Hans[1]) was born Private. She married **Tevas Kahlance** Private. He was born Private.

Child of Sandra Lucenti and Tevas Kahlance is:
    5673   i.   Tara Rose[16] Kahlance, born Private.

5091. Kathryn Ann[15] Mohler (Dorothy Jean[14] Hippensteel, Margaret Elizabeth Alice[13] Goodhart, Theodore[12], Charlotte[11] Farner, Elizabeth[10] Owens, Peter[9] Ober, Elizabeth[8] Stauffer, Johannes[7], Daniel[6] Stouffer, Christian[5] Stauffer, Daniel[4] Stouffer, Christian[3], Hans[2], Hans[1]) was born Private. She married **(1) Colin Crouse** Private. He was born Private. She married **(2) John Daniels** Private. He was born Private.

Child of Kathryn Mohler and Colin Crouse is:
+   5674   i.   Angela Dawn[16] Crouse, born Private.

5092. John Robert[15] Mohler (Dorothy Jean[14] Hippensteel, Margaret Elizabeth Alice[13] Goodhart, Theodore[12], Charlotte[11] Farner, Elizabeth[10] Owens, Peter[9] Ober, Elizabeth[8] Stauffer, Johannes[7], Daniel[6] Stouffer, Christian[5] Stauffer, Daniel[4] Stouffer, Christian[3], Hans[2], Hans[1]) was born Private. He married **Cindy Joan Bloom** Private. She was born Private.

Children of John Mohler and Cindy Bloom are:
    5675   i.   Matthew Robert[16] Mohler, born Private.
    5676   ii. Mark Andrew Mohler, born Private.

5094. Diane Elizabeth[15] **West** (Doris Madeline[14] Hippensteel, Margaret Elizabeth Alice[13] Goodhart, Theodore[12], Charlotte[11] Farner, Elizabeth[10] Owens, Peter[9] Ober, Elizabeth[8] Stauffer, Johannes[7], Daniel[6] Stouffer, Christian[5] Stauffer, Daniel[4] Stouffer, Christian[3], Hans[2], Hans[1]) was born Private. She married **Lynn Richard Wenger** Private. He was born Private.

Children of Diane West and Lynn Wenger are:
- 5677   i. Ethan Richard[16] Wenger, born Private.
- 5678   ii. Seth Jonathan Wenger, born Private.
- 5679   iii. Laura Beth Wenger, born Private.

5095. Barbara Elaine[15] **West** (Doris Madeline[14] Hippensteel, Margaret Elizabeth Alice[13] Goodhart, Theodore[12], Charlotte[11] Farner, Elizabeth[10] Owens, Peter[9] Ober, Elizabeth[8] Stauffer, Johannes[7], Daniel[6] Stouffer, Christian[5] Stauffer, Daniel[4] Stouffer, Christian[3], Hans[2], Hans[1]) was born Private. She married **Barry Lee Batz** Private. He was born Private.

Children of Barbara West and Barry Batz are:
- 5680   i. Jason Barry[16] Batz, born Private.
- 5681   ii. Christy Amanda Batz, born Private.

5100. John Charles[15] **Goodhart** (Charles Dale[14], Clarence Eugene[13], Theodore[12], Charlotte[11] Farner, Elizabeth[10] Owens, Peter[9] Ober, Elizabeth[8] Stauffer, Johannes[7], Daniel[6] Stouffer, Christian[5] Stauffer, Daniel[4] Stouffer, Christian[3], Hans[2], Hans[1]) was born Private. He married **Joy Committus** Private. She was born Private.

Children of John Goodhart and Joy Committus are:
- 5682   i. Dominic Charles[16] Goodhart, born Private.
- 5683   ii. Benjamin Scott Goodhart, born Private.

5105. Margaret H[15] **Harrington** (Almer H[14], Lillie E[13] Hursh, Emma Barbara[12] Ober, David[11], Isaac Huntsberger[10], Christian[9], Elizabeth[8] Stauffer, Johannes[7], Daniel[6] Stouffer, Christian[5] Stauffer, Daniel[4] Stouffer, Christian[3], Hans[2], Hans[1]) was born 1918. She married **Rex Witson**. He was born Abt. 1915.

Child of Margaret Harrington and Rex Witson is:
- 5684   i. Anna L[16] Witson, born 1948.

5143. Nancy L[15] **Bingaman** (B Marie[14] Stevens, Rachael Agnes[13] Duncan, Annie Elizabeth[12] Ober, David[11], Isaac Huntsberger[10], Christian[9], Elizabeth[8] Stauffer, Johannes[7], Daniel[6] Stouffer, Christian[5] Stauffer, Daniel[4] Stouffer, Christian[3], Hans[2], Hans[1]) was born 1927. She married **Edwin D Rhodes**. He was born Abt. 1925.

Children of Nancy Bingaman and Edwin Rhodes are:
- 5685   i. Jacqueline M[16] Rhodes, born 1949.
- 5686   ii. Edwin D Rhodes II, born 1957.

5156. Patricia L[15] **Fink** (Adrian E[14] Duncan, Alvid O[13], Annie Elizabeth[12] Ober, David[11], Isaac Huntsberger[10], Christian[9], Elizabeth[8] Stauffer, Johannes[7], Daniel[6] Stouffer, Christian[5] Stauffer, Daniel[4] Stouffer, Christian[3], Hans[2], Hans[1]) was born 1933. She married **Jack A Brightbill**. He was born 1932.

Child of Patricia Fink and Jack Brightbill is:
- 5687   i. Susan M[16] Brightbill, born 1952.

5178. Private[15] **Rhoads** (Elinor L.[14] Brinser, Mary L.[13] Morning, Annie[12] Ober, Michael Cramer[11], Michael[10], Henry[9], Elizabeth[8] Stauffer, Johannes[7], Daniel[6] Stouffer, Christian[5] Stauffer, Daniel[4] Stouffer, Christian[3], Hans[2], Hans[1]) He married **Private Schillinger**.

Children of Private Rhoads and Private Schillinger are:
- 5688   i. Private[16] Rhoads.
- 5689   ii. Private Rhoads.
- 5690   iii. Private Rhoads.
- 5691   iv. Private Rhoads.
- 5692   v. Private Rhoads.

5186. Jay Earl Franklin[15] **Derr** (Minnie[14] Ober, Daisy Meyers[13], Moses Heagly[12], Moses Ruhl[11], Christian Longnecker[10], David S[9],

The Relations of Milton Snavely Hershey, 4th Ed.

Elizabeth[8] Stauffer, Johannes[7], Daniel[6] Stouffer, Christian[5] Stauffer, Daniel[4] Stouffer, Christian[3], Hans[2], Hans[1]) was born March 24, 1930 in Susquehanna, PA, and died November 17, 1981 in Lewistown, MT. He married **(1) Living Rathgeber**. He married **(2) Living Bortz**.

Children of Jay Derr and Living Rathgeber are:
- 5693 i. Stacey Susan[16] Derr, born in Edgewater, Colorado. She married Living Webber.
- 5694 ii. Jennifer Elizabeth Derr.

5187. Elizabeth Jane Feldser[15] Derr (Minnie[14] Ober, Daisy Meyers[13], Moses Heagly[12], Moses Ruhl[11], Christian Longnecker[10], David S[9], Elizabeth[8] Stauffer, Johannes[7], Daniel[6] Stouffer, Christian[5] Stauffer, Daniel[4] Stouffer, Christian[3], Hans[2], Hans[1]) was born August 06, 1934 in Lancaster, PA, and died April 13, 2000 in New Bloomfield, PA. She married **Living Feldser**.

Children of Elizabeth Derr and Living Feldser are:
- 5695 i. Living[16] Feldser.
- 5696 ii. Living Feldser.
- 5697 iii. Living Feldser.
- 5698 iv. Living Feldser.
- 5699 v. Living Feldser.
- 5700 vi. Living Feldser.

5190. Elvin Ezra[15] Hitz (Elmer Ezra[14], Stella M[13] Ober, Moses Heagly[12], Moses Ruhl[11], Christian Longnecker[10], David S[9], Elizabeth[8] Stauffer, Johannes[7], Daniel[6] Stouffer, Christian[5] Stauffer, Daniel[4] Stouffer, Christian[3], Hans[2], Hans[1]) was born July 01, 1946. He married **Donna Marie Zuver** October 10, 1970. She was born September 05, 1950.

Children of Elvin Hitz and Donna Zuver are:
- + 5701 i. Douglas Wade[16] Hitz, born October 24, 1973.
- + 5702 ii. Bradley Allen Hitz, born December 13, 1977.

5191. Galen D[15] Hitz (Elmer Ezra[14], Stella M[13] Ober, Moses Heagly[12], Moses Ruhl[11], Christian Longnecker[10], David S[9], Elizabeth[8] Stauffer, Johannes[7], Daniel[6] Stouffer, Christian[5] Stauffer, Daniel[4] Stouffer, Christian[3], Hans[2], Hans[1]) was born February 13, 1948. He married **Linda M Hein** August 28, 1971. She was born November 21, 1949.

Children of Galen Hitz and Linda Hein are:
- 5703 i. Lisa Marie[16] Hitz, born May 13, 1973.
- 5704 ii. Crystal Hitz.
- 5705 iii. Jeffrey Hitz.

5192. Jacob Landis[15] Hitz (Elmer Ezra[14], Stella M[13] Ober, Moses Heagly[12], Moses Ruhl[11], Christian Longnecker[10], David S[9], Elizabeth[8] Stauffer, Johannes[7], Daniel[6] Stouffer, Christian[5] Stauffer, Daniel[4] Stouffer, Christian[3], Hans[2], Hans[1]) was born January 24, 1953. He married **Nancy M Kohr** October 06, 1973.

Child of Jacob Hitz and Nancy Kohr is:
- 5706 i. Elizabeth Ashley[16] Hitz, born August 08, 1985.

5287. Private[15] Diehl (Private[14], Percy Ellsworth[13], David Alfred[12], Catherine A.[11] Ober, Jacob[10], Michael[9], Veronica " Frany "[8] Stauffer, Johannes[7], Daniel[6] Stouffer, Christian[5] Stauffer, Daniel[4] Stouffer, Christian[3], Hans[2], Hans[1]) She married **Private Berube**.

Child of Private Diehl and Private Berube is:
- 5707 i. Private[16] Berube.

5288. Private[15] Diehl (Private[14], Percy Ellsworth[13], David Alfred[12], Catherine A.[11] Ober, Jacob[10], Michael[9], Veronica " Frany "[8] Stauffer, Johannes[7], Daniel[6] Stouffer, Christian[5] Stauffer, Daniel[4] Stouffer, Christian[3], Hans[2], Hans[1]) She married **Private Cartier**.

Children of Private Diehl and Private Cartier are:
- 5708 i. Private[16] Cartier.
- 5709 ii. Private Cartier. She married Private Trask.

5289. Private[15] Diehl (Private[14], Percy Ellsworth[13], David Alfred[12], Catherine A.[11] Ober, Jacob[10], Michael[9], Veronica " Frany "[8] Stauffer, Johannes[7], Daniel[6] Stouffer, Christian[5] Stauffer, Daniel[4] Stouffer, Christian[3], Hans[2], Hans[1]) He married **Private Rudolph**.

Children of Private Diehl and Private Rudolph are:

| 5710 | i. | Private[16] Diehl. |
| 5711 | ii. | Private Diehl. |

5291. Private[15] Diehl (Private[14], Percy Ellsworth[13], David Alfred[12], Catherine A.[11] Ober, Jacob[10], Michael[9], Veronica " Frany "[8] Stauffer, Johannes[7], Daniel[6] Stouffer, Christian[5] Stauffer, Daniel[4] Stouffer, Christian[3], Hans[2], Hans[1]) She married **Private McCarrin**.

Child of Private Diehl and Private McCarrin is:
| 5712 | i. | Private[16] McCarrin. |

5292. Private[15] Diehl (Private[14], Percy Ellsworth[13], David Alfred[12], Catherine A.[11] Ober, Jacob[10], Michael[9], Veronica " Frany "[8] Stauffer, Johannes[7], Daniel[6] Stouffer, Christian[5] Stauffer, Daniel[4] Stouffer, Christian[3], Hans[2], Hans[1]) She married **Private Walsh**.

Child of Private Diehl and Private Walsh is:
| 5713 | i. | Private[16] Walsh. |

5293. Private[15] Diehl (Private[14], Percy Ellsworth[13], David Alfred[12], Catherine A.[11] Ober, Jacob[10], Michael[9], Veronica " Frany "[8] Stauffer, Johannes[7], Daniel[6] Stouffer, Christian[5] Stauffer, Daniel[4] Stouffer, Christian[3], Hans[2], Hans[1]) He married **(1) Private Unknown**. He married **(2) Private Unknown**.

Children of Private Diehl and Private Unknown are:
| 5714 | i. | Private[16] Diehl. |
| 5715 | ii. | Private Diehl. |

Child of Private Diehl and Private Unknown is:
| 5716 | i. | Private[16] Diehl. |

5294. Private[15] Diehl (Private[14], Percy Ellsworth[13], David Alfred[12], Catherine A.[11] Ober, Jacob[10], Michael[9], Veronica " Frany "[8] Stauffer, Johannes[7], Daniel[6] Stouffer, Christian[5] Stauffer, Daniel[4] Stouffer, Christian[3], Hans[2], Hans[1]) He married **Private Unknown**.

Children of Private Diehl and Private Unknown are:
| 5717 | i. | Private[16] Diehl. |
| 5718 | ii. | Private Diehl. |

5295. Private[15] Pike (Private[14] Diehl, Percy Ellsworth[13], David Alfred[12], Catherine A.[11] Ober, Jacob[10], Michael[9], Veronica " Frany "[8] Stauffer, Johannes[7], Daniel[6] Stouffer, Christian[5] Stauffer, Daniel[4] Stouffer, Christian[3], Hans[2], Hans[1]) He married **Private Chittenden**.

Child of Private Pike and Private Chittenden is:
| 5719 | i. | Private[16] Pike. |

5296. Private[15] Pike (Private[14] Diehl, Percy Ellsworth[13], David Alfred[12], Catherine A.[11] Ober, Jacob[10], Michael[9], Veronica " Frany "[8] Stauffer, Johannes[7], Daniel[6] Stouffer, Christian[5] Stauffer, Daniel[4] Stouffer, Christian[3], Hans[2], Hans[1]) He married **Private Ackerman**.

Child of Private Pike and Private Ackerman is:
| 5720 | i. | Private[16] Pike. |

5298. Private[15] Bright (Juanita Glada[14] Diehl, Percy Ellsworth[13], David Alfred[12], Catherine A.[11] Ober, Jacob[10], Michael[9], Veronica " Frany "[8] Stauffer, Johannes[7], Daniel[6] Stouffer, Christian[5] Stauffer, Daniel[4] Stouffer, Christian[3], Hans[2], Hans[1]) He married **Private Lichty**.

Children of Private Bright and Private Lichty are:
| + | 5721 | i. | Private[16] Bright. |
| + | 5722 | ii. | Private Bright. |

5299. Private[15] Bright (Juanita Glada[14] Diehl, Percy Ellsworth[13], David Alfred[12], Catherine A.[11] Ober, Jacob[10], Michael[9], Veronica " Frany "[8] Stauffer, Johannes[7], Daniel[6] Stouffer, Christian[5] Stauffer, Daniel[4] Stouffer, Christian[3], Hans[2], Hans[1]) She married **Private Ritter**.

Child of Private Bright and Private Ritter is:
| + | 5723 | i. | Private[16] Ritter. |

5302. Private[15] **Diehl** (Donald[14], Percy Ellsworth[13], David Alfred[12], Catherine A.[11] Ober, Jacob[10], Michael[9], Veronica " Frany "[8] Stauffer, Johannes[7], Daniel[6] Stouffer, Christian[5] Stauffer, Daniel[4] Stouffer, Christian[3], Hans[2], Hans[1]) She married **(1) Takis Lin Pifer**. He was born August 06, 1959 in Adrian, Michigan, and died August 07, 1980 in Traverse City Osteopathic Hospital, Traverse City, Grand Traverse County, Michigan. She married **(2) Private Unknown**.

Child of Private Diehl and Takis Pifer is:
  5724   i.   Private[16] Pifer.

Children of Private Diehl and Private Unknown are:
  5725   i.   Private[16] Unknown.
  5726   ii. Private Unknown.

5313. Private[15] **Mosemann** (Arlene Celeste[14] Brubaker, Allen L[13], Ezra[12], Christian[11], Christian[10], Elizabeth[9] Stauffer, Christian[8], Henry Jacob[7], Hans[6], Christian[5], Daniel[4] Stouffer, Christian[3], Hans[2], Hans[1]) was born Abt. 1942. She married **(1) Private Overly**. He was born Abt. 1942. She married **(2) Dennis Archie Lehman**. He was born August 25, 1949, and died July 26, 1971.

Child of Private Mosemann and Private Overly is:
  5727   i.   Private[16] Overly.

Generation No. 16

5674. Angela Dawn[16] **Crouse** (Kathryn Ann[15] Mohler, Dorothy Jean[14] Hippensteel, Margaret Elizabeth Alice[13] Goodhart, Theodore[12], Charlotte[11] Farner, Elizabeth[10] Owens, Peter[9] Ober, Elizabeth[8] Stauffer, Johannes[7], Daniel[6] Stouffer, Christian[5] Stauffer, Daniel[4] Stouffer, Christian[3], Hans[2], Hans[1]) was born Private. She married **Gordon Woglemuth** Private. He was born Private.

Child of Angela Crouse and Gordon Woglemuth is:
  5728   i.   Sean[17] Woglemuth, born Private.

5701. Douglas Wade[16] **Hitz** (Elvin Ezra[15], Elmer Ezra[14], Stella M[13] Ober, Moses Heagly[12], Moses Ruhl[11], Christian Longnecker[10], David S[9], Elizabeth[8] Stauffer, Johannes[7], Daniel[6] Stouffer, Christian[5] Stauffer, Daniel[4] Stouffer, Christian[3], Hans[2], Hans[1]) was born October 24, 1973. He married **Janet Elaine Pitkin** September 05, 1998. She was born August 11, 1975.

Child of Douglas Hitz and Janet Pitkin is:
  5729   i.   Rachel Emma[17] Hitz, born February 23, 2003.

5702. Bradley Allen[16] **Hitz** (Elvin Ezra[15], Elmer Ezra[14], Stella M[13] Ober, Moses Heagly[12], Moses Ruhl[11], Christian Longnecker[10], David S[9], Elizabeth[8] Stauffer, Johannes[7], Daniel[6] Stouffer, Christian[5] Stauffer, Daniel[4] Stouffer, Christian[3], Hans[2], Hans[1]) was born December 13, 1977. He married **Amanda Klunk** October 12, 2002.

Child of Bradley Hitz and Amanda Klunk is:
  5730   i.   Brayden Joseph[17] Hitz, born August 18, 2005.

5721. Private[16] **Bright** (Private[15], Juanita Glada[14] Diehl, Percy Ellsworth[13], David Alfred[12], Catherine A.[11] Ober, Jacob[10], Michael[9], Veronica " Frany "[8] Stauffer, Johannes[7], Daniel[6] Stouffer, Christian[5] Stauffer, Daniel[4] Stouffer, Christian[3], Hans[2], Hans[1]) He married **Private Hartog**.

Children of Private Bright and Private Hartog are:
  5731   i.   Private[17] Bright.
  5732   ii. Private Bright.

5722. Private[16] **Bright** (Private[15], Juanita Glada[14] Diehl, Percy Ellsworth[13], David Alfred[12], Catherine A.[11] Ober, Jacob[10], Michael[9], Veronica " Frany "[8] Stauffer, Johannes[7], Daniel[6] Stouffer, Christian[5] Stauffer, Daniel[4] Stouffer, Christian[3], Hans[2], Hans[1]) She married **Private Sixberry**.

Child of Private Bright and Private Sixberry is:
  5733   i.   Private[17] Sixberry.

5723. Private[16] **Ritter** (Private[15] Bright, Juanita Glada[14] Diehl, Percy Ellsworth[13], David Alfred[12], Catherine A.[11] Ober, Jacob[10],

Michael⁹, Veronica " Frany "⁸ Stauffer, Johannes⁷, Daniel⁶ Stouffer, Christian⁵ Stauffer, Daniel⁴ Stouffer, Christian³, Hans², Hans¹) He married **Private Lavalley**.

Child of Private Ritter and Private Lavalley is:
    5734   i.   Private¹⁷ Ritter.

The Relations of Milton Snavely Hershey, 4th Ed.

Descendants of George Weber

Generation No. 1

1. George¹ Weber was born Abt. 1578, and died Aft. 1649. He married **Elsbeth Schnebli** Bef. 1621. She died Bef. 1633.

Marriage Notes for George Weber and Elsbeth Schnebli:
[jweaver..FTW]

Marriage was probably before 1617 since oldest child was born abt 1617.

Children of George Weber and Elsbeth Schnebli are:
+ 2   i.   Heinrich² Weber, died Aft. 1670.
   3   ii.   Sara Weber, born Abt. 1617.
   4   iii.   Georg Weber, born Abt. 1623.

Generation No. 2

2. Heinrich² Weber (George¹) died Aft. 1670. He married **Elsbeth Ruggin** January 26, 1640/41 in Baretswil, Switzerland, daughter of Uli Ruggin and Anna Ruegg. She died Bef. 1670.

Children of Heinrich Weber and Elsbeth Ruggin are:
+ 5   i.   Johann Anton³ Weber, died December 17, 1724 in Lancaster Co, PA.
   6   ii.   Jagli Weber.
   7   iii.   Samuel Weber, died Aft. 1700. He married (1) Barbara Pfenniger Bef. 1670; died Bef. 1700. He married (2) Verena Meyer Bef. 1700.
   8   iv.   Anna Weber.
   9   v.   Elsbeth Weber.
   10   vi.   Heinrich Weber.
   11   vii.   Barbeli Weber.
   12   viii.   Georg Weber.
   13   ix.   Hans Rudolf Weber, born 1660. He married Adelheit Pfenniger Bef. 1689.
   14   x.   Verena Weber, born 1664.

Generation No. 3

5. Johann Anton³ Weber (Heinrich², George¹) died December 17, 1724 in Lancaster Co, PA. He married **Maria Margaretha Herr**. She died Aft. November 1725.

Children of Johann Weber and Maria Herr are:
   15   i.   John⁴ Weber, born Abt. 1685; died 1755 in West Lampeter Twp., Lanc Co, Pa. He married Barbara Hauser; died Aft. 1721.
+ 16   ii.   Jacob Weber, born 1688; died January 1746/47.
+ 17   iii.   Henry Weber, born 1690; died June 1745.
+ 18   iv.   George Weber, born 1693; died 1772.
+ 19   v.   Maria Weber, born 1695.
   20   vi.   Anna Weber, born Abt. 1700; died 1727 in at sea on Molly. She married David Martin Bef. 1727; born Abt. 1700; died November 10, 1784 in Earl Twp., Lanc. Co., PA.

        Marriage Notes for Anna Weber and David Martin:
        [jweaver..FTW]

        Family tradition said that his first wife who died at sea on the Molly was Anna Weaver, sister of Henry, George, Jacob, and John Weber of Weber's Thal. However, Darvin Martin argues that this is highly unlikely. He argues in his article that the families probably never knew each other and that it is highly improbable that if he had a wife who was lost at sea, her name was Anna Weber.

        I would like to see more proof before I throw away this wonderful tale which M. G. Weaver quotes in his book. Jay Weaver.

Generation No. 4

16. Jacob[4] **Weber** (Johann Anton[3], Heinrich[2], George[1]) was born 1688, and died January 1746/47. He married **Anna Bauman** Abt. 1721. She was born Abt. 1705, and died February 11, 1771 in Ephrata Cloisters, Ephrata, PA.

Child of Jacob Weber and Anna Bauman is:
    21   i.   Hans[5] Weber, born January 1722/23 in Earl Twp, Lanc Co, PA; died October 11, 1803. He married Barbara Buckwalter; born September 16, 1730; died February 1796.

17. Henry[4] **Weber** (Johann Anton[3], Heinrich[2], George[1]) was born 1690, and died June 1745. He married **Maudlin Kendig**, daughter of Hans Kundig and Susanna Wymann. She was born Abt. 1703, and died Aft. 1744.

Children of Henry Weber and Maudlin Kendig are:
    22   i.   Anna[5] Weber, died 1784. She married John Carpenter; born 1720; died 1786.
+ 23   ii.   Elizabeth Weber, died Aft. March 04, 1771.
    24   iii. Mary Weber. She married John Wanner.
+ 25   iv. Beverly Weber, died October 1788 in Lancaster Co, PA.
    26   v.   Eva Weber. She married John Wistler.
+ 27   vi. Christian Weber, born December 25, 1731 in Earl Twp, Lanc Co, PA; died February 13, 1820.
+ 28   vii. Heine Weber, born 1736; died March 20, 1826.
+ 29   viii. Magdalena Weber, born October 28, 1738; died May 28, 1819.

18. George[4] **Weber** (Johann Anton[3], Heinrich[2], George[1]) was born 1693, and died 1772. He married **Barbara Guth** 1726, daughter of Jacob Gut and Mayer. She was born Abt. 1693, and died 1782.

Children of George Weber and Barbara Guth are:
    30   i.   Magdalena[5] Weber, born January 13, 1726/27.
+ 31   ii.   Johannnes Weber, born February 10, 1727/28; died October 25, 1802.
    32   iii. Anna Weber, born April 30, 1729; died 1780.
    33   iv. Marey Weber, born December 30, 1730; died July 30, 1791. She married Peter Stauffer; died November 20, 1787 in Goodville PA.
    34   v.   Samuel Weber, born August 08, 1732; died 1770. He married Barbara Kauffman; born 1751.
    35   vi. Barbara Weber, born March 11, 1733/34.
+ 36   vii. Heinrich Weber, born October 20, 1738; died September 12, 1787.

19. Maria[4] **Weber** (Johann Anton[3], Heinrich[2], George[1]) was born 1695. She married **Benjamin Landis**, son of Jacob Landes and Ann Witmer. He was born 1697 in Switzerland, and died 1781 in Lancaster Co, PA.

Children of Maria Weber and Benjamin Landis are:
+ 37   i.   Benjamin[5] Landis, born 1730; died October 01, 1787.
    38   ii.   Anna Landis, born January 28, 1729/30; died May 30, 1760. She married John Brackbill; born January 06, 1727/28; died August 20, 1813.
+ 39   iii. Mary Landis, born 1738; died January 29, 1804.
    40   iv. Abraham Landis, born 1739; died 1790. He married Maria Barr; born 1732; died 1802.
+ 41   v.   Jacob Landis, born 1740; died April 08, 1794.
    42   vi. Barbara Landis, born 1747; died 1820. She married Abraham Buckwalter; born August 27, 1740; died January 07, 1819.
+ 43   vii. Henry Landis, born April 10, 1744 in East Lampeter Township, Lancaster County, Pennsylvania; died March 04, 1825 in East Lampeter Township, Lancaster County, Pennsylvania.

Generation No. 5

23. Elizabeth[5] **Weber** (Henry[4], Johann Anton[3], Heinrich[2], George[1]) died Aft. March 04, 1771. She married **(1) Wolfgang Newcomer**, son of Peter Newcomer and Unknown Unknown. He was born Bef. 1710, and died March 04, 1771. She married **(2) Vincent Meyer**, son of John Meyer and Barbara Landis. He was born 1721, and died 1797.

Children of Elizabeth Weber and Wolfgang Newcomer are:
    44   i.   Elizabeth[6] Newcomer.

	45	ii.	Magdalena Newcomer.
	46	iii.	Peter Newcomer. He married Unknown Houser.
	47	iv.	Henry Newcomer, born December 31, 1744; died May 14, 1795. He married Barbara Garver; born December 25, 1746; died February 01, 1818.
	48	v.	Barbara Newcomer, born 1747; died January 26, 1820. She married Abraham Buckwalter; born 1741; died January 07, 1819.
	49	vi.	Christian Newcomer, born January 21, 1748/49; died March 12, 1830. He married Elizabeth Bear March 31, 1772 in Zeltenreich Reformed Church; born 1752; died April 22, 1811.
+	50	vii.	Anna Weber Newcomer, born July 25, 1752; died January 08, 1832.

25. Beverly[5] Weber (Henry[4], Johann Anton[3], Heinrich[2], George[1]) died October 1788 in Lancaster Co, PA. She married **George Anthony Mummah**. He was born 1722, and died 1786 in Hempfield Twp, Lancaster Co, PA.

Children of Beverly Weber and George Mummah are:
	51	i.	Christian[6] Mummah.
	52	ii.	Juliana Mummah. She married David Mellinger.
	53	iii.	David Mummah.
	54	iv.	Magdalena Mummah, born Abt. 1751 in Lancaster Co, PA; died Abt. 1801 in Egypt, Luray, Page Co., VA. She married Jacob Strickler; died 1784.
+	55	v.	Maria Mumma, born Abt. 1759 in Hempfield Twp, Lancaster Co, PA; died Bet. November 1788 - April 1793 in Hempfield Twp, Lancaster Co, PA.
	56	vi.	Henry Mummah, born Abt. 1760 in Lancaster Co, PA; died October 20, 1809 in Sharpsburg, Washington Co., MD. He married Julianna Heckman.
	57	vii.	George Mummah, born December 22, 1762 in Hempfield Twp, Lancaster Co, PA; died May 09, 1835 in Westmoreland Co., PA. He married Catherine Gerber.
	58	viii.	Barbara Mummah, born 1765 in hempfield Twp., Lancaster Co., PA; died in Sharpsburg, Washington Co., MD. She married Joseph Sherrick; born 1769 in Hempfield Twp, Lancaster Co, PA; died March 17, 1845 in Sharpsburg, Washington Co., MD.
	59	ix.	Jacob Mummah, born April 09, 1766 in Lancaster Co, PA; died September 23, 1848 in Sharpsburg, Washington Co., MD. He married Elizabeth Newcomer Hertzler; born October 04, 1764; died February 23, 1635/36 in Sharpsburg, Washington Co., MD.

27. Christian[5] Weber (Henry[4], Johann Anton[3], Heinrich[2], George[1]) was born December 25, 1731 in Earl Twp, Lanc Co, PA, and died February 13, 1820. He married **Magdalena Rutt** September 30, 1749. She was born September 30, 1733, and died February 16, 1804.

Children of Christian Weber and Magdalena Rutt are:
+	60	i.	Henry[6] Weber, died 1827.
	61	ii.	Magdalena Weber. She married Jacob Martin.
+	62	iii.	Esther Weber, died 1830.
	63	iv.	Anna Weber. She married Peter Springer.
	64	v.	Christian Weber, born 1754; died April 13, 1823. He married Anna Long; born 1755; died 1827.
+	65	vi.	Samuel Weber, born May 24, 1759; died February 09, 1825.
+	66	vii.	Jacob Weber, born 1760 in Earl Twp, Lanc Co, PA; died 1846.
+	67	viii.	Peter Weber, born March 07, 1761; died April 07, 1837.
	68	ix.	John Weber, born 1763; died 1823. He married Elizabeth Sensenig; born 1767; died 1846.
	69	x.	Elizabeth Weber, born December 22, 1764; died February 04, 1843. She married (1) Jacob Huber March 1790. She married (2) Wendel Bauman August 17, 1817; born February 25, 1758; died November 20, 1842.
	70	xi.	Joseph Weber, born September 09, 1768; died February 06, 1844. He married Maria Burkholder; born May 16, 1767; died August 23, 1823.
	71	xii.	Barbara Weber, born March 02, 1771; died Bef. 1820. She married Michael Shirk; born September 06, 1749; died June 25, 1829.
+	72	xiii.	Maria Weber, born March 26, 1775; died October 31, 1836.

28. Heine[5] Weber (Henry[4], Johann Anton[3], Heinrich[2], George[1]) was born 1736, and died March 20, 1826. He married **Eve Wenger**, daughter of Christian Wenger and Eva Grabiel. She was born January 07, 1736/37, and died May 07, 1799.

Children of Heine Weber and Eve Wenger are:
	73	i.	Henry[6] Weber, born December 16, 1758; died April 20, 1816. He married Feronica Hershey; born 1766; died 1830.
	74	ii.	Christian Weber, born 1762; died October 08, 1821.
	75	iii.	Barbara Weber, born July 29, 1764; died February 26, 1838. She married Abraham Reiff; born

September 07, 1760; died February 14, 1820.
+ 76   iv. Anna Weber, born September 17, 1766; died June 13, 1823.
   77   v. Michael Weber, born January 21, 1772; died October 15, 1841. He married Catharine Stauffer; born October 30, 1771; died May 15, 1834.
+ 78   vi. Magdalena Weber, born 1776; died 1846 in Horst, Family G.Y..
   79   vii. Eva Weber, born 1783; died 1816. She married John Brubaker; born 1782; died 1863.

29. Magdalena[5] Weber (Henry[4], Johann Anton[3], Heinrich[2], George[1]) was born October 28, 1738, and died May 28, 1819. She married **Frantz Buckwalter**, son of Theodorus Buckwalter and Barbara Landis. He was born April 05, 1732, and died March 06, 1816.

Children of Magdalena Weber and Frantz Buckwalter are:
   80   i. Anna[6] Buckwalter. She married Unknown Siegrist.
   81   ii. Elizabeth Buckwalter. She married Christian W. Sensenig; born March 12, 1757; died January 12, 1832.
+ 82   iii. John Buckwalter, born December 20, 1760; died May 06, 1832.
+ 83   iv. Henry Buckwalter, born June 19, 1765; died September 25, 1844.
   84   v. Magdalena Buckwalter, born January 08, 1784; died August 05, 1858.
   85   vi. Barbara Buckwalter, born 1787; died 1835. She married Peter Landis; born July 09, 1778 in East Lampeter Township, Lancaster County, Pennsylvania; died November 17, 1856 in East Lampeter Township, Lancaster County, Pennsylvania.

31. Johannnes[5] Weber (George[4], Johann Anton[3], Heinrich[2], George[1]) was born February 10, 1727/28, and died October 25, 1802. He married **(1) Magdalena Myers**. He married **(2) Fanny Seachrist**. She was born Abt. 1736 in prob. Hempfield Twp, Lancaster Co, PA, and died May 29, 1803.

Children of Johannnes Weber and Magdalena Myers are:
   86   i. Mary[6] Weber, born May 15, 1757; died December 19, 1822. She married (1) Christian Jenuine. She married (2) William Schoenfield.
+ 87   ii. George Weber, born March 22, 1759; died December 24, 1844.

Children of Johannnes Weber and Fanny Seachrist are:
   88   i. Anna[6] Weber, born December 15, 1760. She married (1) Christian Swartz. She married (2) Christian Ebersole.
   89   ii. David Weber, born September 10, 1762; died 1842. He married Maria Stauffer; born 1785; died 1840.
   90   iii. Barbara Weber, born May 25, 1764; died February 08, 1835. She married Christian Zimmerman; born March 02, 1755; died March 08, 1826.
   91   iv. Fanny Weber, born September 14, 1766.
   92   v. Magdalena Weber, born August 20, 1768; died 1808. She married (1) David Lichty; born 1763; died 1798. She married (2) Christian Sensenig; died 1831.
   93   vi. Samuel Weber, born November 09, 1771; died 1852. He married (1) Magdalena Rutt; born 1770; died 1829. He married (2) Magdalena Eshleman; born 1784; died 1856.
   94   vii. Elizabeth Weber, born August 25, 1774; died 1856. She married Henry Root; born 1771; died 1852.
   95   viii. Catharine Weber, born August 20, 1776; died 1849. She married John Shirk; born 1781; died 1831.
   96   ix. Susanna Weber, born August 20, 1776. She married John Schnader.
   97   x. Aadi Weber, born April 19, 1779. She married John Ebersole.

36. Heinrich[5] Weber (George[4], Johann Anton[3], Heinrich[2], George[1]) was born October 20, 1738, and died September 12, 1787. He married **Elizabeth Unknown**. She was born August 26, 1742, and died June 22, 1815.

Child of Heinrich Weber and Elizabeth Unknown is:
   98   i. Anna[6] Weaver, born January 05, 1780; died February 20, 1816. She married Peter Shirk; born February 08, 1780; died January 16, 1826.

37. Benjamin[5] Landis (Maria[4] Weber, Johann Anton[3], Heinrich[2], George[1]) was born 1730, and died October 01, 1787. He married **Anna Snavely**, daughter of John Schnebele and Anna Unknown.

Children of Benjamin Landis and Anna Snavely are:
   99   i. Maria[6] Landis, born August 14, 1751; died February 15, 1826. She married John Greider; born January 21, 1746/47; died September 25, 1825.
  100   ii. Anna Landis, born July 05, 1753; died 1832. She married John Weaver; born July 04, 1750; died 1832.
+ 101   iii. John Landis, born March 15, 1755; died April 29, 1837.

102	iv.	Benjamin Landis, born May 20, 1755 in Manheim Twp, Lanc Co, PA; died March 08, 1811. He married Elizabeth Brackbill April 08, 1783; born December 10, 1764; died May 28, 1789.
103	v.	Barbara Landis, born February 28, 1758; died 1824. She married Christian Long; born January 26, 1766; died February 27, 1847.
+ 104	vi.	Henry Landis, born December 05, 1760; died February 22, 1839.
105	vii.	Abraham Landis, born December 19, 1762.
106	viii.	Jacob Landis, born January 19, 1765.
107	ix.	Elizabeth Landis, born December 15, 1768; died February 04, 1857. She married John Brackbill; born January 20, 1763; died July 19, 1825.

39. Mary[5] Landis (Maria[4] Weber, Johann Anton[3], Heinrich[2], George[1]) was born 1738, and died January 29, 1804. She married **Abraham Buckwalter** 1756 in Strasburg, Lancaster Co, PA, son of Joseph Buckwalter and Barbara Landis. He was born August 27, 1738, and died January 08, 1820.

Children of Mary Landis and Abraham Buckwalter are:

108	i.	Mary[6] Buckwalter, born 1757.
109	ii.	Abraham Buckwalter, born September 24, 1759.
110	iii.	Susan Buckwalter, born 1763.
+ 111	iv.	Benjamin Buckwalter, born 1764 in East Lampeter Twp, Lancaster Co, PA; died 1804 in East Lampeter Twp, Lancaster Co, PA.

41. Jacob[5] Landis (Maria[4] Weber, Johann Anton[3], Heinrich[2], George[1]) was born 1740, and died April 08, 1794. He married **Esther Barr**. She was born Abt. 1745.

Children of Jacob Landis and Esther Barr are:

112	i.	Mary[6] Landis, born Abt. 1766. She married Jacob Winters June 10, 1780; born in Martic Twp, Rockingham Co, VA.
+ 113	ii.	Johannes Landis, born July 03, 1766; died August 11, 1826.
114	iii.	Abraham Landis, born November 01, 1767; died March 10, 1851. He married (1) Elizabeth Brenneman; born August 11, 1775; died November 15, 1857. He married (2) Elizabeth Houser; born Abt. 1772; died 1795.
115	iv.	Elizabeth Landis, born December 15, 1768; died February 04, 1857. She married Christian L. Houser; born December 09, 1767; died December 29, 1849.
116	v.	Esther Landis, born October 01, 1771; died August 24, 1838. She married John Burkholder; born December 31, 1765; died April 30, 1837.
117	vi.	Magdalena Landis, born Abt. 1775; died 1839.
118	vii.	Barbara Landis, born Abt. 1777; died 1833. She married John Weaver Abt. 1830; born 1777.

43. Henry[5] Landis (Maria[4] Weber, Johann Anton[3], Heinrich[2], George[1]) was born April 10, 1744 in East Lampeter Township, Lancaster County, Pennsylvania, and died March 04, 1825 in East Lampeter Township, Lancaster County, Pennsylvania. He married **Maria Brubaker**. She was born February 08, 1746/47 in Manheim Township, Lancaster County, Pennsylvania, and died September 18, 1828 in East Lampeter Township, Lancaster County, Pennsylvania.

Children of Henry Landis and Maria Brubaker are:

119	i.	Ann[6] Landis, born May 09, 1767 in East Lampeter Township, Lancaster County, Pennsylvania; died November 09, 1852 in Lancaster County, Pennsylvania. She married George Brenner February 28, 1809; born September 29, 1762 in Pennsylvania; died June 26, 1837 in Lancaster County, Pennsylvania.
+ 120	ii.	Benjamin Landis, born May 11, 1769 in East Lampeter Township, Lancaster County, Pennsylvania; died October 24, 1827 in Bareville, Lampeter Township, Lancaster County, ennsylvania.
121	iii.	Maria Landis, born September 22, 1771 in East Lampeter Township, Lancaster County, Pennsylvania; died June 22, 1860 in Pennsylvania. She married Joseph Weaver; born 1765 in Pennsylvania; died September 10, 1824 in East Earl, Pennsylvania.
+ 122	iv.	Rev. John Landis, born August 25, 1775 in East Lampeter Township, Lancaster County, Pennsylvania; died June 21, 1851 in East Lampeter Township, Lancaster County, Pennsylvania.
123	v.	Henry Landis, born May 15, 1777 in East Lampeter Township, Lancaster County, Pennsylvania; died December 24, 1845 in East Lampeter Township, Lancaster County, Pennsylvania. He married Mary Stoner; born October 25, 1778 in East Lampeter Township, Lancaster County, Pennsylvania; died August 14, 1852 in East Lampeter Township, Lancaster County, Pennsylvania.
124	vi.	Peter Landis, born July 09, 1778 in East Lampeter Township, Lancaster County, Pennsylvania; died November 17, 1856 in East Lampeter Township, Lancaster County, Pennsylvania. He married (1) Barbara (Landis); born Abt. 1780 in Pennsylvania; died Abt. 1850 in East Lampeter Township, Lancaster County, Pennsylvania. He married (2) Barbara Buckwalter; born 1787; died 1835.

+ 125 vii. Rev. Abraham Landis, born April 11, 1780 in East Lampeter Township, Lancaster County, Pennsylvania; died April 21, 1861 in East Lampeter Township, Lancaster County, Pennsylvania.
126 viii. Barbara Landis, born March 14, 1782 in East Lampeter Township, Lancaster County, Pennsylvania; died February 1802 in East Lampeter Township, Lancaster County, Pennsylvania.
127 ix. Elizabeth Landis, born September 10, 1785 in East Lampeter Township, Lancaster County, Pennsylvania; died February 1802 in East Lampeter Township, Lancaster County, Pennsylvania.
128 x. Susan Landis, born 1790 in East Lampeter Township, Lancaster County, Pennsylvania; died 1790 in East Lampeter Township, Lancaster County, Pennsylvania.

Generation No. 6

50. Anna Weber[6] Newcomer (Elizabeth[5] Weber, Henry[4], Johann Anton[3], Heinrich[2], George[1]) was born July 25, 1752, and died January 08, 1832. She married **Jacob Snavely Hershey** Abt. 1771 in Pennsylvania, son of Andrew Hershey and Mary Schnabley. He was born 1742 in Hempfield Twp, Lancaster Co, PA, and died April 11, 1825.

Children of Anna Newcomer and Jacob Hershey are:
+ 129 i. John[7] Hershey, born May 21, 1772 in Derry Twp, Dauphin Co, PA; died November 23, 1850.
130 ii. Jacob Hershey, born 1775 in Derry Twp, Dauphin Co, PA; died 1829.
+ 131 iii. Christian Hershey, born June 20, 1780; died August 05, 1843.
132 iv. Elizabeth Hershey, born May 19, 1783 in Derry Twp, Dauphin Co, PA; died June 12, 1875. She married (1) Benedict Brackbill; born June 03, 1779; died May 15, 1827. She married (2) Benedict Brackbill February 12, 1805; born June 08, 1779; died May 15, 1827.
+ 133 v. Abraham Hershey, born January 24, 1787 in Derry Twp, Dauphin Co, PA; died January 09, 1844.
134 vi. Andrew Hershey, born January 24, 1787; died Abt. January 24, 1787.
135 vii. Abraham Hershey, born June 21, 1787 in Derry Twp, Lancaster, PA; died January 09, 1844. He married Anna Eby; born December 15, 1800; died February 29, 1896.
136 viii. Joseph Hershey, born October 10, 1791 in Derry Twp, Dauphin Co, PA; died April 12, 1856. He married Magdelene Rupp; born June 07, 1791; died April 19, 1887.

55. Maria[6] Mumma (Beverly[5] Weber, Henry[4], Johann Anton[3], Heinrich[2], George[1]) was born Abt. 1759 in Hempfield Twp, Lancaster Co, PA, and died Bet. November 1788 - April 1793 in Hempfield Twp, Lancaster Co, PA. She married **Jacob Hertzler**. He was born Abt. 1745 in Switzerland, and died 1794.

Child of Maria Mumma and Jacob Hertzler is:
+ 137 i. John[7] Hertzler, born 1773.

60. Henry[6] Weber (Christian[5], Henry[4], Johann Anton[3], Heinrich[2], George[1]) died 1827. He married **(1) Maria Huber**. She was born 1758, and died 1797. He married **(2) Elizabeth Bauman**. She died 1827.

Child of Henry Weber and Maria Huber is:
+ 138 i. Mary[7] Weber, born September 15, 1788; died October 21, 1865.

62. Esther[6] Weber (Christian[5], Henry[4], Johann Anton[3], Heinrich[2], George[1]) died 1830. She married **Mathias Musser**. He was born November 23, 1764, and died 1834.

Children of Esther Weber and Mathias Musser are:
139 i. Mary[7] Musser, born 1795; died 1868. She married Henry Bauman; born 1789; died 1866.
140 ii. Daniel Musser, born 1798; died 1869. He married Elizabeth Ranck; born 1797; died 1870.
141 iii. Magdalena Musser, born 1802; died 1886.
142 iv. Fronica Musser, born 1803; died 1889. She married Joseph Horning; born 1798; died 1876.
143 v. Esther Musser, born April 27, 1807; died January 11, 1892. She married Jonas Good; born December 30, 1803; died September 21, 1858.
144 vi. Nancy Musser, born 1809; died 1889. She married John Musselman; born 1806; died 1869.
+ 145 vii. Barbara Weber Musser, born February 13, 1811 in Brecknock Twp., Lanc. Co., Pa.; died July 01, 1889.

65. Samuel[6] Weber (Christian[5], Henry[4], Johann Anton[3], Heinrich[2], George[1]) was born May 24, 1759, and died February 09, 1825. He married **Anna Hutwohl**. She was born June 23, 1765, and died October 03, 1808.

Children of Samuel Weber and Anna Hutwohl are:
146 i. Samuel[7] Weber. He married Elizabeth Rhoads; born 1793; died 1875.

	147	ii.	Jacob Weber.
+	148	iii.	Christian Weber, born August 20, 1785; died September 03, 1854.
	149	iv.	Daniel Weber, born 1786; died 1861. He married (1) Elizabeth Buckwalter. He married (2) Ester Andrew; born 1795; died 1838. He married (3) Mary Weaver Kauffman; born 1807; died 1836.
	150	v.	Magdalena Weber, born December 1787; died August 1874. She married Peter Shirk; born February 08, 1780; died January 16, 1826.
	151	vi.	Feronica Weber, born 1789; died 1857. She married Martin Binkley; born 1795; died 1879.
	152	vii.	John Weber, born 1792; died 1850. He married Salome Meyer; born 1788; died 1853.
	153	viii.	Anna Weber, born 1796; died 1876.
+	154	ix.	Isaac Weber, born August 1804; died May 1846.

66. Jacob⁶ Weber (Christian⁵, Henry⁴, Johann Anton³, Heinrich², George¹) was born 1760 in Earl Twp, Lanc Co, PA, and died 1846. He married **Barbara Witwer**. She was born May 1764.

Child of Jacob Weber and Barbara Witwer is:
155   i. Susanna⁷ Weber, born October 22, 1794; died August 02, 1855. She married John Musser; born June 06, 1790; died June 24, 1869.

67. Peter⁶ Weber (Christian⁵, Henry⁴, Johann Anton³, Heinrich², George¹) was born March 07, 1761, and died April 07, 1837. He married **Feronica S. Wenger**. She was born October 17, 1765, and died August 17, 1843.

Children of Peter Weber and Feronica Wenger are:

	156	i.	Maria⁷ Weber, died 1821. She married Jacob Stauffer.
	157	ii.	John Weber, born 1786; died 1854. He married Catharine Gehman; born 1782; died 1864.
	158	iii.	Magdelena Weber, born 1790; died 1872. She married Benjamin Gehman; born 1784; died 1856.
+	159	iv.	Isaac Weaver, born September 11, 1792 in East Earl Twp., Lancaster Co., Pa.; died June 10, 1866.
	160	v.	Anna Weber, born 1797; died 1875. She married Joseph Horst; born 1795; died 1883 in Franklin Co.
	161	vi.	Barbara Weber, born 1798. She married Abraham Gerhart.
	162	vii.	Peter Weaver, born 1801. He married Elizabeth Wenger; born 1805.
	163	viii.	Feronica W Weber, born March 15, 1804. She married Abraham Rife; born March 07, 1798; died February 09, 1879.
	164	ix.	Jacob Weber, born 1809; died January 14, 1871.

72. Maria⁶ Weber (Christian⁵, Henry⁴, Johann Anton³, Heinrich², George¹) was born March 26, 1775, and died October 31, 1836. She married **Jacob Horst**. He was born October 18, 1776, and died August 09, 1863.

Children of Maria Weber and Jacob Horst are:

	165	i.	Magdalena⁷ Horst, born May 26, 1798; died June 21, 1849. She married Peter Shirk; born June 19, 1785; died August 10, 1845.
	166	ii.	Daniel Horst, born March 15, 1799; died February 25, 1854. He married Judith Hoffman; born January 22, 1800; died April 28, 1882.
	167	iii.	Jacob W. Horst, born August 14, 1801; died May 15, 1884. He married Anna Zimmerman; born June 01, 1812; died January 13, 1892.
+	168	iv.	Anna Horst, born January 07, 1803; died September 25, 1857.
	169	v.	Mary Horst, born November 04, 1804; died March 20, 1870.
	170	vi.	Margaret Horst, born January 17, 1806; died March 29, 1875. She married John Hoffman; born April 15, 1794; died April 09, 1842.
	171	vii.	Moses Horst, born February 16, 1813; died April 01, 1899. He married Mary Bauman; born October 30, 1816; died November 14, 1886.

76. Anna⁶ Weber (Heine⁵, Henry⁴, Johann Anton³, Heinrich², George¹) was born September 17, 1766, and died June 13, 1823. She married **David Horst**, son of Joseph Horst and Mary Groff. He was born October 12, 1769, and died May 15, 1845.

Children of Anna Weber and David Horst are:
172   i. Joseph⁷ Horst, born 1795; died 1883 in Franklin Co. He married Anna Weber; born 1797; died 1875.
173   ii. John W. Horst, born September 10, 1797 in Caernarvon Twp, Lanc Co, PA; died March 10, 1877. He married Catharine Witwer; born March 18, 1795 in Earl Twp, Lanc Co, PA; died February 01, 1878.

78. Magdalena⁶ Weber (Heine⁵, Henry⁴, Johann Anton³, Heinrich², George¹) was born 1776, and died 1846 in Horst, Family G.Y.. She married **Joseph Horst**, son of John Horst and Ann Strickler. He was born August 15, 1774, and died November 1856.

Children of Magdalena Weber and Joseph Horst are:
- 174   i. Susanna[7] Horst. She married John Wanner.
- \+ 175   ii. Elizabeth Horst, born October 06, 1802; died November 08, 1829.
- \+ 176   iii. Anna Horst, born 1808; died 1850.
- 177   iv. Fanny Horst, born 1810; died 1879. She married Solomon Martin; born 1808; died 1878.
- 178   v. John W. Horst, born 1816; died 1881. He married Elizabeth Flickinger; born December 26, 1816 in Adamstown, Lancaster Co, PA; died June 26, 1896 in Terre Hill, Lanc Co, PA.

82. John[6] Buckwalter (Magdalena[5] Weber, Henry[4], Johann Anton[3], Heinrich[2], George[1]) was born December 20, 1760, and died May 06, 1832. He married **Anna Eaby** March 09, 1784. She was born March 29, 1763, and died September 10, 1831.

Children of John Buckwalter and Anna Eaby are:
- 179   i. Mary[7] Buckwalter. She married Unknown Siegrist.
- \+ 180   ii. Abraham Buckwalter, born January 24, 1785; died October 14, 1832.
- \+ 181   iii. Judith Buckwalter, born August 10, 1787; died September 28, 1858.

83. Henry[6] Buckwalter (Magdalena[5] Weber, Henry[4], Johann Anton[3], Heinrich[2], George[1]) was born June 19, 1765, and died September 25, 1844. He married **Mary Wenger Sensenig**, daughter of Michael Sensenig and Magdalena Wenger. She was born Abt. 1766 in Lancaster Co, PA.

Child of Henry Buckwalter and Mary Sensenig is:
- 182   i. Magdalena[7] Buckwalter, born January 08, 1784; died August 06, 1855. She married Henry Resh; born 1771; died 1849.

87. George[6] Weber (Johannnes[5], George[4], Johann Anton[3], Heinrich[2], George[1]) was born March 22, 1759, and died December 24, 1844. He married **Catharine Zimmerman**. She was born 1762, and died 1838.

Children of George Weber and Catharine Zimmerman are:
- 183   i. Barbara[7] Weber, born 1787; died 1861. She married Michael Hildabrand; born 1788; died 1880.
- 184   ii. Elizabeth Weber, born 1789; died 1863. She married Francis Sensenig; born 1793; died 1875.
- 185   iii. George Weber, born 1791; died 1862.
- \+ 186   iv. Catharine Weber, born February 01, 1795 in Lancaster Co, PA; died May 10, 1862.
- 187   v. Magdalena Weber, born 1801; died 1837. She married John Plank; born 1802; died 1858.
- 188   vi. Martin C. Weber, born 1805; died 1876. He married Susanna Kurtz; born 1807; died 1881.

101. John[6] Landis (Benjamin[5], Maria[4] Weber, Johann Anton[3], Heinrich[2], George[1]) was born March 15, 1755, and died April 29, 1837. He married **Anna Johns**. She was born 1762, and died October 09, 1823.

Children of John Landis and Anna Johns are:
- 189   i. John[7] Landis, born September 11, 1782; died April 16, 1863 in Landisville, Lancaster Co., PA. He married Anna Bachman; born February 03, 1785; died May 23, 1846.
- \+ 190   ii. Henry Landis, born September 26, 1786; died July 22, 1859.
- \+ 191   iii. Benjamin Landis, born April 30, 1780 in East Lampeter Township, Lancaster County, Pennsylvania; died November 03, 1865 in East Lampeter Township, Lancaster County, Pennsylvania.

104. Henry[6] Landis (Benjamin[5], Maria[4] Weber, Johann Anton[3], Heinrich[2], George[1]) was born December 05, 1760, and died February 22, 1839. He married **Anna Long**, daughter of Isaac Long and Susanna Coffman. She was born March 11, 1766, and died December 10, 1845.

Child of Henry Landis and Anna Long is:
- \+ 192   i. Benjamin L.[7] Landis, born November 06, 1791 in Manheim Twp, Lanc Co, PA; died December 10, 1849.

111. Benjamin[6] Buckwalter (Mary[5] Landis, Maria[4] Weber, Johann Anton[3], Heinrich[2], George[1]) was born 1764 in East Lampeter Twp, Lancaster Co, PA, and died 1804 in East Lampeter Twp, Lancaster Co, PA. He married **Barabara Herr**. She was born 1775, and died 1850 in East Lampeter Twp, Lancaster Co, PA.

Children of Benjamin Buckwalter and Barabara Herr are:
- \+ 193   i. Elizabeth[7] Buckwalter, born March 09, 1789; died February 03, 1865.

194	ii.	Jacob Buckwalter, born 1790.
195	iii.	Abraham Buckwalter, born December 24, 1792.
196	iv.	Mary Buckwalter, born June 12, 1796.
197	v.	Ann Buckwalter, born March 11, 1798.
198	vi.	Benjamin Buckwalter, born May 22, 1804.

113. Johannes[6] Landis (Jacob[5], Maria[4] Weber, Johann Anton[3], Heinrich[2], George[1]) was born July 03, 1766, and died August 11, 1826. He married **(1) Elizabeth Burkholder**. She was born 1768, and died 1795. He married **(2) Barbara Snavely** May 16, 1797, daughter of John Snavely and Elizabeth Barr. She was born October 05, 1779, and died December 25, 1854.

Children of Johannes Landis and Elizabeth Burkholder are:
199	i.	Jacob B.[7] Landis, born October 21, 1792; died January 24, 1835. He married Maria Stauffer; born August 15, 1797; died July 18, 1865.
200	ii.	Anna Landis, born March 04, 1794; died March 10, 1862. She married Abraham Shenk; born May 22, 1795; died February 15, 1844.
201	iii.	John B. Landis, born November 17, 1795; died March 24, 1856. He married Martha Mylin; born February 26, 1791; died October 25, 1803.

Children of Johannes Landis and Barbara Snavely are:
	202	i.	Elizabeth S.[7] Landis, born May 1800; died May 06, 1820.
	203	ii.	Benjamin S. Landis, born September 03, 1801; died September 05, 1872. He married Maria Buchwalter January 29, 1822; born October 28, 1803; died December 16, 1871.
	204	iii.	Abraham S. Landis, born November 12, 1801; died November 12, 1874 in East Lampeter Twp., Lancaster Co., PA. He married Barbara Landis; born January 31, 1779; died August 07, 1881.
+	205	iv.	Christian S. Landis, born June 18, 1803; died December 23, 1870.
	206	v.	Susanna S. Landis, born February 13, 1806; died January 06, 1886. She married Michael Buckwalter; born October 04, 1809; died September 15, 1876.
	207	vi.	Martin S. Landis, born March 09, 1808; died February 10, 1889. He married Elizabeth Rupp February 16, 1835; born January 13, 1814; died May 10, 1889.
	208	vii.	Barbara S. Landis, born December 15, 1810; died September 03, 1887. She married Jacob Stauffer January 28, 1834; born March 14, 1814; died October 1883.
	209	viii.	Daniel S. Landis, born April 02, 1814; died March 30, 1893. He married Elizabeth Landis Huver November 22, 1836; born September 26, 1816; died April 13, 1889.
	210	ix.	David S. Landis, born April 02, 1814; died January 24, 1893. He married Elizabeth Hostetter January 14, 1834; born May 07, 1813; died June 21, 1872.
	211	x.	Mary S. Landis, born 1815; died May 26, 1890. She married Emanuel Groff December 01, 1831; born 1813; died 1889.
	212	xi.	Hettie S. Landis, born November 02, 1819; died March 22, 1902. She married Christian R. Landis December 21, 1837; born January 22, 1814; died March 12, 1894.

120. Benjamin[6] Landis (Henry[5], Maria[4] Weber, Johann Anton[3], Heinrich[2], George[1]) was born May 11, 1769 in East Lampeter Township, Lancaster County, Pennsylvania, and died October 24, 1827 in Bareville, Lampeter Township, Lancaster County, ennsylvania. He married **Barbara Musser** 1790. She was born 1770 in East Hemfield Township, Lancaster County, Pennsylvania, and died Abt. 1840 in Bareville, Lampeter Township, Lancaster County, Pennsylvania.

Child of Benjamin Landis and Barbara Musser is:
213	i.	Maria[7] Landis, born August 27, 1818 in Bareville, Pennsylvania; died June 04, 1878 in West Earl Township, Lancaster County, Pennsylvania.

122. Rev. John[6] Landis (Henry[5], Maria[4] Weber, Johann Anton[3], Heinrich[2], George[1]) was born August 25, 1775 in East Lampeter Township, Lancaster County, Pennsylvania, and died June 21, 1851 in East Lampeter Township, Lancaster County, Pennsylvania. He married **Anna Kreider**. She was born Abt. 1775 in Lancaster, Pennsylvania, and died February 25, 1841 in East Lampeter Township, Lancaster County, Pennsylvania.

Children of John Landis and Anna Kreider are:
214	i.	John K.[7] Landis, born 1797 in East Lampeter Township, Lancaster County, Pennsylvania; died 1797 in East Lampeter Township, Lancaster County, Pennsylvania.
215	ii.	Mary K. Landis, born July 24, 1799 in East Lampeter Township, Lancaster County, Pennsylvania; died September 06, 1875 in Lancaster County, Pennsylvania.
216	iii.	Benjamin Landis, born September 20, 1801 in East Lampeter Township, Lancaster County, Pennsylvania; died November 28, 1863 in Lancaster County, Pennsylvania.

125. Rev. Abraham[6] Landis (Henry[5], Maria[4] Weber, Johann Anton[3], Heinrich[2], George[1]) was born April 11, 1780 in East Lampeter Township, Lancaster County, Pennsylvania, and died April 21, 1861 in East Lampeter Township, Lancaster County, Pennsylvania. He married **Ann Neff**. She was born April 19, 1781 in Manor Township, Lancaster County, Pennsylvania, and died January 11, 1866 in East Lampeter Township, Lancaster County, Pennsylvania.

Child of Abraham Landis and Ann Neff is:

   217   i.   Henry N[7] Landis, born January 20, 1804 in East Lampeter Township, Lancaster County, Pennsylvania; died August 28, 1889 in East Lampeter Township, Lancaster County, Pennsylvania.

Generation No. 7

129. John[7] Hershey (Anna Weber[6] Newcomer, Elizabeth[5] Weber, Henry[4], Johann Anton[3], Heinrich[2], George[1]) was born May 21, 1772 in Derry Twp, Dauphin Co, PA, and died November 23, 1850. He married **(1) Anna Horst**. He married **(2) Anna Horst** March 20, 1802, daughter of John Horst and Ann Strickler. She was born October 03, 1778 in Leacock Twp., Lancaster Co., Pa., and died August 28, 1861.

Children of John Hershey and Anna Horst are:

+ 218   i.   Jacob[8] Hershey, born May 09, 1803 in Lancaster, PA; died July 12, 1883 in Paradise Twp, Lancaster, PA.
   219   ii.   Fronica Hershey, born 1808 in Lancaster, PA; died 1881.
   220   iii. John Hershey, born 1810 in Lancaster, PA; died 1869.
   221   iv. Benjamin Hershey, born 1812 in Lancaster, PA; died 1875.
   222   v.   Joseph Hershey, born 1916 in Lancaster, PA; died 1891.

Children of John Hershey and Anna Horst are:

+ 223   i.   Jacob[8] Hershey, born March 09, 1803 in Paradise Twp., Lancaster Co., PA; died July 12, 1883 in Paradise Twp., Lancaster Co., PA.
   224   ii.   Magdalena Hershey, born August 15, 1804 in Lancaster Co, PA; died July 04, 1857. She married Joseph Snavely; born 1801; died 1871.
+ 225   iii. Nancy Ann Hershey, born October 22, 1805; died September 13, 1885.
+ 226   iv. Veronica Hershey, born August 31, 1808 in Leacock Twp., Lancaster Co., Pa.; died March 19, 1881 in East Earl Twp., Lancaster Co., Pa..
   227   v.   John Hershey, born October 01, 1810 in Salisbury township, Lancaster, PA, USA; died March 19, 1869 in Rohrerstown, Lancaster Co., PA. He married Margaret Musser; born September 06, 1807 in Lancaster Co, PA; died February 24, 1862 in Lancaster Co, PA.
   228   vi. Benjamin Hershey, born April 12, 1812 in Lancaster Co, PA; died February 22, 1875. He married Veronica Musser; born October 26, 1811; died March 15, 1890.
+ 229   vii. Joseph Hershey, born November 20, 1816; died July 17, 1891.

131. Christian[7] Hershey (Anna Weber[6] Newcomer, Elizabeth[5] Weber, Henry[4], Johann Anton[3], Heinrich[2], George[1]) was born June 20, 1780, and died August 05, 1843. He married **Susanna Hershey**, daughter of Jacob Hershey and Elizabeth Eby. She was born November 08, 1785, and died February 08, 1858.

Children of Christian Hershey and Susanna Hershey are:

+ 230   i.   Nancy[8] Hershey, born January 22, 1808; died September 03, 1869.
   231   ii.   Benjamin Hershey, born July 18, 1809.
   232   iii. Jacob L Hershey, born May 03, 1811.
+ 233   iv. Jacob Hershey, born November 27, 1812; died August 24, 1889.
   234   v.   Christian Hershey, born May 07, 1813.
   235   vi. John Hershey, born April 17, 1815.
   236   vii. Elizabeth Hershey, born September 16, 1817.
+ 237   viii. Abraham Hershey, born August 16, 1819; died December 18, 1886.
   238   ix. Susanna Hershey, born July 06, 1822.

133. Abraham[7] Hershey (Anna Weber[6] Newcomer, Elizabeth[5] Weber, Henry[4], Johann Anton[3], Heinrich[2], George[1]) was born January 24, 1787 in Derry Twp, Dauphin Co, PA, and died January 09, 1844. He married **(1) Maria Siegrist**. She was born 1794, and died January 22, 1820. He married **(2) Anna Eby**. She was born December 15, 1800, and died February 29, 1896.

Child of Abraham Hershey and Anna Eby is:

+ 239   i.   Peter E.[8] Hershey, born February 05, 1826; died August 31, 1911.

137. John[7] Hertzler (Maria[6] Mumma, Beverly[5] Weber, Henry[4], Johann Anton[3], Heinrich[2], George[1]) was born 1773. He married **May Brubaker**.

Children of John Hertzler and May Brubaker are:
- 240   i.   Annie[8] Hertzler.
- 241   ii.   Jacob Hertzler.
- 242   iii.   Mary Hertzler.
- 243   iv.   Elizabeth Hertzler.
- 244   v.   John Hertzler.
- 245   vi.   Barbara Hertzler.
- 246   vii.   Christian Hertzler, born 1806; died 1874. He married Barbara Myers; born 1811; died 1880.
- + 247   viii.   Abraham Hertzler, born 1815; died 1898.
- 248   ix.   Rudolph Hertzler, born 1820; died 1855. He married Mary Shupp; born 1823; died 1903.

138. Mary[7] Weber (Henry[6], Christian[5], Henry[4], Johann Anton[3], Heinrich[2], George[1]) was born September 15, 1788, and died October 21, 1865. She married **Peter Good**. He was born March 01, 1778, and died July 04, 1850.

Child of Mary Weber and Peter Good is:
- 249   i.   Benjamin[8] Good, born June 24, 1809 in West Earl Twp, Lanc Co, PA; died 1831. He married (1) Barbara Huber; born November 06, 1809; died January 24, 1838. He married (2) Barbara Bergey.

145. Barbara Weber[7] Musser (Esther[6] Weber, Christian[5], Henry[4], Johann Anton[3], Heinrich[2], George[1]) was born February 13, 1811 in Brecknock Twp., Lanc. Co., Pa., and died July 01, 1889. She married **Jacob Horst** December 18, 1831. He was born December 31, 1804 in Earl Twp, Lanc Co, PA, and died March 09, 1886.

Children of Barbara Musser and Jacob Horst are:
- + 250   i.   Ester[8] Horst, born October 17, 1832; died October 12, 1897.
- 251   ii.   Anna M. Horst, born June 27, 1834; died July 12, 1921. She married Samuel Hollinger; born July 06, 1827; died November 12, 1900.
- 252   iii.   Henry M. Horst, born May 13, 1836; died August 14, 1909. He married Magdalena Weaver; born October 15, 1839; died March 27, 1903.
- 253   iv.   Joseph M. Horst, born January 25, 1840; died February 01, 1916. He married (1) Lizzie Newswanger; born October 24, 1858; died January 07, 1909. He married (2) Anna C. Weaver 1867; born June 29, 1841; died March 07, 1905.
- + 254   v.   Jacob M. Horst, born November 02, 1842 in East Earl Twp., Lancaster Co., Pa.; died September 19, 1919.
- 255   vi.   Mary M. Horst, born June 14, 1845; died November 18, 1919. She married Aaron G. Weaver; born April 21, 1843; died November 02, 1907.
- 256   vii.   Susanna M. Horst, born January 15, 1848; died November 03, 1850.
- 257   viii.   Barbara M. Horst, born September 15, 1851; died June 17, 1924. She married John Z. Burkhart; born August 10, 1847; died March 23, 1936.
- 258   ix.   Mathias M. Horst, born January 18, 1854; died July 21, 1939. He married (1) Mary Weaver; born March 11, 1853; died May 11, 1881. He married (2) Annie Good; born June 06, 1853; died March 12, 1912. He married (3) Leah Bowman; born November 26, 1854; died June 01, 1934.

148. Christian[7] Weber (Samuel[6], Christian[5], Henry[4], Johann Anton[3], Heinrich[2], George[1]) was born August 20, 1785, and died September 03, 1854. He married **Anna Meyer**, daughter of Christian Meyer and Unknown Unknown. She was born January 21, 1787, and died April 21, 1858.

Children of Christian Weber and Anna Meyer are:
- 259   i.   Leah[8] Weber, born 1808; died 1854.
- + 260   ii.   Solomon Weber, born 1810; died 1889.
- 261   iii.   Samuel Weber, born 1813; died 1892. He married Sarah Hoover; born 1816; died 1901.
- + 262   iv.   Gideon Weber, born March 31, 1815; died January 14, 1892.
- 263   v.   Anna Weber, born 1818; died 1838.
- 264   vi.   Isaac Weber, born 1821; died 1889. He married Mary A. Hoffman; born 1831; died 1886.
- 265   vii.   Daniel M. Weber, born 1823; died 1899. He married (1) Mary Fry; born 1829; died 1867. He married (2) Sarah Dooling; born 1839; died 1889.

154. Isaac⁷ Weber (Samuel⁶, Christian⁵, Henry⁴, Johann Anton³, Heinrich², George¹) was born August 1804, and died May 1846. He married **Sarah High**. She was born May 20, 1800, and died December 15, 1878.

Child of Isaac Weber and Sarah High is:
- 266   i.   Fanny⁸ Weaver, born June 16, 1836; died September 08, 1919. She married Joseph S. Martin December 29, 1857; born September 26, 1809 in East Earl Twp., Lancaster Co., Pa.; died September 17, 1891.

159. Isaac⁷ Weaver (Peter⁶ Weber, Christian⁵, Henry⁴, Johann Anton³, Heinrich², George¹) was born September 11, 1792 in East Earl Twp., Lancaster Co., Pa., and died June 10, 1866. He married **Catharine Weber**, daughter of George Weber and Catharine Zimmerman. She was born February 01, 1795 in Lancaster Co, PA, and died May 10, 1862.

Children of Isaac Weaver and Catharine Weber are:
- 267   i.   Tillie⁸ Weaver. She married Joseph Gehman.
- 268   ii.   Feronica Weaver, born 1813; died 1891. She married Daniel Wenger; born 1817; died 1892.
- 269   iii.   George Weaver, born 1818; died January 02, 1883. He married Maria Wenger; born 1819; died 1882.
- 270   iv.   Catharine Weaver, born 1821; died 1888. She married Henry Martin; born 1817; died 1879.
- + 271   v.   Peter Weaver, born 1822; died 1894.
- + 272   vi.   Isaac Weaver, born November 30, 1825; died July 21, 1891.
- 273   vii.   Magdalena Weaver, born 1831; died 1915. She married Reuben Wenger; born 1830; died 1899.
- 274   viii.   Levi Weaver, born May 30, 1832; died March 29, 1913. He married (1) Frances Martin; born October 27, 1831 in Caernarvon Twp, Lanc Co, PA; died 1861. He married (2) Esther Sauder; born 1829; died 1899.
- 275   ix.   Anna Weaver, born 1836; died 1908. She married Daniel S. Burkholder; born 1834; died 1915.
- + 276   x.   Lydia Weaver, born February 09, 1842 in East Earl Twp., Lancaster Co., Pa.; died March 22, 1880.

168. Anna⁷ Horst (Maria⁶ Weber, Christian⁵, Henry⁴, Johann Anton³, Heinrich², George¹) was born January 07, 1803, and died September 25, 1857. She married **Thomas Hollinger** February 15, 1825. He was born December 23, 1799, and died December 06, 1866.

Children of Anna Horst and Thomas Hollinger are:
- 277   i.   Moses⁸ Hollinger.
- 278   ii.   Jacob Hollinger, born 1826; died November 29, 1908.
- 279   iii.   Samuel Hollinger, born July 06, 1827; died November 12, 1900. He married Anna M. Horst; born June 27, 1834; died July 12, 1921.
- + 280   iv.   Johannes Hollinger, born March 29, 1830; died February 28, 1906.
- 281   v.   Anna Hollinger, born June 30, 1839; died May 07, 1920. She married William F. Kern; born December 27, 1840; died April 03, 1917.

175. Elizabeth⁷ Horst (Magdalena⁶ Weber, Heine⁵, Henry⁴, Johann Anton³, Heinrich², George¹) was born October 06, 1802, and died November 08, 1829. She married **Abraham Martin**. He was born May 04, 1799, and died August 18, 1889.

Children of Elizabeth Horst and Abraham Martin are:
- + 282   i.   Joseph Horst⁸ Martin, born December 28, 1823; died September 24, 1900.
- 283   ii.   Frances Horst Martin, born June 09, 1825; died September 22, 1899. She married Daniel N. Lefever; born June 19, 1821; died April 03, 1898.
- 284   iii.   Martha Horst Martin, born December 01, 1826; died December 01, 1900. She married George Zeiset; born June 25, 1828; died March 13, 1907.
- 285   iv.   Abraham Horst Martin, born August 26, 1828 in Salisbury Twp. Lancaster Co, PA; died April 13, 1907. He married (1) Susanna Burkholder September 26, 1849; born November 08, 1828; died November 17, 1851. He married (2) Barbara Wenger December 24, 1852; born January 30, 1829; died February 22, 1906.

176. Anna⁷ Horst (Magdalena⁶ Weber, Heine⁵, Henry⁴, Johann Anton³, Heinrich², George¹) was born 1808, and died 1850. She married **Jonas Weaver**. He was born 1810, and died 1876.

Child of Anna Horst and Jonas Weaver is:
- 286   i.   Magdalena⁸ Weaver, born October 15, 1839; died March 27, 1903. She married Henry M. Horst; born May 13, 1836; died August 14, 1909.

180. Abraham⁷ Buckwalter (John⁶, Magdalena⁵ Weber, Henry⁴, Johann Anton³, Heinrich², George¹) was born January 24, 1785, and died October 14, 1832. He married **Esther Hoover**. She was born May 28, 1792, and died September 25, 1862.

The Relations of Milton Snavely Hershey, 4th Ed.

Children of Abraham Buckwalter and Esther Hoover are:
- 287   i.   Samuel[8] Buckwalter, born September 15, 1816; died January 27, 1897. He married Elizabeth W. Rohrer; born May 02, 1818; died October 04, 1897.
- 288   ii.   Cathrine Buckwalter, born April 20, 1818; died November 03, 1910.
- 289   iii.   Jonas Buckwalter, born December 04, 1820; died May 24, 1912. He married Lydia R. Landis; born January 19, 1827; died December 05, 1889.
- 290   iv.   Moses Buckwalter, born May 26, 1822; died May 26, 1850.
- + 291   v.   Mary Buckwalter, born May 27, 1825; died March 15, 1913.
- + 292   vi.   John Buckwalter, born December 28, 1827; died June 21, 1920.
- 293   vii.   Abraham Buckwalter, born May 23, 1830; died October 28, 1889.

181. Judith[7] **Buckwalter** (John[6], Magdalena[5] Weber, Henry[4], Johann Anton[3], Heinrich[2], George[1]) was born August 10, 1787, and died September 28, 1858. She married **John Buckwalter**, son of Henrich Buckwalter and Barbara Cassel. He was born February 05, 1779, and died November 25, 1844.

Child of Judith Buckwalter and John Buckwalter is:
- + 294   i.   Henry[8] Buckwalter, born Abt. 1810.

186. Catharine[7] **Weber** (George[6], Johannnes[5], George[4], Johann Anton[3], Heinrich[2], George[1]) was born February 01, 1795 in Lancaster Co, PA, and died May 10, 1862. She married **Isaac Weaver**, son of Peter Weber and Feronica Wenger. He was born September 11, 1792 in East Earl Twp., Lancaster Co., Pa., and died June 10, 1866.

Children are listed above under (159) Isaac Weaver.

190. Henry[7] **Landis** (John[6], Benjamin[5], Maria[4] Weber, Johann Anton[3], Heinrich[2], George[1]) was born September 26, 1786, and died July 22, 1859. He married **Maria Rohrer**. She was born March 06, 1784, and died April 25, 1850.

Children of Henry Landis and Maria Rohrer are:
- + 295   i.   Mary Rohrer[8] Landis, born February 13, 1808; died June 08, 1865.
- 296   ii.   Christian R. Landis, born January 22, 1814; died March 12, 1894. He married Hettie S. Landis December 21, 1837; born November 02, 1819; died March 22, 1902.
- 297   iii.   Lydia R. Landis, born January 19, 1827; died December 05, 1889. She married Jonas Buckwalter; born December 04, 1820; died May 24, 1912.

191. Benjamin[7] **Landis** (John[6], Benjamin[5], Maria[4] Weber, Johann Anton[3], Heinrich[2], George[1]) was born April 30, 1780 in East Lampeter Township, Lancaster County, Pennsylvania, and died November 03, 1865 in East Lampeter Township, Lancaster County, Pennsylvania. He married **Barbara Neff**. She was born July 01, 1783 in Manor Township, Lancaster County, Pennsylvania, and died September 02, 1864 in East Lampeter Township, Lancaster County, Pennsylvania.

Children of Benjamin Landis and Barbara Neff are:
- 298   i.   Henry[8] Landis, born January 25, 1808 in East Lampeter Township, Lancaster County, Pennsylvania; died in East Lampeter Township, Lancaster County, Pennsylvania.
- 299   ii.   Esther Landis, born November 28, 1814 in East Lampeter Township, Lancaster County, Pennsylvania; died in East Lampeter Township, Lancaster County, Pennsylvania.

192. Benjamin L.[7] **Landis** (Henry[6], Benjamin[5], Maria[4] Weber, Johann Anton[3], Heinrich[2], George[1]) was born November 06, 1791 in Manheim Twp, Lanc Co, PA, and died December 10, 1849. He married **Anna Long** January 01, 1818, daughter of Benjamin Long and Anna Hershey. She was born May 29, 1800 in Manheim Twp, Lanc Co, PA, and died May 19, 1885.

Child of Benjamin Landis and Anna Long is:
- + 300   i.   Fanny Long[8] Landis, born August 26, 1833 in Manheim Twp, Lanc Co, PA; died July 16, 1898.

193. Elizabeth[7] **Buckwalter** (Benjamin[6], Mary[5] Landis, Maria[4] Weber, Johann Anton[3], Heinrich[2], George[1]) was born March 09, 1789, and died February 03, 1865. She married **Abraham Barr Snavely** January 18, 1809, son of John Snavely and Elizabeth Barr. He was born May 03, 1787, and died March 01, 1866.

Children of Elizabeth Buckwalter and Abraham Snavely are:
- 301   i.   Benjamin[8] Snavely.
- 302   ii.   Martha B Snavely, born 1831.
- 303   iii.   Elizabeth Snavely, born May 11, 1820; died January 19, 1848. She married Abraham S Mylin; born August 09, 1812; died October 31, 1893.
- + 304   iv.   Abraham B Snavely, born December 15, 1824; died November 20, 1901.

+ 305   v. Veronica Buckwalter Snavely, born September 04, 1835 in Pequea Twp, Lancaster Co, PA; died March 11, 1920.

205. Christian S.[7] Landis (Johannes[6], Jacob[5], Maria[4] Weber, Johann Anton[3], Heinrich[2], George[1]) was born June 18, 1803, and died December 23, 1870. He married **Mary Rohrer Landis**, daughter of Henry Landis and Maria Rohrer. She was born February 13, 1808, and died June 08, 1865.

Children of Christian Landis and Mary Landis are:
- 306   i. Katie[8] Landis, born May 20, 1824; died April 16, 1900. She married Christian Risser; born May 30, 1825; died May 20, 1910.
- + 307   ii. Levi L. Landis, born December 31, 1826; died December 14, 1897.
- 308   iii. Elizabeth L. Landis, born February 09, 1828; died January 05, 1918. She married Peter B. Brubaker 1851; born December 22, 1828; died May 01, 1895.
- 309   iv. Annie L. Landis, born December 22, 1829; died June 04, 1918. She married Peter E. Hershey December 05, 1848; born February 05, 1826; died August 31, 1911.
- 310   v. John L. Landis, born July 28, 1832; died July 20, 1914. He married Mary J. Denlinger; born November 24, 1835; died October 01, 1916.
- 311   vi. Hettie Landis, born April 19, 1838; died September 25, 1905. She married Martin R. Herr November 07, 1861; born September 24, 1836; died April 16, 1894.

Generation No. 8

218. Jacob[8] Hershey (John[7], Anna Weber[6] Newcomer, Elizabeth[5] Weber, Henry[4], Johann Anton[3], Heinrich[2], George[1]) was born May 09, 1803 in Lancaster, PA, and died July 12, 1883 in Paradise Twp, Lancaster, PA. He married **Elizabeth Eby**. She was born June 12, 1807 in Paradise Twp., Lancaster Co., PA, and died May 31, 1897 in Paradise Twp., Lancaster Co., PA.

Children of Jacob Hershey and Elizabeth Eby are:
- 312   i. Anna[9] Hershey, born 1824; died 1842.
- 313   ii. Susan Hershey, born 1843; died 1927.
- 314   iii. Unnamed Hershey, born 1851; died 1851.

223. Jacob[8] Hershey (John[7], Anna Weber[6] Newcomer, Elizabeth[5] Weber, Henry[4], Johann Anton[3], Heinrich[2], George[1]) was born March 09, 1803 in Paradise Twp., Lancaster Co., PA, and died July 12, 1883 in Paradise Twp., Lancaster Co., PA. He married **Elizabeth Eby**. She was born June 12, 1807 in Paradise Twp., Lancaster Co., PA, and died May 31, 1897 in Paradise Twp., Lancaster Co., PA.

Children of Jacob Hershey and Elizabeth Eby are:
- 315   i. Anna[9] Hershey, born November 18, 1824; died August 09, 1842.
- 316   ii. Margaret Hershey, born June 23, 1827; died April 14, 1906.
- 317   iii. John Eby Hershey, born January 16, 1830; died May 08, 1906.
- 318   iv. Elizabeth Hershey, born March 08, 1831; died February 13, 1916.
- 319   v. Peter Hershey, born December 25, 1835; died May 27, 1836.
- 320   vi. Elias Hershey, born March 15, 1837; died January 12, 1911.
- + 321   vii. Peter Hershey, born August 02, 1839; died December 17, 1922.
- 322   viii. Maria Hershey, born September 20, 1841; died August 15, 1842.
- 323   ix. Susan Hershey, born January 30, 1843; died May 19, 1927.
- 324   x. David Hershey, born June 01, 1845; died December 20, 1846.
- 325   xi. Jacob Menno Hershey, born October 16, 1847; died December 06, 1923.

225. Nancy Ann[8] Hershey (John[7], Anna Weber[6] Newcomer, Elizabeth[5] Weber, Henry[4], Johann Anton[3], Heinrich[2], George[1]) was born October 22, 1805, and died September 13, 1885. She married **Jonas S. Martin**. He was born January 30, 1806, and died September 11, 1874.

Child of Nancy Hershey and Jonas Martin is:
- 326   i. Frances[9] Martin, born October 27, 1831 in Caernarvon Twp, Lanc Co, PA; died 1861. She married Levi Weaver; born May 30, 1832; died March 29, 1913.

226. Veronica[8] Hershey (John[7], Anna Weber[6] Newcomer, Elizabeth[5] Weber, Henry[4], Johann Anton[3], Heinrich[2], George[1]) was born August 31, 1808 in Leacock Twp., Lancaster Co., Pa., and died March 19, 1881 in East Earl Twp., Lancaster Co., Pa.. She married **Abraham Reiff**, son of Joseph Reiff and Barbara Nolt. He was born November 15, 1803 in West Earl Twp, Lanc Co, PA, and died September 28, 1874.

Children of Veronica Hershey and Abraham Reiff are:
- 327 i. Fanny H.[9] Rife, born February 11, 1836; died March 14, 1900. She married John M. Sauder; born June 29, 1833; died June 11, 1878.
- + 328 ii. Annie Reiff, born October 24, 1842 in West Earl Twp, Lanc Co, PA; died February 23, 1917.
- 329 iii. John A. Reiff, born July 20, 1846; died June 07, 1900.
- 330 iv. Magdalena Reiff, born November 28, 1852; died October 28, 1856.

229. Joseph[8] Hershey (John[7], Anna Weber[6] Newcomer, Elizabeth[5] Weber, Henry[4], Johann Anton[3], Heinrich[2], George[1]) was born November 20, 1816, and died July 17, 1891. He married **Fannie Hartman** January 01, 1839. She was born November 03, 1819, and died April 14, 1894.

Children of Joseph Hershey and Fannie Hartman are:
- 331 i. John[9] Hershey.
- 332 ii. Annie Hershey.
- 333 iii. Henry H Hershey.
- 334 iv. Lydia Hershey.
- 335 v. Catherine Hershey.
- 336 vi. Joseph Hershey.
- 337 vii. Fannie Hershey.
- 338 viii. Magdalena Hershey.
- 339 ix. Elizabeth Hershey.
- 340 x. Margaret Hershey.
- 341 xi. Amos H Hershey, born June 01, 1858; died February 27, 1933.
- 342 xii. Amanda Hershey.

230. Nancy[8] Hershey (Christian[7], Anna Weber[6] Newcomer, Elizabeth[5] Weber, Henry[4], Johann Anton[3], Heinrich[2], George[1]) was born January 22, 1808, and died September 03, 1869. She married **Jacob Frantz Hershey**, son of Isaac Hershey and Anna Frantz. He was born September 22, 1802, and died May 15, 1877.

Children of Nancy Hershey and Jacob Hershey are:
- + 343 i. Henry Hershey[9] Hershey, born January 04, 1829 in Derry Twp, Dauphin Co, PA; died February 18, 1904.
- 344 ii. Joseph Hershey, born January 19, 1830; died August 04, 1855.
- 345 iii. Elizabeth Hershey, born September 26, 1832.
- + 346 iv. Christian Hershey, born March 16, 1836; died September 29, 1884.
- + 347 v. Jacob H Hershey, born October 09, 1839.
- + 348 vi. Elias H Hershey, born December 12, 1841; died November 16, 1925.
- 349 vii. Isaac Hershey, born May 06, 1846; died March 26, 1848.

233. Jacob[8] Hershey (Christian[7], Anna Weber[6] Newcomer, Elizabeth[5] Weber, Henry[4], Johann Anton[3], Heinrich[2], George[1]) was born November 27, 1812, and died August 24, 1889. He married **Maria Martin**. She was born November 17, 1811, and died December 11, 1844.

Child of Jacob Hershey and Maria Martin is:
- 350 i. Elizabeth[9] Hershey, born May 27, 1835; died October 06, 1863.

237. Abraham[8] Hershey (Christian[7], Anna Weber[6] Newcomer, Elizabeth[5] Weber, Henry[4], Johann Anton[3], Heinrich[2], George[1]) was born August 16, 1819, and died December 18, 1886. He married **Martha**. She was born 1824.

Children of Abraham Hershey and Martha are:
- 351 i. Enos[9] Hershey, born 1847.
- + 352 ii. Susan Hershey, born January 14, 1852; died November 24, 1915.
- 353 iii. Levi Hershey, born 1854.
- 354 iv. Mary Hershey, born 1858.
- 355 v. Henry Hershey, born 1862.

239. Peter E.[8] Hershey (Abraham[7], Anna Weber[6] Newcomer, Elizabeth[5] Weber, Henry[4], Johann Anton[3], Heinrich[2], George[1]) was born February 05, 1826, and died August 31, 1911. He married **(1) Annie L. Landis** December 05, 1848, daughter of Christian Landis and Mary Landis. She was born December 22, 1829, and died June 04, 1918. He married **(2) Anna Landis** December 05, 1848. She was born December 22, 1829, and died June 04, 1918.

Children of Peter Hershey and Anna Landis are:
- 356 i. Christian L.[9] Hershey, born May 27, 1850; died January 25, 1868.
- 357 ii. Anna L. Hershey, born August 31, 1852; died September 16, 1877.
- 358 iii. Henry Hershey, born May 19, 1855.
- 359 iv. Mary Hershey, born March 25, 1858.
- 360 v. Landes L. Hershey, born August 24, 1867; died December 14, 1962.

247. Abraham[8] Hertzler (John[7], Maria[6] Mumma, Beverly[5] Weber, Henry[4], Johann Anton[3], Heinrich[2], George[1]) was born 1815, and died 1898. He married **Mary Bender**. She was born 1818, and died 1893.

Children of Abraham Hertzler and Mary Bender are:
- 361 i. Rudolph[9] Hertzler, born 1838; died 1905. He married Mary Zimmerman; born 1841; died 1874.
- 362 ii. Christian Hertzler, born 1840; died 1928 in Mt.Zion Cemetery near Churchtown. He married (1) Suzanne Zimmerman; died 1875. He married (2) Catharine Weaver; died 1925.
- + 363 iii. Michael S. Hertzler, born 1841; died 1928.
- 364 iv. Charles Hertzler, born 1844; died 1926. He married (1) Mary Rupp; born 1842; died 1946. He married (2) Annie Shelly; born 1885; died 1939.
- 365 v. John Hertzler, born 1846; died 1920. He married Martha Bowman; born 1849; died 1935.
- 366 vi. Elizabeth Hertzler, born 1848; died 1913. She married William Brindle; born 1845.
- 367 vii. Daniel Hertzler, born 1849; died 1873.
- 368 viii. Mary Hertzler, born 1851; died 1886.
- 369 ix. Amos Hertzler, born 1856; died 1939. He married Mary Senseman; born 1849; died 1929.

250. Ester[8] Horst (Barbara Weber[7] Musser, Esther[6] Weber, Christian[5], Henry[4], Johann Anton[3], Heinrich[2], George[1]) was born October 17, 1832, and died October 12, 1897. She married **Johannes Hollinger**, son of Thomas Hollinger and Anna Horst. He was born March 29, 1830, and died February 28, 1906.

Children of Ester Horst and Johannes Hollinger are:
- + 370 i. Susanna[9] Hollinger, born July 12, 1852; died April 27, 1935.
- 371 ii. David H. Hollinger, born September 23, 1853; died November 13, 1926.
- 372 iii. Isaias H. Hollinger, born February 03, 1855; died 1945. He married (1) Elizabeth R. Reitz; born August 16, 1856; died 1922. He married (2) Sybilla Hess; born 1854; died 1928.
- 373 iv. Jacob H. Hollinger, born February 24, 1857; died 1933. He married (1) Mary Ann Witmer; born April 07, 1861; died 1890. He married (2) Lydia Sensenig; born November 30, 1863; died 1917.
- 374 v. Maria Ann Hollinger, born January 22, 1859; died April 10, 1930.
- 375 vi. Johannes H. Hollinger, born June 15, 1860; died March 08, 1884. He married Lydia Martin.
- 376 vii. Magdalene Hollinger, born July 04, 1862; died May 21, 1929. She married Harmen Reitz; born June 04, 1859; died October 28, 1937.
- 377 viii. Thomas J. Hollinger, born March 26, 1864; died December 25, 1891. He married Annie W. Martin; born September 21, 1861; died 1926.
- 378 ix. Esther H. Hollinger, born May 24, 1866; died November 24, 1918.
- 379 x. Elisabeth Mae Hollinger, born April 30, 1868; died 1944. She married David Ames Martin; born January 15, 1870; died 1932.
- 380 xi. Anna H. Hollinger, born June 03, 1870; died 1938. She married Jacob W. Martin; born September 16, 1870; died 1931.
- 381 xii. Rebecca H. Hollinger, born December 26, 1872; died 1950. She married Milton H. Hauck; born 1873; died 1943.

254. Jacob M.[8] Horst (Barbara Weber[7] Musser, Esther[6] Weber, Christian[5], Henry[4], Johann Anton[3], Heinrich[2], George[1]) was born November 02, 1842 in East Earl Twp., Lancaster Co., Pa., and died September 19, 1919. He married **(1) Lydia Weaver**, daughter of Isaac Weaver and Catharine Weber. She was born February 09, 1842 in East Earl Twp., Lancaster Co., Pa., and died March 22, 1880. He married **(2) Elizabeth Zimmerman**. She was born March 03, 1841, and died October 15, 1927.

Children of Jacob Horst and Lydia Weaver are:
- 382 i. Frank W.[9] Hurst, born October 30, 1863; died September 13, 1940. He married (1) Lizzie Gehman; born December 23, 1866; died May 06, 1888. He married (2) Lydia B. Martin; born 1862; died 1936.
- 383 ii. Isaac W. Hurst, born November 24, 1864; died January 01, 1941. He married (1) Annie Zimmerman; born June 30, 1861; died April 18, 1925. He married (2) Susie Huber; born January 1885.
- 384 iii. Katie W. Hurst, born November 24, 1865. She married David Zimmerman; born December 26, 1854; died March 10, 1915.
- 385 iv. Jacob W. Hurst, born September 18, 1867. He married Katie Zimmerman; born May 22, 1869.
- + 386 v. Reuben Weaver Horst, born December 05, 1868 in West Earl Twp, Lanc Co, PA; died June 22, 1941.

387	vi.	Barbara W. Hurst, born July 29, 1870; died October 1944. She married Harry Gehman; born October 08, 1868; died April 19, 1923.
388	vii.	Weaver W. Hurst, born May 05, 1872. He married Maggie Auker; born September 28, 1873.
389	viii.	Lydia W. Hurst, born November 03, 1873. She married Samuel S. Gehman; died November 21, 1949.
390	ix.	George W. Hurst, born April 07, 1875; died July 13, 1881.
391	x.	Noah W. Hurst, born January 29, 1877. He married Lydia Z. Martin; born December 20, 1877; died February 1970.
392	xi.	Lizzie W. Hurst, born July 08, 1878; died August 20, 1892.
393	xii.	Susana W. Hurst, born March 10, 1880; died October 05, 1882.

260. Solomon^8 Weber (Christian^7, Samuel^6, Christian^5, Henry^4, Johann Anton^3, Heinrich^2, George^1) was born 1810, and died 1889. He married **Catherine Roose**. She died 1880.

Child of Solomon Weber and Catherine Roose is:
394	i.	Christian^9 Weber, died 1864 in Buffalo, NY.

262. Gideon^8 Weber (Christian^7, Samuel^6, Christian^5, Henry^4, Johann Anton^3, Heinrich^2, George^1) was born March 31, 1815, and died January 14, 1892. He married **Susanna Good** January 02, 1842. She was born May 14, 1818, and died April 11, 1890.

Children of Gideon Weber and Susanna Good are:
	395	i.	Aaron G.^{9} Weaver, born April 21, 1843; died November 02, 1907. He married Mary M. Horst; born June 14, 1845; died November 18, 1919.
	396	ii.	Israel Weaver, born 1845; died 1849.
+	397	iii.	Christian G. Weaver, born September 25, 1847 in East Earl Twp., Lancaster Co., Pa.; died May 20, 1921.
	398	iv.	David G. Weaver, born 1850; died 1904. He married Mary Geigley; born 1860; died 1910.
	399	v.	Daniel G. Weaver, born 1851; died 1927. He married Elizabeth Martin; born 1856; died 1934.
	400	vi.	Anna Weaver, born March 21, 1856; died 1929. She married (1) Daniel Nolt January 08, 1882; born September 26, 1856; died May 01, 1886. She married (2) Noah G. Good October 27, 1895 in Spring Grove, Lanc Co, PA; born 1862; died 1945.
	401	vii.	Martin G. Weaver, born 1859; died 1935. He married (1) Angeline Renninger; born 1862; died 1894. He married (2) Elizabeth Martin; born 1862; died 1939.

271. Peter^8 Weaver (Isaac^7, Peter^6 Weber, Christian^5, Henry^4, Johann Anton^3, Heinrich^2, George^1) was born 1822, and died 1894. He married **(1) Mary Martin**. She was born 1828, and died 1863. He married **(2) Anna Lichty**. She was born 1828, and died 1906.

Child of Peter Weaver and Mary Martin is:
402	i.	Mary^9 Weaver, born March 11, 1853; died May 11, 1881. She married Mathias M. Horst; born January 18, 1854; died July 21, 1939.

272. Isaac^8 Weaver (Isaac^7, Peter^6 Weber, Christian^5, Henry^4, Johann Anton^3, Heinrich^2, George^1) was born November 30, 1825, and died July 21, 1891. He married **Catharine Witwer**. She was born September 14, 1833, and died March 10, 1905.

Children of Isaac Weaver and Catharine Witwer are:
403	i.	John W.^{9} Weaver.
404	ii.	Benjamin Weaver, born 1854; died September 03, 1928.

276. Lydia^8 Weaver (Isaac^7, Peter^6 Weber, Christian^5, Henry^4, Johann Anton^3, Heinrich^2, George^1) was born February 09, 1842 in East Earl Twp., Lancaster Co., Pa., and died March 22, 1880. She married **Jacob M. Horst**, son of Jacob Horst and Barbara Musser. He was born November 02, 1842 in East Earl Twp., Lancaster Co., Pa., and died September 19, 1919.

Children are listed above under (254) Jacob M. Horst.

280. Johannes^8 Hollinger (Anna^7 Horst, Maria^6 Weber, Christian^5, Henry^4, Johann Anton^3, Heinrich^2, George^1) was born March 29, 1830, and died February 28, 1906. He married **Ester Horst**, daughter of Jacob Horst and Barbara Musser. She was born October 17, 1832, and died October 12, 1897.

Children are listed above under (250) Ester Horst.

282. Joseph Horst^8 Martin (Elizabeth^7 Horst, Magdalena^6 Weber, Heine^5, Henry^4, Johann Anton^3, Heinrich^2, George^1) was born December 28, 1823, and died September 24, 1900. He married **(1) Martha H. Oberholtzer** January 18, 1846, daughter of Samuel

Oberholtzer and Martha Hess. She was born August 03, 1828, and died June 05, 1869. He married **(2) Catharine Oberholtzer** September 06, 1870, daughter of Samuel Oberholtzer and Martha Hess. She was born September 26, 1830, and died July 17, 1918.

Children of Joseph Martin and Martha Oberholtzer are:
	405	i.	Elizabeth O.⁹ Martin, born January 15, 1848; died January 10, 1921. She married John B. Keener October 04, 1869; born October 18, 1845.
+	406	ii.	Magdalena O. Martin, born August 15, 1850; died May 09, 1886.
	407	iii.	Anna O. Martin, born August 14, 1853. She married Benjamin Brackbill November 05, 1878; born September 19, 1848.
	408	iv.	Samuel O. Martin, born January 29, 1855; died February 27, 1936. He married Amanda Landis; born September 22, 1854; died August 30, 1931.
	409	v.	Abraham O. Martin, born January 23, 1857; died May 03, 1858.
	410	vi.	Infant1 Martin, born February 19, 1859; died February 24, 1859.
	411	vii.	Joseph O. Martin, born February 24, 1860; died October 31, 1861.
	412	viii.	Henry O. Martin, born June 19, 1862; died December 30, 1876.
	413	ix.	Isaac O. Martin, born October 10, 1864; died October 01, 1872.
	414	x.	David O. Martin, born November 29, 1866; died March 13, 1875.
	415	xi.	Infant2 Martin, born June 03, 1869; died June 03, 1869.

Child of Joseph Martin and Catharine Oberholtzer is:
416	i.	Susanna⁹ Martin, born September 06, 1871; died March 30, 1872.

291. Mary⁸ Buckwalter (Abraham⁷, John⁶, Magdalena⁵ Weber, Henry⁴, Johann Anton³, Heinrich², George¹) was born May 27, 1825, and died March 15, 1913. She married **Levi L. Landis** November 21, 1848, son of Christian Landis and Mary Landis. He was born December 31, 1826, and died December 14, 1897.

Children of Mary Buckwalter and Levi Landis are:
+	417	i.	Elam B.⁹ Landis, born October 06, 1850; died May 06, 1938 in Ephrata Twp, Lanc Co, PA.
	418	ii.	Esther Ann Landis, born November 11, 1852; died August 14, 1874.
	419	iii.	Amanda Landis, born September 22, 1854; died August 30, 1931. She married Samuel O. Martin; born January 29, 1855; died February 27, 1936.
	420	iv.	Emma B. Landis, born February 18, 1861; died May 19, 1947.
	421	v.	Anna Mary Landis, born December 28, 1863; died December 29, 1947.
	422	vi.	Lydia B. Landis, born May 04, 1866; died September 17, 1914.

292. John⁸ Buckwalter (Abraham⁷, John⁶, Magdalena⁵ Weber, Henry⁴, Johann Anton³, Heinrich², George¹) was born December 28, 1827, and died June 21, 1920. He married **Lydia Bressler**. She was born January 15, 1834, and died May 31, 1896.

Children of John Buckwalter and Lydia Bressler are:
423	i.	Salome⁹ Buckwalter, born October 29, 1851; died March 25, 1857.
424	ii.	Bressler Buckwalter, born February 15, 1853; died October 08, 1903. He married Annie Wenger.
425	iii.	Franklin Buckwalter, born May 05, 1854; died May 27, 1945. He married Emma Espenshade.
426	iv.	Morgan Buckwalter, born January 20, 1857; died December 18, 1926. He married Lizzie Hicks.
427	v.	Infant Buckwalter, born February 15, 1859; died February 23, 1859.
428	vi.	Joel B. Buckwalter, born December 25, 1859; died February 09, 1900.
429	vii.	John B. Buckwalter, born October 04, 1870. He married Sallie Blanche Benner.

294. Henry⁸ Buckwalter (Judith⁷, John⁶, Magdalena⁵ Weber, Henry⁴, Johann Anton³, Heinrich², George¹) was born Abt. 1810. He married **Barbara Neff**. She was born Abt. 1810.

Child of Henry Buckwalter and Barbara Neff is:
+	430	i.	Barbara Neff⁹ Buckwalter, born January 23, 1840; died March 29, 1911.

295. Mary Rohrer⁸ Landis (Henry⁷, John⁶, Benjamin⁵, Maria⁴ Weber, Johann Anton³, Heinrich², George¹) was born February 13, 1808, and died June 08, 1865. She married **Christian S. Landis**, son of Johannes Landis and Barbara Snavely. He was born June 18, 1803, and died December 23, 1870.

Children are listed above under (205) Christian S. Landis.

300. Fanny Long⁸ Landis (Benjamin L.⁷, Henry⁶, Benjamin⁵, Maria⁴ Weber, Johann Anton³, Heinrich², George¹) was born August 26, 1833 in Manheim Twp, Lanc Co, PA, and died July 16, 1898. She married **Samuel H Hess**, son of Henry Hess and Catherine Huber.

He was born November 19, 1830 in Elizabeth Twp Lancaster Co, PA, and died December 10, 1871 in Willow Bank Mills, Elizabeth Twp., Lancaster Co., PA.

Child of Fanny Landis and Samuel Hess is:
+   431   i.   Henry L[9] Hess, born January 28, 1857 in Elizabeth Twp Lancaster Co, PA; died December 10, 1919.

304. Abraham B[8] Snavely (Elizabeth[7] Buckwalter, Benjamin[6], Mary[5] Landis, Maria[4] Weber, Johann Anton[3], Heinrich[2], George[1]) was born December 15, 1824, and died November 20, 1901. He married **Catherine Rohrer**. She was born August 29, 1828.

Children of Abraham Snavely and Catherine Rohrer are:
   432   i.   Rohrer[9] Snavely, born 1863.
   433   ii.   Stoner Snavely, born 1866.

305. Veronica Buckwalter[8] Snavely (Elizabeth[7] Buckwalter, Benjamin[6], Mary[5] Landis, Maria[4] Weber, Johann Anton[3], Heinrich[2], George[1]) was born September 04, 1835 in Pequea Twp, Lancaster Co, PA, and died March 11, 1920. She married **Henry Hershey Hershey** January 15, 1856 in Parsonage at Holy Trinity Lutheran Church, Lancaster, PA, son of Jacob Hershey and Nancy Hershey. He was born January 04, 1829 in Derry Twp, Dauphin Co, PA, and died February 18, 1904.

Children of Veronica Snavely and Henry Hershey are:
   434   i.   Milton Snavely[9] Hershey, born September 13, 1857 in Derry Twp, PA; died October 13, 1945 in Hershey, PA. He married Catherine Elizabeth Sweeney May 25, 1898 in St. Patrick's Rectory, New York, NY; born July 06, 1872 in Jamestown, NY; died March 25, 1915 in Philadelphia, PA.
   435   ii.   Sarena Hershey, born April 12, 1862; died March 31, 1867.

307. Levi L.[8] Landis (Christian S.[7], Johannes[6], Jacob[5], Maria[4] Weber, Johann Anton[3], Heinrich[2], George[1]) was born December 31, 1826, and died December 14, 1897. He married **Mary Buckwalter** November 21, 1848, daughter of Abraham Buckwalter and Esther Hoover. She was born May 27, 1825, and died March 15, 1913.

Children are listed above under (291) Mary Buckwalter.

Generation No. 9

321. Peter[9] Hershey (Jacob[8], John[7], Anna Weber[6] Newcomer, Elizabeth[5] Weber, Henry[4], Johann Anton[3], Heinrich[2], George[1]) was born August 02, 1839, and died December 17, 1922. He married **Barbara Neff Buckwalter**, daughter of Henry Buckwalter and Barbara Neff. She was born January 23, 1840, and died March 29, 1911.

Children of Peter Hershey and Barbara Buckwalter are:
   436   i.   Infant[10] Hershey, born May 10, 1862; died May 10, 1862.
+   437   ii.   Sarah Lucinda Hershey, born September 09, 1863; died December 22, 1942.
+   438   iii.   Isaiah B. Hershey, born June 28, 1865; died October 09, 1919.
+   439   iv.   Enos Jacob Hershey, born November 02, 1866; died March 20, 1939.
+   440   v.   Elizabeth Hershey, born September 09, 1868; died September 06, 1934.
   441   vi.   Mary Hershey, born January 01, 1870; died April 08, 1878.
+   442   vii.   Henry Peter Hershey, born March 14, 1872; died December 10, 1949.
+   443   viii.   Martin Eby Hershey, born December 20, 1873; died June 13, 1953.
   444   ix.   Ellen Hershey, born March 29, 1875; died April 16, 1878.
   445   x.   Martha A. Hershey, born August 12, 1876; died August 19, 1968. She married Amos H. Hoover; born November 21, 1852; died October 12, 1941.
   446   xi.   Barbara Hershey, born June 25, 1878; died July 26, 1896.
   447   xii.   Infant Hershey, born December 24, 1879; died December 24, 1879.
+   448   xiii.   Silas N. Hershey, born March 22, 1881; died November 20, 1970.

328. Annie[9] Reiff (Veronica[8] Hershey, John[7], Anna Weber[6] Newcomer, Elizabeth[5] Weber, Henry[4], Johann Anton[3], Heinrich[2], George[1]) was born October 24, 1842 in West Earl Twp, Lanc Co, PA, and died February 23, 1917. She married **Chambers U. Sweigart**. He was born August 23, 1841 in Lancaster Co, PA, and died August 24, 1923.

Children of Annie Reiff and Chambers Sweigart are:
   449   i.   Amos R.[10] Sweigart, born October 06, 1864; died July 15, 1865.
   450   ii.   Abraham R. Sweigart, born November 28, 1865; died October 24, 1934. He married (1) Mary C. Heiney; born September 26, 1863; died March 31, 1895. He married (2) Mary Ann Wenger; born July 29, 1871; died November 16, 1956.
   451   iii.   John R. Sweigart, born June 25, 1867; died November 07, 1928. He married Wynaria M. Geist; born

September 07, 1866; died November 15, 1937.
- + 452   iv.   Frances Reiff Sweigart, born November 03, 1868 in Earl Twp, Lanc Co, PA; died December 12, 1947.
- 453   v.   Martin R. Sweigart, born April 21, 1870; died May 03, 1929. He married Lydia Ann Sauder; born April 20, 1870; died April 05, 1922.
- 454   vi.   Anna R. Sweigart, born January 28, 1872; died January 27, 1948. She married John B. Rutt; born April 27, 1872; died July 13, 1951.
- 455   vii.   Elizabeth R. Sweigart, born September 03, 1873; died May 12, 1936. She married John Kilhefner; born July 19, 1871; died December 16, 1943.
- 456   viii.   Jacob R. Sweigart, born May 18, 1876; died July 20, 1963. He married Hannah G. Shirk; born August 07, 1881; died 1963.
- 457   ix.   Lydia R. Sweigart, born March 25, 1878; died March 08, 1949. She married Frank Kilhefner; born October 02, 1874; died February 21, 1939.
- 458   x.   Amanda R. Sweigart, born February 15, 1879; died November 13, 1940. She married (1) Phares B. Gehman; born September 06, 1875; died March 12, 1898. She married (2) John L. Gockley; born February 26, 1855; died October 03, 1936.
- 459   xi.   Eli R. Sweigart, born October 19, 1885; died August 16, 1957. He married Mary E. Leicy; born February 02, 1889; died September 22, 1968.

343. Henry Hershey[9] Hershey (Nancy[8], Christian[7], Anna Weber[6] Newcomer, Elizabeth[5] Weber, Henry[4], Johann Anton[3], Heinrich[2], George[1]) was born January 04, 1829 in Derry Twp, Dauphin Co, PA, and died February 18, 1904. He married **Veronica Buckwalter Snavely** January 15, 1856 in Parsonage at Holy Trinity Lutheran Church, Lancaster, PA, daughter of Abraham Snavely and Elizabeth Buckwalter. She was born September 04, 1835 in Pequea Twp, Lancaster Co, PA, and died March 11, 1920.

Children are listed above under (305) Veronica Buckwalter Snavely.

346. Christian[9] Hershey (Nancy[8], Christian[7], Anna Weber[6] Newcomer, Elizabeth[5] Weber, Henry[4], Johann Anton[3], Heinrich[2], George[1]) was born March 16, 1836, and died September 29, 1884. He married **Barbara Good**. She was born Abt. 1835.

Children of Christian Hershey and Barbara Good are:
- 460   i.   Virginia[10] Hershey, born 1866; died 1886.
- + 461   ii.   Lorena Hershey, born October 02, 1868.
- 462   iii.   Bessie M Hershey, born April 13, 1874; died August 11, 1911.

347. Jacob H[9] Hershey (Nancy[8], Christian[7], Anna Weber[6] Newcomer, Elizabeth[5] Weber, Henry[4], Johann Anton[3], Heinrich[2], George[1]) was born October 09, 1839. He married **Barbara B Light**. She was born February 13, 1840.

Children of Jacob Hershey and Barbara Light are:
- 463   i.   Morris Light[10] Hershey, born March 04, 1866; died February 05, 1867.
- 464   ii.   Dr. Elmer Light Hershey, born October 27, 1868.
- 465   iii.   Laura Light Hershey, born December 17, 1870; died February 11, 1872.
- 466   iv.   Katie Light Hershey, born July 16, 1872; died August 25, 1918.
- 467   v.   John Adam Light Hershey, born January 22, 1876.
- 468   vi.   Monroe Light Hershey, born January 03, 1878; died March 1907.
- + 469   vii.   Eugene Light Hershey, born October 02, 1880; died August 1966 in 17083 Quentin, Lebanon, PA.
- 470   viii.   Alice Light Hershey, born May 15, 1884; died July 22, 1885.

348. Elias H[9] Hershey (Nancy[8], Christian[7], Anna Weber[6] Newcomer, Elizabeth[5] Weber, Henry[4], Johann Anton[3], Heinrich[2], George[1]) was born December 12, 1841, and died November 16, 1925. He married **Elizabeth Miller Frantz** 1868. She was born December 13, 1844, and died July 09, 1906.

Children of Elias Hershey and Elizabeth Frantz are:
- + 471   i.   Annie[10] Hershey, born November 14, 1869; died May 15, 1916.
- + 472   ii.   Mary Hershey, born November 17, 1872.
- 473   iii.   Jacob Hershey, born March 08, 1876.
- 474   iv.   Christian Hershey, born April 26, 1878.
- + 475   v.   Ezra Frantz Hershey, born September 01, 1879; died 1949.

352. Susan[9] Hershey (Abraham[8], Christian[7], Anna Weber[6] Newcomer, Elizabeth[5] Weber, Henry[4], Johann Anton[3], Heinrich[2], George[1]) was born January 14, 1852, and died November 24, 1915. She married **Oliver Burkholder**, son of Ulrich Burkholder and Mary Kauffman. He was born November 17, 1844, and died March 12, 1921.

Children of Susan Hershey and Oliver Burkholder are:

	476	i.	Annie[10] Burkholder, born 1877.
	477	ii.	Felix Burkholder, born 1879.
+	478	iii.	Abraham H Burkholder, born August 02, 1885; died January 06, 1935.
	479	iv.	Harry Hershey Burkholder, born 1880.

363. Michael S.[9] Hertzler (Abraham[8], John[7], Maria[6] Mumma, Beverly[5] Weber, Henry[4], Johann Anton[3], Heinrich[2], George[1]) was born 1841, and died 1928. He married **Anna Sollenberger** 1866. She was born October 11, 1846, and died October 28, 1886.

Children of Michael Hertzler and Anna Sollenberger are:
	480	i.	May[10] Hertzler.
	481	ii.	Emma Hertzler, born 1867; died 1907.
	482	iii.	Abram Hertzler, born 1870; died 1940. He married Mary Charles; born 1870; died 1942.
	483	iv.	Elizabeth Hertzler, born 1871; died 1871.
	484	v.	Mary Hertzler, born 1874; died 1876.
	485	vi.	Catharine Hertzler, born 1875; died 1921. She married John Neff; born 1871.
	486	vii.	Martha Hertzler, born 1877; died 1938. She married Charles Dougherty; born 1872; died 1932.
	487	viii.	Tobias Hertzler, born 1879; died 1919. He married Mary S. Tritt; born 1879.
+	488	ix.	Gertrude Hertzler, born 1881; died March 1918.
	489	x.	Michael S. Hertzler, born 1883. He married Edna Wilke.

370. Susanna[9] Hollinger (Johannes[8], Anna[7] Horst, Maria[6] Weber, Christian[5], Henry[4], Johann Anton[3], Heinrich[2], George[1]) was born July 12, 1852, and died April 27, 1935. She married **Christian G. Weaver**, son of Gideon Weber and Susanna Good. He was born September 25, 1847 in East Earl Twp., Lancaster Co., Pa., and died May 20, 1921.

Children of Susanna Hollinger and Christian Weaver are:
	490	i.	Amos H.[10] Weaver, born April 26, 1873; died July 11, 1900. He married Lizzie B. Weaver November 29, 1894; born August 21, 1876.
	491	ii.	Anna Mary Weaver, born August 10, 1874; died May 16, 1956. She married Samuel Metzler December 31, 1897; born May 25, 1857; died April 05, 1940.
	492	iii.	Susie Weaver, born April 15, 1878; died April 01, 1946. She married Aaron Martin November 30, 1902; born October 24, 1876.
+	493	iv.	John Hollinger Weaver, born February 23, 1881; died June 06, 1946 in Akron, Lancaster Co, PA.
	494	v.	Hettie Rebecca Weaver, born August 21, 1885; died April 09, 1972. She married James R. Shiffer April 17, 1909; born December 01, 1881; died 1958.
	495	vi.	Barbara Weaver, born January 20, 1888; died January 25, 1888.

386. Reuben Weaver[9] Horst (Jacob M.[8], Barbara Weber[7] Musser, Esther[6] Weber, Christian[5], Henry[4], Johann Anton[3], Heinrich[2], George[1]) was born December 05, 1868 in West Earl Twp, Lanc Co, PA, and died June 22, 1941. He married **Frances Reiff Sweigart** November 18, 1888, daughter of Chambers Sweigart and Annie Reiff. She was born November 03, 1868 in Earl Twp, Lanc Co, PA, and died December 12, 1947.

Children of Reuben Horst and Frances Sweigart are:
+	496	i.	Elam Sweigart[10] Horst, born January 16, 1890; died March 23, 1977.
+	497	ii.	Reuben Sweigart Horst, born August 14, 1891.
+	498	iii.	Amos Sweigart Horst, born July 19, 1893; died January 01, 1963.
+	499	iv.	Eli Sweigart Horst, born January 14, 1896; died September 23, 1980 in Tampa, FL.
	500	v.	Jacob Sweigart Horst, born October 18, 1897; died May 11, 1898.
+	501	vi.	Titus Sweigart Horst, born May 10, 1899; died June 17, 1976.
+	502	vii.	Frances Sweigart Horst, born May 23, 1901; died October 09, 1982.
+	503	viii.	Phares Sweigart Horst, born March 14, 1903.
+	504	ix.	Noah Sweigart Horst, born June 05, 1905; died August 07, 1964.
	505	x.	Anna Sweigart Horst, born July 06, 1907; died November 14, 1999 in Landis Homes, Lancaster Co., PA. She married (1) George Wolf July 1947; born May 10, 1889; died January 01, 1952. She married (2) Jacob G. Herr December 16, 1952; born June 08, 1895 in Lancaster Twp, Lanc Co, PA; died October 15, 1991.
+	506	xi.	Walter Sweigart Horst, born September 04, 1909.
+	507	xii.	Ada Sweigart Horst, born May 30, 1911 in West Earl Twp, Lanc Co, PA; died July 03, 1979 in Akron, Lancaster Co, PA.
+	508	xiii.	Katie Sweigart Horst, born May 30, 1911; died August 20, 1994 in Manheim Twp, Lanc Co, PA.
+	509	xiv.	Lloyd Sweigart Horst, born August 16, 1913.

397. Christian G.⁹ Weaver (Gideon⁸ Weber, Christian⁷, Samuel⁶, Christian⁵, Henry⁴, Johann Anton³, Heinrich², George¹) was born September 25, 1847 in East Earl Twp., Lancaster Co., Pa., and died May 20, 1921. He married **Susanna Hollinger**, daughter of Johannes Hollinger and Ester Horst. She was born July 12, 1852, and died April 27, 1935.

Children are listed above under (370) Susanna Hollinger.

406. Magdalena O.⁹ Martin (Joseph Horst⁸, Elizabeth⁷ Horst, Magdalena⁶ Weber, Heine⁵, Henry⁴, Johann Anton³, Heinrich², George¹) was born August 15, 1850, and died May 09, 1886. She married **Elam B. Landis** November 25, 1875, son of Levi Landis and Mary Buckwalter. He was born October 06, 1850, and died May 06, 1938 in Ephrata Twp, Lanc Co, PA.

Children of Magdalena Martin and Elam Landis are:
- 510   i. Mary M.¹⁰ Landis, born September 07, 1876. She married Benjamin E. Martin June 09, 1900; born June 27, 1875; died February 16, 1927.
- 511   ii. Annie M. Landis, born June 22, 1878; died April 28, 1896.
- 512   iii. Emma M. Landis, born September 13, 1880; died September 17, 1963. She married Michael W. Sensenig January 01, 1899; born December 17, 1877; died 1953.
- + 513 iv. Magdalena M. Landis, born December 22, 1881 in Intercourse, Lanc Co, PA; died October 17, 1946 in Akron, Lancaster Co, PA.
- 514   v. Ada Cathrine Landis, born January 29, 1884; died August 17, 1895.
- 515   vi. Harry M. Landis, born March 28, 1886; died June 21, 1968. He married Emma W. Myers June 03, 1909; born October 24, 1885; died February 18, 1951.

417. Elam B.⁹ Landis (Levi L.⁸, Christian S.⁷, Johannes⁶, Jacob⁵, Maria⁴ Weber, Johann Anton³, Heinrich², George¹) was born October 06, 1850, and died May 06, 1938 in Ephrata Twp, Lanc Co, PA. He married **(1) Magdalena O. Martin** November 25, 1875, daughter of Joseph Martin and Martha Oberholtzer. She was born August 15, 1850, and died May 09, 1886. He married **(2) Mary Ann Bucher** November 13, 1888, daughter of Jonas Bucher and Anna Bollinger. She was born November 05, 1853, and died August 02, 1905. He married **(3) Lizzie O. Oberholtzer** February 07, 1907. She was born March 06, 1866, and died April 05, 1924.

Children are listed above under (406) Magdalena O. Martin.

Children of Elam Landis and Mary Bucher are:
- 516   i. Amanda B.¹⁰ Landis, born August 04, 1890; died July 27, 1962. She married John M. Gockley; born December 26, 1890; died July 05, 1966.
- 517   ii. Alice Ida Landis, born September 10, 1892. She married Isaac B. Witmer December 12, 1911; born November 05, 1883; died July 23, 1950.

Child of Elam Landis and Lizzie Oberholtzer is:
- 518   i. Ruth¹⁰ Landis, born January 05, 1908. She married M. Mose Summers.

430. Barbara Neff⁹ Buckwalter (Henry⁸, Judith⁷, John⁶, Magdalena⁵ Weber, Henry⁴, Johann Anton³, Heinrich², George¹) was born January 23, 1840, and died March 29, 1911. She married **Peter Hershey**, son of Jacob Hershey and Elizabeth Eby. He was born August 02, 1839, and died December 17, 1922.

Children are listed above under (321) Peter Hershey.

431. Henry L⁹ Hess (Fanny Long⁸ Landis, Benjamin L.⁷, Henry⁶, Benjamin⁵, Maria⁴ Weber, Johann Anton³, Heinrich², George¹) was born January 28, 1857 in Elizabeth Twp Lancaster Co, PA, and died December 10, 1919. He married **Sarah Weidler Hess** November 12, 1876, daughter of Joseph Hess and Elizabeth Weidler. She was born February 10, 1859 in Warwick Twp, Lanc Co, PA, and died September 14, 1926.

Child of Henry Hess and Sarah Hess is:
- + 519 i. Harry H¹⁰ Hess, born July 20, 1884 in Manheim Twp, Lanc Co, PA; died January 17, 1958.

Generation No. 10

437. Sarah Lucinda¹⁰ Hershey (Peter⁹, Jacob⁸, John⁷, Anna Weber⁶ Newcomer, Elizabeth⁵ Weber, Henry⁴, Johann Anton³, Heinrich², George¹) was born September 09, 1863, and died December 22, 1942. She married **Henry John Eby**. He was born April 07, 1858, and died September 30, 1922 in New Holland PA.

Children of Sarah Hershey and Henry Eby are:
- + 520 i. Ella Barbara¹¹ Eby, born December 27, 1884; died May 06, 1959.
- + 521 ii. Elizabeth Hershey Eby, born September 15, 1886; died February 16, 1944.
- + 522 iii. Peter Hershey Eby, born August 09, 1889; died February 11, 1919.

+	523	iv.	Enos Jacob Eby, born June 20, 1891; died April 27, 1974.
+	524	v.	Sarah Lucinda Eby, born February 25, 1893; died January 04, 1946.
	525	vi.	John Silas Eby, born October 21, 1894; died December 04, 1912.
+	526	vii.	Henry Musser Eby, born July 14, 1896; died June 15, 1974.
+	527	viii.	Anna Martha Eby, born April 29, 1898; died November 27, 1980.
	528	ix.	Isaac Isaiah Eby, born August 23, 1899; died August 01, 1906.
	529	x.	Mary Edith Eby, born August 26, 1901. She married Ivan M. Sensenig; born March 20, 1898; died August 08, 1983.
+	530	xi.	Aaron Buckwalter Eby, born February 02, 1904; died April 06, 1975.
+	531	xii.	Menno Hershey Eby, born October 27, 1905; died June 22, 1974.
+	532	xiii.	Martin Christian Eby, born July 10, 1910; died March 02, 1986.

438. Isaiah B.[10] Hershey (Peter[9], Jacob[8], John[7], Anna Weber[6] Newcomer, Elizabeth[5] Weber, Henry[4], Johann Anton[3], Heinrich[2], George[1]) was born June 28, 1865, and died October 09, 1919. He married **Katharine Sauder**. She was born July 11, 1863, and died April 04, 1919.

Child of Isaiah Hershey and Katharine Sauder is:
| + | 533 | i. | Galen Warren[11] Hershey, born October 31, 1886; died April 17, 1988. |

439. Enos Jacob[10] Hershey (Peter[9], Jacob[8], John[7], Anna Weber[6] Newcomer, Elizabeth[5] Weber, Henry[4], Johann Anton[3], Heinrich[2], George[1]) was born November 02, 1866, and died March 20, 1939. He married **Susan Eby**. She was born September 29, 1865, and died April 08, 1948.

Children of Enos Hershey and Susan Eby are:
	534	i.	Edith May[11] Hershey, born July 28, 1890; died July 20, 1912.
+	535	ii.	Henry Clay Hershey, born September 01, 1892; died February 20, 1946.
	536	iii.	Grace Elizabeth Hershey, born January 15, 1895. She married Roy Eby Smith; born November 11, 1899; died January 06, 1971.
+	537	iv.	Mark Eby Hershey, born April 13, 1897; died December 19, 1983.
+	538	v.	David Warren Hershey, born November 25, 1899; died July 23, 1985.
+	539	vi.	Mary Helen Hershey, born January 06, 1903.
	540	vii.	Ethel Pauline Hershey, born October 21, 1904; died January 24, 1987. She married (1) Harry R. Lichty; born May 24, 1891; died June 17, 1957. She married (2) Milton S. Horst; born December 23, 1899.

440. Elizabeth[10] Hershey (Peter[9], Jacob[8], John[7], Anna Weber[6] Newcomer, Elizabeth[5] Weber, Henry[4], Johann Anton[3], Heinrich[2], George[1]) was born September 09, 1868, and died September 06, 1934. She married **Henry H. Hess**. He was born April 03, 1862, and died February 07, 1918.

Children of Elizabeth Hershey and Henry Hess are:
+	541	i.	Clyde C.[11] Hess, born April 22, 1888; died March 06, 1957.
+	542	ii.	Harry Hershey Hess, born April 01, 1890; died August 14, 1949.
	543	iii.	Willis Rutter Hess, born December 17, 1891; died March 19, 1968. He married Wilhelmina G. Wederman; born May 18, 1889; died April 22, 1966.
	544	iv.	Harriet Ann Hess, born September 06, 1898.
	545	v.	Mildred Elizabeth Hess, born February 26, 1908; died November 14, 1957. She married Norman Lincoln Towle; born November 24, 1895; died May 15, 1963.

442. Henry Peter[10] Hershey (Peter[9], Jacob[8], John[7], Anna Weber[6] Newcomer, Elizabeth[5] Weber, Henry[4], Johann Anton[3], Heinrich[2], George[1]) was born March 14, 1872, and died December 10, 1949. He married **Anna Keene**. She was born September 05, 1875, and died December 17, 1951.

Children of Henry Hershey and Anna Keene are:
| + | 546 | i. | Paul Keene[11] Hershey, born September 06, 1900; died July 13, 1968. |
| | 547 | ii. | Erma Elizabeth Hershey, born August 12, 1904. She married Charles Wesley Appler; born June 07, 1905. |

443. Martin Eby[10] Hershey (Peter[9], Jacob[8], John[7], Anna Weber[6] Newcomer, Elizabeth[5] Weber, Henry[4], Johann Anton[3], Heinrich[2], George[1]) was born December 20, 1873, and died June 13, 1953. He married **Cora Etta Eaby**. She was born February 27, 1874, and died August 08, 1926.

Children of Martin Hershey and Cora Eaby are:

	548	i.	Esther Elizabeth[11] Hershey, born May 27, 1905.
+	549	ii.	Miriam Clara Hershey, born February 06, 1909; died June 27, 1998.

448. Silas N.[10] Hershey (Peter[9], Jacob[8], John[7], Anna Weber[6] Newcomer, Elizabeth[5] Weber, Henry[4], Johann Anton[3], Heinrich[2], George[1]) was born March 22, 1881, and died November 20, 1970. He married **Lillie Landis Denlinger**. She was born April 13, 1884.

Children of Silas Hershey and Lillie Denlinger are:

	550	i.	Elsie D.[11] Hershey, born December 24, 1905; died July 31, 1987.
+	551	ii.	Frances Hershey, born August 30, 1907.
+	552	iii.	Lester D. Hershey, born February 22, 1910.
+	553	iv.	Barbara Elizabeth Hershey, born March 24, 1912.
+	554	v.	Willis Daniel Hershey, born June 26, 1916; died July 19, 1994.
+	555	vi.	Reba L. Hershey, born July 09, 1922.
+	556	vii.	Doris Mae Hershey, born May 11, 1925.
	557	viii.	Mary Emily Hershey, born January 26, 1928; died March 25, 1928.

452. Frances Reiff[10] Sweigart (Annie[9] Reiff, Veronica[8] Hershey, John[7], Anna Weber[6] Newcomer, Elizabeth[5] Weber, Henry[4], Johann Anton[3], Heinrich[2], George[1]) was born November 03, 1868 in Earl Twp, Lanc Co, PA, and died December 12, 1947. She married **Reuben Weaver Horst** November 18, 1888, son of Jacob Horst and Lydia Weaver. He was born December 05, 1868 in West Earl Twp, Lanc Co, PA, and died June 22, 1941.

Children are listed above under (386) Reuben Weaver Horst.

461. Lorena[10] Hershey (Christian[9], Nancy[8], Christian[7], Anna Weber[6] Newcomer, Elizabeth[5] Weber, Henry[4], Johann Anton[3], Heinrich[2], George[1]) was born October 02, 1868. She married **James B Leithiser**.

Child of Lorena Hershey and James Leithiser is:
558   i.   Margaret[11] Leithiser, born June 02, 1893.

469. Eugene Light[10] Hershey (Jacob H[9], Nancy[8], Christian[7], Anna Weber[6] Newcomer, Elizabeth[5] Weber, Henry[4], Johann Anton[3], Heinrich[2], George[1]) was born October 02, 1880, and died August 1966 in 17083 Quentin, Lebanon, PA. He married **Elizabeth Unknown** 1908. She was born 1883.

Children of Eugene Hershey and Elizabeth Unknown are:
559   i.   Jacob B[11] Hershey, born February 02, 1911; died November 12, 1990.
560   ii.   Leona R Hershey, born 1913.
561   iii.   Freda M Hershey, born 1922.

471. Annie[10] Hershey (Elias H[9], Nancy[8], Christian[7], Anna Weber[6] Newcomer, Elizabeth[5] Weber, Henry[4], Johann Anton[3], Heinrich[2], George[1]) was born November 14, 1869, and died May 15, 1916. She married **Harvey Bitzer**. He was born May 22, 1870.

Children of Annie Hershey and Harvey Bitzer are:

	562	i.	Helen Virginia[11] Bitzer, born February 21, 1891.
+	563	ii.	Elizabeth Gertrude Bitzer, born December 17, 1894.

472. Mary[10] Hershey (Elias H[9], Nancy[8], Christian[7], Anna Weber[6] Newcomer, Elizabeth[5] Weber, Henry[4], Johann Anton[3], Heinrich[2], George[1]) was born November 17, 1872. She married **Monroe Pfautz**. He was born 1857.

Child of Mary Hershey and Monroe Pfautz is:
564   i.   Mildred[11] Pfautz, born November 24, 1896. She married Allen Hammond; born 1894.

475. Ezra Frantz[10] Hershey (Elias H[9], Nancy[8], Christian[7], Anna Weber[6] Newcomer, Elizabeth[5] Weber, Henry[4], Johann Anton[3], Heinrich[2], George[1]) was born September 01, 1879, and died 1949. He married **Mary Amanda Rohrer**. She was born August 04, 1883, and died Aft. 1960.

Children of Ezra Hershey and Mary Rohrer are:

	565	i.	Katherine Rohrer[11] Hershey, born September 30, 1911.
+	566	ii.	Maria Elizabeth Hershey, born June 05, 1913.
	567	iii.	Ezra Frantz Hershey, born March 24, 1916; died May 21, 2003 in Richmond, Henrico, VA.

478. Abraham H[10] Burkholder (Susan[9] Hershey, Abraham[8], Christian[7], Anna Weber[6] Newcomer, Elizabeth[5] Weber, Henry[4], Johann Anton[3], Heinrich[2], George[1]) was born August 02, 1885, and died January 06, 1935. He married **Mabel E Ebersole**. She was born June 05, 1887, and died June 16, 1965.

Children of Abraham Burkholder and Mabel Ebersole are:
	568	i.	Marie[11] Burkholder.
+	569	ii.	Melvin E Burkholder, born January 1909; died 1971.
	570	iii.	Marlin Burkholder.
	571	iv.	A M Burkholder.
	572	v.	Clark A Burkholder.
	573	vi.	Dorothy M Burkholder, born September 17, 1919.
	574	vii.	E J Burkholder.
	575	viii.	George R Burkholder, born 1926.

488. Gertrude[10] Hertzler (Michael S.[9], Abraham[8], John[7], Maria[6] Mumma, Beverly[5] Weber, Henry[4], Johann Anton[3], Heinrich[2], George[1]) was born 1881, and died March 1918. She married **Charles Livengood**. He was born 1881, and died April 1961.

Children of Gertrude Hertzler and Charles Livengood are:
+	576	i.	Martha Anna[11] Livengood, born October 20, 1909 in Mechanics Grove, Lanc Co, PA.
	577	ii.	Mary Elizabeth Livengood, born August 19, 1911 in Quarryville, Lanc Co, PA; died December 18, 1984 in Lancaster, PA. She married Martin M. Wolgemuth.
	578	iii.	Ruth Lydia Livengood, born 1912. She married Chester M. Landis.
	579	iv.	Samuel Livengood, born 1912; died 1912.
	580	v.	Naomi Leah Livengood, born April 08, 1914. She married Russel Jacquet; born September 03, 1908; died January 12, 1986.
	581	vi.	Rhoda Livengood, born March 1918; died March 1918.

493. John Hollinger[10] Weaver (Christian G.[9], Gideon[8] Weber, Christian[7], Samuel[6], Christian[5], Henry[4], Johann Anton[3], Heinrich[2], George[1]) was born February 23, 1881, and died June 06, 1946 in Akron, Lancaster Co, PA. He married **Magdalena M. Landis** August 23, 1903 in Murrel, PA, daughter of Elam Landis and Magdalena Martin. She was born December 22, 1881 in Intercourse, Lanc Co, PA, and died October 17, 1946 in Akron, Lancaster Co, PA.

Children of John Weaver and Magdalena Landis are:
	582	i.	Mabel L.[11] Weaver, born April 12, 1905; died February 25, 2000 in Landis Homes, Lancaster Co., PA. She married Emanuel Marner March 09, 1956; born September 28, 1896 in Kokomo, IN; died February 01, 1983 in Manheim Twp, Lanc Co, PA.
+	583	ii.	John Landis Weaver, born September 04, 1909 in Earl Twp, Lanc Co, PA; died April 30, 1991 in Akron, Lancaster Co, PA.

496. Elam Sweigart[10] Horst (Reuben Weaver[9], Jacob M.[8], Barbara Weber[7] Musser, Esther[6] Weber, Christian[5], Henry[4], Johann Anton[3], Heinrich[2], George[1]) was born January 16, 1890, and died March 23, 1977. He married **(1) Alice Parmer Steffy** November 11, 1911. She was born July 07, 1889, and died November 06, 1952. He married **(2) Rebecca L. Zook** November 25, 1954. She was born May 03, 1919.

Children of Elam Horst and Alice Steffy are:
	584	i.	Martha Steffy[11] Horst, born July 29, 1912; died August 19, 1912.
+	585	ii.	Paul Steffy Horst, born July 26, 1914.
+	586	iii.	William Prichard Horst, born October 03, 1917.
+	587	iv.	Erma Steffy Horst, born April 25, 1924.
+	588	v.	Gordon Steffy Horst, born March 30, 1929.

Children of Elam Horst and Rebecca Zook are:
589	i.	Carl Zook[11] Horst, born August 14, 1955. He married Charlene Tiffany September 11, 1976; born March 12, 1955 in California.
590	ii.	Blaine Zook Horst, born October 24, 1957.

497. Reuben Sweigart[10] Horst (Reuben Weaver[9], Jacob M.[8], Barbara Weber[7] Musser, Esther[6] Weber, Christian[5], Henry[4], Johann Anton[3], Heinrich[2], George[1]) was born August 14, 1891. He married **Ida Snyder Stoner** November 12, 1914. She was born March 05, 1891, and died November 13, 1978.

Children of Reuben Horst and Ida Stoner are:
- 591 i. Ruth Naomi[11] Horst, born September 28, 1915.
- 592 ii. Lois Esther Horst, born June 14, 1917.
- 593 iii. John Alton Horst, born November 08, 1924.

498. Amos Sweigart[10] **Horst** (Reuben Weaver[9], Jacob M.[8], Barbara Weber[7] Musser, Esther[6] Weber, Christian[5], Henry[4], Johann Anton[3], Heinrich[2], George[1]) was born July 19, 1893, and died January 01, 1963. He married **Nora Snyder Stoner** December 12, 1918. She was born February 12, 1895, and died July 08, 1990.

Children of Amos Horst and Nora Stoner are:
- 594 i. John Mark[11] Horst, born December 04, 1919; died February 02, 1935.
- 595 ii. James Albert Horst, born August 01, 1926; died February 22, 1930.

499. Eli Sweigart[10] **Horst** (Reuben Weaver[9], Jacob M.[8], Barbara Weber[7] Musser, Esther[6] Weber, Christian[5], Henry[4], Johann Anton[3], Heinrich[2], George[1]) was born January 14, 1896, and died September 23, 1980 in Tampa, FL. He married **(1) Ruth Campbell**. She died April 10, 1962. He married **(2) Elizabeth Oberholtzer** June 19, 1920.

Children of Eli Horst and Ruth Campbell are:
- 596 i. Henry Reuben[11] Horst, born June 13, 1944.
- 597 ii. Douglas Clyde Horst, born June 06, 1947.
- 598 iii. David Campbell Horst, born June 13, 1951.

Children of Eli Horst and Elizabeth Oberholtzer are:
- 599 i. Quintis[11] Horst, born August 02, 1924; died September 09, 1932.
- 600 ii. Miriam Elizabeth Horst, born August 21, 1927.

501. Titus Sweigart[10] **Horst** (Reuben Weaver[9], Jacob M.[8], Barbara Weber[7] Musser, Esther[6] Weber, Christian[5], Henry[4], Johann Anton[3], Heinrich[2], George[1]) was born May 10, 1899, and died June 17, 1976. He married **Mary Buckwalter Landis** November 24, 1921. She was born January 09, 1899 in Union Grove, Earl Twp, Lanc Co, PA, and died November 18, 1987 in West Earl Twp, Lanc Co, PA.

Children of Titus Horst and Mary Landis are:
- 601 i. John Landis[11] Horst, born January 10, 1923.
- 602 ii. Ray Ernest Horst, born April 23, 1924.
- 603 iii. Martha Frances Horst, born July 22, 1928.
- 604 iv. Titus Glenn Horst, born June 06, 1932.

502. Frances Sweigart[10] **Horst** (Reuben Weaver[9], Jacob M.[8], Barbara Weber[7] Musser, Esther[6] Weber, Christian[5], Henry[4], Johann Anton[3], Heinrich[2], George[1]) was born May 23, 1901, and died October 09, 1982. She married **Lehman Herr Lefever** August 04, 1920. He was born February 22, 1898, and died February 11, 1987.

Children of Frances Horst and Lehman Lefever are:
- 605 i. Harold Horst[11] Lefever, born July 17, 1921.
- 606 ii. Titus Horst Lefever, born April 11, 1923.
- 607 iii. Miriam Horst Lefever, born August 18, 1925.
- 608 iv. Jay Lehman Lefever, born February 22, 1927.
- 609 v. Merle Horst Lefever, born February 22, 1929.
- 610 vi. Frances Violet Lefever, born September 19, 1933.

503. Phares Sweigart[10] **Horst** (Reuben Weaver[9], Jacob M.[8], Barbara Weber[7] Musser, Esther[6] Weber, Christian[5], Henry[4], Johann Anton[3], Heinrich[2], George[1]) was born March 14, 1903. He married **Magdalena Moseman** December 25, 1929. She was born November 01, 1904.

Children of Phares Horst and Magdalena Moseman are:
- 611 i. Jeanne Loraine[11] Horst, born September 16, 1931.
- 612 ii. Lee Sterling Horst, born April 15, 1934.

504. Noah Sweigart[10] **Horst** (Reuben Weaver[9], Jacob M.[8], Barbara Weber[7] Musser, Esther[6] Weber, Christian[5], Henry[4], Johann Anton[3], Heinrich[2], George[1]) was born June 05, 1905, and died August 07, 1964. He married **Ruth Myer** September 19, 1929. She was born September 01, 1906.

Children of Noah Horst and Ruth Myer are:
- 613   i.   Richard M.[11] Horst, born March 30, 1938.
- 614   ii.   Dorothy A. Horst, born July 18, 1944.

506. Walter Sweigart[10] Horst (Reuben Weaver[9], Jacob M.[8], Barbara Weber[7] Musser, Esther[6] Weber, Christian[5], Henry[4], Johann Anton[3], Heinrich[2], George[1]) was born September 04, 1909. He married **(1) Miriam Mosemann** February 29, 1932. She was born June 27, 1912, and died October 03, 1976. He married **(2) Lucy S. Brubaker** December 13, 1979. She was born November 22, 1932.

Children of Walter Horst and Miriam Mosemann are:
- 615   i.   Kenneth Moseman[11] Horst, born January 07, 1933.
- 616   ii.   Walter Dale Horst, born January 27, 1936.
- 617   iii.   Lois Jean Horst, born April 26, 1942.
- 618   iv.   Miriam Darlene Horst, born March 01, 1947.
- 619   v.   Janet Elaine Horst, born June 07, 1949.

507. Ada Sweigart[10] Horst (Reuben Weaver[9], Jacob M.[8], Barbara Weber[7] Musser, Esther[6] Weber, Christian[5], Henry[4], Johann Anton[3], Heinrich[2], George[1]) was born May 30, 1911 in West Earl Twp, Lanc Co, PA, and died July 03, 1979 in Akron, Lancaster Co, PA. She married **John Landis Weaver** January 07, 1932, son of John Weaver and Magdalena Landis. He was born September 04, 1909 in Earl Twp, Lanc Co, PA, and died April 30, 1991 in Akron, Lancaster Co, PA.

Children of Ada Horst and John Weaver are:
- +   620   i.   Jay Donald[11] Weaver, born April 20, 1933 in Ephrata Twp, Lanc Co, PA.
- +   621   ii.   Arvilla Weaver, born July 21, 1934 in Ephrata Twp, Lanc Co, PA.
- +   622   iii.   Donna Lou Weaver, born July 11, 1942 in Akron, Lancaster Co, PA.
- +   623   iv.   John Eric Weaver, born February 11, 1945 in Ephrata, PA.
-      624   v.   Elizabeth Ann Weaver, born January 01, 1947 in Ephrata Twp, Lanc Co, PA. She married (1) Frank Espich. She married (2) James Mcelhenny June 17, 1972 in Ephrata, PA.
- +   625   vi.   Ronald Lee Weaver, born August 16, 1950 in Ephrata, PA.

508. Katie Sweigart[10] Horst (Reuben Weaver[9], Jacob M.[8], Barbara Weber[7] Musser, Esther[6] Weber, Christian[5], Henry[4], Johann Anton[3], Heinrich[2], George[1]) was born May 30, 1911, and died August 20, 1994 in Manheim Twp, Lanc Co, PA. She married **John Kauffman Shenk** June 15, 1930. He was born March 07, 1906 in Penn Twp, Lanc Co, PA, and died December 20, 1986.

Children of Katie Horst and John Shenk are:
- 626   i.   Florence LaVerne[11] Shenk, born March 30, 1932.
- 627   ii.   Frances Geraldine Shenk, born May 08, 1933.
- 628   iii.   John Marlin Shenk, born September 24, 1936.
- 629   iv.   Donald Reuben Shenk, born March 17, 1939.

509. Lloyd Sweigart[10] Horst (Reuben Weaver[9], Jacob M.[8], Barbara Weber[7] Musser, Esther[6] Weber, Christian[5], Henry[4], Johann Anton[3], Heinrich[2], George[1]) was born August 16, 1913. He married **Alice Virginia Heatwole** February 29, 1936. She was born June 14, 1912, and died January 05, 1997.

Children of Lloyd Horst and Alice Heatwole are:
- 630   i.   Joseph Franklin[11] Horst, born March 14, 1938.
- 631   ii.   James Daniel Horst, born July 15, 1940.
- 632   iii.   Amos David Horst, born October 16, 1941.
- 633   iv.   Enos Heatwole Horst, born November 21, 1943.
- 634   v.   Rachel Frances Horst, born November 30, 1945.
- 635   vi.   Reuben Walter Horst, born August 08, 1947.
- 636   vii.   Anna Lois Horst, born November 18, 1950.

513. Magdalena M.[10] Landis (Elam B.[9], Levi L.[8], Christian S.[7], Johannes[6], Jacob[5], Maria[4] Weber, Johann Anton[3], Heinrich[2], George[1]) was born December 22, 1881 in Intercourse, Lanc Co, PA, and died October 17, 1946 in Akron, Lancaster Co, PA. She married **John Hollinger Weaver** August 23, 1903 in Murrel, PA, son of Christian Weaver and Susanna Hollinger. He was born February 23, 1881, and died June 06, 1946 in Akron, Lancaster Co, PA.

Children are listed above under (493) John Hollinger Weaver.

519. Harry H[10] Hess (Henry L[9], Fanny Long[8] Landis, Benjamin L.[7], Henry[6], Benjamin[5], Maria[4] Weber, Johann Anton[3], Heinrich[2],

George¹) was born July 20, 1884 in Manheim Twp, Lanc Co, PA, and died January 17, 1958. He married **Anna Rupp Wolf** August 18, 1910. She was born December 31, 1884 in Millway, Warwick Twp, Lancaster Co, PA, and died October 10, 1958.

Child of Harry Hess and Anna Wolf is:
- 637   i. Ruth Wolf¹¹ Hess, born December 05, 1921 in Millway, Warwick Twp, Lancaster Co, PA. She married Archie L Good May 15, 1943.

Generation No. 11

520. Ella Barbara¹¹ Eby (Sarah Lucinda¹⁰ Hershey, Peter⁹, Jacob⁸, John⁷, Anna Weber⁶ Newcomer, Elizabeth⁵ Weber, Henry⁴, Johann Anton³, Heinrich², George¹) was born December 27, 1884, and died May 06, 1959. She married **Daniel M. Fox**. He was born May 12, 1879, and died June 30, 1971.

Children of Ella Eby and Daniel Fox are:
- + 638   i. Willis Eby¹² Fox, born May 17, 1907.
- + 639   ii. Henry Peter Fox, born September 16, 1909.
- + 640   iii. Sarah Lucinda Fox, born July 06, 1911; died October 19, 1971.
-    641   iv. John David Fox, born June 19, 1913; died January 10, 1971.
-    642   v. Anna Elizabeth Fox, born July 14, 1915.
- + 643   vi. Daniel Hershey Fox, born August 19, 1917; died June 10, 1986.
-    644   vii. Elmer Eby Fox, born May 19, 1920; died February 08, 1921.
-    645   viii. Mary Eby Fox, born September 18, 1923. She married Leo Richard Grant; born February 10, 1925.
- + 646   ix. Ivan Martin Fox, born October 23, 1925; died February 13, 1987.

521. Elizabeth Hershey¹¹ Eby (Sarah Lucinda¹⁰ Hershey, Peter⁹, Jacob⁸, John⁷, Anna Weber⁶ Newcomer, Elizabeth⁵ Weber, Henry⁴, Johann Anton³, Heinrich², George¹) was born September 15, 1886, and died February 16, 1944. She married **Frank W. Mohler**. He was born December 07, 1894, and died February 26, 1967.

Child of Elizabeth Eby and Frank Mohler is:
- 647   i. Graybill Eby¹² Mohler, born March 28, 1922. He married Helen Louise Kochel; born November 19, 1925.

522. Peter Hershey¹¹ Eby (Sarah Lucinda¹⁰ Hershey, Peter⁹, Jacob⁸, John⁷, Anna Weber⁶ Newcomer, Elizabeth⁵ Weber, Henry⁴, Johann Anton³, Heinrich², George¹) was born August 09, 1889, and died February 11, 1919. He married **Anna M. Weaver**. She was born August 18, 1890, and died January 23, 1982.

Children of Peter Eby and Anna Weaver are:
- + 648   i. Franklin W.¹² Eby, born January 31, 1915; died November 14, 1968.
- + 649   ii. Susan W. Eby, born November 16, 1916.
- + 650   iii. Emma Mae Eby, born October 27, 1918.

523. Enos Jacob¹¹ Eby (Sarah Lucinda¹⁰ Hershey, Peter⁹, Jacob⁸, John⁷, Anna Weber⁶ Newcomer, Elizabeth⁵ Weber, Henry⁴, Johann Anton³, Heinrich², George¹) was born June 20, 1891, and died April 27, 1974. He married **Esther Weaver Shirk**. She was born March 13, 1894, and died May 18, 1966.

Children of Enos Eby and Esther Shirk are:
-    651   i. Isaac S.¹² Eby, born November 12, 1916.
- + 652   ii. Rhoda S. Eby, born August 22, 1918.
- + 653   iii. Henry S. Eby, born July 21, 1920.
- + 654   iv. Ezra S. Eby, born October 31, 1922.
- + 655   v. Eli S. Eby, born March 19, 1925; died December 12, 1985.
- + 656   vi. Lydia S. Eby, born March 31, 1927.
-    657   vii. Aaron S. Eby, born August 02, 1929; died October 16, 1929.
-    658   viii. John S. Eby, born March 25, 1932; died March 25, 1932.
-    659   ix. Sarah S. Eby, born January 30, 1935; died April 22, 1960.

524. Sarah Lucinda¹¹ Eby (Sarah Lucinda¹⁰ Hershey, Peter⁹, Jacob⁸, John⁷, Anna Weber⁶ Newcomer, Elizabeth⁵ Weber, Henry⁴, Johann Anton³, Heinrich², George¹) was born February 25, 1893, and died January 04, 1946. She married **Harry H. Gehman**. He was born June 26, 1890, and died March 26, 1947.

Children of Sarah Eby and Harry Gehman are:

- + 660 i. Private[12] Gehman.
- + 661 ii. Private Gehman.
- + 662 iii. Arthur E. Gehman, born January 19, 1920.
- + 663 iv. John E. Gehman, born October 18, 1921.
- + 664 v. Edith Elizabeth Gehman, born March 31, 1923.
- + 665 vi. Lucy E. Gehman, born November 19, 1924.
-    666 vii. Grace Gehman, born October 30, 1926.
- + 667 viii. Harry Jacob Gehman, born November 25, 1929.

526. Henry Musser[11] Eby (Sarah Lucinda[10] Hershey, Peter[9], Jacob[8], John[7], Anna Weber[6] Newcomer, Elizabeth[5] Weber, Henry[4], Johann Anton[3], Heinrich[2], George[1]) was born July 14, 1896, and died June 15, 1974. He married **Anna Mae Zeiset**. She was born January 01, 1900.

Children of Henry Eby and Anna Zeiset are:
- + 668 i. Private[12] Eby.
- + 669 ii. Private Eby.
- + 670 iii. Private Eby.
- + 671 iv. Private Eby.
- + 672 v. Private Eby.
- + 673 vi. Martin Z. Eby, born December 25, 1921.
- + 674 vii. Ethel Z. Eby, born November 25, 1923.
-    675 viii. Warren Z. Eby, born September 23, 1925.
- + 676 ix. Roy Z. Eby, born September 20, 1927.
- + 677 x. Mary Z. Eby, born June 11, 1929.

527. Anna Martha[11] Eby (Sarah Lucinda[10] Hershey, Peter[9], Jacob[8], John[7], Anna Weber[6] Newcomer, Elizabeth[5] Weber, Henry[4], Johann Anton[3], Heinrich[2], George[1]) was born April 29, 1898, and died November 27, 1980. She married **Walter M. Martin**. He was born April 03, 1897, and died April 22, 1975.

Children of Anna Eby and Walter Martin are:
- + 678 i. Private[12] Martin.
- + 679 ii. Private Martin.
- + 680 iii. Clarence E. Martin, born November 13, 1919.
- + 681 iv. Mary E. Martin, born December 22, 1921.
- + 682 v. Paul E. Martin, born September 29, 1923.
- + 683 vi. Earl E. Martin, born November 28, 1926.
- + 684 vii. Wilmer E. Martin, born June 05, 1929.

530. Aaron Buckwalter[11] Eby (Sarah Lucinda[10] Hershey, Peter[9], Jacob[8], John[7], Anna Weber[6] Newcomer, Elizabeth[5] Weber, Henry[4], Johann Anton[3], Heinrich[2], George[1]) was born February 02, 1904, and died April 06, 1975. He married **Edna M. Sensenig**. She was born September 09, 1904.

Children of Aaron Eby and Edna Sensenig are:
- + 685 i. Private[12] Eby.
- + 686 ii. Private Eby.
- + 687 iii. Private Eby.
- + 688 iv. Private Eby.
- + 689 v. Richard S. Eby, born October 08, 1928.
- + 690 vi. Clyde S. Eby, born November 29, 1937; died October 08, 1974.

531. Menno Hershey[11] Eby (Sarah Lucinda[10] Hershey, Peter[9], Jacob[8], John[7], Anna Weber[6] Newcomer, Elizabeth[5] Weber, Henry[4], Johann Anton[3], Heinrich[2], George[1]) was born October 27, 1905, and died June 22, 1974. He married **Helen V. Weaver**. She was born October 11, 1911.

Children of Menno Eby and Helen Weaver are:
- + 691 i. Private[12] Eby.
- + 692 ii. Private Eby.
- + 693 iii. Private Eby.

532. Martin Christian[11] Eby (Sarah Lucinda[10] Hershey, Peter[9], Jacob[8], John[7], Anna Weber[6] Newcomer, Elizabeth[5] Weber, Henry[4],

Johann Anton[3], Heinrich[2], George[1]) was born July 10, 1910, and died March 02, 1986. He married **(1) Helen Stauffer Wenger**. She was born January 20, 1916, and died June 04, 1960. He married **(2) Esta Mae Hershey**. She was born May 13, 1916.

Children of Martin Eby and Helen Wenger are:
+   694   i.   Private[12] Eby.
+   695   ii.   Private Eby.
+   696   iii.   Private Eby.
      697   iv.   Private Eby.
+   698   v.   Private Eby.

533. Galen Warren[11] Hershey (Isaiah B.[10], Peter[9], Jacob[8], John[7], Anna Weber[6] Newcomer, Elizabeth[5] Weber, Henry[4], Johann Anton[3], Heinrich[2], George[1]) was born October 31, 1886, and died April 17, 1988. He married **Margie Eby**. She was born March 30, 1890, and died February 22, 1986.

Children of Galen Hershey and Margie Eby are:
+   699   i.   Erma E.[12] Hershey, born March 08, 1910.
+   700   ii.   Galen Clair Hershey, born February 10, 1914; died July 15, 1992.

535. Henry Clay[11] Hershey (Enos Jacob[10], Peter[9], Jacob[8], John[7], Anna Weber[6] Newcomer, Elizabeth[5] Weber, Henry[4], Johann Anton[3], Heinrich[2], George[1]) was born September 01, 1892, and died February 20, 1946. He married **Edna Hershey**. She was born August 25, 1893, and died April 04, 1939.

Children of Henry Hershey and Edna Hershey are:
+   701   i.   Private[12] Hershey.
+   702   ii.   Private Hershey.
+   703   iii.   Private Hershey.
+   704   iv.   Private Hershey.
+   705   v.   Hazel Pauline Hershey, born August 15, 1914; died March 08, 1985.
      706   vi.   Mildred L. Hershey, born December 22, 1916; died October 31, 1961.
+   707   vii.   Ralph Glenn Hershey, born December 15, 1918; died March 12, 1988.
      708   viii.   William Nelson Hershey, born September 20, 1925.
+   709   ix.   Gladys Edna Hershey, born August 08, 1927.
+   710   x.   Clifford Eby Hershey, born November 17, 1928; died February 06, 1969.

537. Mark Eby[11] Hershey (Enos Jacob[10], Peter[9], Jacob[8], John[7], Anna Weber[6] Newcomer, Elizabeth[5] Weber, Henry[4], Johann Anton[3], Heinrich[2], George[1]) was born April 13, 1897, and died December 19, 1983. He married **Anna Kreider Hershey**. She was born August 10, 1901.

Children of Mark Hershey and Anna Hershey are:
+   711   i.   Private[12] Hershey.
+   712   ii.   Private Hershey.
+   713   iii.   Private Hershey.
+   714   iv.   Private Hershey.
+   715   v.   Private Hershey.
+   716   vi.   Private Hershey.
+   717   vii.   Private Hershey.
      718   viii.   Jean Lois Hershey, born March 23, 1928.

538. David Warren[11] Hershey (Enos Jacob[10], Peter[9], Jacob[8], John[7], Anna Weber[6] Newcomer, Elizabeth[5] Weber, Henry[4], Johann Anton[3], Heinrich[2], George[1]) was born November 25, 1899, and died July 23, 1985. He married **Celeste Edith Denlinger**. She was born October 01, 1901.

Children of David Hershey and Celeste Denlinger are:
+   719   i.   Private[12] Hershey.
+   720   ii.   Vincent Denlinger Hershey, born September 20, 1925.
      721   iii.   Victor Eby Hershey, born April 21, 1927. He married Private Weaver.
      722   iv.   Edith Celeste Hershey, born January 19, 1929. She married Stanley Howard Thomas; born March 21, 1928.

539. Mary Helen[11] Hershey (Enos Jacob[10], Peter[9], Jacob[8], John[7], Anna Weber[6] Newcomer, Elizabeth[5] Weber, Henry[4], Johann Anton[3], Heinrich[2], George[1]) was born January 06, 1903. She married **Edwin Guy Ranck**. He was born January 25, 1902, and died

February 03, 1932.

Children of Mary Hershey and Edwin Ranck are:
+ 723 i. Private[12] Ranck.
+ 724 ii. Lester Hershey Ranck, born April 21, 1924.
+ 725 iii. Arthur Eby Ranck, born September 06, 1925.
+ 726 iv. Donald Edwin Ranck, born June 26, 1927.
   727 v. Enos Raymond Ranck, born December 13, 1929; died August 05, 1930.

541. Clyde C.[11] Hess (Elizabeth[10] Hershey, Peter[9], Jacob[8], John[7], Anna Weber[6] Newcomer, Elizabeth[5] Weber, Henry[4], Johann Anton[3], Heinrich[2], George[1]) was born April 22, 1888, and died March 06, 1957. He married **Catherine L. Price**. She was born June 29, 1888.

Child of Clyde Hess and Catherine Price is:
+ 728 i. Janet Potter[12] Hess, born July 10, 1924.

542. Harry Hershey[11] Hess (Elizabeth[10] Hershey, Peter[9], Jacob[8], John[7], Anna Weber[6] Newcomer, Elizabeth[5] Weber, Henry[4], Johann Anton[3], Heinrich[2], George[1]) was born April 01, 1890, and died August 14, 1949. He married **Manilla Tolemie**. She was born May 20, 1898.

Children of Harry Hess and Manilla Tolemie are:
   729 i. Private[12] Hess.
+ 730 ii. Rhoda Gregory Hess, born September 12, 1926.

546. Paul Keene[11] Hershey (Henry Peter[10], Peter[9], Jacob[8], John[7], Anna Weber[6] Newcomer, Elizabeth[5] Weber, Henry[4], Johann Anton[3], Heinrich[2], George[1]) was born September 06, 1900, and died July 13, 1968. He married **Mabel Corinne Appler**. She was born May 14, 1904, and died December 31, 1987.

Children of Paul Hershey and Mabel Appler are:
+ 731 i. Richard Henry[12] Hershey, born January 10, 1928.
+ 732 ii. Paul Kenneth Hershey, born October 14, 1929.
   733 iii. John Alan Hershey, born June 30, 1931; died September 22, 1958.

548. Esther Elizabeth[11] Hershey (Martin Eby[10], Peter[9], Jacob[8], John[7], Anna Weber[6] Newcomer, Elizabeth[5] Weber, Henry[4], Johann Anton[3], Heinrich[2], George[1]) was born May 27, 1905. She married **William Ralph Pennock**. He was born July 18, 1904, and died March 13, 1984.

Children of Esther Hershey and William Pennock are:
   734 i. Private[12] Pennock.
+ 735 ii. Private Pennock.
+ 736 iii. Betty Louise Pennock, born October 18, 1929.

549. Miriam Clara[11] Hershey (Martin Eby[10], Peter[9], Jacob[8], John[7], Anna Weber[6] Newcomer, Elizabeth[5] Weber, Henry[4], Johann Anton[3], Heinrich[2], George[1]) was born February 06, 1909, and died June 27, 1998. She married **Donald Fink Rodgers**. He was born May 27, 1905, and died October 24, 1966.

Child of Miriam Hershey and Donald Rodgers is:
+ 737 i. Private[12] Rodgers.

550. Elsie D.[11] Hershey (Silas N.[10], Peter[9], Jacob[8], John[7], Anna Weber[6] Newcomer, Elizabeth[5] Weber, Henry[4], Johann Anton[3], Heinrich[2], George[1]) was born December 24, 1905, and died July 31, 1987. She married **Miles Eby Harsh**. He was born February 26, 1893.

Child of Elsie Hershey and Miles Harsh is:
   738 i. Private[12] Harsh.

551. Frances[11] Hershey (Silas N.[10], Peter[9], Jacob[8], John[7], Anna Weber[6] Newcomer, Elizabeth[5] Weber, Henry[4], Johann Anton[3], Heinrich[2], George[1]) was born August 30, 1907. She married **Clarence William Stambaugh**. He was born March 01, 1910.

Child of Frances Hershey and Clarence Stambaugh is:
   739 i. Private[12] Stambaugh. She married John Harold Retallack; born November 24, 1928.

552. Lester D.[11] **Hershey** (Silas N.[10], Peter[9], Jacob[8], John[7], Anna Weber[6] Newcomer, Elizabeth[5] Weber, Henry[4], Johann Anton[3], Heinrich[2], George[1]) was born February 22, 1910. He married **Mary R. Groff**. She was born March 05, 1924.

Children of Lester Hershey and Mary Groff are:
    740   i.   Private[12] Hershey.
+   741   ii.   Private Hershey.

553. Barbara Elizabeth[11] **Hershey** (Silas N.[10], Peter[9], Jacob[8], John[7], Anna Weber[6] Newcomer, Elizabeth[5] Weber, Henry[4], Johann Anton[3], Heinrich[2], George[1]) was born March 24, 1912. She married **Elmer Denlinger Zimmerman**. He was born April 18, 1912.

Children of Barbara Hershey and Elmer Zimmerman are:
+   742   i.   Private[12] Zimmerman.
+   743   ii.   Private Zimmerman.
+   744   iii. Private Zimmerman.

554. Willis Daniel[11] **Hershey** (Silas N.[10], Peter[9], Jacob[8], John[7], Anna Weber[6] Newcomer, Elizabeth[5] Weber, Henry[4], Johann Anton[3], Heinrich[2], George[1]) was born June 26, 1916, and died July 19, 1994. He married **Ella Margaret Newswanger**. She was born October 30, 1918.

Children of Willis Hershey and Ella Newswanger are:
+   745   i.   Private[12] Hershey.
+   746   ii.   Private Hershey.
+   747   iii. Private Hershey.
+   748   iv. Private Hershey.
+   749   v.   Private Hershey.
+   750   vi. Jay Paul Hershey, born April 27, 1941; died November 02, 1996.

555. Reba L.[11] **Hershey** (Silas N.[10], Peter[9], Jacob[8], John[7], Anna Weber[6] Newcomer, Elizabeth[5] Weber, Henry[4], Johann Anton[3], Heinrich[2], George[1]) was born July 09, 1922. She married **Chester B. Nolt**. He was born September 29, 1919.

Children of Reba Hershey and Chester Nolt are:
+   751   i.   Private[12] Nolt.
+   752   ii.   Private Nolt.
    753   iii. Private Nolt.

556. Doris Mae[11] **Hershey** (Silas N.[10], Peter[9], Jacob[8], John[7], Anna Weber[6] Newcomer, Elizabeth[5] Weber, Henry[4], Johann Anton[3], Heinrich[2], George[1]) was born May 11, 1925. She married **(1) Benjamin Franklin Kauffman**. He was born December 15, 1913. She married **(2) Robert Warren Lowry**. He was born March 17, 1920.

Children of Doris Hershey and Benjamin Kauffman are:
+   754   i.   Private[12] Kauffman.
+   755   ii.   Private Kauffman.

Child of Doris Hershey and Robert Lowry is:
+   756   i.   Private[12] Lowry.

562. Helen Virginia[11] **Bitzer** (Annie[10] Hershey, Elias H[9], Nancy[8], Christian[7], Anna Weber[6] Newcomer, Elizabeth[5] Weber, Henry[4], Johann Anton[3], Heinrich[2], George[1]) was born February 21, 1891. She married **Edward W Sigler**. He was born July 15, 1885.

Child of Helen Bitzer and Edward Sigler is:
    757   i.   Anna Elizabeth[12] Sigler, born February 15, 1922.

566. Maria Elizabeth[11] **Hershey** (Ezra Frantz[10], Elias H[9], Nancy[8], Christian[7], Anna Weber[6] Newcomer, Elizabeth[5] Weber, Henry[4], Johann Anton[3], Heinrich[2], George[1]) was born June 05, 1913. She married **Walter Lutz**.

Child of Maria Hershey and Walter Lutz is:
    758   i.   James Hershey[12] Lutz, born Abt. 1940.

569. Melvin E[11] **Burkholder** (Abraham H[10], Susan[9] Hershey, Abraham[8], Christian[7], Anna Weber[6] Newcomer, Elizabeth[5] Weber, Henry[4], Johann Anton[3], Heinrich[2], George[1]) was born January 1909, and died 1971. He married **Marcella Wealand**. She was born January 1910, and died June 1991.

Child of Melvin Burkholder and Marcella Wealand is:
+ 759   i.   Robert Melvin[12] Burkholder, born March 03, 1935.

576. Martha Anna[11] **Livengood** (Gertrude[10] Hertzler, Michael S.[9], Abraham[8], John[7], Maria[6] Mumma, Beverly[5] Weber, Henry[4], Johann Anton[3], Heinrich[2], George[1]) was born October 20, 1909 in Mechanics Grove, Lanc Co, PA. She married **(1) Christian Musser Musser** February 12, 1932. He was born September 01, 1908 in West Hempfield Twp, Lanc Co, PA, and died August 28, 1978 in Lancaster, PA. She married **(2) Clarence Auker** January 25, 1986.

Children of Martha Livengood and Christian Musser are:
+ 760   i.   Mary Naomi[12] Musser, born April 21, 1934 in East Hempfield Twp, Lanc Co, PA.
   761   ii.   Mildred Lois Musser, born January 11, 1938 in East Hempfield Twp, Lanc Co, PA; died November 06, 1999 in Lancaster, Lancaster Co., PA.

583. John Landis[11] **Weaver** (John Hollinger[10], Christian G.[9], Gideon[8] Weber, Christian[7], Samuel[6], Christian[5], Henry[4], Johann Anton[3], Heinrich[2], George[1]) was born September 04, 1909 in Earl Twp, Lanc Co, PA, and died April 30, 1991 in Akron, Lancaster Co, PA. He married **Ada Sweigart Horst** January 07, 1932, daughter of Reuben Horst and Frances Sweigart. She was born May 30, 1911 in West Earl Twp, Lanc Co, PA, and died July 03, 1979 in Akron, Lancaster Co, PA.

Children are listed above under (507) Ada Sweigart Horst.

585. Paul Steffy[11] **Horst** (Elam Sweigart[10], Reuben Weaver[9], Jacob M.[8], Barbara Weber[7] Musser, Esther[6] Weber, Christian[5], Henry[4], Johann Anton[3], Heinrich[2], George[1]) was born July 26, 1914. He married **Sylvia Kauffman**. She was born December 10, 1919.

Children of Paul Horst and Sylvia Kauffman are:
+ 762   i.   Cedric Linn[12] Horst, born March 13, 1942.
   763   ii.   Joan Elaine Horst, born July 27, 1943.
+ 764   iii.   Joann Louise Horst, born July 27, 1943.
+ 765   iv.   Paul Gary Horst, born February 08, 1950.

586. William Prichard[11] **Horst** (Elam Sweigart[10], Reuben Weaver[9], Jacob M.[8], Barbara Weber[7] Musser, Esther[6] Weber, Christian[5], Henry[4], Johann Anton[3], Heinrich[2], George[1]) was born October 03, 1917. He married **Emma Zimmerman Weber** February 06, 1937. She was born June 12, 1916.

Children of William Horst and Emma Weber are:
   766   i.   James Richard[12] Horst, born October 08, 1942.
+ 767   ii.   Mary Louise Horst, born January 27, 1944.
+ 768   iii.   Mark William Horst, born November 08, 1948.

587. Erma Steffy[11] **Horst** (Elam Sweigart[10], Reuben Weaver[9], Jacob M.[8], Barbara Weber[7] Musser, Esther[6] Weber, Christian[5], Henry[4], Johann Anton[3], Heinrich[2], George[1]) was born April 25, 1924. She married **Luke Carvell** February 09, 1946. He was born April 02, 1926.

Children of Erma Horst and Luke Carvell are:
+ 769   i.   Vici Mae[12] Carvell, born March 24, 1948.
+ 770   ii.   Audrey Nadine Carvell, born May 07, 1949.
   771   iii.   Glee Eileen Carvell, born July 29, 1952. She married C. William Usmar March 26, 1977; born September 15, 1934.

588. Gordon Steffy[11] **Horst** (Elam Sweigart[10], Reuben Weaver[9], Jacob M.[8], Barbara Weber[7] Musser, Esther[6] Weber, Christian[5], Henry[4], Johann Anton[3], Heinrich[2], George[1]) was born March 30, 1929. He married **(1) Miriam Galebach** 1947. He married **(2) Barbara Dyer** 1956. He married **(3) Evelyn Mae Neidermyer Shaub** July 17, 1971.

Children of Gordon Horst and Barbara Dyer are:
   772   i.   Diane L.[12] Horst, born October 09, 1956. She married Scott Lee Bachman.
   773   ii.   Randy Paul Horst, born October 07, 1957.
   774   iii.   Rodney William Horst, born February 23, 1959.

775   iv.   Ronald Gregory Horst, born January 20, 1960.

620. Jay Donald[11] Weaver (John Landis[11], John Hollinger[10], Christian G.[9], Gideon[8] Weber, Christian[7], Samuel[6], Christian[5], Henry[4], Johann Anton[3], Heinrich[2], George[1]) was born April 20, 1933 in Ephrata Twp, Lanc Co, PA. He married **Mary Naomi Musser** July 16, 1955 in East Petersburg, PA, daughter of Christian Musser and Martha Livengood. She was born April 21, 1934 in East Hempfield Twp, Lanc Co, PA.

Children of Jay Weaver and Mary Musser are:
- 776   i.   Ellen Sue[12] Weaver, born December 04, 1956 in Reading, Berks Co, PA.
- + 777   ii.   James Edward Weaver, born November 10, 1960 in Lancaster, PA.

621. Arvilla[11] Weaver (John Landis[11], John Hollinger[10], Christian G.[9], Gideon[8] Weber, Christian[7], Samuel[6], Christian[5], Henry[4], Johann Anton[3], Heinrich[2], George[1]) was born July 21, 1934 in Ephrata Twp, Lanc Co, PA. She married **Robert T. Langsdale** March 02, 1958 in Kalamazoo, MI. He was born April 02, 1930 in Pittsburgh, PA.

Children of Arvilla Weaver and Robert Langsdale are:
- + 778   i.   Rae Elizabeth[12] Langsdale, born December 23, 1958 in Ephrata, PA.
- 779   ii.   Edward Jay Langsdale, born June 29, 1960 in Buffalo, NY.
- + 780   iii.   Robert John Langsdale, born September 05, 1965.

622. Donna Lou[11] Weaver (John Landis[11], John Hollinger[10], Christian G.[9], Gideon[8] Weber, Christian[7], Samuel[6], Christian[5], Henry[4], Johann Anton[3], Heinrich[2], George[1]) was born July 11, 1942 in Akron, Lancaster Co, PA. She married **(1) Jerry Foster**. He was born October 25, 1942 in Hartford, CT. She married **(2) David Arthur Bucove** November 05, 1960 in Brownstown, Lancaster Co., PA. He was born January 15, 1941.

Children of Donna Weaver and David Bucove are:
- 781   i.   Andre Maurice[12] Bucove, born August 15, 1961.
- + 782   ii.   Rachel Naomi Bucove, born July 13, 1971.

623. John Eric[11] Weaver (John Landis[11], John Hollinger[10], Christian G.[9], Gideon[8] Weber, Christian[7], Samuel[6], Christian[5], Henry[4], Johann Anton[3], Heinrich[2], George[1]) was born February 11, 1945 in Ephrata, PA. He married **Sandra M. Fritz** October 09, 1965 in Akron, Lancaster Co, PA. She was born December 09, 1944.

Children of John Weaver and Sandra Fritz are:
- + 783   i.   John Michael[12] Weaver, born June 19, 1968 in Ephrata, Lancaster Co., PA.
- 784   ii.   Lisa Rene Weaver, born November 28, 1970.

625. Ronald Lee[11] Weaver (John Landis[11], John Hollinger[10], Christian G.[9], Gideon[8] Weber, Christian[7], Samuel[6], Christian[5], Henry[4], Johann Anton[3], Heinrich[2], George[1]) was born August 16, 1950 in Ephrata, PA. He married **Carolyn Jean Weaver** October 21, 1972. She was born December 21, 1950.

Children of Ronald Weaver and Carolyn Weaver are:
- 785   i.   John Matthew[12] Weaver, born November 29, 1974 in Ephrata, Lancaster Co., PA. He married Krista J. Weber; born March 02, 1974 in Ephrata, Lancaster Co., PA.
- 786   ii.   Jennifer Lynn Weaver, born December 14, 1977 in Ephrata, Lancaster Co., PA. She married Corby M. Burkholder May 16, 1998 in Neffsville Mennonite Church, Manheim Twp., Lancaster Co., PA; born November 09, 1977 in Lancaster, Lancaster Co., PA.
- 787   iii.   Andrew S. Weaver, born July 20, 1979 in Ephrata, Lancaster Co., PA.

Generation No. 12

638. Willis Eby[12] Fox (Ella Barbara[11] Eby, Sarah Lucinda[10] Hershey, Peter[9], Jacob[8], John[7], Anna Weber[6] Newcomer, Elizabeth[5] Weber, Henry[4], Johann Anton[3], Heinrich[2], George[1]) was born May 17, 1907. He married **Vera Weaver Wise**. She was born April 07, 1916.

Children of Willis Fox and Vera Wise are:
- 788   i.   Private[13] Fox. She married Private Hartranft.
- + 789   ii.   Private Fox.
- + 790   iii.   Private Fox.
- + 791   iv.   Private Fox.

	792	v.	Private Fox.
	793	vi.	Private Fox.
+	794	vii.	Private Fox.
	795	viii.	Alta Mae Fox, born September 20, 1959; died September 20, 1959.

639. Henry Peter[12] **Fox** (Ella Barbara[11] Eby, Sarah Lucinda[10] Hershey, Peter[9], Jacob[8], John[7], Anna Weber[6] Newcomer, Elizabeth[5] Weber, Henry[4], Johann Anton[3], Heinrich[2], George[1]) was born September 16, 1909. He married **Ellen Mary Martin**. She was born January 26, 1911.

Children of Henry Fox and Ellen Martin are:

+	796	i.	Private[13] Fox.
	797	ii.	Private Fox. She married Private Gaffney.
+	798	iii.	Private Fox.
+	799	iv.	Private Fox.
	800	v.	Private Fox. She married Private Fellabaum.
+	801	vi.	Private Fox.
	802	vii.	Private Fox.
+	803	viii.	Private Fox.
+	804	ix.	Private Fox.
+	805	x.	Private Fox.
+	806	xi.	Private Fox.

640. Sarah Lucinda[12] **Fox** (Ella Barbara[11] Eby, Sarah Lucinda[10] Hershey, Peter[9], Jacob[8], John[7], Anna Weber[6] Newcomer, Elizabeth[5] Weber, Henry[4], Johann Anton[3], Heinrich[2], George[1]) was born July 06, 1911, and died October 19, 1971. She married **Noah Hoover Zimmerman**. He was born October 13, 1907.

Children of Sarah Fox and Noah Zimmerman are:

+	807	i.	Private[13] Zimmerman.
+	808	ii.	Private Zimmerman.
+	809	iii.	Private Zimmerman.
+	810	iv.	Private Zimmerman.

643. Daniel Hershey[12] **Fox** (Ella Barbara[11] Eby, Sarah Lucinda[10] Hershey, Peter[9], Jacob[8], John[7], Anna Weber[6] Newcomer, Elizabeth[5] Weber, Henry[4], Johann Anton[3], Heinrich[2], George[1]) was born August 19, 1917, and died June 10, 1986. He married **Ruth Esther Winey**. She was born May 12, 1918.

Children of Daniel Fox and Ruth Winey are:

+	811	i.	Private[13] Fox.
+	812	ii.	Private Fox.
+	813	iii.	Private Fox.

646. Ivan Martin[12] **Fox** (Ella Barbara[11] Eby, Sarah Lucinda[10] Hershey, Peter[9], Jacob[8], John[7], Anna Weber[6] Newcomer, Elizabeth[5] Weber, Henry[4], Johann Anton[3], Heinrich[2], George[1]) was born October 23, 1925, and died February 13, 1987. He married **Private Bollinger**.

Children of Ivan Fox and Private Bollinger are:

	814	i.	Private[13] Fox.
+	815	ii.	Private Fox.
+	816	iii.	Private Fox.

648. Franklin W.[12] **Eby** (Peter Hershey[11], Sarah Lucinda[10] Hershey, Peter[9], Jacob[8], John[7], Anna Weber[6] Newcomer, Elizabeth[5] Weber, Henry[4], Johann Anton[3], Heinrich[2], George[1]) was born January 31, 1915, and died November 14, 1968. He married **Mary Martin**. She was born March 26, 1914.

Child of Franklin Eby and Mary Martin is:

+	817	i.	Private[13] Eby.

649. Susan W.[12] **Eby** (Peter Hershey[11], Sarah Lucinda[10] Hershey, Peter[9], Jacob[8], John[7], Anna Weber[6] Newcomer, Elizabeth[5] Weber, Henry[4], Johann Anton[3], Heinrich[2], George[1]) was born November 16, 1916. She married **Aaron K. Martin**. He was born February 24, 1916.

Children of Susan Eby and Aaron Martin are:
  818   i.   Private[13] Martin.
+ 819   ii.   Private Martin.
+ 820   iii. Private Martin.
+ 821   iv.   Private Martin.
+ 822   v.   Private Martin.
+ 823   vi.   Private Martin.
+ 824   vii. Private Martin.
+ 825   viii. Private Martin.
+ 826   ix.   John E. Martin, born May 25, 1949; died February 11, 1984.

650. Emma Mae[12] Eby (Peter Hershey[11], Sarah Lucinda[10] Hershey, Peter[9], Jacob[8], John[7], Anna Weber[6] Newcomer, Elizabeth[5] Weber, Henry[4], Johann Anton[3], Heinrich[2], George[1]) was born October 27, 1918. She married **Carmi R. Stauffer**. He was born November 20, 1913.

Children of Emma Eby and Carmi Stauffer are:
+ 827   i.   Private[13] Stauffer.
+ 828   ii.   Private Stauffer.
+ 829   iii. Private Stauffer.
+ 830   iv.   Private Stauffer.

652. Rhoda S.[12] Eby (Enos Jacob[11], Sarah Lucinda[10] Hershey, Peter[9], Jacob[8], John[7], Anna Weber[6] Newcomer, Elizabeth[5] Weber, Henry[4], Johann Anton[3], Heinrich[2], George[1]) was born August 22, 1918. She married **Daniel B. Stauffer**. He was born September 28, 1920.

Children of Rhoda Eby and Daniel Stauffer are:
  831   i.   Private[13] Stauffer.
+ 832   ii.   Private Stauffer.
+ 833   iii. Private Stauffer.
  834   iv.   Private Stauffer.
  835   v.   Private Stauffer.
  836   vi.   Private Stauffer.
  837   vii. Private Stauffer.
  838   viii. Joe E. Stauffer, born November 14, 1950; died June 04, 1979.

653. Henry S.[12] Eby (Enos Jacob[11], Sarah Lucinda[10] Hershey, Peter[9], Jacob[8], John[7], Anna Weber[6] Newcomer, Elizabeth[5] Weber, Henry[4], Johann Anton[3], Heinrich[2], George[1]) was born July 21, 1920. He married **Emma E. Zeiset**. She was born November 03, 1927.

Children of Henry Eby and Emma Zeiset are:
+ 839   i.   Private[13] Eby.
+ 840   ii.   Private Eby.
+ 841   iii. Private Eby.
+ 842   iv.   Private Eby.
+ 843   v.   Private Eby.
+ 844   vi.   Private Eby.
  845   vii. Private Eby.
  846   viii. James Z. Eby, born August 31, 1960; died February 19, 1961.

654. Ezra S.[12] Eby (Enos Jacob[11], Sarah Lucinda[10] Hershey, Peter[9], Jacob[8], John[7], Anna Weber[6] Newcomer, Elizabeth[5] Weber, Henry[4], Johann Anton[3], Heinrich[2], George[1]) was born October 31, 1922. He married **Ada Zimmerman**. She was born February 02, 1926.

Children of Ezra Eby and Ada Zimmerman are:
  847   i.   Private[13] Eby.
+ 848   ii.   Private Eby.
  849   iii. Private Eby.
+ 850   iv.   Private Eby.
+ 851   v.   Private Eby.
  852   vi.   Private Eby.
+ 853   vii. Private Eby.
+ 854   viii. Private Eby.

655. Eli S.[12] Eby (Enos Jacob[11], Sarah Lucinda[10] Hershey, Peter[9], Jacob[8], John[7], Anna Weber[6] Newcomer, Elizabeth[5] Weber, Henry[4], Johann Anton[3], Heinrich[2], George[1]) was born March 19, 1925, and died December 12, 1985. He married **Private Zimmerman**.

Children of Eli Eby and Private Zimmerman are:
- 855   i.   Private[13] Eby.
- 856   ii.   Private Eby.
- 857   iii.   Private Eby.
- + 858   iv.   Private Eby.
- + 859   v.   Private Eby.
- + 860   vi.   Private Eby.

656. Lydia S.[12] Eby (Enos Jacob[11], Sarah Lucinda[10] Hershey, Peter[9], Jacob[8], John[7], Anna Weber[6] Newcomer, Elizabeth[5] Weber, Henry[4], Johann Anton[3], Heinrich[2], George[1]) was born March 31, 1927. She married **Private Bauman**.

Child of Lydia Eby and Private Bauman is:
- 861   i.   Private[13] Bauman. She married Private Gehman.

660. Private[12] Gehman (Sarah Lucinda[11] Eby, Sarah Lucinda[10] Hershey, Peter[9], Jacob[8], John[7], Anna Weber[6] Newcomer, Elizabeth[5] Weber, Henry[4], Johann Anton[3], Heinrich[2], George[1]) He married **Private Barnhill**.

Children of Private Gehman and Private Barnhill are:
- 862   i.   Private[13] Gehman.
- 863   ii.   Private Gehman.
- + 864   iii.   Private Gehman.
- + 865   iv.   Private Gehman.
- + 866   v.   Private Gehman.

661. Private[12] Gehman (Sarah Lucinda[11] Eby, Sarah Lucinda[10] Hershey, Peter[9], Jacob[8], John[7], Anna Weber[6] Newcomer, Elizabeth[5] Weber, Henry[4], Johann Anton[3], Heinrich[2], George[1]) He married **Mildrfed K. Ebersole**. She was born July 15, 1929.

Children of Private Gehman and Mildrfed Ebersole are:
- + 867   i.   Private[13] Gehman.
- + 868   ii.   Private Gehman.
- 869   iii.   Private Gehman. She married Private Brackbill.
- + 870   iv.   Private Gehman.
- 871   v.   Private Gehman.

662. Arthur E.[12] Gehman (Sarah Lucinda[11] Eby, Sarah Lucinda[10] Hershey, Peter[9], Jacob[8], John[7], Anna Weber[6] Newcomer, Elizabeth[5] Weber, Henry[4], Johann Anton[3], Heinrich[2], George[1]) was born January 19, 1920. He married **Martha Helen Shafer**. She was born February 13, 1919, and died April 21, 1990.

Children of Arthur Gehman and Martha Shafer are:
- + 872   i.   Private[13] Gehman.
- + 873   ii.   Private Gehman.
- + 874   iii.   Private Gehman.

663. John E.[12] Gehman (Sarah Lucinda[11] Eby, Sarah Lucinda[10] Hershey, Peter[9], Jacob[8], John[7], Anna Weber[6] Newcomer, Elizabeth[5] Weber, Henry[4], Johann Anton[3], Heinrich[2], George[1]) was born October 18, 1921. He married **Anna Mae Mull**. She was born July 26, 1920.

Children of John Gehman and Anna Mull are:
- 875   i.   Private[13] Gehman.
- + 876   ii.   Private Gehman.
- 877   iii.   Private Gehman.
- + 878   iv.   Private Gehman.
- + 879   v.   Private Gehman.
- 880   vi.   Private Gehman. She married Private Graybill.
- + 881   vii.   Private Gehman.

664. Edith Elizabeth[12] Gehman (Sarah Lucinda[11] Eby, Sarah Lucinda[10] Hershey, Peter[9], Jacob[8], John[7], Anna Weber[6] Newcomer,

Elizabeth[5] Weber, Henry[4], Johann Anton[3], Heinrich[2], George[1]) was born March 31, 1923. She married **Norman Myer Groff**. He was born March 24, 1924.

Children of Edith Gehman and Norman Groff are:
+ 882   i.   Private[13] Groff.
+ 883   ii.   Private Groff.
+ 884   iii.   Private Groff.
+ 885   iv.   Private Groff.
+ 886   v.   Private Groff.
+ 887   vi.   Private Groff.

665. Lucy E.[12] Gehman (Sarah Lucinda[11] Eby, Sarah Lucinda[10] Hershey, Peter[9], Jacob[8], John[7], Anna Weber[6] Newcomer, Elizabeth[5] Weber, Henry[4], Johann Anton[3], Heinrich[2], George[1]) was born November 19, 1924. She married **John Henry Rudy**. He was born March 06, 1924.

Children of Lucy Gehman and John Rudy are:
   888   i.   Private[13] Rudy.
+ 889   ii.   Private Rudy.
   890   iii.   Private Rudy. He married Private Kiriyama.
   891   iv.   Marjorie Elaine Rudy, born June 16, 1948; died July 19, 1948.

667. Harry Jacob[12] Gehman (Sarah Lucinda[11] Eby, Sarah Lucinda[10] Hershey, Peter[9], Jacob[8], John[7], Anna Weber[6] Newcomer, Elizabeth[5] Weber, Henry[4], Johann Anton[3], Heinrich[2], George[1]) was born November 25, 1929. He married **Private Graybill**.

Children of Harry Gehman and Private Graybill are:
   892   i.   Private[13] Gehman.
   893   ii.   Private Gehman.
+ 894   iii.   Private Gehman.
+ 895   iv.   Private Gehman.
+ 896   v.   Private Gehman.
+ 897   vi.   Private Gehman.
+ 898   vii.   Private Gehman.

668. Private[12] Eby (Henry Musser[11], Sarah Lucinda[10] Hershey, Peter[9], Jacob[8], John[7], Anna Weber[6] Newcomer, Elizabeth[5] Weber, Henry[4], Johann Anton[3], Heinrich[2], George[1]) He married **Private Martin**.

Children of Private Eby and Private Martin are:
   899   i.   Private[13] Eby.
   900   ii.   Private Eby.
   901   iii.   Private Eby.
   902   iv.   Private Eby.

669. Private[12] Eby (Henry Musser[11], Sarah Lucinda[10] Hershey, Peter[9], Jacob[8], John[7], Anna Weber[6] Newcomer, Elizabeth[5] Weber, Henry[4], Johann Anton[3], Heinrich[2], George[1]) She married **Private Penner**.

Children of Private Eby and Private Penner are:
   903   i.   Private[13] Penner.
   904   ii.   Private Penner.

670. Private[12] Eby (Henry Musser[11], Sarah Lucinda[10] Hershey, Peter[9], Jacob[8], John[7], Anna Weber[6] Newcomer, Elizabeth[5] Weber, Henry[4], Johann Anton[3], Heinrich[2], George[1]) She married **Private Hennelly**.

Child of Private Eby and Private Hennelly is:
   905   i.   Private[13] Hennelly.

671. Private[12] Eby (Henry Musser[11], Sarah Lucinda[10] Hershey, Peter[9], Jacob[8], John[7], Anna Weber[6] Newcomer, Elizabeth[5] Weber, Henry[4], Johann Anton[3], Heinrich[2], George[1]) He married **Private Beachy**.

Children of Private Eby and Private Beachy are:
   906   i.   Private[13] Eby.

907 ii. Private Eby.
908 iii. Private Eby.

672. **Private[12] Eby** (Henry Musser[11], Sarah Lucinda[10] Hershey, Peter[9], Jacob[8], John[7], Anna Weber[6] Newcomer, Elizabeth[5] Weber, Henry[4], Johann Anton[3], Heinrich[2], George[1]) He married **Private Stephens**.

Children of Private Eby and Private Stephens are:
909 i. Private[13] Eby.
910 ii. Private Reeves.

673. **Martin Z.[12] Eby** (Henry Musser[11], Sarah Lucinda[10] Hershey, Peter[9], Jacob[8], John[7], Anna Weber[6] Newcomer, Elizabeth[5] Weber, Henry[4], Johann Anton[3], Heinrich[2], George[1]) was born December 25, 1921. He married **Lydia Pearl Heishman**. She was born July 07, 1921.

Children of Martin Eby and Lydia Heishman are:
+ 911 i. Private[13] Eby.
912 ii. Private Eby. He married Private Coakley.

674. **Ethel Z.[12] Eby** (Henry Musser[11], Sarah Lucinda[10] Hershey, Peter[9], Jacob[8], John[7], Anna Weber[6] Newcomer, Elizabeth[5] Weber, Henry[4], Johann Anton[3], Heinrich[2], George[1]) was born November 25, 1923. She married **Edward J. Miller**. He was born November 25, 1921.

Children of Ethel Eby and Edward Miller are:
913 i. Private[13] Miller.
+ 914 ii. Private Miller.
+ 915 iii. Private Miller.
916 iv. Private Miller.

676. **Roy Z.[12] Eby** (Henry Musser[11], Sarah Lucinda[10] Hershey, Peter[9], Jacob[8], John[7], Anna Weber[6] Newcomer, Elizabeth[5] Weber, Henry[4], Johann Anton[3], Heinrich[2], George[1]) was born September 20, 1927. He married **Private Schrock**.

Children of Roy Eby and Private Schrock are:
917 i. Private[13] Eby.
918 ii. Private Eby.
919 iii. Private Eby.
920 iv. Private Eby.

677. **Mary Z.[12] Eby** (Henry Musser[11], Sarah Lucinda[10] Hershey, Peter[9], Jacob[8], John[7], Anna Weber[6] Newcomer, Elizabeth[5] Weber, Henry[4], Johann Anton[3], Heinrich[2], George[1]) was born June 11, 1929. She married **Henry D. Weaver**. He was born May 05, 1928.

Children of Mary Eby and Henry Weaver are:
921 i. Private[13] Weaver.
922 ii. Private Weaver. She married Private Miller.
+ 923 iii. Private Weaver.
+ 924 iv. Private Weaver.

678. **Private[12] Martin** (Anna Martha[11] Eby, Sarah Lucinda[10] Hershey, Peter[9], Jacob[8], John[7], Anna Weber[6] Newcomer, Elizabeth[5] Weber, Henry[4], Johann Anton[3], Heinrich[2], George[1]) He married **Private Unruh**.

Children of Private Martin and Private Unruh are:
925 i. Private[13] Martin.
926 ii. Private Martin.
927 iii. Private Martin.

679. **Private[12] Martin** (Anna Martha[11] Eby, Sarah Lucinda[10] Hershey, Peter[9], Jacob[8], John[7], Anna Weber[6] Newcomer, Elizabeth[5] Weber, Henry[4], Johann Anton[3], Heinrich[2], George[1]) She married **Private Zeiset**.

Child of Private Martin and Private Zeiset is:
+ 928 i. Private[13] Zeiset.

680. Clarence E.[12] **Martin** (Anna Martha[11] Eby, Sarah Lucinda[10] Hershey, Peter[9], Jacob[8], John[7], Anna Weber[6] Newcomer, Elizabeth[5] Weber, Henry[4], Johann Anton[3], Heinrich[2], George[1]) was born November 13, 1919. He married **Lydia Weaver**. She was born May 19, 1920.

Children of Clarence Martin and Lydia Weaver are:
      929   i.   Private[13] Martin.
      930   ii. Private Martin.
+   931   iii. Private Martin.
+   932   iv. Private Martin.
+   933   v.   Private Martin.
+   934   vi. Private Martin.
+   935   vii. Private Martin.

681. Mary E.[12] **Martin** (Anna Martha[11] Eby, Sarah Lucinda[10] Hershey, Peter[9], Jacob[8], John[7], Anna Weber[6] Newcomer, Elizabeth[5] Weber, Henry[4], Johann Anton[3], Heinrich[2], George[1]) was born December 22, 1921. She married **Clarence H. Martin**. He was born December 15, 1919.

Children of Mary Martin and Clarence Martin are:
      936   i.   Private[13] Martin. He married Private Freed.
+   937   ii. Private Martin.

682. Paul E.[12] **Martin** (Anna Martha[11] Eby, Sarah Lucinda[10] Hershey, Peter[9], Jacob[8], John[7], Anna Weber[6] Newcomer, Elizabeth[5] Weber, Henry[4], Johann Anton[3], Heinrich[2], George[1]) was born September 29, 1923. He married **Private High**.

Children of Paul Martin and Private High are:
+   938   i.   Private[13] Martin.
+   939   ii. Private Martin.
+   940   iii. Private Martin.

683. Earl E.[12] **Martin** (Anna Martha[11] Eby, Sarah Lucinda[10] Hershey, Peter[9], Jacob[8], John[7], Anna Weber[6] Newcomer, Elizabeth[5] Weber, Henry[4], Johann Anton[3], Heinrich[2], George[1]) was born November 28, 1926. He married **Private Petersheim**.

Children of Earl Martin and Private Petersheim are:
+   941   i.   Private[13] Martin.
+   942   ii. Private Martin.

684. Wilmer E.[12] **Martin** (Anna Martha[11] Eby, Sarah Lucinda[10] Hershey, Peter[9], Jacob[8], John[7], Anna Weber[6] Newcomer, Elizabeth[5] Weber, Henry[4], Johann Anton[3], Heinrich[2], George[1]) was born June 05, 1929. He married **Private Bollinger**.

Children of Wilmer Martin and Private Bollinger are:
      943   i.   Private[13] Martin.
      944   ii. Private Martin.

685. Private[12] **Eby** (Aaron Buckwalter[11], Sarah Lucinda[10] Hershey, Peter[9], Jacob[8], John[7], Anna Weber[6] Newcomer, Elizabeth[5] Weber, Henry[4], Johann Anton[3], Heinrich[2], George[1]) She married **Private Martin**.

Children of Private Eby and Private Martin are:
      945   i.   Private[13] Martin.
      946   ii. Thomas Dean Martin, born September 30, 1967; died December 28, 1983.

686. Private[12] **Eby** (Aaron Buckwalter[11], Sarah Lucinda[10] Hershey, Peter[9], Jacob[8], John[7], Anna Weber[6] Newcomer, Elizabeth[5] Weber, Henry[4], Johann Anton[3], Heinrich[2], George[1]) He married **Private Brubaker**.

Children of Private Eby and Private Brubaker are:
      947   i.   Private[13] Eby.
      948   ii. Private Eby.

687. Private[12] Eby (Aaron Buckwalter[11], Sarah Lucinda[10] Hershey, Peter[9], Jacob[8], John[7], Anna Weber[6] Newcomer, Elizabeth[5] Weber, Henry[4], Johann Anton[3], Heinrich[2], George[1]) He married **Private Stoltzfus**.

Children of Private Eby and Private Stoltzfus are:
+ 949   i.   Private[13] Eby.
    950   ii.   Private Eby.
    951   iii.   Private Eby.
    952   iv.   Private Eby. She married Private Buckwalter.

688. Private[12] Eby (Aaron Buckwalter[11], Sarah Lucinda[10] Hershey, Peter[9], Jacob[8], John[7], Anna Weber[6] Newcomer, Elizabeth[5] Weber, Henry[4], Johann Anton[3], Heinrich[2], George[1]) He married **Private Lynch**.

Children of Private Eby and Private Lynch are:
    953   i.   Private[13] Eby.
    954   ii.   Private Eby.
    955   iii.   Private Eby. She married Private Breneman.
+ 956   iv.   Private Eby.
    957   v.   Eileen Marie Eby, born March 26, 1958; died October 07, 1967.

689. Richard S.[12] Eby (Aaron Buckwalter[11], Sarah Lucinda[10] Hershey, Peter[9], Jacob[8], John[7], Anna Weber[6] Newcomer, Elizabeth[5] Weber, Henry[4], Johann Anton[3], Heinrich[2], George[1]) was born October 08, 1928. He married **Private Buckwalter**.

Children of Richard Eby and Private Buckwalter are:
+ 958   i.   Private[13] Eby.
    959   ii.   Private Eby.
+ 960   iii.   Private Eby.
+ 961   iv.   Private Eby.
+ 962   v.   Private Eby.
+ 963   vi.   Private Eby.

690. Clyde S.[12] Eby (Aaron Buckwalter[11], Sarah Lucinda[10] Hershey, Peter[9], Jacob[8], John[7], Anna Weber[6] Newcomer, Elizabeth[5] Weber, Henry[4], Johann Anton[3], Heinrich[2], George[1]) was born November 29, 1937, and died October 08, 1974. He married **Private Nauman**.

Children of Clyde Eby and Private Nauman are:
    964   i.   Private[13] Eby.
    965   ii.   Private Eby.
    966   iii.   Private Eby.

691. Private[12] Eby (Menno Hershey[11], Sarah Lucinda[10] Hershey, Peter[9], Jacob[8], John[7], Anna Weber[6] Newcomer, Elizabeth[5] Weber, Henry[4], Johann Anton[3], Heinrich[2], George[1]) He married **Private Kuipers**.

Children of Private Eby and Private Kuipers are:
    967   i.   Private[13] Eby.
    968   ii.   Private Eby.
    969   iii.   Private Eby.

692. Private[12] Eby (Menno Hershey[11], Sarah Lucinda[10] Hershey, Peter[9], Jacob[8], John[7], Anna Weber[6] Newcomer, Elizabeth[5] Weber, Henry[4], Johann Anton[3], Heinrich[2], George[1]) She married **Private Baker**.

Children of Private Eby and Private Baker are:
    970   i.   Private[13] Baker.
    971   ii.   Private Baker.

693. Private[12] Eby (Menno Hershey[11], Sarah Lucinda[10] Hershey, Peter[9], Jacob[8], John[7], Anna Weber[6] Newcomer, Elizabeth[5] Weber, Henry[4], Johann Anton[3], Heinrich[2], George[1]) He married **Private Peters**.

Child of Private Eby and Private Peters is:
    972   i.   Private[13] Eby.

694. Private[12] Eby (Martin Christian[11], Sarah Lucinda[10] Hershey, Peter[9], Jacob[8], John[7], Anna Weber[6] Newcomer, Elizabeth[5] Weber, Henry[4], Johann Anton[3], Heinrich[2], George[1]) He married **Private Martin**.

Children of Private Eby and Private Martin are:
- 973   i.   Private[13] Eby.
- 974   ii.   Private Eby.

695. Private[12] Eby (Martin Christian[11], Sarah Lucinda[10] Hershey, Peter[9], Jacob[8], John[7], Anna Weber[6] Newcomer, Elizabeth[5] Weber, Henry[4], Johann Anton[3], Heinrich[2], George[1]) He married **Private Stoltzfus**.

Children of Private Eby and Private Stoltzfus are:
- 975   i.   Private[13] Eby.
- 976   ii.   Private Eby.

696. Private[12] Eby (Martin Christian[11], Sarah Lucinda[10] Hershey, Peter[9], Jacob[8], John[7], Anna Weber[6] Newcomer, Elizabeth[5] Weber, Henry[4], Johann Anton[3], Heinrich[2], George[1]) She married **Private Ebersole**.

Children of Private Eby and Private Ebersole are:
- 977   i.   Private[13] Ebersole.
- 978   ii.   Private Ebersole.

698. Private[12] Eby (Martin Christian[11], Sarah Lucinda[10] Hershey, Peter[9], Jacob[8], John[7], Anna Weber[6] Newcomer, Elizabeth[5] Weber, Henry[4], Johann Anton[3], Heinrich[2], George[1]) He married **Private Landis**.

Children of Private Eby and Private Landis are:
- 979   i.   Private[13] Eby.
- 980   ii.   Private Eby.
- 981   iii.   Private Eby.

699. Erma E.[12] Hershey (Galen Warren[11], Isaiah B.[10], Peter[9], Jacob[8], John[7], Anna Weber[6] Newcomer, Elizabeth[5] Weber, Henry[4], Johann Anton[3], Heinrich[2], George[1]) was born March 08, 1910. She married **Leo Trostle Crouthamel**. He was born June 22, 1909, and died September 28, 1989.

Children of Erma Hershey and Leo Crouthamel are:
- + 982   i.   Private[13] Crouthamel.
- + 983   ii.   Private Crouthamel.
- + 984   iii.   Private Crouthamel.

700. Galen Clair[12] Hershey (Galen Warren[11], Isaiah B.[10], Peter[9], Jacob[8], John[7], Anna Weber[6] Newcomer, Elizabeth[5] Weber, Henry[4], Johann Anton[3], Heinrich[2], George[1]) was born February 10, 1914, and died July 15, 1992. He married **Martha Louise Acker**. She was born October 25, 1920, and died 1973.

Children of Galen Hershey and Martha Acker are:
- + 985   i.   Private[13] Hershey.
- + 986   ii.   Private Hershey.

701. Private[12] Hershey (Henry Clay[11], Enos Jacob[10], Peter[9], Jacob[8], John[7], Anna Weber[6] Newcomer, Elizabeth[5] Weber, Henry[4], Johann Anton[3], Heinrich[2], George[1]) He married **Private Wenger**.

Children of Private Hershey and Private Wenger are:
- 987   i.   Private[13] Hershey.
- + 988   ii.   Private Hershey.
- 989   iii.   Private Hershey. He married Private Earhart.

702. Private[12] Hershey (Henry Clay[11], Enos Jacob[10], Peter[9], Jacob[8], John[7], Anna Weber[6] Newcomer, Elizabeth[5] Weber, Henry[4], Johann Anton[3], Heinrich[2], George[1]) He married **Private Alter**.

Children of Private Hershey and Private Alter are:

990	i.	Private[13] Hershey.
991	ii.	Private Hershey.
992	iii.	Private Hershey.
993	iv.	Private Hershey.

703. Private[12] Hershey (Henry Clay[11], Enos Jacob[10], Peter[9], Jacob[8], John[7], Anna Weber[6] Newcomer, Elizabeth[5] Weber, Henry[4], Johann Anton[3], Heinrich[2], George[1]) He married **Private Lefever**.

Children of Private Hershey and Private Lefever are:
+ 994   i. Private[13] Hershey.
+ 995   ii. Private Hershey.

704. Private[12] Hershey (Henry Clay[11], Enos Jacob[10], Peter[9], Jacob[8], John[7], Anna Weber[6] Newcomer, Elizabeth[5] Weber, Henry[4], Johann Anton[3], Heinrich[2], George[1]) She married **Private Damiani**.

Children of Private Hershey and Private Damiani are:
996   i. Private[13] Damiani.
997   ii. Private Damiani.

705. Hazel Pauline[12] Hershey (Henry Clay[11], Enos Jacob[10], Peter[9], Jacob[8], John[7], Anna Weber[6] Newcomer, Elizabeth[5] Weber, Henry[4], Johann Anton[3], Heinrich[2], George[1]) was born August 15, 1914, and died March 08, 1985. She married **Elmer Metzler**. He was born March 16, 1916.

Children of Hazel Hershey and Elmer Metzler are:
998   i.   Private[13] Metzler. She married Private Franklin.
+ 999   ii. Private Metzler.
1000   iii. Private Metzler. She married Private Markovich.

707. Ralph Glenn[12] Hershey (Henry Clay[11], Enos Jacob[10], Peter[9], Jacob[8], John[7], Anna Weber[6] Newcomer, Elizabeth[5] Weber, Henry[4], Johann Anton[3], Heinrich[2], George[1]) was born December 15, 1918, and died March 12, 1988. He married **Miriam Lengenecker**. She was born October 15, 1922.

Children of Ralph Hershey and Miriam Lengenecker are:
+ 1001   i.   Private[13] Hershey.
+ 1002   ii. Private Hershey.
+ 1003   iii. Private Hershey.

709. Gladys Edna[12] Hershey (Henry Clay[11], Enos Jacob[10], Peter[9], Jacob[8], John[7], Anna Weber[6] Newcomer, Elizabeth[5] Weber, Henry[4], Johann Anton[3], Heinrich[2], George[1]) was born August 08, 1927. She married **Eby Kreider**. He was born April 22, 1926.

Children of Gladys Hershey and Eby Kreider are:
+ 1004   i.   Private[13] Kreider.
1005   ii. Private Kreider. She married Private Sherid.
+ 1006   iii. Private Kreider.
+ 1007   iv. Private Kreider.
1008   v.   Unknown Kreider, born November 07, 1949; died November 07, 1949.

710. Clifford Eby[12] Hershey (Henry Clay[11], Enos Jacob[10], Peter[9], Jacob[8], John[7], Anna Weber[6] Newcomer, Elizabeth[5] Weber, Henry[4], Johann Anton[3], Heinrich[2], George[1]) was born November 17, 1928, and died February 06, 1969. He married **Private Feister**.

Children of Clifford Hershey and Private Feister are:
1009   i.   Private[13] Hershey.
1010   ii. Private Hershey.
1011   iii. Private Hershey.
+ 1012   iv. Private Hershey.
+ 1013   v.   Private Hershey.

711. Private[12] Hershey (Mark Eby[11], Enos Jacob[10], Peter[9], Jacob[8], John[7], Anna Weber[6] Newcomer, Elizabeth[5] Weber, Henry[4], Johann Anton[3], Heinrich[2], George[1]) He married **Private Lehigh**.

Children of Private Hershey and Private Lehigh are:
- 1014   i.   Private[13] Hershey.
- 1015   ii.   Private Hershey.

712. Private[12] Hershey (Mark Eby[11], Enos Jacob[10], Peter[9], Jacob[8], John[7], Anna Weber[6] Newcomer, Elizabeth[5] Weber, Henry[4], Johann Anton[3], Heinrich[2], George[1]) She married **Private Peachey**.

Children of Private Hershey and Private Peachey are:
- 1016   i.   Private[13] Peachey.
- 1017   ii.   Private Peachey.
- 1018   iii.   Private Peachey.
- 1019   iv.   Private Peachey.

713. Private[12] Hershey (Mark Eby[11], Enos Jacob[10], Peter[9], Jacob[8], John[7], Anna Weber[6] Newcomer, Elizabeth[5] Weber, Henry[4], Johann Anton[3], Heinrich[2], George[1]) She married **Private Lichty**.

Children of Private Hershey and Private Lichty are:
- 1020   i.   Private[13] Lichty.
- 1021   ii.   Private Lichty.
- 1022   iii.   Private Lichty.

714. Private[12] Hershey (Mark Eby[11], Enos Jacob[10], Peter[9], Jacob[8], John[7], Anna Weber[6] Newcomer, Elizabeth[5] Weber, Henry[4], Johann Anton[3], Heinrich[2], George[1]) She married **Private Martin**.

Children of Private Hershey and Private Martin are:
- 1023   i.   Private[13] Martin.
- 1024   ii.   Private Martin. She married Private Frey.
- 1025   iii.   Private Martin. He married Private Yoder.
- + 1026   iv.   Private Martin.

715. Private[12] Hershey (Mark Eby[11], Enos Jacob[10], Peter[9], Jacob[8], John[7], Anna Weber[6] Newcomer, Elizabeth[5] Weber, Henry[4], Johann Anton[3], Heinrich[2], George[1]) He married **Private Kauffman**.

Children of Private Hershey and Private Kauffman are:
- 1027   i.   Private[13] Hershey.
- 1028   ii.   Private Hershey.
- 1029   iii.   Private Hershey. He married Private Unknown.
- 1030   iv.   Private Hershey.
- 1031   v.   Private Hershey.

716. Private[12] Hershey (Mark Eby[11], Enos Jacob[10], Peter[9], Jacob[8], John[7], Anna Weber[6] Newcomer, Elizabeth[5] Weber, Henry[4], Johann Anton[3], Heinrich[2], George[1]) She married **Martin L. Bender**. He was born June 03, 1928.

Children of Private Hershey and Martin Bender are:
- 1032   i.   Private[13] Bender.
- 1033   ii.   Private Bender.
- 1034   iii.   Private Bender.
- 1035   iv.   Private Bender.
- + 1036   v.   Private Bender.

717. Private[12] Hershey (Mark Eby[11], Enos Jacob[10], Peter[9], Jacob[8], John[7], Anna Weber[6] Newcomer, Elizabeth[5] Weber, Henry[4], Johann Anton[3], Heinrich[2], George[1]) He married **Private Singer**.

Children of Private Hershey and Private Singer are:
- + 1037   i.   Private[13] Hershey.
- + 1038   ii.   Private Hershey.
- + 1039   iii.   Private Hershey.
- + 1040   iv.   Private Hershey.

719. Private[12] Hershey (David Warren[11], Enos Jacob[10], Peter[9], Jacob[8], John[7], Anna Weber[6] Newcomer, Elizabeth[5] Weber, Henry[4], Johann Anton[3], Heinrich[2], George[1]) She married **Private Herr**.

Children of Private Hershey and Private Herr are:
+   1041   i.   Private[13] Herr.
      1042   ii.   Private Herr.

720. Vincent Denlinger[12] Hershey (David Warren[11], Enos Jacob[10], Peter[9], Jacob[8], John[7], Anna Weber[6] Newcomer, Elizabeth[5] Weber, Henry[4], Johann Anton[3], Heinrich[2], George[1]) was born September 20, 1925. He married **Mary Ethel Brackbill**. She was born July 24, 1925.

Children of Vincent Hershey and Mary Brackbill are:
      1043   i.   Private[13] Hershey.
+   1044   ii.   Private Hershey.
      1045   iii.   Private Hershey.
+   1046   iv.   Private Hershey.
+   1047   v.   Private Hershey.

723. Private[12] Ranck (Mary Helen[11] Hershey, Enos Jacob[10], Peter[9], Jacob[8], John[7], Anna Weber[6] Newcomer, Elizabeth[5] Weber, Henry[4], Johann Anton[3], Heinrich[2], George[1]) He married **Private Wynia**.

Child of Private Ranck and Private Wynia is:
      1048   i.   Private[13] Ranck.

724. Lester Hershey[12] Ranck (Mary Helen[11] Hershey, Enos Jacob[10], Peter[9], Jacob[8], John[7], Anna Weber[6] Newcomer, Elizabeth[5] Weber, Henry[4], Johann Anton[3], Heinrich[2], George[1]) was born April 21, 1924. He married **Mary Root Todd**. She was born March 05, 1924.

Children of Lester Ranck and Mary Todd are:
      1049   i.   Private[13] Ranck. He married Private Groff.
+   1050   ii.   Private Ranck.
+   1051   iii.   Private Ranck.
      1052   iv.   Private Ranck.

725. Arthur Eby[12] Ranck (Mary Helen[11] Hershey, Enos Jacob[10], Peter[9], Jacob[8], John[7], Anna Weber[6] Newcomer, Elizabeth[5] Weber, Henry[4], Johann Anton[3], Heinrich[2], George[1]) was born September 06, 1925. He married **Phoebe Kennel**. She was born February 27, 1926.

Children of Arthur Ranck and Phoebe Kennel are:
      1053   i.   Private[13] Ranck.
+   1054   ii.   Private Ranck.
      1055   iii.   Private Ranck. He married Private Horst.
      1056   iv.   Jane Elizabeth Ranck, born December 15, 1957; died December 15, 1957.

726. Donald Edwin[12] Ranck (Mary Helen[11] Hershey, Enos Jacob[10], Peter[9], Jacob[8], John[7], Anna Weber[6] Newcomer, Elizabeth[5] Weber, Henry[4], Johann Anton[3], Heinrich[2], George[1]) was born June 26, 1927. He married **Kathleen Martin**. She was born May 07, 1927.

Children of Donald Ranck and Kathleen Martin are:
      1057   i.   Private[13] Ranck.
+   1058   ii.   Private Ranck.

728. Janet Potter[12] Hess (Clyde C.[11], Elizabeth[10] Hershey, Peter[9], Jacob[8], John[7], Anna Weber[6] Newcomer, Elizabeth[5] Weber, Henry[4], Johann Anton[3], Heinrich[2], George[1]) was born July 10, 1924. She married **Ernest Ludwig Daman**. He was born March 14, 1923.

Children of Janet Hess and Ernest Daman are:
      1059   i.   Private[13] Daman.
+   1060   ii.   Private Daman.
+   1061   iii.   Private Daman.

730. Rhoda Gregory[12] Hess (Harry Hershey[11], Elizabeth[10] Hershey, Peter[9], Jacob[8], John[7], Anna Weber[6] Newcomer, Elizabeth[5] Weber, Henry[4], Johann Anton[3], Heinrich[2], George[1]) was born September 12, 1926. She married **Lyle Andrew Briggs**.

Children of Rhoda Hess and Lyle Briggs are:
- 1062   i.   Private[13] Briggs.
- 1063   ii.   Private Briggs. She married Private Heilman.
- 1064   iii.   Private Briggs. She married Private vanWormer.

731. Richard Henry[12] Hershey (Paul Keene[11], Henry Peter[10], Peter[9], Jacob[8], John[7], Anna Weber[6] Newcomer, Elizabeth[5] Weber, Henry[4], Johann Anton[3], Heinrich[2], George[1]) was born January 10, 1928. He married **Private Roush**.

Children of Richard Hershey and Private Roush are:
- 1065   i.   Private[13] Hershey.
- 1066   ii.   Private Hershey.

732. Paul Kenneth[12] Hershey (Paul Keene[11], Henry Peter[10], Peter[9], Jacob[8], John[7], Anna Weber[6] Newcomer, Elizabeth[5] Weber, Henry[4], Johann Anton[3], Heinrich[2], George[1]) was born October 14, 1929. He married **(1) Private Dotts**. He married **(2) Private Hails**.

Children of Paul Hershey and Private Dotts are:
- + 1067   i.   Private[13] Hershey.
- 1068   ii.   Private Hershey.

Children of Paul Hershey and Private Hails are:
- 1069   i.   Private[13] Hershey.
- 1070   ii.   Private Hershey.

735. Private[12] Pennock (Esther Elizabeth[11] Hershey, Martin Eby[10], Peter[9], Jacob[8], John[7], Anna Weber[6] Newcomer, Elizabeth[5] Weber, Henry[4], Johann Anton[3], Heinrich[2], George[1]) She married **Thomas Garrett Hewes**. He was born November 02, 1928.

Children of Private Pennock and Thomas Hewes are:
- + 1071   i.   Private[13] Hewes.
- + 1072   ii.   Private Hewes.
- + 1073   iii.   Private Hewes.
- 1074   iv.   Private Hewes.
- 1075   v.   Private Hewes.
- 1076   vi.   John Martin Hewes, born July 04, 1956; died May 20, 1987. He married Private Unknown.

736. Betty Louise[12] Pennock (Esther Elizabeth[11] Hershey, Martin Eby[10], Peter[9], Jacob[8], John[7], Anna Weber[6] Newcomer, Elizabeth[5] Weber, Henry[4], Johann Anton[3], Heinrich[2], George[1]) was born October 18, 1929. She married **Harry Brisbin Skiles**. He was born January 04, 1929, and died July 09, 1988.

Children of Betty Pennock and Harry Skiles are:
- + 1077   i.   Private[13] Skiles.
- + 1078   ii.   Private Skiles.

737. Private[12] Rodgers (Miriam Clara[11] Hershey, Martin Eby[10], Peter[9], Jacob[8], John[7], Anna Weber[6] Newcomer, Elizabeth[5] Weber, Henry[4], Johann Anton[3], Heinrich[2], George[1]) He married **Private McSeveney**.

Children of Private Rodgers and Private McSeveney are:
- 1079   i.   Private[13] Rodgers.
- + 1080   ii.   Private Rodgers.
- 1081   iii.   Private Rodgers.
- 1082   iv.   Private Rodgers.
- 1083   v.   Private Rodgers.

741. Private[12] Hershey (Lester D.[11], Silas N.[10], Peter[9], Jacob[8], John[7], Anna Weber[6] Newcomer, Elizabeth[5] Weber, Henry[4], Johann Anton[3], Heinrich[2], George[1]) She married **Private Weaver**.

Children of Private Hershey and Private Weaver are:

1084 i. Private[13] Weaver.
1085 ii. Private Weaver.
1086 iii. Private Weaver.
1087 iv. Private Weaver.
1088 v. Private Weaver.

742. Private[12] Zimmerman (Barbara Elizabeth[11] Hershey, Silas N.[10], Peter[9], Jacob[8], John[7], Anna Weber[6] Newcomer, Elizabeth[5] Weber, Henry[4], Johann Anton[3], Heinrich[2], George[1]) She married **Private Stauffer**.

Children of Private Zimmerman and Private Stauffer are:
1089 i. Private[13] Stauffer.
1090 ii. Private Stauffer.

743. Private[12] Zimmerman (Barbara Elizabeth[11] Hershey, Silas N.[10], Peter[9], Jacob[8], John[7], Anna Weber[6] Newcomer, Elizabeth[5] Weber, Henry[4], Johann Anton[3], Heinrich[2], George[1]) He married **Private Lutz**.

Children of Private Zimmerman and Private Lutz are:
1091 i. Private[13] Zimmerman.
1092 ii. Private Zimmerman.
1093 iii. Private Zimmerman.

744. Private[12] Zimmerman (Barbara Elizabeth[11] Hershey, Silas N.[10], Peter[9], Jacob[8], John[7], Anna Weber[6] Newcomer, Elizabeth[5] Weber, Henry[4], Johann Anton[3], Heinrich[2], George[1]) He married **Private Smoker**.

Children of Private Zimmerman and Private Smoker are:
1094 i. Private[13] Zimmerman.
1095 ii. Private Zimmerman.

745. Private[12] Hershey (Willis Daniel[11], Silas N.[10], Peter[9], Jacob[8], John[7], Anna Weber[6] Newcomer, Elizabeth[5] Weber, Henry[4], Johann Anton[3], Heinrich[2], George[1]) She married **(1) Private Richardson**. She married **(2) Private Alexander**.

Children of Private Hershey and Private Richardson are:
+ 1096 i. Private[13] Richardson.
+ 1097 ii. Private Richardson.
  1098 iii. Private Richardson.

746. Private[12] Hershey (Willis Daniel[11], Silas N.[10], Peter[9], Jacob[8], John[7], Anna Weber[6] Newcomer, Elizabeth[5] Weber, Henry[4], Johann Anton[3], Heinrich[2], George[1]) She married **Private Summers**.

Children of Private Hershey and Private Summers are:
+ 1099 i. Private[13] Summers.
+ 1100 ii. Private Summers.

747. Private[12] Hershey (Willis Daniel[11], Silas N.[10], Peter[9], Jacob[8], John[7], Anna Weber[6] Newcomer, Elizabeth[5] Weber, Henry[4], Johann Anton[3], Heinrich[2], George[1]) He married **(1) Private Myers**. He married **(2) Private Gregg**.

Child of Private Hershey and Private Myers is:
+ 1101 i. Private[13] Bomberger.

Child of Private Hershey and Private Gregg is:
+ 1102 i. Private[13] Hershey.

748. Private[12] Hershey (Willis Daniel[11], Silas N.[10], Peter[9], Jacob[8], John[7], Anna Weber[6] Newcomer, Elizabeth[5] Weber, Henry[4], Johann Anton[3], Heinrich[2], George[1]) He married **Private Hoober**.

Children of Private Hershey and Private Hoober are:
+ 1103 i. Private[13] Hershey.
  1104 ii. Private Hershey. He married Private Landis.

749. Private[12] **Hershey** (Willis Daniel[11], Silas N.[10], Peter[9], Jacob[8], John[7], Anna Weber[6] Newcomer, Elizabeth[5] Weber, Henry[4], Johann Anton[3], Heinrich[2], George[1]) She married **Private Miller**.

Children of Private Hershey and Private Miller are:
- 1105   i.   Private[13] Miller.
- 1106   ii.   Private Miller.

750. Jay Paul[12] **Hershey** (Willis Daniel[11], Silas N.[10], Peter[9], Jacob[8], John[7], Anna Weber[6] Newcomer, Elizabeth[5] Weber, Henry[4], Johann Anton[3], Heinrich[2], George[1]) was born April 27, 1941, and died November 02, 1996. He married **Private Boohar**.

Children of Jay Hershey and Private Boohar are:
- + 1107   i.   Private[13] Hershey.
- + 1108   ii.   Private Hershey.
- + 1109   iii.   Private Hershey.

751. Private[12] **Nolt** (Reba L.[11] Hershey, Silas N.[10], Peter[9], Jacob[8], John[7], Anna Weber[6] Newcomer, Elizabeth[5] Weber, Henry[4], Johann Anton[3], Heinrich[2], George[1]) She married **(1) Private Clymer**. She married **(2) Private Swartzendruber**.

Child of Private Nolt and Private Clymer is:
- 1110   i.   Private[13] Clymer.

Child of Private Nolt and Private Swartzendruber is:
- 1111   i.   Private[13] Swartzendruber.

752. Private[12] **Nolt** (Reba L.[11] Hershey, Silas N.[10], Peter[9], Jacob[8], John[7], Anna Weber[6] Newcomer, Elizabeth[5] Weber, Henry[4], Johann Anton[3], Heinrich[2], George[1]) She married **(1) Private Harmon**. She married **(2) Private Kranz**.

Child of Private Nolt and Private Harmon is:
- 1112   i.   Private[13] Harmon.

754. Private[12] **Kauffman** (Doris Mae[11] Hershey, Silas N.[10], Peter[9], Jacob[8], John[7], Anna Weber[6] Newcomer, Elizabeth[5] Weber, Henry[4], Johann Anton[3], Heinrich[2], George[1]) She married **Private Barth**.

Children of Private Kauffman and Private Barth are:
- 1113   i.   Private[13] Barth.
- 1114   ii.   Private Barth.
- 1115   iii.   Private Barth.

755. Private[12] **Kauffman** (Doris Mae[11] Hershey, Silas N.[10], Peter[9], Jacob[8], John[7], Anna Weber[6] Newcomer, Elizabeth[5] Weber, Henry[4], Johann Anton[3], Heinrich[2], George[1]) She married **(1) Private Stover**. She married **(2) Private Haldeman**.

Child of Private Kauffman and Private Stover is:
- 1116   i.   Private[13] Stover.

756. Private[12] **Lowry** (Doris Mae[11] Hershey, Silas N.[10], Peter[9], Jacob[8], John[7], Anna Weber[6] Newcomer, Elizabeth[5] Weber, Henry[4], Johann Anton[3], Heinrich[2], George[1]) She married **Private Wanner**.

Children of Private Lowry and Private Wanner are:
- 1117   i.   Private[13] Wanner.
- 1118   ii.   Private Wanner.

759. Robert Melvin[12] **Burkholder** (Melvin E[11], Abraham H[10], Susan[9] Hershey, Abraham[8], Christian[7], Anna Weber[6] Newcomer, Elizabeth[5] Weber, Henry[4], Johann Anton[3], Heinrich[2], George[1]) was born March 03, 1935. He married **Justina Miller**. She was born March 30, 1935.

Children of Robert Burkholder and Justina Miller are:
- 1119   i.   Robert[13] Burkholder, born February 03, 1957.

1120 ii. Kathleen Burkholder, born February 05, 1959.
1121 iii. Thomas Burkholder, born July 20, 1962.
1122 iv. Lisa Burkholder, born August 07, 1964.
1123 v. Kevin Burkholder, born July 04, 1970. He married Gina Marie D'Ginto.

760. Mary Naomi[12] Musser (Martha Anna[11] Livengood, Gertrude[10] Hertzler, Michael S.[9], Abraham[8], John[7], Maria[6] Mumma, Beverly[5] Weber, Henry[4], Johann Anton[3], Heinrich[2], George[1]) was born April 21, 1934 in East Hempfield Twp, Lanc Co, PA. She married **Jay Donald Weaver** July 16, 1955 in East Petersburg, PA, son of John Weaver and Ada Horst. He was born April 20, 1933 in Ephrata Twp, Lanc Co, PA.

Children are listed above under (620) Jay Donald Weaver.

762. Cedric Linn[12] Horst (Paul Steffy[11], Elam Sweigart[10], Reuben Weaver[9], Jacob M.[8], Barbara Weber[7] Musser, Esther[6] Weber, Christian[5], Henry[4], Johann Anton[3], Heinrich[2], George[1]) was born March 13, 1942. He married **(1) Barbara Carrithers**. She was born March 07, 1951. He married **(2) Cheryl Ann Campbell**. She was born August 28, 1957 in Georgia. He married **(3) Diane Kay Staub** July 07, 1962. She was born December 26, 1945.

Child of Cedric Horst and Barbara Carrithers is:
1124 i. Misty Dawn[13] Horst, born September 22, 1972.

Child of Cedric Horst and Cheryl Campbell is:
1125 i. Jonathan Lynn[13] Horst, born October 22, 1974.

Children of Cedric Horst and Diane Staub are:
1126 i. Paul Howard[13] Horst, born August 17, 1964 in Ohio.
1127 ii. Shelby Lynn Horst, born September 15, 1965 in Ohio.

764. Joann Louise[12] Horst (Paul Steffy[11], Elam Sweigart[10], Reuben Weaver[9], Jacob M.[8], Barbara Weber[7] Musser, Esther[6] Weber, Christian[5], Henry[4], Johann Anton[3], Heinrich[2], George[1]) was born July 27, 1943. She married **Thomas Lyle Adams** July 27, 1962. He was born October 14, 1940 in Ohio.

Child of Joann Horst and Thomas Adams is:
1128 i. Thomas Lyle[13] Adams, born July 30, 1963 in Ohio.

765. Paul Gary[12] Horst (Paul Steffy[11], Elam Sweigart[10], Reuben Weaver[9], Jacob M.[8], Barbara Weber[7] Musser, Esther[6] Weber, Christian[5], Henry[4], Johann Anton[3], Heinrich[2], George[1]) was born February 08, 1950. He married **(1) Milene Sue Ruple Brynmor**. She was born December 30, 1951. He married **(2) Janie Monte Lang** February 04, 1968. She was born December 11, 1951.

Children of Paul Horst and Milene Brynmor are:
1129 i. John Ruple[13] Brynmor, born May 07, 1970 in Ohio.
1130 ii. Shannon Lea Horst, born August 02, 1974 in Pennsylvania.

Children of Paul Horst and Janie Lang are:
1131 i. Gail Marie[13] Horst, born May 16, 1969.
1132 ii. Gary Paul Horst, born June 29, 1972.

767. Mary Louise[12] Horst (William Prichard[11], Elam Sweigart[10], Reuben Weaver[9], Jacob M.[8], Barbara Weber[7] Musser, Esther[6] Weber, Christian[5], Henry[4], Johann Anton[3], Heinrich[2], George[1]) was born January 27, 1944. She married **John W. Farmer** June 17, 1961. He was born July 17, 1937 in Virginia.

Children of Mary Horst and John Farmer are:
1133 i. Mary Elizabeth[13] Farmer, born August 23, 1962.
1134 ii. Cindy Hope Farmer, born February 18, 1968.

768. Mark William[12] Horst (William Prichard[11], Elam Sweigart[10], Reuben Weaver[9], Jacob M.[8], Barbara Weber[7] Musser, Esther[6] Weber, Christian[5], Henry[4], Johann Anton[3], Heinrich[2], George[1]) was born November 08, 1948. He married **Lenora May Gordon** August 05, 1967. She was born November 27, 1946.

Children of Mark Horst and Lenora Gordon are:

1135   i. Christine Marie[13] Horst, born August 23, 1971.
1136   ii. William Mark Horst, born August 09, 1974.

769. Vici Mae[12] Carvell (Erma Steffy[11] Horst, Elam Sweigart[10], Reuben Weaver[9], Jacob M.[8], Barbara Weber[7] Musser, Esther[6] Weber, Christian[5], Henry[4], Johann Anton[3], Heinrich[2], George[1]) was born March 24, 1948. She married **David M. McGowan** September 02, 1967. He was born May 30, 1947 in Massachusets.

Child of Vici Carvell and David McGowan is:
1137   i. Debra Lynne[13] McGown, born June 15, 1973 in New Hampshire.

770. Audrey Nadine[12] Carvell (Erma Steffy[11] Horst, Elam Sweigart[10], Reuben Weaver[9], Jacob M.[8], Barbara Weber[7] Musser, Esther[6] Weber, Christian[5], Henry[4], Johann Anton[3], Heinrich[2], George[1]) was born May 07, 1949. She married **Leon Eugene Buckwalter** July 07, 1973. He was born June 29, 1948.

Child of Audrey Carvell and Leon Buckwalter is:
1138   i. Heidi Rene[13] Buckwalter, born August 02, 1978.

777. James Edward[12] Weaver (Jay Donald[12], John Landis[11], John Hollinger[10], Christian G.[9], Gideon[8] Weber, Christian[7], Samuel[6], Christian[5], Henry[4], Johann Anton[3], Heinrich[2], George[1]) was born November 10, 1960 in Lancaster, PA. He married **Sherry Rittenhouse** May 25, 1985 in Manheim Twp, Lanc Co, PA. She was born in Lancaster, PA.

Child of James Weaver and Sherry Rittenhouse is:
1139   i. Joshua Alan[13] Weaver, born July 18, 1990 in Lancaster, PA.

778. Rae Elizabeth[12] Langsdale (Arvilla[12] Weaver, John Landis[11], John Hollinger[10], Christian G.[9], Gideon[8] Weber, Christian[7], Samuel[6], Christian[5], Henry[4], Johann Anton[3], Heinrich[2], George[1]) was born December 23, 1958 in Ephrata, PA. She married **David A. Burt** April 17, 1990 in Pittsfield, MA.

Child of Rae Langsdale and David Burt is:
1140   i. Caitlin Ann[13] Burt, born October 15, 1991 in Pittsfield, MA.

780. Robert John[12] Langsdale (Arvilla[12] Weaver, John Landis[11], John Hollinger[10], Christian G.[9], Gideon[8] Weber, Christian[7], Samuel[6], Christian[5], Henry[4], Johann Anton[3], Heinrich[2], George[1]) was born September 05, 1965. He married **Ann Marie Giannopolo** September 07, 1991 in Pittsfield, MA. She was born April 16, 1965 in Pittsfield, MA.

Child of Robert Langsdale and Ann Giannopolo is:
1141   i. Tessa Maria[13] Langsdale, born May 28, 1999 in Pittsfield, MA.

782. Rachel Naomi[12] Bucove (Donna Lou[12] Weaver, John Landis[11], John Hollinger[10], Christian G.[9], Gideon[8] Weber, Christian[7], Samuel[6], Christian[5], Henry[4], Johann Anton[3], Heinrich[2], George[1]) was born July 13, 1971. She married **Michael David Hitchcock**. He was born September 17, 1966 in New Haven, CT.

Children of Rachel Bucove and Michael Hitchcock are:
1142   i. Alexander Milton[13] Hitchcock, born January 13, 1993 in Portland, OR.
1143   ii. Zachary Falcon Hitchcock, born September 07, 1995 in Portland, OR.
1144   iii. Jonathan Elliot Hitchcock, born June 07, 1998 in Portland, OR.

783. John Michael[12] Weaver (John Eric[12], John Landis[11], John Hollinger[10], Christian G.[9], Gideon[8] Weber, Christian[7], Samuel[6], Christian[5], Henry[4], Johann Anton[3], Heinrich[2], George[1]) was born June 19, 1968 in Ephrata, Lancaster Co., PA. He married **Jodi Lynn Lied** April 14, 1991.

Children of John Weaver and Jodi Lied are:
1145   i. Rachel Anne[13] Weaver, born January 20, 1998 in Chesapeake, VA.
1146   ii. Benjamin Michael Weaver, born January 26, 2000 in Portsmouth, VA.

Generation No. 13

789. Private[13] Fox (Willis Eby[12], Ella Barbara[11] Eby, Sarah Lucinda[10] Hershey, Peter[9], Jacob[8], John[7], Anna Weber[6] Newcomer, Elizabeth[5] Weber, Henry[4], Johann Anton[3], Heinrich[2], George[1]) She married **Private Zimmerman**.

Children of Private Fox and Private Zimmerman are:
- 1147 i. Private[14] Zimmerman.
- 1148 ii. Private Zimmerman.
- 1149 iii. Christine Renee Zimmerman, born January 19, 1975; died April 17, 1975.
- 1150 iv. Neil Brian Zimmerman, born August 15, 1977; died October 26, 1977.

790. Private[13] Fox (Willis Eby[12], Ella Barbara[11] Eby, Sarah Lucinda[10] Hershey, Peter[9], Jacob[8], John[7], Anna Weber[6] Newcomer, Elizabeth[5] Weber, Henry[4], Johann Anton[3], Heinrich[2], George[1]) He married **Private Trupe**.

Children of Private Fox and Private Trupe are:
- 1151 i. Private[14] Fox.
- 1152 ii. Private Fox.
- 1153 iii. Private Fox.

791. Private[13] Fox (Willis Eby[12], Ella Barbara[11] Eby, Sarah Lucinda[10] Hershey, Peter[9], Jacob[8], John[7], Anna Weber[6] Newcomer, Elizabeth[5] Weber, Henry[4], Johann Anton[3], Heinrich[2], George[1]) She married **Private Newswanger**.

Child of Private Fox and Private Newswanger is:
- 1154 i. Private[14] Newswanger.

794. Private[13] Fox (Willis Eby[12], Ella Barbara[11] Eby, Sarah Lucinda[10] Hershey, Peter[9], Jacob[8], John[7], Anna Weber[6] Newcomer, Elizabeth[5] Weber, Henry[4], Johann Anton[3], Heinrich[2], George[1]) He married **Private Weaver**.

Children of Private Fox and Private Weaver are:
- 1155 i. Private[14] Fox.
- 1156 ii. Private Fox. She married Private Martin.
- + 1157 iii. Private Fox.
- + 1158 iv. Private Fox.
- 1159 v. Marvin Lamar Fox, born December 13, 1962; died March 20, 1980.

796. Private[13] Fox (Henry Peter[12], Ella Barbara[11] Eby, Sarah Lucinda[10] Hershey, Peter[9], Jacob[8], John[7], Anna Weber[6] Newcomer, Elizabeth[5] Weber, Henry[4], Johann Anton[3], Heinrich[2], George[1]) She married **Private Evans**.

Children of Private Fox and Private Evans are:
- 1160 i. Private[14] Evans.
- 1161 ii. Private Evans.
- 1162 iii. Private Evans.
- 1163 iv. Cecile Loren Evans, born July 18, 1985; died November 04, 1985.

798. Private[13] Fox (Henry Peter[12], Ella Barbara[11] Eby, Sarah Lucinda[10] Hershey, Peter[9], Jacob[8], John[7], Anna Weber[6] Newcomer, Elizabeth[5] Weber, Henry[4], Johann Anton[3], Heinrich[2], George[1]) He married **Private Kennel**.

Children of Private Fox and Private Kennel are:
- 1164 i. Private[14] Fox.
- 1165 ii. Private Fox.

799. Private[13] Fox (Henry Peter[12], Ella Barbara[11] Eby, Sarah Lucinda[10] Hershey, Peter[9], Jacob[8], John[7], Anna Weber[6] Newcomer, Elizabeth[5] Weber, Henry[4], Johann Anton[3], Heinrich[2], George[1]) He married **Private Felpel**.

Children of Private Fox and Private Felpel are:
- 1166 i. Private[14] Fox.
- 1167 ii. Private Fox.
- 1168 iii. Private Fox.
- 1169 iv. Private Fox.

801. Private[13] Fox (Henry Peter[12], Ella Barbara[11] Eby, Sarah Lucinda[10] Hershey, Peter[9], Jacob[8], John[7], Anna Weber[6] Newcomer, Elizabeth[5] Weber, Henry[4], Johann Anton[3], Heinrich[2], George[1]) He married **Private Heisey**.

The Relations of Milton Snavely Hershey, 4th Ed.

Children of Private Fox and Private Heisey are:
- 1170   i.   Private[14] Fox.
- 1171   ii.   Private Fox. He married Private Fryberger.

803. Private[13] Fox (Henry Peter[12], Ella Barbara[11] Eby, Sarah Lucinda[10] Hershey, Peter[9], Jacob[8], John[7], Anna Weber[6] Newcomer, Elizabeth[5] Weber, Henry[4], Johann Anton[3], Heinrich[2], George[1]) She married **Private Augsburger**.

Children of Private Fox and Private Augsburger are:
- 1172   i.   Private[14] Augsburger. He married Private Denlinger.
- + 1173   ii.   Private Augsburger.
- + 1174   iii.   Private Augsburger.
- 1175   iv.   Private Augsburger. He married Private Hollinger.

804. Private[13] Fox (Henry Peter[12], Ella Barbara[11] Eby, Sarah Lucinda[10] Hershey, Peter[9], Jacob[8], John[7], Anna Weber[6] Newcomer, Elizabeth[5] Weber, Henry[4], Johann Anton[3], Heinrich[2], George[1]) She married **Private Eberly**.

Children of Private Fox and Private Eberly are:
- 1176   i.   Private[14] Eberly. He married Private Balmer.
- + 1177   ii.   Private Eberly.
- 1178   iii.   Private Eberly. She married Private Hurst.

805. Private[13] Fox (Henry Peter[12], Ella Barbara[11] Eby, Sarah Lucinda[10] Hershey, Peter[9], Jacob[8], John[7], Anna Weber[6] Newcomer, Elizabeth[5] Weber, Henry[4], Johann Anton[3], Heinrich[2], George[1]) She married **Private Good**.

Children of Private Fox and Private Good are:
- 1179   i.   Private[14] Good.
- 1180   ii.   Private Good.
- + 1181   iii.   Private Good.
- + 1182   iv.   Private Good.

806. Private[13] Fox (Henry Peter[12], Ella Barbara[11] Eby, Sarah Lucinda[10] Hershey, Peter[9], Jacob[8], John[7], Anna Weber[6] Newcomer, Elizabeth[5] Weber, Henry[4], Johann Anton[3], Heinrich[2], George[1]) She married **Private Zimmerman**.

Children of Private Fox and Private Zimmerman are:
- + 1183   i.   Private[14] Zimmerman.
- + 1184   ii.   Private Zimmerman.
- + 1185   iii.   Private Zimmerman.

807. Private[13] Zimmerman (Sarah Lucinda[12] Fox, Ella Barbara[11] Eby, Sarah Lucinda[10] Hershey, Peter[9], Jacob[8], John[7], Anna Weber[6] Newcomer, Elizabeth[5] Weber, Henry[4], Johann Anton[3], Heinrich[2], George[1]) He married **Private Long**.

Children of Private Zimmerman and Private Long are:
- 1186   i.   Private[14] Zimmerman.
- 1187   ii.   Private Zimmerman.

808. Private[13] Zimmerman (Sarah Lucinda[12] Fox, Ella Barbara[11] Eby, Sarah Lucinda[10] Hershey, Peter[9], Jacob[8], John[7], Anna Weber[6] Newcomer, Elizabeth[5] Weber, Henry[4], Johann Anton[3], Heinrich[2], George[1]) She married **Private Groff**.

Children of Private Zimmerman and Private Groff are:
- 1188   i.   Private[14] Groff.
- 1189   ii.   Private Groff.
- 1190   iii.   Private Groff.
- 1191   iv.   Private Groff.

809. Private[13] Zimmerman (Sarah Lucinda[12] Fox, Ella Barbara[11] Eby, Sarah Lucinda[10] Hershey, Peter[9], Jacob[8], John[7], Anna Weber[6] Newcomer, Elizabeth[5] Weber, Henry[4], Johann Anton[3], Heinrich[2], George[1]) He married **Private Hostetter**.

Children of Private Zimmerman and Private Hostetter are:
- 1192   i.   Private[14] Zimmerman.

1193 ii. Private Zimmerman.
1194 iii. Private Zimmerman.
1195 iv. Private Zimmerman.
1196 v. Private Zimmerman.
1197 vi. Private Zimmerman.
1198 vii. Private Zimmerman.

810. Private[13] **Zimmerman** (Sarah Lucinda[12] Fox, Ella Barbara[11] Eby, Sarah Lucinda[10] Hershey, Peter[9], Jacob[8], John[7], Anna Weber[6] Newcomer, Elizabeth[5] Weber, Henry[4], Johann Anton[3], Heinrich[2], George[1]) He married **Private Wenger**.

Children of Private Zimmerman and Private Wenger are:
1199 i. Private[14] Zimmerman.
1200 ii. Private Zimmerman.
1201 iii. Private Zimmerman.
1202 iv. Private Zimmerman.
1203 v. Private Zimmerman.
1204 vi. Private Zimmerman.
1205 vii. Private Zimmerman.
1206 viii. Private Zimmerman.
1207 ix. Private Zimmerman.
1208 x. Private Zimmerman.
1209 xi. Private Zimmerman.
+ 1210 xii. Private Zimmerman.
1211 xiii. Private Zimmerman. She married Private Hoover.
1212 xiv. Private Zimmerman.
+ 1213 xv. Private Zimmerman.

811. Private[13] **Fox** (Daniel Hershey[12], Ella Barbara[11] Eby, Sarah Lucinda[10] Hershey, Peter[9], Jacob[8], John[7], Anna Weber[6] Newcomer, Elizabeth[5] Weber, Henry[4], Johann Anton[3], Heinrich[2], George[1]) She married **Private Mall**.

Child of Private Fox and Private Mall is:
1214 i. Private[14] Mall.

812. Private[13] **Fox** (Daniel Hershey[12], Ella Barbara[11] Eby, Sarah Lucinda[10] Hershey, Peter[9], Jacob[8], John[7], Anna Weber[6] Newcomer, Elizabeth[5] Weber, Henry[4], Johann Anton[3], Heinrich[2], George[1]) She married **Private Kilmer**.

Children of Private Fox and Private Kilmer are:
1215 i. Private[14] Kilmer.
1216 ii. Private Kilmer.
1217 iii. Private Kilmer.

813. Private[13] **Fox** (Daniel Hershey[12], Ella Barbara[11] Eby, Sarah Lucinda[10] Hershey, Peter[9], Jacob[8], John[7], Anna Weber[6] Newcomer, Elizabeth[5] Weber, Henry[4], Johann Anton[3], Heinrich[2], George[1])

Child of Private Fox is:
1218 i. Private[14] Fox.

815. Private[13] **Fox** (Ivan Martin[12], Ella Barbara[11] Eby, Sarah Lucinda[10] Hershey, Peter[9], Jacob[8], John[7], Anna Weber[6] Newcomer, Elizabeth[5] Weber, Henry[4], Johann Anton[3], Heinrich[2], George[1]) He married **Private Myers**.

Children of Private Fox and Private Myers are:
1219 i. Private[14] Brown.
1220 ii. Private Brown.

816. Private[13] **Fox** (Ivan Martin[12], Ella Barbara[11] Eby, Sarah Lucinda[10] Hershey, Peter[9], Jacob[8], John[7], Anna Weber[6] Newcomer, Elizabeth[5] Weber, Henry[4], Johann Anton[3], Heinrich[2], George[1]) He married **Private Tangvald**.

Children of Private Fox and Private Tangvald are:
1221 i. Private[14] Fox.
1222 ii. Private Fox.

1223 iii. Private Fox.

817. Private[13] Eby (Franklin W.[12], Peter Hershey[11], Sarah Lucinda[10] Hershey, Peter[9], Jacob[8], John[7], Anna Weber[6] Newcomer, Elizabeth[5] Weber, Henry[4], Johann Anton[3], Heinrich[2], George[1]) She married **(1) Private Groff**. She married **(2) Private Malin**.

Child of Private Eby and Private Groff is:
1224 i. Private[14] Groff.

Child of Private Eby and Private Malin is:
1225 i. Private[14] Malin.

819. Private[13] Martin (Susan W.[12] Eby, Peter Hershey[11], Sarah Lucinda[10] Hershey, Peter[9], Jacob[8], John[7], Anna Weber[6] Newcomer, Elizabeth[5] Weber, Henry[4], Johann Anton[3], Heinrich[2], George[1]) He married **Private Nolt**.

Children of Private Martin and Private Nolt are:
1226 i. Private[14] Martin.
1227 ii. Private Martin.
1228 iii. Private Martin.

820. Private[13] Martin (Susan W.[12] Eby, Peter Hershey[11], Sarah Lucinda[10] Hershey, Peter[9], Jacob[8], John[7], Anna Weber[6] Newcomer, Elizabeth[5] Weber, Henry[4], Johann Anton[3], Heinrich[2], George[1]) She married **Private Martin**.

Children of Private Martin and Private Martin are:
1229 i. Private[14] Martin.
1230 ii. Private Martin.
1231 iii. Private Martin.

821. Private[13] Martin (Susan W.[12] Eby, Peter Hershey[11], Sarah Lucinda[10] Hershey, Peter[9], Jacob[8], John[7], Anna Weber[6] Newcomer, Elizabeth[5] Weber, Henry[4], Johann Anton[3], Heinrich[2], George[1]) She married **Private Weber**.

Children of Private Martin and Private Weber are:
1232 i. Private[14] Weber.
1233 ii. Private Weber.

822. Private[13] Martin (Susan W.[12] Eby, Peter Hershey[11], Sarah Lucinda[10] Hershey, Peter[9], Jacob[8], John[7], Anna Weber[6] Newcomer, Elizabeth[5] Weber, Henry[4], Johann Anton[3], Heinrich[2], George[1]) He married **Private Nolt**.

Children of Private Martin and Private Nolt are:
1234 i. Private[14] Martin.
1235 ii. Private Martin.
1236 iii. Private Martin.
1237 iv. Private Martin.
1238 v. Private Martin.
1239 vi. Private Martin.
1240 vii. Private Martin.
1241 viii. Private Martin. She married Private Good.

823. Private[13] Martin (Susan W.[12] Eby, Peter Hershey[11], Sarah Lucinda[10] Hershey, Peter[9], Jacob[8], John[7], Anna Weber[6] Newcomer, Elizabeth[5] Weber, Henry[4], Johann Anton[3], Heinrich[2], George[1]) He married **Private Nolt**.

Children of Private Martin and Private Nolt are:
1242 i. Private[14] Martin.
1243 ii. Private Martin.
1244 iii. Private Martin.
1245 iv. Private Martin.
1246 v. Private Martin.
1247 vi. Private Martin.
+ 1248 vii. Private Martin.
1249 viii. Rosalea Joy Martin, born January 25, 1979; died January 25, 1979.

824. Private[13] Martin (Susan W.[12] Eby, Peter Hershey[11], Sarah Lucinda[10] Hershey, Peter[9], Jacob[8], John[7], Anna Weber[6] Newcomer, Elizabeth[5] Weber, Henry[4], Johann Anton[3], Heinrich[2], George[1]) He married **Private Mitchell**.

Children of Private Martin and Private Mitchell are:
- 1250   i.   Private[14] Martin.
- 1251   ii. Private Martin.
- 1252   iii. Private Martin. She married Private Gehman.

825. Private[13] Martin (Susan W.[12] Eby, Peter Hershey[11], Sarah Lucinda[10] Hershey, Peter[9], Jacob[8], John[7], Anna Weber[6] Newcomer, Elizabeth[5] Weber, Henry[4], Johann Anton[3], Heinrich[2], George[1]) He married **Private Weaver**.

Children of Private Martin and Private Weaver are:
- 1253   i.   Private[14] Martin.
- 1254   ii.   Private Martin.
- 1255   iii. Private Martin.
- 1256   iv.   Private Martin.
- 1257   v.   Private Martin.
- 1258   vi.   Private Martin.
- 1259   vii. Private Martin.
- 1260   viii. Private Martin. She married Private Stauffer.
- 1261   ix.   Lavone W. Martin, born October 02, 1961; died October 02, 1961.
- 1262   x.   Vernon W. Martin, born October 10, 1962; died October 10, 1962.

826. John E.[13] Martin (Susan W.[12] Eby, Peter Hershey[11], Sarah Lucinda[10] Hershey, Peter[9], Jacob[8], John[7], Anna Weber[6] Newcomer, Elizabeth[5] Weber, Henry[4], Johann Anton[3], Heinrich[2], George[1]) was born May 25, 1949, and died February 11, 1984. He married **Private Good**.

Children of John Martin and Private Good are:
- 1263   i.   Private[14] Martin.
- 1264   ii. Private Martin.
- 1265   iii. Private Martin.

827. Private[13] Stauffer (Emma Mae[12] Eby, Peter Hershey[11], Sarah Lucinda[10] Hershey, Peter[9], Jacob[8], John[7], Anna Weber[6] Newcomer, Elizabeth[5] Weber, Henry[4], Johann Anton[3], Heinrich[2], George[1]) He married **Private Nolt**.

Children of Private Stauffer and Private Nolt are:
- 1266   i.   Private[14] Stauffer.
- 1267   ii. Private Stauffer.
- 1268   iii. Private Stauffer.
- 1269   iv. Private Stauffer.

828. Private[13] Stauffer (Emma Mae[12] Eby, Peter Hershey[11], Sarah Lucinda[10] Hershey, Peter[9], Jacob[8], John[7], Anna Weber[6] Newcomer, Elizabeth[5] Weber, Henry[4], Johann Anton[3], Heinrich[2], George[1]) She married **Private Horst**.

Children of Private Stauffer and Private Horst are:
- 1270   i.   Private[14] Horst.
- 1271   ii.   Private Horst.
- 1272   iii. Private Horst.
- 1273   iv.   Private Horst.
- 1274   v.   Private Horst.
- 1275   vi.   Private Horst.
- 1276   vii. Private Horst.
- 1277   viii. Private Horst.
- 1278   ix.   Private Horst.

829. Private[13] Stauffer (Emma Mae[12] Eby, Peter Hershey[11], Sarah Lucinda[10] Hershey, Peter[9], Jacob[8], John[7], Anna Weber[6] Newcomer, Elizabeth[5] Weber, Henry[4], Johann Anton[3], Heinrich[2], George[1]) She married **Private Horning**.

Children of Private Stauffer and Private Horning are:

1279 i. Private[14] Horning.
1280 ii. Private Horning.
1281 iii. Private Horning.
1282 iv. Private Horning.
1283 v. Private Horning.
1284 vi. Private Horning.
1285 vii. Private Horning.
1286 viii. Private Horning.
1287 ix. Private Horning.
1288 x. Esther Mae Horning, born January 27, 1981; died July 10, 1984.

830. Private[13] Stauffer (Emma Mae[12] Eby, Peter Hershey[11], Sarah Lucinda[10] Hershey, Peter[9], Jacob[8], John[7], Anna Weber[6] Newcomer, Elizabeth[5] Weber, Henry[4], Johann Anton[3], Heinrich[2], George[1]) She married **Private Zimmerman**.

Children of Private Stauffer and Private Zimmerman are:
 1289 i. Private[14] Zimmerman.
 1290 ii. Private Zimmerman.
 1291 iii. Private Zimmerman.
 1292 iv. Private Zimmerman.
 1293 v. Private Zimmerman.
+ 1294 vi. Private Zimmerman.
+ 1295 vii. Private Zimmerman.
+ 1296 viii. Private Zimmerman.
+ 1297 ix. Private Zimmerman.

832. Private[13] Stauffer (Rhoda S.[12] Eby, Enos Jacob[11], Sarah Lucinda[10] Hershey, Peter[9], Jacob[8], John[7], Anna Weber[6] Newcomer, Elizabeth[5] Weber, Henry[4], Johann Anton[3], Heinrich[2], George[1]) She married **Private Martin**.

Children of Private Stauffer and Private Martin are:
 1298 i. Private[14] Martin.
 1299 ii. Private Martin.
 1300 iii. Private Martin.
 1301 iv. Private Martin.

833. Private[13] Stauffer (Rhoda S.[12] Eby, Enos Jacob[11], Sarah Lucinda[10] Hershey, Peter[9], Jacob[8], John[7], Anna Weber[6] Newcomer, Elizabeth[5] Weber, Henry[4], Johann Anton[3], Heinrich[2], George[1]) He married **Private Good**.

Children of Private Stauffer and Private Good are:
 1302 i. Private[14] Stauffer.
 1303 ii. Private Stauffer.
 1304 iii. Private Stauffer.
 1305 iv. Private Stauffer.
 1306 v. Private Stauffer.
 1307 vi. Private Stauffer.

839. Private[13] Eby (Henry S.[12], Enos Jacob[11], Sarah Lucinda[10] Hershey, Peter[9], Jacob[8], John[7], Anna Weber[6] Newcomer, Elizabeth[5] Weber, Henry[4], Johann Anton[3], Heinrich[2], George[1]) She married **Private Weaver**.

Child of Private Eby and Private Weaver is:
 1308 i. Private[14] Weaver.

840. Private[13] Eby (Henry S.[12], Enos Jacob[11], Sarah Lucinda[10] Hershey, Peter[9], Jacob[8], John[7], Anna Weber[6] Newcomer, Elizabeth[5] Weber, Henry[4], Johann Anton[3], Heinrich[2], George[1]) He married **Private Zimmerman**.

Child of Private Eby and Private Zimmerman is:
 1309 i. Private[14] Eby.

841. Private[13] Eby (Henry S.[12], Enos Jacob[11], Sarah Lucinda[10] Hershey, Peter[9], Jacob[8], John[7], Anna Weber[6] Newcomer, Elizabeth[5] Weber, Henry[4], Johann Anton[3], Heinrich[2], George[1]) He married **Private Zimmerman**.

Children of Private Eby and Private Zimmerman are:
- 1310	i.	Private[14] Eby.
- 1311	ii.	Private Eby.

842. Private[13] Eby (Henry S.[12], Enos Jacob[11], Sarah Lucinda[10] Hershey, Peter[9], Jacob[8], John[7], Anna Weber[6] Newcomer, Elizabeth[5] Weber, Henry[4], Johann Anton[3], Heinrich[2], George[1]) He married **Private Zimmerman**.

Child of Private Eby and Private Zimmerman is:
- 1312	i.	Private[14] Eby.

843. Private[13] Eby (Henry S.[12], Enos Jacob[11], Sarah Lucinda[10] Hershey, Peter[9], Jacob[8], John[7], Anna Weber[6] Newcomer, Elizabeth[5] Weber, Henry[4], Johann Anton[3], Heinrich[2], George[1]) He married **Private Auker**.

Children of Private Eby and Private Auker are:
- 1313	i.	Private[14] Eby.
- 1314	ii.	Private Eby.

844. Private[13] Eby (Henry S.[12], Enos Jacob[11], Sarah Lucinda[10] Hershey, Peter[9], Jacob[8], John[7], Anna Weber[6] Newcomer, Elizabeth[5] Weber, Henry[4], Johann Anton[3], Heinrich[2], George[1]) She married **Private Hartzler**.

Child of Private Eby and Private Hartzler is:
- 1315	i.	Private[14] Hartzler.

848. Private[13] Eby (Ezra S.[12], Enos Jacob[11], Sarah Lucinda[10] Hershey, Peter[9], Jacob[8], John[7], Anna Weber[6] Newcomer, Elizabeth[5] Weber, Henry[4], Johann Anton[3], Heinrich[2], George[1]) She married **Private Rissler**.

Child of Private Eby and Private Rissler is:
- 1316	i.	Private[14] Rissler.

850. Private[13] Eby (Ezra S.[12], Enos Jacob[11], Sarah Lucinda[10] Hershey, Peter[9], Jacob[8], John[7], Anna Weber[6] Newcomer, Elizabeth[5] Weber, Henry[4], Johann Anton[3], Heinrich[2], George[1]) He married **Private Horst**.

Child of Private Eby and Private Horst is:
- 1317	i.	Private[14] Eby.

851. Private[13] Eby (Ezra S.[12], Enos Jacob[11], Sarah Lucinda[10] Hershey, Peter[9], Jacob[8], John[7], Anna Weber[6] Newcomer, Elizabeth[5] Weber, Henry[4], Johann Anton[3], Heinrich[2], George[1]) He married **Private Burkholder**.

Children of Private Eby and Private Burkholder are:
- 1318	i.	Private[14] Eby.
- 1319	ii.	Private Eby.
- 1320	iii.	Private Eby.

853. Private[13] Eby (Ezra S.[12], Enos Jacob[11], Sarah Lucinda[10] Hershey, Peter[9], Jacob[8], John[7], Anna Weber[6] Newcomer, Elizabeth[5] Weber, Henry[4], Johann Anton[3], Heinrich[2], George[1]) He married **Private Martin**.

Children of Private Eby and Private Martin are:
- 1321	i.	Private[14] Eby.
- 1322	ii.	Private Eby.
- 1323	iii.	Private Eby.
- 1324	iv.	Private Eby.

854. Private[13] Eby (Ezra S.[12], Enos Jacob[11], Sarah Lucinda[10] Hershey, Peter[9], Jacob[8], John[7], Anna Weber[6] Newcomer, Elizabeth[5] Weber, Henry[4], Johann Anton[3], Heinrich[2], George[1]) He married **Private Sensenig**.

Children of Private Eby and Private Sensenig are:
- 1325	i.	Private[14] Eby.
- 1326	ii.	Private Eby.

1327   iii.   Private Eby.
1328   iv.   Private Eby.
1329   v.   Marsha Eby, born August 18, 1975; died August 18, 1975.

858. Private[13] Eby (Eli S.[12], Enos Jacob[11], Sarah Lucinda[10] Hershey, Peter[9], Jacob[8], John[7], Anna Weber[6] Newcomer, Elizabeth[5] Weber, Henry[4], Johann Anton[3], Heinrich[2], George[1]) She married **Private Sensenig**.

Child of Private Eby and Private Sensenig is:
1330   i.   Private[14] Sensenig.

859. Private[13] Eby (Eli S.[12], Enos Jacob[11], Sarah Lucinda[10] Hershey, Peter[9], Jacob[8], John[7], Anna Weber[6] Newcomer, Elizabeth[5] Weber, Henry[4], Johann Anton[3], Heinrich[2], George[1]) He married **Private Horning**.

Children of Private Eby and Private Horning are:
1331   i.   Private[14] Eby.
1332   ii.   Private Eby.
1333   iii.   Private Eby.
1334   iv.   Private Eby.

860. Private[13] Eby (Eli S.[12], Enos Jacob[11], Sarah Lucinda[10] Hershey, Peter[9], Jacob[8], John[7], Anna Weber[6] Newcomer, Elizabeth[5] Weber, Henry[4], Johann Anton[3], Heinrich[2], George[1]) She married **Private Kurtz**.

Children of Private Eby and Private Kurtz are:
1335   i.   Private[14] Kurtz.
1336   ii.   Private Kurtz.
1337   iii.   Private Kurtz.
1338   iv.   Private Kurtz.

864. Private[13] Gehman (Private[12], Sarah Lucinda[11] Eby, Sarah Lucinda[10] Hershey, Peter[9], Jacob[8], John[7], Anna Weber[6] Newcomer, Elizabeth[5] Weber, Henry[4], Johann Anton[3], Heinrich[2], George[1]) He married **Private Burkett**.

Child of Private Gehman and Private Burkett is:
1339   i.   Private[14] Gehman.

865. Private[13] Gehman (Private[12], Sarah Lucinda[11] Eby, Sarah Lucinda[10] Hershey, Peter[9], Jacob[8], John[7], Anna Weber[6] Newcomer, Elizabeth[5] Weber, Henry[4], Johann Anton[3], Heinrich[2], George[1]) He married **Private Beachy**.

Child of Private Gehman and Private Beachy is:
1340   i.   Private[14] Gehman.

866. Private[13] Gehman (Private[12], Sarah Lucinda[11] Eby, Sarah Lucinda[10] Hershey, Peter[9], Jacob[8], John[7], Anna Weber[6] Newcomer, Elizabeth[5] Weber, Henry[4], Johann Anton[3], Heinrich[2], George[1]) He married **Private Horst**.

Child of Private Gehman and Private Horst is:
1341   i.   Private[14] Gehman.

867. Private[13] Gehman (Private[12], Sarah Lucinda[11] Eby, Sarah Lucinda[10] Hershey, Peter[9], Jacob[8], John[7], Anna Weber[6] Newcomer, Elizabeth[5] Weber, Henry[4], Johann Anton[3], Heinrich[2], George[1]) She married **Private Martin**.

Child of Private Gehman and Private Martin is:
1342   i.   Private[14] Martin.

868. Private[13] Gehman (Private[12], Sarah Lucinda[11] Eby, Sarah Lucinda[10] Hershey, Peter[9], Jacob[8], John[7], Anna Weber[6] Newcomer, Elizabeth[5] Weber, Henry[4], Johann Anton[3], Heinrich[2], George[1]) She married **Private Heimbach**.

Child of Private Gehman and Private Heimbach is:
1343   i.   Private[14] Heimbach.

870. Private[13] Gehman (Private[12], Sarah Lucinda[11] Eby, Sarah Lucinda[10] Hershey, Peter[9], Jacob[8], John[7], Anna Weber[6] Newcomer, Elizabeth[5] Weber, Henry[4], Johann Anton[3], Heinrich[2], George[1]) He married **Private Metzler**.

Children of Private Gehman and Private Metzler are:
- 1344   i. Private[14] Gehman.
- 1345   ii. Private Gehman.
- 1346   iii. Private Gehman.

872. Private[13] Gehman (Arthur E.[12], Sarah Lucinda[11] Eby, Sarah Lucinda[10] Hershey, Peter[9], Jacob[8], John[7], Anna Weber[6] Newcomer, Elizabeth[5] Weber, Henry[4], Johann Anton[3], Heinrich[2], George[1]) He married **Private Rice**.

Children of Private Gehman and Private Rice are:
- 1347   i. Private[14] Gehman.
- 1348   ii. Private Gehman.

873. Private[13] Gehman (Arthur E.[12], Sarah Lucinda[11] Eby, Sarah Lucinda[10] Hershey, Peter[9], Jacob[8], John[7], Anna Weber[6] Newcomer, Elizabeth[5] Weber, Henry[4], Johann Anton[3], Heinrich[2], George[1]) He married **Private Brendle**.

Child of Private Gehman and Private Brendle is:
- 1349   i. Todd Matthew[14] Gehman, born July 26, 1984; died July 26, 1984.

874. Private[13] Gehman (Arthur E.[12], Sarah Lucinda[11] Eby, Sarah Lucinda[10] Hershey, Peter[9], Jacob[8], John[7], Anna Weber[6] Newcomer, Elizabeth[5] Weber, Henry[4], Johann Anton[3], Heinrich[2], George[1]) She married **Private Landis**.

Children of Private Gehman and Private Landis are:
- 1350   i. Private[14] Landis.
- 1351   ii. Private Landis.

876. Private[13] Gehman (John E.[12], Sarah Lucinda[11] Eby, Sarah Lucinda[10] Hershey, Peter[9], Jacob[8], John[7], Anna Weber[6] Newcomer, Elizabeth[5] Weber, Henry[4], Johann Anton[3], Heinrich[2], George[1]) She married **Private Lauver**.

Children of Private Gehman and Private Lauver are:
- 1352   i. Private[14] Lauver.
- 1353   ii. Private Lauver.

878. Private[13] Gehman (John E.[12], Sarah Lucinda[11] Eby, Sarah Lucinda[10] Hershey, Peter[9], Jacob[8], John[7], Anna Weber[6] Newcomer, Elizabeth[5] Weber, Henry[4], Johann Anton[3], Heinrich[2], George[1]) He married **Private Dien**.

Children of Private Gehman and Private Dien are:
- 1354   i. Private[14] Gehman.
- 1355   ii. Private Gehman.

879. Private[13] Gehman (John E.[12], Sarah Lucinda[11] Eby, Sarah Lucinda[10] Hershey, Peter[9], Jacob[8], John[7], Anna Weber[6] Newcomer, Elizabeth[5] Weber, Henry[4], Johann Anton[3], Heinrich[2], George[1]) He married **Private Metzler**.

Children of Private Gehman and Private Metzler are:
- 1356   i. Private[14] Gehman.
- 1357   ii. Private Gehman.
- 1358   iii. Private Gehman.

881. Private[13] Gehman (John E.[12], Sarah Lucinda[11] Eby, Sarah Lucinda[10] Hershey, Peter[9], Jacob[8], John[7], Anna Weber[6] Newcomer, Elizabeth[5] Weber, Henry[4], Johann Anton[3], Heinrich[2], George[1]) She married **Private Eicher**.

Child of Private Gehman and Private Eicher is:
- 1359   i. Private[14] Eicher.

882. Private[13] Groff (Edith Elizabeth[12] Gehman, Sarah Lucinda[11] Eby, Sarah Lucinda[10] Hershey, Peter[9], Jacob[8], John[7], Anna Weber[6]

Newcomer, Elizabeth[5] Weber, Henry[4], Johann Anton[3], Heinrich[2], George[1]) He married **Private Heimbach**.

Child of Private Groff and Private Heimbach is:
    1360   i.   Private[14] Groff.

883. Private[13] Groff (Edith Elizabeth[12] Gehman, Sarah Lucinda[11] Eby, Sarah Lucinda[10] Hershey, Peter[9], Jacob[8], John[7], Anna Weber[6] Newcomer, Elizabeth[5] Weber, Henry[4], Johann Anton[3], Heinrich[2], George[1]) She married **Private Yoder**.

Children of Private Groff and Private Yoder are:
    1361   i.   Private[14] Yoder.
    1362   ii.   Private Yoder.
    1363   iii.   Private Yoder.
    1364   iv.   Private Yoder.

884. Private[13] Groff (Edith Elizabeth[12] Gehman, Sarah Lucinda[11] Eby, Sarah Lucinda[10] Hershey, Peter[9], Jacob[8], John[7], Anna Weber[6] Newcomer, Elizabeth[5] Weber, Henry[4], Johann Anton[3], Heinrich[2], George[1]) He married **Private Yoder**.

Children of Private Groff and Private Yoder are:
    1365   i.   Private[14] Groff.
    1366   ii.   Private Groff.
    1367   iii.   Private Groff.

885. Private[13] Groff (Edith Elizabeth[12] Gehman, Sarah Lucinda[11] Eby, Sarah Lucinda[10] Hershey, Peter[9], Jacob[8], John[7], Anna Weber[6] Newcomer, Elizabeth[5] Weber, Henry[4], Johann Anton[3], Heinrich[2], George[1]) He married **Private Jutzi**.

Children of Private Groff and Private Jutzi are:
    1368   i.   Private[14] Groff.
    1369   ii.   Private Groff.
    1370   iii.   Private Groff.
    1371   iv.   Private Groff.

886. Private[13] Groff (Edith Elizabeth[12] Gehman, Sarah Lucinda[11] Eby, Sarah Lucinda[10] Hershey, Peter[9], Jacob[8], John[7], Anna Weber[6] Newcomer, Elizabeth[5] Weber, Henry[4], Johann Anton[3], Heinrich[2], George[1]) He married **Private Weaver**.

Children of Private Groff and Private Weaver are:
    1372   i.   Private[14] Groff.
    1373   ii.   Private Groff.
    1374   iii.   Private Groff.
    1375   iv.   Private Groff.

887. Private[13] Groff (Edith Elizabeth[12] Gehman, Sarah Lucinda[11] Eby, Sarah Lucinda[10] Hershey, Peter[9], Jacob[8], John[7], Anna Weber[6] Newcomer, Elizabeth[5] Weber, Henry[4], Johann Anton[3], Heinrich[2], George[1]) He married **Private Bomberger**.

Children of Private Groff and Private Bomberger are:
    1376   i.   Private[14] Groff.
    1377   ii.   Private Groff.
    1378   iii.   Private Groff.

889. Private[13] Rudy (Lucy E.[12] Gehman, Sarah Lucinda[11] Eby, Sarah Lucinda[10] Hershey, Peter[9], Jacob[8], John[7], Anna Weber[6] Newcomer, Elizabeth[5] Weber, Henry[4], Johann Anton[3], Heinrich[2], George[1]) He married **Private Jantzi**.

Child of Private Rudy and Private Jantzi is:
    1379   i.   Private[14] Rudy.

894. Private[13] Gehman (Harry Jacob[12], Sarah Lucinda[11] Eby, Sarah Lucinda[10] Hershey, Peter[9], Jacob[8], John[7], Anna Weber[6] Newcomer, Elizabeth[5] Weber, Henry[4], Johann Anton[3], Heinrich[2], George[1]) He married **Private High**.

Child of Private Gehman and Private High is:
    1380   i.   Private[14] Gehman.

895. Private[13] Gehman (Harry Jacob[12], Sarah Lucinda[11] Eby, Sarah Lucinda[10] Hershey, Peter[9], Jacob[8], John[7], Anna Weber[6] Newcomer, Elizabeth[5] Weber, Henry[4], Johann Anton[3], Heinrich[2], George[1]) She married **Private Kreider**.

Children of Private Gehman and Private Kreider are:
- 1381   i.   Private[14] Kreider.
- 1382   ii.   Private Kreider.
- 1383   iii.   Private Kreider.
- 1384   iv.   Private Kreider.

896. Private[13] Gehman (Harry Jacob[12], Sarah Lucinda[11] Eby, Sarah Lucinda[10] Hershey, Peter[9], Jacob[8], John[7], Anna Weber[6] Newcomer, Elizabeth[5] Weber, Henry[4], Johann Anton[3], Heinrich[2], George[1]) He married **Private Kreider**.

Children of Private Gehman and Private Kreider are:
- 1385   i.   Private[14] Gehman.
- 1386   ii.   Private Gehman.

897. Private[13] Gehman (Harry Jacob[12], Sarah Lucinda[11] Eby, Sarah Lucinda[10] Hershey, Peter[9], Jacob[8], John[7], Anna Weber[6] Newcomer, Elizabeth[5] Weber, Henry[4], Johann Anton[3], Heinrich[2], George[1]) He married **Private High**.

Children of Private Gehman and Private High are:
- 1387   i.   Private[14] Gehman.
- 1388   ii.   Private Gehman.

898. Private[13] Gehman (Harry Jacob[12], Sarah Lucinda[11] Eby, Sarah Lucinda[10] Hershey, Peter[9], Jacob[8], John[7], Anna Weber[6] Newcomer, Elizabeth[5] Weber, Henry[4], Johann Anton[3], Heinrich[2], George[1]) He married **Private Shertzer**.

Children of Private Gehman and Private Shertzer are:
- 1389   i.   Private[14] Gehman.
- 1390   ii.   Private Gehman.
- 1391   iii.   Private Gehman.
- 1392   iv.   Private Gehman.
- 1393   v.   Private Gehman.
- 1394   vi.   Private Gehman.

911. Private[13] Eby (Martin Z.[12], Henry Musser[11], Sarah Lucinda[10] Hershey, Peter[9], Jacob[8], John[7], Anna Weber[6] Newcomer, Elizabeth[5] Weber, Henry[4], Johann Anton[3], Heinrich[2], George[1]) He married **Private Greiser**.

Children of Private Eby and Private Greiser are:
- 1395   i.   Private[14] Eby.
- 1396   ii.   Private Eby.

914. Private[13] Miller (Ethel Z.[12] Eby, Henry Musser[11], Sarah Lucinda[10] Hershey, Peter[9], Jacob[8], John[7], Anna Weber[6] Newcomer, Elizabeth[5] Weber, Henry[4], Johann Anton[3], Heinrich[2], George[1]) He married **Private Pickel**.

Children of Private Miller and Private Pickel are:
- 1397   i.   Private[14] Miller.
- 1398   ii.   Private Simpson.
- 1399   iii.   Private Short.
- 1400   iv.   Private Short.

915. Private[13] Miller (Ethel Z.[12] Eby, Henry Musser[11], Sarah Lucinda[10] Hershey, Peter[9], Jacob[8], John[7], Anna Weber[6] Newcomer, Elizabeth[5] Weber, Henry[4], Johann Anton[3], Heinrich[2], George[1]) He married **Private Weng**.

Children of Private Miller and Private Weng are:
- 1401   i.   Private[14] Miller.
- 1402   ii.   Private Miller.
- 1403   iii.   Private Miller.

923. Private[13] Weaver (Mary Z.[12] Eby, Henry Musser[11], Sarah Lucinda[10] Hershey, Peter[9], Jacob[8], John[7], Anna Weber[6] Newcomer, Elizabeth[5] Weber, Henry[4], Johann Anton[3], Heinrich[2], George[1]) She married **Private Aguirre**.

Children of Private Weaver and Private Aguirre are:
- 1404   i.   Private[14] Aguirre.
- 1405   ii. Private Aguirre.

924. Private[13] Weaver (Mary Z.[12] Eby, Henry Musser[11], Sarah Lucinda[10] Hershey, Peter[9], Jacob[8], John[7], Anna Weber[6] Newcomer, Elizabeth[5] Weber, Henry[4], Johann Anton[3], Heinrich[2], George[1]) She married **Private Glick**.

Children of Private Weaver and Private Glick are:
- 1406   i.   Private[14] Glick.
- 1407   ii. Private Glick.

928. Private[13] Zeiset (Private[12] Martin, Anna Martha[11] Eby, Sarah Lucinda[10] Hershey, Peter[9], Jacob[8], John[7], Anna Weber[6] Newcomer, Elizabeth[5] Weber, Henry[4], Johann Anton[3], Heinrich[2], George[1]) He married **Private Dombach**.

Child of Private Zeiset and Private Dombach is:
- 1408   i.   Private[14] Zeiset.

931. Private[13] Martin (Clarence E.[12], Anna Martha[11] Eby, Sarah Lucinda[10] Hershey, Peter[9], Jacob[8], John[7], Anna Weber[6] Newcomer, Elizabeth[5] Weber, Henry[4], Johann Anton[3], Heinrich[2], George[1]) She married **Private Weaver**.

Children of Private Martin and Private Weaver are:
- 1409   i.   Private[14] Weaver.
- 1410   ii. Private Weaver.

932. Private[13] Martin (Clarence E.[12], Anna Martha[11] Eby, Sarah Lucinda[10] Hershey, Peter[9], Jacob[8], John[7], Anna Weber[6] Newcomer, Elizabeth[5] Weber, Henry[4], Johann Anton[3], Heinrich[2], George[1]) He married **Private Zimmerman**.

Children of Private Martin and Private Zimmerman are:
- 1411   i.   Private[14] Martin.
- 1412   ii.   Private Martin.
- 1413   iii. Private Martin.
- 1414   iv.   Private Martin.

933. Private[13] Martin (Clarence E.[12], Anna Martha[11] Eby, Sarah Lucinda[10] Hershey, Peter[9], Jacob[8], John[7], Anna Weber[6] Newcomer, Elizabeth[5] Weber, Henry[4], Johann Anton[3], Heinrich[2], George[1]) She married **Private Kurtz**.

Children of Private Martin and Private Kurtz are:
- 1415   i.   Private[14] Kurtz.
- 1416   ii. Private Kurtz.

934. Private[13] Martin (Clarence E.[12], Anna Martha[11] Eby, Sarah Lucinda[10] Hershey, Peter[9], Jacob[8], John[7], Anna Weber[6] Newcomer, Elizabeth[5] Weber, Henry[4], Johann Anton[3], Heinrich[2], George[1]) He married **Private Hoover**.

Children of Private Martin and Private Hoover are:
- 1417   i.   Private[14] Martin.
- 1418   ii.   Private Martin.
- 1419   iii. Private Martin.
- 1420   iv.   Private Martin.

935. Private[13] Martin (Clarence E.[12], Anna Martha[11] Eby, Sarah Lucinda[10] Hershey, Peter[9], Jacob[8], John[7], Anna Weber[6] Newcomer, Elizabeth[5] Weber, Henry[4], Johann Anton[3], Heinrich[2], George[1]) He married **Private Good**.

Children of Private Martin and Private Good are:
- 1421   i.   Private[14] Martin.
- 1422   ii. Private Martin. He married Private Steffy.

1423   iii.   Private Martin.

937. Private[13] Martin (Mary E.[12], Anna Martha[11] Eby, Sarah Lucinda[10] Hershey, Peter[9], Jacob[8], John[7], Anna Weber[6] Newcomer, Elizabeth[5] Weber, Henry[4], Johann Anton[3], Heinrich[2], George[1]) She married **Private Thomas**.

Children of Private Martin and Private Thomas are:
1424   i.   Private[14] Thomas.
1425   ii.   Private Thomas.

938. Private[13] Martin (Paul E.[12], Anna Martha[11] Eby, Sarah Lucinda[10] Hershey, Peter[9], Jacob[8], John[7], Anna Weber[6] Newcomer, Elizabeth[5] Weber, Henry[4], Johann Anton[3], Heinrich[2], George[1]) He married **Private Nolt**.

Child of Private Martin and Private Nolt is:
1426   i.   Private[14] Martin.

939. Private[13] Martin (Paul E.[12], Anna Martha[11] Eby, Sarah Lucinda[10] Hershey, Peter[9], Jacob[8], John[7], Anna Weber[6] Newcomer, Elizabeth[5] Weber, Henry[4], Johann Anton[3], Heinrich[2], George[1]) She married **Private Hurst**.

Children of Private Martin and Private Hurst are:
1427   i.   Private[14] Hurst.
1428   ii.   Private Hurst.
1429   iii.   Private Hurst.

940. Private[13] Martin (Paul E.[12], Anna Martha[11] Eby, Sarah Lucinda[10] Hershey, Peter[9], Jacob[8], John[7], Anna Weber[6] Newcomer, Elizabeth[5] Weber, Henry[4], Johann Anton[3], Heinrich[2], George[1]) He married **Private Ziegler**.

Children of Private Martin and Private Ziegler are:
1430   i.   Private[14] Martin.
1431   ii.   Private Martin.
1432   iii.   Private Martin.

941. Private[13] Martin (Earl E.[12], Anna Martha[11] Eby, Sarah Lucinda[10] Hershey, Peter[9], Jacob[8], John[7], Anna Weber[6] Newcomer, Elizabeth[5] Weber, Henry[4], Johann Anton[3], Heinrich[2], George[1]) She married **Private Good**.

Child of Private Martin and Private Good is:
1433   i.   Private[14] Good.

942. Private[13] Martin (Earl E.[12], Anna Martha[11] Eby, Sarah Lucinda[10] Hershey, Peter[9], Jacob[8], John[7], Anna Weber[6] Newcomer, Elizabeth[5] Weber, Henry[4], Johann Anton[3], Heinrich[2], George[1]) She married **Private Eberly**.

Children of Private Martin and Private Eberly are:
1434   i.   Private[14] Eberly.
1435   ii.   Private Eberly.

949. Private[13] Eby (Private[12], Aaron Buckwalter[11], Sarah Lucinda[10] Hershey, Peter[9], Jacob[8], John[7], Anna Weber[6] Newcomer, Elizabeth[5] Weber, Henry[4], Johann Anton[3], Heinrich[2], George[1]) She married **Private Groff**.

Child of Private Eby and Private Groff is:
1436   i.   Private[14] Groff.

956. Private[13] Eby (Private[12], Aaron Buckwalter[11], Sarah Lucinda[10] Hershey, Peter[9], Jacob[8], John[7], Anna Weber[6] Newcomer, Elizabeth[5] Weber, Henry[4], Johann Anton[3], Heinrich[2], George[1]) She married **Private Nolt**.

Children of Private Eby and Private Nolt are:
1437   i.   Private[14] Nolt.
1438   ii.   Private Nolt.

958. Private[13] Eby (Richard S.[12], Aaron Buckwalter[11], Sarah Lucinda[10] Hershey, Peter[9], Jacob[8], John[7], Anna Weber[6] Newcomer, Elizabeth[5] Weber, Henry[4], Johann Anton[3], Heinrich[2], George[1]) He married **Private Hershey**.

Children of Private Eby and Private Hershey are:
- 1439   i.   Private[14] Eby.
- 1440   ii.   Private Eby.
- 1441   iii.   Private Eby.

960. Private[13] Eby (Richard S.[12], Aaron Buckwalter[11], Sarah Lucinda[10] Hershey, Peter[9], Jacob[8], John[7], Anna Weber[6] Newcomer, Elizabeth[5] Weber, Henry[4], Johann Anton[3], Heinrich[2], George[1]) She married **Private Delgado**.

Children of Private Eby and Private Delgado are:
- 1442   i.   Private[14] Delgado.
- 1443   ii.   Private Delgado.

961. Private[13] Eby (Richard S.[12], Aaron Buckwalter[11], Sarah Lucinda[10] Hershey, Peter[9], Jacob[8], John[7], Anna Weber[6] Newcomer, Elizabeth[5] Weber, Henry[4], Johann Anton[3], Heinrich[2], George[1]) He married **Private Beachy**.

Child of Private Eby and Private Beachy is:
- 1444   i.   Private[14] Eby.

962. Private[13] Eby (Richard S.[12], Aaron Buckwalter[11], Sarah Lucinda[10] Hershey, Peter[9], Jacob[8], John[7], Anna Weber[6] Newcomer, Elizabeth[5] Weber, Henry[4], Johann Anton[3], Heinrich[2], George[1]) He married **Private Zimmerman**.

Children of Private Eby and Private Zimmerman are:
- 1445   i.   Private[14] Eby.
- 1446   ii.   Private Eby.

963. Private[13] Eby (Richard S.[12], Aaron Buckwalter[11], Sarah Lucinda[10] Hershey, Peter[9], Jacob[8], John[7], Anna Weber[6] Newcomer, Elizabeth[5] Weber, Henry[4], Johann Anton[3], Heinrich[2], George[1]) She married **Private Ober**.

Children of Private Eby and Private Ober are:
- 1447   i.   Private[14] Ober.
- 1448   ii.   Private Ober.
- 1449   iii.   Private Ober.

982. Private[13] Crouthamel (Erma E.[12] Hershey, Galen Warren[11], Isaiah B.[10], Peter[9], Jacob[8], John[7], Anna Weber[6] Newcomer, Elizabeth[5] Weber, Henry[4], Johann Anton[3], Heinrich[2], George[1]) She married **Private Moyer**.

Children of Private Crouthamel and Private Moyer are:
- 1450   i.   Private[14] Moyer.
- 1451   ii.   Private Moyer. She married Private Wood.

983. Private[13] Crouthamel (Erma E.[12] Hershey, Galen Warren[11], Isaiah B.[10], Peter[9], Jacob[8], John[7], Anna Weber[6] Newcomer, Elizabeth[5] Weber, Henry[4], Johann Anton[3], Heinrich[2], George[1]) She married **(1) Private Pier**.   She married **(2) Private O'Connell**.

Child of Private Crouthamel and Private Pier is:
- 1452   i.   Private[14] Pier.

Child of Private Crouthamel and Private O'Connell is:
- 1453   i.   Private[14] O'Connell.

984. Private[13] Crouthamel (Erma E.[12] Hershey, Galen Warren[11], Isaiah B.[10], Peter[9], Jacob[8], John[7], Anna Weber[6] Newcomer, Elizabeth[5] Weber, Henry[4], Johann Anton[3], Heinrich[2], George[1]) He married **Private Baum**.

Children of Private Crouthamel and Private Baum are:
- 1454   i.   Private[14] Crouthamel.
- 1455   ii.   Private Crouthamel.

985. Private[13] **Hershey** (Galen Clair[12], Galen Warren[11], Isaiah B.[10], Peter[9], Jacob[8], John[7], Anna Weber[6] Newcomer, Elizabeth[5] Weber, Henry[4], Johann Anton[3], Heinrich[2], George[1]) He married **Private Manley**.

Children of Private Hershey and Private Manley are:
- 1456 i. Private[14] Hershey.
- 1457 ii. Private Hershey.

986. Private[13] **Hershey** (Galen Clair[12], Galen Warren[11], Isaiah B.[10], Peter[9], Jacob[8], John[7], Anna Weber[6] Newcomer, Elizabeth[5] Weber, Henry[4], Johann Anton[3], Heinrich[2], George[1]) She married **Private Glancey**.

Children of Private Hershey and Private Glancey are:
- 1458 i. Private[14] Glancey.
- 1459 ii. Private Glancey.

988. Private[13] **Hershey** (Private[12], Henry Clay[11], Enos Jacob[10], Peter[9], Jacob[8], John[7], Anna Weber[6] Newcomer, Elizabeth[5] Weber, Henry[4], Johann Anton[3], Heinrich[2], George[1]) She married **Private Nyeholt**.

Child of Private Hershey and Private Nyeholt is:
- 1460 i. Private[14] Nyeholt.

994. Private[13] **Hershey** (Private[12], Henry Clay[11], Enos Jacob[10], Peter[9], Jacob[8], John[7], Anna Weber[6] Newcomer, Elizabeth[5] Weber, Henry[4], Johann Anton[3], Heinrich[2], George[1]) She married **Private Miller**.

Child of Private Hershey and Private Miller is:
- 1461 i. Private[14] Miller.

995. Private[13] **Hershey** (Private[12], Henry Clay[11], Enos Jacob[10], Peter[9], Jacob[8], John[7], Anna Weber[6] Newcomer, Elizabeth[5] Weber, Henry[4], Johann Anton[3], Heinrich[2], George[1]) He married **Private Johnson**.

Children of Private Hershey and Private Johnson are:
- 1462 i. Private[14] Hershey.
- 1463 ii. Private Hershey.

999. Private[13] **Metzler** (Hazel Pauline[12] Hershey, Henry Clay[11], Enos Jacob[10], Peter[9], Jacob[8], John[7], Anna Weber[6] Newcomer, Elizabeth[5] Weber, Henry[4], Johann Anton[3], Heinrich[2], George[1]) He married **Private Grason**.

Children of Private Metzler and Private Grason are:
- 1464 i. Private[14] Metzler.
- 1465 ii. Private Metzler.

1001. Private[13] **Hershey** (Ralph Glenn[12], Henry Clay[11], Enos Jacob[10], Peter[9], Jacob[8], John[7], Anna Weber[6] Newcomer, Elizabeth[5] Weber, Henry[4], Johann Anton[3], Heinrich[2], George[1]) He married **Private McSparron**.

Children of Private Hershey and Private McSparron are:
- 1466 i. Private[14] Hershey.
- 1467 ii. Private Hershey.
- 1468 iii. Private Hershey.

1002. Private[13] **Hershey** (Ralph Glenn[12], Henry Clay[11], Enos Jacob[10], Peter[9], Jacob[8], John[7], Anna Weber[6] Newcomer, Elizabeth[5] Weber, Henry[4], Johann Anton[3], Heinrich[2], George[1]) She married **Private Hershey**.

Children of Private Hershey and Private Hershey are:
- 1469 i. Private[14] Hershey.
- 1470 ii. Private Hershey.

1003. Private[13] **Hershey** (Ralph Glenn[12], Henry Clay[11], Enos Jacob[10], Peter[9], Jacob[8], John[7], Anna Weber[6] Newcomer, Elizabeth[5]

Weber, Henry[4], Johann Anton[3], Heinrich[2], George[1]) He married **Private Long**.

Children of Private Hershey and Private Long are:
- 1471   i. Private[14] Hershey.
- 1472   ii. Private Hershey.
- 1473   iii. Private Hershey.

1004. Private[13] Kreider (Gladys Edna[12] Hershey, Henry Clay[11], Enos Jacob[10], Peter[9], Jacob[8], John[7], Anna Weber[6] Newcomer, Elizabeth[5] Weber, Henry[4], Johann Anton[3], Heinrich[2], George[1]) She married **Private Hoffman**.

Children of Private Kreider and Private Hoffman are:
- 1474   i. Private[14] Hoffman.
- 1475   ii. Private Hoffman.
- 1476   iii. Private Hoffman.

1006. Private[13] Kreider (Gladys Edna[12] Hershey, Henry Clay[11], Enos Jacob[10], Peter[9], Jacob[8], John[7], Anna Weber[6] Newcomer, Elizabeth[5] Weber, Henry[4], Johann Anton[3], Heinrich[2], George[1]) He married **Private Wenger**.

Children of Private Kreider and Private Wenger are:
- 1477   i. Private[14] Kreider.
- 1478   ii. Private Kreider.
- 1479   iii. Private Kreider.

1007. Private[13] Kreider (Gladys Edna[12] Hershey, Henry Clay[11], Enos Jacob[10], Peter[9], Jacob[8], John[7], Anna Weber[6] Newcomer, Elizabeth[5] Weber, Henry[4], Johann Anton[3], Heinrich[2], George[1]) She married **Private Gordley**.

Children of Private Kreider and Private Gordley are:
- 1480   i. Private[14] Gordley.
- 1481   ii. Private Gordley.
- 1482   iii. Private Gordley.

1012. Private[13] Hershey (Clifford Eby[12], Henry Clay[11], Enos Jacob[10], Peter[9], Jacob[8], John[7], Anna Weber[6] Newcomer, Elizabeth[5] Weber, Henry[4], Johann Anton[3], Heinrich[2], George[1]) He married **Private Rutter**.

Children of Private Hershey and Private Rutter are:
- 1483   i. Private[14] Hershey.
- 1484   ii. Private Hershey.

1013. Private[13] Hershey (Clifford Eby[12], Henry Clay[11], Enos Jacob[10], Peter[9], Jacob[8], John[7], Anna Weber[6] Newcomer, Elizabeth[5] Weber, Henry[4], Johann Anton[3], Heinrich[2], George[1]) He married **Private Napoli**.

Children of Private Hershey and Private Napoli are:
- 1485   i. Private[14] Hershey.
- 1486   ii. Private Hershey.

1026. Private[13] Martin (Private[12] Hershey, Mark Eby[11], Enos Jacob[10], Peter[9], Jacob[8], John[7], Anna Weber[6] Newcomer, Elizabeth[5] Weber, Henry[4], Johann Anton[3], Heinrich[2], George[1]) He married **Private Groff**.

Children of Private Martin and Private Groff are:
- 1487   i. Private[14] Martin.
- 1488   ii. Private Martin.

1036. Private[13] Bender (Private[12] Hershey, Mark Eby[11], Enos Jacob[10], Peter[9], Jacob[8], John[7], Anna Weber[6] Newcomer, Elizabeth[5] Weber, Henry[4], Johann Anton[3], Heinrich[2], George[1]) She married **Private Brenneman**.

Children of Private Bender and Private Brenneman are:
- 1489   i. Private[14] Brenneman.
- 1490   ii. Private Brenneman.

1037. Private[13] Hershey (Private[12], Mark Eby[11], Enos Jacob[10], Peter[9], Jacob[8], John[7], Anna Weber[6] Newcomer, Elizabeth[5] Weber, Henry[4], Johann Anton[3], Heinrich[2], George[1]) She married **Private Yoder**.

Children of Private Hershey and Private Yoder are:
- 1491   i.   Private[14] Yoder.
- 1492   ii.   Private Yoder.

1038. Private[13] Hershey (Private[12], Mark Eby[11], Enos Jacob[10], Peter[9], Jacob[8], John[7], Anna Weber[6] Newcomer, Elizabeth[5] Weber, Henry[4], Johann Anton[3], Heinrich[2], George[1]) She married **Private Rohrer**.

Children of Private Hershey and Private Rohrer are:
- 1493   i.   Private[14] Rohrer.
- 1494   ii.   Private Rohrer.

1039. Private[13] Hershey (Private[12], Mark Eby[11], Enos Jacob[10], Peter[9], Jacob[8], John[7], Anna Weber[6] Newcomer, Elizabeth[5] Weber, Henry[4], Johann Anton[3], Heinrich[2], George[1]) She married **Private Lapp**.

Children of Private Hershey and Private Lapp are:
- 1495   i.   Private[14] Lapp.
- 1496   ii.   Private Lapp.

1040. Private[13] Hershey (Private[12], Mark Eby[11], Enos Jacob[10], Peter[9], Jacob[8], John[7], Anna Weber[6] Newcomer, Elizabeth[5] Weber, Henry[4], Johann Anton[3], Heinrich[2], George[1]) He married **Private Saxton**.

Children of Private Hershey and Private Saxton are:
- 1497   i.   Private[14] Hershey.
- 1498   ii.   Private Hershey.

1041. Private[13] Herr (Private[12] Hershey, David Warren[11], Enos Jacob[10], Peter[9], Jacob[8], John[7], Anna Weber[6] Newcomer, Elizabeth[5] Weber, Henry[4], Johann Anton[3], Heinrich[2], George[1]) He married **Private Newlin**.

Child of Private Herr and Private Newlin is:
- 1499   i.   Private[14] Herr.

1044. Private[13] Hershey (Vincent Denlinger[12], David Warren[11], Enos Jacob[10], Peter[9], Jacob[8], John[7], Anna Weber[6] Newcomer, Elizabeth[5] Weber, Henry[4], Johann Anton[3], Heinrich[2], George[1]) He married **Private Stauffer**.

Child of Private Hershey and Private Stauffer is:
- 1500   i.   Private[14] Hershey.

1046. Private[13] Hershey (Vincent Denlinger[12], David Warren[11], Enos Jacob[10], Peter[9], Jacob[8], John[7], Anna Weber[6] Newcomer, Elizabeth[5] Weber, Henry[4], Johann Anton[3], Heinrich[2], George[1]) He married **Private Coates**.

Child of Private Hershey and Private Coates is:
- 1501   i.   Private[14] Hershey.

1047. Private[13] Hershey (Vincent Denlinger[12], David Warren[11], Enos Jacob[10], Peter[9], Jacob[8], John[7], Anna Weber[6] Newcomer, Elizabeth[5] Weber, Henry[4], Johann Anton[3], Heinrich[2], George[1]) He married **Private Buzzard**.

Children of Private Hershey and Private Buzzard are:
- 1502   i.   Private[14] Hershey.
- 1503   ii.   Private Hershey.
- 1504   iii.   Private Hershey.

1050. Private[13] Ranck (Lester Hershey[12], Mary Helen[11] Hershey, Enos Jacob[10], Peter[9], Jacob[8], John[7], Anna Weber[6] Newcomer, Elizabeth[5] Weber, Henry[4], Johann Anton[3], Heinrich[2], George[1]) He married **Private Nissley**.

Children of Private Ranck and Private Nissley are:

1505   i.   Private[14] Ranck.
1506   ii.   Private Ranck.
1507   iii.   Private Ranck.

1051. Private[13] Ranck (Lester Hershey[12], Mary Helen[11] Hershey, Enos Jacob[10], Peter[9], Jacob[8], John[7], Anna Weber[6] Newcomer, Elizabeth[5] Weber, Henry[4], Johann Anton[3], Heinrich[2], George[1]) She married **Private Thomas**.

Children of Private Ranck and Private Thomas are:
1508   i.   Private[14] Thomas.
1509   ii.   Private Thomas.
1510   iii.   Private Thomas.

1054. Private[13] Ranck (Arthur Eby[12], Mary Helen[11] Hershey, Enos Jacob[10], Peter[9], Jacob[8], John[7], Anna Weber[6] Newcomer, Elizabeth[5] Weber, Henry[4], Johann Anton[3], Heinrich[2], George[1]) He married **Private Showalter**.

Children of Private Ranck and Private Showalter are:
1511   i.   Private[14] Ranck.
1512   ii.   Private Ranck.

1058. Private[13] Ranck (Donald Edwin[12], Mary Helen[11] Hershey, Enos Jacob[10], Peter[9], Jacob[8], John[7], Anna Weber[6] Newcomer, Elizabeth[5] Weber, Henry[4], Johann Anton[3], Heinrich[2], George[1]) She married **Private Yoder**.

Child of Private Ranck and Private Yoder is:
1513   i.   Private[14] Yoder.

1060. Private[13] Daman (Janet Potter[12] Hess, Clyde C.[11], Elizabeth[10] Hershey, Peter[9], Jacob[8], John[7], Anna Weber[6] Newcomer, Elizabeth[5] Weber, Henry[4], Johann Anton[3], Heinrich[2], George[1]) She married **Private Hauch**.

Child of Private Daman and Private Hauch is:
1514   i.   Private[14] Hauch.

1061. Private[13] Daman (Janet Potter[12] Hess, Clyde C.[11], Elizabeth[10] Hershey, Peter[9], Jacob[8], John[7], Anna Weber[6] Newcomer, Elizabeth[5] Weber, Henry[4], Johann Anton[3], Heinrich[2], George[1]) She married **Private Gates**.

Children of Private Daman and Private Gates are:
1515   i.   Private[14] Gates.
1516   ii.   Private Gates.

1067. Private[13] Hershey (Paul Kenneth[12], Paul Keene[11], Henry Peter[10], Peter[9], Jacob[8], John[7], Anna Weber[6] Newcomer, Elizabeth[5] Weber, Henry[4], Johann Anton[3], Heinrich[2], George[1]) She married **Private Murphy**.

Child of Private Hershey and Private Murphy is:
1517   i.   Private[14] Murphy.

1071. Private[13] Hewes (Private[12] Pennock, Esther Elizabeth[11] Hershey, Martin Eby[10], Peter[9], Jacob[8], John[7], Anna Weber[6] Newcomer, Elizabeth[5] Weber, Henry[4], Johann Anton[3], Heinrich[2], George[1]) She married **Private Printz**.

Child of Private Hewes and Private Printz is:
1518   i.   Private[14] Printz.

1072. Private[13] Hewes (Private[12] Pennock, Esther Elizabeth[11] Hershey, Martin Eby[10], Peter[9], Jacob[8], John[7], Anna Weber[6] Newcomer, Elizabeth[5] Weber, Henry[4], Johann Anton[3], Heinrich[2], George[1]) He married **Private Lichty**.

Children of Private Hewes and Private Lichty are:
1519   i.   Private[14] Hewes.
1520   ii.   Private Hewes.

1073. Private[13] Hewes (Private[12] Pennock, Esther Elizabeth[11] Hershey, Martin Eby[10], Peter[9], Jacob[8], John[7], Anna Weber[6] Newcomer, Elizabeth[5] Weber, Henry[4], Johann Anton[3], Heinrich[2], George[1]) She married **Private Mohr**.

Child of Private Hewes and Private Mohr is:
- 1521 i. Private[14] Mohr.

1077. Private[13] Skiles (Betty Louise[12] Pennock, Esther Elizabeth[11] Hershey, Martin Eby[10], Peter[9], Jacob[8], John[7], Anna Weber[6] Newcomer, Elizabeth[5] Weber, Henry[4], Johann Anton[3], Heinrich[2], George[1]) He married **Private Loriencz**.

Children of Private Skiles and Private Loriencz are:
- 1522 i. Private[14] Skiles.
- 1523 ii. Private Skiles.
- 1524 iii. Private Skiles.

1078. Private[13] Skiles (Betty Louise[12] Pennock, Esther Elizabeth[11] Hershey, Martin Eby[10], Peter[9], Jacob[8], John[7], Anna Weber[6] Newcomer, Elizabeth[5] Weber, Henry[4], Johann Anton[3], Heinrich[2], George[1]) He married **Private Johndrow**.

Child of Private Skiles and Private Johndrow is:
- 1525 i. Private[14] Skiles.

1080. Private[13] Rodgers (Private[12], Miriam Clara[11] Hershey, Martin Eby[10], Peter[9], Jacob[8], John[7], Anna Weber[6] Newcomer, Elizabeth[5] Weber, Henry[4], Johann Anton[3], Heinrich[2], George[1]) He married **Private Canning**.

Children of Private Rodgers and Private Canning are:
- 1526 i. Private[14] Rodgers.
- 1527 ii. Private Rodgers.

1096. Private[13] Richardson (Private[12] Hershey, Willis Daniel[11], Silas N.[10], Peter[9], Jacob[8], John[7], Anna Weber[6] Newcomer, Elizabeth[5] Weber, Henry[4], Johann Anton[3], Heinrich[2], George[1]) She married **Private Woods**.

Children of Private Richardson and Private Woods are:
- 1528 i. Private[14] Woods.
- 1529 ii. Private Woods.

1097. Private[13] Richardson (Private[12] Hershey, Willis Daniel[11], Silas N.[10], Peter[9], Jacob[8], John[7], Anna Weber[6] Newcomer, Elizabeth[5] Weber, Henry[4], Johann Anton[3], Heinrich[2], George[1]) She married **Private Mercer**.

Children of Private Richardson and Private Mercer are:
- 1530 i. Private[14] Mercer.
- 1531 ii. Private Mercer.
- 1532 iii. Private Mercer.

1099. Private[13] Summers (Private[12] Hershey, Willis Daniel[11], Silas N.[10], Peter[9], Jacob[8], John[7], Anna Weber[6] Newcomer, Elizabeth[5] Weber, Henry[4], Johann Anton[3], Heinrich[2], George[1]) She married **Private Shirk**.

Children of Private Summers and Private Shirk are:
- 1533 i. Private[14] Shirk.
- 1534 ii. Private Shirk.

1100. Private[13] Summers (Private[12] Hershey, Willis Daniel[11], Silas N.[10], Peter[9], Jacob[8], John[7], Anna Weber[6] Newcomer, Elizabeth[5] Weber, Henry[4], Johann Anton[3], Heinrich[2], George[1]) He married **Private Weston**.

Child of Private Summers and Private Weston is:
- 1535 i. Private[14] Summers.

1101. Private[13] Bomberger (Private[12] Hershey, Willis Daniel[11], Silas N.[10], Peter[9], Jacob[8], John[7], Anna Weber[6] Newcomer, Elizabeth[5] Weber, Henry[4], Johann Anton[3], Heinrich[2], George[1]) He married **Private Unknown**.

Children of Private Bomberger and Private Unknown are:

1536 i. Private[14] Bomberger.
1537 ii. Private Bomberger.

1102. Private[13] Hershey (Private[12], Willis Daniel[11], Silas N.[10], Peter[9], Jacob[8], John[7], Anna Weber[6] Newcomer, Elizabeth[5] Weber, Henry[4], Johann Anton[3], Heinrich[2], George[1]) She married **Private Dick**.

Children of Private Hershey and Private Dick are:
1538 i. Private[14] Hershey.
1539 ii. Private Hershey.

1103. Private[13] Hershey (Private[12], Willis Daniel[11], Silas N.[10], Peter[9], Jacob[8], John[7], Anna Weber[6] Newcomer, Elizabeth[5] Weber, Henry[4], Johann Anton[3], Heinrich[2], George[1]) He married **Private Wance**.

Children of Private Hershey and Private Wance are:
1540 i. Private[14] Hershey.
1541 ii. Private Hershey.
1542 iii. Private Hershey.

1107. Private[13] Hershey (Jay Paul[12], Willis Daniel[11], Silas N.[10], Peter[9], Jacob[8], John[7], Anna Weber[6] Newcomer, Elizabeth[5] Weber, Henry[4], Johann Anton[3], Heinrich[2], George[1]) She married **Private Eby**.

Children of Private Hershey and Private Eby are:
1543 i. Private[14] Eby.
1544 ii. Private Eby.
1545 iii. Private Eby.

1108. Private[13] Hershey (Jay Paul[12], Willis Daniel[11], Silas N.[10], Peter[9], Jacob[8], John[7], Anna Weber[6] Newcomer, Elizabeth[5] Weber, Henry[4], Johann Anton[3], Heinrich[2], George[1]) She married **Private Gatto**.

Child of Private Hershey and Private Gatto is:
1546 i. Private[14] Gatto.

1109. Private[13] Hershey (Jay Paul[12], Willis Daniel[11], Silas N.[10], Peter[9], Jacob[8], John[7], Anna Weber[6] Newcomer, Elizabeth[5] Weber, Henry[4], Johann Anton[3], Heinrich[2], George[1]) He married **Private Unknown**.

Children of Private Hershey and Private Unknown are:
1547 i. Private[14] Hershey.
1548 ii. Private Hershey.

Generation No. 14

1157. Private[14] Fox (Private[13], Willis Eby[12], Ella Barbara[11] Eby, Sarah Lucinda[10] Hershey, Peter[9], Jacob[8], John[7], Anna Weber[6] Newcomer, Elizabeth[5] Weber, Henry[4], Johann Anton[3], Heinrich[2], George[1]) He married **Private Eberly**.

Child of Private Fox and Private Eberly is:
1549 i. Private[15] Fox.

1158. Private[14] Fox (Private[13], Willis Eby[12], Ella Barbara[11] Eby, Sarah Lucinda[10] Hershey, Peter[9], Jacob[8], John[7], Anna Weber[6] Newcomer, Elizabeth[5] Weber, Henry[4], Johann Anton[3], Heinrich[2], George[1]) She married **Private Stauffer**.

Children of Private Fox and Private Stauffer are:
1550 i. Private[15] Stauffer.
1551 ii. Private Stauffer.

1173. Private[14] Augsburger (Private[13] Fox, Henry Peter[12], Ella Barbara[11] Eby, Sarah Lucinda[10] Hershey, Peter[9], Jacob[8], John[7], Anna Weber[6] Newcomer, Elizabeth[5] Weber, Henry[4], Johann Anton[3], Heinrich[2], George[1]) She married **Private Hostetter**.

Children of Private Augsburger and Private Hostetter are:

1552   i. Private[15] Hostetter.
1553   ii. Private Hostetter.

1174. Private[14] Augsburger (Private[13] Fox, Henry Peter[12], Ella Barbara[11] Eby, Sarah Lucinda[10] Hershey, Peter[9], Jacob[8], John[7], Anna Weber[6] Newcomer, Elizabeth[5] Weber, Henry[4], Johann Anton[3], Heinrich[2], George[1]) She married **Private Groff**.

Children of Private Augsburger and Private Groff are:
1554   i. Private[15] Groff.
1555   ii. Private Groff.

1177. Private[14] Eberly (Private[13] Fox, Henry Peter[12], Ella Barbara[11] Eby, Sarah Lucinda[10] Hershey, Peter[9], Jacob[8], John[7], Anna Weber[6] Newcomer, Elizabeth[5] Weber, Henry[4], Johann Anton[3], Heinrich[2], George[1]) He married **Private Nafziger**.

Children of Private Eberly and Private Nafziger are:
1556   i. Private[15] Eberly.
1557   ii. Private Eberly.

1181. Private[14] Good (Private[13] Fox, Henry Peter[12], Ella Barbara[11] Eby, Sarah Lucinda[10] Hershey, Peter[9], Jacob[8], John[7], Anna Weber[6] Newcomer, Elizabeth[5] Weber, Henry[4], Johann Anton[3], Heinrich[2], George[1]) He married **Private Weaver**.

Child of Private Good and Private Weaver is:
1558   i. Private[15] Good.

1182. Private[14] Good (Private[13] Fox, Henry Peter[12], Ella Barbara[11] Eby, Sarah Lucinda[10] Hershey, Peter[9], Jacob[8], John[7], Anna Weber[6] Newcomer, Elizabeth[5] Weber, Henry[4], Johann Anton[3], Heinrich[2], George[1]) She married **Private Denlinger**.

Children of Private Good and Private Denlinger are:
1559   i. Private[15] Denlinger.
1560   ii. Private Denlinger.

1183. Private[14] Zimmerman (Private[13] Fox, Henry Peter[12], Ella Barbara[11] Eby, Sarah Lucinda[10] Hershey, Peter[9], Jacob[8], John[7], Anna Weber[6] Newcomer, Elizabeth[5] Weber, Henry[4], Johann Anton[3], Heinrich[2], George[1]) She married **Private Kauffman**.

Child of Private Zimmerman and Private Kauffman is:
1561   i. Private[15] Kauffman.

1184. Private[14] Zimmerman (Private[13] Fox, Henry Peter[12], Ella Barbara[11] Eby, Sarah Lucinda[10] Hershey, Peter[9], Jacob[8], John[7], Anna Weber[6] Newcomer, Elizabeth[5] Weber, Henry[4], Johann Anton[3], Heinrich[2], George[1]) He married **Private Bucher**.

Children of Private Zimmerman and Private Bucher are:
1562   i. Private[15] Zimmerman.
1563   ii. Private Zimmerman.

1185. Private[14] Zimmerman (Private[13] Fox, Henry Peter[12], Ella Barbara[11] Eby, Sarah Lucinda[10] Hershey, Peter[9], Jacob[8], John[7], Anna Weber[6] Newcomer, Elizabeth[5] Weber, Henry[4], Johann Anton[3], Heinrich[2], George[1]) She married **Private Buckwalter**.

Children of Private Zimmerman and Private Buckwalter are:
1564   i. Private[15] Buckwalter.
1565   ii. Private Buckwalter.
1566   iii. Private Buckwalter.

1210. Private[14] Zimmerman (Private[13], Sarah Lucinda[12] Fox, Ella Barbara[11] Eby, Sarah Lucinda[10] Hershey, Peter[9], Jacob[8], John[7], Anna Weber[6] Newcomer, Elizabeth[5] Weber, Henry[4], Johann Anton[3], Heinrich[2], George[1]) She married **Private Hostetter**.

Child of Private Zimmerman and Private Hostetter is:
1567   i. Private[15] Hostetter.

1213. Private[14] Zimmerman (Private[13], Sarah Lucinda[12] Fox, Ella Barbara[11] Eby, Sarah Lucinda[10] Hershey, Peter[9], Jacob[8], John[7], Anna Weber[6] Newcomer, Elizabeth[5] Weber, Henry[4], Johann Anton[3], Heinrich[2], George[1]) She married **Private Hostetter**.

Children of Private Zimmerman and Private Hostetter are:
- 1568   i.   Private[15] Hostetter.
- 1569   ii.   Private Hostetter.
- 1570   iii.   Private Hostetter.
- 1571   iv.   Private Hostetter.

1248. Private[14] Martin (Private[13], Susan W.[12] Eby, Peter Hershey[11], Sarah Lucinda[10] Hershey, Peter[9], Jacob[8], John[7], Anna Weber[6] Newcomer, Elizabeth[5] Weber, Henry[4], Johann Anton[3], Heinrich[2], George[1]) She married **Private Ebersole**.

Child of Private Martin and Private Ebersole is:
- 1572   i.   Private[15] Ebersole.

1294. Private[14] Zimmerman (Private[13] Stauffer, Emma Mae[12] Eby, Peter Hershey[11], Sarah Lucinda[10] Hershey, Peter[9], Jacob[8], John[7], Anna Weber[6] Newcomer, Elizabeth[5] Weber, Henry[4], Johann Anton[3], Heinrich[2], George[1]) She married **Private Garman**.

Child of Private Zimmerman and Private Garman is:
- 1573   i.   Private[15] Garman.

1295. Private[14] Zimmerman (Private[13] Stauffer, Emma Mae[12] Eby, Peter Hershey[11], Sarah Lucinda[10] Hershey, Peter[9], Jacob[8], John[7], Anna Weber[6] Newcomer, Elizabeth[5] Weber, Henry[4], Johann Anton[3], Heinrich[2], George[1]) She married **Private Shirk**.

Children of Private Zimmerman and Private Shirk are:
- 1574   i.   Private[15] Shirk.
- 1575   ii.   Private Shirk.

1296. Private[14] Zimmerman (Private[13] Stauffer, Emma Mae[12] Eby, Peter Hershey[11], Sarah Lucinda[10] Hershey, Peter[9], Jacob[8], John[7], Anna Weber[6] Newcomer, Elizabeth[5] Weber, Henry[4], Johann Anton[3], Heinrich[2], George[1]) She married **Private Zimmerman**.

Children of Private Zimmerman and Private Zimmerman are:
- 1576   i.   Private[15] Zimmerman.
- 1577   ii.   Private Zimmerman.

1297. Private[14] Zimmerman (Private[13] Stauffer, Emma Mae[12] Eby, Peter Hershey[11], Sarah Lucinda[10] Hershey, Peter[9], Jacob[8], John[7], Anna Weber[6] Newcomer, Elizabeth[5] Weber, Henry[4], Johann Anton[3], Heinrich[2], George[1]) She married **Private Burkholder**.

Children of Private Zimmerman and Private Burkholder are:
- 1578   i.   Private[15] Burkholder.
- 1579   ii.   Private Burkholder.
- 1580   iii.   Private Burkholder.

Above: actual photograph of the twisted and burnt wreckage of the B&O trainwreck in Republic, Ohio, Jan. 4, 1887.

Left: The tombstone of David Ober (1827-1887) with epitaph mentioning the fateful train wreck.

The Death of David Ober in the Great B&O Train Wreck in Republic, Ohio, January 4, 1887

A very strange and haunting piece of family history surrounds the ending of David Ober (1827-1887), a sixth cousin to Milton Hershey (3rd great grandfather of the author). David is honored by an obelisk tombstone in the Ober plot in Oberlin Cemetery, Oberlin, PA. When shown it as a youth by my grandmother, I was always intrigued by the epitaph reminding us of David's demise in the "B&O Train Wreck - Republic, Ohio, Jan 4, 1887".

Several years ago, while visiting Oberlin Cemetery again to photograph tombstones, I was reminded of the epitaph. This prompted me to research the circumstances of the wreck. A drawing of the accident can be found in the book "Train Wrecks: A Pictorial History of Accidents on the Main Line" by Robert C. Reed, published by Schiffer Publishing. (Pg. 122). The Tiffin-Seneca (Ohio) Public Library provided newspaper and magazine accounts of the indicent. A railroad buff provided an actual photograph of the wreckage.

Piecing together the accounts, along with what is known about family history, the following sequence of events can be surmised:

About 1855, David married Anna Barbara Brenner (1834-1876). (Anna may be related to Andrew Baer Hackman's wife, Martha Eschbach Brenner - but this has not been proven.)

1876 - Anna dies leaving David a widower at age 49. There are fourteen children ages 0 to 20.

About 1885, David's daughter Agnes Ober married William Murphy and lived in Noblesville, IN.

About 1885, Agnes Ober Murphy gave birth to Eda R Murphy, David's granddaughter.

Early January 1887 - David Ober probably had decided to travel to Indiana to see his recently born granddaughter for the first time. He likely would have left from Middletown or Harrisburg, PA - perhaps on the Pennsylvania Railroad before transferring to the B&O.

Jan 4, 1887 (evening) - The B&O train collides with a freight train coming in the opposite direction on the same track. That train had failed to turn off to the side in time. It was a cold snowy night. As the trains collided, "within minutes the overturned stoves transformed the smoking car into a funeral pyre. The flames leaped high in the air, the roar mingling with cries of anguish of the imprisoned victims."

"George Forrester (from Chicago) had been sleeping in the middle section of the smoker when the collision occurred. He survived and tried to rescue others from the inferno. Earlier that evening he had befriended several of the passengers in the car. He recalled how an old gentleman carrying a crooked cherry-wood cane seemed uneasy in the smoker. (The fellow later was identified as David Ober a widower from Oberlin, PA who was on his way to Michigan to visit his children." (His children actually lived near Indianapolis).

There were fourteen dead in all - and dozens injured. Many of the bodies were unrecognizable - including the body of David Ober.

January 19, 1887 - Four unclaimed bodies including that believed to be David Ober had lain in state in the town of Republic. On that day, the coroner of Seneca County (Edward Lepper) arranged an elaborate mass funeral for the unclaimed dead. At least 800 people turned up in the Republic Town Hall to witness the service dedicated to the memories of David Ober, Frank D Bowman (of Mechanicsburg, PA), Thomas O Pemberton & John S Gortner (all had perished in the smoker car). Several of the Gortner family came from Iowa to attend the services. Their is no record of any Obers attending. Following the service, the mourners drove sleighs or marched on foot to the interment at the Farewell Retreat Cemetery on the edge of town.

Aftermath - David left behind fourteen children, ages 11 to 31. The younger children were taken in by their older siblings. It is not known why no one claimed the body of David Ober. It is likely a memorial service was held in Oberlin, and the tombstone erected in the family plot. However, the body of David Ober was never returned to Oberlin. He was buried in a mass grave in Republic, Ohio. Perhaps because of the gruesomeness of the accident and the uncertainty of the identities of the charred bodies (parts), the family decided to simply remember their father/grandfather.

Summer 2002 - While visiting Columbus, Ohio, I detoured to Republic, Ohio and found many of the old buildings from the period still in existence. The Farewell Retreat Cemetery was easily found on the edge of town - right by the railroad tracks. However, there was no tombstone for the mass grave. There should be.

Interesting Notes Concerning the Kin of Milton Hershey

- Christian Schmidt Hershey (1664-1729) was the first Mennonite bishop of Lancaster Co, PA
- Benjamin Hershey (1730-1812) was a Mennonite bishop.
- Jacob Over/Ober (1729-1804) was a Rev War soldier.
- Henry Ober (1742-1822) was a Rev War soldier.
- John Hess (1768-1830) Mennonite minister.
- Abraham Stouffer (1746/7-1809) founder of Stoufferstown, Franklin Co. and former Rev War soldier.
- Christian Ober (1762-1840) was a Rev War soldier.
- Abraham Hershey Stauffer (1780-1851) founded Stouffville, near Toronto, Canada.
- David Ober (1827-1887) killed in the B&O train wreck 1/4/1887.
- Hiram Hostetter (1844-1863) Civil War soldier memorialized at Gettysburg.
- Lewis Goodhart (1822-1891) adopted a child headed for poor house.
- Ezra Frantz Hershey (b. 1879) - Treasurer of Hershey Chocolate Co.
- Edwin Eshelman (1822-1864) - Gettysburg veteran died in DC.
- Taylor Hostetter (1853-1912) - Candy-maker in Pottsville & Reading
- Sarah B. (Richardson) Snyder (1855-1894) - killed by arsenic in her coffee - daughters also poisoned. Husband Elias innocent?
- David Ober Wolf (1890-1975) - WWI veteran from Highspire.
- Henry Weber (1690-1745) - with brothers Jacob & George, held 3000 acres in "Weber Thal" now known as Weaverland.
- Benjamin Landis (1697-1781) - ordained minister.
- John Hershey (1810-1869) - Deacon, killed at railroad crossing.
- Jacob Hershey (1803-1883) - minister in Paradise.
- Martin G Weaver (1859-1935) - local historian.
- Tommy Herr - former ML baseball player.
- John Kauffman Shenk - Amish taxi-driver.

The Relations of Milton Snavely Hershey, 4th Ed.

Kinship of Milton Snavely Hershey

Name	Relationship with Milton Hershey	Civil	Canon
(Landis), Barbara	Wife of the 1st cousin 3 times removed		
(Meyer), Agatha	Wife of the half 1st cousin 5 times removed		
(Meyer), Maria	Wife of the half 1st cousin 5 times removed		
(Moyer), Hannah	Wife of the half 1st cousin 5 times removed		
(Myer), Anna	Wife of the half 1st cousin 5 times removed		
(Myer), Judith	Wife of the half 1st cousin 5 times removed		
(stoffer), Private	Wife of the 6th cousin twice removed		
?, Anthony	Husband of the 6th cousin 4 times removed		
Abbey, Private	Wife of the 6th cousin 4 times removed		
Abney, Lloyd	Husband of the 6th cousin 3 times removed		
Abney, Neil	6th cousin 4 times removed	XVIII	11
Acker, Amanda	Wife of the 4th cousin once removed		
Acker, Magdelene Polly (Acre)	Wife of the 1st cousin 4 times removed		
Acker, Martha Louise	Wife of the 3rd cousin twice removed		
Ackerman, Elizabeth	Wife of the 6th cousin		
Ackerman, Private	Wife of the 6th cousin 4 times removed		
Adams, Arthur	Husband of the half 3rd cousin 3 times removed		
Adams, E Virginia	Wife of the 6th cousin twice removed		
Adams, Private	Husband of the 6th cousin 3 times removed		
Adams, Private	6th cousin 4 times removed	XVIII	11
Adams, Thomas Lyle	Husband of the 3rd cousin 3 times removed		
Adams, Thomas Lyle	3rd cousin 4 times removed	XII	8
Adams, Unknown	Husband of the 2nd cousin once removed		
Agnew, Charles	6th cousin 3 times removed	XVII	10
Agnew, Donald Robert	6th cousin 3 times removed	XVII	10
Agnew, Harold	6th cousin 3 times removed	XVII	10
Agnew, Harry	Husband of the 6th cousin twice removed		
Agnew, John	6th cousin 3 times removed	XVII	10
Agnew, Mary Elizabeth	6th cousin 3 times removed	XVII	10
Agnew, Private	6th cousin 4 times removed	XVIII	11
Agnew, Private	6th cousin 4 times removed	XVIII	11
Agnew, Private	6th cousin 4 times removed	XVIII	11
Aguirre, Private	Husband of the 3rd cousin 3 times removed		
Aguirre, Private	3rd cousin 4 times removed	XII	8
Aguirre, Private	3rd cousin 4 times removed	XII	8
Aldinger, Mary	Wife of the 6th cousin 3 times removed		
Alexander, Herbert "Jack"	6th cousin twice removed	XVI	9
Alexander, Jay	Husband of the 6th cousin once removed		
Alexander, Minnie B.	Wife of the 6th cousin twice removed		
Alexander, Private	Husband of the 3rd cousin twice removed		
Allebach, Johannes	Husband of the 1st cousin 4 times removed		
Allen, Anna Bell	Wife of the 6th cousin once removed		
Allen, David	Half 3rd cousin 3 times removed	XI	7
Allen, Frances	Wife of the 6th cousin twice removed		
Allen, Hugh	Half 3rd cousin 3 times removed	XI	7
Allen, Jean	Half 3rd cousin 3 times removed	XI	7
Allen, Jennie	Half 3rd cousin 3 times removed	XI	7
Allen, Marjorie	Half 3rd cousin 3 times removed	XI	7
Allen, Phyllis	Half 3rd cousin 3 times removed	XI	7
Allen, Ronald	Half 3rd cousin 3 times removed	XI	7
Allen, William	Husband of the half 3rd cousin twice removed		
Allison, Private	Wife of the 6th cousin 3 times removed		
Allshouse, Private	Wife of the 6th cousin 3 times removed		
Alter, Jacob	Husband of the 2nd cousin 4 times removed		
Alter, John Graham	Husband of the 6th cousin twice removed		
Alter, Private	Wife of the 3rd cousin twice removed		
Alter, Private	6th cousin 3 times removed	XVII	10
Amidon, James A.	6th cousin 3 times removed	XVII	10
Amidon, Julia	Wife of the 6th cousin once removed		
Amidon, Mary L.	6th cousin 3 times removed	XVII	10
Amidon, Mary L.	6th cousin 3 times removed	XVII	10
Amidon, Monroe E.	Husband of the 6th cousin twice removed		
Anderegg, Jeanne D	Wife of the 6th cousin twice removed		
Anderson, Mary	Wife of the half 3rd cousin once removed		

Name	Relationship with Milton Hershey	Civil	Canon
Anderson, Pearl E.	Wife of the half 3rd cousin twice removed		
Andrew, Ester	Wife of the 2nd cousin 3 times removed		
Andrew, Private	Wife of the 2nd cousin 3 times removed		
Anna	Wife of the 6th cousin once removed		
Annett, David	Half 3rd cousin 4 times removed	XII	8
Annett, Helene	Wife of the half 3rd cousin 3 times removed		
Annett, John	Husband of the half 3rd cousin 3 times removed		
Annett, Private	Half 3rd cousin 4 times removed	XII	8
Annett, Private	Half 3rd cousin 4 times removed	XII	8
Annett, Private	Half 3rd cousin 4 times removed	XII	8
Annett, William	Husband of the half 3rd cousin 3 times removed		
Appler, Charles Wesley	Husband of the 3rd cousin once removed		
Appler, Mabel Corinne	Wife of the 3rd cousin once removed		
Applying, Private	Wife of the 6th cousin 3 times removed		
Armstrong, George Irving	Husband of the 6th cousin twice removed		
Armstrong, Private	Husband of the 6th cousin 3 times removed		
Arnold, Emma Iona	Wife of the 6th cousin twice removed		
Arnold, Lilliam	Wife of the half 3rd cousin 3 times removed		
Arnold, Louren E	Husband of the 6th cousin twice removed		
Arnold, Private	6th cousin 3 times removed	XVII	10
Arnold, Private	6th cousin 3 times removed	XVII	10
Arnold, Private	6th cousin 3 times removed	XVII	10
Arthur, John Robert	Husband of the 6th cousin twice removed		
Arthur, Private	6th cousin 3 times removed	XVII	10
Arthur, Private	6th cousin 3 times removed	XVII	10
Arthur, Private	6th cousin 3 times removed	XVII	10
Ash, Mary M.	Wife of the 6th cousin		
Asp, Keith John	Husband of the 6th cousin 3 times removed		
Atkinson, Delma	Wife of the half 3rd cousin 3 times removed		
Atz, Margaret B	Wife of the 6th cousin 3 times removed		
Augsburger, Private	Husband of the 3rd cousin 3 times removed		
Augsburger, Private	3rd cousin 4 times removed	XII	8
Augsburger, Private	3rd cousin 4 times removed	XII	8
Augsburger, Private	3rd cousin 4 times removed	XII	8
Augsburger, Private	3rd cousin 4 times removed	XII	8
Auker, Clarence	Husband of the 5th cousin once removed		
Auker, Maggie	Wife of the 4th cousin once removed		
Auker, Private	Wife of the 3rd cousin 3 times removed		
Auker, Unknown	Husband of the 6th cousin once removed		
Auks, Peter	Husband of the 6th cousin 3 times removed		
Baccus, Gladys	Wife of the half 3rd cousin twice removed		
Bachman, Anna	Wife of the 2nd cousin twice removed		
Bachman, John Zinn	Husband of the 6th cousin		
Bachman, Maria	Wife of the 1st cousin 4 times removed		
Bachman, Maria	Wife of the 1st cousin 4 times removed		
Bachman, Mary	Wife of the 1st cousin once removed		
Bachman, Scott Lee	Husband of the 3rd cousin 3 times removed		
Bachman/Bauman, George M.	Husband of the 5th cousin once removed		
Bacon, Lloyd Frederick	Half 3rd cousin 4 times removed	XII	8
Bacon, Private	Half 3rd cousin 4 times removed	XII	8
Bacon, Private	Half 3rd cousin 4 times removed	XII	8
Bacon, Roy St. Clair	Husband of the half 3rd cousin 3 times removed		
Baer, Alice	6th cousin once removed	XV	8
Baer, Charles	6th cousin once removed	XV	8
Baer, Jesse	6th cousin once removed	XV	8
Baer, Johannes	Husband of the 1st cousin 3 times removed		
Baer, John	6th cousin once removed	XV	8
Baer, John Martin	3rd great-grandfather	V	5
Baer, Martin	4th great-grandfather	VI	6
Baer, Samuel	6th cousin once removed	XV	8
Baer, Unknown	Wife of the 3rd great-grandfather		
Baer, William	Husband of the 6th cousin		
Baier, Elizabeth Catherine Weaver	Wife of the 5th cousin once removed		
Bailey, Helen Josephine Grew	Wife of the 6th cousin twice removed		
Bair, Maria	Wife of the 2nd cousin 3 times removed		
Baird, John	Husband of the half 3rd cousin once removed		

Name	Relationship with Milton Hershey	Civil	Canon
Baker, John Norman	Husband of the 6th cousin twice removed		
Baker, Lowell	6th cousin 3 times removed	XVII	10
Baker, Marian Arlene	Wife of the 4th cousin twice removed		
Baker, Private	Husband of the 3rd cousin twice removed		
Baker, Private	3rd cousin 3 times removed	XI	7
Baker, Private	3rd cousin 3 times removed	XI	7
Baker, Private	6th cousin 4 times removed	XVIII	11
Baker, Private	6th cousin 4 times removed	XVIII	11
Baker, Private	6th cousin 4 times removed	XVIII	11
Baker, Private	6th cousin 4 times removed	XVIII	11
Baker, Private	6th cousin 4 times removed	XVIII	11
Baker, Private	6th cousin 4 times removed	XVIII	11
Ball, Ann Elizabeth	3rd cousin twice removed	X	6
Ball, Gertrude Amelia	3rd cousin twice removed	X	6
Ball, Jacob	Husband of the 2nd cousin 3 times removed		
Ball, Jacob	3rd cousin twice removed	X	6
Ball, Peter Herman	3rd cousin twice removed	X	6
Ball, Stark	Husband of the 6th cousin once removed		
Balmer, Private	Wife of the 3rd cousin 4 times removed		
Balsbaugh, Allen	6th cousin 4 times removed	XVIII	11
Balsbaugh, Clarence	6th cousin 3 times removed	XVII	10
Balsbaugh, Edgar F	6th cousin 3 times removed	XVII	10
Balsbaugh, Erlo R	6th cousin 3 times removed	XVII	10
Balsbaugh, Jayson C	6th cousin 3 times removed	XVII	10
Balsbaugh, Kathryn S	6th cousin 3 times removed	XVII	10
Balsbaugh, Margaret A	6th cousin 3 times removed	XVII	10
Balsbaugh, Ober S	6th cousin 3 times removed	XVII	10
Balsbaugh, Sidney	6th cousin 4 times removed	XVIII	11
Balsbaugh, Solomon S	Husband of the 6th cousin twice removed		
Balsbaugh, William D	6th cousin 3 times removed	XVII	10
Bar, Anna	Wife of the 6th great-grandfather		
Bar, Barbara	Half 2nd cousin 4 times removed	X	7
Bar, Elizabeth	Wife of the 1st cousin 7 times removed		
Bar, Elizabeth	Half 2nd cousin 4 times removed	X	7
Bar, Hannah	Half 2nd cousin 4 times removed	X	7
Bar, Henry	Half 2nd cousin 4 times removed	X	7
Bar, Isaac	Half 2nd cousin 4 times removed	X	7
Bar, John	Half 2nd cousin 4 times removed	X	7
Bar, Martin	Husband of the 4th great-grandmother		
Bar, Mary	Half 2nd cousin 4 times removed	X	7
Bar, Michael	Half 2nd cousin 4 times removed	X	7
Bar, Salome	Half 2nd cousin 4 times removed	X	7
Bar, Samuel	Half 2nd cousin 4 times removed	X	7
Barber, Elisabeth	Wife of the 4th cousin once removed		
Barcome, Unknown	Husband of the half 3rd cousin once removed		
Bardo, Private	Husband of the 6th cousin 3 times removed		
Bardo, Private	6th cousin 4 times removed	XVIII	11
Barger, Jason Howard	Husband of the half 3rd cousin twice removed		
Barker, Audrey Francis	Wife of the 6th cousin twice removed		
Barkey, Alice	Half 3rd cousin 3 times removed	XI	7
Barkey, Arthur C.	Husband of the half 3rd cousin twice removed		
Barkey, Barbara	Half 3rd cousin 3 times removed	XI	7
Barkey, Charles	Half 3rd cousin twice removed	X	6
Barkey, Clarence	Husband of the half 3rd cousin twice removed		
Barkey, Clifford	Half 3rd cousin 3 times removed	XI	7
Barkey, Ella	Half 3rd cousin twice removed	X	6
Barkey, Elmore	Husband of the half 3rd cousin twice removed		
Barkey, Evelyn Maude	Half 3rd cousin twice removed	X	6
Barkey, George	Husband of the half 3rd cousin once removed		
Barkey, Gordon	Half 3rd cousin 3 times removed	XI	7
Barkey, Howard	Half 3rd cousin twice removed	X	6
Barkey, Lawrence	Half 3rd cousin 3 times removed	XI	7
Barkey, Margaret	Wife of the half 3rd cousin twice removed		
Barkey, Marian	Half 3rd cousin 3 times removed	XI	7
Barkey, Mary	Half 3rd cousin twice removed	X	6

Name	Relationship with Milton Hershey	Civil	Canon
Barkey, Mildred	Half 3rd cousin twice removed	X	6
Barkey, Norma	Half 3rd cousin 3 times removed	XI	7
Barkey, Pauline	Half 3rd cousin 3 times removed	XI	7
Barkey, Private	Half 3rd cousin 4 times removed	XII	8
Barkey, Private	Half 3rd cousin 4 times removed	XII	8
Barkey, Private	Half 3rd cousin 4 times removed	XII	8
Barkey, Sarah	Wife of the half 3rd cousin once removed		
Barkey, William	Half 3rd cousin twice removed	X	6
Barkey, Wilmot	Husband of the half 3rd cousin once removed		
Barlow, Vera Luella	Wife of the half 3rd cousin 3 times removed		
Barner, Charles Merle	6th cousin 3 times removed	XVII	10
Barner, Private	6th cousin 4 times removed	XVIII	11
Barner, Private	6th cousin 4 times removed	XVIII	11
Barner, Private	6th cousin 4 times removed	XVIII	11
Barner, Private	6th cousin 4 times removed	XVIII	11
Barner, Private	6th cousin 3 times removed	XVII	10
Barner, Private	6th cousin 4 times removed	XVIII	11
Barner, Private	6th cousin 4 times removed	XVIII	11
Barner, Private	6th cousin 3 times removed	XVII	10
Barner, Private	6th cousin 3 times removed	XVII	10
Barner, Ramona Lee	6th cousin 3 times removed	XVII	10
Barner, Ray J.	Husband of the 6th cousin twice removed		
Barnes, Christina Margaret	Half 3rd cousin 4 times removed	XII	8
Barnes, Unknown	Husband of the 6th cousin twice removed		
Barnes, William	Husband of the half 3rd cousin 3 times removed		
Barnet, Elizabeth	Wife of the 6th cousin		
Barnett, Dale Eugene	6th cousin twice removed	XVI	9
Barnett, Jay Melvin	6th cousin twice removed	XVI	9
Barnett, Paul Eugene	Husband of the 6th cousin once removed		
Barnett, Private	6th cousin 3 times removed	XVII	10
Barnett, Private	6th cousin 3 times removed	XVII	10
Barnett, Private	6th cousin 3 times removed	XVII	10
Barnett, Private	6th cousin 3 times removed	XVII	10
Barnett, Private	6th cousin 4 times removed	XVIII	11
Barnett, Private	6th cousin 4 times removed	XVIII	11
Barnett, Theda Fay	6th cousin twice removed	XVI	9
Barnhill, Private	Wife of the 3rd cousin twice removed		
Barr, Aaron	Half 3rd cousin	VIII	4
Barr, Abraham	Half 1st cousin twice removed	VI	4
Barr, Ann	Half 1st cousin twice removed	VI	4
Barr, Anna	Half 3rd cousin	VIII	4
Barr, Benjamin	Half 3rd cousin	VIII	4
Barr, Catherine	Half 3rd cousin	VIII	4
Barr, Charles S.	Half 3rd cousin once removed	IX	5
Barr, Christian	Half 3rd cousin	VIII	4
Barr, Christina	Half 2nd cousin once removed	VII	4
Barr, Cynthia Odessa	Half 3rd cousin once removed	IX	5
Barr, David	Half 2nd cousin once removed	VII	4
Barr, Elizabeth	Great-grandmother	III	3
Barr, Elizabeth	Half 3rd cousin	VIII	4
Barr, Esther	Wife of the 2nd great-granduncle		
Barr, Esther Christina	Half 3rd cousin once removed	IX	5
Barr, Fanny	Half 1st cousin twice removed	VI	4
Barr, Francis M.	Half 3rd cousin once removed	IX	5
Barr, George Lucas	Half 3rd cousin once removed	IX	5
Barr, Hezekiah	Half 3rd cousin	VIII	4
Barr, Hezekiah	Half 3rd cousin once removed	IX	5
Barr, Infant	Half 3rd cousin once removed	IX	5
Barr, Jacob	2nd great-grandfather	IV	4
Barr, Jacob	Husband of the half 2nd cousin 4 times removed		
Barr, Jacob	Half 1st cousin twice removed	VI	4
Barr, Jacob	Half 2nd cousin once removed	VII	4
Barr, Jacob Cullen	Half 3rd cousin	VIII	4
Barr, James Clement	Half 3rd cousin once removed	IX	5
Barr, Jennie Belle	Half 3rd cousin once removed	IX	5
Barr, John	Half 1st cousin twice removed	VI	4

Name	Relationship with Milton Hershey	Civil	Canon
Barr, John Warren	Half 3rd cousin once removed	IX	5
Barr, Laura A.	Half 3rd cousin once removed	IX	5
Barr, Leona May	Half 3rd cousin once removed	IX	5
Barr, Lorenzo	Half 3rd cousin	VIII	4
Barr, Louis Orin	Half 3rd cousin once removed	IX	5
Barr, Maria	Wife of the 2nd great-granduncle		
Barr, Martin	Half great-granduncle	V	4
Barr, Martin	Half 1st cousin twice removed	VI	4
Barr, Martin James	Half 2nd cousin once removed	VII	4
Barr, Mary	Half 1st cousin twice removed	VI	4
Barr, Mary	Half 3rd cousin	VIII	4
Barr, Mary Elizabeth	Half 3rd cousin once removed	IX	5
Barr, Son1	Half great-granduncle	V	4
Barr, Susan	Half 1st cousin twice removed	VI	4
Barr, Susanna	Half 3rd cousin once removed	IX	5
Barr, Susannah	Wife of the half 2nd cousin once removed		
Barr, Zannie	Half 3rd cousin	VIII	4
Barrett, Earl	Husband of the 6th cousin 3 times removed		
Barrett, Private	6th cousin 4 times removed	XVIII	11
Barricks, Abraham	6th cousin	XIV	7
Barricks, Benjamin	Husband of the 5th cousin once removed		
Barricks, Mary	6th cousin	XIV	7
Barron, George F.	Husband of the 6th cousin		
Bartchey, Bertha	Wife of the 6th cousin twice removed		
Barth, Private	Husband of the 3rd cousin twice removed		
Barth, Private	3rd cousin 3 times removed	XI	7
Barth, Private	3rd cousin 3 times removed	XI	7
Barth, Private	3rd cousin 3 times removed	XI	7
Bartley, Nellie Virginia	Wife of the 6th cousin once removed		
Bassler, Anna	2nd cousin twice removed	VIII	5
Bassler, Christian	2nd cousin twice removed	VIII	5
Bassler, Henry	2nd cousin twice removed	VIII	5
Bassler, Jacob	2nd cousin twice removed	VIII	5
Bassler, John	2nd cousin twice removed	VIII	5
Bassler, John	Husband of the 1st cousin 3 times removed		
Bassler, Maria	2nd cousin twice removed	VIII	5
Bateman, Della	Half 3rd cousin twice removed	X	6
Bateman, I. L.	Husband of the half 3rd cousin once removed		
Bateman, Lydia	Half 3rd cousin twice removed	X	6
Bateman, Mary	Half 3rd cousin twice removed	X	6
Bateman, May	Half 3rd cousin twice removed	X	6
Bateman, Nellie	Half 3rd cousin twice removed	X	6
Bauer, Unknown	Husband of the 6th cousin 3 times removed		
Baughman, Hannah	Wife of the half 4th cousin twice removed		
Baum, Private	Wife of the 3rd cousin 3 times removed		
Bauman, Anna	Wife of the half 6th great-granduncle		
Bauman, Anna	Wife of the 3rd great-granduncle		
Bauman, Elizabeth	Wife of the 1st cousin 4 times removed		
Bauman, Henry	Husband of the 2nd cousin 3 times removed		
Bauman, Mary	Wife of the 2nd cousin 3 times removed		
Bauman, Private	Husband of the 3rd cousin twice removed		
Bauman, Private	3rd cousin 3 times removed	XI	7
Bauman, Wendel	Husband of the 1st cousin 4 times removed		
Baumann, Hans Rudolph	Husband of the half 6th great-grandaunt		
Baumgartner, Kenneth Allen	Husband of the 6th cousin 3 times removed		
Baumgartner, Private	6th cousin 4 times removed	XVIII	11
Baumgartner, Private	6th cousin 4 times removed	XVIII	11
Baumgartner, Private	6th cousin 4 times removed	XVIII	11
Baumgartner, Private	6th cousin 4 times removed	XVIII	11
Baush, George W.	Husband of the 6th cousin		
Baxter, Private	6th cousin 4 times removed	XVIII	11
Baxter, Private	Husband of the 6th cousin 3 times removed		
Bayer, Maurice William	Husband of the 6th cousin twice removed		
Bayleat, Aaron	Husband of the 6th cousin		
Beachy, Private	Wife of the 3rd cousin 3 times removed		
Beachy, Private	Wife of the 3rd cousin twice removed		

Name	Relationship with Milton Hershey	Civil	Canon
Beachy, Private	Wife of the 3rd cousin 3 times removed		
Beam, Frances	Wife of the 1st cousin once removed		
Bear, Barbara	6th cousin	XIV	7
Bear, Catherine	6th cousin	XIV	7
Bear, David	6th cousin	XIV	7
Bear, David	2nd cousin twice removed	VIII	5
Bear, Elizabeth	Wife of the 2nd great-granduncle		
Bear, Elizabeth	2nd cousin twice removed	VIII	5
Bear, Elizabeth	6th cousin	XIV	7
Bear, Ephriam	2nd cousin twice removed	VIII	5
Bear, Gabriel	3rd cousin once removed	IX	5
Bear, Henry	Husband of the half 1st cousin 5 times removed		
Bear, Henry	Husband of the 5th cousin once removed		
Bear, Isaac F	2nd cousin twice removed	VIII	5
Bear, John	3rd cousin once removed	IX	5
Bear, Lea	2nd cousin twice removed	VIII	5
Bear, Lydia	6th cousin	XIV	7
Bear, Magdalena	6th cousin	XIV	7
Bear, Maria	2nd cousin twice removed	VIII	5
Bear, Nancy	6th cousin	XIV	7
Bear, Sarah	6th cousin	XIV	7
Bear, Sophia	6th cousin	XIV	7
Bear, Susanna Frantz	2nd cousin twice removed	VIII	5
Bear, Veronica	2nd cousin twice removed	VIII	5
Beasley, Private	Husband of the 6th cousin 3 times removed		
Beasley, Private	6th cousin 4 times removed	XVIII	11
Bechtal, Nancy	Wife of the 5th cousin once removed		
Bechtel, Daniel Detweiler	Husband of the 4th cousin once removed		
Bechtel, Emanuel	Husband of the 6th cousin		
Bechtel, Henry Landis	5th cousin	XII	6
Bechtel, John Landis	5th cousin	XII	6
Beck, Marjorie Jean	Wife of the 6th cousin 3 times removed		
Beck, Valerie Rishel	Wife of the 6th cousin 3 times removed		
Becker, Arnold	Husband of the 2nd cousin 4 times removed		
Becker, Minnie Mae	Wife of the 4th cousin once removed		
Bedford, Jennie	Wife of the half 3rd cousin once removed		
Beemer, Ellan	Wife of the half 3rd cousin		
Beer, Private	Wife of the 6th cousin 3 times removed		
Begg, John Cameron	Half 3rd cousin 3 times removed	XI	7
Begg, Mildred Louise	Half 3rd cousin 3 times removed	XI	7
Begg, Phyllis Beatrice Mary	Half 3rd cousin 3 times removed	XI	7
Begg, Robert Arthur	Half 3rd cousin 3 times removed	XI	7
Begg, William Arthur	Husband of the half 3rd cousin twice removed		
Behmer, Samuel	Spouse of the 2nd cousin once removed		
Behner, Harold	Husband of the 6th cousin 3 times removed		
Behney, Catharine	Wife of the 6th cousin		
Beidler, Abraham Buckwalter (Beitler)	2nd cousin 3 times removed	IX	6
Beidler, Abraham Landes	3rd cousin twice removed	X	6
Beidler, Anna Buckwalter	2nd cousin 3 times removed	IX	6
Beidler, Catherine Hockman	Wife of the 4th cousin twice removed		
Beidler, Daniel Landes	3rd cousin twice removed	X	6
Beidler, David Buckwalter	2nd cousin 3 times removed	IX	6
Beidler, Eleanor Buckwalter	2nd cousin 3 times removed	IX	6
Beidler, Elizabeth Buckwalter	2nd cousin 3 times removed	IX	6
Beidler, Elizabeth Landes	3rd cousin twice removed	X	6
Beidler, George	4th cousin once removed	XI	6
Beidler, Hannah Buckwalter	2nd cousin 3 times removed	IX	6
Beidler, Hannah Landes	3rd cousin twice removed	X	6
Beidler, Henry	4th cousin once removed	XI	6
Beidler, Israel Landes Rev.	3rd cousin twice removed	X	6
Beidler, Jacob A. Rev. Dr.	4th cousin once removed	XI	6
Beidler, Jacob Buckwalter	2nd cousin 3 times removed	IX	6
Beidler, John Buckwalter	2nd cousin 3 times removed	IX	6
Beidler, John Landes	3rd cousin twice removed	X	6
Beidler, John Moyer (Beitler)	Husband of the 1st cousin 4 times removed		
Beidler, Joseph Buckwalter	2nd cousin 3 times removed	IX	6

The Relations of Milton Snavely Hershey, 4th Ed.

Name	Relationship with Milton Hershey	Civil	Canon
Beidler, Joseph Landes	3rd cousin twice removed	X	6
Beidler, Maria Buckwalter	2nd cousin 3 times removed	IX	6
Beidler, Mary	4th cousin once removed	XI	6
Beidler, Mary Landes	3rd cousin twice removed	X	6
Bell, Cynthia Ann	6th cousin 4 times removed	XVIII	11
Bell, James R	Husband of the 6th cousin 3 times removed		
Bender, Martin L.	Husband of the 3rd cousin twice removed		
Bender, Mary	Wife of the 3rd cousin twice removed		
Bender, Private	3rd cousin 3 times removed	XI	7
Bender, Private	3rd cousin 3 times removed	XI	7
Bender, Private	3rd cousin 3 times removed	XI	7
Bender, Private	3rd cousin 3 times removed	XI	7
Bender, Private	3rd cousin 3 times removed	XI	7
Benjamin, Ober	6th cousin	XIV	7
Benner, Mary	Wife of the 2nd cousin 3 times removed		
Benner, Sallie Blanche	Wife of the 4th cousin once removed		
Bennett, Edith Louise	Wife of the 6th cousin twice removed		
Bennett, Private	Wife of the 6th cousin 4 times removed		
Bennett, Private	Husband of the 6th cousin 3 times removed		
Benson, Private	Husband of the 6th cousin 3 times removed		
Benson, Private	6th cousin 4 times removed	XVIII	11
Benson, Private	6th cousin 4 times removed	XVIII	11
Berg, Barbara	Wife of the 4th cousin twice removed		
Berg, Jacob	Husband of the 3rd cousin 3 times removed		
Berger, Ann Louise	Wife of the 4th cousin 3 times removed		
Berger, Eva	Wife of the 6th cousin twice removed		
Berger, Mabel M	Wife of the 6th cousin once removed		
Berger-Knorr, Abbey	4th cousin 4 times removed	XIV	9
Berger-Knorr, Ann Louise	Wife of the 4th cousin 3 times removed		
Berger-Knorr, Lawrence K	4th cousin 3 times removed	XIII	8
Berger-Knorr, Taylor	4th cousin 4 times removed	XIV	9
Bergey, Barbara	Wife of the 3rd cousin twice removed		
Bergey, John Zieber	Husband of the 5th cousin		
Bergren, Edith Marie	Husband of the 6th cousin 3 times removed		
Berkey, Henry S.	Husband of the 6th cousin		
Berkeybile, Adam Cleveland	Husband of the 6th cousin		
Berkeybile, Ann Elizabeth	Wife of the 5th cousin once removed		
Berridge, Mary	Wife of the 6th cousin once removed		
Berschinger, Verena	Wife of the 7th great-granduncle		
Berube, Private	Husband of the 6th cousin 4 times removed		
Berube, Private	6th cousin 5 times removed	XIX	12
Bessette, Earl Edbert	Half 3rd cousin twice removed	X	6
Bessette, Joseph Edward	Husband of the half 3rd cousin once removed		
Bessette, Merle Edward	Half 3rd cousin twice removed	X	6
Betty	6th cousin 3 times removed	XVII	10
Betzner, Abraham	Half 3rd cousin	VIII	4
Betzner, Albert E.	Half 3rd cousin once removed	IX	5
Betzner, Alice	Half 3rd cousin once removed	IX	5
Betzner, Andrew	Half 3rd cousin once removed	IX	5
Betzner, Annie Agnes	Half 3rd cousin twice removed	X	6
Betzner, Bruce Echlin	Half 3rd cousin 3 times removed	XI	7
Betzner, Cecila La Verne	Half 3rd cousin 3 times removed	XI	7
Betzner, Clancey K.	Half 3rd cousin twice removed	X	6
Betzner, Clare Sadie	Half 3rd cousin 3 times removed	XI	7
Betzner, Clarence	Half 3rd cousin twice removed	X	6
Betzner, David	Husband of the half 2nd cousin once removed		
Betzner, David	Half 3rd cousin once removed	IX	5
Betzner, David S.	Half 3rd cousin	VIII	4
Betzner, David Thomas	Half 3rd cousin once removed	IX	5
Betzner, Donald Temple	Half 3rd cousin 3 times removed	XI	7
Betzner, Doris Madeline	Half 3rd cousin 3 times removed	XI	7
Betzner, Eleanor Ruth	Half 3rd cousin 3 times removed	XI	7
Betzner, Elizabeth	Half 3rd cousin once removed	IX	5
Betzner, Elizabeth Grace	Half 3rd cousin 3 times removed	XI	7
Betzner, Emma Louise	Half 3rd cousin once removed	IX	5
Betzner, Erland Lloyd	Half 3rd cousin 3 times removed	XI	7

Name	Relationship with Milton Hershey	Civil	Canon
Betzner, Erland S.	Half 3rd cousin twice removed	X	6
Betzner, Ethel May	Half 3rd cousin twice removed	X	6
Betzner, Etta	Half 3rd cousin once removed	IX	5
Betzner, Evelyn A.	Half 3rd cousin twice removed	X	6
Betzner, Fanny	Half 3rd cousin once removed	IX	5
Betzner, George David	Half 3rd cousin once removed	IX	5
Betzner, George Washington	Half 3rd cousin once removed	IX	5
Betzner, Harvey Andrew	Half 3rd cousin twice removed	X	6
Betzner, Henry Franklin	Half 3rd cousin twice removed	X	6
Betzner, Ina Louisa	Half 3rd cousin twice removed	X	6
Betzner, Isabella D.	Half 3rd cousin twice removed	X	6
Betzner, Jacob	Half 3rd cousin	VIII	4
Betzner, Jacob	Half 3rd cousin once removed	IX	5
Betzner, Jean	Half 3rd cousin twice removed	X	6
Betzner, John Abram	Half 3rd cousin once removed	IX	5
Betzner, John Elwood	Half 3rd cousin 3 times removed	XI	7
Betzner, John Weir	Half 3rd cousin	VIII	4
Betzner, Joseph	Half 3rd cousin once removed	IX	5
Betzner, Laura G.	Half 3rd cousin twice removed	X	6
Betzner, Mabel T.	Half 3rd cousin twice removed	X	6
Betzner, Mary Claude	Half 3rd cousin twice removed	X	6
Betzner, Mary Elizabeth	Half 3rd cousin once removed	IX	5
Betzner, Muriel Verna	Half 3rd cousin 3 times removed	XI	7
Betzner, Murry Abram	Half 3rd cousin 3 times removed	XI	7
Betzner, Nellie Elizabeth	Half 3rd cousin twice removed	X	6
Betzner, Norman Edwin	Half 3rd cousin twice removed	X	6
Betzner, Private	Half 3rd cousin 4 times removed	XII	8
Betzner, Private	Half 3rd cousin 4 times removed	XII	8
Betzner, Private	Half 3rd cousin 4 times removed	XII	8
Betzner, Private	Half 3rd cousin 4 times removed	XII	8
Betzner, Private	Half 3rd cousin 4 times removed	XII	8
Betzner, Private	Half 3rd cousin 4 times removed	XII	8
Betzner, Rachel Elizabeth	Half 3rd cousin once removed	IX	5
Betzner, Roy Sylvester	Half 3rd cousin twice removed	X	6
Betzner, Samuel	Half 3rd cousin	VIII	4
Betzner, Stanley Bertram	Half 3rd cousin 3 times removed	XI	7
Betzner, Wesley	Half 3rd cousin once removed	IX	5
Betzner, William	Half 3rd cousin once removed	IX	5
Betzner, William	Half 3rd cousin once removed	IX	5
Bever, Eliza	Wife of the 6th cousin		
Biddle, Levi H.	Husband of the 6th cousin		
Bigot, Henry	Husband of the 2nd cousin		
Bill	4th cousin twice removed	XII	7
Bingaman, George M	Husband of the 6th cousin 3 times removed		
Bingaman, John D	6th cousin 4 times removed	XVIII	11
Bingaman, Nancy L	6th cousin 4 times removed	XVIII	11
Binkley, David	3rd cousin twice removed	X	6
Binkley, David	4th cousin once removed	XI	6
Binkley, Henry	Husband of the 3rd cousin twice removed		
Binkley, Henry	Husband of the 2nd cousin 3 times removed		
Binkley, Martin	Husband of the 2nd cousin 3 times removed		
Bishop, Lucinda	Wife of the 5th cousin once removed		
Bishop, Nancy Jane	Wife of the half 3rd cousin once removed		
Bitner, Abraham C.	Husband of the 3rd cousin once removed		
Bitner, Anna	4th cousin	X	5
Bitner, Charles Eby	4th cousin	X	5
Bitner, Clarence	4th cousin	X	5
Bitner, Grace	4th cousin	X	5
Bitner, Herbert	4th cousin	X	5
Bitner, Robert	4th cousin	X	5
Bitner, Walter	4th cousin	X	5
Bitzer, Elizabeth Gertrude	1st cousin once removed	V	3
Bitzer, Harvey	Husband of the 1st cousin		
Bitzer, Helen Virginia	1st cousin once removed	V	3
Blackburn, Mary Rebecca	Wife of the 6th cousin		
Blackman, William	Husband of the 6th cousin 4 times removed		

The Relations of Milton Snavely Hershey, 4th Ed.

Name	Relationship with Milton Hershey	Civil	Canon
Blackwell, Hazel Leona (Dollie)	Wife of the 6th cousin once removed		
Blanier, Adelheed	7th great-grandmother	IX	9
Bleacher, Ester	Wife of the half 2nd cousin once removed		
Blehm, Christian Hackman (Bliem)	Husband of the 4th cousin once removed		
Blehm, J. Stauffer	5th cousin	XII	6
Blehm, William Stauffer	5th cousin	XII	6
Blickenderfer, Private	Husband of the 6th cousin 3 times removed		
Blough, Mary	Wife of the 6th cousin		
Blyth, Joe	Husband of the 6th cousin once removed		
Boale, Sandra	Wife of the 4th cousin 3 times removed		
Boddiger, Private	Husband of the 6th cousin 3 times removed		
Bogdonoff, David L	Husband of the 4th cousin 3 times removed		
Bogdonoff, Eleanor Kate	4th cousin 4 times removed	XIV	9
Bogdonoff, Jacob Alan	4th cousin 4 times removed	XIV	9
Bolender, Arlene	Half 3rd cousin 3 times removed	XI	7
Bolender, Clare	Husband of the half 3rd cousin twice removed		
Bolender, Florence	Half 3rd cousin 3 times removed	XI	7
Bolender, Gladys	Half 3rd cousin 3 times removed	XI	7
Bolender, Grace	Half 3rd cousin 3 times removed	XI	7
Bolender, Howard	Half 3rd cousin 3 times removed	XI	7
Bolender, Lloyd	Half 3rd cousin 3 times removed	XI	7
Bolender, Louie	Half 3rd cousin 3 times removed	XI	7
Bolender, Paul	Half 3rd cousin 3 times removed	XI	7
Bolinger, Walter E	Husband of the 6th cousin once removed		
Bollinger, Anna	Wife of the 6th cousin twice removed		
Bollinger, Benjamin N	Husband of the 3rd cousin once removed		
Bollinger, Private	Wife of the 3rd cousin twice removed		
Bollinger, Private	Wife of the 3rd cousin twice removed		
Bomberger, Abraham	1st cousin 4 times removed	VIII	6
Bomberger, Anna	1st cousin 4 times removed	VIII	6
Bomberger, Annie H	3rd cousin	VIII	4
Bomberger, Barbara	1st cousin 4 times removed	VIII	6
Bomberger, Christian	Husband of the 3rd great-grandaunt		
Bomberger, Christian	1st cousin 4 times removed	VIII	6
Bomberger, Elisabeth	1st cousin 4 times removed	VIII	6
Bomberger, Jacob	1st cousin 4 times removed	VIII	6
Bomberger, Jacob	Husband of the 2nd cousin once removed		
Bomberger, John	1st cousin 4 times removed	VIII	6
Bomberger, Joseph	1st cousin 4 times removed	VIII	6
Bomberger, Mary	1st cousin 4 times removed	VIII	6
Bomberger, Private	Wife of the 3rd cousin 3 times removed		
Bomberger, Private	3rd cousin 3 times removed	XI	7
Bomberger, Private	3rd cousin 4 times removed	XII	8
Bomberger, Private	3rd cousin 4 times removed	XII	8
Bomberger, Sarah	Wife of the 6th cousin		
Bomberger, Susanna	1st cousin 4 times removed	VIII	6
Bonham, Margaret Jean	Half 3rd cousin 3 times removed	XI	7
Bonham, Marion I.	Half 3rd cousin 3 times removed	XI	7
Bonham, Ruth	Half 3rd cousin 3 times removed	XI	7
Bonham, Sanford K.	Husband of the half 3rd cousin twice removed		
Boohar, Private	Wife of the 3rd cousin twice removed		
Boose, Margaret Bucher	Wife of the 4th cousin once removed		
Borough, Amanda Alice	Wife of the 6th cousin once removed		
Borton, Daniel	Husband of the 6th cousin		
Borton, Ellis	6th cousin once removed	XV	8
Borton, Katherine Ann	6th cousin once removed	XV	8
Borton, Ruth Ann	Wife of the 6th cousin twice removed		
Borton, Samuel	6th cousin once removed	XV	8
Bortz, Living	Wife of the 6th cousin 4 times removed		
Bossler, Esther	Wife of the 3rd cousin twice removed		
Bossler, John	Husband of the 1st cousin 3 times removed		
Boughey II, Quincy Edward	Husband of the 6th cousin twice removed		
Bower, John	Husband of the 5th cousin once removed		
Bower, Private	Husband of the 6th cousin 3 times removed		
Bowers, Andrew	6th cousin	XIV	7
Bowers, Barbara	6th cousin	XIV	7

Name	Relationship with Milton Hershey	Civil	Canon
Bowers, Nancy	6th cousin	XIV	7
Bowers, Sarah Rebecca	6th cousin	XIV	7
Bowers, Susan	6th cousin	XIV	7
Bowers, Wilbur Ray	Husband of the 6th cousin twice removed		
Bowman, Anna Margaret	Wife of the 5th cousin once removed		
Bowman, Catherine	Wife of the 3rd cousin twice removed		
Bowman, Leah	Wife of the 3rd cousin twice removed		
Bowman, Mabel	Wife of the half 3rd cousin once removed		
Bowman, Margaret Anna	Wife of the 5th cousin once removed		
Bowman, Martha	Wife of the 4th cousin once removed		
Bowman, Mary A	Wife of the 6th cousin		
Bowman, Mary Louise	Wife of the 6th cousin		
Bowman, Mr.	Husband of the 6th cousin twice removed		
Boyd, Gordon	Husband of the half 3rd cousin twice removed		
Boyd, Private	Half 3rd cousin 3 times removed	XI	7
Boyle, Elgie M	Husband of the 6th cousin twice removed		
Boyle, Patrick	Husband of the half 3rd cousin 3 times removed		
Boyle, Private	6th cousin 3 times removed	XVII	10
Boyle, Private	Half 3rd cousin 4 times removed	XII	8
Brackbill, Benedict	Husband of the great-grandaunt		
Brackbill, Benedict	Husband of the great-grandaunt		
Brackbill, Benjamin	Husband of the 3rd cousin		
Brackbill, Christian	Husband of the half 3rd cousin 3 times removed		
Brackbill, Eliza Ann	Half 4th cousin twice removed	XII	7
Brackbill, Elizabeth	Wife of the 1st cousin 3 times removed		
Brackbill, John	Husband of the 2nd great-grandaunt		
Brackbill, John	Husband of the 1st cousin 3 times removed		
Brackbill, Mary Ethel	Wife of the 3rd cousin twice removed		
Brackbill, Private	Husband of the 3rd cousin 3 times removed		
Bradley, Abraham Shelly	Husband of the 6th cousin		
Brandt, Edna	6th cousin twice removed	XVI	9
Brandt, Sarah	Wife of the 6th cousin		
Brandt, Unknown (spouse of Katie Brubaker)	Husband of the 5th cousin		
Brandt, William H.	Husband of the 6th cousin once removed		
Brant, Ephraim K.	Husband of the 6th cousin		
Break, Private	Wife of the 6th cousin 3 times removed		
Brechbill, Fannie	6th cousin	XIV	7
Brechbill, Henry	Husband of the 5th cousin once removed		
Brechbill, Jacob	Husband of the 5th cousin once removed		
Brechbill, Jacob	Husband of the 6th cousin		
Breitenstein, Mary	4th cousin	X	5
Breitenstein, Moses	Husband of the 3rd cousin once removed		
Brendle, Private	Wife of the 3rd cousin 3 times removed		
Breneman, Amos	4th cousin once removed	XI	6
Breneman, Elisabeth	3rd cousin twice removed	X	6
Breneman, Harry	3rd cousin twice removed	X	6
Breneman, Henry	Husband of the 2nd cousin 3 times removed		
Breneman, Henry	Husband of the 2nd cousin 3 times removed		
Breneman, Jacob	3rd cousin twice removed	X	6
Breneman, Jacob	3rd cousin twice removed	X	6
Breneman, Janice Marie	Wife of the 4th cousin twice removed		
Breneman, John	3rd cousin twice removed	X	6
Breneman, Maria	3rd cousin twice removed	X	6
Breneman, Nancy	3rd cousin twice removed	X	6
Breneman, Private	Husband of the 3rd cousin 3 times removed		
Brenneman, Elizabeth	Wife of the 1st cousin 3 times removed		
Brenneman, Jacob	Husband of the 3rd cousin twice removed		
Brenneman, Melchior	Husband of the great-grandaunt		
Brenneman, Private	Husband of the 3rd cousin 3 times removed		
Brenneman, Private	3rd cousin 4 times removed	XII	8
Brenneman, Private	3rd cousin 4 times removed	XII	8
Brenner, Anna Barabara	Wife of the 6th cousin		
Brenner, George	Husband of the 1st cousin 3 times removed		
Brenner, Martha Eschbach	Wife of the 3rd cousin once removed		
Bressler, Lydia	Wife of the 3rd cousin twice removed		
Bricker, Catherine	Wife of the 2nd great-granduncle		

Name	Relationship with Milton Hershey	Civil	Canon
Briggs, Lyle Andrew	Husband of the 3rd cousin twice removed		
Briggs, Private	3rd cousin 3 times removed	XI	7
Briggs, Private	3rd cousin 3 times removed	XI	7
Briggs, Private	3rd cousin 3 times removed	XI	7
Bright, Private	6th cousin 4 times removed	XVIII	11
Bright, Private	6th cousin 5 times removed	XIX	12
Bright, Private	6th cousin 5 times removed	XIX	12
Bright, Private	6th cousin 6 times removed	XX	13
Bright, Private	6th cousin 6 times removed	XX	13
Bright, Private	6th cousin 4 times removed	XVIII	11
Bright, William Martin	Husband of the 6th cousin 3 times removed		
Brightbill, Jack A	Husband of the 6th cousin 4 times removed		
Brightbill, Susan M	6th cousin 5 times removed	XIX	12
Brindle, William	Husband of the 4th cousin once removed		
Brinser, Elinor L.	6th cousin 3 times removed	XVII	10
Brinser, George A.	Husband of the 6th cousin twice removed		
Brittenstine, Louisa	Wife of the 6th cousin		
Broadway, Jacob	Husband of the half 3rd cousin 3 times removed		
Brock, Private	Wife of the half 3rd cousin 4 times removed		
Brooks, Frederick Henry	Husband of the half 3rd cousin 3 times removed		
Brooks, Gordon E.	Husband of the half 3rd cousin 3 times removed		
Brooks, Private	Half 3rd cousin 4 times removed	XII	8
Brooks, Private	Half 3rd cousin 4 times removed	XII	8
Brooks, Private	Half 3rd cousin 4 times removed	XII	8
Brooks, Velma Donelda	Wife of the 6th cousin twice removed		
Brower, Abraham DeFraine	Husband of the 1st cousin 4 times removed		
Brower, Henry Buckwalter	2nd cousin 3 times removed	IX	6
Brower, Magdelene	2nd cousin 3 times removed	IX	6
Brower, Mary Reiff	Wife of the 2nd cousin 3 times removed		
Brown, Anna	Half 3rd cousin once removed	IX	5
Brown, Eliza	Half 3rd cousin once removed	IX	5
Brown, Marietta	Half 3rd cousin once removed	IX	5
Brown, Mary Louise	Wife of the 6th cousin twice removed		
Brown, Mildred	Wife of the half 3rd cousin twice removed		
Brown, Moses	Husband of the half 3rd cousin		
Brown, Orian	Husband of the 6th cousin 3 times removed		
Brown, Private	3rd cousin 4 times removed	XII	8
Brown, Private	3rd cousin 4 times removed	XII	8
Brown, Private	6th cousin 4 times removed	XVIII	11
Brown, Private	6th cousin 4 times removed	XVIII	11
Brown, Private	6th cousin 4 times removed	XVIII	11
Brown, Private	6th cousin 4 times removed	XVIII	11
Brown, Private	6th cousin 4 times removed	XVIII	11
Brown, Robert Cope	Husband of the 6th cousin 3 times removed		
Brown, Rosa	Half 3rd cousin once removed	IX	5
Brownlee, Ruth	Wife of the 6th cousin twice removed		
Brua, Susan	Wife of the half 4th cousin twice removed		
Brubacher, Augustus	5th cousin once removed	XIII	7
Brubacher, Carolina	6th cousin	XIV	7
Brubacher, Caroline	6th cousin	XIV	7
Brubacher, Catharine D.	6th cousin	XIV	7
Brubacher, David	Husband of the 4th cousin twice removed		
Brubacher, David	6th cousin	XIV	7
Brubacher, David A. Judson	6th cousin	XIV	7
Brubacher, David F.	6th cousin	XIV	7
Brubacher, David N.	6th cousin	XIV	7
Brubacher, David O.	5th cousin once removed	XIII	7
Brubacher, Eliza N.	6th cousin	XIV	7
Brubacher, Elizabeth	6th cousin	XIV	7
Brubacher, Elizabeth D.	6th cousin	XIV	7
Brubacher, George M.	6th cousin	XIV	7
Brubacher, Henry W.	6th cousin	XIV	7
Brubacher, Isaac B.	6th cousin	XIV	7
Brubacher, Jacob D.	6th cousin	XIV	7
Brubacher, Jacob F.	6th cousin	XIV	7
Brubacher, Jacob N.	6th cousin	XIV	7

Name	Relationship with Milton Hershey	Civil	Canon
Brubacher, Jacob O.	5th cousin once removed	XIII	7
Brubacher, John	6th cousin	XIV	7
Brubacher, John D.	6th cousin	XIV	7
Brubacher, John H.	6th cousin	XIV	7
Brubacher, John O.	5th cousin once removed	XIII	7
Brubacher, Joseph D.	6th cousin	XIV	7
Brubacher, Magdalena	Wife of the 4th great-granduncle		
Brubacher, Margaret	6th cousin	XIV	7
Brubacher, Peter	6th cousin	XIV	7
Brubacher, Peter O.	5th cousin once removed	XIII	7
Brubacher, Polly	6th cousin	XIV	7
Brubacher, Priscilla	6th cousin	XIV	7
Brubacher, Samuel F.	6th cousin	XIV	7
Brubacher, Samuel N.	6th cousin	XIV	7
Brubacher, Sarah	6th cousin	XIV	7
Brubacher, Susan N.	6th cousin	XIV	7
Brubacker, Elizabeth	Wife of the 3rd cousin 3 times removed		
Brubaker, Allen L	4th cousin once removed	XI	6
Brubaker, Anna Hiestand	Wife of the 5th great-grandfather		
Brubaker, Arlene Celeste	4th cousin twice removed	XII	7
Brubaker, Arthur J	4th cousin twice removed	XII	7
Brubaker, Charles E	4th cousin twice removed	XII	7
Brubaker, Charles White	4th cousin	X	5
Brubaker, Christian	Husband of the 1st cousin 3 times removed		
Brubaker, Christian	2nd cousin twice removed	VIII	5
Brubaker, Christian	3rd cousin once removed	IX	5
Brubaker, Christopher Scott	5th cousin twice removed	XIV	8
Brubaker, Daniel	Husband of the 1st cousin 3 times removed		
Brubaker, Elias	Husband of the 6th cousin		
Brubaker, Elizabeth	Wife of the half 1st cousin twice removed		
Brubaker, Elizabeth Anna	2nd great-grandmother	IV	4
Brubaker, Elsie	4th cousin twice removed	XII	7
Brubaker, Ezra	4th cousin	X	5
Brubaker, Fannie	4th cousin	X	5
Brubaker, Fanny	3rd cousin once removed	IX	5
Brubaker, Fanny Elizabeth	4th cousin twice removed	XII	7
Brubaker, Florence	4th cousin twice removed	XII	7
Brubaker, Frank Hostetter	4th cousin	X	5
Brubaker, Hans	3rd great-grandfather	V	5
Brubaker, Harold F	4th cousin twice removed	XII	7
Brubaker, Helen	4th cousin twice removed	XII	7
Brubaker, Isaac	3rd cousin once removed	IX	5
Brubaker, Isaac	3rd cousin once removed	IX	5
Brubaker, Isaac	4th cousin	X	5
Brubaker, John	Husband of the 1st cousin 4 times removed		
Brubaker, John	Husband of the 3rd great-grandaunt		
Brubaker, John	Husband of the 1st cousin 4 times removed		
Brubaker, John Gesell	Husband of the 2nd cousin twice removed		
Brubaker, Joseph Stauffer	Husband of the 3rd cousin once removed		
Brubaker, Katie	5th cousin	XII	6
Brubaker, Lucy S.	Wife of the 3rd cousin once removed		
Brubaker, Magdalena	3rd cousin once removed	IX	5
Brubaker, Maria	Wife of the 2nd great-granduncle		
Brubaker, Mary	3rd cousin once removed	IX	5
Brubaker, Mary F	4th cousin twice removed	XII	7
Brubaker, Mary S.	Wife of the 6th cousin		
Brubaker, May	Wife of the 2nd cousin 3 times removed		
Brubaker, Moses S.	Husband of the 6th cousin		
Brubaker, Nathan	4th cousin	X	5
Brubaker, Nathan	5th cousin twice removed	XIV	8
Brubaker, Paul M	5th cousin	XII	6
Brubaker, Peter	2nd cousin twice removed	VIII	5
Brubaker, Peter B.	Husband of the 2nd cousin		
Brubaker, Peter G	Husband of the 4th cousin once removed		
Brubaker, Private	Wife of the 3rd cousin twice removed		
Brubaker, Rheta H	5th cousin	XII	6

The Relations of Milton Snavely Hershey, 4th Ed.

Name	Relationship with Milton Hershey	Civil	Canon
Brubaker, Robert Lee	5th cousin once removed	XIII	7
Brubaker, Rosetta	Wife of the 4th cousin twice removed		
Brubaker, Samuel	Husband of the 2nd cousin twice removed		
Brubaker, Sarah H.	Wife of the 2nd cousin		
Brubaker, Stauffer Joseph	4th cousin	X	5
Brubaker, Susan B	3rd cousin once removed	IX	5
Brubaker, Susanna	3rd cousin once removed	IX	5
Brubaker, Walter F	4th cousin twice removed	XII	7
Brubaker, Warren E	4th cousin twice removed	XII	7
Brubaker, Warren W.	4th cousin once removed	XI	6
Brubashcher, Magdalena	Wife of the 1st cousin 5 times removed		
Bruce, James	Husband of the half 3rd cousin once removed		
Bruderly, Edith	Wife of the 6th cousin twice removed		
Brumbaugh, John Snyder	Husband of the 6th cousin		
Brunk, Ann Mary	4th cousin twice removed	XII	7
Brunk, Barbara	4th cousin twice removed	XII	7
Brunk, Daniel	4th cousin twice removed	XII	7
Brunk, David	4th cousin twice removed	XII	7
Brunk, Elizabeth	4th cousin twice removed	XII	7
Brunk, George	4th cousin twice removed	XII	7
Brunk, Jacob	Husband of the 3rd cousin 3 times removed		
Brunk, Jacob Jr	4th cousin twice removed	XII	7
Brunk, John	4th cousin twice removed	XII	7
Brunk, Joseph	4th cousin twice removed	XII	7
Brunk, Susanna	4th cousin twice removed	XII	7
Bruppacher, Anna	Wife of the 7th great-granduncle		
Bruppacher, Ulrich	Husband of the half 6th great-grandaunt		
Bryant, Marian	Wife of the half 3rd cousin once removed		
Brynmor, John Ruple	3rd cousin 4 times removed	XII	8
Brynmor, Milene Sue Ruple	Wife of the 3rd cousin 3 times removed		
Bucher, Anna	Wife of the 1st cousin 3 times removed		
Bucher, Bonadine Marie	Wife of the 4th cousin twice removed		
Bucher, Elizabeth	Wife of the 3rd cousin once removed		
Bucher, Elizabeth	Wife of the 6th cousin		
Bucher, John B.	7th cousin once removed	XVII	9
Bucher, Jonas	Husband of the 5th cousin 3 times removed		
Bucher, Jonas	6th cousin twice removed	XVI	9
Bucher, Joseph	6th cousin twice removed	XVI	9
Bucher, Mary Ann	7th cousin once removed	XVII	9
Bucher, Private	Wife of the 3rd cousin 4 times removed		
Bucher, Veronica S.	6th cousin	XIV	7
Buchman, Gary Kyle	4th cousin 4 times removed	XIV	9
Buchman, Glenn	Husband of the 4th cousin 3 times removed		
Buchs, Louisa C	Wife of the 6th cousin once removed		
Buchwalter, Maria	Wife of the 1st cousin once removed		
Buck, Charles L.	Husband of the 6th cousin		
Buck, Mildred L.	Wife of the 6th cousin		
Buck, Private	Wife of the 6th cousin 3 times removed		
Buck, Sophia Amanda	Wife of the 6th cousin		
Buckwalter, Abraham	2nd great-grandfather	IV	4
Buckwalter, Abraham	1st cousin 4 times removed	VIII	6
Buckwalter, Abraham	Husband of the 2nd great-grandaunt		
Buckwalter, Abraham	Great-granduncle	V	4
Buckwalter, Abraham	Husband of the 5th cousin 3 times removed		
Buckwalter, Abraham	2nd cousin 3 times removed	IX	6
Buckwalter, Abraham	Granduncle	IV	3
Buckwalter, Abraham	3rd cousin twice removed	X	6
Buckwalter, Anlea	1st cousin 4 times removed	VIII	6
Buckwalter, Ann	Grandaunt	IV	3
Buckwalter, Anna	1st cousin 4 times removed	VIII	6
Buckwalter, Anna	1st cousin 4 times removed	VIII	6
Buckwalter, Anna Buzzard	3rd cousin twice removed	X	6
Buckwalter, Anthony Acker	2nd cousin 3 times removed	IX	6
Buckwalter, Barbara	1st cousin 4 times removed	VIII	6
Buckwalter, Barbara	1st cousin 4 times removed	VIII	6
Buckwalter, Barbara	1st cousin 4 times removed	VIII	6

Name	Relationship with Milton Hershey	Civil	Canon
Buckwalter, Barbara Neff	4th cousin once removed	XI	6
Buckwalter, Barbara Ziegler	2nd cousin 3 times removed	IX	6
Buckwalter, Benjamin	Great-grandfather	III	3
Buckwalter, Benjamin	Granduncle	IV	3
Buckwalter, Bressler	4th cousin once removed	XI	6
Buckwalter, Catherine	1st cousin 4 times removed	VIII	6
Buckwalter, Cathrine	3rd cousin twice removed	X	6
Buckwalter, Christopher Ziegler	2nd cousin 3 times removed	IX	6
Buckwalter, Daniel Longacre	1st cousin 4 times removed	VIII	6
Buckwalter, Daniel Ziegler	2nd cousin 3 times removed	IX	6
Buckwalter, David Johnson Rev.	3rd cousin twice removed	X	6
Buckwalter, David Longenecker	1st cousin 4 times removed	VIII	6
Buckwalter, David Ziegler	2nd cousin 3 times removed	IX	6
Buckwalter, Elisabeth	Wife of the 2nd cousin 3 times removed		
Buckwalter, Elizabeth	1st cousin 4 times removed	VIII	6
Buckwalter, Elizabeth	Wife of the 2nd cousin 3 times removed		
Buckwalter, Elizabeth	1st cousin 4 times removed	VIII	6
Buckwalter, Elizabeth	Grandmother	II	2
Buckwalter, Elizabeth Barbara	Wife of the 2nd cousin 3 times removed		
Buckwalter, Emma Halterman	4th cousin once removed	XI	6
Buckwalter, Esther Longenecker	1st cousin 4 times removed	VIII	6
Buckwalter, Eugene Buzzard	3rd cousin twice removed	X	6
Buckwalter, Francis	4th great-grandfather	VI	6
Buckwalter, Franklin	4th cousin once removed	XI	6
Buckwalter, Frantz	1st cousin 4 times removed	VIII	6
Buckwalter, Frenzi	1st cousin 4 times removed	VIII	6
Buckwalter, George Buzzard	3rd cousin twice removed	X	6
Buckwalter, Hannah	1st cousin 4 times removed	VIII	6
Buckwalter, Hans	1st cousin 4 times removed	VIII	6
Buckwalter, Heidi Rene	3rd cousin 4 times removed	XII	8
Buckwalter, Henrich	1st cousin 4 times removed	VIII	6
Buckwalter, Henry	1st cousin 4 times removed	VIII	6
Buckwalter, Henry	3rd cousin twice removed	X	6
Buckwalter, Henry Heberline	2nd cousin 3 times removed	IX	6
Buckwalter, Infant	4th cousin once removed	XI	6
Buckwalter, Jacob	3rd great-granduncle	VII	6
Buckwalter, Jacob	1st cousin 4 times removed	VIII	6
Buckwalter, Jacob	Granduncle	IV	3
Buckwalter, Jacob Heberline	2nd cousin 3 times removed	IX	6
Buckwalter, Jacob Ziegler	2nd cousin 3 times removed	IX	6
Buckwalter, Joel B.	4th cousin once removed	XI	6
Buckwalter, Johannes	3rd great-granduncle	VII	6
Buckwalter, Johannes Heberline	2nd cousin 3 times removed	IX	6
Buckwalter, Johannes Longenecker	1st cousin 4 times removed	VIII	6
Buckwalter, John	1st cousin 4 times removed	VIII	6
Buckwalter, John	2nd cousin 3 times removed	IX	6
Buckwalter, John	3rd cousin twice removed	X	6
Buckwalter, John B.	4th cousin once removed	XI	6
Buckwalter, John Funk	3rd cousin twice removed	X	6
Buckwalter, John Ziegler	2nd cousin 3 times removed	IX	6
Buckwalter, Jonas	3rd cousin twice removed	X	6
Buckwalter, Joseph	3rd great-grandfather	V	5
Buckwalter, Joseph C. Buzzard	3rd cousin twice removed	X	6
Buckwalter, Joseph Ziegler	2nd cousin 3 times removed	IX	6
Buckwalter, Judith	2nd cousin 3 times removed	IX	6
Buckwalter, Lavina Johnson	3rd cousin twice removed	X	6
Buckwalter, Leon Eugene	Husband of the 3rd cousin 3 times removed		
Buckwalter, Lizzie	1st cousin 4 times removed	VIII	6
Buckwalter, Louisa	1st cousin 4 times removed	VIII	6
Buckwalter, Magdalena	1st cousin 4 times removed	VIII	6
Buckwalter, Magdalena	2nd cousin 3 times removed	IX	6
Buckwalter, Magdalena Longenecker	1st cousin 4 times removed	VIII	6
Buckwalter, Magdelene Heberline	2nd cousin 3 times removed	IX	6
Buckwalter, Marie	1st cousin 4 times removed	VIII	6
Buckwalter, Mary	3rd great-grandaunt	VII	6
Buckwalter, Mary	2nd cousin 3 times removed	IX	6

Name	Relationship with Milton Hershey	Civil	Canon
Buckwalter, Mary	1st cousin 4 times removed	VIII	6
Buckwalter, Mary	Great-grandaunt	V	4
Buckwalter, Mary	Grandaunt	IV	3
Buckwalter, Mary	3rd cousin twice removed	X	6
Buckwalter, Mary Buzzard	3rd cousin twice removed	X	6
Buckwalter, Mary Heberline	2nd cousin 3 times removed	IX	6
Buckwalter, Matleni	1st cousin 4 times removed	VIII	6
Buckwalter, Michael	Husband of the 1st cousin once removed		
Buckwalter, Morgan	4th cousin once removed	XI	6
Buckwalter, Moses	3rd cousin twice removed	X	6
Buckwalter, Nathaniel Halterman	4th cousin once removed	XI	6
Buckwalter, Private	Husband of the 3rd cousin 4 times removed		
Buckwalter, Private	3rd cousin 5 times removed	XIII	9
Buckwalter, Private	3rd cousin 5 times removed	XIII	9
Buckwalter, Private	3rd cousin 5 times removed	XIII	9
Buckwalter, Private	Wife of the 3rd cousin twice removed		
Buckwalter, Private	Husband of the 3rd cousin 3 times removed		
Buckwalter, Rebeccah Francis	2nd cousin 3 times removed	IX	6
Buckwalter, Robert Buzzard	3rd cousin twice removed	X	6
Buckwalter, Salome	4th cousin once removed	XI	6
Buckwalter, Samuel	Husband of the grandaunt		
Buckwalter, Samuel	3rd cousin twice removed	X	6
Buckwalter, Samuel Ziegler	2nd cousin 3 times removed	IX	6
Buckwalter, Sarah (Sallie) Halterman	4th cousin once removed	XI	6
Buckwalter, Susan	Great-grandaunt	V	4
Buckwalter, Susannah	1st cousin 4 times removed	VIII	6
Buckwalter, Theodorus	3rd great-granduncle	VII	6
Bucove, Andre Maurice	2nd cousin 5 times removed	XI	8
Bucove, David Arthur	Ex-husband of the 2nd cousin 4 times removed		
Bucove, Rachel Naomi	2nd cousin 5 times removed	XI	8
Bueler, Barbara	5th great-grandmother	VII	7
Buller, Private	Husband of the 6th cousin 3 times removed		
Bullock, Sarah	Wife of the 3rd cousin twice removed		
Burd, Martha	Wife of the 6th cousin		
Burdett, Private	Husband of the 6th cousin 3 times removed		
Burdett, Private	6th cousin 4 times removed	XVIII	11
Burkett, Private	Wife of the 3rd cousin 3 times removed		
Burkhart, John Z.	Husband of the 3rd cousin twice removed		
Burkheart, Private	6th cousin 3 times removed	XVII	10
Burkheart, Private	6th cousin 3 times removed	XVII	10
Burkheart, Private	6th cousin 3 times removed	XVII	10
Burkheart, Steve	Husband of the 6th cousin twice removed		
Burkholder, A M	2nd cousin once removed	VII	4
Burkholder, Abraham	Husband of the 4th great-grandaunt		
Burkholder, Abraham H	2nd cousin	VI	3
Burkholder, Annie	2nd cousin	VI	3
Burkholder, Barbara	Wife of the 6th cousin		
Burkholder, Christiana	Wife of the 4th cousin 4 times removed		
Burkholder, Clark A	2nd cousin once removed	VII	4
Burkholder, Corby M.	Husband of the 2nd cousin 5 times removed		
Burkholder, Daniel S.	Husband of the 3rd cousin twice removed		
Burkholder, Dorothy M	2nd cousin once removed	VII	4
Burkholder, E J	2nd cousin once removed	VII	4
Burkholder, Elizabeth	Wife of the 1st cousin 3 times removed		
Burkholder, Felix	2nd cousin	VI	3
Burkholder, Fianna	Wife of the 2nd cousin once removed		
Burkholder, Gabriel L.	2nd cousin	VI	3
Burkholder, George R	2nd cousin once removed	VII	4
Burkholder, Harry Hershey	2nd cousin	VI	3
Burkholder, Isaac	2nd cousin	VI	3
Burkholder, John	Husband of the 1st cousin 3 times removed		
Burkholder, John	Husband of the 1st cousin once removed		
Burkholder, Kathleen	2nd cousin 3 times removed	IX	6
Burkholder, Kevin	2nd cousin 3 times removed	IX	6
Burkholder, Lisa	2nd cousin 3 times removed	IX	6
Burkholder, Magdalena	2nd cousin	VI	3

Name	Relationship with Milton Hershey	Civil	Canon
Burkholder, Maria	Wife of the 1st cousin 4 times removed		
Burkholder, Marie	2nd cousin once removed	VII	4
Burkholder, Marlin	2nd cousin once removed	VII	4
Burkholder, Melvin E	2nd cousin once removed	VII	4
Burkholder, Oliver	Husband of the 1st cousin once removed		
Burkholder, Private	Husband of the 3rd cousin 4 times removed		
Burkholder, Private	3rd cousin 5 times removed	XIII	9
Burkholder, Private	3rd cousin 5 times removed	XIII	9
Burkholder, Private	3rd cousin 5 times removed	XIII	9
Burkholder, Private	Wife of the 3rd cousin 3 times removed		
Burkholder, Robert	2nd cousin 3 times removed	IX	6
Burkholder, Robert Melvin	2nd cousin twice removed	VIII	5
Burkholder, Sarah	2nd cousin	VI	3
Burkholder, Susanna	Wife of the 3rd cousin twice removed		
Burkholder, Thomas	2nd cousin 3 times removed	IX	6
Burkholder, Tillie	Wife of the half 3rd cousin twice removed		
Burnham, Lela Berneice	Wife of the 6th cousin twice removed		
Burns, Henry Burt	Husband of the 6th cousin twice removed		
Burns, Private	6th cousin 3 times removed	XVII	10
Burns, Private	6th cousin 3 times removed	XVII	10
Burns, Private	6th cousin 4 times removed	XVIII	11
Burns, Private	6th cousin 4 times removed	XVIII	11
Burns, Private	6th cousin 4 times removed	XVIII	11
Burns, Private	6th cousin 4 times removed	XVIII	11
Burns, Private	6th cousin 4 times removed	XVIII	11
Burns, Private	6th cousin 4 times removed	XVIII	11
Burns, Private	6th cousin 4 times removed	XVIII	11
Burns, Private	Husband of the 6th cousin 3 times removed		
Burns, Private	6th cousin 4 times removed	XVIII	11
Burns, Private	6th cousin 4 times removed	XVIII	11
Burns, Private	6th cousin 4 times removed	XVIII	11
Burnside, Jean Barclay	Wife of the half 3rd cousin 4 times removed		
Burrier, Private	Husband of the 6th cousin 3 times removed		
Burrier, Private	6th cousin 4 times removed	XVIII	11
Burrier, Private	6th cousin 4 times removed	XVIII	11
Burt, Caitlin Ann	2nd cousin 6 times removed	XII	9
Burt, David A.	Ex-husband of the 2nd cousin 5 times removed		
Bush, Private	Wife of the 6th cousin 3 times removed		
Butch, Private	Husband of the 6th cousin 3 times removed		
Butch, Private	6th cousin 4 times removed	XVIII	11
Butterbaugh, R	Husband of the 6th cousin		
Buzzard, Barbara Buckwalter	2nd cousin 3 times removed	IX	6
Buzzard, David High	3rd cousin twice removed	X	6
Buzzard, Elizabeth Buckwalter	2nd cousin 3 times removed	IX	6
Buzzard, Elizabeth High	3rd cousin twice removed	X	6
Buzzard, Esther Buckwalter	2nd cousin 3 times removed	IX	6
Buzzard, Francis High	4th cousin once removed	XI	6
Buzzard, Frederick	Husband of the 1st cousin 4 times removed		
Buzzard, Frederick Buckwalter	2nd cousin 3 times removed	IX	6
Buzzard, Hannah Buckwalter	2nd cousin 3 times removed	IX	6
Buzzard, Harry Thornton	4th cousin once removed	XI	6
Buzzard, Henry High	3rd cousin twice removed	X	6
Buzzard, Jacob Buckwalter	2nd cousin 3 times removed	IX	6
Buzzard, Jacob High	3rd cousin twice removed	X	6
Buzzard, John Buckwalter	2nd cousin 3 times removed	IX	6
Buzzard, John High	3rd cousin twice removed	X	6
Buzzard, John High	4th cousin once removed	XI	6
Buzzard, Jonas High	3rd cousin twice removed	X	6
Buzzard, Magdalena Buckwalter	2nd cousin 3 times removed	IX	6
Buzzard, Margaret High	4th cousin once removed	XI	6
Buzzard, Mary High	4th cousin once removed	XI	6
Buzzard, Mary High	3rd cousin twice removed	X	6
Buzzard, Mazie	5th cousin	XII	6
Buzzard, Private	Wife of the 3rd cousin 3 times removed		
Buzzard, Simeon High	4th cousin once removed	XI	6

Name	Relationship with Milton Hershey	Civil	Canon
Buzzard, Simeon High	3rd cousin twice removed	X	6
Buzzard, Susan High	3rd cousin twice removed	X	6
Buzzard, Susanna Buckwalter	2nd cousin 3 times removed	IX	6
Buzzard, Thornton High	4th cousin once removed	XI	6
Bye, Alton Samuel	Husband of the 6th cousin once removed		
Byers, Dwight	6th cousin 3 times removed	XVII	10
Byers, Evan	Husband of the 6th cousin twice removed		
Byers, Grace	Wife of the half 3rd cousin twice removed		
Byers, Hazel	6th cousin 3 times removed	XVII	10
Byers, James	6th cousin 3 times removed	XVII	10
Byers, Phyllis	6th cousin 3 times removed	XVII	10
Byers, Ralph	6th cousin 3 times removed	XVII	10
Byers, Robert	6th cousin 3 times removed	XVII	10
C, Ella	Wife of the 3rd cousin once removed		
C., Clyde, Jr Stoffer	6th cousin 3 times removed	XVII	10
Cafferty, Florence Anna	Wife of the 6th cousin once removed		
Cain, Betty	Wife of the 6th cousin 3 times removed		
Calaman, Lawrence Delmar	Wife of the 6th cousin twice removed		
Calle, Barbara	Wife of the 5th cousin once removed		
Calvin, Elwood E.	Husband of the 6th cousin twice removed		
Campbell, Angus	Husband of the half 3rd cousin twice removed		
Campbell, Blanche	Half 3rd cousin 3 times removed	XI	7
Campbell, Bruce	Half 3rd cousin 3 times removed	XI	7
Campbell, Cheryl Ann	Wife of the 3rd cousin 3 times removed		
Campbell, James	Half 3rd cousin 3 times removed	XI	7
Campbell, John	Husband of the 6th cousin once removed		
Campbell, Ruth	Wife of the 3rd cousin once removed		
Canfield, Wilma	Wife of the 6th cousin twice removed		
Canning, Private	Wife of the 3rd cousin 3 times removed		
Carbaugh, Adam	Husband of the 6th cousin once removed		
Carbaugh, Unknown	6th cousin twice removed	XVI	9
Carpenter, John	Husband of the 3rd great-grandaunt		
Carpenter, Mary Elizabeth	Wife of the 2nd cousin 6 times removed		
Carper, Fannie	Wife of the 6th cousin		
Carrithers, Barbara	Wife of the 3rd cousin 3 times removed		
Carroll, Catherine	Wife of the 2nd cousin 3 times removed		
Carsey, Private	Husband of the 6th cousin 3 times removed		
Cartier, Private	Husband of the 6th cousin 4 times removed		
Cartier, Private	6th cousin 5 times removed	XIX	12
Cartier, Private	6th cousin 5 times removed	XIX	12
Carvell, Audrey Nadine	3rd cousin 3 times removed	XI	7
Carvell, Glee Eileen	3rd cousin 3 times removed	XI	7
Carvell, Luke	Husband of the 3rd cousin twice removed		
Carvell, Vici Mae	3rd cousin 3 times removed	XI	7
Cassel, Abraham Buckwalter	2nd cousin 3 times removed	IX	6
Cassel, Barbara	Wife of the 1st cousin 4 times removed		
Cassel, Barbara Buckwalter	2nd cousin 3 times removed	IX	6
Cassel, David Buckwalter	2nd cousin 3 times removed	IX	6
Cassel, Esther Veronica Buckwalter	2nd cousin 3 times removed	IX	6
Cassel, John Hershey	3rd cousin twice removed	X	6
Cassel, Joseph Buckwalter	2nd cousin 3 times removed	IX	6
Cassel, Joseph Gochnauer	Husband of the 1st cousin 4 times removed		
Cassel, Mary	Wife of the 2nd cousin twice removed		
Casson, Joseph	Husband of the 5th great-grandaunt		
Caufield, Vaughn	Husband of the 6th cousin 3 times removed		
Cefro, Private	Wife of the 6th cousin 3 times removed		
Censky, Private	Wife of the 6th cousin 3 times removed		
Chadwick, Private	Wife of the 6th cousin 3 times removed		
Charles, Mary	Wife of the 5th cousin		
Chastine, Private	Wife of the 6th cousin 3 times removed		
Chisholm, Private	Husband of the 6th cousin 3 times removed		
Chittenden, Private	Wife of the 6th cousin 4 times removed		
Choflet, Private	6th cousin 3 times removed	XVII	10
Choflet, Private	6th cousin 3 times removed	XVII	10
Choflet, Private	6th cousin 3 times removed	XVII	10
Choflet, Private	6th cousin 3 times removed	XVII	10

Name	Relationship with Milton Hershey	Civil	Canon
Choflet, Rev Kenneth	Husband of the 6th cousin twice removed		
Christen, Bernice	Wife of the 6th cousin twice removed		
Clare, Betty J	Wife of the 6th cousin 3 times removed		
Clark, J. S.	Husband of the half 3rd cousin twice removed		
Clark, Private	Half 3rd cousin 3 times removed	XI	7
Clarke, Bruce	Husband of the half 3rd cousin 3 times removed		
Clarke, Private	Half 3rd cousin 4 times removed	XII	8
Clemons, Lydia	Wife of the half 3rd cousin		
Clymer, Private	Husband of the 3rd cousin twice removed		
Clymer, Private	3rd cousin 3 times removed	XI	7
Coakley, Private	Wife of the 3rd cousin 3 times removed		
Coates, Private	Wife of the 3rd cousin 3 times removed		
Coburn, Martha Asenath	Wife of the 3rd cousin once removed		
Cochran, Private	6th cousin 4 times removed	XVIII	11
Cochran, Private	6th cousin 4 times removed	XVIII	11
Cochran, Virgil William	Husband of the 6th cousin 3 times removed		
Cockburn, Gwen	Wife of the half 3rd cousin 3 times removed		
Cole, Private	Wife of the 6th cousin 3 times removed		
Collard, Alan	Half 3rd cousin twice removed	X	6
Collard, Eric	Half 3rd cousin twice removed	X	6
Collard, George	Husband of the half 3rd cousin once removed		
Collard, Isabel	Half 3rd cousin twice removed	X	6
Collard, Jean	Half 3rd cousin twice removed	X	6
Collard, Private	Half 3rd cousin 3 times removed	XI	7
Colle, Marceline Elodia	Wife of the 6th cousin 3 times removed		
Collingsworth, Oscar Edward	Husband of the 6th cousin 3 times removed		
Connell, Elizabeth Celesta	Wife of the 6th cousin once removed		
Conrad, Clifford	Husband of the 6th cousin 3 times removed		
Conrad, Gerald	6th cousin 4 times removed	XVIII	11
Conrad, Glenn	6th cousin 4 times removed	XVIII	11
Conrad, Marilyn	6th cousin 4 times removed	XVIII	11
Constable, Herbert	Husband of the half 3rd cousin 3 times removed		
Cook, Claud	Half 3rd cousin 3 times removed	XI	7
Cook, Ernest	Half 3rd cousin 3 times removed	XI	7
Cook, Fern	Half 3rd cousin 3 times removed	XI	7
Cook, James	Husband of the half 3rd cousin twice removed		
Cook, Jesse	Husband of the half 3rd cousin once removed		
Cook, Lola	Half 3rd cousin 3 times removed	XI	7
Cook, Private	Half 3rd cousin 4 times removed	XII	8
Cook, Private	Half 3rd cousin 4 times removed	XII	8
Cook, Private	Half 3rd cousin 4 times removed	XII	8
Cook, Private	Half 3rd cousin 4 times removed	XII	8
Cooley, Audrey	Half 3rd cousin 3 times removed	XI	7
Cooley, Bruce	Half 3rd cousin twice removed	X	6
Cooley, Clayton	Half 3rd cousin twice removed	X	6
Cooley, Delores	Half 3rd cousin 3 times removed	XI	7
Cooley, Fern	Half 3rd cousin twice removed	X	6
Cooley, Gerald	Half 3rd cousin twice removed	X	6
Cooley, Harold	Half 3rd cousin twice removed	X	6
Cooley, Jay	Half 3rd cousin twice removed	X	6
Cooley, Marie	Half 3rd cousin twice removed	X	6
Cooley, Myron	Half 3rd cousin twice removed	X	6
Cooley, Nina	Half 3rd cousin twice removed	X	6
Cooley, Unknown	Husband of the half 3rd cousin once removed		
Cooley, Virginia	Half 3rd cousin 3 times removed	XI	7
Cooper, Alan C	6th cousin 4 times removed	XVIII	11
Cooper, Charles David	Husband of the 6th cousin 3 times removed		
Cooper, Donald W	6th cousin 4 times removed	XVIII	11
Cooper, Jerold M	6th cousin 4 times removed	XVIII	11
Cooper, Morris B	Husband of the 6th cousin 3 times removed		
Cooper, Private	6th cousin 4 times removed	XVIII	11
Cope, Kenneth	Husband of the 6th cousin twice removed		
Corbin, Orel Drennan	Husband of the half 3rd cousin once removed		
Cordell	Husband of the half 3rd cousin 3 times removed		
Cordell, Private	Half 3rd cousin 4 times removed	XII	8
Core, Rosina	Wife of the 1st cousin 4 times removed		

Name	Relationship with Milton Hershey	Civil	Canon
Corle, Sarah	Wife of the 6th cousin		
Coughen, Nancy Ann	6th cousin 3 times removed	XVII	10
Coughen, Private	6th cousin 3 times removed	XVII	10
Coughen, Private	6th cousin 3 times removed	XVII	10
Coughen, Private	6th cousin 3 times removed	XVII	10
Coughen, Thomas Phillip	Husband of the 6th cousin twice removed		
Coulter, Dorothy	Wife of the half 3rd cousin 3 times removed		
Court, Virginia M	Wife of the 6th cousin twice removed		
Cowgill, Ewing	Husband of the 2nd cousin 3 times removed		
Cox, Edward L	Husband of the 6th cousin once removed		
Cox, Fredrico	Wife of the 6th cousin 3 times removed		
Cragin, Private	6th cousin 3 times removed	XVII	10
Cragin, Sumner Bowers	Ex-husband of the 6th cousin twice removed		
Craign, Private	6th cousin 3 times removed	XVII	10
Crall, Mary	Wife of the 5th cousin once removed		
Cramer, Mary	Wife of the 5th cousin once removed		
Crantson, Donald	Husband of the 6th cousin twice removed		
Crantson, Private	6th cousin 3 times removed	XVII	10
Crantson, Private	6th cousin 3 times removed	XVII	10
Crefro, Private	Wife of the 6th cousin 3 times removed		
Creighton, Thomas	Husband of the 6th cousin once removed		
Creiner, Christianna	Wife of the 2nd cousin		
Crew, Arnie	Husband of the 6th cousin 3 times removed		
Crew, Arnold	Husband of the 6th cousin 3 times removed		
Crist, Private	Wife of the 6th cousin 3 times removed		
Croisette	Half 3rd cousin twice removed	X	6
Croisette, Eugene	Ex-husband of the half 3rd cousin once removed		
Cross, Daisy Grace	Wife of the 6th cousin once removed		
Crouse, Ellen C.	Wife of the 6th cousin		
Crouse, Jerome	Husband of the 6th cousin		
Crouthamel, Leo Trostle	Husband of the 3rd cousin twice removed		
Crouthamel, Private	3rd cousin 3 times removed	XI	7
Crouthamel, Private	3rd cousin 3 times removed	XI	7
Crouthamel, Private	3rd cousin 3 times removed	XI	7
Crouthamel, Private	3rd cousin 4 times removed	XII	8
Crouthamel, Private	3rd cousin 4 times removed	XII	8
Crowe, Private	Wife of the 6th cousin 3 times removed		
Cruce, Private	Husband of the 6th cousin 3 times removed		
Cruce, Private	6th cousin 4 times removed	XVIII	11
Cruce, Private	6th cousin 4 times removed	XVIII	11
Cruce, Private	6th cousin 4 times removed	XVIII	11
Cruce, Private	6th cousin 4 times removed	XVIII	11
Cruiz, Lucille	Wife of the half 3rd cousin once removed		
Cummings, Private	Husband of the 6th cousin 3 times removed		
Cummings, Private	6th cousin 4 times removed	XVIII	11
Cummings, Private	6th cousin 4 times removed	XVIII	11
Cunningham, Arthur "Murray"	Husband of the 6th cousin 3 times removed		
Cunningham, Private	6th cousin 4 times removed	XVIII	11
Cunningham, Private	6th cousin 4 times removed	XVIII	11
Cunningham, Private	6th cousin 4 times removed	XVIII	11
D'Ginto, Gina Marie	Wife of the 2nd cousin 3 times removed		
Dafoe, Cecil Wilfred	Husband of the half 3rd cousin twice removed		
Dafoe, Kenneth Cecil	Half 3rd cousin 3 times removed	XI	7
Dafoe, Mavis Ruth	Half 3rd cousin 3 times removed	XI	7
Dafoe, Private	Half 3rd cousin 3 times removed	XI	7
Dafoe, Private	Half 3rd cousin 3 times removed	XI	7
Dafoe, Private	Half 3rd cousin 3 times removed	XI	7
Dafoe, Private	Half 3rd cousin 3 times removed	XI	7
Dafoe, Private	Half 3rd cousin 3 times removed	XI	7
Daley, George	Husband of the half 3rd cousin twice removed		
Daman, Ernest Ludwig	Husband of the 3rd cousin twice removed		
Daman, Private	3rd cousin 3 times removed	XI	7
Daman, Private	3rd cousin 3 times removed	XI	7
Daman, Private	3rd cousin 3 times removed	XI	7
Damiani, Private	Husband of the 3rd cousin twice removed		
Damiani, Private	3rd cousin 3 times removed	XI	7

Name	Relationship with Milton Hershey	Civil	Canon
Damiani, Private	3rd cousin 3 times removed	XI	7
Dan, Paradise Tanner	Husband of the half 3rd cousin 3 times removed		
Danherr, Catharina	Wife of the 5th great-granduncle		
Danner, Private	Husband of the 6th cousin 3 times removed		
Danner, Private	6th cousin 4 times removed	XVIII	11
Danson, Private	Husband of the 6th cousin 3 times removed		
Danson, Private	6th cousin 4 times removed	XVIII	11
Danson, Private	6th cousin 4 times removed	XVIII	11
Darr, Matilda Agnes	Wife of the 6th cousin		
Daugherty, Lavinia	Wife of the 6th cousin twice removed		
Daughter, Infant	6th cousin once removed	XV	8
Davenport, Edna Joyce	Wife of the half 3rd cousin 4 times removed		
Davidson, Elsie Ann	Wife of the half 3rd cousin once removed		
Davis, Halleck Charles	Husband of the 6th cousin twice removed		
Davis, Jessie	Wife of the 6th cousin once removed		
Davis, Joella	Wife of the 6th cousin		
Davis, Lucinda	Wife of the 6th cousin		
Davis, Private	6th cousin 3 times removed	XVII	10
Davis, Private	Husband of the 6th cousin 3 times removed		
Davis, Private	6th cousin 4 times removed	XVIII	11
Davis, Private	6th cousin 4 times removed	XVIII	11
Davis, Private	6th cousin 4 times removed	XVIII	11
Deffenbaugh, Mona V	Wife of the 6th cousin once removed		
Deihl, Gideon S.	6th cousin twice removed	XVI	9
Deihl, Harvey A.	6th cousin twice removed	XVI	9
Deihl, Howard B.	6th cousin twice removed	XVI	9
Deihl, James Alfred	6th cousin twice removed	XVI	9
Deihl, Miriam	6th cousin 3 times removed	XVII	10
Deihl, Unknown	6th cousin twice removed	XVI	9
Deihl, Unknown	6th cousin twice removed	XVI	9
Deihl, Unknown	6th cousin twice removed	XVI	9
Deihl, Unknown	6th cousin twice removed	XVI	9
Deihl, Unknown	6th cousin 3 times removed	XVII	10
Deihl, Unknown	6th cousin 3 times removed	XVII	10
Deihl, Unknown	6th cousin 3 times removed	XVII	10
Deihl, Unknown	6th cousin 3 times removed	XVII	10
Deihl, Unknown	6th cousin 3 times removed	XVII	10
Deihl, Unknown	6th cousin 3 times removed	XVII	10
Deihl, Unknown	6th cousin 3 times removed	XVII	10
Deihl, Unknown	6th cousin 3 times removed	XVII	10
Deihl, Unknown	6th cousin 3 times removed	XVII	10
Deimler, Christabel J	Wife of the 6th cousin 3 times removed		
Delebaugh, Maria	Wife of the 4th cousin twice removed		
Delgado, Private	Husband of the 3rd cousin 3 times removed		
Delgado, Private	3rd cousin 4 times removed	XII	8
Delgado, Private	3rd cousin 4 times removed	XII	8
Denlinger, Celeste Edith	Wife of the 3rd cousin once removed		
Denlinger, Lillie Landis	Wife of the 3rd cousin		
Denlinger, Mary J.	Wife of the 2nd cousin		
Denlinger, Private	Husband of the 3rd cousin 4 times removed		
Denlinger, Private	3rd cousin 5 times removed	XIII	9
Denlinger, Private	3rd cousin 5 times removed	XIII	9
Denlinger, Private	Wife of the 3rd cousin 4 times removed		
Dennis, Howard M.	Husband of the 6th cousin 3 times removed		
Dennis, Private	6th cousin 4 times removed	XVIII	11
Denny, Private	Wife of the 6th cousin 3 times removed		
Dentlinger, John	Husband of the 5th cousin 3 times removed		
DePalmo, Ernest	Spouse of the 6th cousin twice removed		
DePalmo, Private	6th cousin 3 times removed	XVII	10
DePalmo, Private	6th cousin 3 times removed	XVII	10
DePalmo, Private	6th cousin 3 times removed	XVII	10
DePalmo, Private	6th cousin 3 times removed	XVII	10
DePalmo, Private	6th cousin 4 times removed	XVIII	11
DePalmo, Private	6th cousin 4 times removed	XVIII	11
DePalmo, Private	6th cousin 4 times removed	XVIII	11
DePalmo, Private	6th cousin 4 times removed	XVIII	11

Name	Relationship with Milton Hershey	Civil	Canon
DePalmo, Private	6th cousin 4 times removed	XVIII	11
DePalmo, Private	6th cousin 4 times removed	XVIII	11
DePalmo, Private	6th cousin 4 times removed	XVIII	11
DePalmo, Private	6th cousin 4 times removed	XVIII	11
DePalmo, Private	6th cousin 3 times removed	XVII	10
DePalmo, Private	6th cousin 3 times removed	XVII	10
DePalmo, Private	6th cousin 3 times removed	XVII	10
DePalmo, Private	6th cousin 4 times removed	XVIII	11
DePalmo, Private	6th cousin 4 times removed	XVIII	11
DePalmo, Private	6th cousin 4 times removed	XVIII	11
DePalmo, Private	6th cousin 4 times removed	XVIII	11
DePalmo, Private	6th cousin 4 times removed	XVIII	11
DePalmo, Private	6th cousin 4 times removed	XVIII	11
DePalmo, Private	6th cousin 4 times removed	XVIII	11
Derr, Cyrus	Husband of the 6th cousin 3 times removed		
Derr, Elizabeth Jane Feldser	6th cousin 4 times removed	XVIII	11
Derr, Goldie Annabell	6th cousin 4 times removed	XVIII	11
Derr, Jay Earl Franklin	6th cousin 4 times removed	XVIII	11
Derr, Jennifer Elizabeth	6th cousin 5 times removed	XIX	12
Derr, Living	6th cousin 4 times removed	XVIII	11
Derr, Living	6th cousin 4 times removed	XVIII	11
Derr, Living	6th cousin 4 times removed	XVIII	11
Derr, Living	6th cousin 4 times removed	XVIII	11
Derr, Luella Mae Ober Anthony	6th cousin 4 times removed	XVIII	11
Derr, Stacey Susan	6th cousin 5 times removed	XIX	12
Detweiler, Elias G.	Husband of the 5th cousin		
Detwiler, Jacob Snowberger	Husband of the 6th cousin		
Deutsch, Abraham	Husband of the 4th great-grandaunt		
Devlin, Gordon	Half 3rd cousin 3 times removed	XI	7
Devlin, Harry	Half 3rd cousin 3 times removed	XI	7
Devlin, John	Husband of the half 3rd cousin twice removed		
Devlin, John	Half 3rd cousin 3 times removed	XI	7
Devlin, Norman	Half 3rd cousin 3 times removed	XI	7
Dice, Amanda E	Wife of the 6th cousin		
Dice, Elizabeth	Wife of the 6th cousin		
Dice, Sarah Ann	Wife of the 6th cousin		
Dick, Cecil E.	Husband of the 6th cousin twice removed		
Dick, Elizabeth	Wife of the 6th cousin		
Dick, Private	Husband of the 3rd cousin 3 times removed		
Dick, Private	6th cousin 4 times removed	XVIII	11
Dicky, Unknown	Husband of the 6th cousin once removed		
Diehl, Anna C.	6th cousin once removed	XV	8
Diehl, Charles A.	6th cousin once removed	XV	8
Diehl, David Alfred	6th cousin once removed	XV	8
Diehl, David R.	6th cousin 3 times removed	XVII	10
Diehl, Donald	6th cousin 3 times removed	XVII	10
Diehl, Elizabeth	Wife of the 6th cousin		
Diehl, Elmer E.	6th cousin once removed	XV	8
Diehl, George	Husband of the 6th cousin		
Diehl, Harold James	6th cousin 3 times removed	XVII	10
Diehl, Harry Lee	6th cousin once removed	XV	8
Diehl, Ida M.	6th cousin once removed	XV	8
Diehl, John Daniel	6th cousin 3 times removed	XVII	10
Diehl, John Reuben	Husband of the 6th cousin		
Diehl, Juanita Glada	6th cousin 3 times removed	XVII	10
Diehl, Kathryn	6th cousin once removed	XV	8
Diehl, Lillian	6th cousin once removed	XV	8
Diehl, Lorraine Louise	6th cousin 3 times removed	XVII	10
Diehl, Myrtle Liliom D.	6th cousin twice removed	XVI	9
Diehl, Percy Ellsworth	6th cousin twice removed	XVI	9
Diehl, Private	6th cousin 4 times removed	XVIII	11
Diehl, Private	6th cousin 4 times removed	XVIII	11
Diehl, Private	6th cousin 4 times removed	XVIII	11
Diehl, Private	6th cousin 4 times removed	XVIII	11
Diehl, Private	6th cousin 4 times removed	XVIII	11

Name	Relationship with Milton Hershey	Civil	Canon
Diehl, Private	6th cousin 4 times removed	XVIII	11
Diehl, Private	6th cousin 4 times removed	XVIII	11
Diehl, Private	6th cousin 4 times removed	XVIII	11
Diehl, Private	6th cousin 4 times removed	XVIII	11
Diehl, Private	6th cousin 4 times removed	XVIII	11
Diehl, Private	6th cousin 4 times removed	XVIII	11
Diehl, Private	6th cousin 4 times removed	XVIII	11
Diehl, Private	6th cousin 4 times removed	XVIII	11
Diehl, Private	6th cousin 4 times removed	XVIII	11
Diehl, Private	6th cousin 5 times removed	XIX	12
Diehl, Private	6th cousin 5 times removed	XIX	12
Diehl, Private	6th cousin 3 times removed	XVII	10
Diehl, Private	6th cousin 3 times removed	XVII	10
Diehl, Private	6th cousin 3 times removed	XVII	10
Diehl, Private	6th cousin 4 times removed	XVIII	11
Diehl, Private	6th cousin 4 times removed	XVIII	11
Diehl, Private	6th cousin 4 times removed	XVIII	11
Diehl, Private	6th cousin 4 times removed	XVIII	11
Diehl, Private	6th cousin 5 times removed	XIX	12
Diehl, Private	6th cousin 5 times removed	XIX	12
Diehl, Private	6th cousin 5 times removed	XIX	12
Diehl, Private	6th cousin 5 times removed	XIX	12
Diehl, Private	6th cousin 5 times removed	XIX	12
Diehl, Thomas E.	6th cousin once removed	XV	8
Diehl, Virginia May	6th cousin twice removed	XVI	9
Diehl, Winifred N.	6th cousin twice removed	XVI	9
Diehl, Zelda F.	6th cousin twice removed	XVI	9
Diehm, Ella Mae	Wife of the 2nd cousin twice removed		
Dien, Private	Wife of the 3rd cousin 3 times removed		
Dietrich, Susan	Wife of the 2nd cousin twice removed		
Diffenbach, Maria	Wife of the half 3rd cousin 3 times removed		
Dilks, Verna	Wife of the 6th cousin 3 times removed		
Dills, Elizabeth	Wife of the 1st cousin 3 times removed		
Dissinger, Catharine	Wife of the 5th cousin once removed		
Ditmars, Harriet	Wife of the 6th cousin		
Docksteader, Tressie Deola	Wife of the half 3rd cousin twice removed		
Dohner, Anna	4th cousin once removed	XI	6
Dohner, Catherine	Wife of the 2nd cousin 3 times removed		
Dohner, Catherine	3rd cousin twice removed	X	6
Dohner, Christian	4th cousin once removed	XI	6
Dohner, Elizabeth	3rd cousin twice removed	X	6
Dohner, Henry	Husband of the 2nd cousin 3 times removed		
Dohner, Jacob	3rd cousin twice removed	X	6
Dohner, John	3rd cousin twice removed	X	6
Dohner, Joseph	Husband of the 2nd cousin 3 times removed		
Dohner, Joseph	3rd cousin twice removed	X	6
Dohner, Joseph	4th cousin once removed	XI	6
Dohner, Lydia	3rd cousin twice removed	X	6
Dohner, Lydia	4th cousin once removed	XI	6
Dohner, Mary Elizabeth	3rd cousin twice removed	X	6
Dohner, Mary Elizabeth	4th cousin once removed	XI	6
Dohner, Michael	4th cousin once removed	XI	6
Dohner, Moses	3rd cousin twice removed	X	6
Dohner, Moses	4th cousin once removed	XI	6
Dohner, Noah	4th cousin once removed	XI	6
Dohner, Susan	3rd cousin twice removed	X	6
Dohner, Susannah	3rd cousin twice removed	X	6
Dollar, Victoria	Wife of the 6th cousin		
Dombach, Private	Wife of the 3rd cousin 3 times removed		
Donaldson, Guy Elmer	Husband of the 6th cousin twice removed		
Donaldson, Mary	Wife of the 2nd cousin 3 times removed		
Donaldson, Mary	Wife of the 2nd cousin 3 times removed		
Doner, Abraham	Husband of the 2nd cousin 4 times removed		
Doner, John	Husband of the 2nd cousin 4 times removed		
Dooling, Sarah	Wife of the 3rd cousin twice removed		
Dotts, Private	Wife of the 3rd cousin twice removed		

Name	Relationship with Milton Hershey	Civil	Canon
Dougherty, Charles	Husband of the 5th cousin		
Doughtery, Ernest	Husband of the half 3rd cousin once removed		
Doughtery, Joseph S.	Husband of the 6th cousin		
Dounell, Anna O.	Wife of the half 3rd cousin twice removed		
Dowdell, Ruth J	Wife of the 6th cousin twice removed		
Downing, Joseph	Husband of the 2nd cousin 3 times removed		
Drexler, Private	Wife of the half 3rd cousin 4 times removed		
Drover, Gertrude	Wife of the 6th cousin twice removed		
Dubble, Mary	Wife of the 4th cousin once removed		
Dubert, Mary	Wife of the 6th cousin once removed		
Dukart, Private	Husband of the 6th cousin 3 times removed		
Dukart, Private	6th cousin 4 times removed	XVIII	11
Duncan, Adrian E	6th cousin 3 times removed	XVII	10
Duncan, Alvid O	6th cousin twice removed	XVI	9
Duncan, Anna B	6th cousin twice removed	XVI	9
Duncan, Delmar A	6th cousin 4 times removed	XVIII	11
Duncan, Delmar M	6th cousin 3 times removed	XVII	10
Duncan, John	Husband of the 6th cousin once removed		
Duncan, Katherine M	6th cousin twice removed	XVI	9
Duncan, Lucille M	6th cousin 4 times removed	XVIII	11
Duncan, Margaret Ann	6th cousin twice removed	XVI	9
Duncan, Rachael Agnes	6th cousin twice removed	XVI	9
Duncan, Shirley A	6th cousin 4 times removed	XVIII	11
Duncan, William Malcolm	Husband of the 6th cousin once removed		
Duncan, William Malcolm	6th cousin twice removed	XVI	9
Dunham, Alvin William	Half 3rd cousin 4 times removed	XII	8
Dunham, Bertha Beatrice	Half 3rd cousin 3 times removed	XI	7
Dunham, Betty Jean Mabel	Half 3rd cousin 4 times removed	XII	8
Dunham, Eleanor Elizabeth	Half 3rd cousin 3 times removed	XI	7
Dunham, Elmer Ray	Half 3rd cousin 3 times removed	XI	7
Dunham, Evert	Husband of the half 3rd cousin twice removed		
Dunham, Frederick Fielding	Half 3rd cousin 3 times removed	XI	7
Dunham, Freedman	Husband of the half 3rd cousin twice removed		
Dunham, Gertie Gibson	Half 3rd cousin 3 times removed	XI	7
Dunham, James Orval	Half 3rd cousin 4 times removed	XII	8
Dunham, Jessie Jean	Half 3rd cousin 3 times removed	XI	7
Dunham, Lorne Milton	Half 3rd cousin 3 times removed	XI	7
Dunham, Mildred Elizabeth	Half 3rd cousin 3 times removed	XI	7
Dunham, Norman Nelson	Half 3rd cousin 3 times removed	XI	7
Dunham, Private	Half 3rd cousin 4 times removed	XII	8
Dunham, Private	Half 3rd cousin 4 times removed	XII	8
Dunham, Private	Half 3rd cousin 4 times removed	XII	8
Dunham, Private	Half 3rd cousin 4 times removed	XII	8
Dunham, Private	Half 3rd cousin 4 times removed	XII	8
Dunham, Private	Half 3rd cousin 4 times removed	XII	8
Dunham, Watson William	Half 3rd cousin 3 times removed	XI	7
Dunham, William Kitchen	Half 3rd cousin 3 times removed	XI	7
Dunk, Living	Husband of the 6th cousin 4 times removed		
Dunn, Mary	Wife of the 6th cousin 3 times removed		
Dupuy, Amy	5th cousin	XII	6
Dupuy, Charles	5th cousin	XII	6
Dupuy, Eleanor	5th cousin	XII	6
Dupuy, Harry Wilford	5th cousin	XII	6
Dupuy, Herbert	Husband of the 4th cousin once removed		
Dupuy, Rosetta	5th cousin	XII	6
Dyer, Barbara	Wife of the 3rd cousin twice removed		
Eaby, Anna	Wife of the 1st cousin 4 times removed		
Eaby, Cora Etta	Wife of the 3rd cousin		
Eager, Private	Husband of the 6th cousin 4 times removed		
Earhart, Private	Wife of the 3rd cousin 3 times removed		
Eberly, Elizabeth	Wife of the 2nd cousin twice removed		
Eberly, Private	Wife of the 3rd cousin 4 times removed		
Eberly, Private	Husband of the 3rd cousin 3 times removed		
Eberly, Private	3rd cousin 4 times removed	XII	8
Eberly, Private	3rd cousin 4 times removed	XII	8
Eberly, Private	3rd cousin 4 times removed	XII	8

Name	Relationship with Milton Hershey	Civil	Canon
Eberly, Private	3rd cousin 5 times removed	XIII	9
Eberly, Private	3rd cousin 5 times removed	XIII	9
Eberly, Private	Husband of the 3rd cousin 3 times removed		
Eberly, Private	3rd cousin 4 times removed	XII	8
Eberly, Private	3rd cousin 4 times removed	XII	8
Eberly, Simon	Husband of the 6th cousin		
Ebersole, Abraham	Husband of the 3rd cousin 3 times removed		
Ebersole, Anna	Wife of the half 1st cousin 5 times removed		
Ebersole, Annie	Wife of the 6th cousin		
Ebersole, Christian	Husband of the 2nd cousin 3 times removed		
Ebersole, Jacob	Husband of the 3rd cousin 3 times removed		
Ebersole, John	Husband of the 3rd cousin 3 times removed		
Ebersole, John	Husband of the 2nd cousin 3 times removed		
Ebersole, Mabel E	Wife of the 2nd cousin		
Ebersole, Mildrfed K.	Wife of the 3rd cousin twice removed		
Ebersole, Private	Husband of the 3rd cousin 4 times removed		
Ebersole, Private	3rd cousin 5 times removed	XIII	9
Ebersole, Private	Husband of the 3rd cousin twice removed		
Ebersole, Private	3rd cousin 3 times removed	XI	7
Ebersole, Private	3rd cousin 3 times removed	XI	7
Eby, Aaron Buckwalter	3rd cousin once removed	IX	5
Eby, Aaron S.	3rd cousin twice removed	X	6
Eby, Andrew	2nd great-granduncle	VI	5
Eby, Anna	2nd great-grandaunt	VI	5
Eby, Anna	Wife of the great-granduncle		
Eby, Anna Martha	3rd cousin once removed	IX	5
Eby, Barabara	2nd great-grandaunt	VI	5
Eby, Candance	Wife of the half 3rd cousin twice removed		
Eby, Catherine	Wife of the 2nd cousin 3 times removed		
Eby, Christian	3rd great-grandfather	V	5
Eby, Christian	2nd great-granduncle	VI	5
Eby, Clyde S.	3rd cousin twice removed	X	6
Eby, Eileen Marie	3rd cousin 3 times removed	XI	7
Eby, Eli S.	3rd cousin twice removed	X	6
Eby, Elizabeth	2nd great-grandmother	IV	4
Eby, Elizabeth	Wife of the 1st cousin twice removed		
Eby, Elizabeth Hershey	3rd cousin once removed	IX	5
Eby, Ella Barbara	3rd cousin once removed	IX	5
Eby, Emma Mae	3rd cousin twice removed	X	6
Eby, Enos Jacob	3rd cousin once removed	IX	5
Eby, Ethel Z.	3rd cousin twice removed	X	6
Eby, Ezra S.	3rd cousin twice removed	X	6
Eby, Franklin W.	3rd cousin twice removed	X	6
Eby, George	3rd great-granduncle	VII	6
Eby, George	2nd great-granduncle	VI	5
Eby, Henry John	Husband of the 3rd cousin		
Eby, Henry Musser	3rd cousin once removed	IX	5
Eby, Henry S.	3rd cousin twice removed	X	6
Eby, Isaac	Husband of the 4th cousin 4 times removed		
Eby, Isaac Isaiah	3rd cousin once removed	IX	5
Eby, Isaac S.	3rd cousin twice removed	X	6
Eby, Jacob	3rd great-granduncle	VII	6
Eby, James Z.	3rd cousin 3 times removed	XI	7
Eby, Johannes	3rd great-granduncle	VII	6
Eby, John	Husband of the 3rd cousin twice removed		
Eby, John Hershey	4th cousin once removed	XI	6
Eby, John S.	3rd cousin twice removed	X	6
Eby, John Silas	3rd cousin once removed	IX	5
Eby, Lydia S.	3rd cousin twice removed	X	6
Eby, Margaret	Wife of the half 3rd cousin 3 times removed		
Eby, Margie	Wife of the 3rd cousin once removed		
Eby, Marsha	3rd cousin 4 times removed	XII	8
Eby, Martin Christian	3rd cousin once removed	IX	5
Eby, Martin Z.	3rd cousin twice removed	X	6
Eby, Mary Edith	3rd cousin once removed	IX	5
Eby, Mary Z.	3rd cousin twice removed	X	6

Name	Relationship with Milton Hershey	Civil	Canon
Eby, Maurice	Husband of the half 3rd cousin twice removed		
Eby, Menno Hershey	3rd cousin once removed	IX	5
Eby, Michael	2nd great-granduncle	VI	5
Eby, Peter	3rd great-granduncle	VII	6
Eby, Peter	2nd great-granduncle	VI	5
Eby, Peter Hershey	3rd cousin once removed	IX	5
Eby, Private	3rd cousin 3 times removed	XI	7
Eby, Private	3rd cousin 3 times removed	XI	7
Eby, Private	3rd cousin 3 times removed	XI	7
Eby, Private	3rd cousin 3 times removed	XI	7
Eby, Private	3rd cousin 3 times removed	XI	7
Eby, Private	3rd cousin 3 times removed	XI	7
Eby, Private	3rd cousin 3 times removed	XI	7
Eby, Private	3rd cousin 3 times removed	XI	7
Eby, Private	3rd cousin 4 times removed	XII	8
Eby, Private	3rd cousin 4 times removed	XII	8
Eby, Private	3rd cousin 4 times removed	XII	8
Eby, Private	3rd cousin 4 times removed	XII	8
Eby, Private	3rd cousin 4 times removed	XII	8
Eby, Private	3rd cousin 4 times removed	XII	8
Eby, Private	3rd cousin 3 times removed	XI	7
Eby, Private	3rd cousin 3 times removed	XI	7
Eby, Private	3rd cousin 3 times removed	XI	7
Eby, Private	3rd cousin 3 times removed	XI	7
Eby, Private	3rd cousin 3 times removed	XI	7
Eby, Private	3rd cousin 3 times removed	XI	7
Eby, Private	3rd cousin 3 times removed	XI	7
Eby, Private	3rd cousin 3 times removed	XI	7
Eby, Private	3rd cousin 4 times removed	XII	8
Eby, Private	3rd cousin 4 times removed	XII	8
Eby, Private	3rd cousin 4 times removed	XII	8
Eby, Private	3rd cousin 4 times removed	XII	8
Eby, Private	3rd cousin 4 times removed	XII	8
Eby, Private	3rd cousin 4 times removed	XII	8
Eby, Private	3rd cousin 4 times removed	XII	8
Eby, Private	3rd cousin 4 times removed	XII	8
Eby, Private	3rd cousin 4 times removed	XII	8
Eby, Private	3rd cousin 4 times removed	XII	8
Eby, Private	3rd cousin 4 times removed	XII	8
Eby, Private	3rd cousin 3 times removed	XI	7
Eby, Private	3rd cousin 3 times removed	XI	7
Eby, Private	3rd cousin 3 times removed	XI	7
Eby, Private	3rd cousin 3 times removed	XI	7
Eby, Private	3rd cousin 3 times removed	XI	7
Eby, Private	3rd cousin 3 times removed	XI	7
Eby, Private	3rd cousin 4 times removed	XII	8
Eby, Private	3rd cousin 4 times removed	XII	8
Eby, Private	3rd cousin 4 times removed	XII	8
Eby, Private	3rd cousin 4 times removed	XII	8
Eby, Private	3rd cousin twice removed	X	6
Eby, Private	3rd cousin twice removed	X	6
Eby, Private	3rd cousin twice removed	X	6
Eby, Private	3rd cousin twice removed	X	6
Eby, Private	3rd cousin twice removed	X	6
Eby, Private	3rd cousin 3 times removed	XI	7
Eby, Private	3rd cousin 3 times removed	XI	7
Eby, Private	3rd cousin 4 times removed	XII	8
Eby, Private	3rd cousin 4 times removed	XII	8
Eby, Private	3rd cousin 3 times removed	XI	7
Eby, Private	3rd cousin 3 times removed	XI	7
Eby, Private	3rd cousin 3 times removed	XI	7
Eby, Private	3rd cousin 3 times removed	XI	7
Eby, Private	3rd cousin 3 times removed	XI	7
Eby, Private	3rd cousin 3 times removed	XI	7
Eby, Private	3rd cousin 3 times removed	XI	7

Name	Relationship with Milton Hershey	Civil	Canon
Eby, Private	3rd cousin 3 times removed	XI	7
Eby, Private	3rd cousin 3 times removed	XI	7
Eby, Private	3rd cousin 3 times removed	XI	7
Eby, Private	3rd cousin 3 times removed	XI	7
Eby, Private	3rd cousin 3 times removed	XI	7
Eby, Private	3rd cousin twice removed	X	6
Eby, Private	3rd cousin twice removed	X	6
Eby, Private	3rd cousin twice removed	X	6
Eby, Private	3rd cousin twice removed	X	6
Eby, Private	3rd cousin 3 times removed	XI	7
Eby, Private	3rd cousin 3 times removed	XI	7
Eby, Private	3rd cousin 3 times removed	XI	7
Eby, Private	3rd cousin 3 times removed	XI	7
Eby, Private	3rd cousin 3 times removed	XI	7
Eby, Private	3rd cousin 4 times removed	XII	8
Eby, Private	3rd cousin 4 times removed	XII	8
Eby, Private	3rd cousin 4 times removed	XII	8
Eby, Private	3rd cousin 4 times removed	XII	8
Eby, Private	3rd cousin 4 times removed	XII	8
Eby, Private	3rd cousin 4 times removed	XII	8
Eby, Private	3rd cousin 3 times removed	XI	7
Eby, Private	3rd cousin 3 times removed	XI	7
Eby, Private	3rd cousin 3 times removed	XI	7
Eby, Private	3rd cousin 3 times removed	XI	7
Eby, Private	3rd cousin 3 times removed	XI	7
Eby, Private	3rd cousin 3 times removed	XI	7
Eby, Private	3rd cousin 3 times removed	XI	7
Eby, Private	3rd cousin 3 times removed	XI	7
Eby, Private	3rd cousin 3 times removed	XI	7
Eby, Private	3rd cousin 3 times removed	XI	7
Eby, Private	3rd cousin 3 times removed	XI	7
Eby, Private	3rd cousin twice removed	X	6
Eby, Private	3rd cousin twice removed	X	6
Eby, Private	3rd cousin twice removed	X	6
Eby, Private	3rd cousin 3 times removed	XI	7
Eby, Private	3rd cousin 3 times removed	XI	7
Eby, Private	3rd cousin 3 times removed	XI	7
Eby, Private	3rd cousin 3 times removed	XI	7
Eby, Private	3rd cousin twice removed	X	6
Eby, Private	3rd cousin twice removed	X	6
Eby, Private	3rd cousin twice removed	X	6
Eby, Private	3rd cousin twice removed	X	6
Eby, Private	3rd cousin twice removed	X	6
Eby, Private	3rd cousin 3 times removed	XI	7
Eby, Private	3rd cousin 3 times removed	XI	7
Eby, Private	3rd cousin 3 times removed	XI	7
Eby, Private	3rd cousin 3 times removed	XI	7
Eby, Private	3rd cousin 3 times removed	XI	7
Eby, Private	3rd cousin 3 times removed	XI	7
Eby, Private	3rd cousin 3 times removed	XI	7
Eby, Private	Husband of the 3rd cousin 3 times removed		
Eby, Private	3rd cousin 4 times removed	XII	8
Eby, Private	3rd cousin 4 times removed	XII	8
Eby, Private	3rd cousin 4 times removed	XII	8
Eby, Rhoda S.	3rd cousin twice removed	X	6
Eby, Richard S.	3rd cousin twice removed	X	6
Eby, Roy Z.	3rd cousin twice removed	X	6
Eby, Samuel	2nd great-granduncle	VI	5
Eby, Sarah Lucinda	3rd cousin once removed	IX	5
Eby, Sarah S.	3rd cousin twice removed	X	6
Eby, Susan	Wife of the 3rd cousin		
Eby, Susan W.	3rd cousin twice removed	X	6
Eby, Theodorus (Durst)	4th great-grandfather	VI	6

The Relations of Milton Snavely Hershey, 4th Ed.

Name	Relationship with Milton Hershey	Civil	Canon
Eby, Warren Z.	3rd cousin twice removed	X	6
Echlin, Annetta	Wife of the half 3rd cousin twice removed		
Eckels, Charles	Husband of the 3rd cousin once removed		
Eckels, Grace	4th cousin	X	5
Eckels, Margery	4th cousin	X	5
Edwards, Mary E	Wife of the 6th cousin twice removed		
Edworthy, Gladys B.	Wife of the half 3rd cousin twice removed		
Edworthy, Louise Norman	Half 3rd cousin 3 times removed	XI	7
Edworthy, Ross Herbert	Husband of the half 3rd cousin twice removed		
Egle, Esther	Wife of the 3rd great-granduncle		
Egli, Adelheid	Wife of the half 6th great-granduncle		
Egli, Barbel	Wife of the 6th great-granduncle		
Eichelberger, Harry D	Husband of the 2nd cousin twice removed		
Eichelberger, Melvin	2nd cousin 3 times removed	IX	6
Eicher, Private	Husband of the 3rd cousin 3 times removed		
Eicher, Private	3rd cousin 4 times removed	XII	8
Eiklor, Private	Wife of the 6th cousin 3 times removed		
Eleftheriades, Sophi	Wife of the 6th cousin twice removed		
Elifdities, Sophi	Wife of the 6th cousin twice removed		
Ellis, Edith Stauffer	5th cousin once removed	XIII	7
Ellis, Edward Stauffer	5th cousin once removed	XIII	7
Ellis, Mary Stauffer	5th cousin once removed	XIII	7
Ellis, Thomas	Husband of the 5th cousin		
Engle, Charles C.	Husband of the 6th cousin 3 times removed		
Engle, Private	6th cousin 4 times removed	XVIII	11
Engle, Private	6th cousin 4 times removed	XVIII	11
Engle, Private	6th cousin 4 times removed	XVIII	11
Erb, Christian	2nd cousin 3 times removed	IX	6
Erb, Christian	Husband of the 2nd cousin 3 times removed		
Erb, Christian	Husband of the 1st cousin 4 times removed		
Erb, Fanny	6th cousin	XIV	7
Erb, Fianna	6th cousin	XIV	7
Erb, Gabrial	6th cousin	XIV	7
Erb, Isaac	6th cousin	XIV	7
Erb, Jacob	2nd cousin 3 times removed	IX	6
Erb, Jacob	3rd cousin twice removed	X	6
Erb, Jacob	Husband of the 5th cousin once removed		
Erb, Maria	2nd cousin 3 times removed	IX	6
Erb, Mary	Wife of the 2nd cousin 4 times removed		
Erb, Mary Louise	6th cousin	XIV	7
Erb, Peter	6th cousin	XIV	7
Erhart, Mary	Wife of the 2nd cousin 3 times removed		
Erisman, Addey	Wife of the half 1st cousin 5 times removed		
Erisman, Albert	3rd cousin once removed	IX	5
Erisman, Amelia	3rd cousin once removed	IX	5
Erisman, Christian	Husband of the 2nd cousin twice removed		
Erisman, Elizabeth	3rd cousin once removed	IX	5
Erisman, Elmer	Husband of the 4th cousin once removed		
Erisman, Elnora	3rd cousin once removed	IX	5
Erisman, Jacob	Husband of the 1st cousin 4 times removed		
Erisman, Mary	3rd cousin once removed	IX	5
Erisman, Mary	Wife of the half 1st cousin 5 times removed		
Erisman, Metz	3rd cousin once removed	IX	5
Erisman, Sarah	3rd cousin once removed	IX	5
Erisman, Susan	3rd cousin once removed	IX	5
Ernest, Private	6th cousin 4 times removed	XVIII	11
Ernst, Private	6th cousin 3 times removed	XVII	10
Ernst, Private	6th cousin 3 times removed	XVII	10
Ernst, Private	6th cousin 3 times removed	XVII	10
Ernst, Private	6th cousin 4 times removed	XVIII	11
Ernst, Private	6th cousin 4 times removed	XVIII	11
Ernst, Private	6th cousin 3 times removed	XVII	10
Ernst, Raymond Hunter	Husband of the 6th cousin twice removed		
Ertzinger, Elizabeth	6th great-grandmother	VIII	8
Ertzinger, Uli	7th great-grandfather	IX	9
Eshelman, Abraham	4th cousin	X	5

Name	Relationship with Milton Hershey	Civil	Canon
Eshelman, Alice	4th cousin	X	5
Eshelman, Edwin	Husband of the 3rd cousin once removed		
Eshelman, Elizabeth	Wife of the 1st cousin 3 times removed		
Eshelman, Frances	Wife of the granduncle		
Eshelman, Hagar	4th cousin	X	5
Eshelman, Isaac	Husband of the 3rd cousin 3 times removed		
Eshelman, Lydia	4th cousin	X	5
Eshelman, Maria	Wife of the 2nd cousin 3 times removed		
Eshelman, Susan	4th cousin	X	5
Eshleman, Annie	Half 4th cousin twice removed	XII	7
Eshleman, Barbara	Wife of the 3rd cousin twice removed		
Eshleman, David	Husband of the half 3rd cousin 3 times removed		
Eshleman, Magdalena	Wife of the 2nd cousin 3 times removed		
Eshleman, Peter	Husband of the 5th cousin 3 times removed		
Espenshade, Emma	Wife of the 4th cousin once removed		
Espich, Frank	Husband of the 2nd cousin 4 times removed		
Evans, Cecile Loren	3rd cousin 4 times removed	XII	8
Evans, Edwin	Husband of the 6th cousin twice removed		
Evans, Ezekiel Owen	Husband of the 2nd cousin 3 times removed		
Evans, Hannah Owen	Wife of the 2nd cousin 3 times removed		
Evans, John	Husband of the half 3rd cousin 3 times removed		
Evans, Private	Husband of the 3rd cousin 3 times removed		
Evans, Private	3rd cousin 4 times removed	XII	8
Evans, Private	3rd cousin 4 times removed	XII	8
Evans, Private	3rd cousin 4 times removed	XII	8
Evans, Private	6th cousin 3 times removed	XVII	10
Evans, Private	6th cousin 3 times removed	XVII	10
Evans, Private	6th cousin 3 times removed	XVII	10
Evans, Private	6th cousin 3 times removed	XVII	10
Evans, Private	6th cousin 3 times removed	XVII	10
Evans, Private	6th cousin 4 times removed	XVIII	11
Evans, Thomas Elijah	Husband of the 6th cousin 3 times removed		
Evans, Viola E.	Wife of the 6th cousin 3 times removed		
Everett, Hugh Munson	Half 3rd cousin 4 times removed	XII	8
Everett, Nelson William	Husband of the half 3rd cousin 3 times removed		
Everett, Private	Half 3rd cousin 5 times removed	XIII	9
Everett, Private	Half 3rd cousin 5 times removed	XIII	9
Everett, Private	Half 3rd cousin 5 times removed	XIII	9
Everett, Private	Half 3rd cousin 5 times removed	XIII	9
Everett, Ralph Avon	Half 3rd cousin 4 times removed	XII	8
Eyer, Harold Ray	6th cousin 3 times removed	XVII	10
Eyer, John Paul	6th cousin 3 times removed	XVII	10
Eyer, Katherine Lucile	6th cousin 3 times removed	XVII	10
Eyer, Lewis Benjamin	6th cousin 3 times removed	XVII	10
Eyer, Mary Belle	6th cousin 3 times removed	XVII	10
Eyer, Private	6th cousin 4 times removed	XVIII	11
Eyer, Private	6th cousin 4 times removed	XVIII	11
Eyer, Private	6th cousin 4 times removed	XVIII	11
Eyer, Private	6th cousin 4 times removed	XVIII	11
Eyer, Private	6th cousin 4 times removed	XVIII	11
Eyer, Private	6th cousin 4 times removed	XVIII	11
Eyer, Private	6th cousin 4 times removed	XVIII	11
Eyer, Private	6th cousin 4 times removed	XVIII	11
Eyers, Isaac	Husband of the 6th cousin twice removed		
Fahlen, Private	Husband of the 6th cousin 3 times removed		
Fahlen, Private	6th cousin 4 times removed	XVIII	11
Fanny	2nd cousin twice removed	VIII	5
Farmer, Cindy Hope	3rd cousin 4 times removed	XII	8
Farmer, John W.	Husband of the 3rd cousin 3 times removed		
Farmer, Mary Elizabeth	3rd cousin 4 times removed	XII	8
Farner, Catharine	6th cousin	XIV	7
Farner, Charlotte	6th cousin	XIV	7
Farner, Conrad	6th cousin	XIV	7
Farner, Daniel	6th cousin	XIV	7
Farner, David	Husband of the 5th cousin once removed		

The Relations of Milton Snavely Hershey, 4th Ed.

Name	Relationship with Milton Hershey	Civil	Canon
Farner, Elizabeth	6th cousin	XIV	7
Farner, Fanny	6th cousin	XIV	7
Farner, Gabriel	6th cousin	XIV	7
Farner, Henry	6th cousin	XIV	7
Farner, John	6th cousin	XIV	7
Farner, Mariah	6th cousin	XIV	7
Farner, Mary	6th cousin	XIV	7
Farner, Peter	6th cousin	XIV	7
Farner, Solomon	6th cousin	XIV	7
Farner, Susannah	6th cousin	XIV	7
Farney, Franey	Wife of the 4th cousin twice removed		
Farsht, Susannah	Wife of the 5th cousin once removed		
Fauher, Private	Wife of the 6th cousin 3 times removed		
Feeser, Anna E	6th cousin 3 times removed	XVII	10
Feeser, John E	6th cousin 3 times removed	XVII	10
Feeser, Martin	Husband of the 6th cousin twice removed		
Feighter, Sarah	Wife of the 5th cousin once removed		
Feister, Private	Wife of the 3rd cousin twice removed		
Feldser, Living	Husband of the 6th cousin 4 times removed		
Feldser, Living	6th cousin 5 times removed	XIX	12
Feldser, Living	6th cousin 5 times removed	XIX	12
Feldser, Living	6th cousin 5 times removed	XIX	12
Feldser, Living	6th cousin 5 times removed	XIX	12
Feldser, Living	6th cousin 5 times removed	XIX	12
Feldser, Living	6th cousin 5 times removed	XIX	12
Felger, June	Wife of the 6th cousin twice removed		
Fellabaum, Private	Husband of the 3rd cousin 3 times removed		
Felpel, Private	Wife of the 3rd cousin 3 times removed		
Fenell, Private	Wife of the 6th cousin 3 times removed		
Ferguson, Victor	Husband of the 6th cousin twice removed		
Ferree, Alice	6th cousin twice removed	XVI	9
Ferree, Anna	Wife of the half 3rd cousin 3 times removed		
Ferree, Rebecca	Wife of the half 3rd cousin 3 times removed		
Ferree, Thomas	Husband of the 6th cousin once removed		
Few, Harriet	Wife of the 6th cousin		
Fidler, Gary	Friend of the 4th cousin 3 times removed		
Fidoe, Private	Husband of the 6th cousin 3 times removed		
Fidoe, Private	6th cousin 4 times removed	XVIII	11
Filyer, Joyce	Wife of the half 3rd cousin twice removed		
Fink, Barbara D	6th cousin 4 times removed	XVIII	11
Fink, James E	6th cousin 4 times removed	XVIII	11
Fink, Joseph A	6th cousin 4 times removed	XVIII	11
Fink, Joseph C	Husband of the 6th cousin 3 times removed		
Fink, Patricia L	6th cousin 4 times removed	XVIII	11
Fink, Richard E	6th cousin 4 times removed	XVIII	11
Finkey, William	Husband of the 6th cousin once removed		
Fisher, Frances	Wife of the 6th cousin twice removed		
Fisher, Henry S.	Husband of the 6th cousin		
Fixter, Private	Wife of the half 3rd cousin 4 times removed		
Flaherty, Billie	Wife of the half 3rd cousin twice removed		
Fleming, Dolly	Wife of the 6th cousin twice removed		
Fleming, Isobel	Wife of the half 3rd cousin 3 times removed		
Fleming, Private	Wife of the 6th cousin 3 times removed		
Fletcher, Ida Mae	Wife of the half 3rd cousin twice removed		
Flickinger, Elizabeth	Wife of the 2nd cousin 3 times removed		
Flickinger, John	Husband of the 6th cousin		
Fluck, John Brallier	Husband of the 6th cousin		
Folliott, Blanche	Wife of the half 3rd cousin twice removed		
Foot, Frank Frederick	Husband of the half 3rd cousin 3 times removed		
Foot, Private	Half 3rd cousin 4 times removed	XII	8
Foot, William Dalton	Husband of the half 3rd cousin 3 times removed		
Foote, Mildred	Wife of the half 3rd cousin twice removed		
Forester, Kenneth Alexander	Husband of the half 3rd cousin 4 times removed		
Forester, Private	Half 3rd cousin 5 times removed	XIII	9
Forney, Betty	Wife of the 4th cousin once removed		
Forney, Elisabeth	Wife of the 2nd cousin twice removed		

Name	Relationship with Milton Hershey	Civil	Canon
Forrer, Anna	Wife of the half 2nd cousin 4 times removed		
Forrest, Howard	Husband of the 6th cousin 3 times removed		
Forrester, Jeremiah	Husband of the 2nd cousin 3 times removed		
Forry, Anna	Wife of the 3rd cousin twice removed		
Forry, Maria	Wife of the 3rd cousin twice removed		
Forsyth, Joe	Husband of the half 3rd cousin twice removed		
Forsyth, Martha	Wife of the half 3rd cousin once removed		
Forsythe, Alice Morene	Half 3rd cousin 3 times removed	XI	7
Forsythe, Floyd	Half 3rd cousin 3 times removed	XI	7
Forsythe, Levi	Husband of the half 3rd cousin twice removed		
Forsythe, Lola Jean	Half 3rd cousin 3 times removed	XI	7
Forsythe, Private	Half 3rd cousin 4 times removed	XII	8
Forsythe, Vera Irene	Half 3rd cousin 3 times removed	XI	7
Fortney, Karen Ann	Wife of the 4th cousin twice removed		
Foster, Elias	Husband of the 5th cousin once removed		
Foster, Jerry	Husband of the 2nd cousin 4 times removed		
Fowler, Dora Maud	Wife of the half 3rd cousin twice removed		
Fox, Alta Mae	3rd cousin 3 times removed	XI	7
Fox, Anna Elizabeth	3rd cousin twice removed	X	6
Fox, Catherine	Wife of the 5th cousin once removed		
Fox, Daniel Hershey	3rd cousin twice removed	X	6
Fox, Daniel M.	Husband of the 3rd cousin once removed		
Fox, Donald	6th cousin 4 times removed	XVIII	11
Fox, Elmer Eby	3rd cousin twice removed	X	6
Fox, Henry Peter	3rd cousin twice removed	X	6
Fox, Howard	Husband of the 6th cousin 3 times removed		
Fox, Ivan Martin	3rd cousin twice removed	X	6
Fox, John David	3rd cousin twice removed	X	6
Fox, Marvin Lamar	3rd cousin 4 times removed	XII	8
Fox, Mary Eby	3rd cousin twice removed	X	6
Fox, Private	3rd cousin 3 times removed	XI	7
Fox, Private	3rd cousin 3 times removed	XI	7
Fox, Private	3rd cousin 3 times removed	XI	7
Fox, Private	3rd cousin 3 times removed	XI	7
Fox, Private	3rd cousin 3 times removed	XI	7
Fox, Private	3rd cousin 3 times removed	XI	7
Fox, Private	3rd cousin 3 times removed	XI	7
Fox, Private	3rd cousin 4 times removed	XII	8
Fox, Private	3rd cousin 4 times removed	XII	8
Fox, Private	3rd cousin 4 times removed	XII	8
Fox, Private	3rd cousin 4 times removed	XII	8
Fox, Private	3rd cousin 5 times removed	XIII	9
Fox, Private	3rd cousin 4 times removed	XII	8
Fox, Private	3rd cousin 4 times removed	XII	8
Fox, Private	3rd cousin 4 times removed	XII	8
Fox, Private	3rd cousin 3 times removed	XI	7
Fox, Private	3rd cousin 3 times removed	XI	7
Fox, Private	3rd cousin 3 times removed	XI	7
Fox, Private	3rd cousin 3 times removed	XI	7
Fox, Private	3rd cousin 3 times removed	XI	7
Fox, Private	3rd cousin 3 times removed	XI	7
Fox, Private	3rd cousin 3 times removed	XI	7
Fox, Private	3rd cousin 3 times removed	XI	7
Fox, Private	3rd cousin 3 times removed	XI	7
Fox, Private	3rd cousin 3 times removed	XI	7
Fox, Private	3rd cousin 4 times removed	XII	8
Fox, Private	3rd cousin 4 times removed	XII	8
Fox, Private	3rd cousin 4 times removed	XII	8
Fox, Private	3rd cousin 4 times removed	XII	8
Fox, Private	3rd cousin 4 times removed	XII	8
Fox, Private	3rd cousin 4 times removed	XII	8
Fox, Private	3rd cousin 4 times removed	XII	8
Fox, Private	3rd cousin 3 times removed	XI	7
Fox, Private	3rd cousin 3 times removed	XI	7

The Relations of Milton Snavely Hershey, 4th Ed.

Name	Relationship with Milton Hershey	Civil	Canon
Fox, Private	3rd cousin 3 times removed	XI	7
Fox, Private	3rd cousin 4 times removed	XII	8
Fox, Private	3rd cousin 3 times removed	XI	7
Fox, Private	3rd cousin 3 times removed	XI	7
Fox, Private	3rd cousin 3 times removed	XI	7
Fox, Private	3rd cousin 4 times removed	XII	8
Fox, Private	3rd cousin 4 times removed	XII	8
Fox, Private	3rd cousin 4 times removed	XII	8
Fox, Richard	6th cousin 4 times removed	XVIII	11
Fox, Sarah Lucinda	3rd cousin twice removed	X	6
Fox, Willis Eby	3rd cousin twice removed	X	6
Frame, Elijah	Husband of the 2nd cousin		
Frame, John L.	2nd cousin once removed	VII	4
Frances	6th cousin twice removed	XVI	9
Franck, Catherine	Wife of the 2nd cousin 3 times removed		
Franck, Lizzie Risser	Wife of the 4th cousin once removed		
Frankfort, Anna	Wife of the 1st cousin once removed		
Franklin, Private	Husband of the 3rd cousin 3 times removed		
Franklin, Private	Husband of the 6th cousin 3 times removed		
Frantz, Anna	1st cousin 3 times removed	VII	5
Frantz, Anna	1st cousin twice removed	VI	4
Frantz, Anna Hostetter	Great-grandmother	III	3
Frantz, Barbara	Great-grandaunt	V	4
Frantz, Christian	2nd great-granduncle	VI	5
Frantz, Christian	1st cousin 3 times removed	VII	5
Frantz, Christian H	Great-granduncle	V	4
Frantz, Elisabeth	Great-grandaunt	V	4
Frantz, Elizabeth	2nd great-grandaunt	VI	5
Frantz, Elizabeth	Wife of the great-granduncle		
Frantz, Elizabeth	1st cousin twice removed	VI	4
Frantz, Elizabeth Miller	Wife of the uncle		
Frantz, Jacob	2nd great-granduncle	VI	5
Frantz, Jacob	Great-granduncle	V	4
Frantz, Jacob	1st cousin 3 times removed	VII	5
Frantz, Jacob Hostetter	1st cousin 3 times removed	VII	5
Frantz, John	Husband of the 2nd great-grandaunt		
Frantz, John	3rd great-grandfather	V	5
Frantz, John	2nd great-grandfather	IV	4
Frantz, John	Great-granduncle	V	4
Frantz, John	1st cousin 3 times removed	VII	5
Frantz, John Miller	2nd cousin twice removed	VIII	5
Frantz, Maria	Great-grandaunt	V	4
Frantz, Michael	2nd great-granduncle	VI	5
Frantz, Samuel	1st cousin 3 times removed	VII	5
Frederick, Philip	Husband of the 1st cousin 4 times removed		
Freed, Private	Wife of the 3rd cousin 3 times removed		
Freitag, Ervin	Husband of the 6th cousin twice removed		
French, Private	Wife of the 6th cousin twice removed		
Freshley, Allen L	Husband of the 6th cousin once removed		
Freshley, Ellen	Wife of the 6th cousin once removed		
Freshley, Eugene A	6th cousin twice removed	XVI	9
Freshley, June	6th cousin twice removed	XVI	9
Freshley, Marjorie	6th cousin twice removed	XVI	9
Freshley, Private	6th cousin 3 times removed	XVII	10
Freshley, Private	6th cousin 3 times removed	XVII	10
Freshley, Private	6th cousin 3 times removed	XVII	10
Freshley, Private	6th cousin 3 times removed	XVII	10
Freshley, Private	6th cousin 3 times removed	XVII	10
Freshley, Private	6th cousin 3 times removed	XVII	10
Freshley, Private	6th cousin 3 times removed	XVII	10
Freshley, Private	6th cousin 3 times removed	XVII	10
Freshley, Robert	6th cousin twice removed	XVI	9
Freshley, William	6th cousin twice removed	XVI	9
Fretz, Sara Schwartz	Wife of the 4th cousin once removed		
Frey, Barbel	Wife of the 6th great-granduncle		
Frey, Private	Husband of the 3rd cousin 3 times removed		

Name	Relationship with Milton Hershey	Civil	Canon
Frick, Anna	Wife of the 1st cousin once removed		
Frick, John	Husband of the 2nd cousin 3 times removed		
Frick, Nancy S	Wife of the granduncle		
Fried, Eliza	Wife of the 5th cousin once removed		
Fritz, Magdalena	Wife of the 3rd great-grandfather		
Fritz, Peter C.	Husband of the 4th cousin once removed		
Fritz, Sandra M.	Wife of the 2nd cousin 4 times removed		
Frock, Sallie J.	Wife of the 5th cousin		
Frost, Alfred DeWitt	Husband of the half 3rd cousin once removed		
Frost, Charles R.	Ex-husband of the 6th cousin twice removed		
Frost, Charles Snyder	6th cousin 3 times removed	XVII	10
Frost, Harry	6th cousin 3 times removed	XVII	10
Frost, Infant	6th cousin 3 times removed	XVII	10
Frost, Oliver	Half 3rd cousin twice removed	X	6
Frost, Private	6th cousin 4 times removed	XVIII	11
Frost, Reginald Joseph	Half 3rd cousin 3 times removed	XI	7
Frost, Reginald Joseph	Half 3rd cousin 4 times removed	XII	8
Fry, Mary	Wife of the 3rd cousin twice removed		
Fryberger, Private	Wife of the 3rd cousin 4 times removed		
Fuchs/Fox, Matilda (Fox)	Wife of the 4th cousin once removed		
Fuller, Florence A.	Wife of the 6th cousin		
Fultz, John	Husband of the 6th cousin		
Fultz, Mark	6th cousin once removed	XV	8
Fultz, Samuel	6th cousin once removed	XV	8
Funk, Barbara	Wife of the 1st cousin 4 times removed		
Funk, Jason	Husband of the 4th cousin 3 times removed		
Funk, Jazmond Hess	4th cousin 4 times removed	XIV	9
Funk, Kate D.	Wife of the 5th cousin		
Funk, Kate Detweiler	Wife of the 4th cousin once removed		
Funk, Margaret	Wife of the 2nd cousin 3 times removed		
Funk, Tyler Ray	4th cousin 4 times removed	XIV	9
Fusilier, Frazier	Husband of the 6th cousin 3 times removed		
Gabel, John Henry	Husband of the 1st cousin 4 times removed		
Gaffney, Private	Husband of the 3rd cousin 3 times removed		
Galbreath, Private	Wife of the 6th cousin twice removed		
Galebach, Miriam	Wife of the 3rd cousin twice removed		
Gallagher, Arthur E	5th cousin	XII	6
Gallagher, Louise E	5th cousin	XII	6
Gallagher, Sherald George	5th cousin	XII	6
Gallagher, William	Husband of the 4th cousin once removed		
Galli, Barbara Neukommet	5th great-grandmother	VII	7
Galli, Ulrich	6th great-grandfather	VIII	8
Gallins, Private	Husband of the 6th cousin 3 times removed		
Gamell, Mamie Dell	Wife of the 6th cousin twice removed		
Games, George	Ex-husband of the half 3rd cousin twice removed		
Games, George Marion	Half 3rd cousin 3 times removed	XI	7
Games, Kenneth Azariah	Half 3rd cousin 3 times removed	XI	7
Garber, Annie L.	Wife of the 6th cousin		
Garber, Sarah A	Wife of the 6th cousin		
Gardner, Benjamin	6th cousin	XIV	7
Gardner, Cyrus	6th cousin	XIV	7
Gardner, Eliza	6th cousin	XIV	7
Gardner, George	6th cousin	XIV	7
Gardner, Henry	6th cousin	XIV	7
Gardner, Infant	Half 3rd cousin twice removed	X	6
Gardner, James	6th cousin	XIV	7
Gardner, John	Half 3rd cousin twice removed	X	6
Gardner, John W.	6th cousin	XIV	7
Gardner, Julia	6th cousin	XIV	7
Gardner, Leah	6th cousin	XIV	7
Gardner, Lewis	6th cousin	XIV	7
Gardner, Mary	6th cousin	XIV	7
Gardner, Nancy	6th cousin	XIV	7
Gardner, Peter	Husband of the 5th cousin once removed		
Gardner, Peter Frederick	6th cousin	XIV	7
Gardner, Rosanna	6th cousin	XIV	7

Name	Relationship with Milton Hershey	Civil	Canon
Gardner, Unknown	Husband of the half 3rd cousin once removed		
Gardner, William	Half 3rd cousin twice removed	X	6
Garman, Private	Husband of the 3rd cousin 4 times removed		
Garman, Private	3rd cousin 5 times removed	XIII	9
Garnes, George A.	Husband of the 5th cousin once removed		
Garren, Hilda	Wife of the 6th cousin twice removed		
Garretson, Sarah	Wife of the 5th cousin once removed		
Garrett, Martha	Wife of the 6th cousin		
Garver, Barbara	Wife of the 2nd great-granduncle		
Gates, Private	Husband of the 3rd cousin 3 times removed		
Gates, Private	3rd cousin 4 times removed	XII	8
Gates, Private	3rd cousin 4 times removed	XII	8
Gatto, Private	Husband of the 3rd cousin 3 times removed		
Gatto, Private	3rd cousin 4 times removed	XII	8
Gatton, Mary Marilla	Wife of the 6th cousin		
Gauthier, Private	Husband of the 6th cousin 4 times removed		
Gaverick, Connie L	Wife of the 6th cousin 3 times removed		
Gearhart, Carroll	6th cousin twice removed	XVI	9
Gearhart, Dayle Kermit	6th cousin twice removed	XVI	9
Gearhart, Don Leedy	6th cousin 3 times removed	XVII	10
Gearhart, Geneva Lucille	6th cousin twice removed	XVI	9
Gearhart, Gladys Estella	6th cousin twice removed	XVI	9
Gearhart, John Fredrick	6th cousin twice removed	XVI	9
Gearhart, Lyle Franklin	6th cousin twice removed	XVI	9
Gearhart, Mable Althea	6th cousin twice removed	XVI	9
Gearhart, Mary Elizabeth	6th cousin twice removed	XVI	9
Gearhart, Mildred Louise	6th cousin twice removed	XVI	9
Gearhart, Pauline Lucille	6th cousin 3 times removed	XVII	10
Gearhart, Private	6th cousin 3 times removed	XVII	10
Gearhart, Private	6th cousin 3 times removed	XVII	10
Gearhart, Ralph Elretus	6th cousin twice removed	XVI	9
Gearhart, Vance Leon	6th cousin twice removed	XVI	9
Gearhart, William Franklin	Husband of the 6th cousin once removed		
Gebraad, John	Husband of the 6th cousin twice removed		
Geckler, Anna Mae	Wife of the 6th cousin twice removed		
Gehman, Arthur E.	3rd cousin twice removed	X	6
Gehman, Benjamin	Husband of the 2nd cousin 3 times removed		
Gehman, Betsy	Wife of the 5th cousin 3 times removed		
Gehman, Catharine	Wife of the 2nd cousin 3 times removed		
Gehman, Edith Elizabeth	3rd cousin twice removed	X	6
Gehman, Grace	3rd cousin twice removed	X	6
Gehman, Harry	Husband of the 4th cousin once removed		
Gehman, Harry H.	Husband of the 3rd cousin once removed		
Gehman, Harry Jacob	3rd cousin twice removed	X	6
Gehman, John E.	3rd cousin twice removed	X	6
Gehman, Joseph	Husband of the 3rd cousin twice removed		
Gehman, Lizzie	Wife of the 4th cousin once removed		
Gehman, Lucy E.	3rd cousin twice removed	X	6
Gehman, Phares B.	Husband of the 3rd cousin		
Gehman, Private	Husband of the 3rd cousin 4 times removed		
Gehman, Private	Husband of the 3rd cousin 3 times removed		
Gehman, Private	3rd cousin twice removed	X	6
Gehman, Private	3rd cousin twice removed	X	6
Gehman, Private	3rd cousin 3 times removed	XI	7
Gehman, Private	3rd cousin 3 times removed	XI	7
Gehman, Private	3rd cousin 3 times removed	XI	7
Gehman, Private	3rd cousin 4 times removed	XII	8
Gehman, Private	3rd cousin 4 times removed	XII	8
Gehman, Private	3rd cousin 3 times removed	XI	7
Gehman, Private	3rd cousin 3 times removed	XI	7
Gehman, Private	3rd cousin 3 times removed	XI	7
Gehman, Private	3rd cousin 3 times removed	XI	7
Gehman, Private	3rd cousin 3 times removed	XI	7
Gehman, Private	3rd cousin 3 times removed	XI	7

Name	Relationship with Milton Hershey	Civil	Canon
Gehman, Private	3rd cousin 4 times removed	XII	8
Gehman, Private	3rd cousin 4 times removed	XII	8
Gehman, Private	3rd cousin 4 times removed	XII	8
Gehman, Private	3rd cousin 4 times removed	XII	8
Gehman, Private	3rd cousin 4 times removed	XII	8
Gehman, Private	3rd cousin 3 times removed	XI	7
Gehman, Private	3rd cousin 3 times removed	XI	7
Gehman, Private	3rd cousin 3 times removed	XI	7
Gehman, Private	3rd cousin 3 times removed	XI	7
Gehman, Private	3rd cousin 3 times removed	XI	7
Gehman, Private	3rd cousin 3 times removed	XI	7
Gehman, Private	3rd cousin 4 times removed	XII	8
Gehman, Private	3rd cousin 4 times removed	XII	8
Gehman, Private	3rd cousin 4 times removed	XII	8
Gehman, Private	3rd cousin 4 times removed	XII	8
Gehman, Private	3rd cousin 4 times removed	XII	8
Gehman, Private	3rd cousin 4 times removed	XII	8
Gehman, Private	3rd cousin 4 times removed	XII	8
Gehman, Private	3rd cousin 4 times removed	XII	8
Gehman, Private	3rd cousin 4 times removed	XII	8
Gehman, Private	3rd cousin 4 times removed	XII	8
Gehman, Private	3rd cousin 3 times removed	XI	7
Gehman, Private	3rd cousin 3 times removed	XI	7
Gehman, Private	3rd cousin 3 times removed	XI	7
Gehman, Private	3rd cousin 3 times removed	XI	7
Gehman, Private	3rd cousin 3 times removed	XI	7
Gehman, Private	3rd cousin 4 times removed	XII	8
Gehman, Private	3rd cousin 4 times removed	XII	8
Gehman, Private	3rd cousin 4 times removed	XII	8
Gehman, Private	3rd cousin 3 times removed	XI	7
Gehman, Private	3rd cousin 3 times removed	XI	7
Gehman, Private	3rd cousin 3 times removed	XI	7
Gehman, Private	3rd cousin 3 times removed	XI	7
Gehman, Private	3rd cousin 3 times removed	XI	7
Gehman, Private	3rd cousin 4 times removed	XII	8
Gehman, Private	3rd cousin 4 times removed	XII	8
Gehman, Private	3rd cousin 4 times removed	XII	8
Gehman, Samuel S.	Husband of the 4th cousin once removed		
Gehman, Todd Matthew	3rd cousin 4 times removed	XII	8
Geib, Anna	2nd cousin	VI	3
Geib, Daniel	Husband of the 1st cousin once removed		
Geib, David L.	2nd cousin	VI	3
Geib, Emma Earhart	Wife of the 4th cousin		
Geib, John L.	2nd cousin	VI	3
Geib, Margaret	2nd cousin	VI	3
Geib, Samuel	2nd cousin	VI	3
Geier	Husband of the 4th cousin 4 times removed		
Geiger, Barbara Ann	6th cousin twice removed	XVI	9
Geiger, Ward	Husband of the 6th cousin once removed		
Geigley, Mary	Wife of the 4th cousin once removed		
Geisinger, Unknown (Kyssinger)	Husband of the 1st cousin 4 times removed		
Geist, Wynaria M.	Wife of the 3rd cousin		
George, Clarence Judson	Half 3rd cousin twice removed	X	6
George, Elizabeth Ann	Half 3rd cousin twice removed	X	6
George, Harold Wideman	Half 3rd cousin twice removed	X	6
George, Nellie Almina	Half 3rd cousin twice removed	X	6
George, Samuel	Husband of the half 3rd cousin once removed		
George, Samuel Ross	Husband of the half 3rd cousin 3 times removed		
Gerber, Catherine	Wife of the 1st cousin 4 times removed		
Gerdes, Miriam	Wife of the 4th cousin once removed		
Gerhart, Abraham	Husband of the 2nd cousin 3 times removed		
Gerlach, Carol Ann	4th cousin 3 times removed	XIII	8
Gerlach, Daryl Eugene	4th cousin 3 times removed	XIII	8
Gerlach, Douglas Scott	4th cousin 3 times removed	XIII	8

The Relations of Milton Snavely Hershey, 4th Ed.

Name	Relationship with Milton Hershey	Civil	Canon
Gerlach, John Henry	Husband of the 4th cousin twice removed		
Germonoff, Private	Wife of the 6th cousin 3 times removed		
Getz, Elizabeth	Wife of the half 1st cousin twice removed		
Giannopolo, Ann Marie	Wife of the 2nd cousin 5 times removed		
Gibbins, Patricia	Half 3rd cousin 3 times removed	XI	7
Gibbins, Peter	Half 3rd cousin 3 times removed	XI	7
Gibbins, Reginald	Husband of the half 3rd cousin twice removed		
Giesbrecht, Ann	Wife of the half 3rd cousin twice removed		
Gilbert, Annielaurie Ruletta	Half 3rd cousin 4 times removed	XII	8
Gilbert, Charles Samuel	Husband of the half 3rd cousin 3 times removed		
Gilbert, George Evert	Half 3rd cousin 4 times removed	XII	8
Gilboyne, Anna Marie	Wife of the half 3rd cousin twice removed		
Gill, Dawn Marie	4th cousin 3 times removed	XIII	8
Gill, John Kennedy	Husband of the 4th cousin twice removed		
Gill, Terry Lee	4th cousin 3 times removed	XIII	8
Gill, Tina Lynn	4th cousin 3 times removed	XIII	8
Gilleland, John	Husband of the 2nd cousin 3 times removed		
Gilleland, Thomas	Husband of the 2nd cousin 3 times removed		
Gingerich, Catherine L.	Wife of the 6th cousin		
Gingrich, Barbara	Wife of the 2nd cousin 5 times removed		
Gingrich, Charles	2nd cousin once removed	VII	4
Gingrich, Fannie	2nd cousin once removed	VII	4
Gingrich, Harry	2nd cousin once removed	VII	4
Gingrich, Katie	2nd cousin once removed	VII	4
Gingrich, LeRoy	2nd cousin once removed	VII	4
Gingrich, Ruth	2nd cousin once removed	VII	4
Gingrich, William	Husband of the 2nd cousin		
Gitters, Private	Wife of the 6th cousin twice removed		
Gittinger, Casper	Husband of the 4th cousin 4 times removed		
Glancey, Private	Husband of the 3rd cousin 3 times removed		
Glancey, Private	3rd cousin 4 times removed	XII	8
Glancey, Private	3rd cousin 4 times removed	XII	8
Glass, John W	Husband of the 6th cousin		
Glick, Private	Husband of the 3rd cousin 3 times removed		
Glick, Private	3rd cousin 4 times removed	XII	8
Glick, Private	3rd cousin 4 times removed	XII	8
Gloss, George M	Husband of the 6th cousin 3 times removed		
Gockley, John L.	Husband of the 3rd cousin		
Gockley, John M.	Husband of the 2nd cousin twice removed		
Gockley, Sarah	Wife of the 3rd cousin twice removed		
Gonzalez, Hilda	Wife of the 6th cousin 3 times removed		
Good, Anna	Wife of the 1st cousin 5 times removed		
Good, Annie	Wife of the 3rd cousin twice removed		
Good, Archie L	Husband of the 3rd cousin twice removed		
Good, Barbara	Wife of the uncle		
Good, Benjamin	3rd cousin twice removed	X	6
Good, Hans	1st cousin 5 times removed	IX	7
Good, Jacob	1st cousin 5 times removed	IX	7
Good, Jonas	Husband of the 2nd cousin 3 times removed		
Good, Lori A	Wife of the 4th cousin 3 times removed		
Good, Noah G.	Husband of the 4th cousin once removed		
Good, Peter	Husband of the 2nd cousin 6 times removed		
Good, Peter	3rd cousin 5 times removed	XIII	9
Good, Peter	Husband of the 2nd cousin 3 times removed		
Good, Private	Husband of the 3rd cousin 3 times removed		
Good, Private	3rd cousin 4 times removed	XII	8
Good, Private	3rd cousin 4 times removed	XII	8
Good, Private	3rd cousin 4 times removed	XII	8
Good, Private	3rd cousin 4 times removed	XII	8
Good, Private	3rd cousin 5 times removed	XIII	9
Good, Private	Husband of the 3rd cousin 4 times removed		
Good, Private	Wife of the 3rd cousin 3 times removed		
Good, Private	Wife of the 3rd cousin 3 times removed		
Good, Private	Wife of the 3rd cousin 3 times removed		
Good, Private	Husband of the 3rd cousin 3 times removed		
Good, Private	3rd cousin 4 times removed	XII	8

Name	Relationship with Milton Hershey	Civil	Canon
good, Susan	Wife of the 2nd cousin 3 times removed		
Good, Susanna	3rd cousin 5 times removed	XIII	9
Good, Susanna	Wife of the 3rd cousin twice removed		
Goodhart, Agnes Bordilla	6th cousin once removed	XV	8
Goodhart, Agnes Druscilla	6th cousin once removed	XV	8
Goodhart, Allan	6th cousin twice removed	XVI	9
Goodhart, Calvin	6th cousin once removed	XV	8
Goodhart, Carl	6th cousin twice removed	XVI	9
Goodhart, Charles Floyd	6th cousin twice removed	XVI	9
Goodhart, Clarence Eugene	6th cousin once removed	XV	8
Goodhart, David Grier McClelland	6th cousin once removed	XV	8
Goodhart, Dellie	6th cousin twice removed	XVI	9
Goodhart, Elizabeth Trough	6th cousin once removed	XV	8
Goodhart, Flora Pauline	6th cousin twice removed	XVI	9
Goodhart, Frances Emma	6th cousin once removed	XV	8
Goodhart, George	6th cousin twice removed	XVI	9
Goodhart, George Grove	6th cousin once removed	XV	8
Goodhart, Henry	6th cousin twice removed	XVI	9
Goodhart, Infant	6th cousin once removed	XV	8
Goodhart, Lettie	6th cousin twice removed	XVI	9
Goodhart, Lewis	Husband of the 6th cousin		
Goodhart, Margaret Elizabeth Alice	6th cousin twice removed	XVI	9
Goodhart, Marian Esther	6th cousin twice removed	XVI	9
Goodhart, Marion Anson	6th cousin once removed	XV	8
Goodhart, Martha	6th cousin twice removed	XVI	9
Goodhart, Mary Elizabeth	6th cousin once removed	XV	8
Goodhart, Mildred	6th cousin twice removed	XVI	9
Goodhart, Newton	6th cousin once removed	XV	8
Goodhart, Nora Griffin	6th cousin once removed	XV	8
Goodhart, Oberdick	6th cousin once removed	XV	8
Goodhart, Pearle Viola	6th cousin twice removed	XVI	9
Goodhart, Ray	6th cousin twice removed	XVI	9
Goodhart, Ruth	6th cousin twice removed	XVI	9
Goodhart, Theodore	6th cousin once removed	XV	8
Goodhart, Theodore	6th cousin twice removed	XVI	9
Goodhart, Theodore Rice	6th cousin 3 times removed	XVII	10
Goodhart, Theodore Riley	6th cousin twice removed	XVI	9
Goodhart, Wilbur	6th cousin twice removed	XVI	9
Goodhart, William	Husband of the 6th cousin		
Goodman, Penelope Hendrickson	5th cousin twice removed	XIV	8
Goodman, Unknown	Husband of the 5th cousin once removed		
Gordley, Private	Husband of the 3rd cousin 3 times removed		
Gordley, Private	3rd cousin 4 times removed	XII	8
Gordley, Private	3rd cousin 4 times removed	XII	8
Gordley, Private	3rd cousin 4 times removed	XII	8
Gordon, Lenora May	Wife of the 3rd cousin 3 times removed		
Goring, Charlotte	3rd cousin twice removed	X	6
Goring, Francis	3rd cousin twice removed	X	6
Goring, Frederick	Husband of the 2nd cousin 3 times removed		
Goring, Frederick Augustus	Husband of the 2nd cousin 3 times removed		
Goring, Frederick Augustus	3rd cousin twice removed	X	6
Goring, Harmon	3rd cousin twice removed	X	6
Goring, James	3rd cousin twice removed	X	6
Goring, John	3rd cousin twice removed	X	6
Goring, Lucretia Caroline	3rd cousin twice removed	X	6
Goring, Sarah	3rd cousin twice removed	X	6
Goring, William	3rd cousin twice removed	X	6
Gorton, Hicks	Ex-husband of the half 3rd cousin once removed		
Goss, Private	Husband of the 6th cousin 3 times removed		
Gottschall, Lottie	Wife of the 6th cousin twice removed		
Gould, Catherine	Wife of the 2nd cousin 3 times removed		
Govier, Cecil Burt	Husband of the half 3rd cousin 3 times removed		
Graby, George	Husband of the 6th cousin		
Grace, Daniel Sverre	4th cousin 4 times removed	XIV	9
Grace, Dorman John	Husband of the 4th cousin twice removed		
Grace, Dorman John III	4th cousin 3 times removed	XIII	8

The Relations of Milton Snavely Hershey, 4th Ed.

Name	Relationship with Milton Hershey	Civil	Canon
Grace, Kathleen Kay	4th cousin 3 times removed	XIII	8
Grace, Nancy Anne	4th cousin 3 times removed	XIII	8
Grace, Robert Joseph	4th cousin 4 times removed	XIV	9
Graeff, Abraham	2nd cousin twice removed	VIII	5
Graeff, Elizabeth	2nd cousin twice removed	VIII	5
Graeff, Jacob	2nd cousin twice removed	VIII	5
Graeff, Kate	2nd cousin twice removed	VIII	5
Graeff, Maria	2nd cousin twice removed	VIII	5
Graeff, Mathias	2nd cousin twice removed	VIII	5
Graeff, Mathias	Husband of the 1st cousin 3 times removed		
Graeff, Susan	2nd cousin twice removed	VIII	5
Graff, Barbara	Wife of the 4th great-granduncle		
Graff, Christian	Husband of the great-grandaunt		
Graham, Mary	Wife of the half 3rd cousin 3 times removed		
Grant, Doris May	Half 3rd cousin 3 times removed	XI	7
Grant, George	Husband of the half 3rd cousin twice removed		
Grant, Leo Richard	Husband of the 3rd cousin twice removed		
Grant, Lola	Half 3rd cousin 3 times removed	XI	7
Grason, Private	Wife of the 3rd cousin 3 times removed		
Graves, Private	Wife of the 6th cousin 3 times removed		
Gray, Charlotte Elizabeth	Wife of the 3rd cousin twice removed		
Gray, Gladys Marie	Wife of the 6th cousin twice removed		
Gray, Robert	Husband of the half 3rd cousin 3 times removed		
Graybill, Martha	Wife of the 2nd cousin once removed		
Graybill, Private	Husband of the 3rd cousin 3 times removed		
Graybill, Private	Wife of the 3rd cousin twice removed		
Green, Private	Husband of the 6th cousin 3 times removed		
Green, Rachael	Wife of the half 3rd cousin once removed		
Green, Winnifred Iva Frances	Wife of the half 3rd cousin 3 times removed		
Greenawald, Joseph	Husband of the 6th cousin		
Greenwalt, Private	Wife of the 6th cousin 3 times removed		
Gregg, Private	Wife of the 3rd cousin twice removed		
Greider, John	Husband of the 1st cousin 3 times removed		
Greiser, Private	Wife of the 3rd cousin 3 times removed		
Grider, Christina	Wife of the half 3rd cousin 3 times removed		
Grieves, Minnie	Wife of the half 3rd cousin once removed		
Griffen, Frank Webb	Husband of the 6th cousin twice removed		
Griffen, Frank Webb	6th cousin 3 times removed	XVII	10
Griffen, Private	6th cousin 3 times removed	XVII	10
Griffith, Deborah	Wife of the half 3rd cousin twice removed		
Griffith, Private	Husband of the 6th cousin 3 times removed		
Griffith, Private	6th cousin 4 times removed	XVIII	11
Groff, Abraham	Half 2nd cousin 4 times removed	X	7
Groff, Anna Elizabeth	3rd great-grandmother	V	5
Groff, Annie	Wife of the half 2nd cousin 4 times removed		
Groff, Barbara	Wife of the 3rd great-granduncle		
Groff, Barbara	3rd cousin 5 times removed	XIII	9
Groff, Barbara	3rd cousin 5 times removed	XIII	9
Groff, Barbara	3rd cousin 5 times removed	XIII	9
Groff, Betsey	Half 3rd cousin 3 times removed	XI	7
Groff, Daniel	2nd cousin 6 times removed	XII	9
Groff, David	2nd cousin 6 times removed	XII	9
Groff, David	3rd cousin 5 times removed	XIII	9
Groff, Elizabeth	Half 2nd cousin 4 times removed	X	7
Groff, Elizabeth	Half 3rd cousin 3 times removed	XI	7
Groff, Elizabeth Betsy	Half 3rd cousin 3 times removed	XI	7
Groff, Emanuel	Husband of the 1st cousin once removed		
Groff, Fronica	2nd cousin 6 times removed	XII	9
Groff, George	Half 4th cousin twice removed	XII	7
Groff, Hannah	2nd cousin 6 times removed	XII	9
Groff, Hans	Husband of the 1st cousin 7 times removed		
Groff, Jacob	Half 2nd cousin 4 times removed	X	7
Groff, John	2nd cousin 6 times removed	XII	9
Groff, John	Husband of the half 1st cousin 5 times removed		
Groff, John	Half 2nd cousin 4 times removed	X	7
Groff, John	Husband of the 4th cousin 4 times removed		

Name	Relationship with Milton Hershey	Civil	Canon
Groff, John	Half 3rd cousin 3 times removed	XI	7
Groff, John	Husband of the half 3rd cousin 3 times removed		
Groff, Marcus	2nd cousin 6 times removed	XII	9
Groff, Margaret	3rd cousin 5 times removed	XIII	9
Groff, Marie	3rd cousin 5 times removed	XIII	9
Groff, Mary	2nd cousin 6 times removed	XII	9
Groff, Mary	3rd cousin 5 times removed	XIII	9
Groff, Mary	Half 3rd cousin 3 times removed	XI	7
Groff, Mary R.	Wife of the 3rd cousin once removed		
Groff, Mathias	Husband of the 1st cousin 3 times removed		
Groff, Norman Myer	Husband of the 3rd cousin twice removed		
Groff, Peter	2nd cousin 6 times removed	XII	9
Groff, Private	Husband of the 3rd cousin 4 times removed		
Groff, Private	3rd cousin 5 times removed	XIII	9
Groff, Private	3rd cousin 5 times removed	XIII	9
Groff, Private	Husband of the 3rd cousin 3 times removed		
Groff, Private	3rd cousin 4 times removed	XII	8
Groff, Private	3rd cousin 4 times removed	XII	8
Groff, Private	3rd cousin 4 times removed	XII	8
Groff, Private	3rd cousin 4 times removed	XII	8
Groff, Private	Husband of the 3rd cousin 3 times removed		
Groff, Private	3rd cousin 4 times removed	XII	8
Groff, Private	3rd cousin 3 times removed	XI	7
Groff, Private	3rd cousin 3 times removed	XI	7
Groff, Private	3rd cousin 3 times removed	XI	7
Groff, Private	3rd cousin 3 times removed	XI	7
Groff, Private	3rd cousin 3 times removed	XI	7
Groff, Private	3rd cousin 3 times removed	XI	7
Groff, Private	3rd cousin 4 times removed	XII	8
Groff, Private	3rd cousin 4 times removed	XII	8
Groff, Private	3rd cousin 4 times removed	XII	8
Groff, Private	3rd cousin 4 times removed	XII	8
Groff, Private	3rd cousin 4 times removed	XII	8
Groff, Private	3rd cousin 4 times removed	XII	8
Groff, Private	3rd cousin 4 times removed	XII	8
Groff, Private	3rd cousin 4 times removed	XII	8
Groff, Private	3rd cousin 4 times removed	XII	8
Groff, Private	3rd cousin 4 times removed	XII	8
Groff, Private	3rd cousin 4 times removed	XII	8
Groff, Private	3rd cousin 4 times removed	XII	8
Groff, Private	3rd cousin 4 times removed	XII	8
Groff, Private	Husband of the 3rd cousin 3 times removed		
Groff, Private	3rd cousin 4 times removed	XII	8
Groff, Private	Wife of the 3rd cousin 3 times removed		
Groff, Private	Wife of the 3rd cousin 3 times removed		
Groff, Samuel	2nd cousin 6 times removed	XII	9
Groff, Susanna	3rd cousin 5 times removed	XIII	9
Groff/Grove, Unknown	Husband of the 3rd cousin twice removed		
Grogg, Private	Wife of the 6th cousin 3 times removed		
Grogg, Robert	Husband of the 6th cousin twice removed		
Groh, Elizabeth	Wife of the 6th cousin		
Gross, Private	Husband of the 6th cousin 3 times removed		
Grossman, Andrew	2nd cousin	VI	3
Grossman, Catharine	2nd cousin	VI	3
Grossman, Daniel	2nd cousin	VI	3
Grossman, David	2nd cousin	VI	3
Grossman, George	2nd cousin	VI	3
Grossman, Henry	2nd cousin	VI	3
Grossman, Jacob	Husband of the 1st cousin once removed		
Grossman, Jacob	2nd cousin	VI	3
Grossman, John	2nd cousin	VI	3
Grossman, Levi	2nd cousin	VI	3
Grossman, Margaret	2nd cousin	VI	3
Grove, Abraham	4th cousin once removed	XI	6

Name	Relationship with Milton Hershey	Civil	Canon
Grove, Ada	Wife of the 6th cousin twice removed		
Grove, Annie	4th cousin once removed	XI	6
Grove, Daniel	4th cousin once removed	XI	6
Grove, George	4th cousin once removed	XI	6
Grove, Henry	4th cousin once removed	XI	6
Grove, Jean	Wife of the half 3rd cousin twice removed		
Grove, John	4th cousin once removed	XI	6
Grove, Martin	4th cousin once removed	XI	6
Grove, Martin	Husband of the 3rd cousin twice removed		
Grove, Mary	4th cousin once removed	XI	6
Grove, Mary	4th cousin once removed	XI	6
Grove, Myrtle	Wife of the half 3rd cousin twice removed		
Grove, Samuel	4th cousin once removed	XI	6
Grove, Samuel	Husband of the 3rd cousin twice removed		
Grubb, Isabelle Stoffer	Wife of the 6th cousin		
Grubb/Krupp, Enos F. Grubb	Husband of the 5th cousin		
Grube, Daniel	Husband of the 1st cousin once removed		
Grube, Daniel	2nd cousin	VI	3
Grube, David	2nd cousin	VI	3
Grube, Elizabeth	2nd cousin	VI	3
Grube, Elsie Maye	Wife of the 6th cousin 3 times removed		
Grube, Isaac	2nd cousin	VI	3
Grube, John	2nd cousin	VI	3
Grube, John	Husband of the 4th cousin		
Grube, Lavina	2nd cousin	VI	3
Grube, Leah	2nd cousin	VI	3
Grube, Margaret	2nd cousin	VI	3
Grube, Margaret	2nd cousin	VI	3
Grube, Peter	Husband of the 1st cousin once removed		
Grube, Peter	2nd cousin	VI	3
Grube, Sarah Ann	2nd cousin	VI	3
Gruber, Irvin	Husband of the 6th cousin 3 times removed		
Gruber, James D	6th cousin 4 times removed	XVIII	11
Gruber, Jihn B	6th cousin 4 times removed	XVIII	11
Grudenroth, Unknown	Husband of the 2nd cousin once removed		
Gruen, David Edward	Husband of the 6th cousin twice removed		
Gruen, Private	6th cousin 3 times removed	XVII	10
Gruen, Private	6th cousin 3 times removed	XVII	10
Gruen, Private	6th cousin 3 times removed	XVII	10
Gruen, Private	6th cousin 3 times removed	XVII	10
Gruen, Private	6th cousin 3 times removed	XVII	10
Gryder, Mary	Wife of the half 4th cousin twice removed		
Gut, Jacob	Husband of the 4th great-grandaunt		
Guth, Barbara	1st cousin 5 times removed	IX	7
Guthrie, Lewin	Husband of the 6th cousin 3 times removed		
Guthrie, Private	6th cousin 4 times removed	XVIII	11
Guthrie, Private	6th cousin 4 times removed	XVIII	11
Guthrie, Private	6th cousin 4 times removed	XVIII	11
Habecker, Christian	Husband of the 3rd cousin twice removed		
Habecker, Christian	4th cousin once removed	XI	6
Habecker, Christian	4th cousin once removed	XI	6
Habecker, Esther	4th cousin once removed	XI	6
Habecker, Esther	4th cousin once removed	XI	6
Hachborn, Alice	Wife of the half 3rd cousin 3 times removed		
Hackman, Aaron	4th cousin	X	5
Hackman, Abraham	Husband of the 3rd cousin 3 times removed		
Hackman, Abraham	4th cousin twice removed	XII	7
Hackman, Abraham Beidler	5th cousin once removed	XIII	7
HACKMAN, ABRAHAM HERR	Husband of the 3rd cousin 3 times removed		
Hackman, Alice Ann B	4th cousin	X	5
Hackman, Alice Lorraine	4th cousin twice removed	XII	7
Hackman, Amy Lynn	4th cousin 3 times removed	XIII	8
Hackman, Andrew	4th cousin	X	5
Hackman, Andrew Baer	3rd cousin once removed	IX	5
Hackman, Andrew Hess	4th cousin once removed	XI	6
Hackman, Anna	5th cousin once removed	XIII	7

Name	Relationship with Milton Hershey	Civil	Canon
Hackman, Anna	3rd cousin once removed	IX	5
Hackman, Anna Maria	5th cousin once removed	XIII	7
Hackman, Annie Marian	4th cousin twice removed	XII	7
Hackman, Augustus Miller	4th cousin	X	5
Hackman, Baby	4th cousin once removed	XI	6
Hackman, Benjamin Beidler	5th cousin once removed	XIII	7
Hackman, Betty Lou	4th cousin twice removed	XII	7
Hackman, Brenda Kay	4th cousin 3 times removed	XIII	8
Hackman, Christian Stauffer	4th cousin twice removed	XII	7
Hackman, Christopher Allen	4th cousin 3 times removed	XIII	8
Hackman, Cindy Lynn	4th cousin 3 times removed	XIII	8
Hackman, Daniel Michael	4th cousin 3 times removed	XIII	8
Hackman, David	4th cousin	X	5
Hackman, David Baer	3rd cousin once removed	IX	5
Hackman, David Hiestand	Husband of the 2nd cousin twice removed		
Hackman, Dennis Ray	4th cousin 3 times removed	XIII	8
Hackman, Dorothy Elaine	4th cousin twice removed	XII	7
Hackman, Elizabeth	Wife of the 2nd cousin 3 times removed		
Hackman, Elizabeth	5th cousin once removed	XIII	7
Hackman, Emma Amelia	4th cousin	X	5
Hackman, Emma Amelia	4th cousin once removed	XI	6
Hackman, Gary Jay	4th cousin 3 times removed	XIII	8
Hackman, Gerald Allen	4th cousin 3 times removed	XIII	8
Hackman, Henry	4th cousin	X	5
Hackman, Henry Hess	4th cousin once removed	XI	6
Hackman, Henry Stauffer (Hockman)	4th cousin twice removed	XII	7
Hackman, Jacob	4th cousin	X	5
Hackman, Jacob Baer	3rd cousin once removed	IX	5
Hackman, John	4th cousin twice removed	XII	7
Hackman, John Allen	4th cousin twice removed	XII	7
Hackman, John Beidler	5th cousin once removed	XIII	7
Hackman, Joseph	4th cousin	X	5
Hackman, Karen Lee	4th cousin 3 times removed	XIII	8
Hackman, Kenneth Lee	4th cousin twice removed	XII	7
Hackman, Kenneth Lee	4th cousin 3 times removed	XIII	8
Hackman, Leonard	4th cousin	X	5
Hackman, Margaret Ann	4th cousin twice removed	XII	7
Hackman, Michael Frederick	4th cousin 3 times removed	XIII	8
Hackman, Mitchell Keith	4th cousin 3 times removed	XIII	8
Hackman, Myrtle	4th cousin once removed	XI	6
Hackman, Randall Lee	4th cousin 3 times removed	XIII	8
Hackman, Ray Donald	4th cousin twice removed	XII	7
Hackman, Rea Ann	4th cousin 3 times removed	XIII	8
Hackman, Richard Forney	4th cousin twice removed	XII	7
Hackman, Richard Hess	4th cousin once removed	XI	6
Hackman, Robert Forney	4th cousin twice removed	XII	7
Hackman, Robert Lorin	4th cousin twice removed	XII	7
Hackman, Romanus Andrew B	4th cousin	X	5
Hackman, Samuel	4th cousin twice removed	XII	7
Hackman, Steven Dean	4th cousin 3 times removed	XIII	8
Hackman, Tammy Sue	4th cousin 3 times removed	XIII	8
Hackman, Terry Lee	4th cousin 3 times removed	XIII	8
Hackman, Thomas Jon	4th cousin 3 times removed	XIII	8
Hackman, Tony Robert	4th cousin 3 times removed	XIII	8
Hackman, Violet Gertrude	4th cousin once removed	XI	6
Hackman, Walter Hess	4th cousin once removed	XI	6
Hackman, Wanda Jean	4th cousin 3 times removed	XIII	8
Hackman, Willard Henry	4th cousin twice removed	XII	7
Hackman, Willis Brenner	4th cousin	X	5
Hackman, Willis Hess	4th cousin once removed	XI	6
Hackman, Willis Martin	4th cousin twice removed	XII	7
Hagar, Hannah	Wife of the 2nd cousin 3 times removed		
Hagey, Christian	Husband of the 3rd cousin 3 times removed		
Haggert, Gertrude	6th cousin 3 times removed	XVII	10
Haggert, Glen	6th cousin 3 times removed	XVII	10
Haggert, Robert	Husband of the 6th cousin twice removed		

The Relations of Milton Snavely Hershey, 4th Ed.

Name	Relationship with Milton Hershey	Civil	Canon
Hahn, Bobby	6th cousin twice removed	XVI	9
Hahn, Earl D.	Husband of the 6th cousin once removed		
Hahn, Leland Eugene	6th cousin twice removed	XVI	9
Hahn, Private	6th cousin 3 times removed	XVII	10
Hahn, Private	6th cousin 3 times removed	XVII	10
Hahn, Private	6th cousin 3 times removed	XVII	10
Hahn, Wayne	6th cousin twice removed	XVI	9
Hails, Private	Wife of the 3rd cousin twice removed		
Haldeman, Abraham Bergey	Husband of the 4th cousin once removed		
Haldeman, Ammond Stauffer	5th cousin	XII	6
Haldeman, Magdelena Funk (Halterman)	Wife of the 3rd cousin twice removed		
Haldeman, Private	Husband of the 3rd cousin twice removed		
Haldeman, Sarah (Sallie) Stauffer (Halteman)	5th cousin	XII	6
Hale, Absalom	Husband of the 5th cousin once removed		
Hale, John	6th cousin	XIV	7
Hall, Benjamin	Husband of the half 3rd cousin once removed		
Hall, Cordelia Abigail	Wife of the half 3rd cousin once removed		
Hall, Faye	Half 3rd cousin twice removed	X	6
Hall, Herman M.	Husband of the half 3rd cousin 3 times removed		
Hall, Lola	Half 3rd cousin twice removed	X	6
Hall, Mildred	Half 3rd cousin twice removed	X	6
Hall, Nellie	Half 3rd cousin twice removed	X	6
Hall, Nettie	Half 3rd cousin twice removed	X	6
Hall, Nina Marie	Wife of the half 3rd cousin 3 times removed		
Hall, Private	Half 3rd cousin 4 times removed	XII	8
Hall, Private	Half 3rd cousin 4 times removed	XII	8
Hall, Vera	Half 3rd cousin twice removed	X	6
Hall, Verna	Half 3rd cousin twice removed	X	6
Halla, Emma	Wife of the half 3rd cousin		
Hallman, Ella Harley	Wife of the 4th cousin once removed		
Hallman, Unknown	Wife of the 4th cousin once removed		
Halwell, Nellie	Wife of the 6th cousin twice removed		
Hambright, Sarah	Wife of the 4th cousin twice removed		
Hamilton, Alice	Wife of the half 3rd cousin once removed		
Hamilton, Aura Titus	6th cousin 3 times removed	XVII	10
Hamilton, Belfry	Husband of the half 3rd cousin twice removed		
Hamilton, Charles Wesley	Husband of the 6th cousin twice removed		
Hamilton, Elton Kenneth	6th cousin 3 times removed	XVII	10
Hamilton, Harold Leon	6th cousin 3 times removed	XVII	10
Hamilton, Private	6th cousin 4 times removed	XVIII	11
Hamilton, Private	6th cousin 4 times removed	XVIII	11
Hamilton, Private	6th cousin 3 times removed	XVII	10
Hamilton, Private	6th cousin 3 times removed	XVII	10
Hamilton, Private	Husband of the 6th cousin 3 times removed		
Hamilton, Private	6th cousin 4 times removed	XVIII	11
Hamilton, Private	6th cousin 4 times removed	XVIII	11
Hamilton, Private	Half 3rd cousin 3 times removed	XI	7
Hamilton, Private	Half 3rd cousin 3 times removed	XI	7
Hamilton, Private	Half 3rd cousin 3 times removed	XI	7
Hamilton, Vera Lucretia	6th cousin 3 times removed	XVII	10
Hamilton, William	Husband of the 4th cousin once removed		
Hamm, Lloyd	Husband of the half 3rd cousin 3 times removed		
Hammond, Allen	Husband of the 1st cousin once removed		
Hammond, George	Husband of the half 3rd cousin once removed		
Hamrick, Private	Wife of the 6th cousin 3 times removed		
Hanesworth, Private	Wife of the 6th cousin 3 times removed		
Hanna, Charles	Husband of the 6th cousin twice removed		
Hansford, Dora Maud	Half 3rd cousin 3 times removed	XI	7
Hansford, William Allen	Ex-husband of the half 3rd cousin once removed		
Hansford, William Allen	Half 3rd cousin twice removed	X	6
Hardgrove, Private	Husband of the 6th cousin 3 times removed		
Hardgrove, Private	6th cousin 4 times removed	XVIII	11
Hardgrove, Private	6th cousin 4 times removed	XVIII	11
Hardgrove, Private	6th cousin 4 times removed	XVIII	11
Hardgrove, Private	6th cousin 4 times removed	XVIII	11
Hardgrove, Private	6th cousin 4 times removed	XVIII	11

Name	Relationship with Milton Hershey	Civil	Canon
Harding, Jessie Bell	Wife of the 6th cousin once removed		
Harding, Mabel Olive	Wife of the half 3rd cousin 3 times removed		
Hardy, Alice Loretta	6th cousin once removed	XV	8
Hardy, George	Husband of the 6th cousin twice removed		
Hardy, Henry Franklin	6th cousin once removed	XV	8
Hardy, Ida May	6th cousin once removed	XV	8
Hardy, Private	6th cousin 3 times removed	XVII	10
Hardy, Private	6th cousin 3 times removed	XVII	10
Hardy, Private	6th cousin 3 times removed	XVII	10
Hardy, Private	6th cousin 3 times removed	XVII	10
Hardy, Private	6th cousin 3 times removed	XVII	10
Hardy, Private	Wife of the 6th cousin 3 times removed		
Hardy, Private	Husband of the 6th cousin 3 times removed		
Hardy, Sylvester	Husband of the 6th cousin		
Hardy, William S	6th cousin once removed	XV	8
Hare, Sarah	Wife of the half 3rd cousin		
Harlan, Iva Martha	Wife of the 6th cousin once removed		
Harlan, Pearl R	Wife of the 6th cousin once removed		
Harley, David Stauffer	4th cousin once removed	XI	6
Harley, Elizabeth Stauffer	4th cousin once removed	XI	6
Harley, Jacob Rev.	Husband of the 3rd cousin twice removed		
Harley, Jacob Stauffer	4th cousin once removed	XI	6
Harley, James A. Stover	Husband of the 4th cousin once removed		
Harley, Jesse Stauffer	4th cousin once removed	XI	6
Harley, John Haldeman	Husband of the 4th cousin once removed		
Harley, John Stauffer Rev.	4th cousin once removed	XI	6
Harley, Joseph Stauffer	4th cousin once removed	XI	6
Harley, Maria Stauffer	4th cousin once removed	XI	6
Harley, Rebecca	Wife of the 4th cousin once removed		
Harley, Rudolph Stauffer	4th cousin once removed	XI	6
Harley, Samuel Buckwalter	5th cousin	XII	6
Harley, Samuel Hoffman	5th cousin once removed	XIII	7
Harley, Thelma Wingert	5th cousin once removed	XIII	7
Harmon, Private	Husband of the 3rd cousin twice removed		
Harmon, Private	3rd cousin 3 times removed	XI	7
Harnish, David	Husband of the grandaunt		
Harnish, Elizabeth	Wife of the granduncle		
Harnish, Private	6th cousin 3 times removed	XVII	10
Harnish, Private	6th cousin 3 times removed	XVII	10
Harnish, Private	6th cousin 3 times removed	XVII	10
Harnish, Private	6th cousin 3 times removed	XVII	10
Harnish, Private	6th cousin 3 times removed	XVII	10
Harnish, Wilbert John	Husband of the 6th cousin twice removed		
Harper, Eleanor Jean	Half 3rd cousin 3 times removed	XI	7
Harper, Gordon Charles	Husband of the half 3rd cousin twice removed		
Harper, Lois Marjorie	Half 3rd cousin 3 times removed	XI	7
Harrington, Alfred	6th cousin 3 times removed	XVII	10
Harrington, Almer H	6th cousin 3 times removed	XVII	10
Harrington, Beryl F	6th cousin 3 times removed	XVII	10
Harrington, Doris J	6th cousin 4 times removed	XVIII	11
Harrington, Frances	6th cousin 3 times removed	XVII	10
Harrington, Frances Anne	6th cousin 4 times removed	XVIII	11
Harrington, Frank B	Husband of the 6th cousin twice removed		
Harrington, Fred	Husband of the 6th cousin twice removed		
Harrington, Grace	6th cousin 3 times removed	XVII	10
Harrington, Jack A	6th cousin 4 times removed	XVIII	11
Harrington, Lillian R	6th cousin 3 times removed	XVII	10
Harrington, Lorene	Wife of the 6th cousin 3 times removed		
Harrington, Lucile	6th cousin 3 times removed	XVII	10
Harrington, Lynn	6th cousin 4 times removed	XVIII	11
Harrington, Margaret H	6th cousin 4 times removed	XVIII	11
Harrop, Mary	Wife of the half 3rd cousin 3 times removed		
Harsh, Miles Eby	Husband of the 3rd cousin once removed		
Harsh, Private	3rd cousin twice removed	X	6
Hart, Private	Wife of the 6th cousin 3 times removed		
Harter, Private	Husband of the 6th cousin 3 times removed		

Name	Relationship with Milton Hershey	Civil	Canon
Harter, Private	6th cousin 4 times removed	XVIII	11
Harter, Private	6th cousin 4 times removed	XVIII	11
Harter, Private	6th cousin 4 times removed	XVIII	11
Hartigan, Joseph Edward	Husband of the 6th cousin 3 times removed		
Hartigan, Private	6th cousin 4 times removed	XVIII	11
Hartigan, Private	6th cousin 4 times removed	XVIII	11
Hartigan, Private	6th cousin 4 times removed	XVIII	11
Hartman, Fannie	Wife of the 1st cousin twice removed		
Hartman, Fern	Husband of the 6th cousin 3 times removed		
Hartman, Living	Husband of the 6th cousin 4 times removed		
Hartog, Private	Wife of the 6th cousin 5 times removed		
Hartranft, Private	Husband of the 3rd cousin 3 times removed		
Hartzler, Private	Husband of the 3rd cousin 3 times removed		
Hartzler, Private	3rd cousin 4 times removed	XII	8
Hasler, Elizabeth	5th great-grandmother	VII	7
Hassler, Michael	6th cousin 4 times removed	XVIII	11
Hassler, William T	Husband of the 6th cousin 3 times removed		
Hastetter, Christiana	4th cousin twice removed	XII	7
Hatfield, Nellie	Ex-wife of the 6th cousin twice removed		
Hauch, Private	Husband of the 3rd cousin 3 times removed		
Hauch, Private	3rd cousin 4 times removed	XII	8
Hauck, Milton H.	Husband of the 4th cousin once removed		
Hauser, Barbara	Wife of the 3rd great-granduncle		
Haverstick, Maria	Wife of the 3rd cousin twice removed		
Hawk, Edgar Paul	Husband of the 6th cousin twice removed		
Hawk, Private	6th cousin 3 times removed	XVII	10
Hawk, Private	6th cousin 3 times removed	XVII	10
Hawkins, Jewell Dean	Wife of the half 3rd cousin twice removed		
Haynes, Agatha E.	6th cousin twice removed	XVI	9
Haynes, Albert W.	Husband of the 6th cousin once removed		
Haynes, Alberta	6th cousin twice removed	XVI	9
Haynes, Dorothy	6th cousin twice removed	XVI	9
Haynes, Ethel	6th cousin twice removed	XVI	9
Haynes, Josephine	6th cousin twice removed	XVI	9
Haynes, Marjorie	6th cousin twice removed	XVI	9
Heagy, Barbara	Wife of the 6th cousin		
Heatwole, Alice Virginia	Wife of the 3rd cousin once removed		
Heavyside, Joan Elizabeth	6th cousin 4 times removed	XVIII	11
Heavyside, Private	6th cousin 4 times removed	XVIII	11
Heavyside, Stuart Joseph Odin	Husband of the 6th cousin 3 times removed		
Hechler, Lillie R. (Heckler)	Wife of the 4th cousin once removed		
Heckman, Julianna	Wife of the 1st cousin 4 times removed		
Heckman, Samuel	Husband of the 6th cousin		
Hedrick, Clarence	Husband of the 6th cousin once removed		
Hedrix, Private	Husband of the 6th cousin 3 times removed		
Heestand, Abraham	Husband of the 5th cousin once removed		
Heestand, Anna	6th cousin	XIV	7
Heestand, Infant	6th cousin	XIV	7
Heestand, Issac S	6th cousin	XIV	7
Heestand, Joseph	6th cousin	XIV	7
Heestand, Levi	6th cousin	XIV	7
Heestand, Samuel	6th cousin	XIV	7
Heffleblower, Henry	Husband of the 6th cousin		
Heilman, Private	Husband of the 3rd cousin 3 times removed		
Heimbach, Private	Wife of the 3rd cousin 3 times removed		
Heimbach, Private	Husband of the 3rd cousin 3 times removed		
Heimbach, Private	3rd cousin 4 times removed	XII	8
Hein, Linda M	Wife of the 6th cousin 4 times removed		
Heinemann, Private	Wife of the 6th cousin 3 times removed		
Heiney, Mary C.	Wife of the 3rd cousin		
Heisey, Private	Wife of the 3rd cousin 3 times removed		
Heishman, Lydia Pearl	Wife of the 3rd cousin twice removed		
Heistand, Abraham	Husband of the 1st cousin 4 times removed		
Heistand, Ann	Wife of the 2nd great-granduncle		
Hemley, Catherine	Wife of the 2nd cousin 3 times removed		
Henderson, Private	Husband of the 2nd cousin 4 times removed		

Name	Relationship with Milton Hershey	Civil	Canon
Hendrickson, Ruth Louise Buzzard	5th cousin once removed	XIII	7
Hendrickson, Unknown	Husband of the 5th cousin		
Hendrix, Jolly A.	Husband of the 6th cousin twice removed		
Hendrix, Private	6th cousin 4 times removed	XVIII	11
Hendrix, Private	6th cousin 4 times removed	XVIII	11
Hendrix, Private	6th cousin 3 times removed	XVII	10
Hendrix, Private	6th cousin 3 times removed	XVII	10
Hennelly, Private	Husband of the 3rd cousin twice removed		
Hennelly, Private	3rd cousin 3 times removed	XI	7
Henry, Fred	Husband of the half 3rd cousin twice removed		
Henry, Private	Half 3rd cousin 3 times removed	XI	7
Henry, Private	Half 3rd cousin 3 times removed	XI	7
Hepler, Private	Husband of the 6th cousin 3 times removed		
Hepler, Private	6th cousin 4 times removed	XVIII	11
Hepler, Private	6th cousin 4 times removed	XVIII	11
Herbein, Maria	Wife of the 1st cousin 4 times removed		
Herbster, William Martin	Husband of the 6th cousin 3 times removed		
Hernley, Abraham	1st cousin 3 times removed	VII	5
Hernley, Anna	2nd great-grandmother	IV	4
Hernley, Isaac	Husband of the 2nd great-grandaunt		
Hernley, John	1st cousin 3 times removed	VII	5
Hernley, Mary	Wife of the 3rd cousin twice removed		
Hernly, Isaac	Husband of the 2nd great-grandaunt		
Herr, Abraham	1st cousin 3 times removed	VII	5
Herr, Abraham	Husband of the 2nd great-grandaunt		
Herr, Abraham	2nd cousin 3 times removed	IX	6
Herr, Abraham	4th cousin once removed	XI	6
Herr, Abraham	Husband of the 2nd great-grandaunt		
Herr, Abraham	3rd cousin twice removed	X	6
Herr, Abraham	3rd cousin twice removed	X	6
Herr, Abraham	6th cousin	XIV	7
Herr, Abram	Husband of the 3rd cousin twice removed		
Herr, Alta	Wife of the 3rd cousin once removed		
Herr, Ann	Wife of the half 1st cousin 5 times removed		
Herr, Ann	1st cousin 5 times removed	IX	7
Herr, Anna	2nd cousin 3 times removed	IX	6
Herr, Anna	1st cousin 3 times removed	VII	5
Herr, Barabara	Great-grandmother	III	3
Herr, Barbara	4th cousin once removed	XI	6
Herr, Barbara	Wife of the half 1st cousin 5 times removed		
Herr, Barbara	1st cousin 3 times removed	VII	5
Herr, Barbara Ann	Wife of the half 2nd cousin 4 times removed		
Herr, Barbara M.	6th cousin	XIV	7
Herr, Benjamin	5th cousin	XII	6
Herr, Benjamin	3rd cousin twice removed	X	6
Herr, Benjamin	4th cousin once removed	XI	6
Herr, C. Bachman	Husband of the 4th cousin once removed		
Herr, Catherine	2nd cousin 3 times removed	IX	6
Herr, Charles S.	5th cousin	XII	6
Herr, Christian	2nd cousin 3 times removed	IX	6
Herr, Christian	Husband of the 4th great-grandaunt		
Herr, Christian	Husband of the 1st cousin 4 times removed		
Herr, Christian	1st cousin 3 times removed	VII	5
Herr, Christian	6th cousin	XIV	7
Herr, Christian B.	Husband of the 5th cousin once removed		
Herr, Daughter2	Wife of the half great-granduncle		
Herr, David	2nd cousin 3 times removed	IX	6
Herr, David	Husband of the 1st cousin 4 times removed		
Herr, David	3rd cousin twice removed	X	6
Herr, David	Husband of the half 2nd cousin 4 times removed		
Herr, Elisabeth	1st cousin 3 times removed	VII	5
Herr, Elizabeth	4th cousin once removed	XI	6
Herr, Elizabeth	6th cousin	XIV	7
Herr, Elizabeth (Betsey)	Half 4th cousin twice removed	XII	7
Herr, Esther	Wife of the great-grandfather		
Herr, Esther	3rd cousin twice removed	X	6

The Relations of Milton Snavely Hershey, 4th Ed.

Name	Relationship with Milton Hershey	Civil	Canon
Herr, Esther	3rd cousin twice removed	X	6
Herr, Esther	1st cousin 3 times removed	VII	5
Herr, Fannie	1st cousin 5 times removed	IX	7
Herr, Fanny	2nd cousin 3 times removed	IX	6
Herr, Fanny	3rd cousin twice removed	X	6
Herr, Fanny	4th cousin once removed	XI	6
Herr, Fronica	2nd cousin 3 times removed	IX	6
Herr, Henry	Husband of the 1st cousin 5 times removed		
Herr, Henry	Husband of the 1st cousin 4 times removed		
Herr, Henry P	4th cousin once removed	XI	6
Herr, Hettie	4th cousin once removed	XI	6
Herr, Jacob G.	Husband of the 3rd cousin once removed		
Herr, Jacob P	4th cousin once removed	XI	6
Herr, Johannes	Husband of the 4th great-grandaunt		
Herr, John	4th cousin once removed	XI	6
Herr, John	Husband of the 2nd cousin 3 times removed		
Herr, John	3rd cousin twice removed	X	6
Herr, John	3rd cousin twice removed	X	6
Herr, Joseph	6th cousin	XIV	7
Herr, Lydia	6th cousin	XIV	7
Herr, Magdalena	Wife of the 3rd cousin twice removed		
Herr, Magdalena	6th cousin	XIV	7
Herr, Magdalene	Half 3rd cousin 3 times removed	XI	7
Herr, Maria	Wife of the half great-granduncle		
Herr, Maria	6th cousin	XIV	7
Herr, Maria Margaretha	4th great-grandmother	VI	6
Herr, Martin R.	Husband of the 2nd cousin		
Herr, Mary	4th cousin once removed	XI	6
Herr, Mary	4th cousin once removed	XI	6
Herr, Mary	1st cousin 5 times removed	IX	7
Herr, Mary	1st cousin 3 times removed	VII	5
Herr, Mary	Wife of the 2nd cousin 3 times removed		
Herr, Minnie P	4th cousin once removed	XI	6
Herr, Nancy	4th cousin once removed	XI	6
Herr, Nancy	6th cousin	XIV	7
Herr, Private	Husband of the 3rd cousin twice removed		
Herr, Private	3rd cousin 3 times removed	XI	7
Herr, Private	3rd cousin 3 times removed	XI	7
Herr, Private	3rd cousin 4 times removed	XII	8
Herr, Rev. John	Husband of the half 3rd cousin 3 times removed		
Herr, Rudolph	Husband of the 2nd cousin 3 times removed		
Herr, Samuel	Husband of the 1st cousin 4 times removed		
Herr, Samuel	6th cousin	XIV	7
Herr, Susanna	Wife of the half 3rd cousin 3 times removed		
Herr, Unnamed	3rd cousin twice removed	X	6
Herr, Veronica	Wife of the granduncle		
Herr, Veronica	6th cousin	XIV	7
Hershberger, Anna	Wife of the 2nd cousin twice removed		
Hershberger, Christian	Husband of the 3rd cousin 3 times removed		
Hershey, Abraham	1st cousin 4 times removed	VIII	6
Hershey, Abraham	2nd cousin 3 times removed	IX	6
Hershey, Abraham	2nd cousin 3 times removed	IX	6
Hershey, Abraham	Great-granduncle	V	4
Hershey, Abraham	Great-granduncle	V	4
Hershey, Abraham	3rd cousin twice removed	X	6
Hershey, Abraham	Granduncle	IV	3
Hershey, Abraham	3rd cousin once removed	IX	5
Hershey, Abraham L.	3rd cousin twice removed	X	6
Hershey, Adah (Ada)	1st cousin 4 times removed	VIII	6
Hershey, Adah Louisa	4th cousin once removed	XI	6
Hershey, Aldus	2nd cousin	VI	3
Hershey, Alice Light	1st cousin	IV	2
Hershey, Amanda	2nd cousin once removed	VII	4
Hershey, Amos F	1st cousin once removed	V	3
Hershey, Amos H	3rd cousin once removed	IX	5
Hershey, Amos H	2nd cousin once removed	VII	4

Name	Relationship with Milton Hershey	Civil	Canon
Hershey, Amy Landis	2nd cousin twice removed	VIII	5
Hershey, Andrew	Great-granduncle	V	4
Hershey, Andrew L K	Husband of the 2nd cousin once removed		
Hershey, Ann	1st cousin 3 times removed	VII	5
Hershey, Ann Elisabeth	3rd great-grandmother	V	5
Hershey, Anna	3rd cousin once removed	IX	5
Hershey, Anna	Wife of the 3rd cousin twice removed		
Hershey, Anna	3rd great-grandaunt	VII	6
Hershey, Anna	2nd cousin 3 times removed	IX	6
Hershey, Anna	Great-grandaunt	V	4
Hershey, Anna	2nd cousin once removed	VII	4
Hershey, Anna	2nd cousin once removed	VII	4
Hershey, Anna	3rd cousin once removed	IX	5
Hershey, Anna Elizabeth	1st cousin 4 times removed	VIII	6
Hershey, Anna Kreider	Wife of the 3rd cousin once removed		
Hershey, Anna L.	2nd cousin once removed	VII	4
Hershey, Annie	2nd cousin once removed	VII	4
Hershey, Annie	1st cousin once removed	V	3
Hershey, Annie	Wife of the 2nd cousin 3 times removed		
Hershey, Annie	1st cousin	IV	2
Hershey, Barbara	3rd cousin twice removed	X	6
Hershey, Barbara	1st cousin 4 times removed	VIII	6
Hershey, Barbara	2nd cousin 3 times removed	IX	6
Hershey, Barbara	3rd cousin	VIII	4
Hershey, Barbara Ann	3rd cousin once removed	IX	5
Hershey, Barbara Elizabeth	3rd cousin once removed	IX	5
Hershey, Barbara Hostetter	Half great-grandaunt	V	4
Hershey, Benjamin	3rd cousin once removed	IX	5
Hershey, Benjamin	1st cousin 3 times removed	VII	5
Hershey, Benjamin	2nd great-granduncle	VI	5
Hershey, Benjamin	Husband of the 2nd cousin 4 times removed		
Hershey, Benjamin	1st cousin 4 times removed	VIII	6
Hershey, Benjamin	Great-granduncle	V	4
Hershey, Benjamin	2nd cousin 3 times removed	IX	6
Hershey, Benjamin	Granduncle	IV	3
Hershey, Benjamin	1st cousin twice removed	VI	4
Hershey, Benjamin	1st cousin twice removed	VI	4
Hershey, Benjamin	3rd cousin twice removed	X	6
Hershey, Benjamin	3rd cousin once removed	IX	5
Hershey, Benjamin H	3rd cousin once removed	IX	5
Hershey, Benjamin Stauffer	3rd great-grandfather	V	5
Hershey, Bessie M	1st cousin	IV	2
Hershey, Catharine	3rd cousin twice removed	X	6
Hershey, Catharine	3rd cousin twice removed	X	6
Hershey, Catherine	2nd cousin once removed	VII	4
Hershey, Catherine	2nd cousin 3 times removed	IX	6
Hershey, Catherine	2nd cousin 3 times removed	IX	6
Hershey, Catherine	3rd cousin twice removed	X	6
Hershey, Chauncey	2nd cousin	VI	3
Hershey, Christian	1st cousin 3 times removed	VII	5
Hershey, Christian	2nd great-grandfather	IV	4
Hershey, Christian	1st cousin 4 times removed	VIII	6
Hershey, Christian	2nd cousin 3 times removed	IX	6
Hershey, Christian	2nd cousin 3 times removed	IX	6
Hershey, Christian	Great-grandfather	III	3
Hershey, Christian	Granduncle	IV	3
Hershey, Christian	Granduncle	IV	3
Hershey, Christian	Uncle	III	2
Hershey, Christian	3rd cousin twice removed	X	6
Hershey, Christian	1st cousin	IV	2
Hershey, Christian B.	3rd cousin once removed	IX	5
Hershey, Christian L.	2nd cousin once removed	VII	4
Hershey, Christian Schmidt	4th great-grandfather	VI	6
Hershey, Christian Stauffer	3rd great-granduncle	VII	6
Hershey, Clifford Eby	3rd cousin twice removed	X	6
Hershey, Cloyd Gray	4th cousin once removed	XI	6

The Relations of Milton Snavely Hershey, 4th Ed.

Name	Relationship with Milton Hershey	Civil	Canon
Hershey, Cora	2nd cousin	VI	3
Hershey, Daniel F	1st cousin once removed	V	3
Hershey, Daniel Webster	3rd cousin twice removed	X	6
Hershey, David	3rd cousin twice removed	X	6
Hershey, David	Husband of the 2nd cousin twice removed		
Hershey, David	3rd cousin twice removed	X	6
Hershey, David	2nd cousin once removed	VII	4
Hershey, David C	3rd cousin once removed	IX	5
Hershey, David Warren	3rd cousin once removed	IX	5
Hershey, Doris Mae	3rd cousin once removed	IX	5
Hershey, Edith Celeste	3rd cousin twice removed	X	6
Hershey, Edith May	3rd cousin once removed	IX	5
Hershey, Edna	Wife of the 3rd cousin once removed		
Hershey, Elias	2nd cousin once removed	VII	4
Hershey, Elias H	Uncle	III	2
Hershey, Elisabeth	1st cousin 4 times removed	VIII	6
Hershey, Elisabeth	Wife of the 2nd cousin twice removed		
Hershey, Elizabeth	2nd cousin once removed	VII	4
Hershey, Elizabeth	1st cousin 3 times removed	VII	5
Hershey, Elizabeth	2nd cousin 3 times removed	IX	6
Hershey, Elizabeth	Wife of the great-granduncle		
Hershey, Elizabeth	Wife of the great-granduncle		
Hershey, Elizabeth	Great-grandaunt	V	4
Hershey, Elizabeth	Grandaunt	IV	3
Hershey, Elizabeth	3rd cousin twice removed	X	6
Hershey, Elizabeth	3rd cousin twice removed	X	6
Hershey, Elizabeth	3rd cousin twice removed	X	6
Hershey, Elizabeth	Grandaunt	IV	3
Hershey, Elizabeth	2nd cousin once removed	VII	4
Hershey, Elizabeth	Aunt	III	2
Hershey, Elizabeth	3rd cousin once removed	IX	5
Hershey, Elizabeth	1st cousin once removed	V	3
Hershey, Elizabeth	1st cousin once removed	V	3
Hershey, Elizabeth	3rd cousin	VIII	4
Hershey, Elizabeth B	2nd cousin	VI	3
Hershey, Elizabeth Frick	1st cousin once removed	V	3
Hershey, Ellen	3rd cousin	VIII	4
Hershey, Elmer Light	1st cousin	IV	2
Hershey, Elsie D.	3rd cousin once removed	IX	5
Hershey, Emily Jane	4th cousin once removed	XI	6
Hershey, Emma	3rd cousin once removed	IX	5
Hershey, Enos	1st cousin once removed	V	3
Hershey, Enos Jacob	3rd cousin	VIII	4
Hershey, Ephraim	3rd cousin once removed	IX	5
Hershey, Erma E.	3rd cousin twice removed	X	6
Hershey, Erma Elizabeth	3rd cousin once removed	IX	5
Hershey, Esta Mae	Wife of the 3rd cousin once removed		
Hershey, Esther	3rd cousin once removed	IX	5
Hershey, Esther	2nd cousin 3 times removed	IX	6
Hershey, Esther	Great-grandaunt	V	4
Hershey, Esther	2nd cousin 3 times removed	IX	6
Hershey, Esther	3rd cousin twice removed	X	6
Hershey, Esther (Hester)	1st cousin 4 times removed	VIII	6
Hershey, Esther Elizabeth	3rd cousin once removed	IX	5
Hershey, Esther G	2nd cousin	VI	3
Hershey, Ethel Pauline	3rd cousin once removed	IX	5
Hershey, Eugene Light	1st cousin	IV	2
Hershey, Ezra Frantz	1st cousin	IV	2
Hershey, Ezra Frantz	1st cousin once removed	V	3
Hershey, Fannie	2nd cousin once removed	VII	4
Hershey, Fanny	1st cousin once removed	V	3
Hershey, Feronica	1st cousin 3 times removed	VII	5
Hershey, Fianna	1st cousin once removed	V	3
Hershey, Frances	3rd cousin once removed	IX	5
Hershey, Francis	1st cousin once removed	V	3
Hershey, Freda M	1st cousin once removed	V	3

Name	Relationship with Milton Hershey	Civil	Canon
Hershey, Frederick	3rd cousin twice removed	X	6
Hershey, Fronica	1st cousin twice removed	VI	4
Hershey, Galen Clair	3rd cousin twice removed	X	6
Hershey, Galen Warren	3rd cousin once removed	IX	5
Hershey, George	3rd cousin twice removed	X	6
Hershey, George Daniel	4th cousin once removed	XI	6
Hershey, Gladys Edna	3rd cousin twice removed	X	6
Hershey, Grace Elizabeth	3rd cousin once removed	IX	5
Hershey, Harriet	Wife of the 3rd cousin once removed		
Hershey, Hazel Pauline	3rd cousin twice removed	X	6
Hershey, Henry	2nd cousin 3 times removed	IX	6
Hershey, Henry	3rd cousin twice removed	X	6
Hershey, Henry	3rd cousin twice removed	X	6
Hershey, Henry	3rd cousin once removed	IX	5
Hershey, Henry	2nd cousin once removed	VII	4
Hershey, Henry	1st cousin once removed	V	3
Hershey, Henry Clay	3rd cousin once removed	IX	5
Hershey, Henry H	2nd cousin once removed	VII	4
Hershey, Henry Hershey	Father	I	1
Hershey, Henry Peter	3rd cousin	VIII	4
Hershey, Hester	3rd cousin once removed	IX	5
Hershey, Hester (Esther)	3rd cousin twice removed	X	6
Hershey, Ida Anne	4th cousin once removed	XI	6
Hershey, Infant	3rd cousin	VIII	4
Hershey, Infant	3rd cousin	VIII	4
Hershey, Isaac	Granduncle	IV	3
Hershey, Isaac	1st cousin once removed	V	3
Hershey, Isaac	Uncle	III	2
Hershey, Isaac Hernley	Great-grandfather	III	3
Hershey, Isaiah B.	3rd cousin	VIII	4
Hershey, Jacob	Husband of the 2nd great-grandaunt		
Hershey, Jacob	2nd great-grandfather	IV	4
Hershey, Jacob	Great-granduncle	V	4
Hershey, Jacob	1st cousin twice removed	VI	4
Hershey, Jacob	1st cousin twice removed	VI	4
Hershey, Jacob	Granduncle	IV	3
Hershey, Jacob	1st cousin once removed	V	3
Hershey, Jacob	3rd cousin twice removed	X	6
Hershey, Jacob	3rd cousin once removed	IX	5
Hershey, Jacob	2nd cousin	VI	3
Hershey, Jacob	1st cousin	IV	2
Hershey, Jacob B	1st cousin once removed	V	3
Hershey, Jacob Frantz	Grandfather	II	2
Hershey, Jacob H	Uncle	III	2
Hershey, Jacob L	Granduncle	IV	3
Hershey, Jacob Menno	2nd cousin once removed	VII	4
Hershey, Jacob Snavely	2nd great-grandfather	IV	4
Hershey, Jay Paul	3rd cousin twice removed	X	6
Hershey, Jean Lois	3rd cousin twice removed	X	6
Hershey, John	2nd cousin once removed	VII	4
Hershey, John	Great-granduncle	V	4
Hershey, John	Great-granduncle	V	4
Hershey, John	2nd cousin 3 times removed	IX	6
Hershey, John	1st cousin twice removed	VI	4
Hershey, John	1st cousin twice removed	VI	4
Hershey, John	Granduncle	IV	3
Hershey, John	3rd cousin twice removed	X	6
Hershey, John	3rd cousin once removed	IX	5
Hershey, John Adam Light	1st cousin	IV	2
Hershey, John Alan	3rd cousin twice removed	X	6
Hershey, John Eby	2nd cousin once removed	VII	4
Hershey, John F	1st cousin once removed	V	3
Hershey, John Frantz	Granduncle	IV	3
Hershey, John Rudy	4th cousin once removed	XI	6
Hershey, Joseph	Husband of the 2nd cousin twice removed		
Hershey, Joseph	3rd cousin once removed	IX	5

The Relations of Milton Snavely Hershey, 4th Ed.

Name	Relationship with Milton Hershey	Civil	Canon
Hershey, Joseph	2nd cousin once removed	VII	4
Hershey, Joseph	Great-granduncle	V	4
Hershey, Joseph	1st cousin twice removed	VI	4
Hershey, Joseph	Uncle	III	2
Hershey, Joseph	1st cousin twice removed	VI	4
Hershey, Joseph B	Husband of the 6th cousin twice removed		
Hershey, Katherine Rohrer	1st cousin once removed	V	3
Hershey, Katie Light	1st cousin	IV	2
Hershey, Landes L.	2nd cousin once removed	VII	4
Hershey, Laura Light	1st cousin	IV	2
Hershey, Lavina	3rd cousin twice removed	X	6
Hershey, Leah	1st cousin once removed	V	3
Hershey, Leona R	1st cousin once removed	V	3
Hershey, Lester D.	3rd cousin once removed	IX	5
Hershey, Levi	1st cousin once removed	V	3
Hershey, Lorena	1st cousin	IV	2
Hershey, Louisa	4th cousin once removed	XI	6
Hershey, Lydia	2nd cousin once removed	VII	4
Hershey, Lydia	1st cousin once removed	V	3
Hershey, Magdalen	1st cousin 3 times removed	VII	5
Hershey, Magdalena	2nd cousin once removed	VII	4
Hershey, Magdalena	1st cousin twice removed	VI	4
Hershey, Malcolm Clarence	4th cousin once removed	XI	6
Hershey, Margaret	2nd cousin once removed	VII	4
Hershey, Margaret	2nd cousin once removed	VII	4
Hershey, Margaret	3rd cousin twice removed	X	6
Hershey, Maria	Half great-grandaunt	V	4
Hershey, Maria	2nd cousin once removed	VII	4
Hershey, Maria	1st cousin once removed	V	3
Hershey, Maria	3rd cousin once removed	IX	5
Hershey, Maria Elizabeth	1st cousin once removed	V	3
Hershey, Mark Eby	3rd cousin once removed	IX	5
Hershey, Martha A.	3rd cousin	VIII	4
Hershey, Martin	1st cousin once removed	V	3
Hershey, Martin Eby	3rd cousin	VIII	4
Hershey, Martin F	1st cousin once removed	V	3
Hershey, Mary	2nd cousin	VI	3
Hershey, Mary	2nd great-grandaunt	VI	5
Hershey, Mary	1st cousin 3 times removed	VII	5
Hershey, Mary	1st cousin 4 times removed	VIII	6
Hershey, Mary	2nd cousin 3 times removed	IX	6
Hershey, Mary	2nd cousin 3 times removed	IX	6
Hershey, Mary	Grandaunt	IV	3
Hershey, Mary	3rd cousin twice removed	X	6
Hershey, Mary	1st cousin once removed	V	3
Hershey, Mary	2nd cousin once removed	VII	4
Hershey, Mary	3rd cousin	VIII	4
Hershey, Mary	1st cousin	IV	2
Hershey, Mary Clyde	4th cousin once removed	XI	6
Hershey, Mary Elizabeth	3rd cousin twice removed	X	6
Hershey, Mary Emily	3rd cousin once removed	IX	5
Hershey, Mary F	2nd cousin	VI	3
Hershey, Mary Helen	3rd cousin once removed	IX	5
Hershey, Mary Katherine Eby	3rd cousin twice removed	X	6
Hershey, May B	2nd cousin	VI	3
Hershey, Menno Frick	1st cousin once removed	V	3
Hershey, Mildred L.	3rd cousin twice removed	X	6
Hershey, Milton Snavely	Self		0
Hershey, Miriam Clara	3rd cousin once removed	IX	5
Hershey, Monroe Light	1st cousin	IV	2
Hershey, Morris Light	1st cousin	IV	2
Hershey, Nancy	Grandmother	II	2
Hershey, Nancy	Grandaunt	IV	3
Hershey, Nancy Ann	1st cousin twice removed	VI	4
Hershey, Nancy Ann	3rd cousin twice removed	X	6
Hershey, Naomi	1st cousin once removed	V	3

Name	Relationship with Milton Hershey	Civil	Canon
Hershey, Naomi B	2nd cousin	VI	3
Hershey, Paul Keene	3rd cousin once removed	IX	5
Hershey, Paul Kenneth	3rd cousin twice removed	X	6
Hershey, Peter	2nd cousin once removed	VII	4
Hershey, Peter	2nd cousin once removed	VII	4
Hershey, Peter E.	1st cousin twice removed	VI	4
Hershey, Priscilla	1st cousin once removed	V	3
Hershey, Private	Wife of the 3rd cousin 3 times removed		
Hershey, Private	3rd cousin 3 times removed	XI	7
Hershey, Private	3rd cousin 3 times removed	XI	7
Hershey, Private	3rd cousin 4 times removed	XII	8
Hershey, Private	3rd cousin 4 times removed	XII	8
Hershey, Private	3rd cousin twice removed	X	6
Hershey, Private	3rd cousin twice removed	X	6
Hershey, Private	3rd cousin twice removed	X	6
Hershey, Private	3rd cousin twice removed	X	6
Hershey, Private	3rd cousin 3 times removed	XI	7
Hershey, Private	3rd cousin 3 times removed	XI	7
Hershey, Private	3rd cousin 3 times removed	XI	7
Hershey, Private	3rd cousin 4 times removed	XII	8
Hershey, Private	3rd cousin 4 times removed	XII	8
Hershey, Private	3rd cousin 4 times removed	XII	8
Hershey, Private	Husband of the 3rd cousin 3 times removed		
Hershey, Private	3rd cousin 4 times removed	XII	8
Hershey, Private	3rd cousin 4 times removed	XII	8
Hershey, Private	3rd cousin 4 times removed	XII	8
Hershey, Private	3rd cousin 4 times removed	XII	8
Hershey, Private	3rd cousin 4 times removed	XII	8
Hershey, Private	3rd cousin 3 times removed	XI	7
Hershey, Private	3rd cousin 3 times removed	XI	7
Hershey, Private	3rd cousin 3 times removed	XI	7
Hershey, Private	3rd cousin 3 times removed	XI	7
Hershey, Private	3rd cousin 3 times removed	XI	7
Hershey, Private	3rd cousin 4 times removed	XII	8
Hershey, Private	3rd cousin 4 times removed	XII	8
Hershey, Private	3rd cousin 4 times removed	XII	8
Hershey, Private	3rd cousin 4 times removed	XII	8
Hershey, Private	3rd cousin 3 times removed	XI	7
Hershey, Private	3rd cousin 3 times removed	XI	7
Hershey, Private	3rd cousin 4 times removed	XII	8
Hershey, Private	3rd cousin 4 times removed	XII	8
Hershey, Private	3rd cousin 3 times removed	XI	7
Hershey, Private	3rd cousin 3 times removed	XI	7
Hershey, Private	3rd cousin 3 times removed	XI	7
Hershey, Private	3rd cousin 3 times removed	XI	7
Hershey, Private	3rd cousin 3 times removed	XI	7
Hershey, Private	3rd cousin 3 times removed	XI	7
Hershey, Private	3rd cousin twice removed	X	6
Hershey, Private	3rd cousin twice removed	X	6
Hershey, Private	3rd cousin twice removed	X	6
Hershey, Private	3rd cousin twice removed	X	6
Hershey, Private	3rd cousin twice removed	X	6
Hershey, Private	3rd cousin twice removed	X	6
Hershey, Private	3rd cousin 3 times removed	XI	7
Hershey, Private	3rd cousin 3 times removed	XI	7
Hershey, Private	3rd cousin 3 times removed	XI	7
Hershey, Private	3rd cousin 3 times removed	XI	7
Hershey, Private	3rd cousin 4 times removed	XII	8
Hershey, Private	3rd cousin 4 times removed	XII	8
Hershey, Private	3rd cousin 3 times removed	XI	7
Hershey, Private	3rd cousin 3 times removed	XI	7
Hershey, Private	3rd cousin 3 times removed	XI	7
Hershey, Private	3rd cousin 3 times removed	XI	7
Hershey, Private	3rd cousin 3 times removed	XI	7

The Relations of Milton Snavely Hershey, 4th Ed.

Name	Relationship with Milton Hershey	Civil	Canon
Hershey, Private	3rd cousin 3 times removed	XI	7
Hershey, Private	3rd cousin 3 times removed	XI	7
Hershey, Private	3rd cousin twice removed	X	6
Hershey, Private	3rd cousin 3 times removed	XI	7
Hershey, Private	3rd cousin 3 times removed	XI	7
Hershey, Private	3rd cousin 3 times removed	XI	7
Hershey, Private	3rd cousin 3 times removed	XI	7
Hershey, Private	3rd cousin 3 times removed	XI	7
Hershey, Private	3rd cousin 4 times removed	XII	8
Hershey, Private	3rd cousin 4 times removed	XII	8
Hershey, Private	3rd cousin 4 times removed	XII	8
Hershey, Private	3rd cousin 4 times removed	XII	8
Hershey, Private	3rd cousin 4 times removed	XII	8
Hershey, Private	3rd cousin 3 times removed	XI	7
Hershey, Private	3rd cousin 3 times removed	XI	7
Hershey, Private	3rd cousin 3 times removed	XI	7
Hershey, Private	3rd cousin 3 times removed	XI	7
Hershey, Private	3rd cousin 3 times removed	XI	7
Hershey, Private	3rd cousin 3 times removed	XI	7
Hershey, Private	3rd cousin twice removed	X	6
Hershey, Private	3rd cousin twice removed	X	6
Hershey, Private	3rd cousin twice removed	X	6
Hershey, Private	3rd cousin twice removed	X	6
Hershey, Private	3rd cousin twice removed	X	6
Hershey, Private	3rd cousin twice removed	X	6
Hershey, Private	3rd cousin twice removed	X	6
Hershey, Private	3rd cousin 3 times removed	XI	7
Hershey, Private	3rd cousin 3 times removed	XI	7
Hershey, Private	3rd cousin 3 times removed	XI	7
Hershey, Private	3rd cousin 4 times removed	XII	8
Hershey, Private	3rd cousin 4 times removed	XII	8
Hershey, Private	3rd cousin 3 times removed	XI	7
Hershey, Private	3rd cousin 4 times removed	XII	8
Hershey, Private	3rd cousin 4 times removed	XII	8
Hershey, Private	3rd cousin 3 times removed	XI	7
Hershey, Private	3rd cousin 3 times removed	XI	7
Hershey, Private	3rd cousin 4 times removed	XII	8
Hershey, Private	3rd cousin 4 times removed	XII	8
Hershey, Private	3rd cousin 4 times removed	XII	8
Hershey, Ralph Glenn	3rd cousin twice removed	X	6
Hershey, Reba L.	3rd cousin once removed	IX	5
Hershey, Richard Henry	3rd cousin twice removed	X	6
Hershey, Robert Landis	2nd cousin once removed	VII	4
Hershey, Rudolph	2nd cousin 3 times removed	IX	6
Hershey, Samuel	Granduncle	IV	3
Hershey, Samuel F	2nd cousin once removed	VII	4
Hershey, Samuel Harnish	1st cousin once removed	V	3
Hershey, Samuel Mark	2nd cousin	VI	3
Hershey, Sarah	3rd cousin twice removed	X	6
Hershey, Sarah Lucinda	3rd cousin	VIII	4
Hershey, Sarena	Sister	II	1
Hershey, Silas N.	3rd cousin	VIII	4
Hershey, Spencer	4th cousin once removed	XI	6
Hershey, Susan	3rd cousin once removed	IX	5
Hershey, Susan	2nd cousin once removed	VII	4
Hershey, Susan	2nd cousin once removed	VII	4
Hershey, Susan	1st cousin once removed	V	3
Hershey, Susanna	Great-grandmother	III	3
Hershey, Susanna	Grandaunt	IV	3
Hershey, Unnamed	2nd cousin once removed	VII	4
Hershey, Unnamed Infant	2nd cousin 3 times removed	IX	6
Hershey, Unnamed Infant	2nd cousin 3 times removed	IX	6
Hershey, Veronica	Great-grandaunt	V	4
Hershey, Veronica	1st cousin twice removed	VI	4
Hershey, Victor Eby	3rd cousin twice removed	X	6
Hershey, Vincent Denlinger	3rd cousin twice removed	X	6

Name	Relationship with Milton Hershey	Civil	Canon
Hershey, Virginia	1st cousin	IV	2
Hershey, William Nelson	3rd cousin twice removed	X	6
Hershey, Willis Daniel	3rd cousin once removed	IX	5
Hertzler, Abraham	3rd cousin twice removed	X	6
Hertzler, Abram	5th cousin	XII	6
Hertzler, Amos	4th cousin once removed	XI	6
Hertzler, Annie	3rd cousin twice removed	X	6
Hertzler, Barbara	3rd cousin twice removed	X	6
Hertzler, Barbara	Wife of the 4th cousin twice removed		
Hertzler, Barbara	Wife of the 2nd cousin 3 times removed		
Hertzler, Catharine	5th cousin	XII	6
Hertzler, Charles	4th cousin once removed	XI	6
Hertzler, Christian	3rd cousin twice removed	X	6
Hertzler, Christian	4th cousin once removed	XI	6
Hertzler, Daniel	4th cousin once removed	XI	6
Hertzler, Elizabeth	3rd cousin twice removed	X	6
Hertzler, Elizabeth	4th cousin once removed	XI	6
Hertzler, Elizabeth	5th cousin	XII	6
Hertzler, Elizabeth Newcomer	Wife of the 1st cousin 4 times removed		
Hertzler, Emma	5th cousin	XII	6
Hertzler, Gertrude	5th cousin	XII	6
Hertzler, Jacob	3rd cousin twice removed	X	6
Hertzler, Jacob	Husband of the 1st cousin 4 times removed		
Hertzler, John	3rd cousin twice removed	X	6
Hertzler, John	2nd cousin 3 times removed	IX	6
Hertzler, John	4th cousin once removed	XI	6
Hertzler, Martha	5th cousin	XII	6
Hertzler, Mary	3rd cousin twice removed	X	6
Hertzler, Mary	4th cousin once removed	XI	6
Hertzler, Mary	5th cousin	XII	6
Hertzler, May	5th cousin	XII	6
Hertzler, Michael S.	4th cousin once removed	XI	6
Hertzler, Michael S.	5th cousin	XII	6
Hertzler, Rudolph	3rd cousin twice removed	X	6
Hertzler, Rudolph	4th cousin once removed	XI	6
Hertzler, Tobias	5th cousin	XII	6
Hess, Anna	3rd cousin 3 times removed	XI	7
Hess, Anna Hess	Wife of the 4th cousin		
Hess, Annie	1st cousin twice removed	VI	4
Hess, Barbara	3rd cousin 3 times removed	XI	7
Hess, Barbara	1st cousin twice removed	VI	4
Hess, Barbara	2nd cousin once removed	VII	4
Hess, Christian	3rd cousin 3 times removed	XI	7
Hess, Christian	1st cousin twice removed	VI	4
Hess, Christian M.	Spouse of the 2nd cousin		
Hess, Clyde C.	3rd cousin once removed	IX	5
Hess, Elizabeth	3rd cousin 3 times removed	XI	7
Hess, Elizabeth	1st cousin twice removed	VI	4
Hess, Esther	1st cousin twice removed	VI	4
Hess, Harold B	Husband of the 2nd cousin 3 times removed		
Hess, Harriet Ann	3rd cousin once removed	IX	5
Hess, Harry H	3rd cousin once removed	IX	5
Hess, Harry Hershey	3rd cousin once removed	IX	5
Hess, Henry	1st cousin twice removed	VI	4
Hess, Henry H.	Husband of the 3rd cousin		
Hess, Henry L	3rd cousin	VIII	4
Hess, Janet Potter	3rd cousin twice removed	X	6
Hess, John	Husband of the 2nd cousin 4 times removed		
Hess, John	3rd cousin 3 times removed	XI	7
Hess, John	1st cousin twice removed	VI	4
Hess, Joseph H	2nd cousin once removed	VII	4
Hess, Judith	3rd cousin 3 times removed	XI	7
Hess, Magdalena	Wife of the 2nd cousin 4 times removed		
Hess, Magdalene	Wife of the half 6th granduncle		
Hess, Margarette	3rd cousin 3 times removed	XI	7
Hess, Martha H.	1st cousin twice removed	VI	4

The Relations of Milton Snavely Hershey, 4th Ed.

Name	Relationship with Milton Hershey	Civil	Canon
Hess, Mary	3rd cousin 3 times removed	XI	7
Hess, Mildred Elizabeth	3rd cousin once removed	IX	5
Hess, Private	3rd cousin twice removed	X	6
Hess, Rhoda Gregory	3rd cousin twice removed	X	6
Hess, Ruth Wolf	3rd cousin twice removed	X	6
Hess, Samuel	1st cousin twice removed	VI	4
Hess, Samuel H	2nd cousin once removed	VII	4
Hess, Sarah Weidler	3rd cousin	VIII	4
Hess, Susanna	3rd cousin 3 times removed	XI	7
Hess, Susanna	1st cousin twice removed	VI	4
Hess, Sybilla	Wife of the 4th cousin once removed		
Hess, Veronica	3rd cousin 3 times removed	XI	7
Hess, Veronica	Wife of the half granduncle		
Hess, Willis Rutter	3rd cousin once removed	IX	5
Hettinger, A C	Husband of the 6th cousin		
Hettinger, Anna	Wife of the 6th cousin once removed		
Hewes, John Martin	3rd cousin 3 times removed	XI	7
Hewes, Private	3rd cousin 3 times removed	XI	7
Hewes, Private	3rd cousin 3 times removed	XI	7
Hewes, Private	3rd cousin 3 times removed	XI	7
Hewes, Private	3rd cousin 3 times removed	XI	7
Hewes, Private	3rd cousin 3 times removed	XI	7
Hewes, Private	3rd cousin 4 times removed	XII	8
Hewes, Private	3rd cousin 4 times removed	XII	8
Hewes, Thomas Garrett	Husband of the 3rd cousin twice removed		
Hewlett, Barbara Rye	Half 3rd cousin 3 times removed	XI	7
Hewlett, James Edward	Half 3rd cousin 3 times removed	XI	7
Hewlett, Wilfred Murison	Half 3rd cousin 3 times removed	XI	7
Hewlett, William	Husband of the half 3rd cousin twice removed		
Hibshman, Sarah	Wife of the 3rd cousin twice removed		
Hicks, Lizzie	Wife of the 4th cousin once removed		
Hiestand, Ann	Wife of the 2nd great-granduncle		
Hiestand, Elisabeth	Wife of the 2nd cousin 3 times removed		
High, Private	Wife of the 3rd cousin 3 times removed		
High, Private	Wife of the 3rd cousin twice removed		
High, Sarah	Wife of the 2nd cousin 3 times removed		
High/Hoch, Elizabeth Pennypacker	Wife of the 3rd cousin twice removed		
Highers(Unknown), Marie	Wife of the 6th cousin 3 times removed		
Higley, Private	6th cousin 3 times removed	XVII	10
Higley, Private	6th cousin 4 times removed	XVIII	11
Higley, Thomas Henson	Husband of the 6th cousin twice removed		
Hildabrand, Michael	Husband of the 3rd cousin twice removed		
Hillman, Margaret	Wife of the half 3rd cousin twice removed		
Hinton, Private	6th cousin 4 times removed	XVIII	11
Hinton, Private	6th cousin 4 times removed	XVIII	11
Hinton, Private	6th cousin 4 times removed	XVIII	11
Hinton, Private	6th cousin 4 times removed	XVIII	11
Hinton, Rev. John Joseph	Husband of the 6th cousin 3 times removed		
Hippensteel, Robert William	Husband of the 6th cousin twice removed		
Hiscox, Carl	Half 3rd cousin 4 times removed	XII	8
Hiscox, Ray	Husband of the half 3rd cousin 3 times removed		
Hiscox, Sharon	Half 3rd cousin 4 times removed	XII	8
Hiscox, Yvonne	Half 3rd cousin 4 times removed	XII	8
Hitchcock, Alexander Milton	2nd cousin 6 times removed	XII	9
Hitchcock, Jonathan Elliot	2nd cousin 6 times removed	XII	9
Hitchcock, Michael David	Husband of the 2nd cousin 5 times removed		
Hitchcock, Zachary Falcon	2nd cousin 6 times removed	XII	9
Hitz, Amanda Elizabeth	6th cousin 3 times removed	XVII	10
Hitz, Amos G	Husband of the 6th cousin twice removed		
Hitz, Ann Marie	6th cousin 4 times removed	XVIII	11
Hitz, Bradley Allen	6th cousin 5 times removed	XIX	12
Hitz, Brayden Joseph	6th cousin 6 times removed	XX	13
Hitz, Crystal	6th cousin 5 times removed	XIX	12
Hitz, Douglas Wade	6th cousin 5 times removed	XIX	12
Hitz, Elizabeth Ashley	6th cousin 5 times removed	XIX	12
Hitz, Elmer Ezra	6th cousin 3 times removed	XVII	10

Name	Relationship with Milton Hershey	Civil	Canon
Hitz, Elvin Ezra	6th cousin 4 times removed	XVIII	11
Hitz, Florence Mae	6th cousin 3 times removed	XVII	10
Hitz, Galen D	6th cousin 4 times removed	XVIII	11
Hitz, George Richard	6th cousin 3 times removed	XVII	10
Hitz, Jacob Amos	6th cousin 3 times removed	XVII	10
Hitz, Jacob Landis	6th cousin 4 times removed	XVIII	11
Hitz, Jay Mark	6th cousin 3 times removed	XVII	10
Hitz, Jeffrey	6th cousin 5 times removed	XIX	12
Hitz, John Amos	6th cousin 4 times removed	XVIII	11
Hitz, Katherine Jane	6th cousin 4 times removed	XVIII	11
Hitz, Lisa Marie	6th cousin 5 times removed	XIX	12
Hitz, Mary Kathryn	6th cousin 3 times removed	XVII	10
Hitz, Rachel Emma	6th cousin 6 times removed	XX	13
Hoch, Mary	Wife of the 2nd cousin 3 times removed		
Hochstetter, Jacob	Husband of the 4th great-grandaunt		
Hochstrasser, Barbara	7th great-grandmother	IX	9
Hochstrasser, Margaretha	Wife of the 7th great-grandfather		
Hofer, John	Husband of the 6th cousin 3 times removed		
Hofer, Private	6th cousin 4 times removed	XVIII	11
Hofer, Private	6th cousin 4 times removed	XVIII	11
Hofer, Private	6th cousin 4 times removed	XVIII	11
Hofer, Private	6th cousin 4 times removed	XVIII	11
Hofer, Private	6th cousin 4 times removed	XVIII	11
Hofer, Private	6th cousin 4 times removed	XVIII	11
Hofer, Private	6th cousin 4 times removed	XVIII	11
Hofer, Private	6th cousin 4 times removed	XVIII	11
Hofer, Private	6th cousin 4 times removed	XVIII	11
Hoffer, Abraham	Husband of the 6th cousin		
Hoffer, Benjamin	Husband of the 6th cousin		
Hoffman, Anna Mary	Wife of the 6th cousin twice removed		
Hoffman, Elisabeth	6th cousin	XIV	7
Hoffman, Elizabeth	Wife of the 2nd cousin		
Hoffman, Elizabeth	Wife of the 5th cousin once removed		
Hoffman, John	Husband of the 2nd cousin 3 times removed		
Hoffman, John	Husband of the 5th cousin once removed		
Hoffman, Judith	Wife of the 2nd cousin 3 times removed		
Hoffman, Mary A.	Wife of the 3rd cousin twice removed		
Hoffman, Matilda	Wife of the 5th cousin		
Hoffman, Nancy	6th cousin	XIV	7
Hoffman, Private	Husband of the 3rd cousin 3 times removed		
Hoffman, Private	3rd cousin 4 times removed	XII	8
Hoffman, Private	3rd cousin 4 times removed	XII	8
Hoffman, Private	3rd cousin 4 times removed	XII	8
Hoffman, Susan	6th cousin	XIV	7
Hoffstetter, Anna	6th great-grandaunt	X	9
Hoffstetter, Anna	1st cousin 8 times removed	XII	10
Hoffstetter, Anna	6th great-grandaunt	X	9
Hoffstetter, Barbel	1st cousin 8 times removed	XII	10
Hoffstetter, Barbel	6th great-grandaunt	X	9
Hoffstetter, Elsi	6th great-grandaunt	X	9
Hoffstetter, Georg	6th great-granduncle	X	9
Hoffstetter, Hans Jacob	6th great-granduncle	X	9
Hoffstetter, Hans Jacob	1st cousin 8 times removed	XII	10
Hoffstetter, Hans Rudolph	1st cousin 8 times removed	XII	10
Hoffstetter, Heini	1st cousin 8 times removed	XII	10
Hoffstetter, Heinrich	7th great-grandfather	IX	9
Hoffstetter, Heinrich	6th great-grandfather	VIII	8
Hoffstetter, Jacob	7th great-granduncle	XI	10
Hoffstetter, Maria	6th great-grandaunt	X	9
Hoffstetter, Mr	8th great-grandfather	X	10
Hoffstetter, Oswald	1st cousin 8 times removed	XII	10
Hoffstetter, Oswald	6th great-granduncle	X	9
Hoffstetter, Verena	1st cousin 8 times removed	XII	10
Hogendobler, Rose	Wife of the 3rd cousin twice removed		
Hoist, Unknown	Husband of the half 3rd cousin once removed		

Name	Relationship with Milton Hershey	Civil	Canon
Holderbaum, Elizabeth	Wife of the 6th cousin		
Holehan, Catherine	Wife of the 6th cousin twice removed		
Hollar, Mary A.	Wife of the 6th cousin		
Hollinger, Anna	3rd cousin twice removed	X	6
Hollinger, Anna H.	4th cousin once removed	XI	6
Hollinger, Colleen	Wife of the 4th cousin 3 times removed		
Hollinger, David H.	4th cousin once removed	XI	6
Hollinger, Elisabeth Mae	4th cousin once removed	XI	6
Hollinger, Esther H.	4th cousin once removed	XI	6
Hollinger, Isaias H.	4th cousin once removed	XI	6
Hollinger, Jacob	3rd cousin twice removed	X	6
Hollinger, Jacob H.	4th cousin once removed	XI	6
Hollinger, Johannes	3rd cousin twice removed	X	6
Hollinger, Johannes H.	4th cousin once removed	XI	6
Hollinger, Magdalene	4th cousin once removed	XI	6
Hollinger, Maria Ann	4th cousin once removed	XI	6
Hollinger, Moses	3rd cousin twice removed	X	6
Hollinger, Private	Wife of the 3rd cousin 4 times removed		
Hollinger, Rebecca H.	4th cousin once removed	XI	6
Hollinger, Samuel	3rd cousin twice removed	X	6
Hollinger, Susanna	4th cousin once removed	XI	6
Hollinger, Thomas	Husband of the 5th cousin 3 times removed		
Hollinger, Thomas	Husband of the 2nd cousin 3 times removed		
Hollinger, Thomas J.	4th cousin once removed	XI	6
Hoober, Private	Wife of the 3rd cousin twice removed		
Hoopes, Private	Wife of the 6th cousin 3 times removed		
Hoover, Abraham	4th cousin once removed	XI	6
Hoover, Amos H.	Husband of the 3rd cousin		
Hoover, Anna	6th cousin	XIV	7
Hoover, Annie	2nd cousin	VI	3
Hoover, Barbara	6th cousin	XIV	7
Hoover, Bella	Half 3rd cousin twice removed	X	6
Hoover, Benjamin	4th cousin once removed	XI	6
Hoover, Benjamin	Husband of the 3rd cousin twice removed		
Hoover, Benjamin	4th cousin once removed	XI	6
Hoover, Betty	Half 3rd cousin 3 times removed	XI	7
Hoover, Blanche	Half 3rd cousin 3 times removed	XI	7
Hoover, Catharine	6th cousin	XIV	7
Hoover, Catharine	Wife of the 6th cousin		
Hoover, Catherine	Wife of the 3rd cousin twice removed		
Hoover, Charles	Husband of the half 3rd cousin twice removed		
Hoover, Charolette	Wife of the half 3rd cousin once removed		
Hoover, Christian	6th cousin	XIV	7
Hoover, Christian	4th cousin once removed	XI	6
Hoover, Christian H.	4th cousin once removed	XI	6
Hoover, Clarence	Husband of the half 3rd cousin twice removed		
Hoover, David	6th cousin	XIV	7
Hoover, Donald	Half 3rd cousin 3 times removed	XI	7
Hoover, Doris	Half 3rd cousin 3 times removed	XI	7
Hoover, Earl	Husband of the half 3rd cousin 3 times removed		
Hoover, Edith	Half 3rd cousin twice removed	X	6
Hoover, Edward	Husband of the half 3rd cousin twice removed		
Hoover, Elizabeth	Wife of the 5th cousin once removed		
Hoover, Elizabeth	4th cousin once removed	XI	6
Hoover, Elizabeth R.	4th cousin once removed	XI	6
Hoover, Emanuel	Husband of the 5th cousin once removed		
Hoover, Esther	Wife of the 2nd cousin 3 times removed		
Hoover, Esther R.	4th cousin once removed	XI	6
Hoover, Flora	Half 3rd cousin twice removed	X	6
Hoover, Florence	Half 3rd cousin 3 times removed	XI	7
Hoover, Frances	Wife of the half 3rd cousin once removed		
Hoover, George	Half 3rd cousin twice removed	X	6
Hoover, Helen	Half 3rd cousin 3 times removed	XI	7
Hoover, Henry	4th cousin once removed	XI	6
Hoover, Herbert	Half 3rd cousin 3 times removed	XI	7
Hoover, Isaac	4th cousin once removed	XI	6

Name	Relationship with Milton Hershey	Civil	Canon
Hoover, Jacob	Husband of the 5th cousin 3 times removed		
Hoover, Jennie	Half 3rd cousin twice removed	X	6
Hoover, John	6th cousin	XIV	7
Hoover, John	Husband of the 3rd cousin twice removed		
Hoover, John D.	4th cousin once removed	XI	6
Hoover, John R.	4th cousin once removed	XI	6
Hoover, Jonathan	4th cousin once removed	XI	6
Hoover, Leah	2nd cousin	VI	3
Hoover, Martin	Husband of the 1st cousin once removed		
Hoover, Mary A.	6th cousin	XIV	7
Hoover, Mary Catherine	4th cousin once removed	XI	6
Hoover, Michael	Husband of the 3rd cousin twice removed		
Hoover, Michael	4th cousin once removed	XI	6
Hoover, Nancy Ann	4th cousin once removed	XI	6
Hoover, Nancy R.	4th cousin once removed	XI	6
Hoover, Private	Husband of the 3rd cousin 4 times removed		
Hoover, Private	Wife of the 3rd cousin 3 times removed		
Hoover, Private	Half 3rd cousin 4 times removed	XII	8
Hoover, Risser	4th cousin once removed	XI	6
Hoover, Ruth	Half 3rd cousin twice removed	X	6
Hoover, Samuel R.	4th cousin once removed	XI	6
Hoover, Sarah	Wife of the 3rd cousin twice removed		
Hoover, Simeon	Husband of the half 3rd cousin once removed		
Hoover, Stephen R.	4th cousin once removed	XI	6
Hoover, Wesley	Half 3rd cousin 4 times removed	XII	8
Hopkins, Barbara G	6th cousin 4 times removed	XVIII	11
Hopkins, Gary Lee	6th cousin 4 times removed	XVIII	11
Hopkins, Unknown	Husband of the 6th cousin 3 times removed		
Horn, Emma A	Wife of the 6th cousin twice removed		
Horning, Alice Celesta	Wife of the half 3rd cousin once removed		
Horning, Esther Mae	3rd cousin 4 times removed	XII	8
Horning, Ida E.	Wife of the half 3rd cousin once removed		
Horning, Joseph	Husband of the 2nd cousin 3 times removed		
Horning, Private	Husband of the 3rd cousin 3 times removed		
Horning, Private	3rd cousin 4 times removed	XII	8
Horning, Private	3rd cousin 4 times removed	XII	8
Horning, Private	3rd cousin 4 times removed	XII	8
Horning, Private	3rd cousin 4 times removed	XII	8
Horning, Private	3rd cousin 4 times removed	XII	8
Horning, Private	3rd cousin 4 times removed	XII	8
Horning, Private	3rd cousin 4 times removed	XII	8
Horning, Private	3rd cousin 4 times removed	XII	8
Horning, Private	3rd cousin 4 times removed	XII	8
Horning, Private	Wife of the 3rd cousin 3 times removed		
Horning, Zilpha	Wife of the half 3rd cousin once removed		
Horst, Ada	Wife of the 4th cousin once removed		
Horst, Ada Sweigart	3rd cousin once removed	IX	5
Horst, Amos David	3rd cousin twice removed	X	6
Horst, Amos Sweigart	3rd cousin once removed	IX	5
Horst, Anna	Wife of the great-granduncle		
Horst, Anna	5th cousin 3 times removed	XV	9
Horst, Anna	2nd cousin 3 times removed	IX	6
Horst, Anna	2nd cousin 3 times removed	IX	6
Horst, Anna	Wife of the 5th cousin 3 times removed		
Horst, Anna	6th cousin	XIV	7
Horst, Anna Lois	3rd cousin twice removed	X	6
Horst, Anna M.	3rd cousin twice removed	X	6
Horst, Anna Sweigart	3rd cousin once removed	IX	5
Horst, Barbara	4th cousin 4 times removed	XIV	9
Horst, Barbara	6th cousin	XIV	7
Horst, Barbara M.	3rd cousin twice removed	X	6
Horst, Blaine Zook	3rd cousin twice removed	X	6
Horst, Carl Zook	3rd cousin twice removed	X	6
Horst, Catharine	6th cousin	XIV	7
Horst, Catherine	5th cousin 3 times removed	XV	9
Horst, Cedric Linn	3rd cousin 3 times removed	XI	7

Name	Relationship with Milton Hershey	Civil	Canon
Horst, Christian	4th cousin 4 times removed	XIV	9
Horst, Christian	5th cousin 3 times removed	XV	9
Horst, Christina	4th cousin 4 times removed	XIV	9
Horst, Christina	5th cousin 3 times removed	XV	9
Horst, Christine Marie	3rd cousin 4 times removed	XII	8
Horst, Daniel	2nd cousin 3 times removed	IX	6
Horst, David	4th cousin 4 times removed	XIV	9
Horst, David Campbell	3rd cousin twice removed	X	6
Horst, Diane L.	3rd cousin 3 times removed	XI	7
Horst, Dorothy A.	3rd cousin twice removed	X	6
Horst, Douglas Clyde	3rd cousin twice removed	X	6
Horst, Elam Sweigart	3rd cousin once removed	IX	5
Horst, Eli Sweigart	3rd cousin once removed	IX	5
Horst, Eliza	6th cousin	XIV	7
Horst, Elizabeth	4th cousin 4 times removed	XIV	9
Horst, Elizabeth	5th cousin 3 times removed	XV	9
Horst, Elizabeth	2nd cousin 3 times removed	IX	6
Horst, Enos Heatwole	3rd cousin twice removed	X	6
Horst, Erma Steffy	3rd cousin twice removed	X	6
Horst, Ester	3rd cousin twice removed	X	6
Horst, Fanny	2nd cousin 3 times removed	IX	6
Horst, Feronica	4th cousin 4 times removed	XIV	9
Horst, Feronica	5th cousin 3 times removed	XV	9
Horst, Frances Sweigart	3rd cousin once removed	IX	5
Horst, Gail Marie	3rd cousin 4 times removed	XII	8
Horst, Gary Paul	3rd cousin 4 times removed	XII	8
Horst, Gordon Steffy	3rd cousin twice removed	X	6
Horst, Henry	5th cousin 3 times removed	XV	9
Horst, Henry M.	3rd cousin twice removed	X	6
Horst, Henry Reuben	3rd cousin twice removed	X	6
Horst, Jacob	Husband of the 1st cousin 4 times removed		
Horst, Jacob	Husband of the 2nd cousin 3 times removed		
Horst, Jacob M.	3rd cousin twice removed	X	6
Horst, Jacob Sweigart	3rd cousin once removed	IX	5
Horst, Jacob W.	2nd cousin 3 times removed	IX	6
Horst, James Albert	3rd cousin twice removed	X	6
Horst, James Daniel	3rd cousin twice removed	X	6
Horst, James Richard	3rd cousin 3 times removed	XI	7
Horst, Janet Elaine	3rd cousin twice removed	X	6
Horst, Jeanne Loraine	3rd cousin twice removed	X	6
Horst, Joan Elaine	3rd cousin 3 times removed	XI	7
Horst, Joann Louise	3rd cousin 3 times removed	XI	7
Horst, John	5th cousin 3 times removed	XV	9
Horst, John	4th cousin 4 times removed	XIV	9
Horst, John Alton	3rd cousin twice removed	X	6
Horst, John Landis	3rd cousin twice removed	X	6
Horst, John Mark	3rd cousin twice removed	X	6
Horst, John W.	2nd cousin 3 times removed	IX	6
Horst, John W.	2nd cousin 3 times removed	IX	6
Horst, Jonathan Lynn	3rd cousin 4 times removed	XII	8
Horst, Joseph	Husband of the 3rd cousin 5 times removed		
Horst, Joseph	5th cousin 3 times removed	XV	9
Horst, Joseph	2nd cousin 3 times removed	IX	6
Horst, Joseph	Husband of the 5th cousin once removed		
Horst, Joseph Franklin	3rd cousin twice removed	X	6
Horst, Joseph M.	3rd cousin twice removed	X	6
Horst, Joseph Shenk	6th cousin	XIV	7
Horst, Katie Sweigart	3rd cousin once removed	IX	5
Horst, Kenneth Moseman	3rd cousin twice removed	X	6
Horst, Lee Sterling	3rd cousin twice removed	X	6
Horst, Lloyd Sweigart	3rd cousin once removed	IX	5
Horst, Lois Esther	3rd cousin twice removed	X	6
Horst, Lois Jean	3rd cousin twice removed	X	6
Horst, Magdalena	5th cousin 3 times removed	XV	9
Horst, Magdalena	2nd cousin 3 times removed	IX	6
Horst, Margaret	2nd cousin 3 times removed	IX	6

Name	Relationship with Milton Hershey	Civil	Canon
Horst, Maria G.	4th cousin 4 times removed	XIV	9
Horst, Mark William	3rd cousin 3 times removed	XI	7
Horst, Martha Frances	3rd cousin twice removed	X	6
Horst, Martha Steffy	3rd cousin twice removed	X	6
Horst, Mary	5th cousin 3 times removed	XV	9
Horst, Mary	2nd cousin 3 times removed	IX	6
Horst, Mary Louise	3rd cousin 3 times removed	XI	7
Horst, Mary M.	3rd cousin twice removed	X	6
Horst, Mathias M.	3rd cousin twice removed	X	6
Horst, Michael	4th cousin 4 times removed	XIV	9
Horst, Milton S.	Husband of the 3rd cousin once removed		
Horst, Miriam Darlene	3rd cousin twice removed	X	6
Horst, Miriam Elizabeth	3rd cousin twice removed	X	6
Horst, Misty Dawn	3rd cousin 4 times removed	XII	8
Horst, Moses	2nd cousin 3 times removed	IX	6
Horst, Nancy	5th cousin 3 times removed	XV	9
Horst, Noah Sweigart	3rd cousin once removed	IX	5
Horst, Paul Gary	3rd cousin 3 times removed	XI	7
Horst, Paul Howard	3rd cousin 4 times removed	XII	8
Horst, Paul Steffy	3rd cousin twice removed	X	6
Horst, Phares Sweigart	3rd cousin once removed	IX	5
Horst, Private	Husband of the 3rd cousin 3 times removed		
Horst, Private	3rd cousin 4 times removed	XII	8
Horst, Private	3rd cousin 4 times removed	XII	8
Horst, Private	3rd cousin 4 times removed	XII	8
Horst, Private	3rd cousin 4 times removed	XII	8
Horst, Private	3rd cousin 4 times removed	XII	8
Horst, Private	3rd cousin 4 times removed	XII	8
Horst, Private	3rd cousin 4 times removed	XII	8
Horst, Private	3rd cousin 4 times removed	XII	8
Horst, Private	Wife of the 3rd cousin 3 times removed		
Horst, Private	Wife of the 3rd cousin 3 times removed		
Horst, Private	Wife of the 3rd cousin 3 times removed		
Horst, Quintis	3rd cousin twice removed	X	6
Horst, Rachel Frances	3rd cousin twice removed	X	6
Horst, Randy Paul	3rd cousin 3 times removed	XI	7
Horst, Ray Ernest	3rd cousin twice removed	X	6
Horst, Reuben Sweigart	3rd cousin once removed	IX	5
Horst, Reuben Walter	3rd cousin twice removed	X	6
Horst, Reuben Weaver	4th cousin once removed	XI	6
Horst, Richard M.	3rd cousin twice removed	X	6
Horst, Rodney William	3rd cousin 3 times removed	XI	7
Horst, Ronald Gregory	3rd cousin 3 times removed	XI	7
Horst, Ruth Naomi	3rd cousin twice removed	X	6
Horst, Samuel	6th cousin	XIV	7
Horst, Shannon Lea	3rd cousin 4 times removed	XII	8
Horst, Shelby Lynn	3rd cousin 4 times removed	XII	8
Horst, Susanna	2nd cousin 3 times removed	IX	6
Horst, Susanna M.	3rd cousin twice removed	X	6
Horst, Susannah	5th cousin 3 times removed	XV	9
Horst, Titus Glenn	3rd cousin twice removed	X	6
Horst, Titus Sweigart	3rd cousin once removed	IX	5
Horst, Walter Dale	3rd cousin twice removed	X	6
Horst, Walter Sweigart	3rd cousin once removed	IX	5
Horst, William Mark	3rd cousin 4 times removed	XII	8
Horst, William Prichard	3rd cousin twice removed	X	6
Hostetter, Aaron	4th cousin once removed	XI	6
Hostetter, Aaron	4th cousin once removed	XI	6
Hostetter, Abner	4th cousin once removed	XI	6
Hostetter, Abraham	1st cousin 4 times removed	VIII	6
Hostetter, Abraham	2nd cousin 3 times removed	IX	6
Hostetter, Abraham	3rd cousin twice removed	X	6
Hostetter, Abraham	1st cousin 4 times removed	VIII	6
Hostetter, Abraham	2nd cousin 3 times removed	IX	6
Hostetter, Abraham	3rd cousin twice removed	X	6

The Relations of Milton Snavely Hershey, 4th Ed.

Name	Relationship with Milton Hershey	Civil	Canon
Hostetter, Abraham	3rd great-granduncle	VII	6
Hostetter, Abraham	2nd cousin 3 times removed	IX	6
Hostetter, Abraham	2nd great-granduncle	VI	5
Hostetter, Abraham	2nd great-granduncle	VI	5
Hostetter, Abraham	1st cousin 3 times removed	VII	5
Hostetter, Abraham	2nd cousin 3 times removed	IX	6
Hostetter, Abraham	2nd cousin 3 times removed	IX	6
Hostetter, Abraham	1st cousin 3 times removed	VII	5
Hostetter, Abraham	2nd cousin 3 times removed	IX	6
Hostetter, Abraham	2nd cousin 3 times removed	IX	6
Hostetter, Abraham	2nd cousin 3 times removed	IX	6
Hostetter, Abraham	2nd cousin twice removed	VIII	5
Hostetter, Abraham	2nd cousin twice removed	VIII	5
Hostetter, Abraham	3rd cousin twice removed	X	6
Hostetter, Abraham	3rd cousin twice removed	X	6
Hostetter, Abraham	3rd cousin twice removed	X	6
Hostetter, Abraham	3rd cousin twice removed	X	6
Hostetter, Abraham	3rd cousin twice removed	X	6
Hostetter, Abraham	4th cousin once removed	XI	6
Hostetter, Abraham	3rd cousin twice removed	X	6
Hostetter, Abraham	3rd cousin once removed	IX	5
Hostetter, Abraham	4th cousin once removed	XI	6
Hostetter, Abraham	4th cousin once removed	XI	6
Hostetter, Abraham F.	3rd cousin twice removed	X	6
Hostetter, Abraham Webster	3rd cousin once removed	IX	5
Hostetter, Abram	5th cousin	XII	6
Hostetter, Abram	4th cousin once removed	XI	6
Hostetter, Adaline	4th cousin	X	5
Hostetter, Adaline	5th cousin	XII	6
Hostetter, Adele	3rd cousin once removed	IX	5
Hostetter, Adella	4th cousin	X	5
Hostetter, Alice	4th cousin once removed	XI	6
Hostetter, Alice M	3rd cousin once removed	IX	5
Hostetter, Alverta	4th cousin once removed	XI	6
Hostetter, Amos	4th cousin once removed	XI	6
Hostetter, Amos	5th cousin	XII	6
Hostetter, Amos	4th cousin once removed	XI	6
Hostetter, Amos	4th cousin once removed	XI	6
Hostetter, Amos	4th cousin once removed	XI	6
Hostetter, Amos J	4th cousin once removed	XI	6
Hostetter, Amy Susette	4th cousin once removed	XI	6
Hostetter, Ann	2nd cousin 3 times removed	IX	6
Hostetter, Ann	4th cousin 3 times removed	XIII	8
Hostetter, Ann	3rd cousin twice removed	X	6
Hostetter, Ann	2nd cousin twice removed	VIII	5
Hostetter, Ann	2nd cousin 3 times removed	IX	6
Hostetter, Ann	2nd cousin 3 times removed	IX	6
Hostetter, Ann	2nd cousin twice removed	VIII	5
Hostetter, Ann	3rd cousin twice removed	X	6
Hostetter, Ann	3rd cousin twice removed	X	6
Hostetter, Ann	3rd cousin twice removed	X	6
Hostetter, Ann Marie	3rd cousin once removed	IX	5
Hostetter, Ann R	4th cousin once removed	XI	6
Hostetter, Anna	3rd great-grandaunt	VII	6
Hostetter, Anna	2nd great-grandaunt	VI	5
Hostetter, Anna	1st cousin 4 times removed	VIII	6
Hostetter, Anna	1st cousin 3 times removed	VII	5
Hostetter, Anna	2nd cousin 3 times removed	IX	6
Hostetter, Anna	4th cousin once removed	XI	6
Hostetter, Anna	3rd cousin twice removed	X	6
Hostetter, Anna	3rd cousin twice removed	X	6
Hostetter, Anna	3rd cousin 4 times removed	XII	8
Hostetter, Anna	3rd cousin twice removed	X	6
Hostetter, Anna	2nd cousin twice removed	VIII	5
Hostetter, Anna	1st cousin 3 times removed	VII	5
Hostetter, Anna	2nd great-grandaunt	VI	5

Name	Relationship with Milton Hershey	Civil	Canon
Hostetter, Anna	2nd cousin 3 times removed	IX	6
Hostetter, Anna	3rd cousin twice removed	X	6
Hostetter, Anna	2nd cousin 3 times removed	IX	6
Hostetter, Anna	5th great-grandaunt	IX	8
Hostetter, Anna	1st cousin 5 times removed	IX	7
Hostetter, Anna	1st cousin 4 times removed	VIII	6
Hostetter, Anna	1st cousin 4 times removed	VIII	6
Hostetter, Anna	1st cousin 3 times removed	VII	5
Hostetter, Anna	2nd cousin 3 times removed	IX	6
Hostetter, Anna	2nd cousin 3 times removed	IX	6
Hostetter, Anna	2nd cousin 3 times removed	IX	6
Hostetter, Anna	2nd cousin 3 times removed	IX	6
Hostetter, Anna	2nd cousin 3 times removed	IX	6
Hostetter, Anna	3rd cousin twice removed	X	6
Hostetter, Anna	3rd cousin twice removed	X	6
Hostetter, Anna	3rd cousin twice removed	X	6
Hostetter, Anna	3rd cousin twice removed	X	6
Hostetter, Anna	3rd cousin twice removed	X	6
Hostetter, Anna	3rd cousin twice removed	X	6
Hostetter, Anna	3rd cousin once removed	IX	5
Hostetter, Anna	4th cousin once removed	XI	6
Hostetter, Anna Magdalena	4th cousin once removed	XI	6
Hostetter, Annali	1st cousin 6 times removed	X	8
Hostetter, Anney	2nd cousin twice removed	VIII	5
Hostetter, Annie	3rd cousin twice removed	X	6
Hostetter, Annie	2nd cousin twice removed	VIII	5
Hostetter, Annie	3rd cousin twice removed	X	6
Hostetter, Annie	3rd cousin once removed	IX	5
Hostetter, Barbara	2nd cousin 3 times removed	IX	6
Hostetter, Barbara	2nd cousin 3 times removed	IX	6
Hostetter, Barbara	3rd cousin twice removed	X	6
Hostetter, Barbara	4th cousin 3 times removed	XIII	8
Hostetter, Barbara	1st cousin 3 times removed	VII	5
Hostetter, Barbara	1st cousin 4 times removed	VIII	6
Hostetter, Barbara	2nd cousin twice removed	VIII	5
Hostetter, Barbara	2nd cousin 3 times removed	IX	6
Hostetter, Barbara	2nd cousin 3 times removed	IX	6
Hostetter, Barbara	3rd cousin twice removed	X	6
Hostetter, Barbara	3rd great-grandaunt	VII	6
Hostetter, Barbara	1st cousin 5 times removed	IX	7
Hostetter, Barbara	2nd great-grandaunt	VI	5
Hostetter, Barbara	2nd great-grandaunt	VI	5
Hostetter, Barbara	1st cousin 4 times removed	VIII	6
Hostetter, Barbara	1st cousin 4 times removed	VIII	6
Hostetter, Barbara	3rd cousin 4 times removed	XII	8
Hostetter, Barbara	2nd cousin 3 times removed	IX	6
Hostetter, Barbara	1st cousin 3 times removed	VII	5
Hostetter, Barbara	2nd cousin twice removed	VIII	5
Hostetter, Barbara	4th cousin once removed	XI	6
Hostetter, Barbara "	Wife of the 2nd cousin 3 times removed		
Hostetter, Barbeli	1st cousin 6 times removed	X	8
Hostetter, Bella	4th cousin	X	5
Hostetter, Benjamin	2nd cousin twice removed	VIII	5
Hostetter, Benjamin	4th cousin once removed	XI	6
Hostetter, Benjamin	4th cousin once removed	XI	6
Hostetter, Benjamin	2nd great-granduncle	VI	5
Hostetter, Benjamin	2nd great-granduncle	VI	5
Hostetter, Benjamin	1st cousin 3 times removed	VII	5
Hostetter, Benjamin	2nd cousin 3 times removed	IX	6
Hostetter, Benjamin	3rd cousin once removed	IX	5
Hostetter, Benjamin	3rd cousin twice removed	X	6
Hostetter, Benjamin	3rd cousin twice removed	X	6
Hostetter, Benjamin	3rd cousin once removed	IX	5
Hostetter, Benjamin	3rd cousin twice removed	X	6
Hostetter, Benjamin	4th cousin	X	5
Hostetter, Benjamin	3rd cousin once removed	IX	5

Name	Relationship with Milton Hershey	Civil	Canon
Hostetter, Benjamin D.	3rd cousin once removed	IX	5
Hostetter, Benjamin F	3rd cousin once removed	IX	5
Hostetter, Benjamin F.	3rd cousin twice removed	X	6
Hostetter, Bert	3rd cousin once removed	IX	5
Hostetter, Bessie Grace	3rd cousin once removed	IX	5
Hostetter, Beth	5th cousin	XII	6
Hostetter, Catharine	1st cousin 3 times removed	VII	5
Hostetter, Catharine	3rd cousin twice removed	X	6
Hostetter, Catharine	4th cousin once removed	XI	6
Hostetter, Catharine	4th cousin once removed	XI	6
Hostetter, Catherine	3rd great-grandaunt	VII	6
Hostetter, Catherine	2nd cousin 3 times removed	IX	6
Hostetter, Catherine	2nd cousin 3 times removed	IX	6
Hostetter, Catherine	2nd cousin 3 times removed	IX	6
Hostetter, Catherine	3rd cousin twice removed	X	6
Hostetter, Catherine	4th cousin once removed	XI	6
Hostetter, Catherine	2nd cousin 3 times removed	IX	6
Hostetter, Catherine	3rd cousin twice removed	X	6
Hostetter, Catherine	2nd cousin 3 times removed	IX	6
Hostetter, Catherine	2nd cousin 3 times removed	IX	6
Hostetter, Catherine	2nd cousin 3 times removed	IX	6
Hostetter, Catherine	3rd cousin twice removed	X	6
Hostetter, Catherine	3rd cousin twice removed	X	6
Hostetter, Catherine	2nd cousin 3 times removed	IX	6
Hostetter, Catherine	3rd cousin twice removed	X	6
Hostetter, Catherine	2nd cousin twice removed	VIII	5
Hostetter, Catherine	3rd cousin twice removed	X	6
Hostetter, Catherine	3rd cousin twice removed	X	6
Hostetter, Catherine	3rd cousin twice removed	X	6
Hostetter, Catherine	3rd cousin twice removed	X	6
Hostetter, Catherine	4th cousin once removed	XI	6
Hostetter, Cathri	5th great-grandaunt	IX	8
Hostetter, Cecilia	3rd cousin once removed	IX	5
Hostetter, Cephas	3rd cousin once removed	IX	5
Hostetter, Charles	3rd cousin twice removed	X	6
Hostetter, Charles E	4th cousin	X	5
Hostetter, Charlotte	2nd cousin 3 times removed	IX	6
Hostetter, Charlotte	2nd cousin 3 times removed	IX	6
Hostetter, Christian	2nd cousin 3 times removed	IX	6
Hostetter, Christian	2nd cousin 3 times removed	IX	6
Hostetter, Christian	3rd cousin twice removed	X	6
Hostetter, Christian	2nd cousin 3 times removed	IX	6
Hostetter, Christian	2nd cousin twice removed	VIII	5
Hostetter, Christian	2nd cousin 3 times removed	IX	6
Hostetter, Christian	1st cousin 4 times removed	VIII	6
Hostetter, Christian	1st cousin 4 times removed	VIII	6
Hostetter, Christian	1st cousin 4 times removed	VIII	6
Hostetter, Christian	2nd cousin 3 times removed	IX	6
Hostetter, Christian	2nd cousin 3 times removed	IX	6
Hostetter, Christian	3rd cousin twice removed	X	6
Hostetter, Christian	3rd cousin twice removed	X	6
Hostetter, Christian	3rd cousin twice removed	X	6
Hostetter, Christian	3rd cousin twice removed	X	6
Hostetter, Christian	2nd cousin twice removed	VIII	5
Hostetter, Christian A.	3rd cousin twice removed	X	6
Hostetter, Christian F.	3rd cousin twice removed	X	6
Hostetter, Christian K.	3rd cousin twice removed	X	6
Hostetter, Christina	3rd cousin once removed	IX	5
Hostetter, Clarence White	4th cousin	X	5
Hostetter, Clement	3rd cousin once removed	IX	5
Hostetter, Cyrus	4th cousin once removed	XI	6
Hostetter, D. Herbert	5th cousin	XII	6
Hostetter, Daniel	3rd cousin twice removed	X	6
Hostetter, Daniel	3rd cousin twice removed	X	6
Hostetter, Daniel	2nd cousin 3 times removed	IX	6
Hostetter, Daniel	3rd cousin twice removed	X	6

Name	Relationship with Milton Hershey	Civil	Canon
Hostetter, Daniel	3rd cousin twice removed	X	6
Hostetter, Daniel M	4th cousin once removed	XI	6
Hostetter, David	3rd cousin twice removed	X	6
Hostetter, David	2nd cousin twice removed	VIII	5
Hostetter, David	3rd cousin twice removed	X	6
Hostetter, David	3rd cousin twice removed	X	6
Hostetter, David	3rd cousin twice removed	X	6
Hostetter, David	2nd cousin twice removed	VIII	5
Hostetter, David	2nd cousin twice removed	VIII	5
Hostetter, David	2nd cousin twice removed	VIII	5
Hostetter, David	3rd cousin twice removed	X	6
Hostetter, David	3rd cousin once removed	IX	5
Hostetter, David	4th cousin	X	5
Hostetter, David F.	3rd cousin twice removed	X	6
Hostetter, David H.	4th cousin once removed	XI	6
Hostetter, David M	3rd cousin once removed	IX	5
Hostetter, David M	4th cousin once removed	XI	6
Hostetter, David R	3rd cousin once removed	IX	5
Hostetter, Deborah	2nd cousin 3 times removed	IX	6
Hostetter, E. Maurice	4th cousin	X	5
Hostetter, Earl W	4th cousin	X	5
Hostetter, Edward	3rd cousin once removed	IX	5
Hostetter, Elam	4th cousin once removed	XI	6
Hostetter, Elias	3rd cousin twice removed	X	6
Hostetter, Elisabeth	2nd cousin 3 times removed	IX	6
Hostetter, Elisabeth	2nd cousin 3 times removed	IX	6
Hostetter, Elisabeth	3rd cousin once removed	IX	5
Hostetter, Elisabeth	3rd cousin twice removed	X	6
Hostetter, Elisabeth	3rd cousin twice removed	X	6
Hostetter, Elisabeth	4th cousin once removed	XI	6
Hostetter, Elisabeth	2nd cousin 3 times removed	IX	6
Hostetter, Elisabeth	3rd great-grandaunt	VII	6
Hostetter, Elisabeth	2nd cousin 3 times removed	IX	6
Hostetter, Elisabeth	1st cousin 3 times removed	VII	5
Hostetter, Elisabeth	2nd cousin 3 times removed	IX	6
Hostetter, Elisabeth	1st cousin 3 times removed	VII	5
Hostetter, Elisabeth	3rd cousin twice removed	X	6
Hostetter, Elisabeth	3rd cousin twice removed	X	6
Hostetter, Elisabeth	3rd cousin twice removed	X	6
Hostetter, Elisabeth	3rd cousin once removed	IX	5
Hostetter, Elisabeth	3rd cousin once removed	IX	5
Hostetter, Elisabeth Ann	4th cousin once removed	XI	6
Hostetter, Elisabeth Jane	3rd cousin twice removed	X	6
Hostetter, Elisabeth Maria	2nd great-grandmother	IV	4
Hostetter, Elizabeth	2nd cousin 3 times removed	IX	6
Hostetter, Elizabeth	2nd cousin twice removed	VIII	5
Hostetter, Elizabeth	3rd cousin twice removed	X	6
Hostetter, Elizabeth	4th cousin 3 times removed	XIII	8
Hostetter, Elizabeth	2nd cousin twice removed	VIII	5
Hostetter, Elizabeth	2nd great-grandaunt	VI	5
Hostetter, Elizabeth	2nd cousin twice removed	VIII	5
Hostetter, Elizabeth	1st cousin 3 times removed	VII	5
Hostetter, Elizabeth	2nd cousin 3 times removed	IX	6
Hostetter, Elizabeth	3rd cousin twice removed	X	6
Hostetter, Elizabeth	2nd cousin 3 times removed	IX	6
Hostetter, Elizabeth	3rd cousin twice removed	X	6
Hostetter, Elizabeth	2nd cousin twice removed	VIII	5
Hostetter, Elizabeth	Wife of the 1st cousin once removed		
Hostetter, Elizabeth	3rd cousin twice removed	X	6
Hostetter, Elizabeth	3rd cousin once removed	IX	5
Hostetter, Elizabeth K.	3rd cousin twice removed	X	6
Hostetter, Ella	4th cousin once removed	XI	6
Hostetter, Elsbeth	5th great-grandaunt	IX	8
Hostetter, Emanuel	3rd cousin twice removed	X	6
Hostetter, Emanuel F	3rd cousin once removed	IX	5
Hostetter, Emanuel H	4th cousin once removed	XI	6

Name	Relationship with Milton Hershey	Civil	Canon
Hostetter, Emanuel P	3rd cousin once removed	IX	5
Hostetter, Emma	4th cousin once removed	XI	6
Hostetter, Emma Elisabeth	4th cousin once removed	XI	6
Hostetter, Emma J	4th cousin once removed	XI	6
Hostetter, Emma Jane	4th cousin once removed	XI	6
Hostetter, Emma Jane	4th cousin once removed	XI	6
Hostetter, Emma M	4th cousin once removed	XI	6
Hostetter, Emmanuel	3rd cousin twice removed	X	6
Hostetter, Emmanuel	2nd cousin twice removed	VIII	5
Hostetter, Emmanuel	3rd cousin twice removed	X	6
Hostetter, Emmanuel	2nd cousin twice removed	VIII	5
Hostetter, Ephraim	3rd cousin once removed	IX	5
Hostetter, Ephraim	4th cousin once removed	XI	6
Hostetter, Ervilla	4th cousin	X	5
Hostetter, Esther	2nd great-grandaunt	VI	5
Hostetter, Esther	1st cousin 3 times removed	VII	5
Hostetter, Esther	2nd great-grandaunt	VI	5
Hostetter, Eva	4th cousin once removed	XI	6
Hostetter, Ezra	4th cousin once removed	XI	6
Hostetter, Ezra	2nd cousin twice removed	VIII	5
Hostetter, Fannie	4th cousin once removed	XI	6
Hostetter, Fanny	2nd cousin twice removed	VIII	5
Hostetter, Fanny	4th cousin once removed	XI	6
Hostetter, Feronica	2nd cousin twice removed	VIII	5
Hostetter, Fianna	3rd cousin once removed	IX	5
Hostetter, Florence	4th cousin	X	5
Hostetter, Florence Ethel	4th cousin	X	5
Hostetter, Floyd R	4th cousin	X	5
Hostetter, Frank L	3rd cousin once removed	IX	5
Hostetter, Franklin	3rd cousin twice removed	X	6
Hostetter, Frederick	5th cousin	XII	6
Hostetter, Fronica	2nd cousin twice removed	VIII	5
Hostetter, George	2nd cousin 3 times removed	IX	6
Hostetter, George Washington	4th cousin	X	5
Hostetter, Grace E	4th cousin	X	5
Hostetter, Hannah	4th cousin once removed	XI	6
Hostetter, Hans	5th great-granduncle	IX	8
Hostetter, Hans	1st cousin 6 times removed	X	8
Hostetter, Hans Heinrich	5th great-granduncle	IX	8
Hostetter, Hans Heinrich	1st cousin 6 times removed	X	8
Hostetter, Hans Jagli	5th great-granduncle	IX	8
Hostetter, Harriet	3rd cousin once removed	IX	5
Hostetter, Harriet A	3rd cousin once removed	IX	5
Hostetter, Harriet Ester	3rd cousin once removed	IX	5
Hostetter, Harry H.	4th cousin once removed	XI	6
Hostetter, Harry Jacob	4th cousin	X	5
Hostetter, Heber	5th cousin	XII	6
Hostetter, Helen	3rd cousin twice removed	X	6
Hostetter, Helen	5th cousin	XII	6
Hostetter, Helen	3rd cousin twice removed	X	6
Hostetter, Henrich	3rd cousin twice removed	X	6
Hostetter, Henry	1st cousin 4 times removed	VIII	6
Hostetter, Henry	3rd cousin once removed	IX	5
Hostetter, Henry	3rd cousin twice removed	X	6
Hostetter, Henry	3rd cousin twice removed	X	6
Hostetter, Henry	4th cousin once removed	XI	6
Hostetter, Henry	3rd cousin twice removed	X	6
Hostetter, Henry	1st cousin 4 times removed	VIII	6
Hostetter, Henry	3rd cousin twice removed	X	6
Hostetter, Henry	3rd cousin twice removed	X	6
Hostetter, Henry	2nd cousin 3 times removed	IX	6
Hostetter, Henry	2nd cousin 3 times removed	IX	6
Hostetter, Henry	3rd cousin twice removed	X	6
Hostetter, Henry	3rd cousin once removed	IX	5
Hostetter, Henry F.	3rd cousin twice removed	X	6
Hostetter, Herman	2nd cousin 3 times removed	IX	6

Name	Relationship with Milton Hershey	Civil	Canon
Hostetter, Herman	1st cousin 4 times removed	VIII	6
Hostetter, Herman	2nd cousin 3 times removed	IX	6
Hostetter, Herman	3rd cousin twice removed	X	6
Hostetter, Herman	3rd cousin twice removed	X	6
Hostetter, Herman Robert	3rd cousin twice removed	X	6
Hostetter, Herman Robert	3rd cousin twice removed	X	6
Hostetter, Hettie	3rd cousin once removed	IX	5
Hostetter, Hetty	4th cousin once removed	XI	6
Hostetter, Hiram	3rd cousin twice removed	X	6
Hostetter, Hiram C.	3rd cousin once removed	IX	5
Hostetter, Hiram H.	3rd cousin twice removed	X	6
Hostetter, Isaac	3rd cousin twice removed	X	6
Hostetter, Isaac	3rd cousin twice removed	X	6
Hostetter, Isaac	2nd cousin 3 times removed	IX	6
Hostetter, Isaac R.	3rd cousin twice removed	X	6
Hostetter, Isabella Victoria	3rd cousin once removed	IX	5
Hostetter, Jacob	1st cousin 3 times removed	VII	5
Hostetter, Jacob	3rd cousin twice removed	X	6
Hostetter, Jacob	3rd cousin twice removed	X	6
Hostetter, Jacob	3rd cousin twice removed	X	6
Hostetter, Jacob	4th cousin once removed	XI	6
Hostetter, Jacob	3rd cousin twice removed	X	6
Hostetter, Jacob	2nd cousin twice removed	VIII	5
Hostetter, Jacob	2nd cousin twice removed	VIII	5
Hostetter, Jacob	1st cousin 3 times removed	VII	5
Hostetter, Jacob	2nd cousin 3 times removed	IX	6
Hostetter, Jacob	3rd cousin twice removed	X	6
Hostetter, Jacob	2nd cousin 3 times removed	IX	6
Hostetter, Jacob	5th great-granduncle	IX	8
Hostetter, Jacob	4th great-grandfather	VI	6
Hostetter, Jacob	3rd great-grandfather	V	5
Hostetter, Jacob	2nd great-granduncle	VI	5
Hostetter, Jacob	1st cousin 4 times removed	VIII	6
Hostetter, Jacob	1st cousin 4 times removed	VIII	6
Hostetter, Jacob	1st cousin 3 times removed	VII	5
Hostetter, Jacob	1st cousin 3 times removed	VII	5
Hostetter, Jacob	2nd cousin 3 times removed	IX	6
Hostetter, Jacob	2nd cousin 3 times removed	IX	6
Hostetter, Jacob	2nd cousin 3 times removed	IX	6
Hostetter, Jacob	2nd cousin 3 times removed	IX	6
Hostetter, Jacob	2nd cousin 3 times removed	IX	6
Hostetter, Jacob	2nd cousin 3 times removed	IX	6
Hostetter, Jacob	2nd cousin twice removed	VIII	5
Hostetter, Jacob	2nd cousin twice removed	VIII	5
Hostetter, Jacob	2nd cousin twice removed	VIII	5
Hostetter, Jacob	3rd cousin twice removed	X	6
Hostetter, Jacob	3rd cousin twice removed	X	6
Hostetter, Jacob	3rd cousin twice removed	X	6
Hostetter, Jacob	3rd cousin twice removed	X	6
Hostetter, Jacob	3rd cousin twice removed	X	6
Hostetter, Jacob	4th cousin once removed	XI	6
Hostetter, Jacob	3rd cousin twice removed	X	6
Hostetter, Jacob D.	3rd cousin once removed	IX	5
Hostetter, Jacob H	4th cousin once removed	XI	6
Hostetter, Jacob H	2nd cousin twice removed	VIII	5
Hostetter, Jacob H	4th cousin once removed	XI	6
Hostetter, Jacob K.	3rd cousin twice removed	X	6
Hostetter, Jacob P	3rd cousin once removed	IX	5
Hostetter, Jageli	5th great-granduncle	IX	8
Hostetter, James	3rd cousin twice removed	X	6
Hostetter, Jenny E	4th cousin	X	5
Hostetter, Jessie Olive	4th cousin	X	5
Hostetter, Johannes	1st cousin 5 times removed	IX	7
Hostetter, John	3rd great-granduncle	VII	6
Hostetter, John	1st cousin 4 times removed	VIII	6
Hostetter, John	2nd cousin 3 times removed	IX	6

The Relations of Milton Snavely Hershey, 4th Ed.

Name	Relationship with Milton Hershey	Civil	Canon
Hostetter, John	4th cousin once removed	XI	6
Hostetter, John	4th cousin once removed	XI	6
Hostetter, John	4th cousin once removed	XI	6
Hostetter, John	4th cousin once removed	XI	6
Hostetter, John	Husband of the 2nd cousin 5 times removed		
Hostetter, John	3rd cousin 4 times removed	XII	8
Hostetter, John	2nd cousin 3 times removed	IX	6
Hostetter, John	3rd cousin twice removed	X	6
Hostetter, John	2nd cousin twice removed	VIII	5
Hostetter, John	2nd cousin 3 times removed	IX	6
Hostetter, John	3rd cousin twice removed	X	6
Hostetter, John	Husband of the 3rd cousin 3 times removed		
Hostetter, John	1st cousin 4 times removed	VIII	6
Hostetter, John	1st cousin 4 times removed	VIII	6
Hostetter, John	2nd cousin 3 times removed	IX	6
Hostetter, John	2nd cousin 3 times removed	IX	6
Hostetter, John	2nd cousin 3 times removed	IX	6
Hostetter, John	2nd cousin 3 times removed	IX	6
Hostetter, John	2nd cousin 3 times removed	IX	6
Hostetter, John	2nd cousin twice removed	VIII	5
Hostetter, John	3rd cousin twice removed	X	6
Hostetter, John	3rd cousin twice removed	X	6
Hostetter, John	3rd cousin twice removed	X	6
Hostetter, John	3rd cousin twice removed	X	6
Hostetter, John	3rd cousin twice removed	X	6
Hostetter, John	3rd cousin twice removed	X	6
Hostetter, John	3rd cousin twice removed	X	6
Hostetter, John	4th cousin once removed	XI	6
Hostetter, John E	4th cousin	X	5
Hostetter, John E.	3rd cousin twice removed	X	6
Hostetter, John E.	3rd cousin twice removed	X	6
Hostetter, John F	3rd cousin once removed	IX	5
Hostetter, John H	4th cousin once removed	XI	6
Hostetter, John H.	3rd cousin twice removed	X	6
Hostetter, John Henry	4th cousin once removed	XI	6
Hostetter, Jonas	4th cousin once removed	XI	6
Hostetter, Jonas	4th cousin once removed	XI	6
Hostetter, Jonas E.	3rd cousin twice removed	X	6
Hostetter, Joseph	1st cousin 3 times removed	VII	5
Hostetter, Joseph	2nd cousin twice removed	VIII	5
Hostetter, Joseph	3rd cousin once removed	IX	5
Hostetter, Joseph	3rd cousin once removed	IX	5
Hostetter, Joseph	4th cousin once removed	XI	6
Hostetter, Josiah	3rd cousin once removed	IX	5
Hostetter, Judith	3rd cousin twice removed	X	6
Hostetter, Kathryn	3rd cousin once removed	IX	5
Hostetter, Kathryn	4th cousin once removed	XI	6
Hostetter, Levi	4th cousin once removed	XI	6
Hostetter, Levi	4th cousin once removed	XI	6
Hostetter, Levi	4th cousin once removed	XI	6
Hostetter, Lewis	3rd cousin twice removed	X	6
Hostetter, Lida Garber	3rd cousin once removed	IX	5
Hostetter, Lidi	3rd cousin twice removed	X	6
Hostetter, Lillie	3rd cousin once removed	IX	5
Hostetter, Linnaeus	4th cousin once removed	XI	6
Hostetter, Lizzie	3rd cousin once removed	IX	5
Hostetter, Lizzie	3rd cousin twice removed	X	6
Hostetter, Lizzie	4th cousin once removed	XI	6
Hostetter, Louisa Jane	4th cousin once removed	XI	6
Hostetter, Lucinda	3rd cousin once removed	IX	5
Hostetter, Luke	3rd cousin twice removed	X	6
Hostetter, Lydia	2nd cousin twice removed	VIII	5
Hostetter, Lydia	3rd cousin twice removed	X	6
Hostetter, Lydia	4th cousin once removed	XI	6

Name	Relationship with Milton Hershey	Civil	Canon
Hostetter, Lydia	2nd cousin twice removed	VIII	5
Hostetter, Lydia	3rd cousin twice removed	X	6
Hostetter, Lydia Ann	3rd cousin once removed	IX	5
Hostetter, Magdalena	1st cousin 3 times removed	VII	5
Hostetter, Magdalena	2nd cousin 3 times removed	IX	6
Hostetter, Magdalena	2nd cousin 3 times removed	IX	6
Hostetter, Magdalena	4th cousin 3 times removed	XIII	8
Hostetter, Magdalena	2nd cousin twice removed	VIII	5
Hostetter, Magdalena	2nd cousin 3 times removed	IX	6
Hostetter, Magdalena	2nd cousin 3 times removed	IX	6
Hostetter, Magdalena	3rd cousin twice removed	X	6
Hostetter, Magdalena	2nd cousin 3 times removed	IX	6
Hostetter, Magdalena	3rd cousin twice removed	X	6
Hostetter, Magdalena	3rd cousin twice removed	X	6
Hostetter, Magdalene	2nd cousin twice removed	VIII	5
Hostetter, Margaret	3rd great-grandaunt	VII	6
Hostetter, Margaret	3rd cousin twice removed	X	6
Hostetter, Margaret	3rd cousin twice removed	X	6
Hostetter, Margaret	3rd cousin twice removed	X	6
Hostetter, Margaret	4th cousin once removed	XI	6
Hostetter, Maria	2nd great-grandaunt	VI	5
Hostetter, Maria	1st cousin 3 times removed	VII	5
Hostetter, Maria	2nd cousin 3 times removed	IX	6
Hostetter, Maria	2nd cousin 3 times removed	IX	6
Hostetter, Maria	2nd cousin 3 times removed	IX	6
Hostetter, Maria	3rd cousin once removed	IX	5
Hostetter, Maria	3rd cousin twice removed	X	6
Hostetter, Maria	2nd cousin 3 times removed	IX	6
Hostetter, Maria	4th cousin 3 times removed	XIII	8
Hostetter, Maria	1st cousin 3 times removed	VII	5
Hostetter, Maria	2nd great-grandaunt	VI	5
Hostetter, Maria	2nd cousin 3 times removed	IX	6
Hostetter, Maria	2nd cousin 3 times removed	IX	6
Hostetter, Maria	1st cousin 3 times removed	VII	5
Hostetter, Maria	2nd cousin 3 times removed	IX	6
Hostetter, Maria	2nd cousin twice removed	VIII	5
Hostetter, Maria	2nd cousin twice removed	VIII	5
Hostetter, Maria	3rd cousin twice removed	X	6
Hostetter, Maria	3rd cousin twice removed	X	6
Hostetter, Maria	Wife of the 2nd cousin once removed		
Hostetter, Martha	2nd cousin twice removed	VIII	5
Hostetter, Martha	3rd cousin once removed	IX	5
Hostetter, Martha	3rd cousin twice removed	X	6
Hostetter, Martha	2nd cousin twice removed	VIII	5
Hostetter, Martha	3rd cousin twice removed	X	6
Hostetter, Martha	3rd cousin twice removed	X	6
Hostetter, Mary	3rd cousin once removed	IX	5
Hostetter, Mary	3rd cousin twice removed	X	6
Hostetter, Mary	4th cousin once removed	XI	6
Hostetter, Mary	4th cousin once removed	XI	6
Hostetter, Mary	2nd cousin twice removed	VIII	5
Hostetter, Mary	2nd cousin 3 times removed	IX	6
Hostetter, Mary	3rd cousin twice removed	X	6
Hostetter, Mary	3rd cousin twice removed	X	6
Hostetter, Mary	2nd cousin 3 times removed	IX	6
Hostetter, Mary	2nd cousin twice removed	VIII	5
Hostetter, Mary	3rd cousin twice removed	X	6
Hostetter, Mary	3rd cousin twice removed	X	6
Hostetter, Mary	3rd cousin twice removed	X	6
Hostetter, Mary	3rd cousin twice removed	X	6
Hostetter, Mary	4th cousin once removed	XI	6
Hostetter, Mary Ann	3rd cousin twice removed	X	6
Hostetter, Mary Ann	3rd cousin twice removed	X	6
Hostetter, Mary Belle	4th cousin	X	5
Hostetter, Mary C	4th cousin once removed	XI	6
Hostetter, Mary Edith	3rd cousin once removed	IX	5

Name	Relationship with Milton Hershey	Civil	Canon
Hostetter, Mary Elisabeth	3rd cousin once removed	IX	5
Hostetter, Mary Elisabeth	4th cousin once removed	XI	6
Hostetter, Mary Ellen	4th cousin once removed	XI	6
Hostetter, Maude Gertrude	3rd cousin once removed	IX	5
Hostetter, Michael	2nd cousin 3 times removed	IX	6
Hostetter, Michael F.	3rd cousin twice removed	X	6
Hostetter, Minnie	4th cousin once removed	XI	6
Hostetter, Miriam Virginia	5th cousin	XII	6
Hostetter, Nathan	3rd cousin once removed	IX	5
Hostetter, Noah	3rd cousin twice removed	X	6
Hostetter, Oliver	3rd cousin once removed	IX	5
Hostetter, Oswald	5th great-grandfather	VII	7
Hostetter, Oswald	4th great-granduncle	VIII	7
Hostetter, Peter	3rd cousin twice removed	X	6
Hostetter, Pharus	3rd cousin once removed	IX	5
Hostetter, Polly	2nd cousin 3 times removed	IX	6
Hostetter, Private	4th cousin	X	5
Hostetter, Private	4th cousin	X	5
Hostetter, Private	4th cousin	X	5
Hostetter, Private	4th cousin	X	5
Hostetter, Private	Husband of the 3rd cousin 4 times removed		
Hostetter, Private	3rd cousin 5 times removed	XIII	9
Hostetter, Private	3rd cousin 5 times removed	XIII	9
Hostetter, Private	Husband of the 3rd cousin 4 times removed		
Hostetter, Private	3rd cousin 5 times removed	XIII	9
Hostetter, Private	3rd cousin 5 times removed	XIII	9
Hostetter, Private	3rd cousin 5 times removed	XIII	9
Hostetter, Private	3rd cousin 5 times removed	XIII	9
Hostetter, Private	Husband of the 3rd cousin 4 times removed		
Hostetter, Private	3rd cousin 5 times removed	XIII	9
Hostetter, Private	Wife of the 3rd cousin 3 times removed		
Hostetter, Rachel	2nd cousin 3 times removed	IX	6
Hostetter, Rebecca	2nd cousin 3 times removed	IX	6
Hostetter, Robert Lynne	4th cousin	X	5
Hostetter, Robert White	4th cousin	X	5
Hostetter, Ross	5th cousin	XII	6
Hostetter, Ross	4th cousin once removed	XI	6
Hostetter, Roy Grant	4th cousin	X	5
Hostetter, Rudolph	2nd cousin twice removed	VIII	5
Hostetter, Rudolph	1st cousin 6 times removed	X	8
Hostetter, Rudolph	1st cousin 3 times removed	VII	5
Hostetter, Salinda	3rd cousin twice removed	X	6
Hostetter, Samuel	2nd cousin twice removed	VIII	5
Hostetter, Samuel	3rd cousin twice removed	X	6
Hostetter, Samuel	2nd cousin twice removed	VIII	5
Hostetter, Samuel	3rd cousin twice removed	X	6
Hostetter, Samuel A.	3rd cousin twice removed	X	6
Hostetter, Samuel E	4th cousin once removed	XI	6
Hostetter, Samuel G	4th cousin once removed	XI	6
Hostetter, Samuel H	4th cousin once removed	XI	6
Hostetter, Sarah	2nd cousin 3 times removed	IX	6
Hostetter, Sarah	3rd cousin once removed	IX	5
Hostetter, Sarah	2nd cousin 3 times removed	IX	6
Hostetter, Sarah	4th cousin once removed	XI	6
Hostetter, Sarah A	3rd cousin once removed	IX	5
Hostetter, Sarah E	4th cousin once removed	XI	6
Hostetter, Sarah J	4th cousin once removed	XI	6
Hostetter, Simon	3rd cousin twice removed	X	6
Hostetter, Simon	4th cousin once removed	XI	6
Hostetter, Susan	3rd cousin twice removed	X	6
Hostetter, Susan	2nd cousin twice removed	VIII	5
Hostetter, Susan	3rd cousin twice removed	X	6
Hostetter, Susan	3rd cousin twice removed	X	6
Hostetter, Susan	2nd cousin twice removed	VIII	5
Hostetter, Susan	3rd cousin twice removed	X	6
Hostetter, Susan	3rd cousin twice removed	X	6

Name	Relationship with Milton Hershey	Civil	Canon
Hostetter, Susan	3rd cousin twice removed	X	6
Hostetter, Susan	3rd cousin twice removed	X	6
Hostetter, Susan	4th cousin once removed	XI	6
Hostetter, Susan A	3rd cousin once removed	IX	5
Hostetter, Susan Alice	4th cousin once removed	XI	6
Hostetter, Susanna	2nd cousin 3 times removed	IX	6
Hostetter, Susanna	2nd cousin 3 times removed	IX	6
Hostetter, Susanna	2nd cousin 3 times removed	IX	6
Hostetter, Susanna	2nd cousin 3 times removed	IX	6
Hostetter, Taylor T	3rd cousin once removed	IX	5
Hostetter, Theodore	4th cousin once removed	XI	6
Hostetter, Thomas	3rd cousin twice removed	X	6
Hostetter, Thomas	3rd cousin twice removed	X	6
Hostetter, Thomas	3rd cousin twice removed	X	6
Hostetter, Tilman N	4th cousin once removed	XI	6
Hostetter, Ulrich	2nd cousin 3 times removed	IX	6
Hostetter, Venich	4th cousin	X	5
Hostetter, Veronica	Wife of the 3rd cousin 3 times removed		
Hostetter, Veronica	1st cousin 5 times removed	IX	7
Hostetter, W. Clyde	3rd cousin once removed	IX	5
Hostetter, Wilfred	4th cousin once removed	XI	6
Hostetter, Wilhelmina	3rd cousin once removed	IX	5
Hostetter, William F	4th cousin	X	5
Hostetter, William H	3rd cousin once removed	IX	5
Hostetter, William H	4th cousin once removed	XI	6
Hostetter, William S	4th cousin	X	5
Hottel, Catherine Stover	Wife of the 5th cousin once removed		
House, Mary	Wife of the 2nd cousin 3 times removed		
Houser, Christian L.	Husband of the 1st cousin 3 times removed		
Houser, Elizabeth	Wife of the 1st cousin 3 times removed		
Houser, Unknown	Wife of the 2nd great-granduncle		
Howard, Ada	Wife of the 6th cousin twice removed		
Howard, Marvin L	Husband of the 6th cousin 3 times removed		
Howe, Jean Marie	Half 3rd cousin 3 times removed	XI	7
Howe, Private	Wife of the 6th cousin 3 times removed		
Howe, Ralph	Half 3rd cousin 3 times removed	XI	7
Howe, Ralph W.	Husband of the half 3rd cousin twice removed		
Howell, Hazel	Wife of the 6th cousin once removed		
Hoyt, Anna	Wife of the 6th cousin		
Hrovatic, Private	Husband of the 6th cousin 3 times removed		
Hrovatic, Private	6th cousin 4 times removed	XVIII	11
Hrovatic, Private	6th cousin 4 times removed	XVIII	11
Hubbard, Eva Graber	Wife of the 6th cousin once removed		
Huber, Abraham	Husband of the 2nd cousin once removed		
Huber, Anna	Wife of the 2nd cousin 6 times removed		
Huber, Anna	Wife of the 7th great-granduncle		
Huber, Anna	Wife of the 3rd great-granduncle		
Huber, Anna	Wife of the granduncle		
Huber, Barbara	Wife of the 1st cousin twice removed		
Huber, Barbara	Wife of the 3rd cousin twice removed		
Huber, Catherine	Wife of the 1st cousin twice removed		
Huber, Christian	Husband of the 1st cousin 4 times removed		
Huber, Christiana	Wife of the 2nd cousin 6 times removed		
Huber, Esther	Wife of the half granduncle		
Huber, Jacob	Husband of the 1st cousin 4 times removed		
Huber, Maria	Wife of the 1st cousin 4 times removed		
Huber, Martin	Husband of the 4th cousin 4 times removed		
Huber, Mary	Wife of the 3rd cousin twice removed		
Huber, Susie	Wife of the 4th cousin once removed		
Huber, Veronica	Wife of the 2nd cousin 3 times removed		
Hubert, Arden	6th cousin 3 times removed	XVII	10
Hubert, Charles	Husband of the 6th cousin once removed		
Hubert, Edgar C	6th cousin twice removed	XVI	9
Hubert, Frank	6th cousin twice removed	XVI	9
Hubert, Helen B	6th cousin twice removed	XVI	9
Hubert, Leonard	6th cousin 3 times removed	XVII	10

The Relations of Milton Snavely Hershey, 4th Ed.

Name	Relationship with Milton Hershey	Civil	Canon
Hubert, Mildred M	6th cousin twice removed	XVI	9
Huffellberg, Barbel	7th great-grandmother	IX	9
Huges, Louise	Wife of the 6th cousin 3 times removed		
Huges, Private	Husband of the 6th cousin 3 times removed		
Huges, Private	6th cousin 4 times removed	XVIII	11
Huges, Private	6th cousin 4 times removed	XVIII	11
Hughes, Rosa	Wife of the half 3rd cousin		
Hummel, J. Maynard	Husband of the 6th cousin twice removed		
Hummel, Julia	6th cousin 3 times removed	XVII	10
Hummerhouser, Agnes R.	Wife of the 6th cousin		
Hunsberger, Susanna	Wife of the 5th cousin 3 times removed		
Hunsicker, Ann Alderfer	Wife of the 3rd cousin twice removed		
Hunsicker, Charles M.	Husband of the 4th cousin once removed		
Hunsperger, Elizabeth	Wife of the 4th cousin twice removed		
Hunter, Charles	Husband of the half 3rd cousin twice removed		
Hunter, Francis M.	Half 3rd cousin 3 times removed	XI	7
Hunter, Shirley	Half 3rd cousin 3 times removed	XI	7
Hunter, Vera	Half 3rd cousin 3 times removed	XI	7
Hursh, Agnes E	6th cousin twice removed	XVI	9
Hursh, Brenner P	6th cousin 3 times removed	XVII	10
Hursh, Clarence B	6th cousin twice removed	XVI	9
Hursh, Diane A	6th cousin 4 times removed	XVIII	11
Hursh, Edna R	6th cousin twice removed	XVI	9
Hursh, Edward M	Husband of the 6th cousin once removed		
Hursh, Emma B	Wife of the 6th cousin twice removed		
Hursh, Frances M	Wife of the 6th cousin 3 times removed		
Hursh, Jay B	6th cousin twice removed	XVI	9
Hursh, Lillie E	6th cousin twice removed	XVI	9
Hursh, Margery B	6th cousin 3 times removed	XVII	10
Hursh, Odille Anne	6th cousin 3 times removed	XVII	10
Hurst, Barbara W.	4th cousin once removed	XI	6
Hurst, Frank W.	4th cousin once removed	XI	6
Hurst, George W.	4th cousin once removed	XI	6
Hurst, Isaac W.	4th cousin once removed	XI	6
Hurst, Jacob W.	4th cousin once removed	XI	6
Hurst, Katie W.	4th cousin once removed	XI	6
Hurst, Lizzie W.	4th cousin once removed	XI	6
Hurst, Lydia W.	4th cousin once removed	XI	6
Hurst, Noah W.	4th cousin once removed	XI	6
Hurst, Private	Husband of the 3rd cousin 4 times removed		
Hurst, Private	Husband of the 3rd cousin 3 times removed		
Hurst, Private	3rd cousin 4 times removed	XII	8
Hurst, Private	3rd cousin 4 times removed	XII	8
Hurst, Private	3rd cousin 4 times removed	XII	8
Hurst, Susana W.	4th cousin once removed	XI	6
Hurst, Weaver W.	4th cousin once removed	XI	6
Huston, Etta Lucinda	Wife of the 6th cousin once removed		
Hutwohl, Anna	Wife of the 1st cousin 4 times removed		
Huver, Elizabeth Landis	Wife of the 1st cousin once removed		
Hyde, Alice Phillipa	Wife of the 6th cousin		
Ickes, Carolyn	6th cousin once removed	XV	8
Ickes, Henry	Husband of the 6th cousin		
Ickes, William	Husband of the 6th cousin		
Ickes, William II	6th cousin once removed	XV	8
Ickis, Susanna	Wife of the 6th cousin		
Imler, Elizabeth	6th cousin	XIV	7
Imler, Hannah	6th cousin	XIV	7
Imler, Joseph	6th cousin	XIV	7
Imler, Margaret	6th cousin	XIV	7
Imler, Mathias	6th cousin	XIV	7
Imler, Sarah	6th cousin	XIV	7
Imler, Solomon	Husband of the 5th cousin once removed		
Imler, Thomas O.	6th cousin	XIV	7
Imler, William	6th cousin	XIV	7
Ingalls, Ann E.	Wife of the 4th cousin once removed		
Ingram, Dora	Wife of the half 3rd cousin twice removed		

Name	Relationship with Milton Hershey	Civil	Canon
Irvin, Susan	Wife of the 6th cousin		
Irvine, Harriet	Wife of the 4th cousin once removed		
Isaacs, Kenneth Eugene	6th cousin 4 times removed	XVIII	11
Isaacs, Private	6th cousin 4 times removed	XVIII	11
Isaacs, Private	6th cousin 4 times removed	XVIII	11
Isaacs, Private	6th cousin 4 times removed	XVIII	11
Isaacs, Robb E.	Husband of the 6th cousin 3 times removed		
Isenschmid, Car W	Husband of the 6th cousin twice removed		
Isenschmid, Carl	Husband of the 6th cousin twice removed		
Isenschmid, Gary	6th cousin 3 times removed	XVII	10
Isenschmid, Private	6th cousin 3 times removed	XVII	10
Jackson, Andrew	Husband of the 3rd cousin once removed		
Jackson, John	4th cousin	X	5
Jackson, Lillian	Ex-wife of the 6th cousin twice removed		
Jackson, Virgil Walton	Husband of the 6th cousin twice removed		
Jacob, Stoffer	5th cousin once removed	XIII	7
Jacobs, Vincent	Husband of the 6th cousin once removed		
Jacoby, Private	Wife of the 6th cousin 3 times removed		
Jacquet, Russel	Husband of the 5th cousin once removed		
Jamieson, Jean	Wife of the half 3rd cousin 3 times removed		
Jane, Private	Wife of the 6th cousin 3 times removed		
Jantzi, Private	Wife of the 3rd cousin 3 times removed		
Jennings, Abbie Mae	Wife of the 6th cousin twice removed		
Jenuine, Christian	Husband of the 2nd cousin 3 times removed		
John, Florence	Wife of the 6th cousin once removed		
John, Myrtle Olive	Wife of the 6th cousin once removed		
Johndrow, Private	Wife of the 3rd cousin 3 times removed		
Johns, Anna	Wife of the 1st cousin 3 times removed		
Johnson, Barbara May	Half 3rd cousin 3 times removed	XI	7
Johnson, Burt	Husband of the 6th cousin once removed		
Johnson, Elvera E.	Wife of the 6th cousin 3 times removed		
Johnson, Garth Wilson	Half 3rd cousin 3 times removed	XI	7
Johnson, Geneva	Half 3rd cousin 3 times removed	XI	7
Johnson, Hannah	Wife of the half 3rd cousin		
Johnson, Harold	Half 3rd cousin 3 times removed	XI	7
Johnson, Henry	Husband of the half 3rd cousin twice removed		
Johnson, Madge Hessel	Wife of the 6th cousin twice removed		
Johnson, Mary Godshall	Wife of the 2nd cousin 3 times removed		
Johnson, Minnie	Wife of the 6th cousin twice removed		
Johnson, Nicholas Sigrid	Husband of the half 3rd cousin twice removed		
Johnson, Private	Wife of the 3rd cousin 3 times removed		
Johnson, Private	Husband of the 6th cousin 3 times removed		
Johnson, Private	Half 3rd cousin 3 times removed	XI	7
Johnson, Private	Half 3rd cousin 3 times removed	XI	7
Johnson, Private	Wife of the 2nd cousin 4 times removed		
Joiner, Private	Wife of the 6th cousin twice removed		
Jones, Annice Hall	Wife of the 6th cousin		
Jones, Dorothy	Wife of the half 3rd cousin		
Jones, George	Half 3rd cousin 3 times removed	XI	7
Jones, John	Husband of the half 3rd cousin twice removed		
Jones, Laura	Half 3rd cousin 3 times removed	XI	7
Jones, Mary	Wife of the half 3rd cousin		
Jones, Overton	Half 3rd cousin 3 times removed	XI	7
Jones, Private	Husband of the 6th cousin 3 times removed		
Jones, Private	6th cousin 4 times removed	XVIII	11
Jones, Private	6th cousin 4 times removed	XVIII	11
Joseph, Kertes	Husband of the 6th cousin 3 times removed		
Josline, Private	Husband of the 6th cousin 4 times removed		
Jr, Private	6th cousin 4 times removed	XVIII	11
Jumper, Oscar John	Husband of the 6th cousin 4 times removed		
Jutzi, Private	Wife of the 3rd cousin 3 times removed		
Kagarise, Andrew Zook	Husband of the 6th cousin		
Kagey, John	Husband of the half 1st cousin 5 times removed		
Kail, Private	Husband of the 6th cousin 3 times removed		
Kail, Private	6th cousin 4 times removed	XVIII	11
Kail, Private	6th cousin 4 times removed	XVIII	11

Name	Relationship with Milton Hershey	Civil	Canon
Kail, Private	6th cousin 4 times removed	XVIII	11
Kalbach, Adam	4th cousin twice removed	XII	7
Kalbach, Daniel	4th cousin twice removed	XII	7
Kalbach, David	4th cousin twice removed	XII	7
Kalbach, Henry	Husband of the 3rd cousin 3 times removed		
Kalbach, Henry	4th cousin twice removed	XII	7
Kalbach, John	4th cousin twice removed	XII	7
Kalbach, Michael	4th cousin twice removed	XII	7
Kalbach, Peter	4th cousin twice removed	XII	7
Kane, Rose Frances	Wife of the 6th cousin twice removed		
Kasper, Dorothy	Wife of the 6th cousin 3 times removed		
Kathy	4th cousin 3 times removed	XIII	8
Kaufer, Stella	Wife of the 6th cousin twice removed		
Kauffman, Ann	2nd cousin 3 times removed	IX	6
Kauffman, Anna K.	Wife of the 2nd cousin twice removed		
Kauffman, Barbara	Wife of the 2nd cousin 5 times removed		
Kauffman, Barbara	Wife of the 1st cousin 4 times removed		
Kauffman, Barbara	2nd cousin 3 times removed	IX	6
Kauffman, Benjamin	2nd cousin 3 times removed	IX	6
Kauffman, Benjamin Franklin	Husband of the 3rd cousin once removed		
Kauffman, Catherine	Wife of the 2nd cousin 3 times removed		
Kauffman, Christian	2nd cousin 3 times removed	IX	6
Kauffman, Christian	Husband of the 1st cousin 4 times removed		
Kauffman, Elizabeth	2nd cousin 3 times removed	IX	6
Kauffman, Magdalena	Wife of the 1st cousin 4 times removed		
Kauffman, Mary	2nd cousin 3 times removed	IX	6
Kauffman, Mary Weaver	Wife of the 2nd cousin 3 times removed		
Kauffman, Private	Husband of the 3rd cousin 4 times removed		
Kauffman, Private	3rd cousin 5 times removed	XIII	9
Kauffman, Private	Wife of the 3rd cousin twice removed		
Kauffman, Private	3rd cousin twice removed	X	6
Kauffman, Private	3rd cousin twice removed	X	6
Kauffman, Susan	2nd cousin 3 times removed	IX	6
Kauffman, Sylvia	Wife of the 3rd cousin twice removed		
Kauffman, Tobias	2nd cousin 3 times removed	IX	6
Keagy, Anna	Wife of the 2nd cousin 3 times removed		
Keagy, Christiana	Wife of the 6th cousin		
Keagy, Nancy Anna	Wife of the 6th cousin		
Keeler, Private	Wife of the 6th cousin 3 times removed		
Keene, Anna	Wife of the 3rd cousin		
Keener, John B.	Husband of the 3rd cousin		
Keener, Trulah	Wife of the 6th cousin once removed		
Kehr, Ruth Susanna	Wife of the 4th cousin twice removed		
Keister, Christina	Wife of the 4th cousin twice removed		
Keister, David	Husband of the 6th cousin once removed		
Keister, Wilson	6th cousin twice removed	XVI	9
Keith, June H	Wife of the 2nd cousin 3 times removed		
Kelker, Luther Reily	Husband of the 6th cousin		
Keller, Magdalena G.	Wife of the 2nd cousin		
Kelley, Private	Husband of the 2nd cousin 4 times removed		
Kelley, Private	2nd cousin 5 times removed	XI	8
Kellner, Private	Wife of the 6th cousin 3 times removed		
Kelly, Edith Maria	Wife of the half 3rd cousin once removed		
Kendall, John	Half 3rd cousin twice removed	X	6
Kendall, Unknown	Husband of the half 3rd cousin once removed		
Kendall, William	Half 3rd cousin twice removed	X	6
Kendig, Abraham	Half 4th great-granduncle	VIII	7
Kendig, Adam	Husband of the half 1st cousin 5 times removed		
Kendig, Alice	Half 2nd cousin 4 times removed	X	7
Kendig, Anna	4th great-grandaunt	VIII	7
Kendig, Anna	Half 2nd cousin 4 times removed	X	7
Kendig, Anna	Half 4th cousin twice removed	XII	7
Kendig, Barbara	4th great-grandaunt	VIII	7
Kendig, Benjamin	Half 4th cousin twice removed	XII	7
Kendig, David	Half 2nd cousin 4 times removed	X	7
Kendig, Elizabeth	4th great-grandaunt	VIII	7

Name	Relationship with Milton Hershey	Civil	Canon
Kendig, Elizabeth	Half 2nd cousin 4 times removed	X	7
Kendig, Elizabeth	Half 4th cousin twice removed	XII	7
Kendig, Elsbeth Alice	Half 1st cousin 5 times removed	IX	7
Kendig, Emanuel	Husband of the half 3rd cousin 3 times removed		
Kendig, Ester	4th great-grandaunt	VIII	7
Kendig, Esther	Half 2nd cousin 4 times removed	X	7
Kendig, Eva	4th great-grandaunt	VIII	7
Kendig, Heinrich	4th great-granduncle	VIII	7
Kendig, Henry	1st cousin 7 times removed	XI	9
Kendig, Henry	Half 1st cousin 5 times removed	IX	7
Kendig, John	Half 1st cousin 5 times removed	IX	7
Kendig, John	Half 2nd cousin 4 times removed	X	7
Kendig, John	Half 3rd cousin 3 times removed	XI	7
Kendig, John	Half 4th cousin twice removed	XII	7
Kendig, John	Half 4th cousin twice removed	XII	7
Kendig, John Jacob	Husband of the half 4th great-grandaunt		
Kendig, Martin	1st cousin 7 times removed	XI	9
Kendig, Martin	Half 1st cousin 5 times removed	IX	7
Kendig, Martin	Half 3rd cousin 3 times removed	XI	7
Kendig, Mary	4th great-grandaunt	VIII	7
Kendig, Mary	Half 4th cousin twice removed	XII	7
Kendig, Mary Eliza	Half 3rd cousin 3 times removed	XI	7
Kendig, Maudlin	4th great-grandmother	VI	6
Kendig, Sarah	Half 4th cousin twice removed	XII	7
Kendig, Susanna	1st cousin 7 times removed	XI	9
Kendig, Veronica	4th great-grandaunt	VIII	7
Kennedy, Ann Newman	Wife of the 1st cousin 4 times removed		
Kennedy, Ann Newman	Wife of the 1st cousin 4 times removed		
Kennel, Phoebe	Wife of the 3rd cousin twice removed		
Kennel, Private	Wife of the 3rd cousin 3 times removed		
Kenneth?Unknown, Private	Husband of the 6th cousin 3 times removed		
Keplinger, Susanna	Wife of the 2nd cousin 3 times removed		
Kern, William F.	Husband of the 3rd cousin twice removed		
Kerns, Maris	Husband of the half 4th cousin twice removed		
Kertes, Private	6th cousin 4 times removed	XVIII	11
Kertes, Private	6th cousin 4 times removed	XVIII	11
Kertes, Private	6th cousin 4 times removed	XVIII	11
Kessler, Leslie	Wife of the 6th cousin 3 times removed		
Kester, Lorne	Husband of the half 3rd cousin once removed		
Kettering, Amanda	6th cousin	XIV	7
Kettering, Elizabeth	6th cousin	XIV	7
Kettering, Henry	6th cousin	XIV	7
Kettering, Jacob	6th cousin	XIV	7
Kettering, John S.	6th cousin	XIV	7
Kettering, Joseph	6th cousin	XIV	7
Kettering, Lydia	6th cousin	XIV	7
Kettering, Mary	6th cousin	XIV	7
Kettering, Philip	6th cousin	XIV	7
Kettering, Private	6th cousin 4 times removed	XVIII	11
Kettering, Private	6th cousin 4 times removed	XVIII	11
Kettering, Private	6th cousin 4 times removed	XVIII	11
Kettering, Ralph	Husband of the 6th cousin 3 times removed		
Kettering, Rebecca	6th cousin	XIV	7
Kettering, Samuel	Husband of the 5th cousin once removed		
Kettering, Samuel	6th cousin	XIV	7
Kettering, Samuel A.	6th cousin	XIV	7
Kettering, Veronica	6th cousin	XIV	7
Kibler, Carl	6th cousin 3 times removed	XVII	10
Kibler, Charles	Husband of the 6th cousin twice removed		
Kibler, Charles C. (Keebler)	Husband of the 4th cousin once removed		
Kibler, Harold	6th cousin 3 times removed	XVII	10
Kibler, Joyce	6th cousin 3 times removed	XVII	10
Kibler, June	6th cousin 3 times removed	XVII	10
Kibler, Lolyd	6th cousin 3 times removed	XVII	10
Kibler, Private	6th cousin 4 times removed	XVIII	11
Kibler, Private	6th cousin 4 times removed	XVIII	11

The Relations of Milton Snavely Hershey, 4th Ed.

Name	Relationship with Milton Hershey	Civil	Canon
Kibler, Private	6th cousin 4 times removed	XVIII	11
Kibler, Private	6th cousin 4 times removed	XVIII	11
Kibler, Private	6th cousin 4 times removed	XVIII	11
Kibler, Private	6th cousin 4 times removed	XVIII	11
Kibler, Private	6th cousin 4 times removed	XVIII	11
Kibler, Private	6th cousin 4 times removed	XVIII	11
Kibler, Private	6th cousin 4 times removed	XVIII	11
Kibler, Private	6th cousin 4 times removed	XVIII	11
Kibler, Private	6th cousin 4 times removed	XVIII	11
Kibler, Private	6th cousin 4 times removed	XVIII	11
Kibler, Private	6th cousin 4 times removed	XVIII	11
Kibler, Private	6th cousin 4 times removed	XVIII	11
Kibler, Private	6th cousin 4 times removed	XVIII	11
Kibler, Private	Husband of the 6th cousin 3 times removed		
Kibler, Robert	6th cousin 3 times removed	XVII	10
Kiefer, Mary	Wife of the 6th cousin		
Kilgore, Private	Wife of the 6th cousin 3 times removed		
Kilhefner, Frank	Husband of the 3rd cousin		
Kilhefner, John	Husband of the 3rd cousin		
Kilmer, Private	Husband of the 3rd cousin 3 times removed		
Kilmer, Private	3rd cousin 4 times removed	XII	8
Kilmer, Private	3rd cousin 4 times removed	XII	8
Kilmer, Private	3rd cousin 4 times removed	XII	8
Kimmel, Susan	Wife of the 5th cousin once removed		
Kindig, Anna	Wife of the 3rd cousin twice removed		
King, Private	Wife of the 6th cousin 3 times removed		
Kinzer, Alfred Glenn	6th cousin 3 times removed	XVII	10
Kinzer, Alfred Lafayette	Husband of the 6th cousin twice removed		
Kinzer, Jesse Arden	6th cousin 3 times removed	XVII	10
Kinzer, Private	6th cousin 4 times removed	XVIII	11
Kinzer, Private	6th cousin 4 times removed	XVIII	11
Kinzer, Wanda Naomi	6th cousin 3 times removed	XVII	10
Kiriyama, Private	Wife of the 3rd cousin 3 times removed		
Kirkpatrick, Barbara	6th cousin 3 times removed	XVII	10
Kirkpatrick, Elmer A	Husband of the 6th cousin twice removed		
Kitch, Anna Catherine	2nd cousin once removed	VII	4
Kitch, Charles L.	2nd cousin once removed	VII	4
Kitch, Cyrus	Husband of the 2nd cousin		
Kitch, Cyrus L.	2nd cousin once removed	VII	4
Kitch, Dora Eve	2nd cousin once removed	VII	4
Kitch, Mary Lizzie	2nd cousin once removed	VII	4
Kitch, Minnie L.	2nd cousin once removed	VII	4
Kitchen, Amos Abraham	Half 3rd cousin twice removed	X	6
Kitchen, Drake	Husband of the half 3rd cousin once removed		
Kitchen, Ellen Ruletta	Half 3rd cousin twice removed	X	6
Kitchen, Harriett	Wife of the half 3rd cousin once removed		
Kitchen, Harry Milton	Half 3rd cousin twice removed	X	6
Kitchen, Lottie Augusta	Half 3rd cousin twice removed	X	6
Kitchen, Mabel Gertrude	Half 3rd cousin twice removed	X	6
Kitchen, Mary Edith	Half 3rd cousin twice removed	X	6
Kiter, George II	Husband of the 2nd cousin 3 times removed		
Kline, Alva	Wife of the 6th cousin 3 times removed		
Kline, Anna Mary	Wife of the 6th cousin		
Kline, Maria	Wife of the half 3rd cousin 3 times removed		
Klunk, Amanda	Wife of the 6th cousin 5 times removed		
Knapp, Andrew Jay	Half 3rd cousin 4 times removed	XII	8
Knapp, Emma Loretta	Half 3rd cousin twice removed	X	6
Knapp, Floyd Everal	Half 3rd cousin twice removed	X	6
Knapp, Victor Ronald	Half 3rd cousin 4 times removed	XII	8
Knapp, Willard Winfield	Husband of the half 3rd cousin once removed		
Knapp, William George	Half 3rd cousin 3 times removed	XI	7
Knight, Barbara J	6th cousin 4 times removed	XVIII	11
Knight, Beverly A	6th cousin 4 times removed	XVIII	11
Knight, Myers W	Husband of the 6th cousin 3 times removed		
Kniveton, Alice	Wife of the 6th cousin twice removed		

Name	Relationship with Milton Hershey	Civil	Canon
Knoll, Chester Larue	Husband of the 6th cousin twice removed		
Knoll, Dorothy Mae	6th cousin 3 times removed	XVII	10
Knoll, June Elizabeth	6th cousin 3 times removed	XVII	10
Knoll, Richard Lee	6th cousin 3 times removed	XVII	10
Knorpp, Betty Ann	6th cousin 3 times removed	XVII	10
Knorpp, Margaret Eda	6th cousin 3 times removed	XVII	10
Knorpp, Mary Jane	6th cousin 3 times removed	XVII	10
Knorpp, Walter Wesley	Husband of the 6th cousin twice removed		
Knorr, Alice Kathleen	4th cousin 3 times removed	XIII	8
Knorr, David Brian	4th cousin 3 times removed	XIII	8
Knorr, Lawrence David	Husband of the 4th cousin twice removed		
Knorr, Lawrence Kevin	4th cousin 3 times removed	XIII	8
Knox, Jean	Wife of the half 3rd cousin 3 times removed		
Knox, Private	Husband of the 6th cousin twice removed		
Knox, Private	6th cousin 3 times removed	XVII	10
Knox, Private	6th cousin 3 times removed	XVII	10
Knupp, Cloyd R	Husband of the 6th cousin twice removed		
Knupp, Cloyd R, Jr	6th cousin 3 times removed	XVII	10
Knupp, Edna M	6th cousin 3 times removed	XVII	10
Knupp, Florence W	6th cousin 3 times removed	XVII	10
Knupp, Jane L	6th cousin 3 times removed	XVII	10
Knupp, John H	6th cousin 3 times removed	XVII	10
Knupp, June A	6th cousin 3 times removed	XVII	10
Knupp, Muriel R	6th cousin 3 times removed	XVII	10
Knupp, Robert O	6th cousin 3 times removed	XVII	10
Koch, Catherine	Wife of the half 4th cousin twice removed		
Kochel, Helen Louise	Wife of the 3rd cousin twice removed		
Koehler, Clayton	4th cousin once removed	XI	6
Koehler, John	Husband of the 4th cousin		
Koffel, Ida M.	Wife of the 6th cousin		
Kohr, Nancy M	Wife of the 6th cousin 4 times removed		
Kolb, Ann Hunsberger (Kulp)	Wife of the 4th cousin once removed		
Kolb, Elizabeth Hunsberger (Kulp)	Wife of the 4th cousin once removed		
Kolb, Jacob Funk (Kulp)	Husband of the 4th cousin once removed		
Konshak, Louise	Wife of the half 3rd cousin once removed		
Kopp, Lillian A	Wife of the 2nd cousin twice removed		
Koppler, Lucille Elizabeth	Wife of the 6th cousin once removed		
Krafft, Dorothy	Wife of the 4th cousin twice removed		
Krall, Sarah	Wife of the 6th cousin		
Kramer, Henrietta	Wife of the 1st cousin once removed		
Krammer, Unknown	Husband of the half 3rd cousin 3 times removed		
Kranz, Private	Husband of the 3rd cousin twice removed		
Kratz, Lizzie Ann Kline	Wife of the 4th cousin once removed		
Krause, Chris W.	Husband of the 6th cousin once removed		
Krause, Glen	6th cousin twice removed	XVI	9
Krause, Herbert Stanton	6th cousin twice removed	XVI	9
Krause, Private	6th cousin twice removed	XVI	9
Krause, Private	6th cousin twice removed	XVI	9
Krause, Private	6th cousin twice removed	XVI	9
Krause, Private	6th cousin 3 times removed	XVII	10
Krause, Private	6th cousin 3 times removed	XVII	10
Krause, Private	6th cousin 3 times removed	XVII	10
Krause, Private	6th cousin 3 times removed	XVII	10
Krause, Private	6th cousin 3 times removed	XVII	10
Krause, Willard D	6th cousin twice removed	XVI	9
Kraybill, Candace M	Wife of the 4th cousin 3 times removed		
Krehmeyer, Kathryn	Wife of the 4th cousin twice removed		
Kreider, Abraham	3rd cousin twice removed	X	6
Kreider, Ann	1st cousin 5 times removed	IX	7
Kreider, Anna	1st cousin 4 times removed	VIII	6
Kreider, Anna	Wife of the 1st cousin 4 times removed		
Kreider, Anna	1st cousin 4 times removed	VIII	6
Kreider, Anna	Wife of the 3rd cousin 4 times removed		
Kreider, Anna	4th great-grandmother	VI	6
Kreider, Anna	1st cousin 5 times removed	IX	7
Kreider, Anna	Wife of the 1st cousin 3 times removed		

Name	Relationship with Milton Hershey	Civil	Canon
Kreider, Anna	2nd cousin 3 times removed	IX	6
Kreider, Barbara	1st cousin 4 times removed	VIII	6
Kreider, Barbara	3rd cousin twice removed	X	6
Kreider, Barbara	4th great-grandaunt	VIII	7
Kreider, Barbara	2nd cousin 3 times removed	IX	6
Kreider, Catherine	2nd cousin 3 times removed	IX	6
Kreider, Catherine	Wife of the 1st cousin 4 times removed		
Kreider, Catherine Louise	1st cousin 4 times removed	VIII	6
Kreider, Christian	2nd cousin 3 times removed	IX	6
Kreider, David	3rd cousin twice removed	X	6
Kreider, Eby	Husband of the 3rd cousin twice removed		
Kreider, Elisabeth	1st cousin 4 times removed	VIII	6
Kreider, Elizabeth	2nd cousin 3 times removed	IX	6
Kreider, Elizabeth	3rd cousin twice removed	X	6
Kreider, Elizabeth	4th cousin 3 times removed	XIII	8
Kreider, Elizabeth	2nd cousin 3 times removed	IX	6
Kreider, George	2nd cousin 3 times removed	IX	6
Kreider, Hans	5th great-granduncle	IX	8
Kreider, Hans Jacob	4th great-granduncle	VIII	7
Kreider, Hans Jacob	1st cousin 5 times removed	IX	7
Kreider, Henry	2nd cousin 3 times removed	IX	6
Kreider, Henry	4th cousin once removed	XI	6
Kreider, Henry Widemoyer	Husband of the 3rd cousin once removed		
Kreider, Jacob	3rd cousin twice removed	X	6
Kreider, Jacob	1st cousin 5 times removed	IX	7
Kreider, Jacob	5th great-grandfather	VII	7
Kreider, Jacob	4th great-granduncle	VIII	7
Kreider, Jacob	Husband of the 1st cousin 4 times removed		
Kreider, Jacob	1st cousin 4 times removed	VIII	6
Kreider, Jacob	2nd cousin 3 times removed	IX	6
Kreider, John	1st cousin 4 times removed	VIII	6
Kreider, John	2nd cousin 3 times removed	IX	6
Kreider, John	3rd cousin twice removed	X	6
Kreider, John	4th cousin 3 times removed	XIII	8
Kreider, John	1st cousin 5 times removed	IX	7
Kreider, John	2nd cousin 3 times removed	IX	6
Kreider, John	Husband of the half 4th cousin twice removed		
Kreider, John	Husband of the 6th cousin		
Kreider, John Funk	Husband of the 4th cousin		
Kreider, Lydia	Wife of the 6th cousin		
Kreider, Lydia Shenk	Wife of the 6th cousin		
Kreider, Magdalena	3rd cousin twice removed	X	6
Kreider, Maria	2nd cousin 3 times removed	IX	6
Kreider, Martin	Husband of the 2nd cousin 3 times removed		
Kreider, Martin	3rd cousin twice removed	X	6
Kreider, Martin	Husband of the 2nd cousin 3 times removed		
Kreider, Martin	Husband of the 2nd cousin 3 times removed		
Kreider, Martin	4th great-granduncle	VIII	7
Kreider, Martin	1st cousin 5 times removed	IX	7
Kreider, Mary Brubaker	4th cousin	X	5
Kreider, Michael	2nd cousin 3 times removed	IX	6
Kreider, Michael	1st cousin 5 times removed	IX	7
Kreider, Michael	6th great-grandfather	VIII	8
Kreider, Michael	4th great-granduncle	VIII	7
Kreider, Michael	Husband of the 1st cousin 4 times removed		
Kreider, Michael	1st cousin 4 times removed	VIII	6
Kreider, Peter	1st cousin 5 times removed	IX	7
Kreider, Peter	1st cousin 4 times removed	VIII	6
Kreider, Private	Wife of the 3rd cousin 3 times removed		
Kreider, Private	Husband of the 3rd cousin 3 times removed		
Kreider, Private	3rd cousin 4 times removed	XII	8
Kreider, Private	3rd cousin 4 times removed	XII	8
Kreider, Private	3rd cousin 4 times removed	XII	8
Kreider, Private	3rd cousin 4 times removed	XII	8
Kreider, Private	3rd cousin 3 times removed	XI	7
Kreider, Private	3rd cousin 3 times removed	XI	7

Name	Relationship with Milton Hershey	Civil	Canon
Kreider, Private	3rd cousin 3 times removed	XI	7
Kreider, Private	3rd cousin 3 times removed	XI	7
Kreider, Private	3rd cousin 4 times removed	XII	8
Kreider, Private	3rd cousin 4 times removed	XII	8
Kreider, Private	3rd cousin 4 times removed	XII	8
Kreider, Rosanna	1st cousin 4 times removed	VIII	6
Kreider, Susanna	1st cousin 4 times removed	VIII	6
Kreider, Tobias	Husband of the 1st cousin 4 times removed		
Kreider, Unknown	3rd cousin 3 times removed	XI	7
Kreider, Veronica	2nd great-grandmother	IV	4
Kreigbaum, Betty L	Wife of the 6th cousin 3 times removed		
Krey, John	Husband of the 2nd cousin 6 times removed		
Kuhns, Mary A.	Wife of the 6th cousin		
Kuhns, Sarah Ann	Wife of the 2nd cousin		
Kuipers, Private	Wife of the 3rd cousin twice removed		
Kundig, Adrian	7th great-granduncle	XI	10
Kundig, Anna	Half 6th great-grandaunt	X	9
Kundig, Anna	5th great-grandaunt	IX	8
Kundig, Barbara	Half 5th great-grandaunt	IX	8
Kundig, Barbel	5th great-grandaunt	IX	8
Kundig, Barbel	6th great-grandaunt	X	9
Kundig, Elizabeth	1st cousin 7 times removed	XI	9
Kundig, Elsbet	7th great-grandaunt	XI	10
Kundig, Elsbeth	5th great-grandaunt	IX	8
Kundig, Felix	9th great-grandfather	XI	11
Kundig, Hans	Half 5th great-granduncle	IX	8
Kundig, Hans	7th great-granduncle	XI	10
Kundig, Hans Heinrich	6th great-grandfather	VIII	8
Kundig, Hans Jacob	5th great-grandfather	VII	7
Kundig, Hans Jagli	6th great-granduncle	X	9
Kundig, Heinrich	6th great-granduncle	X	9
Kundig, Jacob	5th great-granduncle	IX	8
Kundig, Jacob	4th great-granduncle	VIII	7
Kundig, Jagli	Half 6th great-granduncle	X	9
Kundig, Jorg	7th great-grandfather	IX	9
Kundig, Jorg	5th great-granduncle	IX	8
Kundig, Margreth	Half 6th great-grandaunt	X	9
Kundig, Peter	8th great-grandfather	X	10
Kundig, Regula	Half 5th great-grandaunt	IX	8
Kundig, Verena	4th great-grandaunt	VIII	7
Kuntz, Elizabeth	Wife of the 3rd cousin 3 times removed		
Kurtz, Abraham	4th cousin once removed	XI	6
Kurtz, Barbara Ann	4th cousin once removed	XI	6
Kurtz, Christian H.	4th cousin once removed	XI	6
Kurtz, David Harrison	4th cousin once removed	XI	6
Kurtz, Elizabeth	4th cousin once removed	XI	6
Kurtz, Henry Clay	4th cousin once removed	XI	6
Kurtz, Jacob	Husband of the 2nd cousin		
Kurtz, John Erb	Husband of the 3rd cousin twice removed		
Kurtz, John H.	4th cousin once removed	XI	6
Kurtz, Mary	4th cousin once removed	XI	6
Kurtz, Private	Husband of the 3rd cousin 3 times removed		
Kurtz, Private	3rd cousin 4 times removed	XII	8
Kurtz, Private	3rd cousin 4 times removed	XII	8
Kurtz, Private	3rd cousin 4 times removed	XII	8
Kurtz, Private	3rd cousin 4 times removed	XII	8
Kurtz, Private	Husband of the 3rd cousin 3 times removed		
Kurtz, Private	3rd cousin 4 times removed	XII	8
Kurtz, Private	3rd cousin 4 times removed	XII	8
Kurtz, Samuel Albert	4th cousin once removed	XI	6
Kurtz, Sarah	Wife of the 6th cousin		
Kurtz, Susanna	Wife of the 3rd cousin twice removed		
Laber, Michael	Husband of the 3rd cousin 3 times removed		
Lacey, Mary	Wife of the 6th cousin once removed		
Lackey, Patricia A	6th cousin 4 times removed	XVIII	11
Lackey, Richard H, Jr	Husband of the 6th cousin 3 times removed		

The Relations of Milton Snavely Hershey, 4th Ed.

Name	Relationship with Milton Hershey	Civil	Canon
Lackey, Susan J	6th cousin 4 times removed	XVIII	11
Lahodny, Ann	Wife of the half 3rd cousin twice removed		
Lakers, Leone Elizabeth	Wife of the 6th cousin twice removed		
Lambert, Civilla	Wife of the 6th cousin		
Lancaster, Helen Gene	Wife of the 6th cousin twice removed		
Landes, Abraham Beidler	3rd cousin twice removed	X	6
Landes, Abraham Hunsicker	4th cousin once removed	XI	6
Landes, Abraham Lincoln	4th cousin once removed	XI	6
Landes, Benjamin Franklin Hunsicker	4th cousin once removed	XI	6
Landes, Daniel Miller	4th cousin once removed	XI	6
Landes, Davis Miller	4th cousin once removed	XI	6
Landes, Elizabeth Beidler	3rd cousin twice removed	X	6
Landes, Elizabeth Hunsicker	4th cousin once removed	XI	6
Landes, Hannah Beidler	3rd cousin twice removed	X	6
Landes, Hannah Hunsicker	4th cousin once removed	XI	6
Landes, Hattie Hunsicker	4th cousin once removed	XI	6
Landes, Henry Hunsicker	4th cousin once removed	XI	6
Landes, Jacob	4th great-grandfather	VI	6
Landes, James Miller	4th cousin once removed	XI	6
Landes, Jane Miller	4th cousin once removed	XI	6
Landes, John Beidler	3rd cousin twice removed	X	6
Landes, John Horace Hunsicker	4th cousin once removed	XI	6
Landes, John Kolb	Husband of the 2nd cousin 3 times removed		
Landes, Josephine Hunsicker	4th cousin once removed	XI	6
Landes, Katie Hunsicker	4th cousin once removed	XI	6
Landes, Mary Hunsicker	4th cousin once removed	XI	6
Landes, Mary Kolb	Wife of the 2nd cousin 3 times removed		
Landes, Mary Miller	4th cousin once removed	XI	6
Landes, Ralph Kratz	Husband of the 5th cousin once removed		
Landes, William Puhl	4th cousin once removed	XI	6
Landis, Abraham	2nd great-granduncle	VI	5
Landis, Abraham	1st cousin 3 times removed	VII	5
Landis, Abraham	1st cousin 3 times removed	VII	5
Landis, Abraham	1st cousin 3 times removed	VII	5
Landis, Abraham	2nd cousin once removed	VII	4
Landis, Abraham Erb	3rd cousin 3 times removed	XI	7
Landis, Abraham F.	2nd cousin	VI	3
Landis, Abraham S.	1st cousin once removed	V	3
Landis, Ada	2nd cousin once removed	VII	4
Landis, Ada Cathrine	2nd cousin twice removed	VIII	5
Landis, Adeli	Half 6th great-grandaunt	X	9
Landis, Adria	2nd cousin	VI	3
Landis, Agta	7th great-grandaunt	XI	10
Landis, Alice Ida	2nd cousin twice removed	VIII	5
Landis, Alice M	2nd cousin once removed	VII	4
Landis, Amanda	2nd cousin once removed	VII	4
Landis, Amanda	2nd cousin once removed	VII	4
Landis, Amanda B.	2nd cousin twice removed	VIII	5
Landis, Ann	1st cousin 3 times removed	VII	5
Landis, Anna	7th great-grandaunt	XI	10
Landis, Anna	7th great-grandaunt	XI	10
Landis, Anna	7th great-grandaunt	XI	10
Landis, Anna	5th great-grandaunt	IX	8
Landis, Anna	2nd cousin once removed	VII	4
Landis, Anna	3rd great-grandaunt	VII	6
Landis, Anna	2nd great-grandaunt	VI	5
Landis, Anna	2nd cousin 4 times removed	X	7
Landis, Anna	1st cousin 3 times removed	VII	5
Landis, Anna	2nd cousin twice removed	VIII	5
Landis, Anna	Wife of the 1st cousin twice removed		
Landis, Anna	2nd cousin twice removed	VIII	5
Landis, Anna E.	3rd cousin 3 times removed	XI	7
Landis, Anna M	2nd cousin	VI	3
Landis, Anna Mary	2nd cousin once removed	VII	4
Landis, Anna S.	1st cousin once removed	V	3
Landis, Annie	2nd cousin once removed	VII	4

Name	Relationship with Milton Hershey	Civil	Canon
Landis, Annie B.	2nd cousin once removed	VII	4
Landis, Annie E	2nd cousin	VI	3
Landis, Annie L.	2nd cousin	VI	3
Landis, Annie M.	2nd cousin twice removed	VIII	5
Landis, Barbara	4th great-grandaunt	VIII	7
Landis, Barbara	4th great-grandmother	VI	6
Landis, Barbara	2nd cousin 4 times removed	X	7
Landis, Barbara	5th great-grandaunt	IX	8
Landis, Barbara	3rd great-grandmother	V	5
Landis, Barbara	3rd great-grandaunt	VII	6
Landis, Barbara	2nd great-grandaunt	VI	5
Landis, Barbara	1st cousin 3 times removed	VII	5
Landis, Barbara	1st cousin 3 times removed	VII	5
Landis, Barbara	Wife of the 1st cousin once removed		
Landis, Barbara	1st cousin 3 times removed	VII	5
Landis, Barbara S.	1st cousin once removed	V	3
Landis, Benjamin	3rd great-grandfather	V	5
Landis, Benjamin	2nd great-granduncle	VI	5
Landis, Benjamin	1st cousin 3 times removed	VII	5
Landis, Benjamin	1st cousin 3 times removed	VII	5
Landis, Benjamin	2nd cousin twice removed	VIII	5
Landis, Benjamin	2nd cousin twice removed	VIII	5
Landis, Benjamin F	2nd cousin	VI	3
Landis, Benjamin L.	2nd cousin twice removed	VIII	5
Landis, Benjamin S.	1st cousin once removed	V	3
Landis, Betty Jane	2nd cousin 3 times removed	IX	6
Landis, Caspar	5th great-granduncle	IX	8
Landis, Catharina	4th great-grandaunt	VIII	7
Landis, Catharine	2nd cousin	VI	3
Landis, Catherine	2nd cousin 4 times removed	X	7
Landis, Catherine (Kate)	2nd cousin once removed	VII	4
Landis, Chester M.	Husband of the 5th cousin once removed		
Landis, Child	4th great-granduncle	VIII	7
Landis, Christian	1st cousin 6 times removed	X	8
Landis, Christian Creiner	2nd cousin once removed	VII	4
Landis, Christian G.	2nd cousin twice removed	VIII	5
Landis, Christian R.	3rd cousin once removed	IX	5
Landis, Christian S.	1st cousin once removed	V	3
Landis, Christianna	2nd cousin once removed	VII	4
Landis, Christina	2nd cousin 4 times removed	X	7
Landis, Daniel	2nd cousin	VI	3
Landis, Daniel F.	2nd cousin	VI	3
Landis, Daniel S.	1st cousin once removed	V	3
Landis, David	2nd cousin once removed	VII	4
Landis, David B.	2nd cousin once removed	VII	4
Landis, David Erb	3rd cousin 3 times removed	XI	7
Landis, David F.	2nd cousin	VI	3
Landis, David M	2nd cousin	VI	3
Landis, David M.	2nd cousin	VI	3
Landis, David S.	1st cousin once removed	V	3
Landis, David S.	1st cousin once removed	V	3
Landis, Eddie	2nd cousin twice removed	VIII	5
Landis, Elam B.	2nd cousin once removed	VII	4
Landis, Elisabeth	5th great-grandaunt	IX	8
Landis, Eliza F.	2nd cousin	VI	3
Landis, Elizabeth	2nd cousin 4 times removed	X	7
Landis, Elizabeth	1st cousin 3 times removed	VII	5
Landis, Elizabeth	1st cousin 3 times removed	VII	5
Landis, Elizabeth	1st cousin 3 times removed	VII	5
Landis, Elizabeth	2nd cousin	VI	3
Landis, Elizabeth E.	3rd cousin 3 times removed	XI	7
Landis, Elizabeth F.	2nd cousin	VI	3
Landis, Elizabeth H	2nd cousin	VI	3
Landis, Elizabeth L.	2nd cousin	VI	3
Landis, Elizabeth S.	1st cousin once removed	V	3
Landis, Elizabeth S.	1st cousin once removed	V	3

Name	Relationship with Milton Hershey	Civil	Canon
Landis, Ella	2nd cousin once removed	VII	4
Landis, Elsbeth	5th great-grandaunt	IX	8
Landis, Emma	2nd cousin once removed	VII	4
Landis, Emma	2nd cousin twice removed	VIII	5
Landis, Emma B.	2nd cousin once removed	VII	4
Landis, Emma M.	2nd cousin twice removed	VIII	5
Landis, Emma Meashey	Wife of the 6th cousin 3 times removed		
Landis, Ephraim F.	2nd cousin	VI	3
Landis, Esther	1st cousin 3 times removed	VII	5
Landis, Esther	3rd cousin once removed	IX	5
Landis, Esther Ann	2nd cousin once removed	VII	4
Landis, Fanny F.	2nd cousin	VI	3
Landis, Fanny Long	2nd cousin once removed	VII	4
Landis, Felix	Half 6th great-granduncle	X	9
Landis, Frank H	2nd cousin	VI	3
Landis, Franklin	2nd cousin once removed	VII	4
Landis, Franklin Frick	Husband of the 1st cousin once removed		
Landis, Frena	2nd cousin 4 times removed	X	7
Landis, Hans	6th great-grandfather	VIII	8
Landis, Hans	8th great-grandfather	X	10
Landis, Hans	7th great-grandfather	IX	9
Landis, Hans	5th great-granduncle	IX	8
Landis, Hans	4th great-granduncle	VIII	7
Landis, Hans Heinrich	4th great-granduncle	VIII	7
Landis, Hans Heinrich	1st cousin 6 times removed	X	8
Landis, Hans Heinrich	5th great-grandfather	VII	7
Landis, Hans Heinrich (Heini)	7th great-granduncle	XI	10
Landis, Hans Jacob	4th great-granduncle	VIII	7
Landis, Hans Rudolf	5th great-granduncle	IX	8
Landis, Harry Graybill	2nd cousin twice removed	VIII	5
Landis, Harry M.	2nd cousin twice removed	VIII	5
Landis, Harvey	2nd cousin once removed	VII	4
Landis, Heinrich	Half 6th great-granduncle	X	9
Landis, Henry	1st cousin 5 times removed	IX	7
Landis, Henry	2nd great-granduncle	VI	5
Landis, Henry	2nd cousin 4 times removed	X	7
Landis, Henry	1st cousin 3 times removed	VII	5
Landis, Henry	1st cousin 3 times removed	VII	5
Landis, Henry	2nd cousin twice removed	VIII	5
Landis, Henry	3rd cousin once removed	IX	5
Landis, Henry Erb	3rd cousin 3 times removed	XI	7
Landis, Henry Frankfort	2nd cousin	VI	3
Landis, Henry M	2nd cousin	VI	3
Landis, Henry N	2nd cousin twice removed	VIII	5
Landis, Henry S	1st cousin once removed	V	3
Landis, Hettie	2nd cousin	VI	3
Landis, Hettie F.	2nd cousin	VI	3
Landis, Hettie S.	1st cousin once removed	V	3
Landis, Hiram	2nd cousin once removed	VII	4
Landis, Ida May	2nd cousin	VI	3
Landis, Isaac M	2nd cousin	VI	3
Landis, Isaac M.	2nd cousin	VI	3
Landis, Jacob	4th great-granduncle	VIII	7
Landis, Jacob	5th great-granduncle	IX	8
Landis, Jacob	2nd great-granduncle	VI	5
Landis, Jacob	1st cousin 3 times removed	VII	5
Landis, Jacob B.	2nd cousin twice removed	VIII	5
Landis, Jacob M	2nd cousin	VI	3
Landis, Jacob M.	2nd cousin	VI	3
Landis, Jacob S.	1st cousin once removed	V	3
Landis, Jagli	Half 6th great-granduncle	X	9
Landis, Johannes	1st cousin 3 times removed	VII	5
Landis, John	1st cousin 5 times removed	IX	7
Landis, John	1st cousin 3 times removed	VII	5
Landis, John	1st cousin 3 times removed	VII	5
Landis, John	2nd cousin twice removed	VIII	5

Name	Relationship with Milton Hershey	Civil	Canon
Landis, John	2nd cousin twice removed	VIII	5
Landis, John B.	2nd cousin twice removed	VIII	5
Landis, John B.	2nd cousin once removed	VII	4
Landis, John C	2nd cousin once removed	VII	4
Landis, John Erb	3rd cousin 3 times removed	XI	7
Landis, John F.	2nd cousin	VI	3
Landis, John F.	2nd cousin	VI	3
Landis, John K.	2nd cousin twice removed	VIII	5
Landis, John L.	2nd cousin	VI	3
Landis, John M	2nd cousin	VI	3
Landis, John M.	2nd cousin	VI	3
Landis, John Snavely	1st cousin once removed	V	3
Landis, Katie	2nd cousin	VI	3
Landis, Leah	2nd cousin	VI	3
Landis, Leah S.	1st cousin once removed	V	3
Landis, Lester R	2nd cousin 3 times removed	IX	6
Landis, Levi L.	2nd cousin	VI	3
Landis, Lizzie B.	2nd cousin once removed	VII	4
Landis, Ludi	7th great-grandaunt	XI	10
Landis, Lydia B.	2nd cousin once removed	VII	4
Landis, Lydia R.	3rd cousin once removed	IX	5
Landis, Magdalena	2nd cousin 4 times removed	X	7
Landis, Magdalena	1st cousin 3 times removed	VII	5
Landis, Magdalena M.	2nd cousin twice removed	VIII	5
Landis, Magdalena S.	1st cousin once removed	V	3
Landis, Mamie	2nd cousin twice removed	VIII	5
Landis, Margaret	5th great-grandaunt	IX	8
Landis, Margaret	2nd cousin once removed	VII	4
Landis, Margaret	2nd cousin 4 times removed	X	7
Landis, Margaret	2nd cousin	VI	3
Landis, Margaret	2nd cousin	VI	3
Landis, Margaret F.	2nd cousin	VI	3
Landis, Margaret S.	1st cousin once removed	V	3
Landis, Margareth	Half 6th great-grandaunt	X	9
Landis, Margaretha	5th great-grandaunt	IX	8
Landis, Margreth	6th great-grandaunt	X	9
Landis, Maria	1st cousin 3 times removed	VII	5
Landis, Maria	1st cousin 3 times removed	VII	5
Landis, Maria	2nd cousin twice removed	VIII	5
Landis, Mark H	2nd cousin	VI	3
Landis, Marlin R	2nd cousin 3 times removed	IX	6
Landis, Martha A	2nd cousin	VI	3
Landis, Martha G.	2nd cousin twice removed	VIII	5
Landis, Martha M	2nd cousin once removed	VII	4
Landis, Martin S.	1st cousin once removed	V	3
Landis, Mary	2nd cousin 4 times removed	X	7
Landis, Mary	Wife of the 2nd cousin 3 times removed		
Landis, Mary	2nd great-grandmother	IV	4
Landis, Mary	1st cousin 3 times removed	VII	5
Landis, Mary	Wife of the 2nd cousin 3 times removed		
Landis, Mary	Wife of the granduncle		
Landis, Mary	2nd cousin	VI	3
Landis, Mary	2nd cousin	VI	3
Landis, Mary Ann	2nd cousin	VI	3
Landis, Mary Buckwalter	Wife of the 3rd cousin once removed		
Landis, Mary E.	3rd cousin 3 times removed	XI	7
Landis, Mary F.	2nd cousin	VI	3
Landis, Mary Hershey	2nd cousin	VI	3
Landis, Mary Jane	2nd cousin once removed	VII	4
Landis, Mary K.	2nd cousin twice removed	VIII	5
Landis, Mary M.	2nd cousin twice removed	VIII	5
Landis, Mary Rohrer	3rd cousin once removed	IX	5
Landis, Mary S.	1st cousin once removed	V	3
Landis, Mary S.	1st cousin once removed	V	3
Landis, Mervin Glenn	2nd cousin 3 times removed	IX	6
Landis, Milton G.	2nd cousin twice removed	VIII	5

The Relations of Milton Snavely Hershey, 4th Ed.

Name	Relationship with Milton Hershey	Civil	Canon
Landis, Norma Fay	2nd cousin 3 times removed	IX	6
Landis, Peter	1st cousin 3 times removed	VII	5
Landis, Phares M	2nd cousin once removed	VII	4
Landis, Private	Husband of the 3rd cousin 3 times removed		
Landis, Private	3rd cousin 4 times removed	XII	8
Landis, Private	3rd cousin 4 times removed	XII	8
Landis, Private	Wife of the 3rd cousin twice removed		
Landis, Private	Wife of the 3rd cousin 3 times removed		
Landis, Private	2nd cousin 4 times removed	X	7
Landis, Private	2nd cousin 4 times removed	X	7
Landis, Private	2nd cousin 4 times removed	X	7
Landis, Private	2nd cousin twice removed	VIII	5
Landis, Private	2nd cousin 4 times removed	X	7
Landis, Private	2nd cousin 4 times removed	X	7
Landis, Private	2nd cousin 3 times removed	IX	6
Landis, Private	2nd cousin 3 times removed	IX	6
Landis, Private	2nd cousin 5 times removed	XI	8
Landis, Private	2nd cousin 5 times removed	XI	8
Landis, Private	2nd cousin 5 times removed	XI	8
Landis, Private	2nd cousin 5 times removed	XI	8
Landis, Private	2nd cousin 5 times removed	XI	8
Landis, Private	2nd cousin 4 times removed	X	7
Landis, Rodney Lamarr	2nd cousin 4 times removed	X	7
Landis, Rudolf	5th great-granduncle	IX	8
Landis, Rudolf	7th great-granduncle	XI	10
Landis, Rudolf	Half 6th great-granduncle	X	9
Landis, Rudolf	4th great-granduncle	VIII	7
Landis, Rudolph	Half 6th great-granduncle	X	9
Landis, Ruth	2nd cousin twice removed	VIII	5
Landis, Samuel B.	2nd cousin once removed	VII	4
Landis, Samuel F.	2nd cousin	VI	3
Landis, Sarah Ann	2nd cousin once removed	VII	4
Landis, Sarah Ann	2nd cousin	VI	3
Landis, Sarah M	2nd cousin	VI	3
Landis, Susan	1st cousin 3 times removed	VII	5
Landis, Susanna	2nd cousin once removed	VII	4
Landis, Susanna	2nd cousin 4 times removed	X	7
Landis, Susanna	2nd cousin	VI	3
Landis, Susanna S.	1st cousin once removed	V	3
Landis, Susanna S.	1st cousin once removed	V	3
Landis, Suzanna F.	2nd cousin	VI	3
Landis, Ulrich	7th great-granduncle	XI	10
Landis, Verena	5th great-grandaunt	IX	8
Landis, Verena	Half 6th great-grandaunt	X	9
Landis, Victor	2nd cousin twice removed	VIII	5
Landis, Wayne G.	2nd cousin twice removed	VIII	5
Landis, Welti	Half 6th great-granduncle	X	9
Landis, William	2nd cousin once removed	VII	4
Lane, Otto Laurence	Husband of the 6th cousin twice removed		
Lane, Private	6th cousin 3 times removed	XVII	10
Lane, Private	6th cousin 3 times removed	XVII	10
Lane, Private	6th cousin 3 times removed	XVII	10
Lane, Unknown	Husband of the 3rd cousin twice removed		
Lang, Janie Monte	Wife of the 3rd cousin 3 times removed		
Langsdale, Edward Jay	2nd cousin 5 times removed	XI	8
Langsdale, Rae Elizabeth	2nd cousin 5 times removed	XI	8
Langsdale, Robert John	2nd cousin 5 times removed	XI	8
Langsdale, Robert T.	Husband of the 2nd cousin 4 times removed		
Langsdale, Tessa Maria	2nd cousin 6 times removed	XII	9
Lapp, John Reichenbach (NEW YORK) Rev.	Husband of the 2nd cousin 3 times removed		
Lapp, Private	Husband of the 3rd cousin 3 times removed		
Lapp, Private	3rd cousin 4 times removed	XII	8
Lapp, Private	3rd cousin 4 times removed	XII	8
Latscher, Annie Hiestand	Wife of the 4th cousin once removed		
Latscher, Jacob Franz Sauers	Husband of the 1st cousin 4 times removed		
Latscher, John Buckwalter	2nd cousin 3 times removed	IX	6

Name	Relationship with Milton Hershey	Civil	Canon
Latscher, John Rev.	Husband of the 4th cousin once removed		
Latscher, Mary (Latshaw)	Wife of the 3rd cousin twice removed		
Latscher, Mary Buckwalter	2nd cousin 3 times removed	IX	6
Latscher, Susan High	Wife of the 4th cousin once removed		
Latscher, William Stauffer	5th cousin	XII	6
Lauver, Private	Husband of the 3rd cousin 3 times removed		
Lauver, Private	3rd cousin 4 times removed	XII	8
Lauver, Private	3rd cousin 4 times removed	XII	8
Lavalley, Private	Wife of the 6th cousin 5 times removed		
Lavender, Bessie Sitier	Wife of the 6th cousin 3 times removed		
Law, Annie	Wife of the half 3rd cousin twice removed		
Lawless, Private	Wife of the 6th cousin 3 times removed		
Leabo, Cora Alice	Wife of the 6th cousin		
Leacock, Rauchy Ann	Wife of the 3rd cousin twice removed		
Learn, Ethel	Wife of the half 3rd cousin twice removed		
Learn, Evelyn Hershey	4th cousin once removed	XI	6
Learn, Hershey David	4th cousin once removed	XI	6
Learn, Peter	Husband of the 3rd cousin twice removed		
Leary, Margaret	Wife of the 6th cousin twice removed		
Leed, John E	Husband of the 4th cousin		
Leeds, Anna	Wife of the 2nd cousin		
Leedy, Blanche Pauline	Wife of the 6th cousin twice removed		
Lefever, Daniel N.	Husband of the 3rd cousin twice removed		
Lefever, Frances Violet	3rd cousin twice removed	X	6
Lefever, Harold Horst	3rd cousin twice removed	X	6
Lefever, Jay Lehman	3rd cousin twice removed	X	6
Lefever, Lehman Herr	Husband of the 3rd cousin once removed		
Lefever, Merle Horst	3rd cousin twice removed	X	6
Lefever, Miriam Horst	3rd cousin twice removed	X	6
Lefever, Private	Wife of the 3rd cousin twice removed		
Lefever, Titus Horst	3rd cousin twice removed	X	6
LeFevre, Anne	Half 4th cousin twice removed	XII	7
LeFevre, Daniel	Husband of the half 3rd cousin 3 times removed		
LeFevre, Daniel	Half 4th cousin twice removed	XII	7
LeFevre, David W	Half 4th cousin twice removed	XII	7
LeFevre, Elizabeth	Half 4th cousin twice removed	XII	7
LeFevre, Emma Jane	Half 4th cousin twice removed	XII	7
Lefevre, Hannah	Wife of the half 3rd cousin 3 times removed		
LeFevre, Henry W	Half 4th cousin twice removed	XII	7
LeFevre, Hiram	Half 4th cousin twice removed	XII	7
LeFevre, Jacob B	Half 4th cousin twice removed	XII	7
Lefevre, John E.	Husband of the half 3rd cousin 3 times removed		
Lefevre, Nancy	Half 4th cousin twice removed	XII	7
LeFevre, Susan W	Half 5th cousin once removed	XIII	7
Leffler, Catharine	Wife of the 3rd cousin twice removed		
LeGron, Henry D.	Husband of the 6th cousin once removed		
LeGron, Unknown	6th cousin twice removed	XVI	9
LeGron, Unknown	6th cousin twice removed	XVI	9
LeGron, Unknown	6th cousin twice removed	XVI	9
LeGron, Unknown	6th cousin twice removed	XVI	9
Lehigh, Private	Wife of the 3rd cousin twice removed		
Lehman, Dennis Archie	Husband of the 4th cousin 3 times removed		
Lehman, Esther	Wife of the half 2nd cousin once removed		
Lehman, Harold Ray	6th cousin 4 times removed	XVIII	11
Lehman, John	Husband of the half 3rd cousin twice removed		
Lehman, Mildred	Wife of the half 3rd cousin twice removed		
Lehman, Private	6th cousin 4 times removed	XVIII	11
Lehman, Private	6th cousin 4 times removed	XVIII	11
Lehman, Ray C.	Husband of the 6th cousin 3 times removed		
Lehman, Samuel	Husband of the 6th cousin		
Lehman, Sarah	Wife of the half 3rd cousin once removed		
Leichlite, Wilma Ethelyn	Wife of the 6th cousin twice removed		
Leicy, Mary E.	Wife of the 3rd cousin		
Leida, Iva	Wife of the 6th cousin twice removed		
Leipper, Martha Jane	Wife of the 6th cousin once removed		
Leitenberger, John	Husband of the 6th cousin		

Name	Relationship with Milton Hershey	Civil	Canon
Leithiser, James B	Husband of the 1st cousin		
Leithiser, Margaret	1st cousin once removed	V	3
Lemon, Gladys	Wife of the half 3rd cousin twice removed		
Lengenecker, Miriam	Wife of the 3rd cousin twice removed		
Lenhardy, Mary	Wife of the half 4th great-granduncle		
Lesher, Ann	6th cousin	XIV	7
Lesher, Barbara A.	6th cousin	XIV	7
Lesher, Benjamin Franklin	6th cousin once removed	XV	8
Lesher, Caspar	6th cousin	XIV	7
Lesher, Catherine	6th cousin	XIV	7
Lesher, Christian Hertzler	6th cousin once removed	XV	8
Lesher, David	Husband of the 5th cousin once removed		
Lesher, David	6th cousin	XIV	7
Lesher, Elizabeth	6th cousin	XIV	7
Lesher, Fanny	6th cousin	XIV	7
Lesher, Ida Elizabeth	6th cousin once removed	XV	8
Lesher, Jacob	6th cousin	XIV	7
Lesher, Jeremiah	6th cousin once removed	XV	8
Lesher, John	6th cousin	XIV	7
Lesher, Mary	6th cousin	XIV	7
Lesher, Mary Ann	6th cousin once removed	XV	8
Lesher, Naomi Jane	6th cousin once removed	XV	8
Lesher, Peter	6th cousin	XIV	7
Lesher, Susan Alice	6th cousin once removed	XV	8
Lester	6th cousin twice removed	XVI	9
Level, Annie Eliza	6th cousin twice removed	XVI	9
Level, Burgess Coleman	6th cousin twice removed	XVI	9
Level, Cloyd Irwin	6th cousin twice removed	XVI	9
Level, Elizabeth Leone	6th cousin 3 times removed	XVII	10
Level, Frank Marshall	6th cousin twice removed	XVI	9
Level, Ida Mae	6th cousin twice removed	XVI	9
Level, James William	Husband of the 6th cousin once removed		
Level, John Howard	6th cousin twice removed	XVI	9
Level, Private	6th cousin 3 times removed	XVII	10
Level, Private	6th cousin 3 times removed	XVII	10
Level, Private	6th cousin 3 times removed	XVII	10
Level, Unknown	6th cousin 3 times removed	XVII	10
Level, Unknown	6th cousin 3 times removed	XVII	10
Level, Unknown	6th cousin 3 times removed	XVII	10
Level, Unknown	6th cousin 3 times removed	XVII	10
Level, Unknown	6th cousin twice removed	XVI	9
Levison, Private	Husband of the 6th cousin 3 times removed		
Lew	6th cousin 4 times removed	XVIII	11
Lewis, Mary	Wife of the half 3rd cousin twice removed		
Lewis, Moses Owen	Husband of the 2nd cousin 3 times removed		
Lewis, Private	Husband of the 6th cousin twice removed		
LewisStoffer	5th cousin once removed	XIII	7
Liber, Helen	Wife of the 6th cousin twice removed		
Liber, Unknown	Husband of the 6th cousin once removed		
Lichte, Magdalena	Wife of the 3rd cousin twice removed		
Lichty, Anna	Wife of the half 4th great-granduncle		
Lichty, Anna	Wife of the 3rd cousin twice removed		
Lichty, David	Husband of the 2nd cousin 3 times removed		
Lichty, Harry R.	Husband of the 3rd cousin once removed		
Lichty, Jacob	Husband of the 4th great-grandaunt		
Lichty, John	Husband of the 3rd cousin 3 times removed		
Lichty, Magdalena	Wife of the 2nd cousin 3 times removed		
Lichty, Mary	Wife of the 5th cousin once removed		
Lichty, Private	Husband of the 3rd cousin twice removed		
Lichty, Private	3rd cousin 3 times removed	XI	7
Lichty, Private	3rd cousin 3 times removed	XI	7
Lichty, Private	3rd cousin 3 times removed	XI	7
Lichty, Private	Wife of the 3rd cousin 3 times removed		
Lichty, Private	Wife of the 6th cousin 4 times removed		
Lieb, Unknown (Leap)	Husband of the 1st cousin 4 times removed		
Lied, Jodi Lynn	Wife of the 2nd cousin 5 times removed		

Name	Relationship with Milton Hershey	Civil	Canon
Light, Amanda	Wife of the 6th cousin		
Light, Barbara B	Wife of the uncle		
Light, Barbara M.	Wife of the 6th cousin 3 times removed		
Light, Elizabeth	6th cousin	XIV	7
Light, Levi	Husband of the 5th cousin once removed		
Light, Veronica	6th cousin	XIV	7
Lightbody, Ila	Half 3rd cousin 3 times removed	XI	7
Lightbody, Jean	Wife of the half 3rd cousin twice removed		
Lightbody, Matthew	Husband of the half 3rd cousin twice removed		
Lightner, Jane	Wife of the half 3rd cousin 3 times removed		
Lime, Mary J.	Wife of the 6th cousin		
Linda, Private	Wife of the 6th cousin 3 times removed		
Lindsey, Joseph C.	Husband of the 6th cousin		
Line, Clayton Merle	6th cousin 3 times removed	XVII	10
Line, Fauntis May	6th cousin twice removed	XVI	9
Line, Golda Gladys	6th cousin twice removed	XVI	9
Line, Mabel Beatrice	6th cousin twice removed	XVI	9
Line, Sara Margaret	6th cousin twice removed	XVI	9
Line, Stephen Clyde	6th cousin twice removed	XVI	9
Line, Thora Isabelle	6th cousin 3 times removed	XVII	10
Line, Zelorah J.	Husband of the 6th cousin once removed		
Lively, Emma	Ex-wife of the 6th cousin twice removed		
Livengood, Charles	Husband of the 5th cousin		
Livengood, Jacob	Husband of the 5th cousin once removed		
Livengood, Martha Anna	5th cousin once removed	XIII	7
Livengood, Mary Elizabeth	5th cousin once removed	XIII	7
Livengood, Naomi Leah	5th cousin once removed	XIII	7
Livengood, Rhoda	5th cousin once removed	XIII	7
Livengood, Ruth Lydia	5th cousin once removed	XIII	7
Livengood, Samuel	5th cousin once removed	XIII	7
Livingston, Private	6th cousin 3 times removed	XVII	10
Livingston, Private	6th cousin 3 times removed	XVII	10
Livingston, Private	6th cousin 3 times removed	XVII	10
Livingston, William	Husband of the 6th cousin twice removed		
lll, Private	6th cousin 4 times removed	XVIII	11
Locy, Private	Wife of the 6th cousin twice removed		
Loffer, Glen Jackson	Half 3rd cousin twice removed	X	6
Loffer, William J.	Husband of the half 3rd cousin once removed		
Lohr, Catherine	Wife of the 3rd cousin twice removed		
Lohr, Susan N.	Wife of the 6th cousin		
Lonagher, Unknown	Husband of the 6th cousin once removed		
Long, Abraham	2nd cousin 3 times removed	IX	6
Long, Addah	1st cousin 4 times removed	VIII	6
Long, Ann	2nd cousin 3 times removed	IX	6
Long, Anna	1st cousin 4 times removed	VIII	6
Long, Anna	Wife of the 1st cousin 4 times removed		
Long, Anna	Wife of the 1st cousin 3 times removed		
Long, Anna	1st cousin twice removed	VI	4
Long, Barbara	1st cousin 4 times removed	VIII	6
Long, Benjamin	Husband of the great-grandaunt		
Long, Catharine	1st cousin 4 times removed	VIII	6
Long, Christian	1st cousin 4 times removed	VIII	6
Long, Christian	2nd cousin 3 times removed	IX	6
Long, Christian	Husband of the 1st cousin 3 times removed		
Long, David	Husband of the 2nd cousin 3 times removed		
Long, Elizabeth	1st cousin 4 times removed	VIII	6
Long, Elizabeth	2nd cousin 3 times removed	IX	6
Long, Esther	1st cousin 4 times removed	VIII	6
Long, Fronica	1st cousin 4 times removed	VIII	6
Long, Gideon C.	Husband of the 6th cousin		
Long, Herman	1st cousin 4 times removed	VIII	6
Long, Herman	2nd cousin 3 times removed	IX	6
Long, Herman	Husband of the 3rd great-grandaunt		
Long, John	Husband of the 2nd cousin 3 times removed		
Long, John	1st cousin 4 times removed	VIII	6
Long, John	2nd cousin 3 times removed	IX	6

Name	Relationship with Milton Hershey	Civil	Canon
Long, Joseph	2nd cousin 3 times removed	IX	6
Long, Magdalena	1st cousin 4 times removed	VIII	6
Long, Maria	1st cousin 4 times removed	VIII	6
Long, Mary	2nd cousin 3 times removed	IX	6
Long, Private	Wife of the 3rd cousin 3 times removed		
Long, Private	Wife of the 3rd cousin 3 times removed		
Long, Susanna	1st cousin 4 times removed	VIII	6
Longanecker, Rebecca	Wife of the 6th cousin		
Longenecker, Anna (Longacre)	Wife of the 2nd cousin 3 times removed		
Longenecker, Anna F	Wife of the 5th cousin		
Longenecker, Barbara Becker	Wife of the 3rd cousin once removed		
Longenecker, Christian	2nd cousin twice removed	VIII	5
Longenecker, Daniel Ziegler (Longacre)	Husband of the 3rd cousin twice removed		
Longenecker, Elizabeth	Wife of the 4th cousin twice removed		
Longenecker, John	Husband of the 4th great-grandaunt		
Longenecker, Levi Landes (Longacre)	4th cousin once removed	XI	6
Longenecker, Magdelena Clotz	Wife of the 3rd great-granduncle		
Longenecker, Mary Jane (Longacre)	Wife of the 5th cousin		
Longenecker, Peter	2nd cousin twice removed	VIII	5
Longenecker, Samuel	2nd cousin twice removed	VIII	5
Longenecker, Serena	Wife of the 4th cousin		
Longenecker, Solomon	Husband of the 1st cousin 3 times removed		
Longenecker, Unknown	Wife of the 4th cousin once removed		
Loos, Beatrice	Wife of the 6th cousin 3 times removed		
Loose, Carl Gordon	Husband of the 6th cousin twice removed		
Loose, Carl Maurice	6th cousin 3 times removed	XVII	10
Loose, Private	6th cousin 4 times removed	XVIII	11
Loose, Private	6th cousin 4 times removed	XVIII	11
Loose, Private	6th cousin 3 times removed	XVII	10
Loose, Private	6th cousin 3 times removed	XVII	10
Loose, Private	6th cousin 4 times removed	XVIII	11
Loriencz, Private	Wife of the 3rd cousin 3 times removed		
Lotton, Bertha	Wife of the half 3rd cousin twice removed		
Lower, Catherine	Wife of the 6th cousin		
Lowry, Private	3rd cousin twice removed	X	6
Lowry, Robert Warren	Husband of the 3rd cousin once removed		
Lucas, Suzanna	Wife of the half 3rd cousin		
Lucas, Unknown	Husband of the 6th cousin twice removed		
Lucenti, Carmen Joseph	Husband of the 6th cousin 3 times removed		
Luttrell, Robert Larrance	Husband of the 2nd cousin 3 times removed		
Lutz, James Hershey	1st cousin twice removed	VI	4
Lutz, Private	Wife of the 3rd cousin twice removed		
Lutz, Walter	Husband of the 1st cousin once removed		
Lynch, Private	Wife of the 3rd cousin twice removed		
M(Sargent), Private	Wife of the 6th cousin 3 times removed		
Macklem, Jane	Wife of the half 3rd cousin		
Macleod, Alex	Husband of the half 3rd cousin twice removed		
Macleod, Douglas	Half 3rd cousin 3 times removed	XI	7
Macleod, Private	Half 3rd cousin 3 times removed	XI	7
Maggie	6th cousin twice removed	XVI	9
Maglott, Josephine J	Wife of the 6th cousin twice removed		
Makin, Elizabeth	Wife of the 4th cousin once removed		
Malin, Private	Husband of the 3rd cousin 3 times removed		
Malin, Private	3rd cousin 4 times removed	XII	8
Mall, Private	Husband of the 3rd cousin 3 times removed		
Mall, Private	3rd cousin 4 times removed	XII	8
Malone, Daniel	Husband of the 6th cousin		
Manger, Private	Wife of the 6th cousin 3 times removed		
Manley, Private	Wife of the 3rd cousin 3 times removed		
Mann, Patricia	Wife of the 6th cousin twice removed		
Mapes, Private	Husband of the 6th cousin 3 times removed		
Mapes, Private	6th cousin 4 times removed	XVIII	11
Maphis, Mary	Wife of the 5th cousin once removed		
Maples, Private	Husband of the 6th cousin 3 times removed		
Maples, Private	6th cousin 4 times removed	XVIII	11
Margaret Berkey Clark /	Wife of the 6th cousin		

Name	Relationship with Milton Hershey	Civil	Canon
Mark, Sarah	Wife of the 5th cousin once removed		
Mark, Sarah	Wife of the 6th cousin		
Markley, Catherine Landis	5th cousin	XII	6
Markley, Elias Landis	5th cousin	XII	6
Markley, Jacob Landis	5th cousin	XII	6
Markley, John	Husband of the 2nd cousin 3 times removed		
Markley, John Landis	5th cousin	XII	6
Markley, Samuel Moyer	Husband of the 4th cousin once removed		
Markovich, Private	Husband of the 3rd cousin 3 times removed		
Marlow, Andy	Half 3rd cousin twice removed	X	6
Marlow, Jack	Half 3rd cousin twice removed	X	6
Marlow, John	Husband of the half 3rd cousin once removed		
Marlow, Sarah	Half 3rd cousin twice removed	X	6
Marner, Emanuel	Husband of the 2nd cousin 3 times removed		
Marshall, Ann	Wife of the half 3rd cousin		
Martenize, Private	Husband of the 6th cousin 3 times removed		
Martenize, Private	6th cousin 4 times removed	XVIII	11
Martha	Wife of the granduncle		
Martig, Paul	Husband of the 6th cousin twice removed		
Martig, Private	6th cousin 3 times removed	XVII	10
Martig, Private	6th cousin 3 times removed	XVII	10
Martig, Private	6th cousin 3 times removed	XVII	10
Martig, Private	6th cousin 4 times removed	XVIII	11
Martig, Private	6th cousin 4 times removed	XVIII	11
Martig, Private	6th cousin 4 times removed	XVIII	11
Martig, Private	6th cousin 4 times removed	XVIII	11
Martin, Aaron	Husband of the 5th cousin		
Martin, Aaron K.	Husband of the 3rd cousin twice removed		
Martin, Abraham	Husband of the 2nd cousin 3 times removed		
Martin, Abraham Horst	3rd cousin twice removed	X	6
Martin, Abraham M.	4th cousin 4 times removed	XIV	9
Martin, Abraham O.	3rd cousin	VIII	4
Martin, Ada Ann Lucretia	Wife of the 6th cousin once removed		
Martin, Anna	4th cousin 4 times removed	XIV	9
Martin, Anna O.	3rd cousin	VIII	4
Martin, Annie W.	Wife of the 4th cousin once removed		
Martin, Benjamin E.	Husband of the 2nd cousin twice removed		
Martin, Clarence E.	3rd cousin twice removed	X	6
Martin, Clarence H.	Husband of the 3rd cousin twice removed		
Martin, David	Husband of the 3rd great-grandaunt		
Martin, David	Husband of the 3rd cousin 5 times removed		
Martin, David	4th cousin 4 times removed	XIV	9
Martin, David Ames	Husband of the 4th cousin once removed		
Martin, David O.	3rd cousin	VIII	4
Martin, Dorcus Lucinda	4th cousin	X	5
Martin, Earl E.	3rd cousin twice removed	X	6
Martin, Edith	Wife of the 6th cousin twice removed		
Martin, Elizabeth	Half 3rd cousin 3 times removed	XI	7
Martin, Elizabeth	Wife of the 4th cousin once removed		
Martin, Elizabeth	Wife of the 4th cousin once removed		
Martin, Elizabeth O.	3rd cousin	VIII	4
Martin, Ellen Mary	Wife of the 3rd cousin twice removed		
Martin, Frances	2nd cousin once removed	VII	4
Martin, Frances Horst	3rd cousin twice removed	X	6
Martin, Henry	Husband of the 3rd cousin twice removed		
Martin, Henry O.	3rd cousin	VIII	4
Martin, Infant1	3rd cousin	VIII	4
Martin, Infant2	3rd cousin	VIII	4
Martin, Isaac O.	3rd cousin	VIII	4
Martin, Jacob	Husband of the 1st cousin 4 times removed		
Martin, Jacob W.	Husband of the 4th cousin once removed		
Martin, Joab	Husband of the 3rd cousin once removed		
Martin, John	Husband of the half 2nd cousin 4 times removed		
Martin, John E.	3rd cousin 3 times removed	XI	7
Martin, Jonas S.	Husband of the 1st cousin twice removed		
Martin, Joseph Horst	3rd cousin twice removed	X	6

Name	Relationship with Milton Hershey	Civil	Canon
Martin, Joseph O.	3rd cousin	VIII	4
Martin, Joseph S.	Husband of the 3rd cousin twice removed		
Martin, Kathleen	Wife of the 3rd cousin twice removed		
Martin, Lavone W.	3rd cousin 4 times removed	XII	8
Martin, Lucille	Wife of the 6th cousin 3 times removed		
Martin, Lydia	Wife of the 4th cousin once removed		
Martin, Lydia B.	Wife of the 4th cousin once removed		
Martin, Lydia Z.	Wife of the 4th cousin once removed		
Martin, Magdalena O.	3rd cousin	VIII	4
Martin, Margaret	4th cousin	X	5
Martin, Maria	4th cousin 4 times removed	XIV	9
Martin, Maria	Wife of the granduncle		
Martin, Martha Horst	3rd cousin twice removed	X	6
Martin, Martin	Husband of the 3rd cousin 5 times removed		
Martin, Mary	4th cousin	X	5
Martin, Mary	Wife of the 3rd cousin twice removed		
Martin, Mary	Wife of the 3rd cousin twice removed		
Martin, Mary Ann	Wife of the 2nd cousin twice removed		
Martin, Mary E.	3rd cousin twice removed	X	6
Martin, Mary Ebersole	Wife of the 4th cousin once removed		
Martin, Michael	Husband of the 3rd cousin 5 times removed		
Martin, Michael	Husband of the 5th cousin 3 times removed		
Martin, Michael	Husband of the 2nd cousin once removed		
Martin, Nancy	4th cousin	X	5
Martin, Paul	4th cousin	X	5
Martin, Paul E.	3rd cousin twice removed	X	6
Martin, Private	Husband of the 3rd cousin 4 times removed		
Martin, Private	3rd cousin 3 times removed	XI	7
Martin, Private	3rd cousin 3 times removed	XI	7
Martin, Private	3rd cousin 3 times removed	XI	7
Martin, Private	3rd cousin 3 times removed	XI	7
Martin, Private	3rd cousin 3 times removed	XI	7
Martin, Private	3rd cousin 3 times removed	XI	7
Martin, Private	3rd cousin 3 times removed	XI	7
Martin, Private	3rd cousin 4 times removed	XII	8
Martin, Private	3rd cousin 4 times removed	XII	8
Martin, Private	3rd cousin 4 times removed	XII	8
Martin, Private	3rd cousin 4 times removed	XII	8
Martin, Private	3rd cousin 4 times removed	XII	8
Martin, Private	3rd cousin 4 times removed	XII	8
Martin, Private	3rd cousin 4 times removed	XII	8
Martin, Private	3rd cousin 4 times removed	XII	8
Martin, Private	3rd cousin 4 times removed	XII	8
Martin, Private	3rd cousin 4 times removed	XII	8
Martin, Private	3rd cousin 4 times removed	XII	8
Martin, Private	3rd cousin 4 times removed	XII	8
Martin, Private	3rd cousin 4 times removed	XII	8
Martin, Private	3rd cousin 4 times removed	XII	8
Martin, Private	3rd cousin 4 times removed	XII	8
Martin, Private	3rd cousin 4 times removed	XII	8
Martin, Private	3rd cousin 4 times removed	XII	8
Martin, Private	3rd cousin 4 times removed	XII	8
Martin, Private	3rd cousin 4 times removed	XII	8
Martin, Private	3rd cousin 4 times removed	XII	8
Martin, Private	3rd cousin 4 times removed	XII	8
Martin, Private	3rd cousin 4 times removed	XII	8
Martin, Private	3rd cousin 4 times removed	XII	8
Martin, Private	Husband of the 3rd cousin 3 times removed		
Martin, Private	3rd cousin 4 times removed	XII	8

Name	Relationship with Milton Hershey	Civil	Canon
Martin, Private	3rd cousin 4 times removed	XII	8
Martin, Private	3rd cousin 4 times removed	XII	8
Martin, Private	3rd cousin 4 times removed	XII	8
Martin, Private	3rd cousin 4 times removed	XII	8
Martin, Private	3rd cousin 4 times removed	XII	8
Martin, Private	Husband of the 3rd cousin 3 times removed		
Martin, Private	3rd cousin 4 times removed	XII	8
Martin, Private	3rd cousin 4 times removed	XII	8
Martin, Private	3rd cousin 4 times removed	XII	8
Martin, Private	3rd cousin 4 times removed	XII	8
Martin, Private	Wife of the 3rd cousin 3 times removed		
Martin, Private	Husband of the 3rd cousin 3 times removed		
Martin, Private	3rd cousin 4 times removed	XII	8
Martin, Private	Wife of the 3rd cousin twice removed		
Martin, Private	3rd cousin twice removed	X	6
Martin, Private	3rd cousin twice removed	X	6
Martin, Private	3rd cousin 3 times removed	XI	7
Martin, Private	3rd cousin 3 times removed	XI	7
Martin, Private	3rd cousin 3 times removed	XI	7
Martin, Private	3rd cousin 3 times removed	XI	7
Martin, Private	3rd cousin 3 times removed	XI	7
Martin, Private	3rd cousin 3 times removed	XI	7
Martin, Private	3rd cousin 3 times removed	XI	7
Martin, Private	3rd cousin 4 times removed	XII	8
Martin, Private	3rd cousin 4 times removed	XII	8
Martin, Private	3rd cousin 4 times removed	XII	8
Martin, Private	3rd cousin 4 times removed	XII	8
Martin, Private	3rd cousin 4 times removed	XII	8
Martin, Private	3rd cousin 4 times removed	XII	8
Martin, Private	3rd cousin 4 times removed	XII	8
Martin, Private	3rd cousin 4 times removed	XII	8
Martin, Private	3rd cousin 4 times removed	XII	8
Martin, Private	3rd cousin 4 times removed	XII	8
Martin, Private	3rd cousin 3 times removed	XI	7
Martin, Private	3rd cousin 3 times removed	XI	7
Martin, Private	3rd cousin 3 times removed	XI	7
Martin, Private	3rd cousin 3 times removed	XI	7
Martin, Private	3rd cousin 3 times removed	XI	7
Martin, Private	3rd cousin 4 times removed	XII	8
Martin, Private	3rd cousin 4 times removed	XII	8
Martin, Private	3rd cousin 4 times removed	XII	8
Martin, Private	3rd cousin 4 times removed	XII	8
Martin, Private	3rd cousin 3 times removed	XI	7
Martin, Private	3rd cousin 3 times removed	XI	7
Martin, Private	3rd cousin 3 times removed	XI	7
Martin, Private	3rd cousin 3 times removed	XI	7
Martin, Private	3rd cousin 3 times removed	XI	7
Martin, Private	3rd cousin 3 times removed	XI	7
Martin, Private	3rd cousin 3 times removed	XI	7
Martin, Private	Husband of the 3rd cousin twice removed		
Martin, Private	3rd cousin 3 times removed	XI	7
Martin, Private	Wife of the 3rd cousin twice removed		
Martin, Private	Husband of the 3rd cousin twice removed		
Martin, Private	3rd cousin 3 times removed	XI	7
Martin, Private	3rd cousin 3 times removed	XI	7
Martin, Private	3rd cousin 3 times removed	XI	7
Martin, Private	3rd cousin 3 times removed	XI	7
Martin, Private	3rd cousin 4 times removed	XII	8
Martin, Private	3rd cousin 4 times removed	XII	8
Martin, Private	Wife of the 6th cousin 3 times removed		
Martin, Rolandis	3rd cousin once removed	IX	5
Martin, Rosalea Joy	3rd cousin 4 times removed	XII	8
Martin, Rose	4th cousin	X	5
Martin, Samuel O.	3rd cousin	VIII	4
Martin, Solomon	Husband of the 2nd cousin 3 times removed		

The Relations of Milton Snavely Hershey, 4th Ed.

Name	Relationship with Milton Hershey	Civil	Canon
Martin, Susanna	3rd cousin	VIII	4
Martin, Thomas Dean	3rd cousin 3 times removed	XI	7
Martin, Unknown	Husband of the 2nd cousin twice removed		
Martin, Vernon W.	3rd cousin 4 times removed	XII	8
Martin, Walter M.	Husband of the 3rd cousin once removed		
Martin, Wayne	3rd cousin once removed	IX	5
Martin, Wilmer E.	3rd cousin twice removed	X	6
Mary, Unknown	Wife of the 6th cousin twice removed		
Masterson, Alice	Wife of the half 3rd cousin 4 times removed		
Mathews, Private	Wife of the 6th cousin 3 times removed		
Matthews, Unknown	Husband of the half 3rd cousin 3 times removed		
Mattis, Elizabeth	Wife of the 2nd cousin 3 times removed		
Mauzzy, Unknown	Husband of the 2nd cousin 3 times removed		
May, James W	Husband of the 6th cousin 3 times removed		
Mayer	4th great-grandaunt	VIII	7
Mayer, Elisabeth	4th great-grandaunt	VIII	7
Mayer, Elizabeth	3rd great-grandmother	V	5
Mayer, Heinrich	4th great-granduncle	VIII	7
Mayer, John	3rd great-granduncle	VII	6
Mayer, Maria	4th great-grandaunt	VIII	7
Mc Kacken, Private	Wife of the 6th cousin 3 times removed		
Mc Laughlin, Private	Husband of the 6th cousin 3 times removed		
Mc Manas, Betty	Wife of the 6th cousin 3 times removed		
Mc Vay, Neveda Bada	Wife of the 6th cousin once removed		
McAfee, Wilbur	Husband of the 6th cousin 3 times removed		
McCarrin, Private	Husband of the 6th cousin 4 times removed		
McCarrin, Private	6th cousin 5 times removed	XIX	12
McClaughry, Clair	Wife of the 6th cousin twice removed		
McDaniel, Private	Husband of the 6th cousin 3 times removed		
McDanill, Private	6th cousin 4 times removed	XVIII	11
McDonnel, Mildred Burkholder	Wife of the 4th cousin once removed		
McDowell, Clarence	Husband of the half 3rd cousin 3 times removed		
McDowell, Private	Half 3rd cousin 4 times removed	XII	8
McDowell, Private	Half 3rd cousin 4 times removed	XII	8
McDowell, Private	Half 3rd cousin 4 times removed	XII	8
McDowell, Robert	Husband of the half 3rd cousin 3 times removed		
Mcelhenny, James	Ex-husband of the 2nd cousin 4 times removed		
McFarland, Dona Lynn	Ex-wife of the 4th cousin 3 times removed		
McGaw, Henry	Husband of the 6th cousin		
McGee, Private	Wife of the half 3rd cousin 4 times removed		
McGowan, David M.	Husband of the 3rd cousin 3 times removed		
McGown, Debra Lynne	3rd cousin 4 times removed	XII	8
McKain, Harold LeRoy	Husband of the 4th cousin twice removed		
McKain, Sheila Nadine	4th cousin 3 times removed	XIII	8
McKain, Tracy Louise	4th cousin 3 times removed	XIII	8
McKenzie, Alberta	Wife of the half 3rd cousin twice removed		
McKenzie, Private	Husband of the 6th cousin 3 times removed		
McKracken, Private	Wife of the 6th cousin 3 times removed		
McLasty, Margaret	Wife of the half 3rd cousin twice removed		
McLaughlin, Private	Husband of the 6th cousin 3 times removed		
McLemore, William Baird	Ex-husband of the 6th cousin twice removed		
McLeod, Archie	Husband of the half 3rd cousin twice removed		
McLeod, Fern	Half 3rd cousin 3 times removed	XI	7
McLeod, Gerald	Half 3rd cousin 3 times removed	XI	7
McLeod, Jesse	Husband of the half 3rd cousin twice removed		
McLeod, Nina	Half 3rd cousin 3 times removed	XI	7
McMichael, Kyle S	Husband of the 6th cousin 3 times removed		
McMonus, Annie	Wife of the 6th cousin once removed		
McMurray, Everett	Husband of the 6th cousin twice removed		
McQuilkin, Private	Husband of the 6th cousin 3 times removed		
McSeveney, Private	Wife of the 3rd cousin twice removed		
McSparron, Private	Wife of the 3rd cousin 3 times removed		
Meaker, Charles Eldyn	Half 3rd cousin twice removed	X	6
Meaker, Charles Rodney	Husband of the half 3rd cousin once removed		
Meaker, Louis Barr	Half 3rd cousin twice removed	X	6
Meaker, Rodney Eldys	Half 3rd cousin twice removed	X	6

Name	Relationship with Milton Hershey	Civil	Canon
Meili, Elsbeth	Wife of the 6th great-granduncle		
Mellinger, Abraham Kauffman	3rd cousin once removed	IX	5
Mellinger, Anna Kauffman	3rd cousin once removed	IX	5
Mellinger, Benedict	Husband of the 2nd great-grandaunt		
Mellinger, Benjamin	2nd cousin twice removed	VIII	5
Mellinger, Benjamin	3rd cousin once removed	IX	5
Mellinger, Benjamin Kauffman	3rd cousin once removed	IX	5
Mellinger, Christian	1st cousin 3 times removed	VII	5
Mellinger, Christian	2nd cousin twice removed	VIII	5
Mellinger, Christian Kauffman	3rd cousin once removed	IX	5
Mellinger, David	Husband of the 1st cousin 4 times removed		
Mellinger, David	1st cousin 3 times removed	VII	5
Mellinger, David	2nd cousin twice removed	VIII	5
Mellinger, David	2nd cousin twice removed	VIII	5
Mellinger, David	3rd cousin once removed	IX	5
Mellinger, David Kauffman	3rd cousin once removed	IX	5
Mellinger, Elizabeth	2nd cousin twice removed	VIII	5
Mellinger, Elizabeth Kauffman	3rd cousin once removed	IX	5
Mellinger, Fannie Kauffman	3rd cousin once removed	IX	5
Mellinger, Franni	1st cousin 3 times removed	VII	5
Mellinger, Freni	1st cousin 3 times removed	VII	5
Mellinger, Henry	2nd cousin twice removed	VIII	5
Mellinger, Henry Kauffman	3rd cousin once removed	IX	5
Mellinger, Jacob	2nd cousin twice removed	VIII	5
Mellinger, Jacob Kauffman	3rd cousin once removed	IX	5
Mellinger, John	1st cousin 3 times removed	VII	5
Mellinger, John	2nd cousin twice removed	VIII	5
Mellinger, John Kauffman	3rd cousin once removed	IX	5
Mellinger, Magdalena Kauffman	3rd cousin once removed	IX	5
Mellinger, Martin	2nd cousin twice removed	VIII	5
Mellinger, Martin Kauffman	3rd cousin once removed	IX	5
Mellow, Helen	Wife of the half 3rd cousin twice removed		
Meng, Mary Angela	Wife of the 6th cousin 3 times removed		
MenMuir, Helen A	Wife of the 6th cousin twice removed		
Mercer, Bert E	Husband of the 6th cousin once removed		
Mercer, Chester	6th cousin twice removed	XVI	9
Mercer, Glenn A	6th cousin twice removed	XVI	9
Mercer, Hazel Debra	6th cousin twice removed	XVI	9
Mercer, Helen M	6th cousin twice removed	XVI	9
Mercer, Herbert Russell	6th cousin twice removed	XVI	9
Mercer, Isabelle L	Wife of the 6th cousin 3 times removed		
Mercer, Orvie W	6th cousin twice removed	XVI	9
Mercer, Private	Husband of the 3rd cousin 3 times removed		
Mercer, Private	3rd cousin 4 times removed	XII	8
Mercer, Private	3rd cousin 4 times removed	XII	8
Mercer, Private	3rd cousin 4 times removed	XII	8
Mercer, Private	6th cousin 3 times removed	XVII	10
Mercer, Private	6th cousin 3 times removed	XVII	10
Mercer, Private	6th cousin 3 times removed	XVII	10
Mercer, Private	6th cousin 3 times removed	XVII	10
Mercer, Private	6th cousin 3 times removed	XVII	10
Mercer, Private	6th cousin 4 times removed	XVIII	11
Mercer, Private	6th cousin 4 times removed	XVIII	11
Mercer, Private	6th cousin 4 times removed	XVIII	11
Mercer, Private	6th cousin 4 times removed	XVIII	11
Mercer, Private	6th cousin 3 times removed	XVII	10
Mercer, Private	6th cousin 3 times removed	XVII	10
Mercer, Private	6th cousin 3 times removed	XVII	10
Mercer, Private	6th cousin 3 times removed	XVII	10
Mercer, Private	6th cousin 4 times removed	XVIII	11
Mercer, Private	6th cousin 4 times removed	XVIII	11
Mercer, Private	6th cousin 4 times removed	XVIII	11
Mercer, Private	Wife of the 6th cousin 3 times removed		
Mercer, Private	6th cousin 4 times removed	XVIII	11
Mercer, Private	6th cousin 4 times removed	XVIII	11
Mercer, Private	6th cousin 4 times removed	XVIII	11

Name	Relationship with Milton Hershey	Civil	Canon
Mercer, Private	6th cousin 4 times removed	XVIII	11
Mercer, Private	6th cousin 3 times removed	XVII	10
Mercer, Private	6th cousin 3 times removed	XVII	10
Mercer, Ruby	6th cousin 3 times removed	XVII	10
Mercer, Ruth	6th cousin 3 times removed	XVII	10
Mercer, Wilford McKinley	Husband of the 6th cousin twice removed		
Meredith, Private	Half 3rd cousin 4 times removed	XII	8
Meredith, Unknown	Husband of the half 3rd cousin 3 times removed		
Messersmith, Elizabeth Margaret	Wife of the 4th cousin twice removed		
Metcalf, Emma	Wife of the half 3rd cousin twice removed		
Mettler, Christine	Wife of the 5th great-granduncle		
Metz, George R.	Husband of the 6th cousin		
Metzler, Elmer	Husband of the 3rd cousin twice removed		
Metzler, Maria	Wife of the 2nd great-granduncle		
Metzler, Mary Anne	Wife of the 6th cousin		
Metzler, Private	Wife of the 3rd cousin 3 times removed		
Metzler, Private	Wife of the 3rd cousin 3 times removed		
Metzler, Private	3rd cousin 3 times removed	XI	7
Metzler, Private	3rd cousin 3 times removed	XI	7
Metzler, Private	3rd cousin 3 times removed	XI	7
Metzler, Private	3rd cousin 4 times removed	XII	8
Metzler, Private	3rd cousin 4 times removed	XII	8
Metzler, Samuel	Husband of the 5th cousin		
Meyer, Abraham	Half 4th great-granduncle	VIII	7
Meyer, Abraham	Half 1st cousin 5 times removed	IX	7
Meyer, Adam (Myer)	Half 1st cousin 5 times removed	IX	7
Meyer, Adelheit	Wife of the half 6th great-granduncle		
Meyer, Anna	Half 1st cousin 7 times removed	XI	9
Meyer, Anna	1st cousin 7 times removed	XI	9
Meyer, Anna	Wife of the 7th great-grandfather		
Meyer, Anna	2nd cousin 3 times removed	IX	6
Meyer, Anna Magdalena	4th great-grandmother	VI	6
Meyer, Annali	Half 4th great-grandaunt	VIII	7
Meyer, Barbara	Half 2nd cousin 4 times removed	X	7
Meyer, Barbara	Wife of the granduncle		
Meyer, Barbara (Mier)	Half 1st cousin 5 times removed	IX	7
Meyer, Christian	1st cousin 4 times removed	VIII	6
Meyer, Christian	6th great-granduncle	X	9
Meyer, Christian	Half 1st cousin 5 times removed	IX	7
Meyer, Christian	Half 1st cousin 5 times removed	IX	7
Meyer, Christian	Half 2nd cousin 4 times removed	X	7
Meyer, Elias	3rd great-granduncle	VII	6
Meyer, Elizabeth	Half 4th great-grandaunt	VIII	7
Meyer, Elsbeth	Half 1st cousin 7 times removed	XI	9
Meyer, Hans	6th great-granduncle	X	9
Meyer, Hans	5th great-grandfather	VII	7
Meyer, Hans Conrad (Mier)	Half 4th great-granduncle	VIII	7
Meyer, Hans Heinrich	1st cousin 7 times removed	XI	9
Meyer, Hans Jacob	1st cousin 7 times removed	XI	9
Meyer, Heinrich	Half 1st cousin 7 times removed	XI	9
Meyer, Heinrich	1st cousin 7 times removed	XI	9
Meyer, Jacob	Half 1st cousin 5 times removed	IX	7
Meyer, Jacob	Half 1st cousin 5 times removed	IX	7
Meyer, Jacob (Myer)	Half 4th great-granduncle	VIII	7
Meyer, John	4th great-grandfather	VI	6
Meyer, John	Half 4th great-granduncle	VIII	7
Meyer, John	Half 1st cousin 5 times removed	IX	7
Meyer, John (Myer)	Half 1st cousin 5 times removed	IX	7
Meyer, Margret	1st cousin 7 times removed	XI	9
Meyer, Mary	Half 4th great-grandaunt	VIII	7
Meyer, Mary	Wife of the 3rd cousin 3 times removed		
Meyer, Melchior	7th great-grandfather	IX	9
Meyer, Michael	4th great-granduncle	VIII	7
Meyer, Regel	1st cousin 7 times removed	XI	9
Meyer, Regula	Half 1st cousin 7 times removed	XI	9
Meyer, Rev. Hans	Half 1st cousin 5 times removed	IX	7

Name	Relationship with Milton Hershey	Civil	Canon
Meyer, Salome	2nd cousin 3 times removed	IX	6
Meyer, Samuel	4th great-granduncle	VIII	7
Meyer, Ursel	1st cousin 7 times removed	XI	9
Meyer, Verena	Wife of the 4th great-granduncle		
Meyer, Verena	5th great-grandaunt	IX	8
Meyer, Veronica	4th great-grandaunt	VIII	7
Meyer, Vincent	3rd great-granduncle	VII	6
Meyer, Vincenz	6th great-grandfather	VIII	8
Meyer, Vincenz	5th great-grandfather	VII	7
Mezurick, Elizabeth	Wife of the half 3rd cousin 3 times removed		
Migliorsis, Private	Wife of the 6th cousin 3 times removed		
Miller, Anna	Wife of the 1st cousin 3 times removed		
Miller, Anna Miriam	Wife of the 6th cousin		
Miller, Barbara	6th cousin 3 times removed	XVII	10
Miller, Catherine	Wife of the 3rd cousin twice removed		
Miller, Christian	Husband of the 1st cousin 3 times removed		
Miller, Cyrus	Husband of the 6th cousin		
Miller, David	Half 4th cousin twice removed	XII	7
Miller, Delores	Wife of the 6th cousin twice removed		
Miller, Edward J.	Husband of the 3rd cousin twice removed		
Miller, Elisabeth	Wife of the 1st cousin 3 times removed		
Miller, Elizabeth	Wife of the 1st cousin 3 times removed		
Miller, Elizabeth	Wife of the 1st cousin 3 times removed		
Miller, Elizabeth	Wife of the 1st cousin 3 times removed		
Miller, Ethel	Wife of the 6th cousin once removed		
Miller, Ethel	Wife of the 6th cousin twice removed		
Miller, Hannah	Wife of the 3rd cousin twice removed		
Miller, Harriet B	Wife of the 3rd cousin once removed		
Miller, Harvey	Husband of the 6th cousin twice removed		
Miller, Justina	Wife of the 2nd cousin twice removed		
Miller, Kenneth	6th cousin 3 times removed	XVII	10
Miller, Magdalene	Wife of the 5th cousin once removed		
Miller, Mary A.	Wife of the 1st cousin once removed		
Miller, Mary M	Wife of the 6th cousin twice removed		
Miller, Mary Rebecca	Wife of the 2nd cousin twice removed		
Miller, McCelland Edward	Husband of the 6th cousin 3 times removed		
Miller, Michael T.	Husband of the 6th cousin		
Miller, Miley Le Mont	Husband of the 6th cousin twice removed		
Miller, Nettie	Wife of the half 3rd cousin twice removed		
Miller, Peter	Husband of the 5th cousin 3 times removed		
Miller, Private	3rd cousin 3 times removed	XI	7
Miller, Private	3rd cousin 3 times removed	XI	7
Miller, Private	3rd cousin 3 times removed	XI	7
Miller, Private	3rd cousin 3 times removed	XI	7
Miller, Private	3rd cousin 4 times removed	XII	8
Miller, Private	3rd cousin 4 times removed	XII	8
Miller, Private	3rd cousin 4 times removed	XII	8
Miller, Private	3rd cousin 4 times removed	XII	8
Miller, Private	Husband of the 3rd cousin 3 times removed		
Miller, Private	Husband of the 3rd cousin 3 times removed		
Miller, Private	3rd cousin 4 times removed	XII	8
Miller, Private	Husband of the 3rd cousin twice removed		
Miller, Private	3rd cousin 3 times removed	XI	7
Miller, Private	3rd cousin 3 times removed	XI	7
Miller, Private	6th cousin 3 times removed	XVII	10
Miller, Private	6th cousin 3 times removed	XVII	10
Miller, Private	6th cousin 3 times removed	XVII	10
Miller, Private	6th cousin 4 times removed	XVIII	11
Miller, Private	Wife of the 6th cousin 3 times removed		
Miller, Private	6th cousin 4 times removed	XVIII	11
Miller, Private	6th cousin 4 times removed	XVIII	11
Miller, Private	Husband of the 2nd cousin twice removed		
Miller, Private	2nd cousin 3 times removed	IX	6
Miller, Private	2nd cousin 3 times removed	IX	6
Miller, Private	2nd cousin 3 times removed	IX	6
Miller, Private	2nd cousin 3 times removed	IX	6

The Relations of Milton Snavely Hershey, 4th Ed.

Name	Relationship with Milton Hershey	Civil	Canon
Miller, Prudence	Wife of the granduncle		
Miller, Rebecca Nyce	Wife of the 4th cousin once removed		
Miller, Samuel	Husband of the half 3rd cousin 3 times removed		
Miller, Sidney Lincoln	Husband of the 6th cousin twice removed		
Miller, Susan	Half 4th cousin twice removed	XII	7
Miller, Susan	Wife of the 1st cousin once removed		
Miller, Tobias	Husband of the 5th cousin 3 times removed		
Miller, William	Husband of the 2nd cousin 3 times removed		
Minagay, Private	Husband of the 6th cousin 3 times removed		
Minagay, Private	6th cousin 4 times removed	XVIII	11
Minagay, Private	6th cousin 4 times removed	XVIII	11
Minagay, Private	6th cousin 4 times removed	XVIII	11
Mitchell, Private	Wife of the 3rd cousin 3 times removed		
Mitten, Agnes Alverdia	6th cousin twice removed	XVI	9
Mitten, Charlotte	6th cousin twice removed	XVI	9
Mitten, Clarence Edward	6th cousin twice removed	XVI	9
Mitten, James Alexander	Husband of the 6th cousin once removed		
Mitten, Lettie	6th cousin twice removed	XVI	9
Mitten, William L.	6th cousin twice removed	XVI	9
Mizner, Catharine	Wife of the 5th cousin once removed		
Mock, Barbara	Wife of the 6th cousin		
Mohler, Frank W.	Husband of the 3rd cousin once removed		
Mohler, Graybill Eby	3rd cousin twice removed	X	6
Mohr, Private	Husband of the 3rd cousin 3 times removed		
Mohr, Private	3rd cousin 4 times removed	XII	8
Moore, Henry Daniel	6th cousin twice removed	XVI	9
Moore, John Raymond	6th cousin twice removed	XVI	9
Moore, Mary Alice	6th cousin twice removed	XVI	9
Moore, Private	6th cousin 3 times removed	XVII	10
Moore, Private	6th cousin 3 times removed	XVII	10
Moore, Private	6th cousin 3 times removed	XVII	10
Moore, Private	6th cousin 3 times removed	XVII	10
Moore, Private	6th cousin 3 times removed	XVII	10
Moore, Private	6th cousin 3 times removed	XVII	10
Moore, Raymond Niles	Husband of the 6th cousin once removed		
Moore, Richard N	6th cousin twice removed	XVI	9
Moore, Robert	6th cousin twice removed	XVI	9
Mordeau, Private	Husband of the 6th cousin 3 times removed		
Mordeau, Private	6th cousin 4 times removed	XVIII	11
Morgan, Nellie	Wife of the half 3rd cousin twice removed		
Morgan, Private	Husband of the 6th cousin 3 times removed		
Morgan, Private	Wife of the 6th cousin 3 times removed		
Mori, Private	Wife of the 6th cousin twice removed		
Mornhengweig, Private	6th cousin 3 times removed	XVII	10
Mornhengweig, Private	6th cousin 4 times removed	XVIII	11
Mornhengweig, Private	6th cousin 3 times removed	XVII	10
Mornhengweig, Private	6th cousin 3 times removed	XVII	10
Mornhengweig, Private	6th cousin 3 times removed	XVII	10
Mornhingweig, Carl	Husband of the 6th cousin twice removed		
Morning, Mary L.	6th cousin twice removed	XVI	9
Morning, William A.	Husband of the 6th cousin once removed		
Morris, Private	Husband of the 6th cousin 3 times removed		
Morris, Private	6th cousin 4 times removed	XVIII	11
Morris, Private	6th cousin 4 times removed	XVIII	11
Morris, Private	6th cousin 4 times removed	XVIII	11
Morris, Private	6th cousin 4 times removed	XVIII	11
Moseman, Magdalena	Wife of the 3rd cousin once removed		
Mosemann, Luke Musser	Husband of the 4th cousin twice removed		
Mosemann, Miriam	Wife of the 3rd cousin once removed		
Mosemann, Private	4th cousin 3 times removed	XIII	8
Mosemann, Private	4th cousin 3 times removed	XIII	8
Mosemann, Private	4th cousin 3 times removed	XIII	8
Mosemann, Private	4th cousin 3 times removed	XIII	8
Moser, Adolph	Husband of the 6th cousin once removed		
Moser, Stella	6th cousin twice removed	XVI	9
Mosser, Christian	Husband of the 3rd great-grandaunt		

Name	Relationship with Milton Hershey	Civil	Canon
Mossey, Private	Husband of the 6th cousin 3 times removed		
Motheral, Rebecca	Wife of the half 3rd cousin		
Mount, Private	Half 3rd cousin 4 times removed	XII	8
Mount, Private	Half 3rd cousin 4 times removed	XII	8
Mount, Unknown	Husband of the half 3rd cousin 3 times removed		
Mountz, Alta	6th cousin twice removed	XVI	9
Mountz, Jesse	Husband of the 6th cousin once removed		
Mountz, Kathryn	6th cousin twice removed	XVI	9
Mountz, Malvern	6th cousin twice removed	XVI	9
Mountz, Mary	6th cousin twice removed	XVI	9
Mountz, Private	6th cousin 3 times removed	XVII	10
Mountz, Private	6th cousin 4 times removed	XVIII	11
Mountz, Private	6th cousin 4 times removed	XVIII	11
Mountz, Private	6th cousin 3 times removed	XVII	10
Mountz, Private	6th cousin 3 times removed	XVII	10
Mountz, Private	6th cousin 3 times removed	XVII	10
Mountz, Wilfred	6th cousin twice removed	XVI	9
Mowder, Bessie	Wife of the half 3rd cousin twice removed		
Moyer, Abraham	Half 1st cousin 5 times removed	IX	7
Moyer, Barbara	Half 1st cousin 5 times removed	IX	7
Moyer, Barbara	Wife of the 2nd cousin 6 times removed		
Moyer, Barbara	Half 1st cousin 5 times removed	IX	7
Moyer, Eleanor	Half 3rd cousin 3 times removed	XI	7
Moyer, John Haldeman (Meyers)	Husband of the 3rd cousin twice removed		
Moyer, Katherine	Half 3rd cousin 3 times removed	XI	7
Moyer, Lillian	Half 3rd cousin 3 times removed	XI	7
Moyer, Margaret	Half 3rd cousin 3 times removed	XI	7
Moyer, Mary	Half 1st cousin 5 times removed	IX	7
Moyer, Mary	Wife of the 3rd cousin twice removed		
Moyer, Private	Husband of the 3rd cousin 3 times removed		
Moyer, Private	3rd cousin 4 times removed	XII	8
Moyer, Private	3rd cousin 4 times removed	XII	8
Moyer, Roy	Husband of the half 3rd cousin twice removed		
Moyer, Sarah	Wife of the half 3rd cousin twice removed		
Moyer, Warren	Half 3rd cousin 3 times removed	XI	7
Moyer, Willard	Half 3rd cousin 3 times removed	XI	7
Muench, Grace	Wife of the 1st cousin once removed		
Mull, Anna Mae	Wife of the 3rd cousin twice removed		
Muller, Elsbeth	6th great-grandmother	VIII	8
Muller, Ursula	Wife of the 5th great-granduncle		
Mumall, Elizabeth	Wife of the 6th cousin		
Mumma, John	Wife of the 2nd cousin twice removed		
Mumma, Maria	1st cousin 4 times removed	VIII	6
Mumma, Sarah	Wife of the 1st cousin once removed		
Mummah, Barbara	1st cousin 4 times removed	VIII	6
Mummah, Christian	1st cousin 4 times removed	VIII	6
Mummah, David	1st cousin 4 times removed	VIII	6
Mummah, George	1st cousin 4 times removed	VIII	6
Mummah, George Anthony	Husband of the 3rd great-grandaunt		
Mummah, Henry	1st cousin 4 times removed	VIII	6
Mummah, Jacob	1st cousin 4 times removed	VIII	6
Mummah, Juliana	1st cousin 4 times removed	VIII	6
Mummah, Magdalena	1st cousin 4 times removed	VIII	6
Murgas, Joseph	Husband of the 4th cousin 3 times removed		
Murgas, Joseph	4th cousin 4 times removed	XIV	9
Murison, Aileen Ruth	Half 3rd cousin 3 times removed	XI	7
Murison, Anna	Half 3rd cousin twice removed	X	6
Murison, Audrey Jean	Half 3rd cousin 3 times removed	XI	7
Murison, Bessie Louise	Half 3rd cousin twice removed	X	6
Murison, Gordon Ernest	Half 3rd cousin twice removed	X	6
Murison, Isobel Anna	Half 3rd cousin 3 times removed	XI	7
Murison, James	Husband of the half 3rd cousin once removed		
Murison, James Wilfred	Half 3rd cousin 3 times removed	XI	7
Murison, John Alexander	Half 3rd cousin 3 times removed	XI	7
Murison, Private	Half 3rd cousin 3 times removed	XI	7
Murison, Wilfrid Charles	Half 3rd cousin twice removed	X	6

Name	Relationship with Milton Hershey	Civil	Canon
Murison, William Gordon	Half 3rd cousin 3 times removed	XI	7
Murison, William Jacob	Half 3rd cousin twice removed	X	6
Murphy, Eda R	6th cousin twice removed	XVI	9
Murphy, Private	Husband of the 3rd cousin 3 times removed		
Murphy, Private	3rd cousin 4 times removed	XII	8
Murphy, Richard W	6th cousin 3 times removed	XVII	10
Murphy, Robert	Husband of the 6th cousin twice removed		
Murphy, William	Husband of the 6th cousin once removed		
Murray, Donald E	6th cousin 3 times removed	XVII	10
Murray, Ira S	Husband of the 6th cousin twice removed		
Murray, Jack O	6th cousin 3 times removed	XVII	10
Murray, Judy A	6th cousin 4 times removed	XVIII	11
Murray, Richard A	6th cousin 3 times removed	XVII	10
Murray, Sylvan E	6th cousin 3 times removed	XVII	10
Murray, Terry L	6th cousin 4 times removed	XVIII	11
Murrell, Alpha	Half 3rd cousin twice removed	X	6
Murrell, Charles	Husband of the half 3rd cousin once removed		
Murrell, Ernest	Half 3rd cousin twice removed	X	6
Murry, Jean Marie	Half 3rd cousin 3 times removed	XI	7
Murry, Marguerite Elizabeth	Half 3rd cousin 3 times removed	XI	7
Murry, Ralph Sheldon	Husband of the half 3rd cousin twice removed		
Musselman, Henry	Husband of the half 4th great-grandaunt		
Musselman, Henry	Half 1st cousin 5 times removed	IX	7
Musselman, Henry	Husband of the 5th cousin once removed		
Musselman, John	Husband of the 2nd cousin 3 times removed		
Musser, Anna	3rd cousin twice removed	X	6
Musser, Anna	3rd cousin twice removed	X	6
Musser, Barbara	Wife of the 1st cousin 3 times removed		
Musser, Barbara Weber	2nd cousin 3 times removed	IX	6
Musser, Benjamin	3rd cousin twice removed	X	6
Musser, Christian Musser	Husband of the 5th cousin once removed		
Musser, Daniel	3rd cousin twice removed	X	6
Musser, Daniel	2nd cousin 3 times removed	IX	6
Musser, Emma	3rd cousin twice removed	X	6
Musser, Esther	2nd cousin 3 times removed	IX	6
Musser, Fronica	2nd cousin 3 times removed	IX	6
Musser, Gideon	3rd cousin twice removed	X	6
Musser, Henry	3rd cousin twice removed	X	6
Musser, Jacob	3rd cousin twice removed	X	6
Musser, Jacob	3rd cousin twice removed	X	6
Musser, Jacob	Husband of the 2nd great-grandaunt		
Musser, John	Husband of the 2nd cousin 3 times removed		
Musser, John B.	Husband of the 4th cousin 4 times removed		
Musser, Lucretta	3rd cousin twice removed	X	6
Musser, Magdalena	2nd cousin 3 times removed	IX	6
Musser, Margaret	Wife of the 1st cousin twice removed		
Musser, Martha	3rd cousin twice removed	X	6
Musser, Martha	3rd cousin twice removed	X	6
Musser, Martin	3rd cousin twice removed	X	6
Musser, Martin	Husband of the 2nd cousin 3 times removed		
Musser, Mary	2nd cousin 3 times removed	IX	6
Musser, Mary Naomi	5th cousin twice removed	XIV	8
Musser, Mathias	Husband of the 1st cousin 4 times removed		
Musser, Mildred Lois	5th cousin twice removed	XIV	8
Musser, Nancy	2nd cousin 3 times removed	IX	6
Musser, Susan	3rd cousin twice removed	X	6
Musser, Veronica	Wife of the 1st cousin twice removed		
Mustard, Jean	Wife of the half 3rd cousin twice removed		
Myer, Anna	Half 1st cousin 5 times removed	IX	7
Myer, Isaac	Half 1st cousin 5 times removed	IX	7
Myer, Mary	Half 1st cousin 5 times removed	IX	7
Myer, Ruth	Wife of the 3rd cousin once removed		
Myers, Barbara	Wife of the 3rd cousin twice removed		
Myers, Caroline	6th cousin	XIV	7
Myers, Catherine	Wife of the 5th cousin once removed		
Myers, Catherine	Wife of the 5th cousin once removed		

Name	Relationship with Milton Hershey	Civil	Canon
Myers, Daniel	6th cousin	XIV	7
Myers, Elisabeth	6th cousin	XIV	7
Myers, Elizabeth	Wife of the 6th cousin once removed		
Myers, Elizabeth S	Wife of the 6th cousin once removed		
Myers, Emma W.	Wife of the 2nd cousin twice removed		
Myers, Henry	Husband of the 5th cousin once removed		
Myers, Henry O.	6th cousin	XIV	7
Myers, John	Husband of the 5th cousin once removed		
Myers, John O.	6th cousin	XIV	7
Myers, Magdalena	Wife of the 1st cousin 4 times removed		
Myers, Margaret	6th cousin	XIV	7
Myers, Mary A.	6th cousin	XIV	7
Myers, Matilda	6th cousin	XIV	7
Myers, Peter	6th cousin	XIV	7
Myers, Private	Wife of the 3rd cousin 3 times removed		
Myers, Private	Wife of the 3rd cousin twice removed		
Myers, Private	Husband of the 6th cousin 3 times removed		
Myers, Private	6th cousin 4 times removed	XVIII	11
Myers, Private	6th cousin 4 times removed	XVIII	11
Myers, Rebecca	6th cousin	XIV	7
Myers, Susannah	6th cousin	XIV	7
Myers, William O.	6th cousin	XIV	7
Mylin, Abraham S	Husband of the aunt		
Mylin, Anna	Wife of the 3rd great-granduncle		
Mylin, Martha	Wife of the 2nd cousin twice removed		
Myrna, Private	Wife of the 6th cousin 3 times removed		
Naftzinger, Michael	Husband of the 6th cousin		
Nafziger, Private	Wife of the 3rd cousin 4 times removed		
Nagel, Mary	Wife of the 2nd cousin twice removed		
Naples, Private	Husband of the 6th cousin 3 times removed		
Naples, Private	6th cousin 4 times removed	XVIII	11
Napoli, Private	Wife of the 3rd cousin 3 times removed		
Nauman, Ann Elizabeth	Wife of the 5th cousin once removed		
Nauman, Private	Wife of the 3rd cousin twice removed		
Neff, Abraham	Husband of the 1st cousin 4 times removed		
Neff, Ann	Wife of the 1st cousin 3 times removed		
Neff, Barbara	Wife of the 3rd great-granduncle		
Neff, Barbara	Wife of the 2nd cousin twice removed		
Neff, Barbara	Wife of the 3rd cousin twice removed		
Neff, Benjamin	Husband of the 3rd cousin twice removed		
Neff, Catherine	Wife of the 2nd cousin 3 times removed		
Neff, Elizabeth	Wife of the half 1st cousin 5 times removed		
Neff, John	Husband of the 5th cousin		
Neff, Mary V	Wife of the 1st cousin once removed		
Neff, Nellie Louise	Half 3rd cousin twice removed	X	6
Neff, Peter Augustus	Husband of the half 3rd cousin once removed		
Neidig, Christian H.	4th cousin once removed	XI	6
Neidig, Elizabeth	4th cousin once removed	XI	6
Neidig, John	Husband of the 3rd cousin twice removed		
Neidig, Jonathan	Husband of the 3rd cousin twice removed		
Nellie	Wife of the 6th cousin twice removed		
Nelson, Private	Wife of the 6th cousin 3 times removed		
Nessly, Jacob Herr	Husband of the half 2nd cousin 4 times removed		
Neuenschwander, Madlena	7th great-grandmother	IX	9
Neukommet, Barbara	6th great-grandmother	VIII	8
Newcomer, Ann	Wife of the 1st cousin 3 times removed		
Newcomer, Anna Weber	2nd great-grandmother	IV	4
Newcomer, Barbara	6th great-grandmother	VIII	8
Newcomer, Barbara	2nd great-grandaunt	VI	5
Newcomer, Christian	2nd great-granduncle	VI	5
Newcomer, Elizabeth	2nd great-grandaunt	VI	5
Newcomer, Elizabeth	6th cousin	XIV	7
Newcomer, Emmet	Husband of the 6th cousin once removed		
Newcomer, Henry	2nd great-granduncle	VI	5
Newcomer, Henry	Husband of the 5th cousin once removed		
Newcomer, Jacob	6th cousin	XIV	7

Name	Relationship with Milton Hershey	Civil	Canon
Newcomer, Levi	6th cousin	XIV	7
Newcomer, Magdalena	2nd great-grandaunt	VI	5
Newcomer, Mary	6th cousin	XIV	7
Newcomer, Mary	Wife of the 6th cousin		
Newcomer, Pearlie	6th cousin twice removed	XVI	9
Newcomer, Peter	4th great-grandfather	VI	6
Newcomer, Peter	2nd great-granduncle	VI	5
Newcomer, Wolfgang	3rd great-grandfather	V	5
Newkommet, Peter	5th great-grandfather	VII	7
Newlin, Private	Wife of the 3rd cousin 3 times removed		
Newswanger, Ella Margaret	Wife of the 3rd cousin once removed		
Newswanger, Lizzie	Wife of the 3rd cousin twice removed		
Newswanger, Private	Husband of the 3rd cousin 3 times removed		
Newswanger, Private	3rd cousin 4 times removed	XII	8
Nicely, Fred	Husband of the half 3rd cousin twice removed		
Nicely, Private	Half 3rd cousin 3 times removed	XI	7
Nichol, Ruth	Wife of the half 3rd cousin 3 times removed		
Nickey, Edward	6th cousin	XIV	7
Nickey, George	Husband of the 4th cousin twice removed		
Nickey, Mary Jane	6th cousin once removed	XV	8
Nickey, Nancy	6th cousin	XIV	7
Nickey, Samuel	5th cousin once removed	XIII	7
Nigh, Ed	Husband of the half 3rd cousin twice removed		
Nigh, Frances	Half 3rd cousin 3 times removed	XI	7
Nigh, Jack	Half 3rd cousin 3 times removed	XI	7
Nigh, Private	Half 3rd cousin 4 times removed	XII	8
Nigh, Private	Half 3rd cousin 4 times removed	XII	8
Nigh, Private	Half 3rd cousin 4 times removed	XII	8
Nigh, William	Half 3rd cousin 3 times removed	XI	7
Nisley, Rachel H	Wife of the 6th cousin once removed		
Nissley, Annie	Wife of the 6th cousin		
Nissley, Barbara	Wife of the 3rd cousin twice removed		
Nissley, Joseph	Husband of the 6th cousin		
Nissley, Maria	Wife of the 2nd great-granduncle		
Nissley, Private	Wife of the 3rd cousin 3 times removed		
Nissly, Judith	Half 3rd cousin 3 times removed	XI	7
Nolt, Barbara	Wife of the 4th cousin 4 times removed		
Nolt, Chester B.	Husband of the 3rd cousin once removed		
Nolt, Christian	Husband of the 2nd cousin once removed		
Nolt, Daniel	Husband of the 4th cousin once removed		
Nolt, Private	Wife of the 3rd cousin 3 times removed		
Nolt, Private	Wife of the 3rd cousin 3 times removed		
Nolt, Private	Wife of the 3rd cousin 3 times removed		
Nolt, Private	Wife of the 3rd cousin 3 times removed		
Nolt, Private	Wife of the 3rd cousin 3 times removed		
Nolt, Private	Husband of the 3rd cousin 3 times removed		
Nolt, Private	3rd cousin 4 times removed	XII	8
Nolt, Private	3rd cousin 4 times removed	XII	8
Nolt, Private	3rd cousin twice removed	X	6
Nolt, Private	3rd cousin twice removed	X	6
Nolt, Private	3rd cousin twice removed	X	6
Nolt, Susanna	Wife of the 4th cousin 4 times removed		
Novak, Private	Husband of the 6th cousin twice removed		
Novak, Private	6th cousin 3 times removed	XVII	10
Novak, Private	6th cousin 3 times removed	XVII	10
Nusbaum, Elizabeth	Wife of the 6th cousin		
Nussey, Betty	Wife of the 6th cousin 3 times removed		
Nyeholt, Private	Husband of the 3rd cousin 3 times removed		
Nyeholt, Private	3rd cousin 4 times removed	XII	8
Ober, Aaron	6th cousin	XIV	7
Ober, Aaron G.	6th cousin	XIV	7
Ober, Abraham	6th cousin	XIV	7
Ober, Adaline	6th cousin	XIV	7
Ober, Agnes	6th cousin once removed	XV	8
Ober, Agnes Eda	6th cousin once removed	XV	8
Ober, Alfred S.	6th cousin	XIV	7

Name	Relationship with Milton Hershey	Civil	Canon
Ober, Ann	5th cousin once removed	XIII	7
Ober, Ann	6th cousin	XIV	7
Ober, Anna Nancy	5th cousin once removed	XIII	7
Ober, Anne	6th cousin	XIV	7
Ober, Annie	6th cousin	XIV	7
Ober, Annie	6th cousin once removed	XV	8
Ober, Annie	6th cousin once removed	XV	8
Ober, Annie Elizabeth	6th cousin once removed	XV	8
Ober, Arden G	6th cousin twice removed	XVI	9
Ober, Arden G, Jr	6th cousin 3 times removed	XVII	10
Ober, Arthur	6th cousin twice removed	XVI	9
Ober, Augustine	6th cousin	XIV	7
Ober, Barbara	5th cousin once removed	XIII	7
Ober, Barbara	5th cousin once removed	XIII	7
Ober, Barbara	6th cousin	XIV	7
Ober, Barbara	6th cousin	XIV	7
Ober, Barbara	6th cousin	XIV	7
Ober, Barbara Estella	6th cousin once removed	XV	8
Ober, Benjamin	4th cousin twice removed	XII	7
Ober, Benjamin	5th cousin once removed	XIII	7
Ober, Benjamin Franklin	6th cousin	XIV	7
Ober, Benjamin Franklin	6th cousin once removed	XV	8
Ober, Benjamin H.	5th cousin once removed	XIII	7
Ober, Bernard Farren	6th cousin once removed	XV	8
Ober, C Kiefer	6th cousin twice removed	XVI	9
Ober, Caroline	6th cousin	XIV	7
Ober, Catherine	5th cousin once removed	XIII	7
Ober, Catherine	6th cousin	XIV	7
Ober, Catherine	6th cousin	XIV	7
Ober, Catherine A.	6th cousin	XIV	7
Ober, Catherine Rebecca	6th cousin once removed	XV	8
Ober, Cecelia O.	5th cousin once removed	XIII	7
Ober, Cecil S	6th cousin twice removed	XVI	9
Ober, Chambers	5th cousin once removed	XIII	7
Ober, Chandra Kay	6th cousin 3 times removed	XVII	10
Ober, Charlotte	6th cousin	XIV	7
Ober, Christian	4th cousin twice removed	XII	7
Ober, Christian	4th cousin twice removed	XII	7
Ober, Christian	5th cousin once removed	XIII	7
Ober, Christian	6th cousin	XIV	7
Ober, Christian	6th cousin	XIV	7
Ober, Christian J.	6th cousin	XIV	7
Ober, Christian Longnecker	5th cousin once removed	XIII	7
Ober, Cyrus	6th cousin	XIV	7
Ober, Cyrus Henry	5th cousin once removed	XIII	7
Ober, Cyrus Stevens	6th cousin	XIV	7
Ober, Daisy Meyers	6th cousin twice removed	XVI	9
Ober, Daniel	6th cousin	XIV	7
Ober, Daniel	6th cousin	XIV	7
Ober, Daniel M	6th cousin twice removed	XVI	9
Ober, Daniel S.	6th cousin	XIV	7
Ober, David	6th cousin	XIV	7
Ober, David	6th cousin	XIV	7
Ober, David	6th cousin	XIV	7
Ober, David H.	6th cousin	XIV	7
Ober, David S	4th cousin twice removed	XII	7
Ober, David S.	6th cousin	XIV	7
Ober, David W	6th cousin once removed	XV	8
Ober, David W	6th cousin 3 times removed	XVII	10
Ober, David W III	6th cousin 3 times removed	XVII	10
Ober, David W, Jr	6th cousin twice removed	XVI	9
Ober, Delilah O.	6th cousin	XIV	7
Ober, Drusannah	6th cousin	XIV	7
Ober, Edward	6th cousin once removed	XV	8
Ober, Edward	6th cousin 3 times removed	XVII	10
Ober, Edward K.	6th cousin	XIV	7

Name	Relationship with Milton Hershey	Civil	Canon
Ober, Elaine C	6th cousin 3 times removed	XVII	10
Ober, Eleanor V	6th cousin 3 times removed	XVII	10
Ober, Eliza	5th cousin once removed	XIII	7
Ober, Elizabeth	4th cousin twice removed	XII	7
Ober, Elizabeth	5th cousin once removed	XIII	7
Ober, Elizabeth	5th cousin once removed	XIII	7
Ober, Elizabeth	5th cousin once removed	XIII	7
Ober, Elizabeth	5th cousin once removed	XIII	7
Ober, Elizabeth	6th cousin	XIV	7
Ober, Elizabeth	6th cousin	XIV	7
Ober, Elizabeth	6th cousin	XIV	7
Ober, Elizabeth	6th cousin	XIV	7
Ober, Elizabeth	6th cousin	XIV	7
Ober, Elizabeth	6th cousin	XIV	7
Ober, Elizabeth	6th cousin	XIV	7
Ober, Elizabeth Anna	6th cousin	XIV	7
Ober, Elizabeth B.	6th cousin	XIV	7
Ober, Elmer M.	6th cousin twice removed	XVI	9
Ober, Emanuel	6th cousin	XIV	7
Ober, Emma	6th cousin once removed	XV	8
Ober, Emma Barbara	6th cousin once removed	XV	8
Ober, Ephraim B.	6th cousin	XIV	7
Ober, Esther	6th cousin	XIV	7
Ober, Evelyn M	6th cousin 3 times removed	XVII	10
Ober, Fannie O	6th cousin twice removed	XVI	9
Ober, Florence May	6th cousin once removed	XV	8
Ober, Franey	5th cousin once removed	XIII	7
Ober, Fronica	5th cousin once removed	XIII	7
Ober, Gabrielle	6th cousin	XIV	7
Ober, George	6th cousin	XIV	7
Ober, George	6th cousin	XIV	7
Ober, George A	6th cousin twice removed	XVI	9
Ober, Geraldine L	6th cousin 3 times removed	XVII	10
Ober, Hannah	5th cousin once removed	XIII	7
Ober, Hannah Amanda	6th cousin	XIV	7
Ober, Harold	6th cousin twice removed	XVI	9
Ober, Harriet S.	6th cousin	XIV	7
Ober, Harrison Jackson	5th cousin once removed	XIII	7
Ober, Harry F.	6th cousin twice removed	XVI	9
Ober, Henry	5th cousin once removed	XIII	7
Ober, Henry	Husband of the 3rd cousin 3 times removed		
Ober, Henry	4th cousin twice removed	XII	7
Ober, Henry	4th cousin twice removed	XII	7
Ober, Henry	5th cousin once removed	XIII	7
Ober, Henry	5th cousin once removed	XIII	7
Ober, Henry	6th cousin	XIV	7
Ober, Henry	6th cousin	XIV	7
Ober, Henry	6th cousin	XIV	7
Ober, Henry	6th cousin	XIV	7
Ober, Henry	6th cousin	XIV	7
Ober, Henry E.	6th cousin	XIV	7
Ober, Henry Saylor	6th cousin	XIV	7
Ober, Horatio Seymour	6th cousin	XIV	7
Ober, Isaac	6th cousin	XIV	7
Ober, Isaac Huntsberger	5th cousin once removed	XIII	7
Ober, Isaac Newton	6th cousin once removed	XV	8
Ober, Jacob	4th cousin twice removed	XII	7
Ober, Jacob	6th cousin once removed	XV	8
Ober, Jacob	Husband of the 3rd cousin 3 times removed		
Ober, Jacob	5th cousin once removed	XIII	7
Ober, Jacob	5th cousin once removed	XIII	7
Ober, Jacob	5th cousin once removed	XIII	7
Ober, Jacob	5th cousin once removed	XIII	7
Ober, Jacob	6th cousin	XIV	7
Ober, Jacob	6th cousin	XIV	7
Ober, Jacob	6th cousin	XIV	7

Name	Relationship with Milton Hershey	Civil	Canon
Ober, Jacob Myers	6th cousin	XIV	7
Ober, James B.	5th cousin once removed	XIII	7
Ober, James C.	5th cousin once removed	XIII	7
Ober, James C.	6th cousin	XIV	7
Ober, Jean	6th cousin 3 times removed	XVII	10
Ober, Jeremiah	6th cousin	XIV	7
Ober, Joan	6th cousin 3 times removed	XVII	10
Ober, John	4th cousin twice removed	XII	7
Ober, John	5th cousin once removed	XIII	7
Ober, John	5th cousin once removed	XIII	7
Ober, John	6th cousin	XIV	7
Ober, John	6th cousin	XIV	7
Ober, John	6th cousin	XIV	7
Ober, John	6th cousin 3 times removed	XVII	10
Ober, John C.	5th cousin once removed	XIII	7
Ober, John D	6th cousin twice removed	XVI	9
Ober, John D II	6th cousin 3 times removed	XVII	10
Ober, John F.	6th cousin	XIV	7
Ober, John H.	6th cousin	XIV	7
Ober, John J.	6th cousin	XIV	7
Ober, John J.	6th cousin	XIV	7
Ober, John Miller	Husband of the 6th cousin twice removed		
Ober, John Motter	6th cousin once removed	XV	8
Ober, Joseph	6th cousin	XIV	7
Ober, Joseph	5th cousin once removed	XIII	7
Ober, Joseph	6th cousin	XIV	7
Ober, Joseph	6th cousin	XIV	7
Ober, Joseph	6th cousin	XIV	7
Ober, Joseph S.	6th cousin	XIV	7
Ober, Julia Irene	6th cousin once removed	XV	8
Ober, Kain	6th cousin	XIV	7
Ober, Kathleen P	6th cousin 4 times removed	XVIII	11
Ober, Levi	6th cousin	XIV	7
Ober, Levi S.	6th cousin	XIV	7
Ober, Lewis	5th cousin once removed	XIII	7
Ober, Lucy	6th cousin	XIV	7
Ober, Magdalena	5th cousin once removed	XIII	7
Ober, Magdalena	5th cousin once removed	XIII	7
Ober, Margaret	6th cousin	XIV	7
Ober, Margaret	6th cousin	XIV	7
Ober, Margaret	6th cousin	XIV	7
Ober, Margaret R	6th cousin 4 times removed	XVIII	11
Ober, Marilyn E	6th cousin 3 times removed	XVII	10
Ober, Marilyn M	6th cousin 3 times removed	XVII	10
Ober, Marshall	5th cousin once removed	XIII	7
Ober, Martha E.	6th cousin	XIV	7
Ober, Martin	6th cousin	XIV	7
Ober, Mary	5th cousin once removed	XIII	7
Ober, Mary	5th cousin once removed	XIII	7
Ober, Mary	6th cousin	XIV	7
Ober, Mary	6th cousin	XIV	7
Ober, Mary A	6th cousin 3 times removed	XVII	10
Ober, Mary A.	6th cousin	XIV	7
Ober, Mary Adella	6th cousin	XIV	7
Ober, Mary Alice	6th cousin once removed	XV	8
Ober, Mary Ann Or Sue	6th cousin twice removed	XVI	9
Ober, Mary E	6th cousin 3 times removed	XVII	10
Ober, Mary G.	6th cousin	XIV	7
Ober, Mary Or Mattie	6th cousin	XIV	7
Ober, Mary Sue	6th cousin	XIV	7
Ober, Maryann	6th cousin once removed	XV	8
Ober, Melissa G	6th cousin twice removed	XVI	9
Ober, Merritt L	6th cousin twice removed	XVI	9
Ober, Michael	4th cousin twice removed	XII	7
Ober, Michael	5th cousin once removed	XIII	7
Ober, Michael	6th cousin	XIV	7

Name	Relationship with Milton Hershey	Civil	Canon
Ober, Michael Cramer	6th cousin	XIV	7
Ober, Minnie	6th cousin 3 times removed	XVII	10
Ober, Missouri	6th cousin	XIV	7
Ober, Moses Heagly	6th cousin once removed	XV	8
Ober, Moses M.	6th cousin twice removed	XVI	9
Ober, Moses Ruhl	6th cousin	XIV	7
Ober, Nancy	5th cousin once removed	XIII	7
Ober, Nancy	6th cousin	XIV	7
Ober, Nancy Ann	6th cousin	XIV	7
Ober, Nancy Catherine	5th cousin once removed	XIII	7
Ober, Obadiah S.	6th cousin	XIV	7
Ober, Oliver Francis	5th cousin once removed	XIII	7
Ober, Peter	4th cousin twice removed	XII	7
Ober, Peter	4th cousin twice removed	XII	7
Ober, Polly	5th cousin once removed	XIII	7
Ober, Private	Husband of the 3rd cousin 3 times removed		
Ober, Private	3rd cousin 4 times removed	XII	8
Ober, Private	3rd cousin 4 times removed	XII	8
Ober, Private	3rd cousin 4 times removed	XII	8
Ober, Rebecca	6th cousin	XIV	7
Ober, Rebecca	6th cousin	XIV	7
Ober, Rebecca	6th cousin	XIV	7
Ober, Robert H.	6th cousin	XIV	7
Ober, Rosanna	5th cousin once removed	XIII	7
Ober, Sally	5th cousin once removed	XIII	7
Ober, Samuel	5th cousin once removed	XIII	7
Ober, Samuel	6th cousin	XIV	7
Ober, Samuel	5th cousin once removed	XIII	7
Ober, Sarah	5th cousin once removed	XIII	7
Ober, Sarah	6th cousin	XIV	7
Ober, Sarah	6th cousin	XIV	7
Ober, Sarah E.	6th cousin	XIV	7
Ober, Sarah J.	6th cousin	XIV	7
Ober, Sarah Jane	5th cousin once removed	XIII	7
Ober, Sarah Jane	6th cousin	XIV	7
Ober, Solomon Henry	6th cousin once removed	XV	8
Ober, Stella M	6th cousin twice removed	XVI	9
Ober, Susan	5th cousin once removed	XIII	7
Ober, Susan	6th cousin	XIV	7
Ober, Susannah	5th cousin once removed	XIII	7
Ober, Susannah	6th cousin	XIV	7
Ober, Theodore	6th cousin	XIV	7
Ober, Unknown	6th cousin	XIV	7
Ober, Veronica	4th cousin twice removed	XII	7
Ober, Veronica Francis	5th cousin once removed	XIII	7
Ober, Vicky Lee	6th cousin 4 times removed	XVIII	11
Ober, Wilbur C	6th cousin twice removed	XVI	9
Ober, Wilbur C, Jr	6th cousin 3 times removed	XVII	10
Ober, Wilhelmia	6th cousin	XIV	7
Ober, William	5th cousin once removed	XIII	7
Ober, William	6th cousin	XIV	7
Ober, William	6th cousin	XIV	7
Ober, William	6th cousin	XIV	7
Ober, William S.	6th cousin	XIV	7
Oberholtzer, Abraham	Husband of the 6th cousin		
Oberholtzer, Ann	Wife of the 4th cousin twice removed		
Oberholtzer, Anna H.	2nd cousin once removed	VII	4
Oberholtzer, Catharine	2nd cousin once removed	VII	4
Oberholtzer, Catherine	Wife of the 4th cousin twice removed		
Oberholtzer, Elizabeth	Wife of the 3rd cousin once removed		
Oberholtzer, Elizabeth H.	2nd cousin once removed	VII	4
Oberholtzer, Esther H.	2nd cousin once removed	VII	4
Oberholtzer, Henry H.	2nd cousin once removed	VII	4
Oberholtzer, Jacob H.	2nd cousin once removed	VII	4
Oberholtzer, John H.	2nd cousin once removed	VII	4
Oberholtzer, Joseph H.	2nd cousin once removed	VII	4

Name	Relationship with Milton Hershey	Civil	Canon
Oberholtzer, Lizzie O.	Wife of the 2nd cousin once removed		
Oberholtzer, Magdalena	Wife of the half 1st cousin 5 times removed		
Oberholtzer, Martha H.	2nd cousin once removed	VII	4
Oberholtzer, Samuel	Husband of the 1st cousin twice removed		
Oberholtzer, Samuel H.	2nd cousin once removed	VII	4
Oberholtzer, Susanna H.	2nd cousin once removed	VII	4
O'Boyle, Norman	Husband of the half 3rd cousin 3 times removed		
O'Brian, Lily	Wife of the half 3rd cousin once removed		
O'Brien, Jean	Wife of the 6th cousin twice removed		
O'Connell, Private	Husband of the 3rd cousin 3 times removed		
O'Connell, Private	3rd cousin 4 times removed	XII	8
O'Connor, Margaret Cecilia	Wife of the half 3rd cousin twice removed		
Oesch, Susanna Justina	Wife of the 6th cousin		
Offert, Agnes	Wife of the half 3rd cousin 3 times removed		
Oiler, Christopher	Husband of the 6th cousin twice removed		
Oitman, Private	Wife of the 6th cousin 3 times removed		
Oliver, David	Half 3rd cousin 3 times removed	XI	7
Oliver, Earl	Half 3rd cousin 3 times removed	XI	7
Oliver, Edith	Half 3rd cousin 3 times removed	XI	7
Oliver, Edwin	Husband of the half 3rd cousin twice removed		
Oliver, George	Husband of the half 3rd cousin twice removed		
Oliver, Gerald	Half 3rd cousin 3 times removed	XI	7
Oliver, Gladys	Half 3rd cousin 3 times removed	XI	7
Oliver, Jane	Half 3rd cousin 3 times removed	XI	7
Oppliger, Adelfried	6th great-grandmother	VIII	8
Oppliger, Peter	7th great-grandfather	IX	9
Orsbirn, Elmer A	Husband of the 6th cousin 3 times removed		
Orsbirn, Private	6th cousin 4 times removed	XVIII	11
Orsbirn, Private	6th cousin 4 times removed	XVIII	11
Orsbirn, Private	6th cousin 4 times removed	XVIII	11
Orsbirn, Private	6th cousin 4 times removed	XVIII	11
Orsbirn, Private	6th cousin 4 times removed	XVIII	11
Orsbirn, Private	6th cousin 4 times removed	XVIII	11
Osborn, Private	Husband of the 6th cousin 3 times removed		
Osborn, Private	6th cousin 4 times removed	XVIII	11
Osborn, Private	6th cousin 4 times removed	XVIII	11
Oscar, Lloyd	Husband of the half 3rd cousin twice removed		
Outlaw, Katrina Faye	Wife of the 6th cousin twice removed		
Overholtzer, Esther	Wife of the 2nd cousin 3 times removed		
Overly, Private	4th cousin 4 times removed	XIV	9
Overly, Private	Husband of the 4th cousin 3 times removed		
Owen, Wilma Mae	Wife of the 6th cousin twice removed		
Owens, Elizabeth	5th cousin once removed	XIII	7
Owens, Freda I	Wife of the 6th cousin twice removed		
Page, Bessie Bell	Wife of the 6th cousin twice removed		
Palm, Clara Belle	Wife of the 6th cousin once removed		
Palmer, Archie Judson	Husband of the half 3rd cousin twice removed		
Palmer, Darrel Archie	Half 3rd cousin 3 times removed	XI	7
Palmer, Marjorie Ann	Half 3rd cousin 3 times removed	XI	7
Pancake, Bob	Husband of the 6th cousin 3 times removed		
Pancake, Private	6th cousin 4 times removed	XVIII	11
Pancake, Private	6th cousin 4 times removed	XVIII	11
Pancake, Private	6th cousin 4 times removed	XVIII	11
Pancake, Private	6th cousin 4 times removed	XVIII	11
Parker, Helen Ruth	Wife of the half 3rd cousin 3 times removed		
Parker, James	Husband of the 6th cousin		
Parker, Rachel Edith	Wife of the half 3rd cousin once removed		
Parks, Private	Husband of the 6th cousin 3 times removed		
Parry, Antonia Marie	Wife of the 4th cousin twice removed		
Parsons, Ellen	Wife of the half 3rd cousin		
Parsons, Florence	Wife of the half 3rd cousin once removed		
Parsons, Thelma Ruth	Wife of the 6th cousin twice removed		
Partridge, Allan Baker	Husband of the 6th cousin 3 times removed		
Partridge, Charles Allan	6th cousin 4 times removed	XVIII	11
Partridge, Diane Louise	6th cousin 4 times removed	XVIII	11
Patrick	6th cousin 3 times removed	XVII	10

Name	Relationship with Milton Hershey	Civil	Canon
Patterson, Bertram Charles	Husband of the half 3rd cousin 3 times removed		
Patterson, John	Husband of the half 3rd cousin once removed		
Patterson, Lena May	Wife of the half 3rd cousin twice removed		
Patterson, Mary	Wife of the half 3rd cousin once removed		
Patterson, Millard H.	Husband of the 6th cousin 3 times removed		
Patterson, Private	6th cousin 4 times removed	XVIII	11
Patterson, Private	Husband of the 6th cousin 3 times removed		
Paul, Bessie Norene	6th cousin 3 times removed	XVII	10
Paul, Irwin Lee	Husband of the 6th cousin twice removed		
Paul, Private	6th cousin 3 times removed	XVII	10
Pavlovich, Ruth R	Wife of the 6th cousin 3 times removed		
Paxon, Private	Wife of the 6th cousin 3 times removed		
Peachey, Private	Husband of the 3rd cousin twice removed		
Peachey, Private	3rd cousin 3 times removed	XI	7
Peachey, Private	3rd cousin 3 times removed	XI	7
Peachey, Private	3rd cousin 3 times removed	XI	7
Peachey, Private	3rd cousin 3 times removed	XI	7
Pearsol, Agnes Keys	6th cousin	XIV	7
Pearsol, Anna	6th cousin	XIV	7
Pearsol, Charles	6th cousin	XIV	7
Pearsol, Ellen	6th cousin	XIV	7
Pearsol, John H.	Husband of the 5th cousin once removed		
Pearsol, John H.	6th cousin	XIV	7
Pearsol, Unknown	6th cousin	XIV	7
Pearsol, William H.	6th cousin	XIV	7
Peart, Mary	Wife of the 4th cousin once removed		
Peck, Hazel	Wife of the 6th cousin 3 times removed		
Peggie	Wife of the 4th cousin twice removed		
Peifer, Maria	Wife of the 2nd cousin twice removed		
Peiffer, Daniel	Husband of the 3rd cousin twice removed		
Pendergast, John	Husband of the 6th cousin 3 times removed		
Pendergast, Private	6th cousin 4 times removed	XVIII	11
Pengotti, Private	6th cousin 4 times removed	XVIII	11
Pengotti, Private	Husband of the 6th cousin 3 times removed		
Penner, Private	Husband of the 3rd cousin twice removed		
Penner, Private	3rd cousin 3 times removed	XI	7
Penner, Private	3rd cousin 3 times removed	XI	7
Pennock, Betty Louise	3rd cousin twice removed	X	6
Pennock, Private	3rd cousin twice removed	X	6
Pennock, Private	3rd cousin twice removed	X	6
Pennock, William Ralph	Husband of the 3rd cousin once removed		
Pennypacker, Hannah Bergey	Wife of the 3rd cousin twice removed		
Pennypacker, Sophia	Wife of the 4th cousin once removed		
Pentz, John	Husband of the 6th cousin		
Pentz, Mary Ann	6th cousin once removed	XV	8
Pentz, Samuel	6th cousin once removed	XV	8
Pentz, William	6th cousin once removed	XV	8
Pergrem, Private	Wife of the 6th cousin 3 times removed		
Perkins, Alton	Husband of the half 3rd cousin once removed		
Perry, Bonnie K	Wife of the 6th cousin twice removed		
Perry, Eugene	Husband of the 6th cousin once removed		
Peters, Barbara	Wife of the 3rd cousin twice removed		
Peters, George	Husband of the half 3rd cousin 4 times removed		
Peters, Private	Wife of the 3rd cousin twice removed		
Peters, Private	Half 3rd cousin 5 times removed	XIII	9
Petersheim, Private	Wife of the 3rd cousin twice removed		
Peterson, Thelma	Wife of the half 3rd cousin twice removed		
Peveto, Horace	Husband of the 6th cousin once removed		
Pfaltzgraff, Christina Catherine	4th cousin 3 times removed	XIII	8
Pfaltzgraff, David Jasini	4th cousin twice removed	XII	7
Pfaltzgraff, George Hackman	4th cousin twice removed	XII	7
Pfaltzgraff, Kathryn Joyce	4th cousin twice removed	XII	7
Pfaltzgraff, Michael Jasini	4th cousin 3 times removed	XIII	8
Pfaltzgraff, Nevin Mark	4th cousin twice removed	XII	7
Pfaltzgraff, Rebecca	4th cousin 3 times removed	XIII	8
Pfaltzgraff, Renee	4th cousin 3 times removed	XIII	8

Name	Relationship with Milton Hershey	Civil	Canon
Pfaltzgraff, Rhonda	4th cousin 3 times removed	XIII	8
Pfaltzgraff, Roberta	4th cousin 3 times removed	XIII	8
Pfaltzgraff, Roy Edward	Husband of the 4th cousin once removed		
Pfaltzgraff, Roy Edward, Jr	4th cousin twice removed	XII	7
Pfaltzgraff, Timothy David	4th cousin 3 times removed	XIII	8
Pfautz, Mildred	1st cousin once removed	V	3
Pfautz, Monroe	Husband of the 1st cousin		
Pfenniger, Adelheit	Wife of the 4th great-granduncle		
Pfenniger, Barbara	Wife of the 4th great-granduncle		
Pfister, Susanna	Wife of the 5th great-granduncle		
Phillips, Private	Wife of the 6th cousin 3 times removed		
Phillips, Tara	Wife of the 4th cousin 3 times removed		
Pick, Eleanor Gillson	Wife of the half 3rd cousin once removed		
Pickel, Private	Wife of the 3rd cousin 3 times removed		
Pickens, Private	6th cousin 4 times removed	XVIII	11
Pickens, Private	6th cousin 4 times removed	XVIII	11
Pickens, Private	6th cousin 4 times removed	XVIII	11
Pickens, Robert Oliver	Husband of the 6th cousin 3 times removed		
Pier, Private	Husband of the 3rd cousin 3 times removed		
Pier, Private	3rd cousin 4 times removed	XII	8
Pifer, Private	6th cousin 5 times removed	XIX	12
Pifer, Takis Lin	Husband of the 6th cousin 4 times removed		
Pike, Brian K.	6th cousin 4 times removed	XVIII	11
Pike, Private	6th cousin 5 times removed	XIX	12
Pike, Private	6th cousin 5 times removed	XIX	12
Pike, Private	Husband of the 6th cousin 3 times removed		
Pike, Private	6th cousin 4 times removed	XVIII	11
Pike, Private	6th cousin 4 times removed	XVIII	11
Pitkin, Janet Elaine	Wife of the 6th cousin 5 times removed		
Pittman, Cordella	Wife of the 6th cousin twice removed		
Planchock, Dan	Husband of the 6th cousin twice removed		
Planchock, Private	6th cousin 3 times removed	XVII	10
Planchock, Private	6th cousin 3 times removed	XVII	10
Planchock, Private	6th cousin 4 times removed	XVIII	11
Planchock, Private	6th cousin 4 times removed	XVIII	11
Planchock, Private	6th cousin 3 times removed	XVII	10
Planchock, Private	6th cousin 3 times removed	XVII	10
Planchock, Private	6th cousin 3 times removed	XVII	10
Planchock, Private	6th cousin 3 times removed	XVII	10
Plank, John	Husband of the 3rd cousin twice removed		
Pletcher, David M.	Husband of the 6th cousin		
Plock, Private	Wife of the 6th cousin twice removed		
Plonk, David Francis Kauffman	Husband of the 2nd cousin 3 times removed		
Pool, Lydia (Puhl)	Wife of the 3rd cousin twice removed		
Poorman, John	Husband of the 3rd cousin 3 times removed		
Poorman, Veronica	Wife of the 3rd cousin 3 times removed		
Popa, Private	Husband of the 6th cousin 3 times removed		
Popa, Private	6th cousin 4 times removed	XVIII	11
Popa, Private	Husband of the 6th cousin 3 times removed		
Popa, Private	6th cousin 4 times removed	XVIII	11
Pope, Alda	Wife of the 6th cousin 3 times removed		
Porter, Cynthia	Wife of the 4th cousin twice removed		
Porter, Keith	Half 3rd cousin 3 times removed	XI	7
Porter, Kenneth	Half 3rd cousin 3 times removed	XI	7
Porter, Myrtle	Wife of the half 3rd cousin twice removed		
Porter, Roy	Husband of the half 3rd cousin twice removed		
Porter, Verna	Half 3rd cousin 3 times removed	XI	7
Pote, Mary	Wife of the 6th cousin		
Pote, Mary	Wife of the 5th cousin once removed		
Powder, Catherine	6th cousin	XIV	7
Powder, Jacob	6th cousin	XIV	7
Powder, John	Husband of the 5th cousin once removed		
Powder, John	6th cousin	XIV	7
Powder, Michael	6th cousin	XIV	7
Powders, John	Husband of the 6th cousin		
Powell, Betty	Wife of the 6th cousin 3 times removed		

Name	Relationship with Milton Hershey	Civil	Canon
Powell, Private	Husband of the 6th cousin 3 times removed		
Powell, Private	6th cousin 4 times removed	XVIII	11
Powell, Private	6th cousin 4 times removed	XVIII	11
Powell, Private	6th cousin 4 times removed	XVIII	11
Prater, Clifford Jesse	Husband of the 6th cousin twice removed		
Prater, Private	6th cousin 3 times removed	XVII	10
Precise, Private	Wife of the 6th cousin twice removed		
Price, Catherine L.	Wife of the 3rd cousin once removed		
Price, Eliza Rinehart	Wife of the 4th cousin once removed		
Price, Freda Elizabeth	Wife of the 6th cousin once removed		
Price, Hannah	Wife of the half 1st cousin twice removed		
Price, Ora	Wife of the 6th cousin once removed		
Price, Private	Wife of the 2nd cousin 4 times removed		
Prickett, Private	Husband of the 6th cousin 3 times removed		
Prickett, Private	6th cousin 4 times removed	XVIII	11
Prickett, Private	6th cousin 4 times removed	XVIII	11
Printz, Private	Husband of the 3rd cousin 3 times removed		
Printz, Private	3rd cousin 4 times removed	XII	8
Probert, Helen	Wife of the half 3rd cousin once removed		
Pryde, Private	Husband of the half 3rd cousin 4 times removed		
Pryde, Private	Half 3rd cousin 5 times removed	XIII	9
Pullin, George	6th cousin 3 times removed	XVII	10
Pullin, Janet	6th cousin 3 times removed	XVII	10
Pullin, Richard	6th cousin 3 times removed	XVII	10
Pullin, Wilbur	Husband of the 6th cousin twice removed		
Pultz, William	Husband of the 6th cousin twice removed		
Quest, Margaret	Wife of the 2nd cousin 3 times removed		
Rabold, Alvin Kenneth	Husband of the 2nd cousin 3 times removed		
Rabold, Private	2nd cousin 4 times removed	X	7
Rabold, Private	2nd cousin 4 times removed	X	7
Rabold, Private	2nd cousin 5 times removed	XI	8
Rabold, Private	2nd cousin 5 times removed	XI	8
Radcliffe, Private	Wife of the 6th cousin 4 times removed		
Radley, Ruby	Wife of the half 3rd cousin twice removed		
Ramsey, Nellie M	Wife of the 6th cousin once removed		
Ranck, Arthur Eby	3rd cousin twice removed	X	6
Ranck, Donald Edwin	3rd cousin twice removed	X	6
Ranck, Edwin Guy	Husband of the 3rd cousin once removed		
Ranck, Elizabeth	Wife of the 2nd cousin 3 times removed		
Ranck, Enos Raymond	3rd cousin twice removed	X	6
Ranck, Jane Elizabeth	3rd cousin 3 times removed	XI	7
Ranck, Lester Hershey	3rd cousin twice removed	X	6
Ranck, Private	3rd cousin twice removed	X	6
Ranck, Private	3rd cousin 3 times removed	XI	7
Ranck, Private	3rd cousin 3 times removed	XI	7
Ranck, Private	3rd cousin 3 times removed	XI	7
Ranck, Private	3rd cousin 3 times removed	XI	7
Ranck, Private	3rd cousin 4 times removed	XII	8
Ranck, Private	3rd cousin 4 times removed	XII	8
Ranck, Private	3rd cousin 4 times removed	XII	8
Ranck, Private	3rd cousin 3 times removed	XI	7
Ranck, Private	3rd cousin 3 times removed	XI	7
Ranck, Private	3rd cousin 3 times removed	XI	7
Ranck, Private	3rd cousin 4 times removed	XII	8
Ranck, Private	3rd cousin 4 times removed	XII	8
Ranck, Private	3rd cousin 3 times removed	XI	7
Ranck, Private	3rd cousin 3 times removed	XI	7
Ranck, Private	3rd cousin 3 times removed	XI	7
Randall, Cornelius Hall	Husband of the 6th cousin once removed		
Randall, Lowell Orland	6th cousin twice removed	XVI	9
Randall, Private	6th cousin 3 times removed	XVII	10
Randall, Private	6th cousin 3 times removed	XVII	10
Randall, Private	6th cousin 4 times removed	XVIII	11
Randall, Private	6th cousin 4 times removed	XVIII	11
Randels, Alverda	Wife of the 6th cousin		
Rathgeber, Living	Wife of the 6th cousin 4 times removed		

Name	Relationship with Milton Hershey	Civil	Canon
Ray, Gale Emery	Husband of the 6th cousin twice removed		
Ray, Private	6th cousin 3 times removed	XVII	10
Ray, Private	6th cousin 3 times removed	XVII	10
Ray, Private	6th cousin 3 times removed	XVII	10
Ray, Private	6th cousin 3 times removed	XVII	10
Ray, Private	6th cousin 3 times removed	XVII	10
Ray, Private	6th cousin 3 times removed	XVII	10
Ray, Private	6th cousin 3 times removed	XVII	10
Ray, Private	6th cousin 3 times removed	XVII	10
Ray, Private	6th cousin 3 times removed	XVII	10
Ray, Private	6th cousin 4 times removed	XVIII	11
Ray, Private	6th cousin 4 times removed	XVIII	11
Ray, Private	6th cousin 4 times removed	XVIII	11
Ray, Private	6th cousin 4 times removed	XVIII	11
Raymer, Bertie	Half 3rd cousin twice removed	X	6
Raymer, Christian	Husband of the half 3rd cousin once removed		
Raymer, Elmina	Half 3rd cousin twice removed	X	6
Raymer, Magdalena	Wife of the half 2nd cousin once removed		
Raymer, Ruth	Half 3rd cousin twice removed	X	6
Rebecca, Unknown	Wife of the 2nd cousin twice removed		
Reece, Laura	Wife of the 6th cousin		
Reed, James	Husband of the 6th cousin		
Reed, Margaret	Wife of the 6th cousin		
Reen, Charles	Husband of the 5th cousin once removed		
Reese, Elmer	Husband of the 6th cousin twice removed		
Reese, Marion H.	6th cousin 3 times removed	XVII	10
Reese, Neola	6th cousin 3 times removed	XVII	10
Reese, Private	Husband of the 6th cousin 3 times removed		
Reese, Private	6th cousin 4 times removed	XVIII	11
Reese, Private	6th cousin 4 times removed	XVIII	11
Reesor, Anna	Wife of the half 3rd cousin		
Reesor, Christian	2nd cousin 3 times removed	IX	6
Reesor, Elizabeth	Wife of the half 1st cousin twice removed		
Reeves, Private	3rd cousin 3 times removed	XI	7
Reeves, Private	Wife of the 6th cousin 3 times removed		
Reiff, Abraham	Husband of the 3rd cousin 5 times removed		
Reiff, Abraham	4th cousin 4 times removed	XIV	9
Reiff, Abraham	5th cousin 3 times removed	XV	9
Reiff, Anna	4th cousin 4 times removed	XIV	9
Reiff, Anna	5th cousin 3 times removed	XV	9
Reiff, Annie	2nd cousin once removed	VII	4
Reiff, Barbara	4th cousin 4 times removed	XIV	9
Reiff, Benjamin	5th cousin 3 times removed	XV	9
Reiff, Catherine	4th cousin 4 times removed	XIV	9
Reiff, Christina	4th cousin 4 times removed	XIV	9
Reiff, David	4th cousin 4 times removed	XIV	9
Reiff, David	5th cousin 3 times removed	XV	9
Reiff, Elizabeth	5th cousin 3 times removed	XV	9
Reiff, Feronica	4th cousin 4 times removed	XIV	9
Reiff, John A.	2nd cousin once removed	VII	4
Reiff, Jonas N	5th cousin 3 times removed	XV	9
Reiff, Joseph	4th cousin 4 times removed	XIV	9
Reiff, Joseph N	5th cousin 3 times removed	XV	9
Reiff, Magdalena	5th cousin 3 times removed	XV	9
Reiff, Magdalena	2nd cousin once removed	VII	4
Reiff, Mary	4th cousin 4 times removed	XIV	9
Reiff, Mary	5th cousin 3 times removed	XV	9
Reiff, Susanna	4th cousin 4 times removed	XIV	9
Reiff, Susanna	5th cousin 3 times removed	XV	9
Reighart, Abraham	Husband of the 6th cousin		
Reinohl, Maria	Wife of the 2nd cousin twice removed		
Reist, Abraham	Husband of the 2nd cousin 3 times removed		
Reist, Annie	1st cousin 3 times removed	VII	5
Reist, Barbara	Wife of the 1st cousin 4 times removed		
Reist, Barbara	Wife of the 1st cousin 4 times removed		
Reist, Esther	1st cousin 3 times removed	VII	5

Name	Relationship with Milton Hershey	Civil	Canon
Reist, Florence	4th cousin	X	5
Reist, John	1st cousin 3 times removed	VII	5
Reist, John	Husband of the 2nd great-grandaunt		
Reist, John	Husband of the 2nd great-grandaunt		
Reist, John G.	Husband of the 3rd cousin once removed		
Reist, John H.	4th cousin	X	5
Reist, Maria	1st cousin 3 times removed	VII	5
Reist, Maria E.	Wife of the 2nd cousin once removed		
Reist, Naomi	4th cousin	X	5
Reist, Reuben	Husband of the 6th cousin		
Reiter, Private	Husband of the 6th cousin 3 times removed		
Reiter, Private	6th cousin 4 times removed	XVIII	11
Reiter, Private	6th cousin 4 times removed	XVIII	11
Reitober, Private	Wife of the 6th cousin twice removed		
Reitz, Elizabeth R.	Wife of the 4th cousin once removed		
Reitz, Harmen	Husband of the 4th cousin once removed		
Renfro, Private	Husband of the 6th cousin 3 times removed		
Renninger, Angeline	Wife of the 4th cousin once removed		
Resh, Henry	Husband of the 2nd cousin 3 times removed		
Resh, Magdalena	Wife of the 1st cousin 4 times removed		
Ressler, Mary	Wife of the 2nd cousin		
Retallack, John Harold	Husband of the 3rd cousin twice removed		
Rettenmeyer, Carl William	Husband of the 6th cousin 3 times removed		
Reuben, John, Diehl	6th cousin once removed	XV	8
Reuter, Rosella Catherine	Wife of the half 3rd cousin 3 times removed		
Revis, Mary	Wife of the half 3rd cousin		
Reynolds, Elizabeth	Wife of the half 3rd cousin		
Rhoads, Elizabeth	Wife of the 2nd cousin 3 times removed		
Rhoads, James C.	Husband of the 6th cousin 3 times removed		
Rhoads, Private	6th cousin 4 times removed	XVIII	11
Rhoads, Private	6th cousin 4 times removed	XVIII	11
Rhoads, Private	6th cousin 5 times removed	XIX	12
Rhoads, Private	6th cousin 5 times removed	XIX	12
Rhoads, Private	6th cousin 5 times removed	XIX	12
Rhoads, Private	6th cousin 5 times removed	XIX	12
Rhoads, Private	6th cousin 5 times removed	XIX	12
Rhoads, Private	6th cousin 4 times removed	XVIII	11
Rhoda	6th cousin twice removed	XVI	9
Rhode, Mary	3rd great-grandmother	V	5
Rhodes, Edwin D	Husband of the 6th cousin 4 times removed		
Rhodes, Edwin D II	6th cousin 5 times removed	XIX	12
Rhodes, Jacqueline M	6th cousin 5 times removed	XIX	12
Rice, Anna Mabel	Wife of the 6th cousin twice removed		
Rice, Private	Wife of the 3rd cousin 3 times removed		
Rice, Private	Wife of the 6th cousin twice removed		
Richards, Elizabeth	Wife of the half 3rd cousin 3 times removed		
Richardson, Ada Lucretia	6th cousin twice removed	XVI	9
Richardson, Alice Vivian	6th cousin twice removed	XVI	9
Richardson, Andrew Jackson	6th cousin once removed	XV	8
Richardson, Anna	6th cousin once removed	XV	8
Richardson, Carl Andrew	6th cousin 3 times removed	XVII	10
Richardson, Charlotte B.	6th cousin twice removed	XVI	9
Richardson, Dolores Elaine	6th cousin twice removed	XVI	9
Richardson, Emily Pearl	6th cousin twice removed	XVI	9
Richardson, Eva Beatrice	6th cousin twice removed	XVI	9
Richardson, Florence Mildred	6th cousin twice removed	XVI	9
Richardson, Harold	6th cousin twice removed	XVI	9
Richardson, Harriet May	6th cousin once removed	XV	8
Richardson, Leslie Martin	6th cousin twice removed	XVI	9
Richardson, Margaret Ella Blanch	6th cousin twice removed	XVI	9
Richardson, Martha	6th cousin once removed	XV	8
Richardson, Mary Jane	6th cousin once removed	XV	8
Richardson, Mattie Beulah	6th cousin twice removed	XVI	9
Richardson, Melville Jackson	6th cousin twice removed	XVI	9
Richardson, Nancy Ann	6th cousin once removed	XV	8
Richardson, Private	Husband of the 3rd cousin twice removed		

Name	Relationship with Milton Hershey	Civil	Canon
Richardson, Private	3rd cousin 3 times removed	XI	7
Richardson, Private	3rd cousin 3 times removed	XI	7
Richardson, Private	3rd cousin 3 times removed	XI	7
Richardson, Private	6th cousin 4 times removed	XVIII	11
Richardson, Private	6th cousin 4 times removed	XVIII	11
Richardson, Private	6th cousin 4 times removed	XVIII	11
Richardson, Private	6th cousin 4 times removed	XVIII	11
Richardson, Private	6th cousin 4 times removed	XVIII	11
Richardson, Private	6th cousin 3 times removed	XVII	10
Richardson, Private	6th cousin 3 times removed	XVII	10
Richardson, Private	6th cousin 4 times removed	XVIII	11
Richardson, Private	6th cousin 3 times removed	XVII	10
Richardson, Private	6th cousin 3 times removed	XVII	10
Richardson, Private	6th cousin 3 times removed	XVII	10
Richardson, Private	6th cousin 3 times removed	XVII	10
Richardson, Private	6th cousin 3 times removed	XVII	10
Richardson, Private	6th cousin 3 times removed	XVII	10
Richardson, Private	6th cousin 3 times removed	XVII	10
Richardson, Private	6th cousin 3 times removed	XVII	10
Richardson, Private	6th cousin 3 times removed	XVII	10
Richardson, Private	6th cousin 3 times removed	XVII	10
Richardson, Private	6th cousin 3 times removed	XVII	10
Richardson, Private	6th cousin 3 times removed	XVII	10
Richardson, Rebecca Jane	6th cousin once removed	XV	8
Richardson, Reginold	6th cousin twice removed	XVI	9
Richardson, Sarah B.	6th cousin once removed	XV	8
Richardson, Sarah Ruby	6th cousin twice removed	XVI	9
Richardson, Stephen Andrew	6th cousin twice removed	XVI	9
Richardson, Stephen E.	6th cousin once removed	XV	8
Richardson, Stephen R.	Husband of the 6th cousin		
Richardson, Stephen Roscoe	6th cousin twice removed	XVI	9
Richardson, Susan Ann	6th cousin once removed	XV	8
Richardson, Sydney Robert	6th cousin twice removed	XVI	9
Richey, Rosetta Cobb	Wife of the 3rd cousin twice removed		
Rickert, Richard	Husband of the 3rd cousin once removed		
Rider, Marion	Wife of the 6th cousin twice removed		
Rife, Abraham	5th cousin 3 times removed	XV	9
Rife, Fanny H.	2nd cousin once removed	VII	4
Rife, Samuel	4th cousin 4 times removed	XIV	9
Rill, Private	6th cousin 3 times removed	XVII	10
Rill, Private	6th cousin 3 times removed	XVII	10
Rill, Private	6th cousin 3 times removed	XVII	10
Rill, Thpmas Sr	Husband of the 6th cousin twice removed		
Rinehart, Catharine	Wife of the 4th cousin once removed		
Rinehart, John Frick	Husband of the 2nd cousin 3 times removed		
Rinehart, Private	Wife of the 6th cousin 3 times removed		
Rinehart, Rebecca	Wife of the 4th cousin once removed		
Ringer, John	Husband of the 2nd cousin twice removed		
Risser, Abraham H.	2nd cousin 3 times removed	IX	6
Risser, Abraham S.	6th cousin	XIV	7
Risser, Barbara	2nd cousin 3 times removed	IX	6
Risser, Catharine	Wife of the 6th cousin twice removed		
Risser, Catherine	2nd cousin 3 times removed	IX	6
Risser, Christian	Husband of the 2nd cousin		
Risser, Elizabeth	Wife of the 1st cousin 5 times removed		
Risser, Elizabeth	2nd cousin 3 times removed	IX	6
Risser, Elizabeth	Wife of the 5th cousin once removed		
Risser, Elizabeth H.	3rd cousin twice removed	X	6
Risser, Esther	2nd cousin 3 times removed	IX	6
Risser, Jacob H.	2nd cousin 3 times removed	IX	6
Risser, John	2nd cousin 3 times removed	IX	6
Risser, John	Husband of the 5th cousin once removed		
Risser, John H.	Husband of the 6th cousin		
Risser, John S.	6th cousin	XIV	7
Risser, Joseph L.	6th cousin	XIV	7

Name	Relationship with Milton Hershey	Civil	Canon
Risser, Magdalena H.	2nd cousin 3 times removed	IX	6
Risser, Mary M.	Wife of the 2nd cousin once removed		
Risser, Peter	Husband of the 1st cousin 4 times removed		
Risser, Peter	2nd cousin 3 times removed	IX	6
Risser, Samuel S.	6th cousin	XIV	7
Risser, Veronica	6th cousin	XIV	7
Rissler, Private	Husband of the 3rd cousin 3 times removed		
Rissler, Private	3rd cousin 4 times removed	XII	8
Rittenhouse, Sherry	Wife of the 2nd cousin 5 times removed		
Ritter, Benjamin (Riter)	Husband of the 2nd cousin 3 times removed		
Ritter, Private	6th cousin 5 times removed	XIX	12
Ritter, Private	6th cousin 6 times removed	XX	13
Ritter, Private	Husband of the 6th cousin 4 times removed		
Roadt, Magdalena	Wife of the 2nd great-granduncle		
Robb, Frank	Husband of the half 3rd cousin 3 times removed		
Robb, Private	Husband of the 6th cousin 3 times removed		
Roberts, Barbara	Wife of the 6th cousin twice removed		
Robertson, Earl	Husband of the half 3rd cousin twice removed		
Robertson, Ethel	Wife of the half 3rd cousin once removed		
Robertson, Grace	Wife of the half 3rd cousin 3 times removed		
Robertson, Private	Half 3rd cousin 3 times removed	XI	7
Robertson, Private	Half 3rd cousin 3 times removed	XI	7
Robinson, Harry Thomas	Husband of the 6th cousin twice removed		
Robinson, Mabel	Wife of the half 3rd cousin twice removed		
Rockie, Amelia	Wife of the 6th cousin twice removed		
Rockman, Private	Husband of the 6th cousin 3 times removed		
Rockwell, Private	Husband of the 6th cousin 3 times removed		
Rockwell, Private	6th cousin 4 times removed	XVIII	11
Rockwell, Private	6th cousin 4 times removed	XVIII	11
Rode, Murial A	6th cousin 4 times removed	XVIII	11
Rode, Unknown	Husband of the 6th cousin 3 times removed		
Rodgers, Donald Fink	Husband of the 3rd cousin once removed		
Rodgers, Elizabeth	Wife of the 6th cousin 3 times removed		
Rodgers, Leroy	Husband of the 6th cousin 3 times removed		
Rodgers, Private	3rd cousin twice removed	X	6
Rodgers, Private	3rd cousin 3 times removed	XI	7
Rodgers, Private	3rd cousin 3 times removed	XI	7
Rodgers, Private	3rd cousin 3 times removed	XI	7
Rodgers, Private	3rd cousin 3 times removed	XI	7
Rodgers, Private	3rd cousin 3 times removed	XI	7
Rodgers, Private	3rd cousin 4 times removed	XII	8
Rodgers, Private	3rd cousin 4 times removed	XII	8
Rodgers, Private	6th cousin 4 times removed	XVIII	11
Rodgers, Private	6th cousin 4 times removed	XVIII	11
Rogers, Enos Ellis	Husband of the 6th cousin		
Rohaley, Private	Wife of the 6th cousin 3 times removed		
Rohland, Elizabeth	Wife of the 6th cousin		
Rohr, Francis	Wife of the 2nd cousin 3 times removed		
Rohrer, Catherine	Wife of the uncle		
Rohrer, Elizabeth W.	Wife of the 3rd cousin twice removed		
Rohrer, Jacob	Husband of the 2nd cousin 3 times removed		
Rohrer, John	Husband of the 1st cousin 4 times removed		
Rohrer, Maria	Wife of the 2nd cousin twice removed		
Rohrer, Mary Amanda	Wife of the 1st cousin		
Rohrer, Private	Husband of the 3rd cousin 3 times removed		
Rohrer, Private	3rd cousin 4 times removed	XII	8
Rohrer, Private	3rd cousin 4 times removed	XII	8
Roof, Oscar	Husband of the 6th cousin 3 times removed		
Roof, Private	6th cousin 4 times removed	XVIII	11
Roose, Catherine	Wife of the 3rd cousin twice removed		
Root, Adam Frantz	2nd cousin once removed	VII	4
Root, Benjamin B	Husband of the 1st cousin twice removed		
Root, Henry	Husband of the 2nd cousin 3 times removed		
Ross, Daniel	Husband of the half 3rd cousin once removed		
Roth, Irene Loretta	Wife of the 6th cousin 3 times removed		
Roth, Jacob	Husband of the 2nd cousin 3 times removed		

Name	Relationship with Milton Hershey	Civil	Canon
Roush, Private	Wife of the 3rd cousin twice removed		
Rout, Private	Husband of the 6th cousin 3 times removed		
Royer, Ephraim	4th cousin once removed	XI	6
Royer, Jacob	Husband of the 3rd cousin twice removed		
Royer, Jacob	4th cousin once removed	XI	6
Royer, John	4th cousin once removed	XI	6
Royer, Jonas	4th cousin once removed	XI	6
Royer, Leah	4th cousin once removed	XI	6
Royer, Mary	4th cousin once removed	XI	6
Royer, Samuel	4th cousin once removed	XI	6
Royer, Sarah	Wife of the 4th cousin		
Royer, Susannah	4th cousin once removed	XI	6
Royer, William	4th cousin once removed	XI	6
Ruch, John	Husband of the half 3rd cousin		
Ruch, Mary Elizabeth	Half 3rd cousin once removed	IX	5
Rudo, Private	Husband of the 6th cousin 3 times removed		
Rudolph, Private	Wife of the 6th cousin 4 times removed		
Rudy, Charles	Husband of the 2nd cousin twice removed		
Rudy, John Henry	Husband of the 3rd cousin twice removed		
Rudy, Marian A	Wife of the 6th cousin 3 times removed		
Rudy, Marjorie Elaine	3rd cousin 3 times removed	XI	7
Rudy, Private	3rd cousin 3 times removed	XI	7
Rudy, Private	3rd cousin 3 times removed	XI	7
Rudy, Private	3rd cousin 3 times removed	XI	7
Rudy, Private	3rd cousin 4 times removed	XII	8
Rudy, Susanna	Wife of the 2nd cousin 3 times removed		
Ruegg, Anna	6th great-grandmother	VIII	8
Ruesga, Private	Husband of the 6th cousin 3 times removed		
Ruesga, Private	6th cousin 4 times removed	XVIII	11
Ruff, Elizabeth Catherine	Wife of the 6th cousin once removed		
Ruff, Hiram	Husband of the 6th cousin		
Ruff, Nancy	6th cousin once removed	XV	8
Ruggin, Elsbeth	5th great-grandmother	VII	7
Ruggin, Uli	6th great-grandfather	VIII	8
Ruhl, Barbara	Wife of the 5th cousin once removed		
Runion, Betty A	Wife of the 6th cousin twice removed		
Rupert, Donna	Wife of the 6th cousin 3 times removed		
Rupp, Elizabeth	Wife of the 1st cousin once removed		
Rupp, Magdelene	Wife of the great-granduncle		
Rupp, Mary	Wife of the 4th cousin once removed		
Russell, Private	6th cousin 4 times removed	XVIII	11
Russell, Private	Husband of the 6th cousin 3 times removed		
Russell, Private	6th cousin 4 times removed	XVIII	11
Russell, Private	6th cousin 4 times removed	XVIII	11
Russenberger, Anna	Wife of the 6th great-granduncle		
Rutt, John B.	Husband of the 3rd cousin		
Rutt, Magdalena	Wife of the 3rd great-granduncle		
Rutt, Magdalena	Wife of the 2nd cousin 3 times removed		
Rutter, Private	Wife of the 3rd cousin 3 times removed		
Rytz, Annali	8th great-grandmother	X	10
Sager, B. W.	Husband of the half 3rd cousin twice removed		
Sager, Beverly	Half 3rd cousin 3 times removed	XI	7
Sager, Edwin	Half 3rd cousin 3 times removed	XI	7
Sager, Philip	Half 3rd cousin 3 times removed	XI	7
Salisbury, Private	6th cousin 4 times removed	XVIII	11
Salisbury, Private	Husband of the 6th cousin 3 times removed		
Salisbury, Private	6th cousin 4 times removed	XVIII	11
Salisbury, Private	6th cousin 4 times removed	XVIII	11
Salter, Private	Husband of the 6th cousin 3 times removed		
Salter, Private	6th cousin 4 times removed	XVIII	11
Salter, Private	6th cousin 4 times removed	XVIII	11
Salter, Private	6th cousin 4 times removed	XVIII	11
Sanborn, Maria	Wife of the half 3rd cousin		
Sanders, Jamina	Wife of the 3rd cousin once removed		
Sangree, Esther	Wife of the half 3rd cousin 3 times removed		
Sangree, Jacob	Husband of the 6th cousin		

Name	Relationship with Milton Hershey	Civil	Canon
Sanor, Barbara	Wife of the 6th cousin		
Sanor, David	Husband of the 6th cousin		
Sanor, George	Husband of the 5th cousin once removed		
Sanor, Samuel K	Husband of the 6th cousin		
Santee, Betty Jane	Half 3rd cousin 3 times removed	XI	7
Santee, Dorothy	Half 3rd cousin 3 times removed	XI	7
Santee, Kenneth	Half 3rd cousin 3 times removed	XI	7
Santee, Unknown	Husband of the half 3rd cousin twice removed		
Sarciner, Gertrude Y	Wife of the 6th cousin twice removed		
Sartwell, Private	Husband of the 6th cousin 3 times removed		
Sartwell, Private	6th cousin 4 times removed	XVIII	11
Sauder, Esther	Wife of the 3rd cousin twice removed		
Sauder, John M.	Husband of the 2nd cousin once removed		
Sauder, Katharine	Wife of the 3rd cousin		
Sauder, Lydia Ann	Wife of the 3rd cousin		
Sauder, Minnie	Wife of the 6th cousin twice removed		
Saxton, Private	Wife of the 3rd cousin 3 times removed		
Saylor, Anna	Wife of the 5th great-granduncle		
Saylor, Mary Barbara	Wife of the 5th cousin once removed		
Schaak, Elias Kettering	Husband of the 6th cousin		
Schappi, Barbara	Wife of the half 6th great-granduncle		
Scharer, Dorothea	6th great-grandmother	VIII	8
Schell, Clifford	Half 3rd cousin 3 times removed	XI	7
Schell, Esther	Wife of the half 3rd cousin twice removed		
Schell, Gordon	Half 3rd cousin 3 times removed	XI	7
Schell, Miriam	Half 3rd cousin 3 times removed	XI	7
Schell, Robert	Half 3rd cousin 3 times removed	XI	7
Schell, Shirley	Half 3rd cousin 3 times removed	XI	7
Schell, Wilmont	Husband of the half 3rd cousin twice removed		
Schenk, Abraham	4th cousin 3 times removed	XIII	8
Schenk, Andrew K.	3rd cousin 4 times removed	XII	8
Schenk, Anna	3rd cousin 4 times removed	XII	8
Schenk, Anna	3rd cousin 4 times removed	XII	8
Schenk, Barbara	6th great-grandaunt	X	9
Schenk, Barbara	5th great-grandmother	VII	7
Schenk, Barbara	2nd cousin 5 times removed	XI	8
Schenk, Barbara	3rd cousin 4 times removed	XII	8
Schenk, Christian	4th cousin 3 times removed	XIII	8
Schenk, Christian	6th great-granduncle	X	9
Schenk, Christian	5th great-granduncle	IX	8
Schenk, Christian	2nd cousin 5 times removed	XI	8
Schenk, Christian	3rd cousin 4 times removed	XII	8
Schenk, Elisabeth	4th cousin 3 times removed	XIII	8
Schenk, Elisabeth	2nd cousin 5 times removed	XI	8
Schenk, Elisabeth	3rd cousin 4 times removed	XII	8
Schenk, Hans	5th great-granduncle	IX	8
Schenk, Henry	4th cousin 3 times removed	XIII	8
Schenk, Henry	3rd cousin 4 times removed	XII	8
Schenk, Henry	3rd cousin 4 times removed	XII	8
Schenk, Jacob	3rd cousin 4 times removed	XII	8
Schenk, Johannes	6th great-granduncle	X	9
Schenk, John	4th cousin 3 times removed	XIII	8
Schenk, John	1st cousin 6 times removed	X	8
Schenk, John	2nd cousin 5 times removed	XI	8
Schenk, John	3rd cousin 4 times removed	XII	8
Schenk, John	3rd cousin 4 times removed	XII	8
Schenk, Katherine Katrina	Wife of the 2nd cousin 4 times removed		
Schenk, Margaret	6th great-grandaunt	X	9
Schenk, Michael	Husband of the 4th cousin twice removed		
Schenk, Michael	7th great-grandfather	IX	9
Schenk, Michael	6th great-grandfather	VIII	8
Schenk, Michael	5th great-granduncle	IX	8
Schenk, Michael	1st cousin 6 times removed	X	8
Schenk, Michael	2nd cousin 5 times removed	XI	8
Schenk, Michael	3rd cousin 4 times removed	XII	8
Schenk, Michael	3rd cousin 4 times removed	XII	8

Name	Relationship with Milton Hershey	Civil	Canon
Schenk, Niklaus	6th great-granduncle	X	9
Schenk, Ulrich	8th great-grandfather	X	10
Schenk, Ulrich	6th great-granduncle	X	9
Schillinger, Private	Wife of the 6th cousin 4 times removed		
Schinz, Katharina	8th great-grandmother	X	10
Schlichter, Susan	Wife of the 4th cousin once removed		
Schnader, John	Husband of the 2nd cousin 3 times removed		
Schnebli, Elsbeth	6th great-grandmother	VIII	8
Schneider, Elizabeth	Wife of the 1st cousin 4 times removed		
Schneider, Verena	Wife of the 4th great-granduncle		
Schock, Veronica	Wife of the 2nd cousin 3 times removed		
Schoenfield, William	Husband of the 2nd cousin 3 times removed		
Schraeder, Unknown	Husband of the 6th cousin once removed		
Schrantz, John	Husband of the 2nd cousin 4 times removed		
Schreckengast, Private	Husband of the 6th cousin 3 times removed		
Schreiner, George	Husband of the 2nd cousin		
Schrock, Private	Wife of the 3rd cousin twice removed		
Schroeder, Virgile Lewis	Husband of the 6th cousin twice removed		
Schueller, Sarah (Shuler)	Wife of the 3rd cousin twice removed		
Schwarting, Private	Husband of the 6th cousin 3 times removed		
Scogun, Reba A	Wife of the 6th cousin twice removed		
Scott, Aruthur G	6th cousin twice removed	XVI	9
Scott, Harriet	Wife of the 3rd cousin once removed		
Scott, James	6th cousin 3 times removed	XVII	10
Scott, James Little	Husband of the 6th cousin once removed		
Scott, John C	6th cousin twice removed	XVI	9
Scott, Mary A	6th cousin twice removed	XVI	9
Scott, Ralph L	6th cousin twice removed	XVI	9
Scott, Ruth	6th cousin 3 times removed	XVII	10
Scott, Ruth Isabel	6th cousin twice removed	XVI	9
Scott, William	6th cousin 3 times removed	XVII	10
Seachrist, Fanny	Wife of the 1st cousin 4 times removed		
Searle, Ada Elizabeth	Wife of the half 3rd cousin once removed		
Segal, Julia	Wife of the 6th cousin twice removed		
Seibert, Clyde	Husband of the 6th cousin twice removed		
Seibert, Private	6th cousin 3 times removed	XVII	10
Seibert, Private	6th cousin 3 times removed	XVII	10
Selby, Private	Wife of the 6th cousin 3 times removed		
Senseman, Mary	Wife of the 4th cousin once removed		
Sensenderfer, Shelby	Wife of the 4th cousin twice removed		
Sensenig, Christian	Husband of the 2nd cousin 3 times removed		
Sensenig, Christian W.	Husband of the 1st cousin 4 times removed		
Sensenig, Edna M.	Wife of the 3rd cousin once removed		
Sensenig, Elizabeth	Wife of the 1st cousin 4 times removed		
Sensenig, Francis	Husband of the 3rd cousin twice removed		
Sensenig, Ivan M.	Husband of the 3rd cousin once removed		
Sensenig, Lydia	Wife of the 4th cousin once removed		
Sensenig, Mary Wenger	Wife of the 1st cousin 4 times removed		
Sensenig, Michael W.	Husband of the 2nd cousin twice removed		
Sensenig, Private	Wife of the 3rd cousin 3 times removed		
Sensenig, Private	Husband of the 3rd cousin 3 times removed		
Sensenig, Private	3rd cousin 4 times removed	XII	8
Sewell, Ruth	Wife of the 6th cousin 3 times removed		
Shackleton, Private	Husband of the 6th cousin 3 times removed		
Shackleton, Private	6th cousin 4 times removed	XVIII	11
Shackleton, Private	6th cousin 4 times removed	XVIII	11
Shackleton, Private	6th cousin 4 times removed	XVIII	11
Shadrick, Unknown	Husband of the 6th cousin		
Shaeffer, Martin	Husband of the 3rd cousin 5 times removed		
Shafer, Martha Helen	Wife of the 3rd cousin twice removed		
Shaffer, Harriet M.	Wife of the 6th cousin		
Shaner, Elizabeth	Wife of the 5th cousin 3 times removed		
Shank, Carol	Wife of the 5th cousin once removed		
Shank, Christian	Half 1st cousin 5 times removed	IX	7
Shank, Emma	Wife of the half 3rd cousin once removed		
Shank, Glen	Husband of the 6th cousin 3 times removed		

Name	Relationship with Milton Hershey	Civil	Canon
Shank, John	Husband of the half 4th great-grandaunt		
Shanks, Private	Husband of the 6th cousin 3 times removed		
Shanks, Private	6th cousin 4 times removed	XVIII	11
Shanks, Private	6th cousin 4 times removed	XVIII	11
Shapllo, Krenar	Husband of the 6th cousin 3 times removed		
Sharick, Douglas	Half 3rd cousin 3 times removed	XI	7
Sharick, Earl	Half 3rd cousin 3 times removed	XI	7
Sharick, June	Half 3rd cousin 3 times removed	XI	7
Sharick, Mary Elizabeth	Half 3rd cousin 3 times removed	XI	7
Sharick, Patricia	Half 3rd cousin 3 times removed	XI	7
Sharick, Private	Half 3rd cousin 4 times removed	XII	8
Sharick, Unknown	Husband of the half 3rd cousin twice removed		
Sharpe, Charles V	6th cousin 4 times removed	XVIII	11
Sharpe, James W	6th cousin 4 times removed	XVIII	11
Sharpe, Marjorie Ann	6th cousin 4 times removed	XVIII	11
Sharpe, Mary C	6th cousin 4 times removed	XVIII	11
Sharpe, Ruth B	6th cousin 3 times removed	XVII	10
Sharpe, Vernon W	6th cousin 3 times removed	XVII	10
Sharpe, Walter A	Husband of the 6th cousin twice removed		
Shaub, Evelyn Mae Neidermyer	Wife of the 3rd cousin twice removed		
Sheaffer, Alice Margaret	6th cousin twice removed	XVI	9
Sheaffer, Bertie F.	6th cousin twice removed	XVI	9
Sheaffer, Charles M.	6th cousin twice removed	XVI	9
Sheaffer, Doris Madeline	6th cousin 3 times removed	XVII	10
Sheaffer, J. Marion	Husband of the 6th cousin once removed		
Sheaffer, John	Husband of the 2nd cousin twice removed		
Sheaffer, Josiah	3rd cousin once removed	IX	5
Shearer, John	Husband of the 3rd cousin 3 times removed		
Shelley, Veronica	Wife of the 4th cousin 4 times removed		
Shelly, Annie	Wife of the 4th cousin once removed		
Shelly, Ellis Clinton	6th cousin twice removed	XVI	9
Shelly, Jacob S.	Husband of the 6th cousin once removed		
Shelly, John Willis	6th cousin twice removed	XVI	9
Shelly, Magdalene Katherine	6th cousin 3 times removed	XVII	10
Shelly, Mary	Wife of the 1st cousin 5 times removed		
Shelly, Samuel	Husband of the 5th cousin once removed		
Shelly, Viola Lou	6th cousin 3 times removed	XVII	10
Shenfelder, Sarah	Wife of the 4th cousin once removed		
Shenk, Abraham	Husband of the 2nd cousin twice removed		
Shenk, Abraham	6th cousin	XIV	7
Shenk, Anna	Wife of the granduncle		
Shenk, Anna	Wife of the 3rd cousin twice removed		
Shenk, Anna	Wife of the 6th cousin twice removed		
Shenk, Barbara	5th cousin once removed	XIII	7
Shenk, Catherine	5th cousin once removed	XIII	7
Shenk, Catherine	6th cousin	XIV	7
Shenk, Christian	Husband of the 2nd cousin 3 times removed		
Shenk, Christian M.	6th cousin	XIV	7
Shenk, Donald Reuben	3rd cousin twice removed	X	6
Shenk, Elizabeth	5th cousin once removed	XIII	7
Shenk, Florence LaVerne	3rd cousin twice removed	X	6
Shenk, Frances Geraldine	3rd cousin twice removed	X	6
Shenk, Henry	5th cousin once removed	XIII	7
Shenk, Henry	6th cousin	XIV	7
Shenk, Jacob	Husband of the 2nd cousin 3 times removed		
Shenk, Jacob	5th cousin once removed	XIII	7
Shenk, Jacob M.	6th cousin	XIV	7
Shenk, John	5th cousin once removed	XIII	7
Shenk, John Kauffman	Husband of the 3rd cousin once removed		
Shenk, John Marlin	3rd cousin twice removed	X	6
Shenk, John S.	6th cousin	XIV	7
Shenk, Joseph	Husband of the 1st cousin 4 times removed		
Shenk, Joseph	Husband of the 4th cousin twice removed		
Shenk, Joseph	5th cousin once removed	XIII	7
Shenk, Joseph	6th cousin	XIV	7
Shenk, Joseph M.	6th cousin	XIV	7

Name	Relationship with Milton Hershey	Civil	Canon
Shenk, Lydia	5th cousin once removed	XIII	7
Shenk, Magdalena	5th cousin once removed	XIII	7
Shenk, Maria	5th cousin once removed	XIII	7
Shenk, Maria	5th cousin once removed	XIII	7
Shenk, Mary Ann	Wife of the 6th cousin		
Shenk, Michael	Husband of the 2nd cousin 4 times removed		
Shenk, Michael M.	6th cousin	XIV	7
Shenk, Nancy	5th cousin once removed	XIII	7
Shenk, Peter	6th cousin	XIV	7
Shenk, Samuel	6th cousin	XIV	7
Shenk, Sarah	5th cousin once removed	XIII	7
Shenk, Susanna	5th cousin once removed	XIII	7
Shenk, Veronica	5th cousin once removed	XIII	7
Shenk, Veronica	6th cousin	XIV	7
Shepherd, Albert	Husband of the half 3rd cousin twice removed		
Sheraton, George	Husband of the 3rd cousin 3 times removed		
Sherid, Private	Husband of the 3rd cousin 3 times removed		
Sherk, Adam	Husband of the half 3rd cousin		
Sherk, Adgeline	Half 3rd cousin once removed	IX	5
Sherk, Albert	Half 3rd cousin once removed	IX	5
Sherk, Amanda	Half 3rd cousin once removed	IX	5
Sherk, Amos	Husband of the half 3rd cousin		
Sherk, Arvilla	Half 3rd cousin once removed	IX	5
Sherk, Caroline	Half 3rd cousin once removed	IX	5
Sherk, Edward	Half 3rd cousin once removed	IX	5
Sherk, Elizabeth	Half 3rd cousin once removed	IX	5
Sherk, Elizabeth	Wife of the 6th cousin		
Sherk, Franklin	Half 3rd cousin once removed	IX	5
Sherk, Leah	Wife of the 6th cousin		
Sherk, Luella	Half 3rd cousin once removed	IX	5
Sherk, Maria	Half 3rd cousin once removed	IX	5
Sherk, Martha	Half 3rd cousin once removed	IX	5
Sherk, Matilda	Half 3rd cousin once removed	IX	5
Sherk, Reuben	Half 3rd cousin once removed	IX	5
Sherman, Private	Wife of the 6th cousin 3 times removed		
Sherrick, Elizabeth	Wife of the half 3rd cousin		
Sherrick, Joseph	Husband of the 1st cousin 4 times removed		
Shertzer, Baltzer	Husband of the 3rd cousin twice removed		
Shertzer, Baltzer	Husband of the 2nd cousin 3 times removed		
Shertzer, Barbara	4th cousin once removed	XI	6
Shertzer, Barbara	3rd cousin twice removed	X	6
Shertzer, Elizabeth	4th cousin once removed	XI	6
Shertzer, Elizabeth	3rd cousin twice removed	X	6
Shertzer, Private	Wife of the 3rd cousin 3 times removed		
Shiffer, James R.	Husband of the 5th cousin		
Shirk, Esther	Wife of the 5th cousin 3 times removed		
Shirk, Esther Weaver	Wife of the 3rd cousin once removed		
Shirk, Hannah G.	Wife of the 3rd cousin		
Shirk, John	Husband of the 2nd cousin 3 times removed		
Shirk, Michael	Husband of the 1st cousin 4 times removed		
Shirk, Peter	Husband of the 2nd cousin 3 times removed		
Shirk, Peter	Husband of the 2nd cousin 3 times removed		
Shirk, Private	Husband of the 3rd cousin 4 times removed		
Shirk, Private	3rd cousin 5 times removed	XIII	9
Shirk, Private	3rd cousin 5 times removed	XIII	9
Shirk, Private	Husband of the 3rd cousin 3 times removed		
Shirk, Private	3rd cousin 4 times removed	XII	8
Shirk, Private	3rd cousin 4 times removed	XII	8
Shirk, Samuel	Husband of the 5th cousin 3 times removed		
Shissler, Albert	Husband of the 2nd cousin		
Shively, Bonnie Walker	6th cousin 3 times removed	XVII	10
Shively, Florence	6th cousin twice removed	XVI	9
Shively, George W	Husband of the 6th cousin once removed		
Shively, Ray	6th cousin twice removed	XVI	9
Shoemaker, Cora Bell	Wife of the 6th cousin twice removed		
Shore	Husband of the half 3rd cousin 3 times removed		

The Relations of Milton Snavely Hershey, 4th Ed.

Name	Relationship with Milton Hershey	Civil	Canon
Shore, Private	Half 3rd cousin 4 times removed	XII	8
Shore, Private	Half 3rd cousin 5 times removed	XIII	9
Shore, Private	Half 3rd cousin 4 times removed	XII	8
Shore, Private	Half 3rd cousin 4 times removed	XII	8
Shore, Private	Half 3rd cousin 5 times removed	XIII	9
Shore, Private	Half 3rd cousin 5 times removed	XIII	9
Short, Private	3rd cousin 4 times removed	XII	8
Short, Private	3rd cousin 4 times removed	XII	8
Showalter, Private	Wife of the 3rd cousin 3 times removed		
Shreiner, Charles	4th cousin	X	5
Shreiner, Jacob	Husband of the 3rd cousin once removed		
Shreiner, Mary	4th cousin	X	5
Shultz, Eve	Wife of the 1st cousin 5 times removed		
Shultz, Private	Husband of the 6th cousin 3 times removed		
Shultz, Private	6th cousin 4 times removed	XVIII	11
Shultz, Private	6th cousin 4 times removed	XVIII	11
Shultz, Valentine	Husband of the half 1st cousin 5 times removed		
Shumaker, Jacob	Husband of the 2nd cousin 3 times removed		
Shupp, Mary	Wife of the 3rd cousin twice removed		
Shutt, Janet Kaye	Half 3rd cousin 3 times removed	XI	7
Shutt, Mason Simon	Husband of the half 3rd cousin twice removed		
Shutt, Sandra Lee	Half 3rd cousin 3 times removed	XI	7
Siegrist, Maria	Wife of the great-granduncle		
Siegrist, Unknown	Husband of the 2nd cousin 3 times removed		
Siegrist, Unknown	Husband of the 1st cousin 4 times removed		
Sigler, Anna Elizabeth	1st cousin twice removed	VI	4
Sigler, Edward W	Husband of the 1st cousin once removed		
Silver, Edna	Ex-wife of the 6th cousin twice removed		
Simon, Belenia	Wife of the 6th cousin once removed		
Simpson, Private	3rd cousin 4 times removed	XII	8
Sinclair, Metta S.	Wife of the 6th cousin once removed		
Singer, Private	Wife of the 3rd cousin twice removed		
Sisson, Lloyd Hoover	Husband of the half 3rd cousin twice removed		
Sixberry, Private	Husband of the 6th cousin 5 times removed		
Sixberry, Private	6th cousin 6 times removed	XX	13
Skiles, Harry Brisbin	Husband of the 3rd cousin twice removed		
Skiles, Private	3rd cousin 3 times removed	XI	7
Skiles, Private	3rd cousin 3 times removed	XI	7
Skiles, Private	3rd cousin 4 times removed	XII	8
Skiles, Private	3rd cousin 4 times removed	XII	8
Skiles, Private	3rd cousin 4 times removed	XII	8
Skiles, Private	3rd cousin 4 times removed	XII	8
Skinner, Private	Wife of the 6th cousin 3 times removed		
Sleeman, Shirley	Wife of the 6th cousin twice removed		
Sluss, Private	6th cousin 4 times removed	XVIII	11
Sluss, Private	6th cousin 4 times removed	XVIII	11
Sluss, Private	6th cousin 4 times removed	XVIII	11
Sluss, Ray	Husband of the 6th cousin 3 times removed		
Smith, Anna	Wife of the 5th cousin once removed		
Smith, Anna G	6th cousin twice removed	XVI	9
Smith, Anna M.	Wife of the 6th cousin		
Smith, Catherina	Wife of the half 1st cousin 5 times removed		
Smith, Christian	Husband of the 2nd cousin 3 times removed		
Smith, Edna M	6th cousin twice removed	XVI	9
Smith, Emma Jane	Wife of the 3rd cousin twice removed		
Smith, Emma R	6th cousin twice removed	XVI	9
Smith, Esther	Wife of the 6th cousin twice removed		
Smith, George	Husband of the 6th cousin once removed		
Smith, George L	6th cousin twice removed	XVI	9
Smith, Henry	Husband of the half 1st cousin 5 times removed		
Smith, Hugh	Husband of the 6th cousin		
Smith, Margaret Jane	Wife of the 6th cousin once removed		
Smith, Mary	Wife of the 6th cousin twice removed		
Smith, Ober	6th cousin twice removed	XVI	9
Smith, Private	Husband of the 6th cousin 3 times removed		
Smith, Private	Wife of the 6th cousin 3 times removed		

Name	Relationship with Milton Hershey	Civil	Canon
Smith, Private	Husband of the 6th cousin 3 times removed		
Smith, Private	Half 3rd cousin 4 times removed	XII	8
Smith, Roy	Husband of the half 3rd cousin 3 times removed		
Smith, Roy Eby	Husband of the 3rd cousin once removed		
Smoker, Private	Wife of the 3rd cousin twice removed		
Smolizer, Charlotte E	6th cousin 3 times removed	XVII	10
Smolizer, Harry S	Husband of the 6th cousin twice removed		
Snavely, Abraham B	Uncle	III	2
Snavely, Abraham Barr	Grandfather	II	2
Snavely, Anna	Wife of the 2nd great-granduncle		
Snavely, Anna	Great-grandaunt	V	4
Snavely, Anna	Half grandaunt	IV	3
Snavely, Barbara	Grandaunt	IV	3
Snavely, Benjamin	Uncle	III	2
Snavely, Christian	Granduncle	IV	3
Snavely, Daniel	Granduncle	IV	3
Snavely, David	Granduncle	IV	3
Snavely, Elizabeth	Grandaunt	IV	3
Snavely, Elizabeth	Aunt	III	2
Snavely, Henry	Granduncle	IV	3
Snavely, Jacob	2nd great-grandfather	IV	4
Snavely, Jacob	Half granduncle	IV	3
Snavely, John	Great-grandfather	III	3
Snavely, John	Half granduncle	IV	3
Snavely, Joseph	Husband of the 1st cousin twice removed		
Snavely, Margaretta	Grandaunt	IV	3
Snavely, Martha B	Aunt	III	2
Snavely, Martin	Granduncle	IV	3
Snavely, Mary	Great-grandaunt	V	4
Snavely, Rohrer	1st cousin	IV	2
Snavely, Stoner	1st cousin	IV	2
Snavely, Susanna	Granduncle	IV	3
Snavely, Veronica	Grandaunt	IV	3
Snavely, Veronica	Great-grandaunt	V	4
Snavely, Veronica Buckwalter	Mother	I	1
Sneltzer, Joseph	Husband of the 6th cousin twice removed		
Sneltzer, Private	6th cousin 3 times removed	XVII	10
Sneltzer, Private	6th cousin 3 times removed	XVII	10
Sneltzer, Private	6th cousin 3 times removed	XVII	10
Sneltzer, Private	6th cousin 4 times removed	XVIII	11
Sneltzer, Private	6th cousin 4 times removed	XVIII	11
Sneltzer, Private	6th cousin 4 times removed	XVIII	11
Sneltzer, Private	6th cousin 4 times removed	XVIII	11
Sneltzer, Private	6th cousin 3 times removed	XVII	10
Snider, Mary	Wife of the 6th cousin		
Snyder, Amos B	3rd cousin once removed	IX	5
Snyder, Annie B	3rd cousin once removed	IX	5
Snyder, Arlene	2nd cousin 3 times removed	IX	6
Snyder, Barbara B	3rd cousin once removed	IX	5
Snyder, Christian B	3rd cousin once removed	IX	5
Snyder, Elias L.	Husband of the 6th cousin once removed		
Snyder, Goldie May	6th cousin twice removed	XVI	9
Snyder, Harriet Lucretia	6th cousin twice removed	XVI	9
Snyder, Henry G	Husband of the 3rd cousin		
Snyder, Jacob B	3rd cousin once removed	IX	5
Snyder, Johannes	Husband of the 1st cousin 3 times removed		
Snyder, John Henry	2nd cousin twice removed	VIII	5
Snyder, Jonas	Husband of the 6th cousin		
Snyder, Joshua	Husband of the 1st cousin once removed		
Snyder, Lizzie B	3rd cousin once removed	IX	5
Snyder, Mary B	3rd cousin once removed	IX	5
Snyder, Melvin H	2nd cousin 3 times removed	IX	6
Snyder, Private	Husband of the 6th cousin 3 times removed		
Snyder, Private	Wife of the 6th cousin 3 times removed		
Snyder, Ruby	Wife of the half 3rd cousin 3 times removed		
Snyder, Sabina	Wife of the 6th cousin		

The Relations of Milton Snavely Hershey, 4th Ed.

Name	Relationship with Milton Hershey	Civil	Canon
Snyder, Samuel	2nd cousin twice removed	VIII	5
Snyder, Sarah Jane	6th cousin twice removed	XVI	9
Snyder, Simon B.	Husband of the 6th cousin		
Snyder, Veronica	Wife of the great-granduncle		
Snyder, Wanda H	2nd cousin 3 times removed	IX	6
Sollenberger, Anna	Wife of the 4th cousin once removed		
Son, Infant	6th cousin twice removed	XVI	9
Sox, Ward L	Husband of the 6th cousin once removed		
Sparks, Doris M.	Wife of the half 3rd cousin 3 times removed		
Spencer, David	Husband of the 6th cousin		
Spencer, Private	Wife of the 6th cousin 3 times removed		
Spiesterbach, Bertha Etta	Wife of the 6th cousin twice removed		
Spinelli, Rose	Wife of the 6th cousin twice removed		
Sprecher, John S.	Husband of the 6th cousin		
Spring, Joseph M	Husband of the 6th cousin once removed		
Springer, Peter	Husband of the 1st cousin 4 times removed		
St Armond, Private	Wife of the 6th cousin 3 times removed		
St. Clair, Ellen Belle	Spouse of the 2nd cousin once removed		
Stambaugh, Clarence William	Husband of the 3rd cousin once removed		
Stambaugh, Private	3rd cousin twice removed	X	6
Stanton, Lucinda	Wife of the 6th cousin twice removed		
Stark, Gail	Husband of the 6th cousin once removed		
Starns, Dessie May	Wife of the 6th cousin twice removed		
Starr, Charles F.	Husband of the 6th cousin once removed		
Starr, Mabel	6th cousin twice removed	XVI	9
Starr, Ronald(Unknown)	6th cousin twice removed	XVI	9
Starr, Verne E.	6th cousin twice removed	XVI	9
Staub, Diane Kay	Wife of the 3rd cousin 3 times removed		
Staufer, Aesta Blanch	6th cousin 3 times removed	XVII	10
Stauffer, Abraham	Half 3rd cousin	VIII	4
Stauffer, Abraham Hershey	Half 1st cousin twice removed	VI	4
Stauffer, Abraham Hess	Husband of the half great-grandaunt		
Stauffer, Abraham Moyer	4th cousin once removed	XI	6
Stauffer, Agnes Pauline	6th cousin 4 times removed	XVIII	11
Stauffer, Alice Pearl	6th cousin 3 times removed	XVII	10
Stauffer, Andrew Grant	6th cousin twice removed	XVI	9
Stauffer, Andrew Neal	6th cousin 3 times removed	XVII	10
Stauffer, Ann	3rd cousin 3 times removed	XI	7
Stauffer, Anna	2nd cousin 4 times removed	X	7
Stauffer, Anna	7th great-grandmother	IX	9
Stauffer, Anna	6th great-grandmother	VIII	8
Stauffer, Anna	Half 1st cousin twice removed	VI	4
Stauffer, Anna	Wife of the 2nd cousin 3 times removed		
Stauffer, Anna Barbara	3rd cousin 3 times removed	XI	7
Stauffer, Anna Marie	3rd cousin 3 times removed	XI	7
Stauffer, Anna Pearl	6th cousin twice removed	XVI	9
Stauffer, Barbara	4th cousin twice removed	XII	7
Stauffer, Barbara	6th great-grandaunt	X	9
Stauffer, Barbara	3rd cousin 3 times removed	XI	7
Stauffer, Barbara	Half 1st cousin twice removed	VI	4
Stauffer, Barbara Virginia	2nd cousin 4 times removed	X	7
Stauffer, Benjamin Pennypacker	4th cousin once removed	XI	6
Stauffer, Beulah Bell	6th cousin twice removed	XVI	9
Stauffer, Carmi R.	Husband of the 3rd cousin twice removed		
Stauffer, Catharine	Wife of the 1st cousin 4 times removed		
Stauffer, Catharine Latscher	3rd cousin twice removed	X	6
Stauffer, Catharine Moyer	4th cousin once removed	XI	6
Stauffer, Catherina	6th great-grandaunt	X	9
Stauffer, Catherine	Wife of the 2nd cousin 4 times removed		
Stauffer, Catherine	3rd cousin 3 times removed	XI	7
Stauffer, Catherine Pennypacker	4th cousin once removed	XI	6
Stauffer, Charles Albert	6th cousin twice removed	XVI	9
Stauffer, Charles Bennett	6th cousin 3 times removed	XVII	10
Stauffer, Charles Lloyd	6th cousin 3 times removed	XVII	10
Stauffer, Christian	6th great-granduncle	X	9
Stauffer, Christian	4th great-granduncle	VIII	7

Name	Relationship with Milton Hershey	Civil	Canon
Stauffer, Christian	2nd cousin 4 times removed	X	7
Stauffer, Christian	3rd cousin 3 times removed	XI	7
Stauffer, Christian	3rd cousin 3 times removed	XI	7
Stauffer, Christian	Husband of the 4th cousin 4 times removed		
Stauffer, Christian	Half 2nd cousin once removed	VII	4
Stauffer, Christina	3rd cousin 3 times removed	XI	7
Stauffer, Clementine Fox	5th cousin	XII	6
Stauffer, Daniel	3rd cousin 3 times removed	XI	7
Stauffer, Daniel B.	Husband of the 3rd cousin twice removed		
Stauffer, Daniel Latscher	5th cousin	XII	6
Stauffer, David	3rd cousin once removed	IX	5
Stauffer, Earl Evans	6th cousin 4 times removed	XVIII	11
Stauffer, Eleanor	6th cousin 3 times removed	XVII	10
Stauffer, Elias Richardson	6th cousin twice removed	XVI	9
Stauffer, Elisabeth	3rd cousin once removed	IX	5
Stauffer, Elizabeth	3rd cousin 3 times removed	XI	7
Stauffer, Elizabeth	3rd cousin 3 times removed	XI	7
Stauffer, Elizabeth	1st cousin 3 times removed	VII	5
Stauffer, Elizabeth Kulp	5th cousin	XII	6
Stauffer, Elizabeth Latscher	3rd cousin twice removed	X	6
Stauffer, Elizabeth Pennypacker	4th cousin once removed	XI	6
Stauffer, Ella May	6th cousin twice removed	XVI	9
Stauffer, Emma Kulp	5th cousin	XII	6
Stauffer, Eva	3rd cousin 3 times removed	XI	7
Stauffer, Eva	3rd cousin 3 times removed	XI	7
Stauffer, Frederick Latscher	5th cousin	XII	6
Stauffer, Hannah Mary Latscher	5th cousin	XII	6
Stauffer, Hans	7th great-grandfather	IX	9
Stauffer, Hans	6th great-granduncle	X	9
Stauffer, Hans	1st cousin 5 times removed	IX	7
Stauffer, Harriet Moyer	4th cousin once removed	XI	6
Stauffer, Henry	3rd cousin 3 times removed	XI	7
Stauffer, Henry	3rd cousin 3 times removed	XI	7
Stauffer, Henry Jacob	2nd cousin 4 times removed	X	7
Stauffer, Henry Pennypacker	4th cousin once removed	XI	6
Stauffer, Jacob	Husband of the 2nd cousin 3 times removed		
Stauffer, Jacob	2nd cousin 4 times removed	X	7
Stauffer, Jacob	3rd cousin 3 times removed	XI	7
Stauffer, Jacob	3rd cousin 3 times removed	XI	7
Stauffer, Jacob	Half 1st cousin twice removed	VI	4
Stauffer, Jacob	Husband of the 1st cousin once removed		
Stauffer, Jacob Latscher	3rd cousin twice removed	X	6
Stauffer, Jacob Latscher	5th cousin	XII	6
Stauffer, Jacob Moyer	4th cousin once removed	XI	6
Stauffer, Jacob Pennypacker	4th cousin once removed	XI	6
Stauffer, Joe E.	3rd cousin 3 times removed	XI	7
Stauffer, Johannes	2nd cousin 4 times removed	X	7
Stauffer, John	Husband of the 2nd cousin twice removed		
Stauffer, John	Husband of the 1st cousin 4 times removed		
Stauffer, John	3rd cousin 3 times removed	XI	7
Stauffer, John	Half 1st cousin twice removed	VI	4
Stauffer, John Buckwalter Rev.	Husband of the 2nd cousin 3 times removed		
Stauffer, John Latscher	3rd cousin twice removed	X	6
Stauffer, John Milton	6th cousin twice removed	XVI	9
Stauffer, John Moyer	4th cousin once removed	XI	6
Stauffer, John Pennypacker	4th cousin once removed	XI	6
Stauffer, John Wesley	Husband of the 6th cousin once removed		
Stauffer, Joseph Pennypacker	4th cousin once removed	XI	6
Stauffer, Kate Kulp	5th cousin	XII	6
Stauffer, Lavina Moyer	4th cousin once removed	XI	6
Stauffer, Leah Mayford	6th cousin 3 times removed	XVII	10
Stauffer, Madelena	2nd cousin 4 times removed	X	7
Stauffer, Magdalena	2nd cousin 4 times removed	X	7
Stauffer, Magdalena	3rd cousin 3 times removed	XI	7
Stauffer, Magdalena	3rd cousin 3 times removed	XI	7
Stauffer, Magdalena	Half 1st cousin twice removed	VI	4

Name	Relationship with Milton Hershey	Civil	Canon
Stauffer, Margaret Pennypacker	4th cousin once removed	XI	6
Stauffer, Maria	Wife of the 2nd cousin twice removed		
Stauffer, Maria	Wife of the 2nd cousin 3 times removed		
Stauffer, Maria	Wife of the 2nd cousin twice removed		
Stauffer, Maria "Mary"	Wife of the 2nd cousin 3 times removed		
Stauffer, Marie	3rd cousin 3 times removed	XI	7
Stauffer, Martin	2nd cousin 4 times removed	X	7
Stauffer, Mary	3rd cousin 3 times removed	XI	7
Stauffer, Mary Helen	6th cousin 3 times removed	XVII	10
Stauffer, Mary Latscher	3rd cousin twice removed	X	6
Stauffer, Mary Lemmie Ann	6th cousin twice removed	XVI	9
Stauffer, Mary Moyer	4th cousin once removed	XI	6
Stauffer, Michael	3rd cousin 3 times removed	XI	7
Stauffer, Nancy Jane	Half 3rd cousin once removed	IX	5
Stauffer, Paul J.	6th cousin 3 times removed	XVII	10
Stauffer, Peter	Husband of the 1st cousin 4 times removed		
Stauffer, Peter	3rd cousin 3 times removed	XI	7
Stauffer, Private	Husband of the 3rd cousin 4 times removed		
Stauffer, Private	3rd cousin 5 times removed	XIII	9
Stauffer, Private	3rd cousin 5 times removed	XIII	9
Stauffer, Private	Husband of the 3rd cousin 4 times removed		
Stauffer, Private	3rd cousin 3 times removed	XI	7
Stauffer, Private	3rd cousin 3 times removed	XI	7
Stauffer, Private	3rd cousin 3 times removed	XI	7
Stauffer, Private	3rd cousin 3 times removed	XI	7
Stauffer, Private	3rd cousin 4 times removed	XII	8
Stauffer, Private	3rd cousin 4 times removed	XII	8
Stauffer, Private	3rd cousin 4 times removed	XII	8
Stauffer, Private	3rd cousin 4 times removed	XII	8
Stauffer, Private	3rd cousin 3 times removed	XI	7
Stauffer, Private	3rd cousin 3 times removed	XI	7
Stauffer, Private	3rd cousin 3 times removed	XI	7
Stauffer, Private	3rd cousin 3 times removed	XI	7
Stauffer, Private	3rd cousin 3 times removed	XI	7
Stauffer, Private	3rd cousin 3 times removed	XI	7
Stauffer, Private	3rd cousin 4 times removed	XII	8
Stauffer, Private	3rd cousin 4 times removed	XII	8
Stauffer, Private	3rd cousin 4 times removed	XII	8
Stauffer, Private	3rd cousin 4 times removed	XII	8
Stauffer, Private	3rd cousin 4 times removed	XII	8
Stauffer, Private	3rd cousin 4 times removed	XII	8
Stauffer, Private	Wife of the 3rd cousin 3 times removed		
Stauffer, Private	Husband of the 3rd cousin twice removed		
Stauffer, Private	3rd cousin 3 times removed	XI	7
Stauffer, Private	3rd cousin 3 times removed	XI	7
Stauffer, Private	6th cousin 3 times removed	XVII	10
Stauffer, Private	6th cousin 3 times removed	XVII	10
Stauffer, Private	6th cousin 3 times removed	XVII	10
Stauffer, Private	6th cousin 3 times removed	XVII	10
Stauffer, Private	6th cousin 3 times removed	XVII	10
Stauffer, Private	6th cousin 4 times removed	XVIII	11
Stauffer, Private	6th cousin 4 times removed	XVIII	11
Stauffer, Private	6th cousin 4 times removed	XVIII	11
Stauffer, Ray Franklin	6th cousin twice removed	XVI	9
Stauffer, Ray Franklin	6th cousin 3 times removed	XVII	10
Stauffer, Rudolph Pennypacker	4th cousin once removed	XI	6
Stauffer, Russell Lee	6th cousin 3 times removed	XVII	10
Stauffer, Samuel Pennypacker	4th cousin once removed	XI	6
Stauffer, Sara Rebecca	6th cousin twice removed	XVI	9
Stauffer, Sarah Moyer	4th cousin once removed	XI	6
Stauffer, Stephen	6th cousin twice removed	XVI	9
Stauffer, Susanna	3rd cousin 3 times removed	XI	7
Stauffer, Susanna	3rd cousin 3 times removed	XI	7
Stauffer, Susanna	Wife of the 2nd cousin once removed		
Stauffer, Sylvia	6th cousin 3 times removed	XVII	10

Name	Relationship with Milton Hershey	Civil	Canon
Stauffer, Ulrich	6th great-granduncle	X	9
Stauffer, Veronica " Frany "	3rd cousin 3 times removed	XI	7
Stauffer, Veronica Frena	3rd cousin 3 times removed	XI	7
Stauffer, Wesley Richard	6th cousin 3 times removed	XVII	10
Stauffer, William E.	6th cousin twice removed	XVI	9
Stauffer, William Pennypacker	4th cousin once removed	XI	6
Stayer, David S.	Husband of the 6th cousin		
Steele, Marian Taylor	Wife of the 6th cousin twice removed		
Steele, Thelma Lucille	Wife of the 6th cousin 3 times removed		
Steen, Private	Wife of the 6th cousin 3 times removed		
Stees, Luella N.	Wife of the 6th cousin twice removed		
Steffy, Alice Parmer	Wife of the 3rd cousin once removed		
Steffy, Leah	Husband of the 6th cousin		
Steffy, Private	Wife of the 3rd cousin 4 times removed		
Stehman, Elisabeth	Wife of the 3rd cousin twice removed		
Steinman, John	Husband of the great-grandaunt		
Stephens, Asenath	Wife of the 6th cousin twice removed		
Stephens, Private	Wife of the 3rd cousin twice removed		
Stephenson, Margaret Ann	Wife of the half 3rd cousin		
Stevens, Arthur W	6th cousin 3 times removed	XVII	10
Stevens, Arthur W	6th cousin 4 times removed	XVIII	11
Stevens, Arthur W, Jr	6th cousin 4 times removed	XVIII	11
Stevens, B Marie	6th cousin 3 times removed	XVII	10
Stevens, Bryan Keith	6th cousin 4 times removed	XVIII	11
Stevens, Carrell D	6th cousin 3 times removed	XVII	10
Stevens, Clarise	Wife of the 6th cousin 3 times removed		
Stevens, Donna A	6th cousin 4 times removed	XVIII	11
Stevens, F Clair	6th cousin 3 times removed	XVII	10
Stevens, Florida Edwin	Husband of the half 3rd cousin twice removed		
Stevens, Hannah	Wife of the 5th cousin once removed		
Stevens, J Donald	6th cousin 3 times removed	XVII	10
Stevens, John E	6th cousin 4 times removed	XVIII	11
Stevens, Kitty	6th cousin 4 times removed	XVIII	11
Stevens, Linda K	6th cousin 4 times removed	XVIII	11
Stevens, Marlin O	6th cousin 3 times removed	XVII	10
Stevens, Marlin O, Jr	6th cousin 4 times removed	XVIII	11
Stevens, Mary E	6th cousin 4 times removed	XVIII	11
Stevens, Paul A	6th cousin 4 times removed	XVIII	11
Stevens, Private	6th cousin 4 times removed	XVIII	11
Stevens, Private	6th cousin 4 times removed	XVIII	11
Stevens, Private	6th cousin 4 times removed	XVIII	11
Stevens, Richard L	6th cousin 4 times removed	XVIII	11
Stevens, Roger William	Husband of the 6th cousin 3 times removed		
Stevens, Virginia A	6th cousin 4 times removed	XVIII	11
Stevens, Wilbur A	6th cousin 3 times removed	XVII	10
Stevens, William O	Husband of the 6th cousin twice removed		
Stevick, John	Husband of the 6th cousin		
Stiffler, Private	6th cousin 3 times removed	XVII	10
Stiffler, Private	6th cousin 3 times removed	XVII	10
Stiffler, Veron Montell	Husband of the 6th cousin twice removed		
Stitch, Private	Husband of the 6th cousin 3 times removed		
Stitch, Private	6th cousin 4 times removed	XVIII	11
Stitcher, Lydia A.	Wife of the 6th cousin		
Stocker, Jacob	Husband of the 4th great-grandaunt		
Stoever, Jeremiah	Husband of the 6th cousin		
Stoffer, Ada	6th cousin once removed	XV	8
Stoffer, Adaline	6th cousin twice removed	XVI	9
Stoffer, Addie Jane Sherman	Wife of the 6th cousin once removed		
Stoffer, Albert	6th cousin	XIV	7
Stoffer, Albert Lewis	6th cousin once removed	XV	8
Stoffer, Alice Ellen	6th cousin once removed	XV	8
Stoffer, Allie	6th cousin once removed	XV	8
Stoffer, Alva Orlan	6th cousin twice removed	XVI	9
Stoffer, Alveida	6th cousin twice removed	XVI	9
Stoffer, Amanda J	6th cousin once removed	XV	8
Stoffer, Anson Oscar	6th cousin once removed	XV	8

Name	Relationship with Milton Hershey	Civil	Canon
Stoffer, Arnold Leroy	6th cousin twice removed	XVI	9
Stoffer, Barbara Ellen	6th cousin	XIV	7
Stoffer, Barbara Sue	6th cousin 3 times removed	XVII	10
Stoffer, Benjamine Franklin	6th cousin once removed	XV	8
Stoffer, Bertha Cleo	6th cousin once removed	XV	8
Stoffer, Bertha Lorena	6th cousin once removed	XV	8
Stoffer, Beulah Fern	6th cousin twice removed	XVI	9
Stoffer, Blanche	6th cousin twice removed	XVI	9
Stoffer, Blanche Mae	6th cousin once removed	XV	8
Stoffer, Bryan Sewell	6th cousin once removed	XV	8
Stoffer, Buddy Ross	6th cousin twice removed	XVI	9
Stoffer, C Robert	6th cousin 3 times removed	XVII	10
Stoffer, Carl Levy	6th cousin twice removed	XVI	9
Stoffer, Carl T	6th cousin twice removed	XVI	9
Stoffer, Carrie M	6th cousin once removed	XV	8
Stoffer, Catherine	5th cousin once removed	XIII	7
Stoffer, Catherine	6th cousin	XIV	7
Stoffer, Catherine Ann	6th cousin	XIV	7
Stoffer, Cecil F	6th cousin twice removed	XVI	9
Stoffer, Charles Floyd	6th cousin once removed	XV	8
Stoffer, Charles G	6th cousin once removed	XV	8
Stoffer, Charles Henry	6th cousin once removed	XV	8
Stoffer, Chester A	6th cousin once removed	XV	8
Stoffer, Christena	6th cousin	XIV	7
Stoffer, Christina	6th cousin	XIV	7
Stoffer, Christine	6th cousin	XIV	7
Stoffer, Claire Daniel	6th cousin once removed	XV	8
Stoffer, Clara M	6th cousin	XIV	7
Stoffer, Clara M.	6th cousin	XIV	7
Stoffer, Clarence Leward	6th cousin twice removed	XVI	9
Stoffer, Cleo Ruth	6th cousin twice removed	XVI	9
Stoffer, Clifford Lewis	6th cousin twice removed	XVI	9
Stoffer, Clinton	6th cousin once removed	XV	8
Stoffer, Clyde C.	6th cousin twice removed	XVI	9
Stoffer, Cora	6th cousin once removed	XV	8
Stoffer, Cora	6th cousin once removed	XV	8
Stoffer, Cora Alice	6th cousin once removed	XV	8
Stoffer, Corda	6th cousin once removed	XV	8
Stoffer, Curtis Homer	6th cousin once removed	XV	8
Stoffer, Cynthia Idella	6th cousin once removed	XV	8
Stoffer, Dale Milan	6th cousin 3 times removed	XVII	10
Stoffer, Daniel	6th cousin twice removed	XVI	9
Stoffer, Daniel	6th cousin once removed	XV	8
Stoffer, Daniel D	6th cousin	XIV	7
Stoffer, Darl Lincoln	6th cousin once removed	XV	8
Stoffer, David	6th cousin	XIV	7
Stoffer, David	5th cousin once removed	XIII	7
Stoffer, David	6th cousin	XIV	7
Stoffer, David	6th cousin once removed	XV	8
Stoffer, David M	6th cousin	XIV	7
Stoffer, David M.	6th cousin	XIV	7
Stoffer, Debara Ann	6th cousin 3 times removed	XVII	10
Stoffer, Delilah	6th cousin once removed	XV	8
Stoffer, Dennis	6th cousin	XIV	7
Stoffer, Don	6th cousin twice removed	XVI	9
Stoffer, Donald	6th cousin twice removed	XVI	9
Stoffer, Donald Andrew	6th cousin twice removed	XVI	9
Stoffer, Donald Lowell	6th cousin twice removed	XVI	9
Stoffer, Doris May	6th cousin twice removed	XVI	9
Stoffer, Dorothy Ada	6th cousin twice removed	XVI	9
Stoffer, Dwight	6th cousin twice removed	XVI	9
Stoffer, Earl	6th cousin once removed	XV	8
Stoffer, Earl	6th cousin twice removed	XVI	9
Stoffer, Earl Eugene	6th cousin once removed	XV	8
Stoffer, Earl L	6th cousin twice removed	XVI	9
Stoffer, Edith	6th cousin twice removed	XVI	9

Name	Relationship with Milton Hershey	Civil	Canon
Stoffer, Edward	6th cousin twice removed	XVI	9
Stoffer, Edward W	6th cousin once removed	XV	8
Stoffer, Eileen M	6th cousin once removed	XV	8
Stoffer, Elbert R	6th cousin once removed	XV	8
Stoffer, Eldon	6th cousin once removed	XV	8
Stoffer, Elgie	6th cousin once removed	XV	8
Stoffer, Eli	6th cousin	XIV	7
Stoffer, Eli	6th cousin	XIV	7
Stoffer, Eliza	6th cousin	XIV	7
Stoffer, Eliza A	6th cousin	XIV	7
Stoffer, Elizabeth	Half 3rd cousin once removed	IX	5
Stoffer, Elizabeth	5th cousin once removed	XIII	7
Stoffer, Elizabeth Rose	6th cousin	XIV	7
Stoffer, Ella	6th cousin once removed	XV	8
Stoffer, Ellen Ann	6th cousin 3 times removed	XVII	10
Stoffer, Elmer	6th cousin once removed	XV	8
Stoffer, Elmer E	6th cousin once removed	XV	8
Stoffer, Elmer L	6th cousin twice removed	XVI	9
Stoffer, Elurtus Gatton	6th cousin once removed	XV	8
Stoffer, Emmet	6th cousin once removed	XV	8
Stoffer, Emmett	6th cousin twice removed	XVI	9
Stoffer, Enos	6th cousin	XIV	7
Stoffer, Erma Armada	6th cousin twice removed	XVI	9
Stoffer, Erwin William	6th cousin once removed	XV	8
Stoffer, Ester	6th cousin twice removed	XVI	9
Stoffer, Ester	6th cousin twice removed	XVI	9
Stoffer, Ester Leah	6th cousin twice removed	XVI	9
Stoffer, Esther	6th cousin twice removed	XVI	9
Stoffer, Ethel	6th cousin twice removed	XVI	9
Stoffer, Ethel	6th cousin twice removed	XVI	9
Stoffer, Ethel	6th cousin once removed	XV	8
Stoffer, Ethel Marie	6th cousin twice removed	XVI	9
Stoffer, Eva	6th cousin twice removed	XVI	9
Stoffer, Eva	6th cousin once removed	XV	8
Stoffer, Eva Lola	6th cousin once removed	XV	8
Stoffer, Evelyn Ora	6th cousin twice removed	XVI	9
Stoffer, Fannie Pearl	6th cousin once removed	XV	8
Stoffer, Flora Ann	6th cousin once removed	XV	8
Stoffer, Florence Eudora	6th cousin once removed	XV	8
Stoffer, Floyd W	6th cousin twice removed	XVI	9
Stoffer, Frank	6th cousin twice removed	XVI	9
Stoffer, Frank JR	6th cousin 3 times removed	XVII	10
Stoffer, Franklin Eugene	6th cousin twice removed	XVI	9
Stoffer, George	5th cousin once removed	XIII	7
Stoffer, George	6th cousin	XIV	7
Stoffer, George	6th cousin once removed	XV	8
Stoffer, George Allen	6th cousin once removed	XV	8
Stoffer, George D	6th cousin	XIV	7
Stoffer, George O	6th cousin once removed	XV	8
Stoffer, Gladys	6th cousin 3 times removed	XVII	10
Stoffer, Gladys Alice	6th cousin once removed	XV	8
Stoffer, Glen Wilson	6th cousin once removed	XV	8
Stoffer, Goldie Marie	6th cousin once removed	XV	8
Stoffer, Gorman H	6th cousin twice removed	XVI	9
Stoffer, Gwendolyn G	6th cousin twice removed	XVI	9
Stoffer, Harold James	6th cousin twice removed	XVI	9
Stoffer, Harold Walter	6th cousin twice removed	XVI	9
Stoffer, Harry B	6th cousin twice removed	XVI	9
Stoffer, Harvey	6th cousin twice removed	XVI	9
Stoffer, Harvey	6th cousin once removed	XV	8
Stoffer, Harvey W	6th cousin once removed	XV	8
Stoffer, Hazel M	6th cousin twice removed	XVI	9
Stoffer, Helen	6th cousin twice removed	XVI	9
Stoffer, Helen Naomi	6th cousin once removed	XV	8
Stoffer, Herman	6th cousin once removed	XV	8
Stoffer, Homer	6th cousin once removed	XV	8

Name	Relationship with Milton Hershey	Civil	Canon
Stoffer, Homer	6th cousin twice removed	XVI	9
Stoffer, Homer E	6th cousin once removed	XV	8
Stoffer, Horace Raymond	6th cousin once removed	XV	8
Stoffer, Howard H.	6th cousin once removed	XV	8
Stoffer, Ida	6th cousin twice removed	XVI	9
Stoffer, Ida J.	6th cousin once removed	XV	8
Stoffer, Idella	6th cousin once removed	XV	8
Stoffer, Inez Genesta	6th cousin twice removed	XVI	9
Stoffer, Iona Eleanor	6th cousin twice removed	XVI	9
Stoffer, Iris	6th cousin 3 times removed	XVII	10
Stoffer, Jacob	4th cousin twice removed	XII	7
Stoffer, Jacob H	6th cousin twice removed	XVI	9
Stoffer, Jacob L	6th cousin	XIV	7
Stoffer, Jacob S	5th cousin once removed	XIII	7
Stoffer, James	6th cousin	XIV	7
Stoffer, Jean	6th cousin twice removed	XVI	9
Stoffer, Jerome	6th cousin once removed	XV	8
Stoffer, Jesse A	6th cousin	XIV	7
Stoffer, Jimmie Dale	6th cousin twice removed	XVI	9
Stoffer, John	5th cousin once removed	XIII	7
Stoffer, John	6th cousin	XIV	7
Stoffer, John	6th cousin once removed	XV	8
Stoffer, John A	6th cousin twice removed	XVI	9
Stoffer, John Arthur	6th cousin once removed	XV	8
Stoffer, John Jacob	6th cousin	XIV	7
Stoffer, John Ralph	6th cousin once removed	XV	8
Stoffer, John Wallace	6th cousin once removed	XV	8
Stoffer, Joseph	6th cousin	XIV	7
Stoffer, Joseph C	6th cousin twice removed	XVI	9
Stoffer, Kathryn Olive	6th cousin 3 times removed	XVII	10
Stoffer, Kenneth George	6th cousin 3 times removed	XVII	10
Stoffer, Kenneth Lee	6th cousin twice removed	XVI	9
Stoffer, Kenny	6th cousin twice removed	XVI	9
Stoffer, Larry Lee	6th cousin 3 times removed	XVII	10
Stoffer, Laurance L	6th cousin once removed	XV	8
Stoffer, Laurtis W.	6th cousin	XIV	7
Stoffer, Leah	5th cousin once removed	XIII	7
Stoffer, Leander	6th cousin	XIV	7
Stoffer, Lela Catherine	6th cousin twice removed	XVI	9
Stoffer, Leland L	6th cousin twice removed	XVI	9
Stoffer, Lena Viola	6th cousin once removed	XV	8
Stoffer, Leo Lesile	6th cousin once removed	XV	8
Stoffer, Leona Rosa	6th cousin once removed	XV	8
Stoffer, Leonard	6th cousin twice removed	XVI	9
Stoffer, Leslie A	6th cousin once removed	XV	8
Stoffer, Lester Clyde	6th cousin once removed	XV	8
Stoffer, Levi	6th cousin	XIV	7
Stoffer, Levi	6th cousin	XIV	7
Stoffer, Leward	6th cousin twice removed	XVI	9
Stoffer, Lewis John	6th cousin 3 times removed	XVII	10
Stoffer, Lewis Jr	6th cousin	XIV	7
Stoffer, Lida Marrilla	6th cousin once removed	XV	8
Stoffer, Lloyd	6th cousin twice removed	XVI	9
Stoffer, Lola Mae	6th cousin twice removed	XVI	9
Stoffer, Lorin Albert	6th cousin twice removed	XVI	9
Stoffer, Louella	6th cousin	XIV	7
Stoffer, Louella I	6th cousin	XIV	7
Stoffer, Louis J	5th cousin once removed	XIII	7
Stoffer, Loyal	6th cousin twice removed	XVI	9
Stoffer, Lucille	Wife of the 6th cousin twice removed		
Stoffer, Lucille Naomi	6th cousin twice removed	XVI	9
Stoffer, Lula Nora	6th cousin once removed	XV	8
Stoffer, Lydia	6th cousin once removed	XV	8
Stoffer, Mabel	6th cousin twice removed	XVI	9
Stoffer, Mabel Alice	6th cousin once removed	XV	8
Stoffer, Mable Catherine	6th cousin once removed	XV	8

Name	Relationship with Milton Hershey	Civil	Canon
Stoffer, Maggie	Half 3rd cousin once removed	IX	5
Stoffer, Margaret	5th cousin once removed	XIII	7
Stoffer, Margaret Louise	6th cousin twice removed	XVI	9
Stoffer, Marion	6th cousin once removed	XV	8
Stoffer, Marion (Nick)	6th cousin once removed	XV	8
Stoffer, Martha	6th cousin twice removed	XVI	9
Stoffer, Martha Ellen	6th cousin twice removed	XVI	9
Stoffer, Mary Ann	6th cousin	XIV	7
Stoffer, Mary Catherine	6th cousin once removed	XV	8
Stoffer, Mary Catherine	6th cousin once removed	XV	8
Stoffer, Mary Dora	6th cousin once removed	XV	8
Stoffer, Mary Luella	6th cousin once removed	XV	8
Stoffer, Matthew Alan	6th cousin 4 times removed	XVIII	11
Stoffer, Maud E	6th cousin once removed	XV	8
Stoffer, Mauda	6th cousin twice removed	XVI	9
Stoffer, Maude Eve	6th cousin once removed	XV	8
Stoffer, Melinda J	6th cousin	XIV	7
Stoffer, Milan Benjamin	6th cousin twice removed	XVI	9
Stoffer, Milan Leroy	6th cousin once removed	XV	8
Stoffer, Mildred	6th cousin once removed	XV	8
Stoffer, Mildred Louisa	6th cousin 3 times removed	XVII	10
Stoffer, Mildred Marjorie	6th cousin twice removed	XVI	9
Stoffer, Millard	6th cousin once removed	XV	8
Stoffer, Milton C	6th cousin once removed	XV	8
Stoffer, Myrtle	6th cousin once removed	XV	8
Stoffer, Nancy	Half 3rd cousin once removed	IX	5
Stoffer, Nancy	6th cousin	XIV	7
Stoffer, Nancy	6th cousin	XIV	7
Stoffer, Nehariah	6th cousin	XIV	7
Stoffer, Nellie Ione	6th cousin once removed	XV	8
Stoffer, Nettie Pearl	6th cousin once removed	XV	8
Stoffer, Nora	6th cousin twice removed	XVI	9
Stoffer, Nora Olive	6th cousin once removed	XV	8
Stoffer, Odessa	6th cousin once removed	XV	8
Stoffer, Oliver	6th cousin once removed	XV	8
Stoffer, Ora Deliah	6th cousin once removed	XV	8
Stoffer, Orietta	6th cousin once removed	XV	8
Stoffer, Orlan Clifford	6th cousin twice removed	XVI	9
Stoffer, Otis R	6th cousin twice removed	XVI	9
Stoffer, Owen	6th cousin once removed	XV	8
Stoffer, Paul Elmer	6th cousin twice removed	XVI	9
Stoffer, Paul Lawrence	6th cousin twice removed	XVI	9
Stoffer, Pearl	6th cousin once removed	XV	8
Stoffer, Peter	4th cousin twice removed	XII	7
Stoffer, Peter	6th cousin	XIV	7
Stoffer, Peter	6th cousin once removed	XV	8
Stoffer, Private	6th cousin 4 times removed	XVIII	11
Stoffer, Private	6th cousin 4 times removed	XVIII	11
Stoffer, Private	6th cousin 4 times removed	XVIII	11
Stoffer, Private	6th cousin 3 times removed	XVII	10
Stoffer, Private	6th cousin 3 times removed	XVII	10
Stoffer, Private	6th cousin 3 times removed	XVII	10
Stoffer, Private	6th cousin twice removed	XVI	9
Stoffer, Private	6th cousin 4 times removed	XVIII	11
Stoffer, Private	6th cousin 4 times removed	XVIII	11
Stoffer, Private	6th cousin 3 times removed	XVII	10
Stoffer, Private	6th cousin 3 times removed	XVII	10
Stoffer, Private	6th cousin twice removed	XVI	9
Stoffer, Private	6th cousin 3 times removed	XVII	10
Stoffer, Private	6th cousin 3 times removed	XVII	10
Stoffer, Private	6th cousin 4 times removed	XVIII	11
Stoffer, Private	6th cousin 4 times removed	XVIII	11
Stoffer, Private	6th cousin 3 times removed	XVII	10
Stoffer, Private	6th cousin 3 times removed	XVII	10
Stoffer, Private	6th cousin 4 times removed	XVIII	11
Stoffer, Private	6th cousin 4 times removed	XVIII	11

Name	Relationship with Milton Hershey	Civil	Canon
Stoffer, Private	6th cousin 4 times removed	XVIII	11
Stoffer, Private	6th cousin 3 times removed	XVII	10
Stoffer, Private	6th cousin 3 times removed	XVII	10
Stoffer, Private	6th cousin 3 times removed	XVII	10
Stoffer, Private	6th cousin 3 times removed	XVII	10
Stoffer, Private	6th cousin 3 times removed	XVII	10
Stoffer, Private	6th cousin 3 times removed	XVII	10
Stoffer, Private	6th cousin 3 times removed	XVII	10
Stoffer, Private	6th cousin 3 times removed	XVII	10
Stoffer, Private	6th cousin 3 times removed	XVII	10
Stoffer, Private	6th cousin 3 times removed	XVII	10
Stoffer, Private	6th cousin 3 times removed	XVII	10
Stoffer, Private	6th cousin 3 times removed	XVII	10
Stoffer, Private	6th cousin 3 times removed	XVII	10
Stoffer, Private	6th cousin 3 times removed	XVII	10
Stoffer, Private	6th cousin 4 times removed	XVIII	11
Stoffer, Private	6th cousin 4 times removed	XVIII	11
Stoffer, Private	6th cousin 4 times removed	XVIII	11
Stoffer, Private	6th cousin 4 times removed	XVIII	11
Stoffer, Private	6th cousin 4 times removed	XVIII	11
Stoffer, Private	6th cousin 4 times removed	XVIII	11
Stoffer, Private	6th cousin twice removed	XVI	9
Stoffer, Private	6th cousin 3 times removed	XVII	10
Stoffer, Private	6th cousin 3 times removed	XVII	10
Stoffer, Private	6th cousin 3 times removed	XVII	10
Stoffer, Private	6th cousin 3 times removed	XVII	10
Stoffer, Private	6th cousin 3 times removed	XVII	10
Stoffer, Private	6th cousin 3 times removed	XVII	10
Stoffer, Private	6th cousin 3 times removed	XVII	10
Stoffer, Private	6th cousin 3 times removed	XVII	10
Stoffer, Private	6th cousin 3 times removed	XVII	10
Stoffer, Private	6th cousin 3 times removed	XVII	10
Stoffer, Private	6th cousin 3 times removed	XVII	10
Stoffer, Private	6th cousin 3 times removed	XVII	10
Stoffer, Private	6th cousin 3 times removed	XVII	10
Stoffer, Private	6th cousin 3 times removed	XVII	10
Stoffer, Private	6th cousin 3 times removed	XVII	10
Stoffer, Private	6th cousin 3 times removed	XVII	10
Stoffer, Private	6th cousin 3 times removed	XVII	10
Stoffer, Private	6th cousin 4 times removed	XVIII	11
Stoffer, Private	6th cousin 4 times removed	XVIII	11
Stoffer, Private	6th cousin 4 times removed	XVIII	11
Stoffer, Private	6th cousin 3 times removed	XVII	10
Stoffer, Private	6th cousin 4 times removed	XVIII	11
Stoffer, Private	6th cousin 4 times removed	XVIII	11
Stoffer, Private	6th cousin 4 times removed	XVIII	11
Stoffer, Private	6th cousin 4 times removed	XVIII	11
Stoffer, Private	6th cousin 4 times removed	XVIII	11
Stoffer, Private	6th cousin 3 times removed	XVII	10
Stoffer, Private	6th cousin 3 times removed	XVII	10
Stoffer, Private	6th cousin 4 times removed	XVIII	11
Stoffer, Private	6th cousin 3 times removed	XVII	10
Stoffer, Private	6th cousin 4 times removed	XVIII	11
Stoffer, Private	6th cousin 3 times removed	XVII	10
Stoffer, Private	6th cousin 3 times removed	XVII	10
Stoffer, Private	6th cousin 3 times removed	XVII	10
Stoffer, Private	6th cousin twice removed	XVI	9
Stoffer, Private	6th cousin twice removed	XVI	9
Stoffer, Private	6th cousin 3 times removed	XVII	10
Stoffer, Private	6th cousin 3 times removed	XVII	10
Stoffer, Private	6th cousin 3 times removed	XVII	10
Stoffer, Private	6th cousin 4 times removed	XVIII	11

Name	Relationship with Milton Hershey	Civil	Canon
Stoffer, Private	6th cousin 4 times removed	XVIII	11
Stoffer, Private	6th cousin 3 times removed	XVII	10
Stoffer, Private	6th cousin 3 times removed	XVII	10
Stoffer, Private	6th cousin 4 times removed	XVIII	11
Stoffer, Private	6th cousin 4 times removed	XVIII	11
Stoffer, Private	6th cousin twice removed	XVI	9
Stoffer, Private	6th cousin 3 times removed	XVII	10
Stoffer, Private	6th cousin 3 times removed	XVII	10
Stoffer, Private	6th cousin 3 times removed	XVII	10
Stoffer, Private	6th cousin 3 times removed	XVII	10
Stoffer, Private	6th cousin 4 times removed	XVIII	11
Stoffer, Private	6th cousin 4 times removed	XVIII	11
Stoffer, Private	6th cousin 3 times removed	XVII	10
Stoffer, Private	6th cousin 3 times removed	XVII	10
Stoffer, Private	6th cousin twice removed	XVI	9
Stoffer, Private	6th cousin 3 times removed	XVII	10
Stoffer, Private	6th cousin 3 times removed	XVII	10
Stoffer, Private	6th cousin twice removed	XVI	9
Stoffer, Private	6th cousin twice removed	XVI	9
Stoffer, Private	6th cousin twice removed	XVI	9
Stoffer, Private	6th cousin 3 times removed	XVII	10
Stoffer, Private	6th cousin 3 times removed	XVII	10
Stoffer, Private	6th cousin 3 times removed	XVII	10
Stoffer, Private	6th cousin 3 times removed	XVII	10
Stoffer, Private	6th cousin 4 times removed	XVIII	11
Stoffer, Private	6th cousin 4 times removed	XVIII	11
Stoffer, Private	6th cousin 4 times removed	XVIII	11
Stoffer, Private	6th cousin 4 times removed	XVIII	11
Stoffer, Private	6th cousin 4 times removed	XVIII	11
Stoffer, Private	6th cousin 4 times removed	XVIII	11
Stoffer, Private	6th cousin 4 times removed	XVIII	11
Stoffer, Private	6th cousin 4 times removed	XVIII	11
Stoffer, Private	6th cousin 4 times removed	XVIII	11
Stoffer, Private	6th cousin 3 times removed	XVII	10
Stoffer, Private	6th cousin 4 times removed	XVIII	11
Stoffer, Private	6th cousin 3 times removed	XVII	10
Stoffer, Private	6th cousin 3 times removed	XVII	10
Stoffer, Private	6th cousin 3 times removed	XVII	10
Stoffer, Private	6th cousin 3 times removed	XVII	10
Stoffer, Private	6th cousin 3 times removed	XVII	10
Stoffer, Private	6th cousin 3 times removed	XVII	10
Stoffer, Private	6th cousin 4 times removed	XVIII	11
Stoffer, Private	6th cousin 4 times removed	XVIII	11
Stoffer, Private	6th cousin 3 times removed	XVII	10
Stoffer, Private	6th cousin 4 times removed	XVIII	11
Stoffer, Private	6th cousin 4 times removed	XVIII	11
Stoffer, Private	6th cousin 3 times removed	XVII	10
Stoffer, Private	6th cousin 3 times removed	XVII	10
Stoffer, Private	6th cousin 4 times removed	XVIII	11
Stoffer, Private	6th cousin 4 times removed	XVIII	11
Stoffer, Private	6th cousin twice removed	XVI	9
Stoffer, Private	6th cousin twice removed	XVI	9
Stoffer, Private	6th cousin 4 times removed	XVIII	11
Stoffer, Private	6th cousin 4 times removed	XVIII	11
Stoffer, Private	6th cousin 3 times removed	XVII	10
Stoffer, Private	6th cousin 3 times removed	XVII	10
Stoffer, Private	6th cousin 3 times removed	XVII	10
Stoffer, Private	6th cousin 4 times removed	XVIII	11
Stoffer, Private	6th cousin 4 times removed	XVIII	11
Stoffer, Private	6th cousin 4 times removed	XVIII	11
Stoffer, Private	6th cousin 4 times removed	XVIII	11
Stoffer, Private	6th cousin 4 times removed	XVIII	11
Stoffer, Private	6th cousin 4 times removed	XVIII	11
Stoffer, Private	6th cousin 4 times removed	XVIII	11
Stoffer, Private	6th cousin 4 times removed	XVIII	11

Name	Relationship with Milton Hershey	Civil	Canon
Stoffer, Private	6th cousin 4 times removed	XVIII	11
Stoffer, Private	6th cousin 4 times removed	XVIII	11
Stoffer, Private	6th cousin 3 times removed	XVII	10
Stoffer, Private	6th cousin 3 times removed	XVII	10
Stoffer, Private	6th cousin 3 times removed	XVII	10
Stoffer, Private	6th cousin 4 times removed	XVIII	11
Stoffer, Private	6th cousin 4 times removed	XVIII	11
Stoffer, Private	6th cousin 4 times removed	XVIII	11
Stoffer, Private	6th cousin twice removed	XVI	9
Stoffer, Private	6th cousin twice removed	XVI	9
Stoffer, Private	6th cousin 3 times removed	XVII	10
Stoffer, Private	6th cousin 3 times removed	XVII	10
Stoffer, Private	6th cousin 3 times removed	XVII	10
Stoffer, Private	6th cousin 3 times removed	XVII	10
Stoffer, Private	6th cousin 3 times removed	XVII	10
Stoffer, Private	6th cousin twice removed	XVI	9
Stoffer, Private	6th cousin 3 times removed	XVII	10
Stoffer, Private	6th cousin twice removed	XVI	9
Stoffer, Private	6th cousin 3 times removed	XVII	10
Stoffer, Private	6th cousin 3 times removed	XVII	10
Stoffer, Private	6th cousin 3 times removed	XVII	10
Stoffer, Private	6th cousin 3 times removed	XVII	10
Stoffer, Private	6th cousin 3 times removed	XVII	10
Stoffer, Private	6th cousin 3 times removed	XVII	10
Stoffer, Private	6th cousin 3 times removed	XVII	10
Stoffer, Private	6th cousin 3 times removed	XVII	10
Stoffer, Rachel A	6th cousin	XIV	7
Stoffer, Ralph Leo	6th cousin once removed	XV	8
Stoffer, Ralph Norman	6th cousin twice removed	XVI	9
Stoffer, Ray Arnold	6th cousin twice removed	XVI	9
Stoffer, Raymond	6th cousin once removed	XV	8
Stoffer, Raymond	6th cousin twice removed	XVI	9
Stoffer, Rex	6th cousin twice removed	XVI	9
Stoffer, Robert Liewellyn	6th cousin 3 times removed	XVII	10
Stoffer, Robert Price	6th cousin twice removed	XVI	9
Stoffer, Rolandus	6th cousin	XIV	7
Stoffer, Rollin Jr	6th cousin twice removed	XVI	9
Stoffer, Roscoe "Ross"	6th cousin once removed	XV	8
Stoffer, Ross	6th cousin once removed	XV	8
Stoffer, Roy Dean	6th cousin twice removed	XVI	9
Stoffer, Roy Lester	6th cousin once removed	XV	8
Stoffer, Royal	6th cousin once removed	XV	8
Stoffer, Russell D	6th cousin once removed	XV	8
Stoffer, Ruth Anna	6th cousin once removed	XV	8
Stoffer, Ruthanna	6th cousin once removed	XV	8
Stoffer, Samantha	6th cousin once removed	XV	8
Stoffer, Samuel	Half 3rd cousin once removed	IX	5
Stoffer, Samuel	5th cousin once removed	XIII	7
Stoffer, Samuel J	6th cousin	XIV	7
Stoffer, Samuel Jr	6th cousin	XIV	7
Stoffer, Sarah	6th cousin	XIV	7
Stoffer, Sarah	6th cousin once removed	XV	8
Stoffer, Shannon M. Smith	6th cousin 4 times removed	XVIII	11
Stoffer, Sherman	6th cousin	XIV	7
Stoffer, Silvia	6th cousin	XIV	7
Stoffer, Simon Henry	6th cousin	XIV	7
Stoffer, Simon Levi	6th cousin once removed	XV	8
Stoffer, Solomon	6th cousin once removed	XV	8
Stoffer, Stanton Uriah	6th cousin	XIV	7
Stoffer, Susan	6th cousin 3 times removed	XVII	10
Stoffer, Sylvia	6th cousin once removed	XV	8
Stoffer, Thelma R	6th cousin twice removed	XVI	9
Stoffer, Thomas	6th cousin twice removed	XVI	9
Stoffer, Thomas Fredric	6th cousin twice removed	XVI	9
Stoffer, Thomas Lawrence	6th cousin 3 times removed	XVII	10
Stoffer, Vera Lucille	6th cousin once removed	XV	8

Name	Relationship with Milton Hershey	Civil	Canon
Stoffer, Verma Adella	6th cousin twice removed	XVI	9
Stoffer, Veron Roy	6th cousin once removed	XV	8
Stoffer, Virgil Forest	6th cousin twice removed	XVI	9
Stoffer, Virginia	6th cousin twice removed	XVI	9
Stoffer, Wade Orla	6th cousin once removed	XV	8
Stoffer, Wallace Winder	6th cousin once removed	XV	8
Stoffer, Walter George	6th cousin once removed	XV	8
Stoffer, Walter Leon	6th cousin once removed	XV	8
Stoffer, Warren	6th cousin once removed	XV	8
Stoffer, Wesley Emerson	6th cousin once removed	XV	8
Stoffer, Willard Edson	6th cousin once removed	XV	8
Stoffer, William	6th cousin 3 times removed	XVII	10
Stoffer, William	Half 3rd cousin once removed	IX	5
Stoffer, William	6th cousin once removed	XV	8
Stoffer, William Franklin	6th cousin once removed	XV	8
Stoffer, William Stanton	6th cousin twice removed	XVI	9
Stoffer, Wilma E	6th cousin twice removed	XVI	9
Stoffer, Wilma Ruth	6th cousin twice removed	XVI	9
Stoffer, Windfield	6th cousin once removed	XV	8
Stoffer, Zella May	6th cousin once removed	XV	8
Stoffer?, Private	6th cousin 3 times removed	XVII	10
Stoll, Michael H	6th cousin 4 times removed	XVIII	11
Stoll, Richard	Husband of the 6th cousin 3 times removed		
Stoll, Susan L	6th cousin 4 times removed	XVIII	11
Stoltzfus, Private	Wife of the 3rd cousin twice removed		
Stone, Belle	Wife of the 3rd cousin once removed		
Stoneman, Maria	Wife of the 3rd great-granduncle		
Stoner, Abraham L.	2nd cousin	VI	3
Stoner, Anna	2nd cousin	VI	3
Stoner, Daniel L.	2nd cousin	VI	3
Stoner, David L.	2nd cousin	VI	3
Stoner, Eliza L.	2nd cousin	VI	3
Stoner, Emmanuel	2nd cousin	VI	3
Stoner, Ida Snyder	Wife of the 3rd cousin once removed		
Stoner, Isaac L.	2nd cousin	VI	3
Stoner, Jacob	Husband of the 1st cousin once removed		
Stoner, Jacob	2nd cousin	VI	3
Stoner, John L.	2nd cousin	VI	3
Stoner, Maria L.	2nd cousin	VI	3
Stoner, Mary	Wife of the 1st cousin 3 times removed		
Stoner, Nora Snyder	Wife of the 3rd cousin once removed		
Stoner, Private	Husband of the 6th cousin 3 times removed		
Stoudt, Mary Elizabeth	Wife of the 3rd cousin once removed		
Stoudt, Virginia	Wife of the 6th cousin twice removed		
Stouffer, Aaron	Half 3rd cousin once removed	IX	5
Stouffer, Abraham	Half 3rd cousin twice removed	X	6
Stouffer, Abraham	Half 3rd cousin once removed	IX	5
Stouffer, Abraham	Half 2nd cousin once removed	VII	4
Stouffer, Abraham	Half 3rd cousin	VIII	4
Stouffer, Abraham	Half 3rd cousin once removed	IX	5
Stouffer, Abraham Galle	4th great-granduncle	VIII	7
Stouffer, Adelheid Galle	4th great-grandmother	VI	6
Stouffer, Adeline	Half 3rd cousin once removed	IX	5
Stouffer, Agnes	1st cousin 5 times removed	IX	7
Stouffer, Alan	Half 3rd cousin 3 times removed	XI	7
Stouffer, Albert	Half 3rd cousin once removed	IX	5
Stouffer, Alberta	Half 3rd cousin once removed	IX	5
Stouffer, Alden	Half 3rd cousin once removed	IX	5
Stouffer, Alice	Half 3rd cousin 3 times removed	XI	7
Stouffer, Alonz	Half 3rd cousin once removed	IX	5
Stouffer, Andrew	Half 3rd cousin once removed	IX	5
Stouffer, Andrew	6th cousin	XIV	7
Stouffer, Anna Helena	Half 3rd cousin twice removed	X	6
Stouffer, Annie	Half 3rd cousin once removed	IX	5
Stouffer, Archibald	Half 3rd cousin twice removed	X	6
Stouffer, Arthur	Half 3rd cousin twice removed	X	6

Name	Relationship with Milton Hershey	Civil	Canon
Stouffer, Barbara Galle	4th great-grandaunt	VIII	7
Stouffer, Bert Grenfell	Half 3rd cousin 3 times removed	XI	7
Stouffer, Bertha	Half 3rd cousin once removed	IX	5
Stouffer, Bertha	Half 3rd cousin twice removed	X	6
Stouffer, Blanche	Half 3rd cousin twice removed	X	6
Stouffer, Bruce	Half 3rd cousin 3 times removed	XI	7
Stouffer, Carl	Half 3rd cousin twice removed	X	6
Stouffer, Carlton Lee	Half 3rd cousin 3 times removed	XI	7
Stouffer, Carson	Half 3rd cousin 3 times removed	XI	7
Stouffer, Catharine	6th cousin	XIV	7
Stouffer, Charles	Half 3rd cousin twice removed	X	6
Stouffer, Christian	Half 3rd cousin	VIII	4
Stouffer, Christian	Half 3rd cousin once removed	IX	5
Stouffer, Christian	6th great-grandfather	VIII	8
Stouffer, Christian	1st cousin 5 times removed	IX	7
Stouffer, Christian	Husband of the 5th cousin once removed		
Stouffer, Christian	Half 3rd cousin	VIII	4
Stouffer, Christian C.	6th cousin	XIV	7
Stouffer, Christina	Half 3rd cousin once removed	IX	5
Stouffer, Clara	Half 3rd cousin once removed	IX	5
Stouffer, Clarence	Half 3rd cousin twice removed	X	6
Stouffer, Clayton	Half 3rd cousin once removed	IX	5
Stouffer, Clayton Parker	Half 3rd cousin twice removed	X	6
Stouffer, Conrad Ulrick	Half 3rd cousin twice removed	X	6
Stouffer, Daniel	5th great-grandfather	VII	7
Stouffer, Daniel	1st cousin 5 times removed	IX	7
Stouffer, Daniel Ernest	Half 3rd cousin 3 times removed	XI	7
Stouffer, Daniel Galle	4th great-granduncle	VIII	7
Stouffer, David	Half 3rd cousin once removed	IX	5
Stouffer, David	Half 3rd cousin twice removed	X	6
Stouffer, David	Half 3rd cousin	VIII	4
Stouffer, David Abraham	Half 3rd cousin 3 times removed	XI	7
Stouffer, David K.	6th cousin	XIV	7
Stouffer, David Wesley	Half 3rd cousin once removed	IX	5
Stouffer, Delma Izetta	Half 3rd cousin 3 times removed	XI	7
Stouffer, Dianne Louise	Half 3rd cousin 3 times removed	XI	7
Stouffer, Donald	Half 3rd cousin 3 times removed	XI	7
Stouffer, Donna	Half 3rd cousin 3 times removed	XI	7
Stouffer, Donna Maxine	Half 3rd cousin 3 times removed	XI	7
Stouffer, Drusilla	Half 3rd cousin once removed	IX	5
Stouffer, Edna	Half 3rd cousin twice removed	X	6
Stouffer, Edward	Half 3rd cousin once removed	IX	5
Stouffer, Edward Bruce	Half 3rd cousin twice removed	X	6
Stouffer, Edwin	Half 3rd cousin twice removed	X	6
Stouffer, Eldon	Half 3rd cousin 3 times removed	XI	7
Stouffer, Eli	Half 3rd cousin once removed	IX	5
Stouffer, Elias	Half 3rd cousin once removed	IX	5
Stouffer, Elias	Husband of the 6th cousin		
Stouffer, Elizabeth	6th cousin	XIV	7
Stouffer, Elizabeth	Half 2nd cousin once removed	VII	4
Stouffer, Elizabeth	Half 3rd cousin	VIII	4
Stouffer, Elizabeth	Half 3rd cousin	VIII	4
Stouffer, Elizabeth	Half 3rd cousin once removed	IX	5
Stouffer, Elizabeth	Half 3rd cousin once removed	IX	5
Stouffer, Emma Ruth	Half 3rd cousin 3 times removed	XI	7
Stouffer, Ephraim	Half 3rd cousin once removed	IX	5
Stouffer, Erman	Half 3rd cousin twice removed	X	6
Stouffer, Ernest	Half 3rd cousin twice removed	X	6
Stouffer, Ernest	Half 3rd cousin twice removed	X	6
Stouffer, Ernest Albert	Half 3rd cousin twice removed	X	6
Stouffer, Esther	Half 3rd cousin once removed	IX	5
Stouffer, Esther	Half 3rd cousin once removed	IX	5
Stouffer, Esther	Half 3rd cousin once removed	IX	5
Stouffer, Esther	Half 3rd cousin once removed	IX	5
Stouffer, Esther	Half 3rd cousin once removed	IX	5
Stouffer, Evelyn	Half 3rd cousin twice removed	X	6

Name	Relationship with Milton Hershey	Civil	Canon
Stouffer, Fanny	Half 2nd cousin once removed	VII	4
Stouffer, Flavius Jacob	Half 3rd cousin once removed	IX	5
Stouffer, Flora	Half 3rd cousin once removed	IX	5
Stouffer, Florence	Half 3rd cousin 3 times removed	XI	7
Stouffer, Florence	Half 3rd cousin twice removed	X	6
Stouffer, Frances	Half 3rd cousin once removed	IX	5
Stouffer, Francis	Half 3rd cousin once removed	IX	5
Stouffer, Franklin	Half 3rd cousin 3 times removed	XI	7
Stouffer, Fred	Half 3rd cousin once removed	IX	5
Stouffer, Garth	Half 3rd cousin 3 times removed	XI	7
Stouffer, Geraldine	Half 3rd cousin 3 times removed	XI	7
Stouffer, H. Elgin	Half 3rd cousin 3 times removed	XI	7
Stouffer, Hannah	Half 3rd cousin once removed	IX	5
Stouffer, Hans	8th great-grandfather	X	10
Stouffer, Hans	7th great-grandfather	IX	9
Stouffer, Harold	Half 3rd cousin twice removed	X	6
Stouffer, Harry	Half 3rd cousin twice removed	X	6
Stouffer, Harry Norman	Half 3rd cousin twice removed	X	6
Stouffer, Helen	Half 3rd cousin twice removed	X	6
Stouffer, Ida	Half 3rd cousin twice removed	X	6
Stouffer, Infant	Half 3rd cousin once removed	IX	5
Stouffer, Isaac	Half 3rd cousin once removed	IX	5
Stouffer, Isobel	Half 3rd cousin twice removed	X	6
Stouffer, Jacob	6th cousin	XIV	7
Stouffer, Jacob	Half 2nd cousin once removed	VII	4
Stouffer, Jacob	Half 3rd cousin	VIII	4
Stouffer, Jacob	Half 3rd cousin	VIII	4
Stouffer, Jacob	1st cousin 5 times removed	IX	7
Stouffer, Jacob	6th cousin	XIV	7
Stouffer, Jacob Karl	Half 3rd cousin twice removed	X	6
Stouffer, Jared	Half 3rd cousin once removed	IX	5
Stouffer, Jason	Half 3rd cousin twice removed	X	6
Stouffer, Jean	Half 3rd cousin twice removed	X	6
Stouffer, Jean	Half 3rd cousin once removed	IX	5
Stouffer, Jean Carol	Half 3rd cousin 3 times removed	XI	7
Stouffer, Jennie Grace	Half 3rd cousin twice removed	X	6
Stouffer, Joe Karl	Half 3rd cousin 3 times removed	XI	7
Stouffer, John	6th cousin	XIV	7
Stouffer, John	Half 2nd cousin once removed	VII	4
Stouffer, John	Half 3rd cousin once removed	IX	5
Stouffer, John	Half 3rd cousin once removed	IX	5
Stouffer, John	Half 3rd cousin	VIII	4
Stouffer, John	Half 3rd cousin once removed	IX	5
Stouffer, John	Half 3rd cousin 3 times removed	XI	7
Stouffer, John	Husband of the 5th cousin once removed		
Stouffer, John Franklin	Half 3rd cousin once removed	IX	5
Stouffer, John O.	6th cousin	XIV	7
Stouffer, John Reesor	Half 3rd cousin	VIII	4
Stouffer, Josephuine	Half 3rd cousin once removed	IX	5
Stouffer, Katherine E.	Half 3rd cousin 3 times removed	XI	7
Stouffer, Kathleen	Half 3rd cousin twice removed	X	6
Stouffer, Kenneth	Half 3rd cousin twice removed	X	6
Stouffer, Keturah	Half 3rd cousin once removed	IX	5
Stouffer, Lambert	Half 3rd cousin twice removed	X	6
Stouffer, Laura	Half 3rd cousin once removed	IX	5
Stouffer, Lavilla	Half 3rd cousin once removed	IX	5
Stouffer, Leonard	Half 3rd cousin twice removed	X	6
Stouffer, Leslie	Half 3rd cousin twice removed	X	6
Stouffer, Llewellyn	Half 3rd cousin twice removed	X	6
Stouffer, Llewellyn	Half 3rd cousin 3 times removed	XI	7
Stouffer, Lloyd	Half 3rd cousin 3 times removed	XI	7
Stouffer, Lloyd Arthur	Half 3rd cousin twice removed	X	6
Stouffer, Louie	Half 3rd cousin twice removed	X	6
Stouffer, Louis	Half 3rd cousin 3 times removed	XI	7
Stouffer, Luella	Half 3rd cousin twice removed	X	6
Stouffer, Luella	Half 3rd cousin once removed	IX	5

Name	Relationship with Milton Hershey	Civil	Canon
Stouffer, Madeline	Half 3rd cousin 3 times removed	XI	7
Stouffer, Madlena Galle	4th great-grandaunt	VIII	7
Stouffer, Margareth Galle	4th great-grandaunt	VIII	7
Stouffer, Maria	Half 3rd cousin once removed	IX	5
Stouffer, Marian	Half 3rd cousin 3 times removed	XI	7
Stouffer, Marion	Half 3rd cousin 3 times removed	XI	7
Stouffer, Marion	Half 3rd cousin twice removed	X	6
Stouffer, Martha	Half 3rd cousin	VIII	4
Stouffer, Martha	Half 3rd cousin once removed	IX	5
Stouffer, Martha	Half 3rd cousin once removed	IX	5
Stouffer, Martha May	Half 3rd cousin twice removed	X	6
Stouffer, Mary	Half 3rd cousin once removed	IX	5
Stouffer, Mary	Half 3rd cousin 3 times removed	XI	7
Stouffer, Mary	Half 3rd cousin once removed	IX	5
Stouffer, Mary Adrienne	Half 3rd cousin 3 times removed	XI	7
Stouffer, Mary Ann	Half 3rd cousin once removed	IX	5
Stouffer, Matilda	Half 3rd cousin once removed	IX	5
Stouffer, Matilda	Half 3rd cousin once removed	IX	5
Stouffer, Maude	Half 3rd cousin twice removed	X	6
Stouffer, May	Half 3rd cousin twice removed	X	6
Stouffer, Miline	Half 3rd cousin 3 times removed	XI	7
Stouffer, Miline	Half 3rd cousin twice removed	X	6
Stouffer, Minnie	Half 3rd cousin once removed	IX	5
Stouffer, Molly	6th cousin	XIV	7
Stouffer, Myrtle Inez	Half 3rd cousin twice removed	X	6
Stouffer, Neil	Half 3rd cousin 3 times removed	XI	7
Stouffer, Noah	Half 3rd cousin once removed	IX	5
Stouffer, Ora Hilda	Half 3rd cousin twice removed	X	6
Stouffer, Peter	Half 3rd cousin	VIII	4
Stouffer, Phyllis	Half 3rd cousin 3 times removed	XI	7
Stouffer, Phyllis	Half 3rd cousin twice removed	X	6
Stouffer, Private	Half 3rd cousin 3 times removed	XI	7
Stouffer, Private	Half 3rd cousin 3 times removed	XI	7
Stouffer, Private	Half 3rd cousin 3 times removed	XI	7
Stouffer, Private	Half 3rd cousin 3 times removed	XI	7
Stouffer, Private	Half 3rd cousin 3 times removed	XI	7
Stouffer, Private	Half 3rd cousin 3 times removed	XI	7
Stouffer, Private	Half 3rd cousin 3 times removed	XI	7
Stouffer, Private	Half 3rd cousin 3 times removed	XI	7
Stouffer, Private	Half 3rd cousin 3 times removed	XI	7
Stouffer, Private	Half 3rd cousin 3 times removed	XI	7
Stouffer, Private	Half 3rd cousin 3 times removed	XI	7
Stouffer, Private	Half 3rd cousin 3 times removed	XI	7
Stouffer, Private	Half 3rd cousin 3 times removed	XI	7
Stouffer, Ralph Clayton	Half 3rd cousin 3 times removed	XI	7
Stouffer, Reginald	Half 3rd cousin twice removed	X	6
Stouffer, Revis Parsons	Half 3rd cousin once removed	IX	5
Stouffer, Robert	Half 3rd cousin twice removed	X	6
Stouffer, Roxa	Half 3rd cousin once removed	IX	5
Stouffer, Ruth	Half 3rd cousin twice removed	X	6
Stouffer, Samuel	Half 3rd cousin	VIII	4
Stouffer, Samuel	Half 3rd cousin twice removed	X	6
Stouffer, Sarah	Half 3rd cousin once removed	IX	5
Stouffer, Simeon	Half 3rd cousin	VIII	4
Stouffer, Stanley	Half 3rd cousin twice removed	X	6
Stouffer, Stewart W.	Half 3rd cousin twice removed	X	6
Stouffer, Susan	Half 3rd cousin	VIII	4
Stouffer, Thomas	Half 3rd cousin once removed	IX	5
Stouffer, Ulrich	1st cousin 5 times removed	IX	7
Stouffer, Ulrich Galle	4th great-granduncle	VIII	7
Stouffer, Victor	Half 3rd cousin twice removed	X	6
Stouffer, Walter	Half 3rd cousin twice removed	X	6
Stouffer, Walter	Half 3rd cousin twice removed	X	6
Stouffer, Wellington	Half 3rd cousin once removed	IX	5
Stouffer, Wellington	Half 3rd cousin once removed	IX	5

Name	Relationship with Milton Hershey	Civil	Canon
Stouffer, Wesley	Half 3rd cousin 3 times removed	XI	7
Stouffer, Wesley Adrian	Half 3rd cousin twice removed	X	6
Stouffer, Wilbert Gillson	Half 3rd cousin twice removed	X	6
Stouffer, Wilfrid	Half 3rd cousin 3 times removed	XI	7
Stouffer, William	6th cousin	XIV	7
Stouffer, Willis	Half 3rd cousin twice removed	X	6
Stover, Private	Husband of the 3rd cousin twice removed		
Stover, Private	3rd cousin 3 times removed	XI	7
Strain, Sahra Polly	Wife of the 6th cousin twice removed		
Strauss, Millmy	Wife of the 6th cousin once removed		
Streler, Margareth	Wife of the half 6th great-granduncle		
Strickland, Emma	Wife of the 3rd cousin once removed		
Strickler, Abraham	Husband of the 2nd cousin 3 times removed		
Strickler, Abraham	3rd cousin twice removed	X	6
Strickler, Ambrose	2nd cousin	VI	3
Strickler, Ann	Wife of the 4th cousin 4 times removed		
Strickler, Annie	3rd cousin twice removed	X	6
Strickler, Elisabeth	Wife of the 1st cousin 4 times removed		
Strickler, Elisabeth	3rd cousin twice removed	X	6
Strickler, Elizabeth	Wife of the 1st cousin 4 times removed		
Strickler, Elizabeth	Wife of the 6th cousin		
Strickler, Emerson	2nd cousin	VI	3
Strickler, Fannie	2nd cousin	VI	3
Strickler, Fannie	3rd cousin twice removed	X	6
Strickler, Henry	3rd cousin twice removed	X	6
Strickler, Henry B	Husband of the 1st cousin once removed		
Strickler, Jacob	Husband of the 1st cousin 4 times removed		
Strickler, Jacob	3rd cousin twice removed	X	6
Strickler, John	3rd cousin twice removed	X	6
Strickler, Martha	3rd cousin twice removed	X	6
Strickler, Mary	3rd cousin twice removed	X	6
Strickler, Susan	3rd cousin twice removed	X	6
Strite, Abram Joseph	2nd cousin twice removed	VIII	5
Strite, Ada May	2nd cousin twice removed	VIII	5
Strite, Andrew C.	Husband of the 2nd cousin once removed		
Strite, Anrew C.	Husband of the 2nd cousin once removed		
Strite, Cyrus L.	2nd cousin twice removed	VIII	5
Strite, Earl Clarence	2nd cousin twice removed	VIII	5
Strite, Irvin Landis	2nd cousin twice removed	VIII	5
Strite, Lewis Andrew	2nd cousin twice removed	VIII	5
Strome, Mary	Wife of the half 3rd cousin		
Strong, Herbert W, Jr	Husband of the 6th cousin 3 times removed		
Strong, Kirk M	6th cousin 4 times removed	XVIII	11
Stroup, Ada louella	Wife of the 6th cousin once removed		
Stroup, Atlee	6th cousin 3 times removed	XVII	10
Stroup, Earl	6th cousin twice removed	XVI	9
Stroup, Julia Faye	6th cousin 3 times removed	XVII	10
Stroup, June	6th cousin 3 times removed	XVII	10
Stroup, Leola M	Wife of the 6th cousin once removed		
Stroup, Lowell	6th cousin 3 times removed	XVII	10
Stroup, Nellie F.	6th cousin twice removed	XVI	9
Stroup, Private	6th cousin 3 times removed	XVII	10
Stroup, Private	6th cousin 3 times removed	XVII	10
Stroup, Private	6th cousin 3 times removed	XVII	10
Stroup, Private	6th cousin 3 times removed	XVII	10
Stroup, Private	6th cousin 3 times removed	XVII	10
Stroup, Russell	6th cousin 3 times removed	XVII	10
Stroup, William H	Husband of the 6th cousin twice removed		
Stroup, William W.	Husband of the 6th cousin once removed		
Stuart, Dean	6th cousin twice removed	XVI	9
Stuart, Neil	6th cousin twice removed	XVI	9
Stuart, Private	6th cousin twice removed	XVI	9
Stuart, Private	6th cousin 3 times removed	XVII	10
Stuart, Private	6th cousin 3 times removed	XVII	10
Stuart, Private	6th cousin 3 times removed	XVII	10
Stuart, Private	6th cousin 3 times removed	XVII	10

Name	Relationship with Milton Hershey	Civil	Canon
Stuart, Private	6th cousin 3 times removed	XVII	10
Stuart, Private	6th cousin 3 times removed	XVII	10
Stuart, Private	6th cousin 3 times removed	XVII	10
Stuart, Russell	6th cousin twice removed	XVI	9
Stuart, Vernon	Husband of the 6th cousin once removed		
Stuber, Florence Mildred	Wife of the 4th cousin twice removed		
Sturgeon, Sarah Regina	Wife of the 6th cousin		
Stutt, A. Katharine	Half 3rd cousin twice removed	X	6
Stutt, H. Gertrude	Half 3rd cousin twice removed	X	6
Stutt, H. Gordon	Half 3rd cousin twice removed	X	6
Stutt, James E.	Half 3rd cousin twice removed	X	6
Stutt, W. J.	Husband of the half 3rd cousin once removed		
Sukosd, Wilma S	Wife of the 6th cousin twice removed		
Summer, Argus	Husband of the 6th cousin twice removed		
Summer, Bernice Winifred	Wife of the 6th cousin twice removed		
Summers, Bill	Husband of the 6th cousin 3 times removed		
Summers, Clementine	Wife of the 6th cousin		
Summers, Dorothy J	Wife of the 6th cousin twice removed		
Summers, Kathleen Lucille	Wife of the 6th cousin twice removed		
Summers, M. Mose	Husband of the 2nd cousin twice removed		
Summers, Private	Husband of the 3rd cousin twice removed		
Summers, Private	3rd cousin 3 times removed	XI	7
Summers, Private	3rd cousin 3 times removed	XI	7
Summers, Private	3rd cousin 4 times removed	XII	8
Summers, Sarah	Wife of the 6th cousin		
Summy, Aaron	3rd cousin twice removed	X	6
Summy, Abram	3rd cousin twice removed	X	6
Summy, David	3rd cousin twice removed	X	6
Summy, Jacob	3rd cousin twice removed	X	6
Summy, John	Husband of the 2nd cousin 3 times removed		
Summy, John H	3rd cousin twice removed	X	6
Summy, Maria	3rd cousin twice removed	X	6
Summy, Peter	3rd cousin twice removed	X	6
Summy, Peter	Husband of the 6th cousin		
Suner, Jacob	Husband of the half 6th great-grandaunt		
Surerus, Sarah	Wife of the half 3rd cousin		
Sutton, Carrie	Wife of the 6th cousin twice removed		
Swarr, Anna	Wife of the 1st cousin 3 times removed		
Swart, Peter	Husband of the 1st cousin 4 times removed		
Swartz, Christian	Husband of the 2nd cousin 3 times removed		
Swartzendruber, Private	Husband of the 3rd cousin twice removed		
Swartzendruber, Private	3rd cousin 3 times removed	XI	7
Sweeney, Catherine Elizabeth	Wife		
Sweigart, Abraham R.	3rd cousin	VIII	4
Sweigart, Amanda R.	3rd cousin	VIII	4
Sweigart, Amos R.	3rd cousin	VIII	4
Sweigart, Anna R.	3rd cousin	VIII	4
Sweigart, Chambers U.	Husband of the 2nd cousin once removed		
Sweigart, Eli R.	3rd cousin	VIII	4
Sweigart, Elizabeth R.	3rd cousin	VIII	4
Sweigart, Frances Reiff	3rd cousin	VIII	4
Sweigart, Jacob R.	3rd cousin	VIII	4
Sweigart, John R.	3rd cousin	VIII	4
Sweigart, Lydia R.	3rd cousin	VIII	4
Sweigart, Martin R.	3rd cousin	VIII	4
Switzer, John	Husband of the 1st cousin 4 times removed		
Sylvester, Private	Husband of the 6th cousin twice removed		
Taber, Joann	Ex-wife of the 4th cousin twice removed		
Tangvald, Private	Wife of the 3rd cousin 3 times removed		
Taylor, Leighton Robert	Husband of the 6th cousin 3 times removed		
Taylor, Margaret L.	Wife of the 6th cousin		
Taylor, Mary L.	Wife of the 6th cousin		
Teaque, Private	6th cousin 3 times removed	XVII	10
Teaque, Ronald	Husband of the 6th cousin twice removed		
Tedford, Private	Husband of the 6th cousin 3 times removed		
Tedford, Private	6th cousin 4 times removed	XVIII	11

Name	Relationship with Milton Hershey	Civil	Canon
Tedford, Private	6th cousin 4 times removed	XVIII	11
Teeters, Elizabeth	Wife of the 6th cousin		
Temple, Dorothy	Wife of the 6th cousin twice removed		
Temple, Dorothy E.	Wife of the half 3rd cousin twice removed		
Thoman, Geraldine	Wife of the half 3rd cousin twice removed		
Thomas, Bart	Husband of the 6th cousin twice removed		
Thomas, Carol J	6th cousin 4 times removed	XVIII	11
Thomas, Howard	Husband of the 6th cousin 3 times removed		
Thomas, Private	Husband of the 3rd cousin 3 times removed		
Thomas, Private	3rd cousin 4 times removed	XII	8
Thomas, Private	3rd cousin 4 times removed	XII	8
Thomas, Private	Husband of the 3rd cousin 3 times removed		
Thomas, Private	3rd cousin 4 times removed	XII	8
Thomas, Private	3rd cousin 4 times removed	XII	8
Thomas, Private	3rd cousin 4 times removed	XII	8
Thomas, Stanley Howard	Husband of the 3rd cousin twice removed		
Thometz, Anna Theresa	Wife of the 6th cousin twice removed		
Thompson, Ethel Lillian	Wife of the half 3rd cousin 3 times removed		
Thompson, Mary	Wife of the half 3rd cousin once removed		
Thompson, Orin Wesley	Husband of the 6th cousin twice removed		
Thompson, Private	6th cousin 3 times removed	XVII	10
Thornton, Private	6th cousin 3 times removed	XVII	10
Thornton, Private	6th cousin 3 times removed	XVII	10
Thornton, Roy	Husband of the 6th cousin twice removed		
Thorpe, Lulu	Wife of the half 3rd cousin 3 times removed		
Thrope, Helen Edith	Wife of the 6th cousin twice removed		
Tichenon, Margaret	Wife of the 6th cousin 3 times removed		
Tidwell, Mary Dorris	Wife of the 6th cousin 3 times removed		
Tiffany, Charlene	Wife of the 3rd cousin twice removed		
Tinkey, Henry	Husband of the 3rd great-grandaunt		
Tobel, Barbel	Wife of the 7th great-granduncle		
Tobias, Jennie E.	Wife of the 6th cousin once removed		
Todd, A Morris, Jr	Husband of the 6th cousin 3 times removed		
Todd, Marc D	6th cousin 4 times removed	XVIII	11
Todd, Mary Root	Wife of the 3rd cousin twice removed		
Todd, Michael M	6th cousin 4 times removed	XVIII	11
Tolemie, Manilla	Wife of the 3rd cousin once removed		
Tompkins, Bertha Jeanne	Half 3rd cousin 3 times removed	XI	7
Tompkins, J. Daniel S.	Half 3rd cousin 3 times removed	XI	7
Tompkins, James	Husband of the half 3rd cousin twice removed		
Tousignant, Albena May	Wife of the 6th cousin twice removed		
Towle, Norman Lincoln	Husband of the 3rd cousin once removed		
Trask, Private	Husband of the 6th cousin 5 times removed		
Travers, Lewis	Husband of the 2nd cousin 3 times removed		
Trinckler, Elsbeth	Wife of the half 6th great-granduncle		
Tritt, Alice Bell	6th cousin twice removed	XVI	9
Tritt, Alice E.	6th cousin twice removed	XVI	9
Tritt, Christian	6th cousin once removed	XV	8
Tritt, Clarence E.	6th cousin twice removed	XVI	9
Tritt, Clarence Ziegler	6th cousin twice removed	XVI	9
Tritt, Edgar P.	6th cousin twice removed	XVI	9
Tritt, Elizabeth	6th cousin once removed	XV	8
Tritt, Florence E.	6th cousin twice removed	XVI	9
Tritt, John A.	6th cousin once removed	XV	8
Tritt, Lydia Jane	6th cousin once removed	XV	8
Tritt, Maggie T.	6th cousin once removed	XV	8
Tritt, Mary S.	Wife of the 5th cousin		
Tritt, Maud T.	6th cousin twice removed	XVI	9
Tritt, Melvin J.	6th cousin twice removed	XVI	9
Tritt, Peter	Husband of the 6th cousin		
Tritt, Peter Stough	6th cousin once removed	XV	8
Tritt, Samuel John	6th cousin once removed	XV	8
Troutman, Elizabeth	Wife of the 6th cousin 3 times removed		
Truby, Lovina	Wife of the 6th cousin		
Truesdale, Private	Wife of the 6th cousin 3 times removed		
Trump, Anita	6th cousin 3 times removed	XVII	10

Name	Relationship with Milton Hershey	Civil	Canon
Trump, Bessie Pearl	6th cousin twice removed	XVI	9
Trump, Charles Clifford	6th cousin 3 times removed	XVII	10
Trump, Charles Clifford	6th cousin 3 times removed	XVII	10
Trump, Clarence R.	6th cousin twice removed	XVI	9
Trump, Emma Elizabeth	6th cousin twice removed	XVI	9
Trump, Harold	6th cousin 3 times removed	XVII	10
Trump, Jerimiah Washington	Husband of the 6th cousin once removed		
Trump, Jerry	Husband of the 6th cousin once removed		
Trump, Jerry Roosevelt	6th cousin 3 times removed	XVII	10
Trump, John Duane	6th cousin 3 times removed	XVII	10
Trump, John Henry	6th cousin twice removed	XVI	9
Trump, Mary May	6th cousin twice removed	XVI	9
Trump, Oliver Garfield	6th cousin twice removed	XVI	9
Trump, Oscar A.	6th cousin twice removed	XVI	9
Trump, Private	6th cousin 4 times removed	XVIII	11
Trump, Private	6th cousin 4 times removed	XVIII	11
Trump, Private	6th cousin 3 times removed	XVII	10
Trump, Private	6th cousin 3 times removed	XVII	10
Trump, Private	6th cousin 3 times removed	XVII	10
Trump, Private	6th cousin 4 times removed	XVIII	11
Trump, Private	6th cousin 3 times removed	XVII	10
Trupe, Private	Wife of the 3rd cousin 3 times removed		
Turner, Andrew Jackson	Husband of the 6th cousin 3 times removed		
Turner, Elizabeth I.	Wife of the 6th cousin 3 times removed		
Turner, Private	6th cousin 4 times removed	XVIII	11
Tvardek, Private	Wife of the 6th cousin 4 times removed		
Tyner, Bethel Leone	6th cousin 3 times removed	XVII	10
Tyner, Homer	Husband of the 6th cousin twice removed		
Tyner, Kenneth A	6th cousin 3 times removed	XVII	10
Tyner, Saint Elmo Parlette	6th cousin 3 times removed	XVII	10
Unknown	Wife of the 6th cousin 3 times removed		
Unknown	Wife of the 3rd cousin twice removed		
Unknown, Amanda	Wife of the 6th cousin		
Unknown, Ann	Wife of the 3rd cousin 3 times removed		
Unknown, Anna	Wife of the 2nd cousin 6 times removed		
Unknown, Anna	Wife of the 6th cousin		
Unknown, Anna	Wife of the half 3rd cousin once removed		
Unknown, Anna C.	Wife of the 6th cousin		
Unknown, Barbara	Wife of the 3rd great-granduncle		
Unknown, Barbara	Wife of the 5th great-granduncle		
Unknown, Barbara	Wife of the 1st cousin 7 times removed		
Unknown, Barbara	Wife of the 2nd cousin 6 times removed		
Unknown, Barbary	Wife of the half 4th great-granduncle		
Unknown, Barbel/Cherl	Wife of the 6th great-granduncle		
Unknown, Beryl	Wife of the half 3rd cousin 3 times removed		
Unknown, Betty J	Wife of the 6th cousin twice removed		
Unknown, Catharine	3rd great-grandmother	V	5
Unknown, Catharine	Wife of the 5th cousin once removed		
Unknown, Catherine	Wife of the 1st cousin 4 times removed		
Unknown, Catherine	Wife of the 4th cousin twice removed		
Unknown, Elisabeth	Wife of the 5th great-grandfather		
Unknown, Elizabeth	Wife of the 6th cousin		
Unknown, Elizabeth	Wife of the 6th cousin		
Unknown, Elizabeth	Wife of the 4th cousin twice removed		
Unknown, Elizabeth	Wife of the 1st cousin 4 times removed		
Unknown, Elizabeth	Wife of the 1st cousin 4 times removed		
Unknown, Elizabeth	Wife of the 6th cousin		
Unknown, Elizabeth	Wife of the 2nd cousin		
Unknown, Elizabeth	Wife of the 6th cousin		
Unknown, Elizabeth	Wife of the 1st cousin		
Unknown, Ella	Wife of the 6th cousin		
Unknown, Emma	Wife of the half 3rd cousin twice removed		
Unknown, Ethelda	Wife of the 6th cousin twice removed		
Unknown, Eva	Wife of the 3rd cousin 3 times removed		
Unknown, Francis	Wife of the 2nd cousin once removed		
Unknown, Georgiann	Wife of the 6th cousin once removed		

Name	Relationship with Milton Hershey	Civil	Canon
Unknown, Hannah	Wife of the 4th cousin twice removed		
Unknown, Jennie M.	Wife of the 6th cousin twice removed		
Unknown, Julia Ann	Wife of the 6th cousin		
Unknown, Kesiah	Wife of the 5th cousin once removed		
Unknown, Lottie	Wife of the 6th cousin		
Unknown, Lydia	Wife of the 6th cousin		
Unknown, Mae	Wife of the 6th cousin twice removed		
Unknown, Malinda	Wife of the 6th cousin		
Unknown, Malinda B.	Wife of the 6th cousin		
Unknown, Margaret	Wife of the 6th cousin		
Unknown, Margaret	Wife of the 6th cousin		
Unknown, Margaret A.	Wife of the 6th cousin		
Unknown, Margaret D.	Wife of the 6th cousin		
Unknown, Marguerite	Wife of the half 3rd cousin twice removed		
Unknown, Maria	Wife of the 4th great-granduncle		
Unknown, Maria	Wife of the 3rd cousin once removed		
Unknown, Maria Catherine	Wife of the 5th cousin once removed		
Unknown, Mary	4th great-grandmother	VI	6
Unknown, Mary	Wife of the 2nd cousin 6 times removed		
Unknown, Mary	Wife of the 6th cousin		
Unknown, Mary Ann	Wife of the 6th cousin		
Unknown, Matilda	Wife of the 6th cousin		
Unknown, Mina	Wife of the 2nd cousin twice removed		
Unknown, Private	Wife of the 3rd cousin 3 times removed		
Unknown, Private	Wife of the 3rd cousin 3 times removed		
Unknown, Private	Wife of the 3rd cousin 3 times removed		
Unknown, Private	Wife of the 3rd cousin 3 times removed		
Unknown, Private	Wife of the 6th cousin 3 times removed		
Unknown, Private	Wife of the 6th cousin 3 times removed		
Unknown, Private	Wife of the 6th cousin 3 times removed		
Unknown, Private	Wife of the 6th cousin 3 times removed		
Unknown, Private	Wife of the 6th cousin 3 times removed		
Unknown, Private	Wife of the 6th cousin 4 times removed		
Unknown, Private	Wife of the 6th cousin 4 times removed		
Unknown, Private	Wife of the 6th cousin 4 times removed		
Unknown, Private	Husband of the 6th cousin 4 times removed		
Unknown, Private	6th cousin 5 times removed	XIX	12
Unknown, Private	6th cousin 5 times removed	XIX	12
Unknown, Private	Wife of the 6th cousin 3 times removed		
Unknown, Private	Wife of the 6th cousin 3 times removed		
Unknown, Private	Wife of the 6th cousin 3 times removed		
Unknown, Private	Husband of the 6th cousin 3 times removed		
Unknown, Private	Wife of the 6th cousin 3 times removed		
Unknown, Private	Wife of the 6th cousin 3 times removed		
Unknown, Private	Wife of the 6th cousin 3 times removed		
Unknown, Private	Wife of the 6th cousin 3 times removed		
Unknown, Rachel	Wife of the 6th cousin		
Unknown, Sarah	Wife of the 4th cousin twice removed		
Unknown, Sarah	Wife of the 6th cousin		
Unknown, Sarah	Wife of the 6th cousin		
Unknown, Sarah	Wife of the 4th cousin		
Unknown, Sorama	Wife of the 6th cousin once removed		
Unknown, Susan	Wife of the 6th cousin		
Unknown, Unknown	5th great-grandmother	VII	7
Unknown, Unknown	7th great-grandmother	IX	9
Unknown, Unknown	Wife of the 4th great-granduncle		
Unknown, Unknown	5th great-grandmother	VII	7
Unknown, Unknown	Wife of the 3rd great-granduncle		
Unknown, Unknown	Wife of the 4th great-granduncle		
Unknown, Unknown	4th great-grandmother	VI	6
Unknown, Unknown	Wife of the 1st cousin 4 times removed		
Unknown, Unknown	Wife of the 4th cousin twice removed		
Unknown, Unknown	Wife of the 4th cousin twice removed		
Unruh, Private	Wife of the 3rd cousin twice removed		
Urner, Sarah Price	Wife of the 4th cousin once removed		
Usmar, C. William	Husband of the 3rd cousin 3 times removed		

Name	Relationship with Milton Hershey	Civil	Canon
Uts, Ida Ota	Wife of the 6th cousin twice removed		
Valentine, Alma	Wife of the half 3rd cousin twice removed		
Valient, Parthena S	Wife of the 6th cousin 3 times removed		
Van Every, Dinah	Wife of the 3rd cousin twice removed		
Van Hiner, Private	Husband of the 6th cousin 3 times removed		
Van Hiner, Private	6th cousin 4 times removed	XVIII	11
Van Vleck, Henry	Husband of the 1st cousin 4 times removed		
Vansickle, Abram	Husband of the half 3rd cousin 3 times removed		
Vansickle, Barry Learoy	Half 3rd cousin 4 times removed	XII	8
Vansickle, Calvin Learoy	Husband of the half 3rd cousin 3 times removed		
Vansickle, Lloyd	Half 3rd cousin 4 times removed	XII	8
vanWormer, Private	Husband of the 3rd cousin 3 times removed		
Varnes, Mary	Wife of the 5th cousin 3 times removed		
Veith, Robert John	Half 3rd cousin 3 times removed	XI	7
Veith, William J.	Husband of the half 3rd cousin twice removed		
Ventura, Private	Husband of the 6th cousin 3 times removed		
Ventura, Private	6th cousin 4 times removed	XVIII	11
Voelker, Edna	Wife of the 6th cousin 3 times removed		
Vollenweider, Margaret	6th great-grandmother	VIII	8
Wagner, Private	6th cousin 3 times removed	XVII	10
Wagner, Private	6th cousin 3 times removed	XVII	10
Wagner, Private	6th cousin 3 times removed	XVII	10
Wagner, Ross Earl	Husband of the 6th cousin twice removed		
Wagner, Unknown (Wagoner)	Husband of the 1st cousin 4 times removed		
Wagoner, John	Husband of the 6th cousin twice removed		
Wagoner, Private	6th cousin 3 times removed	XVII	10
Wagoner, Private	6th cousin 3 times removed	XVII	10
Wagoner, Private	6th cousin 3 times removed	XVII	10
Walder, Regel	Wife of the 7th great-granduncle		
Walker, Isaac	Husband of the 3rd cousin twice removed		
Walker, Lela	Wife of the 6th cousin twice removed		
Walker, Mary Frances	4th cousin once removed	XI	6
Walker, Private	Husband of the 6th cousin 3 times removed		
Walker, Walter	Husband of the 6th cousin twice removed		
Wall, Lloyd Archer	Husband of the 6th cousin 3 times removed		
Wall, Private	6th cousin 4 times removed	XVIII	11
Wall, Private	6th cousin 4 times removed	XVIII	11
Wall, Private	6th cousin 4 times removed	XVIII	11
Wallace, Claire	Wife of the half 3rd cousin twice removed		
Wallace, Grace	Wife of the half 3rd cousin twice removed		
Walsh, Private	Husband of the 6th cousin 4 times removed		
Walsh, Private	6th cousin 5 times removed	XIX	12
Walters, Grace	Wife of the 6th cousin once removed		
Wance, Private	Wife of the 3rd cousin 3 times removed		
Wanger/Wenger, Iva (Wingert)	Wife of the 5th cousin		
Wanner, John	Husband of the 3rd great-grandaunt		
Wanner, John	Husband of the 2nd cousin 3 times removed		
Wanner, Private	Husband of the 3rd cousin twice removed		
Wanner, Private	3rd cousin 3 times removed	XI	7
Wanner, Private	3rd cousin 3 times removed	XI	7
Waples, Private	Husband of the 6th cousin 3 times removed		
Ward, Albert Ray	Husband of the 6th cousin twice removed		
Ward, James Signor	Husband of the 6th cousin 3 times removed		
Ward, Mary Beemer	Wife of the half 3rd cousin		
Ward, Private	6th cousin 4 times removed	XVIII	11
Ward, Private	6th cousin 3 times removed	XVII	10
Ward, Private	6th cousin 4 times removed	XVIII	11
Ward, Private	6th cousin 4 times removed	XVIII	11
Ward, Private	6th cousin 4 times removed	XVIII	11
Ward, Private	6th cousin 3 times removed	XVII	10
Ward, Unknown	Husband of the 6th cousin twice removed		
Wardecker, Charles A.	Husband of the 6th cousin twice removed		
Warkentine, Agnes	Wife of the half 3rd cousin twice removed		
Warmington, Richard	Husband of the half 3rd cousin twice removed		
Warmington, Richard George	Half 3rd cousin 3 times removed	XI	7
Waugh, Mable	Wife of the 6th cousin twice removed		

Name	Relationship with Milton Hershey	Civil	Canon
Wealand, Marcella	Wife of the 2nd cousin once removed		
Weaver, Aaron G.	4th cousin once removed	XI	6
Weaver, Amos H.	5th cousin	XII	6
Weaver, Andrew S.	2nd cousin 5 times removed	XI	8
Weaver, Anna	2nd cousin 3 times removed	IX	6
Weaver, Anna	3rd cousin twice removed	X	6
Weaver, Anna	4th cousin once removed	XI	6
Weaver, Anna C.	Wife of the 3rd cousin twice removed		
Weaver, Anna M.	Wife of the 3rd cousin once removed		
Weaver, Anna Mary	5th cousin	XII	6
Weaver, Arvilla	2nd cousin 4 times removed	X	7
Weaver, Barbara	5th cousin	XII	6
Weaver, Benjamin	4th cousin once removed	XI	6
Weaver, Benjamin Michael	2nd cousin 6 times removed	XII	9
Weaver, Blanche M	Wife of the 6th cousin twice removed		
Weaver, Carolyn Jean	Wife of the 2nd cousin 4 times removed		
Weaver, Catharine	Wife of the 4th cousin once removed		
Weaver, Catharine	3rd cousin twice removed	X	6
Weaver, Catherine	Wife of the 5th cousin once removed		
Weaver, Christian G.	4th cousin once removed	XI	6
Weaver, Daniel G.	4th cousin once removed	XI	6
Weaver, David G.	4th cousin once removed	XI	6
Weaver, Donna Lou	2nd cousin 4 times removed	X	7
Weaver, Elisabeth	Wife of the 6th cousin		
Weaver, Elizabeth	Wife of the 2nd cousin once removed		
Weaver, Elizabeth Ann	2nd cousin 4 times removed	X	7
Weaver, Ellen Sue	2nd cousin 5 times removed	XI	8
Weaver, Fanny	3rd cousin twice removed	X	6
Weaver, Feronica	3rd cousin twice removed	X	6
Weaver, George	3rd cousin twice removed	X	6
Weaver, Helen V.	Wife of the 3rd cousin once removed		
Weaver, Henry D.	Husband of the 3rd cousin twice removed		
Weaver, Hettie Rebecca	5th cousin	XII	6
Weaver, Isaac	2nd cousin 3 times removed	IX	6
Weaver, Isaac	3rd cousin twice removed	X	6
Weaver, Israel	4th cousin once removed	XI	6
Weaver, James Edward	2nd cousin 5 times removed	XI	8
Weaver, Jay Donald	2nd cousin 4 times removed	X	7
Weaver, Jennifer Lynn	2nd cousin 5 times removed	XI	8
Weaver, John	Husband of the 1st cousin 3 times removed		
Weaver, John	Husband of the 1st cousin 3 times removed		
Weaver, John Eric	2nd cousin 4 times removed	X	7
Weaver, John Hollinger	5th cousin	XII	6
Weaver, John Landis	2nd cousin 3 times removed	IX	6
Weaver, John Matthew	2nd cousin 5 times removed	XI	8
Weaver, John Michael	2nd cousin 5 times removed	XI	8
Weaver, John W	Husband of the 6th cousin		
Weaver, John W.	4th cousin once removed	XI	6
Weaver, Johnathan	Husband of the half 4th cousin twice removed		
Weaver, Jonas	Husband of the 2nd cousin 3 times removed		
Weaver, Joseph	Husband of the 1st cousin 3 times removed		
Weaver, Joshua Alan	2nd cousin 6 times removed	XII	9
Weaver, Levi	3rd cousin twice removed	X	6
Weaver, Lisa Rene	2nd cousin 5 times removed	XI	8
Weaver, Lizzie B.	Wife of the 5th cousin		
Weaver, Lydia	3rd cousin twice removed	X	6
Weaver, Lydia	Wife of the 3rd cousin twice removed		
Weaver, Mabel L.	2nd cousin 3 times removed	IX	6
Weaver, Mable	Wife of the half 3rd cousin twice removed		
Weaver, Magdalena	3rd cousin twice removed	X	6
Weaver, Magdalena	3rd cousin twice removed	X	6
Weaver, Marietta	6th cousin once removed	XV	8
Weaver, Martin G.	4th cousin once removed	XI	6
Weaver, Mary	Wife of the half 4th great-granduncle		
Weaver, Mary	4th cousin once removed	XI	6
Weaver, Mary Grace	Wife of the 6th cousin twice removed		

Name	Relationship with Milton Hershey	Civil	Canon
Weaver, Mary Jane	Wife of the 6th cousin once removed		
Weaver, Odessa May	Wife of the 6th cousin once removed		
Weaver, Peter	2nd cousin 3 times removed	IX	6
Weaver, Peter	3rd cousin twice removed	X	6
Weaver, Private	Wife of the 3rd cousin 3 times removed		
Weaver, Private	Wife of the 3rd cousin 4 times removed		
Weaver, Private	Wife of the 3rd cousin 3 times removed		
Weaver, Private	Husband of the 3rd cousin 3 times removed		
Weaver, Private	3rd cousin 4 times removed	XII	8
Weaver, Private	Wife of the 3rd cousin 3 times removed		
Weaver, Private	3rd cousin 3 times removed	XI	7
Weaver, Private	3rd cousin 3 times removed	XI	7
Weaver, Private	3rd cousin 3 times removed	XI	7
Weaver, Private	3rd cousin 3 times removed	XI	7
Weaver, Private	Husband of the 3rd cousin 3 times removed		
Weaver, Private	3rd cousin 4 times removed	XII	8
Weaver, Private	3rd cousin 4 times removed	XII	8
Weaver, Private	Wife of the 3rd cousin twice removed		
Weaver, Private	Husband of the 3rd cousin twice removed		
Weaver, Private	3rd cousin 3 times removed	XI	7
Weaver, Private	3rd cousin 3 times removed	XI	7
Weaver, Private	3rd cousin 3 times removed	XI	7
Weaver, Private	3rd cousin 3 times removed	XI	7
Weaver, Private	3rd cousin 3 times removed	XI	7
Weaver, Rachel Anne	2nd cousin 6 times removed	XII	9
Weaver, Ronald Lee	2nd cousin 4 times removed	X	7
Weaver, Sarah	Wife of the 2nd cousin		
Weaver, Susie	5th cousin	XII	6
Weaver, Tillie	3rd cousin twice removed	X	6
Weaver, William Shively	Husband of the 6th cousin twice removed		
Webb, Private	Husband of the 6th cousin 3 times removed		
Webb, Private	6th cousin 4 times removed	XVIII	11
Webb, Sarah	Wife of the half 3rd cousin		
Webber, Living	Husband of the 6th cousin 5 times removed		
Weber, Aadi	2nd cousin 3 times removed	IX	6
Weber, Anna	1st cousin 4 times removed	VIII	6
Weber, Anna	3rd great-grandaunt	VII	6
Weber, Anna	4th great-grandaunt	VIII	7
Weber, Anna	3rd great-grandaunt	VII	6
Weber, Anna	1st cousin 4 times removed	VIII	6
Weber, Anna	2nd cousin 3 times removed	IX	6
Weber, Anna	1st cousin 4 times removed	VIII	6
Weber, Anna	2nd cousin 3 times removed	IX	6
Weber, Anna	2nd cousin 3 times removed	IX	6
Weber, Anna	3rd cousin twice removed	X	6
Weber, Barbara	1st cousin 4 times removed	VIII	6
Weber, Barbara	2nd cousin 3 times removed	IX	6
Weber, Barbara	1st cousin 4 times removed	VIII	6
Weber, Barbara	1st cousin 4 times removed	VIII	6
Weber, Barbara	3rd cousin twice removed	X	6
Weber, Barbara	2nd cousin 3 times removed	IX	6
Weber, Barbeli	4th great-grandaunt	VIII	7
Weber, Beverly	3rd great-grandaunt	VII	6
Weber, Catharine	2nd cousin 3 times removed	IX	6
Weber, Catharine	3rd cousin twice removed	X	6
Weber, Christian	4th cousin once removed	XI	6
Weber, Christian	3rd great-granduncle	VII	6
Weber, Christian	1st cousin 4 times removed	VIII	6
Weber, Christian	1st cousin 4 times removed	VIII	6
Weber, Christian	2nd cousin 3 times removed	IX	6
Weber, Daniel	2nd cousin 3 times removed	IX	6
Weber, Daniel M.	3rd cousin twice removed	X	6
Weber, David	2nd cousin 3 times removed	IX	6
Weber, Elizabeth	3rd great-grandmother	V	5
Weber, Elizabeth	1st cousin 4 times removed	VIII	6
Weber, Elizabeth	2nd cousin 3 times removed	IX	6

Name	Relationship with Milton Hershey	Civil	Canon
Weber, Elizabeth	3rd cousin twice removed	X	6
Weber, Elsbeth	4th great-grandaunt	VIII	7
Weber, Emma Zimmerman	Wife of the 3rd cousin twice removed		
Weber, Esther	1st cousin 4 times removed	VIII	6
Weber, Eva	3rd great-grandaunt	VII	6
Weber, Eva	1st cousin 4 times removed	VIII	6
Weber, Fanny	2nd cousin 3 times removed	IX	6
Weber, Feronica	2nd cousin 3 times removed	IX	6
Weber, Feronica W	2nd cousin 3 times removed	IX	6
Weber, Georg	4th great-granduncle	VIII	7
Weber, Georg	5th great-granduncle	IX	8
Weber, George	6th great-grandfather	VIII	8
Weber, George	3rd great-granduncle	VII	6
Weber, George	2nd cousin 3 times removed	IX	6
Weber, George	3rd cousin twice removed	X	6
Weber, Gideon	3rd cousin twice removed	X	6
Weber, Hans	1st cousin 4 times removed	VIII	6
Weber, Hans Rudolf	4th great-granduncle	VIII	7
Weber, Harriet	Wife of the 6th cousin		
Weber, Heine	3rd great-granduncle	VII	6
Weber, Heinrich	5th great-grandfather	VII	7
Weber, Heinrich	4th great-granduncle	VIII	7
Weber, Heinrich	1st cousin 4 times removed	VIII	6
Weber, Henry	1st cousin 4 times removed	VIII	6
Weber, Henry	4th great-grandfather	VI	6
Weber, Henry	Husband of the 1st cousin 3 times removed		
Weber, Henry	1st cousin 4 times removed	VIII	6
Weber, Isaac	2nd cousin 3 times removed	IX	6
Weber, Isaac	3rd cousin twice removed	X	6
Weber, Jacob	2nd cousin 3 times removed	IX	6
Weber, Jacob	3rd great-granduncle	VII	6
Weber, Jacob	1st cousin 4 times removed	VIII	6
Weber, Jacob	2nd cousin 3 times removed	IX	6
Weber, Jagli	4th great-granduncle	VIII	7
Weber, Johann Anton	4th great-grandfather	VI	6
Weber, Johannnes	1st cousin 4 times removed	VIII	6
Weber, John	3rd great-granduncle	VII	6
Weber, John	1st cousin 4 times removed	VIII	6
Weber, John	2nd cousin 3 times removed	IX	6
Weber, John	2nd cousin 3 times removed	IX	6
Weber, Joseph	1st cousin 4 times removed	VIII	6
Weber, Krista J.	Wife of the 2nd cousin 5 times removed		
Weber, Leah	3rd cousin twice removed	X	6
Weber, Lena	Wife of the half 3rd cousin 3 times removed		
Weber, Magdalena	1st cousin 4 times removed	VIII	6
Weber, Magdalena	1st cousin 4 times removed	VIII	6
Weber, Magdalena	3rd great-grandaunt	VII	6
Weber, Magdalena	2nd cousin 3 times removed	IX	6
Weber, Magdalena	1st cousin 4 times removed	VIII	6
Weber, Magdalena	2nd cousin 3 times removed	IX	6
Weber, Magdalena	3rd cousin twice removed	X	6
Weber, Magdelena	2nd cousin 3 times removed	IX	6
Weber, Marey	1st cousin 4 times removed	VIII	6
Weber, Maria	2nd cousin 3 times removed	IX	6
Weber, Maria	3rd great-grandmother	V	5
Weber, Maria	1st cousin 4 times removed	VIII	6
Weber, Martin C.	3rd cousin twice removed	X	6
Weber, Mary	3rd great-grandaunt	VII	6
Weber, Mary	2nd cousin 3 times removed	IX	6
Weber, Mary	2nd cousin 3 times removed	IX	6
Weber, Michael	1st cousin 4 times removed	VIII	6
Weber, Peter	1st cousin 4 times removed	VIII	6
Weber, Private	Husband of the 3rd cousin 3 times removed		
Weber, Private	3rd cousin 4 times removed	XII	8
Weber, Private	3rd cousin 4 times removed	XII	8
Weber, Samuel	4th great-granduncle	VIII	7

Name	Relationship with Milton Hershey	Civil	Canon
Weber, Samuel	2nd cousin 3 times removed	IX	6
Weber, Samuel	1st cousin 4 times removed	VIII	6
Weber, Samuel	1st cousin 4 times removed	VIII	6
Weber, Samuel	2nd cousin 3 times removed	IX	6
Weber, Samuel	3rd cousin twice removed	X	6
Weber, Sara	5th great-grandaunt	IX	8
Weber, Solomon	3rd cousin twice removed	X	6
Weber, Susanna	2nd cousin 3 times removed	IX	6
Weber, Susanna	2nd cousin 3 times removed	IX	6
Weber, Tina	Wife of the 2nd cousin 4 times removed		
Weber, Verena	4th great-grandaunt	VIII	7
Wederman, Wilhelmina G.	Wife of the 3rd cousin once removed		
Weeden, Private	Half 3rd cousin 4 times removed	XII	8
Weeden, Unknown	Husband of the half 3rd cousin 3 times removed		
Weible, Harry	Husband of the 6th cousin		
Weidler, Elizabeth	Wife of the 2nd cousin once removed		
Weidler, Emanuel	Husband of the 2nd cousin twice removed		
Weikert, Mary Swope	Wife of the 3rd cousin twice removed		
Weinhold, Alverta M	Wife of the 2nd cousin 3 times removed		
Weisel, Eliza	6th cousin	XIV	7
Weisel, Israel	6th cousin	XIV	7
Weisel, John	Husband of the 5th cousin once removed		
Weisel, Levi	6th cousin	XIV	7
Welch, Alma	Wife of the half 3rd cousin twice removed		
Weldy, Christian	Husband of the 2nd cousin 3 times removed		
Wellan, Otto	Husband of the half 3rd cousin twice removed		
Wells, Reta	Wife of the half 3rd cousin 3 times removed		
Weng, Private	Wife of the 3rd cousin 3 times removed		
Wenger, Annie	Wife of the 4th cousin once removed		
Wenger, Barbara	Wife of the 3rd cousin twice removed		
Wenger, Daniel	Husband of the 3rd cousin twice removed		
Wenger, Elizabeth	Wife of the 2nd cousin 3 times removed		
Wenger, Eve	Wife of the 3rd great-granduncle		
Wenger, Eve S.	Wife of the 4th cousin 4 times removed		
Wenger, Ezra Meyer	Husband of the 6th cousin		
Wenger, Feronica S.	Wife of the 1st cousin 4 times removed		
Wenger, Helen Stauffer	Wife of the 3rd cousin once removed		
Wenger, John	Husband of the 6th cousin		
Wenger, Joseph G.	Husband of the 4th cousin 4 times removed		
Wenger, Maria	Wife of the 3rd cousin twice removed		
Wenger, Mary Ann	Wife of the 3rd cousin		
Wenger, Michael	Husband of the 3rd cousin 5 times removed		
Wenger, Michael	Husband of the 4th cousin 4 times removed		
Wenger, Private	Wife of the 3rd cousin 3 times removed		
Wenger, Private	Wife of the 3rd cousin 3 times removed		
Wenger, Private	Wife of the 3rd cousin twice removed		
Wenger, Reuben	Husband of the 3rd cousin twice removed		
Wenzel, Private	Wife of the half 3rd cousin 3 times removed		
Wert, Mary Elizabeth	Wife of the 6th cousin		
Werteberger, Mildred R	Wife of the 6th cousin once removed		
Weston, Private	Wife of the 3rd cousin 3 times removed		
Westover, Ann	3rd cousin twice removed	X	6
Westover, Barbara	3rd cousin twice removed	X	6
Westover, Charlotte	3rd cousin twice removed	X	6
Westover, Elizabeth	3rd cousin twice removed	X	6
Westover, George	3rd cousin twice removed	X	6
Westover, Herman	3rd cousin twice removed	X	6
Westover, Hiram	3rd cousin twice removed	X	6
Westover, Horace	3rd cousin twice removed	X	6
Westover, Isaac	3rd cousin twice removed	X	6
Westover, Jacob	3rd cousin twice removed	X	6
Westover, John	3rd cousin twice removed	X	6
Westover, Mahetable	3rd cousin twice removed	X	6
Westover, Ruffus	3rd cousin twice removed	X	6
Westover, William	3rd cousin twice removed	X	6
Westover, William	Husband of the 2nd cousin 3 times removed		

Name	Relationship with Milton Hershey	Civil	Canon
Weyner, Barbel	Wife of the 6th great-grandfather		
Wheeler, Frank Ashley	Husband of the 6th cousin once removed		
Whinery, Private	Husband of the 6th cousin 3 times removed		
Whipple, Pearl	Wife of the 6th cousin once removed		
White, Emily Faline	4th cousin twice removed	XII	7
White, Lydia	Wife of the 2nd cousin twice removed		
White, McKenzie	4th cousin 3 times removed	XIII	8
White, Private	Wife of the 6th cousin 3 times removed		
White, Samuel	Husband of the 2nd cousin		
White, Shelby	4th cousin 3 times removed	XIII	8
White, William Walter	Husband of the 6th cousin twice removed		
White, William Walter	6th cousin 3 times removed	XVII	10
White, William Walter	4th cousin twice removed	XII	7
Whyle, Lola	Half 3rd cousin 3 times removed	XI	7
Whyle, William G.	Husband of the half 3rd cousin twice removed		
Whyle, William George	Half 3rd cousin 3 times removed	XI	7
Wiancko, Bruno	Husband of the half 3rd cousin twice removed		
Wiancko, Eldon	Half 3rd cousin 3 times removed	XI	7
Wiancko, Elmina Jane	Half 3rd cousin 4 times removed	XII	8
Wiancko, Margaret	Half 3rd cousin 3 times removed	XI	7
Wiancko, Paul	Half 3rd cousin 4 times removed	XII	8
Wiancko, Redford	Half 3rd cousin 3 times removed	XI	7
Widdowson, John	Husband of the 6th cousin		
Wideman, Abraham Henry	Half 3rd cousin once removed	IX	5
Wideman, Alan	Half 3rd cousin 3 times removed	XI	7
Wideman, Bruce	Half 3rd cousin 3 times removed	XI	7
Wideman, Carol	Half 3rd cousin 3 times removed	XI	7
Wideman, Carson	Half 3rd cousin twice removed	X	6
Wideman, Clarence	Half 3rd cousin twice removed	X	6
Wideman, David	Husband of the half 3rd cousin		
Wideman, Elizabeth	Half 3rd cousin twice removed	X	6
Wideman, Elizabeth	Half 3rd cousin twice removed	X	6
Wideman, Esther	Half 3rd cousin once removed	IX	5
Wideman, Evelyn	Half 3rd cousin 4 times removed	XII	8
Wideman, Frances	Half 3rd cousin 3 times removed	XI	7
Wideman, Frances E.	Half 3rd cousin 3 times removed	XI	7
Wideman, Glen	Half 3rd cousin 3 times removed	XI	7
Wideman, Harley	Half 3rd cousin 3 times removed	XI	7
Wideman, Harry	Half 3rd cousin twice removed	X	6
Wideman, Harvey	Half 3rd cousin 3 times removed	XI	7
Wideman, Herbert	Half 3rd cousin twice removed	X	6
Wideman, Jacob S.	Half 3rd cousin once removed	IX	5
Wideman, James	Half 3rd cousin 3 times removed	XI	7
Wideman, John	Half 3rd cousin 3 times removed	XI	7
Wideman, Joseph	Half 3rd cousin twice removed	X	6
Wideman, Lloyd	Half 3rd cousin 3 times removed	XI	7
Wideman, Lorne	Half 3rd cousin twice removed	X	6
Wideman, Mabel	Half 3rd cousin twice removed	X	6
Wideman, Martha	Half 3rd cousin twice removed	X	6
Wideman, Martin	Husband of the half 3rd cousin once removed		
Wideman, Muriel	Half 3rd cousin 3 times removed	XI	7
Wideman, Private	Half 3rd cousin 4 times removed	XII	8
Wideman, Private	Half 3rd cousin 4 times removed	XII	8
Wideman, Private	Half 3rd cousin 4 times removed	XII	8
Wideman, Private	Half 3rd cousin 4 times removed	XII	8
Wideman, Private	Half 3rd cousin 4 times removed	XII	8
Wideman, Private	Half 3rd cousin 4 times removed	XII	8
Wideman, Private	Half 3rd cousin 4 times removed	XII	8
Wideman, Private	Half 3rd cousin 4 times removed	XII	8
Wideman, Private	Half 3rd cousin 4 times removed	XII	8
Wideman, Robert	Half 3rd cousin 3 times removed	XI	7
Wideman, Ross	Half 3rd cousin 3 times removed	XI	7
Wideman, Ruby	Half 3rd cousin 3 times removed	XI	7
Wideman, Unknown	Half 3rd cousin 3 times removed	XI	7
Wideman, Vera	Half 3rd cousin 3 times removed	XI	7
Wideman, Wesley	Half 3rd cousin twice removed	X	6

The Relations of Milton Snavely Hershey, 4th Ed.

Name	Relationship with Milton Hershey	Civil	Canon
Wideman, Wilmot	Half 3rd cousin twice removed	X	6
Widemoyer, Christiana	Wife of the 2nd cousin 3 times removed		
Widener, Dorothy Eileen Hawkins	Wife of the 6th cousin twice removed		
Wiggins, Private	Wife of the 6th cousin 3 times removed		
Wilde, Unknown	Husband of the 6th cousin twice removed		
Wilder, Eva Katherine	Wife of the 6th cousin twice removed		
Wiley, Private	Wife of the 6th cousin 3 times removed		
Wilk, Private	Husband of the 6th cousin 3 times removed		
Wilk, Private	6th cousin 4 times removed	XVIII	11
Wilk, Private	6th cousin 4 times removed	XVIII	11
Wilke, Edna	Wife of the 5th cousin		
Williams, Dee Ann	4th cousin 3 times removed	XIII	8
Williams, Donald Everett	4th cousin 3 times removed	XIII	8
Williams, Douglas Thomas	4th cousin 3 times removed	XIII	8
Williams, Elizabeth	Wife of the half 3rd cousin twice removed		
Williams, Elizabeth	Wife of the 6th cousin		
Williams, Howard Jones	Husband of the 6th cousin twice removed		
Williams, Howard Jones	6th cousin 3 times removed	XVII	10
Williams, Leanore	Wife of the 6th cousin 3 times removed		
Williams, Mary	Half 3rd cousin twice removed	X	6
Williams, Ober Wolf	6th cousin 3 times removed	XVII	10
Williams, Ruth L	6th cousin 3 times removed	XVII	10
Williams, Thomas William III	Husband of the 4th cousin twice removed		
Williams, Unknown	Husband of the 6th cousin once removed		
Williams, William	Ex-husband of the half 3rd cousin once removed		
Williamson, Private	Half 3rd cousin 4 times removed	XII	8
Williamson, Private	Half 3rd cousin 4 times removed	XII	8
Williamson, Unknown	Husband of the half 3rd cousin 3 times removed		
Williford, David A	Husband of the 4th cousin twice removed		
Willis, Private	Husband of the 6th cousin twice removed		
Willis, Private	6th cousin 3 times removed	XVII	10
Wilson, Jennie M	Wife of the 6th cousin once removed		
Wilson, Patricia A	6th cousin 4 times removed	XVIII	11
Wilson, Richard	Husband of the 6th cousin 3 times removed		
Wilson, Richard, Jr	6th cousin 4 times removed	XVIII	11
Winder, Abigale	Wife of the 6th cousin		
Winey, Ruth Esther	Wife of the 3rd cousin twice removed		
Winschell, Dorothy	Wife of the 6th cousin once removed		
Winters, Jacob	Husband of the 1st cousin 3 times removed		
Wise, Vera Weaver	Wife of the 3rd cousin twice removed		
Wismer, Elizabeth	Wife of the 5th cousin		
Wissler, Benjamin	3rd cousin once removed	IX	5
Wissler, Christian	Husband of the 2nd cousin twice removed		
Wissler, Elisabeth	3rd cousin once removed	IX	5
Wissler, Jacob	3rd cousin once removed	IX	5
Wissler, Magdalena	Wife of the 2nd great-granduncle		
Wissler, Mary	3rd cousin once removed	IX	5
Wistler, John	Husband of the 3rd great-grandaunt		
Witmer, Abraham	Half 3rd cousin 3 times removed	XI	7
Witmer, Abraham B.	Half 4th cousin twice removed	XII	7
Witmer, Amos L.	Half 4th cousin twice removed	XII	7
Witmer, Ann	4th great-grandmother	VI	6
Witmer, Ann	Half 3rd cousin 3 times removed	XI	7
Witmer, Anna	Wife of the half 2nd cousin 4 times removed		
Witmer, Benjamin	Half 3rd cousin 3 times removed	XI	7
Witmer, David	Husband of the half 2nd cousin 4 times removed		
Witmer, David	Half 3rd cousin 3 times removed	XI	7
Witmer, Edmund	Half 4th cousin twice removed	XII	7
Witmer, Eliza	Wife of the half 2nd cousin 4 times removed		
Witmer, Esther	Half 3rd cousin 3 times removed	XI	7
Witmer, Henry	Half 3rd cousin 3 times removed	XI	7
Witmer, Henry H.	Half 4th cousin twice removed	XII	7
Witmer, Hetty	Half 4th cousin twice removed	XII	7
Witmer, Isaac B.	Husband of the 2nd cousin twice removed		
Witmer, Jacob	Husband of the 4th cousin 4 times removed		
Witmer, Jacob	Half 3rd cousin 3 times removed	XI	7

Name	Relationship with Milton Hershey	Civil	Canon
Witmer, Jane Juliet	Half 4th cousin twice removed	XII	7
Witmer, Lydia	Half 4th cousin twice removed	XII	7
Witmer, Maria Louisa	Half 4th cousin twice removed	XII	7
Witmer, Marie	Wife of the 3rd cousin twice removed		
Witmer, Mary Ann	Wife of the 4th cousin once removed		
Witmer, Mary Emma	Half 4th cousin twice removed	XII	7
Witmer, Michael	Husband of the 1st cousin 4 times removed		
Witmer, Nancy Ann	Half 4th cousin twice removed	XII	7
Witmer, Private	Wife of the 2nd cousin 4 times removed		
Witmer, Samuel Lefevre	Half 4th cousin twice removed	XII	7
Witson, Anna L	6th cousin 5 times removed	XIX	12
Witson, Rex	Husband of the 6th cousin 4 times removed		
Witwer, Barbara	Wife of the 1st cousin 4 times removed		
Witwer, Catharine	5th cousin 3 times removed	XV	9
Witwer, Catharine	Wife of the 3rd cousin twice removed		
Witwer, Daniel	Husband of the 4th cousin 4 times removed		
Witwer, David	Husband of the 4th cousin 4 times removed		
Witwer, Jonas S.	Husband of the 4th cousin 4 times removed		
Witwer, Susan	5th cousin 3 times removed	XV	9
Wolf, Alice K	6th cousin 3 times removed	XVII	10
Wolf, Alice K	6th cousin 4 times removed	XVIII	11
Wolf, Anna B	6th cousin twice removed	XVI	9
Wolf, Anna Rupp	Wife of the 3rd cousin once removed		
Wolf, Barbara Ann	6th cousin 3 times removed	XVII	10
Wolf, Barbara J	6th cousin 3 times removed	XVII	10
Wolf, Catherine	6th cousin	XIV	7
Wolf, Catherine Rebecca	6th cousin twice removed	XVI	9
Wolf, Christena	6th cousin	XIV	7
Wolf, Clarence Franklin	6th cousin 3 times removed	XVII	10
Wolf, Clarence R	6th cousin twice removed	XVI	9
Wolf, Collin	6th cousin	XIV	7
Wolf, David O	6th cousin 3 times removed	XVII	10
Wolf, David Ober	6th cousin twice removed	XVI	9
Wolf, Edgar	6th cousin 3 times removed	XVII	10
Wolf, Franklin Earl	6th cousin twice removed	XVI	9
Wolf, Franklin Earl	6th cousin 3 times removed	XVII	10
Wolf, Franklin LeFevere	Husband of the 6th cousin once removed		
Wolf, George	Husband of the 3rd cousin once removed		
Wolf, George B II	6th cousin	XIV	7
Wolf, George Edgar	6th cousin twice removed	XVI	9
Wolf, Henry	Husband of the 5th cousin once removed		
Wolf, Holly Ann	6th cousin 4 times removed	XVIII	11
Wolf, John S	6th cousin 3 times removed	XVII	10
Wolf, Katherine	Wife of the 5th cousin once removed		
Wolf, Lewis	6th cousin	XIV	7
Wolf, Margaret M	6th cousin 4 times removed	XVIII	11
Wolf, Maria	Wife of the 3rd cousin 3 times removed		
Wolf, Maria	6th cousin 4 times removed	XVIII	11
Wolf, Marian Elizabeth	6th cousin 3 times removed	XVII	10
Wolf, Marjorie Ann	6th cousin 3 times removed	XVII	10
Wolf, Mary	Wife of the 4th great-granduncle		
Wolf, Mary Ann	Wife of the 5th cousin once removed		
Wolf, Mary E	6th cousin 3 times removed	XVII	10
Wolf, Mary E	6th cousin 4 times removed	XVIII	11
Wolf, Mary Estelle	6th cousin twice removed	XVI	9
Wolf, Mary L	6th cousin 3 times removed	XVII	10
Wolf, Nellie I	6th cousin twice removed	XVI	9
Wolf, Ray	6th cousin 4 times removed	XVIII	11
Wolfart, Mary	Wife of the 4th cousin 4 times removed		
Wolgemuth, Martin M.	Husband of the 5th cousin once removed		
Wood, Goldie Lutechia "Lou"	Wife of the 6th cousin twice removed		
Wood, Private	Husband of the 3rd cousin 4 times removed		
Wood, Wilmer	Ex-husband of the 6th cousin twice removed		
Woodburn, Ed	Half 3rd cousin once removed	IX	5
Woodburn, Henry	Husband of the half 3rd cousin		
Woods, Private	Husband of the 3rd cousin 3 times removed		

Name	Relationship with Milton Hershey	Civil	Canon
Woods, Private	3rd cousin 4 times removed	XII	8
Woods, Private	3rd cousin 4 times removed	XII	8
Woods, Private	Husband of the 6th cousin 3 times removed		
Woolf, Analiza Eliza	Wife of the 6th cousin		
Woolf, Florian Charles "Dutch"	Husband of the 6th cousin 3 times removed		
Woolman, Lavilla	Wife of the half 3rd cousin		
Woolridge, Bealah Verdie	Wife of the 6th cousin 3 times removed		
Wymann, Susanna	5th great-grandmother	VII	7
Wynia, Private	Wife of the 3rd cousin twice removed		
Wyss, Audrey Odessa "Audey"	6th cousin twice removed	XVI	9
Wyss, Cleveland Samuel	Husband of the 6th cousin once removed		
Wyss, Darly Leroy	6th cousin 3 times removed	XVII	10
Wyss, Daryl Leroy "Cork"	6th cousin 3 times removed	XVII	10
Wyss, Evelyn	6th cousin twice removed	XVI	9
Wyss, Florian F.	6th cousin twice removed	XVI	9
Wyss, Naomi B.	6th cousin twice removed	XVI	9
Wyss, Private	6th cousin 3 times removed	XVII	10
Wyss, Private	6th cousin 3 times removed	XVII	10
Wyss, Private	6th cousin 3 times removed	XVII	10
Wyss, Ralph Leroy	6th cousin twice removed	XVI	9
Wyss, Richard Adelbert	6th cousin 3 times removed	XVII	10
Wyss, Shirley Ruth	6th cousin 3 times removed	XVII	10
Wyss, Wayne Ralph	6th cousin 3 times removed	XVII	10
Wyss, William	Husband of the 6th cousin once removed		
Wyss, Woodrow	6th cousin twice removed	XVI	9
Yaggi, Agnes Ruth	6th cousin 3 times removed	XVII	10
Yaggi, Irvin Emmanuel	Husband of the 6th cousin twice removed		
Yaggi, Lois Jean	6th cousin 3 times removed	XVII	10
Yaggi, Mary Elizabeth	6th cousin 3 times removed	XVII	10
Yando, Jennie Adelia	Wife of the half 3rd cousin once removed		
Yanosh, Private	Wife of the 6th cousin 3 times removed		
Yarman, Private	Wife of the 6th cousin twice removed		
Yeager, Eva	Wife of the 6th cousin 3 times removed		
Yeager, Mary	Wife of the 6th cousin		
Yeagley, Laura	Wife of the 6th cousin		
Yertz, Susan	Wife of the 3rd cousin twice removed		
Yocum, Albert Shantz	Husband of the 5th cousin		
Yoder, Margaret Sue	Ex-wife of the 4th cousin twice removed		
Yoder, Private	Wife of the 3rd cousin 3 times removed		
Yoder, Private	Husband of the 3rd cousin 3 times removed		
Yoder, Private	3rd cousin 4 times removed	XII	8
Yoder, Private	3rd cousin 4 times removed	XII	8
Yoder, Private	3rd cousin 4 times removed	XII	8
Yoder, Private	3rd cousin 4 times removed	XII	8
Yoder, Private	Husband of the 3rd cousin 3 times removed		
Yoder, Private	3rd cousin 4 times removed	XII	8
Yoder, Private	3rd cousin 4 times removed	XII	8
Yoder, Private	Wife of the 3rd cousin 3 times removed		
Yoder, Private	Husband of the 3rd cousin 3 times removed		
Yoder, Private	3rd cousin 4 times removed	XII	8
Yohe, Delores J	Wife of the 6th cousin twice removed		
Yordy, Elizabeth	Wife of the 2nd cousin 3 times removed		
Yordy, Mary	Wife of the 3rd cousin twice removed		
Yost, Salome Miller	Wife of the 5th cousin		
Young, Bessie Pansy May	Wife of the half 3rd cousin once removed		
Young, Dessie	Wife of the 6th cousin once removed		
Young, Milton	Husband of the 5th cousin once removed		
Young, W. Evart	Husband of the half 3rd cousin twice removed		
Youtsey, Clayton E.	Husband of the 6th cousin twice removed		
Yuengt, Andrew	Husband of the 6th cousin		
Zeigler, George	Husband of the half 1st cousin 5 times removed		
Zeiset, Anna Mae	Wife of the 3rd cousin once removed		
Zeiset, Emma E.	Wife of the 3rd cousin twice removed		
Zeiset, George	Husband of the 3rd cousin twice removed		
Zeiset, Private	Husband of the 3rd cousin twice removed		
Zeiset, Private	3rd cousin 3 times removed	XI	7

Name	Relationship with Milton Hershey	Civil	Canon
Zeiset, Private	3rd cousin 4 times removed	XII	8
Ziegler, Barbara Pawling	Wife of the 1st cousin 4 times removed		
Ziegler, Jacob (Zuglar)	Husband of the 1st cousin 4 times removed		
Ziegler, Private	Wife of the 3rd cousin 3 times removed		
Zimmer, Private	Wife of the 6th cousin 3 times removed		
Zimmerman, Ada	Wife of the 3rd cousin twice removed		
Zimmerman, Anna	Wife of the 2nd cousin 3 times removed		
Zimmerman, Annie	Wife of the 4th cousin once removed		
Zimmerman, Catharine	Wife of the 2nd cousin 3 times removed		
Zimmerman, Christian	Husband of the 2nd cousin 3 times removed		
Zimmerman, Christine Renee	3rd cousin 4 times removed	XII	8
Zimmerman, David	Husband of the 4th cousin once removed		
Zimmerman, Elizabeth	Wife of the 3rd cousin twice removed		
Zimmerman, Elmer Denlinger	Husband of the 3rd cousin once removed		
Zimmerman, Katie	Wife of the 4th cousin once removed		
Zimmerman, Mary	Wife of the 4th cousin once removed		
Zimmerman, Neil Brian	3rd cousin 4 times removed	XII	8
Zimmerman, Noah Hoover	Husband of the 3rd cousin twice removed		
Zimmerman, Private	Husband of the 3rd cousin 3 times removed		
Zimmerman, Private	3rd cousin 4 times removed	XII	8
Zimmerman, Private	3rd cousin 4 times removed	XII	8
Zimmerman, Private	Husband of the 3rd cousin 3 times removed		
Zimmerman, Private	3rd cousin 4 times removed	XII	8
Zimmerman, Private	3rd cousin 4 times removed	XII	8
Zimmerman, Private	3rd cousin 4 times removed	XII	8
Zimmerman, Private	3rd cousin 5 times removed	XIII	9
Zimmerman, Private	3rd cousin 5 times removed	XIII	9
Zimmerman, Private	3rd cousin 3 times removed	XI	7
Zimmerman, Private	3rd cousin 3 times removed	XI	7
Zimmerman, Private	3rd cousin 3 times removed	XI	7
Zimmerman, Private	3rd cousin 3 times removed	XI	7
Zimmerman, Private	3rd cousin 4 times removed	XII	8
Zimmerman, Private	3rd cousin 4 times removed	XII	8
Zimmerman, Private	3rd cousin 4 times removed	XII	8
Zimmerman, Private	3rd cousin 4 times removed	XII	8
Zimmerman, Private	3rd cousin 4 times removed	XII	8
Zimmerman, Private	3rd cousin 4 times removed	XII	8
Zimmerman, Private	3rd cousin 4 times removed	XII	8
Zimmerman, Private	3rd cousin 4 times removed	XII	8
Zimmerman, Private	3rd cousin 4 times removed	XII	8
Zimmerman, Private	3rd cousin 4 times removed	XII	8
Zimmerman, Private	3rd cousin 4 times removed	XII	8
Zimmerman, Private	3rd cousin 4 times removed	XII	8
Zimmerman, Private	3rd cousin 4 times removed	XII	8
Zimmerman, Private	3rd cousin 4 times removed	XII	8
Zimmerman, Private	3rd cousin 4 times removed	XII	8
Zimmerman, Private	3rd cousin 4 times removed	XII	8
Zimmerman, Private	3rd cousin 4 times removed	XII	8
Zimmerman, Private	3rd cousin 4 times removed	XII	8
Zimmerman, Private	3rd cousin 4 times removed	XII	8
Zimmerman, Private	3rd cousin 4 times removed	XII	8
Zimmerman, Private	Husband of the 3rd cousin 3 times removed		
Zimmerman, Private	3rd cousin 4 times removed	XII	8
Zimmerman, Private	3rd cousin 4 times removed	XII	8
Zimmerman, Private	3rd cousin 4 times removed	XII	8
Zimmerman, Private	3rd cousin 4 times removed	XII	8
Zimmerman, Private	3rd cousin 4 times removed	XII	8
Zimmerman, Private	3rd cousin 4 times removed	XII	8
Zimmerman, Private	3rd cousin 4 times removed	XII	8
Zimmerman, Private	3rd cousin 4 times removed	XII	8
Zimmerman, Private	Husband of the 3rd cousin 4 times removed		

Name	Relationship with Milton Hershey	Civil	Canon
Zimmerman, Private	3rd cousin 5 times removed	XIII	9
Zimmerman, Private	3rd cousin 5 times removed	XIII	9
Zimmerman, Private	Wife of the 3rd cousin 3 times removed		
Zimmerman, Private	Wife of the 3rd cousin 3 times removed		
Zimmerman, Private	Wife of the 3rd cousin 3 times removed		
Zimmerman, Private	Wife of the 3rd cousin twice removed		
Zimmerman, Private	Wife of the 3rd cousin 3 times removed		
Zimmerman, Private	Wife of the 3rd cousin 3 times removed		
Zimmerman, Private	3rd cousin twice removed	X	6
Zimmerman, Private	3rd cousin twice removed	X	6
Zimmerman, Private	3rd cousin twice removed	X	6
Zimmerman, Private	3rd cousin 3 times removed	XI	7
Zimmerman, Private	3rd cousin 3 times removed	XI	7
Zimmerman, Private	3rd cousin 3 times removed	XI	7
Zimmerman, Private	3rd cousin 3 times removed	XI	7
Zimmerman, Private	3rd cousin 3 times removed	XI	7
Zimmerman, Private	Husband of the 6th cousin 4 times removed		
Zimmerman, Suzanne	Wife of the 4th cousin once removed		
Zing, Ann	Wife of the 6th cousin twice removed		
Zook, Elizabeth	Wife of the 6th cousin		
Zook, John Kurtz	Husband of the 5th cousin once removed		
Zook, Rebecca L.	Wife of the 3rd cousin once removed		
Zupinger, Elsbeth	Wife of the 7th great-granduncle		
Zuver, Donna Marie	Wife of the 6th cousin 4 times removed		

**Andrew Baer Hackman (1828-1916)
and wife Martha Eschbach Brenner Hackman (1835-1913)
(2nd great grandparents of the author)
Andrew Baer Hackman was related to Milton Hershey three ways - closest being a 3rd cousin once removed. Andrew & Wife lived in the Lancaster, PA area. Photo circa 1860.**

**Willis Brenner Hackman (1877-1947)
and wife Emma Geib Hackman (1880-1958)**

Willis was a son of Andrew Baer Hackman & Martha Brenner Hackman. These are the great grandparents of the author.

About the Author:

Lawrence Berger-Knorr, MBA PMP CCP, born 1964, is an amateur genealogist with deep roots in the Pennsylvania Dutch Region. Lawrence's "real" jobs are as the Chief Information Officer for the Pennsylvania Liquor Control Board and as an adjunct instructor for Wilson College, Chambersburg, PA. Lawrence holds a Bachelor's degree in Business/Economics (History Minor) from Wilson College and a Masters of Business Administration from Penn State. He is also a Certified Computer Professional and Project Management Professional. Lawrence lives with his wife Ann and two daughters in Carlisle, PA.

Lawrence has been involved in genealogical research for fifteen years, and is a member of several related organizations:

>National Genealogical Society
>Pennsylvania German Society
>Berks County Genealogical Society
>Pennsylvania Heritage Society
>Palatines to America - Pennsylvania Chapter
>Sons of the American Revolution
>Mahanoy & Mahantango Historical & Preservation Society
>Derry Township Historical Society
>Manheim Historical Society

Other recently (or soon to be) published works by Lawrence include:

71 Years of Marriage: The Ancestors, Descendents and Relations of George and Alice Knorr of Reading, PA (2002)

The Shellems of Philadelphia (2003)

The Pennsylvania Relations of President Dwight D. Eisenhower (2005)

A Pennsylvania Mennonite and the California Gold Rush: The Journal and Letters of David Baer Hackman (2008)

The Relations of Major General John Fulton Reynolds (to be published 2008/9)

Index of Individuals

(Landis) -
    Barbara: 295, 367
(Meyer) -
    Agatha: 367
    Maria: 367
(Moyer) -
    Hannah: 367
(Myer) -
    Anna: 367
    Judith: 367
(stoffer) -
    Private: 212, 367
? -
    Anthony: 257, 367
Abbey -
    Private: 265, 367
Abney -
    Lloyd: 267, 268, 367
    Neil: 268, 367
Acker -
    Amanda: 367
    Magdelene Polly (Acre): 367
    Maria: 10, 29
    Martha Louise: 171, 332, 367
Ackerman -
    Elizabeth: 83, 367
    Private: 288, 367
Adams -
    Arthur: 161, 367
    E Virginia: 189, 367
    Private: 275, 367
    Private: 275, 367
    Thomas Lyle: 243, 339, 367
    Thomas Lyle: 243, 339, 367
    Unknown: 367
Agnew -
    Charles: 201, 268, 367
    Donald Robert: 202, 268, 367
    Harold: 201, 367
    Harry: 201, 367
    John: 201, 367
    Mary Elizabeth: 201, 267, 268, 367
    Private: 268, 367
    Private: 268, 367
    Private: 268, 367
Aguirre -
    Private: 234, 352, 367
    Private: 234, 352, 367
    Private: 234, 352, 367
Aldinger -
    Mary: 190, 367
Aldridge -
    Private: 247
    Private: 247
Alexander -
    Herbert "Jack": 141, 367
    Jay: 141, 367
    Minnie B.: 197, 367
    Private: 176, 337, 367
Allamong -
    Private: 182
    Private: 182
    Private: 182, 248
    Private: 248
Allan -
    Private: 184
Allebach -
    Johannes: 367
Allen -
    Anna Bell: 132, 367
    David: 154, 367
    Frances: 186, 367
    Hugh: 154, 367
    Jean: 154, 367
    Jennie: 154, 367
    Marjorie: 154, 367
    Phyllis: 154, 367
    Private: 249
    Private: 249
    Private: 249
    Ronald: 154, 367
    William: 154, 367
Allison -
    Private: 271, 367
Allshouse -
    Private: 268, 367
Alter -
    Jacob: 367
    John Graham: 194, 367
    Private: 172, 332, 367
    Private: 194, 262, 367
Amidon -
    James A.: 198, 367
    Julia: 150, 367
    Mary L.: 198, 367
    Mary L.: 198, 367
    Monroe E.: 198, 367
Anderegg -
    Jeanne D: 206, 367
Anderson -
    Mary: 92, 367
    Pearl E.: 150, 368
Andrew -
    Ester: 297, 368
    Private: 368
-
    Anna: 40
    Unnamed: 133, 368
Annett -
    David: 219, 368
    Helene: 219, 220, 368
    John: 220, 368
    Private: 220, 368
    Private: 220, 368
    Private: 220, 368
    William: 219, 368
Appler -
    Charles Wesley: 100, 313, 368
    Mabel Corinne: 124, 321, 368
Applying -
    Private: 262, 368
Armstrong -
    George Irving: 143, 368
    Private: 212, 368
Arnold -
    Emma Iona: 195, 368
    Lilliam: 216, 368
    Louren E: 203, 368
    Private: 203, 368
    Private: 203, 368
    Private: 203, 368
    Private: 130
    II Private: 130, 183, 250
    Private: 183, 250
    Private: 250
    Private: 183, 250
    III Samuel: 130
Arthur -
    Dr. John Robert: 196, 368
    Private: 196, 368
    Private: 196, 368
    Private: 196, 368
Ash -
    Mary M.: 80, 368
Asp -
    Keith John: 211, 368
Atkinson -
    Delma: 159, 368
Atz -
    Margaret B: 254, 368
Augsburger -
    Private: 224, 342, 368
    Private: 224, 342, 368
    Private: 224, 283, 342, 360, 368
    Private: 224, 283, 342, 361, 368
    Private: 224, 342, 368
Auker -
    Clarence: 323, 368
    Maggie: 307, 368
    Private: 229, 347, 368
    Unknown: 112, 368
Auks -
    Peter: 186, 368
Baccus -
    Gladys: 368
Bachman -
    Anna: 298, 368
    John Zinn: 85, 368
    Maria: 368
    Maria: 28, 368
    Mary: 63, 91, 368
    Scott Lee: 178, 323, 368
Bachman/Bauman -
    George M.: 61, 368
Bacon -
    Lloyd Frederick: 215, 368
    Private: 215, 368
    Private: 215, 368
    Roy St. Clair: 215, 368
Baer -
    Alice: 108, 368
    Charles: 108, 368
    Jesse: 108, 368
    Johannes: 48, 368

John: 108, 368
John Martin: 9, 12, 14, 368
Martin: 12, 14, 16, 368
Samuel: 108, 368
Unknown: 13, 368
William: 108, 368

Baier -
Elizabeth Catherine Weaver: 89, 368

Bailey -
Helen Josephine Grew: 213, 368

Bair -
James Dean: 182
Julian Hawthorne: 129
Maria: 50, 55, 368
Private: 129, 182, 248, 249
Private: 182, 248
Private: 182, 249
Private: 182, 249

Baird -
John: 91, 368

Baker -
John Norman: 200, 369
Lowell: 200, 266, 369
Marian Arlene: 221, 369
Private: 171, 331, 369
Private: 171, 331, 369
Private: 171, 331, 369
Private: 266, 369
Private: 266, 369
Private: 266, 369
Private: 266, 369
Private: 266, 369
Private: 266, 369
Private: 266, 369

Ball -
Ann Elizabeth: 52, 369
Gertrude Amelia: 52, 369
Jacob: 37, 52, 369
Jacob: 52, 369
Peter Herman: 52, 369
Stark: 110, 369

Balmer -
Private: 224, 342, 369

Balsbaugh -
Allen: 253, 369
Clarence: 186, 369
Edgar F: 186, 369
Erlo R: 186, 253, 369
Jayson C: 186, 253, 369
Kathryn S: 186, 253, 369
Margaret A: 186, 369
Ober S: 186, 369
Sidney: 253, 369
Solomon S: 186, 369
William D: 186, 369

Bampton -
Bertrand: 129
Private: 129, 181
Private: 129

Bar -
Anna: 19, 369
Barbara: 369
Elizabeth: 369

Elizabeth: 369
Hannah: 369
Henry: 369
Isaac: 369
John: 369
Martin: 16, 369
Mary: 369
Michael: 369
Salome: 369
Samuel: 369

Barber -
Elisabeth: 99, 369

Barcome -
Unknown: 94, 369

Bardo -
Private: 274, 369
Private: 274, 369

Barger -
Jason Howard: 117, 369

Barker -
Audrey Francis: 147, 369

Barkey -
Alice: 160, 369
Arthur C.: 159, 369
Barbara: 161, 369
Charles: 119, 160, 161, 220, 369
Clarence: 160, 369
Clifford: 161, 220, 369
Ella: 119, 369
Elmore: 160, 369
Evelyn Maude: 120, 369
George: 120, 369
Gordon: 160, 369
Howard: 120, 369
Lawrence: 160, 369
Margaret: 161, 369
Marian: 160, 369
Mary: 119, 161, 369
Mildred: 119, 370
Norma: 160, 220, 370
Pauline: 160, 370
Private: 220, 370
Private: 220, 370
Private: 220, 370
Sarah: 116, 370
William: 119, 370
Wilmot: 119, 370

Barlow -
Vera Luella: 151, 370

Barner -
Charles Merle: 194, 262, 370
Private: 262, 370
Private: 262, 370
Private: 262, 370
Private: 262, 370
Private: 194, 262, 370
Private: 262, 370
Private: 262, 370
Private: 194, 370
Private: 194, 370
Ramona Lee: 194, 262, 370
Ray J.: 194, 370

Barnes -
Christina Margaret: 219, 370
Unknown: 142, 370

William: 219, 370

Barnet -
Elizabeth: 81, 370

Barnett -
Dale Eugene: 146, 206, 207, 272, 370
Jay Melvin: 146, 207, 272, 370
Paul Eugene: 146, 370
Private: 207, 272, 370
Private: 207, 272, 370
Private: 207, 272, 370
Private: 207, 272, 370
Private: 272, 370
Private: 272, 370
Theda Fay: 146, 207, 370

Barnhill -
Private: 166, 327, 370

Barr -
Aaron: 370
Abraham: 370
Ann: 370
Anna: 370
Benjamin: 370
Catherine: 370
Charles S.: 370
Christian: 370
Christina: 370
Cynthia Odessa: 370
David: 370
Elizabeth: 6, 7, 9, 299, 303, 370
Elizabeth: 370
Esther: 12, 295, 370
Esther Christina: 370
Fanny: 370
Francis M.: 370
George Lucas: 370
Hezekiah: 370
Hezekiah: 370
Infant: 370
Jacob: 7, 9, 12, 370
Jacob: 370
Jacob: 370
Jacob: 370
Jacob Cullen: 370
James Clement: 370
Jennie Belle: 370
John: 370
John Warren: 371
Laura A.: 371
Leona May: 371
Lorenzo: 371
Louis Orin: 371
Maria: 12, 292, 371
Martin: 371
Martin: 371
Martin James: 371
Mary: 371
Mary: 371
Mary Elizabeth: 371
Son1: 371
Susan: 371
Susanna: 371
Susannah: 371
Zannie: 371

Barrett -

Earl: 279, 371
Private: 279, 371
Private: 182
Barricks -
Abraham: 81, 371
Benjamin: 81, 371
Mary: 81, 371
Barringer -
Jr. Private: 183, 184
III Private: 184
Private: 184
Private: 184
Barron -
George F.: 80, 371
Bartchey -
Bertha: 199, 371
Barth -
Private: 177, 338, 371
Private: 177, 338, 371
Private: 177, 338, 371
Private: 177, 338, 371
Bartley -
Nellie Virginia: 144, 371
Bassler -
Anna: 43, 47, 67, 371
Christian: 47, 371
Henry: 47, 371
Jacob: 47, 371
John: 47, 371
John: 47, 371
Maria: 47, 371
Bateman -
Della: 117, 371
I. L.: 117, 371
Lydia: 117, 371
Mary: 117, 371
May: 117, 371
Nellie: 117, 154, 371
Batz -
Barry Lee: 286
Christy Amanda: 286
Jason Barry: 286
Bauchman -
Magdalena: 10, 29
Bauer -
Unknown: 189, 371
Baugher -
Private: 246
Private: 246
Private: 246
Private: 246
Baughman -
Hannah: 371
Baum -
Private: 237, 354, 371
Bauman -
Anna: 371
Anna: 15, 292, 371
Elizabeth: 296, 371
Henry: 296, 371
Mary: 297, 371
Private: 166, 327, 371
Private: 166, 327, 371
Wendel: 293, 371

Baumann -
Hans Rudolph: 371
Baumgartner -
Kenneth Allen: 269, 371
Private: 269, 371
Private: 269, 371
Private: 269, 371
Private: 269, 371
Baush -
George W.: 80, 371
Baxter -
Private: 272, 371
Private: 272, 371
Bayer -
Maurice William: 208, 371
Bayleat -
Aaron: 83, 371
Beachy -
Private: 231, 348, 371
Private: 168, 328, 371
Private: 236, 354, 372
Beam -
Frances: 64, 372
Bear -
Barbara: 78, 372
Catherine: 78, 372
David: 78, 372
David: 48, 372
Elizabeth: 11, 293, 372
Elizabeth: 48, 372
Elizabeth: 78, 372
Ephriam: 48, 372
Gabriel: 68, 372
Henry: 372
Henry: 78, 372
Isaac F: 48, 68, 372
John: 68, 372
Lea: 48, 68, 372
Lydia: 78, 372
Magdalena: 78, 372
Maria: 48, 372
Martin: 29
Nancy: 78, 372
Sarah: 78, 372
Sophia: 78, 372
Susanna Frantz: 48, 68, 97, 98, 120, 162, 163, 220-223, 282, 283, 372
Veronica (aka: Fanny): 48, 372, 394
Beasley -
Private: 272, 372
Private: 272, 372
Bechtal -
Nancy: 75, 76, 372
Bechtel -
Daniel Detweiler: 372
Emanuel: 77, 372
Henry Landis: 372
John Landis: 372
Beck -
Marjorie Jean: 266, 372
Valerie Rishel: 188, 372
Becker -

Arnold: 372
Minnie Mae: 162, 372
Bedford -
Jennie: 120, 372
Beemer -
Ellan: 91, 372
Beer -
Private: 270, 372
Begg -
John Cameron: 150, 372
Mildred Louise: 150, 372
Phyllis Beatrice Mary: 150, 372
Robert Arthur: 150, 372
William Arthur: 150, 372
Behmer -
Samuel: 372
Behner -
Harold: 201, 372
Behney -
Catharine: 83, 372
Beidler -
Abraham Buckwalter (Beitler): 372
Abraham Landes: 372
Anna Buckwalter: 372
Catherine Hockman: 61, 372
Daniel Landes: 372
David Buckwalter: 372
Eleanor Buckwalter: 372
Elizabeth Buckwalter: 372
Elizabeth Landes: 372
George: 372
Hannah Buckwalter: 372
Hannah Landes: 372
Henry: 372
Israel Landes Rev.: 372
Jacob A. Rev. Dr.: 372
Jacob Buckwalter: 372
John Buckwalter: 372
John Landes: 372
John Moyer (Beitler): 372
Joseph Buckwalter: 372
Joseph Landes: 373
Maria Buckwalter: 373
Mary: 373
Mary Landes: 373
Belhouse -
Private: 129
Bell -
Cynthia Ann: 256, 373
James R: 256, 373
Bender -
Martin L.: 173, 334, 373
Mary: 306, 373
Private: 173, 334, 373
Private: 173, 334, 373
Private: 173, 334, 373
Private: 174, 334, 373
Private: 174, 239, 334, 356, 373
Benham -
Private: 130
Benjamin -
Ober: 82, 373
Benner -
Mary: 373

Sallie Blanche: 308, 373
Bennett -
   Edith Louise: 191, 373
   Private: 264, 373
   Private: 204, 373
Benson -
   Private: 281, 373
   Private: 281, 373
   Private: 281, 373
Berg -
   Barbara: 59, 373
   Jacob: 31, 373
Berger -
   Dr Ann Louise (aka: Ann Louise Berger-Knorr): 283, 373
   Eva: 206, 207, 373
   Mabel M: 148, 373
Berger-Knorr -
   Abbey: 283, 373
   Ann Louise (name: Ann Louise Berger): 283, 373
   Lawrence K (name: Lawrence Kevin Knorr): 223, 283, 373, 440
   Taylor: 283, 373
Bergey -
   Barbara: 301, 373
   John Zieber: 373
Bergren -
   Edith Marie: 261, 373
Berkey -
   Henry S.: 77, 373
Berkeybile -
   Adam Cleveland: 80, 373
   Ann Elizabeth: 79, 80, 373
Bernheisel -
   Michael Scott: 251
   Patrick Alan: 251
   Toni Karen: 251
   Walter J.: 251
Berridge -
   Mary: 111, 373
Berschinger -
   Verena: 21, 373
Berube -
   Private: 287, 373
   Private: 287, 373
Bessette -
   Earl Edbert: 373
   Joseph Edward: 373
   Merle Edward: 373
Betty -
   (name: Bethel Leone Tyner): 197, 264, 373, 501
Betzner -
   Abraham: 65, 91, 114, 151, 215-217, 281, 282, 373
   Albert E.: 92, 115, 152, 217, 373
   Alice: 92, 114, 151, 373
   Andrew: 91, 114, 151, 373
   Annie Agnes: 115, 373
   Bruce Echlin: 151, 217, 373
   Cecila La Verne: 151, 373
   Clancey K.: 114, 151, 373
   Clare Sadie: 151, 216, 373
   Clarence: 115, 373
   David: 64, 373
   David: 92, 373
   David S.: 65, 92, 115, 152, 217, 373
   David Thomas: 92, 115, 152, 217, 373
   Donald Temple: 151, 373
   Doris Madeline: 151, 373
   Eleanor Ruth: 151, 373
   Elizabeth: 91, 114, 151, 215, 216, 281, 282, 373
   Elizabeth Grace: 152, 373
   Emma Louise: 91, 373
   Erland Lloyd: 152, 217, 373
   Erland S.: 115, 152, 217, 374
   Ethel May: 115, 152, 374
   Etta: 92, 115, 374
   Evelyn A.: 115, 152, 374
   Fanny: 91, 374
   George David: 92, 115, 152, 217, 282, 374
   George Washington: 92, 114, 151, 216, 374
   Harvey Andrew: 114, 150, 215, 374
   Henry Franklin: 114, 151, 216, 374
   Ina Louisa: 115, 152, 217, 282, 374
   Isabella D.: 115, 152, 217, 374
   Jacob: 65, 92, 114, 151, 374
   Jacob: 91, 374
   Jean: 115, 374
   John Abram: 92, 115, 152, 374
   John Elwood: 150, 215, 374
   John Weir: 65, 92, 115, 152, 217, 282, 374
   Joseph: 92, 114, 151, 216, 217, 374
   Laura G.: 115, 152, 374
   Mabel T.: 115, 374
   Mary Claude: 114, 374
   Mary Elizabeth: 91, 114, 150, 374
   Muriel Verna: 151, 216, 374
   Murry Abram: 151, 216, 217, 374
   Nellie Elizabeth: 114, 151, 374
   Norman Edwin: 115, 374
   Private: 215, 374
   Private: 215, 374
   Private: 217, 374
   Private: 217, 374
   Private: 217, 374
   Private: 217, 374
   Rachel Elizabeth: 92, 374
   Roy Sylvester: 114, 151, 216, 217, 374
   Samuel: 64, 91, 114, 150, 151, 215, 374
   Stanley Bertram: 150, 374
   Wesley: 91, 114, 150, 215, 374
   William: 91, 374
   William: 92, 374
Bever -
   Eliza: 83, 374
Bickerton -
   Cecelia Beatrice: 101
Biddle -
   Levi H.: 76, 374
Bigot -
   Henry: 374
Bill -
   (name: Willard Henry Hackman): 162, 221, 374, 406
Bingaman -
   George M: 255, 374
   John D: 255, 374
   Nancy L: 255, 286, 374
Binkley -
   David: 31, 374
   David: 42, 374
   Henry: 42, 374
   Henry: 31, 374
   Martin: 297, 374
Bishop -
   Lucinda: 83, 374
   Nancy Jane: 374
Bitner -
   Abraham C.: 97, 374
   Anna: 97, 374
   Charles Eby: 97, 374
   Clarence: 97, 374
   Grace: 97, 374
   Herbert: 97, 374
   Robert: 97, 374
   Walter: 97, 374
Bitzer -
   Elizabeth Gertrude: 90, 314, 374
   Harvey: 90, 314, 374
   Helen Virginia: 90, 113, 314, 322, 374
Bivins -
   Private: 183
Black -
   Sarah Edna: 128
Blackburn -
   Mary Rebecca: 77, 374
Blackman -
   William: 252, 374
Blackwell -
   Hazel Leona (Dollie): 146, 375
Blanier -
   Adelheed: 17, 19, 24, 375
Bleacher -
   Ester: 375
Blehm -
   Christian Hackman (Bliem): 375
   J. Stauffer: 375
   William Stauffer: 375
Blickenderfer -
   Private: 205, 375
Bloom -
   Cindy Joan: 285
Blough -
   Mary: 80, 375
Blyth -
   Joe: 147, 375
Boale -

Sandra: 282, 375
Boddiger -
   Private: 192, 375
Bogdonoff -
   David L: 282, 375
   Eleanor Kate: 283, 375
   Jacob Alan: 282, 375
Bolender -
   Arlene: 159, 375
   Clare: 159, 375
   Florence: 159, 375
   Gladys: 159, 375
   Grace: 159, 375
   Howard: 159, 375
   Lloyd: 159, 375
   Louie: 159, 375
   Paul: 159, 375
Bolinger -
   Walter E: 112, 375
Bollinger -
   Anna: 312, 375
   Benjamin N: 68, 375
   Private: 164, 325, 375
   Private: 169, 330, 375
Bomberger -
   Abraham: 375
   Anna: 36, 375
   Annie H: 62, 89, 90, 113, 375
   Barbara: 375
   Christian: 13, 375
   Christian: 375
   Elisabeth: 375
   Jacob: 375
   Jacob: 62, 375
   John: 375
   Joseph: 375
   Mary: 375
   Private: 233, 350, 375
   Private: 177, 242, 337, 359, 375
   Private: 242, 360, 375
   Private: 242, 360, 375
   Sarah: 84, 375
   Susanna: 375
Bonham -
   Margaret Jean: 152, 375
   Marion I.: 152, 375
   Ruth: 152, 375
   Sanford K.: 152, 375
Boohar -
   Private: 177, 338, 375
Boose -
   Margaret Bucher: 163, 375
   Borkholder (name: Ulrich
      Burkholder): 74, 310
Borough -
   Amanda Alice: 138, 375
Borton -
   Daniel: 109, 375
   Ellis: 109, 375
   Katherine Ann: 109, 375
   Ruth Ann: 202, 375
   Samuel: 109, 375
Bortz -

Living: 287, 375
Bossler -
   Esther: 71, 375
   John: 43, 47, 375
Boughey II -
   Quincy Edward: 138, 375
Bower -
   John: 76, 375
   Private: 214, 375
Bowers -
   Andrew: 76, 375
   Barbara: 76, 375
   Nancy: 76, 376
   Sarah Rebecca: 76, 104, 105, 135-
      137, 190-196, 257-263, 376
   Susan: 76, 376
   Wilbur Ray: 143, 376
Bowman -
   Anna Margaret: 89, 376
   Catherine: 71, 376
   Leah: 301, 376
   Mabel: 117, 376
   Margaret Anna: 89, 376
   Martha: 306, 376
   Mary A: 87, 376
   Mary Louise: 109, 376
   Mr.: 131, 376
Boyd -
   George W.: 58
   Gordon: 161, 376
   Private: 161, 376
Boyer -
   Elizabeth: 41
   Private: 181
   Private: 249
   Private: 249
   Private: 249
Boyle -
   Elgie M: 209, 376
   Patrick: 218, 376
   Private: 209, 376
   Private: 218, 376
Brackbill -
   Benedict: 8, 30, 296, 376
   Benedict: 8, 30, 296, 376
   Benjamin: 62, 308, 376
   Christian: 376
   Eliza Ann: 376
   Elizabeth: 295, 376
   John: 12, 292, 376
   John: 295, 376
   Mary Ethel: 174, 335, 376
   Private: 166, 327, 376
Bradley -
   Abraham Shelly: 83, 376
Brandt -
   Edna: 132, 184, 250, 251, 376
   Sarah: 80, 376
   Unknown (spouse of Katie
      Brubaker): 99, 376
   William H.: 132, 376
Brant -
   Ephraim K.: 77, 376
Break -

Private: 214, 376
Brechbill -
   Fannie: 81, 376
   Henry: 60, 376
   Jacob: 81, 376
   Jacob: 76, 376
Breitenstein -
   Mary: 106, 139, 376
   Moses: 106, 376
Brendle -
   Private: 231, 349, 376
Breneman -
   Amos: 44, 376
   Elisabeth: 376
   Harry: 376
   Henry: 376
   Henry: 376
   Jacob: 376
   Jacob: 376
   Janice Marie: 163, 376
   John: 376
   Maria: 376
   Nancy: 376
   Private: 170, 331, 376
Brenneman -
   Elizabeth: 295, 376
   Jacob: 44, 376
   Melchior: 9, 376
   Private: 239, 356, 376
   Private: 239, 356, 376
   Private: 239, 356, 376
Brenner -
   Anna Barabara: 104, 376
   George: 295, 376
   Martha Eschbach: 98, 376
Bressler -
   Lydia: 308, 376
Bretz -
   Private: 246
   Private: 246
Bricker -
   Catherine: 11, 376
Briggs -
   Lyle Andrew: 175, 336, 377
   Private: 175, 336, 377
   Private: 175, 336, 377
   Private: 175, 336, 377
Bright -
   Private: 265, 288, 289, 377
   Private: 288, 289, 377
   Private: 288, 289, 377
   Private: 289, 377
   Private: 289, 377
   Private: 265, 288, 289, 377
   William Martin: 264, 265, 377
Brightbill -
   Jack A: 286, 377
   Susan M: 286, 377
Brignom -
   Private: 102
Brindle -
   William: 306, 377
Brinser -
   Elinor L.: 190, 257, 286, 377

George A.: 190, 377
Brittenstine -
   Louisa: 84, 377
Broadway -
   Jacob: 161, 377
Brock -
   Private: 282, 377
Brooks -
   Frederick Henry: 216, 377
   Gordon E.: 152, 377
   Private: 216, 377
   Private: 216, 377
   Private: 216, 377
   Velma Donelda: 194, 377
Brower -
   Abraham DeFraine: 377
   Henry Buckwalter: 377
   Magdelene: 377
   Mary Reiff: 377
Brown -
   Anna: 93, 377
   Eliza: 93, 377
   Marietta: 93, 377
   Mary Louise: 208, 377
   Mildred: 377
   Moses: 93, 377
   Orian: 268, 377
   Private: 226, 343, 377
   Private: 226, 343, 377
   Private: 268, 377
   Private: 266, 377
   Private: 267, 377
   Private: 267, 377
   Private: 267, 377
   Robert Cope: 266, 377
   Rosa: 93, 377
Brownlee -
   Ruth: 145, 377
Brua -
   Susan: 377
Brubacher -
   Augustus: 60, 83, 377
   Carolina: 83, 377
   Caroline: 83, 377
   Catharine D.: 83, 377
   David: 60, 377
   David: 83, 377
   David A. Judson: 83, 377
   David F.: 82, 377
   David N.: 83, 377
   David O.: 60, 83, 377
   Eliza N.: 83, 377
   Elizabeth: 83, 377
   Elizabeth D.: 82, 377
   George M.: 83, 377
   Henry W.: 82, 377
   Isaac B.: 83, 377
   Jacob D.: 83, 377
   Jacob F.: 83, 377
   Jacob N.: 83, 377
   Jacob O.: 60, 83, 378
   John: 83, 378
   John D.: 82, 378
   John H.: 83, 378
   John O.: 60, 82, 378

Joseph D.: 82, 378
Magdalena: 15, 24, 378
Margaret: 83, 378
Peter: 83, 378
Peter O.: 60, 83, 378
Polly: 82, 378
Priscilla: 83, 378
Samuel F.: 83, 378
Samuel N.: 83, 378
Sarah: 83, 378
Susan N.: 83, 378
Brubacker -
   Elizabeth: 30, 378
Brubaker -
   Allen L: 139, 198, 265, 289, 378
   Anna Hiestand: 16, 378
   Arlene Celeste: 198, 265, 289, 378
   Arthur J: 198, 378
   Charles E: 198, 378
   Charles White: 96, 378
   Christian: 28, 378
   Christian: 61, 86, 106, 139, 198, 265, 289, 378
   Christian: 86, 106, 139, 198, 265, 289, 378
   Christopher Scott: 163, 378
   Daniel: 61, 378
   Elias: 84, 378
   Elizabeth: 33, 378
   Elizabeth Anna: 7, 9, 12, 378
   Elsie: 198, 378
   Ezra: 106, 139, 198, 265, 289, 378
   Fannie: 106, 378
   Fanny: 68, 378
   Fanny Elizabeth: 198, 378
   Florence: 198, 378
   Frank Hostetter: 96, 378
   Hans: 9, 12, 378
   Harold F: 198, 378
   Helen: 198, 378
   Isaac: 86, 106, 139, 378
   Isaac: 68, 378
   Isaac: 106, 139, 378
   John: 378
   John: 13, 378
   John: 294, 378
   John Gesell: 68, 378
   Joseph Stauffer: 96, 378
   Katie: 99, 378
   Lucy S.: 127, 317, 378
   Magdalena: 86, 106, 139, 378
   Maria: 12, 295, 378
   Mary: 68, 378
   Mary F: 198, 378
   Mary S.: 84, 378
   May: 301, 378
   Moses S.: 84, 378
   Nathan: 106, 378
   Nathan: 163, 378
   Paul M: 99, 121, 163, 378
   Peter: 61, 86, 106, 139, 378
   Peter B.: 304, 378
   Peter G: 99, 378
   Private: 170, 330, 378
   Rheta H: 99, 198, 378
   Robert Lee: 121, 163, 379

Rosetta: 222, 379
Samuel: 48, 379
Sarah H.: 379
Stauffer Joseph: 96, 379
Susan B: 68, 379
Susanna: 86, 106, 139, 379
Walter F: 99, 198, 379
Warren E: 198, 379
Warren W.: 139, 379
Brubashcher -
   Magdalena: 26, 379
Bruce -
   James: 95, 379
Bruderly -
   Edith: 207, 379
Brumbaugh -
   John Snyder: 76, 379
Brunk -
   Ann Mary: 41, 379
   Barbara: 41, 379
   Daniel: 42, 379
   David: 41, 379
   Elizabeth: 41, 379
   George: 41, 379
   Jacob: 41, 379
   Jacob Jr: 41, 379
   John: 41, 379
   Joseph: 42, 379
   Susanna: 41, 379
Bruppacher -
   Anna: 21, 379
   Ulrich: 379
Bryan -
   Jeanette Fredricka: 128, 129
Bryant -
   Marian: 379
Brynmor -
   John Ruple: 243, 339, 379
   Milene Sue Ruple: 243, 339, 379
Bucher -
   Anna: 47, 48, 379
   Bonadine Marie: 222, 379
   Elizabeth: 106, 379
   Elizabeth: 85, 379
   John B.: 379
   Jonas: 86, 379
   Jonas: 312, 379
   Joseph: 86, 379
   Mary Ann: 312, 379
   Private: 284, 361, 379
   Veronica S.: 86, 379
Buchman -
   Gary Kyle: 283, 379
   Glenn: 283, 379
Buchs -
   Louisa C: 142, 379
Buchwalter -
   Maria: 299, 379
Buck -
   Charles L.: 76, 379
   Mildred L.: 77, 379
   Private: 266, 379
   Sophia Amanda: 76, 379
Buckwalter -

Abraham: 8, 9, 12, 295, 379
Abraham: 12, 292, 379
Abraham: 11, 293, 379
Abraham: 9, 295, 379
Abraham: 379
Abraham: 298, 302, 303, 308, 309, 379
Abraham: 8, 299, 379
Abraham: 303, 379
Anlea: 379
Ann: 8, 299, 379
Anna: 294, 379
Anna: 379
Anna Buzzard: 379
Anthony Acker: 379
Barbara: 292, 379
Barbara: 379
Barbara: 294, 295, 379
Barbara Neff: 73, 308, 309, 312, 380
Barbara Ziegler: 380
Benjamin: 6, 8, 9, 295, 298, 303, 309, 380
Benjamin: 8, 299, 380
Bressler: 308, 380
Catherine: 380
Cathrine: 303, 380
Christopher Ziegler: 380
Daniel Longacre: 380
Daniel Ziegler: 380
David Johnson Rev.: 380
David Longenecker: 380
David Ziegler: 380
Elisabeth: 53, 54, 380
Elizabeth: 294, 380
Elizabeth: 297, 380
Elizabeth: 380
Elizabeth: 6-8, 63, 298, 303, 309, 310, 380
Elizabeth Barbara: 55, 380
Emma Halterman: 380
Esther Longenecker: 380
Eugene Buzzard: 380
Francis: 12, 14, 380
Franklin: 308, 380
Frantz: 13, 294, 380
Frenzi: 380
George Buzzard: 380
Hannah: 380
Hans: 380
Heidi Rene: 244, 340, 380
Henrich: 303, 380
Henry: 294, 298, 380
Henry: 73, 303, 308, 309, 312, 380
Henry Heberline: 380
Infant: 308, 380
Jacob: 14, 380
Jacob: 380
Jacob: 8, 299, 380
Jacob Heberline: 380
Jacob Ziegler: 380
Joel B.: 308, 380
Johannes: 14, 380
Johannes Heberline: 380
Johannes Longenecker: 380
John: 294, 298, 302, 303, 308, 312, 380
John: 303, 380
John: 303, 308, 380
John B.: 308, 380
John Funk: 380
John Ziegler: 380
Jonas: 303, 380
Joseph: 9, 12, 14, 295, 380
Joseph C. Buzzard: 380
Joseph Ziegler: 380
Judith: 298, 303, 308, 312, 380
Lavina Johnson: 380
Leon Eugene: 244, 340, 380
Lizzie: 380
Louisa: 380
Magdalena: 294, 380
Magdalena: 298, 380
Magdelena Longenecker: 380
Magdelene Heberline: 380
Marie: 380
Mary: 14, 380
Mary: 298, 380
Mary: 381
Mary: 9, 295, 381
Mary: 8, 299, 381
Mary: 90, 303, 308, 309, 312, 381
Mary Buzzard: 381
Mary Heberline: 381
Matleni: 381
Michael: 299, 381
Morgan: 308, 381
Moses: 303, 381
Nathaniel Halterman: 381
Private: 284, 361, 381
Private: 284, 361, 381
Private: 284, 361, 381
Private: 284, 361, 381
Private: 170, 331, 381
Private: 170, 331, 381
Rebeccah Francis: 381
Robert Buzzard: 381
Salome: 308, 381
Samuel: 7, 381
Samuel: 303, 381
Samuel Ziegler: 381
Sarah (Sallie) Halterman: 381
Susan: 9, 295, 381
Susannah: 381
Theodorus: 14, 294, 381

Bucove -
Andre Maurice: 179, 324, 381
David Arthur: 179, 324, 381
Rachel Naomi: 179, 244, 324, 340, 381

Buehler -
Mary Gertrude: 58

Bueler -
Barbara: 14, 16-18, 381

Buller -
Private: 263, 381

Bullock -
Sarah: 44, 381

Bunora -
Private: 248

Burd -
Martha: 83, 381

Burdett -
Private: 263, 381
Private: 263, 381

Burkett -
Private: 230, 231, 348, 381

Burkhart -
John Z.: 301, 381

Burkheart -
Private: 212, 381
Private: 212, 381
Private: 212, 381
Steve: 212, 381

Burkholder -
A M: 101, 315, 381
Abraham: 16, 381
Abraham H: 74, 101, 128, 179, 311, 315, 323, 338, 381
Annie: 74, 311, 381
Barbara: 86, 381
Christiana: 381
Clark A: 101, 315, 381
Corby M.: 179, 324, 381
Daniel S.: 302, 381
Dorothy M: 101, 315, 381
E J: 101, 315, 381
Elizabeth: 299, 381
Felix: 74, 311, 381
Fianna: 45, 381
Gabriel L.: 381
George R: 101, 315, 381
Harry Hershey: 74, 311, 381
Isaac: 381
John: 295, 381
John: 381
Kathleen: 179, 339, 381
Kevin: 179, 339, 381
Lisa: 179, 339, 381
Magdalena: 381
Maria: 293, 382
Marie: 101, 315, 382
Marlin: 101, 315, 382
Melvin E: 101, 128, 179, 315, 323, 338, 382
Oliver: 74, 310, 382
Private: 285, 362, 382
Private: 285, 362, 382
Private: 285, 362, 382
Private: 285, 362, 382
Private: 230, 347, 382
Robert: 179, 338, 382
Robert Melvin: 128, 179, 323, 338, 382
Sarah: 382
Susanna: 302, 382
Thomas: 179, 339, 382
Tillie: 116, 382
Ulrich (aka: Borkholder): 74, 310

Burnham -
Lela Berneice: 187, 382

Burns -
Henry Burt: 206, 382
Private: 206, 271, 382
Private: 206, 272, 382
Private: 271, 382

Private: 271, 382
Private: 272, 382
Private: 272, 382
Private: 272, 382
Private: 272, 382
Private: 272, 382
Private: 272, 382
Private: 272, 382
Private: 271, 382
Private: 271, 382
Private: 271, 382
Private: 271, 382

Burnside -
Jean Barclay: 282, 382

Burrier -
Private: 272, 382
Private: 272, 382
Private: 272, 382

Burt -
Caitlin Ann: 244, 340, 382
David A.: 244, 340, 382

Bush -
Private: 198, 382

Butch -
Private: 269, 382
Private: 269, 382

Butterbaugh -
R: 88, 382

Buzzard -
Barbara Buckwalter: 382
David High: 382
Elizabeth Buckwalter: 382
Elizabeth High: 382
Esther Buckwalter: 382
Francis High: 382
Frederick: 382
Frederick Buckwalter: 382
Hannah Buckwalter: 382
Harry Thornton: 382
Henry High: 382
Jacob Buckwalter: 382
Jacob High: 382
John Buckwalter: 382
John High: 382
John High: 382
Jonas High: 382
Magdalena Buckwalter: 382
Margaret High: 382
Mary High: 382
Mary High: 382
Mazie: 382
Private: 240, 357, 382
Simeon High: 382
Simeon High: 383
Susan High: 383
Susanna Buckwalter: 383
Thornton High: 383

Bye -
Alton Samuel: 150, 383

Byers -
Dwight: 199, 383
Evan: 199, 383
Grace: 158, 383
Hazel: 199, 383
James: 199, 383
Phyllis: 199, 383
Ralph: 199, 383
Robert: 199, 383

Byram -
Private: 250
Private: 250

Byrne -
Private: 245

C -
Ella: 97, 383

C. -
Clyde , Jr Stoffer: 212, 383

Cafferty -
Florence Anna: 137, 383

Cahill -
Betty Jane: 251, 252

Cain -
Betty: 273, 383

Cake -
Private: 182

Calaman -
Lawrence Delmar: 132, 383

Calle -
Barbara: 58, 383

Calvin -
Elwood E.: 143, 383

Campbell -
Angus: 153, 383
Blanche: 153, 383
Bruce: 153, 383
Cheryl Ann: 243, 339, 383
James: 153, 383
John: 107, 383
Ruth: 126, 316, 383

Canfield -
Wilma: 210, 383

Canning -
Private: 241, 359, 383

Carbaugh -
Adam: 138, 139, 383
Unknown: 139, 383

Carpenter -
John: 13, 292, 383
Mary Elizabeth: 383

Carper -
Fannie: 76, 383

Carrithers -
Barbara: 243, 339, 383

Carroll -
Catherine: 53, 383

Carsey -
Private: 207, 383

Cartier -
Private: 287, 383
Private: 287, 383
Private: 287, 383

Carvell -
Audrey Nadine: 178, 244, 323, 340, 383
Glee Eileen: 178, 323, 383
Luke: 178, 323, 383
Vici Mae: 178, 244, 323, 340, 383

Cary -
Bettie: 128

Cassel -
Abraham Buckwalter: 383
Barbara: 303, 383
Barbara Buckwalter: 383
David Buckwalter: 383
Esther Veronica Buckwalter: 383
John Hershey: 383
Joseph Buckwalter: 383
Joseph Gochnauer: 383
Mary: 65, 383

Casson -
Joseph: 18, 19, 383

Caufield -
Vaughn: 201, 383

Cefro -
Private: 204, 383

Censky -
Private: 270, 383

Chadwick -
Private: 277, 383

Chambers -
Unnamed: 133

Charles -
Mary: 311, 383

Chastine -
Private: 276, 383

Chisholm -
Private: 212, 383

Chittenden -
Private: 288, 383

Choflet -
Private: 205, 383
Private: 205, 383
Private: 205, 383
Private: 205, 383
Rev Kenneth: 205, 384

Christen -
Bernice: 202, 384

Clare -
Betty J: 256, 384

Clark -
J. S.: 151, 384
Private: 152, 384

Clarke -
Bruce: 220, 384
Private: 220, 384

Clemons -
Lydia: 92, 384

Clymer -
Private: 177, 338, 384
Private: 177, 338, 384

Coakley -
Private: 168, 329, 384

Coates -
Private: 240, 357, 384

Coburn -
Martha Asenath: 97, 384

Cochran -
Private: 261, 384
Private: 261, 384
Virgil William: 261, 384

Cockburn -
Gwen: 159, 384

Coffman -
    Susanna: 298
Cole -
    Private: 275, 384
Collard -
    Alan: 118, 158, 384
    Eric: 118, 158, 384
    George: 118, 384
    Isabel: 118, 384
    Jean: 118, 158, 384
    Private: 158, 384
Colle -
    Marceline Elodia: 186, 384
Collingsworth -
    Oscar Edward: 276, 384
Committus -
    Joy: 286
Condie -
    Private: 183
Confer -
    Private: 245
Connell -
    Elizabeth Celesta: 144, 384
Conrad -
    Clifford: 253, 384
    Gerald: 253, 384
    Glenn: 253, 384
    Marilyn: 253, 384
    Private: 245
Constable -
    Herbert: 160, 384
Cook -
    Claud: 153, 218, 384
    Ernest: 153, 218, 384
    Fern: 153, 384
    James: 153, 384
    Jesse: 95, 384
    Lola: 153, 218, 384
    Private: 218, 384
    Private: 218, 384
    Private: 218, 384
    Private: 218, 384
Cooke -
    Private: 248
    Private: 248
    Private: 248
Cooley -
    Audrey: 153, 217, 384
    Bruce: 116, 384
    Clayton: 116, 152, 217, 384
    Delores: 153, 217, 384
    Fern: 116, 384
    Gerald: 116, 384
    Harold: 116, 384
    Jay: 116, 384
    Marie: 116, 153, 218, 384
    Myron: 116, 384
    Nina: 116, 153, 218, 384
    Unknown: 116, 384
    Virginia: 153, 217, 218, 384
Cooper -
    Alan C: 255, 384
    Charles David: 263, 384
    Donald W: 254, 384
    Jerold M: 255, 384
    Morris B: 254, 384
    Private: 263, 384
Cope -
    Kenneth: 142, 384
Copley -
    James: 251
Corbin -
    Orel Drennan: 384
Cordell -
    Unnamed: 217, 384
    Private: 217, 384
Core -
    Rosina: 384
Corle -
    Sarah: 80, 385
Cornelius -
    Private: 247
    Private: 247
    Private: 247
Cottam -
    Private: 180
Coughen -
    Nancy Ann: 208, 385
    Private: 208, 385
    Private: 208, 275, 385
    Private: 208, 275, 385
    Thomas Phillip: 208, 385
Coulter -
    Dorothy: 157, 385
Court -
    Virginia M: 203, 385
Cowgill -
    Ewing: 385
Cox -
    Edward L: 113, 385
    Fredrico: 256, 385
Cragin -
    Private: 195, 385
    Sumner Bowers: 195, 385
Craign -
    Private: 195, 385
Crall -
    Mary: 83, 385
Cramer -
    Mary: 75, 385
Crandell -
    Private: 246
    Jr. Private: 246
Crantson -
    Donald: 213, 385
    Private: 213, 279, 385
    Private: 213, 279, 385
Crefro -
    Private: 204, 385
Creighton -
    Thomas: 111, 385
Creiner -
    Christianna: 385
Crew -
    Arnie: 211, 385
    Arnold: 211, 385
Crist -
    Private: 280, 385
Croisette -
    Unnamed: 385
    Eugene: 385
Cross -
    Daisy Grace: 110, 385
Crouse -
    Angela Dawn: 285, 289
    Colin: 285
    Ellen C.: 79, 385
    Jerome: 77, 385
Crouthamel -
    Leo Trostle: 171, 332, 385
    Private: 171, 237, 332, 354, 385
    Private: 171, 237, 332, 354, 385
    Private: 171, 237, 332, 354, 385
    Private: 237, 354, 385
    Private: 237, 354, 385
Crowe -
    Private: 214, 385
Cruce -
    Private: 271, 385
    Private: 271, 385
    Private: 271, 385
    Private: 271, 385
    Private: 271, 385
Cruiz -
    Lucille: 385
Cummings -
    Private: 274, 385
    Private: 274, 385
    Private: 274, 385
Cunningham -
    Arthur "Murray": 266, 385
    Private: 266, 385
    Private: 266, 385
    Private: 266, 385
D'Ginto -
    Gina Marie: 179, 339, 385
Dafoe -
    Cecil Wilfred: 157, 385
    Kenneth Cecil: 157, 385
    Mavis Ruth: 157, 385
    Private: 157, 385
    Private: 157, 385
    Private: 157, 385
    Private: 157, 385
    Private: 157, 385
Daley -
    George: 117, 385
Daman -
    Ernest Ludwig: 175, 335, 385
    Private: 175, 335, 385
    Private: 175, 240, 335, 358, 385
    Private: 175, 241, 335, 358, 385
Damiani -
    Private: 172, 333, 385
    Private: 172, 333, 385
    Private: 172, 333, 386
Dan -
    Paradise Tanner (name: Daniel LeFevre): 386, 448
Danherr -
    Catharina: 19, 386

Daniels -
    Elmer Clifton: 180
    John: 285
    Private: 180, 245
    Private: 180, 245
    Private: 180, 246
    Private: 245
    Private: 245
    Private: 246
    Private: 246
Danner -
    Private: 281, 386
    Private: 281, 386
Danson -
    Private: 281, 386
    Private: 281, 386
    Private: 281, 386
Darr -
    Matilda Agnes: 77, 386
Daugherty -
    Lavinia: 203, 386
Daughter -
    Infant: 105, 386
Davenport -
    Edna Joyce: 281, 282, 386
Davidson -
    Elsie Ann: 115, 386
Davis -
    Halleck Charles: 194, 386
    Jessie: 109, 386
    Joella: 80, 386
    Lucinda: 80, 386
    Private: 194, 386
    Private: 280, 386
    Private: 280, 386
    Private: 280, 386
    Private: 280, 386
Deffenbaugh -
    Mona V: 149, 386
Deihl -
    Gideon S.: 138, 197, 198, 386
    Harvey A.: 138, 197, 386
    Howard B.: 138, 386
    James Alfred: 138, 197, 386
    Miriam: 197, 386
    Unknown: 139, 386
    Unknown: 139, 386
    Unknown: 139, 386
    Unknown: 139, 386
    Unknown: 197, 386
    Unknown: 197, 386
    Unknown: 197, 386
    Unknown: 197, 386
    Unknown: 197, 386
    Unknown: 197, 386
    Unknown: 197, 386
    Unknown: 198, 386
    Unknown: 198, 386
Deimler -
    Christabel J: 254, 386
Delebaugh -
    Maria: 58, 386
Delgado -
    Private: 236, 354, 386

    Private: 236, 354, 386
    Private: 236, 354, 386
Denlinger -
    Celeste Edith: 123, 320, 386
    Lillie Landis: 101, 314, 386
    Mary J.: 304, 386
    Private: 284, 361, 386
    Private: 284, 361, 386
    Private: 284, 361, 386
    Private: 224, 342, 386
Denninger -
    Catharine: 40
Dennis -
    Howard M.: 260, 386
    Private: 260, 386
Denny -
    Private: 269, 386
Dentlinger -
    John: 386
DePalmo -
    Ernest: 210, 386
    Private: 210, 276, 386
    Private: 210, 276, 277, 386
    Private: 210, 277, 386
    Private: 210, 277, 386
    Private: 277, 386
    Private: 277, 386
    Private: 277, 386
    Private: 276, 386
    Private: 277, 387
    Private: 277, 387
    Private: 276, 387
    Private: 276, 387
    Private: 210, 277, 387
    Private: 210, 277, 387
    Private: 210, 387
    Private: 277, 387
    Private: 277, 387
    Private: 277, 387
    Private: 277, 387
    Private: 276, 387
    Private: 277, 387
    Private: 277, 387
    Private: 277, 387
Derr -
    Cyrus: 257, 387
    Elizabeth Jane Feldser: 257, 287, 387
    Goldie Annabell: 257, 387
    Jay Earl Franklin: 257, 286, 287, 387
    Jennifer Elizabeth: 287, 387
    Living: 257, 387
    Living: 257, 387
    Living: 257, 387
    Living: 257, 387
    Luella Mae Ober Anthony: 257, 387
    Stacey Susan: 287, 387
Detweiler -
    Elias G.: 387
Detwiler -
    Jacob Snowberger: 81, 387
Deutsch -
    Abraham: 16, 387

Devlin -
    Gordon: 153, 387
    Harry: 153, 387
    John: 153, 387
    John: 153, 387
    Norman: 153, 387
DeWitt -
    Private: 183
Dice -
    Amanda E: 107, 140, 387
    Elizabeth: 107, 387
    Sarah Ann: 110, 387
Dick -
    Cecil E.: 137, 259, 387
    Elizabeth: 77, 387
    Private: 242, 360, 387
    Private: 259, 387
Dicky -
    Unknown: 112, 387
Diehl -
    Anna C.: 106, 387
    Charles A.: 105, 387
    David Alfred: 105, 138, 197, 198, 264, 265, 287-289, 387
    David R.: 198, 265, 387
    Donald: 198, 265, 289, 387
    Elizabeth: 76, 387
    Elmer E.: 105, 387
    George: 76, 387
    Harold James: 198, 387
    Harry Lee: 106, 387
    Ida M.: 105, 138, 139, 387
    John Daniel: 198, 387
    John Reuben: 105, 387
    Juanita Glada: 198, 264, 265, 288, 289, 387
    Kathryn: 106, 139, 387
    Lillian: 105, 387
    Lorraine Louise: 198, 387
    Myrtle Liliom D.: 138, 197, 264, 387
    Percy Ellsworth: 138, 198, 264, 265, 287-289, 387
    Private: 265, 289, 387
    Private: 265, 387
    Private: 265, 387
    Private: 265, 387
    Private: 265, 387
    Private: 265, 388
    Private: 265, 388
    Private: 265, 388
    Private: 265, 388
    Private: 264, 288, 388
    Private: 264, 288, 388
    Private: 264, 287, 388
    Private: 264, 287, 388
    Private: 264, 287, 388
    Private: 288, 388
    Private: 288, 388
    Private: 198, 264, 287, 388
    Private: 198, 264, 288, 388
    Private: 198, 264, 288, 388
    Private: 265, 388
    Private: 264, 388
    Private: 264, 288, 388

Private: 264, 288, 388
Private: 288, 388
Private: 288, 388
Private: 288, 388
Private: 288, 388
Private: 288, 388
Thomas E.: 106, 388
Virginia May: 138, 388
Winifred N.: 138, 388
Zelda F.: 138, 198, 388

Diehm -
Ella Mae: 388

Dien -
Private: 232, 349, 388

Dietrich -
Susan: 68, 388

Diffenbach -
Maria: 388

Dilks -
Verna: 253, 388

Dills -
Elizabeth: 35, 388

Dissinger -
Catharine: 82, 388

Ditmars -
Harriet: 77, 388

Docksteader -
Tressie Deola: 157, 388

Dodson -
Private: 183

Dohner -
Anna: 50, 388
Catherine: 29, 388
Catherine: 36, 388
Christian: 50, 388
Elizabeth: 36, 388
Henry: 29, 388
Jacob: 36, 388
John: 36, 388
Joseph: 36, 388
Joseph: 36, 388
Joseph: 50, 388
Lydia: 36, 388
Lydia: 50, 388
Mary Elizabeth: 36, 49, 388
Mary Elizabeth: 50, 388
Michael: 50, 388
Moses: 36, 50, 388
Moses: 50, 388
Noah: 50, 388
Susan: 36, 388
Susannah: 36, 388

Dolan -
John Vincent: 181
Private: 181, 246
Private: 181
Private: 181, 247
Private: 181
Private: 181

Dollar -
Victoria: 83, 388

Dombach -
Private: 234, 352, 388

Donaldson -
Guy Elmer: 136, 388
Mary: 53, 388
Mary: 52, 388

Doner -
Abraham: 388
John: 388

Dooling -
Sarah: 301, 388

Dotts -
Private: 175, 336, 388

Dougherty -
Charles: 311, 389

Doughtery -
Ernest: 94, 389
Joseph S.: 82, 389

Dounell -
Anna O.: 115, 389

Dowdell -
Ruth J: 188, 389

Downing -
Joseph: 389

Downs -
Jr. Private: 128

Dr -
Israel Groff ": 58

Drexler -
Private: 282, 389

Drover -
Gertrude: 189, 389

Drumheller -
James: 180

Drummond -
Douglas: 102

Dubble -
Mary: 163, 389

Dubert -
Mary: 134, 389

Dukart -
Private: 261, 389
Private: 261, 389

Duncan -
Adrian E: 187, 255, 286, 389
Alvid O: 134, 187, 255, 286, 389
Anna B: 134, 188, 256, 389
Delmar A: 255, 389
Delmar M: 187, 255, 389
John: 134, 389
Katherine M: 134, 188, 256, 389
Lucille M: 255, 389
Margaret Ann (aka: Maggie): 133, 186, 253, 389, 451
Rachael Agnes: 134, 187, 255, 286, 389
Shirley A: 255, 389
William Malcolm: 133, 389
William Malcolm: 133, 389

Dunham -
Alvin William: 216, 389
Bertha Beatrice: 151, 215, 216, 281, 389
Betty Jean Mabel: 216, 282, 389
Eleanor Elizabeth: 151, 216, 281, 282, 389
Elmer Ray: 151, 216, 389
Evert: 151, 389
Frederick Fielding: 151, 215, 389
Freedman: 151, 389
Gertie Gibson: 151, 389
James Orval: 216, 389
Jessie Jean: 151, 215, 389
Lorne Milton: 151, 389
Mildred Elizabeth: 151, 216, 389
Norman Nelson: 151, 215, 389
Private: 216, 389
Private: 216, 389
Private: 215, 389
Private: 215, 389
Private: 215, 389
Private: 216, 389
Watson William: 151, 216, 389
William Kitchen: 151, 216, 282, 389

Dunk -
Living: 257, 389

Dunn -
Mary: 259, 389

Dupuy -
Amy: 99, 389
Charles: 99, 389
Eleanor: 99, 389
Harry Wilford: 99, 389
Herbert: 99, 389
Rosetta: 99, 389

Dyer -
Barbara: 178, 323, 389

Eaby -
Anna: 298, 389
Cora Etta: 100, 313, 389

Eager -
Private: 265, 389

Eaken -
John: 251
Norman: 251
Susan: 251

Earhart -
Private: 172, 332, 389

Eberle -
Barbara: 13

Eberly -
Elizabeth: 86, 389
Private: 283, 360, 389
Private: 224, 342, 389
Private: 224, 342, 389
Private: 224, 283, 284, 342, 361, 389
Private: 224, 342, 389
Private: 284, 361, 390
Private: 284, 361, 390
Private: 236, 353, 390
Private: 236, 353, 390
Private: 236, 353, 390
Simon: 83, 390

Ebersole -
Abraham: 30, 390
Anna: 390
Annie: 85, 390
Christian: 294, 390
Jacob: 31, 390
John: 40, 390

John: 294, 390
Mabel E: 101, 315, 390
Mildrfed K.: 166, 327, 390
Private: 284, 362, 390
Private: 285, 362, 390
Private: 171, 332, 390
Private: 171, 332, 390
Private: 171, 332, 390

Eby -
   Aaron Buckwalter: 100, 122, 169, 170, 236, 313, 319, 330, 331, 353, 354, 390
   Aaron S.: 121, 318, 390
   Andrew: 11, 390
   Anna: 11, 41, 390
   Anna: 9, 30, 40, 296, 300, 390
   Anna Martha: 100, 122, 168, 169, 234-236, 313, 319, 329, 330, 352, 353, 390
   Barabara: 11, 390
   Candance: 161, 390
   Catherine: 54, 55, 390
   Christian: 9, 11, 14, 33, 41, 390
   Christian: 11, 390
   Clyde S.: 122, 170, 319, 331, 390
   Eileen Marie: 170, 331, 390
   Eli S.: 121, 166, 230, 318, 327, 348, 390
   Elizabeth: 7, 9, 11, 12, 33, 39, 300, 390
   Elizabeth: 56, 304, 312, 390
   Elizabeth Hershey: 99, 121, 312, 318, 390
   Ella Barbara: 99, 121, 164, 223-226, 283, 284, 312, 318, 324, 325, 340-343, 360-362, 390
   Emma Mae: 121, 165, 228, 285, 318, 326, 345, 346, 362, 390
   Enos Jacob: 99, 121, 165, 166, 228-230, 313, 318, 326, 327, 346-348, 390
   Ethel Z.: 122, 168, 234, 319, 329, 351, 390
   Ezra S.: 121, 165, 166, 229, 230, 318, 326, 347, 390
   Franklin W.: 121, 164, 165, 226, 318, 325, 344, 390
   George: 14, 390
   George: 12, 390
   Henry John: 99, 312, 390
   Henry Musser: 100, 122, 167, 168, 234, 313, 319, 328, 329, 351, 352, 390
   Henry S.: 121, 165, 229, 318, 326, 346, 347, 390
   Isaac: 390
   Isaac Isaiah: 100, 313, 390
   Isaac S.: 121, 318, 390
   Jacob: 14, 390
   James Z.: 165, 326, 390
   Johannes: 14, 390
   John: 43, 390
   John Hershey: 43, 390
   John S.: 121, 318, 390

John Silas: 100, 313, 390
Lydia S.: 121, 166, 318, 327, 390
Margaret: 159, 390
Margie: 123, 320, 390
Marsha: 230, 348, 390
Martin Christian: 100, 123, 171, 313, 319, 320, 332, 390
Martin Z.: 122, 168, 234, 319, 329, 351, 390
Mary Edith: 100, 313, 390
Mary Z.: 122, 168, 234, 319, 329, 352, 390
Maurice: 160, 391
Menno Hershey: 100, 122, 170, 171, 313, 319, 331, 391
Michael: 12, 391
Peter: 14, 391
Peter: 11, 391
Peter Hershey: 99, 121, 164, 165, 226-228, 284, 285, 312, 318, 325, 326, 344-346, 362, 391
Private: 165, 226, 325, 344, 391
Private: 165, 229, 326, 346, 391
Private: 165, 229, 326, 346, 391
Private: 165, 229, 326, 346, 347, 391
Private: 165, 229, 326, 347, 391
Private: 165, 229, 326, 347, 391
Private: 165, 229, 326, 347, 391
Private: 165, 326, 391
Private: 229, 347, 391
Private: 229, 347, 391
Private: 229, 347, 391
Private: 229, 347, 391
Private: 229, 347, 391
Private: 229, 346, 391
Private: 166, 326, 391
Private: 166, 229, 326, 347, 391
Private: 166, 326, 391
Private: 166, 229, 230, 326, 347, 391
Private: 166, 230, 326, 347, 391
Private: 166, 326, 391
Private: 166, 230, 326, 347, 391
Private: 166, 230, 326, 347, 391
Private: 230, 347, 391
Private: 230, 347, 391
Private: 230, 348, 391
Private: 230, 348, 391
Private: 230, 347, 391
Private: 230, 347, 391
Private: 230, 347, 391
Private: 230, 347, 391
Private: 230, 347, 391
Private: 230, 347, 391
Private: 230, 347, 391
Private: 166, 327, 391
Private: 166, 327, 391
Private: 166, 327, 391
Private: 166, 230, 327, 348, 391
Private: 166, 230, 327, 348, 391
Private: 166, 230, 327, 348, 391
Private: 230, 348, 391
Private: 230, 348, 391

Private: 230, 348, 391
Private: 230, 348, 391
Private: 122, 167, 319, 328, 391
Private: 122, 167, 319, 328, 391
Private: 122, 168, 319, 328, 391
Private: 122, 168, 319, 328, 391
Private: 122, 168, 319, 329, 391
Private: 168, 234, 329, 351, 391
Private: 168, 329, 391
Private: 234, 351, 391
Private: 234, 351, 391
Private: 234, 351, 391
Private: 168, 329, 391
Private: 168, 329, 391
Private: 168, 329, 391
Private: 168, 329, 391
Private: 168, 329, 391
Private: 168, 329, 391
Private: 168, 328, 391
Private: 168, 329, 391
Private: 168, 329, 392
Private: 167, 328, 392
Private: 167, 328, 392
Private: 167, 328, 392
Private: 167, 328, 392
Private: 122, 169, 170, 319, 330, 392
Private: 122, 170, 319, 330, 392
Private: 122, 170, 236, 319, 331, 353, 392
Private: 122, 170, 236, 319, 331, 353, 392
Private: 170, 236, 331, 354, 392
Private: 170, 331, 392
Private: 170, 236, 331, 354, 392
Private: 170, 236, 331, 354, 392
Private: 170, 236, 331, 354, 392
Private: 170, 236, 331, 354, 392
Private: 236, 354, 392
Private: 236, 354, 392
Private: 236, 354, 392
Private: 236, 354, 392
Private: 236, 354, 392
Private: 236, 354, 392
Private: 170, 331, 392
Private: 170, 331, 392
Private: 170, 331, 392
Private: 170, 236, 331, 353, 392
Private: 170, 236, 331, 353, 392
Private: 170, 331, 392
Private: 170, 331, 392
Private: 170, 331, 392
Private: 170, 330, 392
Private: 170, 330, 392
Private: 170, 331, 392
Private: 170, 331, 392
Private: 170, 331, 392
Private: 122, 170, 319, 331, 392
Private: 122, 170, 171, 319, 331, 392
Private: 123, 171, 319, 331, 392
Private: 171, 331, 392
Private: 170, 331, 392
Private: 170, 331, 392
Private: 170, 331, 392
Private: 123, 171, 320, 332, 392
Private: 123, 171, 320, 332, 392
Private: 123, 171, 320, 332, 392

Private: 123, 320, 392
Private: 123, 171, 320, 332, 392
Private: 171, 332, 392
Private: 171, 332, 392
Private: 171, 332, 392
Private: 171, 332, 392
Private: 171, 332, 392
Private: 171, 332, 392
Private: 171, 332, 392
Private: 242, 360, 392
Private: 242, 360, 392
Private: 242, 360, 392
Private: 242, 360, 392
Rhoda S.: 121, 165, 228, 229, 318, 326, 346, 392
Richard S.: 122, 170, 236, 319, 331, 354, 392
Roy Z.: 122, 168, 319, 329, 392
Samuel: 12, 392
Sarah Lucinda: 99, 122, 166, 167, 230-233, 313, 318, 327, 328, 348-351, 392
Sarah S.: 121, 318, 392
Susan: 100, 313, 392
Susan W.: 121, 165, 226, 227, 284, 318, 325, 326, 344, 345, 362, 392
Theodorus (Durst): 11, 14, 392
Warren Z.: 122, 319, 393

Echlin -
Annetta: 151, 393

Eckels -
Charles: 96, 393
Grace: 96, 393
Margery: 96, 393

Edwards -
Mary E: 188, 393

Edworthy -
Gladys B.: 152, 393
Louise Norman: 152, 217, 282, 393
Ross Herbert: 152, 393

Egle -
Esther: 12, 25, 393

Egli -
Adelheid: 393
Barbel: 20, 393

Eichelberger -
Harry D: 393
Melvin: 393

Eicher -
Private: 232, 349, 393
Private: 232, 349, 393

Eiklor -
Private: 204, 393

Eleftheriades -
Sophi: 211, 393

Elifdities -
Sophi: 211, 393

Ellis -
Edith Stauffer: 393
Edward Stauffer: 393
Mary Stauffer: 393
Thomas: 393

Emory -
Private: 248

Engle -
Charles C.: 258, 393
Private: 258, 393
Private: 258, 393
Private: 258, 393

Erb -
Christian: 393
Christian: 32, 393
Christian: 36, 393
Fanny: 86, 393
Fianna: 86, 393
Gabrial: 86, 393
Isaac: 86, 393
Jacob: 393
Jacob: 32, 393
Jacob: 86, 393
Maria: 36, 393
Mary: 393
Mary Louise: 86, 393
Peter: 86, 393

Erhart -
Mary: 31, 393

Erisman -
Addey: 393
Albert: 66, 393
Amelia: 66, 393
Christian: 66, 393
Elizabeth: 66, 393
Elmer: 70, 393
Elnora: 66, 393
Jacob: 25, 393
Mary: 66, 393
Mary: 393
Metz: 66, 393
Sarah: 66, 393
Susan: 66, 393

Ernest -
Private: 280, 393

Ernst -
Private: 214, 279, 393
Private: 214, 279, 393
Private: 214, 280, 393
Private: 279, 393
Private: 280, 393
Private: 214, 393
Raymond Hunter: 214, 393

Ertzinger -
Elizabeth: 16, 18, 20, 393
Uli: 18, 20, 393

Eshelman -
Abraham: 96, 393
Alice: 96, 394
Edwin: 96, 394
Elizabeth: 48, 394
Frances: 7, 46, 394
Hagar: 96, 394
Isaac: 30, 394
Lydia: 96, 394
Maria: 50, 394
Susan: 96, 394

Eshenauer -
Fox John Edgar ": 74, 102, 130

Eshleman -
Annie: 394
Barbara: 42, 394
David: 394
Magdalena: 294, 394
Peter: 394

Espenshade -
Emma: 308, 394

Espich -
Frank: 127, 317, 394

Evans -
Cecile Loren: 224, 341, 394
Edwin: 204, 394
Ezekiel Owen: 394
Hannah Owen: 394
John: 394
Private: 223, 224, 341, 394
Private: 224, 341, 394
Private: 224, 341, 394
Private: 224, 341, 394
Private: 204, 394
Private: 204, 394
Private: 204, 394
Private: 204, 394
Private: 204, 394
Private: 272, 394
Thomas Elijah: 272, 394
Viola E.: 258, 394

Everett -
Hugh Munson: 216, 281, 282, 394
Nelson William: 216, 394
Private: 282, 394
Private: 282, 394
Private: 282, 394
Private: 282, 394
Ralph Avon: 216, 282, 394

Eyer -
Harold Ray: 190, 258, 394
John Paul: 190, 258, 394
Katherine Lucile: 190, 258, 394
Lewis Benjamin: 190, 258, 394
Mary Belle: 190, 257, 394
Private: 258, 394
Private: 258, 394
Private: 258, 394
Private: 258, 394
Private: 258, 394
Private: 258, 394
Private: 258, 394
Private: 258, 394
Private: 258, 394

Eyers -
Isaac: 190, 394

Fahlen -
Private: 259, 394
Private: 259, 394

Fanny -
(name: Veronica Bear): 48, 372, 394

Farmer -
Cindy Hope: 243, 339, 394
John W.: 243, 339, 394
Mary Elizabeth: 243, 339, 394

Farner -
Catharine: 75, 394
Charlotte: 75, 103, 131, 132, 184,

185, 250-252, 285, 286,
289, 394
Conrad: 75, 394
Daniel: 75, 394
David: 74, 75, 394
Elizabeth: 75, 395
Fanny: 75, 395
Gabriel: 75, 395
Henry: 75, 395
John: 75, 395
Mariah: 75, 395
Mary: 75, 395
Peter: 75, 395
Solomon: 75, 395
Susannah: 75, 103, 133, 395

Farney -
Franey: 58, 395

Farsht -
Susannah: 83, 395

Fasnacht -
Kathryn Romaine: 129

Fauher -
Private: 260, 395

Feeser -
Anna E: 189, 395
John E: 189, 395
Martin: 189, 395

Feighter -
Sarah: 81, 395

Feister -
Private: 173, 333, 395

Feldser -
Living: 287, 395
Living: 287, 395
Living: 287, 395
Living: 287, 395
Living: 287, 395
Living: 287, 395
Living: 287, 395

Felger -
June: 204, 395

Fellabaum -
Private: 164, 325, 395

Felpel -
Private: 224, 341, 395

Fenell -
Private: 275, 395

Ferguson -
Victor: 144, 395

Ferree -
Alice: 131, 395
Anna: 395
Rebecca: 395
Thomas: 131, 395

Few -
Harriet: 84, 395

Fidler -
Gary: 283, 395

Fidoe -
Private: 274, 395
Private: 274, 395

Filyer -
Joyce: 162, 395

Fink -

Barbara D: 255, 395
James E: 255, 395
Joseph A: 255, 395
Joseph C: 255, 395
Patricia L: 255, 286, 395
Richard E: 255, 395

Finkey -
William: 103, 395

Fisher -
Frances: 188, 395
Henry S.: 79, 395
Private: 128

Fixter -
Private: 282, 395

Flaherty -
Billie: 395

Fleming -
Dolly: 205, 395
Isobel: 218, 219, 395
Private: 269, 395
Private: 183
Jr. Private: 183
Private: 183, 250
Private: 183
Private: 183

Fletcher -
Ida Mae: 395

Flickinger -
Elizabeth: 298, 395
Irene: 252
John: 84, 395

Fluck -
John Brallier: 82, 395

Folliott -
Blanche: 118, 395

Foot -
Frank Frederick: 218, 395
Private: 218, 395
William Dalton: 157, 395

Foote -
Mildred: 118, 395

Forester -
Kenneth Alexander: 282, 395
Private: 282, 395

Forman -
Private: 183

Forney -
Betty: 163, 395
Elisabeth: 65, 395

Forrer -
Anna: 396

Forrest -
Howard: 186, 396

Forrester -
Jeremiah: 37, 396

Forry -
Anna: 69, 396
Maria: 70, 396

Forsyth -
Joe: 155, 396
Martha: 94, 396

Forsythe -
Alice Morene: 159, 396
Floyd: 159, 220, 396

Levi: 159, 396
Lola Jean: 159, 220, 396
Private: 220, 396
Vera Irene: 159, 396

Fortini -
Jr. Private: 245
Private: 245
Private: 245

Fortney -
Karen Ann: 221, 396

Foster -
Elias: 58, 396
Jerry: 179, 324, 396

Fountain -
Kathryn Dorothea: 181
Kristina Diane: 181
Private: 180
Private: 181, 246
Private: 181
Private: 181, 246
Private: 181, 246
Private: 246

Fowler -
Dora Maud: 396

Fox -
Adelaide: 74, 102, 130, 182, 183, 249, 250
Alta Mae: 164, 325, 396
Anna Elizabeth: 121, 318, 396
Beverly: 128
Bryan: 129, 180, 245
Caroline Lee: 74, 102, 130, 183, 250
Catherine: 89, 396
Cecelia Beatrice: 101
Charles Adam: 102, 128, 179, 180, 245
Charles Kunkel: 102, 130
Daniel Hershey: 121, 164, 225, 226, 318, 325, 343, 396
Daniel M.: 121, 318, 396
Diana Lucille: 129, 182, 248
Donald: 252, 396
Dorothy: 129, 180, 246
Elizabeth "Lillie": 74
Elmer Eby: 121, 318, 396
Emilie Karthaus: 103, 130, 183, 250
Ethel Elizabeth: 102
George Francis: 102, 128
George Henry: 129
George Hershey: 74, 103, 130, 131, 183, 184, 250
Henry Peter: 121, 164, 223, 224, 283, 284, 318, 325, 341, 342, 360, 361, 396
Howard: 252, 396
Ivan Martin: 121, 164, 226, 318, 325, 343, 396
James George: 74, 102, 128, 129, 179-182, 244-249
Jr. James George: 102, 129, 130, 182, 249
James Walter: 102
Jeanette Fredricka: 129, 180, 245,

246
John David: 121, 318, 396
John Edward: 102, 128, 129, 180, 181, 245-247
John Edward: 129
Joyce Melinda: 182
Karolyn Diana: 103, 131, 183, 184, 250
Jr. Lawrence Webster: 102, 128
Marjorie: 129, 180, 246
Marvin Lamar: 223, 341, 396
Mary Eby: 121, 318, 396
Mary Elizabeth: 102
Mary Hershey: 74
Mary Virginia: 102, 129, 181
Private: 164, 324, 396
Private: 164, 223, 324, 340, 341, 396
Private: 164, 223, 324, 341, 396
Private: 164, 223, 324, 341, 396
Private: 164, 325, 396
Private: 164, 325, 396
Private: 164, 223, 283, 325, 341, 360, 396
Private: 223, 341, 396
Private: 223, 341, 396
Private: 223, 283, 341, 360, 396
Private: 223, 283, 341, 360, 396
Private: 283, 360, 396
Private: 223, 341, 396
Private: 223, 341, 396
Private: 223, 341, 396
Private: 164, 223, 224, 325, 341, 396
Private: 164, 325, 396
Private: 164, 224, 325, 341, 396
Private: 164, 224, 325, 341, 396
Private: 164, 325, 396
Private: 164, 224, 325, 341, 342, 396
Private: 164, 325, 396
Private: 164, 224, 283, 325, 342, 360, 361, 396
Private: 164, 224, 283, 325, 342, 361, 396
Private: 164, 224, 284, 325, 342, 361, 396
Private: 164, 224, 284, 325, 342, 361, 396
Private: 224, 342, 396
Private: 224, 342, 396
Private: 224, 341, 396
Private: 224, 341, 396
Private: 224, 341, 396
Private: 224, 341, 396
Private: 224, 341, 396
Private: 224, 341, 396
Private: 164, 225, 325, 343, 396
Private: 164, 225, 226, 325, 343, 396
Private: 164, 226, 325, 343, 397
Private: 226, 343, 397
Private: 164, 325, 397
Private: 164, 226, 325, 343, 397
Private: 164, 226, 325, 343, 397
Private: 226, 343, 397
Private: 226, 343, 397
Private: 226, 344, 397
Private: 129, 180, 245
Jr. Private: 102
Private: 128, 179, 244, 245
III Private: 128
Private: 128
Private: 102, 130
Private: 102
Private: 128
Jr. Private: 128
Private: 128
Private: 128, 179, 245
Private: 128, 180, 245
Private: 180
Private: 180, 245
Private: 245
Private: 245
Private: 245
Private: 180
Private: 180, 245
Private: 180
Private: 245
Private: 129, 181, 247
Private: 129, 181, 247
Private: 129, 181, 247
Private: 129, 181, 247, 248
Private: 129
Private: 182
Private: 182, 248
Private: 181, 247
Private: 247
Private: 181, 247
Private: 181, 247
Private: 247
III Private: 130, 182
Private: 130, 182, 249
Private: 182
Private: 182
IV Private: 182
Private: 182
Private: 130
Private: 130
Private: 181, 247
Private: 247
Private: 129, 180
Rachel Virginia: 102, 130
Richard: 252, 397
Jr. Richard Thomas: 180
Robert Thomas: 74
Robert Thomas: 102, 128, 179, 244, 245
Jr. Robert Thomas: 128
Sara Diana: 102, 129, 182, 248, 249
Sarah Lucinda: 121, 164, 225, 284, 318, 325, 342, 343, 361, 362, 397
Thomas Bickerton: 102
Thomas G.: 102, 129, 181, 182, 247, 248
Jr. Thomas G.: 129, 182, 248
Thomas George: 74
Unnamed: 128
Virginia Romaine: 129, 182, 248
Webster: 129
William Webster: 102
Willis Eby: 121, 164, 223, 283, 318, 324, 340, 341, 360, 397

Frame -
Elijah: 397
John L.: 397
Frances -
Unnamed: 133, 397
Franck -
Catherine: 397
Lizzie Risser: 198, 397
Frankfort -
Anna: 397
Franklin -
Private: 172, 333, 397
Private: 213, 397
Frantz -
Anna: 35, 48, 68, 97, 98, 120, 162, 163, 220-223, 282, 283, 397
Anna: 46, 397
Anna Hostetter: 6-8, 33, 34, 46, 57, 305, 397
Barbara: 8, 34, 397
Christian: 10, 397
Christian: 397
Christian H: 8, 34, 397
Elisabeth: 8, 34, 397
Elizabeth: 10, 397
Elizabeth: 8, 28, 397
Elizabeth: 40, 57, 397
Elizabeth Miller: 6, 63, 310, 397
Jacob: 10, 34, 35, 397
Jacob: 8, 34, 46, 397
Jacob: 35, 397
Jacob Hostetter: 35, 49, 397
John: 10, 28, 397
John: 8, 10, 34, 35, 397
John: 7, 8, 10, 33, 34, 40, 397
John: 8, 34, 40, 46, 57, 397
John: 35, 397
John Miller: 49, 397
Maria: 8, 34, 397
Michael: 10, 397
Samuel: 397
Frederick -
Philip: 397
Freed -
Private: 169, 330, 397
Freitag -
Ervin: 144, 397
French -
Private: 211, 397
Freshley -
Allen L: 145, 397
Ellen: 147, 397
Eugene A: 145, 204, 397
June: 145, 204, 205, 397
Marjorie: 145, 204, 397
Private: 204, 397
Private: 204, 397
Private: 204, 397
Private: 204, 397
Private: 204, 397
Private: 204, 397

Private: 204, 397
Private: 204, 397
Private: 204, 397
Robert: 145, 204, 397
William: 145, 397
Fretz -
Sara Schwartz: 397
Frey -
Barbel: 20, 397
Private: 173, 334, 397
Frick -
Anna: 398
John: 27, 398
Nancy S: 7, 45, 398
Fried -
Eliza: 88, 398
Friedel -
Arthur Charles: 130
Jr. Private: 130, 183
Private: 130
III Private: 183
Private: 183
Fritz -
Magdalena: 14, 398
Peter C.: 398
Sandra M.: 179, 324, 398
Frock -
Sallie J.: 398
Frost -
Alfred DeWitt: 115, 398
Charles R.: 193, 398
Charles Snyder: 193, 261, 398
Harry: 193, 398
Infant: 193, 398
Oliver: 115, 152, 217, 398
Private: 261, 398
Reginald Joseph: 152, 217, 398
Reginald Joseph: 217, 398
Fry -
Mary: 301, 398
Fryberger -
Private: 224, 342, 398
Fuchs/Fox -
Matilda (Fox): 398
Fulleman -
Private: 181
Fuller -
Florence A.: 83, 398
Fultz -
John: 109, 398
Mark: 109, 398
Samuel: 109, 398
Funk -
Barbara: 36, 398
Jason: 283, 398
Jazmond Hess: 283, 398
Kate D.: 398
Kate Detweiler: 398
Margaret: 398
Tyler Ray: 283, 398
Fusilier -
Frazier: 185, 398
Gabel -
John Henry: 398

Gaffney -
Private: 164, 325, 398
Galbreath -
Private: 212, 398
Galebach -
Miriam: 178, 323, 398
Gallagher -
Arthur E: 99, 398
Louise E: 99, 398
Private: 246
Sherald George: 99, 398
William: 99, 398
Galli -
Barbara Neukommet: 12, 15, 17, 24, 398
Ulrich: 15, 17, 24, 398
Gallins -
Private: 210, 398
Gamell -
Mamie Dell: 197, 398
Games -
George: 398
George Marion: 398
Kenneth Azariah: 398
Garber -
Annie L.: 85, 398
Sarah A: 88, 398
Gardner -
Benjamin: 80, 398
Cyrus: 80, 398
Eliza: 80, 398
George: 80, 398
Henry: 80, 398
Infant: 116, 398
James: 80, 398
John: 116, 398
John W.: 80, 398
Julia: 80, 398
Leah: 80, 398
Lewis: 80, 398
Mary: 80, 398
Nancy: 80, 398
Peter: 80, 398
Peter Frederick: 80, 398
Rosanna: 80, 398
Unknown: 116, 399
William: 116, 399
Garman -
Private: 285, 362, 399
Private: 285, 362, 399
Garnes -
George A.: 59, 399
Garren -
Hilda: 205, 399
Garretson -
Sarah: 82, 399
Garrett -
Martha: 79, 399
Garver -
Barbara: 11, 293, 399
Gates -
Private: 241, 358, 399
Private: 241, 358, 399
Private: 241, 358, 399

Gatto -
Private: 242, 360, 399
Private: 242, 360, 399
Gatton -
Mary Marilla: 109, 399
Gauthier -
Private: 265, 399
Gaverick -
Connie L: 267, 399
Gay -
Adelaide: 102
Gertrude: 102, 130, 183, 250
John Howard: 102
Jr. John Howard: 102, 130, 182, 183, 249
Margaret: 130
Private: 130, 182, 249
III Private: 130, 183, 249
Private: 183, 249
Private: 183, 249
Private: 183, 249
Gearhart -
Carroll: 143, 399
Dayle Kermit: 143, 201, 267, 399
Don Leedy: 201, 399
Geneva Lucille: 143, 399
Gladys Estella: 143, 399
John Fredrick: 143, 399
Lyle Franklin: 143, 399
Mable Althea: 143, 399
Mary Elizabeth: 143, 399
Mildred Louise: 143, 399
Pauline Lucille: 201, 399
Private: 201, 399
Private: 201, 399
Private: 201, 267, 399
Ralph Elretus: 143, 399
Vance Leon: 143, 399
William Franklin: 143, 399
Gebraad -
John: 138, 399
Geckler -
Anna Mae: 203, 399
Gehman -
Arthur E.: 122, 166, 231, 319, 327, 349, 399
Benjamin: 297, 399
Betsy: 399
Catharine: 297, 399
Edith Elizabeth: 122, 167, 232, 233, 319, 327, 328, 349, 350, 399
Grace: 122, 319, 399
Harry: 307, 399
Harry H.: 122, 318, 399
Harry Jacob: 122, 167, 233, 319, 328, 350, 351, 399
John E.: 122, 166, 167, 231, 232, 319, 327, 349, 399
Joseph: 302, 399
Lizzie: 306, 399
Lucy E.: 122, 167, 233, 319, 328, 350, 399
Phares B.: 74, 310, 399
Private: 227, 345, 399

Private: 166, 327, 399
Private: 122, 166, 230, 231, 319, 327, 348, 399
Private: 122, 166, 231, 319, 327, 348, 349, 399
Private: 166, 231, 327, 349, 399
Private: 166, 231, 327, 349, 399
Private: 166, 231, 327, 349, 399
Private: 231, 349, 399
Private: 231, 349, 399
Private: 167, 327, 399
Private: 167, 231, 232, 327, 349, 399
Private: 167, 327, 399
Private: 167, 232, 327, 349, 399
Private: 167, 232, 327, 349, 399
Private: 167, 327, 399
Private: 167, 232, 327, 349, 399
Private: 232, 349, 400
Private: 232, 349, 400
Private: 232, 349, 400
Private: 232, 349, 400
Private: 232, 349, 400
Private: 167, 328, 400
Private: 167, 328, 400
Private: 167, 233, 328, 350, 400
Private: 167, 233, 328, 351, 400
Private: 167, 233, 328, 351, 400
Private: 167, 233, 328, 351, 400
Private: 167, 233, 328, 351, 400
Private: 233, 351, 400
Private: 233, 351, 400
Private: 233, 351, 400
Private: 233, 351, 400
Private: 234, 351, 400
Private: 234, 351, 400
Private: 233, 351, 400
Private: 233, 351, 400
Private: 233, 351, 400
Private: 233, 351, 400
Private: 233, 350, 400
Private: 166, 231, 327, 348, 400
Private: 166, 231, 327, 348, 400
Private: 166, 327, 400
Private: 166, 231, 327, 349, 400
Private: 166, 327, 400
Private: 231, 349, 400
Private: 231, 349, 400
Private: 231, 349, 400
Private: 166, 327, 400
Private: 166, 327, 400
Private: 166, 230, 231, 327, 348, 400
Private: 166, 231, 327, 348, 400
Private: 166, 231, 327, 348, 400
Private: 231, 348, 400
Private: 231, 348, 400
Private: 231, 348, 400
Samuel S.: 307, 400
Todd Matthew: 231, 349, 400

Geib -
Anna: 400
Daniel: 400
David L.: 400
Emma Earhart: 120, 121, 254, 400
John L.: 400
Margaret: 400
Samuel: 400

Geier -
Unnamed: 400

Geiger -
Barbara Ann: 150, 214, 400
Ward: 150, 400

Geigley -
Mary: 307, 400

Geisinger -
Unknown (Kyssinger): 400

Geist -
Wynaria M.: 73, 309, 400

George -
Clarence Judson: 118, 400
Elizabeth Ann: 118, 157, 400
Harold Wideman: 118, 400
Nellie Almina: 118, 157, 400
Samuel: 118, 400
Samuel Ross: 217, 400

Gerber -
Catherine: 293, 400

Gerdes -
Miriam: 99, 400

Gerhardt -
David Jenkins: 130
Private: 130
Private: 130

Gerhart -
Abraham: 297, 400

Gerlach -
Carol Ann: 222, 400
Daryl Eugene: 222, 400
Douglas Scott: 222, 400
John Henry: 221, 222, 401

Germonoff -
Private: 276, 277, 401

Getz -
Elizabeth: 401

Giannopolo -
Ann Marie: 244, 340, 401

Gibbins -
Patricia: 160, 401
Peter: 160, 401
Reginald: 160, 401

Giesbrecht -
Ann: 156, 401

Gilbert -
Annielaurie Ruletta: 216, 281, 401
Charles Samuel: 216, 401
George Evert: 216, 401

Gilboyne -
Anna Marie: 155, 401

Gill -
Dawn Marie: 221, 401
John Kennedy: 221, 401
Terry Lee: 221, 401
Tina Lynn: 221, 401

Gilleland -
John: 37, 401
Thomas: 37, 401

Gingerich -
Catherine L.: 85, 401

Gingrich -
Barbara: 38, 401
Charles: 91, 401
Fannie: 91, 401
Harry: 91, 401
Katie: 91, 401
LeRoy: 91, 401
Ruth: 91, 401
William: 91, 401

Gitters -
Private: 214, 401

Gittinger -
Casper: 401

Glancey -
Private: 237, 355, 401
Private: 237, 355, 401
Private: 237, 355, 401

Glass -
John W: 88, 401
Private: 246
Private: 246
Private: 246
Private: 246
Private: 246
Jr. Private: 246

Glick -
Private: 234, 352, 401
Private: 234, 352, 401
Private: 234, 352, 401

Gloss -
George M: 201, 401

Glunt -
Private: 181

Gockley -
John L.: 74, 310, 401
John M.: 312, 401
Sarah: 73, 401

Gonzalez -
Hilda: 254, 401

Good -
Anna: 401
Annie: 301, 401
Archie L: 113, 318, 401
Barbara: 6, 63, 310, 401
Benjamin: 301, 401
Hans: 401
Jacob: 401
Jonas: 296, 401
Lori A: 221, 401
Noah G.: 307, 401
Peter: 401
Peter: 401
Peter: 301, 401
Private: 224, 342, 401
Private: 224, 342, 401
Private: 224, 342, 401
Private: 224, 284, 342, 361, 401
Private: 224, 284, 342, 361, 401
Private: 284, 361, 401
Private: 227, 344, 401
Private: 227, 345, 401
Private: 229, 346, 401
Private: 235, 352, 401
Private: 236, 353, 401
Private: 236, 353, 401

Susan: 38, 402
Susanna: 402
Susanna: 307, 311, 402
Goodhart -
   Ada: 133
   Agnes Bordilla: 103, 132, 184, 250, 251, 402
   Agnes Druscilla: 103, 104, 402
   Allan: 132, 402
   Ann Betta: 185
   Argus: 133
   Benjamin Scott: 286
   Calvin: 103, 132, 402
   Carl: 132, 402
   Charles Dale: 185, 251, 252, 286
   Charles Floyd: 132, 402
   Clair: 133
   Clarence Eugene: 103, 104, 402
   Clarence Eugene: 132, 185, 251, 252, 286
   David Grier McClelland: 103, 132, 133, 185, 402
   Della: 133
   Dellie: 132, 402
   Dominic Charles: 286
   Edward Sheaffer: 185
   Elizabeth Trough: 104, 133, 402
   Erik Michael: 252
   Flora Pauline: 132, 402
   Frances Emma: 103, 402
   George: 133, 402
   George Grove: 103, 402
   Henry: 132, 402
   Homer: 185
   Infant: 103, 402
   James Lee: 252
   John Charles: 252, 286
   Lee Piper: 185, 252
   Lester Sheaffer: 132, 185, 252
   Lettie: 132, 402
   Lewis: 103, 184, 402
   Lewis: 133, 185
   Lois: 185
   Lorretta: 133
   Margaret Elizabeth Alice: 132, 184, 251, 285, 286, 289, 402
   Marian Esther: 132, 402
   Marion: 133
   Marion Anson: 103, 402
   Martha: 132, 402
   Mary Elizabeth: 103, 131, 132, 402
   Mildred: 133, 402
   Newton: 104, 133, 402
   Nora Griffin: 104, 133, 402
   Oberdick: 104, 402
   Pearle Viola: 132, 184, 402
   Ray: 132, 402
   Ray: 133
   Robert Michael: 185, 252
   Ruth: 133, 402
   Sharon Agnes: 252
   Theodore: 103, 132, 184, 185, 251, 252, 285, 286, 289, 402
   Theodore: 132, 402
   Theodore Rice: 185, 402
   Theodore Riley: 132, 185, 402
   Traci Diane: 252
   Wilbur: 132, 402
   William: 103, 402
   Winifred Sue: 252
Goodman -
   Penelope Hendrickson: 402
   Unknown: 402
Gordley -
   Private: 238, 356, 402
   Private: 238, 356, 402
   Private: 238, 356, 402
   Private: 238, 356, 402
Gordon -
   Lenora May: 243, 339, 402
Goring -
   Charlotte: 52, 402
   Francis: 52, 402
   Frederick: 37, 402
   Frederick Augustus: 52, 402
   Frederick Augustus: 52, 402
   Harmon: 52, 402
   James: 52, 402
   John: 52, 402
   Lucretia Caroline: 52, 402
   Sarah: 52, 402
   William: 52, 402
Gorton -
   Hicks: 402
Goss -
   Private: 209, 402
Gottschall -
   Lottie: 135, 402
Gould -
   Catherine: 53, 402
Govier -
   Cecil Burt: 151, 402
Grabiel -
   Eva: 293
Graby -
   George: 86, 402
Grace -
   Daniel Sverre: 282, 402
   Dorman John: 220, 402
   Dorman John III: 220, 282, 402
   Kathleen Kay (aka: Kathy): 220, 403, 437
   Nancy Anne: 220, 282, 403
   Robert Joseph: 282, 403
Graeff -
   Abraham: 49, 403
   Elizabeth: 49, 403
   Jacob: 49, 403
   Kate: 49, 403
   Maria: 49, 403
   Mathias: 49, 403
   Mathias: 49, 403
   Susan: 49, 403
Graff -
   Barbara: 15, 403
   Christian: 9, 403
Graham -
   Mary: 220, 403
Grant -
   Doris May: 154, 403
   George: 154, 403
   Leo Richard: 121, 318, 403
   Lola: 154, 403
Grason -
   Private: 238, 355, 403
Graves -
   Private: 201, 403
Gray -
   Charlotte Elizabeth: 42, 403
   Gladys Marie: 206, 403
   Private: 248
   Robert: 153, 403
Graybill -
   Martha: 403
   Private: 167, 327, 403
   Private: 167, 328, 403
Green -
   Private: 205, 403
   Rachael: 114, 403
   Winnifred Iva Frances: 217, 403
Greenawald -
   Joseph: 83, 403
Greenwalt -
   Private: 280, 403
Gregg -
   Private: 177, 337, 403
Greider -
   Zook Elizabeth: 11, 30
   John: 294, 403
   Veronica: 11, 30, 46
Greiner -
   Private: 246
   Private: 246
   Private: 246
   Private: 246
   Private: 246
Greiser -
   Private: 234, 351, 403
Grider -
   Christina: 403
Grieves -
   Minnie: 119, 403
Griffen -
   Frank Webb: 191, 403
   Frank Webb: 192, 403
   Private: 191, 259, 403
Griffith -
   Charles Francis: 101
   Deborah: 403
   Private: 264, 403
   Private: 264, 403
Grill -
   Private: 181
Grimes -
   Private: 247
   Private: 247
   Private: 247
   Private: 247
Groff -
   Abraham: 403
   Anna Elizabeth: 9, 12, 14, 403

Annie: 403
Barbara: 14, 403
Barbara: 403
Barbara: 403
Barbara: 403
Betsey: 403
Daniel: 403
David: 403
David: 403
Elizabeth: 403
Elizabeth: 403
Elizabeth Betsy: 403
Emanuel: 299, 403
Fronica: 27, 403
George: 403
Hannah: 403
Hans: 403
Jacob: 403
John: 403
John: 403
John: 403
John: 403
John: 404
John: 404
Marcus: 404
Margaret: 404
Marie: 404
Mary: 404
Mary: 297, 404
Mary: 404
Mary R.: 125, 322, 404
Mathias: 35, 404
Norman Myer: 167, 328, 404
Peter: 404
Private: 283, 361, 404
Private: 283, 361, 404
Private: 283, 361, 404
Private: 225, 342, 404
Private: 225, 342, 404
Private: 225, 342, 404
Private: 225, 342, 404
Private: 225, 342, 404
Private: 226, 344, 404
Private: 226, 344, 404
Private: 167, 232, 328, 349, 350, 404
Private: 167, 232, 328, 350, 404
Private: 167, 232, 328, 350, 404
Private: 167, 232, 328, 350, 404
Private: 167, 232, 233, 328, 350, 404
Private: 167, 233, 328, 350, 404
Private: 233, 350, 404
Private: 233, 350, 404
Private: 233, 350, 404
Private: 233, 350, 404
Private: 233, 350, 404
Private: 233, 350, 404
Private: 233, 350, 404
Private: 232, 350, 404
Private: 232, 350, 404
Private: 232, 350, 404
Private: 232, 350, 404
Private: 232, 350, 404
Private: 232, 350, 404
Private: 232, 350, 404

Private: 232, 350, 404
Private: 236, 353, 404
Private: 236, 353, 404
Private: 239, 356, 404
Private: 174, 335, 404
Samuel: 404
Susanna: 404
Groff/Grove -
    Unknown: 404
Grogg -
    Private: 276, 277, 404
    Robert: 144, 404
Groh -
    Elizabeth: 84, 404
Gropp -
    Gregorius: 18
Gross -
    Private: 209, 404
Grossman -
    Andrew: 404
    Catharine: 404
    Daniel: 404
    David: 404
    George: 404
    Henry: 404
    Jacob: 404
    Jacob: 404
    John: 404
    Levi: 404
    Margaret: 404
Grove -
    Abraham: 70, 404
    Ada: 210, 405
    Annie: 70, 405
    Daniel: 70, 405
    George: 70, 405
    Henry: 70, 405
    Jean: 162, 405
    John: 70, 405
    Martin: 70, 405
    Martin: 70, 405
    Mary: 70, 405
    Mary: 70, 405
    Myrtle: 159, 405
    Samuel: 70, 405
    Samuel: 70, 405
Grubb -
    Isabelle Stoffer: 109, 405
    Paul: 181
Grubb/Krupp -
    Enos F. Grubb: 405
Grube -
    Daniel: 405
    Daniel: 405
    David: 405
    Elizabeth: 405
    Elsie Maye: 258, 405
    Isaac: 405
    John: 405
    John: 98, 405
    Lavina: 405
    Leah: 405
    Margaret: 405
    Margaret: 405
    Peter: 405

Peter: 405
Sarah Ann: 405
Gruber -
    Irvin: 253, 405
    James D: 253, 405
    Jihn B: 253, 405
Grudenroth -
    Unknown: 405
Gruen -
    David Edward: 215, 405
    Private: 215, 405
    Private: 215, 405
    Private: 215, 405
    Private: 215, 405
    Private: 215, 405
Gryder -
    Mary: 405
Gut -
    Jacob: 16, 292, 405
Guth -
    Barbara: 15, 292, 405
Guthrie -
    Lewin: 259, 405
    Private: 259, 405
    Private: 259, 405
    Private: 259, 405
Habecker -
    Christian: 42, 43, 405
    Christian: 42, 405
    Christian: 43, 405
    Esther: 42, 405
    Esther: 43, 405
Hachborn -
    Alice: 159, 405
Hackman -
    Aaron: 97, 405
    Abraham: 41, 405
    Abraham: 41, 61, 405
    Abraham Beidler: 61, 405
    ABRAHAM HERR: 41, 405
    Alice Ann B: 98, 405
    Alice Lorraine: 163, 221, 222, 405
    Amy Lynn: 222, 405
    Andrew: 97, 405
    Andrew Baer: 68, 98, 120, 162, 163, 220-223, 282, 283, 405
    Andrew Hess: 120, 405
    Anna: 61, 405
    Anna: 68, 406
    Anna Maria: 61, 406
    Annie Marian: 163, 221, 283, 406
    Augustus Miller: 98, 406
    Baby: 120, 406
    Benjamin Beidler: 61, 406
    Betty Lou: 163, 222, 406
    Brenda Kay: 221, 406
    Christian Stauffer: 41, 406
    Christopher Allen: 221, 406
    Cindy Lynn: 221, 406
    Daniel Michael: 221, 406
    David: 97, 406
    David Baer: 68, 97, 98, 406
    David Hiestand: 68, 406
    Dennis Ray: 221, 406

Dorothy Elaine: 162, 220, 282, 406
Elizabeth: 31, 406
Elizabeth: 61, 406
Emma Amelia: 98, 406
Emma Amelia: 121, 163, 223, 254, 406
Gary Jay: 221, 406
Gerald Allen: 221, 406
Henry: 97, 406
Henry Hess: 120, 162, 220, 221, 282, 406
Henry Stauffer (Hockman): 41, 61, 406
Jacob: 97, 406
Jacob Baer: 68, 97, 406
John: 41, 406
John Allen: 162, 406
John Beidler: 61, 406
Joseph: 97, 406
Karen Lee: 222, 406
Kenneth Lee: 163, 221, 406
Kenneth Lee: 221, 406
Leonard: 97, 406
Margaret Ann: 163, 221, 406
Michael Frederick: 221, 406
Mitchell Keith: 222, 406
Myrtle: 120, 406
Randall Lee: 221, 406
Ray Donald: 163, 221, 406
Rea Ann: 221, 406
Richard Forney: 163, 222, 406
Richard Hess: 120, 163, 222, 406
Robert Forney: 163, 406
Robert Lorin: 163, 222, 406
Romanus Andrew B: 98, 406
Samuel: 41, 406
Steven Dean: 222, 406
Tammy Sue: 221, 406
Terry Lee: 221, 406
Thomas Jon: 221, 406
Tony Robert: 222, 406
Violet Gertrude: 121, 163, 222, 406
Walter Hess: 120, 163, 222, 406
Wanda Jean: 221, 406
Willard Henry (aka: Bill): 162, 221, 374, 406
Willis Brenner: 98, 120, 121, 162, 163, 220-223, 254, 282, 283, 406
Willis Hess: 120, 162, 163, 221, 222, 283, 406
Willis Martin: 163, 222, 406

Hagar -
Hannah: 55, 406

Hagey -
Christian: 30, 406

Haggert -
Gertrude: 185, 406
Glen: 185, 406
Robert: 185, 406

Hahn -
Bobby: 149, 407
Earl D.: 149, 407
Leland Eugene: 149, 407
Private: 212, 407
Private: 212, 407
Private: 212, 407
Wayne: 149, 212, 407

Hails -
Private: 175, 336, 407

Haldeman -
Abraham Bergey: 407
Ammond Stauffer: 407
Magdelena Funk (Halterman): 407
Private: 177, 338, 407
Sarah (Sallie) Stauffer (Halteman): 407

Hale -
Absalom: 80, 407
John: 80, 407

Hall -
Benjamin: 116, 407
Cordelia Abigail: 116, 407
Faye: 116, 407
Herman M.: 217, 407
Lola: 116, 154, 407
Mildred: 116, 407
Nellie: 116, 154, 407
Nettie: 116, 154, 407
Nina Marie: 407
Private: 217, 407
Private: 217, 407
Vera: 116, 154, 407
Verna: 116, 407

Halla -
Emma: 92, 407

Hallman -
Ella Harley: 407
Unknown: 407

Halwell -
Nellie: 147, 407

Hambright -
Sarah: 60, 407

Hamilton -
Alice: 119, 407
Aura Titus: 193, 407
Belfry: 162, 407
Charles Wesley: 193, 407
Elton Kenneth: 193, 261, 407
Harold Leon: 193, 407
Private: 261, 407
Private: 261, 407
Private: 193, 261, 407
Private: 193, 407
Private: 210, 277, 407
Private: 277, 407
Private: 277, 407
Private: 162, 407
Private: 162, 407
Private: 162, 407
Vera Lucretia: 193, 407
William: 71, 407

Hamm -
Lloyd: 159, 407

Hammond -
Allen: 91, 314, 407
George: 407

Hamrick -
Private: 207, 407

Hanesworth -
Private: 204, 407

Hanna -
Rev. Charles: 137, 407

Hanrahan -
Private: 182

Hansford -
Dora Maud: 407
William Allen: 407
William Allen: 407

Hardgrove -
Private: 268, 407
Private: 269, 407
Private: 269, 407
Private: 269, 407
Private: 269, 407
Private: 269, 407

Harding -
Jessie Bell: 143, 408
Mabel Olive: 215, 408

Hardy -
Alice Loretta: 107, 408
George: 209, 408
Henry Franklin: 107, 408
Ida May: 107, 408
Private: 209, 408
Private: 209, 408
Private: 209, 408
Private: 209, 408
Private: 209, 408
Private: 280, 408
Private: 271, 408
Sylvester: 107, 408
William S: 107, 408

Hare -
Sarah: 93, 94, 408

Harlan -
Iva Martha: 149, 408
Pearl R: 147, 408

Harley -
David Stauffer: 408
Elizabeth Stauffer: 408
Jacob Rev.: 408
Jacob Stauffer: 408
James A. Stover: 408
Jesse Stauffer: 408
John Haldeman: 408
John Stauffer Rev.: 408
Joseph Stauffer: 408
Maria Stauffer: 408
Rebecca: 408
Rudolph Stauffer: 408
Samuel Buckwalter: 408
Samuel Hoffman: 408
Thelma Wingert: 408

Harmon -
Private: 177, 338, 408
Private: 177, 338, 408

Harnish -
David: 7, 408
Elizabeth: 7, 45, 408
Private: 196, 263, 408
Private: 196, 408
Private: 196, 408
Private: 196, 408

Private: 196, 408
Wilbert John: 196, 408
Harper -
Eleanor Jean: 152, 408
Gordon Charles: 152, 408
Lois Marjorie: 152, 408
Harrington -
Alfred: 185, 252, 408
Almer H: 185, 252, 286, 408
Beryl F: 185, 252, 408
Doris J: 252, 408
Frances: 186, 408
Frances Anne: 252, 408
Frank B: 185, 408
Fred: 185, 408
Grace: 185, 252, 408
Jack A: 252, 408
Lillian R: 185, 252, 408
Lorene: 252, 408
Lucile: 185, 253, 408
Lynn: 252, 408
Margaret H: 252, 286, 408
Harrison -
Private: 247
Private: 247
Private: 247
Private: 247
Harrop -
Mary: 219, 408
Harsh -
Miles Eby: 124, 321, 408
Private: 124, 321, 408
Hart -
Private: 201, 408
Harter -
Private: 193, 260, 408
Private: 260, 409
Private: 260, 409
Private: 260, 409
Hartigan -
Joseph Edward: 260, 409
Private: 260, 409
Private: 260, 409
Private: 260, 409
Hartman -
Fannie: 57, 305, 409
Fern: 190, 409
Living: 257, 409
Hartog -
Private: 289, 409
Hartranft -
Private: 164, 324, 409
Hartzler -
Private: 229, 347, 409
Private: 229, 347, 409
Hasler -
Elizabeth: 14, 16, 18, 409
Hassler -
Michael: 254, 409
William T: 254, 409
Hastetter -
Christiana: 40, 58, 74, 103, 131, 184, 250, 285, 409
Hatfield -

Nellie: 193, 409
Hauch -
Private: 240, 358, 409
Private: 240, 358, 409
Hauck -
Milton H.: 306, 409
Hauser -
Barbara: 15, 291, 409
Haverstick -
Maria: 70, 409
Hawk -
Edgar Paul: 195, 409
Private: 195, 409
Private: 195, 409
Hawkins -
Jewell Dean: 156, 409
Private: 182
Jr. Private: 183, 249
Private: 249
Hawthorne -
Private: 183
Haynes -
Agatha E.: 137, 196, 263, 409
Albert W.: 137, 409
Alberta: 137, 409
Dorothy: 137, 196, 409
Ethel: 137, 409
Josephine: 137, 409
Marjorie: 137, 196, 409
Heagy -
Barbara: 104, 409
Heatwole -
Alice Virginia: 127, 317, 409
Heavyside -
Joan Elizabeth: 263, 409
Private: 263, 409
Stuart Joseph Odin: 263, 409
Hechler -
Lillie R. (Heckler): 409
Heckman -
Julianna: 293, 409
Samuel: 83, 409
Hedrick -
Clarence: 111, 409
Hedrix -
Private: 260, 409
Heestand -
Abraham: 88, 409
Anna: 89, 409
Infant: 89, 409
Issac S: 89, 409
Joseph: 89, 409
Levi: 88, 409
Samuel: 89, 409
Heffleblower -
Henry: 78, 409
Heilman -
Private: 175, 336, 409
Heimbach -
Private: 232, 350, 409
Private: 231, 348, 409
Private: 231, 348, 409
Hein -
Linda M: 287, 409

Heinemann -
Private: 208, 409
Heiney -
Mary C.: 73, 309, 409
Heisey -
Private: 224, 341, 342, 409
Heishman -
Lydia Pearl: 168, 329, 409
Heistand -
Abraham: 25, 409
Ann: 10, 35, 409
Elizabeth: 10, 26
Hemley -
Catherine: 409
Henderson -
Private: 409
Hendrickson -
Ruth Louise Buzzard: 410
Unknown: 410
Hendrix -
Jolly A.: 196, 410
Private: 260, 410
Private: 260, 410
Private: 196, 410
Private: 196, 410
Hennelly -
Private: 168, 328, 410
Private: 168, 328, 410
Henry -
Fred: 162, 410
Private: 162, 410
Private: 162, 410
Hepler -
Private: 274, 410
Private: 274, 410
Private: 274, 410
Herbein -
Maria: 410
Herbster -
William Martin: 192, 410
Hernley -
Abraham: 34, 410
Anna: 7-9, 27, 46, 410
Isaac: 10, 34, 410
John: 34, 410
Mary: 410
Hernly -
Isaac: 10, 28, 410
Herr -
Abraham: 34, 410
Abraham: 10, 33, 34, 410
Abraham: 37, 410
Abraham: 42, 410
Abraham: 10, 28, 410
Abraham: 32, 42, 410
Abraham: 53, 410
Abraham: 84, 410
Abram: 71, 410
Alta: 98, 410
Ann: 410
Ann: 410
Anna: 37, 410
Anna: 34, 410
Barabara: 6, 8, 9, 298, 410

Barbara: 42, 410
Barbara: 410
Barbara: 34, 410
Barbara Ann: 410
Barbara M.: 84, 410
Benjamin: 98, 410
Benjamin: 32, 410
Benjamin: 43, 410
C. Bachman: 98, 410
Catherine: 37, 410
Charles S.: 98, 410
Christian: 37, 410
Christian: 16, 410
Christian: 29, 37, 410
Christian: 34, 410
Christian: 84, 410
Christian B.: 84, 410
Daughter2: 410
David: 37, 410
David: 27, 32, 410
David: 32, 410
David: 410
Elisabeth: 34, 410
Elizabeth: 43, 410
Elizabeth: 84, 410
Elizabeth (Betsey): 410
Esther: 9, 410
Esther: 32, 42, 410
Esther: 32, 43, 411
Esther: 34, 411
Fannie: 411
Fanny: 27, 31, 411
Fanny: 32, 42, 411
Fanny: 43, 411
Fronica: 27, 411
Henry: 411
Henry: 25, 411
Henry P: 71, 411
Hettie: 42, 411
Jacob G.: 101, 311, 411
Jacob P: 71, 411
Johannes: 16, 411
John: 42, 411
John: 38, 411
John: 32, 411
John: 53, 71, 99, 121, 163, 411
Joseph: 84, 411
Lydia: 84, 411
Magdalena: 70, 411
Magdalena: 84, 411
Magdalene: 411
Maria: 411
Maria: 84, 411
Maria Margaretha: 12-14, 17, 291, 411
Martin R.: 304, 411
Mary: 71, 411
Mary: 42, 411
Mary: 411
Mary: 34, 411
Mary: 32, 411
Minnie P: 71, 99, 121, 163, 411
Nancy: 42, 411
Nancy: 84, 411
Private: 174, 335, 411
Private: 174, 239, 335, 357, 411

Private: 174, 335, 411
Private: 240, 357, 411
Rev. John: 411
Rudolph: 38, 53, 411
Samuel: 27, 411
Samuel: 84, 411
Susanna: 411
Unnamed: 32, 411
Veronica: 7, 411
Veronica: 84, 411

Hershberger -
Anna: 86, 411
Christian: 31, 411

Hershey -
Abraham: 25, 27, 32, 42-44, 411
Rev. Abraham: 11, 26, 30, 40, 46
Abraham: 27, 411
Abraham: 27, 32, 411
Abraham: 9, 30, 40, 57, 296, 300, 305, 411
Abraham: 9, 30, 296, 411
Abraham: 32, 43, 68, 411
Abraham: 7, 40, 57, 74, 101, 128, 179, 300, 305, 310, 315, 323, 338, 411
Abraham: 43, 411
Abraham L.: 31, 411
Adah (Ada): 25, 411
Adah Louisa: 42, 411
Adli: 11, 26
Aldus: 64, 411
Alice Light: 63, 310, 411
Amanda: 57, 305, 411
Amos F: 46, 64, 91, 411
Amos H: 67, 411
Amos H: 57, 305, 411
Amy Landis: 113, 412
Andreas: 39, 56
Andrew: 10, 26, 29, 38, 39, 56
Andrew: 29, 39
Andrew: 9, 30, 296, 412
Andrew: 39
Andrew L K: 113, 412
Rev. Andrew Stauffer: 8, 10, 12, 13, 24, 25, 29, 30, 38-40, 56-58, 73, 74, 99-103, 121-131, 164-184, 223-250, 283-285, 296
Ann: 28, 412
Ann Elisabeth: 8-10, 13, 25, 28, 33-35, 46-49, 57, 65-69, 95-98, 120, 162, 163, 220-223, 282, 283, 412
Anna: 66, 412
Anna: 39
Anna: 56
Anna: 32, 412
Anna: 12, 24, 25, 28, 29, 36-38, 49-55, 69-73, 98, 99, 121, 163, 412
Anna: 29
Anna: 27, 412
Anna: 30, 39
Anna: 9, 33, 46, 64, 91, 303, 412
Anna: 39
Anna: 56, 304, 412

Anna: 56, 304, 412
Anna: 43, 412
Anna Elizabeth: 25, 27, 412
Anna Kreider: 123, 320, 412
Anna L.: 57, 306, 412
Annie: 57, 305, 412
Annie: 45, 412
Annie: 412
Annie: 63, 90, 113, 310, 314, 322, 412
Barbara: 56
Barbara: 32, 412
Barbara: 25, 27, 31, 412
Barbara: 27, 32, 42, 43, 412
Barbara: 39
Barbara: 73, 309, 412
Barbara Ann: 43, 412
Barbara Elizabeth: 101, 125, 176, 314, 322, 337, 412
Barbara Hostetter: 11, 28, 33, 41, 412
Benjamin: 66, 412
Benjamin: 38
Benjamin: 56
Benjamin: 28, 412
Benjamin: 9, 25, 28, 412
Benjamin: 10, 26
Benjamin: 412
Benjamin: 25, 27, 32, 44, 412
Benjamin: 8, 27, 412
Benjamin: 27, 412
Benjamin: 7, 39, 300, 412
Benjamin: 39, 300, 412
Benjamin: 39, 300, 412
Benjamin: 32, 412
Benjamin: 43, 412
Benjamin H: 67, 412
Benjamin Stauffer: 8-12, 24, 25, 27, 28, 33-35, 44-49, 57, 62-69, 89-91, 95-98, 113, 120, 150, 162, 163, 178, 179, 220-223, 244, 282, 283, 412
Bessie M: 63, 310, 412
Catharine: 32, 412
Catharine: 11, 26
Catharine: 29
Catharine: 31, 412
Catherine: 57, 305, 412
Catherine: 27, 412
Catherine: 27, 412
Catherine: 39
Catherine: 32, 412
Chauncey: 63, 91, 412
Christian: 28, 412
Christian: 7-9, 11, 13, 25, 27, 28, 33, 41, 44-46, 62-64, 89-91, 113, 150, 178, 179, 244, 412
Christian: 25, 27, 31, 42, 412
Christian: 10, 25
Christian: 27, 412
Christian: 27, 32, 43, 44, 68, 412
Christian: 6-9, 30, 39, 45, 46, 57, 74, 101, 128, 179, 296, 300, 305, 310, 314, 315, 322,

538

323, 338, 412
Christian: 39
Christian: 7, 33, 46, 64, 91, 412
Christian: 7, 40, 300, 412
Christian: 58
Christian: 6, 45, 63, 90, 305, 310, 314, 412
Christian: 31, 412
Christian: 63, 310, 412
Christian B.: 43, 412
Christian L.: 57, 306, 412
Christian Schmidt: 9, 10, 12, 15, 24, 412
Christian Stauffer: 12, 24-27, 31, 32, 42-44, 412
Clifford Eby: 123, 173, 238, 239, 320, 333, 356, 412
Cloyd Gray: 42, 412
Cora: 63, 413
Daniel F: 46, 413
Daniel Webster: 31, 42, 413
David: 32, 413
David: 66, 67, 413
David: 32, 413
David: 56, 304, 413
David C: 67, 413
David Warren: 100, 123, 174, 239, 240, 313, 320, 335, 357, 413
Diana: 58, 74, 101-103, 128-131, 179-184, 244-250
Doris Mae: 101, 125, 177, 178, 314, 322, 338, 413
Edith Celeste: 123, 320, 413
Edith May: 100, 313, 413
Edna: 123, 320, 413
Elias: 56, 304, 413
Elias H: 6, 45, 63, 90, 91, 113, 305, 310, 314, 322, 413
Elisabeth: 25, 26, 31, 42, 413
Elisabeth: 67, 413
Elizabeth: 57, 305, 413
Elizabeth: 39
Elizabeth: 413
Elizabeth: 27, 32, 413
Elizabeth: 8, 46, 413
Elizabeth: 29
Elizabeth: 8, 30, 40, 46, 413
Elizabeth: 8, 30, 296, 413
Elizabeth: 7, 33, 413
Elizabeth: 32, 413
Elizabeth: 32, 44, 413
Elizabeth: 32, 413
Elizabeth: 39
Elizabeth: 7, 40, 300, 413
Elizabeth: 56, 304, 413
Elizabeth: 6, 45, 305, 413
Elizabeth: 43, 413
Elizabeth: 57, 305, 413
Elizabeth: 58
Elizabeth: 58
Elizabeth: 46, 64, 91, 413
Elizabeth: 73, 100, 124, 175, 240, 241, 309, 313, 321, 335, 336, 358, 413
Elizabeth B: 63, 413

Elizabeth Frick: 45, 63, 413
Ellen: 73, 309, 413
Dr. Elmer Light: 63, 310, 413
Elsie D.: 101, 124, 314, 321, 413
Emily Jane: 44, 413
Emma: 44, 413
Enos: 57, 305, 413
Enos Jacob: 73, 100, 123, 124, 172-174, 237-240, 309, 313, 320, 332-335, 355-358, 413
Ephraim: 66, 413
Erma E.: 123, 171, 237, 320, 332, 354, 413
Erma Elizabeth: 100, 313, 413
Esta Mae: 123, 320, 413
Esther: 66, 413
Esther: 27, 413
Esther: 8, 27, 33, 44, 62, 89, 90, 113, 150, 178, 179, 244, 413
Esther: 27, 413
Esther: 39
Esther: 32, 413
Esther (Hester): 25, 413
Esther Elizabeth: 100, 124, 175, 241, 314, 321, 336, 358, 359, 413
Esther G: 64, 413
Ethel Pauline: 100, 313, 413
Eugene Light: 63, 90, 310, 314, 413
Ezra Frantz: 63, 91, 113, 310, 314, 322, 413
Ezra Frantz: 91, 314, 413
Fannie: 57, 305, 413
Fanny: 45, 413
Feronica: 28, 293, 413
Fianna: 46, 64, 413
Frances: 101, 125, 314, 321, 413
Francis: 45, 413
Freda M: 90, 314, 413
Frederick: 32, 414
Fronica: 39, 300, 414
Galen Clair: 123, 171, 237, 320, 332, 355, 414
Galen Warren: 100, 123, 171, 237, 313, 320, 332, 354, 355, 414
George: 32, 44, 414
George Daniel: 42, 414
Gladys Edna: 123, 172, 238, 320, 333, 356, 414
Grace Elizabeth: 100, 313, 414
Harriet: 95, 414
Hazel Pauline: 123, 172, 238, 320, 333, 355, 414
Henrietta: 58
Henry: 39
Henry: 11, 26, 30, 40, 58, 74, 101-103, 128-131, 179-184, 244-250
Henry: 29
Henry: 27, 32, 44, 414
Henry: 40, 58, 74, 101-103, 128-131, 179-184, 244-250
Henry: 40, 58

Henry: 32, 414
Henry: 32, 414
Henry: 43, 414
Henry: 57, 306, 414
Henry: 57, 305, 414
Henry Clay: 100, 123, 172, 173, 237-239, 313, 320, 332, 333, 355, 356, 414
Henry H: 57, 305, 414
Henry Hershey: 6, 45, 63, 305, 309, 310, 414
Henry L: 58
Henry Peter: 73, 100, 124, 175, 241, 309, 313, 321, 336, 358, 414
Hester: 43, 414
Hester (Esther): 32, 44, 414
Ida Anne: 44, 414
Infant: 73, 309, 414
Infant: 73, 309, 414
Isaac: 11, 26
Isaac: 40
Isaac: 7, 33, 414
Isaac: 45, 414
Isaac: 6, 45, 305, 414
Isaac Hernley: 6-8, 27, 33, 45, 46, 57, 63, 64, 90, 91, 113, 305, 414
Isaiah B.: 73, 100, 123, 171, 237, 309, 313, 320, 332, 354, 355, 414
Jacob: 38
Jacob: 11, 414
Jacob: 7, 9, 11, 12, 28, 33, 39, 46, 64, 91, 300, 414
Jacob: 29, 38, 56
Jacob: 8, 30, 296, 414
Jacob: 39, 56, 73, 99-101, 121-125, 164-178, 223-243, 283-285, 300, 304, 309, 312-314, 318-322, 324-338, 340-362, 414
Jacob: 39, 56, 300, 304, 414
Jacob: 40
Jacob: 40
Jacob: 7, 40, 57, 300, 305, 414
Jacob: 56
Jacob: 46, 414
Jacob: 31, 414
Jacob: 43, 414
Jacob: 64, 414
Jacob: 63, 310, 414
Jacob B: 90, 314, 414
Jacob Frantz: 6, 7, 33, 45, 57, 63, 90, 91, 113, 305, 309, 414
Jacob H: 6, 45, 63, 90, 305, 310, 314, 414
Jacob L: 7, 40, 300, 414
Jacob Menno: 56, 304, 414
Jacob Snavely: 7, 8, 11, 26, 30, 39, 40, 46, 56, 57, 73, 74, 99-101, 121-128, 164-179, 223-244, 283-285, 296, 414
Jay Paul: 125, 177, 242, 243, 322, 338, 360, 414
Jean Lois: 123, 320, 414

John: 57, 305, 414
John: 38
John: 11, 26, 30, 39
John: 8, 30, 39, 56, 57, 73, 99-101, 121-127, 164-178, 223-244, 283-285, 296, 300, 304, 305, 309, 312-314, 318-322, 324-338, 340-362, 414
John: 8, 28, 414
John: 29
John: 27, 414
John: 40
John: 40
John: 39, 300, 414
John: 39, 300, 414
John: 7, 40, 300, 414
John: 39
John: 32, 414
John: 43, 414
John: 58
John: 58
John Adam Light: 63, 310, 414
John Alan: 124, 321, 414
John Eby: 56, 304, 414
John F: 46, 64, 414
John Frantz: 7, 33, 45, 63, 414
John Rudy: 42, 414
Joseph: 66, 414
Joseph: 66, 414
Joseph: 57, 305, 415
Joseph: 9, 30, 296, 415
Joseph: 40
Joseph: 40
Joseph: 39, 57, 300, 305, 415
Joseph: 6, 45, 305, 415
Joseph: 39, 300, 415
Joseph B: 133, 415
Katherine Rohrer: 91, 314, 415
Katie Light: 63, 310, 415
Landes L.: 57, 306, 415
Laura Light: 63, 310, 415
Lavina: 31, 415
Leah: 45, 415
Leona R: 90, 314, 415
Lester D.: 101, 125, 176, 314, 322, 336, 415
Levi: 57, 305, 415
Lorena: 63, 90, 310, 314, 415
Louisa: 44, 415
Lydia: 57, 305, 415
Lydia: 45, 415
Magdalen: 28, 415
Magdalena: 57, 305, 415
Magdalena: 39, 300, 415
Magdalena: 39
Malcolm Clarence: 44, 415
Margaret: 57, 305, 415
Margaret: 56, 304, 415
Margaret: 32, 415
Maria: 10, 25
Maria: 11, 28, 415
Maria: 29
Maria: 39
Maria: 56, 304, 415
Maria: 45, 415
Maria: 43, 415

Maria Elizabeth: 91, 113, 114, 314, 322, 415
Mark Eby: 100, 123, 173, 174, 239, 313, 320, 333, 334, 356, 357, 415
Martha A.: 73, 309, 415
Martin: 30, 40, 58, 74, 101-103, 128-131, 179-184, 244-250
Martin: 40
Martin: 45, 415
Martin Eby: 73, 100, 124, 175, 176, 241, 309, 313, 321, 336, 358, 359, 415
Martin F: 46, 64, 415
Mary: 64, 415
Mary: 10, 25, 28, 35, 49, 415
Mary: 28, 415
Mary: 25, 415
Mary: 27, 415
Mary: 27, 415
Mary: 7, 33, 415
Mary: 32, 44, 415
Mary: 57, 305, 415
Mary: 57, 306, 415
Mary: 73, 309, 415
Mary: 63, 90, 310, 314, 415
Mary A: 58
Mary Clyde: 42, 415
Mary Elizabeth: 31, 415
Mary Emily: 101, 314, 415
Mary F: 64, 415
Mary Helen: 100, 124, 174, 240, 313, 320, 321, 335, 357, 358, 415
Mary Katherine Eby: 32, 43, 415
May B: 64, 415
Menno Frick: 45, 415
Mildred L.: 123, 320, 415
Milton Snavely: 6, 63, 309, 415
Miriam Clara: 100, 124, 176, 241, 314, 321, 336, 359, 415
Monroe Light: 63, 310, 415
Morris Light: 63, 310, 415
Nancy: 6, 7, 39, 45, 57, 300, 305, 309, 310, 314, 322, 415
Nancy: 7, 33, 415
Nancy Ann: 39, 56, 300, 304, 415
Nancy Ann: 32, 43, 415
Naomi: 46, 415
Naomi B: 64, 91, 416
Paul Keene: 100, 124, 175, 241, 313, 321, 336, 358, 416
Paul Kenneth: 124, 175, 241, 321, 336, 358, 416
Peter: 11, 26
Peter: 56, 304, 416
Peter: 56, 73, 99-101, 121-125, 164-178, 223-243, 283-285, 304, 309, 312-314, 318-322, 324-338, 340-362, 416
Peter E.: 40, 57, 300, 304-306, 416
Priscilla: 45, 416
Private: 236, 354, 416
Private: 171, 237, 332, 355, 416
Private: 171, 237, 332, 355, 416
Private: 237, 355, 416

Private: 237, 355, 416
Private: 123, 172, 237, 320, 332, 355, 416
Private: 123, 172, 320, 332, 416
Private: 123, 172, 237, 320, 333, 355, 416
Private: 123, 172, 320, 333, 416
Private: 172, 238, 333, 355, 416
Private: 172, 238, 333, 355, 416
Private: 172, 238, 333, 355, 356, 416
Private: 238, 356, 416
Private: 238, 356, 416
Private: 238, 356, 416
Private: 238, 355, 416
Private: 238, 355, 416
Private: 238, 355, 416
Private: 238, 355, 416
Private: 238, 355, 416
Private: 238, 355, 416
Private: 173, 333, 416
Private: 173, 333, 416
Private: 173, 333, 416
Private: 173, 238, 239, 333, 356, 416
Private: 173, 239, 333, 356, 416
Private: 239, 356, 416
Private: 239, 356, 416
Private: 239, 356, 416
Private: 239, 356, 416
Private: 172, 237, 333, 355, 416
Private: 172, 237, 333, 355, 416
Private: 237, 355, 416
Private: 238, 355, 416
Private: 172, 333, 416
Private: 172, 333, 416
Private: 172, 333, 416
Private: 172, 333, 416
Private: 172, 333, 416
Private: 172, 332, 416
Private: 172, 237, 332, 355, 416
Private: 172, 332, 416
Private: 123, 173, 320, 333, 334, 416
Private: 123, 173, 320, 334, 416
Private: 123, 173, 320, 334, 416
Private: 123, 173, 239, 320, 334, 356, 416
Private: 123, 173, 320, 334, 416
Private: 123, 173, 239, 320, 334, 356, 416
Private: 123, 174, 239, 320, 334, 357, 416
Private: 174, 239, 334, 357, 416
Private: 174, 239, 334, 357, 416
Private: 174, 239, 334, 357, 416
Private: 174, 239, 334, 357, 416
Private: 239, 357, 416
Private: 239, 357, 416
Private: 173, 334, 416
Private: 173, 334, 416
Private: 173, 334, 416
Private: 173, 334, 416
Private: 173, 334, 416
Private: 173, 334, 417
Private: 173, 334, 417
Private: 123, 174, 239, 320, 335,

357, 417
Private: 174, 335, 417
Private: 174, 240, 335, 357, 417
Private: 174, 335, 417
Private: 174, 240, 335, 357, 417
Private: 174, 240, 335, 357, 417
Private: 240, 357, 417
Private: 240, 357, 417
Private: 240, 357, 417
Private: 240, 357, 417
Private: 240, 357, 417
Private: 175, 336, 417
Private: 175, 336, 417
Private: 175, 241, 336, 358, 417
Private: 175, 336, 417
Private: 175, 336, 417
Private: 175, 336, 417
Private: 125, 322, 417
Private: 125, 176, 322, 336, 417
Private: 125, 176, 241, 242, 322, 337, 359, 417
Private: 125, 176, 242, 322, 337, 359, 417
Private: 125, 177, 242, 322, 337, 359, 360, 417
Private: 125, 177, 242, 322, 337, 360, 417
Private: 125, 177, 322, 338, 417
Private: 177, 242, 338, 360, 417
Private: 177, 242, 338, 360, 417
Private: 177, 243, 338, 360, 417
Private: 243, 360, 417
Private: 243, 360, 417
Private: 177, 242, 337, 360, 417
Private: 242, 360, 417
Private: 242, 360, 417
Private: 177, 242, 337, 360, 417
Private: 177, 337, 417
Private: 242, 360, 417
Private: 242, 360, 417
Private: 242, 360, 417
Ralph Glenn: 123, 172, 238, 320, 333, 355, 417
Reba L.: 101, 125, 177, 314, 322, 338, 417
Richard Henry: 124, 175, 321, 336, 417
Robert Landis: 91, 417
Rudolph: 27, 31, 42, 417
Samuel: 7, 33, 45, 63, 64, 91, 417
Samuel F: 91, 417
Samuel Harnish: 45, 63, 91, 417
Samuel Mark: 63, 417
Sarah: 32, 417
Sarah Lucinda: 73, 99, 121-123, 164-171, 223-236, 283-285, 309, 312, 318, 319, 324-332, 340-354, 360-362, 417
Sarena: 6, 63, 309, 417
Silas N.: 73, 101, 124, 125, 176-178, 241-243, 309, 314, 321, 322, 336-338, 359, 360, 417
Spencer: 44, 417
Susan: 67, 417
Susan: 56, 304, 417

Susan: 56, 304, 417
Susan: 57, 74, 101, 128, 179, 305, 310, 315, 323, 338, 417
Susanna: 6-9, 33, 39, 45, 46, 300, 417
Susanna: 7, 40, 300, 417
Unnamed: 56, 304, 417
Unnamed Infant: 27, 417
Unnamed Infant: 27, 417
Veronica: 8, 27, 417
Veronica: 39, 56, 73, 101, 125-127, 178, 243, 244, 300, 304, 305, 309, 314, 417
Victor Eby: 123, 320, 417
Vincent Denlinger: 123, 174, 240, 320, 335, 357, 417
Virginia: 63, 310, 418
William Nelson: 123, 320, 418
Willis Daniel: 101, 125, 176, 177, 241-243, 314, 322, 337, 338, 359, 360, 418

Hertzler -
Abraham: 301, 306, 311, 315, 323, 339, 418
Abram: 311, 418
Amos: 306, 418
Annie: 301, 418
Barbara: 301, 418
Barbara: 59, 418
Barbara: 54, 418
Catharine: 311, 418
Charles: 306, 418
Christian: 301, 418
Christian: 306, 418
Daniel: 306, 418
Elizabeth: 301, 418
Elizabeth: 306, 418
Elizabeth: 311, 418
Elizabeth Newcomer: 293, 418
Emma: 311, 418
Gertrude: 311, 315, 323, 339, 418
Jacob: 301, 418
Jacob: 296, 418
John: 301, 418
John: 296, 301, 306, 311, 315, 323, 339, 418
John: 306, 418
Martha: 311, 418
Mary: 301, 418
Mary: 306, 418
Mary: 311, 418
May: 311, 418
Michael S.: 306, 311, 315, 323, 339, 418
Michael S.: 311, 418
Rudolph: 301, 418
Rudolph: 306, 418
Tobias: 311, 418

Hess -
Anna: 418
Anna Hess: 120, 418
Annie: 33, 418
Barbara: 418
Barbara: 33, 418
Barbara: 44, 62, 89, 113, 418
Christian: 418

Christian: 33, 44, 62, 89, 113, 418
Christian M.: 418
Clyde C.: 100, 124, 175, 240, 241, 313, 321, 335, 358, 418
Elizabeth: 418
Elizabeth: 33, 418
Esther: 33, 418
Harold B: 113, 418
Harriet Ann: 100, 313, 418
Harry H: 89, 113, 312, 317, 318, 418
Harry Hershey: 100, 124, 175, 313, 321, 336, 418
Henry: 33, 44, 62, 90, 91, 113, 308, 418
Henry H.: 100, 313, 418
Henry L: 62, 89, 90, 113, 309, 312, 317, 418
Janet Potter: 124, 175, 240, 241, 321, 335, 358, 418
John: 33, 418
John: 8, 33, 418
John: 33, 418
Joseph H: 44, 62, 89, 90, 312, 418
Judith: 418
Magdalena: 31, 33, 418
Magdalene: 418
Margarette: 418
Martha H.: 33, 44, 45, 62, 90, 113, 150, 178, 179, 244, 307, 308, 418
Mary: 419
Mildred Elizabeth: 100, 313, 419
Private: 124, 321, 419
Rhoda Gregory: 124, 175, 321, 336, 419
Ruth Wolf: 113, 318, 419
Samuel: 33, 419
Samuel H: 44, 62, 89-91, 113, 308, 309, 419
Sarah Weidler: 62, 89, 90, 312, 419
Susanna: 419
Susanna: 33, 419
Sybilla: 306, 419
Veronica: 419
Veronica: 419
Willis Rutter: 100, 313, 419

Hesse -
Fred D.: 180

Hettinger -
A C: 88, 419
Anna: 109, 419

Hewes -
John Martin: 175, 336, 419
Private: 175, 241, 336, 358, 419
Private: 175, 241, 336, 358, 419
Private: 175, 241, 336, 359, 419
Private: 175, 336, 419
Private: 175, 336, 419
Private: 241, 358, 419
Private: 241, 358, 419
Thomas Garrett: 175, 336, 419

Hewlett -
Barbara Rye: 157, 419
James Edward: 157, 419

Wilfred Murison: 157, 419
William: 157, 419
Hibshman -
Sarah: 73, 419
Hicks -
Lizzie: 308, 419
Hiestand -
Ann: 10, 35, 419
Elisabeth: 419
Elizabeth: 10, 26
High -
Private: 233, 350, 351, 419
Private: 169, 330, 419
Sarah: 302, 419
High/Hoch -
Elizabeth Pennypacker: 419
Highers(Unknown) -
Marie: 265, 419
Higley -
Private: 192, 259, 260, 419
II Private: 260, 419
Thomas Henson: 192, 419
Hildabrand -
Michael: 298, 419
Hillman -
Margaret: 158, 419
Hines -
Private: 181
Hinton -
Private: 279, 419
Private: 279, 419
Private: 279, 419
Private: 279, 419
Private: 250
Private: 250
Rev. John Joseph: 279, 419
Hippensteel -
Doris Madeline: 184, 251, 286
Dorothy Jean: 184, 251, 285, 289
Infant Son: 251
Judy Ann: 251
Margaret Joanne: 185, 251
Robert Goodhart: 184, 251
Robert William: 184, 419
Sandra Lee: 251
Hiscox -
Carl: 219, 419
Ray: 219, 419
Sharon: 219, 419
Yvonne: 219, 419
Hitchcock -
Alexander Milton: 244, 340, 419
Jonathan Elliot: 244, 340, 419
Michael David: 244, 340, 419
Zachary Falcon: 244, 340, 419
Hitz -
Amanda Elizabeth: 190, 419
Amos G: 190, 419
Ann Marie: 257, 419
Bradley Allen: 287, 289, 419
Brayden Joseph: 289, 419
Crystal: 287, 419
Douglas Wade: 287, 289, 419
Elizabeth Ashley: 287, 419
Elmer Ezra: 190, 257, 287, 289, 419
Elvin Ezra: 257, 287, 289, 420
Florence Mae: 190, 420
Galen D: 257, 287, 420
George Richard: 190, 420
Jacob Amos: 190, 420
Jacob Landis: 257, 287, 420
Jay Mark: 190, 420
Jeffrey: 287, 420
John Amos: 257, 420
Katherine Jane: 257, 420
Lisa Marie: 287, 420
Mary Kathryn: 190, 420
Rachel Emma: 289, 420
Hoch -
Mary: 420
Hochstetter -
Jacob: 16, 420
Hochstrasser -
Barbara: 18, 20, 21, 420
Margaretha: 21, 420
Hockley -
Unnamed: 252
Hofer -
John: 265, 420
Private: 265, 420
Private: 265, 420
Private: 265, 420
Private: 265, 420
Private: 265, 420
Private: 265, 420
Private: 265, 420
Private: 265, 420
Private: 265, 420
Private: 265, 420
Hoffer -
Abraham: 75, 420
Benjamin: 75, 420
Hoffman -
Anna Mary: 140, 420
Elisabeth: 82, 420
Elizabeth: 420
Elizabeth: 87, 420
John: 297, 420
John: 82, 420
Judith: 297, 420
Mary A.: 301, 420
Matilda: 420
Nancy: 82, 420
Private: 238, 356, 420
Private: 238, 356, 420
Private: 238, 356, 420
Private: 238, 356, 420
Susan: 82, 420
Hoffstetter -
Anna: 19, 420
Anna: 420
Anna: 19, 420
Barbel: 420
Barbel: 19, 420
Elsi: 19, 420
Georg: 19, 420
Hans Jacob: 19, 420
Hans Jacob: 420

Hans Rudolph: 420
Heini: 420
Heinrich: 17, 19, 21, 420
Heinrich: 15, 17, 19, 420
Jacob: 21, 420
Maria: 19, 420
Mr: 19, 21, 420
Oswald: 420
Oswald: 19, 420
Verena: 420
Hogendobler -
Rose: 72, 420
Hoist -
Unknown: 116, 420
Holderbaum -
Elizabeth: 76, 421
Holehan -
Catherine: 188, 421
Hollar -
Mary A.: 78, 421
Hollinger -
Anna: 302, 421
Anna H.: 306, 421
Colleen: 221, 421
David H.: 306, 421
Elisabeth Mae: 306, 421
Esther H.: 306, 421
Isaias H.: 306, 421
Jacob: 302, 421
Jacob H.: 306, 421
Johannes: 302, 306, 307, 311, 312, 421
Johannes H.: 306, 421
Magdalene: 306, 421
Maria Ann: 306, 421
Moses: 302, 421
Private: 224, 342, 421
Rebecca H.: 306, 421
Samuel: 301, 302, 421
Susanna: 113, 306, 311, 312, 317, 421
Thomas: 421
Thomas: 302, 306, 421
Thomas J.: 306, 421
Hoober -
Private: 177, 337, 421
Hoopes -
Private: 278, 421
Hoover -
Abraham: 42, 421
Amos H.: 73, 309, 421
Anna: 81, 421
Annie: 63, 421
Barbara: 81, 421
Bella: 119, 160, 421
Benjamin: 42, 421
Benjamin: 42, 421
Benjamin: 43, 421
Betty: 160, 421
Blanche: 160, 421
Catharine: 81, 421
Catharine: 82, 421
Catherine: 50, 421
Charles: 160, 421
Charolette: 94, 421

Christian: 81, 421
Christian: 43, 421
Christian H.: 43, 421
Clarence: 161, 421
David: 81, 421
Donald: 161, 421
Doris: 160, 421
Earl: 220, 421
Edith: 119, 160, 421
Edward: 158, 421
Elizabeth: 81, 421
Elizabeth: 43, 421
Elizabeth R.: 42, 421
Emanuel: 81, 421
Esther: 302, 303, 309, 421
Esther R.: 42, 421
Flora: 119, 160, 421
Florence: 161, 421
Frances: 120, 421
George: 119, 160, 421
Helen: 160, 421
Henry: 43, 421
Herbert: 158, 219, 421
Isaac: 49, 421
Jacob: 422
Jennie: 119, 160, 220, 422
John: 81, 422
John: 49, 422
John D.: 49, 422
John R.: 42, 422
Jonathan: 43, 422
Leah: 63, 422
Magdalena: 11, 30
Martin: 63, 422
Mary A.: 81, 422
Mary Catherine: 43, 422
Michael: 43, 422
Michael: 43, 422
Nancy Ann: 43, 422
Nancy R.: 42, 422
Private: 225, 343, 422
Private: 235, 352, 422
Private: 220, 422
Risser: 42, 422
Ruth: 119, 160, 220, 422
Samuel R.: 42, 422
Sarah: 301, 422
Simeon: 119, 422
Stephen R.: 42, 422
Wesley: 219, 422

Hopkins -
Barbara G: 257, 422
Gary Lee: 257, 422
Unknown: 257, 422

Horn -
Emma A: 189, 422

Horning -
Alice Celesta: 115, 422
Esther Mae: 228, 346, 422
Ida E.: 115, 422
Joseph: 296, 422
Private: 228, 345, 422
Private: 228, 346, 422
Private: 228, 346, 422
Private: 228, 346, 422
Private: 228, 346, 422

Private: 228, 346, 422
Private: 228, 346, 422
Private: 228, 346, 422
Private: 228, 346, 422
Private: 228, 346, 422
Private: 230, 348, 422
Zilpha: 114, 422

Horst -
Ada: 120, 422
Ada Sweigart: 101, 127, 150, 311, 317, 323, 339, 422
Amos David: 128, 317, 422
Amos Sweigart: 101, 126, 311, 316, 422
Anna: 8, 39, 300, 422
Anna: 8, 39, 300, 422
Anna: 297, 302, 306, 307, 311, 422
Anna: 298, 302, 422
Anna: 422
Anna: 84, 422
Anna Lois: 128, 317, 422
Anna M.: 301, 302, 422
Anna Sweigart: 101, 311, 422
Barbara: 422
Barbara: 84, 422
Barbara M.: 301, 422
Blaine Zook: 126, 315, 422
Carl Zook: 126, 315, 422
Catharine: 84, 422
Catherine: 422
Cedric Linn: 178, 243, 323, 339, 422
Christian: 423
Christian: 423
Christina: 423
Christina: 423
Christine Marie: 243, 340, 423
Daniel: 297, 423
David: 297, 423
David Campbell: 126, 316, 423
Diane L.: 178, 323, 423
Dorothy A.: 127, 317, 423
Douglas Clyde: 126, 316, 423
Elam Sweigart: 101, 125, 126, 178, 243, 244, 311, 315, 323, 339, 340, 423
Eli Sweigart: 101, 126, 311, 316, 423
Eliza: 84, 423
Elizabeth: 423
Elizabeth: 423
Elizabeth: 62, 298, 302, 307, 312, 423
Enos Heatwole: 128, 317, 423
Erma Steffy: 126, 178, 244, 315, 323, 340, 423
Ester: 301, 306, 307, 312, 423
Fanny: 298, 423
Feronica: 423
Feronica: 423
Frances Sweigart: 101, 126, 311, 316, 423
Gail Marie: 243, 339, 423
Gary Paul: 243, 339, 423
Gordon Steffy: 126, 178, 315, 323, 423

Henry: 423
Henry M.: 301, 302, 423
Henry Reuben: 126, 316, 423
Jacob: 297, 423
Jacob: 301, 307, 423
Jacob M.: 101, 301, 306, 307, 311, 314-317, 323, 339, 340, 423
Jacob Sweigart: 101, 311, 423
Jacob W.: 297, 423
James Albert: 126, 316, 423
James Daniel: 128, 317, 423
James Richard: 178, 323, 423
Janet Elaine: 127, 317, 423
Jeanne Loraine: 127, 316, 423
Joan Elaine: 178, 323, 423
Joann Louise: 178, 243, 323, 339, 423
John: 423
John: 39, 297, 300, 423
John Alton: 126, 316, 423
John Landis: 126, 316, 423
John Mark: 126, 316, 423
John W.: 297, 423
John W.: 298, 423
Jonathan Lynn: 243, 339, 423
Joseph: 297, 423
Joseph: 297, 298, 423
Joseph: 297, 423
Joseph: 84, 423
Joseph Franklin: 128, 317, 423
Joseph M.: 301, 423
Joseph Shenk: 84, 423
Katie Sweigart: 101, 127, 311, 317, 423
Kenneth Moseman: 127, 317, 423
Lee Sterling: 127, 316, 423
Lloyd Sweigart: 101, 127, 311, 317, 423
Lois Esther: 126, 316, 423
Lois Jean: 127, 317, 423
Magdalena: 423
Magdalena: 297, 423
Margaret: 297, 423
Maria G.: 424
Mark William: 178, 243, 323, 339, 424
Martha Frances: 126, 316, 424
Martha Steffy: 125, 315, 424
Mary: 424
Mary: 297, 424
Mary Louise: 178, 243, 323, 339, 424
Mary M.: 301, 307, 424
Mathias M.: 301, 307, 424
Michael: 424
Milton S.: 100, 313, 424
Miriam Darlene: 127, 317, 424
Miriam Elizabeth: 126, 316, 424
Misty Dawn: 243, 339, 424
Moses: 297, 424
Nancy: 424
Noah Sweigart: 101, 127, 311, 316, 317, 424
Paul Gary: 178, 243, 323, 339, 424

Paul Howard: 243, 339, 424
Paul Steffy: 125, 178, 243, 315, 323, 339, 424
Phares Sweigart: 101, 127, 311, 316, 424
Private: 228, 345, 424
Private: 228, 345, 424
Private: 228, 345, 424
Private: 228, 345, 424
Private: 228, 345, 424
Private: 228, 345, 424
Private: 228, 345, 424
Private: 228, 345, 424
Private: 228, 345, 424
Private: 228, 345, 424
Private: 230, 347, 424
Private: 231, 348, 424
Private: 174, 335, 424
Quintis: 126, 316, 424
Rachel Frances: 128, 317, 424
Randy Paul: 178, 323, 424
Ray Ernest: 126, 316, 424
Reuben Sweigart: 101, 126, 311, 315, 316, 424
Reuben Walter: 128, 317, 424
Reuben Weaver: 101, 150, 306, 311, 314-317, 323, 339, 340, 424
Richard M.: 127, 317, 424
Rodney William: 178, 323, 424
Ronald Gregory: 178, 324, 424
Ruth Naomi: 126, 316, 424
Samuel: 84, 424
Shannon Lea: 243, 339, 424
Shelby Lynn: 243, 339, 424
Susanna: 298, 424
Susanna M.: 301, 424
Susannah: 424
Titus Glenn: 126, 316, 424
Titus Sweigart: 101, 126, 311, 316, 424
Walter Dale: 127, 317, 424
Walter Sweigart: 101, 127, 311, 317, 424
William Mark: 243, 340, 424
William Prichard: 126, 178, 243, 315, 323, 339, 424

Hostetter -
Aaron: 70, 424
Aaron: 69, 424
Abner: 72, 424
Abraham: 29, 36, 50, 69, 70, 424
Abraham: 36, 424
Abraham: 424
Abraham: 29, 38, 55, 424
Abraham: 38, 55, 424
Abraham: 55, 424
Abraham: 13, 29, 425
Abraham: 37, 53, 425
Abraham: 10, 28, 35, 425
Abraham: 10, 28, 35, 49, 425
Abraham: 34, 48, 425
Abraham: 36, 51, 70, 71, 98, 99, 425
Abraham: 37, 51, 425
Abraham: 34, 47, 67, 95-97, 425
Abraham: 37, 53, 54, 71, 425
Abraham: 37, 52, 71, 99, 425
Abraham: 38, 425
Abraham: 48, 425
Abraham: 47, 67, 95-97, 425
Abraham: 51, 425
Abraham: 51, 71, 98, 99, 425
Abraham: 55, 425
Abraham: 50, 425
Abraham: 50, 425
Abraham: 72, 425
Abraham: 54, 72, 425
Abraham: 66, 425
Abraham: 69, 425
Abraham: 70, 425
Abraham F.: 50, 69, 425
Abraham Webster: 67, 97, 425
Abram: 99, 425
Abram: 71, 98, 99, 425
Adaline: 95, 425
Adaline: 99, 425
Adele: 69, 425
Adella: 95, 425
Alice: 72, 425
Alice M: 67, 425
Alverta: 69, 425
Amos: 71, 98, 425
Amos: 98, 425
Amos: 72, 425
Amos: 72, 425
Amos: 72, 425
Amos J: 69, 425
Amy Susette: 71, 99, 425
Ann: 425
Ann: 425
Ann: 425
Ann: 48, 425
Ann: 37, 425
Ann: 37, 52, 425
Ann: 47, 66, 425
Ann: 53, 425
Ann: 53, 425
Ann: 425
Ann Marie: 67, 425
Ann R: 69, 425
Anna: 13, 425
Anna: 10, 28, 33, 34, 425
Anna: 425
Anna: 35, 425
Anna: 36, 425
Anna: 71, 98, 425
Anna: 425
Anna: 425
Anna: 425
Anna: 425
Anna: 47, 425
Anna: 34, 425
Anna: 10, 28, 425
Anna: 36, 426
Anna: 51, 426
Anna: 38, 426
Anna: 17, 426
Anna: 426
Anna: 29, 426
Anna: 29, 37, 426
Anna: 34, 46, 47, 426
Anna: 36, 426
Anna: 426
Anna: 426
Anna: 37, 53, 71, 99, 121, 163, 426
Anna: 426
Anna: 50, 426
Anna: 55, 426
Anna: 50, 426
Anna: 50, 70, 426
Anna: 51, 426
Anna: 426
Anna: 65, 426
Anna: 72, 426
Anna Magdalena: 69, 426
Annali: 426
Anney: 47, 426
Annie: 54, 426
Annie: 48, 426
Annie: 54, 426
Annie: 67, 97, 426
Barbara: 37, 426
Barbara: 426
Barbara: 54, 71, 426
Barbara: 426
Barbara: 34, 47, 426
Barbara: 29, 426
Barbara: 48, 426
Barbara: 36, 426
Barbara: 38, 426
Barbara: 55, 426
Barbara: 9, 11, 13, 27, 28, 41, 426
Barbara: 426
Barbara: 10, 28, 35, 49, 426
Barbara: 10, 28, 34, 35, 48, 68, 97, 98, 120, 162, 163, 220-223, 282, 283, 426
Barbara: 29, 38, 426
Barbara: 426
Barbara: 426
Barbara: 36, 426
Barbara: 34, 43, 47, 67, 426
Barbara: 47, 66, 426
Barbara: 69, 426
Barbara ": 55, 426
Barbeli: 426
Bella: 97, 426
Benjamin: 48, 426
Benjamin: 70, 426
Benjamin: 70, 426
Benjamin: 10, 28, 35, 48, 68, 69, 98, 426
Benjamin: 10, 28, 426
Benjamin: 35, 48, 49, 68, 69, 98, 426
Benjamin: 426
Benjamin: 67, 426
Benjamin: 55, 426
Benjamin: 50, 70, 426
Benjamin: 65, 426
Benjamin: 426
Benjamin: 95, 426
Benjamin: 68, 426
Benjamin D.: 68, 427
Benjamin F: 66, 427
Benjamin F.: 427

Bert: 67, 427
Bessie Grace: 69, 427
Beth: 99, 427
Catharine: 35, 427
Catharine: 54, 427
Catharine: 73, 427
Catharine: 72, 427
Catherine: 13, 427
Catherine: 36, 427
Catherine: 37, 427
Catherine: 36, 427
Catherine: 427
Catherine: 70, 427
Catherine: 427
Catherine: 427
Catherine: 36, 427
Catherine: 37, 427
Catherine: 38, 427
Catherine: 55, 427
Catherine: 56, 427
Catherine: 37, 52, 427
Catherine: 54, 427
Catherine: 47, 66, 427
Catherine: 427
Catherine: 427
Catherine: 53, 427
Catherine: 53, 427
Catherine: 69, 427
Cathri: 17, 427
Cecilia: 67, 427
Cephas: 66, 427
Charles: 54, 427
Charles E: 97, 427
Charlotte: 37, 427
Charlotte: 37, 427
Christian: 427
Christian: 36, 427
Christian: 427
Christian: 427
Christian: 49, 427
Christian: 38, 427
Christian: 29, 38, 54, 55, 72, 73, 427
Christian: 29, 38, 55, 427
Christian: 427
Christian: 38, 427
Christian: 427
Christian: 54, 73, 427
Christian: 50, 427
Christian: 50, 70, 427
Christian: 427
Christian: 49, 427
Christian A.: 55, 427
Christian F.: 427
Christian K.: 427
Christina: 67, 96, 427
Clarence White: 97, 427
Clement: 67, 96, 427
Cyrus: 70, 427
D. Herbert: 99, 427
Daniel: 54, 427
Daniel: 55, 427
Daniel: 38, 54, 427
Daniel: 54, 427
Daniel: 56, 428
Daniel M: 69, 428

David: 53, 428
David: 48, 428
David: 52, 428
David: 55, 428
David: 54, 71, 428
David: 48, 428
David: 47, 67, 97, 428
David: 47, 66, 428
David: 51, 71, 99, 428
David: 67, 95, 428
David: 95, 428
David F.: 428
David H.: 71, 99, 428
David M: 66, 428
David M: 72, 428
David R: 67, 428
Deborah: 37, 428
E. Maurice: 98, 428
Earl W: 97, 428
Edward: 68, 428
Elam: 72, 428
Elias: 54, 428
Elisabeth: 428
Elisabeth: 36, 428
Elisabeth: 65, 428
Elisabeth: 55, 428
Elisabeth: 54, 428
Elisabeth: 71, 428
Elisabeth: 428
Elisabeth: 13, 428
Elisabeth: 36, 428
Elisabeth: 34, 428
Elisabeth: 37, 52, 428
Elisabeth: 35, 49, 428
Elisabeth: 428
Elisabeth: 50, 428
Elisabeth: 50, 70, 428
Elisabeth: 67, 428
Elisabeth: 67, 428
Elisabeth Ann: 73, 428
Elisabeth Jane: 53, 428
Elisabeth Maria: 7, 8, 10, 28, 33, 34, 40, 46, 57, 428
Elizabeth: 428
Elizabeth: 48, 428
Elizabeth: 51, 428
Elizabeth: 428
Elizabeth: 48, 428
Elizabeth: 10, 28, 428
Elizabeth: 48, 428
Elizabeth: 35, 428
Elizabeth: 36, 428
Elizabeth: 52, 428
Elizabeth: 37, 428
Elizabeth: 55, 428
Elizabeth: 47, 428
Elizabeth: 299, 428
Elizabeth: 50, 428
Elizabeth: 67, 428
Elizabeth K.: 55, 428
Ella: 72, 428
Elsbeth: 17, 428
Emanuel: 50, 428
Emanuel F: 65, 428
Emanuel H: 69, 428
Emanuel P: 66, 429

Emma: 70, 429
Emma Elisabeth: 71, 99, 429
Emma J: 69, 429
Emma Jane: 69, 429
Emma Jane: 69, 429
Emma M: 70, 429
Emmanuel: 54, 429
Emmanuel: 48, 429
Emmanuel: 54, 429
Emmanuel: 48, 68, 429
Ephraim: 65, 429
Ephraim: 70, 429
Ervilla: 97, 429
Esther: 10, 28, 34, 429
Esther: 35, 429
Esther: 10, 28, 429
Eva: 71, 429
Ezra: 70, 429
Ezra: 48, 68, 98, 429
Fannie: 72, 429
Fanny: 47, 66, 67, 429
Fanny: 73, 429
Feronica: 48, 429
Fianna: 67, 95, 96, 429
Florence: 95, 429
Florence Ethel: 97, 429
Floyd R: 97, 429
Frank L: 67, 429
Franklin: 55, 429
Frederick: 99, 429
Fronica: 48, 429
George: 36, 50, 429
George Washington: 97, 429
Grace E: 97, 429
Hannah: 72, 429
Hans: 17, 429
Hans: 429
Hans Heinrich: 17, 429
Hans Heinrich: 429
Hans Jagli: 17, 429
Harriet: 65, 429
Harriet A: 67, 96, 429
Harriet Ester: 67, 429
Harry H.: 71, 429
Harry Jacob: 97, 429
Heber: 98, 429
Helen: 52, 429
Helen: 99, 429
Helen: 53, 429
Henrich: 429
Henry: 29, 36, 50, 429
Henry: 65, 429
Henry: 429
Henry: 54, 429
Henry: 70, 429
Henry: 429
Henry: 29, 429
Henry: 55, 429
Henry: 56, 429
Henry: 38, 429
Henry: 38, 429
Henry: 54, 429
Henry: 67, 95, 429
Henry F.: 429
Herman: 37, 429
Herman: 29, 37, 52, 53, 71, 99,

430
Herman: 37, 53, 430
Herman: 53, 430
Herman: 53, 430
Herman Robert: 53, 430
Herman Robert: 52, 430
Hettie: 68, 430
Hetty: 71, 430
Hiram: 53, 430
Hiram C.: 67, 430
Hiram H.: 55, 430
Isaac: 50, 430
Isaac: 54, 430
Isaac: 38, 55, 430
Isaac R.: 54, 430
Isabella Victoria: 67, 96, 430
Jacob: 35, 430
Jacob: 430
Jacob: 430
Jacob: 54, 430
Jacob: 72, 430
Jacob: 430
Jacob: 48, 430
Jacob: 49, 430
Jacob: 35, 430
Jacob: 37, 430
Jacob: 56, 430
Jacob: 38, 55, 430
Jacob: 17, 430
Jacob: 10, 11, 13, 15, 27-29, 430
Jacob: 8-10, 13, 28, 430
Jacob: 10, 28, 34, 46-48, 65-67, 95-97, 430
Jacob: 29, 36, 51, 70, 71, 98, 99, 430
Jacob: 430
Jacob: 34, 47, 65, 66, 430
Jacob: 34, 47, 48, 430
Jacob: 430
Jacob: 36, 51, 71, 99, 430
Jacob: 37, 51, 52, 430
Jacob: 37, 53, 430
Jacob: 38, 54, 430
Jacob: 430
Jacob: 47, 65, 430
Jacob: 48, 430
Jacob: 47, 430
Jacob: 51, 430
Jacob: 51, 70, 71, 98, 430
Jacob: 430
Jacob: 55, 430
Jacob: 53, 430
Jacob: 72, 430
Jacob: 430
Jacob D.: 68, 98, 430
Jacob H: 69, 430
Jacob H: 49, 69, 430
Jacob H: 70, 430
Jacob K.: 50, 69, 430
Jacob P: 66, 430
Jageli: 17, 430
James: 53, 430
Jenny E: 95, 430
Jessie Olive: 97, 430
Johannes: 430
John: 13, 430

John: 430
John: 36, 430
John: 71, 431
John: 72, 431
John: 72, 431
John: 70, 431
John: 431
John: 431
John: 431
John: 431
John: 48, 431
John: 38, 55, 431
John: 55, 431
John: 40, 431
John: 29, 38, 55, 431
John: 29, 37, 53, 54, 71, 72, 99, 121, 163, 431
John: 431
John: 37, 54, 72, 431
John: 38, 55, 431
John: 38, 54, 72, 73, 431
John: 38, 55, 431
John: 36, 50, 69, 70, 431
John: 47, 65, 431
John: 55, 431
John: 50, 69, 431
John: 51, 431
John: 51, 431
John: 56, 431
John: 54, 73, 431
John: 53, 431
John: 53, 431
John: 70, 431
John E: 97, 431
John E.: 55, 431
John E.: 54, 72, 431
John F: 65, 431
John H: 73, 431
John H.: 54, 431
John Henry: 69, 431
Jonas: 72, 431
Jonas: 72, 431
Jonas E.: 54, 72, 431
Joseph: 34, 431
Joseph: 47, 67, 95, 431
Joseph: 67, 95, 431
Joseph: 65, 431
Joseph: 72, 431
Josiah: 66, 431
Judith: 50, 431
Kathryn: 68, 98, 431
Kathryn: 72, 431
Levi: 72, 431
Levi: 73, 431
Levi: 73, 431
Lewis: 53, 431
Lida Garber: 69, 431
Lidi: 50, 431
Lillie: 67, 431
Linnaeus: 71, 98, 431
Lizzie: 66, 431
Lizzie: 431
Lizzie: 72, 431
Louisa Jane: 71, 431
Lucinda: 67, 96, 431
Luke: 53, 431

Lydia: 48, 431
Lydia: 54, 431
Lydia: 73, 431
Lydia: 48, 432
Lydia: 56, 432
Lydia Ann: 67, 432
Magdalena: 35, 432
Magdalena: 37, 432
Magdalena: 432
Magdalena: 432
Magdalena: 48, 432
Magdalena: 37, 432
Magdalena: 38, 432
Magdalena: 55, 432
Magdalena: 36, 51, 432
Magdalena: 54, 432
Magdalena: 432
Magdalene: 47, 432
Margaret: 13, 432
Margaret: 53, 432
Margaret: 53, 432
Margaret: 52, 432
Margaret: 69, 432
Maria: 10, 28, 34, 432
Maria: 35, 432
Maria: 37, 53, 432
Maria: 432
Maria: 432
Maria: 65, 432
Maria: 432
Maria: 432
Maria: 432
Maria: 34, 432
Maria: 10, 28, 432
Maria: 36, 432
Maria: 38, 432
Maria: 34, 432
Maria: 36, 432
Maria: 48, 432
Maria: 47, 432
Maria: 54, 72, 432
Maria: 50, 432
Maria: 45, 432
Martha: 47, 65, 432
Martha: 66, 432
Martha: 432
Martha: 48, 432
Martha: 55, 432
Martha: 54, 432
Mary: 67, 432
Mary: 432
Mary: 72, 432
Mary: 73, 432
Mary: 48, 432
Mary: 37, 432
Mary: 55, 432
Mary: 55, 432
Mary: 37, 432
Mary: 47, 432
Mary: 54, 432
Mary: 432
Mary: 50, 70, 432
Mary: 53, 432
Mary: 72, 432
Mary Ann: 51, 432
Mary Ann: 52, 432

Mary Belle: 95, 432
Mary C: 69, 432
Mary Edith: 69, 432
Mary Elisabeth: 68, 433
Mary Elisabeth: 69, 433
Mary Ellen: 69, 433
Maude Gertrude: 69, 433
Michael: 433
Michael F.: 433
Minnie: 69, 433
Miriam Virginia: 99, 433
Nathan: 66, 433
Noah: 51, 433
Oliver: 67, 433
Oswald: 13, 15, 17, 433
Oswald: 15, 433
Peter: 50, 433
Pharus: 66, 433
Polly: 36, 433
Private: 98, 433
Private: 98, 433
Private: 98, 433
Private: 98, 433
Private: 283, 360, 433
Private: 283, 361, 433
Private: 283, 361, 433
Private: 284, 362, 433
Private: 284, 362, 433
Private: 284, 362, 433
Private: 284, 362, 433
Private: 284, 362, 433
Private: 284, 361, 433
Private: 284, 361, 433
Private: 225, 342, 433
Rachel: 36, 433
Rebecca: 37, 433
Robert Lynne: 97, 433
Robert White: 97, 433
Ross: 99, 433
Ross: 71, 99, 433
Roy Grant: 95, 433
Rudolph: 48, 433
Rudolph: 433
Rudolph: 35, 48, 68, 433
Salinda: 55, 433
Samuel: 47, 433
Samuel: 56, 433
Samuel: 48, 433
Samuel: 54, 73, 433
Samuel A.: 55, 433
Samuel E: 69, 433
Samuel G: 73, 433
Samuel H: 69, 433
Sarah: 36, 433
Sarah: 65, 433
Sarah: 37, 433
Sarah: 71, 433
Sarah A: 66, 433
Sarah E: 69, 433
Sarah J: 69, 433
Simon: 54, 433
Simon: 72, 433
Susan: 433
Susan: 48, 433
Susan: 51, 433
Susan: 55, 433

Susan: 47, 66, 433
Susan: 51, 433
Susan: 54, 433
Susan: 50, 434
Susan: 55, 434
Susan: 71, 434
Susan A: 67, 96, 434
Susan Alice: 69, 434
Susanna: 37, 434
Susanna: 37, 434
Susanna: 38, 434
Susanna: 36, 51, 434
Taylor T: 67, 97, 434
Theodore: 71, 434
Thomas: 55, 434
Thomas: 53, 434
Thomas: 52, 71, 99, 434
Tilman N: 72, 434
Ulrich: 36, 50, 70, 434
Venich: 95, 434
Veronica: 30, 434
Veronica: 434
W. Clyde: 69, 434
Wilfred: 71, 434
Wilhelmina: 68, 434
William F: 95, 434
William H: 67, 434
William H: 73, 434
William S: 97, 434

Hottel -
 Catherine Stover: 61, 434
House -
 Mary: 32, 434
Houser -
 Christian L.: 295, 434
 Elizabeth: 295, 434
 Unknown: 11, 293, 434
Howard -
 Ada: 194, 434
 Marvin L: 186, 434
Howe -
 Jean Marie: 152, 217, 434
 Private: 194, 434
 Ralph: 152, 434
 Ralph W.: 152, 434
Howell -
 Hazel: 146, 434
Hoyt -
 Anna: 83, 434
Hrovatic -
 Private: 269, 434
 Private: 269, 434
 Private: 269, 434
Hubbard -
 Eva Graber: 110, 434
Huber -
 Abraham: 45, 434
 Anna: 434
 Anna: 21, 434
 Anna: 14, 434
 Anna: 7, 434
 Barbara: 44, 434
 Barbara: 301, 434
 Catherine: 44, 91, 308, 434
 Christian: 434

 Christiana: 434
 Esther: 434
 Jacob: 293, 434
 Maria: 296, 434
 Martin: 434
 Mary: 69, 434
 Susie: 306, 434
 Veronica: 54, 55, 434
Hubert -
 Arden: 189, 434
 Charles: 135, 434
 Edgar C: 135, 434
 Frank: 135, 189, 434
 Helen B: 135, 190, 434
 Leonard: 189, 434
 Mildred M: 135, 189, 435
Huffellberg -
 Barbel: 18, 20, 21, 435
Huges -
 Louise: 268, 435
 Private: 279, 435
 Private: 279, 435
 Private: 279, 435
Hughes -
 Rosa: 93, 435
Hummel -
 J. Maynard: 199, 435
 Julia: 200, 435
Hummerhouser -
 Agnes R.: 83, 435
Hunsberger -
 Susanna: 435
Hunsicker -
 Ann Alderfer: 435
 Charles M.: 435
 Private: 248
Hunsperger -
 Elizabeth: 58, 435
Hunter -
 Charles: 154, 435
 Francis M.: 154, 435
 Shirley: 154, 435
 Vera: 154, 435
Hursh -
 Agnes E: 133, 185, 435
 Brenner P: 186, 253, 435
 Clarence B: 133, 435
 Diane A: 253, 435
 Edna R: 133, 185, 252, 253, 435
 Edward M: 133, 435
 Emma B: 133, 435
 Frances M: 253, 435
 Jay B: 133, 186, 253, 435
 Lillie E: 133, 185, 252, 286, 435
 Margery B: 186, 435
 Odille Anne: 186, 435
Hurst -
 Barbara W.: 307, 435
 Frank W.: 306, 435
 George W.: 307, 435
 Isaac W.: 306, 435
 Jacob W.: 306, 435
 Katie W.: 306, 435
 Lizzie W.: 307, 435
 Lydia W.: 307, 435

Noah W.: 307, 435
Private: 224, 342, 435
Private: 235, 353, 435
Private: 235, 353, 435
Private: 235, 353, 435
Private: 235, 353, 435
Susana W.: 307, 435
Weaver W.: 307, 435
Huston -
Etta Lucinda: 110, 435
Hutwohl -
Anna: 296, 435
Huver -
Elizabeth Landis: 299, 435
Hyde -
Alice Phillipa: 111, 435
Ickes -
Carolyn: 107, 140, 435
Henry: 87, 435
William: 106, 107, 140, 435
William II: 107, 435
Ickis -
Susanna: 108, 435
Imler -
Elizabeth: 78, 435
Hannah: 78, 435
Joseph: 78, 435
Margaret: 78, 435
Mathias: 78, 435
Sarah: 78, 435
Solomon: 77, 435
Thomas O.: 78, 435
William: 77, 435
Ingalls -
Ann E.: 435
Ingram -
Dora: 116, 435
Irvin -
Susan: 81, 436
Irvine -
Harriet: 98, 99, 436
Isaacs -
Kenneth Eugene: 261, 436
Private: 261, 436
Private: 261, 436
Private: 261, 436
Robb E.: 261, 436
Isenschmid -
Car W: 209, 436
Carl: 209, 436
Gary: 209, 436
Private: 209, 436
Jackson -
Andrew: 96, 436
Helen Julia: 252
John: 96, 436
Lillian: 191, 436
Virgil Walton: 141, 436
Jacob -
Stoffer: 61, 436
Jacobs -
Vincent: 112, 436
Jacoby -
Private: 267, 436

Jacquet -
Russel: 315, 436
Jamieson -
Jean: 217, 436
Jane -
Private: 269, 436
Jantzi -
Private: 233, 350, 436
Jennings -
Abbie Mae: 195, 436
Jenuine -
Christian: 294, 436
John -
Florence: 148, 436
Myrtle Olive: 144, 436
Johndrow -
Private: 241, 359, 436
Johns -
Anna: 298, 436
Johnson -
Barbara May: 157, 436
Burt: 110, 436
Elvera E.: 261, 436
Garth Wilson: 157, 436
Geneva: 154, 436
Hannah: 93, 436
Harold: 154, 436
Henry: 154, 436
Madge Hessel: 213, 436
Mary Godshall: 436
Minnie: 135, 436
Nicholas Sigrid: 157, 436
Private: 237, 355, 436
Private: 210, 277, 436
Private: 157, 436
Private: 157, 436
Private: 436
Joiner -
Private: 206, 436
Jones -
Annice Hall: 77, 436
Dorothy: 92, 436
George: 154, 436
John: 154, 436
Laura: 154, 436
Mary: 92, 436
Overton: 154, 436
Private: 272, 436
Private: 272, 436
Private: 273, 436
Joseph -
Kertes: 265, 266, 436
Josline -
Private: 265, 436
Jr -
Private: 272, 436
Jumper -
Oscar John: 257, 436
Jutzi -
Private: 232, 350, 436
Kagarise -
Andrew Zook: 76, 436
Kagey -
John: 436

Kahlance -
Tara Rose: 285
Tevas: 285
Kail -
Private: 274, 436
Private: 274, 436
Private: 274, 436
Private: 274, 437
Kalbach -
Adam: 437
Daniel: 437
David: 437
Henry: 437
Henry: 437
John: 437
Michael: 437
Peter: 437
Kane -
Rose Frances: 184, 437
Karthaus -
Emilie: 103
Kasper -
Dorothy: 253, 437
Kathy -
(name: Kathleen Kay Grace): 220, 403, 437
Kaufer -
Stella: 135, 437
Kauffman -
Ann: 437
Anna K.: 49, 437
Barbara: 437
Barbara: 292, 437
Barbara: 437
Benjamin: 437
Benjamin Franklin: 125, 322, 437
Catherine: 437
Christian: 437
Christian: 437
Elizabeth: 437
Esther: 39
Jacob: 13
Magdalena: 27, 437
Mary: 437
Mary E.: 11, 26
Mary Koop (aka: Polly): 74, 310
Mary Weaver: 297, 437
Private: 284, 361, 437
Private: 284, 361, 437
Private: 173, 334, 437
Private: 125, 177, 322, 338, 437
Private: 125, 177, 322, 338, 437
Susan: 437
Sylvia: 178, 323, 437
Tobias: 437
Keagy -
Anna: 50, 55, 437
Christiana: 76, 437
Nancy Anna: 82, 437
Keeler -
Private: 269, 437
Keene -
Anna: 100, 313, 437
Jessica: 128

Keener -
    John B.: 62, 308, 437
    Trulah: 150, 437
Kehr -
    Ruth Susanna: 222, 223, 437
Keister -
    Christina: 61, 437
    David: 143, 437
    Wilson: 143, 437
Keith -
    June H: 437
Kelker -
    Luther Reily: 86, 437
Keller -
    Magdalena G.: 437
Kelley -
    Private: 437
    Private: 437
Kellner -
    Private: 279, 437
Kelly -
    Edith Maria: 114, 437
Kelse -
    Fulton: 133
Kendall -
    John: 116, 437
    Unknown: 116, 437
    William: 116, 437
Kendig -
    Abraham: 437
    Adam: 437
    Alice: 437
    Anna: 16, 437
    Anna: 437
    Anna: 437
    Barbara: 16, 437
    Benjamin: 437
    David: 437
    Elizabeth: 16, 437
    Elizabeth: 438
    Elizabeth: 438
    Elsbeth Alice: 438
    Emanuel: 438
    Ester: 16, 438
    Esther: 438
    Eva: 16, 438
    Heinrich: 16, 438
    Henry: 438
    Henry: 438
    John: 438
    John: 438
    John: 438
    John: 438
    John: 438
    John Jacob: 438
    Martin: 438
    Martin: 438
    Martin: 438
    Mary: 16, 438
    Mary: 438
    Mary Eliza: 438
    Maudlin: 11, 13, 15, 16, 292, 438
    Sarah: 438
    Susanna: 438
    Veronica: 16, 438

Kendrick -
    Private: 181
Kennedy -
    Ann Newman: 37, 438
    Ann Newman: 37, 438
Kennel -
    Phoebe: 174, 335, 438
    Private: 224, 341, 438
Kenneth? Unknown -
    Private: 210, 438
Keplinger -
    Susanna: 50, 438
Kern -
    William F.: 302, 438
Kerns -
    Maris: 438
Kertes -
    Private: 266, 438
    Private: 266, 438
    Private: 266, 438
Kessler -
    Leslie: 190, 438
Kester -
    Lorne: 95, 438
Kettering -
    Amanda: 85, 438
    Elizabeth: 85, 438
    Henry: 85, 438
    Jacob: 85, 438
    John S.: 85, 438
    Joseph: 85, 438
    Lydia: 85, 438
    Mary: 84, 438
    Philip: 85, 438
    Private: 276, 438
    Private: 276, 438
    Private: 276, 438
    Ralph: 276, 438
    Rebecca: 85, 438
    Samuel: 84, 438
    Samuel: 85, 438
    Samuel A.: 85, 438
    Veronica: 85, 438
Keys -
    Private: 181
Kibler -
    Carl: 207, 273, 438
    Charles: 207, 438
    Charles C. (Keebler): 438
    Harold: 207, 438
    Joyce: 207, 273, 438
    June: 207, 273, 438
    Lolyd: 207, 273, 438
    Private: 273, 438
    Private: 273, 438
    Private: 273, 439
    Private: 273, 439
    Private: 273, 439
    Private: 273, 439
    Private: 273, 439
    Private: 273, 439

    Private: 273, 439
    Private: 273, 439
    Private: 273, 439
    Private: 273, 439
    Private: 273, 439
    Private: 210, 439
    Robert: 207, 273, 439
Kiefer -
    Mary: 85, 439
Kilgore -
    Private: 201, 439
Kilhefner -
    Frank: 74, 310, 439
    John: 74, 310, 439
Kilmer -
    Private: 226, 343, 439
    Private: 226, 343, 439
    Private: 226, 343, 439
    Private: 226, 343, 439
Kimmel -
    Susan: 79, 439
Kindig -
    Anna: 69, 439
King -
    Alice Gordon: 180
    Private: 271, 439
Kinney -
    Private: 250
Kinzer -
    Alfred Glenn: 193, 439
    Alfred Lafayette: 193, 439
    Jesse Arden: 193, 261, 439
    Private: 261, 439
    Private: 261, 439
    Wanda Naomi: 193, 261, 439
Kiriyama -
    Private: 167, 328, 439
Kirkpatrick -
    Barbara: 187, 254, 439
    Elmer A: 187, 439
Kitch -
    Anna Catherine: 439
    Charles L.: 439
    Cyrus: 439
    Cyrus L.: 439
    Dora Eve: 439
    Mary Lizzie: 439
    Minnie L.: 439
Kitchen -
    Amos Abraham: 114, 439
    Drake: 114, 439
    Ellen Ruletta: 114, 151, 215, 216, 281, 282, 439
    Harriett: 114, 439
    Harry Milton: 114, 439
    Lottie Augusta: 114, 439
    Mabel Gertrude: 114, 151, 216, 282, 439
    Mary Edith: 114, 439
Kiter -
    George II: 439
Klein -
    Private: 245
Kline -

Alva: 255, 439
Anna Mary: 80, 439
Maria: 439
Klunk -
Amanda: 289, 439
Knapp -
Andrew Jay: 439
Emma Loretta: 439
Floyd Everal: 439
Victor Ronald: 439
Willard Winfield: 439
William George: 439
Knight -
Barbara J: 256, 439
Beverly A: 256, 439
Myers W: 256, 439
Kniveton -
Alice: 199, 439
Knoll -
Chester Larue: 200, 440
Dorothy Mae: 200, 267, 440
June Elizabeth: 200, 440
Richard Lee: 200, 440
Knorpp -
Betty Ann: 192, 440
Margaret Eda: 192, 440
Mary Jane: 192, 440
Walter Wesley: 192, 440
Knorr -
Alice Kathleen: 223, 283, 440
David Brian: 223, 440
Lawrence David: 223, 440
Lawrence Kevin (aka: Lawrence K Berger-Knorr): 223, 283, 373, 440
Knox -
Jean: 216, 440
Private: 215, 440
Private: 215, 440
Private: 215, 440
Knupp -
Cloyd R: 189, 440
Cloyd R , Jr: 189, 440
Edna M: 189, 257, 440
Florence W: 189, 440
Jane L: 189, 440
John H: 189, 440
June A: 189, 440
Muriel R: 189, 257, 440
Robert O: 189, 440
Koch -
Catherine: 440
Kochel -
Helen Louise: 121, 318, 440
Koehler -
Clayton: 140, 440
John: 139, 440
Koffel -
Ida M.: 111, 440
Kohr -
Nancy M: 287, 440
Kolb -
Ann Hunsberger (Kulp): 440
Elizabeth Hunsberger (Kulp): 440

Jacob Funk (Kulp): 440
Konshak -
Louise: 117, 440
Kopp -
Lillian A: 440
Koppler -
Lucille Elizabeth: 150, 440
Krafft -
Dorothy: 223, 440
Krall -
Sarah: 83, 440
Kramer -
Henrietta: 46, 440
Krammer -
Unknown: 153, 440
Kranz -
Private: 177, 338, 440
Kratz -
Lizzie Ann Kline: 440
Krause -
Chris W.: 149, 440
Glen: 149, 440
Herbert Stanton: 149, 212, 440
Private: 149, 212, 440
Private: 149, 440
Private: 149, 440
Private: 212, 440
Private: 212, 440
Private: 212, 440
Private: 212, 440
Private: 212, 440
Willard D: 149, 440
Kraybill -
Candace M: 221, 440
Krehmeyer -
Kathryn: 222, 440
Kreider -
Abraham: 51, 440
Ann: 440
Anna: 440
Anna: 440
Anna: 440
Anna: 440
Anna: 10, 11, 13, 15, 27-29, 440
Anna: 440
Anna: 299, 440
Anna: 29, 36, 49, 50, 441
Barbara: 441
Barbara: 51, 441
Barbara: 15, 441
Barbara: 29, 441
Catherine: 441
Catherine: 441
Catherine Louise: 441
Christian: 441
David: 51, 441
Eby: 172, 333, 441
Elisabeth: 441
Elizabeth: 441
Elizabeth: 51, 441
Elizabeth: 441
Elizabeth: 29, 441
George: 441
Hans: 18, 441

Hans Jacob: 15, 441
Hans Jacob: 441
Henry: 29, 441
Henry: 139, 441
Henry Widemoyer: 106, 441
Jacob: 51, 441
Jacob: 441
Jacob: 13, 15, 18, 441
Jacob: 15, 441
Jacob: 29, 441
Jacob: 441
Jacob: 29, 441
John: 441
John: 441
John: 51, 441
John: 441
John: 13, 441
John: 29, 441
John: 441
John: 85, 441
John Funk: 139, 441
Lydia: 85, 441
Lydia Shenk: 85, 441
Magdalena: 51, 441
Maria: 29, 441
Martin: 51, 441
Martin: 51, 441
Martin: 37, 441
Martin: 38, 441
Martin: 15, 441
Martin: 441
Mary Brubaker: 106, 139, 441
Michael: 441
Michael: 441
Michael: 15, 18, 441
Michael: 15, 441
Michael: 441
Michael: 441
Peter: 441
Peter: 441
Private: 233, 351, 441
Private: 233, 351, 441
Private: 233, 351, 441
Private: 233, 351, 441
Private: 233, 351, 441
Private: 233, 351, 441
Private: 172, 238, 333, 356, 441
Private: 172, 333, 441
Private: 172, 238, 333, 356, 442
Private: 172, 238, 333, 356, 442
Private: 238, 356, 442
Private: 238, 356, 442
Private: 238, 356, 442
Rosanna: 442
Susanna: 442
Tobias: 442
Unknown: 172, 333, 442
Veronica: 7, 9, 442
Kreigbaum -
Betty L: 188, 442
Krey -
John: 442
Kuhns -
Mary A.: 85, 442
Sarah Ann: 442
Kuipers -

Private: 170, 331, 442
Kundig -
   Adrian: 21, 442
   Anna: 442
   Anna: 18, 442
   Barbara: 442
   Barbel: 18, 442
   Barbel: 20, 442
   Elizabeth: 442
   Elsbet: 21, 442
   Elsbeth: 18, 442
   Felix: 21, 442
   Hans: 442
   Hans: 21, 442
   Hans Heinrich: 16, 18, 20, 442
   Hans Jacob: 13, 16, 18, 292, 442
   Hans Jagli: 20, 442
   Heinrich: 20, 442
   Jacob: 18, 442
   Jacob: 16, 442
   Jagli: 442
   Jorg: 18, 20, 21, 442
   Jorg: 18, 442
   Margreth: 442
   Peter: 20, 21, 442
   Regula: 442
   Verena: 16, 442
Kunkel -
   Rachel Beverlina: 102
Kuntz -
   Elizabeth: 41, 442
Kurtz -
   Abraham: 44, 442
   Barbara Ann: 44, 442
   Christian H.: 44, 442
   David Harrison: 44, 442
   Elizabeth: 44, 442
   Henry Clay: 44, 442
   Jacob: 442
   John Erb: 44, 442
   John H.: 44, 442
   Mary: 44, 442
   Private: 230, 348, 442
   Private: 230, 348, 442
   Private: 230, 348, 442
   Private: 230, 348, 442
   Private: 230, 348, 442
   Private: 235, 352, 442
   Private: 235, 352, 442
   Private: 235, 352, 442
   Samuel Albert: 44, 442
   Sarah: 84, 442
   Susanna: 298, 442
Laber -
   Michael: 30, 442
Lacey -
   Mary: 131, 442
Lackey -
   Patricia A: 253, 442
   Richard H , Jr: 253, 442
   Susan J: 253, 443
Lafayette -
   Webster Fox Lawrence ": 74, 101, 128
Lahodny -
   Ann: 156, 443
Lakers -
   Leone Elizabeth: 197, 443
Lambert -
   Civilla: 80, 443
Lancaster -
   Helen Gene: 187, 443
Landes -
   Abraham Beidler: 443
   Abraham Hunsicker: 443
   Abraham Lincoln: 443
   Benjamin Franklin Hunsicker: 443
   Daniel Miller: 443
   Davis Miller: 443
   Elizabeth Beidler: 443
   Elizabeth Hunsicker: 443
   Hannah Beidler: 443
   Hannah Hunsicker: 443
   Hattie Hunsicker: 443
   Henry Hunsicker: 443
   Jacob: 12, 14, 17, 292, 443
   James Miller: 443
   Jane Miller: 443
   John Beidler: 443
   John Horace Hunsicker: 443
   John Kolb: 443
   Josephine Hunsicker: 443
   Katie Hunsicker: 443
   Mary Hunsicker: 443
   Mary Kolb: 443
   Mary Miller: 443
   Ralph Kratz: 443
   William Puhl: 443
Landis -
   Abraham: 12, 292, 443
   Abraham: 295, 443
   Abraham: 295, 443
   Rev. Abraham: 296, 300, 443
   Abraham: 443
   Abraham Erb: 443
   Abraham F.: 443
   Abraham S.: 299, 443
   Ada: 443
   Ada Cathrine: 90, 312, 443
   Adeli: 443
   Adria: 64, 443
   Agta: 21, 443
   Alice Ida: 312, 443
   Alice M: 443
   Amanda: 62, 308, 443
   Amanda: 443
   Amanda B.: 312, 443
   Ann: 295, 443
   Anna: 21, 443
   Anna: 21, 443
   Anna: 21, 443
   Anna: 18, 443
   Anna: 443
   Anna: 14, 443
   Anna: 12, 292, 443
   Anna: 443
   Anna: 294, 443
   Anna: 299, 443
   Anna: 57, 305, 306, 443
   Anna: 443
   Anna E.: 443
   Anna M: 443
   Anna Mary: 308, 443
   Anna S.: 443
   Annie: 443
   Annie B.: 444
   Annie E: 64, 444
   Annie L.: 57, 304, 305, 444
   Annie M.: 90, 312, 444
   Barbara: 17, 444
   Barbara: 11, 14, 16, 292, 444
   Barbara: 444
   Barbara: 19, 444
   Barbara: 9, 12, 14, 295, 444
   Barbara: 14, 294, 444
   Barbara: 12, 292, 444
   Barbara: 295, 444
   Barbara: 295, 444
   Barbara: 299, 444
   Barbara: 296, 444
   Barbara S.: 299, 444
   Benjamin: 9, 12, 14, 15, 292, 444
   Benjamin: 12, 292, 294, 298, 303, 308, 312, 317, 444
   Benjamin: 295, 444
   Benjamin: 295, 299, 444
   Benjamin: 298, 303, 444
   Benjamin: 299, 444
   Benjamin F: 64, 444
   Benjamin L.: 62, 64, 298, 303, 308, 312, 317, 444
   Benjamin S.: 299, 444
   Betty Jane: 444
   Caspar: 19, 444
   Catharina: 17, 444
   Catharine: 444
   Catherine: 27, 444
   Catherine (Kate): 444
   Chester M.: 315, 444
   Child: 17, 444
   Christian: 444
   Christian: 58
   Christian Creiner: 444
   Christian G.: 444
   Christian R.: 299, 303, 444
   Christian S.: 57, 299, 304, 305, 308, 309, 312, 317, 444
   Christianna: 444
   Christina: 444
   Daniel: 444
   Daniel F.: 444
   Daniel S.: 299, 444
   David: 444
   David B.: 444
   David Erb: 444
   David F.: 444
   David M: 444
   David M.: 444
   David S.: 444
   David S.: 299, 444
   Eddie: 444
   Elam B.: 90, 308, 312, 315, 317, 444
   Elisabeth: 19, 444
   Eliza F.: 444
   Elizabeth: 27, 444

Elizabeth: 295, 444
Elizabeth: 295, 444
Elizabeth: 40
Elizabeth: 296, 444
Elizabeth: 444
Elizabeth E.: 444
Elizabeth F.: 444
Elizabeth H: 64, 91, 444
Elizabeth L.: 304, 444
Elizabeth S.: 299, 444
Elizabeth S.: 444
Ella: 445
Elsbeth: 19, 445
Emma: 445
Emma: 445
Emma B.: 308, 445
Emma M.: 90, 312, 445
Emma Meashey: 257, 445
Ephraim F.: 445
Esther: 295, 445
Esther: 303, 445
Esther Ann: 308, 445
Fanny F.: 445
Fanny Long: 62, 64, 89, 91, 303, 308, 309, 312, 317, 445
Felix: 445
Frank H: 64, 445
Franklin: 445
Franklin Frick: 64, 91, 445
Frena: 445
Hans: 16, 18, 20, 445
Hans: 20, 21, 445
Hans: 18, 20, 21, 445
Hans: 19, 445
Hans: 17, 445
Hans Heinrich: 17, 445
Hans Heinrich: 445
Hans Heinrich: 14, 16-18, 445
Hans Heinrich (Heini): 21, 445
Hans Jacob: 17, 445
Hans Rudolf: 19, 445
Harry Graybill: 445
Harry M.: 90, 312, 445
Harvey: 445
Heinrich: 445
Henry: 27, 445
Henry: 12, 292, 295, 299, 300, 445
Henry: 445
Henry: 64, 295, 298, 303, 308, 312, 317, 445
Henry: 295, 445
Henry: 298, 303, 304, 308, 445
Henry: 303, 445
Henry Erb: 445
Henry Frankfort: 445
Henry M: 445
Henry N: 300, 445
Henry S: 445
Hettie: 304, 445
Hettie F.: 445
Hettie S.: 299, 303, 445
Hiram: 445
Ida May: 64, 445
Isaac M: 445
Isaac M.: 445
Jacob: 17, 445

Jacob: 19, 445
Jacob: 12, 292, 295, 299, 304, 309, 312, 317, 445
Jacob: 295, 445
Jacob B.: 299, 445
Jacob M: 445
Jacob M.: 445
Jacob S.: 445
Jagli: 445
Johannes: 7, 295, 299, 304, 308, 309, 312, 317, 445
John: 445
John: 294, 298, 303, 308, 445
Rev. John: 295, 299, 445
John: 298, 445
John: 446
John B.: 299, 446
John B.: 446
John C: 446
John Erb: 7, 446
John F.: 446
John F.: 446
John K.: 299, 446
John L.: 304, 446
John M: 446
John M.: 446
John Snavely: 446
Katie: 304, 446
Leah: 446
Leah S.: 446
Lester R: 446
Levi L.: 90, 304, 308, 309, 312, 317, 446
Lizzie B.: 446
Ludi: 21, 446
Lydia B.: 308, 446
Lydia R.: 303, 446
Magdalena: 446
Magdalena: 295, 446
Magdalena M.: 90, 113, 127, 150, 178, 179, 244, 312, 315, 317, 446
Magdalena S.: 446
Mamie: 446
Margaret: 19, 446
Margaret: 446
Margaret: 446
Margaret: 446
Margaret: 446
Margaret F.: 446
Margaret S.: 446
Margareth: 446
Margaretha: 18, 446
Margreth: 20, 446
Maria: 294, 446
Maria: 295, 446
Maria: 299, 446
Mark H: 64, 446
Marlin R: 446
Martha A: 446
Martha G.: 446
Martha M: 113, 446
Martin S.: 299, 446
Mary: 446
Mary: 51, 52, 446
Mary: 8, 9, 12, 292, 295, 298, 303, 309, 446

Mary: 295, 446
Mary: 51, 446
Mary: 7, 33, 446
Mary: 446
Mary: 446
Mary (Nancy): 58
Mary Ann: 446
Mary Buckwalter: 126, 316, 446
Mary E.: 446
Mary F.: 446
Mary Hershey: 64, 446
Mary Jane: 446
Mary K.: 299, 446
Mary M.: 90, 312, 446
Mary Nancy: 58
Mary Rohrer: 57, 303-305, 308, 446
Mary S.: 446
Mary S.: 299, 446
Mervin Glenn: 446
Milton G.: 446
Norma Fay: 447
Peter: 294, 295, 447
Phares M: 447
Private: 231, 349, 447
Private: 231, 349, 447
Private: 231, 349, 447
Private: 171, 332, 447
Private: 177, 337, 447
Private: 447
Private: 447
Private: 447
Private: 447
Private: 447
Private: 447
Private: 447
Private: 447
Private: 447
Private: 447
Private: 447
Private: 447
Private: 447
Rodney Lamarr: 447
Rudolf: 18, 447
Rudolf: 21, 447
Rudolf: 447
Rudolf: 17, 447
Rudolph: 447
Ruth: 312, 447
Samuel B.: 447
Samuel F.: 447
Sarah Ann: 447
Sarah Ann: 447
Sarah M: 447
Susan: 296, 447
Susanna: 447
Susanna: 33, 447
Susanna: 447
Susanna S.: 299, 447
Susanna S.: 447
Suzanna F.: 447
Ulrich: 21, 447
Verena: 19, 447
Verena: 447

Victor: 447
Wayne G.: 447
Welti: 447
William: 447

Lane -
Otto Laurence: 194, 447
Private: 194, 262, 447
Private: 194, 447
Private: 194, 447
Unknown: 447

Lang -
Janie Monte: 243, 339, 447
Johannes: 13

Langsdale -
Edward Jay: 179, 324, 447
Rae Elizabeth: 179, 244, 324, 340, 447
Robert John: 179, 244, 324, 340, 447
Robert T.: 179, 324, 447
Tessa Maria: 244, 340, 447

Lapp -
John Reichenbach (NEW YORK) Rev.: 447
Private: 239, 357, 447
Private: 239, 357, 447
Private: 239, 357, 447

Latscher -
Annie Hiestand: 447
Jacob Franz Sauers: 447
John Buckwalter: 447
John Rev.: 448
Mary (Latshaw): 448
Mary Buckwalter: 448
Susan High: 448
William Stauffer: 448

Lauver -
Private: 231, 232, 349, 448
Private: 232, 349, 448
Private: 232, 349, 448

Lavalley -
Private: 290, 448

Lavender -
Bessie Sitier: 259, 448
Private: 249
Private: 249

Law -
Annie: 153, 448

Lawless -
Private: 194, 448

Leabo -
Cora Alice: 80, 448

Leacock -
Rauchy Ann: 448

Learn -
Ethel: 119, 448
Evelyn Hershey: 44, 448
Hershey David: 44, 448
Peter: 44, 448

Leary -
Margaret: 205, 448

Lee -
Harry Foster: 130
Jr. Private: 130, 183, 250
Private: 183, 250
Private: 250
Private: 250
Private: 183

Leed -
John E: 98, 448

Leeds -
Anna: 448

Leedy -
Blanche Pauline: 201, 448

Lefever -
Daniel N.: 302, 448
Frances Violet: 127, 316, 448
Harold Horst: 126, 316, 448
Jay Lehman: 126, 316, 448
Lehman Herr: 126, 316, 448
Merle Horst: 127, 316, 448
Miriam Horst: 126, 316, 448
Private: 172, 333, 448
Titus Horst: 126, 316, 448

LeFevre -
Anne (aka: Nancy Lefevre): 448
Daniel (aka: Paradise Tanner Dan): 386, 448
Daniel: 448
David W: 448
Elizabeth: 448
Emma Jane: 448
Hannah: 448
Henry W: 448
Hiram: 448
Jacob B: 448
John E.: 448
Nancy (name: Anne LeFevre): 448
Susan W: 448

Leffler -
Catharine: 73, 448

Lefoon -
Margaret: 184

LeGron -
Henry D.: 139, 448
Unknown: 139, 448
Unknown: 139, 448
Unknown: 139, 448
Unknown: 139, 448

Lehigh -
Private: 173, 333, 334, 448

Lehman -
Dennis Archie: 289, 448
Esther: 65, 448
Harold Ray: 258, 448
John: 118, 448
Mildred: 160, 448
Private: 258, 448
Private: 258, 448
Ray C.: 257, 448
Samuel: 83, 448
Sarah: 118, 448

Leichlite -
Wilma Ethelyn: 208, 448

Leicy -
Mary E.: 74, 310, 448

Leida -
Iva: 203, 448

Leipper -
Martha Jane: 148, 448

Leitenberger -
John: 80, 448

Leithiser -
James B: 90, 314, 449
Margaret: 90, 314, 449

Lemon -
Gladys: 120, 449

Lengenecker -
Miriam: 172, 333, 449

Lenhardy -
Mary: 449

Lesher -
Ann: 78, 79, 449
Barbara A.: 78, 449
Benjamin Franklin: 105, 449
Caspar: 78, 449
Catherine: 78, 449
Christian Hertzler: 105, 449
David: 78, 449
David: 78, 105, 137, 138, 196, 197, 263, 264, 449
Elizabeth: 78, 449
Fanny: 78, 449
Ida Elizabeth: 105, 449
Jacob: 78, 449
Jeremiah: 105, 449
John: 78, 449
Mary: 78, 449
Mary Ann: 105, 137, 138, 196, 197, 263, 264, 449
Naomi Jane: 105, 138, 449
Peter: 78, 449
Private: 247
Private: 247
Private: 247
Susan Alice: 105, 449

Lester -
Unnamed: 133, 449

Level -
Annie Eliza: 138, 449
Burgess Coleman: 138, 196, 449
Cloyd Irwin: 138, 196, 449
Elizabeth Leone: 197, 449
Frank Marshall: 138, 449
Ida Mae: 138, 449
James William: 137, 138, 449
John Howard: 138, 197, 263, 264, 449
Private: 197, 263, 449
Private: 197, 264, 449
Private: 197, 264, 449
Unknown: 196, 449
Unknown: 196, 449
Unknown: 197, 449
Unknown: 197, 449
Unknown: 138, 449

Levison -
Private: 207, 449

Lew -
Unnamed: 264, 449

Lewis -
Mary: 161, 449
Moses Owen: 449

Lewis (cont.)
  Private: 148, 449
LewisStoffer -
  Unnamed: 61, 449
Liber -
  Helen: 201, 449
  Unknown: 108, 449
Lichte -
  Magdalena: 32, 449
Lichty -
  Anna: 449
  Anna: 307, 449
  David: 294, 449
  Harry R.: 100, 313, 449
  Jacob: 16, 449
  John: 449
  Magdalena: 51, 449
  Mary: 77, 449
  Private: 173, 334, 449
  Private: 173, 334, 449
  Private: 173, 334, 449
  Private: 173, 334, 449
  Private: 241, 358, 449
  Private: 288, 449
Lieb -
  Unknown (Leap): 449
Lied -
  Jodi Lynn: 244, 340, 449
Light -
  Amanda: 85, 450
  Barbara B: 6, 63, 310, 450
  Barbara M.: 263, 450
  Elizabeth: 85, 450
  Levi: 85, 450
  Veronica: 85, 450
Lightbody -
  Ila: 154, 450
  Jean: 120, 450
  Matthew: 154, 450
Lightner -
  Jane: 450
Lime -
  Mary J.: 83, 450
Linda -
  Private: 277, 450
Lindsey -
  Joseph C.: 78, 450
Line -
  Clayton Merle: 195, 450
  Fauntis May: 137, 450
  Golda Gladys: 137, 196, 450
  Isabelle: 252
  Mabel Beatrice: 137, 195, 263, 450
  Sara Margaret: 137, 196, 263, 450
  Stephen Clyde: 137, 195, 263, 450
  Thora Isabelle: 195, 263, 450
  Zelorah J.: 137, 450
Lively -
  Emma: 191, 450
Livengood -
  Charles: 315, 450
  Jacob: 59, 450
  Martha Anna: 178, 315, 323, 324, 339, 450
  Mary Elizabeth: 315, 450
  Naomi Leah: 315, 450
  Rhoda: 315, 450
  Ruth Lydia: 315, 450
  Samuel: 315, 450
Livingston -
  Private: 205, 450
  Private: 205, 450
  Private: 205, 450
  William: 204, 205, 450
lll -
  Private: 270, 450
Locy -
  Private: 211, 450
Loffer -
  Glen Jackson: 450
  William J.: 450
Lohr -
  Catherine: 69, 450
  Susan N.: 80, 450
Lonagher -
  Unknown: 112, 450
Long -
  Abraham: 29, 450
  Addah: 25, 450
  Ann: 29, 450
  Anna: 25, 450
  Anna: 293, 450
  Anna: 64, 298, 450
  Anna: 46, 62, 64, 91, 303, 450
  Barbara: 25, 450
  Sr Benjamin: 46
  Jr Benjamin: 9, 46, 303, 450
  Catharine: 13, 25, 29, 36-38, 50-55, 69-73, 98, 99, 121, 163, 450
  Christian: 25, 450
  Christian: 29, 450
  Christian: 295, 450
  David: 27, 450
  Elizabeth: 25, 450
  Elizabeth: 29, 450
  Esther: 25, 450
  Fronica: 25, 450
  Gideon C.: 76, 450
  Herman: 25, 450
  Herman: 28, 450
  Herman: 12, 25, 450
  Isaac: 298
  John: 27, 450
  John: 25, 28, 450
  John: 28, 450
  Joseph: 29, 451
  Magdalena: 25, 451
  Maria: 25, 451
  Mary: 29, 451
  Private: 225, 342, 451
  Private: 238, 356, 451
  Private: 278
  Susanna: 25, 29, 36, 49, 50, 451
Longanecker -
  Rebecca: 87, 451
Longenecker -
  Anna (Longacre): 451
  Anna F: 121, 451
  Barbara Becker: 106, 451
  Christian: 451
  Daniel Ziegler (Longacre): 451
  Elizabeth: 59, 451
  John: 16, 451
  Levi Landes (Longacre): 451
  Magdelena Clotz: 14, 451
  Mary Jane (Longacre): 451
  Peter: 451
  Samuel: 451
  Serena: 139, 451
  Solomon: 451
  Unknown: 451
Loos -
  Beatrice: 272, 451
Loose -
  Carl Gordon: 195, 451
  Carl Maurice: 195, 263, 451
  Private: 263, 451
  Private: 263, 451
  Private: 195, 263, 451
  Private: 195, 263, 451
  Private: 263, 451
Loriencz -
  Private: 241, 359, 451
Lotrek -
  Private: 249
Lotton -
  Bertha: 156, 451
Lower -
  Catherine: 88, 451
Lowry -
  Private: 125, 178, 322, 338, 451
  Robert Warren: 125, 322, 451
Lucas -
  Suzanna: 451
  Unknown: 144, 451
Lucenti -
  Carmen Joseph: 250, 451
  Sandra Marie: 250, 285
  Teresa Rose Charlene: 250, 285
Luttrell -
  Robert Larrance: 451
Lutz -
  James Hershey: 114, 322, 451
  Private: 176, 337, 451
  Walter: 114, 322, 451
Lynch -
  Private: 170, 331, 451
M(Sargent) -
  Private: 275, 451
MacCallum -
  Private: 182
Machamer -
  Gladford Doris: 130
Macklem -
  Jane: 95, 451
Macleod -
  Alex: 158, 451
  Douglas: 158, 451
  Private: 158, 451
Maggie -
  (name: Margaret Ann Duncan): 133, 186, 253, 389, 451

Maglott -
   Josephine J: 143, 451
Makin -
   Elizabeth: 451
Malin -
   Private: 226, 344, 451
   Private: 226, 344, 451
Mall -
   Private: 225, 343, 451
   Private: 225, 343, 451
Malone -
   Daniel: 80, 451
Manger -
   Private: 265, 451
Manley -
   Private: 237, 355, 451
Mann -
   Patricia: 204, 451
Mapes -
   Private: 269, 270, 451
   Private: 270, 451
Maphis -
   Mary: 61, 451
Maples -
   Private: 281, 451
   Private: 281, 451

   Margaret Berkey Clark /: 80, 451
Mark -
   Sarah: 83, 452
   Sarah: 84, 452
Markley -
   Catherine Landis: 452
   Elias Landis: 452
   Jacob Landis: 452
   John: 38, 452
   John Landis: 452
   Samuel Moyer: 452
Markovich -
   Private: 172, 333, 452
Marlow -
   Andy: 115, 452
   Jack: 115, 452
   John: 115, 452
   Sarah: 115, 452
Marner -
   Emanuel: 113, 315, 452
Marshall -
   Ann: 92, 452
Martenize -
   Private: 271, 452
   Private: 271, 452
Martha -
   Unnamed: 7, 57, 305, 452
Martig -
   Paul: 207, 452
   Private: 207, 274, 452
   Private: 208, 274, 452
   Private: 208, 452
   Private: 274, 452
   Private: 274, 452
   Private: 274, 452
   Private: 274, 452

Martin -
   Aaron: 311, 452
   Aaron K.: 165, 325, 326, 452
   Abraham: 62, 302, 452
   Abraham Horst: 302, 452
   Abraham M.: 452
   Abraham O.: 62, 308, 452
   Ada Ann Lucretia: 136, 452
   Anna: 452
   Anna O.: 62, 308, 452
   Annie W.: 306, 452
   Benjamin E.: 90, 312, 452
   Clarence E.: 122, 169, 234, 235, 319, 330, 352, 452
   Clarence H.: 169, 330, 452
   David: 15, 291, 452
   David: 452
   David: 452
   David Ames: 306, 452
   David O.: 62, 308, 452
   Dorcus Lucinda: 96, 452
   Earl E.: 122, 169, 236, 319, 330, 353, 452
   Edith: 188, 452
   Elizabeth: 452
   Elizabeth: 307, 452
   Elizabeth: 307, 452
   Elizabeth O.: 62, 308, 452
   Ellen Mary: 164, 325, 452
   Frances: 56, 302, 304, 452
   Frances Horst: 302, 452
   Henry: 302, 452
   Henry O.: 62, 308, 452
   Infant1: 62, 308, 452
   Infant2: 62, 308, 452
   Isaac O.: 62, 308, 452
   Jacob: 293, 452
   Jacob W.: 306, 452
   Joab: 96, 452
   John: 452
   John E.: 165, 227, 326, 345, 452
   Jonas S.: 56, 304, 452
   Joseph Horst: 62, 302, 307, 308, 312, 452
   Joseph O.: 62, 308, 453
   Joseph S.: 302, 453
   Kathleen: 174, 175, 335, 453
   Lavone W.: 227, 345, 453
   Lucille: 268, 453
   Lydia: 306, 453
   Lydia B.: 306, 453
   Lydia Z.: 307, 453
   Magdalena O.: 62, 90, 113, 150, 178, 179, 244, 308, 312, 315, 453
   Margaret: 96, 453
   Maria: 453
   Maria: 7, 57, 305, 453
   Martha Horst: 302, 453
   Martin: 453
   Mary: 96, 453
   Mary: 307, 453
   Mary: 164, 165, 325, 453
   Mary Ann: 453
   Mary E.: 122, 169, 235, 319, 330, 353, 453

   Mary Ebersole: 163, 453
   Michael: 453
   Michael: 453
   Michael: 45, 453
   Nancy: 96, 453
   Paul: 96, 453
   Paul E.: 122, 169, 235, 319, 330, 353, 453
   Private: 223, 341, 453
   Private: 165, 326, 453
   Private: 165, 226, 326, 344, 453
   Private: 165, 226, 326, 344, 453
   Private: 165, 226, 326, 344, 453
   Private: 165, 227, 326, 344, 453
   Private: 165, 227, 284, 326, 344, 362, 453
   Private: 165, 227, 326, 345, 453
   Private: 165, 227, 326, 345, 453
   Private: 227, 345, 453
   Private: 227, 345, 453
   Private: 227, 345, 453
   Private: 227, 345, 453
   Private: 227, 345, 453
   Private: 227, 345, 453
   Private: 227, 345, 453
   Private: 227, 345, 453
   Private: 227, 345, 453
   Private: 227, 345, 453
   Private: 227, 344, 453
   Private: 227, 344, 453
   Private: 227, 344, 453
   Private: 227, 344, 453
   Private: 227, 344, 453
   Private: 227, 344, 453
   Private: 227, 344, 453
   Private: 227, 284, 344, 362, 453
   Private: 227, 344, 453
   Private: 227, 344, 453
   Private: 227, 344, 453
   Private: 227, 344, 453
   Private: 227, 344, 453
   Private: 227, 344, 453
   Private: 227, 344, 453
   Private: 227, 344, 453
   Private: 227, 345, 453
   Private: 227, 345, 453
   Private: 227, 345, 453
   Private: 226, 344, 453
   Private: 226, 344, 453
   Private: 226, 344, 454
   Private: 226, 344, 454
   Private: 226, 344, 454
   Private: 226, 344, 454
   Private: 226, 344, 454
   Private: 228, 346, 454
   Private: 228, 346, 454
   Private: 228, 346, 454
   Private: 228, 346, 454
   Private: 228, 346, 454
   Private: 230, 347, 454
   Private: 231, 348, 454
   Private: 231, 348, 454
   Private: 167, 328, 454
   Private: 122, 168, 169, 319, 329, 454
   Private: 122, 169, 234, 319, 329,

352, 454
　　Private: 169, 330, 454
　　Private: 169, 330, 454
　　Private: 169, 234, 330, 352, 454
　　Private: 169, 234, 330, 352, 454
　　Private: 169, 235, 330, 352, 454
　　Private: 169, 235, 330, 352, 454
　　Private: 169, 235, 330, 352, 454
　　Private: 235, 352, 454
　　Private: 235, 352, 454
　　Private: 235, 353, 454
　　Private: 235, 352, 454
　　Private: 235, 352, 454
　　Private: 235, 352, 454
　　Private: 235, 352, 454
　　Private: 235, 352, 454
　　Private: 235, 352, 454
　　Private: 235, 352, 454
　　Private: 235, 352, 454
　　Private: 169, 330, 454
　　Private: 169, 235, 330, 353, 454
　　Private: 169, 235, 330, 353, 454
　　Private: 169, 235, 330, 353, 454
　　Private: 169, 235, 330, 353, 454
　　Private: 235, 353, 454
　　Private: 235, 353, 454
　　Private: 235, 353, 454
　　Private: 235, 353, 454
　　Private: 169, 236, 330, 353, 454
　　Private: 169, 236, 330, 353, 454
　　Private: 169, 330, 454
　　Private: 169, 330, 454
　　Private: 169, 329, 454
　　Private: 169, 329, 454
　　Private: 169, 329, 454
　　Private: 169, 170, 330, 454
　　Private: 170, 330, 454
　　Private: 171, 332, 454
　　Private: 173, 334, 454
　　Private: 173, 334, 454
　　Private: 173, 334, 454
　　Private: 173, 334, 454
　　Private: 173, 239, 334, 356, 454
　　Private: 239, 356, 454
　　Private: 239, 356, 454
　　Private: 278, 454
　　Rolandis: 68, 454
　　Rosalea Joy: 227, 344, 454
　　Rose: 96, 454
　　Samuel O.: 62, 308, 454
　　Solomon: 298, 454
　　Susanna: 62, 308, 455
　　Thomas Dean: 170, 330, 455
　　Unknown: 68, 455
　　Vernon W.: 227, 345, 455
　　Walter M.: 122, 319, 455
　　Wayne: 68, 455
　　Wilmer E.: 122, 169, 319, 330, 455
Mary -
　　Unknown: 213, 455
Mascutti -
　　Jr. Private: 129
Mason -
　　C.W.: 128
Masterson -

　　Alice: 216, 455
Mathews -
　　Private: 279, 455
Matthews -
　　Unknown: 218, 455
Mattis -
　　Elizabeth: 455
Mauzzy -
　　Unknown: 455
May -
　　James W: 186, 455
Mayer -
　　Unnamed: 16, 292, 455
　　Elisabeth: 16, 455
　　Elizabeth: 9, 11, 14, 33, 41, 455
　　Heinrich: 16, 455
　　John: 14, 455
　　Maria: 16, 455
Mc Kacken -
　　Private: 204, 455
Mc Laughlin -
　　Private: 275, 455
Mc Manas -
　　Betty: 273, 455
Mc Vay -
　　Neveda Bada: 149, 455
McAfee -
　　Wilbur: 190, 455
McCarrin -
　　Private: 288, 455
　　Private: 288, 455
McClaughry -
　　Clair: 191, 455
McCreary -
　　Mabel: 102
McDaniel -
　　Private: 262, 455
McDanill -
　　Private: 262, 455
McDonnel -
　　Mildred Burkholder: 162, 455
McDowell -
　　Clarence: 220, 455
　　Private: 220, 455
　　Private: 220, 455
　　Private: 220, 455
　　Robert: 160, 455
Mcelhenny -
　　James: 127, 317, 455
McFarland -
　　Dona Lynn: 221, 455
McGaw -
　　Henry: 81, 455
McGee -
　　Private: 282, 455
McGowan -
　　David M.: 244, 340, 455
McGown -
　　Debra Lynne: 244, 340, 455
McKain -
　　Harold LeRoy: 221, 455
　　Sheila Nadine: 221, 455
　　Tracy Louise: 221, 283, 455

McKenzie -
　　Alberta: 155, 455
　　Private: 206, 455
McKitrick -
　　Private: 181
　　Private: 181, 247
　　Jr. Private: 181
　　Private: 181
McKracken -
　　Private: 204, 455
McLasty -
　　Margaret: 155, 455
McLaughlin -
　　Private: 274, 455
McLemore -
　　William Baird: 136, 455
McLeod -
　　Archie: 116, 455
　　Fern: 154, 455
　　Gerald: 154, 455
　　Jesse: 154, 455
　　Nina: 154, 455
McMichael -
　　Kyle S: 186, 455
McMonus -
　　Annie: 131, 455
McMurray -
　　Everett: 137, 455
McNulty -
　　Private: 250
　　Private: 250
McQuilkin -
　　Private: 208, 455
McSeveney -
　　Private: 176, 336, 455
McSparron -
　　Private: 238, 355, 455
Meacham -
　　Private: 183
Meaker -
　　Charles Eldyn: 455
　　Charles Rodney: 455
　　Louis Barr: 455
　　Rodney Eldys: 455
Meili -
　　Elsbeth: 20, 456
Melchiorin -
　　Anna: 15, 18
Mellinger -
　　Abraham Kauffman: 49, 456
　　Anna Kauffman: 49, 456
　　Benedict: 10, 28, 456
　　Benjamin: 35, 456
　　Benjamin: 49, 456
　　Benjamin Kauffman: 49, 456
　　Christian: 28, 456
　　Christian: 35, 456
　　Christian Kauffman: 49, 456
　　David: 293, 456
　　David: 28, 35, 49, 456
　　David: 35, 456
　　David: 35, 49, 456
　　David: 49, 456
　　David Kauffman: 49, 456

Elizabeth: 36, 456
Elizabeth Kauffman: 49, 456
Fannie Kauffman: 49, 456
Franni: 28, 456
Freni: 28, 456
Henry: 35, 456
Henry Kauffman: 49, 456
Jacob: 35, 456
Jacob Kauffman: 49, 456
John: 28, 35, 49, 456
John: 35, 456
John Kauffman: 49, 456
Magdalena Kauffman: 49, 456
Martin: 35, 49, 456
Martin Kauffman: 49, 456

Mellow -
Helen: 120, 456

Meng -
Mary Angela: 266, 456

Mengel -
Private: 182
Private: 182, 248
Private: 248
Private: 248
Private: 248

MenMuir -
Helen A: 188, 456

Mercer -
Bert E: 144, 456
Chester: 144, 202, 268, 269, 456
Glenn A: 144, 203, 270, 456
Hazel Debra: 144, 202, 203, 269, 456
Helen M: 144, 203, 456
Herbert Russell: 144, 202, 269, 456
Isabelle L: 267, 456
Orvie W: 144, 202, 268, 456
Private: 242, 359, 456
Private: 242, 359, 456
Private: 242, 359, 456
Private: 242, 359, 456
Private: 202, 268, 456
Private: 202, 456
Private: 202, 268, 456
Private: 202, 269, 456
Private: 202, 269, 456
Private: 269, 456
Private: 269, 456
Private: 269, 456
Private: 269, 456
Private: 203, 270, 456
Private: 214, 280, 456
Private: 214, 280, 456
Private: 214, 456
Private: 280, 456
Private: 280, 456
Private: 280, 456
Private: 214, 456
Private: 268, 456
Private: 268, 456
Private: 268, 456
Private: 268, 457
Private: 202, 269, 457
Private: 202, 269, 457

Ruby: 202, 268, 457
Ruth: 202, 268, 457
Wilford McKinley: 214, 457

Meredith -
Private: 218, 457
Unknown: 218, 457

Messersmith -
Elizabeth Margaret: 60, 457

Metcalf -
Emma: 457

Mettler -
Christine: 18, 457

Metz -
George R.: 81, 457

Metzler -
Elmer: 172, 333, 457
Maria: 10, 34, 457
Mary Anne: 104, 457
Private: 232, 349, 457
Private: 231, 349, 457
Private: 172, 333, 457
Private: 172, 238, 333, 355, 457
Private: 172, 333, 457
Private: 238, 355, 457
Private: 238, 355, 457
Samuel: 311, 457

Meyer -
Abraham: 457
Abraham: 457
Adam (Myer): 457
Adelheit: 457
Anna: 457
Anna: 457
Anna: 21, 457
Anna: 301, 457
Anna Magdalena: 12, 14, 16, 457
Annali: 457
Barbara: 457
Barbara: 7, 457
Barbara (Mier): 457
Christian: 301, 457
Christian: 20, 457
Christian: 457
Christian: 457
Christian: 457
Elias: 14, 457
Elizabeth: 457
Elsbeth: 457
Hans: 20, 457
Hans: 14, 16, 457
Hans Conrad (Mier): 457
Hans Heinrich: 457
Hans Jacob: 457
Heinrich: 457
Heinrich: 457
Jacob: 457
Jacob: 457
Jacob (Myer): 457
John: 11, 14, 16, 292, 457
John: 457
John: 457
John (Myer): 457
Margret: 457
Mary: 457
Mary: 457

Melchior: 18, 20, 457
Michael: 16, 457
Regel: 457
Regula: 457
Rev. Hans: 457
Salome: 297, 458
Samuel: 16, 458
Ursel: 458
Verena: 17, 291, 458
Verena: 18, 458
Veronica: 16, 458
Vincent: 13, 14, 292, 458
Vincenz: 16, 18, 20, 458
Vincenz: 14, 16, 18, 458

Mezurick -
Elizabeth: 215, 458

Migliorsis -
Private: 201, 458

Miller -
Anna: 49, 458
Anna Miriam: 111, 458
Barbara: 189, 458
Catherine: 71, 458
Christian: 34, 458
Cyrus: 77, 458
David: 458
Delores: 210, 212, 458
Edward J.: 168, 329, 458
Elisabeth: 47, 458
Elizabeth: 48, 458
Elizabeth: 48, 49, 458
Elizabeth: 47, 48, 458
Ethel: 146, 458
Ethel: 209, 458
Hannah: 458
Harriet B: 97, 98, 458
Harvey: 189, 458
Justina: 179, 338, 458
Kenneth: 189, 458
Magdalene: 84, 458
Mary A.: 458
Mary M: 186, 458
Mary Rebecca: 69, 458
McCelland Edward: 266, 458
Michael T.: 78, 458
Miley Le Mont: 132, 458
Nettie: 159, 458
Peter: 458
Private: 168, 329, 458
Private: 168, 234, 329, 351, 458
Private: 168, 234, 329, 351, 458
Private: 168, 329, 458
Private: 234, 351, 458
Private: 234, 351, 458
Private: 234, 351, 458
Private: 234, 351, 458
Private: 168, 329, 458
Private: 237, 355, 458
Private: 237, 355, 458
Private: 177, 338, 458
Private: 177, 338, 458
Private: 177, 338, 458
Private: 194, 458
Private: 194, 458
Private: 194, 458
Private: 263, 458

Private: 276, 458
Private: 266, 458
Private: 266, 458
Private: 458
Private: 458
Private: 458
Private: 458
Private: 458
Private: 179
Private: 179, 244
Private: 179, 245
Private: 244
Prudence: 8, 459
Rebecca Nyce: 459
Samuel: 459
Sidney Lincoln: 193, 194, 459
Susan: 459
Susan: 459
Tobias: 459
William: 37, 459

Minagay -
Private: 279, 459
Private: 279, 459
Private: 279, 459
Private: 279, 459

Minishka -
Private: 181

Mitchell -
Private: 227, 345, 459

Mitten -
Agnes Alverdia: 132, 459
Charlotte (aka: Lettie Mitten): 132, 459
Clarence Edward: 132, 459
James Alexander: 131, 132, 459
Lettie (name: Charlotte Mitten): 132, 459
William L.: 132, 459

Mizner -
Catharine: 87, 459

Mock -
Barbara: 82, 459

Mohler -
David Ralph: 251
Frank W.: 121, 318, 459
Graybill Eby: 121, 318, 459
John Robert: 251, 285
Kathryn Ann: 251, 285, 289
Mark Andrew: 285
Matthew Robert: 285
Ralph E.: 251

Mohr -
Private: 241, 359, 459
Private: 241, 359, 459
Private: 249
Private: 249

Molly -
Fox Mary Eliza ": 129, 181, 246, 247

Moore -
Henry Daniel: 146, 459
John Raymond: 146, 206, 459
Mary Alice: 146, 459
Private: 206, 459
Private: 206, 459

Private: 206, 459
Private: 206, 459
Private: 206, 459
Private: 206, 459
Private: 248
Raymond Niles: 146, 459
Richard N: 146, 459
Robert: 146, 459

Mooseberger -
Private: 246
Private: 246

Mordeau -
Private: 276, 459
Private: 276, 459

Morgan -
Nellie: 157, 459
Private: 259, 459
Private: 201, 459

Mori -
Private: 208, 459

Mornhengweig -
Private: 196, 263, 459
Private: 263, 459
Private: 196, 459
Private: 196, 263, 459
Private: 196, 459

Mornhingweig -
Carl: 196, 459

Morning -
Mary L.: 135, 190, 257, 286, 459
William A.: 135, 459

Morris -
Private: 264, 459
Private: 264, 459
Private: 264, 459
Private: 264, 459
Private: 264, 459

Moseman -
Magdalena: 127, 316, 459

Mosemann -
Luke Musser: 265, 459
Miriam: 127, 317, 459
Private: 265, 459
Private: 265, 459
Private: 265, 459
Private: 265, 289, 459

Moser -
Adolph: 143, 459
Stella: 143, 201, 267, 268, 459

Mosser -
Christian: 14, 459

Mossey -
Private: 210, 460

Motheral -
Rebecca: 93, 460

Mount -
Private: 218, 460
Private: 218, 460
Unknown: 218, 460

Mountz -
Alta: 147, 207, 273, 460
Jesse: 146, 460
Kathryn: 147, 207, 274, 460
Malvern: 147, 460

Mary: 147, 207, 274, 460
Private: 207, 273, 460
Private: 273, 460
Private: 274, 460
Private: 207, 274, 460
Private: 207, 460
Private: 207, 274, 460
Wilfred: 147, 207, 273, 274, 460

Mowder -
Bessie: 160, 161, 460

Moyer -
Abraham: 460
Barbara: 460
Barbara: 460
Barbara: 460
Eleanor: 160, 460
John Haldeman (Meyers): 460
Katherine: 160, 220, 460
Lillian: 160, 460
Margaret: 160, 460
Mary: 460
Mary: 460
Private: 237, 354, 460
Private: 237, 354, 460
Private: 237, 354, 460
Roy: 160, 460
Sarah: 159, 460
Warren: 160, 460
Willard: 160, 460

Muench -
Grace: 64, 460

Mull -
Anna Mae: 166, 167, 327, 460

Muller -
Elsbeth: 16, 18, 20, 460
Ursula: 18, 460

Mumall -
Elizabeth: 103, 460

Mumma -
Fanny: 58
John: 47, 460
Maria: 293, 296, 301, 306, 311, 315, 323, 339, 460
Sarah: 64, 460

Mummah -
Barbara: 293, 460
Christian: 293, 460
David: 293, 460
George: 293, 460
George Anthony: 13, 293, 460
Henry: 293, 460
Jacob: 293, 460
Juliana: 293, 460
Magdalena: 293, 460

Munroe -
Lawrence Robertson: 129

Murgas -
Joseph: 283, 460
Joseph: 283, 460

Murison -
Aileen Ruth: 156, 460
Anna: 117, 460
Audrey Jean: 157, 460
Bessie Louise: 118, 157, 460
Gordon Ernest: 118, 156, 460

Isobel Anna: 156, 460
James: 117, 460
James Wilfred: 156, 460
John Alexander: 156, 460
Private: 157, 460
Wilfrid Charles: 118, 460
William Gordon: 156, 461
William Jacob: 118, 461

Murphy -
Eda R: 134, 187, 254, 461
Private: 241, 358, 461
Private: 241, 358, 461
Richard W: 189, 461
Robert: 189, 461
William: 134, 461

Murray -
Donald E: 188, 256, 461
Ira S: 188, 461
Jack O: 188, 461
Judy A: 256, 461
Richard A: 188, 461
Sylvan E: 188, 256, 461
Terry L: 256, 461

Murrell -
Alpha: 117, 154, 461
Charles: 117, 461
Ernest: 117, 461

Murry -
Jean Marie: 151, 461
Marguerite Elizabeth: 151, 461
Ralph Sheldon: 151, 461

Musselman -
Henry: 461
Henry: 461
Henry: 61, 461
John: 296, 461

Musser -
Anna: 461
Anna: 461
Barbara: 299, 461
Barbara Weber: 296, 301, 306, 307, 311, 315-317, 323, 339, 340, 461
Benjamin: 461
Christian Musser: 178, 323, 324, 461
Daniel: 461
Daniel: 296, 461
Emma: 461
Esther: 296, 461
Fronica: 296, 461
Gideon: 461
Henry: 461
Jacob: 461
Jacob: 461
Jacob: 10, 28, 461
John: 297, 461
John B.: 461
Lucretta: 461
Magdalena: 296, 461
Margaret: 39, 300, 461
Martha: 461
Martha: 461
Martin: 461
Martin: 461

Mary: 296, 461
Mary Naomi: 178, 323, 324, 339, 461
Mathias: 296, 461
Mildred Lois: 323, 461
Nancy: 296, 461
Susan: 461
Veronica: 39, 300, 461

Mustard -
Jean: 158, 461

Mutch -
Private: 246
Private: 246
Private: 246

Myer -
Anna: 461
Isaac: 461
Mary: 461
Ruth: 127, 316, 317, 461

Myers -
Barbara: 301, 461
Caroline: 77, 461
Catherine: 75, 461
Catherine: 78, 79, 461
Daniel: 77, 462
Elisabeth: 77, 462
Elizabeth: 104, 462
Elizabeth S: 135, 462
Emma W.: 90, 312, 462
Henry: 58, 462
Henry O.: 77, 462
John: 77, 462
John O.: 77, 462
Magdalena: 294, 462
Margaret: 77, 462
Mary A.: 77, 462
Matilda: 77, 462
Peter: 77, 462
Private: 226, 343, 462
Private: 177, 337, 462
Private: 276, 462
Private: 276, 462
Private: 276, 462
Rebecca: 77, 462
Susannah: 77, 462
William O.: 77, 462

Mylin -
Abraham S: 6, 303, 462
Anna: 14, 462
Martha: 299, 462

Myrna -
Private: 268, 462

Naftzinger -
Michael: 84, 462

Nafziger -
Private: 284, 361, 462

Nagel -
Mary: 462

Naples -
Private: 281, 462
Private: 281, 462

Napoli -
Private: 239, 356, 462

Nauman -
Ann Elizabeth: 83, 462

Private: 170, 331, 462

Neff -
Abraham: 25, 462
Ann: 300, 462
Barbara: 14, 462
Barbara: 303, 462
Barbara: 73, 308, 309, 462
Benjamin: 70, 462
Catherine: 462
Elizabeth: 462
John: 311, 462
Mary V: 64, 462
Nellie Louise: 114, 150, 462
Peter Augustus: 114, 462

Neidig -
Christian H.: 43, 462
Elizabeth: 43, 462
John: 43, 462
Jonathan: 32, 462

Nellie -
(name: Helen Edith Thrope): 192, 193, 462, 500

Nelson -
Private: 206, 462

Nessly -
Jacob Herr: 462

Neuenschwander -
Madlena: 18, 20, 462

Neukommet -
Barbara (aka: Barbara Newcomer): 15, 17, 24, 462

Newberry -
Private: 250

Newcomer -
Ann: 35, 462
Anna Weber: 7, 8, 11, 30, 46, 293, 296, 300, 304, 305, 309, 310, 312-315, 318-338, 340-362, 462
Barbara (name: Barbara Neukommet): 15, 17, 24, 462
Barbara: 11, 293, 462
Christian: 11, 293, 462
Elizabeth: 11, 292, 462
Elizabeth: 87, 462
Emmet: 143, 462
Henry: 11, 293, 462
Henry: 86, 462
Jacob: 87, 462
Levi: 87, 463
Magdalena: 11, 293, 463
Mary: 87, 463
Mary: 112, 113, 463
Pearlie: 143, 463
Peter: 11, 13, 16, 292, 463
Peter: 11, 293, 463
Wolfgang: 8, 11, 13, 30, 292, 463

Newell -
Jr. Private: 249
Private: 249
Private: 249
Private: 250

Newkommet -
Peter: 13, 16, 463

Newlin -
    Private: 239, 357, 463
Newswanger -
    Ella Margaret: 125, 322, 463
    Lizzie: 301, 463
    Private: 223, 341, 463
    Private: 223, 341, 463
Nicely -
    Fred: 162, 463
    Private: 162, 463
Nichol -
    Ruth: 218, 463
Nickey -
    Edward: 74, 103, 463
    George: 58, 463
    Mary Jane: 103, 463
    Nancy: 74, 103, 131, 184, 250, 285, 463
    Samuel: 58, 74, 103, 131, 184, 250, 285, 463
Nigh -
    Ed: 158, 463
    Frances: 158, 463
    Jack: 158, 218, 219, 463
    Private: 219, 463
    Private: 219, 463
    Private: 219, 463
    William: 158, 463
Nisley -
    Rachel H: 134, 463
Nissley -
    Annie: 75, 463
    Barbara: 72, 463
    John Paul: 102
    Rev Joseph: 75, 463
    Katherine: 102, 130, 183, 250
    Maria: 10, 463
    Private: 240, 357, 463
Nissly -
    Judith: 463
Noble -
    Maybelle: 185
Nolt -
    Barbara: 56, 304, 463
    Chester B.: 125, 322, 463
    Christian: 45, 463
    Daniel: 307, 463
    Private: 227, 344, 463
    Private: 227, 344, 463
    Private: 226, 344, 463
    Private: 228, 345, 463
    Private: 235, 353, 463
    Private: 236, 353, 463
    Private: 236, 353, 463
    Private: 236, 353, 463
    Private: 125, 177, 322, 338, 463
    Private: 125, 177, 322, 338, 463
    Private: 125, 322, 463
    Susanna: 463
Novak -
    Private: 205, 463
    Private: 205, 463
    Private: 205, 463
Nusbaum -
    Elizabeth: 82, 463
Nussey -
    Betty: 256, 463
Nyeholt -
    Private: 237, 355, 463
    Private: 237, 355, 463
Ober -
    Aaron: 75, 463
    Aaron G.: 82, 463
    Abraham: 82, 463
    Adaline: 79, 463
    Agnes: 104, 463
    Agnes Eda: 104, 134, 187, 254, 463
    Alfred S.: 76, 463
    Ann: 59, 78, 464
    Ann: 81, 464
    Anna Nancy: 60, 81, 464
    Anne: 75, 464
    Annie: 75, 464
    Annie: 104, 135, 190, 257, 286, 464
    Annie: 104, 464
    Annie Elizabeth: 104, 134, 187, 188, 255, 256, 286, 464
    Arden G: 134, 189, 256, 464
    Arden G, Jr: 189, 256, 464
    Arthur: 134, 464
    Augustine: 80, 464
    Barbara: 60, 80, 464
    Barbara: 59, 78, 105, 137, 138, 196, 197, 263, 264, 464
    Barbara: 75, 464
    Barbara: 76, 464
    Barbara: 75, 464
    Barbara Estella: 104, 135, 189, 190, 464
    Benjamin: 41, 60, 86, 464
    Benjamin: 60, 82, 464
    Benjamin Franklin: 81, 464
    Benjamin Franklin: 104, 134, 187, 254, 464
    Benjamin H.: 61, 464
    Bernard Farren: 104, 134, 464
    C Kiefer: 134, 189, 464
    Caroline: 76, 464
    Catherine: 59, 78, 464
    Catherine: 75, 464
    Catherine: 82, 464
    Catherine A.: 79, 105, 138, 139, 197, 198, 264, 265, 287-289, 464
    Catherine Rebecca: 104, 133, 186, 187, 253, 254, 283, 464
    Cecelia O.: 60, 86, 464
    Cecil S: 134, 188, 256, 464
    Chambers: 59, 464
    Chandra Kay: 189, 464
    Charlotte: 82, 464
    Christian: 40, 58, 75, 104, 133-135, 185-190, 252-257, 283, 286, 464
    Christian: 41, 59, 60, 79, 80, 464
    Christian: 59, 77, 464
    Christian: 75, 464
    Christian: 75, 464

    Christian J.: 76, 464
    Christian Longnecker: 59, 75, 104, 135, 190, 257, 286, 287, 289, 464
    Cyrus: 77, 464
    Cyrus Henry: 59, 464
    Cyrus Stevens: 76, 464
    Daisy Meyers: 135, 190, 257, 286, 287, 464
    Daniel: 76, 464
    Daniel: 79, 464
    Daniel M: 135, 464
    Daniel S.: 80, 464
    David: 79, 464
    David: 81, 464
    David: 75, 104, 133-135, 185-190, 252-257, 283, 286, 464
    David H.: 76, 464
    David S: 40, 59, 75, 104, 135, 190, 257, 286, 287, 289, 464
    David S.: 77, 464
    David W: 104, 134, 188, 256, 464
    David W: 188, 464
    David W III: 188, 464
    David W, Jr: 134, 188, 464
    Delilah O.: 76, 464
    Drusannah: 77, 464
    Edward: 104, 464
    Edward: 188, 464
    Edward K.: 79, 464
    Elaine C: 189, 256, 465
    Eleanor V: 189, 465
    Eliza: 59, 465
    Elizabeth: 41, 60, 82, 83, 465
    Elizabeth: 59, 79, 465
    Elizabeth: 60, 82, 465
    Elizabeth: 59, 465
    Elizabeth: 58, 465
    Elizabeth: 81, 465
    Elizabeth: 82, 465
    Elizabeth: 76, 465
    Elizabeth: 82, 465
    Elizabeth: 76, 465
    Elizabeth: 77, 465
    Elizabeth: 80, 465
    Elizabeth Anna: 75, 465
    Elizabeth B.: 77, 465
    Elmer M.: 135, 465
    Emanuel: 82, 465
    Emma: 104, 465
    Emma Barbara: 104, 133, 185, 186, 252, 253, 286, 465
    Ephraim B.: 79, 465
    Esther: 76, 465
    Evelyn M: 189, 465
    Fannie O: 134, 187, 254, 465
    Florence May: 104, 134, 135, 189, 257, 465
    Franey: 59, 77, 465
    Fronica: 59, 465
    Gabrielle: 80, 465
    George: 81, 465
    George: 80, 465
    George A: 135, 465
    Geraldine L: 189, 465
    Hannah: 59, 465

Hannah Amanda: 76, 465
Harold: 134, 465
Harriet S.: 76, 465
Harrison Jackson: 59, 465
Harry F.: 135, 465
Henry: 60, 465
Henry: 40, 465
Henry: 41, 59, 75-77, 104, 135-137, 190-196, 257-263, 465
Henry: 40, 58, 75, 104, 135, 190, 257, 286, 465
Henry: 60, 81, 465
Henry: 59, 465
Henry: 81, 465
Henry: 76, 465
Henry: 81, 465
Henry: 76, 465
Henry: 75, 465
Henry E.: 75, 104, 465
Henry Saylor: 77, 465
Horatio Seymour: 80, 465
Isaac: 75, 465
Isaac Huntsberger: 58, 75, 104, 133-135, 185-190, 252-257, 283, 286, 465
Isaac Newton: 104, 134, 188, 189, 256, 465
Jacob: 41, 465
Jacob: 40
Jacob: 104, 465
Jacob: 40, 465
Jacob: 58, 465
Jacob: 59, 78, 79, 105, 138, 139, 197, 198, 264, 265, 287-289, 465
Jacob: 60, 81, 465
Jacob: 59, 76, 465
Jacob: 81, 465
Jacob: 77, 465
Jacob: 77, 465
Jacob Myers: 78, 79, 466
James B.: 61, 466
James C.: 59, 466
James C.: 80, 466
Jean: 188, 466
Jeremiah: 75, 466
Joan: 188, 256, 466
John: 41, 60, 81, 82, 466
John: 59, 75, 76, 466
John: 60, 82, 466
John: 81, 466
John: 76, 466
John: 82, 466
John: 188, 466
John C.: 60, 79, 80, 466
John D.: 134, 188, 466
John D II: 188, 466
John F.: 79, 466
John H.: 81, 466
John J.: 79, 466
John J.: 80, 466
John Miller: 190, 466
John Motter: 104, 466
Joseph: 77, 466
Joseph: 59, 76, 466
Joseph: 81, 466

Joseph: 76, 466
Joseph: 77, 466
Joseph S.: 77, 466
Julia Irene: 104, 466
Kain: 80, 466
Kathleen P: 256, 466
Levi: 76, 466
Levi S.: 82, 466
Lewis: 59, 79, 466
Lucy: 77, 466
Magdalena: 60, 466
Magdalena: 59, 79, 466
Margaret: 82, 466
Margaret: 82, 466
Margaret: 80, 466
Margaret R: 256, 466
Marilyn E: 188, 466
Marilyn M: 189, 466
Marshall: 59, 466
Martha E.: 79, 466
Martin: 81, 466
Mary (aka: Polly Ober): 58, 466, 467
Mary: 59, 77, 466
Mary: 82, 466
Mary: 79, 466
Mary A: 188, 466
Mary A.: 77, 466
Mary Adella: 80, 466
Mary Alice: 104, 466
Mary Ann Or Sue: 135, 466
Mary E: 188, 256, 466
Mary G.: 82, 466
Mary Or Mattie: 75, 466
Mary Sue: 76, 466
Maryann: 104, 466
Melissa G: 134, 466
Merritt L: 134, 188, 466
Michael: 41, 59, 78, 79, 105, 137-139, 196-198, 263-265, 287-290, 466
Michael: 59, 75, 104, 135, 190, 257, 286, 466
Michael: 75, 466
Michael Cramer: 75, 104, 135, 190, 257, 286, 467
Minnie: 190, 257, 286, 287, 467
Missouri: 77, 467
Moses Heagly: 104, 135, 190, 257, 286, 287, 289, 467
Moses M.: 135, 467
Moses Ruhl: 75, 104, 135, 190, 257, 286, 287, 289, 467
Nancy: 60, 80, 467
Nancy: 76, 467
Nancy Ann: 82, 467
Nancy Catherine: 60, 81, 467
Obadiah S.: 76, 467
Oliver Francis: 59, 467
Peter: 41, 59, 467
Peter: 40, 58, 74, 103, 131-133, 184, 185, 250-252, 285, 286, 289, 467
Polly (name: Mary Ober): 58, 466, 467
Private: 236, 354, 467

Private: 236, 354, 467
Private: 237, 354, 467
Private: 237, 354, 467
Rebecca: 81, 467
Rebecca: 76, 467
Rebecca: 80, 467
Robert H.: 80, 467
Rosanna: 59, 467
Sally (name: Sarah Ober): 58, 467
Samuel: 59, 79, 467
Samuel: 75, 467
Samuel: 59, 77, 467
Sarah (aka: Sally Ober): 58, 467
Sarah: 76, 467
Sarah: 81, 467
Sarah E.: 77, 467
Sarah J.: 80, 467
Sarah Jane: 59, 467
Sarah Jane: 79, 467
Solomon Henry: 104, 467
Stella M: 135, 190, 257, 287, 289, 467
Susan: 61, 467
Susan: 82, 467
Susannah: 59, 76, 104, 135-137, 190-196, 257-263, 467
Susannah: 82, 467
Theodore: 79, 467
Unknown: 77, 467
Veronica: 41, 60, 84-86, 467
Veronica Francis: 60, 81, 467
Vicky Lee: 256, 467
Wilbur C: 134, 188, 256, 467
Wilbur C , Jr: 188, 256, 467
Wilhelmia: 80, 467
William: 59, 467
William: 82, 467
William: 77, 467
William: 80, 467
William S.: 76, 467

Oberholtzer -
Abraham: 84, 467
Ann: 60, 467
Anna H.: 45, 467
Catharine: 45, 62, 308, 467
Catherine: 59, 467
Elizabeth: 126, 316, 467
Elizabeth H.: 45, 467
Esther H.: 45, 467
Henry H.: 45, 467
Jacob H.: 45, 467
John H.: 45, 467
Joseph H.: 45, 467
Lizzie O.: 312, 468
Magdalena: 468
Martha H.: 45, 62, 90, 113, 150, 178, 179, 244, 307, 308, 312, 468
Samuel: 45, 307, 308, 468
Samuel H.: 45, 468
Susanna H.: 45, 468

O'Boyle -
Norman: 158, 468

O'Brian -
Lily: 120, 468

O'Brien -

Jean: 199, 468
O'Connell -
    Private: 237, 354, 468
    Private: 237, 354, 468
O'Connor -
    Margaret Cecilia: 152, 468
Oesch -
    Susanna Justina: 112, 468
Offert -
    Agnes: 219, 468
Oiler -
    Christopher: 133, 468
Oitman -
    Private: 262, 468
Oliver -
    David: 155, 468
    Earl: 155, 468
    Edith: 155, 468
    Edwin: 155, 468
    George: 117, 468
    Gerald: 155, 468
    Gladys: 155, 468
    Jane: 155, 468
Oppliger -
    Adelfried: 15, 17, 19, 24, 468
    Peter: 17, 19, 24, 468
Orsbirn -
    Elmer A: 273, 468
    Private: 273, 468
    Private: 273, 468
    Private: 273, 468
    Private: 273, 468
    Private: 273, 468
    Private: 273, 468
Osborn -
    Private: 262, 468
    Private: 262, 468
    Private: 262, 468
Osborne -
    Mabel: 128
Oscar -
    Lloyd: 116, 468
Outlaw -
    Katrina Faye: 206, 468
Overholtzer -
    Esther: 38, 468
Overly -
    Private: 289, 468
    Private: 289, 468
Owen -
    Wilma Mae: 210, 468
Owens -
    Elizabeth: 58, 74, 75, 103, 131-
        133, 184, 185, 250-252,
        285, 286, 289, 468
    Freda I: 209, 468
Page -
    Bessie Bell: 143, 468
Palm -
    Clara Belle: 104, 468
Palmer -
    Archie Judson: 156, 468
    Darrel Archie: 156, 468
    Marjorie Ann: 156, 468

Private: 250
Private: 250
Pancake -
    Bob: 268, 468
    Private: 268, 468
    Private: 268, 468
    Private: 268, 468
    Private: 268, 468
Parker -
    Helen Ruth: 217, 468
    James: 78, 468
    Rachel Edith: 118, 468
Parks -
    Private: 213, 468
Parry -
    Antonia Marie: 163, 468
Parsons -
    Ellen: 95, 468
    Florence: 120, 468
    Thelma Ruth: 208, 468
Partridge -
    Allan Baker: 254, 468
    Charles Allan: 254, 468
    Diane Louise: 254, 468
Patrick -
    (name: Wilbur A Stevens): 187,
        468, 486
Patterson -
    Bertram Charles: 151, 469
    John: 94, 469
    Lena May: 156, 469
    Mary: 95, 469
    Millard H.: 258, 469
    Private: 258, 469
    Private: 214, 469
Paul -
    Bessie Norene: 192, 260, 469
    Irwin Lee: 192, 469
    Private: 192, 260, 469
Pavlovich -
    Ruth R: 256, 469
Paxon -
    Private: 274, 469
Peachey -
    Private: 173, 334, 469
    Private: 173, 334, 469
    Private: 173, 334, 469
    Private: 173, 334, 469
    Private: 173, 334, 469
Pearsol -
    Agnes Keys: 86, 469
    Anna: 86, 469
    Charles: 86, 469
    Ellen: 86, 469
    John H.: 86, 469
    John H.: 86, 469
    Unknown: 86, 469
    William H.: 86, 469
Peart -
    Mary: 98, 469
Peck -
    Hazel: 255, 469
Peggie -
    Unnamed: 222, 469

Peifer -
    Maria: 66, 469
Peiffer -
    Daniel: 32, 469
Pendergast -
    John: 259, 469
    Private: 259, 469
Pengotti -
    Private: 279, 469
    Private: 279, 469
Penner -
    Private: 167, 328, 469
    Private: 167, 328, 469
    Private: 167, 328, 469
Pennock -
    Betty Louise: 124, 175, 241, 321,
        336, 359, 469
    Private: 124, 321, 469
    Private: 124, 175, 241, 321, 336,
        358, 359, 469
    William Ralph: 124, 321, 469
Pennypacker -
    Hannah Bergey: 469
    Sophia: 469
Pentz -
    John: 109, 469
    Mary Ann: 109, 469
    Samuel: 109, 469
    William: 109, 469
Pergrem -
    Private: 194, 469
Perkins -
    Alton: 94, 469
Perry -
    Bonnie K: 134, 469
    Eugene: 109, 469
Peters -
    Barbara: 71, 469
    George: 281, 469
    Private: 171, 331, 469
    Private: 281, 469
Petersheim -
    Private: 169, 330, 469
Peterson -
    Thelma: 469
Peveto -
    Horace: 111, 469
Pfaltzgraff -
    Christina Catherine: 222, 469
    David Jasini: 163, 222, 223, 469
    George Hackman: 163, 222, 469
    Kathryn Joyce: 163, 469
    Michael Jasini: 223, 469
    Nevin Mark: 163, 469
    Rebecca: 222, 469
    Renee: 222, 469
    Rhonda: 222, 470
    Roberta: 222, 470
    Roy Edward: 163, 470
    Roy Edward , Jr: 163, 222, 470
    Timothy David: 223, 470
Pfautz -
    Mildred: 91, 314, 470
    Monroe: 90, 314, 470

Pfenniger -
    Adelheit: 17, 291, 470
    Barbara: 17, 291, 470
Pfister -
    Susanna: 19, 470
Phillips -
    Private: 277, 470
    Tara: 223, 470
Pick -
    Eleanor Gillson: 117, 470
Pickel -
    Private: 234, 351, 470
Pickens -
    Private: 267, 470
    Private: 267, 470
    Private: 267, 470
    Robert Oliver: 267, 470
Pier -
    Private: 237, 354, 470
    Private: 237, 354, 470
Pifer -
    Private: 289, 470
    Takis Lin: 289, 470
Pike -
    Brian K.: 264, 470
    Private: 288, 470
    Private: 288, 470
    Private: 264, 470
    Private: 264, 288, 470
    Private: 264, 288, 470
Piper -
    Mary Mildred: 185
Pitkin -
    Janet Elaine: 289, 470
Pittman -
    Cordella: 209, 470
Planchock -
    Dan: 207, 470
    Private: 207, 274, 470
    Private: 207, 274, 470
    Private: 274, 470
    Private: 274, 470
    Private: 207, 470
    Private: 207, 274, 470
    Private: 207, 470
    Private: 207, 470
Plank -
    John: 298, 470
Pletcher -
    David M.: 77, 470
Plock -
    Private: 211, 470
Plonk -
    David Francis Kauffman: 470
Pohl -
    Private: 183
 -
    Polly (name: Mary Koop
        Kauffman): 74, 310
Pool -
    Lydia (Puhl): 470
Poorman -
    John: 31, 470
    Veronica: 41, 470

Popa -
    Private: 275, 470
    Private: 275, 470
    Private: 275, 470
    Private: 275, 470
Pope -
    Alda: 195, 470
Porter -
    Cynthia: 222, 470
    Keith: 155, 470
    Kenneth: 155, 470
    Myrtle: 155, 470
    Roy: 155, 470
    Verna: 155, 470
Pote -
    Mary: 81, 470
    Mary: 82, 470
Powder -
    Catherine: 78, 470
    Jacob: 78, 470
    John: 78, 470
    John: 78, 470
    Michael: 78, 470
Powders -
    John: 78, 470
Powell -
    Betty: 273, 470
    Private: 280, 471
    Private: 280, 471
    Private: 280, 471
    Private: 280, 471
Prater -
    Clifford Jesse: 211, 471
    Private: 211, 471
Precise -
    Private: 205, 471
Price -
    Catherine L.: 124, 321, 471
    Eliza Rinehart: 471
    Freda Elizabeth: 145, 146, 471
    Hannah: 33, 471
    Ora: 106, 471
    Private: 471
Prickett -
    Private: 280, 281, 471
    Private: 281, 471
    Private: 281, 471
Printz -
    Private: 241, 358, 471
    Private: 241, 358, 471
 -
    Private: 250
Probert -
    Helen: 95, 471
Pryde -
    Private: 282, 471
    Private: 282, 471
Pullin -
    George: 190, 471
    Janet: 190, 471
    Richard: 190, 471
    Wilbur: 190, 471
Pultz -
    William: 138, 471

Quest -
    Margaret: 471
Rabold -
    Alvin Kenneth: 471
    Private: 471
    Private: 471
    Private: 471
    Private: 471
Radcliffe -
    Private: 265, 471
Radley -
    Ruby: 153, 471
Rakestron -
    Unnamed: 252
Ramsey -
    Nellie M: 134, 471
Ramsies -
    Mary Jane: 185
Ranck -
    Arthur Eby: 124, 174, 240, 321,
        335, 358, 471
    Donald Edwin: 124, 174, 175, 240,
        321, 335, 358, 471
    Edwin Guy: 124, 320, 321, 471
    Elizabeth: 296, 471
    Enos Raymond: 124, 321, 471
    Jane Elizabeth: 174, 335, 471
    Lester Hershey: 124, 174, 240,
        321, 335, 357, 358, 471
    Private: 124, 174, 321, 335, 471
    Private: 174, 335, 471
    Private: 174, 240, 335, 357, 471
    Private: 174, 240, 335, 358, 471
    Private: 174, 335, 471
    Private: 240, 358, 471
    Private: 240, 358, 471
    Private: 240, 358, 471
    Private: 174, 335, 471
    Private: 174, 240, 335, 358, 471
    Private: 174, 335, 471
    Private: 240, 358, 471
    Private: 240, 358, 471
    Private: 175, 335, 471
    Private: 175, 240, 335, 358, 471
    Private: 174, 335, 471
Randall -
    Cornelius Hall: 145, 471
    Lowell Orland: 145, 205, 270, 471
    Private: 205, 270, 471
    Private: 205, 270, 471
    Private: 270, 471
    Private: 270, 471
Randels -
    Alverda: 111, 471
Rathgeber -
    Living: 287, 471
Ray -
    Gale Emery: 214, 472
    Private: 214, 280, 472
    Private: 214, 280, 472
    Private: 214, 280, 472
    Private: 214, 280, 472
    Private: 214, 280, 281, 472
    Private: 214, 281, 472
    Private: 214, 281, 472

Private: 214, 281, 472
Private: 214, 472
Private: 280, 472
Private: 280, 472
Private: 280, 472
Private: 280, 472

Raymer -
Bertie: 118, 472
Christian: 118, 472
Elmina: 118, 158, 219, 472
Magdalena: 65, 472
Ruth: 118, 158, 219, 472

Rebecca -
Unknown: 67, 472

Reece -
Laura: 109, 472

Reed -
James: 87, 472
Margaret: 79, 472

Reen -
Charles: 59, 472

Reese -
Adam George: 184
Dana Everett: 184
Elmer: 184, 472
Herman Wilson: 184, 251
Marion H.: 184, 472
Mary Esther Katherine: 184, 251
Neola: 184, 472
Ola: 184
Private: 270, 472
Private: 270, 472
Private: 270, 472
Ricky: 251
Velva Grace: 184, 250, 251

Reesor -
Anna: 94, 472
Christian: 26, 472
Elizabeth: 46, 472

Reeves -
Private: 168, 329, 472
Private: 262, 472

Reiff -
Abraham: 472
Abraham: 293, 472
Abraham: 56, 304, 305, 472
Anna: 472
Anna: 472
Annie: 56, 73, 101, 125-127, 178, 243, 244, 305, 309, 311, 314, 472
Barbara: 472
Benjamin: 472
Catherine: 472
Christina: 472
David: 472
David: 472
Elizabeth: 472
Feronica: 472
John A.: 57, 305, 472
Jonas N: 472
Joseph: 56, 304, 472
Joseph N: 472
Magdalena: 472
Magdalena: 57, 305, 472

Mary: 472
Mary: 472
Susanna: 472
Susanna: 472

Reiffer -
Private: 181
Private: 181

Reighart -
Abraham: 76, 472

Reinohl -
Maria: 67, 472

Reist -
Abraham: 472
Annie: 34, 472
Barbara: 38, 472
Barbara: 38, 472
Esther: 34, 472
Florence: 98, 473
John: 34, 473
John: 10, 28, 473
John: 10, 34, 473
John G.: 98, 473
John H.: 98, 473
Maria: 34, 473
Maria E.: 45, 473
Naomi: 98, 473
Reuben: 84, 473

Reiter -
Private: 262, 473
Private: 262, 473
Private: 262, 473

Reitober -
Private: 206, 473

Reitz -
Elizabeth R.: 306, 473
Harmen: 306, 473

Renfro -
Private: 210, 277, 473

Renninger -
Angeline: 307, 473

Resh -
Henry: 298, 473
Magdalena: 37, 38, 473

Ressler -
Mary: 473

Retallack -
John Harold: 125, 321, 473

Rettenmeyer -
Carl William: 186, 473

Reuben -
John, Diehl: 105, 139, 473

Reuter -
Rosella Catherine: 217, 473

Revis -
Mary: 95, 473

Reynolds -
Elizabeth: 92, 473

Rhoads -
Elizabeth: 296, 473
James C.: 257, 473
Private: 257, 286, 473
Private: 257, 473
Private: 286, 473
Private: 286, 473

Private: 286, 473
Private: 286, 473
Private: 286, 473
Private: 257, 473

Rhoda -
Unnamed: 133, 473

Rhode -
Mary: 8-12, 25, 473

Rhodes -
Edwin D: 286, 473
Edwin D II: 286, 473
Jacqueline M: 286, 473

Rice -
Anna Mabel: 185, 473
Private: 231, 349, 473
Private: 149, 212, 473

Richards -
Elizabeth: 215, 473

Richardson -
Ada Lucretia: 137, 193, 194, 473
Alice Vivian: 137, 473
Andrew Jackson: 105, 136, 193, 194, 261, 262, 473
Anna: 105, 473
Carl Andrew: 193, 261, 473
Charlotte B.: 137, 195, 473
Dolores Elaine: 137, 473
Emily Pearl: 136, 473
Eva Beatrice: 137, 194, 262, 473
Florence Mildred: 137, 194, 473
Harold: 137, 473
Harriet May: 105, 137, 195, 196, 263, 473
Leslie Martin: 137, 194, 473
Margaret Ella Blanch: 137, 194, 262, 473
Martha: 105, 137, 196, 263, 473
Mary Jane: 105, 135, 190-192, 257-259, 473
Mattie Beulah: 137, 194, 262, 473
Melville Jackson: 137, 194, 262, 473
Nancy Ann: 105, 473
Private: 176, 337, 473
Private: 176, 241, 337, 359, 474
Private: 176, 242, 337, 359, 474
Private: 176, 337, 474
Private: 261, 474
Private: 261, 474
Private: 261, 474
Private: 262, 474
Private: 262, 474
Private: 194, 262, 474
Private: 194, 262, 474
Private: 262, 474
Private: 194, 474
Private: 194, 474
Private: 195, 474
Private: 195, 474
Private: 195, 474
Private: 195, 474
Private: 195, 474
Private: 195, 474
Private: 195, 474
Private: 195, 474

Private: 195, 474
Private: 195, 474
Private: 195, 474
Rebecca Jane: 105, 136, 192, 260, 474
Reginold: 137, 474
Sarah B.: 105, 136, 193, 261, 474
Sarah Ruby: 136, 474
Stephen Andrew: 136, 193, 261, 474
Stephen E.: 105, 137, 194, 195, 474
Stephen R.: 104, 105, 474
Stephen Roscoe: 137, 195, 474
Susan Ann: 105, 136, 192, 260, 474
Sydney Robert: 137, 195, 474

Richey -
Rosetta Cobb: 71, 474

Rickert -
Richard: 68, 474

Rider -
Marion: 188, 474

Rife -
Abraham: 297, 474
Fanny H.: 56, 305, 474
Samuel: 474

Rill -
Private: 203, 474
Private: 203, 474
Private: 203, 474
Thpmas Sr: 203, 474

Rinehart -
Catharine: 474
John Frick: 474
Private: 201, 474
Rebecca: 474

Ringer -
John: 68, 474

Risser -
Abraham H.: 26, 31, 42, 474
Abraham S.: 85, 474
Barbara: 26, 474
Catharine: 474
Catherine: 26, 474
Christian: 304, 474
Elizabeth: 26, 474
Elizabeth: 26, 474
Elizabeth: 85, 474
Elizabeth H.: 31, 42, 474
Esther: 26, 474
Jacob H.: 26, 474
John: 26, 474
John: 85, 474
John H.: 85, 474
John S.: 85, 474
Joseph L.: 85, 474
Magdalena H.: 26, 475
Mary M.: 45, 475
Peter: 26, 475
Peter: 26, 475
Samuel S.: 85, 475
Veronica: 85, 475

Rissinger -
Sandra: 252

Rissler -
Private: 229, 347, 475
Private: 229, 347, 475

Rittenhouse -
Sherry: 244, 340, 475

Ritter -
Benjamin (Riter): 475
Private: 288-290, 475
Private: 290, 475
Private: 288, 475

Roach -
Private: 244

Roadt -
Magdalena: 9, 28, 475

Robb -
Frank: 156, 475
Private: 201, 475

Roberts -
Barbara: 203, 475

Robertson -
Earl: 158, 475
Ethel: 95, 475
Grace: 157, 475
Private: 158, 475
Private: 158, 475

Robinson -
Harry Thomas: 143, 475
Mabel: 475

Rockie -
Amelia: 213, 475

Rockman -
Private: 210, 475

Rockwell -
Private: 259, 475
Private: 259, 475
Private: 259, 475

Rode -
Murial A: 257, 475
Unknown: 257, 475

Rodgers -
Donald Fink: 124, 321, 475
Elizabeth: 253, 475
Leroy: 273, 475
Private: 124, 176, 241, 321, 336, 359, 475
Private: 176, 336, 475
Private: 176, 241, 336, 359, 475
Private: 176, 336, 475
Private: 176, 336, 475
Private: 176, 336, 475
Private: 241, 359, 475
Private: 241, 359, 475
Private: 273, 475
Private: 273, 475

Rogers -
Carolyn: 251
Enos Ellis: 82, 475

Rohaley -
Private: 280, 475

Rohland -
Elizabeth: 82, 475

Rohr -
Francis: 475

Rohrer -
Catherine: 6, 309, 475
Elizabeth W.: 303, 475
Jacob: 36, 475
John: 25, 475
Maria: 303, 304, 475
Mary Amanda: 91, 314, 475
Private: 239, 357, 475
Private: 239, 357, 475
Private: 239, 357, 475

Roof -
Oscar: 268, 475
Private: 268, 475

Roose -
Catherine: 307, 475

Root -
Adam Frantz: 58, 475
Benjamin B: 57, 475
Henry: 294, 475

Ross -
Daniel: 475

Roth -
Irene Loretta: 258, 475
Jacob: 475

Rounck -
Witmer C.: 58

Rourke -
Robert: 251

Roush -
Private: 175, 336, 476

Rout -
Private: 281, 476

Rowland -
Margaret: 130

Royer -
Ephraim: 72, 476
Jacob: 72, 476
Jacob: 72, 476
John: 72, 476
Jonas: 72, 476
Leah: 72, 476
Mary: 72, 476
Samuel: 72, 476
Sarah: 139, 476
Susannah: 72, 476
William: 72, 476

Ruch -
John: 476
Mary Elizabeth: 476

Rudo -
Private: 214, 476

Rudolph -
Private: 287, 476

Rudy -
Charles: 48, 476
Christina: 46
John Henry: 167, 328, 476
Marian A: 255, 476
Marjorie Elaine: 167, 328, 476
Private: 167, 328, 476
Private: 167, 233, 328, 350, 476
Private: 167, 328, 476
Private: 233, 350, 476
Susanna: 54, 476

Ruegg -

Anna: 17, 19, 291, 476
Ruesga -
   Private: 281, 476
   Private: 281, 476
Ruff -
   Elizabeth Catherine: 142, 476
   Hiram: 107, 476
   Nancy: 107, 140, 199, 265, 266, 476
Ruggin -
   Elsbeth: 14, 17, 19, 291, 476
   Uli: 17, 19, 291, 476
Ruhl -
   Barbara: 75, 476
Runion -
   Betty A: 213, 476
Rupert -
   Donna: 270, 476
Rupp -
   Elizabeth: 299, 476
   Magdelene: 9, 30, 296, 476
   Mary: 306, 476
Russell -
   Private: 278, 476
   Private: 277, 476
   Private: 278, 476
   Private: 278, 476
Russenberger -
   Anna: 20, 476
Rutherford -
   John: 179
   Private: 179, 245
   Private: 180, 245
   Private: 245
   Private: 245
   Private: 245
   Private: 245
   Private: 245
Rutt -
   John B.: 74, 310, 476
   Magdalena: 13, 293, 476
   Magdalena: 294, 476
Rutter -
   Private: 238, 239, 356, 476
Rytz -
   Annali: 20, 21, 476
Sager -
   B. W.: 155, 476
   Beverly: 155, 476
   Edwin: 155, 476
   Philip: 155, 476
Salisbury -
   Private: 267, 476
   Private: 267, 476
   Private: 267, 476
   Private: 267, 476
Salter -
   Private: 280, 476
   Private: 280, 476
   Private: 280, 476
   Private: 280, 476
Sanborn -
   Maria: 92, 476
Sanders -

Jamina: 95, 476
Sangree -
   Esther: 476
   Jacob: 78, 476
Sanor -
   Barbara: 108, 477
   David: 88, 477
   George: 88, 477
   Samuel K: 87, 477
Santee -
   Betty Jane: 153, 218, 477
   Dorothy: 153, 477
   Kenneth: 153, 477
   Unknown: 153, 477
Sarciner -
   Gertrude Y: 187, 477
Sartwell -
   Private: 274, 477
   Private: 274, 477
Sauder -
   Esther: 302, 477
   John M.: 56, 305, 477
   Katharine: 100, 313, 477
   Lydia Ann: 73, 310, 477
   Minnie: 135, 477
Saxton -
   Private: 239, 357, 477
Saylor -
   Anna: 18, 477
   Mary Barbara: 77, 477
Schaak -
   Elias Kettering: 86, 477
Schappi -
   Barbara: 477
Scharer -
   Dorothea: 16, 18, 20, 477
Schell -
   Clifford: 159, 477
   Esther: 160, 477
   Gordon: 159, 477
   Miriam: 159, 219, 477
   Robert: 159, 477
   Shirley: 159, 477
   Wilmont: 159, 477
Schenk -
   Abraham: 38, 477
   Andrew K.: 477
   Anna: 477
   Anna: 477
   Barbara: 20, 477
   Barbara: 13, 15, 18, 477
   Barbara: 477
   Barbara: 477
   Christian: 38, 477
   Christian: 20, 477
   Christian: 18, 477
   Christian: 477
   Christian: 477
   Elisabeth: 38, 477
   Elisabeth: 13, 477
   Elisabeth: 477
   Hans: 18, 477
   Henry: 38, 477
   Henry: 477

Henry: 38, 477
   Jacob: 477
   Johannes: 20, 477
   John: 38, 477
   John: 477
   John: 38, 477
   John: 477
   John: 477
   Katherine Katrina: 30, 477
   Margaret: 20, 477
   Michael: 41, 477
   Michael: 18, 20, 21, 477
   Michael: 15, 18, 20, 477
   Michael: 18, 477
   Michael: 477
   Michael: 477
   Michael: 477
   Michael: 477
   Niklaus: 20, 478
   Ulrich: 20, 21, 478
   Ulrich: 20, 478
Schillinger -
   Private: 286, 478
Schinz -
   Katharina: 20, 21, 478
Schlichter -
   Susan: 478
Schmidt -
   Private: 247
Schmutz -
   Barbara: 10, 26
Schnabley -
   Mary Catharine (aka: Mary Catherine Snavely): 8, 10, 12, 13, 25, 296
Schnader -
   John: 294, 478
Schnebel -
   Philip: 18
Schnebele -
   Anna: 13
   Eva: 13
   Felix: 18
   Heinrich: 18
   Jacob: 15, 18
   Jakob: 13, 15, 16, 18
   Johann Jacob: 18
   Johann Jacob: 10, 13, 16, 25
   Johann Jacob: 13
   John: 13, 294
   Regula: 18
Schnebli -
   Elsbeth: 17, 19, 291, 478
Schneider -
   Elizabeth: 478
   Jacob Bauman: 10, 25
   Verena: 17, 478
Schock -
   Veronica: 38, 478
Schoenfield -
   William: 294, 478
Schraeder -
   Unknown: 105, 478
Schrantz -

John: 478
Schreckengast -
　Private: 279, 478
Schreiner -
　George: 478
Schrock -
　Private: 168, 329, 478
Schroeder -
　Virgile Lewis: 143, 478
Schueller -
　Sarah (Shuler): 478
Schuyler -
　George: 250, 251
　George: 251
　Grace: 251
Schwarting -
　Private: 259, 478
Scogun -
　Reba A: 146, 478
Scott -
　Aruthur G: 140, 478
　Harriet: 95, 478
　James: 199, 478
　James Little: 140, 478
　John C: 140, 199, 478
　Mary A: 140, 199, 478
　Ralph L: 140, 199, 478
　Ruth: 199, 478
　Ruth Isabel: 140, 199, 265, 266, 478
　William: 199, 478
Seachrist -
　Fanny: 294, 478
　Jr. Private: 181
　Private: 181, 247
　Private: 181, 247
　III Private: 182, 248
　Private: 182, 248
　Private: 182, 248
　Private: 182, 248
　Private: 248
　Private: 248
　Private: 248
　Private: 248
Searle -
　Ada Elizabeth: 478
Segal -
　Julia: 191, 478
Seibert -
　Clyde: 196, 478
　Private: 196, 478
　Private: 196, 478
Selby -
　Private: 270, 478
Senseman -
　Mary: 306, 478
Sensenderfer -
　Shelby: 221, 478
Sensenig -
　Christian: 294, 478
　Christian W.: 294, 478
　Edna M.: 122, 319, 478
　Elizabeth: 293, 478
　Francis: 298, 478

Ivan M.: 100, 313, 478
Lydia: 306, 478
Mary Wenger: 298, 478
Michael Krey: 298
Michael W.: 90, 312, 478
Private: 230, 347, 478
Private: 230, 348, 478
Private: 230, 348, 478
Sewell -
　Ruth: 252, 478
Shackleton -
　Private: 270, 478
　Private: 270, 478
　Private: 270, 478
　Private: 270, 478
Shadrick -
　Unknown: 81, 478
Shaeffer -
　Martin: 478
Shafer -
　Martha Helen: 166, 327, 478
Shaffer -
　Harriet M.: 80, 478
Shaner -
　Elizabeth: 478
Shank -
　Carol: 163, 478
　Christian: 478
　Emma: 119, 478
　Glen: 190, 478
　John: 479
Shanks -
　Private: 272, 479
　Private: 272, 479
　Private: 272, 479
Shapllo -
　Krenar: 186, 479
Sharick -
　Douglas: 153, 479
　Earl: 153, 479
　June: 153, 479
　Mary Elizabeth: 153, 218, 479
　Patricia: 153, 218, 479
　Private: 218, 479
　Unknown: 153, 479
Sharpe -
　Charles V: 254, 479
　James W: 254, 479
　Marjorie Ann: 254, 479
　Mary C: 254, 479
　Ruth B: 187, 254, 479
　Vernon W: 187, 254, 479
　Walter A: 187, 479
Shaub -
　Evelyn Mae Neidermyer: 178, 323, 479
Shay -
　Jenny: 129
Sheaffer -
　Alice Margaret: 131, 132, 184, 479
　Bertie F.: 131, 479
　Charles M.: 131, 184, 250, 285, 479
　Doris Madeline: 184, 250, 285,

479
　J. Marion: 131, 132, 479
　John: 66, 479
　Josiah: 66, 479
Shearer -
　John: 31, 479
Shelley -
　Veronica: 479
Shelly -
　Annie: 306, 479
　Ellis Clinton: 136, 192, 260, 479
　Jacob S.: 136, 479
　John Willis: 136, 479
　Magdalene Katherine: 192, 260, 479
　Mary: 479
　Samuel: 58, 479
　Viola Lou: 192, 479
Shenfelder -
　Sarah: 479
Shenk -
　Abraham: 299, 479
　Abraham: 85, 479
　Anna: 7, 479
　Anna: 32, 479
　Anna: 479
　Barbara: 60, 84, 479
　Catherine: 60, 85, 86, 479
　Catherine: 84, 479
　Christian: 36, 479
　Christian M.: 84, 479
　Donald Reuben: 127, 317, 479
　Elizabeth: 60, 84, 479
　Florence LaVerne: 127, 317, 479
　Frances Geraldine: 127, 317, 479
　Henry: 60, 479
　Henry: 84, 479
　Jacob: 36, 479
　Jacob: 60, 84, 479
　Jacob M.: 84, 479
　John: 60, 479
　John Kauffman: 127, 317, 479
　John Marlin: 127, 317, 479
　John S.: 84, 479
　Joseph: 479
　Joseph: 60, 479
　Joseph: 60, 85, 479
　Joseph: 85, 479
　Joseph M.: 84, 479
　Lydia: 60, 480
　Magdalena: 60, 85, 480
　Maria: 60, 480
　Maria: 60, 85, 480
　Mary Ann: 85, 480
　Michael: 480
　Michael M.: 84, 480
　Nancy: 60, 86, 480
　Peter: 85, 480
　Samuel: 85, 480
　Sarah: 60, 480
　Susanna: 60, 480
　Veronica: 60, 84, 480
　Veronica: 84, 480
Shepherd -
　Albert: 115, 480

Sheraton -
    George: 480
Sherid -
    Private: 172, 333, 480
Sherk -
    Adam: 92, 480
    Adgeline: 92, 480
    Albert: 93, 480
    Amanda: 93, 480
    Amos: 93, 480
    Arvilla: 93, 480
    Caroline: 92, 480
    Edward: 93, 480
    Elizabeth: 93, 480
    Elizabeth: 85, 480
    Franklin: 92, 480
    Leah: 85, 480
    Luella: 93, 480
    Maria: 93, 480
    Martha: 92, 480
    Matilda: 93, 480
    Reuben: 93, 480
Sherman -
    Private: 264, 480
Sherrick -
    Elizabeth: 94, 480
    Joseph: 293, 480
Shertzer -
    Baltzer: 42, 480
    Baltzer: 31, 480
    Barbara: 42, 480
    Barbara: 31, 480
    Elizabeth: 42, 480
    Elizabeth: 31, 480
    Private: 233, 351, 480
Shiffer -
    James R.: 311, 480
Shiffler -
    Private: 180
Shirk -
    Esther: 480
    Esther Weaver: 121, 318, 480
    Hannah G.: 74, 310, 480
    John: 294, 480
    Michael: 293, 480
    Peter: 294, 297, 480
    Peter: 297, 480
    Private: 285, 362, 480
    Private: 285, 362, 480
    Private: 285, 362, 480
    Private: 242, 359, 480
    Private: 242, 359, 480
    Private: 242, 359, 480
    Samuel: 480
Shirley -
    Private: 247
    Private: 247
    Private: 247
Shissler -
    Albert: 480
Shively -
    Bonnie Walker: 202, 480
    Florence: 144, 480
    George W: 144, 480
    Ray: 144, 202, 480

Shoemaker -
    Cora Bell: 195, 480
Shope -
    Private: 245
    Private: 245
    Private: 245
Shopp -
    Christian: 39
    Johannes: 39
Shore -
    Unnamed: 217, 480
    Private: 217, 282, 481
    Private: 282, 481
    Private: 217, 282, 481
    Private: 217, 282, 481
    Private: 282, 481
    Private: 282, 481
Short -
    Private: 234, 351, 481
    Private: 234, 351, 481
Shotzer -
    Blanche: 185
Showalter -
    Private: 240, 358, 481
Shreiner -
    Charles: 96, 481
    Jacob: 96, 481
    Mary: 96, 481
Shultz -
    Eve: 481
    Private: 279, 481
    Private: 280, 481
    Private: 280, 481
    Valentine: 481
Shumaker -
    Jacob: 27, 481
Shupp -
    Mary: 301, 481
Shutt -
    Janet Kaye: 156, 481
    Mason Simon: 156, 481
    Sandra Lee: 156, 481
Siegrist -
    Maria: 9, 40, 300, 481
    Unknown: 298, 481
    Unknown: 294, 481
Sigler -
    Anna Elizabeth: 113, 322, 481
    Edward W: 113, 322, 481
Silver -
    Edna: 195, 481
    Private: 182
    Private: 182, 249
    Private: 182, 249
    Private: 182
    Private: 249
    Private: 249
    Private: 249
Simon -
    Belenia: 138, 481
Simpson -
    Private: 234, 351, 481
Sinclair -
    Metta S.: 109, 481

Singer -
    Private: 174, 334, 481
Sisson -
    Lloyd Hoover: 115, 481
Sixberry -
    Private: 289, 481
    Private: 289, 481
Skiles -
    Harry Brisbin: 175, 336, 481
    Private: 175, 241, 336, 359, 481
    Private: 175, 241, 336, 359, 481
    Private: 241, 359, 481
    Private: 241, 359, 481
    Private: 241, 359, 481
    Private: 241, 359, 481
Skinner -
    Private: 206, 481
Sleeman -
    Shirley: 210, 481
Slothour -
    Private: 247
Sluss -
    Private: 270, 481
    Private: 270, 481
    Private: 270, 481
    Ray: 270, 481
Smith -
    Anna: 76, 481
    Anna G: 135, 481
    Anna M.: 77, 481
    Catherina: 481
    Christian: 36, 481
    Edna M: 135, 189, 257, 481
    Emma Jane: 71, 481
    Emma R: 135, 189, 481
    Esther: 201, 481
    George: 134, 135, 481
    George L: 135, 481
    Henry: 481
    Hugh: 78, 481
    Margaret Jane: 132, 133, 481
    Mary: 135, 481
    Ober: 135, 481
    Private: 193, 481
    Private: 273, 481
    Private: 280, 482
    Private: 218, 482
    Private: 181
    Private: 248
    Roy: 218, 482
    Roy Eby: 100, 313, 482
Smoker -
    Private: 176, 337, 482
Smolizer -
    Charlotte E: 188, 256, 482
    Harry S: 188, 482
Snavely -
    Abraham B: 6, 303, 309, 482
    Abraham Barr: 6-8, 63, 303, 310, 482
    Anna: 12, 294, 482
    Anna: 9, 482
    Anna: 482
    Barbara: 7, 299, 308, 482
    Benjamin: 6, 303, 482

Christian: 7, 482
Daniel: 7, 482
David: 8, 482
Elizabeth: 7, 482
Elizabeth: 6, 303, 482
Henry: 7, 482
Jacob: 7, 9, 482
Jacob: 482
John: 6, 7, 9, 299, 303, 482
John: 482
Joseph: 39, 300, 482
Margaretta: 7, 482
Martha B: 6, 303, 482
Martin: 7, 482
Mary: 9, 482
Mary Catherine (name: Mary Catharine Schnabley): 8, 10, 12, 13, 25, 296
Rohrer: 309, 482
Stoner: 309, 482
Susanna: 7, 482
Veronica: 7, 482
Veronica: 9, 482
Veronica Buckwalter: 6, 63, 304, 309, 310, 482

Sneltzer -
Joseph: 202, 203, 482
Private: 203, 269, 482
Private: 203, 269, 482
Private: 203, 269, 482
Private: 269, 482
Private: 269, 482
Private: 269, 482
Private: 269, 482
Private: 203, 269, 270, 482

Snider -
Mary: 77, 482

Snowd -
Private: 278

Snyder -
Amos B: 90, 113, 482
Annie B: 90, 482
Arlene: 113, 482
Barbara B: 90, 482
Betty Knoll: 129
Christian B: 90, 482
Elias L.: 136, 482
Goldie May: 136, 193, 261, 482
Harriet Lucretia: 136, 193, 261, 482
Henry G: 90, 482
Jacob B: 90, 482
Johannes: 34, 46, 47, 482
John Henry: 47, 482
Jonas: 84, 482
Joshua: 482
Lizzie B: 90, 482
Mary B: 90, 482
Melvin H: 113, 482
Private: 203, 482
Private: 201, 482
Ruby: 219, 482
Sabina: 84, 482
Samuel: 47, 483
Sarah Jane: 136, 193, 261, 483
Simon B.: 86, 483

Veronica: 8, 27, 483
Wanda H: 113, 483

Solga -
Private: 245

Sollenberger -
Anna: 311, 483

Son -
Infant: 136, 483

Soper -
John Keith: 180
Private: 180, 245
Private: 180
Private: 245
Private: 245

Sox -
Ward L: 113, 483

Sparks -
Doris M.: 152, 483

Spencer -
David: 78, 483
Private: 213, 483

Spiesterbach -
Bertha Etta: 143, 483

Spinelli -
Rose: 148, 483

Sprecher -
John S.: 85, 483

Spring -
Joseph M: 111, 483

Springer -
Peter: 293, 483

St Armond -
Private: 271, 483

St. Clair -
Ellen Belle: 483

Stackhouse -
Private: 249
Private: 249
Private: 249

Stambaugh -
Clarence William: 125, 321, 483
Private: 125, 321, 483

Stancer -
O. P.: 251

Stanton -
Lucinda: 206, 483

Stark -
Gail: 111, 483

Starns -
Dessie May: 191, 483

Starr -
Charles F.: 138, 483
Mabel: 138, 483
Ronald(Unknown): 138, 483
Verne E.: 138, 483

Staub -
Diane Kay: 243, 339, 483

Staufer -
Aesta Blanch: 191, 259, 483

Stauffer -
Abraham: 65, 92, 115, 152, 217, 483
Abraham Hershey: 33, 46, 64, 65, 91-95, 114-120, 150-162, 215-220, 281, 282, 483
Abraham Hess: 11, 31, 33, 41, 46, 64, 65, 91-95, 114-120, 150-162, 215-220, 281, 282, 483
Abraham Moyer: 483
Agnes Pauline: 258, 483
Alice Pearl: 191, 259, 483
Andrew Grant: 135, 190, 191, 258, 259, 483
Andrew Neal: 191, 483
Ann: 30, 483
Anna: 26, 483
Anna: 18, 20, 21, 483
Anna: 15, 18, 20, 483
Anna: 33, 483
Anna: 483
Anna Barbara: 30, 40, 58, 74, 103, 131, 184, 250, 285, 483
Anna Marie: 31, 41, 483
Anna Pearl: 136, 192, 483
Barbara: 41, 483
Barbara: 20, 483
Barbara: 31, 483
Barbara: 11, 26
Barbara: 33, 483
Barbara Virginia: 26, 483
Benjamin Pennypacker: 483
Beulah Bell: 136, 483
Carmi R.: 165, 326, 483
Catharine: 294, 483
Catharine Latscher: 483
Catharine Moyer: 483
Catherina: 20, 483
Catherine: 30, 483
Catherine: 30, 483
Catherine Pennypacker: 483
Charles Albert: 135, 191, 259, 483
Charles Bennett: 191, 483
Charles Lloyd: 191, 259, 483
Christian: 20, 483
Christian: 15, 24, 26, 30, 31, 40, 41, 46, 58-61, 64, 65, 74-89, 91-95, 103-112, 114-120, 131-162, 184-220, 250-283, 285-290, 483
Christian: 26, 484
Christian: 11, 31, 41, 61, 86, 106, 139, 198, 265, 289, 484
Christian: 30, 484
Christian: 484
Christian: 46, 65, 92, 93, 115, 152, 217, 484
Christina: 30, 484
Clementine Fox: 484
Daniel: 31, 484
Daniel B.: 165, 326, 484
Daniel Latscher: 484
David: 65, 484
Earl Evans: 258, 484
Eleanor: 191, 484
Elias Richardson: 135, 191, 259, 484
Elisabeth: 65, 484
Elizabeth: 31, 41, 61, 484

Elizabeth: 30, 40, 58, 59, 74, 75, 103, 104, 131-135, 184-190, 250-257, 283, 285-287, 289, 484
Elizabeth: 41, 61, 86, 106, 139, 198, 265, 289, 484
Elizabeth Kulp: 484
Elizabeth Latscher: 484
Elizabeth Pennypacker: 484
Ella May: 135, 190, 257, 258, 484
Emma Kulp: 484
Eva: 30, 484
Eva: 31, 484
Frederick Latscher: 484
Hannah Mary Latscher: 484
Hans: 18, 20, 484
Hans: 20, 484
Hans: 25, 26, 31, 41, 46, 61, 64, 65, 86-89, 91-95, 106-112, 114-120, 139-162, 198-220, 265-282, 289, 484
Harriet Moyer: 484
Henry: 30, 484
Henry: 31, 484
Henry Jacob: 26, 31, 33, 41, 46, 61, 64, 65, 86-89, 91-95, 106-112, 114-120, 139-162, 198-220, 265-282, 289, 484
Henry Pennypacker: 484
Jacob: 297, 484
Jacob: 26, 484
Jacob: 31, 41, 61, 86-89, 106-112, 140-150, 199-215, 265-281, 484
Jacob: 30, 484
Jacob: 33, 484
Jacob: 299, 484
Jacob Latscher: 484
Jacob Latscher: 484
Jacob Moyer: 484
Jacob Pennypacker: 484
Joe E.: 165, 326, 484
Johannes: 26, 30, 40, 58-60, 74-86, 103-105, 131-139, 184-198, 250-265, 283, 285-290, 484
John: 65, 484
John: 484
John: 30, 484
John: 33, 484
John Buckwalter Rev.: 484
John Latscher: 484
John Milton: 135, 484
John Moyer: 484
John Pennypacker: 484
John Wesley: 135, 484
Joseph Pennypacker: 484
Kate Kulp: 484
Lavina Moyer: 484
Leah Mayford: 191, 484
Madelena: 26, 484
Magdalena: 26, 484
Magdalena: 31, 484
Magdalena: 31, 484
Magdalena: 33, 484
Margaret Pennypacker: 485

Maria: 65, 485
Maria: 294, 485
Maria: 299, 485
Maria "Mary": 29, 485
Marie: 30, 485
Martin: 26, 485
Mary: 31, 485
Mary Helen: 191, 259, 485
Mary Latscher: 485
Mary Lemmie Ann: 136, 192, 259, 485
Mary Moyer: 485
Michael: 30, 485
Nancy Jane: 92, 115, 152, 217, 485
Paul J.: 191, 258, 485
Peter: 292, 485
Peter: 31, 485
Private: 283, 360, 485
Private: 283, 360, 485
Private: 283, 360, 485
Private: 227, 345, 485
Private: 165, 228, 326, 345, 485
Private: 165, 228, 326, 345, 485
Private: 165, 228, 326, 345, 485
Private: 165, 228, 285, 326, 346, 362, 485
Private: 228, 345, 485
Private: 228, 345, 485
Private: 228, 345, 485
Private: 228, 345, 485
Private: 165, 326, 485
Private: 165, 228, 326, 346, 485
Private: 165, 229, 326, 346, 485
Private: 165, 326, 485
Private: 165, 326, 485
Private: 165, 326, 485
Private: 165, 326, 485
Private: 229, 346, 485
Private: 229, 346, 485
Private: 229, 346, 485
Private: 229, 346, 485
Private: 229, 346, 485
Private: 229, 346, 485
Private: 240, 357, 485
Private: 176, 337, 485
Private: 176, 337, 485
Private: 176, 337, 485
Private: 191, 258, 485
Private: 191, 259, 485
Private: 191, 259, 485
Private: 191, 485
Private: 191, 485
Private: 258, 485
Private: 259, 485
Private: 259, 485
Ray Franklin: 136, 191, 259, 485
Ray Franklin: 191, 485
Rudolph Pennypacker: 485
Russell Lee: 191, 485
Samuel Pennypacker: 485
Sara Rebecca: 136, 191, 259, 485
Sarah Moyer: 485
Stephen: 135, 485
Susanna: 31, 485
Susanna: 30, 485

Susanna: 45, 485
Sylvia: 191, 485
Ulrich: 20, 486
Veronica " Frany ": 30, 40, 59, 60, 75-86, 104, 105, 135-139, 190-198, 257-265, 287-290, 486
Veronica Frena: 31, 486
Wesley Richard: 191, 486
William E.: 135, 486
William Pennypacker: 486

Stayer -
David S.: 77, 486

Steele -
Marian Taylor: 186, 486
Thelma Lucille: 260, 486

Steen -
Private: 204, 486

Stees -
Luella N.: 192, 486

Steffy -
Alice Parmer: 125, 315, 486
Leah: 76, 486
Private: 235, 352, 486

Stehman -
Elisabeth: 72, 486

Steinman -
John: 9, 486

Stengel -
Private: 249
Private: 249
Private: 249

Stephens -
Asenath: 133, 486
Private: 168, 329, 486

Stephenson -
Margaret Ann: 95, 486

Stetson -
Private: 250

Stevens -
Arthur W: 187, 255, 486
Arthur W: 255, 486
Arthur W , Jr: 255, 486
B Marie: 187, 255, 286, 486
Bryan Keith: 267, 486
Carrell D: 187, 486
Clarise: 187, 486
Donna A: 255, 486
F Clair: 187, 486
Florida Edwin: 486
Hannah: 76, 486
J Donald: 187, 255, 486
John E: 255, 486
Kitty: 255, 486
Linda K: 255, 486
Marlin O: 187, 255, 486
Marlin O , Jr: 255, 486
Mary E: 255, 486
Paul A: 255, 486
Private: 267, 486
Private: 267, 486
Private: 267, 486
Richard L: 255, 486
Roger William: 267, 486
Virginia A: 255, 486

Wilbur A (aka: Patrick): 187, 468, 486
William O: 187, 486

Stevick -
John: 78, 486

Stiffler -
Private: 214, 281, 486
Private: 214, 281, 486
Veron Montell: 214, 486

Stitch -
Private: 275, 486
Private: 275, 486

Stitcher -
Lydia A.: 84, 486

Stocker -
Jacob: 17, 486

Stoever -
Jeremiah: 85, 486

Stoffer -
Ada: 110, 143, 201, 267, 268, 486
Adaline: 148, 486
Addie Jane Sherman: 147, 486
Albert: 88, 486
Albert Lewis: 107, 141, 142, 486
Alice Ellen: 111, 146, 206, 486
Allie: 107, 486
Alva Orlan: 148, 210, 486
Alveida: 140, 486
Amanda J: 108, 486
Anson Oscar: 113, 149, 213, 279, 486
Arnold Leroy: 148, 487
Barbara Ellen: 87, 107, 487
Barbara Sue: 200, 266, 487
Benjamin Franklin II: 211
Benjamine Franklin: 112, 147, 148, 209-211, 275-278, 487
Bertha Cleo: 112, 149, 212, 487
Bertha Lorena: 111, 146, 207, 273, 274, 487
Beulah Fern: 141, 200, 267, 487
Blanche: 144, 487
Blanche Mae: 112, 487
Bryan Sewell: 110, 145, 146, 206, 270, 487
Buddy Ross: 148, 487
C Robert: 201, 267, 487
Carl Levy: 143, 487
Carl T: 142, 487
Carrie M: 110, 487
Catherine: 61, 86, 487
Catherine: 88, 487
Catherine Ann: 88, 109, 487
Cecil F: 145, 204, 487
Charles Floyd: 113, 487
Charles G: 110, 145, 205, 487
Charles Henry: 112, 487
Chester A: 111, 147, 487
Christena: 88, 487
Christina: 87, 108, 487
Christine: 87, 487
Claire Daniel: 111, 146, 487
Clara M: 89, 487
Clara M.: 89, 487
Clarence Leward: 148, 209, 275, 487
Cleo Ruth: 148, 210, 276, 277, 487
Clifford Lewis: 148, 209, 275, 276, 487
Clinton: 109, 487
Clyde C.: 148, 212, 487
Cora: 107, 487
Cora: 109, 487
Cora Alice: 106, 487
Corda: 108, 487
Curtis Homer: 112, 148, 212, 487
Cynthia Idella: 109, 143, 201, 267, 487
Dale Milan: 210, 276, 487
Daniel: 149, 487
Daniel: 108, 487
Daniel D: 88, 487
Darl Lincoln: 113, 150, 215, 487
David: 87, 487
David: 62, 487
David: 88, 487
David: 108, 142, 201, 267, 487
David M: 89, 487
David M.: 89, 487
Debara Ann: 211, 487
Delilah: 108, 487
Dennis: 88, 109, 487
Don: 146, 487
Donald: 149, 487
Donald Andrew: 148, 210, 487
Donald Lowell: 149, 213, 279, 487
Doris May: 149, 214, 280, 281, 487
Dorothy Ada: 141, 200, 201, 267, 487
Dwight: 145, 205, 487
Earl: 112, 487
Earl: 142, 487
Earl Eugene: 111, 487
Earl L: 149, 213, 487
Edith: 148, 212, 487
Edward: 142, 488
Edward W: 112, 488
Eileen M: 112, 488
Elbert R: 110, 488
Eldon: 113, 488
Elgie: 112, 488
Eli: 87, 488
Eli: 87, 108, 488
Eliza: 88, 109, 488
Eliza A: 87, 488
Elizabeth: 93, 488
Elizabeth: 61, 488
Elizabeth Rose: 88, 488
Ella: 108, 488
Ellen Ann: 203, 270, 488
Elmer: 108, 488
Elmer E: 110, 488
Elmer L: 145, 205, 488
Elurtus Gatton: 109, 488
Emmet: 107, 488
Emmett: 140, 488
Enos: 88, 488
Erma Armada: 141, 488
Erwin William: 110, 144, 203, 488
Ester: 145, 204, 488
Ester: 143, 488
Ester Leah: 149, 213, 279, 488
Esther: 144, 488
Ethel: 144, 488
Ethel: 143, 488
Ethel: 112, 488
Ethel Marie: 144, 488
Eva: 144, 488
Eva: 110, 488
Eva Lola: 111, 488
Evelyn Ora: 149, 214, 280, 488
Fannie Pearl: 111, 488
Flora Ann: 110, 488
Florence Eudora: 106, 488
Floyd W: 145, 204, 488
Frank: 142, 201, 267, 488
Frank JR: 201, 267, 488
Franklin Eugene: 148, 211, 278, 488
George: 62, 89, 110-112, 143-150, 201-215, 267-281, 488
George: 88, 488
George: 109, 488
George Allen: 111, 146, 206, 271, 272, 488
George D: 89, 111, 146, 147, 207, 208, 273-275, 488
George O: 109, 488
Gladys: 201, 488
Gladys Alice: 110, 145, 204, 488
Glen Wilson: 113, 149, 213, 214, 279-281, 488
Goldie Marie: 113, 150, 214, 488
Gorman H: 144, 203, 488
Gwendolyn G: 147, 488
Harold James: 143, 488
Harold Walter: 143, 202, 268, 488
Harry B: 142, 201, 488
Harvey: 144, 488
Harvey: 108, 488
Harvey W: 110, 488
Hazel M: 143, 488
Helen: 143, 488
Helen Naomi: 112, 488
Herman: 107, 488
Homer: 107, 488
Homer: 149, 213, 489
Homer E: 109, 142, 489
Horace Raymond: 106, 489
Howard H.: 107, 140, 489
Ida: 140, 489
Ida J.: 107, 140, 199, 489
Idella: 110, 144, 202, 489
Inez Genesta: 141, 200, 266, 489
Iona Eleanor: 149, 214, 281, 489
Iris: 201, 489
Jacob: 41, 61, 86-89, 106-112, 140-150, 199-215, 265-281, 489
Jacob H: 145, 489
Jacob L: 87, 108, 142, 201, 267, 489
Jacob S: 61, 87, 106, 489
James: 87, 489
Jean: 144, 489
Jerome: 107, 489

Jesse A: 87, 107, 489
Jimmie Dale: 147, 489
John: 62, 88, 109, 143, 201, 267, 489
John: 87, 106, 489
John: 108, 142, 489
John A: 142, 489
John Arthur: 109, 489
John Jacob: 88, 109, 143, 201, 267, 489
John Ralph: 111, 489
John Wallace: 110, 144, 203, 489
Joseph: 88, 489
Joseph C: 145, 489
Kathryn Olive: 200, 266, 489
Kenneth George: 200, 266, 489
Kenneth Lee: 148, 489
Kenny: 148, 489
Larry Lee: 209, 275, 489
Laurance L: 110, 143, 202, 268, 489
Laurtis W.: 89, 110, 144, 145, 203-206, 270, 489
Leah: 62, 88, 489
Leander: 89, 112, 113, 149, 150, 213-215, 279-281, 489
Lela Catherine: 142, 489
Leland L: 142, 489
Lena Viola: 111, 489
Leo Lesile: 112, 149, 213, 489
Leona Rosa: 112, 489
Leonard: 148, 212, 489
Leslic A: 109, 489
Lester Clyde: 110, 144, 145, 204, 489
Levi: 88, 489
Levi: 89, 110, 143, 144, 201-203, 267-270, 489
Leward: 148, 489
Lewis John: 200, 266, 489
Lewis Jr: 87, 107, 140, 141, 199, 200, 266, 267, 489
Lida Marrilla: 110, 489
Lloyd: 146, 489
Lola Mae: 146, 206, 271, 272, 489
Lorin Albert: 148, 211, 212, 278, 279, 489
Louella: 89, 489
Louella I: 89, 489
Louis J: 61, 87, 106, 107, 140, 141, 199, 200, 265-267, 489
Loyal: 144, 203, 489
Lucille: 207, 489
Lucille Naomi: 149, 214, 279, 280, 489
Lula Nora: 111, 489
Lydia: 108, 489
Mabel: 140, 489
Mabel Alice: 113, 489
Mable Catherine: 111, 489
Maggie: 92, 490
Margaret: 62, 88, 490
Margaret Louise: 148, 211, 490
Marion: 108, 490
Marion (Nick): 110, 490

Martha: 145, 205, 490
Martha Ellen: 148, 490
Mary Ann: 87, 107, 140, 199, 265, 266, 490
Mary Catherine: 107, 141, 490
Mary Catherine: 110, 145, 205, 270, 490
Mary Dora: 111, 490
Mary Luella: 110, 490
Matthew Alan: 268, 490
Maud E: 113, 490
Mauda: 140, 490
Maude Eve: 113, 490
Melinda J: 87, 108, 109, 490
Milan Benjamin: 148, 210, 276, 490
Milan Leroy: 112, 490
Mildred: 109, 490
Mildred Louisa: 201, 490
Mildred Marjorie: 149, 490
Millard: 110, 490
Milton C: 110, 490
Myrtle: 110, 490
Nancy: 92, 490
Nancy: 87, 106, 107, 140, 490
Nancy: 87, 108, 490
Nehariah: 88, 490
Nellie Ione: 106, 490
Nettie Pearl: 111, 490
Nora: 144, 490
Nora Olive: 110, 490
Odessa: 112, 490
Oliver: 108, 490
Ora Deliah: 112, 147, 208, 209, 490
Orietta: 112, 490
Orlan Clifford: 147, 208, 274, 275, 490
Otis R: 142, 490
Owen: 107, 490
Paul Elmer: 143, 490
Paul Lawrence: 144, 203, 270, 490
Pearl: 110, 144, 202, 203, 268-270, 490
Peter: 41, 490
Peter: 87, 108, 142, 490
Peter: 108, 142, 490
Private: 278, 490
Private: 278, 490
3rd Private: 278, 490
Private: 211, 490
Private: 211, 278, 490
Private: 211, 278, 490
Private: 148, 490
Private: 278, 490
Private: 278, 490
Private: 211, 490
Private: 212, 490
Private: 146, 206, 490
Private: 211, 277, 490
Private: 211, 278, 490
Private: 211, 278
Private: 278, 490
Private: 278, 490
Private: 278
Private: 278

Private: 278
Private: 209, 275, 490
Private: 209, 275, 490
Private: 275, 490
Private: 275, 490
Private: 275, 491
Private: 210, 491
Private: 210, 491
Private: 210, 491
Private: 210, 491
Private: 210, 276, 491
Private: 210, 491
Private: 210, 491
Private: 210, 491
Private: 210, 491
Private: 210, 491
Private: 210, 491
Private: 211, 491
Private: 206, 491
Private: 212, 279, 491
Private: 212, 279, 491
Private: 275, 491
Private: 275, 491
Private: 275, 491
Private: 276, 491
Private: 276, 491
Private: 278, 491
Private: 146, 206, 271, 491
Private: 206, 272, 491
Private: 206, 491
Private: 206, 272, 491
Private: 206, 491
Private: 206, 271, 491
Private: 206, 271, 491
Private: 206, 271, 491
Private: 206, 271, 491
Private: 206, 271, 491
Private: 206, 271, 491
Private: 209, 276, 491
Private: 210, 491
Private: 210, 276, 491
Private: 210, 276, 491
Private: 210, 491
Private: 210, 491
Private: 210, 491
Private: 211, 491
Private: 211, 278, 491
Private: 211, 278, 491
Private: 275, 491
Private: 275, 491
Private: 278, 491
2nd Private: 211, 278, 491
Private: 270, 491
Private: 270, 491
Private: 270, 491
Private: 270, 491
Private: 270, 491
Private: 203, 491
Private: 204, 491
Private: 275, 491
Private: 204, 491
Private: 276, 491
Private: 204, 491
Private: 205, 491
Private: 205, 491
Private: 145, 205, 491

Private: 145, 205, 491	Private: 271, 492	Solomon: 108, 493
Private: 205, 491	Private: 271, 492	Stanton Uriah: 89, 111, 112, 147-149, 208-212, 275-279, 493
Private: 205, 491	Private: 271, 492	Susan: 211, 493
Private: 205, 491	Private: 271, 492	Sylvia: 112, 493
Private: 270, 491	Private: 271, 492	Thelma R: 142, 493
Private: 278, 492	Private: 271, 493	Thomas: 148, 493
Private: 208, 274, 492	Private: 271, 493	Thomas Fredric: 146, 493
Private: 208, 275, 492	Private: 203, 493	Thomas Lawrence: 203, 270, 493
Private: 275, 492	Private: 203, 493	Vera Lucille: 111, 146, 206, 207, 272, 493
Private: 275, 492	Private: 203, 493	Verma Adella: 147, 208, 275, 494
Private: 147, 208, 492	Private: 276, 493	Veron Roy: 110, 145, 205, 494
Private: 213, 492	Private: 276, 493	Virgil Forest: 141, 200, 266, 494
Private: 213, 492	Private: 276, 493	Virginia: 144, 203, 494
Private: 213, 492	Private: 146, 493	Wade Orla: 113, 150, 214, 494
Private: 213, 279, 492	Private: 146, 493	Wallace Winder: 106, 494
Private: 279, 492	Private: 212, 493	Walter George: 107, 140, 141, 200, 266, 267, 494
Private: 279, 492	Private: 212, 493	Walter Leon: 110, 494
Private: 213, 492	Private: 201, 493	Warren: 107, 494
Private: 213, 279, 492	Private: 201, 493	Wesley Emerson: 111, 147, 208, 274, 275, 494
Private: 150, 214, 492	Private: 201, 493	Willard Edson: 109, 494
Private: 214, 492	Private: 148, 493	William: 201, 494
Private: 214, 492	Private: 212, 493	William: 92, 494
Private: 150, 215, 492	Private: 149, 493	William: 108, 494
Private: 150, 215, 492	Private: 213, 493	William Franklin: 110, 144, 203, 270, 494
Private: 150, 215, 492	Private: 213, 493	William Stanton: 148, 209, 210, 494
Private: 215, 492	Private: 213, 493	Wilma E: 147, 494
Private: 215, 492	Private: 213, 493	Wilma Ruth: 149, 213, 279, 494
Private: 215, 492	Private: 213, 493	Windfield: 110, 494
Private: 215, 492	Private: 213, 493	Zella May: 111, 147, 208, 494
Private: 278, 492	Private: 213, 493	*Stoffer?* -
Private: 268, 492	Private: 213, 493	Private: 206, 494
Private: 266, 492	Rachel A: 88, 493	*Stoll* -
Private: 266, 492	Ralph Leo: 112, 493	Michael H: 252, 494
Private: 266, 492	Ralph Norman: 143, 493	Richard: 252, 494
Private: 276, 492	Ray Arnold: 148, 210, 276, 493	Susan L: 252, 494
Private: 266, 492	Raymond: 110, 493	*Stoltzfus* -
Private: 266, 492	Raymond: 142, 493	Private: 170, 171, 331, 332, 494
Private: 266, 492	Rex: 146, 493	*Stone* -
Private: 266, 492	Robert Liewellyn: 203, 270, 493	Belle: 96, 494
Private: 202, 268, 492	Robert Price: 146, 206, 270, 493	Private: 180
Private: 270, 492	Rolandus: 89, 111, 146, 206, 207, 272, 493	*Stoneman* -
Private: 204, 492	Rollin Jr: 148, 211, 277, 278, 493	Maria: 12, 25, 494
Private: 205, 492	Roscoe "Ross": 112, 148, 211, 212, 278, 279, 493	*Stoner* -
Private: 205, 492	Ross: 112, 493	Abraham L.: 494
Private: 206, 270, 492	Roy Dean: 146, 206, 272, 493	Anna: 494
Private: 214, 492	Roy Lester: 111, 493	Daniel L.: 494
Private: 214, 492	Royal: 107, 493	David L.: 494
Private: 267, 492	Russell D: 111, 147, 208, 493	Eliza L.: 494
Private: 267, 492	Ruth Anna: 112, 149, 212, 493	Emmanuel: 494
Private: 201, 492	Ruthanna: 112, 148, 149, 212, 493	Ida Snyder: 126, 315, 316, 494
Private: 267, 492	Samantha: 108, 493	Isaac L.: 494
Private: 267, 492	Samuel: 93, 493	Jacob: 494
Private: 206, 271, 492	Samuel: 61, 87, 108, 109, 142, 201, 267, 493	Jacob: 494
Private: 205, 492	Samuel J: 87, 493	John L.: 494
Private: 267, 492	Samuel Jr: 88, 109, 142, 493	Maria L.: 494
Private: 270, 492	Sarah: 87, 493	Mary: 295, 494
Private: 145, 205, 492	Sarah: 108, 493	Nora Snyder: 126, 316, 494
Private: 146, 492	Shannon M. Smith: 278, 493	Private: 208, 494
Private: 268, 492	Sherman: 89, 112, 149, 213, 493	*Stoudt* -
Private: 266, 492	Silvia: 87, 493	
Private: 208, 275, 492	Simon Henry: 89, 110, 111, 146, 206, 271, 272, 493	
Private: 204, 492	Simon Levi: 111, 146, 206, 493	
Private: 204, 492		
Private: 275, 492		
Private: 267, 492		
Private: 267, 492		

Mary Elizabeth: 97, 494
Virginia: 202, 494

Stouffer -
Aaron: 94, 116, 153, 218, 494
Abraham: 119, 161, 494
Abraham: 94, 117, 156, 494
Abraham: 46, 65, 93-95, 116-120, 152-162, 217-220, 494
Abraham: 65, 94, 118, 119, 158-161, 219, 220, 494
Abraham: 95, 119, 161, 494
Abraham Galle: 15, 24, 494
Adelheid Galle: 9, 10, 12, 15, 24-40, 42-58, 62-74, 89-91, 95-103, 113, 120-131, 150, 162-184, 220-250, 282-285, 494
Adeline: 95, 494
Agnes: 25, 494
Alan: 161, 494
Albert: 93, 494
Alberta: 95, 120, 494
Alden: 93, 494
Alice: 155, 494
Alonz: 93, 494
Andrew: 95, 120, 162, 494
Andrew: 79, 494
Anna Helena: 117, 156, 494
Annie: 93, 494
Archibald: 119, 161, 494
Arthur: 120, 494
Barbara Galle: 15, 24, 495
Bert Grenfell: 161, 495
Bertha: 94, 116, 152, 153, 217, 218, 495
Bertha: 119, 495
Blanche: 116, 153, 495
Bruce: 155, 495
Carl: 120, 495
Carlton Lee: 156, 495
Carson: 154, 495
Catharine: 79, 495
Charles: 119, 495
Christian: 65, 93, 495
Christian: 95, 495
Christian: 15, 17, 19, 24-290, 495
Christian: 25, 495
Christian: 79, 495
Christian: 65, 95, 119, 120, 161, 162, 495
Christian C.: 79, 495
Christina: 95, 118, 158, 219, 495
Clara: 93, 495
Clarence: 116, 495
Clayton: 94, 495
Clayton Parker: 118, 157, 218, 495
Conrad Ulrick: 117, 156, 495
Daniel: 12, 15, 17, 24-290, 495
Daniel: 25, 26, 30, 40, 58-60, 74-86, 103-105, 131-139, 184-198, 250-265, 283, 285-290, 495
Daniel Ernest: 156, 495
Daniel Galle: 15, 24, 495
David: 95, 120, 162, 495
David: 120, 162, 495

David: 65, 95, 495
David Abraham: 161, 495
David K.: 79, 495
David Wesley: 94, 117, 155, 156, 218, 495
Delma Izetta: 157, 218, 495
Dianne Louise: 156, 495
Donald: 155, 495
Donna: 161, 495
Donna Maxine: 156, 495
Drusilla: 93, 495
Edna: 117, 154, 495
Edward: 95, 495
Edward Bruce: 120, 162, 495
Edwin: 117, 155, 495
Eldon: 153, 495
Eli: 94, 116, 153, 495
Elias: 94, 495
Elias: 78, 495
Elizabeth: 79, 495
Elizabeth: 46, 64, 91, 92, 114, 115, 150-152, 215-217, 281, 282, 495
Elizabeth: 65, 92, 495
Elizabeth: 65, 94, 118, 157, 158, 218, 495
Elizabeth: 94, 117, 154, 495
Elizabeth: 95, 495
Emma Ruth: 156, 218, 495
Ephraim: 93, 495
Erman: 117, 495
Ernest: 119, 495
Ernest: 116, 495
Ernest Albert: 117, 156, 495
Esther: 94, 116, 495
Esther: 95, 495
Esther: 94, 495
Esther: 94, 495
Esther: 95, 495
Evelyn: 117, 155, 495
Fanny: 46, 496
Flavius Jacob: 94, 118, 157, 218, 496
Flora: 93, 496
Florence: 153, 496
Florence: 120, 162, 496
Frances: 95, 119, 159, 219, 220, 496
Francis: 93, 496
Franklin: 155, 496
Fred: 94, 118, 496
Garth: 155, 496
Geraldine: 160, 496
H. Elgin: 161, 496
Hannah: 94, 116, 154, 496
Hans: 19, 21, 24-290, 496
Hans: 17, 19, 21, 24-290, 496
Harold: 118, 496
Harry: 119, 160, 496
Harry Norman: 118, 496
Helen: 120, 162, 496
Ida: 116, 153, 218, 496
Infant: 92, 496
Isaac: 94, 496
Isobel: 117, 155, 496
Jacob: 79, 496

Jacob: 46, 496
Jacob: 65, 92, 496
Jacob: 65, 94, 117, 118, 154-157, 218, 496
Jacob: 25, 496
Jacob: 79, 496
Jacob Karl: 117, 156, 218, 496
Jared: 93, 496
Jason: 116, 153, 496
Jean: 119, 161, 496
Jean: 94, 496
Jean Carol: 156, 496
Jennie Grace: 118, 157, 496
Joe Karl: 156, 496
John: 79, 496
John: 46, 496
John: 92, 496
John: 93, 496
John: 65, 93, 94, 116, 152, 153, 217, 218, 496
John: 94, 496
John: 161, 496
John: 79, 496
John Franklin: 94, 117, 154, 155, 496
John O.: 79, 496
John Reesor: 65, 93, 496
Josephuine: 95, 119, 160, 220, 496
Katherine E.: 161, 496
Kathleen: 117, 155, 496
Kenneth: 117, 155, 496
Keturah: 94, 117, 156, 157, 496
Lambert: 119, 161, 496
Laura: 94, 118, 158, 496
Lavilla: 94, 117, 154, 496
Leonard: 118, 496
Leslie: 117, 496
Llewellyn: 117, 496
Llewellyn: 155, 496
Lloyd: 155, 496
Lloyd Arthur: 117, 156, 496
Louie: 119, 159, 220, 496
Louis: 155, 496
Luella: 119, 161, 496
Luella: 94, 496
Madeline: 153, 497
Madlena Galle: 15, 24, 497
Margareth Galle: 15, 24, 497
Maria: 92, 497
Marian: 161, 497
Marion: 154, 497
Marion: 120, 162, 497
Martha: 65, 93, 497
Martha: 93, 497
Martha: 95, 119, 160, 161, 220, 497
Martha May: 118, 157, 497
Mary: 94, 497
Mary: 161, 497
Mary: 94, 497
Mary Adrienne: 156, 497
Mary Ann: 95, 497
Matilda: 94, 116, 497
Matilda: 94, 497
Maude: 118, 497
May: 116, 153, 497

Miline: 161, 497
Miline: 116, 497
Minnie: 93, 497
Molly: 79, 497
Myrtle Inez: 117, 497
Neil: 155, 497
Noah: 95, 119, 159, 160, 220, 497
Ora Hilda: 117, 156, 497
Peter: 65, 93, 497
Phyllis: 155, 497
Phyllis: 117, 497
Private: 161, 497
Private: 161, 497
Private: 161, 497
Private: 161, 497
Private: 155, 497
Private: 157, 497
Private: 157, 497
Private: 157, 497
Private: 162, 497
Private: 162, 497
Private: 162, 497
Private: 162, 497
Private: 162, 497
Private: 162, 497
Ralph Clayton: 157, 497
Reginald: 119, 161, 497
Revis Parsons: 95, 497
Robert: 120, 497
Roxa: 92, 497
Ruth: 117, 497
Samuel: 65, 94, 116, 117, 153, 154, 497
Samuel: 116, 153, 154, 497
Sarah: 94, 497
Simeon: 65, 94, 118, 158, 497
Stanley: 117, 155, 497
Stewart W.: 119, 162, 497
Susan: 65, 93, 497
Thomas: 95, 120, 162, 497
Ulrich: 25, 497
Ulrich Galle: 15, 24, 497
Victor: 120, 497
Walter: 118, 497
Walter: 119, 497
Wellington: 92, 497
Wellington: 95, 119, 161, 162, 497
Wesley: 156, 498
Wesley Adrian: 117, 155, 498
Wilbert Gillson: 117, 156, 498
Wilfrid: 155, 498
William: 79, 498
Willis: 116, 498

Stover -
Private: 177, 338, 498
Private: 178, 338, 498

Strain -
Sahra Polly: 211, 212, 498

Strauss -
Millmy: 134, 498

Streler -
Margareth: 498

Strickland -
Emma: 95, 498

Strickler -
Abraham: 38, 53, 498
Abraham: 53, 498
Ambrose: 64, 498
Ann: 39, 297, 300, 498
Annie: 53, 498
Elisabeth: 36, 498
Elisabeth: 53, 498
Elizabeth: 38, 498
Elizabeth: 105, 498
Emerson: 64, 498
Emma Brightbill: 102
Fannie: 64, 498
Fannie: 53, 498
Henry: 53, 498
Henry B: 64, 498
Jacob: 293, 498
Jacob: 53, 498
John: 53, 498
Martha: 53, 498
Mary: 53, 498
Susan: 53, 498

Strite -
Abram Joseph: 498
Ada May: 498
Andrew C.: 498
Anrew C.: 498
Cyrus L.: 498
Earl Clarence: 498
Irvin Landis: 498
Lewis Andrew: 498

Strome -
Mary: 93, 498

Strong -
Herbert W , Jr: 254, 498
Kirk M: 254, 498

Stroup -
Ada louella: 142, 498
Atlee: 199, 498
Earl: 140, 199, 498
Julia Faye: 199, 498
June: 199, 498
Leola M: 142, 498
Lowell: 199, 498
Nellie F.: 140, 199, 498
Private: 204, 498
Private: 204, 498
Private: 199, 498
Private: 199, 498
Private: 199, 498
Russell: 199, 498
William H: 204, 498
William W.: 140, 498

Stuart -
Dean: 147, 208, 498
Neil: 147, 498
Private: 147, 208, 498
Private: 208, 498
Private: 208, 498
Private: 208, 498
Private: 208, 498
Private: 208, 499
Private: 208, 499
Private: 208, 499
Russell: 147, 208, 499
Vernon: 147, 499

Stuber -
Florence Mildred: 222, 499

Sturgeon -
Sarah Regina: 111, 112, 499

Stutt -
A. Katharine: 115, 151, 499
H. Gertrude: 115, 499
H. Gordon: 114, 499
James E.: 115, 499
W. J.: 114, 499

Sukosd -
Wilma S: 142, 499

Summer -
Argus: 144, 499
Bernice Winifred: 200, 499

Summers -
Bill: 202, 499
Clementine: 89, 499
Dorothy J: 204, 499
Kathleen Lucille: 202, 499
M. Mose: 312, 499
Private: 176, 337, 499
Private: 176, 242, 337, 359, 499
Private: 176, 242, 337, 359, 499
Private: 242, 359, 499
Sarah: 89, 499

Summy -
Aaron: 51, 499
Abram: 51, 499
David: 51, 499
Jacob: 51, 499
John: 37, 51, 499
John H: 51, 499
Maria: 51, 499
Peter: 51, 499
Peter: 78, 499

Suner -
Jacob: 499

Surerus -
Sarah: 91, 499

Sutton -
Carrie: 199, 499

Swarr -
Anna: 35, 499

Swart -
Peter: 25, 499

Swartz -
Christian: 294, 499

Swartzendruber -
Private: 177, 338, 499
Private: 177, 338, 499

Sweeney -
Catherine Elizabeth: 6, 63, 309, 499

Sweigart -
Abraham R.: 73, 309, 499
Amanda R.: 74, 310, 499
Amos R.: 73, 309, 499
Anna R.: 74, 310, 499
Chambers U.: 73, 309, 311, 499
Eli R.: 74, 310, 499
Elizabeth R.: 74, 310, 499
Frances Reiff: 73, 101, 125-127, 150, 178, 243, 244, 310,

311, 314, 323, 499
Jacob R.: 74, 310, 499
John R.: 73, 309, 499
Lydia R.: 74, 310, 499
Martin R.: 73, 310, 499

Switzer -
John: 499

Sykes -
Paul Jay: 129
Jr. Private: 129, 181

Sylvester -
Private: 200, 499

Taber -
Joann: 162, 499

Tangvald -
Private: 226, 343, 499

Taylor -
James Alfred: 131
Jr. James Alfred: 131, 184, 250
Lawrence R.: 285
Leighton Robert: 260, 499
Margaret L.: 80, 499
Mary L.: 82, 499
Private: 184, 250
Private: 184, 250
Private: 131, 183, 250
Private: 131, 183, 184
Jr. Private: 183
Private: 183, 250
Jr. Private: 250
Traci Ann: 285

Teaque -
Private: 212, 499
Ronald: 212, 499

Tedford -
Private: 271, 499
Private: 271, 499
Private: 271, 500

Teeters -
Elizabeth: 76, 500

Teets -
Private: 180

Temple -
Dorothy: 204, 500
Dorothy E.: 151, 500

Thoman -
Geraldine: 160, 500

Thomas -
Bart: 136, 500
Carol J: 256, 500
Howard: 256, 500
Private: 235, 353, 500
Private: 235, 353, 500
Private: 235, 353, 500
Private: 240, 358, 500
Private: 240, 358, 500
Private: 240, 358, 500
Private: 240, 358, 500
Stanley Howard: 123, 320, 500

Thometz -
Anna Theresa: 192, 500

Thompson -
Ethel Lillian: 216, 500
Mary: 115, 500

Orin Wesley: 213, 500
Private: 213, 279, 500

Thornton -
Private: 207, 500
Private: 207, 500
Roy: 207, 500

Thorpe -
Lulu: 218, 500

Thrope -
Helen Edith (aka: Nellie): 192, 193, 462, 500

Tichenon -
Margaret: 252, 500

Tidwell -
Mary Dorris: 186, 500

Tiffany -
Charlene: 126, 315, 500

Tinkey -
Henry: 14, 500

Tobel -
Barbel: 21, 500

Tobias -
Jennie E.: 131, 500

Todd -
A Morris , Jr: 256, 500
Marc D: 256, 500
Mary Root: 174, 335, 500
Michael M: 256, 500

Tolemie -
Manilla: 124, 321, 500

Tolman -
Private: 248
Private: 248
Private: 248
Private: 248

Tomilson -
Robert: 251

Tompkins -
Bertha Jeanne: 161, 500
J. Daniel S.: 161, 500
James: 161, 500

Toomey -
Private: 245

Tousignant -
Albena May: 198, 500

Towle -
Norman Lincoln: 100, 313, 500

Trask -
Private: 287, 500

Travers -
Lewis: 37, 500

Trinckler -
Elsbeth: 500

Tritt -
Alice Bell: 131, 500
Alice E.: 131, 500
Christian: 103, 500
Clarence E.: 131, 500
Clarence Ziegler: 131, 500
Edgar P.: 131, 500
Elizabeth: 103, 131, 500
Florence E.: 131, 500
John A.: 103, 131, 500
Lydia Jane: 103, 131, 132, 184,

250, 285, 500
Maggie T.: 103, 500
Mary S.: 311, 500
Maud T.: 131, 500
Melvin J.: 131, 500
Peter: 103, 500
Peter Stough: 103, 131, 500
Samuel John: 103, 131, 500

Troutman -
Elizabeth: 187, 500

Truby -
Lovina: 82, 500

Truesdale -
Private: 271, 500

Trump -
Anita: 193, 260, 261, 500
Bessie Pearl: 136, 501
Charles Clifford: 193, 501
Charles Clifford: 193, 501
Clarence R.: 136, 501
Emma Elizabeth: 136, 192, 260, 501
Harold: 192, 501
Jerimiah Washington (aka: Jerry Trump): 136, 501
Jerry (name: Jerimiah Washington Trump): 136, 501
Jerry Roosevelt: 193, 260, 501
John Duane: 193, 501
John Henry: 136, 192, 193, 260, 501
Mary May: 136, 501
Oliver Garfield: 136, 192, 260, 501
Oscar A.: 136, 192, 501
Private: 260, 501
Private: 260, 501
Private: 193, 501
Private: 192, 260, 501
Private: 192, 501
Private: 260, 501
Private: 193, 260, 501

Trupe -
Private: 223, 341, 501

Turner -
Andrew Jackson: 262, 501
Elizabeth I.: 258, 501
Private: 262, 501

Tvardek -
Private: 265, 501

Tyner -
Bethel Leone (aka: Betty): 197, 264, 373, 501
Homer: 197, 501
Kenneth A: 197, 501
Saint Elmo Parlette: 197, 501

Uhl -
Private: 181

Uihlein -
Frederick W.: 130
Jr. Private: 130
Private: 130

Unknown -
Unnamed: 194, 501
Unnamed: 501

Amanda: 80, 501
Ann: 30, 501
Anna: 13, 294
Anna: 501
Anna: 84, 501
Anna: 501
Anna C.: 79, 501
Barbara: 14, 501
Barbara: 18, 501
Barbara: 501
Barbara: 501
Barbary: 501
Barbel/Cherl: 20, 501
Beryl: 155, 501
Betty J: 212, 501
Catharine: 8, 10, 34, 35, 501
Catharine: 84, 501
Catherine: 501
Catherine: 59, 60, 501
Elisabeth: 18, 501
Elizabeth: 78, 501
Elizabeth: 79, 501
Elizabeth: 61, 501
Elizabeth: 294, 501
Elizabeth: 501
Elizabeth: 82, 501
Elizabeth: 501
Elizabeth: 77, 501
Elizabeth: 90, 314, 501
Ella: 81, 501
Emma: 156, 501
Ethelda: 196, 501
Eva: 31, 501
Francis: 501
Georgiann: 139, 501
Hannah: 59, 502
Jennie M.: 197, 198, 502
Julia Ann: 81, 502
Kesiah: 79, 502
Lottie: 77, 502
Lydia: 81, 502
Mae: 196, 502
Malinda: 84, 502
Malinda B.: 84, 502
Margaret: 81, 502
Margaret: 78, 502
Margaret A.: 83, 502
Margaret D.: 79, 502
Marguerite: 502
Maria: 15, 502
Maria: 97, 502
Maria Catherine: 79, 502
Mary: 12, 14, 502
Mary: 502
Mary: 84, 502
Mary Ann: 79, 502
Matilda: 80, 502
Mina: 68, 502
Private: 173, 334, 502
Private: 175, 336, 502
Private: 243, 360, 502
Private: 242, 359, 502
Private: 264, 502
Private: 198, 502
Private: 198, 502
Private: 198, 502

Private: 264, 502
Private: 288, 502
Private: 288, 502
Private: 288, 502
Private: 289, 502
Private: 289, 502
Private: 289, 502
Private: 275, 502
Private: 276, 502
Private: 276, 502
Private: 212, 502
Private: 268, 502
Private: 271, 502
Private: 272, 502
Private: 272, 502
Rachel: 78, 502
Sarah: 59, 502
Sarah: 78, 502
Sarah: 81, 502
Sarah: 106, 502
Sorama: 142, 502
Susan: 81, 502
Unknown: 10, 13, 16, 25
Unknown: 13
Unknown: 13, 15, 16, 18
Unknown: 13, 16, 502
Unknown: 18, 20, 502
Unknown: 16, 502
Unknown: 14, 16, 502
Unknown: 14, 502
Unknown: 17, 502
Unknown: 11, 13, 16, 292, 502
Unknown: 301, 502
Unknown: 60, 502
Unknown: 221, 502
Unruh -
   Private: 169, 329, 502
Urner -
   Sarah Price: 502
Usmar -
   C. William: 178, 323, 502
Uts -
   Ida Ota: 190, 191, 503
Valentine -
   Alma: 161, 503
Valient -
   Parthena S: 255, 503
Van Every -
   Dinah: 53, 503
Van Hiner -
   Private: 275, 503
   Private: 275, 503
Van Vleck -
   Henry: 503
Vanasco -
   Deanna: 180
   James Marten: 180
   John Michael: 180
   Laureen: 180
   Private: 180
   Private: 180
   Private: 180, 246
   Private: 180, 246
Vansickle -
   Abram: 216, 503

   Barry Learoy: 216, 503
   Calvin Learoy: 216, 503
   Lloyd: 216, 503
vanWormer -
   Private: 175, 336, 503
Varnes -
   Mary: 503
Veith -
   Robert John: 152, 503
   William J.: 152, 503
Ventura -
   Private: 279, 503
   Private: 279, 503
Voelker -
   Edna: 193, 503
Vogelsong -
   Glenda: 252
Vollenweider -
   Margaret: 15, 17, 19, 503
Wada -
   Private: 247
Wagner -
   Private: 214, 503
   Private: 214, 503
   Private: 214, 503
   Ross Earl: 214, 503
   Unknown (Wagoner): 503
Wagoner -
   John: 205, 503
   Private: 205, 503
   Private: 205, 503
   Private: 205, 503
Wakely -
   Susan: 251
Walder -
   Regel: 21, 503
Walker -
   Isaac: 503
   Lela: 202, 503
   Mary Frances: 503
   Private: 276, 503
   Walter: 194, 503
Wall -
   Lloyd Archer: 259, 503
   Private: 259, 503
   Private: 259, 503
   Private: 259, 503
Wallace -
   Claire: 115, 503
   Grace: 156, 503
Walley -
   Private: 245
Wallower -
   Private: 102
Walsh -
   Private: 288, 503
   Private: 288, 503
Walters -
   Grace: 144, 145, 503
Walton -
   Lillie Sophia: 128
   Private: 245
Wance -
   Private: 242, 360, 503

Wanger/Wenger -
   Iva (Wingert): 503
Wanner -
   John: 13, 292, 503
   John: 298, 503
   Private: 178, 338, 503
   Private: 178, 338, 503
   Private: 178, 338, 503
Waples -
   Private: 194, 503
Ward -
   Albert Ray: 200, 201, 503
   James Signor: 263, 503
   Mary Beemer: 91, 503
   Private: 263, 503
   Private: 201, 267, 503
   Private: 267, 503
   Private: 267, 503
   Private: 267, 503
   Private: 201, 267, 503
   Unknown: 144, 503
Wardecker -
   Charles A.: 132, 503
Warkentine -
   Agnes: 119, 503
Warmington -
   Richard: 157, 503
   Richard George: 157, 503
Waugh -
   Mable: 193, 503
Wealand -
   Marcella: 128, 323, 504
Weaver -
   Aaron G.: 301, 307, 504
   Amos H.: 311, 504
   Andrew S.: 179, 324, 504
   Anna: 294, 504
   Anna: 302, 504
   Anna: 307, 504
   Anna C.: 301, 504
   Anna M.: 121, 318, 504
   Anna Mary: 311, 504
   Arvilla: 127, 178, 179, 244, 317, 324, 340, 504
   Barbara: 311, 504
   Benjamin: 307, 504
   Benjamin Michael: 244, 340, 504
   Blanche M: 201, 504
   Carolyn Jean: 179, 324, 504
   Catharine: 306, 504
   Catharine: 302, 504
   Catherine: 89, 504
   Christian G.: 113, 307, 311, 312, 315, 317, 323, 324, 340, 504
   Daniel G.: 307, 504
   David G.: 307, 504
   Donna Lou: 127, 179, 244, 317, 324, 340, 504
   Elisabeth: 108, 504
   Elizabeth: 45, 504
   Elizabeth Ann: 127, 317, 504
   Ellen Sue: 178, 324, 504
   Fanny: 302, 504
   Feronica: 302, 504
   George: 302, 504
   Helen V.: 122, 319, 504
   Henry D.: 168, 329, 504
   Hettie Rebecca: 311, 504
   Isaac: 297, 302, 303, 306, 307, 504
   Isaac: 302, 307, 504
   Israel: 307, 504
   James Edward: 178, 244, 324, 340, 504
   Jay Donald: 127, 178, 244, 317, 324, 339, 340, 504
   Jennifer Lynn: 179, 324, 504
   John: 294, 504
   John: 295, 504
   John Eric: 127, 179, 244, 317, 324, 340, 504
   John Hollinger: 113, 127, 311, 315, 317, 323, 324, 340, 504
   John Landis: 113, 127, 150, 178, 179, 244, 315, 317, 323, 324, 339, 340, 504
   John Matthew: 179, 324, 504
   John Michael: 179, 244, 324, 340, 504
   John W: 108, 504
   John W.: 307, 504
   Johnathan: 504
   Jonas: 302, 504
   Joseph: 295, 504
   Joshua Alan: 244, 340, 504
   Levi: 56, 302, 304, 504
   Lisa Rene: 179, 324, 504
   Lizzie B.: 311, 504
   Lydia: 101, 302, 306, 307, 314, 504
   Lydia: 169, 330, 504
   Mabel L.: 113, 315, 504
   Mable: 151, 504
   Magdalena: 302, 504
   Magdalena: 301, 302, 504
   Marietta: 108, 504
   Martin G.: 307, 504
   Mary: 504
   Mary: 301, 307, 504
   Mary Grace: 132, 504
   Mary Jane: 110, 505
   Odessa May: 140, 141, 505
   Peter: 297, 505
   Peter: 302, 307, 505
   Private: 223, 341, 505
   Private: 284, 361, 505
   Private: 227, 345, 505
   Private: 229, 346, 505
   Private: 229, 346, 505
   Private: 233, 350, 505
   Private: 168, 329, 505
   Private: 168, 329, 505
   Private: 168, 234, 329, 352, 505
   Private: 168, 234, 329, 352, 505
   Private: 234, 352, 505
   Private: 234, 352, 505
   Private: 234, 352, 505
   Private: 123, 320, 505
   Private: 176, 336, 505
   Private: 176, 337, 505
   Private: 176, 337, 505
   Private: 176, 337, 505
   Private: 176, 337, 505
   Private: 176, 337, 505
   Rachel Anne: 244, 340, 505
   Ronald Lee: 127, 179, 317, 324, 505
   Sarah: 505
   Susie: 311, 505
   Theodore Floyd: 184
   Tillie: 302, 505
   William Shively: 184, 505
Webb -
   Private: 260, 505
   Private: 260, 505
   Sarah: 94, 505
Webber -
   Living: 287, 505
Weber -
   Aadi: 294, 505
   Anna: 293, 505
   Anna: 13, 292, 505
   Anna: 17, 291, 505
   Anna: 15, 291, 505
   Anna: 292, 505
   Anna: 294, 505
   Anna: 294, 297, 505
   Anna: 297, 505
   Anna: 297, 505
   Anna: 301, 505
   Barbara: 292, 505
   Barbara: 294, 505
   Barbara: 293, 505
   Barbara: 293, 505
   Barbara: 298, 505
   Barbara: 297, 505
   Barbeli: 17, 291, 505
   Beverly: 13, 292, 293, 296, 301, 306, 311, 315, 323, 339, 505
   Catharine: 294, 505
   Catharine: 298, 302, 303, 306, 505
   Christian: 307, 505
   Christian: 13, 292, 293, 296, 297, 301, 302, 306, 307, 311, 312, 315-317, 323, 324, 339, 340, 505
   Christian: 293, 505
   Christian: 293, 505
   Christian: 297, 301, 307, 312, 315, 323, 324, 340, 505
   Daniel: 297, 505
   Daniel M.: 301, 505
   David: 294, 505
   Elizabeth: 8, 11, 13, 14, 30, 292, 296, 300, 304, 305, 309, 310, 312-315, 318-338, 340-362, 505
   Elizabeth: 293, 505
   Elizabeth: 294, 505
   Elizabeth: 298, 506
   Elsbeth: 17, 291, 506
   Emma Zimmerman: 178, 323, 506
   Esther: 293, 296, 301, 306, 311, 315-317, 323, 339, 340, 506

Eva: 13, 292, 506
Eva: 294, 506
Fanny: 294, 506
Feronica: 297, 506
Feronica W: 297, 506
Georg: 17, 291, 506
Georg: 19, 291, 506
George: 17, 19, 291-362, 506
George: 15, 291, 292, 294, 298, 303, 506
George: 294, 298, 302, 303, 506
George: 298, 506
Gideon: 301, 307, 311, 312, 315, 323, 324, 340, 506
Hans: 292, 506
Hans Rudolf: 17, 291, 506
Harriet: 104, 506
Heine: 13, 292, 293, 297, 302, 307, 312, 506
Heinrich: 14, 17, 19, 291-362, 506
Heinrich: 17, 291, 506
Heinrich: 292, 294, 506
Henry: 293, 296, 301, 506
Henry: 11, 13, 15, 16, 291-294, 296-298, 300-362, 506
Henry: 28, 506
Henry: 28, 293, 506
Isaac: 297, 302, 506
Isaac: 301, 506
Jacob: 297, 506
Jacob: 15, 291, 292, 506
Jacob: 293, 297, 506
Jacob: 297, 506
Jagli: 17, 291, 506
Johann Anton: 12-14, 17, 291-362, 506
Johannnes: 292, 294, 298, 303, 506
John: 15, 291, 506
John: 293, 506
John: 297, 506
John: 297, 506
Joseph: 293, 506
Krista J.: 179, 324, 506
Leah: 301, 506
Lena: 219, 506
Magdalena: 293, 506
Magdalena: 292, 506
Magdalena: 13, 292, 294, 298, 302, 303, 308, 312, 506
Magdalena: 294, 506
Magdalena: 294, 297, 298, 302, 307, 312, 506
Magdalena: 297, 506
Magdalena: 298, 506
Magdelena: 297, 506
Marey: 292, 506
Maria: 297, 506
Maria: 9, 12, 14, 15, 291, 292, 294, 295, 298-300, 303, 304, 308, 309, 312, 317, 506
Maria: 293, 297, 302, 307, 311, 506
Martin C.: 298, 506
Mary: 13, 292, 506

Mary: 294, 506
Mary: 296, 301, 506
Michael: 294, 506
Peter: 293, 297, 302, 303, 307, 506
Private: 226, 344, 506
Private: 226, 344, 506
Private: 227, 344, 506
Samuel: 17, 291, 506
Samuel: 296, 507
Samuel: 292, 507
Samuel: 293, 296, 301, 302, 307, 312, 315, 323, 324, 340, 507
Samuel: 294, 507
Samuel: 301, 507
Sara: 19, 291, 507
Solomon: 301, 307, 507
Susanna: 294, 507
Susanna: 297, 507
Tina: 507
Verena: 17, 291, 507
Wederman -
   Wilhelmina G.: 100, 313, 507
Weeden -
   Private: 217, 507
   Unknown: 217, 507
Weible -
   Harry: 80, 507
Weidler -
   Elizabeth: 62, 90, 312, 507
   Emanuel: 47, 507
Weigle -
   Carolyn Ann: 251
Weikert -
   Mary Swope: 69, 507
Weinhold -
   Alverta M: 507
Weisel -
   Eliza: 82, 507
   Israel: 82, 507
   John: 81, 507
   Levi: 82, 507
Welch -
   Alma: 507
Weldy -
   Christian: 36, 507
Wellan -
   Otto: 118, 507
Wells -
   Reta: 220, 507
Weng -
   Private: 234, 351, 507
Wenger -
   Annie: 308, 507
   Barbara: 302, 507
   Christian: 293
   Daniel: 302, 507
   Elizabeth: 297, 507
   Ethan Richard: 286
   Eve: 13, 293, 507
   Eve S.: 507
   Ezra Meyer: 85, 507
   Feronica S.: 297, 303, 507

   Helen Stauffer: 123, 320, 507
   John: 85, 507
   Joseph G.: 507
   Laura Beth: 286
   Lynn Richard: 286
   Magdalena Graybill: 298
   Maria: 302, 507
   Mary Ann: 73, 309, 507
   Michael: 507
   Michael: 507
   Private: 225, 343, 507
   Private: 238, 356, 507
   Private: 172, 332, 507
   Reuben: 302, 507
   Seth Jonathan: 286
Wengert -
   Diane: 252
Wenzel -
   Private: 157, 507
Wert -
   Mary Elizabeth: 83, 507
Werteberger -
   Mildred R: 145, 507
West -
   Adam Leroy: 251
   Barbara Elaine: 251, 286
   Diane Elizabeth: 251, 286
Weston -
   Private: 242, 359, 507
Westover -
   Ann: 52, 507
   Barbara: 52, 507
   Charlotte: 52, 507
   Elizabeth: 52, 507
   George: 52, 507
   Herman: 52, 507
   Hiram: 52, 507
   Horace: 52, 507
   Isaac: 52, 507
   Jacob: 52, 507
   John: 52, 507
   Mahetable: 52, 507
   Ruffus: 52, 507
   William: 52, 507
   William: 37, 52, 507
Weyner -
   Barbel: 20, 508
Wheeler -
   Frank Ashley: 110, 508
Whinery -
   Private: 209, 508
Whipple -
   Pearl: 110, 508
White -
   Emily Faline: 163, 223, 283, 508
   Lydia: 67, 508
   McKenzie: 223, 508
   Private: 280, 508
   Samuel: 508
   Shelby: 223, 508
   William Walter: 163, 187, 508
   William Walter: 163, 187, 254, 283, 508
   William Walter: 163, 223, 508

Whyle -
    Lola: 157, 508
    William G.: 157, 508
    William George: 157, 508
Wiancko -
    Bruno: 158, 508
    Eldon: 159, 508
    Elmina Jane: 219, 508
    Margaret: 159, 219, 508
    Paul: 219, 508
    Redford: 158, 219, 508
Widdowson -
    John: 81, 508
Wideman -
    Abraham Henry: 94, 508
    Alan: 159, 219, 220, 508
    Bruce: 159, 508
    Carol: 158, 508
    Carson: 118, 158, 508
    Clarence: 118, 158, 508
    David: 94, 508
    Elizabeth: 119, 508
    Elizabeth: 118, 158, 218, 508
    Esther: 94, 118, 157, 508
    Evelyn: 219, 508
    Frances: 159, 508
    Frances E.: 159, 508
    Glen: 158, 508
    Harley: 159, 219, 508
    Harry: 118, 157, 508
    Harvey: 159, 219, 508
    Herbert: 119, 159, 219, 508
    Jacob S.: 94, 118, 157, 158, 218, 508
    James: 158, 508
    John: 158, 508
    Joseph: 119, 159, 219, 220, 508
    Lloyd: 159, 508
    Lorne: 118, 508
    Mabel: 119, 159, 219, 508
    Martha: 119, 159, 508
    Martin: 119, 508
    Muriel: 159, 219, 508
    Private: 219, 508
    Private: 219, 508
    Private: 219, 508
    Private: 219, 508
    Private: 220, 508
    Private: 220, 508
    Private: 220, 508
    Private: 220, 508
    Private: 219, 508
    Private: 219, 508
    Robert: 158, 508
    Ross: 159, 508
    Ruby: 159, 508
    Unknown: 158, 508
    Vera: 159, 220, 508
    Wesley: 119, 508
    Wilmot: 119, 159, 219, 509
Widemoyer -
    Christiana: 29, 509
Widener -
    Dorothy Eileen Hawkins: 208, 509
Wiggins -
    Private: 263, 509

Wild -
    Private: 182
Wilde -
    Unknown: 149, 509
Wilder -
    Eva Katherine: 192, 509
Wiley -
    Private: 276, 277, 509
Wilk -
    Private: 281, 509
    Private: 281, 509
    Private: 281, 509
Wilke -
    Edna: 311, 509
Will -
    Louis: 102
Williams -
    Dee Ann: 222, 509
    Donald Everett: 222, 509
    Douglas Thomas: 222, 509
    Elizabeth: 153, 154, 509
    Elizabeth: 82, 509
    Howard Jones: 186, 509
    Howard Jones: 186, 509
    Leanore: 261, 509
    Mary: 509
    Ober Wolf: 186, 509
    Ruth L: 186, 509
    Thomas William III: 222, 509
    Unknown: 112, 509
    William: 509
Williamson -
    Private: 218, 509
    Private: 218, 509
    Unknown: 217, 218, 509
Williford -
    David A: 163, 509
Willis -
    Private: 208, 509
    Private: 208, 509
Wilson -
    Jennie M: 146, 509
    Patricia A: 254, 509
    Richard: 254, 509
    Richard, Jr: 254, 509
Winder -
    Abigale: 106, 509
Windsor -
    Catharine: 40
Winey -
    Ruth Esther: 164, 325, 509
Winschell -
    Dorothy: 146, 509
Winters -
    Jacob: 295, 509
Wise -
    Vera Weaver: 164, 324, 509
Wismer -
    Elizabeth: 509
Wissler -
    Benjamin: 66, 509
    Christian: 66, 509
    Elisabeth: 66, 509
    Jacob: 66, 509

    Magdalena: 10, 28, 35, 509
    Mary: 66, 509
Wistler -
    John: 13, 292, 509
Witmer -
    Abraham: 509
    Abraham B.: 509
    Amos L.: 509
    Ann: 12, 14, 17, 292, 509
    Ann: 509
    Anna: 509
    Benjamin: 509
    David: 509
    David: 509
    Edmund: 509
    Eliza: 509
    Esther: 509
    Henry: 509
    Henry H.: 509
    Hetty: 509
    Isaac B.: 312, 509
    Jacob: 509
    Jacob: 509
    Jane Juliet: 510
    Lydia: 510
    Maria Louisa: 510
    Marie: 70, 71, 510
    Mary Ann: 306, 510
    Mary Emma: 510
    Michael: 25, 510
    Nancy Ann: 510
    Private: 510
    Samuel Lefevre: 510
Witson -
    Anna L: 286, 510
    Rex: 286, 510
Witwer -
    Barbara: 297, 510
    Catharine: 297, 510
    Catharine: 307, 510
    Daniel: 510
    David: 510
    Jonas S.: 510
    Susan: 86, 510
Woglemuth -
    Gordon: 289
    Sean: 289
Wolf -
    Alice K: 186, 510
    Alice K: 253, 510
    Anna B: 133, 510
    Anna Rupp: 113, 318, 510
    Barbara Ann: 186, 510
    Barbara J: 187, 254, 510
    Catherine: 88, 510
    Catherine Rebecca: 134, 163, 187, 254, 283, 510
    Christena: 88, 510
    Clarence Franklin: 186, 253, 510
    Clarence R: 133, 186, 253, 510
    Collin: 88, 510
    David O: 186, 510
    David Ober: 134, 186, 253, 510
    Edgar: 187, 510
    Franklin Earl: 134, 187, 254, 510

Franklin Earl: 187, 254, 510
Franklin LeFevere: 133, 510
George: 101, 311, 510
George B II: 88, 510
George Edgar: 134, 187, 254, 510
Henry: 88, 510
Holly Ann: 253, 510
John S: 186, 253, 510
Katherine: 87, 510
Lewis: 88, 510
Margaret M: 253, 510
Maria: 510
Maria: 254, 510
Marian Elizabeth: 186, 510
Marjorie Ann: 186, 253, 254, 510
Mary: 16, 510
Mary Ann: 87, 510
Mary E: 186, 510
Mary E: 253, 510
Mary Estelle: 134, 186, 510
Mary L: 187, 254, 510
Nellie I: 134, 510
Ray: 253, 510

Wolfart -
Mary: 510

Wolff -
Albert Nathan: 130
Private: 130, 183
Private: 131, 183, 250
Private: 183
Private: 183
Private: 183

Wolgemuth -
Martin M.: 315, 510

Wolk -
Pearl Lorraine: 182

Wood -
Goldie Lutechia "Lou": 211, 510
Private: 237, 354, 510
Wilmer: 196, 510

Woodburn -
Ed: 94, 510
Henry: 94, 510

Woods -
Private: 241, 359, 510
Private: 241, 359, 511
Private: 241, 359, 511
Private: 214, 511

Woolf -
Analiza Eliza: 110, 511
Florian Charles"Dutch": 201, 511

Woolman -
Lavilla: 94, 511

Woolridge -
Bealah Verdie: 261, 511

Wymann -
Susanna: 13, 16, 18, 292, 511

Wynia -
Private: 174, 335, 511

Wyss -
Audrey Odessa "Audey": 147, 209, 511
Cleveland Samuel: 147, 511
Darly Leroy: 209, 511

Daryl Leroy "Cork": 209, 511
Evelyn: 147, 511
Florian F.: 147, 209, 511
Naomi B.: 147, 209, 511
Private: 208, 511
Private: 209, 511
Private: 209, 511
Ralph Leroy: 147, 208, 511
Richard Adelbert: 209, 511
Shirley Ruth: 209, 511
Wayne Ralph: 209, 511
William: 145, 511
Woodrow: 147, 511

Yaggi -
Agnes Ruth: 199, 265, 266, 511
Irvin Emmanuel: 199, 511
Lois Jean: 199, 265, 511
Mary Elizabeth: 199, 266, 511

Yando -
Jennie Adelia: 117, 511

Yanosh -
Private: 274, 511

Yarman -
Private: 215, 511

Yeager -
Eva: 190, 511
Mary: 88, 511

Yeagley -
Laura: 112, 113, 511

Yertz -
Susan: 32, 511

Yocum -
Albert Shantz: 511

Yoder -
Margaret Sue: 162, 511
Private: 232, 350, 511
Private: 232, 350, 511
Private: 232, 350, 511
Private: 232, 350, 511
Private: 232, 350, 511
Private: 232, 350, 511
Private: 239, 357, 511
Private: 239, 357, 511
Private: 239, 357, 511
Private: 173, 334, 511
Private: 240, 358, 511
Private: 240, 358, 511

Yohe -
Delores J: 211, 212, 511

Yohn -
Private: 248
Private: 248

Yordy -
Elizabeth: 32, 68, 511
Mary: 31, 511

Yost -
Salome Miller: 511

Young -
Bessie Pansy May: 511
Dessie: 145, 511
Milton: 59, 511
W. Evart: 115, 511

Youtsey -
Clayton E.: 193, 511

Yuengt -
Andrew: 83, 511

Zeigler -
George: 511

Zeiset -
Anna Mae: 122, 319, 511
Emma E.: 165, 326, 511
George: 302, 511
Private: 169, 329, 511
Private: 169, 234, 329, 352, 511
Private: 234, 352, 512

Ziegler -
Barbara Pawling: 512
Edna Snyder: 129, 130
Jacob (Zuglar): 512
Private: 235, 353, 512

Zimmer -
Private: 264, 512

Zimmerman -
Ada: 165, 166, 326, 512
Anna: 297, 512
Annie: 306, 512
Catharine: 298, 302, 512
Christian: 294, 512
Christine Renee: 223, 341, 512
David: 306, 512
Elizabeth: 306, 512
Elmer Denlinger: 125, 322, 512
Katie: 306, 512
Mary: 306, 512
Neil Brian: 223, 341, 512
Noah Hoover: 164, 325, 512
Private: 223, 340, 341, 512
Private: 223, 341, 512
Private: 223, 341, 512
Private: 224, 342, 512
Private: 225, 284, 342, 361, 512
Private: 225, 284, 342, 361, 512
Private: 225, 284, 342, 361, 512
Private: 284, 361, 512
Private: 284, 361, 512
Private: 164, 225, 325, 342, 512
Private: 164, 225, 325, 342, 512
Private: 164, 225, 325, 342, 512
Private: 164, 225, 284, 325, 343, 361, 362, 512
Private: 225, 343, 512
Private: 225, 343, 512
Private: 225, 343, 512
Private: 225, 343, 512
Private: 225, 343, 512
Private: 225, 343, 512
Private: 225, 343, 512
Private: 225, 343, 512
Private: 225, 343, 512
Private: 225, 343, 512
Private: 225, 343, 512
Private: 225, 284, 343, 361, 512
Private: 225, 343, 512
Private: 225, 343, 512
Private: 225, 284, 343, 362, 512
Private: 225, 342, 512
Private: 225, 343, 512
Private: 225, 343, 512
Private: 225, 343, 512

    Private: 225, 343, 512
    Private: 225, 343, 512
    Private: 225, 343, 512
    Private: 225, 342, 512
    Private: 225, 342, 512
    Private: 228, 346, 512
    Private: 228, 346, 512
    Private: 228, 346, 512
    Private: 228, 346, 512
    Private: 228, 346, 512
    Private: 228, 346, 512
    Private: 228, 285, 346, 362, 512
    Private: 228, 285, 346, 362, 512
    Private: 228, 285, 346, 362, 512
    Private: 228, 285, 346, 362, 512
    Private: 285, 362, 512
    Private: 285, 362, 513
    Private: 285, 362, 513
    Private: 229, 347, 513
    Private: 229, 346, 347, 513
    Private: 229, 346, 513
    Private: 166, 327, 513
    Private: 234, 352, 513
    Private: 236, 354, 513
    Private: 125, 176, 322, 337, 513
    Private: 125, 176, 322, 337, 513
    Private: 125, 176, 322, 337, 513
    Private: 176, 337, 513
    Private: 176, 337, 513
    Private: 176, 337, 513
    Private: 176, 337, 513
    Private: 176, 337, 513
    Private: 265, 513
    Suzanne: 306, 513

Zing -
    Ann: 143, 513

Zook -
    Elizabeth: 76, 513
    John Kurtz: 61, 513
    Rebecca L.: 125, 126, 315, 513

Zupinger -
    Elsbeth: 21, 513

Zuver -
    Donna Marie: 287, 513

www.ingramcontent.com/pod-product-compliance
Lightning Source LLC
Chambersburg PA
CBHW080529300426
44111CB00017B/2655